The New York Times Company

v.

United States

A Documentary History

The Pentagon Papers Litigation

Compiled and with an introduction by James C. Goodale,
General Counsel of The Times.

Volume I

*A complete record of this case, arranged chrono-
logically, starting with the motion by the Government
on June 15, 1971, in Federal Court, for a temporary
restraining order and ending with the opinion of the
Supreme Court on June 30, 1971. Contains all the legal
papers and briefs filed in the District Court, Court of
Appeals and Supreme Court, as well as transcripts of
all arguments except for those proceedings held in
camera. Also included are reprints of articles in* The
Times *covering this case and the companion case,*
United States v. The Washington Post Company *et al.*

*The only complete record of this case, since, be-
cause of pressure of time, no printed record was filed
with the Court.*

ARNO PRESS

A New York Times Company

Library of Congress Catalog Card Number: 72-173288

ISBN: 0-405-00100-2

Manufactured in the United States of America

THE NEW YORK TIMES COMPANY

v.

UNITED STATES OF AMERICA

Table of Contents

---

    a. Annexed affidavit of Melvin Wulf
    b. Annexed affidavit of Aryeh Neier
    c. Annexed affidavit of Edwin Oppenheimer, Jr.
    d. Pleadings of defendant intervenor
    e. Defendant Intervenors Memo of Points and Authorities in Support of their motion to Intervene.
    f. Memorandum in behalf of Amici Curiae
    g. Annexed proposed Order

    a. Brief in Support of Motion for intervention
    b. Proposed answer of intervenors
    c. Proposed Order

An Introduction

On June 13 and June 14, 1971, *The New York Times* published two articles based on the 47-volume study, History of U.S. Decision-Making Process on Vietnam Policy (the *Pentagon Papers*).

On June 14, John N. Mitchell, Attorney General of the United States, sent a telegram to The Times requesting it to cease publishing further information from the Pentagon Papers. The Times refused this request and published a third installment of its series the next day, June 15.

On the morning of the 15th, the Government began a court action in New York City, *The United States* v. *The New York Times Company et al*, which, eleven days later, reached the Supreme Court.

This volume is a reprint of all the papers that were filed with the Supreme Court in this case. An index of the district court papers filed with the Court appears on page 687 of this volume. We reproduced these papers chronologically and not in the order submitted to the Court since they were never put in sequence for the Court because of the pressure of time.

An index of the Second Circuit papers filed with the Court appears on page 700 of this volume. We have not reproduced these papers in the form submitted to the Court since they too were filed out of order with the Court. We have, however, rearranged them chronologically. At this printing, the Court had not prepared its index for the papers filed by the parties with it such as Supreme Court briefs, etc., and, accordingly, these papers too have been produced in chronological order.

If reconstruction of the precise record in the form submitted to the Court is deemed necessary, it may be done by referring to the two indexes on page 687 and 700 and rearranging the papers in the order set forth in those indexes.

Ordinarily, the record of a case in the Supreme Court contains excerpts of the proceedings in the lower courts, as agreed upon by counsel for the opposing parties, and it is then reprinted and filed with the Court. Because of the accelerated timetable for this case, there never was an opportunity to print such a record. In addition, only one copy of the record was filed with the Court, whereas the rules require that forty copies be filed.

When this introduction was written, no plans had been made for a formal printing of the Record; therefore, this volume may be the only "record" generally available to the public for its study of this historic decision.

All papers filed in this proceeding were filed either in typewritten or Xerox form. Forty copies of the briefs prepared by The Times and the United States were filed with the Court, and only one copy of The Washington Post's brief was filed.

As this volume went to press, the Court requested that the briefs filed with it on the day of argument (June 26) be refiled in printed form. This volume, however, has reproduced such briefs in the form originally filed with the Court.

In reviewing the District Court index, it appeared to us that it did not contain a full listing of the papers filed by those parties who sought intervention in this proceeding. We believe this may be an error of omission and that in fact such papers were filed with both the Court of Appeals and the Supreme Court. Accordingly, these papers have been included in this volume.

The table of contents of this volume contains page numbers that we have supplied. There is also an index at the end of this volume. It will be noted that some of the briefs refer to page numbers of transcripts. Examination of these transcripts will show that they have individual page numbers that we have not changed for ease of reference. We have, however, given an additional page number for each page of such transcripts so that the transcripts will be numbered consecutively with the rest of the pages of this volume.

Inserted at appropriate places in this volume are reprints of *The Times*'s articles that covered this litigation. None of the material published in *The Times* concerning the *Pentagon Papers* has been inserted, except the first three installments published by *The Times* before the lawsuit began. All of these articles are reprinted verbatim in *The Pentagon Papers* by Neil Sheehan, Hedrick Smith, E. W. Kenworthy and Fox Butterfield (Bantam Books, Inc., New York: July, 1971).

Since the litigation proceeded at such an accelerated pace, I have taken the liberty of summarizing below its progress, as well as that of The Washington Post's litigation, which was proceeding roughly at the same time as The Times's case. No part of The Washington Post record is reprinted in this volume.

The case began formally when the Government moved on June 15, 1971, in the United States District Court for the Southern District of New York for a temporary restraining order to prevent *The Times* and certain named defendants from printing any part of the *Pentagon Papers*. Mr. Mitchell's telegram was

received by The Times at approximately 6 P.M. June 14. At approximately 8:30 P.M. Harding F. Bancroft, Executive Vice President of The Times, called Assistant Attorney General Robert Mardian, to tell him that The Times was not going to comply with the Government's request (pages xiii, xiv).

The next morning, at approximately 10:15 A.M., Michael Hess, Assistant United States Attorney for the Southern District, called me to say that the Government was going to move before District Judge Murray I. Gurfein for a temporary restraining order, and asked me to be in court before noon. The previous evening, I had engaged Prof. Alexander Bickel of the Yale Law School and Floyd Abrams of the New York City law firm of Cahill, Gordon, Sonnett, Reindel & Ohl, to represent The Times in court. Professor Bickel argued this motion after lunch on that day. No transcript of this argument was made, but The Times's article of the next day reporting the argument is reproduced on page 62 of this volume.

After hearing argument, Judge Gurfein in a memorandum opinion granted the temporary restraining order (pages 27 to 29). Judge Gurfein set Friday, June 18, as the day for a formal hearing on this motion.

On the 16th, the Government moved by order to show cause requiring The Times and the other named defendants to produce its copy of the Pentagon Papers for inspection and copying by the United States Government. This motion was heard the next day, June 17, and was argued by Mr. Abrams. This argument appears on pages 256 to 291 and The Times story covering this argument appears on page 295.

Judge Gurfein declined to act on this motion and, instead, The Times gave the Court and the Justice Department a list of descriptive headings for those portions of the Pentagon Papers in the Time's possession. This list appears on page 292.

On the morning of June 18, The Washington Post carried parts of the Pentagon Papers covering the years 1954 to 1955. Also that morning in New York, the hearing began concerning a preliminary injunction. The Times moved at the opening of that hearing for a dismissal of the action for mootness because of the publication by The Post. This motion was not granted. Later in the day, the Government brought an action against The Washington Post in Washington, D.C., also seeking to enjoin it. A hearing on this request commenced at 6 P.M. before Judge Gerhard A. Gesell of the District of Columbia District Court.

Judge Gesell heard The Washington Post's case from 6 to 7 P.M. At 8 P.M., Judge Gesell rendered his opinion and decided not to grant the Government's motion for temporary restraining order. In the New York case, the hearing before Judge Gurfein began at 9:30 A.M. Following the adjournment for lunch, an in camera hearing was held by Judge Gurfein, and that hearing is not part of this record. Final arguments began before Judge Gurfein at 9 P.M. and ended at 10:30 P.M.; the transcript of this hearing begins on page 447.

That night, in Washington, the Government appealed Judge Gesell's decision to the Court of Appeals for the D.C. Circuit and that Circuit, by a 2-to-1 vote, granted the Government's request for a temporary restraining order and sent the case back to Judge Gesell for further hearing on the morning of Monday June 21. Newspaper clippings on that action and The Times proceedings that day are on pages 645 and 646.

On Saturday, June 19, at 1:30 in the afternoon, Judge Gurfein, in an opinion that is reproduced on pages 654 to 669, denied the Government's motion for a preliminary injunction. A few minutes following this decision, the Government appealed the case to Judge Irving R. Kaufman of the Second Circuit. Judge Kaufman granted a stay pending a meeting of a three-judge Court on Monday, June 21 (pages 675 to 677). Relevant clippings follow these pages.

On June 21, a three-judge court met to hear the appeal of the Government and decided to continue the stay. The three-judge court postponed argument until the following day, Tuesday, June 22, in order that a full panel of the Second Circuit could hear the case. At the hearing on June 21, the Government asked to submit additional secret affidavits concerning the Government's case on the Pentagon Papers. The court granted this request.

On the same day, June 21, a hearing commenced before Judge Gesell on the Pentagon Papers, based in part on the same affidavits as submitted in the Court of Appeals in New York. After this hearing, Judge Gesell refused to grant a preliminary injunction and the Government appealed this decision to the Court of Appeals for the District of Columbia. The Appeals Court granted a stay pending argument before that court at 2 P.M. on June 22. (Clippings on this action, including Judge Gesell's decision appear on pages 883 and 884.)

On the same day, at the same time, argument on The Times case was heard in the Second Circuit in New York before an eight-judge panel comprising Chief Justice Henry J. Friendly, J. Edward Lumbard, J. Joseph Smith, Judge Kaufman, Walter R. Mansfield, Wilfred Feinberg, James L. Oakes and Paul R. Hays. The

transcript of this argument appears on pages 885 to 967. In addition, part of the argument was held *in camera*, which does not appear in this record. (Newspaper clippings are on pages 968 to 971.)

At 5 P.M. June 23, the Court of Appeals for the Second Circuit, by a 5-to-3 vote, remanded the case to Judge Gurfein for further hearing based on the affidavits submitted by the Government on June 21 (see page 973), and any additional evidence that the Government wished to designate by 5 P.M. Friday, June 25.

At 8:15 P.M., the same day, the Court of Appeals for the District of Columbia affirmed Judge Gesell, but granted a stay until 6 P.M. June 25 (see clippings on pages 976, 977).

On the morning of June 24, The Times filed a petition for certiorari (pages 984 and 1027). On that day, the Government moved before the District of Columbia Circuit for reargument, requesting that Circuit to conform its opinion with the opinion of the Second Circuit. On the night of June 24, the Government was denied that motion by a 7-to-2 decision; and, the next day, June 25, the Government petitioned for certiorari in The Washington Post case.

On the morning of June 25, the Supreme Court granted certiorari in both The Times and Post cases by a 5-4 decision (see pages 1050 to 1051). The Court also permitted the Government to designate by 5 P.M. that day additional parts of the *Pentagon Papers* that would inflict "grave and immediate danger" to the nation's security if disclosed. This ruling was consonant with the ruling of the Second Circuit, which had also set a 5 P.M. deadline the same day for the same purpose.

At 5 P.M., June 25, The Times was served, in Washington, D.C., with such a designation. This list was made part of the *in camera* record for the Supreme Court. At 5 P.M., in New York City, The Times was served with another set of designations under the Court of Appeals ruling. This set also became a part of the *in camera* record before the Supreme Court.

Argument was set on the case before the Supreme Court at 11 A.M. on Saturday, June 26. At 10:30 A.M., The Times filed its brief with the Court and served it on the Government; and, in addition, served an *in camera* brief, which is not part of this record.

The Government, at the same time, served its copy of the brief, an *in camera* brief, as well as two further sets of designated items from the *Pentagon Papers*, one prepared by the State Department and one prepared by the Department of Defense. In addition, the *in camera* brief made further designations within the *Pentagon Papers* and the Solicitor General made reference to these designations on oral argument (page 1218).

The oral argument before the Supreme Court was reprinted in full in *The Times* (pages 1218 to 1232) on June 27. At the time of printing, the official transcript had not been printed, but it should not vary from that published in *The Times*.

On June 30, 1971 the Court handed down its decision upholding The Times and The Post by a 6-3 vote. This is printed on pages 1235 to 1290.

JAMES C. GOODALE

MITCHELL SEEKS TO HALT SERIES ON VIETNAM BUT TIMES REFUSES

COURT STEP LIKELY

Return of Documents Asked in Telegram To Publisher

By MAX FRANKEL
Special to The New York Times

WASHINGTON, June 14—Attorney General John N. Mitchell asked The New York Times this evening to refrain from further publication of documents drawn from a Pentagon study of the Vietnam war on the ground that such disclosures would cause "irreparable injury to the defense interests of the United States."

If the paper refused, another Justice Department official said, the Government would try to forbid further publication by court action tomorrow. The Times refused to halt publication voluntarily.

The Justice Department's request and intention to seek a court enjoinder were conveyed by Robert C. Mardian, Assistant Attorney General in charge of the internal security division, to Harding F. Bancroft, executive vice president of The Times.

Spoke by Telephone

They spoke by telephone at about 7:30 P.M., which was some two hours before tomorrow's first edition of the paper was scheduled to go to press with the third installment of the articles about the Pentagon study.

An hour later, a telegram from Mr. Mitchell asked that The Times halt further publication of the material and return the documents to the Pentagon.

The Times then issued the following statement:

"We have received the telegram from the Attorney General asking The Times to cease further publication of the Pentagon's Vietnam study.

"The Times must respectfully decline the request of the Attorney General, believing that it is in the interest of the people of this country to be informed of the material contained in this series of articles.

"We have also been informed of the Attorney General's intention to seek an injunction against further publication. We believe that it is properly a matter for the courts to decide. The Times will oppose any request for an injunction for the same reason that led us to publish the articles in the first place. We will of course abide by the final decision of the court."

Telegram From Mitchell

The telegram from Attorney General Mitchell, addressed to Arthur Ochs Sulzberger, president and publisher of The Times, said:

"I have been advised by the Secretary of Defense that the material published in The New York Times on June 13, 14, 1971, captioned 'Key Texts From Pentagon's Vietnam Study' contains information relating to the national defense of the United States and bears a top secret classification.

"As such, publication of this information is directly prohibited by the provisions of the Espionage Law, Title 18, United States Code, Section 793.

"Moreover, further publication of information of this character will cause irreparable injury to the defense interests of the United States.

"Accordingly, I respectfully request that you publish no further information of this character and advise me that you have made arrangements for the return of these documents to the Department of Defense.

Espionage Law Cited

The section cited by the Attorney General is labeled "gathering, transmitting or losing defense information."

The laws governing the disclosure of secret documents were described earlier in the day by a Pentagon spokesman as containing "certain ambiguities" about whether they apply to publications or only to their sources of information. Government lawyers were divided on the matter, the spokesman indicated, because there appeared to be no precedent for application of the law to a publication.

Both Mr. Mitchell and the Pentagon spokesman, Jerry W. Friedheim, cited sections of the Espionage and Censorship Chapter of the Federal criminal code. Mr. Friedheim mentioned Section 798, entitled "Disclosure of Classified Information." The Attorney General mentioned Section 793, headed "Gathering, Transmitting or Losing Defense Information."

Much of Section 793 refers to spying on defense installations and to obtaining code books, blueprints, maps or other defense-related documents.

Selections From Section

It goes on to state that "whoever having unauthorized possession of, access to, or control over any document, writing, code book . . . or information relating to the national defense which information the possessor has reason to believe could be used to the injury of the United States or to the advantage of any foreign nation, willfully communicates, delivers, transmits . . . the same to any person not entitled to receive it, or willfully retains the same and fails to deliver it to the officer or employee of the United States entitled to receive it . . . shall be fined not more than $10,000 or imprisoned not more than ten years, or both."

The Justice Department's request conveyed by Mr. Mardian was the first direct contact between the Government and The Times about the publication of the Pentagon papers.

The first group of materials, published in the Sunday issue of the paper, dealt with the clandestine warfare carried on against North Vietnam before the Tonkin Gulf incident in August, 1964. The second installment, in this morning's issue, covered the Johnson Administration's decision to begin open bombing of North Vietnam in February, 1965.

Before Mr. Mardian's call, the Administration had said only that the Justice Department was investigating the disclosures, at the request of the Defense Department.

Laird Sees 'Violation'

Secretary of Defense Melvin R. Laird said the disclosure "violated the security regulations of the United States."

The Secretary implied a difference between the violation of security regulations—by officials subject to these regulations—and violation of law. He said he had asked the Justice Department to determine the legal implications.

This morning, a formal Pentagon statement expressed concern about "this violation of security" but left determination of legal action to the Justice Department.

At the Justice Department this afternoon, a spokesman said the subject was still under consideration by Attorney General Mitchell. "We have yet to determine whether or not there is something to investigate," the spokesman added, explaining that Mr. Mitchell was dealing during the day with a statement on housing discrimination and had not yet considered the matter fully.

As of that time, there was said to have been no order for any Justice investigation, but other agencies of government reported intensive inquiries into the affair.

Authority Unchallenged

Mr. Mitchell, Secretary Laird and White House officials began to confer on Sunday on the disclosures in The Times.

No official here challenged the authenticity of the account of the Pentagon study and of the documents printed in The Times. Only a few members of Congress commented on their content.

The White House referred to the Pentagon all questions on the circumstances of the disclosure. Under vigorous questioning about the documents, it chose to emphasize that President Nixon had developed a "new Vietnam policy" and decided when he took office in 1969 "not to engage ourselves in a continuation or justification" of the policies of earlier administrations, which are the subject of the Pentagon papers.

Ronald L. Ziegler, the President's press secretary, said that a copy of the 1967-68 Pentagon study was brought to the White House this morning from the Defense Department.

Although Mr. Nixon and his aides were said to be unfamiliar with this "internal" archive, Mr. Ziegler stressed that the basic documents and information contained in them had been available to the new Administration and were fully considered in its own policy review in early 1969.

Asked whether The Times had informed the White House of its publishing plans, Mr. Ziegler said the newspaper "did not at any time check with us." Asked whether the President was concerned about the publication of secret documents, he replied:

"I'm not going to build up, by White House comment, the exposure of classified information."

The only formal public statement was that by the Pentagon referring the matter to the Justice Department. This came after Secretary Laird was drawn into a discussion of the affair by Senator Stuart Symington, Democrat of Missouri, at a hearing of the Senate Foreign Relations Committee on foreign aid.

Data Called Still 'Sensitive'

Senator Symington announced his intention to propose a "full examination of the origins of the war" for the benefit of future generations. Mr. Laird opposed the idea, arguing that a debate of the past "would not serve the interests of the country and would not help us disengage from Vietnam."

Stating a theme that he apparently hoped would dominate the reaction to The Times' disclosures, Mr. Laird said that "the divisions caused by debate of the past actions would not serve a useful purpose today." He has been trying to shift focus away from "Why Vietnam?" to the means of disengaging in an honorable way, he declared.

Mr. Laird said the disclosure of the Pentagon papers was "unauthorized" and "violates the security regulations of our Government." Although the study covers information only to 1968, he added, the information "remains sensitive" and its publication does not serve "a useful purpose." The Secretary said the documents would remain classified and would not be made available to the Foreign Relations Committee.

Senator Symington observed that the committee had tried several times to obtain the material, on a confidential basis. He said it was "shocking" that Congress had been kept ignorant of the materials and that even now he had to read about them in the newspapers.

Asked whether he knew who might have passed the materials to The Times, Mr. Laird said, "No, I don't yet know." But since there were so few copies, he added, "it won't be hard to track down whoever was responsible.

"This is highly sensitive information and should not have been made public," he declared.

Legal Distinction Implied

Shortly afterward, Mr. Friedheim, the Pentagon briefing officer, read a statement that had been worked out after a full day of consultation among

Mr. Mitchell, Mr. Laird, some White House officials and lawyers of the Defense and Justice Departments. Inferentially, the statement made a distinction between violation of Government security regulations and possible violations of law. It said:

"The Department of Defense must be and is concerned about the disclosure of publication of highly classified information affecting national security.

"The material remains classified and sensitive despite the fact that it covers a period that ended in 1968.

"It is our responsibility to call this violation of security to the attention of the Justice Department. We have done so.

"The Government has the responsibility to determine what individual or individuals, if any, violated the laws relating to national security information by unauthorized disclosure of classified material."

Mr. Friedheim said officials of the Justice and Defense Departments had had various discussions of the matter, face to face and also by telephone, since Sunday, when The Times began publication of its series of articles.

He said the relevant law was Title 18 of the United States Code, Section 798, noting that it contained "certain ambiguities" as to whether it applies to publications or only to their sources of secret information.

"Some lawyers are of the opinion that the publication is liable to prosecution as well as the official [source]," the spokesman said. "but there appears no precedent to establish that point. Justice is studying the whole matter to decide who, if anyone, to charge with law violation."

Classified Data Defined

The section that he cited states: "Whoever knowingly and willfully communicates, furnishes, transmits, or otherwise makes available to an unauthorized person, or publishes, or uses in any manner prejudicial to the safety or interest of the United States or for the benefit of any foreign government to the detriment of the United States any classified information . . . shall be fined not more than $10,000 or imprisoned not more than 10 years, or both."

The section contains a list and definition of classified information as bearing on codes, weapons and materials, intelligence activities and material obtained from the communications of foreign governments.

Mr. Friedheim said the Pentagon had determined that there were "a dozen or so" copies of the papers and that half of these, at the Defense Department, "have remained under extremely tight control." He said he did not believe the Pentagon's copies had either been duplicated or shown to unauthorized persons. He refused to say where the other copies had been kept.

7,000 Pages of Material

There is a possibility, the spokesman remarked, that unauthorized duplicate copies were made at some point, "or even that a set of the study was stolen at some point." The materials run to about 7,000 pages of analysis and documentation.

As a practical matter, Mr. Friedheim said, the Pentagon regards individuals with authorized clearance to handle classified information as primarily responsible for the protection of such information.

He said Secretary Laird had been aware of the secret Pentagon study since he came into office in 1969 and had even once referred to its existence in public testimony before the Senate Foreign Relations Committee.

The spokesman then emphasized again Mr. Laird's "philosophical" conviction that it was more important to consider ways of disengaging from Vietnam than to "rake over the coals" of past policies.

At the State Department, a spokesman said he could not comment "on the accuracy of —or make any useful comment on the substance of — these papers until we have had an opportunity to check the original."

Checking was difficult, the spokesman, Charles W. Bray 3d, said this morning, because the department had not had time to locate its copy of the report, or even to determine whether it had one.

Several hours later, according to Mr. Bray, the papers were found in personal files that had been left behind by William P. Bundy, who served as Assistant Secretary of State for East Asian and Pacific Affairs during the Johnson Administration.

Secretary of State William P. Rogers had no comment on the matter today, but he is likely to be asked about the materials at a news conference scheduled for tomorrow.

In Congress, there were only a few other comments on the matter and no indication that disclosure of the Vietnam materials would significantly influence the Senate vote Wednesday on legislation that would require withdrawal of American forces from the war zone by the end of this year.

Materials Called 'Instructive'

Senator George S. McGovern of South Dakota, a cosponsor of that measure and candidate for the Democratic Presidential nomination, said the documents told a story of "almost incredible deception" of Congress and the American people by the highest officials in Government, including the President.

He said that he did not see how any Senator could ever again believe it was safe to permit the executive branch to make foreign policy alone, and added:

"We would make a serious mistake to assume the kind of deception revealed in these documents began and ended with the Johnson Administration."

Senator Hugh Scott of Pennsylvania, the Republican leader, said that the "release" of the documents was "a bad thing, it's a federal crime." But he described their content as "very instructive and somewhat shocking."

"I think the American people have never been told as much as they could digest about the war until President Nixon assumed office," he added. "He has been more than candid. This President has taken the people into his confidence more than anyone else."

Asked whether The Times should continue publication of its articles, Senator Scott said the paper would have to decide "on its good judgment."

Representative Paul N. McCloskey Jr. of California, who has talked of challenging Mr Nixon for the Presidency in th Republican primaries next year discussed The Times article and underlying Pentagon paper on the floor of the House.

Deception Is Charged

He said "the issue of truthfulness in Government is a problem as serious as that of ending the war itself." He also complained of "deceptive," "incomplete" and "misleading" briefings given to him during a recent visit to Southeast Asia, often, he said, with officers who knew the statements to be incorrect standing mute in his presence.

"This deception is not a matter of protecting secret information from the enemy," Mr. McCloskey said. "The intention is to conceal information from the people of the United State as if we were the enemy."

Robert S. McNamara, the former Secretary of Defense, who commissioned the Pentagon study in 1967, was reported to have sent the copy later delivered to him to the National Archives.

Mr. McNamara turned down several invitations to make a public comment today on the ground that this was inappropriate to his present duties as President of the International Bank for Reconstruction and Development—the World Bank.

UNITED STATES DISTRICT COURT
SOUTHERN DISTRICT OF NEW YORK
- - - - - - - - - - - - - - - - - - - -X

UNITED STATES OF AMERICA,   :

                          Plaintiff,   :   ORDER TO SHOW
                                                      CAUSE
                                             :   _____

              -v-   :   71 Civ. 2662

                                             :
NEW YORK TIMES COMPANY, ARTHUR
OCHS SULZBERGER, HARDING F. BANCROFT,   :
IVAN VEIT, FRANCIS A. COX, JAMES C.
GOODALE, SYDNEY GRUSON, WALTER   :
MATTSON, JOHN McCABE, JOHN MORTIMER,
JAMES RESTON, JOHN B. OAKES, A. M.   :
ROSENTHAL, DANIEL SCHWARZ, CLIFTON
DANIEL, TOM WICKER, E. W. KENWORTHY,   :
FOX BUTTERFIELD, GERALD GOLD, ALLAN
M. SIEGAL, SAMUEL ABT, NEIL SHEEHAN   :
and HEDRICK SMITH,
                                             :

                          Defendants.   :
- - - - - - - - - - - - - - - - - - - -X

     Upon the motion of plaintiff, United States of America,

for a Temporary Restraining Order and Preliminary Injunction

the verified Compalint in this action, the annexed affidavits

of J. Fred Buzhardt, General Counsel of the Department of

Defense, and Robert C. Mardian, Assistant Attorney General

of the United States, sworn to June 15, 1971, and all other

pleadings and proceedings heretofore had herein, and

sufficient cause appearing therefor, it is hereby

     ORDERED, that defendants show cause, if any there be,

before this Court at Room 506, United States Court House,

Foley Square, New York, N. Y. on the 18th day of June, 1971,

at 10 A.M.   , or as soon thereafter as counsel

can be heard, why an order of this Court should not be made (i)

enjoining and restraining the defendants; New York Times

Company, Sulzberger, Bancroft, Veit, Cox, Goodale, Gruson, Mattson, McCabe, Mortimer, Reston, Oakes, Rosenthal, Schwarz, Daniel, Wicker, Kenworthy, Butterfield, Gold, Siegal, Abt, Sheehan, and Smith, their agents, servants, and employees, and all other persons in active concert or participation with them, and each of them, from further dissemination, disclosure or divulgence of the Top Secret or Secret documents referred to in said verified Complaint, or any portions thereof, and (ii) directing the aforesaid defendants to deliver to this Court forthwith all the aforementioned documents and any copies, excerpts, duplications, or other tangible evidence of such documents to be held by this Court pending the final determination of this cause, and for such other and further relief as is just; and it is further

ORDERED, that service of a copy of this order, and of all the papers upon which it is based, in the manner provided for by the Federal Rules of Civil Procedure for the service of a summons, shall be made on or before the 15th day of June 1971, at 5:30 P.M.

Dated: New York, N. Y.
        June 15th, 1971.

_____
              U. S. D. J.

2

UNITED STATES DISTRICT COURT
FOR THE
SOUTHERN DISTRICT OF NEW YORK

UNITED STATES OF AMERICA,
    Plaintiff   )
)
)
         v.   )   <u>AFFIDAVIT</u>
)
NEW YORK TIMES COMPANY, et al.,)
    Defendants   )

J. FRED BUZHARDT, being duly sworn, deposes and says:

1. I am the General Counsel of the Department of
Defense.

2. I have reviewed the 47-volume study entitled:
"History of U. S. Decision - Making Process on Vietnam
Policy," also known as "United States - Vietnam Relations"
covering the period 1945-1967, which was prepared in 1967-
1968 at the direction of then Secretary of Defense Robert
McNamara. The aforesaid study is currently classified
"Top Secret - Sensitive," pursuant to the provisions of
Executive Order 10501 and the contents thereof relate to
the national defense of the United States. The excerpts
appearing in the New York <u>Times</u>' editions of June 13 and
14, 1971, under the caption "Key Texts From Pentagon's
Vietnam Study", contains the source material from which
the 47-volume study was drawn, and that source material is
variously classified as "Top Secret" and "Secret"; pursuant
to the aforesaid Executive Order. Publication of the said
exerpts has prejudiced the defense interests of the United
States and publication of additional excerpts or material
from the aforesaid study would further prejudice the defense

interests of the United States and result in irreparable injury to the national defense.

3. Deponent further says that the New York <u>Times</u> edition of June 13, 1971, asserts the New York <u>Times</u> has also in its possession a summary of a document entitled "The Command and Control Study of the Tonkin Gulf incident done by the Defense Department's Weapons System Evaluation Group in 1965,"; that this document is currently classified "Top Secret," pursuant to the provision of Executive Order 10501 and the contents thereof relate to the national defense of the United States; that publication of the aforesaid document would prejudice the defense interests of the United States and result in irreparable injury to the national defense.

4. Deponent further says that the New York <u>Times</u> was not authorized by the United States Government or any authorized officer thereof to have possession of the aforesaid 47-volume study, the internal documents from which it was drawn, or the study of the Gulf of Tonkin incident, or to publish the contents of the same.

J. FRED BUZHARDT
General Counsel
Department of Defense

Subscribed and sworn to
before me this 15 day of
June , 1971.

Notary Public

RALPH I. LEE
Notary Public, State of New York
No. 41-252838   Queens County
Term Expires March 30, 1973

UNITED STATES DISTRICT COURT
FOR THE
SOUTHERN DISTRICT OF NEW YORK

UNITED STATES OF AMERICA,   )
    Plaintiff   )
)
)
    v.   )   Affidavit
)
)
NEW YORK TIMES COMPANY, et al.,)
    Defendants   )

ROBERT C. MARDIAN, Being duly sworn, deposes and says:

1. I am the Assistant Attorney General of the United States, in charge of the Internal Security Division of the Department of Justice.

2. At or about 7:00 p.m. on June 14, 1971, I placed a call to Harding F. Bancroft, Executive Vice President of the New York _Times_ and in response to said call, I talked to a person who identified himself as Harding F. Bancroft, Executive Vice President of the New York _Times_, hereinafter referred to as defendant Bancroft.

3. I identified myself to said defendant Bancroft and informed him of the fact that the Attorney General of the United States had transmitted a telegram, a copy of which is attached hereto as Exhibit A, which is incorporated by reference as though fully set forth in this affidavit. I read the said telegram to the said defendant Bancroft and requested that he and the New York _Times_ comply with the request of the Attorney General set forth therein.

4. Defendant Bancroft informed me he would consider the request and advise me of the decision of the New York <u>Times</u> within an hour. At or about 8:30 p.m. on day aforesaid, I received a call from a person identifying himself as defendant Bancroft, who told me that a decision had been reached to the effect hereinafter set forth and introduced a person whom he identified as Sidney Gruson, one of the defendants herein.

5. Defendant Gruson read me a statement to the effect that the New York <u>Times</u> had received the telegram, attached as Exhibit A and had concluded that the New York <u>Times</u> must respectfully deny the request of the Attorney General and unless enjoined, would continue to publish the balance of the series of articles announced in the June 13, 1971 issue of their newspaper.

(signature)

ROBERT C. MARDIAN
Assistant Attorney General of
the United States

Subscribed and sworn to before me _in Alexandria, Virginia,_
on the ___15th___ day of _July_, 1971.

(signature)
Notary Public

My Commission Expires: August 24, 1974

UNITED STATES OF AMERICA,
    Plaintiff

          v.

NEW YORK TIMES COMPANY, ARTHUR
OCHS SULZBERGER, HARDING F.
BANCROFT, IVAN VEIT, FRANCIS A.
COX, JAMES C. GOODALE, SYDNEY
GRUSON, WALTER MATTSON, JOHN
McCABE, JOHN MORTIMER, JAMES
RESTON, JOHN B. OAKES, A.M.
ROSENTHAL, DANIEL SCHWARZ,
CLIFTON DANIEL, TOM WICKER,
E.W. KENWORTHY, FOX BUTTERFIELD,
GERALD GOLD, ALLAN M. SIEGAL,
SAMUEL ABT, NEIL SHEEHAN and
HEDRICK SMITH,
    Defendants

71 CIV. 2662

Complaint

The United States of America, by its attorney, Whitney

North Seymour, Jr., United States Attorney for the Southern

District of New York, at the direction of the Attorney

General of the United States, brings this action against the

defendants and alleges as follows:

    1. This Court has jurisdiction over the subject matter

of this action pursuant to Title 28, United States Code,

Section 1345.

    2. This is a civil action to obtain an Order enjoining

the dissemination, disclosure or divulgence without authority

by the defendants of official information classified "Top

or Secret

Secret"/in the interests of the national defense under the authority and pursuant to the requirements of Executive Order 10501 entitled "Safeguarding Classified Information".

3. Defendant New York _Times_ Company is a corporation with its principal place of business in the City and State of New York and which publishes a daily newspaper under the title of the New York _Times_. The individual defendants are employees and/or officers of the aforementioned company, serving in the following capacities: Arthur Ochs Sulzberger, President and Publisher; Harding F. Bancroft, Executive Vice President; Ivan Veit, Executive Vice President; Francis A. Cox, Vice President; James C. Goodale, Vice President, Sydney Gruson, Vice President; Walter Mattson, Vice President; John McCabe, Vice President; John Mortimer, Vice President; James Reston, Vice President; John B. Oakes, Editorial Page Editor; A.M. Rosenthal, Managing Editor; Daniel Schwarz, Sunday Editor; Clifton Daniel, Associate Editor; Tom Wicker, Associate Editor. Defendants Neil Sheehan, Hedrick Smith, E.W. Kenworthy, Fox Butterfield, Gerald Gold, Allan M. Siegal and Samuel Abt are employees and/or reporters for the aforementioned publication.

4. At a time and place and in a manner unknown to the plaintiff the defendants without lawful authority obtained a copy of certain documents consisting of 47 volumes entitled

"History of U.S. Decision-Making Process on Vietnam Policy",
covering the period 1945-1967, prepared in 1967-1968 at the
direction of then Secretary of Defense Robert McNamara and
which is and at all times material herein has been classified
"Top Secret-Sensitive", and the internal documents from which
the said study was drawn are variously classified as "Top Secret"
and "Secret," pursuant to the aforementioned Executive Order 10501
as evidenced by the attached affidavit of J. Fred Buzhardt,
General Counsel of the United States Department of Defense.

5. Also, at a time and place and in a manner unknown to
the plaintiff the defendants without lawful authority obtained
a copy of a document described as a "one-volume command and
control study of the Gulf of Tonkin incident" dated February 26,
1965, prepared for the Joint Chiefs of Staff by the Weapons
Systems Evaluation Group of the United States Department of
Defense which is and at all times material herein has been
classified "Top Secret" pursuant to the aforementioned Executive
Order 10501, as evidenced by the aforementioned attached affidavit.

6. As defined in Executive Order 10501 "Top Secret"
information is ". . . that information or material the defense
aspect of which is paramount, and the unauthorized disclosure
of which could result in exceptionally grave damage to the
Nation such as leading to a definite break in diplomatice
relations affecting the defense of the United States, an armed
attack against the United States or its allies, a war, or the
compromise of military or defense plans, or intelligence operations, or scientific or technological developments vital to the
national defense,"and   "Secret" information is defined as

" . . . defense information or material the unauthorized disclosure of which could result in serious damage to the Nation,
such as by jeopardizing the international relations of the United
States, endangering the effectiveness of a program or policy of
vital importance to the national defense, or compromising important military or defense plans, scientific or technological
developments important to national defense, or information
revealing important intelligence operations."

7. On June 13, 1971, the New York Times published an
article entitled "Vietnam Archive: Pentagon Study Traces Three
Decades of Growing U.S. Involvement," authoried by defendant
Sheehan and an article entitled "Vast Study of War Took a
Year", authored by defendant Smith. These articles were represented to be the initial article in a series written by defendants Sheehan, Smith, defendant E. W. Kenworthy and defendant
Fox Butterfield. The series was represented to be one reporting on [a history of] the United States' decision making process
on Vietnam policy for the period 1945-1967. The articles in the
series and the classified documents upon which they are based
were edited by defendants Gold, Siegal, and Abt. In the aforementioned article, authored by the defendant Sheehan, it is
asserted that "most of the study (described in the article as
"a massive study of how the United States went to war in Indochina, conducted by the Pentagon three years ago") and many
of the appended documents have been obtained by the New
York Times and will be described and presented in a series
of articles beginning today." It was also asserted in the
June 13 issue of the New York Times with respect to the

aforementioned "one-volume command and control study" that

the <u>Times</u> had obtained a summary of that study.

8. On June 13 and 14, the defendants have without

authority intentionally and knowingly published excerpts and

other portions of the aforementioned classified defense

information knowing that such information had been classi-
                        or "Secret"
fied "Top Secret"/pursuant to the authority of Executive

Order 10501. At the time of such publication the said

defendants, and each of them, knew, or had reason to believe,

that such information could be used to the injury of the
                        and
United States/to the advantage of a foreign nation and

notwithstanding such knowledge and belief did willfully

communicate, deliver and transmit said information by the

publication thereof, to persons not entitled to receive such

information.

9. The publication of the information published as

aforesaid on June 13 and June 14, 1971, has prejudiced the

defense interests of the United States and the publication of

additional excerpts from the documents hereinbefore referred

to would further prejudice the defense interests of the United

States and result in irreparable injury to the United States.

10. The defendants have publicly announced their avowed

determination to continue publishing excerpts and other
                                        or Secret
portions of the aforementioned "Top Secret"/documents relating

to the national defense and unless the defendants, and all persons in active concert and participation with the defendants are enjoined from such, the national defense interests of the United States and the nation's security will suffer immediate and irreparable harm, for which injury plaintiff has no adequate remedy at law.

WHEREFORE, the plaintiff, the UNITED STATES OF AMERICA, prays:

1. That this Court enter its Order enjoining the defendants, their agents, servants, and employees and all persons acting in concert with them, from further dissemination, disclosure or divulgence of the information heretofore described in paragraphs 4 and 5 of this complaint, or any excerpt, portion or summary thereof.

2. That the Court order the defendants and each of them having possession of the documents referred to in the complaint to deliver said documents and any copies, excerpts, duplications, or other tangible evidence of such documents to the plaintiff herein.

3. That this Court, pending the final determination of this cause, issue a preliminary injunction, restraining and enjoining the defendants in the manner and form aforesaid.

4. That, pending the issuance of the aforesaid preliminary injunction, this Court issue forthwith a temporary restraining order restraining and enjoining the defendants in the manner and form aforesaid and further ordering said defendants to deliver to this Court all the documents and

materials referred to in paragraph 2 of the prayer herein to be held by this Court <u>in</u> <u>camera</u> pending a final order of this Court.

5. That this Court grant such other, further, and different relief as the Court may deem just and equitable.

                    JOHN N. MITCHELL
                    Attorney General of the United States

                    WHITNEY NORTH SEYMOUR, JR.
                    United States Attorney

By: _____
                    MICHAEL D. HESS
                    Chief, Civil Division

NY K TIMES NY

X

NY K TIMES NY

ARTHUR OCHSSULZBERGER

PRESIDENT AND PUBLISHER

THE NEW YORK TIMES

NEW YORK, NEW YORK

I HAVE BEEN ADVISED BY THE SECRETARY OF DEFENSE THAT THE MATERIAL PUBLISHED IN THE NEW YORK TIMES ON JUNE L3, 14, 1971 CAPTIONED "KEY TEXTS FROM PENTAGON'S VIETNAM STUDY" CONTAINS INFORMATION RELATING TO THE NATIONAL DEFENSE OF THE UNITED STATES AND BEARS A TOP SECRET CLASSIFICATION.

AS, SUCH, PUBLICATION OF THIS INFORMATION IS DIRECTLY PROHIBITED BY THE PROVISIONS OF THE ESPIONAGE LAW, TITLE 18, UNITED STATES CODE, SECTION 793.

MOREOVER, FURTHER PUBLICATION OF INFORMATION OF THIS CHARACTER WILL CAUSEIREXXX IRREPARABLE INJURY TO THE DEFENSE INTERESTS OF THE UNITED STATES.

14

ACCORDINGLY, I RESPECTFULLY REQUEST THAT YOU PUBLISH NO
FURTHER INFORMATION OF THIS CHARACTER AND ADVISE ME THAT
YOU HAVE MADE ARRANGEMENTS FOR THE RETURN OF THESE
DOCUMENTS TO THE DEPARTMENT OF DEFENSE.

JOHN N. MITCHELL
ATTORNEY GENERAL

ACK PLS

NEW YP
NEW YORK TIMES RECED WELL THANKS
FBI WASH DC

15

UNITED STATES DISTRICT COURT
SOUTHERN DISTRICT OF NEW YORK

- - - - - - - - - - - - - - - - - - - -x

UNITED STATES OF AMERICA,   :

                                    Plaintiff, :

                                             :

            v.   :

                                             :

NEW YORK TIMES COMPANY, ARTHUR   :
OCHS SULZBERGER, HARDING F.
BANCROFT, IVAN VEIT, FRANCIS A. COX,   :
JAMES C. GOODALE, SYDNEY GRUSON,
WALTER MATTSON, JOHN McCABE, JOHN   :
MORTIMER, JAMES RESTON, JOHN B. OAKES,
A. M. ROSENTHAL, DANIEL SCHWARZ,   :
CLIFTON DANIEL, TOM WICKER, E. W.
KENWORTHY, FOX BUTTERFIELD, GERALD   :
GOLD, ALLAN M. SIEGAL, SAMUEL ABT,
NEIL SHEEHAN and HEDRICK SMITH,   :

                                    Defendants. :

- - - - - - - - - - - - - - - - - - - -x

MEMORANDUM OF LAW

Preliminary Statement

This action has been commenced to preliminarily
and permanently enjoin defendants and their agents from
further disseminating documents consisting of forty-seven
volumes entitled "History of U. S. Decision-Making Process

16

on Vietnam Policy". Plaintiffs further seek to gain
the recovery of the aforementioned documents from
defendants. This memorandum is submitted in support
of plaintiff's application for an Order temporarily
restraining the defendants from further disseminating
the aforementioned documents and requiring the delivery
of the documents to this Court pending the determination
of plaintiff's motion for a preliminary injunction.

Statute Relied Upon

Section 793(d) of Title 18 of the United
States Code provides as follows:

> "Whoever, lawfully having poss-
> ession of, access to, control over, or
> being entrusted with any document, writing,
> code book, signal book, sketch, photograph,
> photographic negative, blueprint, plan,
> map, model, instrument, appliance, or note
> relating to the national defense, or
> information relating to the national defense
> which information the possessor has reason
> to believe could be used to the injury of the
> United States or to the advantage of any
> foreign nation, willfully communicates,
> delivers, transmits or causes to be com-
> municated, delivered, or transmitted or

2

> attempts to communicate, deliver,
> transmit or cause to be communicated,
> delivered or transmitted the same to
> any person not entitled to receive it,
> or willfully retains the same and fails
> to deliver it on demand to the officer or
> employee of the United States entitled to
> receive it;"

ARGUMENT

Defendants are in possession of a forty-seven volume study entitled "History of United States Decision-Making Process on Vietnam Policy". This study is currently classified as "Top Secret-Sensitive"* pursuant to the provisions of Executive Order 10501. As defined in the Executive Order, top secret information is "that information or material the defense aspect of which is paramount, and the unauthorized disclosure of which could result in exceptionally grave damage to the nation . . . ."

---

* In determining whether information properly has been classified top secret, the test to be applied by the Court is whether the classifying authority acted capriciously. Epstein v. Resor, 296 F. Supp. 214 (N.D. Calif. 1969).

3

On June 13, 14 and 15, 1971, defendants published documents contained in the study. By telegram dated June 14, 1971, defendants were advised by the Attorney General of the United States that further publication of the contents of the study will cause irreparable injury to the defense interests of the United States. In the telegram, defendants were requested to cease publication of the contents of the study and to return the study to the Department of Defense. Defendants have expressed the intention to continue to publish documents contained in the study until they are restrained from doing so by an Order of this Court.

Section 793(d) of Title 18 of the United States Code provides for criminal penalties against a person who, while lawfully in possession of information relating to the national defense which could be used to the injury of the United States, willfully communicates that information to persons not entitled to receive it or willfully fails to deliver it, on demand, to the officer of the United States entitled to receive it. The applicability of Section 793(d)

4

has not been restricted to criminal actions. Dubin v. United States, 289 F.2d 651 (Ct. Cl. 1961).

Further publication of the contents of the study and defendants' continued refusal to return all of the papers to the Department of Defense, will constitute a violation of Section 793(d). Moreover, such publication will result in irreparable injury to the interests of the United States, for which there is no adequate remedy at law. An injury is deemed irreparable when it cannot be adequately compensated in damages due to the nature of the injury itself or where there exists no pecuniary standard for the measurement of the damages. Luckenbach S.S. Co. v. Norton, 21 F. Supp. 707. 709 (E.D. Pa. 1937). Irreparable injury also means "that species of damage, whether great or small, that ought not to be submitted to on the one hand or inflicted on the other". Anderson v. Sooza, 38 Cal. 2d 825, 243 P.2d 497, 503 (1952). The inadequacy of a remedy at law exists where the circumstances demand preventive relief. Cruikshank v. Bidwell, 176 U.S. 73, 81 (1900).

5

In the instant case, defendants will suffer

no injury if they cease to publish the contents of the

study in their possession pending the determination of

plaintiff's motion for a preliminary injunction. On the

other hand, the national interest of the United States

may be seriously damaged if the defendants continue to

publish the contents of the study. Under circumstances

in which no injury will result to defendants from the

cessation of publication of the study in their possession

and irreparable injury may result to the United States,

the granting of a temporary restraining Order is appropriate.

CONCLUSION

For the foregoing reasons, the plaintiff's

application for a temporary restraining Order pending the

determination of its motion for a preliminary injunction

should be granted.   Plaintiff's application for an

Order temporarily restraining the further publication

of the contents of the study in defendants' possession

should be granted.

Dated: New York, New York

June 15, 1971.   Respectfully submitted,

                        WHITNEY NORTH SEYMOUR, JR.
                        United States Attorney for the
                        Southern District of New York,
                        Attorney for the Plaintiff
                        United States of America.

MICHAEL D. HESS
HOWARD S. SUSSMAN
MILTON SHERMAN,
Assistant United States Attorneys,

    Of Counsel.

UNITED STATES DISTRICT COURT

SOUTHERN DISTRICT OF NEW YORK

--------------------------------------x

UNITED STATES OF AMERICA,

                Plaintiff,

    -against-

NEW YORK TIMES COMPANY, ARTHUR
OCHS SULZBERGER, HARDING F.
BANCROFT, IVAN VEIT, FRANCIS A.
COX, JAMES C. GOODALE, SYDNEY
GRUSON, WALTER MATTSON, JOHN
MC CABE, JOHN MORTIMER, JAMES
RESTON, JOHN B. OAKES, A. M.
ROSENTHAL, DANIEL SCHWARZ,
CLIFTON DANIEL, TOM WICKER,
E. W. KENWORTHY, FOX BUTTER-
FIELD, GERALD GOLD, ALLAN M.
SIEGAL, SAMUEL ABT, NEIL
SHEEHAN and HEDRICK SMITH,

                Defendants.

71 Civ. 2662

--------------------------------------x

MEMORANDUM

GURFEIN, D. J.

The United States seeks a temporary restraining order
and a preliminary injunction against The New York Times,
its publisher and other officers and employees to restrain
them from further dissemination or disclosure of certain
alleged top secret or secret documents of the United States
referred to in a verified complaint filed therewith.

I have granted the order to show cause as to why a
preliminary injunction against the defendants should not be
entered and have made it returnable Friday morning, June 18.
Preliminarily thereto the Government has requested a
temporary restraining order and also a direction from
this Court to require the defendants to deliver to the
Court certain documents and other tangible evidence to be
held by the Court pending final determination of the cause.
At this stage of the proceeding I do not direct The New York
Times or the other defendants to produce the documents pending the outcome of the litigation. I do not believe that
The New York Times will wilfully disregard the spirit of
our restraining order. I am restraining The New York Times
and the other defendants, however, from publishing or further
disseminating or disclosing the documents consisting of 47
volumes entitled "HISTORY OF UNITED STATES DECISION MAKING
PROCESS ON VIETNAM POLICY" covering the period 1945-67, prepared in 1967-1968 at the direction of the then Secretary of
Defense Robert McNamara, the internal documents from which
the aforesaid documents were prepared, and a one volume
"COMMAND AND CONTROL STUDY OF THE TONKIN GULF INCIDENT" prepared in 1965 for the Joint Chiefs of Staff by the Weapon
System Evaluation Group of the United States Department of

-2-

Defense, pending the hearing of the Government's application for a preliminary injunction.

The questions raised by this action are serious and fundamental. They involve not only matters of procedure, but matters of substance and presumptively of constitutional implication as well. I have, in effect, been asked by the parties to pass upon the merits of the litigation upon the arguments made on the order to show cause. I believe that the matter is so important and so involved with the history of the relationship between the security of the Government and a free press that a more thorough briefing than the parties have had an opportunity to do is required. I have granted the restraining order because in my opinion any temporary harm that may result from not publishing during the pendency of the application for a preliminary injunction is far outweighed by the irreparable harm that could be done to the interests of the United States Government if it should ultimately prevail. I have intentionally expressed no opinion on the merits, but I believe this matter is brought in good faith by the United States and that on the balancing of interests mentioned, both parties deserve a full consideration of the issues raised.

-3-

Accordingly, the restraining order will be in effect until Saturday afternoon at one o'clock unless the Court directs otherwise.

The parties are requested to brief as thoroughly as possible the points adverted to in the oral argument by 5 p.m. Thursday, June 17, 1971.

                                    _____
                                              U.S.D.J.

Dated: June 15, 1971.

-4-

UNITED STATES DISTRICT COURT
FOR THE
SOUTHERN DISTRICT OF NEW YORK

UNITED STATES OF AMERICA,
    Plaintiff   )
)
)
       v.   )
)

NEW YORK TIMES COMPANY, ARTHUR)
OCHS SULZBERGER, HARDING F.   )
BANCROFT, IVAN VEIT, FRANCIS A.) TEMPORARY RESTRAINING
COX, JAMES C. GOODALE, SYDNEY   )   ORDER
GRUSON, WALTER MATTSON, JOHN   )
McCABE, JOHN MORTIMER, JAMES   )
RESTON, JOHN B. OAKES, A. M.   )
ROSENTHAL, DANIEL SCHWARZ,   )
CLIFTON DANIEL, TOM WICKER,   )
E. W. KENWORTHY, FOX BUTTERFIELD,)
GERALD GOLD, ALLAN M. SIEGAL,   )
SAMUEL ABT, NEIL SHEEHAN and   )
HEDRICK SMITH,   )
    Defendants   )

WHEREAS, in the above-named cause, it has been made to

appear, by the Motion of the United States of America for

a Temporary Restraining Order, as supported by the affidavits

of J. Fred Buzhardt and Robert C. Mardian, the verified

Complaint herein, and by the Motion for Preliminary Injunction,

which were on this _____ day of _____, 1971, presented to

the Honorable _____ Judge of the United

States District Court for the Southern District of New York,

that a Restraining Order preliminary to a hearing upon a

motion for a preliminary injunction should issue because

immediate and irreparable injury, loss or damage will result

to the plaintiff and to the national defense before a

hearing can be had thereon, in that the defendants New York

Times Company, Sulzberger, Bancroft, Veit, Cox, Goodale,

Gruson, Mattson, McCabe, Mortimer, Reston, Oakes,
Rosenthal, Schwarz, Daniel, Wicker, Kenworthy, Butterfield,
Gold, Siegal, Abt, Sheehan, and Smith have publicly
announced their avowed determination to continue publishing excerpts and other portions of Top Secret /documents or Secret
relating to the national defense, namely: certain documents
consisting of 47 volumes entitled "History of U.S. Decision-
Making Process on Vietnam Policy", covering the period 1945-1967,
prepared in 1967-1968 at the direction of than Secretary of
Defense Robert McNamara, the internal documents from which
the aforementioned document was prepared, and a one-volume
"Command and Control Study of the Tonkin Gulf Incident",
prepared in 1965 for the Joint Chiefs of Staff by the
Weapons Systems Evaluation Group of the United States Department
of Defense.

NOW, THEREFORE, on the motion of the plaintiff, it is:

ORDERED that the defendants New York Times Company,
Sulzberger, Bancroft, Veit, Cox, Goodale, Gruson, Mattson,
McCabe, Mortimer, Reston, Oakes, Rosenthal, Schwarz, Daniel,
Wicker, Kenworthy, Butterfield, Gold, Siegal, Abt, Sheehan,
and Smith, their agents, servants, and employees, and all other
persons in active concert or participation with them, and
each of them, be, and they hereby are, restrained from further
dissemination, disclosure or divulgence of the documents
heretofore referred to, or any portions thereof, pending
a hearing on plaintiff's Motion for Preliminary Injunction.

FURTHER ORDERED that the aforesaid defendants deliver
to this Court forthwith all the aforementioned documents and
any copies, excerpts, duplications. or other tangible evidence
of such documents to be held by this Court pending the
final determination of this cause.

FURTHER ORDERED that plaintiff's Motion for Preliminary
Injunction be, and the same hereby is, set for hearing in this
Court on _Wednesday_. 1971, at _16_ o'clock _A_.m.;
and it is

FURTHER ORDERED that the above and foregoing Temporary
Restraining Order shall expire on _Friday June 18_. 1971, _at_
unless it is further extended by order of this Court.

Issued at _4:15_ o'clock _P_.m., this _15th_ day of
June, 1971.

_____
UNITED STATES DISTRICT JUDGE

Vietnam Archive: Pentagon Study Traces 3 Decades of Growing U. S. Involvement

By NEIL SHEEHAN

A massive study of how the United States went to war in Indochina, conducted by the Pentagon three years ago, demonstrates that four administrations progressively developed a sense of commitment to a non-Communist Vietnam, a readiness to fight the North to protect the South, and an ultimate frustration with this effort—to a much greater extent than their public statements acknowledged at the time.

The 3,000-page analysis, to which 4,000 pages of official documents are appended, was commissioned by Secretary of Defense Robert S. McNamara and covers the American involvement in Southeast Asia from World War II to mid-1968—the start of the peace talks in Paris after President Lyndon B. Johnson had set a limit on further military commitments and revealed his intention to retire. Most of the study and many of the appended documents have been obtained by The New York Times and will be described and presented in a series of articles beginning today.

Though far from a complete history, even at 2.5 million words, the study forms a great archive of government decision-making on Indochina over three decades. The study led its 30 to 40 authors and researchers to many broad conclusions and specific findings, including the following:

¶That the Truman Administration's decision to give military aid to France in her colonial war against the Communist-led Vietminh "directly involved" the United States in Vietnam and "set" the course of American policy.

¶That the Eisenhower Administration's decision to rescue a fledgling South Vietnam from a Communist takeover and attempt to undermine the new Communist regime of North Vietnam gave the Administration a "direct role in the ultimate breakdown of the Geneva settlement" for Indochina in 1954.

¶That the Kennedy Administration, though ultimately spared from major escalation decisions by the death of its leader, transformed a policy of "limited-risk gamble," which it inherited, into a "broad commitment" that left President Johnson with a choice between more war and withdrawal.

¶That the Johnson Administration, though the President was reluctant and hesitant to take the final decisions, intensified the covert warfare against North Vietnam and began planning in the spring of 1964 to wage overt war, a full year before it publicly revealed the depth of its involvement and its fear of defeat.

¶That this campaign of growing clandestine military pressure through 1964 and the expanding program of bombing North Vietnam in 1965 were begun despite the judgment of the Government's intelligence community that the measures would not cause Hanoi to cease its support of the Vietcong insurgency in the South, and that the bombing was

Continued on Page 38, Col. 1

Vietnam Archive: Pentagon Study Traces 3 Decades of Rising U.S. Involvement

Continued From Page 1, Col. 7

deemed militarily ineffective within a few months.

¶That these four succeeding administrations built up the American political, military and psychological stakes in Indochina, often more deeply than they realized at the time, with large-scale military equipment to the French in 1950; with acts of sabotage and terror warfare against North Vietnam beginning in 1954; with moves that encouraged and abetted the overthrow of President Ngo Dinh Diem of South Vietnam in 1963; with plans, pledges and threats of further action that sprang to life in the Tonkin Gulf clashes in August, 1964; with the careful preparation of public opinion for the years of open warfare that were to follow; and with the calculation in 1965, as the planes and troops were openly committed to sustained combat, that neither accommodation inside South Vietnam nor early negotiations with North Vietnam would achieve the desired result.

The Pentagon study also ranges beyond such historical judgments. It suggests that the predominant American interest was at first containment of Communism and later the defense of the power, influence and prestige of the United States, in both stages irrespective of conditions in Vietnam.

And it reveals a great deal about the ways in which several administrations conducted their business on a fateful course, with much new information about the roles of dozens of senior officials of both major political parties and a whole generation of military commanders.

The Pentagon study was divided into chronological and thematic chapters of narrative and analysis, each with its own documentation attached. The Times —which has obtained all but one of nearly 40 volumes—has collated these materials into major segments of varying chronological length, from one that broadly covers the two decades before 1960 to one that deals intensively with the agonizing debate in the weeks following the 1968 Tet offensive.

The months from the beginning of 1964 to the Tonkin Gulf incident in August were a pivotal period, the study makes clear, and The Times begins its series with this phase.

The Covert War

The Pentagon papers disclose that in this phase the United States had been mounting clandestine military attacks against North Vietnam and planning to obtain a Congressional resolution that the Administration regarded as the equivalent of a declaration of war. The papers make it clear that these far-reaching measures were not improvised in the heat of the Tonkin crisis.

When the Tonkin incident occurred, the Johnson Administration did not reveal these clandestine attacks, and pushed the previously prepared resolution through both houses of Congress on Aug. 7.

Within 72 hours, the Administration, drawing on a prepared plan, then secretly sent a Canadian emissary to Hanoi. He warned Premier Pham Van Dong that the resolution meant North Vietnam must halt the Communist-led insurgencies in South Vietnam and Laos or "suffer the consequences." [See text, Page 36.]

The section of the Pentagon study dealing with the internal debate, planning and action in the Johnson Administration from the beginning of 1964 to the August clashes between North Vietnamese PT boats and American destroyers—portrayed as a critical period when the groundwork was laid for the wider war that followed—also reveals that the covert military operations had become so extensive by August, 1964, that Thai pilots flying American T-28 fighter planes apparently bombed and strafed North Vietnamese villages near the Laotian border on Aug. 1 and 2.

Moreover, it reports that the Administration was able to order retaliatory air strikes on less than six hours' notice during the Tonkin incident because planning had progressed so far that a list of targets was available for immediate choice. The target list had been drawn up in May, the study reports, along with a draft of the Congressional resolution—all as part of a proposed "scenario" that was to build toward openly acknowledged air attacks on North Vietnam.

Simultaneously, the papers reveal, Secretary McNamara and the Joint Chiefs of Staff also arranged for the deployment of air strike forces to Southeast Asia for the opening phases of the bombing campaign. Within hours of the retaliatory air strikes on Aug. 4 and three days before the passage of the Congressional resolution, the squadrons began their planned moves. [See text.]

'Progressively Escalating Pressure'

What the Pentagon papers call "an elaborate program of covert military operations against the state of North Vietnam" began on Feb. 1, 1964, under the code name Operation Plan 34A. President Johnson ordered the program, on the recommendation of Secretary McNamara, in the hope, held very faint by the intelligence community, that "progressively escalating pressure" from the clandestine attacks might eventually force Hanoi to order the Vietcong guerrillas in Vietnam and the Pathet Lao in Laos to halt their insurrections.

In a memorandum to the President on Dec. 21, 1963, after a two-day trip to Vietnam, Mr. McNamara remarked that the plans, drawn up by the Central Intelligence Agency station and the military command in Saigon, were "an excellent job."

"They present a wide variety of sabotage and psychological operations against North Vietnam from which I believe we should aim to select those that provide maximum pressure with minimum risk," Mr. McNamara wrote. [See text.]

President Johnson, in this period, showed a preference for steps that would remain "noncommitting" to combat, the study found. But weakness in South Vietnam and Communist advances kept driving the planning process. This, in turn, caused the Saigon Government and American officials in Saigon to demand ever more action.

Through 1964, the 34A operations ranged from flights over North Vietnam by U-2 spy planes and kidnappings of North Vietnamese citizens for intelligence information, to parachuting sabotage and psychological-warfare teams into the North, commando raids from the sea to blow up rail and highway bridges and the bombardment of North Vietnamese coastal installations by PT boats.

These "destructive undertakings," as they were described in a report to the President on Jan. 2 1964, from Maj. Gen. Victor H. Krulak of the Marine Corps, were designed "to result in substantial destruction, economic loss and harassment." The tempo and magnitude of the strikes were designed to rise in three phases through 1964 to "targets identified with North Vietnam's economic and industrial well-being."

The clandestine operations were directed for the President by Mr. McNamara through a section of the Joint Chiefs organization called the Office of the Special Assistant for Counterinsurgency and Special Activities. The study says that Mr. McNamara was kept regularly informed of planned and conducted raids by memorandums from General Krulak, who first held the position of special assistant, and then from Maj. Gen. Rollen H. Anthis of the Air Force, who succeeded him in February, 1964. The Joint Chiefs themselves periodically evaluated the operations for Mr. McNamara.

Secretary of State Dean Rusk was also informed, if in less detail.

The attacks were given "interagency clearance" in Washington, the study says, by coordinating them with the State Department and the Central Intelligence Agency, including advance monthly schedules of the raids from General Anthis.

The Pentagon account and the documents show that William P. Bundy, the Assistant Secretary of State for Far Eastern Affairs, and John T. McNaughton, head of the Pentagon's politico-military operations as the Assistant Secretary of Defense for International Security Affairs, were the senior civilian officials who supervised the distribution of the schedules and the other aspects of interagency coordination for Mr. McNamara and Mr. Rusk.

The analyst notes that the 34A program differed in a significant respect from the relatively low-level and unsuccessful intelligence and sabotage operations that the C.I.A. had earlier been carrying out in North Vietnam.

Air Raids Were Planned Jointly

The 34A attacks were a military effort under the control in Saigon of Gen. Paul D. Harkins, chief of the United States Military Assistance Command there. He ran them through a special branch of his command called the Studies and Observations Group. It drew up the advance monthly schedules for approval in Washington. Planning was done jointly with the South Vietnamese and it was they or "hired personnel," apparently Asian mercenaries, who performed the raids, but General Harkins was in charge.

The second major segment of the Administration's covert war against North Vietnam consisted of air operations in Laos. A force of propeller-driven T-28 fighter-bombers, varying from about 25 to 40 aircraft, had been organized there. The planes bore Laotian Air Force markings, but only some belonged to that air force. The rest were manned by pilots of Air America (a pseudo-private airline run by the C.I.A.) and by Thai pilots under the control of Ambassador Leonard Unger. [See text.]

Reconnaissance flights by regular United States Air Force and Navy jets, code-named Yankee Team, gathered photographic intelligence for bombing raids by the T-28's against North Vietnamese and Pathet Lao troops in Laos.

The Johnson Administration gradually stepped up these air operations in Laos through the spring and summer of 1964 in what became a kind of preview of the bombing of the North. The escalation occurred both because of ground advances by the North Vietnamese and the Pathet Lao and because of the Administration's desire to bring more military pressure against North Vietnam.

As the intensity of the T-28 strikes rose, they crept closer to the North Vietnamese border. The United States Yankee Team jets moved from high-altitude reconnaissance at the beginning of the year to low-altitude reconnaissance in May. In June, armed escort jets were added to the reconnaissance missions. The escort jets began to bomb and strafe North Vietnamese and Pathet Lao troops and installations whenever the reconnaissance planes were fired upon.

The destroyer patrols in the Gulf of Tonkin, code-named De Soto patrols, were the third element in the covert military pressures against North Vietnam. While the purpose of the patrols was mainly psychological, as a show of force, the destroyers collected the kind of intelligence on North Vietnamese warning radars and coastal defenses that would be useful to 34A raiding parties or, in the event of a bombing campaign, to pilots. The first patrol was conducted by the destroyer Craig without incident in February and March, in the early days of the 34A operations.

Separate Chain of Command

The analyst states that before the August Tonkin incident there was no attempt to involve the destroyers with the 34A attacks or to use the ships as bait for North Vietnamese retaliation. The patrols were run through a separate naval chain of command.

Although the highest levels of the Administration sent the destroyers into the gulf while the 34A raids were taking place, the Pentagon study, as part of its argument that a deliberate provocation was not intended, in effect says that the Administration did not believe that the North Vietnamese would dare to attack the ships.

But the study makes it clear that the physical presence of the destroyers provided the elements for the Tonkin clash. And immediately after the reprisal air strikes, the Joint Chiefs of Staff and Assistant Secretary of Defense McNaughton put forward a "provocation strategy" proposing to repeat the clash as a pretext for bombing the North.

Of the three elements of the covert war, the analyst cites the 34A raids as the most important. The "unequivocal" American responsibility for them "carried with it an implicit symbolic and psychological intensification of the U.S. commitment," he writes. "A firebreak had been crossed."

The fact that the intelligence community and even the Joint Chiefs gave the program little chance of compelling Hanoi to stop the Vietcong and the Pathet Lao, he asserts, meant that "a demand for more was stimulated and an expectation of more was aroused."

The accompanying article, as well as the rest of the series on the Pentagon's study of the Vietnam war, was a result of investigative reporting by Neil Sheehan of The New York Times Washington bureau. The series has been written by Mr. Sheehan, Hedrick Smith, E. W. Kenworthy and Fox Butterfield. The articles and documents were edited by Gerald Gold, Allan M. Siegal and Samuel Abt.

Warning by the Joint Chiefs

On Jan. 22, 1964, a week before the 34A raids started, the Joint Chiefs warned Mr. McNamara in a memorandum signed by the Chairman, Gen. Maxwell D. Taylor, that while "we are wholly in favor of executing the covert actions against North Vietnam . . . it would be idle to conclude that these efforts will have a decisive effect" on Hanoi's will to support the Vietcong. [See text.]

The Joint Chiefs said the Administration "must make ready to conduct increasingly bolder actions," including "aerial bombing of key North Vietnam targets, using United States resources under Vietnamese cover," sending American ground troops to South Vietnam and employing "United States forces as necessary in direct actions against North Vietnam."

And, after a White House strategy meeting on Feb. 20, President Johnson ordered that "contingency planning for pressures against North Vietnam should be speeded up."

"Particular attention should be given to shaping such pressures so as to produce the maximum credible deterrent effect on Hanoi," the order said.

The impelling force behind the Administration's desire to step up the action during this period was its recognition of the steady deterioration in the positions of the pro-American governments in Laos and South Vietnam, and the corresponding weakening of the United States hold on both countries. North Vietnamese and Pathet Lao advances in Laos were seen as having a direct impact on the morale of the anti-Communist forces in South Vietnam, the primary American concern.

This deterioration was also concealed from Congress and the public as much as possible to provide the Administration with maximum flexibility to determine its moves as it chose from behind the scenes.

The United States found itself particularly unable to cope with the Vietcong insurgency, first through the Saigon military regime of Gen. Duong Van Minh and later through that of Gen. Nguyen Khanh, who seized power in a coup d'état on Jan. 30, 1964. Accordingly, attention focused more and more on North Vietnam as "the root of the problem," in the words of the Joint Chiefs.

Walt W. Rostow, the dominant intellectual of the Administration, had given currency to this idea and provided the theoretical framework for escalation. His concept, first enunciated in a speech at Fort Bragg, N.C., in 1961, was that a revolution could be dried up by cutting off external sources of support and supply.

Where North Vietnam was concerned, Mr. Rostow had evolved another theory —that a credible threat to bomb the industry Hanoi had so painstakingly constructed out of the ruins of the French Indochina War would be enough to frighten the country's leaders into ordering the Vietcong to halt their activities in the South.

'No Longer a Guerrilla Fighter'

In a memorandum on Feb. 13, 1964, Mr. Rostow told Secretary of State Rusk that President Ho Chi Minh "has an industrial complex to protect: he is no longer a guerrilla fighter with nothing to lose."

The Administration was firmly convinced from interceptions of radio traffic between North Vietnam and the guerrillas in the South that Hanoi controlled and directed the Vietcong. Intelligence analyses of the time stated, however, that "the primary sources of Communist strength in South Vietnam are indigenous," arising out of the revolutionary social aims of the Communists and their identification with the nationalist cause during the independence struggle against France in the nineteen-fifties.

The study shows that President Johnson and most of his key advisers would not accept this intelligence analysis that bombing the North would have no lasting effect on the situation in the South, although there was division — even among those who favored a bombing campaign if necessary—over the extent to which Vietcong fortunes were dependent on the infiltration of men and arms from North Vietnam.

William Bundy and Mr. Rusk mentioned on several occasions the need to obtain more evidence of this infiltration to build a case publicly for stronger actions against North Vietnam.

Focus Turns to Bombing

As the Vietcong rebellion gathered strength, so did interest in bombing the North as a substitute for successful prosecution of the counterinsurgency campaign in the South, or at least as an effort to force Hanoi to reduce guerrilla activity to a level where the feeble Saigon Government could handle it.

This progression in Administration thinking was reflected in Mr. McNamara's reports to President Johnson after the Secretary's trips to Vietnam in December and March.

In his December memorandum recommending initiation of the covert 34A raids, Mr. McNamara painted a "gloomy picture" of South Vietnam, with the Vietcong controlling most of the rice and population heartland of the Mekong Delta south and west of Saigon. "We should watch the situation very carefully," he concluded, "running scared, hoping for the best, but preparing for more forceful moves if the situation does not show early signs of improvement."

Then, in his memorandum of March 16 on his latest trip, Mr. McNamara reported that "the situation has unquestionably been growing worse" and recommended military planning for two programs of "new and significant pressures upon North Vietnam."

The first, to be launched on 72 hours' notice, was described as "Border Control and Retaliatory Actions." These would include assaults by Saigon's army against infiltration routes along the Ho Chi Minh Trail network of supply lines through southeastern Laos, "hot pursuit" of the guerrillas into Cambodia, "retaliatory bombing strikes" into North Vietnam by the South Vietnamese Air Force "on a tit-for-tat basis" in response to guerrilla attacks, and "aerial mining. . .(possibly with United States assistance) of the major. . .ports in North Vietnam." The words in parentheses are Mr. McNamara's.

Beyond a Tit-for-Tat Basis

The second program, called "Graduated Overt Military Pressure," was to be readied to begin on 30 days' notice. "This program would go beyond reacting on a tit-for-tat basis," Mr. McNamara told the President. "It would include air attacks against military and possibly industrial targets." The raids would be carried out by Saigon's air force and by an American air commando squadron code-named Farmgate, then operating in South Vietnam with planes carrying South Vietnamese markings. To conduct the air strikes, they would be reinforced by three squadrons of United States Air Force B-57 jet bombers flown in from Japan.

President Johnson approved Mr. McNamara's recommendations at a National Security Council meeting on March 17, 1964, directing that planning "proceed energetically."

Mr. McNamara had advocated trying a number of measures to improve the

Continued on Following Page

Study Traces Growing U.S. Will to Use Force in North as Effort in South Flagged

Continued from Preceding Page

Saigon Government's performance first, before resorting to overt escalation. "There would be the problem of marshaling the case to justify such action, the problem of Communist escalation and the problem of dealing with pressures for premature or 'stacked' negotiations," he remarked in his March memorandum.

His description of negotiations echoed a belief in the Administration that the Government of General Khanh was incapable of competing politically with the Communists. Therefore, any attempt to negotiate a compromise political settlement of the war between the Vietnamese themselves was to be avoided because it would result in a Communist take-over and the destruction of the American position in South Vietnam.

Similarly, any internal accommodation between the opposing Vietnamese forces under the vague "neutralization" formula for Vietnam that had been proposed by President de Gaulle of France that June was seen as tantamount to the same thing, a Communist victory. In his March memorandum, Mr. McNamara mentioned the dangerous growth of "neutralist sentiment" in Saigon and the possibility of a coup by neutralist forces who might form a coalition government with the Communists and invite the United States to leave.

A 'Solution' in Disfavor

William Bundy would later refer to this possibility as a "Vietnam solution" that must be prevented.

In a glimpse into the President's thoughts at this time, the study shows he was concerned with the problem. Mr. Johnson told Ambassador Henry Cabot Lodge in a cablegram to Saigon on March 20, 1964, that he was intent on "knocking down the idea of neutralization wherever it rears its ugly head, and on this point I think nothing is more important than to stop neutralist talk wherever we can by whatever means we can." [See text.]

Mr. Lodge was opposed to planning for "massive destruction actions" before trying what he described as "an essentially diplomatic carrot and stick approach, backed by covert military means."

This plan, which Mr. Lodge had been proposing since the previous October, involved sending a secret non-American envoy to Hanoi with an offer of economic aid, such as food imports to relieve the rice shortages in North Vietnam, in return for calling off the Vietcong. If the North Vietnamese did not respond favorably, the stick—unpublicized and unacknowledged air strikes, apparently with unmarked planes—would be applied until they did.

The President's message of March 20 shared Mr. Lodge's opinion that it was still too early for open assaults on the North.

"As we agreed, in our previous messages to each other," Mr. Johnson cabled, "judgment is reserved for the present on overt military action in view of the consensus from Saigon conversations of McNamara mission with General Khanh and you on judgment that movement against the North at the present would be premature. We . . . share General Khanh's judgment that the immediate and essential task is to strengthen the southern base. For this reason, our planning for action against the North is on a contingency basis at present, and immediate problem in this area is to develop the strongest possible military and political base for possible later action."

Mr. Johnson added that the Administration also expected a "showdown" soon in the Chinese-Soviet dispute "and action against the North will be more practicable" then.

Pushing, Yet Hesitating

This and the other sporadic insights the study gives into Mr. Johnson's thoughts and motivations during these months leading up to the Tonkin Gulf incident in August indicate a President who was, on the one hand, pushing his Administration to plan energetically for escalation while, on the other, continually hesitating to translate these plans into military action.

The glimpses are of a Chief Executive who was determined to achieve the goal of an "independent, non-Communist South Vietnam" he had enunciated in a national security action memorandum in March, yet who was holding back on actions to achieve that goal until he believed they were absolutely necessary.

Above all, the narrative indicates a President who was carefully calculating international and domestic political conditions before making any of his moves in public.

By the latter half of April, 1964, accordingly, planning for further attacks against the North had matured sufficiently through several scenarios for Secretary Rusk, William Bundy and Gen. Earle G. Wheeler, the Army Chief of Staff, to review the plans with Ambassador Lodge at a Saigon strategy meeting on April 19 and 20.

The scenario envisioned escalation in three stages from intensification of the current clandestine 34A raids, to "covert U.S. support of overt . . . aerial mining and air strike operations" by Saigon to "overt joint . . . aerial reconnaissance, naval displays, naval bombardments and air attacks" by the United States and South Vietnam.

The analyst does not mention any provision in the April planning scenario for a Congressional resolution that would constitute authority to wage war; he refers instead to "Presidential consultations with key Congressional leaders." But the idea of a resolution was already current by then. The author reports its first emergence in discussions in the State Department in mid-February, 1964, "on the desirability of the President's requesting a Congressional resolution, drawing a line at the borders of South Vietnam." He cites a Feb. 13 letter to Secretary Rusk to this effect from Mr. Rostow, then chairman of the State Department's Policy Planning Council.

At the April Saigon meeting and in the weeks immediately afterward, the author says, "a deliberate, cautious pacing of our actions" prevailed over a near-term escalation approach being pressed by the Joint Chiefs and Mr. Rostow.

One reason for this, the study explains, was that the Administration recognized that it "lacked adequate information concerning the nature and magnitude" of infiltration of trained guerrilla leaders and arms from the North and was beginning a major effort to try to gather enough concrete evidence to justify escalation if this became necessary.

"For example," the study reports, "citing the 'lack of clarity' on the 'role of external intrusion' in South Vietnam, Walt Rostow urged William Sullivan [chairman of the interagency Vietnam coordinating committee] on the eve of [a] March visit to attempt to 'come back from Saigon with as lucid and agreed a picture' as possible on the extent of the infiltration and its influence on the Vietcong."

The direct outcome of Mr. Rusk's April visit to Saigon was his agreement to try Ambassador Lodge's carrot-and-stick approach. On April 30, 1964, the Secretary flew to Ottawa and arranged with the Canadian Government for J. Blair Seaborn, Canada's new representative on the International Control Commission, to convey the offer of United States economic aid to Premier Dong when Mr. Seaborn visited Hanoi in June.

On May 4 General Khanh, sensing a decline in his fortunes and beginning to abandon the idea of strengthening his government to the point where it could defeat the Vietcong in the South, told Ambassador Lodge that he wanted to declare war quickly on North Vietnam, have the United States start bombing and send 10,000 Special Forces troops of the United States Army into the South "to cover the whole Cambodian - Laotian border." Mr. Lodge deflected the suggestions.

Secretary McNamara, on a visit to Saigon May 13, was instructed to tell General Khanh that while the United States did not "rule out" bombing the North, "such actions must be supplementary to and not a substitute for successful counter-insurgency in the South" and that "we do not intend to provide military support nor undertake the military objective of 'rolling back' Communist control in North Vietnam."

But on May 17, when the Pathet Lao launched an offensive on the Plaine des Jarres that threatened to collapse the pro-American Government of Premier Souvanna Phouma and with it "the political underpinning of United States-Laotian policy," the study declares, this "deliberate, cautious approach" to escalation planning was suddenly thrown into "crisis management."

The Administration immediately turned the Laotian air operations up a notch by intensifying the T-28 strikes and, on May 21, by starting low-altitude target reconnaissance by United States Navy and Air Force jets over areas held by the Pathet Lao and the North Vietnamese.

30-Day Program Is Worked Up

In Washington, the chief planner, William Bundy, assisted by Mr. McNaughton and Mr. Sullivan, worked up a 30-day program culminating in full-scale bombing of the North. He submitted it as a formal draft Presidential memorandum for consideration by an executive committee of the National Security Council.

For a number of reasons, this May 23 scenario was never carried out as written. The President, in fact, delayed another nine months the scenario's dénouement in an air war.

But the document is important because it reveals how far the Administration had progressed in its planning by this point and because a number of the steps in the scenario were carried out piecemeal through June and July and then very rapidly under the political climate of the Tonkin Gulf clash.

For the military side of the scenario, the President's order of March 17 to plan for retaliatory air strikes on 72 hours' notice and for full-scale air raids on 30 days' notice had borne fruit in Operation Plan 37-64.

This plan had been prepared in the Honolulu headquarters of Adm. Harry D. Felt, commander in chief of Pacific forces, or CINCPAC, and had been approved by the Joint Chiefs on April 17. It tabulated how many planes and what bomb tonnages would be required for each phase of the strikes, listed the targets in North Vietnam with damage to be achieved, and programed the necessary positioning of air forces for the raids. A follow-up operation plan, designated 32-64, calculated the possible reactions of China and North Vietnam and the American ground forces that might be necessary to meet them.

The Joint Staff had refined the bombing plan with more target studies. These estimated that an initial category of targets associated with infiltration, such as bridges and depots of ammunition and petroleum, could be destroyed in only 12 days if all the air power in the western Pacific were used.

For the political side of the scenario, recommendations from William Bundy and Mr. Rusk had produced more evidence of infiltration by the North for public release to justify escalation. William J. Jorden, a former correspondent of The New York Times who had become a State Department official, had gone to South Vietnam and had pulled together the data available there for a possible new State Department white paper.

Pentagon Version of Scenario

Here is the scenario as the Pentagon analyst quotes it. The words in parentheses—and the numbers designating the length of time to "D-day"—were in the original scenario and the words in brackets were inserted by the analyst for clarification:

"1. Stall off any 'conference [Laos or] Vietnam until D-Day.'

"2. Intermediary (Canadian?) tell North Vietnam in general terms that U.S. does not want to destroy the North Vietnam regime (and indeed is willing 'to provide a carrot') but is determined to protect South Vietnam from North Vietnam.

"3. (D-30) Presidential speech in general terms launching Joint Resolution.

"4. (D-20) Obtain joint resolution approving past actions and authorizing whatever is necessary with respect to Vietnam.

"Concurrently: An effort should be made to strengthen the posture in South Vietnam. Integrating (interlarding in a single chain of command) the South Vietnamese and U.S. military and civilian elements critical to pacification, down at least to the district level, might be undertaken.

"5. (D-16) Direct CINCPAC to take all prepositioning and logistic actions that can be taken 'quietly' for the D-Day forces. . . .

"6. (D-15) Get Khanh's agreement to start overt South Vietnamese air attacks against targets in the North (see D-Day item 15 below), and inform him of U.S. guarantee to protect South Vietnam in the event of North Vietnamese and/or Chinese retaliation.

"7. (D-14) Consult with Thailand and the Philippines to get permission for U.S. deployments; and consult with them plus U.K., Australia, New Zealand and Pakistan, asking for their open political support for the undertaking and for their participation in the re-enforcing action to be undertaken in anticipation of North Vietnamese and/or Chinese retaliation.

"8. (D-13) Release an expanded 'Jorden Report,' including recent photography and evidence of the communication nets, giving full documentation of North Vietnamese supply and direction of the Vietcong.

"9. (D-12) Direct CINCPAC to begin moving forces and making specific plans on the assumption that strikes will be made on D-Day (see Attachment B* in backup materials for deployments).

"10. (D-10) Khanh makes speech demanding that North Vietnam stop aggression, threatening unspecified military action if he does not. (He could refer to a "carrot.')

"11. (D-3) Discussions with allies not covered in Item above.

"12. (D-3) President informs U.S. public (and thereby North Vietnam) that action may come, referring to Khanh speech (Item 10 above) and declaring support for South Vietnam.

"13. (D-1) Khanh announces that all efforts have failed and that attacks are imminent. (Again he refers to limited goal and possibly to 'carrot.')

"14. (D-Day) Remove U.S. dependents.

"15. (D-Day) Launch first strikes. . . . Initially, mine their ports and strike North Vietnam's transport and related ability (bridge, trains) to move south; and then against targets which have maximum psychological effect on the North's willingness to stop insurgency—POL (petroleum, oil and lubricants) storage, selected airfields, barracks/training areas, bridges, railroad yards, port facilities, communications, and in-

dustries. Initially, these strikes would be by South Vietnamese aircraft; they could then be expanded by adding Farmgate, or U.S. aircraft, or any combination of them.

"16. (D-Day) Call for conference on Vietnam (and go to U.N.). State the limited objective: Not to overthrow the North Vietnam regime nor to destroy the country, but to stop D.R.V.-directed efforts in the South. Essential that it be made clear that attacks on the North will continue (i.e., no cease-fire) until (a) terrorism, armed attacks, and armed resistance to pacification efforts in the South stop, and (b) communications on the networks out of the North are conducted entirely in uncoded form."

The Analyst's Definition

The last paragraph was to provide a capsule definition of what the Administration meant when it later spoke publicly about "negotiations," a definition the analyst describes as "tantamount to unconditional surrender" for the other side.

The covering memorandum on the scenario pointed out that military action would not begin until after "favorable action" on the joint Congressional resolution. William Bundy drafted the resolution on May 25.

Attached to the scenario were assessments of possible Soviet, Chinese and North Vietnamese reactions. These included a provision for reinforcing the South Vietnamese Army "by U.S. ground forces prepositioned in South Vietnam or on board ship nearby" if Hanoi reacted by intensifying Vietcong activity in the South.

After meetings on May 24 and 25, the Executive Committee of the National Security Council—including Secretaries Rusk and McNamara, John A. McCone, Director of Central Intelligence, and McGeorge Bundy, Presidential assistant for national security—decided to recommend to the President only piecemeal elements of the scenario. Among these were the sending of the Canadian emissary to Hanoi and the move for a joint Congressional resolution.

The documents do not provide a clear explanation for their decision, the analyst says, although an important factor seems to have been concern that "our limited objectives might have been obscured" if the Administration had begun a chain of actions to step up the war at this point.

Whether political considerations in an election year also prompted the President to limit the proposed escalation is a question that is not addressed by the study here. The narrative does attribute such motives to Mr. Johnson's similar hesitation to take major overt actions in the following month, June.

In any case, the account explains, the urgency was taken out of the Laos crisis by a Polish diplomatic initiative on May 27 for a new Laos conference that would not include discussions of Vietnam, a major fear of the Administration. The President instructed his senior advisers to convene another strategy conference in Honolulu at the beginning of June "to review for . . . final approval a series of plans for effective action."

On his way to the conference, after attending the funeral of Prime Minister Jawaharlal Nehru in New Delhi, Secretary Rusk stopped off in Saigon for conversations with General Khanh and Ambassador Lodge.

Strategy Session in Honolulu

The Ambassador and Gen. William C. Westmoreland, who was replacing General Harkins as chief of the Military Assistance Command in Saigon, flew to Honolulu with Secretary Rusk for the strategy session at Admiral Felt's headquarters there on June 1 and 2, 1964. They were joined by William Bundy, Mr. McNamara, General Taylor, Mr. McCone and Mr. Sullivan.

While he had previously counseled patience, Mr. Lodge's chief recommendation at Honolulu reflected his growing nervousness over the shakiness of the Saigon regime. He argued for bombing the North soon.

The analyst writes: "In answer to Secretary Rusk's query about South Vietnamese popular attitudes, which supported Hanoi's revolutionary aims, the Ambassador stated his conviction that most support for the VC would fade as soon as some 'counterterrorism measures' were begun against the D.R.V."—the Democratic Republic of (North) Vietnam.

Admiral Felt's record of the first day's session quotes Mr. Lodge as predicting that "a selective bombing campaign against military targets in the North" would "bolster morale and give the population in the South a feeling of unity."

The Honolulu discussions concentrated on an air war, ranging over its entire implications, down to such details as the kind of antiaircraft guns North Vietnam had and how difficult these defenses might make attacks on particular targets. By now the Joint Chiefs had improved on Admiral Felt's Operation Plan 37-64 to the point of producing the first version of a comprehensive list of 94 targets, from bridges to industries, that Mr. McNamara and President Johnson would use to select the actual sites to be struck when sustained air raids began in the coming year.

Obtaining a Congressional resolution "prior to wider U. S. action in Southeast Asia" was a major topic. The analyst paraphrases and quotes from William Bundy's memorandum of record on the second day's talks to summarize the discussion concerning the resolution:

"Ambassador Lodge questioned the need for it if we were to confine our actions to 'tit-for-tat' air attacks against North Vietnam: However, Secretaries McNamara and Rusk and C.I.A. Director McCone all argued in favor of the resolution. In support, McNamara pointed to the need to guarantee South Vietnam's defense against retaliatory air attacks and against more drastic reactions by North Vietnam and Communist China. He added that it might be necessary, as the action unfolded . . . to deploy as many as seven divisions. Rusk noted that some of the military requirements might involve the calling up of reserves, always a touchy Congressional issue. He also stated that public opinion on our Southeast Asia policy was badly divided in the United States at the moment and that, therefore, the President needed an affirmation of support."

"General Taylor noted that there was a danger of reasoning ourselves into inaction," the memorandum goes on. "From a military point of view, he said the U.S. could function in Southeast Asia about as well as anywhere in the world except Cuba."

The upshot of the conference, however, was that major actions "should be delayed for some time yet," the historian says. A separate briefing paper that William Bundy prepared for Secretary Rusk to use in communicating the conference's findings to the President at a White House meeting late on the afternoon of June 3 counseled more time "to refine our plans and estimates." Mr. Bundy emphasized the need for an "urgent" public relations campaign at home to "get at the basic doubts of the value of Southeast Asia and the imporance of our stake there."

Secretary McNamara, General Taylor and Mr. McCone joined Secretary Rusk in making the June 3 report to the President on the Honolulu conference. A documentary record of this White House meeting is not available, but the study deduces the President's reaction and decisions from the subsequent actions taken by his senior advisers.

Where decisive military actions were concerned, "the President apparently recognized the need for more and better information, but did not convey a sense of urgency regarding its acquisition," the analyst says. He notes that on the same day as the White House meeting, "possibly just following," Secretary Mc-

Namara told the Joint Chiefs that he wanted to meet with them on June 8, five days later, "to discuss North Vietnamese targets and troop movement capabilities."

But one element of the May 23 scenario, the positioning of forces for later action, began to fall into place right after the White House meeting. The Pentagon study says that "noncommitting military actions . . . were given immediate approval."

On June 4 Mr. McNamara directed the Army to take "immediate action . . . to improve the effectiveness and readiness status of its matériel prestocked for possible use in Southeast Asia."

The Secretary's directive specifically ordered the Army to augment stocks previously placed with Thailand's agreement at Korat, a town south of the Laotian border, to support potential combat operations by a United States Army infantry brigade and to give "first priority at the Okinawa Army Forward Depot to stocking non-air-transportable equipment" that would be required by another Army infantry brigade flown to the island staging base on sudden notice.

The President also "apparently encouraged" the intensified public-relations campaign recommended by William Bundy and the other Honolulu conference participants, the study asserts.

"In June, State and Defense Department sources made repeated leaks to the press affirming U.S. intentions to support its allies and uphold its treaty commitments in Southeast Asia," the analyst explains, citing several articles that month in The New York Times. The Administration also focused pub-licity through June and into July on its military prepositioning moves. The augmentation of the Army war stocks at Korat in Thailand was given "extensive press coverage," the account says, citing a dispatch in The Times on June 21, 1964.

And what the analyst calls "the broad purpose" of these positioning moves—to serve as steps in the operation plans—was not explained to the public.

Downing of Two Navy Jets

The Administration did openly step up its air operations in Laos in mid-June, after the enemy provided it with a rationale of self-defense. On June 6 and 7 two Navy jets on low-altitude target reconnaissance flights were shot down by enemy ground fire. Washington immediately added armed escort jets to the reconnaissance flights and on June 9 the escort jets struck Pathet Lao gun positions and attacked a Pathet Lao headquarters.

A similar escalation of the T-28 operations and the involvement of Thai pilots was unofficially acknowledged in Washington, although the responsibility for these operations was laid to the Laotian Government. And subsequent strikes by the American escort jets against enemy positions were not made public.

At the end of June the Royal Laotian Air Force was secretly strengthened with more T-28's, and American planes began conducting troop transport operations and night reconnaissance flights for a successful counteroffensive by the Laotian Army to protect the key position of Muong Soui.

Firmness, but Restraint

President Johnson was projecting an image of firmness but moderation, the study notes. In early June, he first requested and then rejected a draft from Mr. Rostow for a major policy speech on Southeast Asia that took an "aggressive approach," and instead relied "on news conferences and speeches by other officials to state the official view," the account continues. "In contrast to the Rostow approach, [the President's] news conference on 23 June and Secretary Rusk's speech at Williams College, 14 June, emphasized the U.S. determination to support its Southeast Asian allies, but avoided any direct challenge to Hanoi and Peking or any hint of intent to increase our military commitment."

A formal question the President submitted to the C.I.A. in June also indicated what was on his mind. "Would the rest of Southeast Asia necessarily fall if Laos and South Vietnam came under North Vietnamese control?" he asked. The agency's reply on June 9 challenged the domino theory, widely believed in one form or another within the Administration.

"With the possible exception of Cambodia," the C.I.A. memorandum said, "it is likely that no nation in the area would quickly succumb to Communism as a result of the fall of Laos and South Vietnam. Furthermore, a continuation of the spread of Communism in the area would not be inexorable, and any spread which did occur would take time —time in which the total situation might change in any number of ways unfavorable to the Communist cause."

The C.I.A. analysis conceded that the loss of South Vietnam and Laos "would be profoundly damaging to the U.S. position in the Far East" and would raise the prestige of China "as a leader of world Communism" at the expense of a more moderate Soviet Union. But the analysis argued that so long as the United States could retain its island bases, such as those on Okinawa, Guam, the Philippines and Japan, it could wield enough military power in Asia to deter China and North Vietnam from overt military aggression against Southeast Asia in general.

Some Leverage Available

Even in the "worst case," if South Vietnam and Laos were to fall through "a clear-cut Communist victory," the United States would still retain some leverage to affect the final outcome in Southeast Asia, according to the analysis.

It said that "the extent to which individual countries would move away from the U.S. towards the Communists would be significantly affected by the substance and manner of U.S. policy in the period following the loss of Laos and South Vietnam."

As in the case of the earlier C.I.A. analysis stating that the real roots of Vietcong strength lay in South Vietnam, the study shows that the President and his senior officials were not inclined to adjust policy along the lines of this analysis challenging the domino theory.

Only the Joint Chiefs, Mr. Rostow and General Taylor appear to have accepted the domino theory in its literal sense—that all of the countries of Southeast Asia, from Cambodia to Malaysia, would tumble automatically into the Communist camp if the linchpin, South Vietnam, were knocked out, and that the United States position in the rest of the Far East, from Indonesia through the Philippines to Japan and Korea, would also be irrevocably harmed.

Yet the President and most of his closest civilian advisers—Mr. Rusk, Mr. McNamara and McGeorge Bundy—seem to have regarded the struggle over South Vietnam in more or less these terms. [See text.]

In 1964, the Administration also feared an outbreak of other "wars of national liberation" in the Asian, African and Latin American countries, and, Mr. McNamara wrote in his March 16 memorandum to the President, "the South Vietnam conflict is regarded as a test case."

The Threat of China

The struggle in South Vietnam was likewise bound up with the idea of "containing China," whose potential shadow over Southeast Asia was viewed as a palpable threat by Mr. Rusk because of his World War II exprience in Asia and the victory of Mao Tse-tung's revolution in China.

But behind these foreign-policy axioms about domino effects, wars of liberation and the containment of China, the study reveals a deeper perception among the President and his aides that the United States was now the most powerful nation in the world and that the outcome in South Vietnam would demonstrate the will and the ability of the United States to have its way in world affairs.

The study conveys an impression that the war was thus considered less important for what it meant to the South Vietnamese people than for what it meant to the position of the United States in the world.

Mr. McNaughton would later capsulize this perception in a memorandum to Mr. McNamara seeking to apportion American aims in South Vietnam:

"70 pct.—To avoid a humiliating U.S. defeat (to our reputation as a guarantor).

"20 pct.—To keep SVN (and then adjacent) territory from Chinese hands.

"10 pct.—To permit the people of SVN to enjoy a better, freer way of life.

"Also—To emerge from crisis without unacceptable taint from methods used.

"NOT—To 'help a friend,' although it would be hard to stay in if asked out."

The words in parentheses are Mr. McNaughton's.

Thus, he had reasoned in another memorandum, even if bombing North Vietnam did not force Hanoi to call off the Vietcong, "it would demonstrate that U.S. was a 'good doctor' willing to keep promises, be tough, take risks, get bloodied and hurt the enemy badly."

Confidence at the Top

And while the study shows doubt and worry in the Administration, it also reveals an underlying confidence among the decision makers at the top, whose attitude would count, that if this mightiest nation resolved to use its vast power, the other side would buckle.

Mr. Rostow would articulate this confidence in a memorandum to Secretary Rusk that fall: "I know well the anxieties and complications on our side of the line. But there may be a tendency to underestimate both the anxieties and complications on the other side and also to underestimate that limited but real margin of influence on the outcome

'64 Air Strikes Deepened U.S. Commitment and Reduced Choices, Survey Finds

that flows from the simple fact that we are the greatest power in the world—if we behave like it."

Accordingly, in mid-June, the Administration carried out another element of the May 23 scenario, the element that had first been formulated by Ambassador Lodge as his "carrot and stick." On June 18, at the Administration's request, Mr. Seaborn, the new Canadian representative on the International control Commission, paid the first of his two secret calls on Premier Dong in Hanoi.

Washington sought to convey to North Vietnam through Mr. Seaborn the more precise and threatening meaning of the preparatory military deployments to Southeast Asia that it was publicizing on a vaguer level in public. Back in May, Mr. Lodge had urged an unacknowledged air strike on some target in the North "as a prelude to his [Mr. Seaborn's] arrival" if the Vietcong had recently committed some terrorist act "of the proper magnitude" in the South, but the President apparently did not see fit to act on the suggestion by June.

The analyst says Mr. Seaborn stressed to Premier Dong that while the United States' ambition in Southeast Asia were limited and its intentions "essentially peaceful," its patience was not limitless. The United States was fully aware of the degree to which Hanoi controlled the Vietcong, Mr. Seaborn said, and "in the event of escalation the greatest devastation would of course result for the D.R.V. itself."

No Report on the 'Carrot'

The North Vietnamese Premier, the study relates," fully understood the seriousness and import of the warning conveyed by Seaborn." Whether Mr. Seaborn also proferred the "carrot" of food and other economic aid is not reported.

At the June 3 meeting at the White House, the President had also apparently approved continued work for the Congressional resolution, the historian says, because planning for it continued apace. "Its intended purpose," the historian comments, "was to dramatize and make clear to other nations the firm resolve of the United States Government in an election year to support the President in taking whatever action was necessary to resist Communist aggression in Southeast Asia."

By June 10, there was "firm support" from most of the foreign-policy-making machinery of the Government for obtaining the resolution, although the account notes that at an interagency meeting that day "five basic 'disagreeable questions' were identified for which the Administration would have to provide convincing answers to assure public support."

"These included: (1) Does this imply a blank check for the President to go to war in Southeast Asia? (2) What kinds of force could he employ under this authorization? (3) What change in the situation (if any) requires the resolution now? (4) Can't our objectives be attained by means other than U.S. military force? (5) Does Southeast Asia mean enough to U.S. national interests?"

Despite the prospect of having to answer these questions publicly, William Bundy wrote in a memorandum for a second interagency meeting on June 12, the Administration required a Congressional resolution immediately as "a continuing demonstration of U.S. firmness and for complete flexibility in the hands of the executive in the coming political months." While the United States did not expect "to move in the near future to military action against North Vietnam," he said, events in South Vietnam or Laos might force it to reconsider this position.

But in the opinion of the analyst, the President in June, 1964, already felt "the political conventions just around the corner and the election issues regarding Vietnam clearly drawn," and so he recoiled at this time from the repercussions of major escalation and of seeking a Congressional resolution. At a high-level meeting on both subjects June 15, McGeorge Bundy, the historian says, brought Presidential guidance to Secretaries Rusk and McNamara in the form of a White House memorandum that postponed a decision for the present.

Washington's efforts to achieve some political stability in Saigon and to hold the line militarily against the guerrillas were coming to naught, however, under the blows of the Vietcong. In his fear and nervousness, General Khanh broke a promise he had made to Ambassador Lodge and Secretary Rusk in their May meeting to consult with Washington before publicly announcing any intention to declare war on the North and to start a bombing campaign.

On July 19, he started a "March North" campaign of militant slogans and oratory at a "unification rally" in Saigon. The same day, as the analyst puts it, Air Marshal Nguyen Cao Ky, then chief of the South Vietnamese Air Force, "spilled the beans to reporters" on joint planning that the United States and the Saigon Government had secretly been conducting since June, with President Johnson's approval, for ground and air assaults in Laos.

In an emotional meeting on July 23 with General Taylor, who had just replaced Mr. Lodge as Ambassador, General Khanh asserted that North Vietnamese draftees had been taken prisoner with Vietcong guerrillas in fighting in the northern provinces. The United States should realize, he said, that the war had entered a new phase that called for new measures.

Another Heated Meeting

During another heated meeting on July 24, General Khanh asked Ambassador Taylor whether to resign. The Ambassador asked him not to do so and cabled Washington urging that the United States undertake covert joint planning with the South Vietnamese for bombing the North.

The State Department, the study says, immediately authorized Ambassador Taylor "to tell Khanh the U. S. G. had considered attacks on North Vietnam that might begin, for example, if the pressure from dissident South Vietnamese factions became too great. He must keep this confidential."

The Pentagon narrative skims over the last few days in July, 1964, but a summary of a command and control study of the Tonkin Gulf incident done by the Defense Department's Weapons System Evaluation Group in 1965, which The Times obtained along with the Pentagon narratives, fills in the events of these few days.

The study discloses that after a National Security Council meeting called on July 25, apparently to discuss these critical developments in Saigon, the Joint Chiefs proposed air strikes by unmarked planes flown by non-American crews against several targets in North Vietnam, including the coastal bases for Hanoi's flotilla of torpedo boats.

Assistant Secretary McNaughton sent the Joint Chiefs' memorandum to Secretary Rusk on July 30, the study reports, the same day that a chain of events was to unfold that would make it unnecessary to carry out the Joint Chiefs' plan, even if the President had wanted to accept it.

The Pentagon narrative now remarks that the clandestine 34A raids against North Vietnam—after getting off to what the Joint Chiefs had called "a slow beginning" in a report to Mr. McNamara on May 19—picked up in tempo and size during the summer, although the analyst provides few details. The Joint Chiefs had informed Mr. McNamara that trained sabotage teams, electronic intelligence-gathering equipment, C-123 transports for the air-drops and fast PT boats for the coastal raids were giving the program "growing operational capabilities. [See text.]

Attack on Two Islands

At midnight on July 30, South Vietnamese naval commandos under General Westmoreland's command staged an amphibious raid on the North Vietnamese islands of Hon Me and Hon Nieu in the Gulf of Tonkin.

While the assault was occurring, the United States destroyer Maddox was 120 to 130 miles away, heading north into the gulf on the year's second De Soto intelligence-gathering patrol. Her sailing orders said she was not to approach closer than eight nautical miles to the North Vietnamese coast and four nautical miles to North Vietnamese islands in the gulf.

The account does not say whether the captain of the Maddox had been informed about the 34A raid. He does state that the Maddox altered course twice on Aug. 2 to avoid a concentration of three North Vietnamese torpedo boats and a fleet of junks that were still searching the seas around the islands for the raiders.

The destroyer reached the northernmost point of her assigned patrol track the same day and headed south again.

"When the [North Vietnamese] PT boats began their high-speed run at her, at a distance of approximately 10 miles, the destroyer was 23 miles from the coast and heading further into international waters," the study says. "Apparently," it explains, "these boats . . . had mistaken Maddox for a South Vietnamese escort vessel."

In the ensuing engagement, two of the torpedo boats were damaged by planes launched from the aircraft carrier Ticonderoga, stationed to the south for reasons the study does not explain. A third PT boat was knocked dead in the water, sunk by a direct hit from one of the Maddox's five-inch guns.

New Orders for Maddox

The next day, Aug. 3, President Johnson ordered the Maddox reinforced by the destroyer C. Turner Joy and directed that both destroyers be sent back into the gulf, this time with instructions not to approach closer than 11 nautical miles to the North Vietnamese coast. A second aircraft carrier, the Constellation, on a visit to Hong Kong, was instructed to make steam and join the Ticonderoga as quickly as possible.

The study terms these reinforcing actions "a normal precaution" in the light of the first attack on the Maddox and not an attempt to use the destroyers as bait for another attack that would provide a pretext for reprisal airstrikes against the North. "Moreover," it comments, "since the augmentation was coupled with a clear [public] statement of intent to continue the patrols and a firm warning to the D.R.V. that a repetition would bring dire consequences, their addition to the patrol could be expected to serve more as a deterrent than a provocation."

The study gives a clear impression that the Administration at this moment did not believe the North Vietnamese would dare to attack the reinforced destroyer patrol.

For on the night of Aug. 3, while the De Soto patrol was resuming, two more clandestine 34A attacks were staged. PT boats manned by South Vietnamese crews bombarded the Rhon River estuary and a radar installation at Vinhson. This time the Maddox and the Turner Joy were definitely warned that the clandestine assaults were going to take place, the documents show.

Apparently expecting the President to order a resumption of the patrol, the admiral commanding the Seventh Fleet asked General Westmoreland on Aug. 2 to furnish him the general location of the planned raids so that the destroyers could steer clear of the 34A force. There was a good deal of cable traffic back and forth between the two commanders through the Pentagon communications center in Washington to modify the patrol's course on Aug. 3 to avoid any interference with the raiders.

On the night of Aug. 4, Tonkin Gulf time, approximately 24 hours after this second 34A assault, North Vietnamese torpedo boats then attacked both the Maddox and the Turner Joy in what was to be the fateful clash in the gulf.

Motives Still Unclear

The Pentagon account says that Hanoi's motives for this second attack on he destroyers are still unclear. The narrative ties the attack to the chain of events set off by the 34A raids of July 30, but says that Hanoi's precise motive may have been to recover from the embarrassment of having two torpedo boats damaged and another sunk in the first engagement with the Maddox, without any harm to the American destroyer.

"Perhaps closer to the mark is the narrow purpose of prompt retaliation for an embarrassing and well-publicized rebuff by a much-maligned enemy," the narrative says. "Inexperienced in modern naval operations, D.R.V. leaders may have believed that under the cover of darkness it would be possible to even the score or to provide at least a psychological victory by severely damaging a U.S. ship."

The study does not raise the question whether the second 34A raid on the night of Aug. 3, or the apparent air strikes on North Vietnamese villages just across the Laotian border on Aug. 1 and 2 by T-28 planes, motivated the Hanoi leadership in any way to order the second engagement with the destroyers.

Marshall Green, then the Deputy Assistant Secretary of State for Far Eastern Affairs, mentioned the apparent bombing of the villages in a lengthy memorandum to William Bundy dated Nov. 7, 1964, on United States covert activities in Indochina. [See text.]

Listing complaints that North Vietnam had been making to the International Control Commission over the T-28 operations with Thai pilots, Mr. Green noted charges by Hanoi that "T-28's have violated North Vietnamese airspace and bombed/strafed NVN villages on Aug. 1 and 2, and on Oct. 16 and 17 and again on Oct. 28. The charges are probably accurate with respect to the first two dates (along Route 7) and the last one (Mugia Pass area)." The words in parentheses are Mr. Green's.

Raids Possibly Inadvertent

The context of the memorandum indicates that the raids on the North Vietnamese villages may have been inadvertent. But neither the narrative nor Mr. Green's memorandum says whether Hanoi thought this at the time the air strikes occurred.

Whatever the North Vietnamese motives for the second clash, President Johnson moved quickly now to carry out what the analyst calls "recommendations made . . . by his principal advisers earlier that summer and subsequently placed on the shelf."

Because of the Pacific time difference, the Pentagon received the first word that an attack on the Maddox and the Turner Joy might be imminent at 9:20

A.M. on the morning of Aug. 4, after the destroyers had intercepted North Vietnamese radio traffic indicating preparations for an assault. The flash message that the destroyers were actually engaged came into the communications center at 11 A.M.

The Joint Chiefs' staff began selecting target options for reprisal air strikes from the 94-target list, the first version of which was drawn up at the end of May. Adm. U.S. Grant Sharp, who had replaced Admiral Felt as commander in chief of Pacific forces, telephoned from Honolulu to suggest bombing the coastal bases for the torpedo boats.

Within 10 minutes, Mr. McNamara convened a meeting with the Joint Chiefs in his conference room on the third floor of the Pentagon to discuss possibilities for retaliation. Secretary Rusk and McGeorge Bundy came over to join them.

Meeting Already Scheduled

Twenty-five minutes later the two secretaries and Mr. Bundy left for a previously scheduled National Security Council meeting at the White House. They would recommend reprisal strikes to the President, while the Joint Chiefs stayed at the Pentagon to decide on specific targets.

At 1:25 P.M., two and a half hour after the flash message of the engagement and possibly while Mr. McNamara, Mr. Rusk, Mr. McCone and McGeorge Bundy were still at lunch with the President, the director of the Joint Staff telephone Mr. McNamara to say that the Chiefs had unanimously agreed on the targets. Fighter-bombers from the carriers Constellation and Ticonderoga should strike four torpedo boat bases at Hongay, Lochau, Phucloi and Quangkhe, and an oil storage depot near Vinh that held some 10 per cent of North Vietnam's petroleum supply.

At a second National Security Council meeting that afternoon, President Johnson ordered the reprisals, decided to seek the Congressional resolution immediately and discussed with his advisers the swift Southeast Asia deployment of the air strike forces designated in Operation Plan 37-64 for the opening blows in a possible bombing campaign against the North. His approval for these preparatory air deployments, and for the readiness of Marine Corps and Army units planned to meet any Chinese or North Vietnamese retaliation to a bombing campaign, was apparently given later that day, the study shows.

Mr. McNamara returned to the Pentagon at 3 P.M. to approve the details of the reprisal strikes, code-named Pierce Arrow. An execution order was prepared by the Joint Staff, but at 4 P.M. Mr. McNamara learned from Admiral Sharp in a telephone conversation that there was now confusion over whether an attack on the destroyers had actually taken place.

Admiral Instructed to Check

The Secretary told Admiral Sharp that the reprisal order would remain in effect, but that the admiral was to check and make certain that an attack had really occurred before actually launching the planes. At 4:49 P.M., less than six hours after the first message of the attack had flashed into the Pentagon communications center, the formal execution order for the reprisals was transmitted to Honolulu. Admiral Sharp had not yet called back with confirming details of the attack. The order specified that the carriers were to launch their planes within about two and a half hours.

The admiral called back at 5:23 P.M. and again a few minutes after 6 o'clock to say that he was satisfied, on the basis of information from the task group commander of the two destroyers, that the attack had been genuine. The study says that in the meantime Mr. McNamara and the Joint Chiefs had also examined the confirming evidence, including intercepted radio messages from the North Vietnamese saying that their vessels were engaging the destroyers and that two torpedo boats had been

sunk.

By now Mr. McNamara and the Chiefs had moved on to discussing the pre-positioning of the air strike forces under Operation Plan 37-64.

At 6:45 P.M., President Johnson met with 16 Congressional leaders from both parties whom he had summoned to the White House. He told them that because of the second unprovoked attack on the American destroyers, he had decided to launch reprisal air strikes against the North and to ask for a Congressional resoluion, the study says.

The Pentagon study gives no indication that Mr. Johnson informed the Congressional leaders of United States responsibility for and command of the covert 34A raids on July 30 and Aug. 3.

Nor does the history give any indication that Mr. Johnson told the Congressional leaders of what the historian describes as "the broader purpose of the deployments" under Operation Plan 37-64, which Mr. McNamara was to announce at a Pentagon news conference the next day and describe as a precautionary move.

"It is significant," the analyst writes, "that few of these additional units were removed from the western Pacific when the immediate crisis subsided. In late September the fourth attack aircraft carrier was authorized to resume its normal station in the eastern Pacific as soon as the regularly assigned carrier completed repairs. The other forces remained in the vicinity of their August deployment."

Planes Leave Ticonderoga

At 8:30 P.M. on Aug. 4, Mr. McNamara returned to the Pentagon and at 11:30 P.M., after several telephone calls to Admiral Sharp, he learned that the Ticonderoga had launched her bomb-laden aircraft at 10:43 P.M. They were expected to arrive over their targets in about an hour and 50 minutes.

The carriers had needed more time to get into launching position than the execution order had envisioned. The Constellation, steaming from Hong Kong, was not to launch her planes for another couple of hours.

The President did not wait. Sixteen minutes after Mr. McNamara's last phone call to Admiral Sharp, at 11:36 P.M., he went on television to tell the nation of the reprisal strikes. He characterized his actions as a "limited and fitting" response. "We still seek no wider war," he said.

Almost simultaneously, the air deployments under Operation Plan 37-64 had begun.

The first F-102 Delta Dagger jet fighters were landing at Saigon's airport around the time Mr. McNamara described the deployments at a Pentagon news conference on Aug. 5. He had given a brief post-midnight conference the same day to describe the reprisal strikes. He reported now that 25 North Vietnamese patrol craft had been destroyed or damaged along with 90 per cent of the oil storage tanks near Vinh.

"Last night I announced that moves were under way to reinforce our forces in the Pacific area," he continued. "These moves include the following actions:

"First, an attack carrier group has been transferred from the First Fleet on the Pacific coast to the western Pacific. Secondly, interceptor and fighter-bomber aircraft have been moved into South Vietnam. Thirdly, fighter-bomber aircraft have been moved into Thailand. Fourthly, interceptor and fighter-bomber squadrons have been transferred from the United States into advance bases in the Pacific. Fifthly, and antisubmarine task force group has been moved into the South China Sea. And finally, selected Army and Marine forces have been alerted and readied for movement."

Fulbright a Senate Sponsor

The study notes that the Administration drafted the Congressional resolution for the two men who would sponsor its passage through both houses for the

President: Senator J. W. Fulbright of Arkansas, chairman of the Senate Foreign Relations Committee, and Representative Thomas E. Morgan of Pennsylvania, chairman of the House Foreign Affairs Committee.

Precisely who drafted this final version of the resolution is not mentioned. The wording was less precise than that of the resolution drafted by William Bundy for the May 23 scenario, but the key language making the resolution in effect a declaration of war remained:

"Resolved by the Senate and House of Representatives of the United States of America in Congress assembled, That the Congress approve and support the determination of the President, as Commander in Chief, to take all necessary measures to repel any armed attack against the forces of the United States and to prevent further aggression.

"Sec. 2. The United States regards as vital to its national interest and to world peace the maintenance of international peace and security in Southeast Asia. Consonant with the Constitution of the United States and the Charter of the United Nations and in accordance with its obligations under the Southeast Asia Collective Defense Treaty, the United States is, therefore, prepared, as the President determines, to take all necessary steps, including the use of armed force, to assist any member or protocol state of the Southeast Asia Collective Defense Treaty requesting assistance in defense of its freedom."

Mr. McNamara and Secretary Rusk both testified on behalf of the resolution in secret sessions of the Senate and House foreign relations committees on Aug. 6. In his narrative, the Pentagon analyst occasionally quotes from and refers to portions of their testimony that have never been made public by the Pentagon. Along with the study, The Times also obtained more extensive quotations from this portion of the hearing transcript. The following account of the testimony on Aug. 6 thus contains both quotations used by the Pentagon analyst and the fuller quotations obtained by The Times.

Morse Learns of Attacks

Senator Wayne Morse of Oregon had learned that boats manned by South Vietnamese crews had attacked the two North Vietnamese islands on July 30. Mr. Morse, one of two Senators who were to vote against the Tonkin Gulf resolution — the other was Ernest L. Gruening of Alaska — alleged during the secret hearing on Aug. 6 that Mr. McNamara had known about the raids and that the destroyers had been associated with it.

"First," Mr. McNamara replied, "our Navy played absolutely no part in, was not associated with, was not aware of, any South Vietnamese actions, if there were any. . . . The Maddox was operating in international waters, was carrying out a routine patrol of the type we carry out all over the world at all times."

"I did not have knowledge at the time of the attack on the island," he said. "There is no connection between this patrol and any action by South Vietnam."

Mr. McNamara contended that whatever action had taken place against these North Vietnamese islands had been part of an anti-infiltration operation being conducted by a fleet of coastal patrol junks the United States had helped South Vietnam to organize in December, 1961.

"In the first seven months of this year they have searched 149,000 junks, some 570,000 people," he is quoted as telling the committee in this secret session. "This is a tremendous operation endeavoring to close the seacoasts of over 900 miles. In the process of that action, as the junk patrol has increased in strength, they have moved farther and farther north endeavoring to find the source of the infiltration.

"As part of that, as I reported to you earlier this week, [Mr. McNamara had testified before the committee in a secret session on Aug. 3 after the first attack on the Maddox], we understand that the South Vietnamese sea force carried out patrol action around these islands and actually shelled the parts they felt were associated with this infiltration.

"Our ships had absolutely no knowledge of it, were not connected with it; in no sense of the word can be considered to have backstopped the effort," he said.

Senator Frank Church of Idaho then asked Secretary Rusk at the same secret session: "I take it that our government which supplied these boats . . . . did know that the boats would be used for attacks on North Vietnamese targets, and that we acquiesced in that policy, is that correct?"

". . . In the larger sense, that is so, but as far as any particular detail is concerned we don't from Washington follow that in great detail," Mr. Rusk replied.

Church Presses Questions

"They are doing it with our acquiescence and consent, is that correct?" Senator Church continued.

"But within very limited levels as far as North Vietnam is concerned," Mr. Rusk said.

At a Pentagon news conference after his testimony before the committee, Mr. McNamara spoke about the coastal patrol junks again and avoided any specific mention of the July 30 raid:

Q. Mr. Secretary

A. Yes?

Q. Have there been any incidents that you know involving the South Vietnamese vessels and the North Vietnamese?

A. No, none that I know of, although I think that I should mention to you the South Vietnamese naval patrol activities that are carried on to prevent in the infiltration of men and matériel from the North into the South.

In the last seven months of 1961, for example, about 1,400 men were infiltrated across the 17th Parallel from North Vietnam into South Vietnam. To prevent further infiltration of that kind, the South Vietnamese with our assistance have set up a naval patrol which is very active in that area which continues to inspect and examine junks and their personnel.

In one eight-month period that I can recall they discovered 140 Vietcong infiltrators.

Q. They operate on their own?

A. They operate on their own. They are part of the South Vietnamese Navy, commanded by the South Vietnamese Navy, operating in the coastal waters inspecting suspicious incoming junks, seeking to deter and prevent the infiltration of both men and matériel from North Vietnam into South Vietnam.

Q. Mr. Secretary. Do these junks go north into North Vietnam areas?

A. They have advanced closer and closer to the 17th Parallel and in some cases I think have moved beyond that in an effort to stop the infiltration closer to the point of origin.

Q. Do our naval vessels afford any cover for these operations?

A. Our naval vessels afford no cover whatsoever. Our naval personnel do not participate in the junk operations.

McGovern Raised the Issue

When Senator George S. McGovern of South Dakota subsequently brought up the July 30 attack on the islands during the Senate floor debate on the resolution, Senator Fulbright replied that he had been assured by the Administration that "our boats did not convoy or support or back up any South Vietnamese naval vessels" and that the destroyer patrol "was entirely unconnected

or unassociated with any coastal forays the South Vietnamese themselves may have conducted."

The Congressional resolution passed on Aug. 7 by a vote of 88 to 2 in the Senate and 416 to 0 in the House.

The history shows that besides the May 19 progress report from the Joint Chiefs on the 34A Operations, Mr. McNamara had received other memorandums on the clandestine attacks from General Anthis, the special assistant to the Joint Chiefs, on June 13, July 1 and July 28, 1964. General Anthis drew up the advance monthly schedules of the covert operations for approval by William Bundy and Mr. McNaughton.

Where Mr. Rusk is concerned, the study reveals that he was kept reasonably well informed.

The study also makes it clear that there was no connection between the 34A raids and the coastal patrol junk fleet described by Mr. McNamara and referred to by Mr. Rusk.

Thus, in the space of three days, the Administration had put firmly into place two key elements of the May 23 scenario—prepositioning of major air strike forces and Congressional authorization for wider action.

Internal Administration planning for Congressional authorization to escalate also now disappears from the documentary record. The account notes that during the next round of planning "the question of Congressional authority for open acts of war against a sovereign nation was never seriously raised."

There was confusion in Congress, however, over precisely what the resolution meant, the account says, commenting:

"Despite the nearly unanimous votes of support for the resolution, Congressional opinions varied as to the policy implications and the meaning of such support. The central belief seemed to be that the occasion necessitated demonstrating the nation's unity and collective will in support of the President's action and affirming U.S. determination to oppose further aggression. However, beyond that theme, there was a considerable variety of opinion. . . . Several spokesmen stressed that the resolution did not constitute a declaration of war, did not abdicate Congressional responsibility for determining national policy commitments and did not give the President carte blanche to involve the nation in a major Asian war."

The Administration would now communicate the meaning of the resolution to Hanoi by carrying out in a more significant manner an element of the May 23 scenario that Washington had already used once in June when the Canadian emissary had paid his first visit to Hanoi.

Second Seaborn Mission

On Aug. 10, Mr. Seaborn was sent back with a second message for Premier Dong, which concluded:

"a. That the events of the past few days should add credibility to the statement made last time, that 'U.S. public and official patience with North Vietnamese aggression is growing extremely thin.'

"b. That the U.S. Congressional resolution was passed with near unanimity, strongly reaffirming the unity and determination of the U.S. Government and people not only with respect to any further attacks on U.S. military forces but more broadly to continue to oppose firmly, by all necessary means, D.R.V. efforts to subvert and conquer South Viet-Nam and Laos.

"c. That the U.S. has come to the view that the D.R.V. role in South Vietnam and Laos is critical. If the D.R.V. persists in its present course, it can expect to continue to suffer the consequences. [The word "continue" referred to the reprisal air strikes that followed the Tonkin incident.]

"d. That the D.R.V. knows what it must do if the peace is to be restored.

"e. That the U.S. has ways and means of measuring the D.R.V.'s participation in, and direction and control of, the

war on South Vietnam and in Laos and will be carefully watching the D.R.V.'s response to what Mr. Seaborn is telling them." [See text.]

Mr. McNaughton had drafted the message on the day the resolution was passed.

During this, as in his first meeting with Mr. Seaborn in June, the history says, "Pham Van Dong showed himself utterly unintimidated and calmly resolved to pursue the course upon which the D.R.V. was embarked to what he confidently expected would be its successful conclusion."

In the heat of the Tonkin clash, the Administration had also accomplished one of the major recommendations of the June strategy conference at Honolulu—preparing the American public for escalation.

'An Important Firebreak'

"The Tonkin Gulf reprisal constituted an important firebreak and the Tonkin Gulf resolution set U. S. public support for virtually any action," the study remarks.

Almost none of the "disagreeable questions" the Administration might have to answer about the resolution, which had given the President pause in mid-June, had been asked in the emotional atmosphere of the crisis."

And inside the Administration the planners were moving more quickly now.

On Aug. 10, three days after passage of the resolution, Ambassador Taylor cabled the President a situation report on South Vietnam. It said that the Khanh regime had only "a 50-50 chance of lasting out the year." Therefore, a major objective of the United States Mission in Saigon was to "be prepared to implement contingency plans against North Vietnam with optimum readiness by Jan. 1, 1965."

On Aug. 11, four days after passage of the resolution, William Bundy drew up a memorandum for a high-level State-Defense Departments policy meeting.

The memorandum outlined graduated steps towards a possible full-scale air war against North Vietnam with "a contingency date, as suggested by Ambassador Taylor, of 1 January 1965." But until the end of August, Mr. Bundy said, there should be "a short holding phase, in which we would avoid actions that would in any way take the onus off the Communist side for escalation." [See text.]

Summary Sent to Taylor

On Aug. 14, a lengthy summary of Mr. Bundy's memorandum was cabled to Ambassador Taylor, Ambassador Unger in Vientiane, and to Admiral Sharp in Honolulu for comments that would permit "further review and refinement."

The Tonkin Gulf reprisal air strikes, the analyst writes, "marked the crossing of an important threshold in the war, and it was accomplished with virtually no domestic criticism, indeed, with an evident increase in public support for the Administration. The precedent for strikes against the North was thus established and at very little apparent cost."

"There was a real cost, however," he concludes, in that the Administration was psychologically preparing itself for further escalation. "The number of unused measures short of direct military action against the North had been depleted. Greater visible commitment was purchased at the price of reduced flexibility." And "for all these reasons, when a decision to strike the North was faced again, it was much easier to take."

Admiral Sharp, in his cable to Washington on Aug. 17 commenting on Mr. Bundy's memorandum, "candidly" summed up this psychological commitment, the analyst says.

"Pressures against the other side once instituted should not be relaxed by any actions or lack of them which would destroy the benefits of the rewarding steps previously taken," the admiral wrote.

Tomorrow: Planning the bombing of North Vietnam.

Vietnam Archive: A Consensus to Bomb Developed Before '64 Election, Study Says

By NEIL SHEEHAN

The Johnson Administration reached a "general consensus" at a White House strategy meeting on Sept. 7, 1964, that air attacks against North Vietnam would probably have to be launched, a Pentagon study of the Vietnam war states. It was expected that "these operations would begin early in the new year."

"It is important to differentiate the consensus of the principals at this September meeting," the study says, "from the views which they had urged on the President in the preceding spring. In the spring the use of force had been clearly contingent on a major reversal—principally in Laos—and had been advanced with the apparent assumption that military actions hopefully would not be required. Now, however, their views were advanced with a sense that such actions were inevitable."

The administration consensus on bombing came at the height of the Presidential election contest between President Johnson and Senator Barry Goldwater, whose advocacy of full-scale air attacks on North Vietnam had become a major issue. That such a consensus had been reached as early as September is a major disclosure of the Pentagon study.

The consensus was reflected, the analysis says, in the final paragraph of a formal national security action memorandum issued by the President three days later, on Sept. 10. This paragraph spoke of "larger decisions" that might be "required at any time."

The last round of detailed planning of various political and military strategies for a bombing campaign began "in earnest," the study says, on Nov. 3, 1964, the day that Mr. Johnson was elected President in his own right.

Less than 100 days later, on Feb. 8, 1965, he ordered new reprisal strikes against the North. Then, on Feb. 13, the President gave the order for the sustained bombing of North Vietnam, code-named Rolling Thunder.

This is the second in a series of articles on a secret study, made in the Pentagon, of American participation in the Vietnam war. The study was obtained from other sources by The New York Times through the investigative reporting of Mr. Sheehan. The series was researched and written over three months by Mr. Sheehan and other staff members.

This period of evolving decision to attack North Vietnam, openly and directly, is shown in the Pentagon papers to be the second major phase of President Johnson's defense of South Vietnam. The same period forms the second phase of the presentation of those papers by The New York Times.

The papers, prepared by a team of 30 to 40 authors in 1967-68 as an official study of how the United States went to war in Indochina, consist of 3,000 pages of analysis and 4,000 pages of supporting documents. The study covers nearly three decades of American policy on Southeast Asia. Yesterday The Times's first report on this study, and presentation of key documents, covered the period of clandestine warfare and planning before the Tonkin Gulf incidents in 1964.

In its glimpses into Lyndon B. Johnson's personal thoughts and motivations between the fateful September meeting and his decision to embark on an air war, the Pentagon study shows a President moving and being moved toward war, but reluctant and hesitant to act until the end.

But, the analyst explains, "from the September meeting forward, there was little basic disagreement among the prin-

Continued on Page 30, Column 1

Vietnam Archive: Consensus to Bomb Evolved Before '64 Election, Study Says

Continued From Page 1, Col. 5

cipals [the term the study uses for the senior policy makers] on the need for military operations against the North. What prevented action for the time being was a set of tactical considerations."

The first tactical consideration, the analyst says, was that "the President was in the midst of an election campaign in which he was presenting himself as the candidate of reason and restraint as opposed to the quixotic Barry Goldwater," who was publicly advocating full-scale bombing of North Vietnam. The historian also mentions other "temporary reasons of tactics":

¶The "shakiness" of the Saigon Government.

¶A wish to hold the line militarily and diplomatically in Laos.

¶The "need to design whatever actions were taken so as to achieve maximum public and Congressional support..."

¶The "implicit belief that overt actions at this time might bring pressure for premature negotiations—that is negotiations before the D.R.V. [Democratic Republic of (North) Vietnam] was hurting."

Assistant Secretary of Defense John T. McNaughton, the head of the Pentagon's Office of International Security Affairs, summed up these tactical considerations in the final paragraph of a Sept. 3 memorandum to Secretary of Defense Robert S. McNamara, in preparation for the crucial White House strategy session four days later:

"Special considerations during the next two months. The relevant audiences of U. S. actions are the Communists (who must feel strong pressures), the South Vietnamese (whose morale must be buoyed), our allies (who must trust us as 'underwriters'), and the U.S. public (which must support our risk-taking with U. S. lives and prestige). During the next two months, because of the lack of 'rebuttal time' before election to justify particular actions which may be distorted to the U. S. public, we must act with special care—signaling to the D.R.V. that initiatives are being taken, to the G.V.N. [Government of (South) Vietnam] that we are behaving energetically despite the restraints of our political season, and to the U. S. public that we are behaving with good purpose and restraint." The words in parentheses are Mr. McNaughton's.

'Not to Enlarge the War'

The President was already communicating this sense of restraint to the voters. On the night of Aug. 29, in an address to a crowd at an outdoor barbecue a few miles from his ranch in Texas, when two tons of beef were served in a belated celebration of his 56th birthday, he made a statement that he was to repeat in numerous election speeches.

"I have had advice to load our planes with bombs," the President said, "and to drop them on certain areas that I think would enlarge the war and escalate the war, and result in our committing a good many American boys to fighting a war that I think ought to be fought by the boys of Asia to help protect their own land."

The policy of the United States toward Vietnam, the President explained later in his speech, was "to furnish advice, give counsel, express good judgment, give them trained counselors, and help them with equipment to help themselves."

'It Is a War and a Big War'

"We are doing that," he said. "We have lost less than 200 men in the last several years, but to each one of those 200 men—and we lost about that many in Texas on accidents on the Fourth of July—to each of those 200 men who have given their life to preserve freedom, it is a war and a big war and we recognize it.

"But we think it is better to lose 200 than to lose 200,000. For that reason we have tried very carefully to restrain ourselves and not to enlarge the war."

Eleven days earlier, on Aug. 18, Ambassador Maxwell D. Taylor had cabled from Saigon that he agreed with an "assumption" now held in the Administration in Washington that the Vietcong guerrillas—the VC, as they were usually termed—could not be defeated and the Saigon Government preserved by a counterguerrilla war confined to South Vietnam itself.

"Something must be added in the coming months," the Ambassador said in his message. What General Taylor proposed to add was "a carefully orchestrated bombing attack on NVN [North Vietnam], directed primarily at infiltration and other military targets" with "Jan. 1, 1965, as a target D-Day."

The bombing should be undertaken under either of two courses of action, the Ambassador said. The first course would entail using the promise of the air attacks as an inducement to persuade the regime of Gen. Nguyen Khanh to achieve some political stability and get on seriously with the pacification program. Under the second course, the United States would bomb the North, regardless of whatever progress General Khanh made, to prevent "a collapse of national morale" in Saigon.

For the Ambassador cautioned that "it is far from clear at the present moment that the Khanh Government can last until Jan. 1, 1965." The Ambassador said that before bombing the North the United States would also have to send Army Hawk antiaircraft missile units to the Saigon and Danang areas to protect the airfields there against retaliatory Communist air attacks—assumed possible from China or North Vietnam — and to land a force of American Marines at Danang to protect the air base there against possible ground assaults.

His cable was designated a joint United States mission message, meaning that Deputy Ambassador U. Alexis Johnson and Gen. William C. Westmoreland, chief of the United States Military Assistance Command, had concurred with the Ambassador's views.

On Aug. 26, three days before the President's speech at the barbecue in Stonewall, Tex., the Joint Chiefs of Staff submitted a memorandum to Secretary McNamara agreeing with Ambassador Taylor. They said that bombing under his second criterion, to stave off a breakdown in Saigon, was "more in accord with the current situation" in their view and added that an air war against the North was now "essential to prevent a complete collapse of the U.S. position in Southeast Asia."

The Joint Chiefs' memorandum was the first appearance, the account says, of a "provocation strategy" that was to be discussed at the Sept. 7 White House session—in the words of the narrative, "deliberate attempts to provoke the D. R. V. into taking actions which could then be answered by a systematic U.S. air campaign."

The memorandum itself is not this explicit, although it does seem to suggest attempting to repeat the Tonkin Gulf clashes as a pretext for escalation.

In a Sept. 3 memorandum to Secretary McNamara, however, Mr. McNaughton was specific. He outlined several means of provocation that could culminate in a sustained air war. In the meantime, they could be employed to conduct reprisal air strikes that would help hold the situation in South Vietnam together and, the analyst notes, permit postponing "probably until November or December any decision as to serious escalation."

Defines Serious Escalation

This serious escalation Mr. McNaughton defined as "a crescendo of GVN-U.S. military actions against the D.R.V.," such as mining harbors and gradually escalating air raids.

He described his provocation program to Mr. McNamara as "an orchestration of three classes of actions, all designed to meet these five desiderata—(1) From the U.S., GVN and hopefully allied points of view they should be legitimate things to do under the circumstances, (2) they should cause apprehension, ideally increasing apprehension, in the D.R.V., (3) they should be likely at some point to provoke a military D.R.V. response, (4) the provoked response should be likely to provide good grounds for us to escalate if we wished, and (5) the timing and crescendo should be under our control, with the scenario capable of being turned off at any time." [See text, McNaughton plan, Sept. 3.]

The classes of actions were:

¶South Vietnamese air strikes at enemy infiltration routes through southeastern Laos that would "begin in Laos near the South Vietnamese border and slowly 'march' up the trails and eventually across the North Vietnamese border."

¶A resumption of the covert coastal raids on North Vietnam under Operation Plan 34A, which President Johnson had temporarily suspended since the Tonkin Gulf incident. The South Vietnamese Government would announce them publicly, declaring them "fully justified as necessary to assist in interdiction of infiltration by sea."

¶A resumption of patrols in the Gulf of Tonkin by United States destroyers, code-named De Soto patrols, although these would still be physically "disassociated" from the 34A attacks. Mr. McNaughton noted that "the U.S. public is sympathetic to reasonable insistence on the right of the U.S. Navy to ply international waters."

Majority in Disagreement

But a majority of the officials at the Sept. 7 White House strategy meeting disagreed. They decided for the present against adopting a provocation strategy for reprisal air attacks, precisely because the Khanh regime was so weak and vulnerable and the morale-lifting benefits of such strikes might be offset by possible Communist retaliation, the analyst says. The meeting was attended by the President; Secretary of State Dean Rusk; Secretary McNamara; Gen. Earle G. Wheeler, the new Chairman of the Joint Chiefs; Ambassador Taylor, who had flown in from Saigon, and John A. McCone, the Director of Central Intelligence.

"We believe such deliberately provocative elements should not be added in the immediate future while the GVN is still struggling to its feet," Assistant Secretary of State William P. Bundy wrote in a memorandum recording the consensus recommendations formally made to the President after the meeting.

"By early October, however, we may recommend such actions depending on GVN progress and Communist reaction in the meantime, especially to U.S. naval patrols." A resumption of the destroyer patrols was one outcome of the Sept. 7 meeting.

The analyst says that a similar reason was given for the decision against beginning a sustained bombing campaign against the North, with or without a provocation strategy, in the near future. "The GVN over the next 2-3 months will be too weak for us to take any major deliberate risks of escalation that would involve a major role for, or threat to, South Vietnam," the Bundy memorandum states.

Ambassador Taylor had acknowledged in his cable of Aug. 18 that bombing the North to prevent a collapse in the South if the Khanh regime continued to decline "increases the likelihood of U.S. involvement in ground action since Khanh will have almost no available ground forces which can be released from pacification employment to mobile resistance of D.R.V. attacks."

'A Base for Wider Action'

The Pentagon account concludes from the Sept. 7 strategy discussions that by now the Saigon regime was being regarded less and less as a government capable of defeating the Vietcong insurgency than "in terms of its suitability as a base for wider action."

Despite the pessimistic analyses of Ambassador Taylor and the Joint Chiefs for future escalation, some of those at the White House meeting hoped the Khanh regime could be somewhat stabilized. Citing handwritten notes of the meeting in the Pentagon files, the analyst quotes Mr. McNamara as saying that he understood "we are not acting more strongly because there is a clear hope of strengthening the GVN."

"But he went on," the account continues, "to urge that the way be kept open for stronger actions even if the GVN did not improve or in the event the war were widened by the Communists."

The handwritten notes of the meeting quote the President as asking, "Can we really strengthen the GVN?"

And in his memorandum of the consensus, William Bundy wrote: "Khanh will probably stay in control and may make some headway in the next 2-3 months in strengthening the Government (GVN). The best we can expect is that he and the GVN will be able to maintain order, keep the pacification program ticking over (but not progressing markedly), and give the appearance of a valid government."

On Sept. 10, therefore, the President ordered a number of interim measures in National Security Action Memorandum 314, issued over the signature of his special assistant, McGeorge Bundy. These were intended, in the words of William Bundy's memorandum of consensus, "to assist morale in SVN and show the Communists we still mean business, while at the same time seeking to keep the risks low and under our control at each stage."

A Reflection of Consensus

The most important orders Mr. Johnson gave dealt with covert measures. The final paragraph in the President's memorandum also reflected the consensus, the analyst finds, of the Sept. 7 meeting and other strategy discussions of the time—"the extent to which the new year was anticipated as the occasion for beginning overt military operations against North Vietnam."

This final paragraph read: "These decisions are governed by a prevailing judgment that the first order of business at present is to take actions which will help to strengthen the fabric of the Government of South Vietnam; to the extent that the situation permits, such action should precede larger decisions. If such larger decisions are required at any time by a change in the situation, they will be taken." [See text, McGeorge Bundy memo, Sept. 10.]

The interim measures Mr. Jonnson ordered included these:

¶Resumption of the De Soto patrols by American destroyers in the Tonkin Gulf. They would "operate initially well beyond the 12-mile limit and be clearly disassociated from 34A maritime operations," but the destroyers "would have air cover from carriers."

¶Reactivation of the 34A coastal raids, this time after completion of the first De Soto patrol. The directive added that "we should have the GVN ready to admit they are taking place and to justify and legitimize them on the basis of the facts of VC infiltration by sea." The account explains, "It was believed that this step would be useful in establishing a climate of opinion more receptive to expanded (air) operations against North Vietnam when they became necessary." The word in parentheses is the study's.

¶An arrangement with the Laotian Government of Premier Souvanna Phouma to permit "limited GVN air and ground operations into the corridor areas of [southeastern] Laos, together with Lao air strikes and possible use of U.S. armed aerial reconnaissance." Armed aerial reconnaissance is a military operation in which the pilot has authority to attack unprogramed targets, such as gun installations or trucks, at his own discretion.

¶The United States "should be prepared" to launch "tit for tat" reprisal air strikes like those during the Tonkin Gulf incident "as appropriate against the D.R.V. in the event of any attack on U.S. units or any special D.R.V.-VC action against SVN."

The President also ordered "economic and political actions" in South Vietnam, such as pay raises for Vietnamese civil servants out of American funds, to try to strengthen the Saigon regime.

The United States destroyers Morton

and Edwards resumed the De Soto patrols in the Tonkin Gulf on Sept. 12, two days after Mr. Johnson's directive. They were attacked in a third Tonkin incident on the night of Sept. 18, and the President glossed over it.

However, he went ahead with his decision to resume the 34A coastal raids, still covertly, the account says. The order to reactivate them was issued by Mr. Johnson on Oct. 4, with the specification that they were to be conducted under tightened American controls.

Each operation on the monthly schedules now had to be "approved in advance" by Deputy Secretary of Defense Cyrus R. Vance for Secretary McNamara, Llewellyn A. Thompson, acting Deputy Under Secretary of State for Political Affairs, for Secretary Rusk, and McGeorge Bundy at the White House for the President.

During October, a subsequent report to William Bundy on covert activities said, the 34A coastal raids consisted of two shallow probes of North Vietnamese defenses, an attempt to capture a junk, and successful shellings of the radar station at Vinhson and the observation post at Muidao.

2 Sabotage Actions

Two of the sabotage teams that had previously been parachuted into the North also "carried out successful actions during October," the report said. "One demolished a bridge, the other ambushed a North Vietnamese patrol. Both teams suffered casualties, the latter sufficient to cast doubt on the wisdom of the action."

The U-2 spy plane flights over North Vietnam and the parachuting of supplies and reinforcements to sabotage and psychological warfare teams in the North continued throughout this period and had not been affected by the President's suspension of the coastal raids after the original Tonkin Gulf incident.

The covert step-up in the air operations in Laos ordered by the President did not take place until mid-October. The Pentagon account says that one reason for the delay was the Administration's need to "await the uncertain outcome" of negotiations then taking place in Paris between the right-wing, neutralist and pro-Communist factions in Laos. The objective of the talks was to arrange a cease-fire that might lead to a new 14-nation Geneva conference to end the Laotian civil war.

"However, a Laotian cease-fire was not compatible with current perceptions of U.S. interest," the analyst writes.

The Administration feared that during an ensuing Geneva conference on Laos, international pressures, particularly from the Communist countries, might force the discussions onto the subject of Vietnam. Negotiations in the present circumstances were considered certain to unravel the shaky anti-Communist regime in Saigon.

The Administration also believed that even the convening of a conference on Laos might create an impression in Saigon that Washington was going to seek a negotiated withdrawal from South Vietnam and set off a political collapse there and the emergence of a neutralist coalition regime that would ask the United States to leave.

The account notes that in his Aug. 11 high-level policy memorandum on Southeast Asia, William Bundy had "characterized U.S. strategy" toward the Paris talks with the statement that "we should wish to slow down any progress toward a conference and to hold Souvanna to the firmest possible position." Mr. Bundy had referred to a suggestion by Ambassador Leonard Unger that Prince Souvanna Phouma insist on three-faction administration of the Plaine des Jarres as "a useful delaying gambit."

"Significantly," the analyst says, "this proposal was advanced at Paris by Souvanna Phouma on 1 September— illustrating the fact that Souvanna was carefully advised by U.S. diplomats both prior to and during the Paris meetings. Other features of Souvanna's nego-

tiating posture which apparently were encouraged as likely to have the effect of drawing out the discussions were insistence on Communist acceptance of (1) Souvanna's political status as Premier and (2) unhampered operations by the I.C.C. [International Control Commission]."

"Insistence on Souvanna's position is another point on which he should insist, and there would also be play in the hand on the question of free I.C.C. operations," Mr. Bundy wrote in his Aug. 11 memorandum.

Breakdown in Negotiations

"It will be recalled that the latter point was the issue on which progress toward a cease-fire became stalled," the analyst remarks. The negotiations broke down in Paris late in September.

American mission representatives from Bangkok and Vientiane met in Saigon on Sept. 11 under Ambassador Taylor's auspices, however, and decided that the South Vietnamese Air Force should not participate in the stepped-up air action in Laos authorized by the President in his directive of Sept. 10.

A list of 22 targets in the Laotian panhandle had been drawn up during the summer for the possibility of such raids, including one on a control point at the Mugia Pass, just across the North Vietnamese border.

South Vietnamese air strikes would offend Premier Souvanna Phouma by complicating his political position, the meeting determined, so the air attacks would be confined to clandestine raids by the T-28's in Laos and the United States Navy and Air Force jets—codenamed Yankee Team—operating over Laos. Accord was also reached that South Vietnamese troops, possibly accompanied by American advisers, would also make ground forays into Laos up to a depth of 20 kilometers, or 12 miles.

"The mission representatives agreed that, once the [air and ground] operations began, they should not be acknowledged publicly," the analyst writes. "In effect, then, they would supplement the other covert pressures being exerted against North Vietnam. Moreover, while the Lao Government would of course know about the operations of their T-28's, Souvanna was not to be informed of the GVN/U.S. [ground] operations. The unacknowledged nature of these operations would thus be easier to maintain."

Joint Departmental Message

On Oct. 6, a joint State and Defense Department message authorized Ambassador Unger in Laos to obtain Premier Souvanna Phouma's approval for the T-28 strikes "as soon as possible."

But as the analyst points out, the message showed that the President had decided to postpone the accompanying strikes by Yankee Team jets, the "U.S. armed aerial reconnaissance" mentioned in Mr. Johnson's National Security Action Memorandum 314.

Five of the targets in the Laotian panhandle, well-defended bridges, had been specifically marked for the American jets, and fire by the Yankee Team planes would also be required against antiaircraft batteries defending the Mugia Pass. The message from Washington excluded these targets from the list of 22.

"You are further authorized to inform Lao that Yankee Team suppressive-fire strikes against certain difficult targets in panhandle, interspersing with further T-28 strikes, are part of the over-all concept and are to be anticipated later, but that such U.S. strikes are not repeat not authorized at this time," the cable said. [See text, cable on Laos Strikes, Sept. 10.]

Ambassadors Unger and Taylor both warned that the Laotian Government, without some participation by the American jets, would not persevere in attacking targets on the Communist infiltration routes. Accordingly, the day before the T-28 strikes began on Oct. 14 with Premier Souvanna Phouma's approval, Washington authorized the

Yankee Team jets to fly combat air patrol over the T-28's to raise morale and protect them from any interference by North Vietnamese MIG's.

'Minor Extension' Only

Ambassador Taylor said in his cable that the combat air patrol missions could be achieved by "a relatively minor extension" of the current rules of engagement for American aircraft in Indochina.

The President also postponed for the present the planned ground forays into Laos by the South Vietnamese. Ambassador Taylor pointed out in a cable on Oct. 9 that these would not be possible "in forseeable future" in any case because the South Vietnamese Army was so tied down fighting the guerillas in its own country.

Several eight-man South Vietnamese reconnaissance teams were parachuted into Laos in an operation called Leaping Lena, but the Nov. 7 report to William Bundy on covert operations would note that "all of these teams were located by the enemy and only four survivors returned. . . . "

On Nov. 1, two days before the election, the Vietcong struck with a devastating mortar barrage on American planes and facilities at Bienhoa airfield near Saigon. The attack put the

President under great internal pressure, the analyst says, to strike back openly, as he had said in his directive of Sept. 10 that he was prepared to do "in the event of any attack on U.S. units or any special D.R.V./VC action against SVN."

In the enemy's barrage, four Americans were killed, five B-57 bombers were destroyed and eight damaged. These were some of the B-57's that had earlier been sent from Japan to the Philippines at Mr. McNamara's suggestion as part of the preparations for possible bombing of the North. They had since been moved into South Vietnam, however, to try to shore up the Khanh Government's military position by bringing more air power to bear upon the Vietcong.

"As of the end of October (in anticipation of resumed De Soto patrols), elements of our Pacific forces were reported as 'poised and ready' to execute reprisals for any D.R.V. attacks on our naval vessels. Thus, there was a rather large expectancy among Administration officials that the United States would do something in retaliation," the analyst writes. The words in parentheses are his.

'Change of Ground Rules'

The Joint Chiefs told Mr. McNamara

that the Bienhoa attack had been "a deliberate act of escalation and a change of the ground rules under which the VC had operated up to now." Asserting that "a prompt and strong response is clearly justified," they proposed, on the same day as the incident, "that the following specific actions be taken" (the words in parentheses are those of the Joint Chiefs; words in brackets have been inserted by The Times for clarification):

"a. Within 24-36 hours Pacific Command (PACOM) forces take initial U.S. military actions as follows:

"(1) Conduct air strikes in Laos against targets No. 3 (Tchepone barracks, northwest), No. 4 (Tchepone military area), No. 19 (Banthay military area), No. 8 (Nape highway bridge), and the Banken bridge on Route 7.

"(2) Conduct low-level air reconnaissance of infiltration routes and of targets in North Vietnam south of Latitude 19 degrees.

"b. Prior to air attacks on the D.R.V., land the Marine special landing forces at Danang and airlift Army or Marine units from Okinawa to the Saigon-Tansonnhut-Bienhoa area, to provide increased security for US personnel and installations.

"c. Use aircraft engaged in airlift (subparagraph b, above) to assist in evacuation of U.S. dependents from

Continued on Following Page

Survey Reports That Basic Commitment Went Unquestioned by Top U.S. Officials

Continued from Preceding Page

Saigon, to commence concurrently with the daylight air strikes against the D.R.V. (subparagraph d, below).

"d. Assemble and prepare necessary forces so that:

"(1) Within 60 to 72 hours, 30 B-52's from Guam conduct a night strike on D.R.V. target No. 6 (Phucyen airfield). [Phucyen, 13 miles from Hanoi, is the principal North Vietnamese air base].

"(2) Commencing at first light on the day following subparagraph (1) above, PACOM air and naval forces conduct air strikes against D.R.V. targets No. 6 (Phucyen airfield) (daylight follow-up on the above night strike), No. 3 (Hanoi Gialam airfield), No. 8 (Haiphong Catbi airfield), No. 48 (Haiphong POL), and No. 49 (Hanoi POL). [POL is a military abbreviation for petroleum, oil and lubricants.]

"(3) Concurrently with subparagraph (2). above the Vietnamese Air Force (VNAF) will strike DRV target No. 36 (Vitthulu barracks).

"(4) Combat air patrols (CAP), flak suppressive fire, strike photographic reconnaissance, and search and rescue operations (S.A.R.) are conducted as appropriate.

"(5) The above actions are followed by:

"(a) Armed reconnaissance on infiltration routes in Laos.

"(b) Air strikes against infiltration routes and targets in the D.R.V.

"(c) Progressive PACOM and SAC [Strategic Air Command] strikes against the targets listed in 94 Target Study.

"(e) Thai bases be used as necessary in connection with the foregoing, with authority to be obtained through appropriate channels. . . .

"Recognizing that security of this plan is of critical importance, they [the Joint Chiefs] consider that external agencies, such as the VNAF, should be apprised only of those parts of the plan necessary to insure proper and effective coordination. The same limited revelation of plans should govern discussions with the Thais in securing authority for unlimited use of Thai bases."

Caution From Saigon

From Saigon, Ambassador Taylor cabled for a more restrained response consisting of "retaliation bombing attacks on selected D.R.V. targets" using both American and South Vietnamese planes and for a "policy statement that we will act similarly in like cases in the future."

But the President felt otherwise for the moment. "Apparently, the decision was made to do nothing," the analyst says, adding that the documentary evidence does not provide an adequate explanation.

At a White House meeting the same day, the account continued, the President expressed concern that United States retaliatory strikes might bring counterretaliation by North Vietnam or China against American bases and civilian dependents in the South.

In briefing the press, Administration officials, unidentified in the study, drew a contrast "between this incident and the Tonkin Gulf attacks where our destroyers were 'on United States business.' "

"A second [White House] meeting to discuss possible U.S. actions was 'tentatively scheduled' for 2 November, but the available materials contain no evidence that it was held," the account continues. "President Johnson was scheduled to appear in Houston that afternoon, for his final pre-election address, and it may be that the second White House meeting was called off."

"One thing is certain," the writer concludes. "There were no retaliatory strikes authorized following the attack on the U.S. bomber base."

A Panel Under Bundy

But the President had not altogether declined to act on Nov. 1. He had appointed an interagency working group under William Bundy to draw up various political and military options for direct action against North Vietnam. This was the one "concrete result" of the Nov. 1 mortar raid on Bienhoa, the account reports.

The Bundy working group, as it would be unofficially called in the Government, held its first meeting at 9:30 A.M. on

Nov. 3, the day that Mr. Johnson was elected to the Presidency in his own right by a huge landslide.

"Bienhoa may be repeated at any time," Mr. Bundy wrote in a memorandum to the group on Nov. 5. "This would tend to force our hand, but would also give us a good springboard for any decision for stronger action. The President is clearly thinking in terms of maximum use of a Gulf of Tonkin rationale, either for an action that would show toughness and hold the line till we can decide the big issue, or as a basis for starting a clear course of action under the broad options." [See text, McGeorge Bundy draft, Nov. 5.]

Ostensibly, the Bundy group had a mandate to re-examine the entire American policy toward Vietnam and to recommend to the National Security Council a broad range of options. Its membership represented the entire foreign-policy-making machine of the Government—Mr. Bundy; Marshall Green; Michael V. Forrestal, head of the interagency Vietnam coordinating committee, and Robert Johnson of the State Department; Mr. McNaughton from the civilian hierarchy of the Pentagon; Vice Adm. Lloyd M. Mustin from the Joint Chiefs' staff and Harold Ford of the Central Intelligence Agency.

But, the account says, "there appears to have been, in fact, remarkably little latitude for reopening the basic question about U.S. involvement in the Vietnam struggle."

The basic national objective of "an independent, non-Communist South Vietnam," established by the President's National Security Action Memorandum 288 of the previous March, "did not seem open to question."

The Options Harden

The September discussions had established a consensus that bombing of the North "would be required at some proximate future date for a variety of reasons" and individual and institutional pressures all tended to harden the options toward this end as they were finally presented to the National Security Council and then the President.

The analyst gives a number of examples of this stiffening process from the successive draft papers developed by the group during its three weeks of deliberations.

"The extreme withdrawal option was rejected almost without surfacing for consideration" because of its conflict with the policy memorandums. "Fallback positions" outlined in an original working-group draft suffered a similar fate.

First Fallback Position

The first fallback position, the study says, "would have meant holding the line — placing an immediate, low ceiling on the number of U.S. personnel in SVN, and taking vigorous efforts to build on a stronger base elsewhere, possibly Thailand."

"The second alternative would have been to undertake some spectacular, highly visible supporting action like a limited-duration selective bombing campaign as a last effort to save the South; to have accompanied it with a propaganda campaign about the unwinnability of the war given the GVN's ineptness and, then, to have sought negotiations through compromise and neutralization when the bombing failed."

But because of "forceful objections" by Admiral Mustin, the Joint Chiefs representative, both of these possibilities were downgraded in the final paper presented to the National Security Council on Nov. 21. In effect they were "rejected before they were fully explored," the study says.

Thus all three options, labeled A, B and C, entailed some form of bombing, with "the distinctions between them" tending to blur as they evolved during the group's three weeks of deliberations, the analyst says. Mr. McNaughton and William Bundy collaborated closely on their formulation.

A similar convergence occurred on the question of negotiations.

The Minimum Position

Here the minimum United States position was defined as forcing Hanoi to halt the insurgency in the South and to agree to the establishment of a secure, non-Communist state there, a position the analyst defines as "acceptance or else." Moreover, talks of any kind with Hanoi were to be avoided until the effects of bombing had put the United States into a position to obtain this minimum goal in negotiations.

"The only option that provided for bargaining in the usual sense of the word was Option C," the study says. Here the United States would be willing to bargain away international supervisory machinery to verify Hanoi's agreement.

"The policy climate in Washington simply was not receptive to any suggestion that U.S. goals might have to be compromised," the study comments.

These are the options in their final form as the study summarizes them:

OPTION A—Conduct U.S. reprisal air strikes on North Vietnam "not only against any recurrence of VC 'spectaculars' such as Bienhoa," intensify the coastal raids of Operation Plan 34A, resume the destroyer patrols in the gulf, step up the air strikes by T-28's against infiltration targets in Laos and seek reforms in South Vietnam.

OPTION B—What Mr. McNaughton called "a fast/full squeeze." Bomb the North "at a fairly rapid pace and without interruption," including early air raids on Phucyen Airfield near Hanoi and key bridges along the road and

rail links with China until full American demands are met. "Should pressures for negotiations become too formidable to resist and discussion begin before a Communist agreement to comply," the analyst writes, "it was stressed that the United States should define its negotiating position 'in a way which makes Communist acceptance unlikely.' In this manner it would be 'very likely that the conference would break up rather rapidly,' thus enabling our military pressures to be resumed."

OPTION C—Mr. McNaughton's "slow squeeze"; the option he and William Bundy favored. Gradually increasing air strikes "against infiltration targets, first in Laos and then in the D.R.V., and then against other targets in North Vietnam" intended to "give the impression of a steady deliberate approach . . . designed to give the United States the option at any time to proceed or not, to escalate or not and to quicken the pace or not." This option also included the possibility of a "significant ground deployment to the northern part of South Vietnam" as an additional bargaining counter.

A Select Committee Meets

On Nov. 24, a select committee of the National Security Council met to discuss the option papers formally presented to the council three days earlier. This group comprised Secretaries Rusk and McNamara, Mr. McCone, General Wheeler, McGeorge Bundy and Under Secretary of State George W. Ball. William Bundy attended to keep a record and to represent the working group.

In the account of this meeting, Mr. Ball makes his first appearance in the Pentagon history as the Administration dissenter on Vietnam. William Bundy's memorandum of record says Mr. Ball "indicated doubt" that bombing the North in any fashion would improve the situation in South Vietnam and "argued against" a judgment that a Vietcong victory in South Vietnam would have a falling-domino effect on the rest of Asia.

While the working-group sessions had been in progress, the study discloses, Mr. Ball had been writing a quite different policy paper "suggesting a U.S. diplomatic strategy in the event of an imminent GVN collapse."

"In it, he advocated working through the U.K. [United Kingdom, or Britain] who would in turn seek cooperation from the U.S.S.R., in arranging an international conference (of smaller proportions than those at Geneva) which would work out a compromise political settlement for South Vietnam," the analyst says. The words in parentheses are the analyst's.

Of those present at the November 24 meeting, the memorandum of record indicates, only Mr. Ball favored Option A. The study gives the impression this was conceived as a throwaway option by the Working Group. The group's analysis labeled it "an indefinite course of action" whose "sole advantages" were these:

"(a) Defeat would be clearly due to GVN failure, and we ourselves would be less implicated than if we tried Option B or Option C, and failed.

"(b) The most likely result would be a Vietnamese negotiated deal, under which an eventually unified Communist Vietnam would reassert its traditional hostility to Communist China and limit its own ambitions to Laos and Cambodia."

Secretary Rusk Disagrees

At the Nov. 24 meeting, however, Mr. Rusk said that while he favored bombing North Vietnam he did not accept an analysis by Mr. McNaughton and William Bundy that if the bombing failed to save South Vietnam "we would obtain international credit merely for trying."

"In his view," the analyst writes, "the harder we tried and then failed, the worse our situation would be."

McGeorge Bundy demurred to some extent, the account goes on, but Mr. Ball "expressed strong agreement with the last Rusk point."

General Wheeler, reflecting the viewpoint of the Joint Chiefs, argued that the hard, fast bombing campaign of Option B actually entailed "less risk of a major conflict before achieving success," in words of the study, than the gradually rising air strikes of Option C.

The study adds that Mr. Bundy and Mr. McNaughton may have deliberately loaded the language of Option B to try to frighten the President out of adopting it lest it create severe international pressure for quick negotiations.

General Wheeler's argument presaged a running controversy between the Joint Chiefs and the civilian leadership after the bombing campaign began in the coming year.

The meeting on Nov. 24 ended without a clear majority decision on which option should be recommended to the President. The principals resumed when Ambassador Taylor reached Washington to join the strategy talks on Nov. 27, 1964.

Taylor's Three Purposes

In a written briefing paper, he told the conferees:

"If, as the evidence shows, we are playing a losing game in South Vietnam . . . it is high time we change and find a better way." He proposed gradually increasing air strikes against the North for a threefold purpose:

"First, establish an adequate government in SVN; second, improve the conduct of the counterinsurgency campaign; finally persuade or force the D.R.V. to stop its aid to the Vietcong and to use its directive powers to make the Vietcong desist from their efforts to overthrow the Government of South Vietnam."

To improve anti-Communist prospects in the South, the Ambassador proposed using the lever of American air strikes

against the North to obtain promises from the Saigon leaders that they would achieve political stability, strengthen the army and the police, suppress dissident Buddhist and student factions, replace incompetent officials and get on with the war effort.

The analyst says that the Ambassador had thus revised his earlier view that Washington should bomb the North merely to prevent "a collapse of national morale" in Saigon. He still favored some form of bombing in an emergency, but now he wanted something solid from the Saigon leaders in exchange for a coherent program of rising air war.

In the course of discussions on Nov. 27, however, the Ambassador acknowledged that while bombing "would definitely have a favorable effect" in South Vietnam, ". . . he was not sure this would be enough really to improve the situation," the analyst reports, again quoting from William Bundy's memorandum of record.

"Others, including McNamara, agreed with Taylor's evaluation, but the Secretary [Mr. McNamara] added that 'the strengthening effect of Option C could at least buy time, possibly measured in years.'"

Ambassador Taylor proposed that the Administration therefore adopt a two-phase program culminating in the bombing of infiltration facilities south of the 19th Parallel in North Vietnam, in effect Option A plus the first stages of Option C. Phase I would consist of 30 days of the Option A type of actions, such as intensification of the coastal raids on the North, air strikes by American jets at infiltration routes and one or two reprisal raids against the North. Meanwhile, Ambassador Taylor would obtain the promises of improvement from the Saigon leadership.

'When You Crawl Out . . .'

At the end of the 30 days, with the promises in hand, the United States would then move into Phase II, the air war. The air raids were to last two to six months, during which Hanoi was apparently expected to yield.

The others agreed, and the proposal was redefined further at a meeting on Nov. 28. William Bundy was assigned the task of drawing up a formal policy paper outlining the proposal. The Cabinet-level officials agreed to recommend it to the President at a White House meeting scheduled for Dec. 1, right after Mr. Johnson's Thanksgiving holiday at his ranch.

On Nov. 28, the same day that his closest advisers made their decision to advise him to bomb North Vietnam, Mr. Johnson was asked at a news conference at the ranch:

"Mr. President, is expansion of the Vietnam war into Laos or North Vietnam a live possibility at this moment?"

"I don't want to give you any particular guide posts as to your conduct in the matter," Mr. Johnson told the newsmen about their articles. "But when you crawl out on a limb, you always have to find another one to crawl back on.

"I have just been sitting here in this serene atmosphere of the Pedernales for the last few days reading about the wars that you [speculating newsmen] have involved us in and the additional undertakings that I have made decisions on or that General Taylor has recommended or that Mr. McNamara plans or Secretary Rusk envisages. I would say, generally speaking, that some people are speculating and taking positions that I think are somewhat premature."

"At the moment," he concluded, "General Taylor will report to us on developments. We will carefully consider these reports. . . . I will meet with him in the early part of the week. I anticipate there will be no dramatic announcement to come out of these meetings except in the form of your speculation."

William Bundy's draft policy paper, written the next day, said the bombing campaign "would consist principally of progressively more serious air strikes, of a weight and tempo adjusted to the situation as it develops (possibly running from two to six months)." The words in parentheses are Mr. Bundy's.

The draft paper added: "Targets in the D.R.V. would start with infiltration targets south of the 19th Parallel and work up to targets north of that point. This could eventually lead to such measures as air strikes on all major military-related targets, aerial mining of D.R.V. ports, and a U.S. naval blockade of the D.R.V.

"Concurrently," it continued, "the U.S. would be alert to any sign of yielding by Hanoi, and would be prepared to explore negotiated solutions that attain U.S. objectives in an acceptable manner." [See text, working group's draft, Nov. 29.]

Apparently at Mr. McNamara's suggestion, the analyst says, a final sentence in this paragraph was deleted; it read, "The U.S. would seek to control any negotiations and would oppose any independent South Vietnamese efforts to negotiate." Also removed, possibly during a final meeting of the top officials on Nov. 30 to review the policy paper and "apparently on the advice of McGeorge Bundy," was a proposal that the President make a major speech indicating the new direction that Washington's policy was taking.

Likewise deleted was a provision to brief "available Congressional leaders . . . (no special leadership meeting will be convened for this purpose)" on new evidence being compiled on North Vietnamese infiltration into the South, as a public justification of the bombing.

A separate recommendation from the Joint Chiefs for a series of major raids —like those in their retaliation proposal for the Vietcong mortar strike at Bienhoa air base on Nov. 1—was deleted for unspecified reasons, the analyst says, "in effect, presenting a united front to the President."

The paper that was sent to the President made no mention of American ground troops to provide security for airfields in the South when the bombing began, as General Wheeler had reminded the conferees on Nov. 24 would be necessary.

The writer notes the "gap" between the drastic concessions expected from Hanoi and the relatively modest bombing campaign that was expected to break Hanoi's will. He puts forward "two by no means contradictory explanations of this gap." This is the first:

Calculated 'Doses of Force'

"There is some reason to believe that the principals thought that carefully calculated doses of force could bring about predictable and desirable responses from Hanoi. Underlying this optimistic view was a significant underestimate of the level of the D.R.V. commitment to victory in the South and an overestimate of the effectiveness of U.S. pressures in weakening that resolve."

A related factor, the account says, "which, no doubt, commended the proposal to the Administration was the relatively low cost—in political terms— of such action." The context here indicates that the Administration thought the public would find an air war less repugnant than a ground war.

The President seems to have shared the view of his chief advisers, the analyst writes, that "the threat implicit in minimum but increasing amounts of force ('slow squeeze') would . . . ultimately bring Hanoi to the table on terms favorable to the U.S."

"McGeorge Bundy, as the President's assistant for national security affairs, was in a position to convey President Johnson's mood to the group," the account goes on. It adds that notes taken at a White House meeting on Dec. 1 when the senior officials met with Mr. Johnson to present the bombing plan "tend to confirm that the President's mood was more closely akin to the measures recommended" than to other, harsher bombing plans.

"A second explanation of the gap between ends and means is a more simple one," the account comments. "In a phrase, we had run out of alternatives other than pressures."

A memorandum by Assistant Secretary McNaughton on Nov. 6, 1964, made the point succinctly: "Action against North Vietnam is to some extent a substitute for strengthening the Government in South Vietnam. That is, a less active VC (on orders from D.R.V.) can be matched by a less efficient GVN. We therefore should consider squeezing North Vietnam." The words in parentheses are Mr. McNaughton's. [See text.]

Doubts at Two Poles

The two dissenters from the view that "calculated doses of force" would bring Hanoi around were, at opposite poles, the Joint Chiefs and the intelligence agencies.

"The J.C.S. differed from this view on the grounds that if we were really interested in affecting Hanoi's will, we would have to hit hard at its capabilities," the account says. The Joint Chiefs wanted the United States to demonstrate a willingness to apply unlimited force.

Their bombing plan, deleted from the position paper before it was presented to the President, asserted that the destruction of all of North Vietnam's major airfields and its petroleum supplies "in the first three days" was intended to "clearly . . . establish the fact that the U.S. intends to use military force to the full limits of what military force can contribute to achieving U.S. objectives in Southeast Asia . . . The follow-on military program—involving armed reconnaissance of infiltration routes in Laos, air strikes on infiltration targets in the D.R.V. and then progressive strikes throughout North Vietnam — could be suspended short of full destruction of the D.R.V. if our objectives were achieved earlier."

The analyst remarks that the Joint Chiefs' plan was "shunted aside because both its risks and costs were too high," but the author does not attempt to evaluate the possible effect of his plan on Hanoi's will.

Analysis of Enemy Policy

Like Mr. Ball, the account says, the intelligence community "tended toward a pessimistic view" of the effect of bombing on the Hanoi leaders.

The intelligence panel within the Bundy working group, composed of representatives from the three leading intelligence agencies—the C.I.A., the State Department's Bureau of Intelligence and Research and the Pentagon's Defense Intelligence Agency—"did not concede very strong chances for breaking the will of Hanoi," the author writes.

"The course of actions the Communists have pursued in South Vietnam over past few years implies a fundamental estimate on their part that the difficulties facing the U.S. are so great that U.S. will and ability to maintain resistance in that area can be gradually eroded—without running high risks that this would wreak heavy destruction on the D.R.V. or Communist China," the panel's report said.

If the United States now began bombing, the panel said, the Hanoi leadership would have to ask itself "a basic question" about how far the United States was willing to step up the war "regardless of the danger of war with Communist China and regardless of the international pressures that could be brought to bear. . . ." The decision of the Hanoi leadership was thus uncertain for a number of reasons, the panel cautioned, and "in any event, comprehension of the other's intentions

[w]ould almost certainly be difficult on [both] sides, and especially as the scale [of] hostilities mounted."

The panel then cast doubt on the so-called Rostow thesis of how much Hanoi feared destruction of its industry. This thesis, named for its proponent, Walt W. Rostow, chairman of the State Department's Policy Planning Council, underlay much of the Administration's hope for the success of a bombing campaign.

The panel said: "We have many indications that the Hanoi leadership is acutely and nervously aware of the extent to which North Vietnam's transportation system and industrial plant is vulnerable to attack. On the other hand, North Vietnam's economy is over

whelmingly agricultural and, to a large extent, decentralized in a myriad of more or less economically self-sufficient villages. Interdiction of imports and extensive destruction of transportation facilities and industrial plants would cripple D.R.V. industry. These actions would also seriously restrict D.R.V. military capabilities, and would degrade, though to a lesser extent, Hanoi's capabilities to support guerrilla warfare in South Vietnam and Laos. We do not believe that such actions would have a crucial effect on the daily lives of the overwhelming majority of the North Vietnam population. We do not believe that attacks on industrial targets would so greatly exacerbate current economic difficulties as to create unmanageable control problems. It is reasonable to infer that the D.R.V. leaders have a psychological investment in the work of reconstruction they have accomplished over the last decade. Nevertheless, they would probably be willing to suffer some damage to the country in the course of a test of wills with the U. S. over the course of events in South Vietnam."

No Change of Policy

As in the case of earlier intelligence findings that contradicted policy intentions, the study indicates no effort on the part of the President or his most trusted advisers to reshape their policy along the lines of this analysis.

One part of the intelligence panel's report that the Administration did accept was a prediction that China would not react in any major way to a bombing campaign unless American or South Vietnamese troops invaded North Vietnam or northern Laos. The study indicates that, this analysis eased Administration fears on this point.

Chinese reaction to systematic bombing of North Vietnam was expected to be limited to providing Hanoi with antiaircraft artillery, jet fighters and naval patrol craft. The panel predicted that the Soviet role was "likely to remain a minor one," even where military equipment was concerned. However, the Russians subsequently sent large-scale shipments of formidable antiaircraft equipment to North Vietnam.

'Cautious and Equivocal'

Now that a decision to bomb North Vietnam was drawing near, the study says, Mr. Johnson became "cautious and equivocal" in approaching it. Two analysts of this period, in fact, differ in their characterization of his decision at the two-and-a-half-hour White House meeting on Dec. 1, 1964, a month after the election, when the bombing plan was presented to him.

One analyst says that at this meeting the President "made a tentative decision" to bomb, ordering the preparatory Phase I put into effect and approving Phase II, the air war itself, "in principle."

The second analyst says that while the President approved the entire bombing plan "in general outline at least

Continued on Following Page

Pentagon Study Says Shakiness in Saigon Hampered Planning for Step-Up

Continued from Preceding Page

it is also clear that he gave his approval to implement only the first phase of the concept."

The President tied the actual waging of air war to reforms by the Saigon Government, this analyst says, and left an impression by the end of the meeting that he was "considerably less than certain that future U. S. actions against North Vietnam [the air war] would be taken, or that they would be desirable."

No Following Memorandum

The study notes that "the precise nature of the President's decisions" at the meeting is not known because a national security action memorandum was not issued afterward.

"However," the study continues, "from handwritten notes of the meeting, from instructions issued to action agencies and from later reports of diplomatic and military actions taken, it is possible to reconstruct the approximate nature of the discussion and the decisions reached." The footnotes do not indicate who made the handwritten notes found in the Pentagon files, although the indication is that it was Mr. McNaughton or Mr. McNamara.

After a briefing by Ambassador Taylor on the situation in South Vietnam, the discussion turned to a draft statement, prepared by William Bundy, that the Ambassador was to deliver to the Saigon leaders. The statement explained the two-phase bombing plan and tied

Phase II to a serious attempt by the Saigon leadership to achieve some political stability and get on with the war effort against the Vietcong.

In Saigon, General Khanh had nominally surrendered authority to a civilian cabinet headed by Premier Tran Van Huong. The general was intriguing against the Huong Cabinet, however, as the ostensible commander in chief of the armed forces and head of a Military Revolutionary Committee of South Vietnamese generals. Within this council, a group headed by Air Vice Marshal Nguyen Cao Ky, the chief of the air force, was intriguing both with and against General Khanh.

Against this background, the study says of the White House meeting:

"The President made it clear that he considered that pulling the South Vietnamese together was basic to anything else the United States might do. He asked the Ambassador specifically which groups he [Ambassador Taylor] might talk to and what more we might do to help bring unity among South Vietnam's leaders. He asked whether we could not say to them 'we just can't go on' unless they pulled together. To this, Taylor replied that we must temper our insistence somewhat . . . ."

Which Ones to Brief

The meeting then moved into a discussion of which allied countries were to be briefed on the proposed air war. The President said he wanted "new, dramatic effective" forms of assistance from several, specifically mentioning Australia, New Zealand, Canada and the Philippines. These briefings by special

envoys were included in the draft position paper laying out the bombing plan as the important diplomatic element in Phase I.

"In each case," the study says, "the representative was to explain our concept and proposed actions and request additional contributions by way of forces in the event the second phase of U.S. actions were entered."

The plan made no provision for similar consultations with Congressional leaders and there is no evidence in the study that Mr. Johnson conducted any.

In approving the statement General Taylor was to make to the Saigon leaders, the President also gave his assent to ready the military signal that was formally to sound the beginning of the 30 days of Phase I—Operation Barrel Roll, air strikes by United States Air Force and Navy jets of Yankee Team against infiltration routes and facilities in the Laotian panhandle, which was to be the final step-up in the Laos air operations.

At the end of the meeting, the account continues, Ambassador Taylor "slipped out the White House rear entrance" to avoid the press and "only a brief, formal statement" was issued. The analyst, remarks that the White House press statement released immediately afterward "contained only two comments regarding any determinations that had been reached."

Instructions for Taylor

One said, "The President instructed Ambassador Taylor to consult urgently with the South Vietnamese Government as to measures that should be taken to

improve the situation in all its aspects."

The other, the concluding paragraph, said the President had "reaffirmed the basic U.S. policy of providing all possible and useful assistance to the South Vietnamese people and Government in their struggle to defeat the externally supported insurgency and aggression being conducted against them."

The final sentence in this paragraph, the analyst notes, was one "specifically linking this policy" with Congress's Tonkin Gulf resolution. The sentence read: "It was noted that this policy accords with the terms of the Congressional joint resolution of Aug. 10, 1964, which remains in full force and effect."

Then, on Dec. 3, emerging from a second meeting with Mr. Johnson, "presumably having received the final version of his instructions," the account goes on, Ambassador Taylor told reporters assembled at the White House "that he was going to hold 'across-the-board' discussions with the GVN."

"Asserting that U..S. policy for South Vietnam remained the same, he stated that his aim would be to improve the deteriorating situation in South Vietnam. Although he hinted at changes 'in tactics and method,' he quite naturally did not disclose the kind of operations in which the United States was about to engage or any future actions to which immediate activity could lead."

The Administration now moved quickly. William Bundy left for Australia and New Zealand the next day, Dec. 4, to brief their governments on both phases of the bombing plan, the writer says.

Wilson Visits Washington

Prime Minister Harold Wilson of Britain was "thoroughly briefed on the forthcoming U.S. actions" during a state visit to Washington Dec. 7 to 9, the narrative continues, while other envoys briefed the Canadians and the Asian allies. The writer notes that while Britain, Australia and New Zealand were given "the full picture," the Canadians were "told slightly less" and the Philippines, South Korea and the Chinese Nationalist Government on Taiwan were "briefed on Phase I only." What the Thais and the Laotians were told is not made explicit.

The New Zealand Government "expressed grave doubts" that the bombing would break Hanoi's will, the writer says, and predicted that it might increase infiltration to South Vietnam.

In meetings in Saigon on Dec. 7 and 9 with General Khanh and Premier Huong, Ambassador Taylor exacted the desired promises in exchange for the bombing. At the second meeting, the Ambassador presented them with a draft press release describing the desired improvements, including strengthening of the army and the police, which the Saigon Government released in its own name, at the United States' request, on Dec. 11.

William H. Sullivan, newly appointed as Ambassador to Laos, obtained Premier Souvanna Phouma's agreement on Dec. 10 to the American air strikes at infiltration routes along the Ho Chi Minh Trail supply network through the Laotian panhandle, and Operation Barrel Roll got under way on Dec. 14 with attacks by American jets on "targets of opportunity"—that is, unprogramed targets sighted by the pilots.

At a meeting of the National Security Council on Dec. 12, when the final details for Barrel Roll were reviewed and approved, the study reports, it was "agreed that there would be no public operations statements about armed reconnaissance in Laos unless a plane were lost."

"In such an event, the principals stated, the Government should continue to insist that we were merely escorting reconnaissance fights as requested by the Laotian Government."

Level of Attacks Set

McGeorge Bundy was quoted in the memorandum of record as stating that the agreed plan "fulfilled precisely the President's wishes."

On Dec. 18 Secretary McNamara set the level of Barrel Roll attacks for the 30 days of Phase I—the analyst indicates that he did so at the President's wishes—at two missions of four aircraft apiece each week.

The Administration also stepped up the raids by T-28 fighter planes in Laos with a joint mesage on Dec. 8 from Secretaries McNamara and Rusk to Ambassador Sullivan. The cable instructed him to have the Laotians intensify bombing "in the corridor areas and close to the D.R.V. border."

The analyst reports that in the three months between the beginning of October and the end of December there were 77 sorties by the T-28's in the panhandle area—a sortie is a strike by a single plane—and that by early December the air raids had "already precipitated several complaints from the D.R.V." to the International Control Commission "alleging U.S.-sponsored air attacks on North Vietnamese territory."

Events in Saigon had meanwhile gone awry. Political turmoil broke out there again with Buddhist and student demonstrations against Premier Huong's Cabinet.

On Dec. 20, in defiance of Ambassador Taylor's wishes, General Khanh, in a temporary alliance with the so-called Young Turks—the young generals led by Marshal Ky—announced the dissolution of the High National Council, a body that was supposed to be functioning as a temporary legislature to draw up a constitution for a permanent civilian government. They also made a large number of political arrests by night, seizing several members of the High National Council.

That day, Ambassador Taylor summoned the Young Turks to the embassy and, in the writer's words, read them "the riot act." They included Gen. Nguyen Van Thieu, now President of South Vietnam.

According to the embassy's cable to Washington, the conversation began like this:

Ambassador Taylor: Do all of you understand English? (Vietnamese officers indicated they did ...)

I told you all clearly at General Westmoreland's dinner we Americans were tired of coups. Apparently I wasted my words. Maybe this is because something is wrong with my French because you evidently didn't understand. I made it clear that all the military plans which I know you would like to carry out are dependent on government stability. Now you have made a real mess. We cannot carry you forever if you do things like this.

Marshal Ky and other Vietnamese generals denied that they had staged a coup and said they were trying to achieve unity by getting rid of divisive elements, the account goes on.

The Ambassador tried to persuade them to support the civilian regime of Premier Huong and apparently to restore the High National Council. The Vietnamese officers would not agree.

The embassy cable describes the end of the conversation:

"In taking a friendly leave, Ambassador Taylor said: 'You people have broken a lot of dishes and now we have to see how we can straighten out this mess.'" [See text, Taylor message, Dec. 12.]

By the end of the month, Ambassador Taylor, Deputy Ambassador Johnson and General Westmoreland had apparently despaired of trading a bombing campaign against the North for a stable Saigon Government that would prosecute the war in the South. On Dec. 31, the account continues, they sent a joint message to Washington saying, in effect, that the United States should go ahead with the air campaign against the North "under any conceivable alliance condition short of complete abandonment of South Vietnam."

A Firmer Base Sought

The account indicates, however, that the President was reluctant to proceed into Phase II without at least the appearance of a firmer base in Saigon since the turmoil there was making it more difficult for him to justify escalation to the American public.

The writer remarks that at the meeting of the senior National Security Council Members on Dec. 24, Secretary Rusk "raised an issue that was high among Administration concerns—namely that the American public was worried about the chaos in the GVN, and particularly with respect to its viability as an object of increased U. S. commitment."

On Christmas Eve, the Vietcong planted a bomb in the Brinks, an officers billet in Saigon, killing two Americans in the blast and wounding 58 others; the President declined to authorize reprisal air strikes against the North, despite vigorous recommendations from Ambassador Taylor, Admiral Sharp in Honolulu and the Joint Chiefs, who were now pressing hard for escalation.

"Highest levels today reached negative decision on proposal . . . for reprisal action," Mr. Rusk cabled the Ambassador on Dec. 29.

Five days earlier, Mr. Rusk had also instructed Ambassador Taylor to halt, until the turmoil in Saigon subsided, the planned, piecemeal release to the press of evidence of a major increase in infiltration from the North during 1964, the writer says. The Ambassador had first reported the increase to Washington in October, along with a report of the appearance of individual North Vietnamese Army regulars, and the Administration began leaking the information in November through background briefings.

Making a Case in Public

By this time, the Administration felt that it had sufficient information on infiltration to make a public case for bombing the North. The intelligence community had obtained evidence that a minimum of 19,000 and a maximum of 34,000 infiltrators, mostly former southerners who had fought against the French in the Vietminh, had entered the South since 1959. Chester L. Cooper, a former intelligence officer, had put together a major report on Hanoi's support and direction of the guerrillas, but the Administration had decided earlier in December against public disclosure of the document itself because this might create "undesirable speculation," and had instead instructed the Ambassador to continue the piecemeal approach. Now, the analyst says, Mr. Rusk wanted this halted as well for fear that more publicity might create pressure for action prematurely.

Debate Grows in Congress

The political upheaval in Saigon, the writer continues, was fueling a Vietnam debate in Congress, which, while it did not exhibit much antiwar sentiment, did show considerable confusion and dismay, the writer says.

Secretary Rusk, on television on Jan. 3, 1965, felt it necessary to defend the Administration "in the context of a year-end foreign policy report," the account adds.

Mr. Rusk did not hint at the Administration's plans for possible bombing of the North. "Ruling out either a U. S. withdrawal or a major expansion of the war," the writer says, "Rusk gave assurances that with internal unity, and our aid and persistence the South Vietnamese could themselves defeat the insurgency."

On Jan. 14, however, as a result of the loss of two American jets over Laos in Operation Barrel Roll, "accounts of U.S. air operations against Laotian infiltration routes gained wide circulation for the first time," the writer says. A dispatch from Laos by United Press International, he adds, "in effect blew the lid on the entire Yankee Team operation in Laos since May of 1964."

"Despite official State or Defense refusal to comment on the nature of the Laotian air missions, these disclosures added new fuel to the public policy debate," the writer continues. The disclosures were complicating matters for the President by giving ammunition to the very small minority of antiwar senators who were taking seriously the press speculation that the United States might be getting ready to bomb the North.

In a Senate speech on Jan. 19, the account goes on, Senator Wayne Morse of Oregon charged that the Yankee Team air strikes had ignored the 1962 Geneva accords on Laos and "violated the nation's belief in 'substituting the rule of law for the jungle law of military might.' Broadening his attack, he warned, that 'there is no hope of avoiding a massive war in Asia' if U. S. policy towards Southeast Asia were to continue without change."

Within the Administration in Washington, key policy makers were coming to the same conclusion that Ambassador Taylor and his colleagues had reached in Saigon—that it was desirable to bomb the North regardless of what state of government existed in the South.

The political turmoil in Saigon, the narrative says, appears "to have been interpreted in Washington as an impending sellout" to the National Liberation Front. Fear increased that a neutralist coalition government would emerge and invite the United States to leave.

Victory for the Vietcong

Washington's sense of crumbling in the military situation was heightened when Saigon's army suffered a "highly visible" setback in a ferocious battle at Binhgia, southeast of the capital, between Dec. 26 and Jan. 2. Vietcong guerrillas nearly destroyed two South Vietnamese Marine battalions.

"All evidence pointed to a situation in which a final collapse of the GVN appeared probable and a victorious consolidation of VC power a distinct possibility," the narrative says.

The Hour Approaches

William Bundy communicated the feeling in a memorandum he wrote to Secretary Rusk on Jan. 6 for a meeting Mr. Rusk was to have with the President that afternoon. Mr. Bundy explained that the memorandum encompassed, besides his own thoughts, those of Mr. Forrestal, head of the interagency committee, and Ambassador Unger, who had recently been transferred back to Washington from Vientiane.

"I think we must accept that Saigon morale in all quarters is now very shaky indeed," he said in part, "and that this relates directly to a widespread feeling that the U.S. is not ready for stronger action and indeed is possibly looking for a way out. We may regard this feeling as irrational and contradicted by our repeated statements, but Bill Sullivan was very vivid in describing the existence of such feelings in October, and we must honestly concede that our actions and statements since the election have not done anything to offset it. The blunt fact is that we have appeared to the Vietnamese (and to wide circles in Asia and even in Europe) to be insisting on a more perfect government than can reasonably be expected, before we consider any additional action—and that we might even pull out our support unless such a government emerges.

"In key parts of the rest of Asia, notably Thailand, our present posture also appears weak. As such key parts of Asia see us, we looked strong in May and early June, weaker in later June and July, and then appeared to be taking a quite firm line in August with the Gulf of Tonkin. Since then we must have seemed to be gradually weakening — and, again, insisting on perfectionism in the Saigon Government before we moved.

"The sum total of the above seems to us to point—together with almost certainly stepped-up Vietcong actions in the current favorable weather — to a prognosis that the situation in Vietnam is now likely to come apart more rapidly than we had anticipated in November. We would still stick to the estimate that the most likely form of coming apart would be a government of key groups starting to negotiate covertly with the Liberation Front or Hanoi, perhaps not asking in the first instance that we get out, but with that necessarily following at a fairly early stage. In one sense this would be a 'Vietnam solution,' with some hope that it would produce a Communist Vietnam that would assert its own degree of independence from Peiping and that would produce a pause in Communist pressure in Southeast Asia. On the other hand, it would still be virtually certain than [sic] Laos would then become unten-

able and that Cambodia would accommodate in some way. Most seriously, there is grave question whether the Thai in these circumstances would retain any confidence at all in our continued support. In short, the outcome would be regarded in Asia, and particularly among our friends, as just as humiliating a defeat as any other form. As events have developed, the American public would probably not be too sharply critical, but the real question would be whether Thailand and other nations were weakened and taken over thereafter.

'Grave Difficulties' Are Foreseen

"The alternative of stronger action obviously has grave difficulties. It commits the U.S. more deeply, at a time when the picture of South Vietnamese will is extremely weak. To the extent that it included actions against North Vietnam, it would be vigorously attacked by many nations and disapproved initially even by such nations as Japan and India, on present indications. Most basically, its stiffening effect on the Saigon political situation would not be at all sure to bring about a more effective government, nor would limited actions against the southern D.R.V. in fact sharply reduce infiltration or, in present circumstances, be at all likely to induce Hanoi to call it off.

"Nonetheless, on balance we believe that such action would have some faint hope of really improving the Vietnamese situation, and, above all, would put us in a much stronger position to hold the next line of defense, namely Thailand. Accepting the present situation—or any negotiation on the basis of it—would be far weaker from this latter key standpoint. If we moved into stronger actions, we should have in mind that negotiations would be likely to emerge from some quarter in any event, and that under existing circumstances, even with the additional element of pressure, we could not expect to get an outcome that would really secure an independent South Vietnam. Yet even on an outcome that produced a progressive deterioration in South Vietnam and an eventual Communist take-over, we would still have appeared to Asians to have done a lot more about it.

"In specific terms, the kinds of action we might take in the near future would be:

"a. An early occasion for reprisal action against the D.R.V.

"b. Possibly beginning low-level reconnaissance of the D.R.V. at once.

"Concurrently with a or b, an early orderly withdrawal of our dependents [from Saigon, but only if] stronger ac-

tion [is contemplated]. If we are to clear our decks in this way—and we are more and more inclined to think we should—it simply must be, for this reason alone, in the context of some stronger action. . . .

"Introduction of limited U.S. ground forces into the northern area of South Vietnam still has great appeal to many of us, concurrently with the first air attacks into the D.R.V. It would have a real stiffening effect in Saigon, and a strong signal effect to Hanoi. On the disadvantage side, such forces would be possible attrition targets for the Vietcong."

A Similar Memorandum

Mr. McNaughton, Mr. Bundy's counterpart at the Pentagon, had given Mr. McNamara a similar memorandum three days earlier.

"The impact of these views can be seen in the policy guidance emanating from Washington in mid and late January, 1965," the Pentagon's narrative says.

In a cablegram to Saigon on Jan. 11, the writer goes on, Secretary Rusk instructed Ambassador Taylor "to avoid actions that would further commit the United States to any particular form of political solution" to the turmoil there. If another military regime emerged from the squabbling "we might well have to swallow our pride and work with it," Mr. Rusk said.

Another memorandum to Mr. McNamara from Mr. McNaughton, on Jan. 27, along with Mr. McNamara's penciled comments on it, "adds perspective to this viewpoint," the historian says. Mr. McNaughton stated "and Mr. McNamara agreed" that the United States objective in South Vietnam was "not to 'help friend' but to contain China," and "both favored initiating strikes against North Vietnam."

Paraphrasing the memorandum and Mr. McNamara's comments, the writer says, "At first they believed these [air attacks] should take the form of reprisals; beyond that, the Administration would have to 'feel its way' into stronger, graduated pressures. McNaughton doubted that such strikes would actually help the situation in South Vietnam, but thought they should be carried out anyway. McNamara believed they probably would help the situation, in addition to their broader impacts on the U.S. position in Southeast Asia."

"Clear indication that the Administration was contemplating some kind of increased military activity" had gone out to Saigon two days earlier in another cablegram from Mr. Rusk, the account goes on. "Ambassador Taylor was asked to comment on the 'departmental view'

that U.S. dependents should be withdrawn to 'clear the decks' in Saigon and enable better concentration of U.S. efforts on behalf of South Vietnam."

The Signal for 'D-Day'

Ever since the original bombing scenario of May 23, 1964, the evacuation of American women and children had been the signal for "D-Day."

"The Rusk cable made specific reference to a current interest in reprisal actions," the analyst says.

The initial blow came in about two weeks. The Vietcong attacked the United States military advisers' compound at Pleiku in the Central Highlands and an Army helicopter base at Camp Holloway, four miles away. Nine Americans were killed and 76 wounded.

"The first flash from Saigon about the assault came on the ticker at the National Military Command Center at the Pentagon at 2:38 P.M. Saturday, Feb. 6, Washington time," the narrative says. "It triggered a swift, though long-contemplated Presidential decision to give an 'appropriate and fitting' response. Within less than 14 hours, by 4 P.M. Sunday, Vietnam time, 49 U.S. Navy jets—A-4 Skyhawks and F-8 Crusaders from the Seventh Fleet carriers U.S.S. Coral Sea and U.S.S. Hancock—had penetrated a heavy layer of monsoon clouds to deliver their bombs and rockets upon North Vietnamese barracks and staging areas at Donghoi, a guerrilla training garrison 40 miles north of the 17th Parallel.

"Though conceived and executed as a limited one-shot tit-for-tat reprisal, the drastic U.S. action, long on the military planners' drawing boards under the operational code name Flaming Dart precipitated a rapidly moving sequence of events that transformed the character of the Vietnam war and the U.S. role in it."

Then the guerrillas attacked an American barracks at Quinhon, on the central coast, and on Feb. 11, the President launched a second and heavier reprisal raid, Flaming Dart II.

Two days later, on Feb. 13, he decided to begin Operation Rolling Thunder, the sustained air war against North Vietnam.

"As is readily apparent," the analyst concludes, "there was no dearth of reasons for striking North. Indeed, one almost has the impression that there were more reasons than were required. But in the end, the decision to go ahead with the strikes seems to have resulted as much from the lack of alternative proposals as from any compelling logic in their favor."

Tomorrow: The President orders a ground-combat mission.

49

Vietnam Archive: Study Tells How Johnson Secretly Opened Way to Ground Combat

By NEIL SHEEHAN

President Johnson decided on April 1, 1965, to use American ground troops for offensive action in South Vietnam because the Administration had discovered that its long-planned bombing of North Vietnam—which had just begun—was not going to stave off collapse in the South, the Pentagon's study of the Vietnam war discloses. He ordered that the decision be kept secret.

"The fact that this departure from a long-held policy had momentous implications was well recognized by the Administration leadership," the Pentagon analyst writes, alluding to the policy axiom since the Korean conflict that another land war in Asia should be avoided.

Although the President's decision was a "pivotal" change, the study declares, "Mr. Johnson was greatly concerned that the step be given as little prominence as possible."

The decision was embodied in National Security Action Memorandum 328, on April 6, which included the following paragraphs:

"5. The President approved an 18-20,000 man increase in U.S. military support forces to fill out existing units and supply needed logistic personnel.

"6. The President approved the deployment of two additional Marine Battalions and one Marine Air Squadron and associated headquarters and support elements.

"7. The President approved a change of mission for all Marine Battalions deployed to Vietnam to permit their more active use under conditions to be established and approved by the Secretary of Defense in consultation with the Secretary of State."

The paragraph stating the President's concern about publicity gave stringent orders in writing to members of the National Security Council:

"11. The President desires that with respect to the actions in paragraphs 5 through 7, premature publicity be avoided by all possible precautions. The actions themselves should be taken as rapidly as practicable, but in ways that should minimize any appearance of sudden changes in policy, and official statements on these troop movements will be made only with the direct approval of the Secretary of Defense, in consultation with the Secretary of State. The President's desire is that these movements and changes should be understood as being gradual and wholly consistent with existing policy." [See text, action memorandum on change of mission, April 6, 1965, Page 21.]

The period of increasing ground-combat involvement is shown in the Pentagon papers to be the third major phase of President Johnson's commitment to South Vietnam. This period forms another section of the presentation of those papers by The New York Times.

The papers, prepared by a large team of authors in 1967-68 as an official study of how the United States went to war in Indochina, consist of 3,000 pages of analysis and 4,000 pages of supporting documents. The study covers nearly three decades of American policy toward Southeast Asia. Thus far The Times's reports on the study, with presentation of key documents, have covered the

> This is the third in a series of articles on a secret study, made in the Pentagon, of American participation in the Vietnam war. The study was obtained from other sources by The New York Times through the investigative reporting of Mr. Sheehan. The series was researched and written over three months by Mr. Sheehan and other staff members.

Continued on Page 22, Col. 1

Vietnam Archive: Study Tells How Johnson Secretly Paved Way to Combat Use

Continued From Page 1, Col. 7

period of clandestine warfare before the Tonkin Gulf incidents in 1964 and the planning for sustained bombing of North Vietnam to begin early the next year.

In the spring of 1965, the study discloses, the Johnson Administration pinned its hopes on air assaults against the North to break the enemy's will and persuade Hanoi to stop the Vietcong insurgency in the South. The air assaults began on a sustained basis on March 2.

"Once set in motion, however, the bombing effort seemed to stiffen rather than soften Hanoi's backbone, as well as the willingness of Hanoi's allies, particularly the Soviet Union, to work toward compromise," the study continues.

"Official hopes were high that the Rolling Thunder program . . . would rapidly convince Hanoi that it should agree to negotiate a settlement to the war in the South. After a month of bombing with no response from the North Vietnamese, optimism began to wane," the study remarks.

"The U.S. was presented essentially with two options: (1) to withdraw unilaterally from Vietnam leaving the South Vietnamese to fend for themselves, or (2) to commit ground forces in pursuit of its objectives. A third option, that of drastically increasing the scope and scale of the bombing, was rejected because of the concomitant high risk of inviting Chinese intervention."

And so within a month, the account continues, with the Administration recognizing that the bombing would not work quickly enough, the crucial decision was made to put the two Marine battalions already in South Vietnam on the offensive. The 3,500 marines had landed at Danang on March 8—bringing the total United States force in South Vietnam to 27,000 — with their mission restricted to the static defense of the Danang airfield.

Orders Put in Writing

As a result of the President's wish to keep the shift of mission from defense to offense imperceptible to the public, the April 1 decision received no publicity "until it crept out almost by accident in a State Department release on 8 June," in the words of the Pentagon study.

The day before, the hastily improvised static security and enclave strategies of the spring were overtaken by a request from Gen. William C. Westmoreland, the American commander in Saigon, for nearly 200,000 troops. He wanted these forces, the Pentagon study relates, to hold off defeat long enough to make possible a further build-up of American troops.

"Swiftly and in an atmosphere of crisis," the study says, President Johnson gave his approval to General Westmoreland's request a little more than a month later, in mid-July. And once again, the study adds, Mr. Johnson concealed his decision.

New Warnings of Failure

Before the opening of the air war in the spring warnings were sounded high in the Administration that it would not succeed. Now there were warnings that a ground war in the South might prove fruitless. The warnings came not only from Under Secretary of State George W. Ball, long known as a dissenter on Vietnam, but also from John A. McCone, Director of Central Intelligence, who felt the actions planned were not strong enough.

On April 2 Mr. McCone circulated a memorandum within the National Security Council asserting that unless the United States was willing to bomb the North "with minimum restraint" to break Hanoi's will, it was unwise to commit ground troops to battle.

"In effect," he said, "we wil find ourselves mired down in combat in the jungle in a military effort that we cannot win and from which we will have extreme difficulty extracting ourselves." [See text, McCone memorandum, April 2, 1965.]

It is not clear from the documentary record whether President Johnson read this particular memorandum, but the Pentagon study says Mr. McCone expressed these same views in a personal memorandum to the President on April 28.

In a separate intelligence estimate for the President on May 6, Vice Adm. William F. Raborn Jr., Mr. McCone's successor, indicated agreement with Mr. McCone.

Mr. Ball's dissent came from the opposite side. He believed that neither bombing the North nor fighting the guerrillas in the South nor any combination of the two offered a solution and said so in a memorandum circulated on June 28, the study reports.

"Convinced that the U.S. was pouring its resources down the drain in the wrong place," the account goes on, Mr. Ball proposed that the United States "cut its losses" and withdraw from South Vietnam.

Ball Offers 'a Compromise'

"Ball was cold-blooded in his analysis," the study continues, describing the memorandum. "He recognized that the U.S. would not be able to avoid losing face before its Asian allies if it staged some form of conference leading to withdrawal of U.S. forces. The losses would be of short-term duration, however, and the U.S. could emerge from this period of travail as a 'wiser and more mature nation.'"

On July 1, the analyst says, Mr. Ball reiterated his proposal for withdrawal in a memorandum to the President entitled "A Compromise Solution for South Vietnam." [See text, Ball memorandum, July 1, 1965.]

But the President, the narrative continues, was now heeding the counsel of General Westmoreland to embark on a full-scale ground war. The study for this period concludes that Mr. Johnson and most of his Administration were in no mood for compromise on Vietnam.

As an indication of the Administration's mood during this period, the study cites "a marathon public-information campaign" conducted by Secretary of State Dean Rusk late in February and early in March as sustained bombing was getting under way.

Mr. Rusk, the study says, sought "to signal a seemingly reasonable but in fact quite tough U.S. position on negotiations, demanding that Hanoi 'stop doing what it is doing against its neighbors' before any negotiations could prove fruitful.

"Rusk's disinterest in negotiations at this time was in concert with the view of virtually all of the President's key advisers, that the path to peace was not then open," the Pentagon account continues. "Hanoi held sway over more than half of South Vietnam and could see the Saigon Government crumbling before her very eyes. The balance of power at this time simply did not furnish the U.S. with a basis for bargaining and Hanoi had no reason to accede to the hard terms that the U.S. had in mind. Until military pressures on North Vietnam could tilt the balance of forces the other way, talk of negotiation could be little more than a hollow exercise."

A Position of Compromise

The study also says that two of the President's major moves involving the bombing campaign in the spring of 1965 were designed, among other aims, to quiet critics and obtain public support for the air war by striking a position of compromise. But in fact, the account goes on, the moves masked publicly unstated conditions for peace that "were not 'compromise' terms, but more akin to a 'cease and desist' order that, from the D.R.V./VC point of view, was tantamount to a demand for their surrender." "D.R.V." denotes the Democratic Republic of Vietnam; "VC" the Vietcong.

In Mr. Johnson's first action, his speech at the Johns Hopkins University in Baltimore on April 7, he offered to negotiate "without posing any preconditions" and also held out what the study calls a "billion-dollar carrot" in the form of an economic-development program for the Mekong River Basin financed by the United States, in which North Vietnam might participate.

The second action was the unannounced five-day pause in bombing in May, during which the President called upon Hanoi to accept a "political solution" in the South. This "seemed to be aimed more at clearing the decks for a subsequent intensified resumption than it was at evoking a reciprocal act of de-escalation by Hanoi," the study says. Admiral Raborn, in his May 6 memorandum, had suggested a pause for this purpose and as an opportunity for Hanoi "to make concessions with some grace."

The air attacks had begun Feb. 8 and Feb. 11 with reprisal raids, code-named Operations Flaming Dart I and II, announced as retaliation for Vietcong attacks on American installations at Pleiku and Quinhon.

In public Administration statements on the air assaults, the study goes on, President Johnson broadened "the reprisal concept as gradually and imperceptibly as possible" into sustained air raids against the North, in the same fashion that the analyst describes him blurring the shift from defensive to offensive action on the ground during the spring and summer of 1965.

The study declares that the two February strikes—unlike the Tonkin Gulf reprisals in August, 1964, which were tied directly to a North Vietnamese attack on American ships—were publicly associated with a "larger pattern of aggression" by North Vietnam. Flaming Dart II, for example, was characterized as "a generalized response to 'continued acts of aggression,'" the account notes.

"Although discussed publicly in very muted tones," it goes on, "the second Flaming Dart operation constituted a sharp break with past U.S. policy and set the stage for the continuing bombing program that was now to be launched in earnest."

In another section of the study, a Pentagon analyst remarks that "the

6/15/71

Page 22, 23

change in ground rules . . . posed serious public-information and stage-managing problems for the President."

It was on Feb. 13, two days after this second reprisal, that Mr. Johnson ordered Operation Rolling Thunder. An important influence on his unpublicized decision was a memorandum from his special assistant for national security affairs, McGeorge Bundy, who was heading a fact-finding mission in Vietnam when the Vietcong attack at Pleiku occurred on Feb. 7. With Mr. Bundy were Assistant Secretary of Defense John T. McNaughton and Deputy Assistant Secretary of State Leonard Unger.

"A policy of sustained reprisal against North Vietnam" was the strategy advocated by Mr. Bundy in his memorandum, drafted on the President's personal Boeing 707, Air Force One, while returning from Saigon the same day." [See text, Bundy memorandum, Feb. 7, 1965.]

The memorandum explained that the justification for the air attacks against the North, and their intensity, would be keyed to the level of Vietcong activity in the South.

'Sustained Pressure' Sought

"We are convinced that the political values of reprisal require a continuous operation," Mr. Bundy wrote. "Episodic responses geared on a one-for-one basis to 'spectacular' outrages would lack the persuasive force of sustained pressure. More important still, they would leave it open to the Communists to avoid reprisals entirely by giving up only a small element of their own program. . . . It is the great merit of the proposed scheme that to stop it the Communists would have to stop enough of their activity in the South to permit the probable success of a determined pacification effort."

The analyst notes, however, that Mr. Bundy's memorandum was a "unique articulation of a rationale for the Rolling Thunder policy" because Mr. Bundy held out as the immediate benefit an opportunity to rally the anti-Communist elements in the South and achieve some political stability and progress in pacification. "Once such a policy is put in force," Mr. Bundy wrote, in summary conclusions to his memorandum," we shall be able to speak in Vietnam on many topics and in many ways, with growing force and effectiveness."

It was also plausible, he said, that bombing in the North, "even in a low key, would have a substantial depressing effect upon the morale of Vietcong cadres in South Vietnam."

Mr. Bundy, the study remarks, thus differed from most other proponents of bombing. These included Ambassador Maxwell D. Taylor, who despaired of improving the Saigon Government's effectiveness and who wanted bombing primarily as a will-breaking device "to inflict such pain or threat of pain upon the D.R.V. that it would be compelled to order a stand-down of Vietcong violence," in the study's words.

As several chapters of the Pentagon study show, a number of Administration strategists—particularly Walt W. Rostow, chairman of the State Department's Policy Planning Council—had assumed for years that "calculated doses" of American air power would accomplish this end.

Mr. Bundy, while not underrating the bombing's "impact on Hanoi" and its use "as a means of affecting the will of Hanoi," saw this as a "longer-range purpose."

'This Program Seems Cheap'

The bombing might not work. Mr. Bundy acknowledged. "Yet measured against the costs of defeat in Vietnam," he wrote, "this program seems cheap. And even if it fails to turn the tide— as it may—the value of the effort seems to us to exceed its cost."

President Johnson informed Ambassador Taylor of his Rolling Thunder decision in a cablegram drafted in the White House and transmitted to Saigon late in the afternoon of Sunday, Feb. 13.

The cable told the Ambassador that "we will execute a program of measured and limited air action jointly with the GVN [the Government of Vietnam] against selected military targets in D.R.V., remaining south of the 19th Parallel until further notice."

"Our current expectation," the message added, "is that these attacks might come about once or twice a week and involve two or three targets on each day of operation." [See text of White House cable, Feb. 13, 1965.]

Mr. Johnson said he hoped "to have appropriate GVN concurrence by Monday if possible. . . ."

The study recounts that "Ambassador Taylor received the news of the President's new program with enthusiasm. In his response, however, he explained the difficulties he faced in obtaining authentic GVN concurrence 'in the condition of virtual nongovernment' which existed in Saigon at that moment."

Gen. Nguyen Khanh, the nominal commander of the South Vietnamese armed forces, had ousted the civilian

Continued on Following Page

Saigon Governmental Situation Chaotic
as Bombing Began, Survey Reports

Continued on Following Page

cabinet of Premier Tran Van Huong on Jan. 27. Led by Air Vice Marshal Nguyen Cao Ky, a group of young generals—the so-called Young Turks— were in turn intriguing against General Khanh.

(A footnote in the account of the first reprisal strikes, on Feb. 8, says that Marshal Ky, who led the South Vietnamese planes participating in the raid, caused "consternation" among American target controllers by dropping his bombs on the wrong targets. "In a last minute switch," the footnote says, Marshal Ky "dumped his flight's bomb loads on an unassigned target in the Vinhlinh area, in order, as he later explained, to avoid colliding with U.S.A.F. aircraft which, he claimed, were striking his originally

assigned target when his flight arrived over the target area." Adm. U.S. Grant Sharp, commander of United States forces in the Pacific, reported the incident to the Joint Chiefs.)

Cables to the Embassies

Referring to the political situation in Saigon, the account says: "This Alice-in-Wonderland atmosphere notwithstanding, Taylor was undaunted."

"It will be interesting to observe the effect of our proposal on the internal political situation here," the Ambassador cabled back to Mr. Johnson in Washington about the bombing. "I will use the occasion to emphasize that a dramatic change is occurring in U.S. policy, one highly favorable to GVN interests but demanding a parallel dramatic change of attitude on the part of the GVN. Now is the time to install the best possible Government as we are clearly approaching a climax in the

next few months."

Ambassador Taylor apparently obtained what concurrence was possible and on Feb. 8 another cable went out from the State Department to London and eight United States Embassies in the Far East besides the one in Saigon. The message told the ambassadors of the forthcoming bombing campaign and instructed them to "inform head of government or State (as appropriate) of above in strictest confidence and report reactions." [See text, cable to U.S. envoys, Feb. 18, 1965.]

Both McGeorge Bundy and Ambassador Taylor had recommended playing down publicity on the details of the raids. "Careful public statements of U.S.G. [United States Government], combined with fact of continuing air actions, are expected to make it clear that military action will continue while aggression continues," the cable said.

"But focus of public attention will be kept as far as possible on D.R.V. aggression; not on joint GVN/US military operations.

The President had scheduled the first of the sustained raids, Rolling Thunder I, for Feb. 20. Five hours after the State Department transmitted that cable, a perennial Saigon plotter, Col. Pham Ngoc Thao, staged an unsuccessful "semi-coup" against General Khanh and "pandemonium reigned in Saigon," the study recounts. "Ambassador Taylor promptly recommended cancellation of the Feb. 20 air strikes and his recommendation was equally promptly accepted" by Washington, the Pentagon study says.

The State Department sent a cablegram to the various embassies rescinding the instructions to notify heads of government or state of the planned air war until further notice "in view of the disturbed situation in Saigon."

The situation there, the study says, remained "disturbed" for nearly a week while the Young Turks also sought to get rid of General Khanh.

"The latter made frantic but unsuccessful efforts to rally his supporters," the study says, and finally took off in his plane to avoid having to resign as commander in chief. "Literally running out of gas in Nhatrang shortly before dawn on Feb. 21, he submitted his resignation, claiming that a 'foreign hand' was behind the coup. No one, however, could be quite certain that Khanh might not 're-coup' once again, unless he were physically removed from the scene."

This took three more days to accomplish, and on Feb. 25 General Khanh finally went into permanent exile as an ambassador at large, with Ambassador Taylor seeing him off at the airport, "glassily polite," in the study's words.

"It was only then that Taylor was able to issue, and Washington could accept, clearance for the long-postponed and frequently rescheduled first Rolling Thunder strike."

Less than three weeks earlier, in his memorandum to the President predicting that "a policy of sustained reprisal" might bring a better government in Saigon, McGeorge Bundy had said he did not agree with Ambassador Taylor that General Khanh "must somehow be removed from the . . . scene."

"We see no one else in sight with anything like his ability to combine military authority with some sense of politics," the account quotes Mr. Bundy as having written.

In the meantime two more Rolling Thunder strikes—II and III— had also been scheduled and then canceled because, the study says, the South Vietnamese Air Force was on "coup alert," in Saigon.

During part of this period, air strikes against North Vietnam were also inhibited by a diplomatic initiative from the Soviet Union and Britain. They moved to reactivate their co-chairmanship of the 1954 Geneva conference on Indochina to consider the current Vietnam crisis. Secretary Rusk cabled Ambassador Taylor that the diplomatic initiative would not affect Washington's decision to begin the air war, merely its timing.

According to the Pentagon study, the Administration regarded the possibility of reviving the Geneva conference of 1954, which had ended the French Indochina War, "not as a potential negotiating opportunity, but as a convenient vehicle for public expression of a tough U.S. position."

But, the account adds, this "diplomatic gambit" had "languished" by the time General Khanh left Saigon, and the day of his departure Mr. Johnson scheduled a strike, Rolling Thunder IV, for Feb. 26.

The pilots had been standing by, for nearly a week, with the orders to execute a strike being canceled every 24 hours.

But the order to begin the raid was again canceled, a last time, by monsoon weather for four more days.

Rolling Thunder finally rolled on March 2, 1965, when F-100 Super Sabre and F-105 Thunderchief jets of the United States Air Force bombed an ammunition depot at Xombang while 19 propeller-driven A-1H fighter-bombers of South Vietnam struck the Quangkhe naval base.

The various arguments in the Administration over how the raids ought to be conducted, which had developed during the planning stages, were now revived in sharper form by the opening blow in the actual air war.

Secretary McNamara, whose attention to management of resources and cost-effectiveness is cited repeatedly by the study, was concerned about improving the military efficacy of the bombing even before the sustained air war got under way.

He had received bomb damage assessments on the two reprisal strikes in February, reporting that of 491 buildings attacked, only 47 had been destroyed and 22 damaged. The information "caused McNamara to fire off a rather blunt memorandum" to Gen. Earle G. Wheeler, Chairman of the Joint Chiefs of Staff, on Feb. 17, the account says.

'I Am Quite Satisfied'

"Although the four missions [flown during the two raids] left the operations at the targets relatively unimpaired, I am quite satisfied with the results," Mr. McNamara began. "Our primary objective, of course, was to communicate our political resolve. This I believe we did. Future communications or resolve, however, will carry a hollow ring unless we accomplish more military damage than we have to date. . . . Surely we cannot continue for months accomplishing no more with 267 sorties than we did on these four missions." A sortie is a flight by a single plane.

General Wheeler replied that measures were being taken to heighten the destructiveness of the strikes and said that one way to accomplish this was to give the operational commander on the scene "adequate latitude" to attack the target as he saw fit, rather than seeking to control the details from Washington.

One measure approved by the President on March 9 was the use of napalm in North Vietnam.

And the day before, the day that 3,500 marines came ashore at Danang to protect the airfield there, Ambassador Taylor had already expressed, in two cables to Washington, what the historian describes as "sharp annoyance" with the "unnecessarily timid and ambivalent" way in which the air war was being conducted.

No air strikes had been authorized by the President beyond the initial Rolling Thunder raids that began on March 2, and, according to the study, the Ambassador was irritated at "the long delays between strikes, the marginal weight of the attacks and the great ado about behind-the-scenes diplomatic feelers."

General Westmoreland Concurs

With the concurrence of General Westmoreland, Ambassador Taylor proposed "a more dynamic schedule of strikes, a several week program relentlessly marching north" beyond the 19th Parallel, which President Johnson had so far set as a limit, "to break the will of the D.R.V."

Ambassador Taylor cabled: "Current feverish diplomatic activity particularly by French and British" was interfering with the ability of the United States to "progressively turn the screws on D.R.V."

"It appears to me evident that to date D.R.V. leaders believe air strikes at present levels on their territory are meaningless and that we are more susceptible to international pressure for negotiations than they are," the Ambassador said. He cited as evidence a report from J. Blair Seaborn, the Canadian member of the International Control Commission, who, in Hanoi earlier that month, had performed one of a series of secret diplomatic missions for the United States.

Mr. Seaborn had been sent back to convey directly to the Hanoi leaders an American policy statement on Vietnam that had been delivered to China on Feb. 24 through its embassy in Warsaw.

'No Designs' on the D.R.V.

In essence, the Pentagon study reports, the policy statement said that while the United States was determined to take whatever measures w..re necessary to maintain South Vietnam, it "had no designs on the territory of North Vietnam, nor any desire to destroy the D.R.V."

The delivery of the message to the Chinese was apparently aimed at helping to stave off any Chinese intervention as a result of the forthcoming bombing campaign.

But the purpose in sending Mr. Seaborn back, the study makes clear, was to convey the obvious threat that Hanoi now faced "extensive future destruction of . . . military and economic investments" if it did not call off the Vietcong guerrillas and accept a separate, non-Communist South.

Premier Pham Van Dong of North Vietnam, who had seen Mr. Seaborn on two earlier visits, declined this time, and the Canadian had to settle for the chief North Vietnamese liaison officer for the commission, to whom he read Washington's statement.

The North Vietnamese officer, the account says, commented that the message "contained nothing new and that the North Vietnamese had already received a briefing on the Warsaw meeting" from the Chinese Communists.

This treatment led the Canadian to sense "a mood of confidence" among the Hanoi leaders, Ambassador Taylor told Washington in a cablegram, and Mr. Seaborn felt "that Hanoi has the impression that our air strikes are a limited attempt to improve our bargaining position and hence are no great cause for immediate concern."

"Our objective should be to induce in D.R.V. leadership an attitude favorable to U.S. objectives in as short a time as possible in order to avoid a build-up of international pressure to negotiate," the Ambassador said.

To Dispel Any Illusions

Therefore, he went on, it was necessary to "begin at once a progression of U.S. strikes north of 19th Parallel in a slow but steadily ascending movement" to dispel any illusions in Hanoi.

"If we tarry too long in the south [below the 19th Parallel], we will give Hanoi a weak and misleading signal which will work against our ultimate purpose," he said.

The next Rolling Thunder strikes, on March 14 and 15, were the heaviest of the air war so far, involving 100 American and 24 South Vietnamese planes against barracks and depots on Tiger Island off the North Vietnamese coast and the ammunition dump near Phuqui, 100 miles southwest of Hanoi.

For the first time, the planes used napalm against the North, a measure approved by Mr. Johnson to achieve the more efficient destruction of the targets that Mr. McNamara was seeking and to give the pilots protection from antiaircraft batteries.

But the Ambassador regarded these, too, as an "isolated, stage-managed joint U.S./GVN operation," the Pentagon study says. He sent Washington another cable, saying that "through repeated delays we are failing to give the mounting crescendo to Rolling Thunder which is necessary to get the desired results."

Meanwhile, Admiral Sharp in Honolulu and the Joint Chiefs in Washington were quickly devising a number of other programs to broaden and intensify the air war now that it had begun.

Meanwhile, Admiral Sharp in Honolulu and the Joint Chiefs in Washington were quickly devising a number of other programs to broaden and intensify the air war now that it had begun.

On March 21, Admiral Sharp proposed a "radar busting day" to knock out the North Vietnamese early-warning system, and a program "to attrite harass and interdict the D.R.V south" of the 20th Parallel by cutting lines of communication, "LOC" in official terminology.

The "LOC cut program" would choke off traffic along all roads and rail lines through southern North Vietnam by bombing strikes and would thus squeeze the flow of supplies into the South.

"All targets selected are extremely difficult or impossible to bypass," the admiral said in a cable to the Joint Chiefs. "LOC network cutting in this depth will degrade tonnage arrivals at the main 'funnels' and will develop a broad series of new targets such as backed-up convoys, offloaded matériel dumps and personnel staging areas at one or both sides of cuts."

These probable effects might in turn "force major D.R.V. log flow to seacarry and into surveillance and attack by our SVN [South Vietnamese] coastal sanitization forces," the admiral added.

In Washington at this time, the narrative goes on, the Joint Chiefs were engaged in an "interservice division" over potential ground-troop deployments to Vietnam and over the air war itself.

Gen. John P. McConnell, Chief of Staff of the Air Force adopted a "maverick position" and was arguing for a short and violent 28-day bombing campaign. All of the targets on the original 94-target list drawn up in May, 1964, from bridges to industries, would be progressively destroyed.

"He proposed beginning the air strikes in the southern part of North Vietnam and continuing at two-to six-day intervals until Hanoi was attacked," the study continues.

The raids would be along the lines of the mighty strikes, including the use of B-52 bombers, that the Joint Chiefs had proposed in retaliation for the Vietcong mortar attack in Beinhoa airfield on Nov. 1, 1964, the narrative says. General McConnell contended that his plan was consistent with previous bombing proposals by the Joint Chiefs.

The general abandoned his proposal, however, when the other members of the Joint Chiefs decided to incorporate Admiral Sharp's "LOC cut program" and some of General McConnell's individual target concepts into a bombing program of several weeks. They proposed this to Mr. McNamara on March 27.

This plan proposed an intense bombing campaign that would start on road and rail lines south of the 20th Parallel and then "march north" week by week to isolate North Vietnam from China gradually by cutting road and rail lines above Hanoi. In later phases upon which the Joint Chiefs had not yet fully decided, the port facilities were to be destroyed to isolate North Vietnam from the sea. Then industries outside populated areas would be attacked "leading up to a situation where the enemy will realize that the Hanoi and Haiphong areas will be the next logical targets in our continued air campaign."

But the President and Mr. McNamara declined to approve any multiweek program, the study relates. "They clearly preferred to retain continual personal control over attack concepts and individual target selection."

Alternate Targets Approved

In mid-March, after a Presidential fact-finding trip to Vietnam by Gen. Harold K. Johnson, the Army Chief of Staff, the President did regularize the bombing campaign and relaxed some of the restrictions. Among the innovations was the selection of the targets in weekly packages with the precise timing of the individual attacks left to the commanders on the scene. Also, "the strikes were no longer to be specifically related to VC atrocities" and "publicity on the strikes was to be progressively reduced," the study says.

The President did not accept two recommendations from General Johnson relating to a possible ground war. They were to dispatch a division of American troops to South Vietnam to hold coastal enclaves or defend the Central Highlands in order to free Saigon Government forces for offensive action against the Vietcong. The second proposal was to create a four-division force of American and Southeast Asia Treaty Organization troops, who, to interdict infiltration, would patrol both the demilitarized zone along the border separating North and South Vietnam and the Laotian border region.

Better organization for the air war meant that concepts such as Admiral Sharp's "LOC cut program" and his "radar busting" were now incorporated into the weekly target packages. But President Johnson and Secretary McNamara continued to select the targets and to communicate them to the Joint Chiefs—and thus, eventually, to the operating strike forces—in weekly Rolling Thunder planning messages issued by the Secretary of Defense.

Hopes Were Waning

Operation Rolling Thunder was thus being shifted from an exercise in air power "dominated by political and psychological considerations" to a "militarily more significant, sustained bombing program" aimed at destroying the capabilities of North Vietnam to support a war in the South.

But the shift also meant that "early hopes that Rolling Thunder could succeed by itself" in persuading Hanoi to call off the Vietcong were also waning.

"The underlying question that was being posed for the Administration at this time was well formulated," the study says, by Mr. McNaughton in a memorandum drafted on March 24 for Secretary McNamara in preparation for the April 1-2 National Security Council meetings.

"Can the situation inside SVN be bottomed out (a) without extreme measures against the DRV and/or (b) without deployment of large numbers of U.S. (and other) combat troops inside SVN?"

Mr. McNaughton's answer was "perhaps, but probably no." [See Text, McNaughton action plan, March 24, 1965.]

General Westmoreland stated his conclusions in a half-inch-thick report labeled "Commander's Estimate of the situation in SVN." The document, "a classic Leavenworth-style analysis," the analyst remarks, referring to the Command and General Staff College, was completed in Saigon on March 26 and delivered to Washington in time for the April 1-2 strategy meeting.

The Saigon military commander and his staff had begun working on this voluminous report on March 13, the day after General Johnson left Vietnam with his ground war proposals of an American division to hold enclaves and a four-division American and SEATO force along the borders, the study notes.

General Westmoreland predicted that the bombing campaign against the North would not show tangible results until June at the earliest, and that in the meantime the South Vietnamese Army needed American reinforcements to hold the line against growing Vietcong strength and to carry out an "orderly" expansion of its own ranks.

And, paraphrasing the report, the study says that the general warned that the Saigon troops, "although at the moment performing fairly well, would

not be able in the face of a VC summer offensive to hold in the South long enough for the bombing to become effective."

General Westmoreland asked for reinforcements equivalent to two American divisions, a total of about 70,000 troops, counting those already in Vietnam.

They included 17 maneuver battalions. The general proposed adding two more Marine battalion landing teams to the two battalions already at Danang in order to establish another base at the airfield at Phubai to the north; putting an Army brigade into the Bienhoa-Vungtau area near Saigon, and using two more Army battalions to garrison the central coastal ports of Quinhon and Nhatrang as logistics bases. These bases would sustain an army division that General Westmoreland proposed to send into active combat in the strategic central highlands inland to "defeat" the Vietcong who were seizing control there.

General Westmoreland said that he wanted the 17 battalions and their initial supporting elements in South Vietnam by June and indicated that more troops might be required thereafter if the bombing failed to achieve results.

The Saigon military commander and General Johnson were not alone in pressing for American ground combat troops to forestall a Vietcong victory, the study points out.

On March 20, the Joint Chiefs as a body had proposed sending two American divisions and one South Korean division to South Vietnam for offensive combat operations against the guerrillas.

Secretary McNamara, the Joint Chiefs and Ambassador Taylor all discussed the three-division proposal on March 29, the study relates, while the Ambassador was in Washington for the forthcoming White House strategy conference.

The Ambassador opposed the plan, the study says, because he felt the South Vietnamese might resent the presence of so many foreign troops—upwards of 100,000 men—and also because he believed there was still no military necessity for them.

The Joint Chiefs "had the qualified support of McNamara," however, the study continues, and was one of the topics discussed at the national security council meeting.

Concern With Deployment

Thus, the study says, at the White House strategy session of April 1-2, "the principal concern of Administration policy makers at this time was with the prospect of major deployment of U.S. and third-country combat forces to SVN."

A memorandum written by McGeorge Bundy before the meeting, which set forth the key issues for discussion and decision by the President, "gave only the most superficial treatment to the complex matter of future air pressure policy," the Pentagon analyst remarks.

The morning that Ambassador Taylor left Saigon to attend the meeting, March 29, the Vietcong guerrillas blew up the American Embassy in Saigon in what the study calls "the boldest and most direct Communist action against the U.S. since the attacks at Pleiku and Quinhon which had precipitated the Flaming Dart reprisal airstrikes."

Admiral Sharp requested permission to launch a "spectacular" air raid on North Vietnam in retaliation, the narrative continues, but the "plea . . . did not fall on responsive ears" at the White House.

"At this point, the President preferred to maneuver quietly to help the nation get used to living with the Vietnam crisis. He played down any drama intrinsic in Taylor's arrival" and refused to permit a retaliation raid for the embassy bombing.

"After his first meeting with Taylor and other officials on March 31, the President responded to press inquiries concerning dramatic new developments by saying: "I know of no far-reaching strategy that is being suggested or promulgated."

"But the President was being less than candid," the study observes. "The

proposals that were at that moment being promulgated, and on which he reached significant decision the following day, did involve a far-reaching strategy change: acceptance of the concept of U.S. troops engaged in offensive ground operations against Asian insurgents. This issue greatly overshadowed all other Vietnam questions then being reconsidered."

The analyst is referring to the President's decision at the White House strategy conference on April 1-2 to change the mission of the Marine battalions at Danang from defense to offense.

McGeorge Bundy embodied the decision in National Security Action Memorandum 328, which he drafted and signed on behalf of the President on April 6. The analyst says that this "pivotal document" followed almost "verbatim" the text of another memorandum that Mr. Bundy had written before the N.S.C. meeting to outline the proposals for discussion and decision by the President.

The Pentagon study notes that the actual landing of 3,500 marines at Danang the previous month had "caused surprisingly little outcry."

Secretary of State Rusk had explained on a television program the day before the marines came ashore that their mission was solely to provide security for the air base and "not to kill the Vietcong," in the words of the study. This initial mission for the marines was later to be referred to as the short-lived strategy of security that would apply only to this American troop movement into South Vietnam.

'A Dead Letter' Quickly

The President's decision to change their mission to offense now made the strategy of base security "a dead letter," the study says, when it was less than a month old.

At the April 1-2 meeting, Mr. Johnson had also decided to send ashore two more Marine battalions, which General Westmoreland had asked for in a separate request on March 17. Mr. Johnson further decided to increase support forces in South Vietnam by 18,000 to 20,000 men.

The President was "doubtless aware" of the general's additional request for the equivalent of two divisions, and of the Joint Chiefs' for three divisions, the Pentagon account says, but Mr. Johnson took no action on them.

"The initial steps in ground build-up appear to have been grudgingly taken," the study says, "indicating that the President . . . and his advisers recognized the tremendous inertial complications of ground troop deployments. Halting ground involvement was seen to be a manifestly greater problem than halting air or naval activity.

"It is pretty clear, then, that the President intended, after the early April N.S.C. meetings, to cautiously and carefully experiment with the U. S. forces in offensive roles," the analyst concludes.

National Security Action Memorandum 328 did not precisely define or limit the offensive role it authorized, and Ambassador Taylor, who had attended the National Security Council meeting during his visit to Washington, was not satisfied with the guidance he received from the State Department. Therefore, on his way back to Saigon on April 4, the Ambassador, formerly President John F. Kennedy's military adviser and Chairman of the Joint Chiefs, sent a cable from the Honolulu headquarters of the commander of Pacific forces to the State Department, saying:

"I propose to describe the new mission to [Premier Pham Huy] Quat as the use of marines in a mobile counterinsurgency role in the vicinity of Danang for the improved protection of that base and also in a strike role as a reserve in support of ARVN operations anywhere within 50 miles of the base. This latter employment would follow acquisition of experience on local counter-insurgency missions."

55

Confusion and Suspicion

Ambassador Taylor's 50-mile limit apparently became an accepted rule-of-thumb boundary for counterinsurgency strikes.

And so, the analyst sums up, with the promulgation of National Security Action Memorandum 328, "the strategy of security effectively becomes a dead letter on the first of April," and the strategy of enclave begins.

There was some confusion, suspicion and controversy about the President's approval of an 18,000-20,000 increase in support troops, which, he explained, was meant "to fill out existing units and supply needed logistic personnel."

On April 21, Secretary McNamara told the President that 11,000 of these new men would augment various existing forces, while 7,000 were logistic troops to support "previously approved forces."

"It isn't entirely clear from the documents exactly what the President did have in mind for the support troop add-ons," the study comments. "What is clear, however, . . . was that the J.C.S. were continuing to plan for the earliest possible introduction of two to three divisions into RVN." The analyst cites a memorandum from Mr. McNamara to General Wheeler on April 6 as evidence of this planning.

Later, on May 5, the study continues, Assistant Secretary of Defense McNaughton would send a memorandum to Deputy Secretary of Defense Cyrus R. Vance, saying that "the J.C.S. misconstrued the [support] add-ons to mean logistic build-up for coastal enclaves and the possible later introduction of two to three divisions." (These were the divisions the Joint Chiefs had requested on March 20.)

'Relatively Low Risk'

The enclave strategy had as its object the involvement of United States combat units at "relatively low risk." It proposed "that U. S. troops occupy coastal enclaves, accept full responsibility for enclave security, and be prepared to go to the rescue of the RVNF as far as 50 miles outside the enclave. . . . The intent was not to take the war to the enemy but rather to deny him certain critical areas," the study says.

To prove the viability of its "reserve reaction," the analyst goes on, the enclave strategy required testing, but the rules for committing United States troops under it had not been worked out by the time it was overtaken by events—a series of major military victories by the Vietcong in May and June that led to the adoption of the search-and destroy strategy.

Search and destroy, the account says, was "articulated by Westmoreland and the J.C.S. in keeping with sound military principles garnered by men accustomed to winning. The basic idea . . . was the desire to take the war to the enemy, denying him freedom of movement anywhere in the country . . . and deal him the heaviest possible blows." In the meantime, the South Vietnamese Army "would be free to concentrate their efforts in populated areas."

From April 11 through April 14, the additional two Marine battalions were deployed at Hue-Phubai and at Danang, bringing the total maneuver battalions to four.

"The marines set about consolidating and developing their two coastal base areas, and, although they pushed their patrol perimeters out beyond their tactical wire and thereby conducted active rather than passive defense, they did not engage in any offensive operations in support of ARVN for the next few months," the study says.

At this point, the Defense Department, the Joint Chiefs and General Westmoreland collaborated—as it turned out, successfully—in what the study calls "a

little cart-before-horsemanship." It involved the deployment to South Vietnam of the 173d Airborne Brigade, two battalions that were then situated on Okinawa in a reserve role.

General Westmoreland had had his eye on the 173d for some time. On March 26, in his "Commander's Estimate of the Situation," in which he requested the equivalent of two divisions, he also recommended that the 173d Airborne Brigade be deployed to the Bienhoa-Vungtau areas "to secure vital U.S. installations." This recommendation, like that for two divisions, was not acted upon by the National Security Council in the April 1-2 meeting.

On April 11, General Westmoreland cabled Admiral Sharp, the Pacific commander, that he understood from the National Security Council's meetings and Ambassador Taylor's discussions in Washington at the beginning of the month that his requested divisions were not in prospect. But, he said, he still wanted the 173d Airborne Brigade.

Ahead in Two Areas

This message, the study says, set in motion "a series of cables, proposals and false starts which indicated that Washington was well ahead of Saigon in its planning and in its anxiety."

The upshot of all this communication was that at a meeting in Honolulu of representatives of the Joint Chiefs and the Pacific command from April 10 to April 12, the deployment of the 173d Airborne Brigade was recommended. On April 14, the Joint Chiefs of Staff ordered the deployment to Bienhoa-Vungtau, and the replacement of the brigade by one from the United States.

"This decision to deploy the 173d apparently caught the Ambassador flat-footed," the study says, "for he had quite obviously not been privy to it."

On the day of the Joint Chiefs' decision, Ambassador Taylor cabled the State Department that "this [decision on the deploying the brigade] comes as a complete surprise in view of the understanding reached in Washington [during his visit] that we would experiment with the marines in a counterinsurgency role before bringing in other U.S. contingents." He asked that deployment of the brigade be held up until matters were sorted out.

However, the study notes, Ambassador Taylor "held the trump card" because the proposed action had to be cleared with Premier Quat, and the Ambassador told his superiors on April 17 that he did not intend to tell the Premier "without clearer guidance explaining Washington's Intentions." [See text, Taylor cable, April 17, 1965.]

"That Washington was determined, with the President's sanction, to go beyond what had been agreed to and formalized in NSAM 328 was manifested unmistakably in a cable under joint Defense/State auspices by Mr. McNaughton to the Ambassador on 15 April," the Pentagon study says.

In the cablegram, Mr. McNaughton said: "Highest authority [the President] believes the situation in South Vietnam has been deteriorating and that, in addition to actions against the North, something new must be added in the South to achieve victory." He then listed seven recommended actions, including the introduction of military-civil affairs personnel into the air effort and the deployment of the 173d Airborne Brigade to Bienhoa-Vungtau "as a security force for our installations and also to participate in counterinsurgency combat operations" according to General Westmoreland's plans.

Reacting to that cable on April 17, Ambassador Taylor protested to McGeorge Bundy in the White House against the introduction of military-civilian affairs personnel into the aid effort. The Ambassador's cablegram con-

56

Pressure From Military

tinued by saying that the McNaughton message "shows a far greater willingness to get into the ground war than I had discerned in Washington during my recent trip."

"Mac, can't we be better protected from our friends?" the Ambassador asked. "I know that everyone wants to help, but there's such a thing as killing with kindness." [See text, Taylor cable, April 17, 1965.]

Exact Date Is Uncertain

Discussing the contretemps between the Pentagon and General Taylor, the study says: "The documents do not reveal just exactly when Presidential sanction was obtained for the expanded scope of the above [McNaughton] proposals. It is possible that [on the approval for deploying the brigade] the Ambassador may have caught the Defense Department and the J.C.S. in a little cart-before-horsemanship."

In any event, on April 15, the day after it had ordered the deployment of the brigade, the J.C.S. sent a memorandum to Secretary McNamara dealing with the Ambassador's objections and still insisting that the brigade was needed.

"Whether or not the J.C.S. wrote that memorandum with red faces," the study remarks, "the Secretary of Defense dates approval for final deployment of the 173d as of the 30th of April."

The strategy of base security having been ended by National Security Action Memorandum 328, a high-level meeting began in Honolulu on April 20 to "sanctify" and "structure", as the Pentagon analyst puts it, "an expanded enclave strategy."

Present at the meeting were Secretary of Defense McNamara; William Bundy, Assistant Secretary of State for Far Eastern Affairs; Assistant Secretary of Defense McNaughton; Ambassador Taylor; Admiral Sharp; General Wheeler and General Westmoreland.

"Some of these men had helped produce the current optimism in situation reports and cables," the Pentagon study says, "and yet the consensus of their meeting was that the then-present level of Vietcong activity was nothing but the lull before the storm.

"The situation which presented itself to the Honolulu conferees was in many ways the whole Vietnam problem in microcosm. What was needed to galvanize everyone to action was some sort of dramatic event within South Vietnam itself. Unfortunately, the very nature of the war precluded the abrupt collapse of a front or the loss of large chunks of territory in lightning strokes by the enemy. The enemy in this war was spreading his control and influence slowly and inexorably but without drama. The political infrastructure from which he derived his strength took years to create, and in most areas the expansion of control was hardly felt until it was a fait accompli."

In a Rear-Guard Action

Of the conferees, the study says, "by far the most dogged protagonist of the enclave strategy was Ambassador Taylor." It had already become apparent, however, and was to become manifestly clear at Honolulu, that the Ambassador was fighting a rear-guard action against both civilian and military officials in the Pentagon who were bent on expansion of U.S. forces in South Vietnam and an enlargement of their combat mission.

On March 18, in a message to Washington, Ambassador Taylor had suggested that if a division were sent to South Vietnam as had been proposed by the Army Chief of Staff, General Johnson, then consideration should be given to deploying it in either a highland or coastal enclave.

When he got no response, Ambassador Taylor sent another message on March 27, stating that if United States forces were to come, his preference was, as the study says, that they be used in a combination of defensive or offensive enclave plus reserve for an emergency, rather than in "territorial clear and hold" operations.

The Ambassador, the study notes, interpreted the pivotal National Security Action Memorandum as supporting his position, because in it the President seemed to make plain that he "wanted to experiment very carefully with a small amount of force before deciding whether or not to accept any kind of ground war commitment."

For Guerrillas, Tanks

Therefore, the study says, "the Ambassador was surprised to discover that the marines [the two additional battalions that landed April 11-14] had come ashore with tanks, self-propelled artillery, and various other items of weighty equipment not 'appropriate for counterinsurgency operations.'"

In his April 17 cable to McGeorge Bundy, Ambassador Taylor had also protested the "hasty and ill-conceived" proposals for the deployment of more forces with which he was being flooded.

"Thus was the Ambassador propelled into the conference of 20 April 1965, only one step ahead of the Washington juggernaut, which was itself fueled by encouragement from Westmoreland in Saigon," the study comments. "Taylor was not opposed to the U.S. build-up per se, but rather was concerned to move slowly with combat troop deployments . . . He was overtaken in Honolulu."

According to Mr. McNaughton's minutes, the conference in preliminary discussions on April 20 agreed that:

"(1) The D.R.V. was not likely to quit within the next six months; and in any case, they were more likely to give up because of VC failure in the South than because of bomb-induced 'pain' in the North. It could take up to two years to demonstrate VC failure.

"(2) The level of air activity through Rolling Thunder was about right. The U.S. did not, in Ambassador Taylor's words, want 'to kill the hostage.' Therefore, Hanoi and environs remained on the restricted list. It was recognized that air activity would not do the job alone.

"(3) Progress in the South would be slow, and great care should be taken to avoid dramatic defeat. The current lull in Vietcong activity was merely the quiet before a storm.

"(4) The victory strategy was to 'break the will of the D.R.V./VC by denying them victory.' Impotence would lead eventually to a political solution."

At the time of the Honolulu conference, the study notes, "the level of approved U.S. forces for Vietnam was 40,200," but 33,500 were actually in the country at that time.

"To accomplish the 'victory strategy' described above," the study continues, the conferees agreed that U.S. ground forces should be increased from 4 to 13 maneuver battalions and to 82,000 men. The United States, they agreed, should also seek to get additional troops from Australia and South Korea that would bring the so-called third-country strength to four maneuver battalions and 7,250 men.

Detailed Deployment Plan

Thus, the Honolulu conferees proposed raising the recommended United States-third country strength to 17 battalions.

The conferees also mentioned but did not recommend a possible later deployment of 11 U.S. and 6 South Korean battalions, which, when added to the ap-

57

The Enemy Responds

proved totals, would bring the United States-third country combat capability to 34 battalions. In this later possible deployment was included an Army airmobile division.

Secretary McNamara forwarded the Honolulu recommendations to the President on April 21, together with a notation on possible later deployment of the airmobile division and the Third Marine Expeditionary Force.

On April 30 the Joint Chiefs presented a detailed program for deployment of some 48,000 American and 5,250 third-country soldiers. "Included were all the units mentioned in the Honolulu recommendations plus a healthy support package," the study says.

The Joint Chiefs said that these additional forces were "to bolster GVN forces during their continued build-up, secure bases and installations, conduct counterinsurgency combat operations in coordination with the RVNAF, and prepare for the later introduction of an airmobile division to the central plateau, the remainder of the third M.E.F. [the marine force] to the Danang area, and the remainder of a ROK [Republic of Korea] division to Quangngai."

From the thrust of this memorandum by the Joint Chiefs, the analyst comments, "it is apparent that the enclave strategy was no stopping place as far as the Chiefs were concerned. They continued to push hard for the earliest possible input of three full divisions of troops. They were still well ahead of the pack in that regard."

The question of final Presidential approval of the 17-battalion recommendations now became academic as the enemy started attacks that provided the Pentagon and General Westmoreland with a battlefield rationale for their campaign to have American troops take over the major share of the ground war.

As the manpower debates continued in March and April, the study portrays the military situation: "The Vietcong were unusually inactive throughout March and April. There had been no major defeat of the enemy's forces and no signs of any major shift in strategy on his part. Hence it was assumed that he was merely pausing to regroup and to assess the effect of the changed American participation in the war embodied in air strikes and in the marines," the first two battalions deployed at Danang on March 8.

"There were, however, plenty of indications in the early spring of 1965 of what was to come," the study continues. . . . "From throughout the country came reports that Vietcong troops and cadres were moving into central Vietnam and into areas adjacent to the ring of provinces . . . around Saigon."

'A Sobering Harbinger'

"Finally and most ominous of all," the study says, a memorandum by the Central Intelligence Agency and the Defense Intelligence Agency on April 21, 1965, "reflected the acceptance into the enemy order of battle of one regiment of the 325th PAVN [People's Army of Vietnam] division said to be located in Kontum province. The presence of this regular North Vietnamese unit, which had been first reported as early as February, was a sobering harbinger. . . ."

On May 11, when the Vietcong attacked Songbe, the capital of Phuoclong Province, using more than a regiment of troops, "the storm broke in earnest," the study says. The enemy overran the town and the American advisers' compound, causing heavy casualties. After holding the town for a day, the Vietcong withdrew, the study relates.

Later in May, in Quangngai Province in the northern part of South Vietnam, a battalion of Government troops—the Army of the Republic of Vietnam—was ambushed and overrun near Bagia, west of Quangngai. Reinforcements were also ambushed.

"The battle," the study says, "dragged on for several days and ended in total defeat for the ARVN. Two battalions were completely decimated. . . . From Bagia came a sense of urgency, at least among some of the senior U.S. officers who had been witness to the battle."

Two Regiments Attack

Then in June, two Vietcong regiments attacked an outpost at Dongxoai and when Government reinforcements were committed "piecemeal" they were "devoured by the enemy" the Pentagon study says.

"By mid-June, 1965," it asserts, "the Vietcong summer offensive was in full stride." By mid-July, the Vietcong were "systematically forcing the GVN to yield what little control it still exercised in rural areas outside the Mekong Delta."

On June 7, after the attack on Bagia, General Westmoreland sent a long message on the military situation and his needs to the Pacific Commander for relay to the Joint Chiefs.

"In pressing their campaign," the general said, "the Vietcong are capable of mounting regimental-size operations in all four ARVN corps areas, and at least battalion-sized attack in virtually all provinces. . . .

"ARVN forces on the other hand are already experiencing difficulty in coping with this increased VC capability. Desertion rates are inordinately high. Battle losses have been higher than expected; in fact, four ARVN battalions have been rendered ineffective by VC action in the I and II Corps zones. . . .

"Thus, the GVN/VC force ratios upon which we based our estimate of the situation, in March have taken an adverse trend. You will recall that I recommended the deployment of a U.S. division in II Corps to cover the period of the RVNAF build-up and to weight the force ratios in that important area. We assumed at that time that the ARVN battalions would be brought to full strength by now and that the force build-up would proceed on schedule. Neither of these assumptions has materialized. . . .

"In order to cope with the situation outlined above, I see no course of action open to us except to reinforce our efforts in SVN with additional U.S. or third country forces as rapidly as is practical during the critical weeks ahead."

The '44-Battalion Request'

What General Westmoreland asked for added up to a total force of 44 battalions and the June 7 message became known as the "44-battalion request."

Just as intense internal debate was beginning on the request, there was a "credibility" flare-up deriving from President Johnson's injunction of secrecy on the change of missions for the marines authorized on April 1 in National Security Action Memorandum 328.

"The long official silence between the sanction for U.S. offensive operations contained in NSAM 328 and the final approval [in negotiations with Saigon] of the conditions under which U.S. troops could be committed was not without cost," the study asserts. "The President had admonished each of the N.S.C. members not to allow release of provisions of the NSAM, but the unduly long interregnum inevitably

led to leaks." In addition, the marines had 200 casualties, including 18 killed, as they went about "tidying up," as the study puts it, their newly assigned area in April and May.

"The Commandant of the Marine Corps," the study continues, "raised the tempo of speculation by saying to the press during an inspection trip to Vietnam in April that the marines were not in Vietnam to 'sit on their dittyboxes'—and they were there to 'kill Vietcong.'

"An honest and superficially innocuous statement by Department of State Press Officer Robert McCloskey on 8 June to the effect that 'American forces would be available for combat support together with Vietnamese forces when and if necessary' produced an immediate response [in the press]."

'By Its Own Petard'

"The White House was hoisted by its own petard. In an attempt to quell the outcry, a statement was issued on the 9th of June which, because of its ambiguity, only served to exacerbate the situation and to widen what was being described as 'the credibility gap'."

The White House statement said: "There has been no change in the mission of United States ground combat units in Vietnam in recent days or weeks. The President has issued no order of any kind in this regard to General Westmoreland recently or at any other time. The primary mission of these troops is to secure and safeguard important military installations like the air base at Danang. They have the associated mission of . . . patrolling and securing actions in and near the areas thus safeguarded.

"If help is requested by the appropriate Vietnamese commander, General Westmoreland also has authority within the assigned mission to employ those troops in support of Vietnamese forces faced with aggressive attack when other effective reserves are not available and when, in his judgment, the general military situation urgently requires it."

Discussing this statement, the Pentagon analyst says: "The documents do not reveal whether or not the ground rules for engagement of U.S. forces had actually been worked out to everyone's satisfaction at the time of the White House statement. There is good indication that they had not." The analyst also notes that during the battles of Bagia and Dongxoai, the Government forces "were desperately in need of assistance," but that United States forces were not committed although the marines were available for Bagia and the 173d Airborne Brigade for Dongxoai.

The study reports that the first major ground action by United States forces took place northwest of Saigon from June 27 to June 30, and involved the 173d Airborne Brigade, an Australian battalion and South Vietnamese forces.

"The operation could by no stretch of definition have been described as a reserve reaction," the study says. "It was a search and destroy operation into Vietcong base areas. . . . The excursion was a direct result of the sanction given to General Westmoreland . . . [as a result of National Security Action Memorandum 328 and the enemy offensive] to 'commit U.S. troops to combat, independent of or in conjunction with GVN forces in any situation in which the use of such troops is requested by an appropriate GVN commander and when in [General Westmoreland's] judgment, their use is necessary to strengthen the relative position of GVN forces'." The wording of this sanction came in a State Department message.

'Overcome by Events'

However, as the study notes, "At that juncture the 44-battalion debate was in full swing and the enclave strategy, as a means to limit the amount and use of U.S. combat force in Vietnam, was certainly overcome by events." and by "a much more ambitious strategy sanctioned by the President."

Recapitulating the situation just before the debate, the study gives this picture of deployment: At the beginning of June, the enclave strategy was in its first stages with Marine Corps forces at Phubai, Danang and Chulai, and Army forces in Vungtau. Other enclaves were under consideration. Approved for deployment—but not all arrived in South Vietnam yet—were approximately 70,000 troops in 13 maneuver battalions; with third-country forces the total came to 77,250 men and 17 maneuver battalions.

This was the situation when, on June 7, General Westmoreland asked for reinforcements "as rapidly as possible."

General Westmoreland's message, the Pentagon study says, "stirred up a veritable hornet's nest in Washington," because his request for large reinforcements and his proposed strategy to go on the offensive "did not contain any of the comfortable restrictions and safeguards which had been part of every strategy debated to date."

"In such a move," the study continues "the specter of U.S. involvement in a major Asian ground war was there for all to see."

Just as Ambassador Taylor had consistently resisted involvement of United States forces, the study says, so General Westmoreland had been equally determined to get the troops into the war and have "a free hand" in using them.

At the time of his message, the general had available in Vietnam seven Marine and 2 Army maneuver battalions, plus an Australian battalion. Now,

he was asking for a total of 33 battalions, and if the 173d Airborne Brigade's two battalions—which were on temporary assignment—were added, the total came to 35. But in a subparagraph, General Westmoreland also identified nine other United States battalions that he might request at a later date. Thus the total of 44 battalions, and hence the name given the request. In the total was included an airmobile division of nine battalions to be formed later.

Admiral Sharp favored the request in a message to the Joint Chiefs on June 7, saying, "We will lose by staying in enclaves defending coastal areas."

The Chiefs in Favor

The Joint Chiefs, the Pentagon analyst says, favored bolstering the United States troop commitment. As far back as March 20, the Joint Chiefs had advocated sending three divisions—two American and one Korean—with the objective of "destroying the Vietcong."

Now, the study states, General Westmoreland's request "altered drastically the role of the J.C.S. in the build-up debate.

"Up to that time," the study continues, "the J.C.S. had, if anything, been ahead of General Westmoreland in advocating allied forces for Vietnam. The 27 battalions of their three-division plan were in themselves more than Westmoreland ever requested until 7 June. After that date, the big push came from Westmoreland in Saigon, and the J.C.S were caught in the middle between the latter and the powerful and strident opposition his latest request for forces had surfaced in Washington."

On June 11, the Joint Chiefs cabled Admiral Sharp that something less than General Westmoreland's request was

59

Divergent Views at Home

close to approval, but they wanted to know, the study says, "where Westmoreland intended to put this force in Vietnam."

He replied on June 13 in detail and the study comments: "This message was extremely important, for in it [he] spelled out the concept of keeping U.S.

forces away from the people. The search and destroy strategy for U.S. and third country forces which continues to this day and the primary focus of RVNAF on pacification both stem from that concept. In addition, Westmoreland made a big pitch in this cable for a free hand to maneuver the troops around inside the country. . . ."

Confirmation by Taylor

Ambassador Taylor, in a report on June 17, "confirmed the seriousness of the military situation as reported by General Westmoreland and also pointed up the very tenuous hold the new government had on the country." This was the Government of President Nguyen Van Thieu and Premier Nguyen Cao Ky.

"This report apparently helped to remove the last obstacles to consideration of all of the forces mentioned in Westmoreland's request of 7 June," the analyst says.

On June 22, General Wheeler cabled General Westmoreland and asked if the 44 battalions were enough to convince the enemy forces that they could not win. General Westmoreland replied, the study says, "that there was no evidence the VC/DRV would alter their plans regardless of what the U.S. did in the next six months."

"The 44-battalion force should, however, establish a favorable balance of power by the end of the year," the study quotes the general as having said. "If the U.S. was to seize the initiative from the enemy, then further forces would be required into 1966 and beyond. . . ."

On June 26, the general was given authority to commit U.S. forces to battle when he decided they were necessary "to strengthen the relative position of GVN forces."

"This was about as close to a free hand in managing the forces as General Westmoreland was likely to get," the analyst says. "The strategy was finished, and the debate from then on centered on how much force and to what end."

The opposition to General Westmoreland had "its day in court," late in June and early in July, the study says. The embassy in Saigon, "while recognizing the seriousness of the situation in South Vietnam, was less then sanguine about the prospects for success if large numbers of foreign troops were brought in."

Another critic of General Westmoreland's recommendations, the account reports, was Under Secretary of State Ball who was "convinced that the U.S. was pouring its resources down the drain in the wrong place."

"In Ball's view, the account continues," there was absolutely no assurance that the U.S. could with the provision of more ground forces achieve its political objectives in Vietnam. Instead, the U.S. risked involving itself in a costly and indeterminate struggle. To further complicate matters, it would be equally impossible to achieve political objectives by expanding the bombing of the North. . . ." [See text, George Ball memorandum, July 1, 1965.]

William Bundy in the Middle

Assistant Secretary William P. Bundy, the study says, "like so many others found himself in between Westmoreland and Ball."

In a memorandum to the President on July 1, Mr. Bundy gave his position, as summarized in the Pentagon study:

"The U.S. needed to avoid the ultimatum aspects of the 44 battalions and also the Ball withdrawal proposal. . . . The U.S. should adopt a policy which would allow it to hold on without risking disasters of scale if the war were lost despite deployment of the full 44 battalions. For the moment, according to Bundy, the U.S. should complete planned deployments to bring in-country forces to 18 maneuver battalions and 85,000 men. . . . The forces in Vietnam, which Bundy assumed would be enough to prevent collapse, would be restricted to reserve reaction in support of RVNAF. This would allow for some experimentation without taking over the war effort —a familiar theme."

As for Secretary McNamara's views, the study comments: "It is difficult to be precise about the position of the Secretary of Defense during the build-up debate because there is so little of him in the files."

"There are plenty of other indications in the files that the Secretary was very carefully and personally insuring that the Defense Establishment was ready to provide efficient and sufficient support to the fighting elements in Vietnam," the study continues. "From the records, the Secretary comes out much more clearly for good management than he does for any particular strategy."

The Secretary went to South Vietnam for a four-day inspection starting July 16. The study says that while he was in Saigon on July 17, he received a cable from Deputy Secretary of Defense Vance informing him that the President had decided to go ahead with the plan to deploy 34 battalions.

"The debate was over," the analyst says. "McNamara left Saigon bearing Westmoreland recommendations for an even greater increase in forces. . . ."

The study says 34 battalions. This is not entirely clear, because in his request General Westmoreland had asked for a total of 33, and if the battalions of the 173rd Airborne Brigade were added, the total would be 35. The explanation apparently is that when the Airmobile Division was finally organized, it had eight rather than nine battalions. The 34 battalions were, of course, to be supplied immediately. The nine others were to be requested later if needed.

The Pentagon analyst apparently did not have access to White House memoranda, so he is able to give only a sketchy account of Mr. Johnson's role. But he says: "There is no question that

the key figure in the early 1965 build-up was the President."

On May 4, the President asked Congress for a $700-million supplemental appropriation "to meet mounting military requirements in Vietnam."

"Nor can I guarantee this will be the last request," he said in a message. "If our need expands I will turn again to the Congress. For we will do whatever must be done to insure the safety of South Vietnam from aggression. This is the firm and irrevocable commitment of our people and nation."

On July 28, the President held a press conference in which he said, "The lesson of history dictated that the U.S. commit its strength to resist aggression in South Vietnam."

As for the troop increases, the President said:

"I have asked the commanding general, General Westmoreland, what more he needs to meet this mounting aggression. He has told me. We will meet his needs.

"I have today ordered to Vietnam the Airmobile Division and certain other forces which will raise our fighting strength from 75,000 to 125,000 men almost immediately. Additional forces will be needed later, and they will be sent as requested . . . .

"I have concluded that it is not essential to order Reserve units into service now."

'It Does Not Imply Change'

During the questioning after the announcement, this exchange took place:

"Q. Mr. President, does the fact that you are sending additional forces to Vietnam imply any change in the existing policy of relying mainly on the South Vietnamese to carry out offensive operations and using American forces to guard installations and to act as emergency back-up?

"A. It does not imply any change in policy whatever. It does not imply change of objective."

On July 30, the Joint Chiefs approved 44 maneuver battalions for deployment, involving a total of 193,887 United States troops. By the end of the year, United States forces in South Vietnam numbered 184,314.

"The major participants in the decision knew the choices and understood the consequences," the study says in summation. The decision taken in mid-July to commit 44 battalions of troops to battle in South Vietnam "was perceived as a threshold—entrance into an Asian land war. The conflict was seen to be long, with further U.S. deployments to follow. The choice at that time was not whether or not to negotiate, it was not whether to hold on for a while or let go—the choice was viewed as winning or losing South Vietnam."

Accompanying this decision to give General Westmoreland enough troops to embark on the first phase of his search-and-destroy strategy "was a subtle change of emphasis," the study says, adding:

"Instead of simply denying the enemy victory and convincing him that he could not win, the thrust became defeating the enemy in the South. This was sanctioned implicitly as the only way to achieve the U.S. objective of a non-Communist South Vietnam.

"The acceptance of the search-and-destroy strategy...left the U.S. commitment to Vietnam open-ended. The implications in terms of manpower and money are inescapable.

"Final acceptance of the desirability of inflicting defeat on the enemy rather than merely denying him victory opened the door to an indeterminate amount of additional force."

Precisely what President Johnson and Secretary of Defense McNamara expected their decisions of July to bring within the near term "is not clear," the study says, "but there are manifold indications that they were prepared for a long war."

JUDGE, AT REQUEST OF U.S., HALTS TIMES VIETNAM SERIES FOUR DAYS PENDING HEARING ON INJUNCTION

ARGUMENT FRIDAY

Court Here Refuses to Order Return of Documents Now

By FRED P. GRAHAM

United States District Judge Murray I. Gurfein yesterday ordered The New York Times to halt publication of material from a secret Pentagon study of the Vietnam war for four days. Argument on publication thereafter will be heard Friday.

The judge granted a request by the Justice Department for temporary relief, but he gave no hint as to how he would

Texts of complaint and court restraining order, Page 18.

eventually rule. He also refused to order The Times to return the massive report immediately to the Government.

Declaring that the case could be an important one in the history of relations between the Government and the press, Judge Gurfein said that any temporary harm done to The Times by his order "is far outweighed by the irreparable harm that could be done to the interests of the United States" if more articles and documents in the series were published while the case was in progress.

Times Says It Will Comply

The Times, in a statement issued after the hearing, said:

"The Times will comply with the restraining order issued by Judge Murray I. Gurfein. The Times will present its arguments against a permanent injunction at the hearing scheduled for Friday."

Lawyers for The Times and the Justice Department told the judge, at the proceedings in the Federal District Court House at Foley Square, that this appeared to be the first time in the nation's history that a newspaper was being restrained by a court from publishing an article.

Meanwhile, the Justice Department disclosed in Washington that the Federal Bureau of Investigation was investigating possible violations of federal criminal laws in connection with publication of the secret documents.

The bureau was known to be checking all who had access to the document, of which Justice Department sources said there were 15 copies.

Judge Gurfein, in his first day on the bench after having taken his oath of office last week, acted upon the Justice Department's argument that the publication of further articles by The Times would cause serious injury to the nation's international relations.

The 63-year-old judge deferred until Friday's hearing a decision on the Government's request that The Times be ordered immediately to return the voluminous documents from which its Vietnam series has been drawn.

Order Expires Saturday

The temporary restraining order issued by Judge Gurfein yesterday expires at 1 P.M. Saturday.

His action came a day after Attorney General John N. Mitchell had requested that The Times cease publishing the documents and The Times had refused to do so voluntarily.

Yesterday afternoon, the Justice Department filed a civil suit seeking to permanently enjoin The Times and 22 of its officers, editors and reporters from going forward with the series of articles and documents on the origins of the Indochina war. Three installments had been published and The Times had said that the series was to continue.

Word filtered through the city's legal community yesterday that the Government had requested an afternoon hearing on a temporary restraining order against The Times, and the courtroom was packed—mostly with young lawyers and spectators — when the mustached judge took his seat in Room 605 of the United States Court House.

The arguments pitted a 30-year-old staff member of the United States Attorney's office, Michael D. Hess, against Prof. Alexander M. Bickel of the Yale Law School, a 46-year-old constitutional authority who has been mentioned as a possible Supreme Court nominee. Prof. Bickel represented The Times and its personnel.

The gist of the Government's argument was that The Times had violated a statute that makes it a crime for persons having "unauthorized possession" of Government documents to disclose their contents under circumstances that "could be used to the injury of the United States or to the advantage of any foreign nation."

In his argument, Mr. Hess asserted that "serious injuries are being inflicted on our foreign relations, to the benefit of other nations opposed to our form of government." He told the judge that Secretary of State William P. Rogers had said that several friendly nations had expressed concern over the disclosures in the articles.

With the Government facing the prospect of "irreparable injury" in its international relations, Mr. Hess said, The Times should be required to suffer a "slight delay" in its publication schedule until the case could be heard on Friday.

Otherwise, he said, the case would be mooted by publication of the material before a decision could be reached.

Professor Bickel, a tanned, dapper man in a brown suit and blue shirt, replied that this was a "classic case of censorship" that is forbidden by the First Amendment's free-press guarantee. He also insisted that the statute being invoked by the Government was an anti-espionage law that had never been intended by Congress to be used against the press.

The law, Title 18 of the United States Code, Section 793, provides for a maximum punishment of 10 years' imprisonment and a $10,000 fine against:

"Whoever having unauthorized possession of, access to, or control over any document . . . relating to the national defense, or information relating to the national defense which information the possessor has reason to believe could be used to the injury of the United States or to the advantage of any foreign nation, willfully communicates . . . the same to any person not entitled to receive it, or willfully retains the same and fails to deliver it to the officer or employe of the United States entitled to receive it."

Mr. Bickel contended that to rely upon this wording to bar a newspaper from publishing certain matter "for the first time in this history of the republic" would set an unfortunate precedent. "A newspaper exists to publish, not to submit its publishing schedule to the United States Government," he argued.

During a final discussion in his chambers, Judge Gurfein heard brief statements from two civil liberties groups that asked to be heard as friends of the court. Norman Dorsen, general counsel of the American Civil Liberties Union, and Kristin Booth Glen of the Emergency Civil Liberties Committee made the statements and asked to be heard again on Friday.

Judge Gurfein instructed them to file briefs and reserved judgment on their request to be heard.

He urged The Times to consent to a restraining order, but Mr. Bickel refused, saying that to do so would invite future Government efforts to curb news publications. The order was issued over Mr. Bickel's objections.

Order Not Appealed

The Times could have attempted to appeal the order to the United States Court of Appeals for the Second Circuit. However, such extraordinary appeals of temporary restraining orders are rarely granted, and The Times elected to have the issue tried on its merits before Judge Gurfein.

Mr. Bickel was accompanied in court by Floyd Abrams, a partner in the New York law firm of Cahill, Gordon, Sonnett, Reindel and Ohl.

The Justice Department named the following defendants in addition to The New York Times Company in today's injunction: Arthur Ochs Sulzberger, president and publisher, who will return today from a trip to London; Harding F. Bancroft and Ivan Veit, executive vice presidents; and Francis A. Cox, James C. Goodale, Sydney Gruson, Walter Mattson, John McCabe, John Mortimer and James Reston, vice presidents.

Also, John B. Oakes, editorial page editor; A. M. Rosenthal, managing editor; Daniel Schwarz, Sunday editor; Clifton Daniel and Tom Wicker, associate editors; Gerald Gold and Allan M. Siegal, assistant foreign editors; Neil Sheehan, Hedrick Smith, E. W. Kenworthy and Fox Butterfield, reporters; and Samuel Abt, a foreign desk copy editor.

Texts of Government Papers in Complaint Against The Times and Judge's Order

Following are the texts of a United States Government complaint and a United States District Court temporary restraining order served on The New York Times Company, its officers and several of its employes yesterday in connection with a series of articles and documents on the Vietnam war that The New York Times has been publishing. Also included is the text of a memorandum of law submitted by the Government in support of its petition for the restraining order.

Complaint

UNITED STATES OF AMERICA, Plaintiff

v.

NEW YORK TIMES COMPANY, ARTHUR OCHS SULZBERGER, HARDING F. BANCROFT, IVAN VEIT, FRANCIS A. COX, JAMES C. GOODALE, SYDNEY GRUSON, WALTER MATTSON, JOHN McCABE, JOHN MORTIMER, JAMES RESTON, JOHN B. OAKES, A. M. ROSENTHAL, DANIEL SCHWARZ, CLIFTON DANIEL, TOM WICKER, E. W. KENWORTHY, FOX BUTTERFIELD, GERALD GOLD, ALLAN M. SIEGAL, SAMUEL ABT, NEIL SHEEHAN and HEDRICK SMITH, Defendants

The United States of America, by its attorney, Whitney North Seymour Jr., United States Attorney for the Southern District of New York, at the direction of the Attorney General of the United States, brings this action against the defendants and alleges as follows:

[1]

This Court has jurisdiction over the subject matter of this action pursuant to Title 28, United States Code, Section 1345.

[2]

This is a civil action to obtain an order enjoining the dissemination, disclosure or divulgence without authority by the defendants of official information classified "Top Secret" or "Secret" in the interests of the national defense under the authority and pursuant to the requirements of Executive Order 10501 entitled "Safeguarding Classified Information."

[3]

Defendant New York Times Company is a corporation with its principal place of business in the City and State of New York and which publishes a daily newspaper under the title of The New York Times. The individual defendants are employees and/or officers of the aforementioned company, serving in the following capacities: Arthur Ochs Sulzberger, President and Publisher; Harding F. Bancroft, Executive Vice President; Ivan Veit, Executive Vice President; Francis A. Cox, Vice President; James C. Goodole, Vice President; Sydney Gruson, Vice President; Walter Mattson, Vice President; John McCabe, Vice President; John Mortimer, Vice President; James Reston, Vice President; John B. Oakes, Editorial Page Editor; A. M. Rosenthal, Managing Editor; Daniel Schwarz, Sunday Editor; Clifton Daniel, Associate Editor; Tom Wicker; Associate Editor. Defendants Neil Sheehan, Hedrick Smith, E. W. Kenworthy, Fox Butterfield, Gerald Gold, Allan M. Siegal and Samuel Abt are employees and/or reporters for the aforementioned publication.

[4]

At a time and place and in a manner unknown to the plaintiff the defendants without lawful authority obtained a copy of certain documents consisting of 47 volumes entitled "History of U.S. Decision-Making Process on Vietnam Policy", covering the period 1945-1967, prepared in 1967-1968 at the direction of then Secretary of Defense Robert McNamara and which is and at all times material herein has been classified "Top Secret-Sensitive," and the internal documents from which the said study was drawn are variously classified as "Top Secret" and "Secret," pursuant to the aforementioned Executive Order 10501 as evidenced by the attached affidavit of J. Fred Buzhardt, General Counsel of the United States Department of Defense.

[5]

Also, at a time and place and in a manner unknown to the plaintiff the defendants without lawful authority obtained a copy of a document described as a "one-volume command and control study of the Gulf of Tonkin incident" dated Feb. 26, 1965, prepared for the Joint Chiefs of Staff by the Weapons Systems Evaluation Group of the United States Department of Defense which is and at all times material herein has been classified "Top Secret" pursuant to the aforementioned Executive Order 10501, as evidenced by the aforementioned attached affidavit.

[6]

As defined in Executive Order 10501 "Top Secret" information is ". . . that information or material the defense aspect of which is paramount, and the unauthorized disclosure of which could result in exceptionally grave damage to the nation such as leading to a definite break in diplomatic relations affecting the defense of the United States, an armed attack against the United States or its allies, a war, or the compromise of military or defense plans, or intelligence operations, or scientific or technological developments vital to the national defense," and "Secret" information is defined as ". . . defense information or material the unauthorized disclosure of which could result in serious damage to the nation, such as by jeopardizing the international relations of the United States, endangering the effectiveness of a program or policy of vital importance to the national defense, or compromising important military or defense plans, scientific or technological developments important to national defense, or information revealing important intelligence operations."

[7]

On June 13, 1971, The New York Times published an article entitled "Vietnam Archive: Pentagon Study Traces Three Decades of Growing U.S. Involvement," authored by defendant Sheehan, and an article entitled "Vast Study of War Took a Year," authored by defendant Smith. These articles were represented to be the initial articles in a series written by defendants Sheehan, Smith, defendant E. W. Kenworthy and defendant Fox Butterfield. The series was represented to be one reporting on [a history of] the United States' decision making process on Vietnam policy for the period 1945-1967. The articles in the series and the classified documents upon which they are based were edited by defendants Gold, Siegal, and Abt. In the aforementioned article, authored by the defendant Sheehan, it is asserted that "most of the study (described in the article as 'a massive study of how the United States went to war in Indochina, conducted by the Pentagon three years ago') and many of the appended documents have been obtained by The New York Times and will be described and presented in a series of articles beginning today." It was also asserted in the June 13 issue of The New York Times with respect to the aforementioned "one-volume command and control study" that the Times had obtained a summary of that study.

[8]

On June 13 and 14, the defendants have without authority intentionally and knowingly published excerpts and other portions of the aforementioned classified defense information knowing that such information had been classified "Top Secret" or "Secret" pursuant to the authority of Executive Order 10501. At the time of such publication the said defendants, and each of them, knew, or had reason to believe, that such information could be used to the injury of the United States and to the advantage of a foreign nation and notwithstanding such knowledge and belief did willfully communicate, deliver and transmit said information by the publication thereof, to persons not entitled to receive such information.

[9]

The publication of the information published as aforesaid on June 13 and June 14, 1971, has prejudiced the defense interests of the United States and the publication of additional excerpts from the documents hereinbefore referred to would further prejudice the defense interests of the United States and result in irreparable injury to the United States.

[10]

The defendants have publicly announced their avowed determination to continue publishing excerpts and other portions of the aforementioned "Top Secret" or "Secret" documents relating to the national defense and unless the defendants, and all persons in active concert and participation with the defendants are enjoined from such, the national defense interests of the United States and the nation's security will suffer immediate and irreparable harm, for which injury plaintiff has no adequate remedy at law.

WHEREFORE, the plaintiff, the UNITED STATES OF AMERICA, prays:

[1]

That this Court enter its order enjoining the defendants, their agents, servants and employees and all persons acting in concert with them from further dissemination, disclosure or divulgence of the information heretofore described in paragraphs 4 and 5 of this complaint, or any excerpt, portion or summary thereof.

[2]

That the Court order the defendants and each of them having possession of the documents referred to in the complaint to deliver said documents and any copies, excerpts, duplications or other tangible evidence of such documents to the plaintiff herein.

[3]

That this Court, pending the final determination of this cause, issue a preliminary injunction, restraining and enjoining the defendants in the manner and form aforesaid.

[4]

That, pending the issuance of the aforesaid preliminary injunction, this Court issue forthwith a temporary restraining order restraining and enjoining the defendants in the manner and form aforesaid and further ordering said defendants to deliver to this Court all the documents and materials referred to in paragraph 2 of the prayer herein to be held

by this Court in camera pending a final order of this Court.

[5]

That this Court grant such other, further, and different relief as the Court may deem just and equitable.

JOHN N. MITCHELL
Attorney General
of the United States

WHITNEY NORTH SEYMOUR Jr.
United States Attorney

By: MICHAEL D. HESS
Chief, Civil Division

Temporary Restraining Order

#71 Civ. 2662

UNITED STATES OF AMERICA, Plaintiff

v.

NEW YORK TIMES COMPANY, ARTHUR OCHS SULZBERGER, HARDING F. BANCROFT, IVAN VEIT, FRANCIS A. COX, JAMES C. GOODALE, SYDNEY GRUSON, WALTER MATTSON, JOHN McCABE, JOHN MORTIMER, JAMES RESTON, JOHN B. OAKES, A. M. ROSENTHAL, DANIEL SCHWARZ, CLIFTON DANIEL, TOM WICKER, E. W. KENWORTHY, FOX BUTTERFIELD, GERALD GOLD, ALLAN M. SIEGAL, SAMUEL ABT, NEIL SHEEHAN and HEDRICK SMITH, Defendants

MEMORANDUM

The United States seeks a temporary restraining order and a preliminary injunction against The New York Times, its publisher and other officers and employes to restrain them from further dissemination or disclosure of certain alleged top secret or secret documents of the United States referred to in a verified complaint filed herewith. I have granted the order to show cause as to why a preliminary injunction against the defendants should not be entered and have made it returnable Friday morning, June 18.

Preliminary thereto the Government has requested a temporary restraining order and also a direction from this Court to require the defendants to deliver to the Court certain documents and other tangible evidence to be held by the Court pending final determination of the cause. At this stage of the proceedings I do not direct The New York Times or the other defendants to produce the documents pending the outcome of the litigation. I do not believe that The New York Times will wilfully disregard the spirit of our restraining order. I am restraining The New York Times and the other defendants, however, from publishing or further disseminating or disclosing the documents consisting of 47 volumes entitled "History of United States Decision-Making Process on Vietnam Policy," covering the period 1945-67, prepared in 1967-68 at the direction of the then Secretary of Defense, Robert

McNamara, the internal documents from which the aforesaid documents were prepared, and a one-volume "Command and Control Study of the Tonkin Gulf Incident," prepared in 1965 for the Joint Chiefs of Staff by the Weapon System Evaluation Group of the United States Department of Defense, pending the hearing of the Government's application for a preliminary injunction.

The questions raised by this action are serious and fundamental. They involve not only matters of procedure, but matters of substance and presumptively of constitutional implication as well. I have, in effect, been asked by the parties to pass on the merits of the litigation upon the arguments made on the order to show cause. I believe that the matter is so important and so involved with the history of the relationship between the security of the Government and of a free press that a more thorough briefing than the parties have had an opportunity to do is required. I have granted the restraining order because in my opinion any temporary harm that may result from not publishing during the pendency of the application for a preliminary injunction is far outweighed by the irreparable harm that could be done to the interests of the United States Government if it should ultimately prevail. I have intentionally expressed no opinion on the merits, but I believe this matter is brought in good faith by the United States and that on the balancing of interests mentioned, both parties deserve a full consideration of the issues raised.

Accordingly, the restraining order will be in effect until Saturday afternoon at 1 o'clock unless the Court directs otherwise.

The parties are requested to brief as thoroughly as possible the points adverted to in the oral arguments by 5 P.M. Thursday, June 17, 1971.

M. I. GURFEIN
U.S.D.J.

Dated: June 15, 1971.

Memorandum of Law

PRELIMINARY STATEMENT

This action has been commenced to preliminarily and permanently enjoin defendants and their agents from further disseminating documents consisting of 47 volumes entitled "History of U.S. Decision-Making Process on Vietnam Policy." Plaintiff further seeks to gain the recovery of the aforementioned documents from defendants. This memorandum is submitted in support of plaintiff's application for an order temporarily restraining the defendants from further disseminating the aforementioned documents and requiring the delivery of the documents to this court pending the determination of

plaintiff's motion for a preliminary injunction.

STATUTE RELIED UPON

Section 793 (d) of Title 18 of the United States Code provides as follow: "Whoever, lawfully having possession of, access to, control over, or being entrusted with any document, writing, code book, signal book, sketch, photograph, photographic negative, blueprint, plan, map, model, instrument, appliance, or note relating to the national defense, or information relating to the national defense which information the possessor has reason to believe could be used to the injury of the United States or to the advantage of any foreign nation, willfully communicates, delivers, transmits or causes to be communicated, delivered, or transmitted or attempts to communicate, deliver, transmit or cause to be communicated, delivered or transmitted the same to any person not entitled to receive or willfully retains the same and fails to deliver it upon demand to the officer or employe of the United States entitled to receive it. . . ."

ARGUMENT

Defendants are in possession of a 47-volume study entitled "History of the United States Decision-Making Process on Vietnam Policy." This study is currently classified as "Top Secret-sensitive"* pursuant to the provisions of Executive Order 10501. As defined in the Executive Order, top-secret information is "that information or material the defense aspect of which is paramount, and the unauthorized disclosure of which could result in exceptionally grave damage to the nation. . . ."

On June 13, 14 and 15, 1971, defendants published documents contained in the study. By telegram dated June 14, 1971, defendants were advised by the Attorney General of the United States that further publication of the contents of the study will cause irreparable injury to the defense interests of the United States. In the telegram, defendants were requested to cease publication of the contents of the study and to return the study to the Department of Defense. Defendants have expressed the intention to continue to publish documents contained in the study until they are restrained from doing so by an order of this Court.

Section 793 (d) of Title 18 of the United States Code provides for criminal penalties against a person who, while lawfully in possession of information relating to the national defense which could be used to the injury of the United States, willfully communicates that information to persons not en-

titled to receive it or willfully fails to deliver it, on demand, to the officer of the United States entitled to receive it. The applicability of Section 793 (d) has not been restricted to criminal actions. *Dubin v. United States*, 289 F. 2d 651 (Ct. Cl. 1961).

Further publication of the contents of the study and defendants' continued refusal to return all of the papers to the Department of Defense will constitute a violation of Section 793 (d). Moreover, such publication will result in irreparable injury to the interests of the United States, for which there is no adequate remedy at law. An injury is deemed irreparable when it cannot be adequately compensated in damages due to the nature of the injury itself or where there exists no pecuniary standard for the measurement of the damages. *Luckenbach S. S. Co. v. Norton*, 12 F. Supp. 707,709 (E. D. Pa. 1937). Irreparable injury also means "that species of damage, whether great or small, that ought not to be submitted to on the one hand or inflicted on the other." *Anderson v. Sooza*, 38 Cal. 2d, 825,243 P. 2d 497,503 (1952). The inadequacy of a remedy at law exists where the circumstances demand preventive relief. *Cruikshank v. Bidwell* 176 U.S. 73,81 (1900).

In the instant case, defendants will suffer no injury if they cease to publish the contents of the study in their possession pending the determination of plaintiff's motion for a preliminary injunction. On the other hand, the national interest of the United States may be seriously damaged if the defendants continue to publish the contents of the study. Under circumstances in which no injury will result to defendants from the cessation of publication of the study in their possession and irreparable injury may result to the United States, the granting of a temporary restraining order is appropriate.

CONCLUSION

For the foregoing reasons, the plaintiff's application for a temporary restraining order pending the determination of its motion for a preliminary injunction should be granted. Plaintiff's application for an order temporarily restraining the further publication of the contents of the study in defendant's possession should be granted.

Dated: New York, New York
June 15, 1971

Respectfully submitted,

WHITNEY NORTH SEYMOUR Jr.
United States Attorney for the Southern District of New York, Attorney for the plaintiff, United States of America.

MICHAEL D. HESS
HOWARD S. SUSSMAN
MILTON SHERMAN
Assistant United States Attorneys, United of Counsel.

---

*In determining whether information properly has been classified top secret, the test to be applied by the court is whether the classifying authority acted capriciously. Epstein v. Resor, 296 F. Supp. 214 (N. D. Calif. 1969).

UNITED STATES DISTRICT COURT
FOR THE SOUTHERN DISTRICT OF NEW YORK
- - - - - - - - - - - - - - - - - - -

EDWARD J. ENNIS, EDWARD I. KOCH,
ARYEH NEIER, IRA GLASSER, EDWIN J.
OPPENHEIMER, JR., and NANCY LEE ENNIS,

        Defendant-Intervenors,

           v.

UNITED STATES OF AMERICA,

        Plaintiff,

           v.

NEW YORK TIMES COMPANY, ARTHUR OCHS
SULZBERGER, HARDING F. BANCROFT, IVAN
VEIT, FRANCIS A. COR, JAMES C. GOODALE,
SYDNEY GRUSON, WALTER MATTSON,
JOHN McCABE, JOHN MORTIMER, JAMES RESTON,
JOHN B. OAKES, A. M. ROSENTHAL, DANIEL
SCHWARZ, CLIFTON DANIEL, TOM WICKER,
W. E. KENWORTHY, FOX BUTTERFIELD,
GERALD GOLD, ALLAN M. SIEGAL, SAMUEL ABT,
NEIL SHEEHAN, and HENDRICK SMITH,

        Defendants.

- - - - - - - - - - - - - - - - - - -

MOTION TO INTERVENE
AS DEFENDANTS

71 Civ. 2662

TO THE HONORABLE JUDGES OF THE UNITED STATES DISTRICT COURT

FOR THE SOUTHERN DISTRICT OF NEW YORK:

    1. Upon the annexed pleading of the intervenors and

affidavits of Melvin L. Wulf, Esq., Aryeh Neier, and Edwin J.

Oppenheimer, Jr., the aforecaptioned defendant-intervenors

hereby move this Court to intervene as parties defendant

pursuant to F.R.Civ.P. 24(a)(2) and/or 24(b) with all the rights provided by said rule(s) on the grounds that (1) the defendant-intervenors claim interests relating to the property or transaction which is the subject of the action and that they are so situated that the disposition of the action will as a practical matter impair or impede their ability to protect their interests and (2) that the intervenors' defense and the main action involve common questions of law and fact relating to the constitutionality of the application of certain Acts of Congress which affect the public interest.

2. Annexed hereto in accordance with Rule 24(c) of the F.R.Civ.P. is a pleading entitled "Pleading of Defendant-Intervenors." Defendant-intervenors move that said pleading be deemed the appearance of the defendant-intervenors in opposition to the application of the statutes herein drawn into question (18 U.S.C. §§ 793, 794, 798) and in opposition to all pleadings and motions of the plaintiff that have been or may be filed in so far as said pleadings or motions are based on the contention that said Acts of Congress are being constitutionally applied to the defendants, New York Times, et al. or to the defendant-intervenors.

3. Defendant-intervenors further move this Court to fix a time in which the parties thereto may plead to the Pleading of the Defendant-Intervenors, in default of which, or

- 2 -

to the extent not denied in such responsive pleadings as the
parties may file and serve, the averments thereof shall be
deemed admitted; and to the extent that the same may be denied,
the defendant-intervenors offer to prove the same and move to
present arguments and evidence in support thereof.

Respectfully submitted,

MELVIN L. WULF
American Civil Liberties Union
   Foundation
156 Fifth Avenue
New York, N. Y. 10010

NORMAN DORSEN
New York University School of Law
Washington Square South
New York, N. Y. 10003

BURT NEUBORNE
BRUCE J. ENNIS
New York Civil Liberties Union
84 Fifth Avenue
New York, N. Y. 10011

EDWIN J. OPPENHEIMER, JR.
c/o New York Civil Liberties Union
84 Fifth Avenue
New York, N. Y. 10011
Pro Se

Attorneys for Defendant-Intervenors

UNITED STATES DISTRICT COURT
FOR THE SOUTHERN DISTRICT OF NEW YORK
- - - - - - - - - - - - - - - - - - - -

EDWARD J. ENNIS, EDWARD I. KOCH,   :
ARYEH NEIER, IRA GLASSER, EDWIN J.   :
OPPENHEIMER, JR., and NANCY LEE ENNIS,   :

                Defendant-Intervenors,   :

                                                    :   ORDER
                                                            TO SHOW CAUSE
                v.   :

UNITED STATES OF AMERICA,   :

                Plaintiff,   :   71 Civ. 2662

                                                    :
                v.
                                                    :

NEW YORK TIMES COMPANY, ARTHUR OCHS   :
SULZBERGER, HARDING F. BANCROFT, IVAN   :
VEIT, FRANCIS A. COX, JAMES C. GOODALE,   :
SYDNEY GRUSON, WALTER MATTSON,   :
JOHN McCABE, JOHN MORTIMER, JAMES RESTON,   :
JOHN B. OAKES, A. M. ROSENTHAL, DANIEL   :
SCHWARZ, CLIFTON DANIEL, TOM WICKER,   :
W. E. KENWORTHY, FOX BUTTERFIELD,   :
GERALD GOLD, ALLAN M. SIEGAL, SAMUEL ABT,   :
NEIL SHEEHAN, and HENDRICK SMITH,   :

                Defendants.   :

- - - - - - - - - - - - - - - - - - - -

        Upon the Pleading of Defendant-Intervenors and the

affidavits attached thereto and the annexed affidavit of

Melvin L. Wulf, Esq., one of the attorneys for the Defendant-

Intervenors herein, it is hereby

        ORDERED, that the parties hereto show cause before

the Hon. Murray I. Gurfein, U.S.D.J., at the United States

Courthouse, Foley Square, New York, New York, in   Part

June 16, 1971

Defendant Times

68

thereof, on June   1971 at   o'clock in the   noon or as

soon thereafter as counsel can be heard why an ORDER pursuant

to Rule 24(a)(2) and/or 24(b) of the F.R.Civ.P. should not be

entered allowing the aforecaptioned Defendant-Intervenors

to appear in the above-entitled action as Defendant-Intervenors,

and it is further

ORDERED, that service of this order together with a

copy of the papers on which it is granted be served upon the

parties on or before June   1971 at   o'clock in the

noon of that day and that such service may be deemed good and

sufficient.

_____
Hon. Murray I. Gurfein
U.S.D.J.

Dated:

UNITED STATES DISTRICT COURT
FOR THE SOUTHERN DISTRICT OF NEW YORK
- -

EDWARD J. ENNIS, EDWARD I. KOCH,
ARYEH NEIER, IRA GLASSER, EDWIN J.
OPPENHEIMER, JR., and NANCY LEE ENNIS,

              Defendant-Intervenors,

                  v.

UNITED STATES OF AMERICA,

              Plaintiff,

                  v.

NEW YORK TIMES COMPANY, ARTHUR OCHS
SULZBERGER, HARDING F. BANCROFT, IVAN
VEIT, FRANCIS A. COR, JAMES C. GOODALE,
SYDNEY GRUSON, WALTER MATTSON,
JOHN McCABE, JOHN MORTIMER, JAMES RESTON,
JOHN B. OAKES, A. M. ROSENTHAL, DANIEL
SCHWARZ, CLIFTON DANIEL, TOM WICKER,
W. E. KENWORTHY, FOX BUTTERFIELD,
GERALD GOLD, ALLAN M. SIEGAL, SAMUEL ABT,
NEIL SHEEHAN, and HENDRICK SMITH,

              Defendants

- -

AFFIDAVIT

71 Civ. 2662

STATE OF NEW YORK)
) ss.:
COUNTY OF NEW YORK)

     MELVIN L. WULF, being duly sworn, deposes and says:

     1. That I am one of the attorneys for the defendant-intervenors herein and I make this affidavit for the purpose of showing, pursuant to Rule 9(c)(4) of the General Rules of this Court, good and sufficient reasons for bringing on defendant-

intervenors' motion to intervene by order to show cause rather than by notice of motion.

2. The issues in this case raise questions of the highest constitutional magnitude. The United States is seeking to permanently enjoin the New York Times and its employees and agents from publishing certain documents excerpted from a purportedly classified report prepared by the Department of Defense on the history of the escalation of the war in Vietnam. Such a request for judicially enforced censorship immediately brings into question the most serious First Amendment issues relating to the freedom of the press.

3. However, during arguments before this Court on the plaintiff's application for a Temporary Restraining Order, it became apparent that issues of equally far reaching constitutional significance are presented by this case, to wit, the right of the public at large to read accounts of purported deception and decision making rendered in the early years of America's engagement in the war in Vietnam.

4. Neither of the parties presently before the Court are in a position to adequately protect the First Amendment rights of the defendant-intervenors to acquire information about the conduct of the United States Government vital to their interests as American citizens. The right of defendant-intervenors to know what the New York Times, et al. have to

- 2 -

tell them in the press is equally as compelling from a constitutional standpoint as the right of the defendants to publish
the documents in question.

5. The "Pleading of the Defendant-Intervenors" and
the affidavits attached thereto further clarify the specialized
interests of the defendant-intervenors as individuals in
seeking vindication of their right to be recipients of vital
political information free of governmental censorship.

6. The reason that the within motion for leave to
intervene is brought on by order to show cause rather than
notice of motion is because of the limited time factors involved.
A hearing on plaintiff's motion for a preliminary injunction is
scheduled for Friday, June 18, 1971. Defendant-intervenors are
presently preparing a brief to present to the Court on the substantive issues herein in anticipation of the granting of this
motion.

WHEREFORE, it is respectfully requested that defendant-
intervenors' motion pursuant to Rule 24(a)(2) and/or Rule 24(b),
F.R.Civ.P., be granted.

_____
Melvin L. Wulf

Sworn to before me this
16th day of June 1971

BELLA GREENE
Notary Public, State of New York
No. 21-1551210
Qualified in Kings County
Commission Expires March 30, 1973

- 3 -

UNITED STATES DISTRICT COURT
FOR THE SOUTHERN DISTRICT OF NEW YORK
- -

EDWARD J. ENNIS, EDWARD I. KOCH,
ARYEH NEIER, IRA GLASSER, EDWIN J.
OPPENHEIMER, JR., and NANCY LEE ENNIS,

          Defendant-Intervenors,

             v.

UNITED STATES OF AMERICA,

          Plaintiff,

             v.

NEW YORK TIMES COMPANY, ARTHUR OCHS
SULZBERGER, HARDING F. BANCROFT, IVAN
VEIT, FRANCIS A. COR, JAMES C. GOODALE,
SYDNEY GRUSON, WALTER MATTSON,
JOHN McCABE, JOHN MORTIMER, JAMES RESTON,
JOHN B. OAKES, A. M. ROSENTHAL, DANIEL
SCHWARZ, CLIFTON DANIEL, TOM WICKER,
W. E. KENWORTHY, FOX BUTTERFIELD,
GERALD GOLD, ALLAN M. SIEGAL, SAMUEL ABT,
NEIL SHEEHAN, and HENDRICK SMITH,

          Defendants.

- -

AFFIDAVIT

71 Civ. 2662

STATE OF NEW YORK)
) ss.:
COUNTY OF NEW YORK)

      ARYEH NEIER, being duly sworn, deposes and says:

      1. I am one of the movant defendant-intervenors herein and I make this affidavit in support of defendant-intervenors' motion pursuant to Rule 24(a)(2) and/or 24(b) of the F.R.Civ.P. for leave to intervene as parties defendant.

2. I have been a reader of the New York Times for twenty years .

3. I am employed as Executive Director of the American Civil Liberties Union.

4. In the course of my employment as Director of the American Civil Liberties Union I am constantly engaged in discussion and debate over the history and propriety of American engagement in the war in Vietnam. No issue has been more hotly debated within the American Civil Liberties Union than whether the organization should oppose the war as an infringement of civil liberties because of presidential usurpation of the constitutional power of Congress to engage the nation in war. The American Civil Liberties Union is engaged in continued review of its view of the war and in presentation of its views in courts, before Congress and to the general public. The material thus far presented in the New York Times' series is of critical importance in reviewing, refining and presenting our views and I believe that the information contained in the remaining articles will be of similar importance. Therefore, I consider it of great importance that I have an opportunity to see the remaining articles.

5. In addition, I believe that as a citizen exercizing my responsibilities of citizenship it' is important for me to see the remaining articles in the series so that I might make informal

- 2 -

74

judgments on American engagement in the Indo-China war.

_____
Aryeh Neier

Sworn to before me this
16th day of June 1971

UNITED STATES DISTRICT COURT
FOR THE SOUTHERN DISTRICT OF NEW YORK

- -

EDWARD J. ENNIS, EDWARD I. KOCH,
ARYEH NEIER, IRA GLASSER, EDWIN J.
OPPENHEIMER, JR., and NANCY LEE ENNIS,

        Defendant-Intervenors,   AFFIDAVIT

            v.   71 Civ. 2662

UNITED STATES OF AMERICA,

        Plaintiff,

            v.

NEW YORK TIMES COMPANY, ARTHUR OCHS
SULZBERGER, HARDING F. BANCROFT, IVAN
VEIT, FRANCIS A. COR, JAMES C. GOODALE,
SYDNEY GRUSON, WALTER MATTSON,
JOHN McCABE, JOHN MORTIMER, JAMES RESTON,
JOHN B. OAKES, A. M. ROSENTHAL, DANIEL
SCHWARZ, CLIFTON DANIEL, TOM WICKER,
W. E. KENWORTHY, FOX BUTTERFIELD,
GERALD GOLD, ALLAN M. SIEGAL, SAMUEL ABT,
NEIL SHEEHAN, and HENDRICK SMITH,

        Defendants.

- -

STATE OF NEW YORK)
) ss.:
COUNTY OF NEW YORK)

      EDWIN J. OPPENHEIMER, JR., being duly sworn, deposes
and says:

      1. I am one of the movant defendant-intervenors herein
and I make this affidavit in support of defendant-intervenors
motion pursuant to Rule 24(a)(2) and/or 24(b) of the F.R. of
Civ. P. for leave to intervene as parties defendant.

2. I have been a reader of the New York Times for
over ten years.

3. I am employed as a law clerk, apprenticed to an
attorney admitted to the practice of law in the State of New
York pursuant to applicable provisions of the New York CPLR.

4. In the course of my employment as a law clerk I
am currently engaged in extensive research regarding the formulation of American policy and involvement in the war in Vietnam;
said research to be used in the preparation of a petition for a
writ of certiorari to the United States Court of Appeals for
the Second Circuit in the cases of Berk v. Laird, ____F.2d ____,
No. 35535 (2nd Cir. 1971), and Orlando v. Laird, ____F.2d ____,
No. 35270 (2nd Cir. 1971) both of which are the first cases
testing the constitutionality of the war in Vietnam which have
been held to present justiciable issues. The material contained
in the first three installments of the New York Times' articles
here in question present issues absolutely essential to the
resolution of the issues presented by the Berk and Orlando
cases. I believe that the information contained in the remaining
articles of the series will be of equal importance and I therefore
have a desire to read those articles still remaining to be
published.

5. In addition, I desire to read the articles remaining
to be published from the series so that I may acquire a greater

knowledge of the events surrounding my country's involvement

in the war in Vietnam.

Edwin J. Oppenheimer, Jr.

Sworn to before me this
16th day of June 1971

78

UNITED STATES DISTRICT COURT
FOR THE SOUTHERN DISTRICT OF NEW YORK

- - - - - - - - - - - - - - - - - - - -

EDWARD J. ENNIS, EDWARD I. KOCH,
ARYEH NEIER, IRA GLASSER, EDWIN J.
OPPENHEIMER, JR., and NANCY LEE ENNIS,

        Defendant-Intervenors,

              v.

UNITED STATES OF AMERICA,

        Plaintiff,

              v.

NEW YORK TIMES COMPANY, ARTHUR OCHS
SULZBERGER, HARDING F. BANCROFT, IVAN
VEIT, FRANCIS A. COR, JAMES C. GOODALE,
SYDNEY GRUSON, WALTER MATTSON,
JOHN McCABE, JOHN MORTIMER, JAMES RESTON,
JOHN B. OAKES, A. M. ROSENTHAL, DANIEL
SCHWARZ, CLIFTON DANIEL, TOM WICKER,
W. E. KENWORTHY, FOX BUTTERFIELD,
GERALD GOLD, ALLAN M. SIEGAL, SAMUEL ABT,
NEIL SHEEHAN, and HENDRICK SMITH,

        Defendants.

:   **PLEADING OF DEFENDANT INTERVENORS**

:   71 Civ. 2662

- - - - - - - - - - - - - - - - - - - -

The defendant-intervenors above named allege for

their pleading pursuant to Rule 24(c), F.R.Civ.P.,

PARTIES

1. EDWARD J. ENNIS, is a citizen of the United States

and a resident of the City of New York. He has been a constant

reader of the New York Times for more than forty years. The

New York Times is one of his principal sources of factual information regarding the conduct of the United States Government and of political affairs in general. He has read the excerpts of a forty-seven volume report known as the "History of U.S. Decision-Making Process on Vietnam Policy" which were printed in the New York Times on June 12, 13 and 14 and believes that the information set out in those excerpts is of vital importance to all citizens of the United States. He believes that completion of the series by the New York Times will serve the vital interests of the nation. He also believes that the information does not endanger the national security of the United States.

2. EDWARD I. KOCH, a member of the United States House of Representatives, is a citizen of the United States and a resident of the City of New York. He has been a constant reader of the New York Times for thirty years. The New York Times is a principal source of factual information relevant to the discharge of his responsibilities as a member of the House of Representatives and relevant to his responsibility to vote upon all the measures presented to the members of the House. He has read the excerpts of a forty-seven volume report known as the "History of U.S. Decision-Making Process on Vietnam Policy" which were printed in the New York Times on June 12, 13 and 14 and believes that the information set out in those

- 2 -

excerpts is of vital importance and relevance to his responsibilities as a member of the House of Representatives. That information will affect the decisions he makes on how to vote upon measures related to the war in Vietnam, and upon the views he communicates to the residents of his Congressional District. He is vitally interested in reading the remaining unpublished portions of the study which the New York Times intends to print so that he may have a more complete picture of the history of the involvement of the United States in the war in Vietnam.

3. ARYEH NEIER is a citizen of the United States and a resident of the City of New York. He has been a constant reader of the New York Times for twenty-five years. The New York Times is one of his principal sources of information regarding the conduct of the United States Government and of political affairs in general. He has read the excerpts of a forty-seven volume report entitled "History of U.S. Decision-Making Process on Vietnam Policy" which were printed in the New York Times on June 12, 13 and 14 and believes the information set out in those excerpts is of vital importance to all citizens of the United States and to his own interest in being fully informed about the history of the involvement of the United States in the Vietnam War.

4. IRA GLASSER is a citizen of the United States and a resident of the City of New York. , He has been a constant reader of the New York Times for twenty-five years. The New

- 3 -

York Times is one of his principal sources of information regarding the conduct of the United States Governmand and of political affairs in general. He has read the excerpts of a forty-seven volume report entitled "History of U.S. Decision-Making Process on Vietnam Policy" which were printed in the New York Times on June 12, 13 and 14 and believes the information set out in those excerpts is of vital importance to all citizens of the United States and to his own interest in being fully informed about the history of the involvement of the United States in the Vietnam War.

5. NANCY LEE ENNIS is a citizen of the United States and a resident of the City of New York. She has been a constant reader of the New York Times for over five years. The New York Times is one of her principal sources of information regarding the conduct of the United States Government and of political affairs in general. She has read the excerpts of a forty-seven volume report entitled "History of U.S. Decision-Making Process on Vietnam Policy" which were printed in the New York Times on June 12, 13 and 14 and believes the information set out in those excerpts is of vital importance to all citizens of the United States and to her own interest in being fully informed about the history of the involvement of the United States in the Vietnam War.

6. EDWIN J. OPPENHEIMER, JR. is a citizen of the United States and a resident of White Plains, New York, in the Southern District of New York, and has been a reader of the New York Times for over ten years. The New York Times is one of his principal sources of information regarding the conduct of the United States Government and of political affairs in general. He has read the excerpts of a forty-seven volume report entitled "History of U.S. Decision-Making Process on Vietnam Policy" which were printed in the New York Times on June 12, 13 and 14 and believes the information set out in those excerpts is of vital importance to all citizens of the United States and to his own interest in being fully informed about the history of the involvement of the United States in the Vietnam War. At the present time, as a function of his employment as a law clerk apprenticed to an attorney on the staff of the New York Civil Liberties Union, he is engaged in extensive research regarding the legality of the war in Vietnam for inclusion in a petition for certiorari in a case presently being brought to the Supreme Court as more fully set out in his affidavit annexed hereto.

7. The New York Times Company, Arthur Ochs Sulzberger, Harding F. Bancroft, Ivan Veit, Francis A. Cor, James C. Goodale, Sydney Gruson, Walter Mattson, John McCabe, John Mortimer, James Reston, John B. Oakes, A. M. Rosenthal, Daniel Schwarz,

- 5 -

Clifton Daniel, Tom Wicker, W. E. Kenworthy, Fox Butterfield, Gerald Gold, Allan M. Siegal, Samuel Abt, Neil Sheehan, and Hendrick Smith are parties defendant.

8. The United States of America is the party plaintiff.

ANSWER TO PLAINTIFF'S COMPLAINT

9. Defendant-intervenors admit the allegations contained in paragraphs 3, 6, 7.

10. Defendant-intervenors deny the allegations contained in paragraphs 1, 9, 10.

11. Defendant-intervenors deny the allegations contained in paragraph 2 of the complaint to the extent that plaintiff alleges that the documents in question are "classified Top Secret or Secret" or that they are documents properly coming within the restrictive purview of Executive Order 10501

12. Defendant-intervenors lack sufficient knowledge upon which to base an answer to the allegation contained in paragraph 4 of the complaint.

13. Defendant-intervenors lack sufficient knowledge upon which to base an answer to the allegation contained in paragraph 5 of the complaint.

14. Defendant-intervenors lack sufficient knowledge upon which to base an answer to the allegation contained in paragraph 8 of the complaint.

- 6 -

15. Defendant-intervenors deny that this Court has subject matter jurisdiction over the defendants New York Times, et al.

16. Defendant-intervenors deny that this Court has jurisdiction over the defendants New York Times, et al.

17. The complaint fails to state a claim upon which relief can be granted.

18. 18 U.S.C. §§ 793, 794, 798 and Executive Order 10501, on their face or as applied in this case, violate the First Amendment of the United States Constitution, are over-broad, and unconstitutionally interfere with the right of defendant-intervenors to acquire information regarding the conduct of the United States Government.

19. 18 U.S.C. §§ 793, 794, 798 and Executive Order 10501 violate the Due Process Clause of the Fifth Amendment because they are vague and uncertain.

20. The documents in question here have been invalidly classified in violation of the First and Fifth Amendments to the Constitution of the United States and Executive Order 10501.

WHEREFORE, defendant-intervenors demand that this Court grant relief dismissing plaintiff's complaint in accordance

- 7 -

with defendant-intervenors answer to the complaint and upon

each and every affirmative defense thereto and for such other

relief as this Court may deem just and proper.

MELVIN L. WULF
American Civil Liberties Union
   Foundation
156 Fifth Avenue
New York, N. Y. 10010

NORMAN DORSEN
New York University School of Law
Washington Square South
New York, N. Y. 10003

BURT NEUBORNE
BRUCE J. ENNIS
New York Civil Liberties Union
84 Fifth Avenue
New York, N. Y. 10011

EDWIN J. OPPENHEIMER, JR.
c/o New York Civil Liberties Union
84 Fifth Avenue
New York, N. Y. 10011
Pro Se

Attorneys for Defendant-Intervenors

UNITED STATES DISTRICT COURT
FOR THE SOUTHERN DISTRICT OF NEW YORK

EDWARD J. ENNIS, et al

                Defendant-Intervenors,

      v.

UNITED STATES OF AMERICA,

                Plaintiff,

      v.

NEW YORK TIMES COMPANY, et al,

                Defendants.

: 71 Civ. 2662

DEFENDANT-INTERVENORS'MEMORANDUM OF POINTS
AND AUTHORITIES IN SUPPORT OF THEIR MOTION
TO INTERVENE AS PARTIES DEFENDANT.

MELVIN L. WULF
American Civil Liberties Union
  Foundation
156 Fifth Avenue
New York, N.Y. 10010

NORMAN DORSEN
New York University School of Law
Washington Square South
New York, N.Y. 10003

BURT NEUBORNE
BRUCE J. ENNIS
New York Civil Liberties Union
84 Fifth Avenue
New York, N.Y. 10011

EDWIN J. OPPENHEIMER, JR.
c/o New York Civil Liberties Union
84 Fifth Avenue
New York, N.Y. 10011
Pro se

    Attorneys for Defendant-Intervenors

87

UNITED STATES DISTRICT COURT
FOR THE SOUTHERN DISTRICT OF NEW YORK

EDWARD J. ENNIS, EDWARD I. KOCH,
ARYEH NEIER, IRA GLASSER, EDWIN J.
OPPENHEIMER, JR., and NANCY LEE ENNIS,   :

        Defendant-Intervenors,   :

      v.   :

UNITED STATES OF AMERICA,   :   71 Civ. 2662

        Plaintiff,   :

      v.   :

NEW YORK TIMES COMPANY, ARTHUR OCHS
SULZBERGER, HARDING F. BANCROFT, IVAN
VEIT, FRANCIS A. COR, JAMES C. GOODALE,   :
SYDNEY GRUSON, WALTER MATTSON,
JOHN McCABE, JOHN MORTIMER, JAMES RESTON,   :
JOHN B. OAKES, A. M. ROSENTHAL, DANIEL
SCHWARZ, CLIFTON DANIEL, TOM WICKER,   :
W.E. KENWORTHY, FOX BUTTERFIELD,
GERALD GOLD, ALLAN M. SIEGAL, SAMUEL ABT,   :
NEIL SHEEHAN, and HENDRICK SMITH,   :

        Defendants.   :

DEFENDANT-INTERVENORS' MEMORANDUM OF POINTS AND
AUTHORITIES IN SUPPORT OF THEIR MOTION TO
INTERVENE AS PARTIES DEFENDANT.

I.
INTERVENORS CLAIM AN INTEREST OF CONSTITUTIONAL MAGNITUDE

AND SHOULD THUS BE PERMITTED TO INTERVENE.

Should this Court issue a preliminary or permanent

injunction as requested by the Government, the First Amendment rights

of the Intervenors to enjoy a free and unabridged press would be

materially effected and thus Intervenors claim a clearly

requisite interest to be permitted to intervene. Atlantis

Development v. United States, 319 F.2d 818(5th Cir.1957);

Neuessen v. Camp,385 F.2d 694(D.C. Cir. 1967);   Cf. Flast

v. Cohen, 392 U.S. 83 (1968); International Mortgage and

Investment Corp. v. Von Clemm, 301 F.2d 857 (2nd Cir. 1962);

United States v. First National Bank and Trust Co., 263 F.Supp.

268 (E.D.Ky. 1967).

II.
THE RIGHTS OF THE INTERVENORS TO READ THE MATERIAL

IN QUESTION WOULD BE BOUND BY A DECISION FOR PLAINTIFFS

AND THE MOVANTS SHOULD THUS BE PERMITTED TO INTERVENE.

In International Mortgage and Investment Corp v.Von Clemm,

supra,   the Second Circuit liberally established a standard

for intervention coupled with judicial economy for a settlement

of interests in a single action where the intervening party

might or "may" be bound by a decision between the original

parties. It is clear that if the Government prevails, the

right of the Intervenors to read the documents in question would

be foreclosed. Thus, upon the rationale of International Mortgage

and Investment Corp. v. Von Clemm, supra, Defendant-Intervenors'

motion should be granted. United States v. Utica, C and S. V.

Ry. Co., et al 48 F.Supp. 903 at 905(S.D.N.Y. 1942)

-2-

III.
THE INTERESTS OF THE DEFENDANT-INTERVENORS ARE NOT
ADEQUATELY REPRESENTED BY THE NAMED DEFENDANTS HEREIN.

The First Amendment right of the Defendant-Intervenors
to read the documents at issue here is separate and distinct
from the rights of the named Defendants to engage in unabridged
press activities. Defendant-Intervenors submit that while
this is not a class action, they are representative of the diverse
numbers of persons throughout the United States and, indeed,
throughout the world, who are readers of the New York Times
and who believe they have a right to read the documents in
question. While the New York Times seeks to protect its own
press activities, it was apparent to counsel by their presence
at oral argument that the thrust of the named Defendants' arguments in opposition to the Plaintiffs' motion are not sufficiently
broad to clearly and conclusively protect the rights of the
Defendant-Intervenors who set forth a related, but distinct
First Amendment defense. Thus, Defendant-Intervenors' motion
should be granted as to this ground. Stell v. Savanah-Chatham
County Board of Education, Harris v. Gibson, 333 F.2d 55 5th
Cir. 1954).

-3-

IV.
A COMMON QUESTION OF LAW AND FACT EXISTS BETWEEN
THE PARTIES AND DEFENDANT-INTERVENORS.

The basic issue presented by this case is whether or not the Government of the United States on the barest of allegations may effectively suppress and suspend the First Amendment guarantee of the right of the people to enjoy a free and un-abridged press. While it has been previously noted (See Section III, supra) that the right of the press to carry on its activities in an unencumbered fashion and the right of the people to read the end product of the press' work are in one manner distinct because of the difference in emphasis with respect to the exercise of the First Amendment franchise by the respective parties, an obvious constitutional vein runs through both the cases of the Defendants and the Defendant-Intervenors. Both the people and the press benefit from the basic First Amendment guarantee of a free working press. For example, see Caldwell v. United States, 434 F.2d 1081(9th Cir. 1970). The disposition of the First Amendment issue as to the Defendants New York Times, et al, will act as an estoppel on the exercise of the First Amendment right of the Defendant-Intervenors as well. It is hard to conceive of a more basic or important common question. As to this ground, Defendant-Intervenors' motion should be granted for the foregoing reason.

-4-

See generally <u>Champ v. Atkins</u>, 128 F.2d 601(D.C. Cir.

1942); <u>Ruby v. Pan American World Airways, Inc.</u>, 252 F.Supp.

393(S.D.N.Y. 1966); cf. <u>International Mortgage and Investment</u>

<u>Corp. v. Von Clemm</u>, <u>supra</u>; <u>O'Keefe v. Boeing Company</u>, 38 F.R.D. 329

(S.D.N.Y. 1965); and see generally Moore's Federal Practice

volume 3B, pages 24-354 through 24-358.

    For all of the aforementioned reasons, the Defendant-

Intervenors' motion should be granted.

MELVIN L. WULF
American Civil Liberties Union
  Foundation
156 Fifth Avenue
New York, N.Y. 10010

NORMAN DORSEN
New York University School of Law
Washington Square South
New York, N.Y. 10003

BURT NEUBORNE
BRUCE J. ENNIS
New York Civil Liberties Union
84 Fifth Avenue
New York, N.Y. 10011

EDWIN J. OPPENHEIMER, JR.
c/o New York Civil Liberties Union
84 Fifth Avenue
New York, N.Y. 10011
Pro se

Attorneys for Defendant-Intervenors

UNITED STATES DISTRICT COURT
SOUTHERN DISTRICT OF NEW YORK

- - - - - - - - - - - - - - - - - - :

UNITED STATES OF AMERICA,
     Plaintiff, :

    -v-   :

NEW YORK TIMES COMPANY, et al, :
     Defendants.

- - - - - - - - - - - - - - - - - - :

MEMORANDUM IN BEHALF OF
AMICI CURIAE
AMERICAN CIVIL LIBERTIES UNION AND
<u>NEW YORK CIVIL LIBERTIES UNION.</u>

NORMAN DORSEN
New York University School of Law
Washington Square South
New York, New York

MELVIN L. WULF
American Civil Liberties Union
156 Fifth Avenue
New York, New York

OSMOND K. FRAENKEL
120 Broadway
New York, New York

BURT NEUBORNE
BRUCE J. ENNIS
New York Civil Liberties Union
84 Fifth Avenue
New York, New York

Attorneys for Amici Curiae.

INDEX

94

INDEX

i

For fifty years the American Civil Liberties Union, and its New York State affiliate, the New York Civil Liberties Union, have sought to preserve the freedoms enshrined in our Bill of Rights. Amici believe that the instant case poses questions of critical importance to the continued existence of an informed citizenry and a free press. Amici respectfully submit the following brief in the hope that it will aid the Court in resolving the fundamental constitutional issues raised herein.

I. DEFENDANTS' PUBLICATION OF MATERIAL DETAILING THE HIS-TORICAL BACKGROUND OF OUR NATION'S INVOLVEMENT IN THE VIETNAM WAR IS ABSOLUTELY PROTECTED AGAINST GOVERNMENTAL INTERFERENCE BY THE FIRST AMENDMENT

A. The Constitutionally Protected Nature of the Material Which the New York Times seek to Publish.

In this action the executive, relying upon Title 18 U.S.C. §793 (the Espionage Act) seeks to prevent the New York Times from publishing excerpts from a study commissioned by the Secretary of Defense detailing the his-torical background of the political decisions from 1945-

1968 which culminated in our nation's involvement in the

Vietnam war. The material contains no hint of future

diplomatic or military policy, nor does it reveal current

tactical, technological or strategic information.* The

Vietnam Study does contain, however, information which

casts doubt upon the integrity of the process by which

Congress and the nation were induced to acquiesce in an

ever increasing military commitment in Vietnam.

Occurring, as it does, in the midst of a national

debate over the continuation of the war in Vietnam, the

publication of the Defense Department's account of the

process by which we became engaged militarily in Vietnam

constitutes a dissemination of information critically

necessary for the proper functioning of a representative

---

*It is important to specify at the outset what this case
is not about. The "Vietnam Study" and appended documents
so far published do not describe, and contain no information
concerning, "military" or "naval installations or equipment"
or about the "movement, numbers, description, condition,
or disposition of any of the Armed Forces, ships, aircraft,
or war materials of the United States." The study has
nothing to do with battle plans or defense fortifications
or code books, signals, photographs, blueprints, maps,
models, instruments, appliances or electronic equipment.
That is, no doubt, why the Government has elected not to
proceed under Sections 794-797 of the Espionage Act prohibiting the dissemination of such "hard" defense information.
The study involves solely, in the words of former Vice President Humphrey, "matters relating to what I call political
decisions."

democracy. Indeed, it is difficult to comprehend how a citizen can be expected to reach informed and rational decisions on the myriad issues raised by the war in Vietnam if he is denied access to the basic historical data relating to its origin.

It requires no great knowledge of either political science or constitutional law to recognize that information of the type which The New York Times seeks to publish in this case constitutes the lifeblood of a functioning democracy. Our courts have consistently emphasized that the free dissemination of information relevant to political questions of "public or general interest" is an indispensible pre-condition to effective representative democracy. As early as 1890, Warren and Brandeis singled out such information for special constitutional protection. Warren and Brandeis, The Right to Privacy, 4 Harv. L. Rev. 193, 214 (1890).

Our national commitment to affording maximum constitutional protection to the dissemination of information relevant to political questions "of public or general interest" has never slackened and was recently reaffirmed by the Supreme Court in Rosenbloom v. Metromedia, Inc., ____ U.S. ____, 39 USLW 4694 (June 7, 1971), when Mr. Justice Brennan, speaking for himself, the Chief Justice and Mr. Justice Blackmun,

reaffirming our "profound national commitment to the prin-

ciple that debate on public issues should be uninhibited,

robust and wide-open."* stated:

> We honor the commitment to robust debate on public
> issues, which is embodied in the First Amendment,
> by extending constitutional protection to all
> discussion and communication involving matters of
> public or general concern..." 39 U.S.L.W. 4694 at
> 4699.

Despite the fact that the dissemination of the his-

torical and political material at issue in this case is

central to the proper functioning of a representative

democracy and is, therefore, entitled to the highest

quantum of constitutional protection, the Executive argues

that it possesses power to suppress the report on its

conclusory and unsupported assertion that its publication

might be detrimental to our national interest.

Although the Executive has couched his objection to

publication in terms of national defense, no allegation has

been made that the nation's military or security posture,

as those terms are commonly understood, would be compromised

by the publication of the remainder of the Vietnam Study.

The "irreparable injury" which the Executive claims would

flow from the Study's publication is acute embarrassment

over revelations of moral astigmation, mendacity and arrogant

disregard of the truth on the part of high government

---

*New York Times Co. v. Sullivan, 376 U.S. 254 (1964), at 270

officials involved in the decisions leading up to the escalation of the war in Vietnam.

Although the Executive's contentions are phrased in the parlance of the 20th century, they raise ominous echoes of an earlier era when the United States asserted the power to suppress the publishing of documents which it believed would be detrimental to the national interest by tending to bring the Government "into contempt or disrepute." 1 Stat 596 (July 14, 1798) (The Sedition Act).

Stripped to its essentials, the Government's case is little more than a 20th century exhumation of the unlamented Sedition Act, condemned by the Supreme Court-- and by history--as contrary to the basic tenets of a free society. See New York Times v. Sullivan, 376 U.S. 254, 273-276 (1964). When measured against the constitutional imperatives of an adequately informed citizenry and a free press, the Executive's attempt to "classify" history must be categorically rejected.

   B.   The Constitutional Right to Receive Information
        Concerning Questions of "Public or General
        Interest."

The proud assertion in our Declaration of Independence that governments "derive their just powers from the consent of the governed" would ring hollow if the "consent" involved were something less than the informed consent of the governed.

Accordingly, it has been universally recognized that as a
condition to the functioning of a robust representative
democracy, American citizens must be endowed with a constitutional right to receive information necessary to an
exercise of informed political judgment on issues of
public or general interest. See Symposium, Community
Security vs. Man's Right to Knowledge, 54 Col.L.Rev. 667
(1954).

In a long series of decisions, the Supreme Court has
enunciated the doctrine that citizens in a free society
possess an inalienable right to receive precisely the type
of political information on public issues which the Executive now seeks to suppress. In Thornhill v. Alabama,
310 U.S. 88 (1940), the Court stated:

> Freedom of discussion, if it would fulfill its
> historic function in this nation, must embrace
> all issues about which information is needed
> or appropriate to enable the members of our
> society to cope with the exigencies of their
> period. 310 U.S. at 102.

In Lamont v. Postmaster General, 381 U.S. 301 (1965),
the Supreme Court struck down a postal regulation which
impeded the free flow of information from Iron Curtain
countries to addressees in the United States.

In a concurring opinion, Mr. Justice Brennan explicitly
recognized that the First Amendment necessarily protects

the right to receive information as well as the right to

disseminate it.   Citing Martin v. Struthers, 319 U.S. 141,

143 (1943), and in language strikingly apt to this case,

Mr. Justice Brennan concluded:

> That the governments which originate this pro-
> paganda themselves have no equivalent guarantees
> only highlights the cherished values of our con-
> stitutional framework; it can never justify
> emulating the practice of restrictive regimes in
> the name of expediency.   381 U.S. at 310.

In Stanley v. Georgia, 394 U.S. 557 (1969), Mr.

Justice Marshall, writing for the Court, recognized the

existence of a constituional right to receive information

when he wrote:

> It is now well established that the Constitution
> protects the right to receive information and
> ideas.   "This freedom [of speech and press]...
> necessarily protects the right to receive..."
> [omitting cases].   This right to receive infor-
> mation and ideas, regardless of their social
> worth, see Winters v. New York, 333 U.S. 507,
> 510 (1948), is fundamental to our free society.
> 394 U.S. at 564.

The Courts of Appeal have also enforced the First

Amendment right to receive information on public issues.

Thus, the Second Circuit in United States v. Dellapia,

433 F.2d 1252, 1258, n. 25 (2nd Cir. 1970); the Ninth

Circuit in Caldwell v. United States, 434 F.2d 1081, 1089

(9th Cir. 1970); and the Fifth Circuit in Hiett v. United

States, 415 F.2d 664, 671 (5th Cir. 1968) and Brooks v.

<u>Auburn University</u>, 412 F.2d 1171, 1172 (5th Cir. 1969),
have each explicitly recognized that the Government may
not seek to insulate individuals from the free flow of
information and opinion on public issues.

District Courts in both the Southern and Eastern
Districts of New York have concurred. E.g., <u>Fortune Society</u>
<u>v. McGinnis</u>, 319 F.Supp. 901, 904 (S.D.N.Y. 1970); <u>Mandell</u>
<u>v. Mitchell</u>, _____F.Supp._____, (E.D.N.Y. 1971), 39 LW 2531.
See also <u>United States v. B. & H Dist. Corp.</u>, 319 F.Supp.
1231 (W.D.Wisc. 1970); <u>ACLU v. Radford College</u>, 315 F.Supp.
893 (W.D.Va. 1970); <u>Williams v. Blount</u>, 314 F.Supp. 1356
(D.D.C. 1970); <u>Smith v. University of Tennessee</u>, 300 F.Supp.
777 (E.D.Tenn. 1969).

In <u>Mandel v. Mitchell</u>, <u>supra</u>, where plaintiffs successfully challenged the Government's refusal to grant a
visitor's visa to a Marxist scholar, Judge Dooling, writing
for a majority of the three judge court, stated:

> Since the First Amendment is not in its primary
> and most significant aspect a grant by the Con-
> stitution to the citizens of individual rights
> of self-expression but on the contrary reflects
> the total retention by the people as sovereign
> themselves of the right to free and open debate
> of political questions, the issue of 'standing
> to sue' is immediately seen to be unreal. The
> concern of the First Amendment is not with a
> non-resident alien's individual and personal

interest in being heard, but with the rights of
the citizens of the country to have the alien
enter and to hear him explain and seek to defend
his views. 39 LW at 2531.

Given the nature of the historical material which

The New York Times wishes to publish--its unquestioned

relevance to current political issues of the highest magni-

tude; and its manifest failure to create even a remote danger

to the security of the United States--the citizens of the

United States, as participants in a free democractic

society, possess a constitutional right to receive the

information at issue in this case.*

---

*Even apart from the Constitution, Federal law expressly
prohibits the classification of documents for the purpose
of "withholding of information, otherwise releasable, because its release might tend to reveal administrative error
or inefficiency, or might be embarrassing." 32 CFR (1971)
section 505.4 (a)(3). The initial classification was also
contrary to the letter and spirit of Executive Order 10501:
"It is essential that the citizens of the United States be
informed concerning the activities of their government."

Furthermore, even if national defense at one time required
classification of these materials, a point we dispute, it
is clear that most, and probably all, of them could long
ago have been declassified without jeopardizing national
defense. Section 4 of Executive Order 10501, the only
authority for classification, expressly mandates frequent
review of classified material in order "to eliminate accu-
mulation of classified material which no longer requires
protection in the defense interest." Had that requirement
been observed, there would be no basis for the present
action. Plaintiff is thus in the inequitable posture of
asking this Court to enjoin publication of materials whose
classified status results solely from plaintiff's violation
of both constitutional and Federal law.

C. The Constitutional Right of a Free Press to
Disseminate Information Relevant to Questions
of "Public or General Interest."

In 1799, James Madison wrote:

Among those principles deemed sacred in America,
among those sacred rights considered as forming
the bulwark of their liberty, which the Government contemplates with awful reverence and would
approach only with the most cautious circums-
pection, there is no one of which the importance
is more deeply impressed on the public mind than
the liberty of the press. VI Writings of James
Madison, 1790-1802, 336 (Hunt ed. 1906).

Madison's perception that a free society is ultimately

dependent for its survival upon a vigorous free press has

been reflected in the virtually unbroken line of judicial

decisions upholding the right of a free press to disseminate

information on public issues free from governmental restraint,

even when such dissemination may be shown to impinge on

competing societal interests. E.g., Bridges v. California,

314 U.S. 252 (1941); Pennekamp v. Florida, 328 U.S. 331

(1946); Craig v. Harney, 331 U.S. 367 (1947); Wood v. Georgia,

370 U.S. 375 (1962); Rosenbloom v. Metromedia, Inc.,____U.S.

____, 39 USLW 4694 (June 7, 1971); Ocala Star-Banner Company

v. Damron, 91 S.Ct. 628 (1971); Monitor Patriot Company v.

Roy, 31 S.Ct. 621 (1970); Time, Inc. v. Pape, 91 S.Ct. 633

(1971); Greenbelt Coop. Pub. Assn. v. Bresler, 398 U.S. 6

(1970); Beckley Newspaper Corp. v. Hanks, 389 U.S. 81 (1967);

Curtis Publishing Co. v. Butts, 388 U.S. 130 (1967);

Associated Press v. Walker, 388 U.S. 130 (1967); New York Times Co. v. Sullivan, 376 U.S. 254 (1964); see also, Rosenblatt v. Baer, 383 U.S. 75 (1966); St. Amant v. Thompson, 390 U.S. 727 (1968); Garrison v. Louisiana, 379 U.S. 64 (1964); Time, Inc. v. Hill, 385 U.S. 374 (1967).

The First Amendment itself was adopted against the background of widespread use of the common law of seditious libel to suppress the dissemination of information embarrassing to the Government. From the trial of John Peter Zenger, 17 How.St.Tr. 675 (1735), to the passage of Fox's Libel Act by Parliament in 1792, the founders wrestled with the intolerable burdens which the law of seditious libel imposed upon a free press. See generally, Z. Chafee, Free Speech in the United States (1941) Ch. XIII; T. Emerson, The System of Free Expression in the United States (1970), Ch. V. With the expiration of the Sedition Act in 1801, one would have hoped that the attempts to muzzle a free press in this country would have expired as well. Indeed, in New York Times v. Sullivan, 376 U.S. 254, 273 (1964), the Sedition Act was posthumously condemned as contrary to "the central meaning of the First Amendment." Unfortunately, however, the attempt by the Executive to prevent the publication of the historical documents on the ground that publication would be embarrassing to the national interest is frighteningly

reminiscent of the twenty-five prosecutions which took place under the Sedition Act. See generally, <u>United States v. Lyon</u>, Wharton's St.Tr. 684 (1800); <u>United States v. Cooper</u> Wharton's St.Tr. 688 (1800). If the free press guaranty of the First Amendment was intended to cure any evil at all, it was intended to prevent overzealous Government officials from jeopardizing the operation of a free press in the misguided belief that they were stamping out information detrimental to the national interest. The overzealous government officials are motivated by the age-old belief that they are protecting us by keeping us ignorant. The First Amendment protects us from the consequences of their misguided zeal.

D.   The Danger to a Free Society Inherent In
     The Government's Contentions

The bitter colonial experience with the British licensing laws, imposing prior restraints on the dissemination of information, left us with a healthy fear of any system of Governmental regulation of political information.

In 1586 the Star Chamber promulgated the first licensing regulations restricting domestic printing and controlling the importation of books from abroad. Tanner, <u>Tudor Constitutional Documents</u> A.D. 1485-1603, 279-84 (1903). In

In 1637, motivated by the fear of Puritan agitation and foreign competition, the Star Chamber directive was dramatically expanded and became the model for an act of the Restoration Parliament for the licensing of books. 14 Car. II, c. 33. Even after the lapse of the licensing act in 1694, the law of seditious libel continued to render it impossible to print material tending to cast contempt upon the Government. With the decision in the Zenger case and the enactment of the First Amendment, free men believed that the State had lost the power to regulate the flow of political information. The assertion by the Executive that in the name of "national defense", it may determine what political information may be disseminated is nothing short of an attempt to resurrect the colonial licensing system in its classic form.

Indeed, if the Government can suppress historical information of a political, rather than a tactical or techno-logical, nature merely by invoking the shibboleth of national defense, the basic commitment of this nation to the maintenance of free trade in ideas will have been struck a serious, if not a mortal, blow. Under such a doctrine, the flow of information concerning controversial and sensitive political issues would be controlled solely by the Executive branch of the Government. The people would be permitted to know only what the then current administration

believes would be in the national defense interest for them
to know. If such a doctrine seems terrifying alien to the
"central purpose of the First Amendment," it is because it
is the heart of totalitarianism. Would it not be tragically
ironic if, in the name of protecting us from totalitarianism,
we permitted to erosion of the very First Amendment Freedoms
which characterize our free society, and make it worth
defending?

II THE FIRST AMENDMENT PROHIBITION AGAINST PRIOR RESTRAINT WILL NOT TOLERATE THE ISSUANCE OF AN INJUNCTION PRIOR TO THE PUBLICATION OF A NEWS ARTICLE

The abhorrence of prior restraint is firmly established in the law of the First Amendment. For reasons of overriding public importance, the Supreme Court has laid down the broad and immutable rule that government may not restrict free speech--particularly the dissemination of newspapers and periodicals--prior to publication.

The narrow issue presented here is whether the prohibition against prior restraint will tolerate the issuance of an injunction prior to publication. The leading case, Near v. Minnesota 283 U.S. 697 (1931) held that the State's prayer for an injunction to prevent publication by a newspaper constituted an unconstitutional abridgement of the First Amendment prohibition against prior restraints. Near involved a statute--known as the Minnesota Gag Law--which permitted prospective injunctions to prevent the publication of "malicious scandalous and defamatory" newspapers. 283 U.S. at 701.

-15-

Focusing on that provision of the Minnesota statute which permitted injunctive proceedings prior to publication, Chief Justice Hughes, speaking for the Court in _Near_, reviewed the historical considerations and policies inherent in the First Amendment:

> "In determining the extent of the constitutional protection, it has been generally, if not universally, considered that it is the chief purpose of the guaranty to prevent previous restraints upon publication. The struggle in England, directed against the legislative power of the licenser, resulted in renunciation of the censorship of the press. The liberty deemed to be established was thus described by Blackstone: 'The liberty of the press is indeed essential to the nature of a free state; but this consists in laying no _previous_ restraints upon publications, and not in freedom from censure for criminal matter when published. Every freeman has an undoubted right to lay what sentiments he pleases before the public; to forbid this, is to destroy the freedom of the press; but if he publishes what is improper, mischievous or _illegal_, he must take the consequence of his own temerity.' 4 Bl. Com. 151, 152; see Story on the Constitution §§ 1884, 1889." _Ibid._ at 713-714 (emphasis added).

The Court in _Near_ concluded that "liberty of the

-16-

press historically considered and taken up by the
Federal Constitution, has meant, principally, although
not exclusively, immunity from previous restraints or
censorship." Ibid. at 717.

Since Near v. Minnesota, supra, the prohibition
against prior restraint has been consistently reaffirmed
where the issue has involved the freedom of the press.
In Grosjean v. American Press Co., 297 U.S. 233 (1936),
the Supreme Court invalidated a licensing tax on newspapers
partially because it constituted a prior restraint. The
Court reiterated the holding in Near and concluded that:

> "...the First Amendment...was meant
> to preclude the national government...
> from adopting any form of previous
> restraint upon printed publications, or
> their circulation....
>
> "Judge Cooley has laid down the test
> to be applied--'The evils to be
> prevented were not the censorship of
> the press merely, but any action of
> the government by means of which it
> might prevent such free and general
> discussion of public matters as seems
> absolutely essential to prepare the
> people for an intelligent exercise of
> their rights as citizens.' 2 Cooley,
> Const. Lim. 8th ed. p. 886,"Ibid at
> 249-250. (emphasis added).

Lovell v. Griffin, 303 U.S. 444 (1938) similarly involved the

-17-

constitutionality of a licensing ordinance. In declaring

the ordinance unconstitutional, the court stated that

"[w]hile...freedom from previous restraint upon publication

cannot be regarded as exhausting the guaranty of liberty,

the prevention of that restraint was a leading purpose

in the adoptionn of the constitutional provision."

Ibid at 451-452. The principle embodied in these cases

has been followed in a long line of authorities. See

e.g., Stuab v. City of Baxley, 355 U.S. 319 (1958) and

most recently, Hull v. Petrillo, 439 F2d 1184 (2nd Cir.

1971).

The prior restraint which the Executive

seeks to impose here is a restraint upon the dissemination

of political information on matters of general interest.

When communication less central to the proper functioning

of our form of government has been at issue, we have

tolerated carefully regulated limitations on its dissemination,

with the government bearing a heavy burden of justification.

See Bantam Books v. Sullivan, 372 U.S. 58, 70 (1963); Freedman

v. Maryland, 380 U.S. 51 (1965). But, in the history of

-18-

the Republic, no prior restraint has ever been permitted in the area of political speech. Even the infamous Sedition Act did not authorize such a means of censorship.

There are compelling reasons of constitutional polity that underly this unbroken pattern of opposition to previous restraints. As Professor Emerson carefully describes in his recent book:

> "[a] system of prior restraint is in many
> ways more inhibiting than a system of sub-
> sequent punishment: It is likely to bring
> under government scrutiny a far wider range
> of expression; it shuts off communication before
> it takes place; suppression by a stroke
> of the pen is more likely to be applied than
> suppression through criminal process; the
> procedures to not require attention to
> the safeguards of the criminal process;
> the system allows less opportunity
> for public appraisal and criticism; the
> dynamics of the system drive toward excesses,
> as the history of all censorship shows."
> T. Emerson, The System of Freedom of
> Expression at 506. See also Emerson, "The
> Doctrine of Prior Restraint", 20 Law and
> Contemp. Probs. 648 (1955); Monaghan, First
> Amendment "Due Process", 83 Harv. L. Rev.
> 518, 543 (1970).

For the above reasons, all rooted in the core policies of the First Amendment, the Government's attempt to restrain publication here should be denied as plainly

-19-

inconsistent with the constitutional command. Any
other result would lead to an impairment of liberty in
the name of a spurious and unsupported concern with national
defense.

III. THE ONLY STATUTE RELIED UPON BY PLAINTIFF,
      18 U.S.C.A., SECTION 793, PROVIDES NO
      AUTHORITY FOR RELIEF IN THIS CASE.

A. The Act Does Not Authorize Prior Restraint
    Of The Press.

The only statutory authority cited by plaintiff

for the extraordinary relief sought herein is 18 U.S.C. §793.

That statute, in its present form and wording, was enacted on

September 23, 1950 by section 18 of Chapter 1024 of the acts

of the 81st Congress, 2nd Session, reported at 64 Stat. 987, 1003-

1005.* Section 1(b), of the act, reported at 64 Stat. 987, pro-

vides:

> "Nothing in this Act shall be construed to
> authorize, require, or establish military
> or civilian censorship or in any way to
> limit or infringe upon freedom of the press
> or of speech as guaranteed by the Constitution
> of the United States and no regulation shall
> be promulgated hereunder having that effect."

Congress, sensitive to the importance of a free

press**, carefully prefaced the act with an express disavowal

of any intent to authorize a prior restraint, or in any way to

limit freedom of the press. Plaintiff may, if it chooses,

---

*Chapter 1024 was known as the "Internal Security Act of
1950," and was divided into two Titles. Title I, of which
section 18, now section 793 of the Code, was a part, was known
as the "Subversive Activities Control Act of 1950".

**Indeed, the express purpose of the act was to protect this
country from "totalitarian" forms of government which would
deny those "fundamental rights and liberties which are characteristic of a representative form of government, such as freedom of speech, of the press..." Chapter 1024, section 2(2),
64 Stat. 987.

-21-

attempt to prosecute defendants under section 793, but it may not invoke section 793 as authority for an entirely different type of remedy, a remedy which Congress expressly proscribed.

The legislative history, reported in 2 <u>U.S. Code Congressional Service,</u> 81st Cong., 2nd Sess. (1950), at pp. 3886-3922 (cited hereafter as "Code Service"), reveals that the act's prohibition of prior restraint was a carefully considered legislative response to problems which Congress realized were of constitutional dimension, as we have demonstrated in Point II of this brief. House Report No. 2980 phrased the problem as follows (Code Service, p. 3888):

> "The [House] committee approached the problem with care and restraint because it is believed essential that any legislation recommended be strictly in accordance with our constitutional traditions. How to protect freedom from those who would destroy it, without infringing upon the freedom of all our people, presents a question fraught with constitutional and practical difficulties. We must not mortally wound our democratic framework in attempting to protect it from those who threaten to destroy it."

But the House bill, though it was careful not to <u>authorize</u> prior restraint, did not expressly prohibit it, an omission the Senate considered objectionable. The Senate therefore passed a bill containing the language now found in section 1(a) of the Act, the "managers on the part of the House" (Code Service, p. 3899), one of whom was the Hon., now President, Richard Nixon (Code Service, p. 3922), agreed to

-22-

117

the Senate's language, and the Conference Report recommended the enactment of the Senate language (Code Service, p. 3900).*

B. Section 793 Does Not Authorize Relief.

Even if the Act which enacted section 793 in its present form could be construed to authorize prior restraint of the press, section 793 would still not authorize relief.

1. Subdivision (d) of section 793 is, by its terms, inapplicable.

The plaintiff's own papers demonstrate conclusively that subdivision (d) is inapplicable. Subdivision (d) applies only to persons "lawfully having possession of", or lawfully intrusted with documents "relating to the national defense." The complaint, paragraphs "4" and "5", alleges that defendants "without lawful authority obtained" the documents at issue herein. And paragraph "4" of the Buzhardt affidavit alleges that the Times "was not authorized . . . to have possession" of said documents. Accordingly, plaintiff cannot even claim, much less prove, that defendants' possession was "lawful", the prerequisite to relief under subdivision (d).

2. Subdivision (e) of section 793 is, by its terms, inapplicable.

a. Subdivision (e) does not purport to cover classified documents or information.

An entirely different section of the Act--section 798--deals expressly and exclusively with dissemination of

---

*The Conference Report and the report of the House Mangers were eventually read on the floor of the House. Congressional Record-House, Vol. 96, Part II (September 20, 1950, pp. 15265, 15279-15280.)

"classified" material. Subdivision (e) of §793, which carefully specifies the types of subject matter proscribed, does
not use the word "classified." Clearly that subdivision is
inapplicable when the very essence of plaintiff's case is that
the Vietnam Study is a classified document.*

b. Subdivision (e) does not purport to cover publications.

Both subdivision (e) and section 798 proscribe any
attempt to "communicate" or "transmit" certain types of information, but subdivision (e), unlike section 798, does not
expressly proscribe "publication." Congress clearly viewed
"communicate," "transmit" and "publish" as distinct acts, and
whatever Congress intended to proscribe by the word "publish",
a question difficult enough in itself, it did not intend to
proscribe under subdivision (e). If the acts which plaintiff
seeks to enjoin would constitute "publication", then plaintiff's
reliance upon §793 (e) is misplaced. Although §798, which
speaks of the "publication" of "classified information" would
seem, at first blush, to be the more applicable of the two
sections, plaintiff no doubt decided not to rely upon §798
because the materials at issue here do not even arguably fall
within one or more of the four types of classified information
whose publication is proscribed by §798.

_____

*"Where Congress has laid down specific procedures to deal with
the type of crisis confronting the President, he must follow
those procedures in meeting the crisis", and no other. Youngstown
Sheet & Tube Co. v. Sawyer, 343 U.S. 579, 662 (1952) (Clark,
J., concurring).

C. IF SECTION 793 (e) IS APPLICABLE, IT IS UNCONSTITUTIONAL.

Section 793 (e) is, for a criminal statute, remarkably vague. The first part of the statute is predicated upon unauthorized possession of various "documents" and other tangible items. The second part speaks of unauthorized possession of "information". The "information" clause expressly requires that the possessor of the information have "reason to believe" that the information he possesses "could be used to the injury of the United States or to the advantage of any foreign nation", but the "document" clause does not expressly require "reason to believe" that the documents "could be used to the injury of the United States", etc. If the "reason to believe" requirement does not modify the "document" clause, then the "document" clause either establishes a criminal presumption that the possessor intends injury -- a presumption which would clearly be unconstitutional under the test for criminal presumptions announced in Leary v. United States, 395 U.S. 6, 33 (1969) -- or the "document" clause proscribes the possession and communication of things which the possessor need not even suspect could, or would, be injurious to the United States.

On the other hand, if the "reason to believe" requirement does modify the document clause, then plaintiff must come forward with evidence, not mere assertions, sufficient to prove that the defendants (that is, in effect, The New York Times), not just the plaintiff, had reason to believe that the

-25-

documents (or information) could be used to the injury of the United States.

Both the "document" clause and the "information" clause proscribe only documents or information "relating to the national defense." Is a secretary who steals a ball-point pen from the desk of her boss in the Pentagon to be imprisoned for delivering that pen to a third person? The hypothetical is absurd, but so is the statute. If ever a phrase in a criminal statute was void for vagueness, "relating to" is such a phrase. <u>Coates</u> v. <u>City of Cincinnati</u>, 39 U.S. L.W. 4630 (United States Supreme Court, June 1, 1971); <u>Connally</u> v. <u>General Construction Co.</u>, 269 U.S. 385, 391 (1926). The same can be said of "could be used."

D. <u>PLAINTIFF'S UNCERTAINTY CONCERNING THE APPLICABILITY OF SECTION 793 IS, IN ITSELF, SUFFICIENT REASON TO DENY PRE-LIMINARY RELIEF.</u>

Here, of course, the applicability of §793 is so <u>improbable</u>, that even Pentagon spokesman openly acknowledge "certain ambiguities" about whether it applies "to publications or only to their sources of information." <u>The New York Times</u>, June 15, 1971, p. 18, column 1 (reported by Max Frankel), and "government lawyers" are "divided on the matter" (<u>Id</u>.). The Attorney General seems to think 793 is the applicable statute (<u>Id</u>.), but the "Pentagon briefing officer . . . said the relevant law is . . . Section 798" (<u>Id</u>., column 2). To further compound the confusion, at the argument on the temporary re-

-26-

121

straining order, plaintiffs attorneys were not even able to decide which subdivision of 793 they were relying upon. Their complaint does not disclose _any_ statutory authority for the action, and their brief relies exclusively upon §793(d). At oral argument, however, they relied, for the first time, upon §793(e). In the future they may assert liability under still other subdivisions or sections. The point is obvious: if the lawyers for plaintiff cannot even agree among themselves which sections or subdivisions are or are not applicable to this case, they certainly cannot establish the "probable" applicability of a given section of the statute.

-27-

IV. PUBLICATION OF THE REMAINING
DOCUMENTS WOULD PROMOTE THE
NATIONAL INTEREST WITHOUT
PREJUDICING NATIONAL DEFENSE.

Executive Order 10501, upon which plaintiff principally relies, was issued for the limited purpose of safeguarding "national defense," which is described in the Order as "the ability of the United States to protect and defend itself against all hostile or destructive action by covert or overt means, including espionage as well as military action." Thus, a mere showing of embarrassment or even serious diplomatic inconvenience would not suffice. Plaintiff must show that publication of the remaining documents would jeopardize the ability of the United States to defend against hostile acts.

A. The Documents Published Thus Far Do Not
Jeopardize the Ability of the United
States to Defend Against Hostile Acts.

There is absolutely nothing in the documents published thus far that even arguably compromises this nation's security, or that threatens the life or safety of one single United States soldier or civilian. Given the non-prejudicial nature of the previous disclosures, this Court must examine with particular care the plaintiff's claim, which must be, in essence, that the remaining documents will somehow prejudice the national security, even though publication of the previously published documents, taken from the same study, did not. Had plaintiff

-28-

filed suit last Saturday, before publication of the first documents, we could have said that plaintiff's claim of prejudice was speculative. In retrospect, however, it is clear, at least with respect to those documents published thus far, that any such claim would have been not only speculative but frivolous. Thus, this Court should not seriously consider plaintiff's claim that publication of the remaining documents will be prejudicial until after plaintiff has _specified_ those documents whose publication plaintiff deems prejudicial, and until after this Court has, _in camera_, examined those specified documents to determine whether their publication would, in fact, create a danger so great as to justify an unprecedented abridgment of the press.

> B. Plaintiff's Claim that Publication of the Remaining Documents Would Jeopardize National Defense is Subject to Close Judicial Scrutiny.

For almost two decades, the law has been quite clear: A mere _claim_ by the Government that disclosure of documents or information would jeopardize national defense, is not enough. _United States v. Reynolds_, 345 U.S. 1 (1953). The first requirement is that "there must be a formal claim," which can only be "lodged by the head of the department which has control over the matter, after actual personal consideration

-29-

by that officer" (345 U.S. at 7-8)* It is not clear in the
present case whether the claim should be lodged by the Secretary
of Defense or by the Secretary of State, or both, but it is
clear that _neither_ has done so. Instead, the claim has been
lodged only by the General Counsel of the Department of
Defense and, inferentially, by an Assistant Attorney General.
The "head of the department" rule announced in United States
v. Reynolds arose in the context of a tort action, not involving,
on the non-government side, any constitutionally protected
interest, and certainly not an interest as important as freedom
of the press or the public's right to know. Certainly,
therefore, in a case of this importance, Reynolds compels
the conclusion that the present claim is not only insufficient
for preliminary relief, but would not ultimately authorize
relief on the merits.

Second, even if the Government had lodged a
formal claim by the head of the relevant department (or in
future does so), "the court itself must determine whether the

*The Supreme Court thus followed the English precedent announced
in Ducan v. Cammell, Laird & Co., (1942) A.C. 624, 638: "The
essential matter is that the decision to object should be taken
by the minister who is the political head of the department,
and that he should have seen and considered the contents of
the documents and himself have formed the view that on grounds
of public interest they ought not to be produced" (quoted in
345 U.S. 8, note 20).

-30-

circumstances are appropriate for the claim" (345 U.S. at 8).*

Cognizant that "a complete abandonment of judicial control would lead to intolerable abuses", (345 U.S. at 8), and that "judicial control over the evidence in a case cannot be abdicated to the caprice of executive officers" (345 U.S. 9-10), the Supreme Court held that the trial court "must be satisfied from all the evidence and circumstances...that there is a reasonable danger that compulsion [or publication] of the evidence will expose military matters which, in the interest of national security, should not be divulged" (345 U.S. 9-10). That, then, is the burden the Government must bear even in a civil case not involving the First Amendment.

Reynolds not only authorizes but requires the trial judge to look behind the conclusory allegations of a government affidavit, and to determine, from all the circumstances, whether disclosure of the information would jeopardize national defense. We turn, then, to the circumstances of this case.

> C. The Documents Which the Plaintiff Seeks to Suppress do not Describe on-going Policies of Our Government and do not Jeopardize National Defense.

---

*Again, the Supreme Court quoted with approval from Duncan: "...the decision ruling out such documents is the decision of the judge...It is the judge who is in control of the trial, not the executive" (quoted in 345 U.S. 8, note 21).

-31-

As demonstrated supra, point I, the materials here do not deal with troop movements, military installations, codes, or other "hard" defense data. They involve, rather, only disclosure of governmental policies, and not even on-going policies at that.

The Vietnam Study describes only policies of the past. More important, those policies, which involved, primarily, escalation of the war in Vietnam, have expressly been repudiated by the present Administration. On June 14th, in response to questions about the Vietnam Study, the "White House... chose to emphasize that President Nixon had developed a 'new Vietnam policy' and decided when he took office in 1969 'not to engage ourselves in a continuation or justification' of the policies of earlier administrations, which are the subject of the Pentagon Papers." The New York Times, June 15, 1971, p. 18, column 1 (reported by Max Frankel). The same day, Secretary Laird told the Senate Foreign Relations Committee that the "Times' disclosures" related only to "past actions" (Id., at column 2).

On June 15, 1971, the Presidential Press Secretary, Ronald L. Ziegler, "refused to be drawn into a discussion of the contents of the report on the ground that the study dealt

-32-

with 'something that occurred in the previous administration'.
He said that the Nixon Administration had developed a new
policy on Vietnam." The New York Times, June 16, 1971, p.
18, column 6 (reported by John W. Finney). And Hugh Scott,
the Senate Republican leader, said disclosure of the Vietnam
Study was "not harmful to this Administration", because the
Nixon Administration, when it took office, undertook a "reassessment"
of Vietnam policy. (Id., columns 6-7).

The same day, Secretary of State Rogers remarked
at a news conference that the study "was completed before this
Administration took office" and that the study described our
"involvement" in the war, while the concern of the present
administration is not involvement but "how to get out of the
war" The New York Times, June 16, 1971, p. 15, column 1.

Indeed, so irrelevnat is the Vietnam Study to the
on-going policies of this nation, that neither the President
nor the Secretary of State had ever seen it. Ronald L. Ziegler
stated that it was only after the initial disclosures on Sunday
that "a copy of the 1967-68 Pentagon study was brought to the
White House," and that previously President Nixon "and his
aides" had been "unfamiliar" with the study. The New York
Times, June 15, 1971 p. 18, columns 1 and 2 (reported by Max
Frankel).* Similarly, when asked about the documents, Secretary

---

*The same unfamiliarity with the study was reported in the

of State Rogers said: "I saw them for the first time yesterday [June 14th] because they were not part of our files." The New York Times, June 16, 1971, p. 16, columns 1-2.

It is our position that the disclosure of information which relates only to policies of previous administrations, which policies have been not only abandoned but expressly repudiated by the present government, cannot, as a matter of law, be prejudicial to the current and on-going security interests of this nation. Certainly they cannot be so prejudicial as to justify the unprecedented granting of injunctive relief against a newspaper. Any realistic appraisal of the circumstances of this case compels the conclusion that the claim of "national security" is a bogus claim. Plaintiff waited almost three days before requesting injunctive relief. And it is clear that the request was ultimately made not because the national security required it, but because the Attorney General felt a "statutory responsibility" to act:

> "Under questioning by reporters, Mr. Ziegler also sought to emphasize that the Administration, in seeking a court injunction against further publication of the study, was seeking neither to quash the report nor to harrass The New York Times.
>
> "Rather, Mr. Ziegler took the position that the

New York Post of June 15, 1971 p. 5, columns 4-5: "Presidential press secretary Ronald L. Ziegler said President Nixon was unaware of the report until the Times started to run it on Sunday."

Administration had a statutory responsibility once 'highly classified material had been published, to seek the prevention of further publication of the material.

"Mr. Ziegler said that President Nixon had not ordered Attorney General John N. Mitchell to ask The New York Times to refrain from further publication of the study. The Attorney General, the press secretary said, informed the President that it was necessary to take the step so that the Government would not waive its responsibility to carry out the law...and the President accepted that judgment.'" The New York Times, June 16, 1971, p. 18, column 6 (reported by John W. Finney) (emphasis added).

There is no indication, or even claim, that the President, the Secretary of Defense, or the Secretary of State, requested the relief sought here. Rather, the decision to seek injunctive relief emanated from the Attorney General, whose report to the President on his proposed action did not even mention national security, and relied, instead, on the Attorney General's statutory responsibility to "carry out the law" as he reads the law. "After a White House meeting," Senate Republican leader Hugh Scott said not one word about White House concern for national security; rather he "told reporters that there was a general feeling at the White House that the report was made public as a result of 'an intraparty dispute' within the Democratic Party." The New York Times, June 16, 1971, p. 18, column 7 (reported by John W. Finney). And, fresh from the White House, Senator Scott expressly declined to criticize the Times for what he called its "editorial decision" to publish the Vietnam

-35-

Study, hardly apt language to express concern for the national

security. (Id.).

        D.   Publication of the Study is in the
              National Interest.

Scores of prominent citizens, including Senators,

Congressmen and former members of the executive department,

have hailed the publication of the Vietnam Study as a "public

service" of the highest order, and have stated unequivocally

that the national interest mandates publication, not suppression,

of the remaining documents.

Senator Mike Mansfield, the Senate Majority Leader,

was "delighted" that the Times had been publishing the study,

and announced that a Senate committee would hold hearings in

order to "lay-out the whole story before Congress and the

American people." The New York Times, June 16, 1971, p. 18,

column 6 and page 1, column 7 (reported by John W. Finney).

Earlier, Senator Scott, the Minority Leader of the Senate,

though of the opinion that "release" of the information was

probably a "crime," nevertheless described the reports

published by the Times as "very instructive and somewhat

shocking." When asked whether the Times should "continue

publication," Senator Scott declined a negative response and

replied that the Times would have to decide "on its good

judgment." The New York Times, June 15, 1971, p. 18, column

5 (reported by Max Frankel).

-36-

131

The list does not stop with the majority and minority
leaders. Senator Hubert H. Humphrey said he believed "in
freedom of information and the right to know," and that "matters
relating to what I call political decisions ought not to be
secret." The New York Times June 16, 1971, p. 18, column 8
(reported by John Finney).

Senator J.W. Fulbright "said the information that
had been printed had not breached the national security and
that it was within The Times' right under the First Amendment,"
adding that "too often national security as an excuse for secrecy
has been invoked solely to prevent personal embarrassment."
The New York Times, June 17, 1971, p. 18, column 6 (reported
by David E. Rosenbaum). Senator George S. McGovern said
plaintiff's attempt to "harry the New York Times" violated
freedom of the press and "also shuts off a free flow of
vital information to the public." (Id. column 8).

In the House, Representative John E. Moss, the
ranking member of the House Freedom of Information Committee,
and author of the Freedom of Information Act, praised the
disclosures as a "public service," and criticized the current
attempt to suppress the remaining documents: "There is
no basis for bringing a case against a newspaper. What that
amounts to is censorship." The New York Post, June 16, 1971,
p. 4, column 2 (reported by Antony Prisendorf).

-37-

Representative Roman C. Pucinski agreed that issuance
of the restraining order was "incredible and indefensible."
New York Post, June 16, 1971,p. 4, column 2 (reported by
Antony Prisendorf). Similar sentiments were expressed by
Senator George Aiken (Id., at column 1). Representative Seymour
Halpern explicitly disagreed with plaintiff's "national security"
claim: "I believe it is more of a danger to American security
to force a curb of such information than to inform the American
people of the facts of our involvement" (Id.). Representative
William S. Moorhead concurred: "The classification of these
reports, which are three to four years old, was done not so
much to save the security of the United States, but to save
some red faces" (Id.).

And sixty-two members of the House sent joint letters
to the Secretary of Defense and to the Attorney General, "protesting"
the "harrassment" of The New York Times. (Id., column 6).

Other Senators and Representatives could be quoted,
but most of their sentiments are contained in the apt statement
of Senator Gaylord P. Nelson:

> "These documents do not contain any information that
> would endanger the national security," he said, "and
> it would be a disservice for any court to enjoin
> their further publication. Quite obviously these
> documents contain information embarrassing to the
> political and military leadership of the country,
> but that is no reason to deny the public information
> it is clearly entitled to have." New York Times,
> June 16, 1971, p. 18, column 7 (reported by John
> W. Finney).

-38-

133

Given this broad consensus of opinion, in the highest echelons of our government, it would be astonishing for this Court to accept as true the contrary claim of the plaintiff, supported, as it is at present, by two conclusory affidavits from lesser governmental officials. Certainly preliminary relief, which is justified only if plaintiff can prove "probable" success on the merits, could not conceivably be justified by the present record. A contrary ruling would put this Court in the position of siding with some representatives of government rather than others, in determining whether publication of the materials at issue herein would or would not prejudice national security. Certainly, absent procedural standards for identifying who in government is authorized to determine the national interest, and absent substantive standards for guiding that person in the exercise of his authority, this Court should not, on a mere claim of prejudice by some government officials, vigorously disputed by others, interfere with a right so fundamental to the very process of determining national interest as freedom of the press, and the public's paramount concern with information relating to the policies of its government.

CONCLUSION

<u>PLAINTIFF'S MOTION FOR PRELIMINARY</u>
<u>RELIEF MUST BE DENIED.</u>

Dated: New York, New York
June 18, 1971   Respectfully submitted,

                                 NORMAN DORSEN
                                 New York University School of La
                                 Washington Square South
                                 New York, New York

                                 MELVIN L. WULF
                                 American Civil Liberties Union
                                 156 Fifth Avenue
                                 New York, New York

                                 OSMOND K. FRAENKEL
                                 120 Broadway
                                 New York, New York

Of Counsel,
JAMES PARVER   BURT NEUBORNE
                                 BRUCE J. ENNIS
                                 New York Civil Liberties Union
                                 84 Fifth Avenue
                                 New York, New York

                    Attorneys for Amici Curiae,*

---

*The attorneys herein wish to acknowledge the assistance of
Arthur N. Eisenberg and Edwin J. Oppenheimer, Jr., in the
research and preparation of this brief.

-40-

135

UNITED STATES DISTRICT COURT

FOR THE SOUTHERN DISTRICT OF NEW YORK

UNITED STATES OF AMERICA)
)
PLAINTIFF)
)
V.)   71 CIV. 2662
)
THE NEW YORK TIMES CO., ET AL.)
)
DEFENDANTS)

MOTION FOR INTERVENTION

Now come Phillip Burton, John Dow, Bob Eckhardt, Don
Edwards, Michael Harrington, Robert Kastenmeier, Edward Koch,
Abner Mikva, Benjamin Rosenthal, William F. Ryan, James Abourezk,
Bella S. Abzug, William R. Anderson, Herman Badillo, Jonathan B.
Bingham, William Clay, Ronald V. Dellums, Sam Gibbons, Ella T.
Grasso, Seymour Halpern, Peter Kyros, Parren Mitchell, Bertram L.
Podell, Charles B. Rangel, Donald W. Riegle, Jr., James H. Scheuer,
and Lester L. Wolff and ask leave to intervene in this cause in
order to assert the defenses set forth in their proposed answer
of which a copy is hereto attached, on the grounds that:

1. Movants are all Members of Congress and are affected
by this litigation. If this litigation prevents the defendant New
York Times from publishing material from the Defense Department's
1968 Task Force Study on Vietnam, they will be denied important
information, known to be in existence, which bears strongly on
the following extremely important policy questions (among others):

136

(1) The definition and extent of the authority of
Congress and of the Presidency with regard to
the war-making power as respects:

    (a) the power of Congress to declare
war and exercise other authority
under Article I, Section 8, of the
Constitution; and

    (b) the power of the President to act
as Commander-in Chief of the Army
and Navy of the United States and
to exercise other authority under
Article II, Section 2, of the Constitution.

(2) The manner in which the power of the Presidency has
been conducted as respects the war-making power;

(3) whether or not Congress should enact further
statutory provisions providing processes designed
to prevent the President from overstepping constitutional authority or initiate further statutory or constitutional provisions delineating
with greater precision the boundaries between
presidential and constitutional authority;

(4) the conduct of foreign affairs bearing on the
subject;

(5) the matter of governmental organization bearing
on the subject; and

(6) all questions relating to the right of the people
to secure information necessary to the effective
exercise of their function as citizens in a
democracy.

137

2. A prior restraint upon the defendant New York Times preventing the publishing of material from the Defense Department's 1968 Task Force Study on Vietnam would, and does (as respects the temporary restraining order), constitute prior restraint on the exercise of the right of free speech and freedom of the press as guaranteed by the First and Fourteenth Amendments to the Constitution of the United States.

3. Movants have suffered, and do suffer, injury in fact by virtue of the temporary restraining order. H. R. 8687, the Military Procurement Authorization Bill, is being debated in the House at the time of the preparation of this motion and during the period while the temporary restraining order herein is in effect. The debate upon such bill (as exemplified for instance by that of the Honorable John J. Flynt, Jr. of Georgia, on June 17, 1971) dealt heavily with the policy questions set out in items (1) and (2) of paragraph 1 above. Enjoining further publication of matter contained in the Defense Department's 1968 Task Force Study on Vietnam will deny to these movants important facts which constitute their tools for dealing with the important policy questions listed in items (1) through (6) of paragraph 1 above.

4. The interest of these movants is one protected by law in that

(1) Section 8 of Article I of the Constitution places upon them, together with other Members of Congress, duties requiring access to a wide range of information concerning, among other matters, the declaration of war, the raising and support of armies, the regulation of the land and naval forces, the providing for organizing, arming, governing and disciplining the militia, and

138

(2) The First and Fourteenth Amendments to the

Constitution protect and guarantee movants'

right to access to information unrestricted

by abridgement of the freedom of speech, or

of the press.

These and other provisions of the Constitution, and laws passed

pursuant to them, were designed, in part, to protect the interests

asserted by these movants. Because of the duties placed upon them

as described in (1), above, the interests of these movants are

distinct and different from those of the members of the public

generally. Movants are so situated that the disposition of this

action may, as a practical matter, impair their ability to protect

their interests, and the representation of their interest by

existing parties may be inadequate. Movants' defense also has

common questions of law and fact with the main action. Intervention

by movants will not unduly delay or prejudice the adjudication of the

rights of the original parties.

WHEREFORE, these movants pray that

(1) They be permitted to intervene in this cause,

(2) That the temporary restraining order granted

against defendant New York Times be vacated,

and

(3) That no further injunction be issued depriving

them of information which they would otherwise

receive through newspaper coverage were it not

for a prior restraint against publication of

the said Task Force Study.

Thomas Emerson
Attorney for Movants

139

4

UNITED STATES DISTRICT COURT

FOR THE SOUTHERN DISTRICT OF NEW YORK

UNITED STATES OF AMERICA   )
)
          PLAINTIFF   )
)
    V.   )   71 CIV. 2662
)
THE NEW YORK TIMES CO., ET AL.)
)
          DEFENDANTS)

BRIEF IN SUPPORT OF MOTION FOR INTERVENTION

There is, of course, no question but that the case before
this Court falls within the constitutional grant of jurisdiction
to federal courts of certain "cases, in law and equity" and
"certain controversies." The United States has contended that
the New York Times is wrongfully in possession of certain
governmental documents and should be enjoined from publishing
them. As a result the Court has granted a temporary restraining
order. The New York Times asserts that it is entitled to publish
the materials as a part of its exercise of freedom of speech and
freedom of the press. There being, therefore, a case or controversy before this Court, the only question respecting these
movants' intervention is the question of their standing to enter
such case.

The New York Times' interest in freedom of speech and of
the press here is the interest of the speaker or the publisher
not to be restricted by governmental action abridging freedom
of speech. The interest of the Members of Congress seeking
to intervene is the other side of the coin: The interest
in not being deprived of information which   would normally
flow to them but for an intervening act of government restraining that flow.

The United States District Court for the Eastern District of New York has recently recognized the interest of those deprived of information or of viewpoints which they could have received had it not been for an unconstitutional prevention of the exercise of free speech. In the case of Mandel v. Mitchell, 39 LW 2530, certain university professors complained of the refusal to permit an alien, Mandel, to come into the country and express certain economic, international, and governmental doctrines of world communism. Mandel was denied a non-immigrant visitor's visa under the asserted authority of Section 212(a)(28) of the Immigration and Nationality Act. The professors alleged that they and other citizens desired to have Mandel speak at universities and other forums to hear his views and to engage in free and open academic exchange and they charged that the section of the Act excluding from admission to the United States aliens who are or at any time were members of described classes of aliens identified with certain leftist and extremist political doctrines is invalid under the 1st and 5th Amendments and that it imposes a prior restraint on constitutionally protected communication.

In response to defendant's attack on the professors' "standing to sue" the Court said:

> Since the First Amendment is not in its primary and most significant aspect a grant by the Constitution to the citizens of individual rights of self-expression but on the contrary reflects the total retention by the people as sovereign to themselves of the right to free and open debate of political questions, the issue of "standing to sue" is immediately seen to be unreal. The concern of the First Amendment is not with a non-resident alien's individual and personal interest in entering and being heard, but with the rights of the citizens of the country to have the alien enter and to hear him explain and seek to defend his views. * * *

141

2

Mandel's status as a party does not rest
on any individual right to enter (for he has
none) but exists only as against the efforts
to exclude him on a ground that denies to
citizens of this country their primary rights
to hear Mandel and debate with him. Here the
plaintiffs other than Mandel are directly
involved with Mandel's entry because they
have invited him, and they expect to participate in meetings with him or expect
to be among his auditors. No more is required
to establish their standing. Cf. Snyder v.
Board of Trustees, 286 F. Supp. at 931-932
(N.D. Ill. 1968); Smith v. University of
Tennessee, 300 F. Supp. 777 (E.D. Tenn.
1969).

It was held in Data Processing Service Organizations v. Camp,

90 S. Ct. 827 at p. 829, that the question of standing concerns

"the question whether the interest sought to be protected by the

complainant is arguably within the zone of interest to be protected

or regulated by the statute or constitutional guarantee in question."

[Emphasis added.]

Though it is quite clear that the contention of the defendant

New York Times is in fact within the constitutional guarantee of

free speech and that, therefore, it is not constitutionally per-

missible to apply a prior restraint to the exercise of that right,

it is not really necessary to determine the merits of the case in

deciding that these movants have standing to intervene. Clearly

their interests are as much within the zone of interest to be

protected or regulated by the constitutional guarantee as are the

interests of the New York Times.

The four leading cases establishing present law of standing

are: Hardin v. Kentucky Utilities Company, 390 U. S. 1 (1968);

Flast v. Cohen, 392 U. S. 83 (1968); Data Processing Service

Organizations v. Camp, 90 S. Ct. 827 (1970); and Barlow v.

Collins, 90 S. Ct. 832 (1970).

142

3

Professor Kenneth Culp Davis has pointed out that, as a result of these cases,

> A huge portion of the former foundation of the law of standing was . . . knocked out. The old test of a "recognized legal interest" was specifically rejected. In its place were two new tests. The first, based on Article III, was "injury in fact, economic or otherwise." . . . The second test . . . was "whether the interest sought to be protected by the complainant is arguably within the zone of interest to be protected or regulated by the statute or constitutional guarantee in question."[*]

Even under traditional standards, these intervenors have standing. Their status is even more secure under the new standards. Let us examine them:

1. There Was "Injury In Fact, Economic or Otherwise."

Congress has been currently dealing with matters related to the power of the Presidency and of Congress related to the making of war, the financing of the war effort, and the termination of the Indochinese involvement.

The subject matter of the New York Times articles has been widely accepted by Members of Congress as pertinent to these issues before Congress. Note, for instance, that Congressmen McCloskey and Harrington inserted the New York Times installments of Sunday and Monday in the Congressional Record on June 14, 1971 (H-5096 - 5136; E-5794 - 5832). On the same day Senator McGovern inserted the same documentation (S-8977 - 9015). On

---

[*] The Liberalized Law of Standing, Kenneth Culp Davis, 37 U. of Chicago Law Rev. 450, at p. 452.

143

4

the next day Senator McGovern inserted the third installment

in the Tuesday New York Times in the Congressional Record

(S-9111 - 9130), and Congressmen McCloskey and Harrington

inserted the same article in the Record (H-5202 - 5222;

E-5878 - 5896).

During the very period during which the temporary restrain-

ing order was in effect and was blocking further installments,

both the House and Senate were dealing with legislative topics

whose subject matter made the content of the Task Force Study

germane to the Congressional debate. On June 16, 1971, 6

votes were taken in the Senate and 4 in the House on topics

to which the study is germane. In the Senate these were the

Chiles Amendment to S. 9275 and the Hatfield-McGovern Amendment

to S. 9279. The House was on the same day acting on the Mili-

tary Procurement Authorization Bill (H. R. 8687). The House

continued consideration of the Military Procurement Authoriza-

tion Bill on June 17, 1971, taking up the Nedzi-Whalen Amendment

(providing a deadline after which funds under the procurement
                    for Indochina war support):
act should not be used /the Harrington Amendment (which deleted
                                                        to

a title of H. R. 8687 providing an authorization for Vietnamese

forces and their allies, and local forces in Laos and Thailand),

and considering several other amendments variously establishing

cutoff dates and restrictions respecting funds which might find

their way into support of the Indochina war.

Debate on these amendments was wide-ranging. For instance, Congressman John F. Flynt, Jr., of Georgia, reviewed what he called the mistaken premise upon which the Tonkin Gulf Resolution was enacted, the misinformation that was afforded the public and the Congress in that connection, the circumstances of its repeal, and the fact that the present war is being waged without a Congressional declaration of war. The question of candor of public officials during the development and the conduct of the war was a prominent feature of the debate on the Procurement Act, and such question of candor, or lack of it, was related to the desirability of Congressional action or Congressional expression calculated to bring the war to an end.

In debate in the House on June 16, 1971, at least three Representatives discussed the New York Times documents: Congressman McCloskey (H-5305), Congressman Podell (H-5311) and Congressman Abourezk (H-5331).

Nor have the issues which arose in these bills become moot by the defeat of the Hatfield-McGovern Amendment and the passage of the Military Procurement Authorization Act. There are at least four classes of legislation in the House in which the issue will undoubtedly be raised again:

Foreign Aid Appropriations and Authorization Bills

Military Construction Authorization Bill

Defense Appropriation Bill

Vietnam Disengagement Act

Also, there is presently a discharge petition on the Speaker's desk for the discharge of the Vietnam Disengagement Act (H. R. 4101).

6

If this litigation prevents the defendant New York Times
from publishing material from the Defense Department's 1968
Task Force Study on Vietnam, intervenors will be denied important
information, known to be in existence, which bears strongly on
the various important policy questions listed in the motion
for intervention: (1) The definition and extent of the authority
of Congress and of the Presidency with regard to the war-making
power, (2) the manner in which the Presidential power has been
exercised, (3) the desirability of statutory or constitutional
changes, (4) questions related to the conduct of foreign affairs
and of matters of governmental organization, and (5) all questions
relating to the right of the people to secure information necessary
to the effective exercise of their function as citizens in
a democracy.

Thus the granting of an injunction would cause injury in
fact to these intervenors in limiting their resources and their
tools for solving such problems. In addition, it would injure
them in this respect: Even if it were possible for Members of
Congress to obtain similar information through private and confidential
sources, these intervenors would have to act on this information
without their constituents knowing the same basic facts. Such is
not only directly injurious to a person called upon to represent
a constituency but also tends to undermine the entire representative process. The right of the people to secure information
necessary to the effective exercise of their function as citizens
in a democracy is interrelated with the right of their representative
to act on information commonly available to himself and to those
whom he represents.

7

2. The Interest Sought to be Protected by Intervenors
   is Arguably Within the Zone of Interest to be Protected or Regulated by the Constitutional Guarantee
   in Question.

Section 8 of Article I of the Constitution places upon

intervenors, together with other Members of Congress, duties

requiring access to a wide range of information concerning,

among other matters, the declaration of war, the raising and

support of armies, the regulation of the land and naval forces,

and the providing for, organizing, arming, governing and dis-

ciplining the militia.

The 1st and 14th Amendments to the Constitution protect

and guarantee movants' right to access to this information un-

restricted by abridgement of freedom of speech or of the press.

These and other provisions of the Constitution, and laws

passed pursuant to them, were designed in part to protect

the interests asserted by these intervenors. Because of the

duties placed upon them as described above, the interests of

these intervenors are distinct and different from those of the

members of the public generally.

These intervenors are within precisely the same zone of

interest as the professor plaintiffs in the Mandell case. Both

are within the zone of interest protecting the right of citizens

to enjoy the product of free speech. Persons who are so

deprived because of a prior restraint by government in violation

of the First Amendment are among those intended to be protected

by that amendment just as are those who are silenced by the

restraint.

147

The case of <u>Office of Communications of United Church of</u>
<u>Christ</u> v. <u>Federal Communications Commission</u>, 359 F. 2d 994 (D.C.
Cir. 1966) should also be noted as one in which the right to <u>hear</u>
was involved. Certain individuals and organizations sought to
intervene in a hearing before the Federal Communications Commission to contest the renewal of a broadcast license. The Commission denied intervention, stating that the individuals and
groups had no "standing" to appear. Action was then brought
under the A.P.A. to review this decision, and the standing of
Plaintiffs was challenged. Plaintiff individuals and organizations constituting a listening public were held to have standing.
The Court said:

> Since the concept of standing is a practical
> and functional one designed to assure that
> <u>only those with a genuine and legitimate</u>
> <u>interest can participate in a proceeding,</u>
> we can see no reason to exclude those with
> such an obvious and acute concern as the
> listening audience.

A less direct and specific interest in the subject matter
existed in the case of the plaintiffs in the following environmental protection cases:

> <u>Scenic Hudson Preservation Conference</u> v.
> <u>Federal Power Commission</u>, 354 F. 2d 608
> (2nd Cir. 1965), cert. den., 384 U. S.
> 941, 16 L. Ed. 2d 540, 86 Sup. Ct. 1462
> (1966).

> <u>Road Review League, Town of Bedford</u> v. <u>Boyd</u>,
> 270 F. Supp. 650 (S.D. N.Y. 1967).

> <u>Parker</u> v. <u>United States</u>, 307 F. Supp. 685
> (D. Col. 1969).

> <u>Pennsylvania Environmental Council</u> v.
> <u>Bartlett</u>, 315 F. Supp. 238 (M.D. Pa. 1970).

> <u>Citizens Committee for Hudson Valley</u> v.
> <u>Volpe</u>, 425 F. 2d 97 (2nd Cir. 1970).

Yet the Court held that the parties, complaining usually as little more than interested citizens against governmental action, had standing to sue.

It is respectfully urged that movants have standing in this case and that they should be permitted to intervene.

Respectfully submitted,

_____
Thomas Emerson
Attorney for Movants

149

UNITED STATES DISTRICT COURT

FOR THE SOUTHERN DISTRICT OF NEW YORK

UNITED STATES OF AMERICA)	
)	
PLAINTIFF)	
)	
V.)	71 CIV. 2662
)	
THE NEW YORK TIMES CO., ET AL.)	
)	
DEFENDANTS)	

Proposed
ANSWER OF INTERVENORS

Intervenors who have intervened in this action with
leave of the Court, answer the complaint herein as follows:

FIRST DEFENSE

The complaint fails to state a claim on which relief
can be granted.

SECOND DEFENSE

The court lacks jurisdiction over the subject matter
of this action.

THIRD DEFENSE

Plaintiffs's claim is barred by the First Amendment
to the Constitution of the United States.

FOURTH DEFENSE

Plaintiff's claim is an unconstitutional interference
with the powers of Congress under Article I of the Constitution
of the United States.

FIFTH DEFENSE

1. Paragraph 1 of the complaint states a conclusion of
law and intervenors are not required to respond thereto.
Intervenors deny that any Court of the United States has
jurisdiction to enjoin a newspaper from publishing information.

150

2. Intervenors admit that plaintiff makes the averments that are made in Paragraph 2 of the complaint, but deny them insofar as they are factual averments.

3. Intervenors are without knowledge or information sufficient to form a belief as to the truth of the averments in Paragraph 3 of the complaint.

4. Intervenors are without knowledge or information sufficient to form a belief as to the truth of the averments in Paragraph 4 of the complaint, except that intervenors deny that defendants' actions were without lawful authority.

5. Intervenors are without knowledge or information sufficient to form a belief as to the truth of the averments in Paragraph 5 of the complaint, except that intervenors deny that defendants' actions were without lawful authority.

6. Paragraph 6 states a matter of law and intervenors are not required to respond thereto. Executive Order 10501 speaks for itself.

7. Intervenors are without knowledge or information sufficient to form a belief as to the truth of the averments in Paragraph 7 of the complaint.

8. Intervenors deny the averments of Paragraph 8 of the complaint.

9. Intervenors deny the averments of Paragraph 9 of the complaint.

. 10. Intervenors deny the allegations of Paragraph 10 of the complaint.

Thomas Emerson
Attorney for Intervenors

151

UNITED STATES DISTRICT COURT

FOR THE SOUTHERN DISTRICT OF NEW YORK

UNITED STATES OF AMERICA)
)
PLAINTIFF)
)
V.) 71 CIV. 2662
)
THE NEW YORK TIMES CO., ET AL.)
)
DEFENDANTS)

Proposed
O R D E R

On this the _____ day of _____, 1971, came on
to be heard the Motion of Phillip Burton, John Dow, Bob Eckhardt,
Don Edwards, Michael Harrington, Robert Kastenmeier, Edward Koch,
Abner Mikva, Benjamin Rosenthal, William F. Ryan, James Abourezk,
Bella S. Abzug, William R. Anderson, Herman Badillo, Jonathan B.
Bingham, William Clay, Ronald V. Dellums, Sam Gibbons, Ella T.
Grasso, Seymour Halpern, Peter Kyros, Parren Mitchell, Bertram L.
Podell, Charles B. Rangel, Donald W. Riegle, Jr., James H. Scheuer,
and Lester L. Wolff, intervenors in the above styled and numbered
cause, and it appearing to the Court that the same are entitled
to intervene in this cause, it is hereby:

ORDERED, ADJUDGED AND DECREED that the above listed persons
are granted leave to intervene in the above styled and numbered
cause.

_____
Judge

152

UNITED STATES DISTRICT COURT FOR THE
SOUTHERN DISTRICT OF NEW YORK

United States of America,
Plaintiff,

v.

#71 Civ. 2662

New York Times Co., et al.,
Defendants.

MOTION FOR LEAVE TO FILE BRIEF AS AMICI CURIAE

The Members of Congress, whose names are set forth below,
hereby respectfully move for leave to file as amici curiae the
brief annexed hereto.

The Members of Congress, on whose behalf this motion is
made, have a vital interest in the outcome of this case, distinct
from that of the plaintiff, the defendants, or the general
public. As members of the national legislature they must have
information of the kind involved in this suit in order to carry
out their law-making and other functions in the legislative
branch of the government. They seek to vindicate here a
legislative right to know.

In addition as elected representatives of the people in
their districts, Members of Congress have a particular and
profound interest in having their constituents obtain all the
information necessary to perform their functions as voters and
citizens. More than any other officials of government, Members
of Congress have relations with the public that gives them a
crucial concern with the public's right to know.

(i)

For these reasons leave is requested to file the attached brief in opposition to the Government's motion for a temporary restraining order.

Respectfully submitted,

Thomas I. Emerson

Dated: June 17, 1971

Thomas I. Emerson
127 Wall Street
New Haven, Connecticut
06520

Submitted in behalf of:

Bella S. Abzug
Herman Badillo
Phillip Burton
William Clay
Ronald Dellums
John G. Dow
Bob Eckhardt
Don Edwards
Michael Harrington
Robert W. Kastenmeier
Edward Koch
Abner Mikva
Parren Mitchell
Bertram Podell
Charles Rangel
Benjamin S. Rosenthal
William F. Ryan
James Scheuer
Lester Wolff

(ii)

UNITED STATES DISTRICT COURT FOR THE

SOUTHERN DISTRICT OF NEW YORK

    United States of America,
    Plaintiff,

          v.   #71 Civ. 2662

    New York Times Co., et. al.,
    Defendants

BRIEF AS AMICI CURIAE

    Members of Congress have a particular interest in the free circulation of information which is essential to the performance of their function as legislators and to their relations with the public in the districts from which they are elected. To a substantial extent these interests coincide with those of the defendants in this case, since freedom of the press is necessary to any democratic system. The basic arguments in support of the defendants' right to publish the material in question have been put forward by them, and this brief will not attempt to elaborate upon them here. The main position we wish to urge upon the Court is that it should apply those principles with particular stringency in this case in order to protect the crucial interests of Members of Congress in freedom of information for themselves and their constituents.

(1)

155

I. ESTABLISHED FIRST AMENDMENT DOCTRINES REQUIRE DISMISSAL OF THE COMPLAINT

The principal constitutional doctrines that support the right of defendants to be free from injunctive interference in the publication of the materials in question may be stated in summary form as follows:

1. The rule against prior restraint has been a vital part of our constitutional structure since the Supreme Court's decision in Near v. Minnesota, 283 U.S. 697 (1931). Exception has been permitted in the case of motion picture censorship boards to the extent of upholding laws which require advance screening of films against possible illegal obscenity. Times Film Corp. v. City of Chicago, 365 U.S. 43 (1961). But the doctrine has been otherwise reaffirmed, and in the exceptional case of motion picture films the censorship process has been surrounded with strict procedural safeguards. Freedman v. Maryland, 380 U.S. 51 (1965); Carroll v. President and Commissioners of Princess Anne, 393 U.S. 175 (1968).

There is no sound reason why the doctrine of prior restraint should not apply in the case at bar. So far in the history of this country there have been no occasions where the security of the country has been in danger because of the inability of the courts to restrain publication in advance. Certainly there is no reason to believe, from that part of the publication which already has taken place, that the vital interests of the nation

(2)

156

would be impaired by remanding the Government to the provisions of the criminal law or to other post-publication sanctions. On the other hand to relax the doctrine of prior restraint here, on a general allegation by the Government that publication would "further prejudice the defense interests of the United States" or that the "national security will suffer immediate and irreparable harm", wo`'. open the door to extensive Government control over all kinds of information deemed harmful to the interests of the administration then in power.

2. Apart from prior restraint, whatever limits might eventually be placed on the press by way of subsequent punishment, the First Amendment would clearly not permit them to extend to a prohibition on the publication of material that in some vague way merely "prejudiced defense interests" or adversely affected "national security." Materials published every day have such an impact. Wherever the line is to be drawn it would have to be very close to the point where publication would directly affect military operations. Information about "national security" and "defense interests" are well within the protection of the First Amendment. No system of freedom of expression could exist under any less stringent rule. See Bond v. Floyd, 385 U.S. 116 (1966); Brandenburg v. Ohio, 395 U.S. 444 (1969).

It is not necessary to consider here other constitutional objections to issuance of an injunction against these defendants.

(3)

We proceed to the point that the special interests of Members of Congress in the legislative right to know and in the public's right to know demand that these basic doctrines be applied with particular strictness in the circumstances of this case.

II. THE LEGISLATIVE RIGHT TO KNOW AND THE PUBLIC'S RIGHT TO KNOW REQUIRE FULL AND FREE COMMUNICATION OF INFORMATION ON ALL MATTERS OF LEGISLATIVE INTEREST

The legislative right to know derives from the position and function of the legislative branch in the general structure of our government. It has been recognized many times in the decisions of the Supreme Court.   See, e.g., Watkins v. U.S., 354 U.S. 178 (1957). The public right to know has likewise been repeatedly recognized by the Supreme Court as a vital aspect of our system of freedom of expression. Lamont v. Postmaster General, 381 U.S. 301 (1965); Griswold v. Connecticut, 381 U.S. 479 (1965); Red Lion Broadcasting Co. v. F.C.C., 395 U.S. 367 (1969).

It is impossible, within the time limits imposed at this stage of the case, to consider in full detail how these rights would be impaired by a decision to enjoin publication of the materials involved. We call the attention of the Court, however, to the following points:

(4)

1. Congress has before it now a complex series of
questions dealing with the war in Vietnam, relations between
Congress and the Executive, and other similar matters.
Members of the legislature must have all the information
available if they are to know how to cast their vote on
these issues.   Clearly the material which is now the
subject of this litigatio   s very relevant to an intelligent
resolution of these questions. Access to such information
goes to the very heart of the decision-making process in
Congress.

2. Factors which the Court may consider important on
the issue of whether a newspaper should publish material
obtained in an unauthorized manner are not necessarily applicable
to the question whether the Congress should be permitted access
to such materials. The materials are known to exist, and to be
no longer in the possession of the Executive. It would thwart
common sense to say that private persons may have access to
materials which are withheld from Members of Congress.

3. Members of Congress have methods of obtaining information from the Executive Department apart from publication in
the press. The limits of Congressional power to obtain such
materials are the subject of debate at the present time.   A
decision by this Court which considered only the specific
interests of the present parties, might adversely affect the
ability of the legislature to obtain information from the
Executive directly.

(5)

4. Members of Congress have special relationships with the persons in the district they represent. It is vital to the functioning of a democracy that such persons understand the issues upon which their representatives are voting. It is likewise vital to the Member of Congress that he relate to the ideas and responses of his constituents. All this is not possible unless both legislator and constituent have full access to the relevant information. The public's right to know, therefore, takes on particular importance when it concerns issues pending before the legislature.

5. In general, if power is upheld in the Executive to suppress information which leaks out of the Executive Department, on the general claim that "national security" is affected, the Executive is given a degree of control over information circulating at the seat of government, and to the public at large, that approaches totalitarian control.

For these reasons we respectfully submit that the request for an injunction be denied and the complaint dismissed.

Respectfully submitted,

Thomas I. Emerson

Dated: June 17, 1971.

Thomas I. Emerson
127 Wall Street
New Haven, Connecticut
06520

(6)

UNITED STATES DISTRICT COURT
SOUTHERN DISTRICT OF NEW YORK

--x
                                          :
UNITED STATES OF AMERICA,   :
                                          :
                 Plaintiff,   :
                                          :
           -against-   :
                                          :
THE NEW YORK TIMES,   :
                                          :
                 Defendant.   : Index #71 Civ. 2662
                                          :
NOAM CHOMSKY; ALEXANDER ERLICH;   : Response to Plaintiff's
RICHARD FALK; ROBERT JAY LIFTON;   : Motion for a Preliminary
SEYMOUR MELMAN; HANS MORGENTHAU;   : Injunction
CARL SCHORSKE; FRANZ SCHURMANN;   :
GEORGE WALD; HOWARD ZINN,   :
                                          :
           Intervenor Defendants.   :
                                          :
--x

    For their response Intervenor Defendants respectfully
show the following:

    1. They are citizens of the United States and are eligible
and registered to vote in the upcoming federal, state and local
elections;

    2. They are members of the academic community in this
country and have studied, investigated and published articles
and books concerning the origin, nature and consequences of
United States involvement in the Vietnam and Indo-China Wars.

    3. They believe the United States involvement in these
wars and the policies which have caused and maintained this
involvement to be wrong. Intervenors have sought to convince
other scholars and the American people generally of the validity of their beliefs, and they have cast their votes and participated in political campaigns in an effort to elect public
officials who share these beliefs.

    4. On June 13, 14 and 15th, 1971, the New York Times,
defendant in this action, published a series of documents
referred to as the "Pentagon's Vietnam Study," which are of

161

unparalleled historical and political importance.

5. These documents reveal a gross disparity between the policies and actions our government says that it has followed and taken in Vietnam and Indo-China and the actual policies and actions our government has followed and taken.

6. The information contained in and revealed by these documents will greatly assist Intervenors in formulating their academic and political views on the Vietnam War, in selecting public officials who will implement these views and in convincing other scholars and the American people of the validity of these views.

7. Moreover, Intervenors believe that the remaining documents in the "Pentagon's Vietnam Report," which the New York Times intends to publish will be of equal value in furthering free and intelligent assessment of this nation's role in Vietnam.

8. The plaintiff contends that it has both the constitutional and statutory authority to suppress and restrain the publication of any and all parts of the "Pentagon's Vietnam Study."

9. To accomplish this end, plaintiff has instituted and threatened to institute criminal and civil actions under § 793(d),(e) against anyone possessing, disseminating, publishing or republishing any or all of the Pentagon's Vietnam Study.

10. Plaintiff seeks a preliminary injunction in this action restraining further possession and publication by the New York Times of any or all of the Pentagon's Vietnam Study.

11. Intervenors will suffer grave and irreparable injury if plaintiffs requested relief is granted, in that

a. they will be denied their right to know the contents of that portion of the Pentagon's Vietnam Study which remains to be published by the New York Times;

b. they will be placed in fear that when they re-

publish, use, comment upon and disseminate the portions of the Pentagon's Vietnam Study which have been published by the New York Times, they will be subjected to criminal prosecution or civil sanctions under 18 U.S.C. § 793(d),(e) by plaintiff thereby inhibiting and preventing Intervenors from freely exercising their political and academic rights; and

    c. they will be afraid to/and/deterred from using,
                           use will be
disseminating and publishing controversial information, particularly that which disparages United States policy in Vietnam, because plaintiff, in its unbounded discretion, may deem the possession and use of such information to be "unauthorized," to be "[related] to the national defense" and the possessor to "have reason to believe [such information] could be used to the injury of the United States or to the advantage of any foreign nation" in violation of 18 U.S.C. § 793(d),(e).

    THEREFORE, plaintiff's motion for a preliminary injunction should be denied on the grounds that it seeks to and will deprive Intervenor Defendants of their rights under the First, Fourth, Fifth, Ninth and Tenth Amendments to the Constitution to hear, know and have access to critical information relating to public issues; to freely, intelligently and voluntarily exercise their voting franchise; and to conduct and participate in open, free and meaningful academic inquiry and debate, in that

    1. § 793(d),(e) is vague and overbroad on its face and permits plaintiff to punish and suppress the lawful publication of information;

    2. § 793(d),(e) is unconstitutional as applied to the possession and publication of information which the government has no overriding or, indeed any valid interest in keeping secret,

    3. the imposition of an injunction against the New York Times, further possession and publication of any and all of the Pentagon's Vietnam Study constitutes prior censorship and restraint, which never in our history has been sanctioned

against a newspaper, and

   4. § 793 (d),(e) does not authorize plaintiff to institute this or any action to suppress the possession and publication by the New York Times of the Pentagon's Vietnam Study.

                                    Respectfully submitted,

                                    Rabinowitz, Boudin & Standard
                                    (Emergency Civil Liberties Union)
Dated: New York,   30 East 42nd Street
        New York   New York, New York 10017

        June 16, 1971
                                    Charles R. Nesson
                                    David Rosenberg
                                    Langdell Hall
                                    Cambridge, Massachusetts 02138

UNITED STATES DISTRICT COURT
SOUTHERN DISTRICT OF NEW YORK

```
-----------------------------------x
UNITED STATES OF AMERICA,            :

                      Plaintiff,     :

           -against-                 :

THE NEW YORK TIMES,                  :
                                         Index #71 Civ. 2662
                      Defendant.     :
                                         Intervenor Defendants'
NOAM CHOMSKY; ALEXANDER ERLICH;      :   Motion for Preliminary
RICHARD FALK; ROBERT JAY LIFTON;         Injunction and for the
SEYMOUR MELMAN; HANS MORGENTHAU;     :   Convening of a Three-
CARL SCHORSKE; FRANZ SCHURMANN;          Judge Court
GEORGE WALD; HOWARD ZINN,            :

                 Intervenor Defendants.  :

-----------------------------------x
```

Intervenor Defendants, through their undersigned counsel, hereby move this Court for an order

a.) granting a preliminary injunction pursuant to Rule 65 of the Federal Rules of Civil Procedure restraining the plaintiff from enforcing or implementing 18 U.S.C. § 793(d),(e) on its face or insofar as it may be applied to penalize and suppress the possession and publication by the defendant and the intervenor defendants of any or all portions of the Pentagon's Vietnam Study; and

b.) convening a three-judge Federal District Court pursuant to 28 U.S.C. § 2281 et seq. to hear and decide the substantial constitutional questions presented with respect to the validity of 18 U.S.C. § 793(d),(e).

                              Respectfully submitted,

Dated: New York,   Rabinowitz, Boudin & Standard
        New York   (Emergency Civil Liberties Union)
                            30 East 42nd Street
        June 16, 1971   New York, New York 10017

                            Charles R. Nesson
                            David Rosenberg

UNITED STATES DISTRICT COURT
SOUTHERN DISTRICT OF NEW YORK

------------------------------------x

UNITED STATES OF AMERICA,   :

                          Plaintiff,   :

                 -against-   :

THE NEW YORK TIMES,   :

                          Defendant.   :   Index #71 Civ. 2662

NOAM CHOMSKY; ALEXANDER ERLICH;   :   Order to Show Cause
RICHARD FALK; ROBERT JAY LIFTON;
SEYMOUR MELMAN; HANS MORGENTHAU;   :
CARL SCHORSKE; FRANZ SCHURMANN;
GEORGE WALD; HOWARD ZINN,   :

          Intervenor Defendants.   :

------------------------------------x

          Upon the annexed affidavit of David Rosenberg, Esq., the

annexed response to plaintiff's motion for a preliminary in-

junction and the annexed motion for an order preliminarily

enjoining plaintiff from enforcing or implementing 18 U.S.C.

§793(d),(e) and for an order pursuant to 28 U.S.C. §2281 et seq.

convening a three-judge Federal District Court, and

          It appearing that the Intervenor Defendants claim an inter-

est relating to the property or transaction which is the subject

of the main action and that they are so situated that the dis-

position of that action may as a practical matter impair or

impede their ability to protect that interest, and it further

appearing that the Intervenor Defendants' interest will not be

adequately represented by the existing parties, *in Room 506*

          Let the plaintiff show cause to this Court/on the 22nd

day of June, 1971, at 10:00 o'clock in the   m. at the

Federal District Court House, Foley Square, why an order

should not be entered pursuant to Rule 24(a)(2) of the Federal

Rules of Civil Procedure permitting the Intervenor Defendants

to intervene in this action as a matter of right and upon such

intervention, to file a response on their behalf to the

plaintiff's motion for a preliminary injunction and to further

166

file a motion for a preliminary injunction and for the convening of a three-judge Federal District Court; and alternatively,

Let the plaintiff show cause why an order should not be entered pursuant to Rule 24(b) of the Federal Rules of Civil Procedure permitting the Intervenor Defendants to intervene in this action in the discretion of this Court, and

Let service of this order, along with the supporting papers, upon the United States Attorney for the Southern District of New York and the *attorney for the* defendant, New York Times Company, at its principal office located at ~~229 West 43rd~~ *80 Pine* Street in the City of New York on or before ~~5 o'clock p.m.~~ *11 A.M.* of the *18th* day of June, 1971, be deemed good and sufficient service.

M. Gurfein
_____
U.S.D.J.

Dated New York, New York
June *17th* 1971

UNITED STATES DISTRICT COURT
SOUTHERN DISTRICT OF NEW YORK

---------------------------------------x

UNITED STATES OF AMERICA,   :

                    Plaintiff,   :

              -against-   :

THE NEW YORK TIMES,   :

                    Defendant.   :   Index #71 Civ. 2662

NOAM CHOMSKY; ALEXANDER ERLICH;   :
RICHARD FALK; ROBERT JAY LIFTON;
SEYMOUR MELMAN; HANS MORGENTHAU;   :
CARL SCHORSKE; FRANZ SCHURMANN;
GEORGE WALD; HOWARD ZINN,   :

                                            :

          Intervenor Defendants.

---------------------------------------x

STATE OF NEW YORK)
)   ss.:
COUNTY OF NEW YORK)

        DAVID ROSENBERG, being duly sworn deposes and says:

        I am one of the attorneys for the above-named Intervenor

Defendants and I make this affidavit in support of the annexed

motion for intervention as of right under Rule 24(a) of the

Federal Rules of Civil Procedure. This affidavit is also

submitted in support of Intervenor Defendants' annexed motion

for a preliminary injunction restraining Plaintiff, its agents

and representatives from enforcing and implementing through

civil or criminal proceedings or otherwise 18 U.S.C. §793(d),(e)

on its face or in so far as it may be applied to punish and

suppress the possession and publication by the New York Times

and the Intervenor Defendants of the Pentagon's Vietnam Study.

        Intervenors are citizens of the United States, eligible

and registered to vote. They are members of the academic

community who have investigated and published numerous art-

icles and books concerning the origin, nature, and conse-

quences of the United States' involvement in the Indo-China

War.

        The intervenors are as follows

Noam Chomsky of Lexington, Massachusetts is Professor of Modern Language and Linguistics at the Massachusetts Institute of Technology. He has published, among other works: <u>American Power and the New Mandarins</u>, 1969; <u>At War With Asia</u>, 1970.

Alexander Erlich, New York, New York is Professor of Economics and Russian Institute, Columbia University. He has published <u>The Soviet Industrialization Debate 1924-1928</u>, 1960.

Richard Falk, Princeton, New Jersey is Professor of International Law, Princeton University. He has published: <u>This Endangered Plan</u>, 1971; <u>Crimes of War</u>, co-editor, 1971; <u>Legal Order in a Violent World</u>, 1968.

Robert Jay Lifton, New Haven, Connecticut is Professor of Psychiatry, Yale University. He has published: <u>Crimes of War</u>, co-editor, 1971; <u>History and Human Survival</u>, 1970; <u>Boundaries: Psychological Man and Revolution</u>, 1970; <u>Death and Life: Survivors of Hiroshima</u>, 1968.

Seymour Melman, New York, New York is Professor of Industrial Engineering, Columbia University. He has published: <u>Pentagon Capitalism</u>; <u>The War Economy of the United States</u>; <u>In the Name of America</u>, editor; <u>Our Depleted Society</u>.

Hans Morgenthau of Chicago, Illinois is Professor of Political Science and Modern History at University of Chicago. He has published, among other works: <u>Politics in the 20th Century</u>, 1962; <u>A New Foreign Policy for the United States</u>, 1967.

Carl Schorski, Princeton, New Jersey is Professor of History Princeton University. He has published: <u>The Politics of Escalation in Vietnam</u>, contributor 1960; <u>The Problem of Germany</u>, 1947.

Franz Schurmann, Berkeley, California is Professor of Sociology and Chinese Studies. He has published: <u>Politics of Escalation in Vietnam</u>, contributor 1960; <u>Ideology and Organization in Communist China</u>.

George Wald, Cambridge, Massachusetts is Professor of Biology Harvard University; Nobel Laureate in Medicine, 1967; author of numerous articles and speeches.

Howard Zinn, Boston, Massachusetts is Professor of Political Science, Boston University. He has published: <u>The Politics of History</u>, 1970; <u>Vietnam. The Logic of Withdrawal</u>, 1967; <u>Disobedience</u>

be a prelude and precedent for criminal prosecution against Intervenors who intend to analyze, comment and elaborate upon the Study.

3. The New York Times is likely to maintain that a distinction exists between its factual reportage which does not disparage United States policy and the Intervenors' use of information in their efforts to demonstrate the immorality of the Government's war policy and the Government's deception in presenting its policies to the American electorate. Such a distinction would benefit the defendant's case to the Intervenors' detriment.

4. The Intervenors do not believe and the court cannot assume that defentant New York Times' corporate management will fight to the fullest extent of its resources for the public's right to know. The Intervenors have at times in the past been frustrated by the defendant's reportage of events relating to the War because this reportage did not present a complete picture. Intervenors should not be required to rely on the defendant New York Times now to fully represent their interests.

In the alternative, if this Court should find that the Intervenor Defendants are not eligible for intervention as of right pursuant to Rule 24(a), we respectfully request that they be permitted to intervene in the discretion of this Court pursuant to Rule 24(b). Intervenors' claim and defense and the main action have a question of law in common. There will be no prejudice to the original parties or interruption or delay in the proceedings caused by such intervention.

This Motion is brought on by Order to Show Cause since the Plaintiff's motion of preliminary injunction is presently scheduled for hearing on Friday, June 18th, at 2:00 p.m. Intervenors desire to be heard at that time on their motions and on the merits of the issues presented by this case. In

addition, it is necessary to proceed by the most expeditious process because the continued threat of civil and criminal sanctions pursuant to 18 U.S.C. § 793(d),(e) has a substantial deterrent effect on the exercise by Intervenors of their constitutional rights to speak and to freely and openly engage in academic inquiry.

No prior application has been made for the relief requested herein.

David Rosenberg
David Rosenberg

SWORN to before me this
16th day of June, 1971.

JEANETTE ROSENFELD
Notary Public, State of New York
No. 31-3355935
Qualified in New York County
Commission Expires March 30, 1973

UNITED STATES DISTRICT COURT
SOUTHERN DISTRICT OF NEW YORK

------------------------------------x

UNITED STATES OF AMERICA,   :

            Plaintiff   :

    - against -   :   Index #71 Civ. 2662

THE NEW YORK TIMES, et al.,   :

            Defendants   :

------------------------------------x

BRIEF ON BEHALF OF NATIONAL EMERGENCY
CIVIL LIBERTIES COMMITTEE AS AMICUS CURIAE

        This brief is submitted pursuant to leave of

the court by National Emergency Civil Liberties Committee,

an organization whose purpose is to assist in the preservation

of the civil rights and civil liberties of the American people,

with specific reference to the First Amendment rights of

free speech, press and assembly.   In that capacity the

Committee has engaged in litigation in all of the courts of

the United States and New York State as well as elsewhere and

has carried on for many years an active educational campaign

throughout the country in support of the Bill of Rights.

                        - 1 -

It is, of course, elementary that the right of free press guaranteed by the First Amendment is a right, not only of the publisher but of those would read the material published. This principle is well recognized and hardly needs extensive argument at this point. See, for example, Lamont v. Postmaster General, 381 U.S. 301; New York Times v. Sullivan, 376 U.S. 254; Garrison v. Louisiana, 379 U.S. 64; Stanley v. Georgia, 394 U.S. 557; Red Lion Broadcasting Co. v. F.C.C., 395 U.S. 367, and United States v. Sweezy, 254 U.S. 234, 250, 262.

A three-judge court sitting in the United States District Court for the Eastern District of New York has recently decided that a group of college professors, historians and other students of public affairs had a sufficient interest in hearing an alien who wished to enter the United States and speak to them to enable them to bring an action challenging the political exclusionary provisions of 8 U.S.C. 1182(a)(2) [The McCarran Act of 1952]. Mandell v. Mitchell, ____ F. Supp. ____, 70 Civ. 344 (March 18, 1971). The court in that case, after extended discussion, came to the conclusion that the statute was unconstitutional because it deprived the plaintiffs of rights, even though the alien himself had no right to complain.

- 2 -

It is for the purpose of presenting to the
court a consideration of the rights of those who read in
addition to the rights of those that print that this brief
is submitted.

POINT I

THERE IS NO JURISDICTION TO
GRANT THE RELIEF REQUESTED

Rule 8(a) of the Rules of Civil Procedure provides
that "a pleading which sets forth a claim for relief . . .
shall contain (1) a short and plain statement of the grounds
upon which the Court's jurisdiction depends. . ." The complaint
in this case did not allege any such statement of grounds. The
only reference in the complaint was to § 1345 of Title 28, which
provides only that the Government has the right to act as a
plaintiff; it does not provide a basis for jurisdiction.

Similarly, Executive Order 10501 cannot provide a
basis for jurisdiction. Youngstown Sheet & Tube Co. v. Sawyer,
343 U.S. 579 (1952).

Subsequent to the filing of the complaint, the
Government placed its reliance on § 793(d) and (e) as the basis
for jurisdiction, but that statute merely defines a crime. It
does not provide a basis for jurisdiction in a court of equity
to entertain the civil action now before the Court.

One of the most venerable principles in Anglo-American
law is contained in Lord Elden's pronouncement that equity has
no jurisdiction to prevent the commission of a crime. Gee v.

- 4 -

Pritchard 2 Swans 402, 413, 36 Eng. Rep. 670, 674 (1818).

The reasons for such prohibition in the present circumstances are twofold.

First, the issuance of an injunction, followed by performance of the act sought to be enjoined, would subject the actor to contempt charges and thus deprive him of his Fifth and Sixth Amendment rights to trial by jury for the act complained of. See generally 5 Moore, Federal Practice ¶38.24(3) at 192 (2d ed. 1968).

The other reason, of course, is the general prohibition of the First Amendment against prior censorship discussed more fully, infra at Point II, a prohibition which in this situation means, colloquially, that "you pay your money and take your chances". In other words, a citizen is protected by the First Amendment up to the point at which he executes his choice as to action which he may deem to be legal, but which the Government may not. If he is right, free speech has been preserved and vindicated, and no harm has befallen the Government. If he is wrong, he is liable to criminal prosecution for his acts and the Government will be vindicated.

The interests protected by the prohibition against

- 5 -

enjoining an alleged criminal act are so strong that the prohibition relaxes only in three narrowly defined situations, (1) national emergencies, (2) widespread public nuisances,*/ and (3) where a specific statutory grant of power exists. e.g. United States v. Jalas, 409 F. 2d 358, 360 (7th Cir. 1969).

The leading, and indeed one of the very few cases dealing with this issue, In re Debs, 158 U.S. 564, 15 S. Ct. 900 (1895) relied upon the first two situations. See also United States v. United Mineworkers of America, 330 U.S. 258 (1947). Even in these cases, there were civil statutes which were directly applicable to the offenses alleged. The third generally encompasses areas of economic regulation such as securities, commerce and the like, overtly inapplicable here.

The instant case, notwithstanding the unsupported statements of counsel, comes under none of these exceptions. The publication of the documents in question may have created

---

*/ Although we doubt that the instant case even arguably falls under (2), we note the Supreme Court's statement that ". . . characterizing publication as a business, and the business as a nuisance, does not permit an invasion of the constitutional immunity against [prior] restraint." Near v. Minnesota, 283 U.S. 697, 720, 51 S. Ct. 632

- 6 -

a national embarrassment, although even that seems unlikely, see generally New York Times June 17, 1971, p. 19, cols. 1 - 8; 18 "European Allies Make No. Complaints", col. 3 - 5. It has certainly not created an emergency in either the common meaning of the word or the meaning as exemplified by the Debs and Mineworkers cases, supra.

The Government's citation of Dubin v. United States, 289 F. 2d 651 (Ct. Cl.) in no way supports its contention that the statute is anything but criminal. In fact, that case, dealing of course with a wholly different situation where the Government was the defendant, specifically considered the options open to the Government upon discovering unauthorized possession pursuant to § 793. The Court found only one, that which we argue is the only constitutionally permissible option, i.e. a demand for return which, if indeed, could be followed by a criminal, not civil or injunctive proceeding.

In Jalas, 409 F. 2d 358 (7th Cir. 1969), the Court considered a problem substantially identical to the one before the Court here. There also the Government sought to enjoin an alleged criminal act relying for jurisdiction solely upon a criminal statute. The 7th Circuit held that the sole remedy

for the complained wrong was a criminal prosecution and, in dismissing the action for lack of jurisdiction, specifically declined to decide an important issue of criminal law "in the context of a civil action."

Before this Court can act, it must find, somewhere, jurisdiction to entertain the complaint. No such jurisdiction appears, and the complaint should be dismissed.

- 8 -

POINT II

THE OTHERWISE IMPERMISSIBLE INJUNCTION WOULD ALSO ACT AS A PRIOR RESTRAINT IN VIOLATION OF THE FIRST AMENDMENT

As previously alluded to, an injunction in this case would not only violate one of the most basic principles of equity, but also would constitute a prior restraint impermissible under the First Amendment.

The Supreme Court has consistently struck down all forms of prior restraint, especially in the area of freedom of the press, as repugnant to and destructive of the most basic rights guaranteed by the First Amendment, e.g., Near v. Minnesota, 283 U.S. 697, Grosjean v. American Press Co., 297 U.S. 233 and most recently in Organization for a Better Austin v. Jerome Keefe, 39 U.S.L.W. 4577 (May 17, 1971).

As the Supreme Court wrote in Near:

> "The fact that the liberty of the press may be abused...does not make any the less necessary the immunity of the press from previous restraint ...Subsequent punishment for such abuses as may exist is the appropriate remedy, consistent with constitutional privilege." Id. at 283 U.S. 719, 51 S.Ct. 632.

Where, in a factual situation like that in the instant case, the First Amendment policy against prior restraint coincides with the Fifth and Sixth Amendment

- 9 -

prohibition against injunction of a criminal act, Point I supra, the already overwhelming arguments against equitable action are doubted, and compel the conclusion that an injunction may not constitutionally issue

18 U.S.C. §793(e) IS UNCONSTITUTIONALLY VAGUE
AND VOID FOR OVERBREADTH IN THAT IT PROSCRIBES
CONDUCT PROTECTED BY THE FIRST AMENDMENT TO
THE CONSTITUTION OF THE UNITED STATES.

The complaint in this action makes no reference
to any statute and the Executive Order upon which the complaint
does rely is insufficient as a base for the injunction here
sought.   The Order itself makes no reference to any statute,
and we do not know what, if any, authority is claimed for it.
See Youngstown Sheet & Tube v. Sawyer 343 U.S. 579.

In response to this point the plaintiff has
referred to Title 18 U.S.C. §§793(d) and 793(e).   The former
section seems to have no relevance in view of the Government's
contention that the defendants have unauthorized possession
of the papers in question and this memorandum will therefore
be confined to a discussion of §793(e).   That section is
void because it fails to define precisely the nature of the
crime described therein and because the breadth of its
language (insofar as its vague terms are possible of construction
at all) encompasses conduct protected by the Constitution of
the United States.

- 11 -

A. The Statute Violates Due Process of Law
under the Fifth Amendment Because it
Fails to Specify with Reasonable Precision
Acts Constituting a Crime.

The section in question reads as follows:

"(e) Whoever having unauthorized possession
of, access to, or control over any document, writing,
code book, signal book, sketch, photograph,
photographic negative, blueprint, plan, map, model,
instrument, appliance, or note relating to the national
defense, or information relating to the national
defense which information the possessor has reason
to believe could be used to the injury of the United
States or to the advantage of any foreign nation,
wilfully communicates, delivers, transmits or causes
to be communicated, delivered, or transmitted, or
attempts to communicate, deliver, transmit or cause
to be communicated, delivered, or transmitted the
same to any person not entitled to receive it, or
wilfully retains the same and fails to deliver it to
the officer or employee of the United States
entitled to receive it".

That section fails to meet the most rudimentary

tests of specification and precision necessary to the creation

and definition of a crime under our constitutional scheme.

N.A.A.C.P. v. Button, 371 U.S. 415 (1963); Dombrowski v. Pfister,

380 U.S. 479 (1965); Shelton v. Tucker, 364 U.S. 439 (1965);

Lanzetta v. New Jersey, 306 U.S. 451, 453 (1939). A criminal

statute must be "clear and positive" and must give "unequivocal

warning" of conduct which is punishable; it must be "informative

on its face". People v. Firth, 3 N.Y. 2d 472 (1957).

The infirmity of §793(e) is immediately apparent.

Basically there are two elements to the crime defined by that

section which are relevant to this discussion: The first is the

"unauthorized possession" by the defendant of documents, notes

or information and the second is that the documents must be

"relating to the national defense".   Both of these elements

are overbroad and vague, and if permitted to stand would raise

the potential of a censorship in the United States totally

inconsistent with all of our history and with the provisions

of the First Amendment.

The statute makes possession of a document legal or

illegal depending upon whether that possession is "authorized"

or "unauthorized".   We are referred to no provision of law

setting up standards on the basis of which possession of a

document may be "authorized" or "unauthorized".   The purported

standards set forth in Executive Order 10501 are themselves

vague, and the plaintiff has made not the slightest effort to

show how the documents in question come even within those

improper standards.   It is obviously inconsistent with a free

press that the Government or any officer thereof should have

the right, without effective limitation, to withhold authorization

for the publication of documents.   On the basis of the statute

there is not even any suggestion as to who has the right to give

or withhold the authority which will make possession an

- 13 -

innocent act or a criminal one.   Is this authority lodged

in the President of the United States, the Secretary of

Defense or some clerk in the Pentagon equipped with a rubber

stamp?   The breadth of the statute in this respect is so

extraordinary that it cannot possibly stand consistent with

established law.

The other key expression, namely, that the

document or information must relate to the national defense

is equally broad and vague.   In the instant case the plaintiff

is contending that materials three to five years old relate

to "the national defense".   We suppose that it might also be

claimed that the documents relating to the Korean War or to

World War II might also "relate to national defense".   The

materials in question are not battle plans, technical devices,

war secrets or any other similar material, the disclosure of

which might affect some current strategy of the Armed Forces

of the United States.   At least if any of the documents in

question do contain any such material, the plaintiff has not

so alleged.   Instead, it has proceeded to seek an injunction

of the broadest possible scope to prevent the disclosure

- 14 -

185

of many volumes of historical material of the greatest

importance to the American people.*

          B. The Statute in Question is Unconstitutional
              on its Face because it is Overbroad and
              Punishes Conduct Protected by the First
              <u>Amendment to the United States Constitution</u>.

The statute is unconstitutional because it broadly

proscribes conduct protected by the First Amendment to the

United States Constitution. The vice of vagueness, described

in Point A above, is compounded where the subject matter of a

criminal statute involves conduct with/the confines of
                                   in

traditionally protected constitutional freedoms. This is

especially true where the First Amendment considerations are

present - as is evident here. "Because First Amendment

freedoms need breathing space to survive, government may

regulate in the area only with narrow specificity."

<u>N.A.A.C.P.</u> v. <u>Button</u>, 371 U.S. 415, 433 (1963).

---

*The statute is unclear even as a matter of simple use of the
English language. We have assumed that the words "which
information the possessor has reason to believe could be used
to the injury of the United States or to the advantage of any
foreign nation" modify the word "information" which immediately
precedes them and that it does not modify specific words such as
"document, writing, code book, signal book, sketch", etc.
If our construction is wrong and if the words "which information
the possessor has reason to believe ...any foreign nation" modify
"document, writing, code book", etc., the statute is even more
vague and overbroad than we have suggested since it uses
additional language, the meaning of which is quite unclear.

- 15 -

Where First Amendment freedoms are at issue, the courts have erected numerous barriers against state vindication of even legitimate interests where such vindication is not narrowly conceived and defined. It would take a volume to analyze the nature of the restraints placed upon the state's power to define, prohibit and punish anti-social conduct where free speech considerations predominate. The State (i.e., all government) has been subjected to increased and increasing judicial scrutiny when it attempts to punish obscenity (Roth v. United States, 354 U.S. 476, 1957; Memoirs v. Attorney General, 383 U.S. 413, 1966), libel (New York Times v. Sullivan, 376 U.S. 254, 1964; Near v. Minnesota, 283 U.S. 625, 1931; Garrison v. Louisiana, 379 U.S. 64, 1964), membership in "subversive organizations" (Dombrowski v. Pfister, supra, and the illegal practice of law (N.A.A.C.P. v. Button, supra). State attempts to impose and enforce loyalty oaths - especially of the disclaimer variety - have engendered sharply negative judicial responses (Shelton v. Tucker, supra; Keyishian v. United States, 385 U.S. 589; Cramp v. Board of Instruction, 368 U.S. 278; Elfbrandt v. Russell, 384 U.S. 918) as have efforts to elicit information in connection with admission to and practice of licensed

- 16 -

professions (<u>Koenigsberg</u> v. <u>State Bar</u>, 353 U.S. 252; <u>Schware</u> v. <u>Board of Bar Examiners</u>, 353 U.S. 32). These restraints have become virtually routine and have been reaffirmed in recent weeks by the United States Supreme Court. <u>Time, Inc.</u> v. <u>Pape</u>, 401 U. S. 279; <u>Baird</u> v. <u>State Bar of Arizona</u>, 401 U.S. 1.

The doctrines of vagueness and overbreadth are applied with particular care in these areas where First Amendment rights are involved. "Standards of permissible statutory vagueness are strict in the area of free expression." <u>N.A.A.C.P.</u> v. <u>Button</u>, <u>supra</u>, at 432. The <u>Button</u> standard for determination of the validity of <u>any</u> curtailment of free speech has been repeated <u>ad infinitum</u>:

> "Broad prophylactic rules in the area of
> free expression are suspect. . . Precision
> of regulation must be the touchstone in
> an area so closely touching our most precious
> freedoms." <u>Supra</u>, at 438.

Although the Supreme Court has countenanced some flexibility where speech is combined with conduct, it has permitted none where "pure speech" is involved. <u>Tinker</u> v. <u>Des Moines Independent School District</u>, 393 U.S. 503. Where

- 17 -

"pure speech" of a politically inflammatory nature is

   it

involved,/has resurrected doctrines such as "clear and

present danger" to assure that maximum protection is afforded.

Brandenberg v. Ohio, 395 U.S. 444.   Indeed, it is inconceivable

that any doctrine short of "clear and present danger" would

be appropriate to define the interests of the government in

enforcing the statute in question, since the statute is a

clear prohibition upon the dissemination of "pure" "Political"

information.

   The vices of vagueness and overbreadth so tellingly

present in the "loyalty oath" cases and in Dombrowski v.

Pfister, supra, operate here to mandate the same result, the

invalidation of the statute at issue.   Just as the loyalty

oath in Whitehill v. Elkins, supra, could not constitutionally

be "so vague and broad as to make men of common intelligence

speculate at their peril on its meaning" (at 58-9), so must

the proscription upon dissemination of information herein

not require such men to so fruitlessly speculate.   Prohibition

of transmission of information which "could injure" the

United States is as clearly unconstitutional as was the

Whitehill oath requiring attestation that deponent was not

"in one way or another" attempting to overthrow the government.

- 18 -

189

POINT IV

THE PUBLIC INTEREST WILL BE IRREPARABLY INJURED IF A PRELIMINARY INJUNCTION IS GRANTED.

Delay in the publication of the materials in question will irreparably injure the public interest even though it may not result in similar or equal injury to the New York Times.

The Times is a commercial enterprise. Its financial wellbeing is not likely to be affected by a delay in the publication of these documents. Whether they are published Sunday or a month from Sunday or 6 months hence, the circulation of the Times is not likely to be seriously affected and it may therefore well be concluded that no irreparable injury, in a legal sense, will result from such delay.

But the public interest is quite another matter. We are engaged now in a great national debate concerning the war in Vietnam and the origins of that war play an important role in that debate. Whether the war was in fact legal or not legal, whether or not the President usurped his power, whether or not Congress was misled as to the facts giving rise to hostilities, whether or not the public

- 19 -

was given misleading information — all of these issues and
many others are central to this great national debate.

And the papers which are the subject of this
action are central to these questions.

Yesterday, June 16, the Senate of the United
States voted on the McGovern-Hatfield Amendment calling for
a December 31 deadline to hostilities in Vietnam.   That
amendment was defeated by a margin of only a few votes.
It may be that revelation of further information such as that
which the Times has already published could have influenced
the votes of 5 or 6 Senators and affected the outcome in the
Senate.   Irreparable injury may therefore already have
occurred to the public interest as a result of the temporary
restraining order.

But the debate is not over and will undoubtedly
continue and even increase in intensity as long as the war
continues.   The House equivalent of the McGovern-Hatfield
Amendment is still pending.   Congress still has before it
appropriation bills, a bill for the extension of the draft
and numerous other important items of legislation which have
a close relationship to the conduct of hostilities in Vietnam.

- 20 -

191

Every day that passes during which vital information is

kept from the Congress and the public, serious irreparable

injury is suffered by the public interest.

                        Respectfully submitted,

                        RABINOWITZ, BOUDIN & STANDARD

                        Attorneys for National Emergency Civil
                            Liberties Committee, Amicus Curiae

VICTOR RABINOWITZ,
KRISTIN BOOTH GLEN,

        Of Counsel

June 17, 1971

                        - 21 -

UNITED STATES DISTRICT COURT
FOR THE SOUTHERN DISTRICT
OF NEW YORK

UNITED STATES OF AMERICA,

        Plaintiff,

v.

THE NEW YORK TIMES COMPANY,
et al.,

        Defendants.

VIETNAM VETERANS AGAINST THE
WAR, AMERICAN FRIENDS SERVICE
COMMITTEE, WAR RESISTERS
LEAGUE, PEOPLE'S PEACE TREATY,
PEOPLE'S COALITION FOR PEACE
AND JUSTICE, NATIONAL STUDENT
ASSOCIATION OF THE UNITED
STATES, all being corporations
or unincorporated associations;
CONGRESSMAN RONALD DELLUMS,
JOHN KERRY, DICK GREGORY,
ABBOTT SIMON, KATHERINE L.
CAMP, ROBERT GREENBLATT,
DR. SIDNEY PECK, STUART
MEACHEM, MIKE OLIVER,
MORTON A. MEYERS, M.D., MRS.
BERNARD JACKOWITZ, MR. AND
MRS. LEONARD AMSTERDAM,
SAMUEL SCHEINKMAN, M.D.,
MR. AND MRS. EDWARD
WAGNER, JOSEPH G. SWEETING,
M.D., BRONSON T. CLARK,
DAVID IFSHIN, SISTER
ELIZABETH McALISTER, and
EQBAL AHMAD, DELIA ALVAREZ,
and MRS. JANE DUDLEY,

        Intervenors.

#71 Civ. 2662

MOTION TO INTERVENE
AS DEFENDANTS

Intervenors, Vietnam Veterans Against the War, American

Friends Service Committee, War Resisters League, People's Peace

Treaty, People's Coalition for Peace and Justice, and National

Student Association of the United States, all being corporations

or unincorporated associations;

193

Congressman Ronald Dellums, of the Seventh Congressional District California; John Kerry, residing in New York, N. Y.; Dick Gregory, residing in Chicago, Illinois; Bronson T. Clark, residing in Philadelphia, Pa.; Abbott Simon, residing in New York, N.Y.; Katherine L. Camp, residing in Philadelphia, Pa.; Robert Greenblatt, residing in New York, N.Y.; Dr. Sidney Peck, residing in Cambridge, Mass.; Stuart Meachem, residing in Philadelphia, Pa.; Mike Oliver, residing in New York, N.Y.; Morton A. Meyers, M.D., residing in New York, N.Y.; Mrs. Bernard Jackowitz, residing in New York, N.Y.; Mr. and Mrs. Samuel Herzfeld, residing in New York, N.Y.; Mr. and Mrs. Leonard Amsterdam, residing in New York, N.Y.; Samuel Scheinkman, M.D., residing in New York, N.Y.; Mr. and Mrs. Edward Wagner, residing in New York, N.Y.; Joseph G. Sweeting, M.D., residing in New York, N.Y.; David Ifshin, residing in Washington, D.C.;

Sister Elizabeth McAlister, residing in New York, N.Y.; and Mrs. Delia Alvarez, Santa Clara, Calif.; and Jane Dudley, Honolulu, Eqbal Ahmad, residing in Chicago Ill.;/move for leave to intervene as defendants in this action in order to assert the defenses set forth in the proposed Answer, a copy of which is hereto attached, on the ground that (1) movants are entitled to do so under Rule 24(a)(2) in that the representation of their interest by the defendants is or may be inadequate for the reason that the interest asserted by proposed intervenors is different from that of the defendant NEW YORK TIMES and its staff as hereinafter appears, and (2) in the event the Court should deny intervention as of right under Rule 24(a)(2), movants seek intervention under Rule 24(b)(2) in that the proposed intervenors have a question of law or fact in common with that before the Court.

The intervention here sought will not delay or prejudice the rights of the original parties and will assure the full representation of interests before the Court which may otherwise not be fully represented in the proceedings.

The attorneys representing the proposed intervenors are all associated with the Center for Constitutional Rights, a charitable corporation of the State of New Jersey authorized to do business in New York. Attorneys associated with the Center have participated actively in major constitutional litigation, particularly in the area of the First Amendment, and their representation of the proposed intervenors will emphasize the unique and special constitutional rights of such intervenors which, it is submitted, appear to be different from those of the NEW YORK TIMES. The interest of the several intervenors and the difference between their interest and that of the NEW YORK TIMES appears as follows:

Vietnam Veterans Against the War is an organization designed to contribute to the ending of the war in Southeast Asia by developing the ability of members to collect and disseminate information to the public and to effect peace in Southeast Asia by the use of the knowledge and experience of the membership. They have banded together for the purpose of exercising their rights under the First Amendment, to effect a change in the policies of the United States government in order to terminate the said war.

American Friends Service Committee is an organization which believes that creative action can overcome hate, prejudice and fear. It operates programs of relief, service and education, and stands in opposition to war, oppression, and racism. Its members exercise their constitutional rights to bring about a termination of the Vietnam war.

War Resisters League is a 47-year-old pacifist organization devoted to finding nonviolent ways of resolving conflict. Its members exercise their constitutional rights to affect the policies of the United States government in order to bring the Vietnam war to an end.

People's Peace Treaty is an organization of persons throughout the country who have concluded that it is appropriate to establish direct relations between the people of the United States and the people of Vietnam so as to effect peace. They have prepared a document which sets forth realistic conditions under which the war could end honorably for the people of both nations, and are coordinating a nationwide effort to bring the document to the people. The force of their movement depends upon the number of people who sign the proposed treaty, and that in turn will depend upon their conviction that the war should terminate.

People's Coalition for Peace and Justice is a multi-issue, multi-tactical coalition which sees the war abroad and the racism, repression and exploitation at home as one and the same. Through the use of nonviolent tactics, they exercise their constitutional rights to affect the policies of the government in the direction of ending the Vietnam war.

National Student Association of the United States is the largest national student association in the world, composed of over 500 student bodies through their democratically elected student governments. Since students are among those called upon to bear the brunt of war, the NSA has understandably had a special interest in the termination of the war in Vietnam and exercises its constitutional rights in opposition thereto.

Each of the organizations above is exercising its rights under the First Amendment and its right to petition the government of the United Snates to effect a change in the policies of the government in order to terminate the war in Vietnam. Essential to the exercise of the foregoing constitutional rights is the availability of the truth with respect to the program and policies of the United States in regard to the war, and inter-venors assert that they have a constitutional right to a truthful statement of such programs and policies. Heretofore the

executive branch has failed and refused to disclose the true facts with respect to the development and implementation of policies of the United States with regard to American participation in the war in Southeast Asia and the people of the United States have accordingly not been in a position fully to exercise their constitutional right to affect the policies of their government. The facts already disclosed in the articles appearing in the NEW YORK TIMES on June 13, 14 and 15 reveal that statements heretofore made by the executive branch are not in accord with the truth, and upon information and belief the additional facts which will be disclosed from the publication of the full series of articles proposed to be published by the defendant TIMES will reveal additional vital facts. These intervenors will therefore press before the Court their constitutional right to obtain the truth in order that they may exercise their constitutional right to organize to influence the policies of their government.

Congressman Ronald Dellums is a member of the Congress of the United States, representing the Seventh Congressional District in California. He has a constitutional responsibility to consider proposed legislation and appropriate funds for the management of the government of the United States, including specifically, with respect to the matter at hand, the power to declare war. Essential to the performance of these functions is the obtaining of truthful and accurate information as to programs, policies, and practices of the executive branch, and especially with respect to the continuation of the war in Vietnam.

John Kerry, Dick Gregory, Abbott Simon, Katherine L. Camp, Robert Greenblatt, Dr. Sidney Peck, Stuart Meachem, Mike Oliver, Morton A. Meyers, M.D., Mrs. Bernard Jackowitz, Mr. and Mrs. Leonard Amsterdam, Smauel Scheinkman, M.D., Mr. and Mrs. Edward Wagner, Joseph G. Sweeting, M.D., Bronson T. Clark and David

Ifshin are each citizens of the United States who in varying manner are seeking to exercise their rights under the Constitution to influence the policies of their government so as to effect a termination of the war in Vietnam. Some of said individuals have acted individually and some through organizations of their own choosing, but all of them have a common objective in effecting a change in the policies of the United States in regard to the Vietnam war.

Sister Elizabeth McAlister and Eqbal Ahmad are citizens of the United States strongly opposed to the war in Vietnam and have been desirous of exercising their rights under the Constitution to effect a change in the policies of the United States in respect to the war in Vietnam. By reason of their identification with such activity they have been indicted by a grand jury of the United States acting in Pennsylvania, in which false and fraudulent charges have been brought against them. In the course of the trial of such charges, it will become important to the defense to establish the illegality and contrived nature of the war in Vietnam for the purpose of showing that the indictments have been motivated solely for the purpose of throttling opposition to the war.

Delia Alvarez is the sister of Everett Alvarez, a member of the armed forces of the United States and now a prisoner of war in North Vietnam. Mrs. Jane Dudley is the mother of George G. McKnight, a member of the armed forces of the United States and now a prisoner of war in North Vietnam. As appears from recent statements of the government of North Vietnam, that country has no intention of releasing the prisoners of war unless and until the United States announces a firm and fixed date for the withdrawal of its forces from Vietnam. Delia Alvarez and Jane Dudley have joined with many other persons in the United States, including relatives of other prisoners of war in North Vietnam, and seek to shape the policy of the United States so as to effect the

termination of the war and the release of the prisoners.

Congressman Dellums and each of the individual intervenors will join the organizational intervenors in pressing before this Court their constitutional right to obtain the truth in order that they may exercise their constitutional right to influence the policies of the government of the United States; the individual intervenors McAlister and Ahmad will further press for the true facts as to the Vietnam war to bolster their defense.

Intervenors state that their interests in this litigation will not be fully represented by the defendants and that their intervention will not interfere with the proceedings but will simply assure the proper representation of all interests.

WHEREFORE, intervenors move that they be granted leave to intervene as parties defendant; that they be permitted to participate in all proceedings herein; and they have leave to file the Answer annexed hereto.

Attorneys for Intervenors:

WILLIAM CUNNINGHAM
ARTHUR KINOY
WILLIAM M. KUNSTLER
JAMES REIF
MORTON STAVIS
NANCY STEARNS
PETER WEISS
  c/o Center for Constitutional Rights
    588 Ninth Ave.
    New York, N. Y. 10036
    (212) 265-2500

By: _____
          Morton Stavis

UNITED STATES OF AMERICA,

        Plaintiff,

   VS.

THE NEW YORK TIMES COMPANY,
et al.,

        Defendants.

#71 Civ. 2662

Proposed

ANSWER

VIETNAM VETERANS AGAINST THE WAR,
AMERICAN FRIENDS SERVICE COMMITTEE,
WAR RESISTERS LEAGUE, PEOPLE'S
PEACE TREATY, PEOPLE'S COALITION
FOR PEACE AND JUSTICE, NATIONAL
STUDENT ASSOCIATION OF THE UNITED
STATES, all being corporations or
unincorporated associations;
CONGRESSMAN RONALD DELLUMS, JOHN
KERRY, DICK GREGORY, ABBOTT SIMON,
KATHERINE L. CAMP, ROBERT GREENBLATT,
DR. SIDNEY PECK, STUART MEACHEM,
MIKE OLIVER, MORTON A. MEYERS, M.D.,
MRS. BERNARD JACKOWITZ, MR. AND
MRS. LEONARD AMSTERDAM, SAMUEL
SCHEINKMAN, M.D., MR. AND MRS. EDWARD
WAGNER, JOSEPH G. SWEETING, M.D.,
BRONSON T. CLARK, DAVID IFSHIN,
SISTER ELIZABETH McALISTER, and
EQBAL AHMAD, DELIA ALVAREZ, and MRS.
JANE DUDLEY,

        Intervenors.

    Intervenors, answering the Complaint, say:

    1.   They admit the allegations of paragraph 1.

    2.   As to the allegations of paragraph 2, they admit only that this is a civil action seeking to enjoin the disclosure of information.

    3.   They admit the allegations of paragraph 3.

    4.   They admit so much of paragraph 4 as alleges that the defendants obtained a copy of certain documents but they deny that the same was without lawful authority in that there was no lawful authority to deny access to such documents.

    5.   They admit so much of paragraph 5 as alleges that

defendants obtained a copy of certain documents but they deny that the same was without lawful authority in that there was no lawful authority to deny access to such documents.

6. They admit that the executive order is accurately quoted but deny that such executive order has been properly applied to the documents here in question.

7. They admit the allegations of paragraph 7.

8. They deny the allegations of paragraphs 8, 9, and 10.

AFFIRMATIVE DEFENSES

1. The Plaintiff, in violation of constitutional rights of intervenors, seeks to deny the rights of the intervenors to know of the facts which have shaped the policies and practices of the United States government with respect to the war in Vietnam, so that the intervenors may influence such policy in the direction of the termination of the war in Vietnam.

2. Representatives of the Plaintiff have falsely and fraudulently led the people of the United States into a war which has no constitutional or moral justification, and in order to conceal the facts, the Plaintiff is now falsely claiming that the interests of the government of the United States will be damaged by disclosure of the truth, when in fact the only persons who will be damaged by such disclosure are officials responsible for the illegal and immoral war.

3. Plaintiff, having mistated the facts and having denied the truth to the American people, comes into Court with unclean hands and is not entitled to injunctive relief under any circumstances and certainly not to achieve censorship.

- 2 -.

WHEREFORE, intervenors demand dismissal of the

Complaint.

Attorneys for Intervenors:

WILLIAM CUNNINGHAM
ARTHUR KINOY
WILLIAM M. KUNSTLER
JAMES REIF
MORTON STAVIS
NANCY STEARNS
PETER WEISS
  c/o Center for Constitutional Right:
    588 Ninth Avenue
    New York, N. Y. 10036
    (212) 265-2500

By: _____
      Morton Stavis

UNITED STATES DISTRICT COURT
FOR THE SOUTHERN DISTRICT OF
NEW YORK

UNITED STATES OF AMERICA,

        Plaintiff,

v.   #71 Civ. 2662

THE NEW YORK TIMES COMPANY,
et al.,

        Defendants.

VIETNAM VETERANS AGAINST THE
WAR, et al.,

        Intervenors.

MEMORANDUM ON BEHALF OF THE INTERVENORS

This memorandum is submitted in support of the motion
for intervention on behalf of a group of peace organizations which
have been seeking to influence American policy towards termination of the war in Vietnam; a Congressman of the United States
and a group of individuals similarly directed; two individuals
having an interest by reason of their being prosecuted by the
government because of their activity in opposition to the war;
and the sister of one prisoner of war and the mother of another.

The intervention is sought for the reason, among others,
that the interest of the proposed intervenors is different from
that of the New York Times. The latter's interest is the dissemination of news, certainly an important constitutional interest,

which, however, is consistent with a stance of neutrality as to the political or legal consequences of such news. The intervenors have a point of view and seek the truth for the specific purpose of either influencing the policies of the government or, in the case of intervenors McAlister and Ahmade, for the purpose of preparing their defense.

I.

> "Truth is the only ground upon which [men's] wishes safety can be carried out."

Mr. Justice Holmes in <u>Abrams</u> v. <u>United States</u>, 250 U.S. 616, 624.

> "If there be time to expose through discussion the falsehood and fallacies, to avert the evil by the process of education, the remedy to be applied is more speech, not enforced silence."

Mr. Justice Brandeis in <u>Whitney</u> v. <u>California</u>, 274 U.S. 357, 377.

The transcendant point that emerges from the facts already published by the <u>New York Times</u> shows that the government of the United States has attempted to hide the truth from the people. The object of the present proceeding brought by the government is to employ the courts to further that objective. The foregoing is such an affront to the entire fabric of the democratic process that the Court must strike it down, not merely for the neutral interests of those who wish to disseminate knowledge, but precisely to allow those who wish to influence government policy or further their own defense to have the facts upon which they may base their programs.

Nor may the Court accept the general, unsupported claims of the government that the security of the United States can be

affected by the publication of the documents in question. The only security that is threatened is the political security of the originators of the Vietnam war, as well as that of those who continue it. This appears on the face of the documents. To accept the government's bald claim that national security is affected, when the facts are to the contrary, is to ignore both the Constitution and one of the vital roles of the courts, i.e., to protect the people from the excesses of the executive.

II.

> "The power of the licensor against which John Milton directed his assault by his "Appeal for the Liberty of Unliscensed Printing' is pernicious not merely by reason of the censure of particular comments but by reason of the threat tocensure comments on matters of public concern."

Mr. Justice Murphy in Thornhill v. Alabama, 310 U.S. 88, 97.

Never before his this country been so openly faced with the threat of censorship -- prior restraints -- such as the government seeks here. The intervenors would wish to present to the Court the extraordinary context in which this effort at censorship is presented.

We live in a period where many constitutional rights are being threatened by unusual assertion of executive authority, including the power to conduct war without Congressional approval, the power to wiretap in violation of Fourth Amendment rights, the power to make mass arrests without justification, a program of preventive detention of persons not convicted of crime, and now

the power to exercise censorship. This program collectively constitutes so fundamental a change in the fabric of our society that the intervenors seek to present their views to the Court on the extraordinary threat of the proposed censorship to the basic democratic process of this nation.

Conclusion

The issues involved here affect the people of the United States in different ways. Intervenors have a special concern that their constitutional right to obtain facts is protected so that they may contribute to shaping the policy of the United States. Their motion to intervene should be granted.

Attorneys for Intervenors:

WILLIAM CUNNINGHAM
ARTHUR KINOY
WILLIAM M. KUNSTLER
JAMES REIF
MORTON STAVIS
NANCY STEARNS
PETER WEISS
  c/o Center for Constitutional Rights
     588 Ninth Ave.
     New York, N. Y. 10036
     (212) 265-2500

By: _____
     Morton Stavis

6/17/71

UNITED STATES DISTRICT COURT
SOUTHERN DISTRICT OF NEW YORK
-------------------------------------X
                                       :
UNITED STATES OF AMERICA,   :   AFFIDAVIT
                        Plaintiff,   :   71 Civ. 2662
                                       :
        -v-   :
                                       :
NEW YORK TIMES COMPANY, et al.,   :
                        Defendants.   :
------------------------------------- X

STATE OF NEW YORK   )
COUNTY OF NEW YORK   (ss.:
SOUTHERN DISTRICT OF NEW YORK)

        Michael D. Hess, being duly sworn, deposes and says:

        1. I am an Assistant United States Attorney and
Chief of the Civil Division in the office of Whitney North
Seymour, Jr., United States Attorney for the Southern District of New York. As such, I am in charge of and familiar
with this action.

        2. I submit this affidavit in opposition to the
motion of Edward J. Ennis, Edward I. Koch, Aryeh Neier,
Ira Glasser, Edwin J. Oppenheimer, Jr., and Nancy Lee
Ennis to intervene in this action as parties defendant.

        3. This is an action by the United States to enjoin
the publication by the New York Times of certain secret
Government documents, the disclosure of which would be

detrimental to the national defense of the United States.

3. Intervention by the movants herein will create serious problems for the parties and the Court in this complex case. Secret classified documents are the heart of this lawsuit. They will have to be examined and discussed by the participants in this proceeding. Portions of the proceedings herein may have to be held in camera. Many substantive and procedural problems are already present in this lawsuit and the addition of numerous parties will merely delay and complicate the disposition of this case.

4. It is important to note that the movants have shown no special interests which would permit them to intervene herein. Their moving papers state that they should be able to intervene because their right to read the documents at issue will be decided in this case. That is the ultimate question in this lawsuit and the movants merely have the same interest as every other newspaper reader. Every citizen is interested in questions relating to the Vietnam War. However, this Court cannot permit every citizen or every newspaper reader to intervene as a party in this action.

5. An examination of the movants' affidavits and memorandum of law shows their lack of special competence or interest to intervene herein. Movants "submit that while this is not a class action, they are representative

- 2 -

of the diverse numbers of persons throughout the United States and, indeed, throughout the world, who are readers of the _New York Times_ and who believe they have a right to read the documents in question. While the _New York Times_ seeks to protect its own press activities, it was apparent to counsel by their presence at oral argument that the thrust of the named Defendants' arguments in opposition to the Plaintiff's motion are not sufficiently broad to clearly and conclusively protect the rights of the Defendant-Intervenors. . . ." Merely because they read the _New York Times_ or because they are somehow displeased with the arguments of defendants' counsel is not enough to permit formal intervention herein.

WHEREFORE, your deponent prays that the motion to intervene be denied in all respects.

/s/
_____

MICHAEL D. HESS
Assistant United States Attorney.

SWORN TO BEFORE ME

this 17th day of June, 1971.

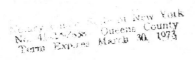

Form No. USA-38a-270
(Rev. 10-25-65)

United States District Court

SOUTHERN DISTRICT OF NEW YORK

UNITED STATES OF AMERICA,

Plaintiff,

"v"

NEW YORK TIMES COMPANY, et al.,

Defendants.

ORDER TO SHOW CAUSE AND AFFIDAVIT

71 Civ. 2662

Whitney North Seymour, Jr.
United States Attorney
Attorney for **Plff.**
TEL. 264-3311

Due service of a copy of the within is hereby admitted.

New York,——————, 19——

——————
Attorney for-

To ——————

Attorney for-

Sir:

Please take notice that the within ——
will be presented for settlement and signature to the Honorable ——
United States District Judge, at the office of
the Clerk, Room 601, United States Courthouse, Foley Square, Borough of Manhattan,
City of New York, on the —— day of ——,
19 ——, at 10:30 o'clock in the —— noon,
or as soon thereafter as counsel can be heard.

Dated, N. Y.,——————, 19——

Yours, etc.,

——————
United States Attorney
Attorney for ——

To ——————

Attorney for ——

Sir:

You will please take notice that a ——
of which the within is a copy, was this day
duly entered in the office of the Clerk of this Court.

Dated, N. Y.,——————, 19——

Yours, etc.,

——————
United States Attorney
Attorney for ——

To ——————

Attorney for ——

UNITED STATES DISTRICT COURT
SOUTHERN DISTRICT OF NEW YORK
------------------------------------X

UNITED STATES OF AMERICA,   :

           Plaintiff,   :

          -v-   :

NEW YORK TIMES COMPANY, et al.,   :

          Defendants.   :

------------------------------------X

ORDER TO SHOW CAUSE

71 Civ. 2662

Upon the annexed affidavit of Michael D. Hess, Assistant United States Attorney and Chief of the Civil Division in the office of Whitney North Seymour, United States Attorney for the Southern District of New York, and upon all of the pleadings and proceedings heretofore had herein, and sufficient cause appearing therefor, it is

ORDERED, that defendants show cause, if any there be, before this Court at Room 506, United States Court House, Foley Square, New York, N. Y., on the 17th day of June, 1971, at 10:00 A. M. in the forenoon, or as soon thereafter as counsel can be heard, why an order of this Court should not be made pursuant to Rules 26, 34, and 37 of the Federal Rules of Civil Procedure, directing defendants to produce and permit plaintiff to inspect and copy the documents designated in plaintiff's Notice for Production of Documents in this matter, dated June 16, 1971, a copy of which is annexed to said affidavit as Exhibit "A", and granting plaintiff such other and further relief as is just; and it is further

ORDERED, that service of a copy of this order and
of the affidavit annexed hereto shall be made by personal
delivery to the offices of Messrs. Cahill, Gordon, Sonnett,
Reindel & Ohl, 80 Pine Street, New York, N. Y., 10005,
on or before June 16, 1971, at 6:30 P. M. *MIG*

Dated: New York, N. Y.

      June 16, 1971, at

      _5:15_ P. M.

                      MI Gurfein
                        U.   S.   D.   J.

UNITED STATES DISTRICT COURT
SOUTHERN DISTRICT OF NEW YORK
-----------------------------------X

UNITED STATES OF AMERICA,   :

               Plaintiff,   :

                           :

         -v-

                           :

NEW YORK TIMES COMPANY, et al.,

                           :

          Defendants.

----------------------------------- X

AFFIDAVIT	
71 Civ. 2662	

STATE OF NEW YORK   )
COUNTY OF NEW YORK   (ss.:
SOUTHERN DISTRICT OF NEW YORK)

     Michael D. Hess, being duly sworn, deposes and says:

     1. I am an Assistant United States Attorney and Chief
of the Civil Division in the office of Whitney North Seymour, United States Attorney for the Southern District of
New York. As such, I am in charge of and familiar with
the above captioned action.

     2. This affidavit is submitted in support of plain-
tiff's motion for an order directing defendant, the New
York Times Company, to produce and permit plaintiff to
inspect and copy certain designated documents pursuant to
the provisions of Rule 34 of the Federal Rules of Civil
Procedure. The documents which plaintiff desires to inspect and copy are designated in a Notice for Production
of Documents, pursuant to said Rule 34, a copy of which is
annexed hereto as Exhibit "A".

3. This is an action to enjoin the publication by
the New York Times of certain documents, the disclosure
of which would be detrimental to the national defense of
the United States. At the present time, plaintiff does
not know what documents defendants have in their possession,
custody and control. By the admission of defendant, New
York Times Company, those documents include a 47 volume
study entitled "History of U. S. Decision-Making Process
on Vietnam Policy" and a summary of a document entitled
"The Command and Control Study of the Tonkin Gulf incident
done by the Defense Department's Weapons System Evaluation
Group in 1965". The production of these documents is
called for by the first two items of plaintiff's said
Notice for Production of Documents.

4. Plaintiff also believes that defendants have in
their possession, custody or control other classified
documents belonging to plaintiff which defendants are not
authorized to have. Plaintiff is unable to specify these
documents with precision but believes that defendants well
know what documents they are.

5. Although defendants' time to respond to plaintiff's
Notice for Production of Documents has not expired, we
believe defendants will refuse to produce any of these
documents voluntarily. As we believe that their production
is important to the proper presentation of the Government's
case, and to the proper protection of the national interest, we believe that this Court should order defendants
to produce these documents if they will not produce them

- 2 -

215

voluntarily.

6. Plaintiff has sought the production of these documents in compliance with Rule 34 of the Federal Rules of Civil Procedure. Because plaintiff's motion for a preliminary injunction is returnable on Friday morning, June 18, 1971, the 30-day time provision contained in that Rule is inappropriate. For the reasons set forth in the accompanying memorandum of law, this Court has the power to direct defendants to produce those documents for inspection and copying.

MICHAEL D. HESS,
Assistant United States Attorney.

SWORN TO BEFORE ME

this 16th day of June, 1971.

RALPH I. LEE
Notary Public, State of New York
No. 41-2292838   Queens County
Term Expires March 30, 1973

UNITED STATES DISTRICT COURT
SOUTHERN DISTRICT OF NEW YORK
------------------------------------X

UNITED STATES OF AMERICA,   :

           Plaintiff,   :

             -v-   :

NEW YORK TIMES COMPANY, ARTHUR   :   NOTICE FOR PRODUCTION
OCHS SULZBERGER, HARDING F.   OF DOCUMENTS
BANCROFT, IVAN VEIT, FRANCIS A.   :   _____
COX, JAMES C. GOODALE, SYDNEY
GRUSON, WALTER MATTSON, JOHN Mc-   :   71 Civ. 2662
CABE, JOHN MORTIMER, JAMES RESTON,
JOHN B. OAKES, A. M. ROSENTHAL,   :
DANIEL SCHWARZ, CLIFTON DANIEL,
TOM WICKER, E. W. KENWORTHY,
FOX BUTTERFIELD, GERALD GOLD, ALLAN
M. SIEGAL, SAMUEL ABT, NEIL   :
SHEEHAN and HEDRICK SMITH,

                 :

          Defendants.   :

                 :
------------------------------------X

S I R S :

       PLEASE TAKE NOTICE that pursuant to Rule 34 of

the Federal Rules of Civil Procedure plaintiff hereby re-

quests that you produce and permit plaintiff, or persons

acting on its behalf, to inspect and copy the following

documents:

       1. Each of the 47 volumes of the classified study

entitled "History of U. S. Decision-Making Process on Viet-

nam Policy" referred to in the decision of the Hon. Murray

I. Gurfein, United States District Judge, dated June 15,

1971, and all copies of any of said volumes, or any part

thereof.

       2. The classified document entitled "The Command and

EXHIBIT "A"

Control Study of the Tonkin Gulf incident done by the Defense Department's Weapons System Evaluation Group in 1965" likewise referred to in Judge Gurfein's said decision, and all copies and summaries of said classified document, or any part thereof.

3. Each and every other classified document in the possession, custody, or control of defendants, or any of them.

PLEASE TAKE FURTHER NOTICE that the said documents shall be produced at 10:00 A. M. on June 17, 1971, in Room 401 of the United States Court House, Foley Square, New York, N. Y., at which time and place they will be inspected and copied as aforesaid.

Dated: New York, N. Y.

June 16, 1971.

Yours, etc.

WHITNEY NORTH SEYMOUR, Jr.
United States Attorney for the
Southern District of New York,
Attorney for Plaintiff.

By _____

MICHAEL D. HESS,
Assistant United States Attorney.
Office & Post Office Address:
United States Court House, Foley
Square, New York, N. Y. 10007.
Tel. 264:6318

TO:
MESSRS. CAHILL, GORDON, SONNETT, REINDEL & OHL
Attorneys for Defendant,
New York Times Company,
80 Pine Street,
New York, N. Y. 10005.

UNITED STATES DISTRICT COURT
SOUTHERN DISTRICT OF NEW YORK
--x

UNITED STATES OF AMERICA,   :

                     Plaintiff,   :

                              :

        v.   :

                              :

NEW YORK TIMES COMPANY, et al.,   :   71 Civ. 2662

                  Defendants.   :

--x

PLAINTIFF'S MEMORANDUM IN SUPPORT OF ITS MOTION FOR THE PRODUCTION OF DOCUMENTS

                                    WHITNEY NORTH SEYMOUR, JR.
                                    United States Attorney for the
                                    Southern District of New York,
                                    Attorney for Plaintiff
                                    United States of America.

MICHAEL D. HESS
HOWARD S. SUSSMAN
MILTON SHERMAN,
Assistant United States Attorneys,

        Of Counsel.

UNITED STATES DISTRICT COURT
SOUTHERN DISTRICT OF NEW YORK
--x

UNITED STATES OF AMERICA,   :

                              Plaintiff,   :

                                                   :

          v.   :

                                                   :   71 Civ. 2662

NEW YORK TIMES COMPANY, et al.,   :

                              Defendants.   :

--x

PLAINTIFF'S MEMORANDUM IN
SUPPORT OF ITS MOTION FOR
THE PRODUCTION OF DOCUMENTS

Preliminary Statement

This is an action for a preliminary and
permanent injunction to prevent publication by defendant,
New York Times Company, of documents the disclosure of which
would be detrimental to the national defense of the
United States.   By Order of the Honorable Murray I. Gurfein,
United States District Judge, dated June 15, 1971,

221

defendants have been temporarily restrained from publishing certain documents. Plaintiff believes that defendants have in their possession, custody or control other classified documents not mentioned in that temporary restraining Order.

In order to ascertain what documents defendants have in their possession, custody and control so that the national defense interests of the United States may be properly protected, plaintiff has served a notice for production of documents pursuant to Rule 34 of the Federal Rules of Civil Procedure. Although defendants' time to respond to that notice has not yet expired, plaintiff believes that defendants will not voluntarily produce the documents described in it. Plaintiff, therefore, requests this Court to order defendants to produce those documents.

ARGUMENT

THIS COURT HAS POWER TO GRANT THE ORDER PLAINTIFF SEEKS.

Although the 30-day period which Rule 34 allows for response to a notice for production has not yet expired,

this Court has power to "allow a shorter or a longer time." Rule 34(b). In addition, Rule 26(c) empowers this Court to "make any order which justice requires to protect a party or person from annoyance, embarrassment, oppression or undue burden or expense * * *." Of course, Rule 37(a)(2) authorizes a motion for an Order compelling inspection if a party, in response to a request for inspection under Rule 34, fails to permit an inspection as requested.

In all the circumstances, this Court should order defendants to produce, permit plaintiff to inspect and copy, the documents designated in plaintiff's notice for production of documents dated June 16, 1971.

CONCLUSION

The Order plaintiff seeks should be granted.

Dated: New York, New York
       June 16, 1971.

Respectfully submitted,

WHITNEY NORTH SEYMOUR, JR.
United States Attorney for the
Southern District of New York,
Attorney for Plaintiff
United States of America.

MICHAEL D. HESS
HOWARD S. SUSSMAN
MILTON SHERMAN,
Assistant United States Attorneys,

Of Counsel.

223

U.S. ASKING COURT FOR ORDER TO SEE TIMES DOCUMENTS

A HEARING TODAY

Newspaper Asserts It Fears Its Sources Will Be Exposed

By FRED P. GRAHAM

The Justice Department asked United States District Judge Murray I. Gurfein yesterday to order The New York Times to turn over for the Government's inspection the secret Pentagon study from which its Vietnam series has been drawn.

Late yesterday Judge Gurfein signed an order instructing The Times to appear in his court at 10 A.M. today to give reasons why it should not be ordered to produce the huge document.

The action came at about 5:30 P.M. after a lawyer for The Times, Floyd Abrams, met with Government attorneys in the United States Attorney's office here and told them that The Times would not voluntarily surrender the documents.

Called Important to Case

The Government asserted in papers filed with Judge Gurfein that examination of the papers "is important to the proper presentation of the Government's case" in proceedings for an injunction pending before the judge.

On Tuesday, the judge granted a temporary restraining order barring The Times from publishing further material from the documents for four days, and ordering a hearing for tomorrow morning on whether the publication ban should be continued thereafter.

In arguments before Judge Gurfein Tuesday, a lawyer for The Times insisted that to turn the documents over to the Government might permit agents to trace the source that had given the documents to the newspaper.

First Amendment Cited

The Judge was told that The Times feared that scientific tests of the study and its accompanying documents might permit the Government to trace the copying machine used to duplicate them, exposing the source. Arguing that the First Amendment shields newspapers from being forced to disclose their confidential sources, The Times's lawyer asserted that the Constitution thus protects the newspaper from having to surrender the documents.

The Times's lawyer, Prof. Alexander M. Bickel of the Yale Law School, also argued that the Government had its own copies of the 7,000-page work, which were available for the Government lawyers' inspection. Government sources have said that at least 15 copies were initially made when the study was written in 1968.

These arguments were made in opposition to the Justice De-

Continued on Page 18, Column 1

U.S. Asks Court Order to Allow Inspection

and Copying of Times Documents

NEWSPAPER GIVES ITS REPLY TODAY

Government Says It Must See Archive to Prepare Case for Injunction

Continued From Page 1, Col. 8

partment's effort to get The Times to give the archive back to the Government permanently. Judge Gurfein refused to order The Times to return them, and the Government returned to him yesterday with the demand that it be permitted to "inspect and copy" the papers.

Affidavit With Demand

The demand was accompanied by an affidavit by Michael D. Hess, the chief of the civil division in the United States Attorney's office here. In it, he said that the Government did not know precisely what documents The Times had, and that it needed to know to argue its case properly tomorrow.

Mr. Hess said that The Times had admitted having a multi-volume study entitled "History of U.S. Decision-Making Process on Vietnam Policy," plus a summary of a document on the Tonkin Gulf incidents. He said that the Government also suspected that The Times had additional secret papers, and he demanded that all be delivered to the United States Attorney's office for inspection.

Under the Federal Rules of Civil Procedure, the Government was required to ask The Times to turn over the papers voluntarily before it could ask for an order requiring that they be yielded. Mr. Abrams, a partner in the New York law firm of Cahill, Gordon, Sonnett, Reindel & Ohl, went to the United States Attorney's office and refused to comply voluntarily. Mr. Hess then obtained the show-cause order from Judge Gurfein yesterday.

In a related development, Representative Edward I. Koch, Manhattan Democrat, and five other persons asked permission to join the suit as defendants, to represent the interests of the reading public.

Filed by A.C.L.U.

The action, which was filed by lawyers for the American Civil Liberties Union, asserted that neither the Government nor The Times was in a position to protect the readers' right "to acquire information about the conduct of the United States Government [that is] vital to their interests as American citizens."

The others in the action are Aryeh Neier, executive director of the A.C.L.U., Edwin J. Oppenheimer, a law clerk who is preparing a legal brief challenging the constitutionality of the Vietnam war, and Edward J. Ennis, Ira Glasser and Nancy Lee Ennis, who said they depended upon The Times for much of their information on world affairs.

Judge Gurfein will also hear arguments on their request to join the suit at the hearing this morning.

James C. Goodale, vice president and general counsel of The Times, said that the newspaper would not oppose the motion of Mr. Koch and the others to join the suit. It was understood that The Times would not support the motion either, but would leave the matter to Judge Gurfein's discretion.

In Washington, the Department of Justice said yesterday that it had not ruled out filing criminal charges in the case.

Refuses to speculate

John W. Hushen, the department's spokesman, said in response to a question that "we would not rule out the filing of criminal charges." The department has thus far taken only civil actions.

Mr. Hushen would not speculate on the question of whom criminal charges might be brought against. He said only "against people who have violated Federal law." Asked what Federal laws, he mentioned these possibilities: "Theft of Government property, removal of Government property, unlawful publication of classified documents, or conspiracy to commit any one of the three."

In the meantime, reliable sources report that lawyers in the State Department were making their way through the study of the war to determine what foreign policy interests might be damaged by the publication of more material.

State Department Involved

State Department lawyers are reported working in cooperation with the Justice Department in preparation for the hearing on the issuance of a permanent injunction. They are trying to provide the Government with evidence to support the claim that the interest of the United States would be irreparably damaged.

A spokesman for the Defense Department said that 15 official copies of the archive had been prepared at the Pentagon and were now at various places.

The statements of several Government officials have identified their locations as: The Pentagon, six copies; the White House, one copy; the State Department, two copies (in the files of Nicholas DeB. Katzenbach, former Under Secretary, and William P. Bundy, former Assistant Secretary for Asia and the Far East); the Lyndon B. Johnson Library in Austin, one copy; the National Archives, two copies; the Rand Corporation, two copies, and Clark M. Clifford, former Secretary of Defense, one copy.

Pentagon sources confirmed that the chairman of the group that wrote the study was Leslie H. Gelb, a former Deputy Assistant Secretary of Defense for International Security Affairs. Mr. Gelb, now at the Brookings Institution here, could not be reached yesterday.

UNITED STATES DISTRICT COURT
SOUTHERN DISTRICT OF NEW YORK

---------------------------------------X

UNITED STATES OF AMERICA,   :

                        Plaintiff,   :

            -v-   :

NEW YORK TIMES COMPANY, et al.,   :

                        Defendants.   :

---------------------------------------X

**MEMORANDUM OF DEFENDANT
NEW YORK TIMES COMPANY
IN OPPOSITION TO MOTION
FOR PRODUCTION OF DOCU-
MENTS**

CAHILL, GORDON, SONNETT, REINDEL & OHL
Attorneys for Defendant New York
    Times Company
80 Pine Street
New York, N. Y. 10005

Of Counsel:

        Alexander M. Bickel
        Floyd Abrams
        William E. Hegarty

UNITED STATES DISTRICT COURT
SOUTHERN DISTRICT OF NEW YORK

---------------------------------------x

UNITED STATES OF AMERICA,   :

                Plaintiff,   :

         -v-   :   71 Civ. 2662

NEW YORK TIMES COMPANY, et al.,   :

              Defendants.   :

---------------------------------------x

MEMORANDUM OF DEFENDANT NEW YORK TIMES COMPANY IN OPPOSITION TO MOTION FOR PRODUCTION OF DOCUMENTS

This memorandum is submitted on behalf of the defendant New York Times Company ("the New York Times") in opposition to the motion of plaintiff, United States of America, seeking production of documents pursuant to Rule 34 of the Federal Rules of Civil Procedure. Defendant respectfully submits that the demand for production is in conflict with the Constitution of the United States, the Federal Rules of Civil Procedure and the Civil Rights Law of the State of New York and that it should not be granted.

THE ACTION

In this action, the United States seeks to bar

the New York Times from publishing significant newsworthy stories with respect to the single most controversial issue of the day - the Vietnam war. The government seeks to enjoin The Times from "further dissemination, disclosure or divulgence" from a 47 volume history completed in 1968 entitled "History of U. S. Decision-Making Process on Vietnam Policy" and a summary of a document relating to the Tonkin Gulf incident prepared by the Defense Department in 1965.

The action was commenced by the service upon The Times of a proposed order to show cause on June 15, 1971. On that date the Court entered a temporary restraining order, effective until 1:00 P.M. on June 19, 1971, restraining The Times from disclosing "the documents" referred to "or any portions thereof". Simultaneously, the Court denied the motion of the United States seeking to require The Times to "deliver to this Court forthwith all the aforementioned documents . . ." In its opinion, the Court observed that:

> "At this stage of the proceedings, I do not direct The New York Times or the other defendants to produce the documents pending the outcome of the litigation."

THE INSTANT MOTION

This instant motion was brought on, on one day's notice, on June 16, 1971 by an order to show cause seeking production of the volumes relating to the "History of the U.S. Decision-Making Process on Vietnam Policy", the 1965 summary relating to the Tonkin Gulf incident and "each and every other classified document in the possession, custody or control of the defendants, or any of them."* In the face of this Court's decision one day earlier declining to order The Times to place the documents in court, the United States now, again, seeks production of the documents-not in court but in its offices.

ARGUMENT

I.

THE UNITED STATES HAS NO LEGITIMATE NEED FOR PRODUC- TION OF THE DOCUMENTS

At the outset, we turn to the utter and total failure of the United States to demonstrate <u>any</u> legitimate

---

* The United States, however, has not made the slightest effort to demonstrate why it needs to view the documents - if at all - prior to the hearing on June 18, 1971 with respect to the granting of a preliminary injunction.

need for production of the sought documents. Since the
United States, by its own statements in court and in the
press, already has some 15 original copies of the documents,
it surely cannot require The Time's xerox copy to learn the
contents of the documents. As for the basis for the government's request, we are only told, by counsel, and in language
as broad and conclusory as can be drafted, that the production "is important to the proper presentation of the Government's case, and to the proper protection of the national
interest . . . ." What the importance is, why the documents
are needed, why the government cannot read its originals instead of The Time's xerox copy, is not disclosed in the
government's papers.

In such circumstances, even absent the constitutional
and statutory bars (to be discussed _infra_), to requiring The
Times to produce the documents to the United States, it is
self-evident that the sought production is improper. Discovery is not available to parties to obtain information already in their possession. Hefter v. National Airlines,
Inc., 14 F.R.D. 78 (S.D.N.Y. 1952); Grogan v. Pennsylvania
R. Co., 10 F.R.D. 456 (W.D.N.Y. 1950); Moss v. Lane, 50 F.R.D.
122 (W.D. Va. 1970).

As for the government's demand for "classified"

documents in the possession of The Times which it is "not authorized to have" other than the 1968 history relating to Vietnam and the 1965 Tonkin Gulf summary, one need turn no farther than Mr. Hess's affidavit for a clear demonstration of the impropriety of the government's demands. According to Mr. Hess, the government "is unable to specify these documents with precision but believes that defendants well know what documents they are." To say the very least, the Federal Rules do not permit documents to be demanded on so flimsy - if frank - a statement. "Other" classified documents are not referred to in the complaint of the United States. They have not been referred to in Mr. Hess's oral presentation to the Court. There is absolutely no basis for concluding that, in the language of Rule 26(b) of the Federal Rules, they are "relevant" to the subject matter of this case. See, e.g., Union Carbide Corp. v. Filtrol Corp., 12 F.R. Serv. 2d, 34.13, Case 4 (D. C. C. D. Cal. 1967); E. L. Bruce Co. v. Empire Millwork Corp., 1 F.R. Serv. 2d, 34.41, Case 1 (S.D.N.Y. 1958); Hanover Shoe, Inc. v. United Shoe Machinery Corp., 6 F.R. Serv. 2d, 34.41, Case 1 (D.C. M.D. Pa. 1962); Green Valley Products, Inc. v. Sterwood Corp., 13 F.R. Serv. 2d, 26b.31, Case 3, 308 Fed. Supp. (E.D.N.Y. 1969).

Nor, as Mr. Hess's affidavit candidly admits, are th.. sought documents specified "with precision". That being true, the case law is plain that production cannot be ordered. See, e.g., Camco, Inc. v. Baker Oil Tools, Inc., 12 F.R. Serv. 2d, 34.11, Case 8; 45 F.R.D. 384.

II

THE PRODUCTION SOUGHT BY THE UNITED STATES IS BARRED BY THE FIRST AMENDMENT

Since it is apparent that the United States cannot desire to view a sixteenth copy of the papers involved simply for historical reasons, it is apparent that another purpose must be present. The annexed affidavit of James Greenfield, Foreign Editor of The Times, makes perfectly clear what that purpose is: the Government's hope that examination by it of the documents will lead it to the Times' source for the documents. As Mr. Greenfield's affidavit demonstrates, production of the documents could well lead to such disclosure.

The entry of the United States into this area places it squarely at the heart of a constitutional issue the Supreme Court will apparently decide later this year. The question of when, if ever, journalists may be required to disclose their confidential sources is one which goes to the core of the First Amendment. That First Amendment rights are not easily to be dismissed or "balanced" out of existence is plain from a

plethora of Supreme Court opinions. Balancing with respect to the First Amendment does not commence with the party relying on the Amendment--speaker, writer or whatever--being obliged to prove that his interest in exercising his First Amendment right outweighs the interest of the state. The contrary is true. First Amendment rights are uniquely "preferred" in the Constitution, Thomas v. Collins, 323 U.S. 516, 530 (1945), Marsh v. Alabama, 326 U.S. 501, 509 (1946) and the courts thus "look even more closely" than usual when those rights are threatened. Ashton v. Kentucky, 384 U.S. 195, 200 (1966). For this reason, the Supreme Court has held that it is the state which must show "the gravest abuses, endangering paramount interests . . . and [that] no alternative regulation would combat such abuses without infringing First Amendment rights" before restrictions on free speech will be permitted. Sherbert v. Verner, 374 U.S. 398, 406-07 (1963); Thomas v. Collins, supra, at 530. And, where the state seeks information the disclosure of which can limit First Amendment freedoms, it must show "a substantial relation between the information sought and a subject of overriding and compelling state interest." Gibson v. Florida

Legislative Investigative Comm., 372 U.S. 539, 546 (1963).
See, NAACP v. Button, 371 U.S. 415, 438 (1963); Bates v.
Little Rock, 361 U.S. 516, 522-24 (1960). "A free press,"
the Supreme Court has observed, "stands as one of the
great interpreters between the government and the people.
To allow it to be fettered is to fetter ourselves."
Grosjean v. American Press Company, 297 U.S. 233, 250
(1936).

Constitutional interests of the highest order
are threatened by the effort of the United States to discover the source of The Times' Vietnam news stories. While
these rights are here defended by The Times, they are, in
fact, those of the public generally to "receive suitable
access to social, political, esthetic, moral and other
ideas." Red Lion Broadcasting Co. v. FCC, 395 U.S. 367,
390 (1969). For the First Amendment "rests on the assumption that the widest possible dissemination of information
from diverse and antagonistic sources is essential to the
welfare of the public. . . ." Associated Press v. United
States, 326 U.S. 1, 20 (1945). And that "[a]ny inroad made
upon the constitutional protection of a free press tends
to undermine the freedom of all men to print and to read

the truth." Craig v. Harney, 331 U.S. 367, 383 (1947)
(Murphy, J. concurring). As the Supreme Court observed
in its classic decision in Grosjean v. American Press
Co., Inc., supra:

> "The predominant purpose of the . . .
> [First Amendment] was to preserve an un-
> trammeled press as a vital source of public
> information. The newspapers, magazines and
> other journals of the country, it is safe
> to say, have shed and continue to shed, more
> light on the public and business affairs of
> the nation than any other instrumentality
> of publicity; and since informed public
> opinion is the most potent of all restraints
> upon misgovernment, the suppression or
> abridgement of the publicity afforded by a
> free press cannot be regarded otherwise than
> with grave concern." (297 U.S. at 250).

See, Thornhill v. Alabama, 310 U.S. 88, 102 (1940);
New York Times v. Sullivan, 376 U.S. 254, 269 (1964);
Time, Inc. v. Hill, 385 U.S. 374 (1967).

All this being said, it is hardly surprising
that the courts have increasingly recognized that substantive impediments to the gathering of news are as
violative of the First Amendment as would be statutes
providing for direct censorship of news. See, e.g.
Associated Press v. United States, 326 U.S. 1, 20 (1945);
Associated Press v. KVOS, Inc., 80 F.2d 575, 581 (9th Cir.
1935), rev'd on jurisdictional grounds, 299 U.S. 269 (1936).

In the area of the confidential relationship
between journalists and their sources, this has resulted
in ever-growing judicial protection so as to protect the
public's opportunity to know. Of the cases in this area,
Application of Caldwell, 434 F.2d 1081 (9th Cir. 1970)
stands pre-eminent. Caldwell, the only recent decision
of a Federal Court of Appeals,* the Court of Appeals had
before it a District Court opinion granting a protective
order to a New York Times reporter with respect to his
testimony before a Grand Jury. Caldwell, the reporter,
had argued before the District Court that he should
not be required to appear before the Grand Jury to
testify as to his communications from the Black
Panthers and that, alternatively, if his appearance
were to be required, an appropriate protective order should
be entered to preserve Caldwell's confidential relationship
with his news sources. The Court denied the first branch
of Caldwell's motion but did extend protective relief to

---

* In two state court cases, differing results have been
   reached. In both those cases, In Re Pappas, 266 N.E.2d 297
   (Mass. 1971) and Branzburg v. Hayes (Ct.App.Ky. 1970),
   the Supreme Court first granted a stay of enforcement of
   an order directing a reporter to testify to confidential
   source material and then granted certiorari. The cases
   are on the October, 1971 docket of the Supreme Court.

the extent of providing that Caldwell would not be obliged
to:

> ". . . reveal confidential associations that
> impinge upon the effective exercise of his
> First Amendment right to gather news for
> dissemination to the public through the press
> or other recognized media until such time as
> a compelling and overriding national interest
> which cannot be alternatively served has been
> established to the satisfaction of the Court."
> (Emphasis added; 311 F.Supp. at 360).

Upon Caldwell's refusal to appear before the Grand Jury
at all, he was held in contempt and appealed his conviction to the Court of Appeals for the Ninth Circuit. In
light of the United States' position in this Court, it
is noteworthy that the United States did not appeal from
the District Court's order. Nor, in the petition for
certiorari filed with the Supreme Court on December 16,
1970 by the United States, did the United States quarrel
with the scope or nature of the protective order granted
by the District Court. The Court of Appeals approved the
granting of the protective order, while reversing the
decision below with respect to the question of whether
Caldwell was obliged even to appear before the Grand Jury.
Holding that he did not, the Court concluded that:

"The very concept of a free press requires
that the news media be accorded a measure
of autonomy; that they should be free to
pursue their own investigations to their
own ends without fear of governmental interference, and that they should be able to
protect their investigative processes. To
convert news gatherers into Department of
Justice investigators is to invade the
autonomy of the press by imposing a governmental function upon them. To do so where
the result is to diminish their future
capacity as news gatherers is destructive
of their public function. To accomplish
this where it has not been shown to be
essential to the Grand Jury inquiry simply
cannot be justified in the public interest."
(Emphasis added; 434 F.2d at

The Court of Appeals in Caldwell further held

that the Government cannot obtain disclosure of materials

before a grand jury which could lead to the disclosure

of a confidential source absent proof of a crime, proof

that the information sought is essential to prove the

crime, and that it has made unsuccessful efforts to obtain

the information elsewhere. Whatever may be said of the

applicability of these tests in a grand jury context in

which a crime is under investigation,* in the present

---

* In our brief due to be submitted tomorrow with respect
  to the motion of the United States for a preliminary
  injunction, we will demonstrate that the Government
  cannot meet any of the three Caldwell tests.

context it is at least inescapable that "the information" sought by the Government--e.g. the xeroxes held by The Times--is already in the hands of the United States. There can thus be no justification, consistent with Caldwell, sufficient to warrant production of the documents.

Apart from its apparent acquiescence to the protective order granted by the District Court in Caldwell* the United States has itself issued "guidelines" with respect to the issuance of subpoenas which, if applied, plainly bar the current demand of the Government. The guidelines (39 U.S.L.W. 2111 (August 25, 1970)) provide that:

> "The Department of Justice does not consider the press 'an investigative arm of the government.' Therefore, all reasonable attempts should be made to obtain information from non-press sources before there is any consideration of sub- poenaing the press."

---

* Numerous other similar holdings have recently issued. See People v. Dohrn, Cir. Ct., Cook County, Illinois, No. 69-3808) [in criminal action, Government barred from issuing subpoenas to media absent prior judicial approval]; Alioto v. Cowles Communications, Inc., U.S.D.C., N.D. Cal., No. 52150, trans- cript of December 4, 1969, pp. 165-67 [in libel action court refused to hold authors of magazine article in contempt for failure to disclose sources]; Air Transport Ass'n. et al., and United States v. Air Professional Air Traffic Controllers Organization, et al., U.S.D.C., E.D.N.Y., Nos. 70-C-400-410, transcript of April 6, 1970, pp. 18-24, 36; transcript of April 7, 1970, pp. 21, 38-39, 149-51 [in contempt proceeding reporter not required to produce notes which were basis of article]; People v. Rios (Cal.Super.Ct., No. 75129, July 15, 1970) [in criminal case, subpoena demanding television "out-takes" quashed].

The guidelines thus provide that subpoenas will not be issued prior to first negotiating with the press and, if the negotiations fail, then receiving the Attorney General's approval for the issuance of the subpoenas. In requesting the Attorney General's authorization for a subpoena, the guidelines provide:

"C. The government should have unsuccessfully attempted to obtain the information from alternative non-press sources.

"D. Authorization requests for subpoenas should normally be limited to the verification of published information and to such surrounding circumstances as relate to the accuracy of the published information.

"E. Great caution should be observed in requesting subpoena authorization by the Attorney General for unpublished information, or where an orthodox First Amendment defense is raised or where a serious claim of confidentiality is alleged.

"F. Even subpoena authorization requests for publicly disclosed information should be treated with care because, for example, cameramen have recently been subjected to harassment on the grounds that their photographs will become available to the government.

"G. In any event, subpoenas should, wherever possible, be directed at material information regarding a limited subject matter, should cover a reasonably limited period of time, and should avoid requiring production of a large volume of unpublished material. They should give reasonable and timely notice of the demand for documents."

In light of the fact that the United States possesses the documents, copies of which it now seeks, it is plain that its demand for production served on The Times is flatly inconsistent with the guidelines themselves.

Finally, even if the Government could meet the stern Caldwell tests and even if it could meet the tests of its own guidelines, we submit that in this case--a classic one of political reporting on the basis of information obtained in confidence--the documents could not properly be ordered produced. As we will demonstrate in our brief to be submitted tomorrow, the very fact that publication of this information could not be punished under the Espionage Act demonstrates that there is no "overriding national interest" here such as could possibly justify forcing a reporter to breach his confidence. There is indeed, in a case such as this, if there ever is, an overriding national interest in protecting the confidence and thus making this sort of reporting possible. Government officials are here trying by injunctive process and disguised subpoenas to shield other Government officials, past and present, from searching scrutiny in precisely the way in which New York Times v. Sullivan, 376 U.S. 254 (1964)

held the law of libel cannot protect them consistently with the First Amendment.

The First Amendment is not so fragile as the United States in this case would have it. The demand for documents violates the First Amendment.

III

COMPULSORY PRODUCTION OF THE
DOCUMENTS WOULD VIOLATE THE
NEW YORK CIVIL RIGHTS LAW

In addition to the impropriety of the government's
demand for documents under the Constitution and the Federal
Rules, the demand is also violative of Section 79-h of the
Civil Rights Law of New York.*

This section in its relevant part provides that:

"Notwithstanding the provisions of any
general or specific law to the contrary, no
professional journalist or newscaster employed
or otherwise associated with any newspaper,
magazine, news agency, press association, wire
service, radio or television transmission station
or network, shall be adjudged in contempt by any
court, the legislature or other body having
contempt powers, for refusing or failing to disclose any news or the source of any such news
coming into his possession in the course of
gathering or obtaining news for publication or
to be published in a newspaper, magazine, or for
broadcast by a radio or television transmission station or network, by which he is

---

* While the issue is not free from doubt, the prevailing
view is that state statutes govern with respect to
testimonial "privileges" or the like. See, e.g., Mass.
Mut. Life Insc. Co. v. Brei, 311 F.2d 463 (2d Cir. 1962);
Krijak v. W. C. Brooks & Sons, Inc., 320 F.2d 37 (4th
Cir. 1963); Merlin v. Aetna Life Insc. Co., 180 F.Supp.
90 (S.D.N.Y. 1960); Stiles v. Clifton Springs Sanitorium,
74 F.Supp. 907 (W.D.N.Y. 1947); Cepeda v. Cohane, 233
F.Supp. 465 (S.D.N.Y. 1964); Munzer v. Swedish American
Line, 35 F.Supp. 493 (S.D.N.Y. 1940).

professionally employed or otherwise associated
in a news gathering capacity."

The legislative history of Section 79-h demonstrates its applicability to the present case. In his
official statement, released by his press secretary on
May 12, 1970, Nelson A. Rockefeller, the Governor of New
York, approved Section 79-h, stating that:

"This 'Freedom of Information Bill for
Newsmen' will make New York State - the
Nation's principal center of news gathering
and dissemination - the only state that clearly
protects the public's right to know and the
First Amendment rights of all legitimate newspapermen, reporters and television and radio
broadcasters.

"The bill protects journalists and news-
casters from charges of contempt in any proceeding brought under State law for refusing
or failing to disclose information or sources
of information obtained in the course of
gathering news for publication.

"The types of information that need not
be disclosed by newsmen are written, oral and
pictorial information and communications concerning local, national or world-wide events
or any other matter of public concern or public
interest or affecting the public welfare.

"Freedom on the press is one of the foundations upon which our form of government is based.
A representative democracy, such as ours, cannot
exist unless there is a free press both willing
and able to keep the public informed of all the
news.

"The threat to a newsman of being charged
with contempt and of being imprisoned for

failing to disclose his information or its sources
can significantly reduce his ability to gather
vital information. That this is a real and
imminent threat has been demonstrated by the
statements of several prominent reporters that
valuable sources of information have been cut
off because of recent attempts by the Federal
Government to require the disclosure of information obtained by reporters in confidence."

Compulsory production of the documents sought by
the United States would thus violate this state statute,
as well as the Constitution and the Federal Rules.

CONCLUSION

The demand of the United States for the production of documents should be denied.

.

Respectfully submitted,

CAHILL, GORDON, SONNETT,
 REINDEL & OHL
Attorneys to The New York
 Times Company
Office and P.O. Address
80 Pine Street
New York, New York 10005
212-944-7400

Of Counsel:

Alexander M. Bickel
Floyd Abrams
William E. Hegarty

UNITED STATES DISTRICT COURT
SOUTHERN DISTRICT OF NEW YORK

------------------------------------X

UNITED STATES OF AMERICA,   :

                    Plaintiff,   :

           -v-   :   71 Civ. 2662

NEW YORK TIMES COMPANY, et al.,   :

                    Defendants.   :

------------------------------------X

STATE OF NEW YORK)
                  : SS.:
COUNTY OF NEW YORK)

          FLOYD ABRAMS, being duly sworn, deposes and says:

          1. I am a member of the firm of Cahill, Gordon,
Sonnett, Reindel & Ohl, counsel to defendant New York Times
Company. I submit this affidavit in opposition to the motion
of the United States, brought on on one day's notice by order to
show cause, seeking production of documents. I respectfully
submit that plaintiff's extraordinary demand is in conflict with
the Constitution of the United States, the Federal Rules of Civil
Procedure and the Civil Rights Law of the State of New York and
that it should not be granted.

          2. In this action, the United States seeks to bar the
New York Times from reporting a news story of the utmost import
relating to the single most controversial public issue of the
day--the war in Vietnam. The United States maintains that
The Times should be enjoined from "further dissemination,
disclosure or divulgence" of materials contained in a 47 volume

historical study completed in 1968 entitled "History of U. S. Decision-Making Process on Vietnam Policy" and a summary of a document entitled "The Command and Control Study of the Tonkin Gulf incident done by the Defense Department's Weapons System Evaluation Group in 1965". The United States has conceded both in its oral argument to this Court earlier this week, and in a variety of statements to the press, that it already has some 15 copies of the documents it now seeks to force the New York Times to produce. On this motion, it seeks a sixteenth copy -- that in the possession of The Times.

3. On Tuesday, June 15, 1971, this Court, inter alia, denied the motion of the United States seeking a temporary restraining order directing The Times to deliver to this Court the documents sought. By the present motion made on Wednesday, June 16, 1971, the United States seeks all this Court denied it the day before and more. One day after this Court declined to order The Times to produce the documents in Court, the United States seeks to have them produced in their offices. There is no basis for this Court to change its ruling on this critical issue.

The Lack of Need for Production

4. Entirely apart from the grave constitutional questions posed by the efforts of the United States, contrary to all precedent, to suppress publication by the New York Times of its newsworthy articles, I respectfully submit the motion should peremptorily be denied because of its evident lack of merit.

If what the United States seeks to learn is what the documents say, it need only read one of the many sets in its possession and not the xerox copy held by The Times.

5. The United States has not made the slightest effort to justify its need for the production of duplicate sets of that which it already has. The sole attempted showing of need is Mr. Hess' assertion in his affidavit that the production "is important to the proper presentation of the Government's case, and to the proper protection of the national interest . . . ." Mr. Hess has not favored us with even the most amorphous explanation of the basis of his conclusory statement, nor any factual justification which could suggest the desirability of production of the documents.

The Constitutional Vice of Production

6. Since the United States cannot want to "inspect" the documents to relearn its printed contents, it is evident that its purpose is different in nature--that of a disguised subpoena seeking what leads the copies may have as to the identity of The Times' source. As the accompanying affidavit of James Greenfield, Foreign Editor of The Times, demonstrates, production might well result in disclosure of the source. That being true, the demand poses a most substantial constitutional problem for the Government. Three cases are now pending before the United States Supreme Court awaiting argument this fall as to the constitutional propriety of requiring disclosure of confidential sources. In Application of Caldwell, 434 F.2d 1081 (9th Cir. 1970), the only one of the three decided by a United States

-3-

Court of Appeals, the court held that such disclosure could only
be required where the Government demonstrated, _inter alia_, that
it could not obtain the sought information elsewhere. The United
States has not appealed from that part of the decision of the
Court of Appeals. Since it has the originals of the documents
it seeks from The Times, it plainly cannot meet this essential
element of the Caldwell test.

The Statutory Vice of Production

7. As our memorandum of law demonstrates, the demand
for production also violates the laws of New York State. Section 79-h of the Civil Rights Law of New York is explicit in
permitting a newsman to decline to disclose "any news or the
source of any such news coming into his possession . . . ."

The Third Demand of the United States

8. I turn in conclusion to plaintiff's additional
catch-all demand for all classified documents held by The Times,
apart from the studies referred to above. As to this demand,
Mr. Hess observes that the United States "is unable to specify
these documents with precision but believes that defendants well
know what documents they are." While the frankness of the
Government is to be commended, the Federal Rules could hardly be
clearer in providing that only documents which are of relevance
to litigation and which can be specified "with precision" must
be produced. That the additional category of documents sought
by the United States is irrelevant is demonstrated by the briefest review of its complaint which is based entirely upon the 47
volume study and the Tonkin Gulf summary. That the documents

-4-

have not been specified with sufficient precision is demonstrable by a mere reading of Mr. Hess' affidavit.

9. In essence, what the Government seeks by this motion is the production of documents which it already has, which it does not need, and which, if ordered produced, could result in a most serious violation of the First Amendment, as well as the law of New York. There is no basis in law for the granting of the Government's demand.

_____
Floyd Abrams

Sworn to before me this
17th day of June, 1971.

_____
Notary Public

-5-

71 Civ. No. 2662

UNITED STATES DISTRICT COURT
SOUTHERN DISTRICT OF NEW YORK

UNITED STATES OF AMERICA,

Plaintiff,

-against-

NEW YORK TIMES COMPANY, et al.,

Defendants.

AFFIDAVIT

CAHILL, GORDON, SONNETT, REINDEL & OHL

Attorneys for Defendant
New York Times Company

Office and Post Office Address,
80 Pine Street,
Borough of Manhattan, New York, N.Y. 10005
WHitehall 4-7400

To ....

....
Attorney for ....

Due and timely service of a copy of the within
is hereby admitted.

Dated, N.Y., ..., 19 ......

....
Attorneys for ....

252

UNITED STATES DISTRICT COURT

SOUTHERN DISTRICT OF NEW YORK

--x
UNITED STATES OF AMERICA,   :

                        Plaintiff,   :

        -against-   :   71 Civil 2662

THE NEW YORK TIMES COMPANY, ET AL.,   :

                        Defendants.   :

--x

STATE OF NEW YORK   )
                       : SS.:
COUNTY OF NEW YORK   )

        JAMES L. GREENFIELD, being duly sworn, deposes
and says:

        1.   I am Foreign Editor of The New York Times.
I make this affidavit in opposition to the motion made on
behalf of the United States Government by order to show
cause, dated June 16, 1971, for an order requiring The New
York Times and the other defendants named in the above-
entitled action to produce the documents which are the
subject matter of this action for inspection and copying
by the plaintiff.

        2.   In my capacity as Foreign Editor of The New
York Times, I have examined these documents. They consist
of xeroxed copies of the documents referred to in the

articles which have appeared in The New York Times.
Many of the xeroxed copies bear handwritten notations.

     3. Production of these documents in accordance
with the plaintiff's application would facilitate identification by the plaintiff, or certain of its agencies, of the
confidential source of the material which has been the basis
for the articles published in The New York Times and which
The New York Times proposes to publish.

     4. The effective exercise of the freedom of the
press guaranteed to The New York Times by the First
Amendment requires that we protect the identity of the
sources of such material.

Jams L. Gufeld

Sworn to before me the
17th day of June, 1971.

Mary Ann C. Simpson
Notary Public

MARY ANN C. SIMPSON
Notary Public, State of New York
No. 41-3682775
Qualified in Queens County
Commission Expires March 30, 1973

Sir :- Please take notice that the within is a *(certified)* true copy of a duly entered in the office of the clerk of the within named court on 19

Dated,

Yours, etc.,

Attorney for

Office and Post Office Address

To

Attorney(s) for

Sir :- Please take notice that an order of which the within is a true copy will be presented for settlement to the Hon.

one of the judges of the within named Court, at

on the day of 19

at M.

Dated,

Yours, etc.,

Attorney for

Office and Post Office Address

To

Attorney(s) for

Index No. 71 Civil 2662 Year 19

UNITED STATES DISTRICT COURT
SOUTHERN DISTRICT OF NEW YORK

UNITED STATES OF AMERICA,

Plaintiff,

-against-

THE NEW YORK TIMES COMPANY,
ET AL.,

Defendants.

AFFIDAVIT

CAHILL, GORDON, SONNETT,
REINDEL
Attorney for Defendant The New
York Times Company

Office and Post Office Address, Telephone

80 Pine Street
New York, N. Y. 10005
WH 4-7400

To

Attorney(s) for

Service of a copy of the within

is hereby admitted.

Dated,

....

....

Attorney(s) for

1500- © 1963, JULIUS BLUMBERG, INC., 80 EXCHANGE PLACE, N. Y. 4

255

UNITED STATES DISTRICT COURT

SOUTHERN DISTRICT OF NEW YORK

- x
                                          :
UNITED STATES OF AMERICA,
                                          :
                                                    71 Civ. 2662
                                          :
            Plaintiff,
                                          :
        -vs-
                                          :

                                          :
NEW YORK TIMES COMPANY, et al.,
                                          :
            Defendants.
- x

Before:

                HON. MURRAY I. GURFEIN,

                            District Judge

                    New York, June 17, 1971
                        10: a.m.

                APPEARANCES:

WHITNEY NORTH SEYMOUR, JR., ESQ. United States Attorney,
                    for the government;
        Michael D. Hess, Esq and
        Silvio J. Molli, Esq, Assistant United States Attorneys,

CAHILL, GORDON, SONNETT, REINDEL & OHL, ESQS.,
                    Attorneys for Defendant New York
                    Times Company;
        Floyd Abrams, Esq.,
        Lawrence J. McKay, Esq., and
        Eugene R. Scheilman, Esq., of Counsel

MELVIN L. WULF, ESQ.,
                    Attorney for Edward Ennis, et al.,
    -and-
NORMAN D. DORSEN, ESQ.

STEPHEN SCHUMAN, ESQ.,
                    Appearing pro se.

                              - -

            THE COURT: Which matter is this, Mr. Hess?

            MR. HESS: Does your Honor want to take up

our discovery motion first or the intervention motion?

            THE COURT: I think the intervention first,

I would guess.

            How many intervenors are there?   I am not

going to hear oral argument on this?

            MR. WULF: Just one.

            THE COURT: The American Civil Liberties

Union.

            I have read your papers.   I told you the

other day that I would be delighted to have the American

Civil Liberties Union file a brief as amicus.   I am

going to deny your motion for intervention.

            MR. WULF: Won't you hear us, your Honor?

            THE COURT: I can't hear you on this because

I don't think there is anything to argue.   Do you claim

you have an intervention as of right or as of discretion?

MR. WULF: As of right, your Honor.

THE COURT: As of right?   I deny that.

Next.   As of discretion.

MR. WULF: We also move under that provision, your Honor.

THE COURT: I know you do, and I am trying to say now that although you may have standing to start a separate action, which you are at liberty to do, I believe that the counsel for the New York Times can adequately represent the interests of the times and the public.   I don't think they are in conflict.

In other words, I don't believe that the Times is in here avowedly for the purpose of selling newspapers but for the purpose of asserting that the general public has a right to read and hear.   In that sense it is exactly the same problem that you would pose as an inter-venor.

Now let me explain to you what the practical difficulties would be.   We are now at the threshold of the litigation.   If I permit you to intervene now, it requires pleading.   Nothing is done in this court orally.   It requires an opportunity for you to submit evidence.   It requires a complication beyond what I consider the necessities of the case.

In denying your motion to intervene formally,
I will say that you may have leave to apply to intervene
as the proceeding proceeds further and if it should come
to the stage of a trial.

MR. WULF: We have already filed pleadings,
your Honor, and I don't think to that extent that our
intervention would unduly delay or prejudice the proceedings.

THE COURT: I know that.   But if I let
you in, I would have to let every citizen in.   The only
ground you have is that you read the New York Times and
you have a constitutional right to read it.   But there
are 200 million people with the same right.

MR. WULF: But we assert that that right
should be represented in the proceedings through a party,
your Honor, not because the New York Times will not
represent those interests adequately, but that they won't
represent them fully and that the readers have a supplementary and substantial constitutional right that should
be heard and presented vigorously to the Court in order
that the full breadth of the profound constitutional
issues in this case are presented to the Court.

THE COURT: If there are profound constitutional issues - I said that without any prompting - that

I will allow you to file briefs with the parties. You may tell me anything on the constitutional subject.

What I am doing is I am saying I will not allow you to bring independent evidence or try to control the proceedings, which I will leave to the adversary parties, namely, the United States and the New York Times.

MR. WULF: We wouldn't try to control the proceedings. Of course, we would want to work closely with the New York Times.

THE COURT: I am very sympathetic with your point of view as trying to represent the people.of the United States and raising very important constitutional issues. In my judgment, in my discretion, I believe that you will adequately represent those interests by the filing of briefs. And, as I said, I reserve the right also to let you argue orally, which I have not yet determined, but I do not wish any other parties in the case and I don't think that you come within the rule which makes it compulsory for me to have you intervene. That is my ruling.

MR. WULF: May I argue to that question of our eligibility as of right, your Honor?

THE COURT: Yes, you may argue to that.

MR. WULF: I think that under the rule we as applicants do have standing.   The 24(a)(2) has three elements to it: The party seeking to intervene must have an interest relating to the transaction; the disposition of the action may as a practical matter impair or impede the ability to protect that interest; and the third element is the question of adequacy of representation.

As representatives of the public who read the New York Times, it is our position that their interest in a sense is even dominant to that of the New York Times because the purpose of the First Amendment's right of free press is not merely to allow the press to publish daily --

THE COURT: Let me ask you a simple question. Should I allow 200 million people to intervene?

MR. WULF: No, sir. · I would be quite satisfied if you just allowed our motion to intervene and denied any others which might be filed.

THE COURT: Suppose the other 199 million come in tomorrow?   What do I do?

MR. WULF: You can deny those, your Honor.

THE COURT: I see.   Good answer.

I don't read Rule 24(a), "Intervention of Right,"

to go that far.   And there is also the case ---

MR. WULF: The problem is that they generally arise in a commercial context where, of course, it is easier to describe the interest in a concrete and palpable way.   But the interest here, of course, is one of a constitutional dimension, which doesn't involve tangible assets as a commercial case would.   And it is a little bit more difficult ---

THE COURT: It is more difficult.   I'm interested in hearing all parties and anybody who has a real interest, but I have to be limited to some extent by judicial necessity, that is, the court requirements, the necessity for a careful but speedy determination in view of the nature of the matter.

The only case I can see that is really in point is Hatton v. County Board of Education, which is recorded in 422 F. 2d 457, which is a decision of the United States Court of Appeals for the Sixth Circuit on February 26, 1970, in which they held that where a school teacher, Negro school teacher, claimed that she was discharged for discriminatory racial reasons, that the parents of the school children did not, I repeat not, have a right to intervene as a matter of right.

That's pretty close to this, in a sense.   If

it were a matter of first impression, that is another

story.   But I agree with the reasoning for the reasons

I have already stated and therefore I will deny the

intervention on both grounds under (a) and (b).

    But I hope you will file an amicus brief.

    MR. WULF: We shall, your Honor.

    MR. HESS: With your Honor's permission, we

would like to file an affidavit with regard to the

intervention question.

    THE COURT: Yes.

    MR. SCHUMAN: Your Honor, I have submitted

papers in support of a motion to appear as amicus curiae.

I do this as a citizen of the United States deeply

concerned that my rights under the Constitution to read

the New York Times and to find out what our government

is doing are being compromised, and I respectfully

request your Honor to grant me permission to submit a

brief in support --

    THE COURT: Whom do you represent?   Any

organization?

    MR. SCHUMAN: I represent myself as a citizen

of the United States of America.

    THE COURT: The motion is denied.

    MR. SCHUMAN: May I speak to that?

THE COURT: No.

Does that dispose of the interventions?

MR. HESS: I believe it does, your Honor.

THE COURT: Let's proceed to the motion by the government -- order to show cause, rather.

MR. HESS: Your Honor, the government brought on an order to show cause yesterday before your Honor late in the afternoon, asking that this motion be brought on today and asking for inspection of the documents in the hands of the New York Times.   This is pursuant to Rule 34 of the Federal Rules of Civil Procedure.

Your Honor, the Federal Rules of Civil Procedure were amended in 1970, effective July 1st.   They were made more liberal and several of the amendments related to discovery procedures.   Under Rule 34 of the amended rules, a party need serve a notice of production on the other party to obtain documents.   We have done this.   The relevancy is a major criteria with regard to this rule and here, your Honor, it is self-evident, the documents are the heart of this case.

Your Honor, it is important to remember in this matter that we are talking about documents that are the property of the United States.   They are stolen or embezzled property by their very nature.   They are

top-secret, confidential documents.

The government feels that we have a right to identify what was taken from us, we have a right to identify what the New York Times has in its possession. They admit that they have a secret study; they don't particularize how much of that study they have.   We are not asking today for its return and we are not asking today that it be given to your Honor.   We are merely asking that we have proper inspection under the Civil Rules of Procedure of the documents that they hold.

As your Honor recently indicated this morning, we are on the threshold of this case.   Tomorrow we have a preliminary injunction hearing.   The government will have a burden, as the plaintiff, at that hearing but we can't be forced to go ahead and litigate in the dark. The Times cannot ask this Court or the government to decide and yet hide the evidence from the Court.

Your Honor, if the government carries the day tomorrow your Honor will be faced with the problem of framing an injunction.   The Court cannot frame an injunction unless the Court knows what needs to be enjoined. The government cannot properly proceed to prove its case unless we know what documents the Times has in its possession.

THE COURT: Let me ask you this: Why is it not a fishing expedition in the sense of seeking general discovery which is normally constitutionally prohibited?

MR. HESS: Well, your Honor, we feel it is not a fishing expedition because we want to show why these documents, or we will have to show, your Honor, why these documents should not be published, why they should be enjoined, why it will hurt the national interest to have them published.   In order to do that we have to know what documents the Times has and what documents they intend to publish.   They have stated they intend to publish additional articles in the series but they have not stated with particularity what documents they have.

THE COURT: Couldn't you do that by interrogatory tomorrow, by asking the representative of the Times to testify and ask him what he has and what he intends to publish?

MR. HESS: That is what we would like to find out, your Honor, and if the Times would state with particularity to us.

THE COURT: Let me hold that in abeyance. That is a thought I had as you went along.

rma

MR. HESS: This has occurred to us as well, your Honor, but under Rule 34 we felt we should proceed as the rule spells out for production and inspection.

THE COURT: Do we know -- I say "we" -- I mean does the government know or can it tell the Court, are these original documents or are they photostats or Xerox copies of the documents? Does anybody know that?

MR. HESS: We are not sure, your Honor, but we think they are original documents.

THE COURT: You think they are?

MR. HESS: Yes. We think it is somewhat ironic that the Times is coming into court stating that they want openness, they want freedom for the right of people to know, and yet they are refusing to let the people or the government or this Court know exactly what documents they have in their possession. That is why we have made our motion today.

Your Honor, I am reminded of the fact that the Times has a motto, "All the news that's fit to print," and they publish that every day in their paper for the last 75 years, and, your Honor, I can't imagine that any news that the Times would consider unfit to be inspected would truly be fit to be printed, and they state they want to print it and under the rules of discovery and

for our enlightenment and for the enlightenment of the

Court, so that the proceeding can go ahead in an or-

ganized manner, we feel production and inspection of these

documents is necessary.

THE COURT: I suppose one of the questions

is would the government agree, if I should grant this

motion, to have the documents kept secret.   I suppose

it would?

MR. HESS: Yes, your Honor, it would.   We

would just like to see ---

THE COURT: I can see the Times not wanting --

I won't mention any other newspapers -- others getting

hold of it before anything happens and they can be

enjoined.

MR. HESS: I can understand that consideration,

but we just want to inspect and we will inspect in the

presence of representatives from the New York Times

and see what documents they have.

THE COURT: I will hear the other side.

MR. ABRAMS: Your Honor, my name is Floyd

Abrams.   I am a member of the firm of Cahill, Gordon,

Sonnett, Reindel & Ohl.

As Mr. Hess indicates, this motion, as the

earlier motion this week, came on late in the day and I

should like to ask leave of the Court to submit certain

papers in response to that motion at this time.

THE COURT: The Rule 34 to show cause?

MR. ABRAMS: Yes, sir.

Your Honor, this has been an astonishing week in the history of journalism. It is astonishing because the United States has chosen to bring the New York Times to Court in an effort to enjoin publication of obviously newsworthy articles. It is astonishing in the manner in which this has been timed and the amount of time that has been given, indeed the lack of time that has been given throughout these proceedings.

THE COURT: Lack of time for what?

MR. ABRAMS: Lack of time to reflect upon the issues, your Honor.

THE COURT: I asked The New York Times whether it would consent not to publish for a limited time so that these very issues could be discussed, and The Times refused.

MR. ABRAMS: Yes, sir, The Times refused and would continue to do so.

THE COURT: That is why I don't understand --

MR. ABRAMS: I am speaking of a motion such as the one before you this morning, your Honor, which was brought on by order to show cause yesterday in circumstances in which I hope I can persuade you, sir, that there is absolutely no need whatever for the Government to have these papers, with a single exception which I will come to in a moment.

Your Honor Mr. Hess has said that his purpose is to let the people know, and I would think that comes with no small irony in a situation such as the present.

What this motion is, your Honor, is an attempt to require The New York Times to make available to the United States Xeroxes, which is what The Times has, of certain papers which the United States in its complaint

purported to specify.

In its complaint in this action, your Honor, the United States did not come in and say, "We don't know what the documents are, we don't know what The Times has."

It filed a complaint, it referred to certain documents, this case is going to go on.   There is absolutely no need, No. 1, your Honor, for any urgency with respect to the production of documents by The New York Times.

THE COURT: Let's be practical about it:

Does The Times have a fundamental objection and, if so, what is it, to letting the Government know what it has?

MR. ABRAMS: The Times has a very fundamental objection, your Honor.   Apart from the fact the Government has the papers it wants --

THE COURT: That is another point.

MR. ABRAMS: The Times has a most substantial constitutional problem with respect to production of these papers.

THE COURT: I am not asking about production. Listen to me very carefully.   I am asking you now, and it has nothing to do with production, whether The Times

would object to giving the Government a list, with

description, only of the documents which it has in its

possession coming from the Pentagon.

MR. ABRAMS: The Times, your Honor, in response

to the complaint in this action has been prepared to

respond in terms of which documents it has, yes, sir.

The Times is not prepared, your Honor, to allow the

Government to inspect the documents which The New York

Times has.

THE COURT: Let's take one thing at a time

then. You now say on behalf of The Times that you will

give a list to the Government of the documents which you

have with sufficient description so that they can identify

them as against their own?

MR. ABRAMS: The Times will give a list which

sets forth the documents that it has.

May I turn to the disclosure --

THE COURT: That, if you want to, can be made

into the form of an order, but if you say you will produce

it by, let's say, five o'clock today, I will accept that.

Is that all right?

MR. ABRAMS: We would be prepared to advise the

Government this afternoon of the documents.

THE COURT: So that would then limit the question

of whether there are other documents -- that will be under

some kind of affirmation by somebody or other --

MR. ABRAMS: Wait a minute, sir, I want to make

sure I am making my position very clear.

The Government has filed a complaint here and

referred to two kinds of documents, your Honor, one

supposed 47-volume series and one summary with respect

to the Tonkin Gulf.   That is the issue as framed by the

Government in this case.

With respect to that issue as framed, we will

be prepared to advise what we have.   We are absolutely

unprepared, sir, to go through our files and make avail-

able to the Government, or to advise the Government of

anything else which is outside the scope of those issues

as framed in the complaint.

THE COURT: Why is that?

MR. ABRAMS: Why is that?   Because that would

be an ultimate fishing expedition through files of a

newspaper, which are as protected by the First Amendment

as one could imagine.

THE COURT: I am trying to be practical about

this thing.   The Government has the documents.   You

are not disclosing anything to them --

MR. ABRAMS: I am not sure we are talking about

the same documents, your Honor.   To the extent you are

speaking about the documents which the Government refers

to in its complaint, I have said that we will advise what

we have.

THE COURT: Without deciding anything at this

moment, I just want to put this question to The New York

Times through you:

It is claimed that The New York Times has an

unauthorized possession of documents purportedly taken by

somebody or through somebody from the files of the

Pentagon.   The Government apparently in its complaint

knew of certain documents only because The New York Times

disclosed that in its article.   Therefore, apparently

when they drew their complaint the Government mentioned

those articles which The New York Times had admitted it

had.

The question now is, does The New York Times,

so that the whole matter can be adjudicated, have any

other documents besides those mentioned in the complaint

which came from the same source?

MR. ABRAMS: Your Honor, The New York Times

is not prepared to advise the Government with respect to

any documents whatsoever, with the exception of the docu-

ments referred to in the complaint in this action and

which were referred to in the stories published in The

New York Times.

THE COURT: I ask you again, why is that?

MR. ABRAMS: Why is that? The answer to that,

your Honor, is that a newspaper has a great many sources

of information, a great many documents, a great many

employees, a great many secrets, which is the essence in

good part, your Honor, of journalism.

THE COURT: No question about that.

MR. ABRAMS: And The Times absolutely cannot

make available --

THE COURT: The question is more limited.

Nobody would tolerate a fishing expedition into the files

of a newspaper.

MR. ABRAMS: What then is the Government talking

about, your Honor?

THE COURT: Unauthorized or stolen documents,

the Government is talking about. There is a big

difference.

MR. ABRAMS: The Government is talking about

documents which were referred to in The New York Times,

which they have made a subject of this inquiry.

THE COURT: I am not going to belabor the point because I can't force you, sitting here, from the bench to do it. But I am wondering, and I must wonder, why, limiting the category as I have to unauthorized documents and avoiding by all means any fishing expedition into the files of The New York Times or any other newspaper, there could not be merely a listing and not a turning over -- we are not talking about that now -- or an answer to the question of are there any other documents that came from the Pentagon, so that the Court can view the entire matter. That's all I am asking you.

It is your privilege to answer it, if you want to.

MR. ABRAMS: May I say this, your Honor:

My present inclination, and it is a very strong one, is to adhere to the position that I have set forth to you today. This is a case, as your Honor has pointed out and as we are very well aware, sir, of immense magnitude. Issues of this sort are ones which I as counsel wish to talk to my client about.

THE COURT: All right.

MR. ABRAMS: I will tell you, sir, that it is my inclination now to say that the issue --

THE COURT: Then I misunderstood you before and

I am glad we carried on this colloquy.   Talk to them

and find out what they want to do.

            MR. ABRAMS: I will do that, sir.   But I do

want the position that I express now to be made clear,

and perhaps I haven't done so.

            THE COURT: In communicating to them, I wish

you would say for the Court that I am not tolerating any

fishing expedition into the files of any newspaper.

            MR. ABRAMS: Your Honor, I must say, sir, I am

not clear.   I think I follow you, sir, but I am not

sure I follow what the Government wants.

            THE COURT: I am not interested in what the

Government wants, now.   This is my suggestion.

            MR. ABRAMS: You are asking The New York Times ---

            THE COURT: Let me put it this way:

The Government has asked for very broad relief,

namely the actual production for inspection and copying

of your documents, which I am taking under advisement,

which you are now arguing.

            There is a second branch to th Government's

request, which is that that discovery and inspection

include documents beyond those already disclosed to be

in the possession of The New York Times.

            Without discussing the merits or whether or not

I will grant the motion by the Government for the actual

production and inspection of the documents, I ask whether

you have any objection to making a list available to the

Government of what you have.

At first I thought you said you had no objection.

Then I thought you said that you objected to anything

beyond what the Government already knew through the

publication of The New York Times.   And I therefore

ask you, without revealing the documents at this point

or bringing them into Court, whether The New York Times

is willing, in order to get the issues in this matter in

some perspective, to tell the Government what else it

has which is by way of unauthorized documents, by way of

an unauthorized document.   That you can answer me

MR. MOLLO: Your Honor, may I just add that

other, extra, word, namely the unauthorized documents from

the same source?

THE COURT: From the same source.   I thank you

for that correction.   That is what I said before, the

same source.

In other words, we are not engaged in any

fishing expedition, nor will this Court permit one.   But

within the limits of the pleading, it seems to me that

rather than rustle with the difficult question of inspection

at the outset, let us first see whether we can determine

what else the Times has.

MR. ABRAMS: Your Honor, I have already advised

you on that and, as I have advised you, sir, I will

speak to my clients with respect to that.

THE COURT: Do it by this afternoon. I am

going to reserve on this motion anyhow, gentlemen.

MR. ABRAMS: Before I turn to the question

of the disclosure to the Government and the permission

to the Government to inspect the documents in question,

may I just focus on one point, your Honor?

Everything else aside here, when Mr. Hess tells

you that the Government must know these things in order

to come into this court tomorrow for a preliminary

injunction, I disagree with him. It is not so, in my

view, that the Government must know with precision every

single matter that it believes it is talking about in that

area.

If your Honor chooses to enter an order at some

time with respect to the New York Times, with respect to

the documents in its possession, that would be one thing.

It is a very different thing, sir, for the Government to

come in here and tell you today that it must know tomorrow

or today of these documents, which as we have previously

advised the Court and as the Government has been able to

read in the New York Times, it has in its entirety.

Moreover, your Honor ---

THE COURT: Let me understand your argument.

Do you say they are not relevant, these

documents, to the issue?

MR. ABRAMS: I am saying that what the Government is saying in this action is that it has reason to believe that there are certain unauthorized documents held by the New York Times and that it wants certain action taken with respect to them.

THE COURT: And I take it the Times does not seriously controvert that, is that correct?

MR. ABRAMS: Your Honor, we will controvert that.

THE COURT: That makes a difference.

MR. ABRAMS: Come the preliminary hearing.

THE COURT: Yes.

MR. ABRAMS: I don't think we have reached that point now, sir.

THE COURT: No. By the way, if I ask you any questions that you feel you should not answer at this stage, just tell me so.

MR. ABRAMS: Surely.

I think that the most significant aspect of the

motion before your Honor today relates to the basic

request made by the Government of this Court.   That

request is that the Government be permitted to inspect

the documents in the possession of the New York Times in

what Mr. Hess calls an organized manner.

We have submitted today, your Honor, an affidavit

from James L. Greenfield, the Foreign Editor of the New

York Times, in which Mr. Greenfield says to this Court,

under oath, that in his capacity as Foreign Editor of the

New York Times he has examined these documents, that they

consist of Xerox copies of the documents referred to in

the articles which have appeared in the New York Times,

and that many of the Xerox copies bear handwritten

notations.

Production of these documents in accordance

with the plaintiff's application, Mr. Greenfield says,

would facilitate identification by the plaintiff or certain

of its agencies of the confidential source of the material

which has been the basis for the articles published in

the New York Times.

THE COURT: I don't see anything about hand-

writing in this affidavit.   Are you sure it is there?

MR. ABRAMS: Yes, sir, the second line of the

second page of Mr. Greenfield's affidavit:

"Many of the Xerox copies bear handwritten

notations."

THE COURT: All right.

MR. ABRAMS: Your Honor, this case, then, among

other things, imposes many of the same problems that the

case of Earl Caldwell, a New York Times reporter, posed.

That case is now in the United States Supreme Court.

And I may say that the United States, as our

brief points out, has not appealed from the kind of

protective order that Mr. Caldwell received at the

District Court level in San Francisco. Indeed, your

Honor, as our memorandum of law points out, the very

guide lines issued by the Attorney General of the United

States with respect to the issuance of subpoenas would,

in our view, not be met by the Government in this

equivalent of a subpoena.

Entirely apart, your Honor, from what the

Government's position is with respect to its guide lines,

it may be said at the very least that the Caldwell case

and its progeny pose the most serious, the most signifi-

cant and some of the most difficult judicial issues for

resolution.

We believe, your Honor, that those decisions

will be rendered this Fall term of the United States

Supreme Court.   We think there are three cases as to

which certiorari has been granted.

We submit to your Honor that nothing should be

done in this case which could compromise the confidential

source --

THE COURT: Let me ask you something.

Do you see any distinction between Caldwell,

where first there was a grand jury investigation in a

criminal sense and, second, where the sources purportedly

of Caldwell were a private organization, the Panthers,

whereas here the Government claimed that the source had

to be, by virtue of the statute and the Executive order,

an unauthorized source? .   Do you make any distinction?

I am not passing on it yet.   I just want to hear your

view on it.

MR. ABRAMS: I make one distinction and that is, as your Honor correctly points out, Caldwell was a criminal case.   I would say that if the courts had to choose between requiring production of documents in criminal cases and civil cases, they would be more likely to require them in criminal cases.

This is not, sir, a criminal case.   This is a case of an injunction.

Your Honor, we are submitting this afternoon a lengthy brief with respect to the pending motion for a preliminary injunction as is the government, I take it.   That brief will deal in some detail with many of the issues.

THE COURT: You answered one part of my question and, if you want to, you may answer the other part, and that is: is there a difference between a source which by statute is illegal and the Panthers, which are free citizens of the United States?

MR. ABRAMS: Your Honor, as you will see tomorrow, or this afternoon, sir, we very vigorously take the position that the Times has done nothing illegal whatsoever.

THE COURT: All right.   Maybe I am jumping ahead.

MR. ABRAMS: That there has been no violation of statute whatsoever.

THE COURT: I did not say the Times committed a violation necessarily -- I am not passing on that -- but whether the person who gave it to the Times did.

MR. ABRAMS: What was involved, your Honor, in the Caldwell case was an investigation of the Black Panthers, which the United States Government tied into an alleged assassination plot of the President of the United States.

THE COURT: I am conscious of that.

MR. ABRAMS: I think, in terms of the gravity of what is being talked about here, the government could not underestimate what it was saying at least but, in the Caldwell case, unsuccessfully.

I would say, in conclusion, sir, two things: First, the issues posed by the current motion before the Court even go beyond the constitutional ones I have raised. There is a New York State statute in effect. We maintain that that New York statute, Section 79(h) of the Civil Rights Law, also provides complete protection to the New York Times and bars the government from obtaining the documents it now seeks.

THE COURT: Do you have any case indicating

that the Federal Rules are limited by a state statute of

that kind?

MR. ABRAMS: Your Honor, we cite cases at

page 18 of our brief, in a footnote, to the effect that

while the issue that your Honor raises is not free

from doubt, the prevailing view, in our view, your Honor,

and we believe what the case law says, is that state

statutes do govern with respect to testimonial "privi-

leges" and the like.

It is not our position, your Honor, that on

the constitutional issue here we are asserting a privi-

lege in the sense that there is a lawyer-client privilege.

We are asserting the rights of the New York Times and

its public under the First Amendment.

THE COURT: You are talking of the Caldwell

right?

MR. ABRAMS: Yes, sir.   But with respect

to Section 79(h) of the Civil Rights Law, that is a

privilege statute which, as Governor Rockefeller pointed

out in his message, is based upon and was premised upon

the Constitution.

THE COURT: That is a difficult area, you

are right.

MR. ABRAMS: If your Honor has no further

questions ---

THE COURT: No.

Do you have anything further to say, Mr. Hess?

MR. HESS: If I may just have a moment, I would like to emphasize two distinctions in the Caldwell case.

First, there we had an appearance before a grand jury.   The case speaks, the Ninth Circuit decision speaks, of the scope of the grand jury's investigatory power.   Here, as Mr. Abrams has stated, we are concerned with a civil proceeding and with an often used discovery rule of civil procedure.

The Caldwell case, the circuit judge on page 1089 narrows his ruling and says that the government there had to make a compelling showing of need.   That was a different context, a criminal grand jury investigatory proceeding.

Here we feel we have shown the need, although it is a different type of proceeding --

THE COURT: But there, too, the investigation and suppression of crime was held to be subordinate to the privilege of the newspaper, because obviously if the reporter had been compelled to testify and to give his sources, it might well have led to indictments. And yet the Court held that the First Amendment privilege

was so strong that it would not do it.

MR. HESS: Here, your Honor, we jump to the point that you were discussing with Mr. Abrams, that there the source was different. Here we are talking about government papers. There they were not talking about stolen or embezzled papers. Here we are. And there, despite Mr. Abrams' representation, I disagree, they were not dealing with papers that bore on the security of the nation and here we are.

If I might add one more thing, we would have no objection, with regard to the notation in Mr. Greenfield affidavit, if the New York Times wanted to block out any handwritten notations on the papers.

THE COURT: Let me ask one question. The thing I am troubled about a little bit, and I would like to hear you on it while I think about this, is: is there a difference between revealing a source directly, as in the Caldwell case, and turning over a paper which is otherwise the subject of discovery only because, looking at the paper or the ink or some handwriting, something else might be discovered? Is there a difference there?

MR. ABRAMS: Your Honor, we don't believe that there could be a difference there. The constitu-

tional right which journalists have with respect to

the protection of their sources would, in our view, be

equally applicable no matter how the source became known.

I could imagine, your Honor, a case where the

possibility of a source becoming known was so obscure,

where the situation was so unlikely, that a court might

in its judgment make one decision or the other on that

factual issue.   But that is not the case here, that

is not what our sworn affidavit says here.

May I just return, sir, to the point made

by Mr. Hess, really two final points?

First, the Caldwell case, your Honor, did not

involve papers at all.   It involved testimony and it

involved identification of people, what they were doing,

what Mr. Caldwell saw.

With respect to the distinction, your Honor,

between civil and criminal actions, I would strongly

urge upon the Court reference to the New York Times vs.

Sullivan case, which in our view states --

THE COURT: There are only two things

that are troublesome.   Otherwise there is a tremendous

privilege that Caldwell created for newspapers.   There

is no doubt about it.

The question is --

MR. ABRAMS: We would like to think the First Amendment created the privilege.

THE COURT: I said "for newspapers."   I didn't say "by newspapers."   For newspapers.

But I am troubled by two things.   Is there any case that you know of -- and again I am assuming a hypothetical fact -- where the documents were obtained illegally and, second, where the only lead to the source is indirect and not direct?

MR. ABRAMS: I believe, sir, that there is a Pennsylvania case.

THE COURT: Have you got the citation here?

MR. ABRAMS: No, sir.   The issue had not, in our mind, arisen.   In re Taylor is the name of the case.   I believe that that related to documents which were obtained illegally by a newspaper in the City of Philadelphia.

THE COURT: I know that case.   But that is not from the government.   That was obtained from a private organization or person.   Wasn't that the one with the Liberty League or something like that?

MR. ABRAMS: No, your Honor.   My recollection, at least, of the Taylor case, and I haven't read it in a while, is that it involved a person in the city

jga

government of Philadelphia who provided a Philadelphia

newspaper with information and, I believe, documents

relating to the city corruption.

THE COURT: I would like to see that case.

There is another Philadelphia case, I think, involved

in the stealing of documents from a private organization

by some people who gave it to the newspapers.

MR. ABRAMS: We would be happy, of course,

to supply your Honor with that authority.

THE COURT: All right.   Give me that author-

ity when you find it.

MR. ABRAMS: I take it your Honor will re-

serve decision.

THE COURT: I will reserve decision.   Thank

you very much.

- -

The following is an inventory list of materials in The New York Times possession relating to the Vietnam Archive commissioned by Secretary of Defense McNamara. The Times has no other materials in its possession relating to this Archive.

United States Policy in Indochina 1940 to 1950.

United States Aid for France in Indochina 1950 to 1954.

United States Involvement in the French-Indochina War 1950 to 1954.

The United States and France's Withdrawal from Vietnam 1954 to 1956.

Geneva Conference of 1954.

Origins of the Insurgency in South Vietnam 1954 to 1960.

The Kennedy Commitments and Programs 1961 to 1963.

The Coup Against Ngo Dinh Diem 1963.

The Advisory Buildup 1961 to 1967.

The Strategic Hamlet Program 1961 to 1963.

Phased Withdrawal of United States Forces 1962 to 1964.

United States-South Vietnamese Relations 1963 to 1967.

-1-

United States Programs in South Vietnam 1963 to 1965.

The First Phase in the Buildup of United States Forces
     March to July 1965.

Marine Combat Units Go To Danang - March 1965.

Pacification Programs 1965 to 1967.

The Ground War in South Vietnam 1965 to 1968
     in three volumes.

The Military Pressures Against North Vietnam
     in three volumes - February 1964 to January 1965.

The Beginning Stage of the Bombing Campaign Against
     North Vietnam - January 1965 to June 1965.

The Air Campaign Against North Vietnam
     in two volumes - July 1965 to March 31, 1968.

Internal Policy Commitments
     A chronological list and summary of major internal
     policy documents for the Roosevelt, Truman,
     Eisenhower, Kennedy and Johnson Administrations
     on Indochina.

Public Policy Statements on Indochina for Four
     Administrations, Truman, Eisenhower, Kennedy
     and Johnson.

Documents Relating to Studies covering the period
     1950 to 1954 including the Geneva Conference
     of 1954.

Documents Relating to the Kennedy Period
    including the Coup Against President Diem
    and covering the years from 1961 to 1963
    plus two documents for this period not
    cited in the narrative, a message from
    President Kennedy to Ambassador Lodge and
    Mr. Lodge's reply, in late 1963.

Documents Relating to the Study of Military Pressures
    Against North Vietnam February 1964 to January 1965.

Documents Relating to the Study of the Beginning Stage
    of the Air War Against North Vietnam January 1965
    to June 1965.

Documents Relating to the Studies on the Ground and
    Air Wars for 1965 to 1968.

A Summary of the Command and Control Study on the
    Tonkin Gulf Incident.

U.S. Fails to Get Immediate Court Order To Force Times to Turn Over Documents

Paper Gives List Identifying Material It Has

By FRED P. GRAHAM

The Justice Department failed yesterday — at least for the present — to obtain a court order forcing The New York Times to turn over for the Government's inspection the secret Pentagon study from which the newspaper's series on the Vietnam war has been drawn.

Instead, The Times gave the Court and the Justice Department a list of descriptive head-

Excerpts from the argument appear on Page 14.

ings for those portions of the archive in The Times's possession.

The purpose of this procedure was to permit the Government to identify the portions of the 7,000-page study that The Times has, without giving officials actual possession of The Times's copies.

Suggested by Judge

This result appeared to satisfy United States District Judge Murray I. Gurfein, who had withheld any immediate action on the Government's demand to see The Times's documents.

Judge Gurfein had suggested this resolution of the dispute over the papers after ruling out the Government's demand for all classified material in the newspaper's possession. "I am not tolerating any fishing expedition into the files of any newspaper," he said.

At about midnight last night the Government filed with Judge Gurfein a 30-page brief outlining the argument that will be made today in support of its efforts to block publication of the material.

Although the Government had based its initial request for an injunction upon the allegation that the national interest would be harmed by further publications, the brief depended heavily upon the claim that The Times could not have obtained the documents if it had requested them under the Freedom of Information Act of 1966.

The Washington Post in its late editions this morning began what it described as a series of articles based on "sections" of a Pentagon study "made available to The Washington Post." The article quoted from summary papers done by Pentagon researchers as part of the study.

Contained Notations

The Times's Vietnam series was halted by a temporary order on Tuesday. Articles published on Sunday, Monday and Tuesday dealt with events leading to the Tonkin Gulf incident, the decision to wage an air war against North Vietnam, and the first use of American ground troops in South Vietnam.

Each part of the series con-

Continued on Page 14, Column 1

U.S. Fails to Get Court Order on Study

Continued From Page 1, Col. 6

sisted of articles as well as documentary material.

During the court arguments yesterday, lawyers for The Times insisted that if the newspaper's own copies were turned over to the Justice Department, Government agents might be able to use them to discover the identity of the source of the material that The Times has.

The lawyer, Floyd Abrams, disclosed that the documents were Xeroxed and contained handwritten notations. He implied that the handwriting might be identified, or the copying machine might be traced, and declared that therefore The Times would not give up its copies.

In response, the Government insisted that it needed to see the papers to prepare for the hearing set for 10 A.M. today at the Federal Court House on Foley Square on its suit to permanently enjoin The Times from publishing further material from the papers.

Michael D. Hess, chief of the civil division in the United States Attorney's office here, protested to Judge Gurfein that the Government could not support its claim that publication would harm the national interest unless it knew what The Times had planned to publish.

Also, he said, "the court cannot frame an injunction unless the court knows what needs to be enjoined." At one point Mr. Hess offered to let representatives of The Times be present when the documents were being examined by the Government, but the suggestion was not taken up by the judge or The Times's lawyers.

Mr. Abrams' argument had two basic points. One was that the Government did not need The Times's documents, because at least 15 copies were known to have been made when the study was completed in 1968.

The second was that because surrender of the papers might compromise The Times's source, the First Amendment's free press guarantee shielded the newspaper from having to give up the documents.

Copies Bear Notations

Mr. Abrams introduced a sworn affidavit by James L. Greenfield, foreign editor of The Times, who said that "many of the Xeroxed copies bear handwritten notations" and that to give them up would "facilitate identification," by the Government of "the confidential source of the material."

This, Mr. Abrams argued, made the situation fall within the decision handed down several months ago by the United States Court of Appeals in San Francisco regarding a New York Times reporter, Earl

Caldwell. That court said that the First Amendment shielded Mr. Caldwell from having to answer a subpoena to give grand jury testimony about Black Panther activities, because this would destroy his contacts with his sources and undermine his capacity to gather news.

Judge Gurfein skirted the issue by suggesting that The Times furnish its list. It did so later in the day, but refused requests by reporters to release the list for publication—partly because to do so might be a violation of the temporary order against further publication of the material.

The Times replied to reporters' questions with the following statement:

"The Times today continued to oppose the Government's demand to produce any part of the study on the ground it would prejudice the sources.

"The Times did not object to a court request that it give to the court and the Government its own typewritten list of descriptive headings for those parts of the Pentagon study it possesses."

Yesterday afternoon a Government copy of the study and its supporting documents arrived from Washington and was delivered to Mr. Hess.

Earlier yesterday, the judge rejected the petitions of two groups who asked to join the case as defendants to represent the interests of readers.

One petition, which was dismissed without a hearing, was brought in the names of 10 academic figures who are known for their criticism of United States Vietnam policy, and who sought to represent academicians' rights to receive the unpublished materials.

They were Noam Chomsky of the Massachusetts Institute of Technology, Alexander Erlich and Seymour Melman of Columbia University, Richard Falk and Carl Schorski of Princeton, Robert Jay Lifton of Yale, Hans Morgenthau of the University of Chicago, Franz Shurmann of Berkley, George Wald of Harvard and Howard Zinn of Boston University.

Hearing for Readers

Judge Gurfein did grant a hearing to a group of readers of The Times, which included Representative Edward I. Koch, Manhattan Democrat. Melvin L. Wulf, legal director of the American Civil Liberties Union, argued that readers' First Amendment rights to receive information needed to be protected, because the Times lawyers "won't represent them fully."

"I don't believe that The Times is in here avowedly for the purpose of selling newspapers but for the purpose of asserting that the general pub-

lic has a right to read and hear," Judge Gurfein replied. He said that the A.C.L.U. could file a friend-of-the-court brief for the group, but that it could not join as defendants because "there are 200 million people with the same right," and the case might be swamped with defendants.

Both groups of would-be intervenors appealed immediately to the United States Court of Appeals for the Second Circuit, which sits in the United States Court House on Foley Square, where Judge Gurfein's court is located.

A three-judge panel composed of Judge J. Edward Lumbard, Irving R. Kaufman and William H. Timbers of the Federal District Court of Connecticut heard a half-hour of arguments in the early afternoon.

At the conclusion of the arguments Judge Lumbard pulled out and read a unanimous opinion in which the appeal was dismissed because "there is no practical impairment of the intervenors' interests."

Court Rulings Cited

The brief filed late last night by the Government conceded that "of course, the First Amendment to the Constitution guarantees the freedoms of speech and press." But it cited Supreme Court rulings that held that the First Amendment must give way to "compelling governmental need."

In arguing that such need exists in this case, the brief asserted that the papers are all classified, and that under the Freedom of Information Act, such papers could not have been obtained by The Times unless they had been "purloined."

An "equally compelling" reason cited in the brief was that "The Times cannot claim any greater right to these documents and materials because they are presently in the unlawful and unauthorized possession of The Times."

The brief repeated the argument made at Tuesday's hearing, that the Federal court was given legal grounds to enjoin the publication because the documents were allegedly held in violation of the "espionage act."

A second legal basis was added in the brief. It was that the Constitution entrusts the conduct of foreign affairs to the Government and that publication of the materials might interfere with it.

Lawyers for The New York Times filed copies of a brief with the court and opposing counsel about midnight, but did not make copies available to reporters.

Excerpts From Oral Arguments on U.S. Effort to Obtain Documents From Times

Following are excerpts from the oral argument before United States District Judge Murray I. Gurfein yesterday, by Michael D. Hess, Assistant United States attorney, and Floyd Abrams, representing The New York Times, on the Justice Department's request for a court order compelling The Times to turn over the classified documents to the Government for inspection:

MR. HESS: Your Honor, the Government brought on an order to show cause yesterday before your Honor late in the afternoon, asking that this motion be brought on today and asking for inspection of the documents in the hand of The New York Times. This is pursuant to Rule 34 of the Federal Rules of Civil Procedure.

Under Rule 34, a party need serve a notice of production on the other party to obtain documents. We have done this. The relevancy is a major criteria and here, your Honor, it is self-evident; the documents are the heart of this case. They are stolen or embezzled property by their very nature. They are top-secret, confidential documents.

The Government feels that we have a right to identify what was taken from us, we have a right to identify what The New York Times has in its possession.

THE COURT: Let me ask you this: Why is it not a fishing expedition in the sense of seeking general discovery, which is normally constitutionally prohibited?

MR. HESS: Well, your Honor, we feel it is not a fishing expedition because we want to show why these documents, or we will have to show, your Honor, why these documents should not be published, why they should be enjoined, why it will hurt the national interest to have them published. In order to do that we have to know what documents The Times has and what documents they intend to publish.

Suggests Interrogation

THE COURT: Couldn't you do that by interrogatory tomorrow, by asking the representative of The Times to testify and ask him what he has and what he intends to publish?

MR. HESS: That is what we would like to find out, your Honor, and if The Times would state with particularity to us.

THE COURT: Let me hold that in abeyance. That is a thought I had as you went along. I will hear the other side.

MR. ABRAMS: Your Honor, this has been an astonishing week in the history of journalism. It is astonishing because the United States has chosen to bring The New York Times to Court in an effort to enjoin publication of obviously newsworthy articles.

I am speaking of a motion such as the one before you this morning, your Honor, which was brought on by order to show cause yesterday in circumstances in which I hope I can persuade you, sir, that there is absolutely no need whatever for the Government to have these papers, with a single exception which I will come to in a moment.

What this motion is, your Honor, is an attempt to require The New York Times to make available to the United States Xeroxes, which is what The Times has, of certain papers which the United States in its complaint purported to specify.

Cites U.S. Complaint

In its complaint in this action, your Honor, the United States did not come in and say, "We don't know what the documents are, we don't know what The Times has." It filed a complaint, it referred to certain documents.

THE COURT: Does The Times have a fundamental objection and, if so, what is it, to letting the Government know what it has?

MR. ABRAMS: The Times has a most substantial constitutional problem with respect to production of these papers.

THE COURT: I am not asking about production. Listen to me very carefully. I am asking you now whether The Times would object to giving the Government a list, with description, only of the documents which it has in its possession coming from the Pentagon.

MR. ABRAMS: The Times is not prepared, Your Honor, to allow the Government to inspect the documents which The New York Times has. The Times will give a list which sets forth the documents that it has.

THE COURT: That, if you want to, can be made into the form of an order, but if you say you will produce it by, let's say, 5 o'clock today, I will accept that. Is that all right?

The New York Times/Meyer Liebowitz

LAWYERS FOR THE TIMES: Floyd Abrams, left, and Lawrence McKay leaving U.S. Court House yesterday.

MR. ABRAMS: We would be prepared to advise the Government this afternoon of the documents.

Would Limit Question

THE COURT: So that would then limit the question of whether there are other documents—that will be under some kind of affirmation by somebody or other—

MR. ABRAMS: Wait a minute, sir. The Government has filed a complaint here and referred to two kinds of documents, Your Honor, one supposed 47-volume series and one summary with respect to the Tonkin Gulf. That is the issue as framed by the Government in this case.

With respect to that issue as framed, we will be prepared to advise what we have. We are absolutely unprepared, sir, to go through our files and make available to the Government, or to advise the Government of anything else which is outside the scope of those issues as framed in the complaint.

THE COURT: Why is that?

MR. ABRAMS: Why is that? Because that would be an ultimate fishing expedition through files of a newspaper, which are as protected by the First Amendment as one could imagine.

THE COURT: Without deciding anything at this moment, I just want to put this question: does The New York Times, so that the whole matter can be adjudicated, have any other documents besides those mentioned in the complaint which came from the same source?

MR. ABRAMS: Your Honor, The New York Times is not prepared to advise the Government with respect to any documents whatsoever, with the exception of the documents referred to in the complaint in this action and which were referred to in the stories published in The New York Times. A newspaper has a great many sources of information, a great many documents, a great many employes, a great many secrets, which is the essence in good

part, your Honor, of journalism.

THE COURT: I must wonder, why, limiting the category as I have to unauthorized documents and avoiding by all means any fishing expedition into the files of The New York Times or any other newspaper, there could not be merely a listing and not a turning over—we are not talking about that now—or an answer to the question of are there any other documents that came from the Pentagon, so that the Court can view the entire matter. That's all I am asking you.

MR. ABRAMS: This is a case, as your Honor has pointed out and as we are very well aware, sir, of immense magnitude. Issues of this sort are ones which I as counsel wish to talk to my client about.

THE COURT: All right. Let me put it this way:

The Government has asked for very broad relief, namely the actual production for inspection and copying of your documents, which I am taking under advisement, which you are now arguing.

There is a second branch to the Government's request, which is that discovery and inspection include documents beyond those already disclosed to be in the possession of The New York Times.

Without discussing the merits or whether or not I will grant the motion by the Government for the actual production and inspection of the documents, I ask whether you have any objection to making a list available to the Government of what you have.

Would Consult Client

At first I thought you said you had no objection. Then I thought you said that you objected to anything beyond what the Government already knew through the publication of The New York Times. And I therefore ask you, without revealing the documents at this point or bringing them into Court, whether The New York Times is willing, in order to get the issues in this matter in some perspective, to tell the Government what else it has which is by way of unauthorized documents from the same source.

MR. ABRAMS: Your Honor, sir, I will speak to my clients with respect to that.

I think that the most significant aspect of the motion before your Honor today relates to the basic request that the Government be permitted to inspect the docu-

ments in the possession of The New York Times in what Mr. Hess calls an organized manner.

We have submitted today, your Honor, an affidavit from James L. Greenfield, the Foreign Editor of The New York Times, in which Mr. Greenfield says to this Court, under oath, that he has examined these documents, that they consist of Xerox copies of the documents referred to in the articles which have appeared in The New York Times, and that many of the Xerox copies bear handwritten notations.

Production of these documents in accordance with the plaintiff's application, Mr. Greenfield says, would facilitate identification by the plaintiff or certain of its agencies of the confidential source of the material which has been the basis for the articles published in The New York Times.

Your Honor, this case, then, among other things, imposes many of the same problems that the case of Earl Caldwell, a New York Times reporter, posed. That case is now in the United States Supreme Court.

And I may say that the United States, as our brief points out, has not appealed from the kind of protective order that Mr. Caldwell received at the District Court level in San Francisco. Indeed, your Honor, as our memorandum of law points out, the very guide lines issued by the Attorney General of the United States with respect to the issuance of subpoenas would, in our view, not be met by the Government in this equivalent of a subpoena.

We submit to your Honor that nothing should be done in this case which could compromise the confidential source—

THE COURT: Do you see any distinction between Caldwell, where first there was a grand jury investigation in a criminal sense and, second, where the sources purportedly of Caldwell were a private organization, the Panthers, whereas here the Government claimed that the source had to be, by virtue of the statute and the Executive order, an unauthorized source? Do you make any distinction? I am not passing on it yet. I just want to hear your view on it.

MR. ABRAMS: I make one distinction and that is, as your Honor correctly points out, Caldwell was a criminal case. I would say that if the courts had to choose between requiring production of documents in criminal cases and

The New York Times

REPRESENTS THE U.S.: Michael D. Hess, chief of the civil division of the U.S. Attorney's office.

civil cases, they would be more likely to require them in criminal cases.

THE COURT: You answered one part of my question and, if you want to, you may answer the other part, and that is: is there a difference between a source which by statute is illegal and the Panthers, which are free citizens of the United States?

MR. ABRAMS: Your Honor, as you will see tomorrow, or this afternoon, sir, we very vigorously take the position that The Times has done nothing illegal whatsoever.

THE COURT: All right. Maybe I am jumping ahead.

MR. ABRAMS: That there has been no violation of statute whatsoever.

THE COURT: I did not say The Times committed a violation necessarily—I am not passing on that—but whether the person who gave it to The Times did.

MR. ABRAMS: What was involved, your Honor, in the Caldwell case was an investigation of the Black Panthers, which the United States Government tied into an alleged assassination plot of the President of the United States. I think, in terms of

the gravity of what is being talked about here, the government could not underestimate what it was saying at least but, in the Caldwell case, unsuccessfully.

It is not our position, your Honor, that on the constitutional issue here we are asserting a privilege in the sense that there is a lawyer-client privilege. We are asserting the rights of The New York Times and its public under the First Amendment.

THE COURT: You are talking of the Caldwell right?

MR. ABRAMS: Yes, sir. If your Honor has no further questions.

THE COURT: No.

Do you have anything further to say, Mr. Hess?

MR. HESS: If I may just have a moment, I would like to emphasize two distinctions in the Caldwell case.

First, there we had an appearance before a grand jury. The decision speaks of the scope of the grand jury's investigatory power. Here, as Mr. Abrams has stated, we are concerned with a civil proceeding and with an often-used discovery rule of civil procedure.

Says Ruling Was Narrow

The Caldwell case, the circuit judge on Page 1089 narrows his ruling and says that the Government there had to make a compelling showing of need. That was a different context, a criminal grand jury investigatory proceeding.

Here we feel we have shown the need, although it is a different type of proceeding—

THE COURT: But there, too, the investigation and suppression of crime was held to be subordinate to the privilege of the newspaper, because obviously if the reporter had been compelled to testify and to give his sources, it might well have led to indictments. And yet the Court held that the First Amendment privilege was so strong that it would not do it.

MR. HESS: There they were not talking about stolen or embezzled papers. Here we are. And there, despite Mr. Abrams' representation, I disagree, they were not dealing with papers that bore on the security of the nation and here we are.

If I might add one more thing, we would have no objection, with regard to the notation in Mr. Greenfield's affidavit, if The New York Times wanted to block out any handwritten notations on the papers.

HSS:mn
71-1697

UNITED STATES DISTRICT COURT
SOUTHERN DISTRICT OF NEW YORK

--x

UNITED STATES OF AMERICA,   :

                                 Plaintiff,   :

                                                   :

                 v.   :

NEW YORK TIMES COMPANY, ARTHUR   :
OCHS SULZBERGER, HARDING F.   71 Civ. 2662
BANCROFT, IVAN VEIT, FRANCIS A. COX,   :
JAMES C. GOODALE, SYDNEY GRUSON,
WALTER MATTSON, JOHN McCABE, JOHN   :
MORTIMER, JAMES RESTON, JOHN B. OAKES,
A. M. ROSENTHAL, DANIEL SCHWARZ,   :
CLIFTON DANIEL, TOM WICKER, E. W.
KENWORTHY, FOX BUTTERFIELD, GERALD   :
GOLD, ALLAN M. SIEGAL, SAMUEL ABT,
NEIL SHEEHAN and HEDRICK SMITH,   :

                             Defendants.   :

--x

                          MEMORANDUM IN SUPPORT
                          OF PLAINTIFF'S MOTION
                          FOR A PRELIMINARY
                          INJUNCTION

Preliminary Statement

This is an action by the United States to enjoin defendant, New York Times Company (the "Times"), and the individual defendants who are officers and employees of the Times, from the further dissemination, disclosure or divulgence of classified documents which the Times has in its possession without authority. These documents were stolen from the possession of the Federal government. In addition to preliminary and permanent injunctive relief, plaintiff seeks the return of these documents.

The pending motion for a preliminary injunction was brought on by Order To Show Cause signed on June 15, 1971, by Hon. Murray I. Gurfein, United States District Judge.

Statement of Facts

On June 13, 14 and 15, the Times published extensive articles dealing with United States involvement in Vietnam. Underlying these articles are Top Secret and Secret documents obtained by the Times without authority, including a 47-volume study entitled "History of U.S. Decision-Making Process on Vietnam Policy" and another document entitled "The Command and Control Study of the

2

Tonkin Gulf incident done by the Defense Department's Weapons System Evaluation Group in 1965" (Compl. para. 7, 8; Buzhardt aff., pars. 2-4.) The Times admits to having the whole of the first of these studies, and a summary of the second. It also admits to having in its possession other classified documents so numerous that it requires many pages simply to list them.*

Responsible officials of the United States have informed the Times that publication of these documents will cause irreparable injury to the national defense (Mardian aff. and Ex. A). Evidence to be introduced before this Court will substantiate that statement.

When the Times, notwithstanding the demands of the national defense, refused voluntarily to halt publication of this material, the United States sought and obtained from Judge Gurfein a temporary restraining

---

* The Times has admitted possession of these documents only in response to plaintiff's Notice for Production of Documents under Rule 34 of the Federal Rules of Civil Procedure, and a related motion for an order directing such production.

3

order preventing further publication pending a

hearing on its motion for injunctive relief.

For the reasons set forth below,

this Court has power to grant the United States the

relief it seeks.   That relief should be granted in

this case.

POINT I

THIS COURT HAS POWER TO
GRANT THE INJUNCTION THE
UNITED STATES SEEKS IN
THIS ACTION

There is no question that this Court can

grant the injunction the United States seeks, whether or

not the conduct of defendants constitutes a crime under

18 U.S.C. § 793(e).   Two well established grounds

support that power: one is the equitable principles enun-

ciated in In re Debs, 158 U.S. 564 (1895), and its progeny.

The second is the rule of cases such as Wyandotte

Transportation Co. v. United States, 389 U.S. 191, 201-202

(1967), implying civil remedies from criminal statutes

when the criminal sanctions provided are "inadequate to

ensure the[ir] full effectiveness".

      A.   In re Debs and its Progeny
          Authorize the Injunction
          Plaintiff Seeks

In re Debs recognized the salutary principle

that the United States may resort to the courts to protect

5

the public interest "in respect to matters which

by the Constitution are entrusted to the care of the

Nation" (158 U.S. at 586).   After discussing earlier

cases, the Supreme Court said (ibid.):

> "It is obvious from these
> decisions that while it is not the
> province of the government to inter-
> fere in any mere matter of private
> controversy between individuals, or
> to use its great powers to enforce
> the rights of one against another,
> yet, whenever the wrongs complained
> of are such as affect the public at
> large, and are in respect of matters
> which by the Constitution are entrusted
> to the care of the Nation, and concerning
> which the Nation owes the duty to all
> the citizens of securing to them their
> common rights, then the mere fact that
> the government has no pecuniary interest
> in the controversy is not sufficient
> to exclude it from the courts, or
> prevent it from taking measures therein
> to fully discharge those constitutional
> duties."

In re Debs involved the power of Congress

to regulate interstate commerce, and the injunction

issued there enjoined a railroad strike which had grossly

interfered with that commerce, including the movement of

the mails.   The doctrine of the Debs case, however,

has not been restricted to interstate commerce.   It has

more recently been applied to sustain the right of the
United States to injunctions in aid of its performance of
other Constitutional duties.

United States v. Arlington County, 326 F.2d
929, 932-933 (4th Cir. 1964), provides an example. There
the Court of Appeals held the United States entitled to
restrain the collection of a tax imposed in contravention
of the Soldiers' and Sailors' Civil Relief Act of 1940
because "the interest of the national government in the
proper implementation of its policies and programs involving
the national defense is such as to vest in it the non-
statutory right to maintain this action."

The same rationale was applied in United
States v. Brittain, 319 F. Supp. 1058, 1061 (N.D. Ala. 1970),
where the United States obtained an injunction against
the State of Alabama and those acting in its behalf from
enforcing the miscegenation laws of that State. The
Court observed that the "United States, in appropriate cases,
has standing to sue irrespective of specific statutory
mandates." It found that the case before it was such a

case because there "is a special interest which the
United States has respecting the exercise, without
undue frustration by the States, of its military
powers."

Recently, in United States v. Brand
Jewelers, Inc., 318 F. Supp. 1293, 1299 (S.D.N.Y. 1970),
Judge Frankel relied on the Debs rationale to support the
right of the United States to an injunction to correct
widespread deprivations by state action of the citizens'
right not to be deprived of property without due process
of law.   Judge Frankel's careful opinion collects and
analyzes the cases (id., at 1297-1299).

Thus, although Congress can expressly
authorize the issuance of injunctions in certain cases
by explicit statute, as it has done, for example, in
the case of certain Internal Revenue laws, there is nothing
unusual or novel about the United States obtaining an
injunction in the absence of an explicit statutory
direction that an injunction issue.   To the contrary,
it is well settled, as the cases just discussed show, that
when a vital interest of the United States, entrusted to

8

the national government by the Constitution, is involved,
an injunction will lie to protect the interest of the
United States and its citizens.*

The conduct of the Nation's foreign affairs
is, of course, a matter entrusted by the Constitution to
the Federal government.   See, e.g., Oetjen v. Central
Leather Co., 246 U.S. 297, 302 (1918); United States v.
Belmont, 301 U.S. 324, 328 (1937); United States v. Pink,
315 U.S. 203, 222-223 (1942); Zemel v. Rusk, 381 U.S. 1,
17 (1965).   Provision for the Nation's defense is likewise
entrusted by the Constitution to the Federal government,

---

* That the conduct sought to be enjoined may also constitute
  a crime is no reason to deny the injunction.   "The law
  is full of instances in which the same act may give rise
  to a civil action and a criminal prosecution.   * * * and
  it is no defence to the civil action that the same act by
  the defendant exposes him also to indictment and punishment in a court of criminal jurisdiction."   In re Debs,
  supra, 158 U.S., at 594.   The rule "that the United States
  may sue to protect its interests" is "not necessarily
  inapplicable when the particular governmental interest
  sought to be protected is expressed in a statute carrying
  criminal penalties for its violation."   Wyandotte
  Transportation Co. v. United States, 389 U.S. 191, 201-202
  (1967).

as the provisions of Article I, Section 8 make

abundantly plain.

There is no reason of principle why

the rationale of the Debs case should not be applied

to allow an injunction at the suit of the United States

in furtherance of its duty to provide for the Nation's

defense and conduct its foreign relations. Reason and

authority support the view that such an injunction can

and should be granted in a proper case. As we shall

demonstrate below, this is a proper case for the granting

of an injunction.

B. The Injunction The United States
Seeks Is Likewise Supported By
Implication From 18 U.S.C. 793(e)

As we have said, we believe that no statutory

authority is necessary for the issuance of the injunction

the United States seeks. If such authority were thought

necessary, however, the need is easily filled by implication

from the provisions of 18 U.S.C. § 793(e). Wyandotte

Transportation Co. v. United States, supra, recognizes the

well-established rule that a civil suit for an injunction

10

will lie when the criminal liability established by statute "is inadequate to ensure the full effectiveness of the statute which Congress had intended" (389 U.S., at 202).

Congress has not been reticent in expressing its policy against the disclosure of classified information. The public is not entitled to obtain such information under the Freedom of Information Act, 5 U.S.C. § 552 (Supp. V 1969), as the express provisions of 5 U.S.C. § 552(b)(1) make unambiguously clear. The provisions of 18 U.S.C. c. 37 make unlawful the improper handling of classified information and of information "relating to the national defense," whether classified or not.

Of particular interest here is one part of c. 37, 18 U.S.C. § 793(e), which provides:

> "Whoever having unauthorized possession of, access to, or control over any document, writing, code book, signal book, sketch, photograph, photographic negative, blueprint, plan, map, model, instrument, appliance, or note relating to the national defense, or information relating to the national defense which information the possessor has reason to believe could be used to the injury of the United States or to the advantage of any foreign nation,

11

willfully communicates, delivers,
transmits or causes to be communicated,
delivered, or transmitted, or attempts
to communicate, deliver, transmit or
cause to be communicated, delivered or
transmitted the same to any person not
entitled to receive it, or willfully
retains the same and fails to deliver it
to the officer or employee of the United
States entitled to receive it;

* * *

"Shall be fined not more than
$10,000 or imprisoned not more than
ten years, or both."

There can be no meaningful doubt that

defendants have "unauthorized possession of . . . [a]

document relating to the national defense, or information

relating to the national defense which information the

possessor has reason to believe could be used to the injury

of the United States or to the advantage of any foreign

nation * * * ." Defendants are not authorized by

competent authority to have possession of any classified

12

document. "The purpose of the classification system is to safeguard information from becoming known to potential enemies of the United States in the interest of national defense." Dubin v. United States, 363 F.2d 938, 942 (Ct. Cl. 1966). The mere fact of classification must give the possessor "reason to believe" that the classified document "could be used to the injury of the United States or to the advantage of any foreign nation * * * ." See S. Rep. No. 427, at 7 (80th Cong., 1st Sess.); H. R. Rep. No. 3112, 52-53 (81st Cong., 2d Sess.). Classification is presumptive evidence that the document is one "relating to the national defense * * * ."

Likewise, there can be no meaningful doubt that one who intentionally publishes classified documents in a newspaper of international circulation "willfully communicates, delivers, transmits" those documents, or "causes [them] to be communicated, delivered or transmitted" to a * * * person not entitled to receive" them, within the meaning of Section 793(e)*.

---

* The absence of the word "publish" from Section 793 does not suggest the contrary. Manifestly, one who publishes a document in a newspaper "communicate[s]" that document. The use of the word "publish" in Sections 794, 797 and 798 of Chapter 37 of 18 U.S. Code, discloses no contrary Congressional intent It seems apparent from the face of the statute that the word "publish" in those sections is used in some other sense, for example, in the sense which the word has in the law of libel.

13

(cont'd) ...

Again, defendants' refusal to return the
classified material of which they have unauthorized
possession must come within the language "willfully retains"
a document "and fails to deliver it to the officer or
employee of the United States entitled to receive it * * * ."

The criminal sanction imposed for unlawful
communication of such defense-related documents is clearly
"inadequate to ensure the full effectiveness of the statute."
It requires no unusual acuity to understand that the
communication of such information can irreparably damage
the national wellbeing, and that criminal sanctions imposed
against the wrongdoer--no matter how severe--cannot repair
that damage.   If the prospective wrongdoer's sense of

---

* Section 794(b) covers the acts of one who "collects, records,
publishes or communicates," war materials of the United States
Section 797 covers the acts of one who "reproduces, publishes
sells or gives away" visual representations of certain
military installations. Section 798 covers the acts of one
who "communicates, furnishes, transmits, or otherwise makes
available to an unauthorized person, or publishes, or uses
in any manner prejudicial to the safety or interest of the
United States or for the benefit of any foreign government
to the detriment of the United States" certain classified
information. No rational basis appears for excluding
"publish" from "communicate" as used in Section 793(e),
particularly in light of the expansive legislative history
referred to in the text above.

14

civic duty, and the existence of criminal sanctions, do

not provide a sufficient disincentive to its communication

of such information, the courts' exercise of their power

to enjoin such conduct becomes essential to the effectuation

of the Congressional policy.

HSS:mn
71-1697

POINT II

THE INJUNCTION THE UNITED STATES
SEEKS CAN BE GRANTED EVEN THOUGH
IT WILL PREVENT A NEWSPAPER FROM
PUBLISHING INFORMATION IN ITS
POSSESSION

Of course, the First Amendment to the

Constitution guarantees the freedoms of speech and

press.   But it is equally clear that these freedoms

are not absolute.   Justice Holmes expressed the point

forcefully in his now-famous dictum, Schenck v. United

States, 249 U.S. 47, 52 (1918):

> "The most stringent protection
> of free speech would not protect a
> man in falsely shouting fire in a
> theatre and causing a panic.   It
> does not even protect a man from an
> injunction against uttering words
> that have all the effect of force."

Instead, what is involved in every case

is a balancing of interests for, as the Supreme Court has

consistently recognized in numerous cases, under certain

circumstances the freedoms of speech and press must give

16

way to compelling governmental need.   As the Court

put it in <u>Dennis</u> v. <u>United States</u>, 341 U.S. 494 (1950),

what is required is an examination of "whether the gravity

of the evil, discounted by its improbability, justifies

such invasion of free speech as is necessary to avoid the

danger" (341 U.S., at 510).

The underlying principle is not different

when what is involved is a prior restraint instead of

the subsequent imposition of a sanction.   <u>Near</u> v. <u>Minnesota</u>,

283 U.S. 697 (1931), which outlaws prior restraints as a

general proposition, nonetheless recognizes that in certain

highly unusual circumstances they are constitutionally

permissible (283 U.S., at 715-716):

> "The objection has also been made
> that the principle as to immunity from
> previous restraint is stated too broadly,
> if every such restraint is deemed to be
> prohibited. That is undoubtedly true;
> the protection even as to previous res-
> traint is not absolutely unlimited. But
> the limitation has been recognized only
> in exceptional cases: 'When a nation is
> at war many things that might be said in
> time of peace are such a hindrance to its
> effort that their utterance will not be
> endured so long as men fight and that no
> Court could regard them as protected by
> any constitutional right.'   <u>Schenck</u> v. <u>United</u>
> <u>States</u>, 249 U.S. 47, 52.   No one would
> question but that a government might prevent

17

actual obstruction to its recruiting service or the publication of the
sailing dates of transports or the
number and location of troops."

It is hardly rational to suppose that
the meager listing given in Near v. Minnesota—which was
a libel case—was intended to be an exhaustive catalogue
of the exception. Other compelling examples come
readily to mind: publishing the plans of weapons
systems, the revelation of military codes, secret
communications between allied governments, to mention but
a few. Instead, Near recognizes a principle that seems to
us beyond dispute. The issue to be decided in any
particular case is whether the projected disclosure
involved is so damaging to the national interest that prior
restraint is permissible.

The principle has been more recently
recognized in Liberty Lobby, Inc. v. Pearson, 390 F.2d
489 (D.C. Cir. 1968). There the Court of Appeals, in an
opinion by Judge (now Chief Justice) Burger, affirmed
the District Court's denial of an injunction against Drew
Pearson, a publisher of a syndicated newspaper column.

18

315

Pearson had obtained copies of documents removed from the files of plaintiff, an organization devoted to political lobbying and the dissemination of information on highly controversial subjects.

Although the Court affirmed the denial of the prior restraint, it recognized that prior restraints are permissible in some circumstances, even when the freedom of the press is involved (_id._, at 490-491):

> "Any claim which seeks prior restraint
> on publication bears a heavy burden.
> The validity of any such claim depends
> on a balance of the interests sought to be
> protected by the limitation against the
> injury to free utterance."

The balancing which _Liberty Lobby_ recognizes as applicable to prior restraints of the press has been applied to uphold the constitutionality of prior restraints in the obscenity field, _Times Film Corp._ v. _Chicago_, 365 U.S. 43 (1960), provided procedural safeguards are present and observed, _Freedman_ v. _Maryland_, 380 U.S. 51 (1964). Manifestly, procedural safeguards are present and will be observed in the present case.

What remains, therefore, is the question whether in this case this Court should grant the injunction plaintiff seeks. To that question we now turn.

19

POINT III

THE INJUNCTION THE UNITED STATES
SEEKS IN THIS CASE SHOULD BE GRANTED

The Times would not be able by lawful
means to secure the documents in question under the
Freedom of Information Act.   Surely, it cannot contend
that it has any greater right to possession and
dissemination of those documents because of the illegal
manner in which they were purloined and received.* Cf.
Maas v. United States, 371 F.2d 348 (D.C. Cir. 1966)

The materials and documents at issue
have been classified by the Department of Defense as
Top Secret pursuant to the authority delegated to that
Department by Executive Order 10501** - "Safeguarding
Official Information in the Interests of the Defense of
the United States".*** The documents and materials were
designated as Top Secret pursuant to Section 1(a) of the
Order, which states in pertinent part as follows:

---

*   The right of the Government to obtain documents stolen
    from it is sustainable under the common law action of
    replevin, and under its common law copyright 17 U.S.C. § 2.
** Title 3, Code of Federal Regulations, Chapter IV, Page 280.
*** The authority granted to the Secretary of Defense or his
    duly designated representative to effect such a classifica-
    tion is found in Section 2 of the Executive Order.

20

> "The Top Secret classification
> shall be applied only to that
> information or material the defense
> aspect of which is paramount, and
> the unauthorized disclosure of which
> could result in exceptionally grave
> damage to the Nation such as leading
> to a definite break in diplomatic
> relations affecting the defense of the
> United States, an armed attack against
> the United States or its allies, a war,
> or the compromise of military or defense
> plans, or intelligence operations . . ."

The classification given to the entire group of documents

and materials in question was required to be "as high as

that of the most highly classified document therein."

Section 3(b).

Having been so designated, it is clear that

these documents and materials would be exempt from public

disclosure under the Freedom of Information Act,* if the

documents and materials were still in the possession of the

Department of Defense. This statute constitutes the most

comprehensive and expansive Congressional statement of the

availability of governmental documents to the public. An

---

* Title 5, U.S.C. § 552, Pub. L. 89-554, (September 6,
  1966), 89 Stat. 383.

21

examination of the Act's legislative history establishes

that the "primary purpose of the Freedom of Information Act

was to increase the citizens' access to Government records".

Bristol-Myers Company v. Federal Trade Commission, 424

F.2d 935, 938 (D.C. Circuit 1970). Nevertheless,

throughout the twelve-year Congressional study which preceded

the passage of the "Freedom of Information" Act, the need to

exempt certain categories of documents from public disclosure

was recognized and ultimately given expression. Nine

exemptions are set forth in subparagraph (b) of 5 U.S.C.

§ 552.

Of particular relevance is Section (b)(1)

of the Act which exempts from disclosure matters that are:

> "Specifically required by Executive
> order to be kept secret in the
> interest of the national defense or
> foreign policy . . . "

The critical importance assigned by the Congress to this

exemption pervades the legislative history of the

22

Act.*   The rationale for the exemption was succinctly

stated in the following terms:

>"Citizens, both in and out of
>Government can agree to restric-
>tions of categories of information
>which the President has determined
>must be kept secret to protect the
>national defense or to advance foreign
>policy, such as materials classified
>pursuant to Executive Order 10501."**

In a parallel expression, the United States Senate observed

that "there is, of course, a certain need for confidentiality

in some aspects of Government operations and these are

protected specifically . . . " ***

In addition to the above-mentioned legis-

lative expressions respecting the importance of this

---

*   See, Hearings, "Freedom of Information and Secrecy in
Government," Part I, Subcommittee on Constitutional
Rights of the Committee on the Judiciary, U. S. Senate,
85th Congress, 2nd Session (March 6, 1958).

** H. Rep. No. 1497, 89th Cong., 2nd Sess. (1966),
CLARIFYING AND PROTECTING THE RIGHT OF THE PUBLIC TO
INFORMATION, Committee on Government Operations.

***S. Report No. 813, 89th Cong., 1st Sess. 1965.

23

exemption, the Executive Branch has also underscored

its essential character.   President Lyndon B. Johnson,

upon signing this Act into law on July 4, 1966, stated:

> " . . . This bill in no way impairs
> the President's power under our
> Constitution to provide for
> confidentiality when the national
> interests so requires . . .. I have
> always believed that freedom of
> information is so vital that only
> the national security, not the desire
> of public officials or private
> citizens should determine when it must
> be restricted."

Under <u>Epstein</u> v. <u>Resor</u>, 421 F.2d 930, 932-33

(9th Cir. 1970), the only decision construing the exemption

conferred by Section (b)(1), a Court in passing upon the

availability of documents designated as classified is

limited to the very narrow inquiry of whether the challenged

classification is arbitrary and capricious.

> "Section (b)(1) is couched in terms
> significantly different from the
> other exemptions.   Under the others
> . . . the very basis of the agency
> determination--the underlying factual
> contention--is open to judicial review
> . . .. Under (b)(1) this is not so.
> The function of determining whether
> secrecy is required in the national

24

interest, is expressly assigned to
the Executive. The judicial inquiry
is limited to the question whether an
appropriate Executive order has been
made as to the material in question."

The District Court in Epstein, 296 F. Supp. 214, 217
(N.D. Cal. 1969), more particularly delineated the
Court's role as involving a determination of "whether
classifications within the first exemption is clearly
arbitrary and unsupportable". The Epstein decision
places in proper perspective and defines the awesome
burden which confronts the defendants in resisting the
Government's application.

The Ninth Circuit cogently articulated the
reasons which necessitate the limited review to be exercised
by the judiciary in this area.

"It simply recognizes the proposition
that the question of what is desirable
in the interest of national defense and
foreign policy is not the sort of
question that the Courts are designed
to deal with. As has been stated, the
judiciary has neither the 'aptitude,
facilities, nor responsibility' to
review these essentially political
decisions" 421 F.2d at 933.

25

Quite obviously, the predicate for the Court's decision was its recognition of the primacy and expertise of the executive branch in the conduct of this nation's foreign affairs and in matters relating to national security.

It is further submitted that the materials and documents at issue would also be exempt from disclosure under the exemption contained in paragraph (b)(5) of the Act, which excludes:

> (5) Inter-agency or intra-agency memorandums or letters which would not be available by law to a party other than an agency in litigation with the agency.

The rationale for this exemption was set forth before the United States Senate in the following terms:

> "This exemption was made upon the strong urging of virtually every Government agency. It is their contention, and one that the Committee believes has merit, that there are certain government processes relating to legal and policy matters which cannot be carried out efficiently if they must be carried out 'in a goldfish bowl.' Government officials would

be most hesitant to give their
frank and conscientious opinion
on legal and policy matters to
their superiors and co-workers if
they knew that at any future date,
their opinions of the moment would
be spread on the public record.
The Committee is of the opinion that
the Government cannot operate
effectively and honestly under such
circumstances."*

The exemption contained in Section (b)(5)

covers the type of documents and materials referred to in

Stiftung v. Zeiss, 40 FRD 318, 324 (D.D.C. 1966).

There, the District Court held that the following category

of documents was clearly covered by an executive privilege

and therefore non-obtainable:

". . . Intra-governmental documents
reflecting advisory opinions,
recommendations, and deliberations
comprising part of a process by

---

* Senate Report No. 1219, United States Senate, 88th
Congress, 2nd Session (1964).

27

324

> which governmental decisions and
> policies are formulated."

Section (b)(5) of the Act expressly incorporated the
prior case law of which Stiftung v. Zeiss, supra, is a
recent example.

Under the Freedom of Information Act,
Section (b)(5), the Courts have afforded the above-mentioned
material the same exemption from disclosure.   See
Freeman v. Seligson, 405 F.2d 326, 339 (D.C. Cir. 1968).
The judicial inquiry under (b)(5) involves a determination
as to whether the documents in question were part of an
agency's deliberate process "that must precede any well-
taken decision or policy statement".   Consumer's Union of
the United States, Inc. v. Veterans Administration, 301 F.
Supp. 796, 804-805 (S.D.N.Y. 1969).

It is clear that of the documents and
materials in question, the 3,000 page analysis unquestionably
comes within the (b)(5) exemption, in that the decision-
making process of a Government agency is analyzed at the
instance of the Secretary of Defense.   Many of the 4,000
pages of official documents clearly also come within the
(b)(5) exemption.   The Times in its edition of June 13,

28

1971, refers to the documents and materials in question
as a "highly unusual report of Government self-analysis".
It also refers to the study as a "great archive of
Government decision-making on Indochina over three decades".
A vast portion of the documents and materials in question
thus contain "advisory opinions, recommendations,
deliberations, comprising part of a process by which
governmental decisions and policies are formulated."

President Johnson, when signing into law
the Freedom of Information Act, recognized the importance
of the (b)(5) exemption when he stated:

> "Officials within Government must
> be able to communicate with one
> another fully and frankly and without
> publicity."

This principle has been judicially recognized in Bristol-
Myers Company v. Federal Trade Commission, supra, at Page 939
when the Court noted that (b)(5) "encourages the free
exchange of ideas among Government policy-makers . . ."
If an exemption from disclosure is not afforded the documents and materials in question under (b)(5), the willingness
and motivation of an agency of the Federal Government to

29

voluntarily analyze, and freely criticize its policies and decision-making processes will no doubt be curtailed in the future.

Under the foregoing analysis it is clear that if the documents and materials in question were in the Government's possession, a private party, such as the Times, could not lawfully compel their production; the exemptions contained sections (b)(1) and (b)(5) of the Act compel this conclusion. Equally compelling is the conclusion that the Times cannot claim any greater right to these documents and materials because they are presently in the unlawful and unauthorized possession of the Times.

CONCLUSION

Plaintiff's motion for a preliminary

30

injection should be in all respects granted.

Dated: New York, New York
June 17, 1971

Respectfully submitted,

WHITNEY NORTH SEYMOUR, JR.
United States Attorney for the
Southern District of New York,
Attorney for Plaintiff
United States of America.

MICHAEL D. HESS
JOSEPH D. DANAS
DANIEL RIESEL
MICHAEL I. SALTZMAN
MILTON SHERMAN
HOWARD S. SUSSMAN,
Assistant United States Attorneys,

Of Counsel.

UNITED STATES DISTRICT COURT

SOUTHERN DISTRICT OF NEW YORK

- - - - - - - - - - - - - - - - - - x

UNITED STATES OF AMERICA,   :

                    Plaintiff,   :

            -v-   :   71 Civ. 2662

NEW YORK TIMES COMPANY, et al.,   :

                    Defendants.   :

- - - - - - - - - - - - - - - - - - x

MEMORANDUM OF DEFENDANT NEW YORK TIMES COMPANY IN OPPOSITION TO ISSUANCE OF PRELIMINARY INJUNCTION

        This memorandum is submitted on behalf of defendant
New York Times Company in opposition to the motion of the
United States of America for a preliminary injunction.

        This action is a unique one in the history of the
nation. The United States here seeks to enjoin The New York
Times from performing its function as a newspaper. It seeks to
do so with respect to news articles dealing with the single most
controversial war in American history, which is today the single
most controversial issue in American life. Against the background of a First Amendment which, in the words of the Supreme

Court, "rests on the assumption that the widest possible
dissemination of information from diverse and antagonistic
sources is essential to the welfare of the public, [and]
that a free press is a condition of a free society",* the
United States here seeks to suppress further publication
of historical data of direct import to every citizen.

The Facts

On June 12, June 13 and June 14, 1971, The New
York Times published summaries and portions of the texts
of two highly significant historical documents. The documents,
certain volumes from a 1968 Pentagon study relating to Vietnam
and a summary of a 1965 Defense Department study relating to
the Tonkin Gulf incident, were made available to The Times
by a confidential source. The three articles, published at
a time of continuing widespread public debate as to the
Vietnam War, have been widely reported upon and commented
on throughout the world.

The United States seeks to enjoin The Times from
"further dissemination, disclosure or divulgence" of materials
contained in the 1968 study of the decision-making process

---

* Associated Press v. United States, 326 U.S. 1, 20 (1945).

with respect to Vietnam and the summary of the 1965 Tonkin Gulf study. It also seeks to require The Times to furnish to the United States all copies of the above documents held by The Times.

The action was commenced by the service upon The Times of a proposed order to show cause on June 15, 1971. On that day, this Court entered a temporary restraining order, effective until 1:00 P.M. on June 19, 1971, restraining The Times from disclosing "the documents" referred to "or any portions thereof." Simultaneously, the Court denied the motion of the United States seeking to require The Times to "deliver to this Court forthwith all the aforementioned documents. . . ."

The News Articles
In Question

As The Times stated in the first of its articles about the Pentagon study, what is involved in this case is a massive history of how the United States went to war in Indochina. The 3,000 page analysis to which 4,000 pages of official documents were appended was commissioned by Secretary of Defense McNamara in 1967 and completed in 1968. The

analysis is historical. Portions of it relate as far back as 40 years. None of it relates to a time period later than 1968.*

Publication of portions of the studies in question must be viewed against the background of Washington set forth in the uncontradicted affidavits of The Times personnel involved. There is before this Court a lengthy affidavit from Max Frankel relating to practices in Washington. There are before this Court affidavits from Messrs. Walter Rugaber, Hedrick Smith, John W. Finney, Tad Szulc and William Beecher, each of whom has sworn that numerous articles appended to his affidavit were obtained as a result of supposedly "classified" information being released to him.

---

* For the information of the Court the annexed affidavit of Max Frankel, Washington Bureau Chief and Washington correspondent of The Times, sets forth in detail some of the broad conclusions and specific findings of The Times with respect to the study. See, Frankel Aff., ¶¶ 29-37.

The Government's Case

The United States here seeks the remedy of a
temporary injunction on the basis that it will assertedly
suffer "irreparable harm" to its "defense interests" if
the New York Times is not judicially forbidden to publish
further articles such as those previously published. The
moving papers of the United States purport to support the
proposition that publication by the Times of further
excerpts will "prejudice the defense interests of the
United States and result in irreparable injury to the
national defense." (Buzhardt aff., ¶¶ 2,3). Beyond those
general allegations, thus far unsupported by a single _fact_
presented to this Court, the United States has not made
the slightest effort to prove that defense interests

of the nation would in fact be harmed by publication of the
series. The United States has not suggested that the
articles thus far published have revealed information
which can in any way endanger or injure American armed forces
or that there is any prospect of future articles having this
effect. The Times has not published sailing dates of troop
transports, not published secret plans of future military
maneuvers, not published data relating to weapons systems or
the like. It has instead published part of an historical
·record and, we submit, in doing so has served the nation as
the First Amendment intended it to.

First Amendment in Historical Perspective

This case lies at the core of First Amendment concern, namely, the interest in open and "robust debate" with respect to public affairs. New York Times Co. v. Sullivan, 378 U.S. 254, 269-70 (1964). The United States attempts, moreover, to impose a prior restraint on newspaper publications and prior restraints, as we shall show further, have an especially disfavored position under the First Amendment. Conflicting interests are pressed by the Government, and we need not and do not contend that the First Amendment always carries all before it, regardless of countervailing considerations. But "[a]ny claim which seeks prior restraint on publication bears a heavy burden." Liberty Lobby Inc. v. Pearson, 390 F.2d 489 (D.C.Cir. 1968) (Burger, J.).

In Liberty Lobby, plaintiffs sought a preliminary injunction against two syndicated newspaper columnists to prohibit "dissemination or publication" of letters and documents copied and removed from their files. The district court denied the motion, and the Court of Appeals affirmed, per Judge (now Chief Justice) Burger. In the court below, District Judge Holtzoff wrote:

"It would be a far-reaching limitation
on the freedom of the press if courts
were endowed with power to review the
manner in which the press obtains its
information and could restrain the
publication of news that is obtained
in a way that the Court does not aprove. [sic]
If such were the law we would not have a
free press; we would have a controlled
press. Such, however, is not the law.

"Cases involving publication of
letters in violation of a property right
in them or in violation of a copyright
are not in point. Here we are dealing
with the freedom of the press." Liberty
Lobby, Inc. v. Pearson, D.C.D.C., 261 F. Supp.
726, 727-728 (1966).

L

A half-century ago, in the years immediately during
and after World War I, the nation experienced a wave of re-
pressive prosecutions and Governmental actions directed against
"seditious" speech or speech otherwise thought to endanger the
national security. To this period belong cases decided under
earlier versions of the Espionage Act. But even decisions as
highly restrictive of freedom of speech and press as Schenck v.
United States, 249 U.S. 47 (1919) and Abrams v. United States,
250 U.S. 616 (1919), did not involve or sanction prior restraint.

And Chafee, Government and Mass Communications (1947)
notes that "Unlike the Sedition Act of 1798, the Espionage Act
was not used against newspapers of general circulation . . . ."
(Id. at 448).

Modern decisions have overruled most of the landmark cases of that time. See, e.g., Brandenburg, v. Ohio, 395 U.S. 444 (1969) overruling Whitney v. California, 274 U.S. 357 (1927). Other precedents dating back to that period, even when not overruled, are at best quiescent, being plainly out of tune with more recent authoritative judicial statements. Compare, Milwaukee Publishing Company v. Burleson, 255 U.S. 407 (1921) with Lamont d/b/a Basic Pamphlets v. Postmaster General, 381 U.S. 301 (1965) and Hannegan v. Esquire, Inc., 327 U.S. 146 (1946).

In the 1950s, First Amendment problems centered on speech inciting to violent overthrow of the Government, and on Congressional investigations of alleged subversive activities and associations. These developments are scarcely relevant to the instant case, but what may be deemed a re-latively harsh and overbroad approach in such a case as Dennis v. United States, 341 U.S. 494 (1951), was ameliorated and brought into line with other First Amendment developments in subsequent decisions, such as Yates v. United States, 354 U.S. 298 (1957) and Noto v. United States, 367 U.S. 290 (1961). See, also, Spock v. United Stated, 416 F.2d 165 (1st Cir. 1969) and, more recently, Brandenburg v. Ohio, supra.

The liberalizing trend is even more evident in legislative investigation cases, which are much more nearly analogous to the instant case. Compare, Barenblatt v. United States, 360 U.S. 109 (1959), with Gibson v. Florida Legislative Investigation Committee, 372 U.S. 539 (1963); and DeGregory v. Attorney General of New Hampshire, 383 U.S. 825 (1966).

The mainstream of modern First Amendment law relevant to the instant case is represented by New York Times Co. v. Sullivan, 376 U.S. 254 (1964) and the cases following it, culminating in Rosenbloom v. Metromedia Inc., 39 U.S.L.W. 4694 (U.S.Sup.Ct. June 7, 1971). In that case, the Supreme Court restated the governing principle in terms immediately applicable to the instant case. Quoting from Thornhill v. Alabama, 310 U.S. 88, 102 (1941), the court said:

> "Freedom of discussion if it would fulfill
> its inherent function in this nation, must
> embrace all issues about which information
> is needed or appropriate to enable the
> members of society to cope with the exigencies
> of their period." Rosenbloom v. Metromedia,
> Inc., B2656.

II.

Concerning specifically prior restraints, we start, as the Constitution itself started, with Blackstone, who wrote that "the liberty of the press. . . consists in laying no _previous_ restraints upon publications and not in freedom from censure for criminal matter when published." Blackstone, Commentaries IV, p. 151. The second half of this sentence has long since fallen into thorough disrepute, insofar as it is read to suggest that the criminal sanction may freely be imposed after publication. But ever since it was uttered, that sentence has been regarded as characterizing the especially disfavored position of prior restraints under the First Amendment. Blackstone's statement on prior restraints, and the repression in Stuart England and under George I, are the immediate formative background of the First Amendment. There may be debate about just how absolutely prohibited prior restraints should be. "The total prohibition of previous restraint", wrote Chafee in 1941, "would not allow the Government to prevent a newspaper from publishing the sailing dates of transports or the number of troops in a sector. It would forbid the removal of an indecent poster from a billboard. Censorship of moving pictures before exhibiting has been held valid under a free speech clause." Chafee, _Free Speech in the United States_, 10 (5th printing 1954). Under current decisions, the indecent

poster is likely to stay on the billboard, and censorship
of motion pictures, as allowed by <u>Mutual Film Corporation</u>
v. <u>Industrial Commission of Ohio</u>, 236 U.S. 230 (1915),
would not be possible today. <u>See</u>, <u>Freedman</u> v. <u>Maryland</u>,
380 U.S. 51 (1965), though as a general proposition it may
be conceded that the publication of sailing dates of transports or the number of troops in a sector of a war zone
could be prevented. But Chafee is the first to assert that
the purpose of the framers of the Bill of Rights was to
codify Blackstone's radical aversion to prior restraints,
which had ultimately prevailed in England as well, and then
to go further and prevent most subsequent restraints imposed
by criminal sanctions also. "In short, the framers of the
First Amendment sought to preserve the fruits of the old
victory abolishing the censorship and to achieve a new victory
abolishing sedition prosecutions." Chafee, <u>Free Speech in the</u>
<u>United States</u>, p. 22.

It has been clear, at least since the decision
in Near v. Minnesota, 203 U.S. 687 (1931), that whatever
the Government may do in the way of punishing a publisher
for his utterances, it cannot stifle that utterance prior
to publication except in the most narrowly defined circumstances. The Supreme Court has repeatedly and clearly
stated that any prior governmental restrictions on the
publication by the press of information bearing on public
affairs and questions of legitimate public interest are
completely incompatible with the public's freedom of speech
and with freedom of the press.

As Mr. Justice Harlan observed in Curtis Publ. Co.
v. Butts, 388 U.S. 130, 149 (1967), ". . . we have rejected
all manner of prior restraint on publication, Near v. Minnesota,
283 U.S. 697, 75 L.Ed. 1357, 51 S.Ct. 625, despite strong
arguments that if the material was unprotected the time of
suppression was immaterial." And as the Court stated in
Bantam Books, Inc. v. Sullivan, 372 U.S. 58, 70 (1963): "Any
system of prior restraints of expression comes to this Court
hearing a heavy presumption against its constitutional validity."

The crucial principle is that the utterances involved must be permitted entrance to the free market place of ideas. If the speaker has abused his right to speak he is, of course, liable to pay the penalties pre-scribed by law. See Near v. Minnesota, 283 U.S. 697 (1931).

The unprecedented nature of the relief sought by the Government here is sharply revealed by its inability to cite a simple case authorizing such a pre-publication injunction. We have found none*, and thus far the United States has cited none.

The Government Has to Have A Specific Statutory Basis For the Relief It Seeks

As the Government conceded in oral argument on June 15, no non-statutory, or inherent, authority exists or can be claimed for its prayer in this case. Youngstown Sheet

---

* It is true that in some cases the State may enjoin the publication of obscene books where the statutory procedure provides for prompt judicial review and determination -- see Bantam Books Inc. v. Sullivan, 372 U.S. 58, 70 (1963). However, obscene speech is not protected by the First Amendment at all - Roth v. United States, 354 U.S. 476 (1953), whereas the protection afforded to free speech on public affairs and politics lies at the very heart of the First Amendment.

and Tube Company v. Sawyer; Cf., United States v. United States District Court Eastern District of Michigan, 6th Cir., April 8, 1971, 37 U.S. Law Week 2574.

We have surveyed all statutory provisions which
might, by their terms, prohibit the dissemination (to use
the broadest term) of sensitive government information. The
only statutory provision which is not, by its very terms,
conclusively inapplicable in this case is 18 U.S.C. § 793(e).*

---

* The other statutory provisions directed to the prohibition
of or punishment for the dissemination of such data are
42 U.S.C. §§ 2161 through 2166 relating to the authority of
the Atomic Energy Commission to classify and declassify
"Restricted Data" ["Restricted Data" is a term of art employed uniquely by the Atomic Energy Act]. Specifically,
42 U.S.C. § 2162 authorizes the Atomic Energy Commission to
classify certain information. 42 U.S.C. Chapter 23, Sub-
chapter XVII prohibits the unlawful dissemination of
"Restricted Data". 42 U.S.C. § 2274, subsection (a) provides penalties for a person who "communicates, transmits,
or discloses . . . with intent to injure the United States
or an intent to secure an advantage to any foreign nation
. . ." "Restricted Data". Subsection (b) of § 2274 provides
lesser penalties for one who "communicates, transmits, or
discloses" such information "with reason to believe such
data will be utilized to injure the United States or to
secure an advantage to any foreign nation . . . ." Other
sections of Title 42 of the U.S.C. dealing with atomic energy
prohibit and punish acquisition, removal, concealment,
tampering with, alteration, mutilation or destruction of
documents incorporating "Restricted Data" and provide penalties for employees and former employees of the Atomic Energy
Commission, the armed services, contractors and licensees of
the Atomic Energy Commission. 42 U.S.C. §§ 2276, 2277 - the
foregoing statutes are clearly not applicable in this case
because there has been no claim that the study in question
contains any "Restricted Data" within the meaning of the
Atomic Energy Act. Title 50 appendix of the U.S.C., § 781
prohibits the making of any sketch or other representation
of military installations or any military equipment located
on any military installation, as specified. This section is,
by its terms, not relevant to this case. 50 U.S.C. § 783(b)
makes it unlawful for any officers or employee of the United
States or any corporation which is owned by the United States
to communicate material which has been "classified" by the
President to any person whom that governmental employee knows
or has reason to believe is an agent or representative of any
foreign government or any communist organization. This section is clearly inapplicable, by its terms, to any of the
defendants in this action.

In his telegram to the New York Times of June 14, the only statutory authority asserted by the Attorney General was section 793. The Government's memorandum in support of its motion for a temporary restraining order relied on 793(d). But in oral argument the Government shifted reliance to 793(e). Subsection 793(e) is indeed the only statutory provision that is even colorably applicable, although, as we shall show, even it is not on analysis capable of meeting the Government's purposes in this case. Our contention is that there is no statutory basis for the Government's action which must therefore fail. We contend also that if subsection 793(e) is construed to support the claims the Government makes under it in this case, it must be held unconstitutional as applied.

Any Statute Allegedly Applicable
To This Case Must Be Framed In
Specific and Clear Language to
Avoid Being Held Unconstitutional
For Vagueness or Excessive Delegation

The limited area of leeway left to the Government under the First Amendment to impose restraints on speech is tolerated only in context of a strict requirement that the greatest precision be used in defining these restraints.

General rules of vagueness and of the need of standards in
legislative delegation have particular application in this
area. United States v. Rumely, 345 U.S. 41 (1953);
Watkins v. United States, 354 U.S. 178 (1957); Kent v.
Dulles, 357 U.S. 116 (1958); Aptheker v. United States,
378 U.S. 500 (1964); Gojack v. United States, 384 U.S. 702
(1966); Zemel v. Rusk, 381 U.S. 1 (1965). "The tradition
of English-speaking freedom has depended in no small part
upon the merely procedural requirement that the state point
with exactness to just that conduct which violates the law."
Masses Publishing Co. v. Patten, 244 Fed. 535 (   )
(L. Hand, J.) (S.D.N.Y. 1917), reversed on other grounds,
245 Fed. 102 (2d Cir. 1917).

Moreover, 18 U.S.C. 793 is a criminal statute, and
although it is at the moment not invoked in the attempt to
impose the criminal sanctions, its construction in this extraordinary civil action can hardly be different than the construction which would be given it if it were used to achieve its
prime end, namely, imposition of the criminal sanction. Criminal
statutes of all sorts, let alone those affecting First Amendment
rights, must, of course, also be read closely and narrowly, so as

to avoid the vice of vagueness. United States v. Sullivan,
332 U.S. 689 (1948); Winters v. New York, 333 U.S. 507 (1948);
Lanzetta v. New Jersey, 306 U.S. 451 (1939); Connally v.
General Construction Co., 269 U.S. 385 (1926).

It is in this spirit that 18 U.S.C. section 793
must be read. It is, indeed, in this spirit that the predecessor statute of section 793 was read in Gorin v. U.S.,
312 U.S. 19 (1941), a case which does not settle the construction of Section 793 for our purposes, although we will return
to a further discussion of it presently.

The Inapplicability of § 793 of the Espionage Act

The United States relies upon 18 U.S.C. § 793(d) and (e) in its effort to locate a statute as to which it may assert against The Times a colorable claim of breach. The argument will not withstand analysis.

Subsections (d) and (e) of 18 U.S.C. § 793, as amended in 1950, were plainly intended to be complementary. Subsection (d) deals with persons having lawful possession of the materials referred to, while subsection (e) deals with "unauthorized possession."

As the Government conceded in oral argument on its motion for a temporary restraining order, subsection (d) can scarcely apply to the instant case. The section is obviously directed at Government officials, or consultants and the like, and intended to regulate their conduct in dealing with documents, other materials, and information relating to the national defense, by forbidding them to communicate, deliver or transmit to persons outside the Government, and requiring them to surrender possession on demand to other officials. If the attempt is to apply it to the New York Times or to any other private person having no quasi-official connection with the Government, the absurdity that results is

that the premise of lawful possession by such private
person negates any allegation of a relationship to
the national defense in the document or material in
question, or of the classified nature of such material.
Else the section has to be read as conceiving the possibility of _lawful_ private possession by non-government
connected persons of information relating to the national
defense which it is a crime for Government officials to
communicate or transmit to precisely such private persons.
Unlawful or unauthorized possession of such documents or
information by private persons may be another matter.
Assuming, nevertheless, that subsection (d) deals with
lawful possession of information related to the national
defense by private persons, the equally absurd and legally
untenable result would be that the section punishes communication, and, as it would have to be read for purposes of this
case, publication of material lawfully in private hands, such
as a press release or a government publication.

It is certainly unnecessary to extend the argument about subsection (d) any further, and it was perhaps
unnecessary to enter upon it to begin with. We believe
we can safely take it that section (d) is inapplicable.
Hence, we direct our argument at 18 U.S.C. § 793(e).

The operative terms of subsection (e) are
(1) "unauthorized possession," (2) "relating to the
national defense," (3) "wilfully communicates, delivers,
transmits or causes to be communicated, delivered or
transmitted," and (4) "wilfully retains the same and
fails to deliver it to the officer or employee of the
United States entitled to receive it."

In analyzing the subsection, and endeavoring
to discover in it the close and precise drafting required
in a criminal statute affecting the freedom of the press,
we will deal separately and first with the provisions
under which the Government attempts to enjoin publication,
and then with the last quoted language on which the Government bases its demand for delivery.

"Unauthorized Possession"

We start with the word "unauthorized". It is
undefined and has no point of reference, and it is not
helped much by being read to mean simply "unlawful." The
difficulty is that it is nowhere indicated under what
statutory provision possession is to be deemed authorized
or unauthorized, lawful or unlawful.

18 U.S.C. § 798 defines possession of Government documents or official information as unlawful, and then punishes their communication, transmission or -- what is of the first importance, as we shall argue further -- its publication. (18 U.S.C. § 798) The Government does not rely on this section because it cannot. The section applies to four specified categories of classified information, none of which fit the Government's allegations about the documents in issue in this case. In view of the explicit use and definition in section 798 of the term "classified information", it is not possible to argue that "unauthorized possession" in subsection (e) means simpliciter possession by a private person of classified information. For when Congress meant to refer to classified information it knew how to do so, not only in 18 U.S.C. § 798, but in numerous other statutes not here applicable, in all of which classified information is called by that name, or alternatively designated as restricted information, that term being duly defined.*

.

---

* See 50 U.S.C. § 783(b), which makes it unlawful for any officer or employee of the United States to communicate with an agent or representative of any foreign government or an officer or member of any communist organization any information of a kind which shall have been classified by the president or under the authority of the president as affecting the security of the United States. See also 42 U.S.C. §§ 2161-2166, 42 U.S.C. § 2274-2277 where the defined term "Restricted Data" is used. 42 U.S.C. § 2014(y) defines "Restricted Data" as all data concerning the design, manufacture or utilization of atomic weapons, the production of special nuclear material (as defined in 42 U.S.C. § 4(aa)) and the use of special nuclear material in the producti of energy.

The word "unauthorized" is too vague for valid use in a criminal statute affecting First Amendment rights. It recalls nothing so much as the use of the word "may", which was held to constitute a vague and invalid delegation in Kent v. Dulles, supra. The contrary contention is an arbitrary attempt to amalgamate two separate sections of the statute, 793 and 798, which must have been intended to deal with separate kinds of conduct. The attempt is understandable, because by its own terms, section 798 is inapplicable to this case. While understandable from the Government's point of view, however, the attempt is inadmissible.

"Relating to the National Defense"

The core concept of subsection (e) is embodied in the phrase "relating to the national defense." The phrase has a certain definite look about it, but the appearance is delusive. The merest glance at the Federal Register, for example, will show some 18 inches of text relating to the national defense, and so captioned, including such disparate matters as procurement and promotion procedures, and paternity suits in cases involving the military.

In Gorin v. United States, 312 U.S. 19 (1941), the vice of vagueness in this phrase, as it appeared in a

predecessor statute, was dealt with by the Supreme Court
in a way which is probably not open in this case, or which,
if it is open, must result in a denial of the Government's
motion. An element of the offense in Gorin was "intent or
reason to believe [on the part of the defendants] that the
information to be obtained is to be used to the injury of
the United States or to the advantage of any foreign nation."
The language just quoted, the Court held, required the defendants to have acted in bad faith. Hence, the Court said,
the sanctions "apply only when scienter is established." 312
U.S. at 28. Similar language requiring that the possessor of
information relating to the national defense have "reason to
believe [that it] could be used to the injury of the United
States or to the advantage of any foreign nation," appears in
subsection (e). But it seems to us likely that in subsection
(e), this language modifies only the word "information," not
the words "any document, writing, code book, etc." appearing
earlier in the subsection. There is an indication to this effect
in the legislative history. S.Rep. 2369, 81st Cong., 2d Sess. 9
(1950). Scienter cannot therefore be imputed as an element in
the phrase "relating to the national defense," so far as it relates to documents and writings, which under the Government's
allegations are in issue in this case. Without the element of
scienter, the holding of Gorin that the phrase is not void for
vagueness is inapplicable.

In this connection it is to be noted also that
Gorin construed the predecessor statute of section 793(e)
in an ordinary espionage case concerning the delivery of
documents to an agent of a foreign nation. It did not deal
with a newspaper publication, and thus was decided wholly
outside any First Amendment context. The vice of vagueness
is at its gravest in statutory language affecting First
Amendment rights.

If, on the other hand, the clause requiring the
possessor to believe that what he had in his possession
"could be used to the injury of the United States or to
the advantage of any foreign nation" is deemed applicable
to this case, then the clause emphasizes and renders even
more conclusive an argument concerning the state of mind of
the defendant in this case which we shall elaborate further
on. Suffice it to say here that if this clause is inapplicable, the court needs to find wilfulness in the communication
and retention of the documents obtained by the New York Times.
If the clause is applicable, it is necessary to find also
that the New York Times had "reason to believe" that the documents "could be used to the injury of the United States or to
the advantage of any foreign nation." But as our affidavits
show, the New York Times had every reason to believe that

these documents contained nothing but historical materials compiled over a period of time ending in 1968, that most of them run back several years and some of them several decades, and that none deal with events less than three years old. The Times had no reason to surmise injury to the United States or advantage to any foreign nation, unless we are to accept the preposterous and plainly unconstitutional construction that any discomfiture caused the Government of the United States by political opposition at home qualifies as an injury to the United States and an advantage to a foreign nation within the meaning of subsection (e).

Quite aside from any requirement of scienter, and all the more so if such a requirement is applicable, the concept of documents or information "relating to the national defense" must be restricted to a meaning that can fairly be expected to have been in the minds of, or at least accessible to, persons situated as is the defendant in this case. We believe the concept is clearly unconstitutionally vague if it is read to go beyond both decided cases that have construed it in the past, and the common understanding exhibited in the practices of newspapers

and publishers of other materials.

We have found no case beyond a single civil action* -- which was not a prosecution or other action initiated by the Government -- in which this subsection, or indeed any part of section 793, was applied to anything but an ordinary espionage situation. At no time until the Government's motion was filed in this Court on June 15 has the Government used this section to move criminally or civilly against a publication -- not communication or transmittal or delivery, but publication -- of any materials or information in a newspaper or magazine or book or any other medium addressed internally within the United States to the American public. This has been the unbroken administrative practice, which we submit is conclusive against the attempted application of section 793 in this case. See, e.g., Poe v. Ullman, 367 U.S. 497 (1961); Louisville C. & St. L. Ry. v. Browning , 310 U.S. 262 (1960).

There might be some question about the conclusive application of the administrative practice rule of construction here if it were true that no or few recent occasions had arisen, or come to the Government's attention, which presented the need for an application of the

---

* Dubin v. United States, 289 F.2d 651 (Ct. of Claims 1961) (a civil action brought by a private citizen to recover the fair market value of radar equipment purchased as "surplus" which the Government reclaimed under an assertion that said devices were "classified" and mistakenly sold for surplus.)

statute, if such an application were thought possible,
beyond the ordinary espionage situation. But the overwhelming fact, demonstrated by Max Frankel's affidavit
(e.g., Frankel affidavit ¶¶ 15, 16, 20) and other affidavits and by our appendix, is that numerous publications
similar and even precisely equivalent to the publications
made and still contemplated by The New York Times, have
been common in newspapers, magazines and books in the
United States for many years. The unbroken practice on
the part of the government of moving only against what
may properly be defined as espionage - a practice bespeak-
ing the construction of section 793 as applying only to
what may accurately be described as espionage - has prevailed, then, in a context of public discourse in which
the supposed offense now charged to The New York Times
under section 793 was an entirely common occurrence in
newspapers, magazines and books published to the American
people. This is the context of public discourse in which
former President Lyndon Johnson, appearing on a CBS television program, brandished a document of the same vintage
and on the same subject as the documents now in the possession of The New York Times (and no doubt equally classified).

---

*   See also affidavit of Walter Rugaber, ¶ 2 and annexed
      exhibits; affidavit of Hedrick Smith, ¶ 2 and annexed
      exhibits; affidavit of John W. Finney, ¶ 2 and annexed
      exhibits, affidavit of Tad Szule, ¶ 2 and annexed exhi-
      bits and affidavit of William Beecher, ¶ 2 and annexed
      exhibits.

and read from it to the public. It is the context in which
memoirists who formerly held high government office and
various journalists and others have published books going
over the same ground as the publications of The New York Times,
and using in part materials included in the documents now in
the possession of The New York Times.*

Vagueness is held to be the vice in part because
application of a vague statute necessarily takes place without notice. It punishes or regulates with the same degree
of surprise to those on whom it falls as an ex post facto
law. A vague statute is applied without prior notice of the
conduct that is suddenly made subject to the law, and in the
sense of running counter to justifiably held expectations,
and imposing a legal sanction by surprise, it is, like an
ex post facto statute, a law that did not exist at the time
the supposed offense was committed. In the circumstances,
the law the government now seeks to apply to The New York
Times was written for the first time in the government's
complaint.

---

* See Frankel affidavit ¶¶ 27, 28; see also Matthew B. Ridgeway,
The Korean War, pp. 267, 268 (containing texts of letters of
instruction to air and naval forces of the United States;
Theodore C. Sorenson, Kennedy, p. 612 (relating to the
"missile gap"), p. 642 (relating to U.S. intervention in
Laos), p. 659 (paraphrasing cable relating to overthrow of
Diem), p. 712 (relating to Cuban missile crisis; John
Bartlow Martin, Overtaken by Events, p. 757 (revealing the
author's sources of information to be private notes and files
accumulated while in government service, p. 235 (paraphrasing
a "top priority - top secret" cable on communist involvement
in Dominican Republic in 1965).

It may be contended that Attorney General
Mitchell's telegram to The New York Times of June 14th
authoritatively defines the phrase "relating to the national
defense" for purposes of this case, and cures its vagueness.
Among other difficulties with this contention, the
decisive one is that it would repose untrammeled discretion
in the Attorney General or in the Secretary of Defense or
in some other officers of the Government to define the
terms of a statute which imposes criminal penalties,
and which in this unprecedented instance is being used to
impose a prior restraint upon a newspaper. Such a delegation would without doubt be unconstitutional under Kent v.
Dulles, supra; Rumely v. United States, supra; Watkins v.
United States, 354 U.S. 178 (1957); Sweezy v. New Hampshire,
354 U.S. 234 (1957). See also, Schechter Poultry Company v.
United States, 295 U.S. 495 (1965).

There is no warrant for defining the concept,
"relating to the national defense," as coterminous with the
concept of classified information. Nor would it be possible
in this fashion to cure the vagueness of the phrase as applied
in this case, since no expectation can be imputed to the defendant that any classified material, no matter what its nature,
would be considered, to relate to the national defense within
the meaning of this statute. It is notorious that numerous
papers having no proper relation to the national defense, or
no longer having any, and in no sense dangerous or injurious

to the national security if published, are or remain
nevertheless classified, despite the perhaps more restrictive criteria for classification contained in the
President's Executive Order No. 10501. (18 Fed. Reg.
7049, Nov. 10, 1953). The late Professor Chafee wrote:

> "Of course, state secrets are nothing new. Military
> information was always guarded from the enemy, and
> bureaucrats have often invoked public safety as a
> protection from criticism. What is significant is
> the enormous recent expansion of the subjects which
> officials are seeking to hide from publication until
> they give the signal. If persuasion fails to pre-
> vent leaks, they are tempted to use threats. The
> result may be a hush-hush attitude, likely to extend
> beyond the real public need for silence. . . . A
> direct consequence of secrecy in the ordinary press
> may be great activity of the subsidiary press in
> disseminating the concealed material, and this is
> more dangerous than frank discussion in the general
> press. . . . Too often we get as gossip what
> ought to reach us as regular news." Chafee, Government
> and mass communications 13 (Archon ed. 1965).

It may be true, and it does not in any event,
affect our position in this case, that as was held in
Epstein v. Resor, 296 F. Supp. 214 (D.C.N.D. Calif. 1969),
no elaborate inquiry into the justification for a classification will be undertaken by a court in response to a suit
by a private individual seeking to have the Government declassify
material so that the plaintiff can obtain it under section 3
of the Administrative Procedure Act, 5 U.S.C. § 552. That
statute by its terms does not apply to materials kept
secret in the interest of national defense or foreign
policy. What may be judicially acceptable as a criterion

for classification when the classification comes under attack in a suit by a plaintiff wanting to obtain material from the Government is one thing. But there is a vast difference when application to a private person of a criminal statute is questioned, or when as here the Government, acting under a criminal statute, seeks to impose a prior restraint on publication. Under these conditions, the judicial function in passing on criteria for classification is infinitely more crucial. Yet it is notable that even in the Epstein case, the Court did not accept without question and without judicial review any classification simply because it was placed on a document in the regular order by a Government official. The Court undertaook rather to make an independent judicial inquiry at least whether a classification is "clearly arbitrary and unsupportable." The Court said:

> "Otherwise, the agencies could easily frustrate the purpose of full disclosure intended by Congress merely by labelling the information to fall within the exemption." 296 F. Supp. at 217.

Other cases in addition to Epstein conclusively refute any assertion that the question of whether a classification is valid is a political question, and that the act of classification is an exercise of executive discretion not subject to

judicial review. To the contrary, like other equally and
sometimes even more serious exercises of executive discretion relating to the internal and external security of the
country, the act of classifying a document is subject to
judicial review, even as the ultimate act of declaring
martial law is under our system of government subject to
judicial review. Sterling v. Constantine, 287 U.S. 378 (1932);
 Duncan v. Kohonamaku, 327 U.S. 304 (1946);

United States v. Reynolds, 345 U.S. 1 (1953);

United
States v. U.S. Dist. Ct. E.D. Mich., 39 U.S.L.W. 2574 (6th
Cir. 1971); United States v. Hilliard, 39 U.S.L.W. 2680
(U.S. Dist. Ct. Cal. 1971); Dubin v. United States, supra. In
United States v. Drummond, 354 F.2d 132 (2d Cir. 1965) which
affirmed a conviction under the Federal Espionage Act, the
Second Circuit held that the classification of certain documents as "Top Secret" or as "containing information affecting
the national security of the United States" was not sufficient
for a conviction. Rather, the Second Circuit ruled that the
defendant had a "right to a jury determination on the character
of the documents," pointing out that the trial court had
properly charged the jury that:

> "Whether any given document relates to the
> national defense of the United States is a
> question of fact for you to decide. It is not
> a question of how they are marked." Id. at 152.

In a case arising under a criminal statute in which a prior
restraint on publication is sought, it is all the more
essential that judicial review of a classification be full,
even to the extent of imposing the burden of proof on the
Government.

We contend that it is not permissible to read
the statutory phrase "relating to the national defense" as
synonymous with the phrase classified materials in view of
the use by Congress of the express term classification in
18 U.S.C. 798 and other statutes. Without conceding the
possibility of such a construction, we believe furthermore
that even if it were possible, and the concept of classification were read into the statutory phrase, "relating to
the national defense," so as to constitute a sufficient
definition of it, the considerations aduced in the previous
paragraph would strengthen our contention that the statutory
language as applied in this case is unconstitutionally vague.
We have demonstrated that the notorious misuse and indiscriminate use of classifications, which would have made it
impossible for any newspaper to conclude that the mere fact
of a classification appearing on a document proves that
that document relates to the national defense in the terms
of section 793(e) -- this misuse and indiscriminate use of

classification is reflected in the practice of the courts in exercising judicial review of classification;in cases in which they become relevant. A person picking up a classified document and asking himself the question whether the classification it bears brings it within the category of materials "relating to the national defense" in the terms of section 793(e) would be disabled from arriving at a definite answer to that question, which could govern his conduct. Not only is it notorious that officials often lightly affix classifications to documents, but the ultimate determination of the bearing of the classification on liability under section 793(e) remains for a court to make on judicial review. In the First Amendment area, such vagueness is not tolerated. See e.g. Burstyn v. Wilson, 393 U.S. 495 (1952).

As this court pointed out at the argument on the Government's motion for a temporary restraining order, and as is of course true, the general rule is that federal courts "have no power to enjoin the commission of a crime." United States v. Jalas, 409 F.2d 358 (7th Cir. 1969). Among the reasons underlying this general rule is that when it enjoins a prospective criminal act, as it is asked to do in this case, the court initiates a procedure whereby the defendant, by performing the criminal act prohibited by the court becomes a contemnor and is punished for his crime by the court. The criminal process is thus short-circuited, and the defendant-contemnor deprived of his right to a jury trial for

offenses, as the law now stands, for which a punishment of no
more than six months is imposed. He is deprived also, of course,
of the right to indictment by a grand jury.

The bearing of the general rule that equity will not
enjoin commission of a crime on the present case is that the
exceptions to the rule are generally given as three: the presence
of a national emergency, existence of a widespread public nuisance,
or existence of a specific statutory power to issue the injunction.
The first exception, on which In re Debs, 158 U.S. 564 (1⁢), and
United States v. United Mine Workers of America, 330 U.S. 259
(1947) rested, is obviously the only one that could be applicable
in this case. In order to issue the preliminary injunction
prayed for, the court would therefore have to find not
merely that documents or information "relating to the national
defense" in some attenuated or remote way were in issue,
but that further publication of these documents - - further
publication, since that is all the court is asked to enjoin
and that is all this case is about -- would so relate to the
national defense as to give rise to a national emergency, comparable to the railroad and mine strikes that were involved in
the two cited cases. In those cases the finding of a national
emergency was supported by very concrete facts concerning the effect
of the strikes, not only on the economy in general, but on the
health and well-being of millions of people. Whatever else it has
vouchsafed us in its generalities about the long-range effect of
further publication of these documents, about supposed subtle effect:
not immediately apparent to even close observers of our affairs,

including foreign officials, historians, and members of
Congress, as our affidavits show -- whatever allegations of
that sort the Government has framed in general terms, it has
of course shown nothing remotely comparable to the concrete-
ness of the facts on which a finding of national emergency
was supported in the Debs and United Mine Workers cases.
Yet such a finding is required of the court by the only
exception here applicable to the rule that equity will not
enjoin a prospective criminal act. We cannot conceive how
a simple equation of the phrase "relating to the national
defense" with the concept of classification could suffice
to constitute a finding, not only that section 793(e) is
applicable to this case, but also -- as is indispensable --
that a national emergency is in the offing, which justifies
enjoining the commission of an alleged prospective criminal
act.

"Communicates, Delivers, Transmits . . ."

The phrase "communicates, delivers, transmits
or causes to be . . ." is a wholly inapt reference to
the act of publishing. What it does aptly describe is
the ordinary espionage situation, as for example in
Gorin v. United States, supra, and in all other cases
we have been able to find, without exception, to which
in the past the Government has applied section 793.*

---

* Boeckenhaupt v. U.S., 392 F.2d 24 (4th Cir. 1968); U.S.
v. Rosenberg, 195 F.2d 583 (2d Cir. 1952); U.S. v.
Drummond, supra, and U.S. v. Butenko, 384 F.2d 554
(3rd Cir. 1967), vacated sub. nom Alderman v. U.S.,
394 U.S. 165 (1969).

This is evident as a matter of common English. Communicating, delivering, transmitting -- these are actions that take place between one and another individual or groups of individuals. In common usage they do not denote the act of printing and publishing. No doubt the jargon of the day refers to "communications media," but we do not say that anyone communicates a newspaper or a book, or that anyone communicates an article or even information in a newspaper or a book, let alone deliver or transmit it.

The only case we have found, which in a somewhat different but tellingly relevant context delineates the distinction between communicating and publishing is United States v. Baltimore Post Co., 22 F.2d 761 (D.C. Md. 1924). In this case, the Baltimore Post Company was indicted for violating Revised Statutes, Section 3167, as re-enacted by section 1018 of the Revenue Act of June 2, 1924 (43 Stat. 253, 254), by publishing that portion of a citizen's federal income tax return which showed his name and the amount of his tax. The newspaper defended on the ground that the statute did not apply to it, and that if it was forbidden to publish, the statute abridged the freedom

of the press guaranteed by the First Amendment. The
Court held the statute inapplicable, avoiding the constitutional issue, and in meeting an argument by the government, necessary for purposes of the government's proposed
statutory construction, that the words communicate and
publish were synonymous, the court said:

> "To 'publish' is to make public; to make
> known to people in general. In the statute,
> it does not cover the private communication
> by one person to another. It is not synonymous
> with 'communicate' as it may be in the law
> of libel or slander." 2 F.2d at 764.

Whatever doubts might nonetheless be legitimately
entertained on the question whether Section 793(e) covers
the act of publishing are disspelled by an examination of
the entire Espionage Act and of its legislative history.
The striking fact is that when Congress wanted to proscribe
the act of publishing as well as communicating, delivering
or transmitting, it knew how to do so, and insisted on doing
so.

When it wanted to proscribe publishing, as well
as communicating, delivering or transmitting, it said so,
and used the specific term. This is what Congress did in

18 U.S.C. Sections 794, 797 and 798. In other words,
when Congress dealt in Section 794 with the highly
dangerous act of revealing to the enemy, in war time,
information on troop movements and dispositions, on
ships, aircraft and war materials, on operations plans
fortifications and other [which would be construed to
mean similar] information relating to public defense,
which it made a capital offense, Congress spoke of whoever, in time of war, "collects, records, publishes, or
communicates." (Italics supplied) Again, when in
Section 797 Congress dealt with special military and
naval installations so denominated by the President,
Congress spoke of "whoever reproduces, publishes, sells,
or gives away any photograph, sketch, picture, etc."
(Italics supplied) Finally, when in Section 798, which
we have referred to previously, Congress very specifically
defined and listed, and then punished the disclosure of,
four categories of classified information, it spoke of
whoever "knowingly and wilfully communicates, furnishes,
transmits, or otherwise makes available to an unauthorized
person, or publishes . . . ." (Italics supplied)

Section 798, then, as well as the other
sections referred to, unmistakably demonstrate
Congress' practice of distinguishing carefully among
actions such as communicating, furnishing, making
available and transmitting, on the one hand, and on
the other hand the act of publishing. When Congress
wished to cover the latter, it named it. And under
a Constitution that includes a First Amendment, which
in turn places the act of publishing to the people at
large in a specially protected category, it is natural
for a legislative body to take nice distinctions between
words (e.g. communicate, transmit) aptly characterizing
the ordinary espionage transaction, and the single term
which describes with precision the activities of those
who issue to the public its daily newspapers, its books,
and, by extension, its radio and TV broadcasts. And
it is doubly natural, given the First Amendment, for
Congress to have used the word "publish" sparingly,
and only when it thought it crucial, on particular
occaions or with respect to particular matters, to
attempt to reach this far.

Thus in the extended debates in the first session of the 65th Congress in 1917 on the predecessor espionage act to present Sections 793 and 794 of Title 18 U.S.C., both the House bill (H.R. 291), which ultimately was enacted as Sections 31, 32, 34 and 36 of Title 50 U.S.C.,* and the parallel (but more broadly drawn) Senate Bill (S.2), contained provisions empowering the President in time of war or threat of war to directly prohibit by proclamation the publication of information relating to national defense which might be useful to the enemy. The provision in H.R. 291 was as follows:

> "SEC. 4. During any national emergency resulting from a war to which the United States is a party, or from threat of such a war, the President may, by proclamation, prohibit the publishing or communicating of, or the attempting to publish or communicate any information relating to the national defense which, in his judgment, is of such character that it is or might be useful to the enemy. Whoever violates any such prohibition shall be punished by a fine of not more than $10,000 or by imprisonment for not more than 10 years, or both: <u>Provided</u>, That nothing in this section shall be construed to limit or restrict any discussion, comment, or criticism of the acts or policies of the Government or its representatives or the publication of the same." (55 Cong. Rec. 1763)

---

* Act of June 15, 1917, ch 30, Title I, §§ 1, 2, 4, 6, 40 Stat. 217, 218, 219

Since war had already been declared on Germany, Congress

was under great pressure to grant whatever emergency powers

the executive requested. Yet from the beginning, the issue

of freedom of the press was considered of paramount importance,

and was felt by the sponsors of the espionage acts to require

the most precise and careful draftsmanship. This attitude

was expressed by Representative Webb of North Carolina,

Chairman of the House Committee on the Judiciary, in introducing

H.R. 291:

> "Mr. WEBB. Mr. Speaker and gentlemen
> of the House, what the gentleman from Illinois
> [Mr. MADDEN] has said is in large part true,
> in that this is a very important measure. I
> think it has been magnified somewhat by a lot
> of misinformation that has been printed about
> it in the newspapers, and they have created
> the impression that the committee or somebody
> was undertaking to unduly abridge the freedom
> of the press and the freedom of speech. There
> might have been some little warrant for that
> suggestion if some provisions for the various
> bills introduced during the last six months
> had been recommended to this House; but I
> desire to say to the House that the bill as
> originally introduced has been practically
> rewritten by your committee. We sat around
> the committee table for practically three
> weeks in an effort to clarify every ambiguous
> and uncertain term used in the original bill.
> We wanted to make each offense definite, so that
> the public would know when it was committing
> a crime; and, section by section, patiently,
> all day long often, the committee have gone
> over every line of the bill and have rewritten
> it, and therefore we offer you a substitute
> for the bill as originally introduced; and,
> at the risk of being a little tiresome possibly,
> I will explain in a running way each section
> of the bill." (55 Cong. Rec. 1590)

Similarly Senator Ashurst spoke at length on the question of freedom of the press in supporting this amendment to S.2:

"Mr. ASHURST. Mr. President, I have submitted an amendment of Chapter II of the pending bill because I am unable to support that chapter in its present form. I am opposed to a censorship of the press as we have come to know that expression, and I oppose it on two grounds-upon the ground of public policy and upon the ground of constitutionality. I shall discuss the present chapter, reviewing both aspects of the same as they present themselves to me; that is, from the standpoint of public policy and from the standpoint of its constitutionality.

"Press censorships in every government have invariably brought unhappy and in many instances disastrous results. The evil that a censorship creates is more malignant than the evil it seeks to avoid and conceal. If, during the ensuing war, the press should be censored and information as to the progress of the war should go to the public filtered through a censor, we would soon be living in a vapor of suspicion, a cloud of misinformation, a miasma of rumor.

"A censorship of the press results in the diffusion and spread of misinformation and idle tales. Under a censorship sensational stories fly apparently on the wings of the wind. The ordinary citizen is practically helpless and knows not what or whom to believe. I do not mean to say that the press is always accurate in its gathering and presentation of facts, or always correct in its interpretation of facts, but in the main it attempts to be correct and seldom is willfully and wantonly unjust. A censorship proposed

to be established with the intention and
for the purpose of preventing our enemies
from obtaining information as to the position
and movement of our troops and fleets and the
location of munition factories, machine shops,
and details of coast defenses would, and no
doubt should, meet with general approval.

"The people composing the United States
Government are now just about to enter upon a
most stupendous struggle. Events of world-wide
importance are following each other so rapidly
that they tread upon each other's heels; and
sufficient events are transpiring each day to
make volumes of history for the historian of
the future.

"I wish first to present my view as to
the censorship in respect to its being an
unconstitutional statute as proposed.

"The first amendment to the Federal
Constitution reads as follows:

"Congress shall make no law
respecting an establishment of
religion, or prohibiting the free
exercise thereof; or abriding the
freedom of speech, or of the press; * * *

"Or abridging, omitting the parenthetical
matter-

"the freedom * * * of the press.

"Everyone here knows what the word 'abridging'
means. I need not pause to consider or discuss
the meaning of 'abridgment.'

"What does 'freedom of the press' mean? It
is amazing to note the amount of loose talk -
not in the Senate, but throughout the country
and in the newspapers themselves - as to what
is 'freedom of the press' as used in the
Constitution of the United States. The average

citizen of this Republic, the ordinary publisher
in our country who is not a lawyer, thinks that
'freedom of the press' means the right to publish
his sentiments just as he pleases. In a large
sense, that may be true; but in a legalistic
sense, and from a constitutional standpoint,
that is not entirely accurate. 'Freedom of
the press' means simply, solely, and only the
right to be free from a precensorship, the
right to be free from the restraints of a censor.
In other words, under the Constitution as amended
by amendment No. 1, 'freedom of the press' means
nothing except that the citizen is guaranteed
that he may publish whatever he sees fit and
not be subjected to pains and penalties because
he did not consult the censor before doing so.
The citizen is left to publish just what he
pleases, and must take his chances before a
court of his country as to whether or not he
has published anything libelous or anything
that may bring any human being to disrepute or
ridicule, or whether he has published anything
of a treasonable or obscene nature. I undertake
to say upon the floor of the Senate that any sort
of censorship which even the necessities of
war may apparently cast upon us would not
be in keeping with the Constitution of the
United States." (Cong. Rec. 2004)

On May 4, 1917, Representative Graham rose

in the House to speak to his amendment to strike Section 4

of Title I of H.R. 291, quoted above, and supported his

position specifically on the basis of infringement of

freedom of the press:

"The people of the counrty are the
sovereigns in this land, and they have a
right to know about their own war, the
war to which they will have to contribute
the means and the men, and make the
sacrifices that will bring the conflict
to a right conclusion. Any attempt to
hamper, any attempt to prevent proper
communication, any attempt to prevent
the right interchange of thought, is
an attempt that will be productive of
ill and can not accomplish any good.

"I wish to have this section stricken
from the law because of these manifold
objections to its text, because its purposes
can not be accomplished without injury to
the cause.

"During the entire Civil War, when
there was danger of the communication and
publication of evil things, there was never
such a bill as this attempted to be put upon
the statute books of our country. Why should
we attempt it now? Let us make this piece
of otherwise useful legislation valuable
to the country and valuable to the administration by striking out section 4 and passing
the rest of it with such amendments as you
may deem proper to make it perfect. [Applause.]"
(55 Cong. Rec. 1808)

Thereafter, by a roll call vote of 221 to 167, Representative
Graham's amendment was passed and Section 4 stricken from
H.R. 291.

While the present language of 18 U.S.C. §§ 793-794
is not exactly the same as that passed upon by Congress in 1917,
§ 793, which alone is relevant to this case, does not include
the word "publish", and is thus faithful to the legislative
history we have cited.

When it enacted the second of the two sections numbered 798 in Title 18, continuing in effect the wartime penalties of Section 794, Congress had before it a report from a Senate committee which analyzed some of the sections we are concerned with. The committee pointed out that the prohibition of Section 794 on gathering or publishing certain information in time of war with intent to communicate it to the enemy could be invoked only in time of war. However, the committee pointed out that Section 793 of Title 18 prohibits "similar acts of gathering or communicating defense information at any time (in wartime or peacetime), under penalty of a fine . . . or imprisonment . . . or both." S. Rep. No. 409, 83rd Cong., 1st Sess.2 (1953). (Italics supplied) The committee thus carefully noted and brought to the attention of Congress the differences between the two sections, and the omission in Section 793 of the act of publishing, although "similar acts of gathering or communicating" were covered. The committee did not suggest, and Congress did not, supply this omission. But nothing could be clearer than that Congress was aware of it and of its significance. What the committee did suggest, and what Congress did do, was to continue in effect the wartime penalties of Section 794 - which does punish publishing.

The omission of the word "publish" in Section 793, and the fact, therefore, that newspapers were not covered by it, continued to be noticed in Congress. In 1957, the Senate had before it S. 2417, introduced on June 27, 1957, by Senator Cotton (for himself and Senator Stennis), expressly to implement certain of the recommendations of the Commission on Government Security for revision, inter alia., of the espionage laws. (85th Cong., 1st Sess., 103 Cong. Rec. 10447). The Commission specifically focused on the problem of unauthorized publication of classified information as being not covered by the espionage acts:

> "The Commission found to its dismay that one frustrating aspect of this overall security problem is the frequent unauthorized disclosure without subversive intent of classified information affecting national security. Several instances were noted where information emanating from the Department of Defense, and subsequently determined to have been classified, has found its way through various media into the public domain, when in deference to the interests of national security more restraint should have been exercised before dissemination. Airplane journals, scientific periodicals, and even the daily newspaper have featured articles containing information and other data which should have been deleted in whole or in part for security reasons.

"In many instances the chief culprits responsible
for any unauthorized publication of classified material
are persons quite removed from Government service and
therefore not amenable to applicable criminal statutes
or other civil penalties. Congressional inaction in
this particular area can be traced to the genuine fear
of imposing undue censorship upon the bulk of information
flowing from the various governmental agencies, and
which the American people, for the most part, have the
right to know. Any statute designed to correct this
difficulty must necessarily minimize constitutional
objections by maintaining the proper balance between
the guarantee of the first amendment, on one hand, and
required measures to establish a needed safeguard
against any real danger to our national security."
(Report of the United States Commission on Government
Security 619-20 (1957)

.That the Commission's Bill S. 2418 was intended to extend the

.applicability of Sec. 793 to newsmen as well as others outside

the Government was reaffirmed in a colloquy on the Senate

floor between Senator Humphrey and Senator Cotton, a sponsor

of the bill. Senator Humphrey stated:

". . . . The proposed new criminal penalties
against disclosure of secret information by newsmen
seem to be superfluous in view of current statutory
provisions . . . ."

Senator Cotton then advised Mr. Humphrey:

"Mr. COTTON. I note that the Senator refers to disclosure of information by newsmen.

"Mr. HUMPHREY. Yes.

"Mr. COTTON. Which would imply that the report and the recommendation concerned itself only with newsmen. To the contrary, it was not confined to newsmen. The recommendation extended to all those outside the Government. I am not defending that recommendation at this time, and I am not at all sure that it is entirely correct. We shall go into it fully, of course, but it should be made crystal clear that at the present time penalties for the disclosure of secret information can only be applied against those employed by the Government. The recommendation extended such control over those outside the Government.

"I would not want the impression to be left that it was directed at newsmen. That is not correct.

"Mr. HUMPHREY. I accept the thoughts of the Senator from New Hampshire; but I must confess that there was obviously some emphasis placed in the public mind on the news media in connection with the matter of restraint of information, particularly if the information had been classified as either confidential or secret or top secret. I believe a re-evaluation is required of what we mean by confidential information or classified information.

"Mr. COTTON. I agree with the Senator. I should like to add a further thought, if the Senator will be kind enough to yield for that purpose. In the first place I believe the impression about this recommendation, which caused great concern among journalists and other newspaper people-and justifiably so, I may say-came fully as much from the comments of some of the members of the commission and other sources as it did from the report itself.

* * *

"The recommended action by the Commission
could affect, for instance, a Member of the
Senate or a Member of the House who disclosed
secret information off the floor and outside
his committee as much as it would any other
individual who came into possession of secret
information and then disclosed it, rather
than just someone connected with the press.
I think in fairness to the press and the
Commission that fact should be made clear."
(85th Cong., 1st Sess., 103 Cong. Rec. at
10449 (1957))

The bill was, of course, not acted upon, but it demonstrates yet again that until the present action against the New York Times, no one supposed that Congress, despite the First Amendment, and in the teeth of common English usage, had meant to cover the act of publishing by using such words as "communicate, deliver or transmit." The ommission of the word "publish" in Section 793 was noted, and its significance clearly understood. There were those who wished to cure the omission and cover newspapers, but happily for the liberties of the people, they were unsuccessful. This prosecution cannot be allowed to do what Congress itself declined to do.

The Government's Demand for the Documents

All the contentions we have made earlier in this brief concerning the operative phrases, "unauthorized possession" and "relating to the national defense" are fully applicable to this portion of the Government's case, and are entirely sufficient to dispose of it.

It is true that in demanding production of the documents, the Government is not required to perform the impossible feat of reading the word "publish" into section 793(e), as it must in order to obtain its injunction. But section 793(e) has to be read as a whole. The offense of willfully retaining or failing to deliver cannot be deemed to have been committed in circumstances in which the offense of communicating could not be made out. The reason, as this case demonstrates, is that otherwise the Government, by getting possession, would be allowed to do indirectly what it cannot do directly, namely, stop publication. If to stop publication under section 738(e) would in this case be an unconstitutional act of censorship, as we believe we have demonstrated it would be, then the Government cannot come in by the back door and exercise unconstitutional censorship by confiscating the documents.

If the documents the Government demands had been stolen from it by The New York Times, if they were the originals, or copies removed from the Government's files,

one could conceive of a claim that the Government was simply
demanding return of its property. Even then, as we shall show,
the Government would not prevail against what we believe to
be a First Amendment right of the press to protect the identity of its sources. In re Taylor, 412 Pa. 32, 193 A.2d 181
(1963); Cf., Liberty Lobby Inc. v. Pearson, supra. But what
the Times has is a xerox copy. The Times does not hold anything that was taken from Government files. And it is not
arguable that the Government is demanding delivery because
it needs the documents for its own use, since the Government
has made it clear that it has in its possession numerous copies.

The demand for delivery can, therefore, be made
for only two reasons: (i) to prevent further publication,
which is to say, to achieve indirect censorship, and (ii)
as a disguised subpoena seeking whatever leads the xerox
copies may yield on the identity of the Times' source.
The first objective cannot be attained independently. The
Government can have the documents only if this court holds
that the Government is entitled to an injunction against
further publication, which, we believe, dannot constitutionally be done. Viewed in the alternative as a disguised
subpoena, seeking whatever leads the xerox copies may yield
to the identity of the Times' source, the demand for delivery
is fatally vulnerable to First Amendment considerations, which
equally with those mentioned in the earlier part of the brief,
go to the heart of the guarantee of freedom of the press.

Like the First Amendment rights asserted in the earlier part of the brief, those here involved, though defended by The Times, belong in fact to the public generally. They are the public's right to "receive suitable access to social, political, esthetic, moral and other ideas." Red Lion Broadcasting Company v. FCC, 395 U.S. 367, 390 (1969). As the Supreme Court observed in Grosjean v. American Press Co., Inc., supra:

> "The predominant purpose of the . . .
> [First Amendment] was to preserve an un-
> trammeled press as a vital source of public
> information. The newspapers, magazines and
> other journals of the country, it is safe
> to say, have shed and continue to shed, more
> light on the public and business affairs of
> the nation than any other instrumentality
> of publicity; and since informed public
> opinion is the most potent of all restraints
> upon misgovernment, the suppression or
> abridgement of the publicity afforded by a
> free press cannot be regarded otherwise than
> with grave concern." (297 U.S. at 250).

All this being said, it is hardly surprising that the courts have increasingly recognized that substantive impediments to the gathering of news are as violative of the First Amendment as would be statutes providing for direct censorship of news. See, e.g. Associated Press v. United States, 326 U.S. 1, 20 (1945); Associated Press v. KVOS, Inc., 80 F.2d 575, 581 (9th Cir. 1935), rev'd on jurisdictional grounds, 299 U.S. 269 (1936).

In the area of the confidential relationship
between journalists and their sources, this has resulted
in ever-growing judicial protection of the public's opportunity to know. Of the cases in this area, Application of
Caldwell, 434 F.2d 1081 (9th Cir. 1970) stands pre-eminent.
In Caldwell, the only recent decision of a Federal Court
of Appeals,* the Court of Appeals had before it a District
Court opinion granting a protective order to a New York Times
reporter with respect to his testimony before a Grand Jury.
Caldwell, the reporter, had argued before the District Court
that he should not be required to appear before the Grand
Jury to testify as to his communications from the Black
Panthers and that, alternatively, if his appearance were
to be required, an appropriate protective order should be
entered to preserve Caldwell's confidential relationship
with his news sources. The Court denied the first branch
of Caldwell's motion but did extend protective relief to

---

* In two state court cases, differing results have been
  reached. In both those cases, In Re Pappas, 266 N.E.2d
  297 (Mass. 1971) and Branzburg v. Hayes (Ct. App.Ky. 1970),
  the Supreme Court first granted a stay of enforcement to
  an order directing a reporter to testify to confidential
  source material and then granted certiorari. The cases
  are on the October, 1971 docket of the Supreme Court.

the extent of providing that Caldwell would not be obliged
to:

> ". . . reveal confidential associations that
> impinge upon the effective exercise of his
> First Amendment right to gather news for
> dissemination to the public through the press
> or other recognized media until such time as
> a compelling and overriding national interest
> which cannot be alternatively served has been
> established to the satisfaction of the Court."
> (Emphasis added; 311 F.Supp. at 360).

Upon Caldwell's refusal to appear before the Grand Jury
at all, he was held in contempt and appealed his conviction to the Court of Appeals for the Ninth Circuit. In
light of the United States' position in this Court, it
is noteworthy that the United States did not appeal from
the District Court's order. Nor, in the petition for
certiorari filed with the Supreme Court on December 16,
1970 by the United States, did the United States quarrel
with the scope or nature of the protective order granted
by the District Court. The Court of Appeals approved the
granting of the protective order, while reversing the
decision below with respect to the question of whether
Caldwell was obliged even to appear before the Grand Jury.
Holding that he did not, the Court concluded that:

"The very concept of a free press requires
that the news media be accorded a measure
of autonomy; that they should be free to
pursue their own investigations to their
own ends without fear of governmental interference, and that they should be able to
protect their investigative processes. To
convert news gatherers into Department of
Justice investigators is to invade the
autonomy of the press by imposing a governmental function upon them. To do so where
the result is to diminish their future
capacity as news gatherers is destructive
of their public function. To accomplish
this where it has not been shown to be
essential to the Grand Jury inquiry simply
cannot be justified in the public interest."
(Emphasis added; 434 F.2d at

The Court of Appeals in Caldwell further held
that the Government cannot obtain disclosure of materials
before a grand jury which could lead to the disclosure
of a confidential source absent proof of a crime, proof
that the information sought is essential to prove the
crime, and that it has made unsuccessful efforts to obtain
the information elsewhere. Whatever may be said of the
applicability of these tests in a grand jury context in
which a crime is under investigation,* in the present

---

* In our brief due to be submitted tomorrow with respect
to the motion of the United States for a preliminary
injunction, we will demonstrate that the Government
cannot meet any of the three Caldwell tests.

context it is at least inescapable that "the information"
sought by the Government--e.g. the xeroxes held by The
Times--is already in the hands of the United States. There
can thus be no justification, consistent with Caldwell,
sufficient to warrant production of the documents.

Apart from its apparent acquiescence to the
protective order granted by the District Court in Caldwell*
the United States has itself issued "guidelines" with
respect to the issuance of subpoenas which, if applied,
plainly bar the current demand of the Government.   The
guidelines (39 U.S.L.W. 2111 (August 25, 1970)) provide
that:

> "The Department of Justice does not
> consider the press 'an investigative arm
> of the government.' Therefore, all
> reasonable attempts should be made to
> obtain information from non-press sources
> before there is any consideration of sub-
> poenaing the press."

---

* Numerous other similar holdings have recently issued. See
People v. Dohrn, Cir. Ct., Cook County, Illinois, No. 69-3808)
[in criminal action, Government barred from issuing subpoenas
to media absent prior judicial approval]; Alioto v. Cowles
Communications, Inc., U.S.D.C., N.D. Cal., No. 52150, transcript of December 4, 1969, pp. 165-67 [in libel action court
refused to hold authors of magazine article in contempt for
failure to disclose sources]; Air Transport Ass'n. et al.,
and United States v. Air Professional Air Traffic Controllers
Organization, et al., U.S.D.C., E.D.N.Y., Nos. 70-C-400-410,
transcript of April 6, 1970, pp. 18-24, 36; transcript of
April 7, 1970, pp. 21, 38-39, 149-51 [in contempt proceeding
reporter not required to produce notes which were basis of
article]; People v. Rios (Cal.Super.Ct., No. 75129, July 15,
1970) [in criminal case, subpoena demanding television
"out-takes" quashed].

The guidelines thus provide that subpoenas will not be issued prior to first negotiating with the press and, if the negotiations fail, then receiving the Attorney General's approval for the issuance of the subpoenas. In requesting the Attorney General's authorization for a subpoena, the guidelines provide:

"C. The government should have unsuccessfully attempted to obtain the information from alternative non-press sources.

"D. Authorization requests for subpoenas should normally be limited to the verification of published information and to such surrounding circumstances as relate to the accuracy of the published information.

"E. Great caution should be observed in requesting subpoena authorization by the Attorney General for unpublished information, or where an orthodox First Amendment defense is raised or where a serious claim of confidentiality is alleged.

"F. Even subpoena authorization requests for publicly disclosed information should be treated with care because, for example, cameramen have recently been subjected to harassment on the grounds that their photographs will become available to the government.

"G. In any event, subpoenas should, wherever possible, be directed at material information regarding a limited subject matter, should cover a reasonably limited period of time, and should avoid requiring production of a large volume of unpublished material. They should give reasonable and timely notice of the demand for documents."

In light of the fact that the United States
possesses the documents, copies of which it now seeks,
it is plain that its demand for production served on
The Times is flatly inconsistent with the guidelines
themselves.

Finally, even if the Government could meet the
stern Caldwell tests and even if it could meet the tests
of its own guidelines, we submit that in this case--a
classic one of political reporting on the basis of
information obtained in confidence--the documents could
not properly be ordered produced. As we will demonstrate
in our brief to be submitted tomorrow, the very fact that
publication of this information could not be punished
under the Espionage Act demonstrates that there is no
"overriding national interest" here such as could possibly
justify forcing a reporter to breach his confidence. There
is indeed, in a case such as this, if there ever is, an
overriding national interest in protecting the confidence
and thus making this sort of reporting possible. Government
officials are here trying by injunctive process and disguised subpoenas to shield other Government officials,
past and present, from searching scrutiny in precisely the
way in which New York Times v. Sullivan, 376 U.S. 254 (1964)

held the law of libel cannot protect them consistently with the First Amendment.

The First Amendment is not so fragile as the United States in this case would have it. The demand for documents violates the First Amendment.

CONCLUSION

The preliminary injunction sought by the United States should not be granted. Given the grave constitutional questions posed and the failure of the government - in a variety of ways - to prove its case, we respectfully submit that the demand of the United States should, in all respects, be denied.

Respectfully submitted,

CAHILL, GORDON, SONNETT, REINDEL & OHL
Attorneys to The New York Times
    Company
Office and P. O. Address
80 Pine Street
New York, New York 10005
212-944-7400

Of·Counsel:

    Alexander M. Bickel
    Floyd Abrams
    William E. Hegarty

UNITED STATES DISTRICT COURT

SOUTHERN DISTRICT NEW YORK

--X

UNITED STATES OF AMERICA,

       Plaintiff

          v.   71 Civ. 2662

THE NEW YORK TIMES COMPANY, et al,

       Defendants.

--X

AFFIDAVIT of ARTHUR OCHS SULZBERGER

STATE OF NEW YORK)
                 : ss.:
COUNTY OF NEW YORK)

      ARTHUR OCHS SULZBERGER, being duly sworn, deposes and says:

      1. I am President of The New York Times Company, the principal defendant herein, and Publisher of The New York Times.

      2. I make this affidavit in opposition to the motion made on behalf of the United States Government for a preliminary injunction restraining The New York Times from publishing any further articles based upon the Pentagon study of the events relating to this country's intervention in the Vietnam war and requiring The New York Times to surrender material upon which the articles which it has published and proposes to publish have been and will be based.

392

3. The decision of The New York Times to publish
this series of articles was made with the conviction that such
publication was not only right and proper, but was an obligation
by The New York Times to its readers, to the citizens of this
country, and indeed to this country's government, including
not simply members of the Executive Branch, but also the Congress
and the Judiciary.   The reasoning which led to this decision
has been accurately stated in an editorial which appeared in the
issue of The New York Times on June 16, 1971, from which I
quote the following:

> "What was the reason that impelled The Times
> to publish this material in the first place?
> The basic reason is, as was stated in our
> original reply to Mr. Mitchell, that we
> believe 'that it is in the interest of the
> people of this country to be informed....'
> A fundamental responsibility of the press
> in this democracy is to publish information
> that helps the people of the United States
> to understand the processes of their own
> government, especially when those processes
> have been clouded over in a hazy veil of
> public dissimulation and even deception.
>
> "As a newspaper that takes seriously its
> obligation and its responsibilities to the
> public, we believe that, once this material
> fell into our hands, it was not only in the
> interests of the American people to publish
> it but, even more emphatically, it would

-2-

have been an abnegation of responsibility
and a renunciation of our obligations under
the First Amendment not to have published it.
Obviously, The Times would not have made this
decision if there had been any reason to
believe that publication would have endangered
the life of a single American soldier or in
any way threatened the security of our country
or the peace of the world.

"The documents in question belong to history.
They refer to the development of American
interest and participation in Indochina from
the post-World War II period up to mid-1968,
which is now almost three years ago.   Their
publication could not conceivably damage
American security interests, much less the
lives of Americans or Indochinese.   We
therefore felt it incumbent to take on ourselves the responsibility for their publication, and in doing so raise once again the
question of the Government's propensity for
over-classification and mis-classification
of documents that by any reasonable scale
of values have long since belonged in the
public domain.

"We publish the documents and related running
account not to prove any debater's point about
the origins and development of American

-3-

participation in the war, not to place the
finger of blame on any individuals, civilian
or military, but to present to the American
public a history--admittedly incomplete--of
decision-making at the highest levels of
government on one of the most vital issues
that has ever affected 'our lives, our
fortunes and our sacred honor'--an issue
on which the American people and their duly
elected representatives in Congress have
been largely curtained off from the truth.

"It is the effort to expose and elucidate
that truth that is the very essence of
freedom of the press."

4) We at The New York Times continue to believe that
our reasoning and our decision was and is right.

Sworn to before me
this _17th_ day of
June 1971

Notary Public

ARTHUR H. KROLLAGE
NOTARY PUBLIC, State of New York
No. 41-2205825 Queens County
Cert. Filed in New York County
Term Expires March 30, 1973

-4-

UNITED STATES DISTRICT COURT
SOUTHERN DISTRICT OF NEW YORK

---x

UNITED STATES OF AMERICA,   :

                        Plaintiff,   :

            -v-   :   71 Civ. 2662

NEW YORK TIMES COMPANY, et al.,   :

                        Defendants. :

---x

STATE OF NEW YORK)
                   : ss.:
COUNTY OF NEW YORK)

        MAX FRANKEL, being duly sworn, deposes and says:

        1. I am the Washington Bureau Chief and the Washington
correspondent of The New York Times. I have been a reporter on
The Times for 20 years, including 5 years as a foreign correspondent, mostly in Moscow, and 10 years in Washington. In our
capital, I have been successively The Times' diplomatic correspondent, White House correspondent and, currently, chief correspondent, supervising the work of 35 editors and reporters,
including most of those who prepared the disputed series of
articles.

        2. I submit this affidavit in opposition to the
pending motion by the United States for an injunction barring
The Times, among other things, from printing further documents
relating to its current series of articles on the Vietnam war.

3.   The Government's unprecedented challenge to The Times in the case of the Pentagon papers, I am convinced, cannot be understood, or decided, without an appreciation of the manner in which a small and specialized corps of reporters and a few hundred American officials regularly make use of so-called classified, secret, and top secret information and documentation. It is a cooperative, competitive, antagonistic and arcane relationship. I have learned, over the years, that it mystifies even experienced professionals in many fields, including those with Government experience, and including the most astute politicians and attorneys.

4.   Without the use of "secrets" that I shall attempt to explain in this affidavit, there could be no adequate diplomatic, military and political reporting of the kind our people take for granted, either abroad or in Washington and there could be no mature system of communication between the Government and the people. That is one reason why the sudden complaint by one party to these regular dealings strikes us as monstrous and hypocritical--unless it is essentially perfunctory, for the purpose of retaining some discipline over the Federal bureaucracy.

5.   I know how strange all this must sound. We have been taught, particularly in the past generation of spy scares and Cold War, to think of secrets as secrets--varying in their

"sensitivity" but uniformly essential to the private conduct of diplomatic and military affairs and somehow detrimental to the national interest if prematurely disclosed. By the standards of official Washington--Government and press alike--this is an antiquated, quaint and romantic view. For practically everything that our Government does, plans, thinks, hears and contemplates in the realms of foreign policy is stamped and treated as secret-- and then unraveled by that same Government, by the Congress and by the press in one continuing round of professional and social contacts and cooperative and competitive exchanges of information

6. The governmental, political and personal interests of the participants are inseparable in this process. Presidents make "secret" decisions only to reveal them for the purposes of frightening an adversary nation, wooing a friendly electorate, protecting their reputations. The military services conduct "secret" research in weaponry only to reveal it for the purpose of enhancing their budgets, appearing superior or inferior to a foreign army, gaining the vote of a congressman or the favor of a contractor. The Navy uses secret information to run down the weaponry of the Air Force. The Army passes on secret informa- tion to prove its superiority to the Marine Corps. High of- ficials of the Government reveal secrets in the search for sup- port of their policies, or to help sabotage the plans and policies of rival departments. Middle-rank officials of govern- ment reveal secrets so as to attract the attention of their superiors or to lobby against the orders of those superiors. Though not the only vehicle for this traffic in secrets--the

Congress is always eager to provide a forum--the press is probably the most important.

7. In the field of foreign affairs, only rarely does our Government give full public information to the press for the direct purpose of simply informing the people. For the most part, the press obtains significant information bearing on foreign policy only because it has managed to make itself a party to confidential materials, and of value in transmitting these materials from government to other branches and offices of government as well as to the public at large. This is why the press has been wisely and correctly called The Fourth Branch of Government.

8. I remember during my first month in Washington, in 1961, how President Kennedy tried to demonstrate his "toughness" toward the Communists after they built the Berlin wall by having relayed to me some direct quotations of his best arguments to Foreign Minister Gromyko. We were permitted to quote from this conversation and did so. Nevertheless, the record of the conversation was then, and remains today, a "secret."

9. I remember a year later, at the height of the Cuban missile crises, a State Department official concluding that it would surely be in the country's interest to demonstrate the perfidy of the same Mr. Gromyko as he denied any knowledge of those missiles in another talk with the President; the official returned within the hour and let me take verbatim notes of the Kennedy-Gromyko transcript--providing only that I would not use direct quotations. We printed the conversation between the President and the Foreign Minister in the third person, even though the record probably remains a "secret."

10. I remember President Johnson standing beside me, waist-deep in his Texas swimming pool, recounting for more than an hour his conversation the day before, in 1967, with Prime Minister Kosygin of the Soviet Union at Glassboro, N. J., for my "background" information, and subsequent though not immediate use in print, with a few special off-the record sidelights that remain confidential.

11. I remember Secretary of State Dean Rusk telling me at my first private meeting with him in 1961 that Laos is not worth the life of a single Kansas farm boy and that the SEATO treaty, which he sould later invoke so elaborately in defense of the intervention in Vietnam, was a useless instrument that should be retained only because it would cause too much diplomatic difficulty to abolish it.

12. Similar dealings with high officials continue to this day.

13. We have printed stories of high officials of this Administration berating their colleagues and challenging even the President's judgment about Soviet activities in Cuba last year.

14. We have printed official explanations of why American intelligence gathering was delayed while the Russians moved missiles toward the Suez Canal last year.

15. These random recollections are offered here not as a systematic collection of secrets made known to me for many, usually self-evident (and often self-serving) reasons. Respect for sources and for many of the secrets prevents a truly detailed

accounting, even for this urgent purpose. But I hope I have begun to convey the very loose and special way in which "classified" information and documentation is regularly employed by our government. Its purpose is not to amuse or flatter a reporter whom many may have come to trust, but variously to impress him with their stewardship of the country, to solicit specific publicity, to push out diplomatically useful information without official responsibility, and, occasionally, even to explain and illustrate a policy that can be publicly described in only the vaguest terms.

16. This is the coin of our business and of the officials with whom we regularly deal. In almost every case, it is secret information and much of the time, it is top secret. But the good reporter in Washington, in Saigon, or at the United Nations, gains access to such information and such sources because they wish to use him for loyal purposes of government while he wishes to use them to learn what he can in the service of his readers. Learning always to trust each other to some extent, and never to trust each other fully--for their purposes are often contradictory or downright antagonistic--the reporter and the official trespass regularly, customarily, easily and unself-consciously (even unconsciously) through what they both know to be official "secrets." The reporter knows always to protect his sources and is expected to protect military secrets about troop movements and the like. He also learns to cross-check his information and to nurse it until an insight or story has turned ripe. The official knows, if he wishes to preserve this valuable

channel and outlet, to protect his credibility and the deeper
purpose that he is trying to serve.

The Role of "Classified" Information

17.   I turn now in an attempt to explain, from a
reporter's point of view, the several ways in which "classified"
information figures in our relations with government. The
Government's complaint against The Times in the present case
comes with ill-grace because Government itself has regularly and
consistently, over the decades, violated the conditions it suddenly seeks to impose upon us--in three distinct ways:

First, it is our regular partner in the informal
but customary traffic in secret information, without even the
pretense of legal or formal "declassification." Presumably,
many of the "secrets" I cited above, and all the "secret" documents and pieces of information that form the basis of the many
newspaper stories that are attached hereto, remain "secret" in
their official designation.

Second, the Government and its officials regularly
and customarily engage in a kind of ad hoc, de facto "declassification" that normally has no bearing whatever on considerations
of the national interest. To promote a political, personal,
bureaucratic or even commerical interest, incumbent officials
and officials who return to civilian life are constantly revealing

-7-

the secrets entrusted to them. They use them to barter with the Congress or the press, to curry favor with foreign governments and officials from whom they seek information in return. They use them freely, and with a startling record of impunity, in their memoirs and other writings.

Third, the Government and its officials regularly and routinely misuse and abuse the "classification" of information, either by imposing secrecy where none is justified or by retaining it long after the justification has become invalid, for simple reasons of political or bureaucratic convenience. To hide mistakes of judgment, to protect reputations of individuals, to cover up the loss and waste of funds, almost everything in government is kept secret for a time and, in the foreign policy field, classified as "secret" and "sensitive" beyond any rule of law or reason. Every minor official can testify to this fact.

18. Obviously, there is need for some secrecy in foreign and military affairs. Considerations of secruity and tactical flexibility require it, though usually for only brief periods of time. The Government seeks with secrets not only to protect against enemies but also to serve the friendship of allies. Virtually every mature reporter respects that necessity and protects secrets and confidences that plainly serve it.

19. But for the vast majority of "secrets," there has developed between the Government and the press (and Congress) a

-8-

rather simple _rule of thumb_: The Government hides what it can,
pleading necessity as long as it can, and the press pries out
what it can, pleading a need and right to know. Each side in
this "game" regularly "wins" and "loses" a round or two. Each
fights with the weapons at its command. When the Government
loses a secret or two, it simply adjusts to a new reality. When
the press loses a quest or two, it simply reports (or misreports)
as best it can. Or so it has been, until this moment.

Some Examples

20. Some of the most powerful examples of the widespread traffic in secret information that I describe were found
by a few colleagues in the Washington bureau in a most perfunctory search of our files. Even as I write this affidavit I can
glance at the Times of June 16, 1971 and find, beside the headline of the Court's temporary restraining order in this case, a
sample from our military correspondent, William Beecher:

> WASHINGTON--June 15--The Nixon Administration
> is engaged in a broad policy review aimed at de-
> termining courses of action that might improve
> South Vietnam's ability to withstand military
> assaults next year, after most American forces
> have been withdrawn...
>
> Other key developments include an estimate
> by the National Security Council that North
> Vietnam is building toward a new offensive in
> the South next year....
>
> Well-placed Administration sources disclose
> that, against the expected North Vietnamese threat,
> officials are focusing on the following major
> questions....
>
> Many planners expect President Nixon to scale
> down to a residual force of 30,000 to 70,000 men
> by July 1, 1972, but to leave enough flexibility
> in the pace of reductions so that many of them can
> be timed for May and June...

-9-

Should this residual force include many
helicopter and artillery units to "stiffen"
South Vietnamese defenses....

Not a single source of that information is identified by name,
either because sources are peddling information for which they
have asked not to be held responsible or because they are revealing information without authorization. Either way, they are
relaying secret data which we, judging by other confidential
contacts, deem reasonably reliable.

21. Some of the best examples of the regular traffic
I describe may be found in the Pentagon papers that the Government asks us not to publish. The uses of top secret information
by our Government in deliberate leaks to the press for the purposes of influencing public opinion are recorded, cited and commented upon in several places of the study. Also cited and
analyzed are numerous examples of how the Government tried to
control the release of such secret information so as to have it
appear at a desired time, or in a desired publication, or in a
deliberately loud or soft manner for maximum or minimum impact,
as desired.

22. The temporary restraining order currently in effect precludes me from citing and quoting these passages in the
Pentagon study. Examples of my point are so numerous that
despite the great bulk of the papers, we were able to locate more
than a dozen different kinds of such passages in less than an hour.

23. Extensive samples of stories plainly based on
supposedly secret information are annexed to this affidavit.
They include not only regular, daily articles but also major

contemporary analyses of Government decision-making at several
key stages of the Vietnam war, right after the Cuban missile
crisis, and shortly after the invasion of Cambodia. They include
major journalistic investigations of secret institutions, like
the Central Intelligence Agency. They combine known facts,
pried-out secrets and deliberate disclosures of secrets. They
are recognized within the profession and among readers as the
most valuable kind of journalism and have never been shown to
cause "irreparable" harm to the national security. They have
occasionally prompted investigations inside the Government to
determine the sources of information, the possible presence of
disloyal or dissenting officials or the existence of information
not previously given any weight or credibility by higher
authority. None of these articles could be fairly described as
less "sensitive" or more innocuous than the materials now challenged. None of them ever produced a legal challenge or a request for new legislation.

24. Samples of the second kind of traffic in secrets
that I mentioned--the ad hoc, de facto (but by no means authorized,
official or "legal") declassification of documents--are simply
too numerous and too voluminous to collect in this format and on
such short notice.

25. George Christian of Austin, Tex., former press
secretary to President Johnson, who had free admission to all
foreign and domestic discussions involving the President, at any
level and in any forum, has already published his memoir. It
includes 70 pages of narrative on the decisions to end the bombing of North Vietnam in late 1968, with many direct quotations of

the President and other officials, many unflattering references to our allies in South Vietnam and a great deal of detailed information, all still highly classified, about the secret negotiations with North Vietnam in Paris. This book, entitled, "The President Steps Down," (MacMillan, 1970), actually covers a period more recent than that discussed in the Pentagon papers, and at a much higher level of government and secrecy.

26. Recently, a book of top *Containing* secret documents from members of the Joint Chiefs of Staff about the very same period covered by The Times' materials was published. The book, entitled "Roots of Involvement," by Marvin Kalb and Elie Abel (pp. 208-212) includes telegram exchanges between General Westmoreland and General Wheeler in early 1968. We are advised that these texts were taken from privately circulated analyses and histories of phases of the war by leading military commanders still on active duty!

27. Theodore C. Sorensen's "Kennedy," written within a year of the death of his President, reveals dozens upon dozens of actions, meetings, reports and documents, all still treated as "classified" by the Government and unavailable for more objective journalistic analysis. Sorensen treated the Kennedy-Khrushchev correspondence as private, to protect future channels of communication with Soviet leaders, but the most "secret" of these letters, during the Cuban missile crisis, were fully revealed in two subsequent books, one by Elie Abel and one by Robert F. Kennedy. Sorensen also observes that while Kennedy was still alive he invited Professor Richard Neustadt into

-12-

Government archives for a contemporary analysis of decision-making of the "Skybolt" affair, the secrets of which were later revealed by the professor in a public account of this minor-missile crisis with Britain.

28. Arthur Schlesinger, Jr., kept notes in the White House for his history of the Kennedy years entitled "A Thousand Days." Roger Hilsman, an intelligence officer and then Assistant Secretary of State for the Far East poured his files and secrets into a quick memoir entitled "To Move a Nation" (Doubleday 1967). John Martin, special ambassador during the Dominican Republic invasion of 1965, wrote "Overtaken by Events," (Doubleday, 1966) recounting numerous confidential messages and communications. Chester Cooper, a C.I.A. official involved in Vietnam policy for two decades left the White House to produce what was probably the most complete and best-documented history until the Pentagon papers became available to The Times. "The Secret Search for Peace in Vietnam," by David Kraslow and Stuart Loory of The Los Angeles Times, remains to this day the most thorough newspaper (and book) account of the diplomacy surrounding the war--through channels that are still deemed "live".

The Pentagon Study

29. As The Times indicated in the first of its articles about the Pentagon study that is in question here, it is a massive history of how the United States went to war in Indochina. Its 3,000-page analysis, to which 4,000 pages of official documents are appended, was commissioned by Secretary of Defense Robert S. McNamara in 1967 and completed in 1968, by which time

he had been replaced by Clark M. Clifford. The analysis covers a historical record, as The Times said, from World War II to May, 1968--the start of the peace talks in Paris, by which time President Johnson had set a limit on further military commitments and revealed his intention to retire. We said that "though far from a complete history, even at 2.5 million words, the study forms a great archive of government decision-making on Indochina over three decades." That was the most concise journalistic definition we could give to the materials. Examination of our report thus far on the study and presentation of its documentation confirms the accuracy of that definition.

30. Moreover, the material was treated by The Times as an historical record that was of importance not only to our daily readers but also to the community of scholars that we have long served with a record of events. Our presentation was subjected to the most careful editing so that our report would remain faithful to the Pentagon record itself.

31. It is difficult, while publication is suspended, to describe the content and scope of the material. But our first article has already established the framework for our readers. We said the authors of the study reached many broad conclusions and specific findings, including the following:

(a) "--That the Truman Administration's decision to give military aid to France in her colonial war against the Communist led Vietminh 'directly involved' the United States in Vietnam and 'set' the course of American policy.

-14-

(b) "--That the Eisenhower Administration's decision
to rescue a fledgling South Vietnam from a Communist take-
over and attempt to undermine the new Communist regime of
North Vietnam gave the Administration a 'direct role in the
ultimate breakdown of the Geneva settlement' for Indochina
in 1954.

(c) "--That the Kennedy Administration, though ultimately spared from major escalation decisions by the death
of its leader, transformed a policy of 'limited-risk gamble,'
which it inherited, into a 'broad commitment' that left
President Johnson with a choice between more war and withdrawal.

(d) "--That the Johnson Administration, though the
President was reluctant and hesitant to take the final
decision, intensified the covert warfare against North
Vietnam and began planning in the spring of 1964 to wage
overt war, a full year before it publicly revealed the
depth of its involvement and its fear of defeat.

(e) "--That this campaign of growing clandestine
military pressure through 1964 and the expanding program of
bombing North Vietnam in 1965 were begun despite the judgment of the Government's intelligence community that the
measures would not cause Hanoi to cease its support of the
Vietcong insurgency in the South, and that the bombing was
deemed militarily ineffective within a few months.

(f) "--That these four succeeding Administrations

-15-

410

built up the American political, military and psychological stakes in Indochina, often more deeply than they realized at the time, with large-scale military equipment to the French in 1950; with acts of sabotage and terror warfare against North Vietnam beginning in 1954; with moves that encouraged and abetted the overthrow of President Ngo Dinh Diem of South Vietnam in 1963; with plans, pledges and threats of further action that sprang to life in the Tonkin Gulf clashes in August, 1964; with the careful preparation of public opinion for the years of open warfare that were to follow; and with the calculation in 1965, as the planes and troops were openly committed to sustain combat, that neither accommodation inside South Vietnam nor early negotiations with North Vietnam would achieve the desired result."

(g) Further characterizing the materials, our introduction also indicated revelations "about the ways in which several administrations conducted their business on a fateful course, with much new information about the roles of dozens of senior officials of both major political parties and a whole generation of military commanders."

32. The Times found the history to be concerned primarily with the decision-making process in Washington and the thoughts, motives, plans, debates and calculations of the decisionmakers. I have seen no materials bearing on future plans of a diplomatic or military nature.

-16-

The Times' interest throughout, like that of the study itself, in the words of our opening line, was in "how the United States went to war in Indochina."

33. In considering the remainder of the material, in preparation for publication, it is difficult to be precise, without compromising our deep conviction that no agency of Government ought to be placed in the position of approving, or being asked to approve, prior to publication, any article or other materials that we plan to publish in the exercise of our profession.

34. But it may be helpful to affirm to the Court what is already plain from what we have published so far. The remaining articles will be of the same historical character as the first three, similarly dealing with the decision-making process and the thoughts, debates and calculations of the decision-makers.

35. Of the numbered paragraphs in our original introduction to the first article, the materials and accounts bearing on paragraphs (4) and (5) and a part of (6) -- covering the period from early 1964 to the middle of 1965 -- have already appeared in print. The remainder of that introduction was deemed by us to be a fair journalistic summary of the remainder of our story.

36. Within the limits we have set on discussion of our unpublished articles, we can state that the stories will cover, as we have indicated, the origins of the United States

-17-

involvement in Southeast Asia from World War II forward, in the broad context of our evolving policy for the Pacific, through the period of the Eisenhower Administration and the Geneva conference on Indochina. They will cover the history of policy-making inherited by President Kennedy and the Kennedy years, including the broad perspective of those years, which involved the specific problem of political stability culminating in the overthrow of President Ngo Dinh Diem. Among other things, our stories will also cover the history of other policy decisions through early 1968, including the personal disillusionment with policy felt by Secretary McNamara and the roles of other policy-makers.

37. The Pentagon papers published and to be published by the Times and a bureaucratic history and analysis of the interaction of events and policy decisions are an invaluable historical record of a momentous era in our history. We cannot believe they should or will be suppressed.

_____
Max Frankel

Sworn to before me this
17th day of June, 1971

MARY ANN C. SIMPSON
Notary Public, State of New York
No. 41-3682775
Qualified in Queens County
Commission Expires March 30, 1973

[The following pages contain copies of exhibits submitted with Mr. Frankel's affidavit, articles copied from various publications.]]

-18-

CIA Series 1966 New York Times
written by Max Frankel, Tom Wicker,
John W. Finney, E. W. Kenworthy
and others

Survey Finds Widely Feared Agency Is Tightly Controlled

Following is the first of five articles on the Central Intelligence Agency. The articles are by a team of New York Times correspondents consisting of Tom Wicker, John W. Finney, Max Frankel, E. W. Kenworthy and other Times staff members.

Special to The New York Times

WASHINGTON, April 24— One day in 1960 an agent of the Central Intelligence Agency caught a plane in Tokyo, flew to Singapore and checked into a hotel room in time to receive a visitor. The agent plugged a lie detector into an overloaded electrical circuit and blew out the lights in the building.

In the investigation that followed, the agent and a C.I.A. colleague were arrested and jailed as American spies.

The result was an international incident that infuriated London, not once but twice. It embarrassed an American Ambassador. It led an American Secretary of State to write a rare letter of apology to a foreign Chief of State.

Five years later that foreign leader was handed an opportunity to denounce the perfidy of all Americans and of the C.I.A. in particular, thus increasing the apprehension of his Oriental neighbors about the agency and enhancing his own political position.

Ultimately, the incident led the United States Government to tell a lie in public and then to admit the lie even more publicly.

Persistent Questions

The lie was no sooner disclosed than a world predisposed to suspicion of the C.I.A. and unaware of what really had happened in Singapore five years earlier began to repeat questions that have dogged the agency and the United States Government for years:

¶Was this secret body, which was known to have overthrown governments and installed others, raised armies, staged an invasion of Cuba, spied and counterspied, established airlines, radio stations and schools and supported books, magazines and businesses, running out of the control of its supposed political master?

¶Was it in fact damaging, while it sought to advance, the national interest? Could it spend huge sums for ransoms, bribes and subversion without check or regard for the consequences?

¶Did it lie to or influence the political leaders of the United States to such an extent that it really was an "invisible government" more powerful than even the President?

These are questions constantly asked around the world. Some of them were raised again recently when it was disclosed that Michigan State University was the cover for some C.I.A. agents in South Vietnam during a multimillion-dollar technical assistance program the university conducted for the regime of the late President Ngo Dinh Diem.

Last week, it also became known that an Estonian refugee who was being sued for slander in a Federal District Court in Baltimore was resting his defense on the fact that the alleged slander had been committed in the course of his duties as a C.I.A. agent.

In a public memorandum addressed to the court, the C.I.A. stated that it had ordered the agent, Juri Raus, to disclose no further details of the case, in order to protect the nation's foreign intelligence apparatus. Mr. Raus is claiming complete legal immunity from the suit on the ground that he had acted as an official agent of the Federal Government.

Such incidents, bringing the activities of the C.I.A. into dim and often dismaying public view, have caused members of Congress and many publications to question ever more persistently the role and propriety of one of Washington's most discussed and least understood institutions. Some of the misgivings have been shared by at least two American Presidents, Harry S. Truman and John F. Kennedy.

A Wide Examination

To seek reliable answers to these questions; to sift, where possible, fact from fancy and theory from condition; to determine what real questions of public policy and international relations are posed by the existence and operations of the C.I.A., The New York Times has compiled information and opinions from informed Americans throughout the world.

It has obtained reports from 20 foreign correspondents and editors with recent service in more than 35 countries and from reporters in Washington who interviewed more than 50 present and former Government officials, members of Congress and military officers.

This study, carried out over several months, disclosed, for instance, that the Singapore affair resulted not from a lack of political control or from recklessness by the C.I.A., but from bad fortune and diplomatic blundering.

It found that the C.I.A., for all its fearsome reputation, is under far more stringent political and budgetary control than most of its critics know or concede, and that since the Bay of Pigs disaster in Cuba in 1961 these controls have been tightly exercised.

The consensus of those interviewed was that the critics' favorite recommendation for a stronger rein on the agency — a Congressional committee to oversee the C.I.A.—would probably provide little more real control than now exists and might both restrict the agency's effectiveness and actually shield it from those who desire more knowledge about its operations.

A Matter of Will

Other important conclusions of the study include the following:

¶While the institutional *forms* of political control appear effective and sufficient, it is really the *will* of the political officials who must exert control that is important and that has most often been lacking.

¶Even when control is tight and effective, a more important question may concern the extent to which C.I.A. information and policy judgments affect political decisions in foreign affairs.

¶Whether or not political control is being exercised, the more serious question is whether the very existence of an efficient C.I.A. causes the United States Government to rely too much on clandestine and illicit activities, back-alley tactics, subversion and what is known in official jargon as "dirty tricks."

¶Finally, regardless of the facts, the C.I.A.'s reputation in the world is so horrendous and its role in events so exaggerated that it is becoming a burden on American foreign policy, rather than the secret weapon it was intended to be.

The Singapore incident, with its bizarre repercussions five years later, is an excellent lesson in how that has happened, although none of the fears of the critics are justified by the facts of the particular case.

Problem in Singapore

The ill-fated agent who blew out the lights flew from Tokyo to Singapore only after a prolonged argument inside the C.I.A. Singapore, a strategic Asian port with a large Chinese population, was soon to get its independence from Britain and enter the Malaysian Federation. Should C.I.A. recruit some well-placed spies, or should it, as before, rely on MI-6, the British secret service, and on Britain's ability to maintain good relations and good sources in Singapore?

Allen W. Dulles, then director of the C. I. A., decided to infiltrate the city with its own agents, to make sure that the British were sharing everything they knew. Although the decision was disputed, it is not uncommon in any intelligence service to bypass or double-check on an ally.

(On Vice President Humphrey's visit late last year to the capitals of Japan, South Korea, Taiwan, and the Philippines, Secret Service agents found at least three "bugs," or listening devices, hidden in his private quarters by one of his hosts.)

The agent who flew from Tokyo to Singapore was on a recruiting mission, and the lie detector, an instrument used by the C.I.A. on its own employes, was intended to test the reliability of a local candidate for a spy's job.

When the machine shorted out the lights in the hotel, the visiting agent, the would-be spy and another C.I.A. man were discovered. They wound up in a Singapore jail. There they were reported to have been "tortured" —either for real, or to extract a ransom.

The Price Was High

Secret discussions—apparently through C.I.A. channels— were held about the possibility of buying the agents' freedom with increased American foreign aid, but Washington eventually decided Singapore's price was too high. The men were subsequently released.

Secretary of State Dean Rusk — the Kennedy Administration had succeeded to office in January, 1961—wrote a formal apology to Premier Lee Kuan Yew of Singapore and promised to discipline the culprits.

That appeared to have ended the matter until last fall, when Premier Lee broke away from the Malaysian Federation and sought to establish himself for political reasons as more nearly a friend of Britain than of the United States, although his anti-Americanism was short of pro-Communism.

To help achieve this purpose, Mr. Lee disclosed the 1960 "affront" without giving any details, except to say that he had been offered a paltry $3.3-million bribe when he had demanded $33-million.

The State Department, which had been routinely fed a denial of wrongdoing by C.I.A. officials who did not know of the Rusk apology, described the charge as false. Mr. Lee then published Mr. Rusk's letter of 1961 and threatened also to play some interesting tape recordings for the press.

connected with the incident, or to the incident itself, but to having done something that had merited an apology.

London, infuriated in the first instance by what it considered the C.I.A.'s mistrust of MI-6, now fumed a second time about clumsy tactics in Washington.

Acting on Orders

Errors of bureaucracy and mishaps of chance can easily be found in the Singapore incident, but critics of the C.I.A. cannot easily find in it proof of the charges so often raised about the agency—"control," "making policy" and "undermining policy."

The agent in Singapore was acting on direct orders from Washington. His superiors in the C.I.A. were acting within the directives of the President and the National Security Council. The mission was not contrary to American foreign policy, was not undertaken to change or subvert that policy, and was not dangerously foolhardy. It was not much more than routine—and would not have been unusual in any intelligence service in the world.

Nevertheless, the Singapore incident — the details of which have been shrouded in the C.I.A.'s enforced secrecy—added greatly to the rising tide of dark suspicion that many people throughout the world, including many in this country, harbor about the agency and its activities.

Carl Rowan, the former director of the United States Information Agency and former Ambassador to Finland, wrote last year in his syndicated column that "during a recent tour of East Africa and Southeast Asia, it was made clear to me that suspicion and fear of the C.I.A. has become a sort of Achilles heel of American foreign policy."

President Sukarno of Indonesia, Prince Norodom Sihanouk, Cambodia's Chief of State, President Jomo Kenyatta of Kenya, former President Kwame Nkrumah of Ghana and many other leaders have repeatedly insisted that behind the regular American government there is an "invisible government," the C.I.A., threatening them all with infiltration, subversion and even war. Communist China and the Soviet Union sound this theme endlessly.

"The Invisible Government" was the phrase applied to American intelligence agencies, and particularly the C.I.A., in a book of that title by David Wise and Thomas B. Ross. It was a best-seller in the United States and among many government officials abroad.

Subject of Humor

So prevalent is the C.I.A. reputation of menace in so much of the world that even humorists have taken note of it. The New Yorker magazine last December printed a cartoon showing two natives of an unspecified country watching a volcano erupt. One native is saying to the other: "The C.I.A. did it. Pass it along."

In Southeast Asia, even the most rational leaders are said to be ready to believe anything about the C.I.A.

"Like Dorothy Parker and the things she said," one observer notes, "the C.I.A. gets credit or blame both for what it does and for many things it has not even thought of doing."

Many earnest Americans, too, are bitter critics of the C.I.A. Senator Eugene J. McCarthy, Democrat of Minnesota, has charged that the agency "is making foreign policy and in so doing is assuming the roles of President and Congress." He has introduced a proposal to create a special Foreign Relations subcommittee to make a "full and complete" study of the effects of C.I.A. operations on United States foreign relations.

Senator Stephen M. Young, Democrat of Ohio, has proposed that a joint Senate-House committee oversee the C.I.A. because, "wrapped in a cloak of secrecy, the C.I.A. has, in effect, been making foreign policy."

Mayor Lindsay of New York, while a Republican member of Congress, indicted the C.I.A. on the House floor for a long series of fiascos, including the most famous blunder in recent American history—the Bay of Pigs invasion of Cuba.

Former President Truman, whose Administration established the C.I.A. in 1947, said in 1963 that by then he saw "something about the way the C.I.A. has been functioning that is casting a shadow over our historic positions, and I feel that we need to correct it."

Kennedy's Bitterness

And President Kennedy, as the enormity of the Bay of Pigs disaster came home to him, said to one of the highest officials of his Administration that he wanted "to splinter the C.I.A. in a thousand pieces and scatter it to the winds."

Even some who defend the C.I.A. as the indispensable eyes and ears of the Government—for example Allen Dulles, the agency's most famous director—now fear that the cumulative criticism and suspicion, at home and abroad, have impaired the C.I.A.'s effectiveness and therefore the nation's safety.

They are anxious to see the criticisms answered and the suspicions allayed, even if—in some cases—the agency should thus become more exposed to domestic politics and to compromises of security.

"If the establishment of a Congressional committee with responsibility for intelligence would quiet public fears and restore public confidence in the C.I.A.," Mr. Dulles said in an interview, "then I now think it would be worth doing despite some of the problems it would cause the agency."

Because this view is shared in varying degree by numerous friends of the C.I.A. and because its critics are virtually unanimous in calling for more "control," most students of the problem have looked to Congress for a remedy.

In the 19 years that the C.I.A. has been in existence, 150 resolutions for tighter Congressional control have been introduced—and put aside. The statistic in itself is evidence of widespread uneasiness about the C.I.A. and of how little is known about the agency.

For the truth is that despite the C.I.A.'s international reputation, few persons in or out of the American Government know much about its work, its organization, its supervision or its relationship to the other arms of the executive branch.

A former chairman of the Joint Chiefs of Staff, for instance, had no idea how big the C.I.A. budget was. A Senator, experienced in foreign affairs, proved, in an interview, to know very little about, but to fear very much, its operations.

Many critics do not know that virtually all C.I.A. expenditures must be authorized in advance—first by an Administration committee that includes some of the highest-ranking political officials and White House staff assistants, then by officials in the Bureau of the Budget, who have the power to rule out or reduce an expenditure.

They do not know that, instead of a blank check, the C.I.A. has an annual budget of a little more than $500-million—only one-sixth the $3-billion the Government spends on its overall intelligence effort. The National Security Agency, a cryptographic and code-breaking operation run by the Defense Department, and almost never mentioned by outsiders, spends twice as much as the C.I.A.

[illegible] about the fact that President Kennedy, after the most rigorous inquiry into the agency's affairs, methods and problems after the Bay of Pigs, did not "splinter" it after all and did not recommend Congressional supervision.

They may be unaware that since then supervision of intelligence activities has been tightened. When President Eisenhower wrote a letter to all Ambassadors placing them in charge of all American activities in their countries, he followed it with a secret letter specifically *exempting* the C.I.A.; but when President Kennedy put the Ambassadors in command of all activities, he sent a secret letter specifically *including* the C.I.A. It is still in effect but, like all directives, variously interpreted.

Out of a Spy Novel

The critics, quick to point to the agency's publicized blunders and setbacks, are not mollified by its genuine achievements—its precise prediction of the date on which the Chinese Communists would explode a nuclear device; its fantastic world of electronic devices; its use of a spy, Oleg Penkovskiy, to reach into the Kremlin itself; its work in keeping the Congo out of Communist control; or the feat—straight from a spy novel—of arranging things so that when Gamal Abdel Nasser came to power in Egypt the "management consultant" who had an office next to the Arab leader's and who was one of his principal advisers was a C.I.A. operative.

When the U-2 incident is mentioned by critics, as it always is, the emphasis is usually on the C.I.A.'s—and the Eisenhower Administration's—blunder in permitting Francis Gary Powers's flight over the Soviet Union in 1960 just before a scheduled summit conference. Not much is usually said of the incalculable intelligence value of the undisturbed U-2 flights between 1956 and 1960 over the heartland of Russia.

And when critics frequently charge that C.I.A. operations contradict and sabotage official American policy, they may not know that the C.I.A. is often overruled in its policy judgments.

As an example, the C.I.A. strongly urged the Kennedy Administration not to recognize the Egyptian-backed Yemeni regime and warned that President Nasser would not quickly pull his troops out of Yemen. Ambassador John Badeau thought otherwise. His advice was accepted, the republic was recognized, President Nasser's troops remained—and much military and political trouble followed that the C.I.A. had foreseen and the State Department had not.

Nor do critics always give the C.I.A. credit where it is due for its vital and daily service as an accurate and encyclopedic source of quick news, information, analysis and deduction about everything from a new police chief in Mozambique to an aid agreement between Communist China and Albania, from the state of President Sukarno's health to the meaning of Nikita S. Khrushchev's fall from power.

Yet the critics' favorite indictments are spectacular enough to explain the world's suspicions and fears of the C.I.A. and its operations.

A sorry episode in Asia in the early nineteen-fifties is a frequently cited example. C.I.A. agents gathered remnants of the defeated Chinese Nationalist armies in the jungles of northwest Burma, supplied them with gold and arms and encouraged them to raid Communist China.

One aim was to harrass Peking to a point where it might retaliate against Burma, forcing the Burmese to turn to the United States for protection.

Actually, few raids occurred, and the army became a troublesome and costly burden. The C.I.A. had enlisted the help of Gen. Phao Sriyanod, the police chief of Thailand—and a leading narcotics dealer. The Nationalists, with the planes and gold furnished them by the agents, went into the opium business. By the time the "anti-Communist" force could be disbanded, and the C.I.A. could wash its hands of it, Burma had renounced American aid, threatened to quit the United Nations and moved closer to Peking.

Moreover, some of the Nationalist Chinese are still in northern Burma, years later, and still fomenting trouble and infuriating governments in that area, although they have not been supported by the C.I.A. or any American agency for a decade.

In 1958, a C.I.A.-aided operation involving South Vietnamese agents and Cambodian rebels was interpreted by Prince Sihanouk as an attempt to overthrow him. It failed but drove him farther down the road that ultimately led to his break in diplomatic relations with Washington.

Indonesian Venture

In Indonesia in the same year, against the advice of American diplomats, the C.I.A. was authorized to fly in supplies from Taiwan and the Philippines to aid army officers rebeling against President Sukarno in Sumatra and Java. An American pilot was shot down on a bombing mission and was released only at the insistent urging of the Kennedy Administration in 1962. Mr. Sukarno, naturally enough, drew the obvious conclusions; how much of his fear and dislike of the United States can be traced to those days is hard to say.

In 1960, C.I.A. agents in Laos, disguised as "military advisers," stuffed ballot boxes and engineered local uprisings to help a hand-picked strongman, Gen. Phoumi Nosavan, set up a "pro-American" government that was desired by President Eisenhower and Secretary of State John Foster Dulles.

This operation succeeded—so much so that it stimulated Soviet intervention on the side of leftist Laotians, who counterattacked the Phoumi government. When the Kennedy Administration set out to reverse the policy of the Eisenhower Administration, it found the C.I.A. deeply committed to Phoumi Nosovan and needed two years of negotiations and threats to restore the neutralist regime of Prince Souvanna Phouma.

Pro-Communist Laotians, however, were never again driven from the border of North Vietnam, and it is through that region that the Vietcong in South Vietnam have been supplied and replenished in their war to destroy still another C.I.A.-aided project, the non-Communist government in Saigon.

Catalogue of Charges

It was the C.I.A. that built up Ngo Dinh Diem as the pro-American head of South Vietnam after the French, through Emperor Bao Dai, had found him in a monastery cell in Belgium and brought him back to Saigon as Premier. And it was the C.I.A. that helped persuade the Eisenhower and Kennedy Administrations to ride out the Vietnamese storm with Diem—probably too long.

These recorded incidents not only have prompted much soul-searching about the influence of an instrument such as the C.I.A. on American policies but also have given the C.I.A. a reputation for deeds and misdeeds far beyond its real intentions and capacities.

Through spurious reports, gossip, misunderstandings, deep-seated fears and forgeries and falsifications, the agency has been accused of almost anything anyone wanted to accuse it of.

It has been accused of:

- Plotting the assassination of Jawaharlal Nehru of India.
- Provoking the 1965 war between India and Pakistan.
- Engineering the "plot" that became the pretext for the murder of leading Indonesia generals last year.
- Supporting the rightist army plots in Algeria.
- Murdering Patrice Lumumba in the Congo.
- Kidnapping Moroccan agents in Paris.
- Plotting the overthrow of President Kwame Nkrumah of Ghana.

All of these charges and many similar to them are fabrications, authoritative officials outside the C.I.A. insist.

The C.I.A.'s notoriety even enables some enemies to recover from their own mistakes. A former American official unconnected with the agency recalls that pro-Chinese elements in East Africa once circulated a document urging revolts against several governments. When this inflammatory message backfired on its authors, they promptly spread the word that it was a C.I.A. forgery designed to discredit them—and some believed the falsehood.

Obvious Deduction

"Many otherwise rational African leaders are ready to take forgeries at face value," one observer says, "because deep down they honestly fear the C.I.A. Its image in this part of the world couldn't be worse."

The image feeds on the rankest of fabrications as well as on the wildest of stories—for the simple reason that the wildest of stories are not always false, and the C.I.A. is often involved and all too often obvious.

When an embassy subordinate in Lagos, Nigeria, known to be the C.I.A. station chief had a fancier house than the United States Ambassador, Nigerians made the obvious deduction about who was in charge.

When President João Goulart of Brazil fell from power in 1964 and C.I.A. men were accused of being among his most energetic opponents, exaggerated conclusions as to who had ousted him were natural.

It is not only abroad that such C.I.A. involvements—real or imaginery—have aroused dire fears and suspicions. Theodore C. Sorensen has written, for instance, that the Peace Corps in its early days strove manfully, and apparently successfully, to keep its ranks free of C.I.A. infiltration.

Other Government agencies, American newspapers and business concerns, charitable foundations, research institutions and universities have, in some cases, been as diligent as Soviet agents in trying to protect themselves from C.I.A. penetration. They have not always been so successful as the Peace Corps.

Some of their fear has been misplaced; the C.I.A. is no longer so dependent on clandestine agents and other institutions' resources. But as in the case of its overseas reputation, its actual activities in the United States—for instance, its aid in financing a center for international studies at the Massachusetts Institute of Technology—have made the fear of infiltration real to many scholars and businesses.

The revelation that C.I.A. agents served among Michigan State University scholars in South Vietnam from 1955 to 1959 has contributed to the fear. The nature of the agents' work and the circumstances of their employment are in dispute, but their very involvement, even relatively long ago, has aroused concern that hundreds of schol- [illegible]

efforts abroad will be tainted and hampered by the suspicions of other governments.

Thus, it is easy for sincere men to believe deeply that the C.I.A. must be brought "to heel" in the nation's own interest. Yet every well-informed official and former official with recent knowledge of the C.I.A. and its activities who was interviewed confirmed what Secretary of State Rusk has said publicly—that the C.I.A. "does not initiate actions unknown to the high policy leaders of the Government."

The New York Times survey left no doubt that, whatever its miscalculations, blunders and misfortunes, whatever may have been the situation during its bumptious early days and during its over-hasty expansion in and after the Korean War, the agency acts today not on its own but with the approval and under the control of the political leaders of the United States Government.

But that virtually undisputed fact raises in itself the central questions that emerge from the survey: What is control? And who guards the guards?

For it is upon information provided by the C.I.A. itself that those who must approve its activities are usually required to decide.

It is the C.I.A. that has the money (not unlimited but ample) and the talent (as much as any agency) not only to conceive but also to carry out projects of great importance—and commensurate risk.

Action, If Not Success

It is the C.I.A., unlike the Defense Department with its service rivalries, budget concerns and political involvements, and unlike the State Department with its international diplomatic responsibilities and its vulnerability to criticism, that is freest of all agencies to advocate its projects and press home its views; the C.I.A. can promise action, if not success.

And both the agency and those who must pass upon its plans are shielded by security from the outside oversight and review under which virtually all other officials operate, at home and abroad.

Thus, while the survey left no doubt that the C.I.A. operates under strict *forms* of control, it raised the more serious question whether there was always the *substance* of control.

In many ways, moreover, public discussion has become too centered on the question of control. A more disturbing matter may be whether the nation has allowed itself to go too far in the grim and sometimes deadly business of espionage and secret operations.

One of the best-informed men on this subject in Washington described that business as "ugly, mean and cruel." The agency loses men and no one ever hears of them again, he said, and when "we catch one of them" (a Soviet or other agent), it becomes necessary "to get everything out of them and we do it with no holds barred."

Secretary Rusk has said publicly that there is "a tough struggle going on in the back alleys all over the world." "It's a tough one, it's unpleasant, and no one likes it, but that is not a field which can be left entirely the other side," he said.

The back-alley struggle, he concluded, is "a never-ending war, and there's no quarter asked and none given."

'Struggle for Freedom'

But that struggle, Mr. Rusk insisted, is "part of the struggle for freedom."

No one seriously disputes that the effort to gain intelligence about real or potential enemies, even about one's friends, is a vital part of any government's activities, particularly a government so burdened with responsibility as the United States Government in the 20th century.

But beyond their need for information, how far should the political leaders of the United States go in approving the clandestine violation of treaties and borders, financing of coups, influencing of parties and governments, without tarnishing and retarding those ideas of freedom and self-government they proclaim to the world?

And how much of the secrecy and autonomy necessary to carry out such acts can or should be tolerated by a free society?

There are no certain or easy answers. But these questions cannot even be discussed knowledgeably on the basis of the few glimpses — accidental or intentional—that the public has so far been given into the private world of the C.I.A.

That world is both dull and lurid, often at the same time.

A year ago, for instance, it was reported that some of the anti-Castro Cuban survivors of the Bay of Pigs were flying in combat in deepest, darkest Africa. Any Madison Avenue publisher would recognize that as right out of Ian Fleming and James Bond.

But to the bookish and tweedy men who labor in the pastoral setting of the C.I.A.'s huge building on the banks of the Potomac River near Langley, Va., the story was only a satisfying episode in the back-alley version of "Struggle for Freedom."

Tomorrow: Who and what is the C.I.A.?

Intervention or Spying All in a Day's Work

Following is the second of five articles on the Central Intelligence Agency. The articles are by a team of New York Times correspondents consisting of Tom Wicker, John W. Finney, Max Frankel, E. W. Kenworthy and other Times staff members.

Special to The New York Times

WASHINGTON, April 25—At the Itari River, eight miles south of Nia Nia in the northeast Congo, a government column of 600 Congolese troops and 100 white mercenaries had been ambushed by a rebel force and was under heavy fire. Suddenly, three B-26's skimmed in over the rain forest and bombed and strafed a path through the rebel ranks for the forces supported by the United States.

At the controls of the American-made planes were anti-Castro Cubans, veterans of the Bay of Pigs invasion of Cuba in 1961, three years before. They had been recruited by a purportedly private company in Florida. Servicing their planes were European mechanics solicited through advertisements in London newspapers. Guiding them into action were American "diplomats" and other officials in apparently civilian positions.

The sponsor, paymaster and director of all of them, however, was the Central Intelligence Agency, with headquarters in Langley, Va. Its rapid and effective provision of an "instant air force" in the Congo was the climax of the agency's deep involvement there.

The C.I.A.'s operation in the Congo was at all times responsible to and welcomed by the policy-makers of the United States.

It was these policy-makers who chose to make the agency the instrument of political and military intervention in another nation's affairs, for in five years of strenuous diplomatic effort it was only in Langley that the White House, the State Department and the Pentagon found the peculiar combination of talents necessary to block the creation of a pro-Communist regime, recruit the leaders for a pro-American government and supply the advice and support to enable that government to survive.

In Dark and Light

From wiretapping to influencing elections, from bridge-blowing to armed invasions, in the dark and in the light, the Central Intelligence Agency has become a vital instrument of American policy and a major component of American government.

It not only gathers information but also rebuts an adversary's information. It not only organizes its own far-flung operations but also resists an adversary's operation.

Against the Soviet Union alone, it performs not only certain of the services performed in Moscow by the K.G.B., the Committee for State Security, but also many of the political intelligence and military services performed by pro-Soviet Communist parties around the world.

When the Communist and Western worlds began to wrestle for control of the vast undeveloped Congo in 1960 after it had gained independence from Belgium, a modest little C.I.A. office in Leopoldville mushroomed overnight into a virtual embassy and miniature war department.

This was not to compete with the real United States Embassy and military attachés but to apply the secret, or at least discreet, capacities of the C.I.A. to a seething contest among many conflicting forces.

Starting almost from scratch because the Belgians had forbidden Americans even to meet with Congolese officials, the C.I.A. dispersed its agents to learn Congolese politics from the bush on up, to recruit likely leaders and to finance their bid for power.

Capable of quickly gathering information from all sources, of buying informants and disbursing funds without the bureaucratic restraints imposed on other government agencies, the C.I.A. soon found Joseph Mobutu, Victor Nendaka and Albert Ndele. Their eventual emergence as President of the country, Minister of Transportation and head of the national bank, respectively, proved a tribute to the Americans' judgment and tactics.

So pervasive was the C.I.A. influence that the agency was widely accused of the assassination of Moscow's man, Premier Patrice Lumumba. Correspondents who were in the Congo are convinced the C.I.A. had nothing to do with the murder, though it did play a major role in establishing Cyrille Adoula as Mr. Lumumba's successor for a time.

Money and shiny American automobiles, furnished through the logistic wizardry of Langley, are said to have been the deciding factors in the vote that brought Mr. Adoula to power. Russian, Czechslovak, Egyptian and Ghanaian agents were simply outbid where they could not be outmaneuvered.

In one test after Mr. Adoula had been elected, rival agents of East and West almost stumbled over each other rushing in and out of parliamentary delegates' homes. On the day of the roll-call, American and Czech representatives sat one seat apart in the gallery with lists of members, winking at each other in triumph whenever a man pledged to the one turned out to have been picked off by the other. Ultimately Mr. Adoula won by four votes.

More Than Money

By the Congo period, however, the men at Langley say they had learned that their earlier instincts to try to solve nasty political problems with money alone had been overtaken by the recognition of the need for far more sophisticated and enduring forms of influence.

"Purchased?" one American commented. "You can't even rent these guys for the afternoon."

And so the C.I.A. kept growing in size and scope.

By the time Moise Tshombe had returned to power in the Congo — through American acquiescence, if not design — it became apparent that hastily supplied arms and planes, as well as dollars and cars, would be needed to protect the American-sponsored government in Leopoldville.

This, apparently, was a job for the Defense Department, but to avoid a too obvious American involvement, and in the interests of speed and efficiency, the Government again turned to the C.I.A.

The agency had the tools. It knew the Cubans in Miami and their abilities as pilots. It had the front organizations through which they could be recruited, paid and serviced.

It could engage 20 British mechanics without legal complications and furnish the tactical expertise from its own ranks or from Americans under contract.

Moreover, some C.I.A. agents eventually felt compelled to fly some combat missions themselves in support of South African and Rhodesian mercenaries. The State Department denied this at first — then insisted the Americans be kept out of combat.

But it was pleased by the overall success of the operation, in which no planes were lost and all civilian targets were avoided.

Meanwhile, in Other Areas . . .

In the years of the Congo effort, the C.I.A. was also smuggling Tibetans in and out of Communist China, drawing secrets from Col. Oleg Penkovsky of Soviet military intelligence, spying on Soviet missile build-ups and withdrawals in Cuba, masterminding scores of lesser operations, analyzing the world's press and radio broadcasts, predicting the longevity of the world's major political leaders, keeping track of the world's arms traffic and of many arms manufacturing enterprises and supplying a staggering flow of information, rumor, gossip and analysis to the President and all major departments of government.

For all this, the C.I.A. employs about 15,000 persons and spends about a half billion dollars a year.

Its headquarters, the brain and nerve center, the information repository of this sprawling intelligence and operations system, is a modern, eight-story building of precast concrete and inset windows — a somewhat superior example of the faceless Federal style — set in 140 acres of lawn and woodland overlooking the south bank of the Potomac eight miles from downtown Washington.

In this sylvan setting, somewhat resembling an English deer park, about 8,000 C.I.A. employes — the top managers, the planners and the analysts —live, if not a cloistered life, at least a kind of academic one with the materials they are studying or the plans they may be hatching.

Formerly, the C.I.A. was scattered through many buildings in downtown Washington, which increased the problems and expense of security.

In the early nineteen-fifties, a $30-million appropriation for a new, unitary headquarters was inserted without identification in the budget of another agency—and promptly knocked out by a Congressional committee so befuddled by C.I.A. secrecy that it did not know what the item was for.

When Allen W. Dulles, then director of the C.I.A., came back in 1956 with more candor, he asked for $50-million, and Congress gave him $46-million. He justified the bite that he proposed to take out of a 750-acre Government reservation on the Potomac by saying the site with "its isolation, topography and heavy forestation" would provide the agency with the required security.

While the whitish-gray building is undoubtedly as secure as fences, guards, safes and elaborate electronic devices can make it, the location is hardly a secret. A large sign on the George Washington Parkway pointing to "Central Intelligence Agency" has been removed, but thousands of people know you can still get to the same building by turning off on the same road, now marked by the sign "BPR"—"Bureau of Public Roads."

There, beyond the affable guard at the gate, is the large, rectangular structure with four wings, the ground-level windows barred, which stands as the visible symbol of what is supposed to be an invisible operation.

For organizational purposes, C.I.A. headquarters is divided into four divisions, each under a deputy director — plans, intelligence, science and technology, and support.

What the Divisions Do

The Division of Science and Technology is responsible for keeping current on developing techniques in science and weapons, including nuclear weapons, and for analyzing photos taken by U-2 reconnaissance planes and by space satellites.

The Division of Support is responsible for procuring equipment and for logistics, communications and security, including the C.I.A. codes.

The Division of Plans and the Division of Intelligence perform the basic functions of the agency. They represent the alpha and omega, the hand and brain, the dagger and the lamp, the melodrama and the monograph of the intelligence profession. Their presence under one roof has caused much of the controversy that has swirled about the C.I.A. since the Bay of Pigs.

It is the responsibility of the Intelligence Division to assemble, analyze and evaluate information from all sources, and to produce daily and periodical intelligence reports on any country, person or situation for the President and the National Security Council, the President's top advisory group on defense and foreign policy.

All information — military, political, economic, scientific, industrial — is grist for this division's mill. Perhaps no more than one-fifth — by volume and not necessarily importance — comes from agents overseas under varying depths of cover.

Most information is culled from foreign newspapers, scientific journals, industry publications, the reports of other Government departments and intelligence services and foreign broadcasts monitored by C.I.A. stations around the world.

All Sorts of Experts

The Intelligence Division is organized by geographical sections that are served by resident specialists from almost every profession and discipline — linguists, chemists, physicists, biologists, geographers, engineers, psychiatrists and even agronomists, geologists and foresters.

Some of the achievements of these experts are prodigious, if reports filtering through the secrecy screen are even half accurate. For instance:

¶From ordinarily available information, reliable actuarial and life-expectancy studies have been prepared on major foreign leaders.

¶In the case of one leader, from not-so-ordinarily available information, physicians gleaned important health data: They made a urinalysis from a specimen stolen from a hospital in Vienna where the great man was being treated.

¶C.I.A. shipping experts, through sheer expertise, spot-

ted the first shipment of Soviet arms to Cuba before the vessels had cleared the Black Sea.

Some anthropologists at C.I.A. headquarters devote their time to helpful studies of such minor — but strategically crucial — societies as those of the hill tribes of Laos and Vietnam.

One woman has spent her professional lifetime in the agency doing nothing but collecting, studying, collating, analyzing and reporting on everything that can be learned about President Sukarno of Indonesia — "and I mean everything," one official reported.

Heavy With Ph.D.'s

It is the agency's boast that it could staff any college from its analysts, 50 per cent of whom have advanced degrees and 30 per cent of whom have doctorates.

Sixty per cent of the Intelligence Division personnel have served 10 years. Twenty-five per cent have been with the C.I.A. since 1947, when the agency was established. The heaviest recruiting occurred during the Korean War — primarily, but by no means exclusively, among Ivy League graduates.

The Division of Plans is a cover title for what is actually the division of secret operations, or "dirty tricks." It is charged with all those stratagems and wiles — some as old as those of Rahab and some as new as satellites — associated with the black and despised arts of espionage and subversion.

The operations of the C.I.A. go far beyond the hiring and training of spies who seek out informers and defectors.

It was the Plans Division that set up clandestine "black" radio stations in the Middle East to counter the propaganda and the open incitements to revolution and murder by President Gamal Abdel Nasser's Radio Cairo.

It was the Plans Division that masterminded the ouster of the Arbenz government in Guatemala in 1954, the overthrow of Premier Mohammed Mossadegh in Iran in 1953 (two notable successes) and the Bay of Pigs invasion in 1961 (a resounding failure).

Among the triumphs of the Plans Division are the development of the U-2 high-altitude plane, which, between 1956 and May, 1960, when Francis Gary Powers was shot down by a Soviet rocket, photographed much of the Soviet Union; the digging of a tunnel into East Berlin from which C.I.A. agents tapped telephone cables leading to Soviet military headquarters in the Eastern Zone and the acquisition of a copy of Premier Khrushchev's secret speech to the 20th party congress in 1956 denouncing Stalin's excesses and brutalities.

Liberals in the C.I.A.

The C.I.A. analysts of the Intelligence Division, in the opinion of many experts, are aware of the embedded antagonisms and frustrations of peoples just emerging into nationhood. Thus they are likely to be more tolerant than the activists in the Plans Division of the flamboyant nationalism and socialist orientation of the leaders in former colonies and more flexible than many of the State Department's cautious and legalistic diplomats.

In discussing the Portuguese territories of Angola or Mozambique, for example, the analysts are said to take the attitude that change is inevitable, that the United States has to deal with a pluralistic world. The State Department, on the other hand, tends to be diverted by Portuguese sensitivities and the North Atlantic Treaty Organization base in the Azores, a Portuguese territory.

Regarding the C.I.A. analysts, one State Department officer said: "there are more liberal intellectuals per square inch at ... than anywhere else in ... overnment."

The operators and agents of the Plans Division, on the other hand, are described as more conservative in their economic outlook and more single-minded in their anti-Communism. This is particularly true of those engaged in deep-cover operations, many of whom are ex-military people or men formerly in the Office of Strategic Services or the Federal Bureau of Investigation.

It has been said, however, that many of the agents who are essentially information gatherers and who work under transparent cover are as sophisticated as the analysts back home, and like them are sympathetic to the "anti-Communist left" in underdeveloped countries.

The C.I.A. agents abroad fall into two groups — both under the Plans Division.

First, there are those engaged in the really dirty business — the spies and counterspies, the saboteurs, the leaders of paramilitary operations, the suborners of revolution. Such agents operate under deepest cover, and their activities become known only when they are unfortunate enough to be caught and "surfaced" for political or propaganda purposes.

While such operatives may be known to "the chief of station" — the top C.I.A. officer in any country — they are rarely known to the American Ambassador, although he may sometimes be aware of their mission. In fact, these deep agents are not known to the C.I.A.'s Intelligence Division in Washington, and their reports are not identified to it by name.

Correspondents of The New York Times say they have never, with certainty, been able to identify one of these agents, although they have on occasion run across some unaccountable American of whom they have had their suspicions. Often unknown to each other, the deep agents masquerade as businessmen, tourists, scholars, students, missionaries or charity workers.

Second, there are those agents, by far the larger number, who operate under the looser cover of the official diplomatic mission. In the mission register they are listed as political or economic officers, Treasury representatives, consular officers or employes of the Agency for International Development (the United States foreign aid agency) or United States Information Agency. The C.I.A. chief of station may be listed as a special assistant to the Ambassador or as the top political officer.

A Thin Cover

This official cover is so thin as to be meaningless except to avoid embarrassment for the host government. These agents usually are readily identifiable.

The chief of station is recognized as the man with a car as big as the Ambassador's and a house that is sometimes — as in Lagos, Nigeria — better.

In practically all the allied countries the C.I.A. agents identify themselves to host governments, and actually work in close cooperation with Cabinet officials, local intelligence and the police.

In some embassies the C.I.A. agents outnumber the regular political and economic officers. In a few they have made up as much as 75 per cent of the diplomatic mission.

The chief of station often has more money than the Ambassador. Sometimes he has been in the country longer and is better informed than the Ambassador.

For all these reasons the host government, especially in underdeveloped areas of the world, may prefer to deal with the chief of station rather than the Ambassador, believing him to have readier access to top policy-making officials in Washington.

was Kept Secret

Obviously the number of agents abroad is a closely held secret, kept from even such close Presidential advisers in the past as the historian, Arthur M. Schlesinger Jr. In his book "A Thousand Days," Mr. Schlesinger states that those "under official cover overseas" number almost as many as State Department employes. This would be roughly 6,000. The actual number, however, is believed to be considerably less, probably around 2,200.

The secrecy of identification can lead to some amusing situations. Once when Allen Dulles, then C.I.A. director, visited New Delhi, every known "spook" (C.I.A. man) was lined up in an anteroom of the embassy to greet him. At that moment a newspaper correspondent who had been interviewing Mr. Dulles walked out of the inner office. A look of bewilderment crossed the faces of the C.I.A. men, plainly asking, "Is this one we didn't know about?"

Mr. Schlesinger has written that "in some areas the C.I.A. had outstripped the State Department in the quality of its personnel."

Almost without exception, correspondents of The New York Times reported that the men at the top overseas were men of "high competence and discipline," "extremely knowing," "imaginative," "sharp and scholarly" and "generally somewhat better than those in State in work and dedication."

But they also found that below the top many C.I.A. people were "a little thin" and did not compare so favorably with Foreign Service officers on the same level.

The C.I.A. screens and rescreens applicants, because it is quite aware of the attraction that secrecy holds for the psychopath, the misfit and the immature person.

The greatest danger obviously lies in the area of special operations. Although it is generally agreed that the agents — overt and covert — have been for the most part men of competence and character, the C.I.A. has also permitted some of limited intelligence and of emotional instability to get through its screen and has even assigned them to sensitive tasks, with disastrous results.

One example was the assignment of a man known as "Frank Bender" as contact with Cuban exile leaders during the preliminaries of the Bay of Pigs operation. A German refugee with only a smattering of Spanish and no understanding of Latin America or Latin character, Bender antagonized the more liberal of the leaders by his bullying and his obvious partiality for the Cuban right.

Offices in This Country

The C.I.A. maintains field offices in 30 American cities. These offices are overt but discreet. Their telephone numbers are listed under "Central Intelligence Agency" or "United States Government," but no address is given. Anyone wanting the address must know the name of the office director, whose telephone number and address are listed.

At one time these field offices sought out scholars, businessmen, students and even ordinary tourists whom they knew to be planning a trip behind the Iron Curtain and asked them to record their observations and report to the C.I.A. on their return.

Very little of this assertedly is done any more, probably because of some embarrassing arrests and imprisonment of tourists and students. While the C.I.A. deals frankly with businessmen, it reputedly does not compromise their traveling representatives.

Most of the work of domestic field agents involves contacts with industry and universities. For example, an agent, on instructions from headquarters, will seek evaluation of captured equipment, analysis of the color of factory smoke as a clue to production, an estimate of production capacity from the size of a factory, or critiques of articles in technical and scientific journals.

The Human Inadequacy

In greater secrecy, the C.I.A. subsidizes, in whole or in part, a wide range of enterprises — "private" foundations, book and magazine publishers, schools of international studies in universities, law offices, "businesses" of various kinds and foreign broadcasting stations. Some of these perform real and valuable work for the C.I.A. Others are not much more than "mail drops."

Yet all these human activities, all the value received and the dangers surmounted, all the organization and secrecy, all the trouble averted and all the setbacks encountered, still do not describe the work of the C.I.A. For the most gifted of analysts, the most crafty of agents — like all human beings — have their limitations.

At the time when the Americans were successfully keeping the Congo out of the Communist orbit, it still took the same men several months to slip an African agent into Stanleyville in the Congo to check on the lives and fate of some arrested Americans.

Men are fallible and limited, and the demands on the C.I.A. are almost infinite; that is why, today, some of the most valuable spies and some of the most omnipotent agents hum through the heavens, and above.

Tomorrow: The C.I.A. in action.

Electronic Prying Grows

Following is the third of five articles on the Central Intelligence Agency. The articles are by a team of New York Times correspondents consisting of Tom Wicker, John W. Finney, Max Frankel, E. W. Kenworthy and other Times staff members.

Special to The New York Times.

WASHINGTON, April 26 — To the men most privy to the secrets of the Central Intelligence Agency, it sometimes seems that the human spies, the James Bonds and Mata Haris, are obsolete. Like humans everywhere, they are no match for the computers, cameras, radars and other gadgets by which nations can now gather the darkest secrets of both friends and foes.

With complex machines circling the earth at 17,000 miles an hour, C.I.A. agents are able to relax in their carpeted offices beside the Potomac and count the intercontinental missiles poised in Soviet Kazakhstan, monitor the conversations between Moscow and a Soviet submarine near Tahiti, follow the countdown of a sputnik launching as easily as that of a Gemini capsule in Florida, track the electronic imprint of an adversary's bombers and watch for the heat traces of his missiles.

Only a half dozen years ago, at least one human pilot was still required to guide a black U-2 jet across the Soviet Union from Pakistan to Norway, or over Cuba or Communist China from bases in Florida and Taiwan.

His cameras and listening devices, capable of picking out a chalk line or a radar station from 13 miles up, were incredible in their day, the product of imaginative C.I.A. research and development. But spies in the sky now orbiting the earth do all this as well from 100 miles.

Missile Espionage

Both the United States and the Soviet Union are vying with each other in cosmic spying. The American Samos and Soviet Cosmos satellites gather more data in one 90-minute orbit than an army of earthbound spies.

Other gadgets of the missile age have taken over the counter-spy function. Secretary of Defense Robert S. McNamara gave a Congressional committee a strong hint about that last spring when he mentioned "inspection of orbiting objects in the satellite interceptor Thor program as well as in the two large ground-based optical programs at Cloudcroft, N. M."

His testimony suggested that the United States could orbit a satellite capable of photographing and otherwise "inspecting" Soviet space spies, while other equipment could photograph them from the ground with remarkable detail.

Such electronic eyes, ears, noses and nerve ends — and similar ones aboard ships and submarines — are among the nation's most vital secrets. They are not exclusively the property or inspiration of the C.I.A.

C.I.A. cameras and other snooping equipment are riding in spacecraft that are otherwise the responsibility of the Defense Department.

No clear breakdown of responsibilities and cost is available, but, altogether, the annual cost of the United States intelligence effort exceeds $3-billion a year — more than six times the amount specifically allocated to the C.I.A. and more than 2 per cent of the total Federal budget.

Bugging From Afar

Not all the gadgetry is cosmic. The agency is now developing a highly sensitive device that will pick up from afar indoor conversations, by recording the window vibrations caused by the speakers' voices.

This is only one of many nefarious gadgets that have made the word "privacy" an anachronism. It is possible, for instance, with equipment so tiny as to be all but invisible, to turn the whole electric wiring system of a building into a quivering transmitter of conversation taking place anywhere within.

Picking up information is one thing; getting it "home" and doing something with it is another. Some satellites, for instance, are rigged to emit capsules bearing photos and other readings; as they float to earth by parachute, old C-130 aircraft dash across the Pacific from Hawaii and snare the parachutes with long, dangling, trapeze-like cables. The planes have a 70 per cent catching average.

Sometimes the intelligence wizards get carried away by their imaginations. Several years ago they spent tens of millions of dollars on the construction of a 600-foot radio telescope designed to eavesdrop on the Kremlin. It was to pick up radio signals, such as those emitted when a Soviet Premier called his chauffeur by radio-telephone, as they bounced off the moon.

The project turned into an engineering fiasco, but technology came to the rescue by providing "ferret" satellites that can tune in on the same short-range radio signals as they move straight up to the ionosphere.

Overlooking the rights of territorial sovereignty and national and human privacy, officials throughout the United States Government praise the C.I.A.'s gadgetry as nothing short of "phenomenal." The atmosphere everywhere, they say, is full of information, and the objective of a technological intelligence service is to gather and translate it into knowledge.

At C.I.A. headquarters in Langley, Va., other intricate machines, some unknown a decade or even a few years ago, read, translate, interpret, collate, file and store the information. Sometimes months or years later, the data can be retrieved from tens of millions of microfilmed categories.

This effort has paid off monumentally, according to those who know most about it.

It was aerial reconnaissance by the U-2 spy plane — succeeded in many ways by satellites in 1961 — that enabled Washington to anticipate and measure the Soviet Union's capacity to produce missiles in the nineteen-fifties. These estimates, in turn, led to the so-called "missile gap," which became a prime political issue in the 1960 Presidential campaign. But it was also the U-2 that later produced proof that the Russians were not turning out missiles as fast as they could, thus dispelling the "missile gap" from Washington's thinking and jargon.

Still later, C.I.A. devices discovered missiles being emplaced underground in the Soviet Union. U-2's spotted the preparation of missile sites in Cuba in 1962. They also sampled the radioactive fallout of Soviet nuclear tests in 1961. Highly secret techniques, including aerial reconnaissance, allowed the C.I.A. to predict the Chinese nuclear explosion in 1964 with remarkable accuracy.

Purloined Messages

Countless conversations and messages the world over have been purloined; even subtler signals and indications, once detected by the marvels of science, can be read and combined into information of a kind once impossible to obtain.

The first duty of the C.I.A. is to collect, interpret and disseminate what it learns from its worldwide nerve system — weaving together, into the "intelligence" the government needs, every electronic blip, squeak and image and the millions of other items that reach its headquarters from more conventional, often public, sources: random diplomatic contacts, press clippings, radio monitor reports, books and research projects and eyewitness evidence. (Even some of these "open" sources, such as a regional newspaper from Communist China, must be smuggled or bought at a stiff price.)

Every hour of every day, about 100 to 150 fresh items of news, gossip and research reach the C.I.A.'s busy headquarters in Virginia and are poured into the gigantic human-and-technological computer that its analysis section resembles.

Four of every five of these items, it is said, now come either from "open" sources or inanimate devices. But in many important instances it is still the human agent, alerted to make a particular arrangement or to chase a specific piece of information, who provides the link that makes all else meaningful and significant; sometimes, now as in the 18th century, it is men alone who do the job in danger and difficulty.

When it was discovered, for instance, that Premier Khrushchev had shaken the Communist world with a secret speech denouncing Stalin in 1956, it was a C.I.A. agent who finally came up with the text, somewhere in Poland, and other analysts who determined that it was genuine.

A Rebellion Hastened

This feat of human spying in an electronic age yielded vital information and, leaked to the press in Europe and elsewhere, hastened the anti-Stalin rebellions in many Communist countries and probably contributed to upheavals in Poland and Hungary that are still among the heaviest liabilities of Communist history.

It takes a sub-agent in Tibet, personally recruited by a C.I.A. man there and paid either a retainer or by the piece, to deliver a sheaf of secret army documents circulating among regimental commanders of Communist China's People's Liberation Army.

Only his counterpart in Algeria can provide some drawings of the design of the interior of Peking's embassy (although such designs can often be obtained with no more effort than asking' for them at the offices of the American who constructed the building).

And beyond this large remaining value of the human being in the humming world of espionage, it is also the human brain in the C.I.A. that gives information its real importance by supplying interpretations for the President and his men.

The end product is a series of papers, handsomely printed and often illustrated with fancy maps to gain a bureaucratic advantage over rival pieces of paper from other agencies.

The agency produces intelligence reports almost hourly, and sweeping summaries every weekday. It provides a special news report for President Johnson's nightly bedtime reading, sometimes containing such juicy tidbits as the most recent playboy activities of the indefatigable President Sukarno of Indonesia.

More elaborate reports and projections are prepared on such matters at the rate of Soviet economic growth.

The State Department has sometimes published these, without credit to their origin.

Piqued by these announcements, the C.I.A. called its first news conference in 1964 to put out the latest readings on Soviet prosperity. The idea of the "spooks," as C.I.A. men are called, summoning reporters caused so much amusement in Washington—and perhaps displeasure in other agencies—that the C.I.A. has never held another news conference.

Still more important subjects, such as Soviet nuclear capabilities or Communist Chinese intentions in Southeast Asia, are dealt with in formal national intelligence estimates. These encompass all information available on a given subject and reflect the final judgment of the Board of National Estimates, a group of 14 analysts in the C.I.A.

National estimate intelligence is intended to reach a definite conclusion to guide the President. But as other departments are consulted and the various experts express their views, their disagreements, caveats and dissents are noted and recorded by footnotes in the final document. These signs of dispute are likely to herald important uncertainties, and some officials believe the footnotes to be the best-read lines of all the millions committed to paper in the Government every month.

The C.I.A. also produces rapid analyses and predictions on request — say, about the likelihood of the Soviet Union's going to war over the Cuban missile crisis, or about the consequences of different courses of action contemplated at a particular moment by the United States in Vietnam.

How Good Are the Reports?

How effective these reports have been, and how well they are heeded by the policy-makers, are questions of lively debate in the intelligence community.

In recent years, the C.I.A. is generally believed to have been extremely good in furnishing information about Soviet military capabilities and orders of battle, about the Chinese nuclear weapons program and, after constant goading from the White House, about the progress of India, the United Arab Republic, Israel and other nations toward a capacity to build nuclear weapons.

Reports from inside Indonesia, Algeria and the Congo during recent fast-moving situations are also said to have been extremely good.

On the other hand, the C.I.A. has been criticized for not having known more in advance about the construction of the Berlin Wall in 1961, about the divorce of the United Arab Republic and Syria in 1961, about the political leanings of various leaders in the Dominican Republic and about such relatively public matters as party politics in Italy.

Some — including Dwight D. Eisenhower — have criticized the agency for not having recognized in time Fidel Castro's Communist leanings or the possibility that the Soviet Union would ship missiles to Cuba.

Almost everyone, however, generally concedes the necessity for gathering intelligence to guide the Government in its worldwide involvements. Criticism goes beyond the value or accuracy of C.I.A. reports. For information-gathering often spills over at the scene of action into something else — subversion, counteractivity, sabotage, political and economic intervention and other kinds of "dirty tricks." Often the intelligence gatherer, by design or force of circumstance, becomes an activist in the affairs he was set to watch.

On-the-Scene Action

C.I.A. analysts reading the punchcards of their computers in Virginia can determine that

a new youth group in Bogotá appears to have fallen under the control of suspected Communists, but it takes an agent on the spot to trade information with the local police, collect photographs and telephone taps of those involved, organize and finance a countermovement of, say, young Christians or democratic labor youth, and help them erect billboards and turn mimeograph machines at the next election.

Dozens — at times hundreds — of C.I.A. men have been employed on Taiwan to train men who will be smuggled into Communist China and to interview defectors and refugees who come out; to train Chinese Nationalists to fly the U-2; to identify and befriend those who will move into power after the departure of the Nationalists' President, Chiang Kai-shek; to beam propaganda broadcasts at the mainland; to organize harassing operations on the islands just off the shore of the mainland, and to provide logistic support for other C.I.A. operations in Laos, Thailand, Vietnam, the Philippines and Indonesia.

In these and dozens of other instances, an agent who is merely ostensibly gathering intelligence is in reality an activist attempting to create or resolve a situation.

Because a great many such activists are also in the field for a variety of purposes other than open or clandestine information gathering, the involvement of fallible human beings in the most dangerous and murky areas of C.I.A. operations causes most of the agency's failures and difficulties and gives it its fearsome reputation.

Men, by and large, can control machines but not events, and not always themselves. It was not, after all, the shooting down of a U-2 inside the Soviet Union in 1960 that caused worldwide political repercussions and a Soviet-American crisis; each side could have absorbed that in some sort of "cover." It was rather the Soviet capture of a living American pilot, Francis Gary Powers, that could not be explained away and that Russians did not want explained away.

But the C.I.A. invariably develops an interest in its projects and can be a formidable advocate in the Government.

When it presented the U-2 program in 1956, fear of detection and diplomatic repercussions led the Eisenhower Administration to run some "practice" missions over Eastern Europe. The first mission to the Soviet Union, in mid-1956, over Moscow and Leningrad, was detected but not molested. It did, however, draw the first of a number of secret diplomatic protests.

After six missions the Administration halted the flights, but the C.I.A pressed for their resumption. Doubts were finally overcome, and 20 to 25 more flights were conducted, with Soviet fighter planes in vain pursuit of at least some of them.

The Powers plane is thought to have been crippled by the nearby explosion of an antiaircraft missile developed with the U-2's in mind.

Risky and Often Profitable

The simplest and most modest of such risky, often profitable, sometimes disastrous human efforts are reported to be carried out in the friendly nations of Western Europe.

In Britain, for instance, C.I.A. agents are said to be little more than contact men with British intelligence, with British Kremlinologists and other scholars and experts.

With MI-6, its London counterpart, the C.I.A. compares notes and divides responsibilities on targets of mutual interest. The agency, having come a painful cropper in Singapore a few years ago, now leaves spying in Malaysia, for instance, to the old Commonwealth sleuths while probably offering in return the C.I.A.'s [illegible]

Generally cooperative arrangements also prevail in countries such as Canada and Italy and, to a somewhat lesser degree, in France. In West Germany, a major cold-war battleground, the C.I.A. is much more active.

The C.I.A. runs an office in Bonn for general coordination. Another in Berlin conducts special activities such as the famous wiretap tunnel under East Berlin, a brilliant technical hookup that eavesdropped on Soviet Army headquarters. It was exposed in 1956 when East German workmen, digging on another project, struck a weak spot in the tunnel and caused it to collapse.

A C.I.A. office in Frankfurt supervises some of the United States' own espionage operations against the Soviet Union, interviews defectors and recruits agents for service in Communist countries.

In Munich, the C.I.A. supports a variety of research groups and such major propaganda outlets as Radio Free Europe, which broadcasts to Eastern Europe, and Radio Liberty, aimed at the Soviet Union.

Jobs for Refugees

Besides entertaining and informing millions of listeners in Communist nations, these nominally "private" outlets provide employment for many gifted and knowledgeable refugees from Russia, Poland, Hungary and other countries.

They also solicit the services of informers inside the Communist world, monitor Communist broadcasts, underwrite anti-Communist lectures and writings by Western intellectuals and distribute their research materials to scholars and journalists in all continents.

But there is said to be relatively little direct C.I.A. spying upon the United States' allies. Even in such undemocratic countries as Spain and Portugal, where more independent C.I.A. activity might be expected, the operation is reliably described as modest.

The American agency has a special interest, for instance, in keeping track in Spain of such refugees from Latin America as Juan Perón of Argentina. Nevertheless, it relies so heavily on the information of the Spanish police that American newspapermen are often a better source for American Embassy officials than the C.I.A. office.

In much of Africa, too, despite the formidable reputation it has among governments, the C.I.A. takes a back seat to the intelligence agencies of the former colonial nations, Britain and France, and concentrates on gathering information about Soviet, Chinese and other Communist efforts there. (The Congo has been the major exception. The agency compiles lists of travelers to Moscow, Prague or Peking, attempts to infiltrate their embassies and checks on arms and aid shipments through African airfields.

An Eye on Potential Rebels

The agency is thought to have attempted to infiltrate the security services of some African countries but only with mixed success. It gathers special dossiers on the activities of various nationalist and liberation movements and befriends opposition leaders in such countries as Algeria and the United Arab Republic, in the hope that it can predict upheavals or at least be familiar with new rulers if their bids for power are successful.

The C.I.A., long in advance, had information on the plan by which Algerian Army officers overthrew Ahmed Ben Bella last June — but it did not know the month in which the officers would make their move, and it had nothing to do with plotting or carrying out the coup.

Thanks to contacts with Gamal Abdel Nasser before he seized power in Egypt, the C.I.A. had almost intimate dealings with the Nasser government before the United States drew his ire by reneging on [illegible]

Some of these Egyptian ties lingered even through the recent years of strained relations. Through reputed informants like Mustafa Amin, a prominent Cairo editor, the C.I.A. is said in the United Arab Republic to have obtained the details of a Soviet-Egyptian arms deal in 1964 and other similar information. Thus, Mr. Amin's arrest last fall may have closed some important channels and it gave the United Arab Republic the opportunity to demand greater American aid in return for playing down its "evidence" of C.I.A. activity in Cairo.

A Talent for Secret War

The C.I.A.'s talent for secret warfare is known to have been tested twice in Latin America. It successfully directed a battle of "liberation" against the leftist government of Col. Jacobo Arbenz Guzman in Guatemala in 1954. Seven years later, a C.I.A.-sponsored army jumped off from secret bases in Guatemala and Nicaragua for the disastrous engagement at Cuba's Bay of Pigs.

Not so melodramatically, the agency runs dozens of other operations throughout the hemisphere.

It provides "technical assistance" to most Latin nations by helping them establish anti-Communist police forces. It promotes anti-Communist front organizations for students, workers, professional and business men, farmers and political parties. It arranges for contact between these groups and American labor organizations, institutes and foundations.

It has poured money into Latin-American election campaigns in support of moderate candidates and against leftist leaders such as Cheddi Jagan of British Guiana.

It spies upon Soviet, Chinese and other Communist infiltrators and diplomats and attempts to subvert their programs. When the C.I.A. learned last year that a Brazilian youth had been killed in 1963, allegedly in an auto accident, while studying on a scholarship at the Lumumba University in Moscow, it mounted a massive publicity campaign to discourage other South American families from sending their youngsters to the Soviet Union.

In Southeast Asia over the last decade, the C.I.A. has been so active that the agency in some countries has been the principal arm of American policy.

It is said, for instance, to have been so successful at infiltrating the top of the Indonesian government and army that the United States was reluctant to disrupt C.I.A. covering operations by withdrawing aid and information programs in 1964 and 1965. What was presented officially in Washington as toleration of President Sukarno's insults and provocations was in much larger measure a desire to keep the C.I.A. fronts in business as long as possible.

Though it is not thought to have been involved in any of the maneuvering that has curbed President Sukarno's power in recent months, the agency was well poised to follow events and to predict the emergence of anti-Communist forces.

Links to Power

After helping to elect Ramón Magsaysay as president of the Philippines in 1953, buttressing the family government of Ngo Dinh Diem and Ngo Dinh Nhu in South Vietnam in 1954 and assisting in implanting the regime of the strong-man Phoumi Nosavan in Laos in 1960, the C.I.A. agents responsible obviously became for long periods much more intimate advisers and effective links to Washington than the formally designated American Ambassadors in those countries.

And when the Kennedy administration came into office in 1961, the President concluded that the C.I.A. had so mortgaged American interests to Phoumi Nosavan that there was at first no alternative to dealing with him

Moreover, the C.I.A.'s skill at moving quickly and in reasonable secrecy drew for it many assignments in Southeast Asia that would normally be given to the Defense Department. It was able, for instance, to fly supplies to the Meo tribesmen in Laos to help them fight against the pro-Communist Pathet Lao at a time when treaty obligations forbade the assignment of American military advisers to the task.

In South Vietnam, the C.I.A.'s possession of energetic young men with political and linguistic talents proved much more successful in wresting mountain and jungle villages from Communist control than the Pentagon's special forces.

But the C.I.A. was also deeply committed to the Ngo brothers and was tricked by them into supporting their private police forces. These were eventually employed against the Buddhist political opposition, thus provoking the coup d'état by military leaders in 1963 that brought down the Ngos.

In Thailand, the C.I.A. has now begun a program of rural defense against Communist subversion. Acting through foreign aid offices and certain airlines, agents are working with hill tribes along the Burmese and Laos borders and helping to build a provincial police network along the borders of Laos and Cambodia.

Furtive Operations

Few Americans realize how such operations as these may affect innocent domestic situations — the extent to which the dispatch of a planeload of rice by a subsidized carrier, Air America, in Laos causes the agency to set furtive operations in motion within the United States.

When Air America or any other false-front organization has run into financial difficulties, the agency has used its influence in Washington and throughout the United States to drum up some legitimate sources of income.

Unknown to most of the directors and stockholders of an airline, for instance, the C.I.A. may approach the leading officials of the company, explain its problem and come away with some profitable air cargo contracts.

In other domestic offshoots of the C.I.A.'s foreign dealings, American newspaper and magazine publishers, authors and universities are often the beneficiaries of direct or indirect C.I.A. subsidies.

A secret transfer of C.I.A. funds to the State Department or United States Information Agency, for example, may help finance a scholarly inquiry and publication. Or the agency may channel research and propaganda money through foundations—legitimate ones or dummy fronts.

The C.I.A. is said to be behind the efforts of several foundations that sponsor the travel of social scientists in the Communist world. The vast majority of independent foundations have warned that this practice casts suspicion on all traveling scholars, and in the last year the C.I.A. is said to have curtailed these activities somewhat.

Congressional investigation of tax-exempt foundations in 1964 showed that the J. M. Kaplan Fund, Inc., among others, had disbursed at least $400,000 for the C.I.A. in a single year to a research institute. This institute, in turn, financed research centers in Latin America that drew other support from the Agency for International Development (the United States foreign aid agency), the Ford Foundation and such universities as Harvard and Brandeis.

Among the Kaplan Fund's other previous contributors there had been eight funds or foundations unknown to experts on tax-exempt charitable organizations. Five of them were not even listed on the Internal Revenue Service's list of foundations entitled to tax exemp-

An even greater amount of
C.I.A. money apparently was
spent on direct, though often
secret, support of American
scholars. The Massachusetts Institute of Technology opened a
Center of International Studies
with a grant of $300,000 from
the C.I.A. in 1951 and continued
to take agency funds until the
link was exposed, causing great
embarrassment to M.I.T.'s
scholars working in India and
other countries.

The agency's support for
M.I.T projects gradually dwin-
... ..., for the fear of compro-
...sing publicity led the university to decide a year ago to
...p no new C.I.A. contracts.
... further embarrassment was
... to Michigan State Univer-
...y over the recent disclosure
... C.I.A. agents had served
... payroll in a foreign-aid
...ject in South Vietnam from
...53 to 1959. The university,
...tended that no secret intel-
...gence work was done by the
...ants, but ...fended that a
... other overseas projects
... under way would be ham-
...ed by the suspicions of other
...vern ments.

The C.I.A. was among the
first Government agencies to
seek the valuable services of
American scholars — an idea
now widely emulated. Many
scholars continue to serve the
agency as consultants, while
others work on research proj-

...ects mainly presented to their
superiors as C.I.A. assignments.

At a meeting of the American
Political Science Foundation
here last fall, however, at least
two speakers said too many
scholars were still taking on
full-time intelligence services.
They also warned that the part-
time activities of others could
influence their judgments or
reputations.

Radio Free Europe and Radio
Liberty provide cover for C.I.A.-
financed organizations that
draw upon the research talents
of American scholars and also
service scholars with invaluable
raw material. The Free Europe
Committee even advertises for
public contributions without revealing its ties to the United
States Government.

Radio Swan, a C.I.A. station
in the Caribbean that was particularly active during the Bay
of Pigs invasion, maintains unpublicized contacts with private
American broadcasters.

The C.I.A. at times has addressed the American people
directly through public relations men and nominally independent citizens committees.
Many other C.I.A.-run fronts
and offices, however, exist primarily to gather mail from and
to provide credentials for its
overseas agents.

Thus, the ramifications of
C.I.A. activities, at home and
abroad, seem almost endless.
Though satellites, electronics
and gadgets have taken over
much of the sheer drudgery of
espionage, there remains a deep
involvement of human beings,
who project the agency into
awkward diplomatic situations,
raising many issues of policy
and ethics.

That is why many persons
are convinced that in the C.I.A.
a sort of Frankenstein's mon-
ster has been created that no
one can fully control.

By its clandestine nature, the
C.I.A. has few opportunities to
explain, justify or defend itself.
It can don the cloak of secrecy
and label all its works as necessary to further some "national
interest." And it can quietly
lobby for support inside the
Government and among influential members of Congress and
with the President.

But a "national interest" that
is not a persuasive defense to
men who have their own ideas
of the "national interest" —
along with secrecy itself — has
the inevitable effect of convincing critics that the agency has
plenty to hide besides its code-
books.

The imaginations and con-
sciences of such critics are certainly not set at rest when they
learn, for instance, that in 1962
an outrage President Kennedy
— obviously differing with the
agency about the "national interest" — forced the C.I.A. to
undo a particularly clumsy
piece of sabotage that might
have blackened the nation's
name all around the world.

Tomorrow: How the C.I.A.
is "controlled."

M.I.T. Cuts Agency Ties

Special to The New York Times

WASHINGTON, April 26—
The Center of International
Studies at the Massachusetts
Institute of Technology dis-
closed today that it would "re-
luctantly" sever connections
with the Central Intelligence
Agency at the end of June.

The agency helped to establish the center with a $300,000
grant in 1951 and since then
has supported much of its research, mostly in Communist
affairs.

A spokesman for the center
said it was decided a year ago
that, "for practical and not
moral reasons," no further contracts should be accepted
from the C.I.A. Although the
work supported by agency funds
has done much good and has
involved nothing improper, the
relationship had been "misunderstood" and has "caused sufficient difficulty," he said.

Existing contracts are being
allowed to run their course but
no further work will be performed with the agency's support after July 1, the spokesman said.

In its early years, the center performed a great deal of
research work for the intelligence agency, supplying
analyses of events and trends

Continued on Page 28, Column 6

M.I.T. Research Center to Cut Its Ties With C.I.A. After June

Continued From Page 1, Col. 3

in the Communist world but
insisting upon the right to publish the results of the work.
In recent years, after faculty
members and others criticized
the arrangement, the number
of C.I.A. projects is said to
have been sharply restricted.

In the last two or three years,
the spokesman said, the agency
contributed no more than 15
per cent, or $112,500, of the cen-
ter's $750,000 budget. The
exact amounts are classified as
secret by the agency, he said.

One early beneficiary of the
agency's support was a research team on Soviet affairs
headed by Prof. Walt W. Rostow, who later became chairman of the Policy Planning
Council at the State Department and is now a special assistant to President Johnson.
Prof. Max Millikan, an assistant director of the intelligence agency in 1951-52, has
been director of the center
since 1952.

The authorities at M.I.T. have
tried in recent days to make
clear that they have not conducted any overseas operations
and that the center's work in
India and other nations to help
promote economic development
has not been supported by the
intelligence agency.

Some "confusion" was caused,
the spokesman explained, by
the disclosure that at least five
C.I.A. agents worked among
Michigan State University
scholars on a foreign aid proj-

ect in South Vietnam from 1955
to 1959.

Some embarrassment is also
said to have been caused to
M.I.T. scholars earlier in their
dealings with foreign governments when it was disclosed
that the agency had helped to
create their center. Faculty
opinion about the link was described as divided until Mr. Millikan passed word of the decision to accept no more research
contracts with the agency.

The center's spokesman said
the university had always protected itself adequately against
direct involvement with or control of its work by the intelligence agency. It considered
the research for the agency to
be not only consistent with the
traditions of academic freedom,
he said, but also a fulfillment
of the university's duty to contribute to the Government's
intelligence "with a small 'i.'"

There has been a "rigid rule"
that no field work be undertaken with C.I.A. funds, he said.
When it was decided in March,
1965, to sever all connections,
he added, there was thought
to be no reason to withdraw
abruptly. Thus, the last contracts, running through June,
1966, were honored, he said.

Individual scholars will continue to have the right to act
as consultants to the agency or
to accept any other kind of
Government assignment. This
right has been enjoyed by most
American scholars, even those
at institutions, such as Harvard,
that have refused to accept
direct contracts from the intelligence agency.

C.I.A. OPERATIONS: A PLOT SCUTTLED

[illegible] '66

Plan to Doctor Cuban Sugar Depicts Control Problem

Following is the fourth of five articles on the Central Intelligence Agency. The articles are the work of New York Times correspondents consisting of Tom Wicker, John W. Finney, Max Frankel, E. W. Kenworthy and other Times staff members.

Special to The New York Times

WASHINGTON, April 27—On Aug. 22, 1962, the S.S. Streatham Hill, a British freighter under Soviet lease, crept into the harbor of San Juan, Puerto Rico, for repairs. Bound for a Soviet port with 80,000 bags of Cuban sugar, she had damaged her propeller on a reef.

The ship was put in drydock, and 14,135 sacks were off-loaded to facilitate repairs. Because of the United States embargo on Cuban imports, the sugar was put under bond in a customs warehouse.

Sometime during the lay-up, agents of the Central Intelligence Agency entered the customs shed and contaminated the off-loaded sugar with a harmless but unpalatable substance.

Later, a White House official, running through some intelligence reports, came upon a paper indicating the sabotage. He investigated, had his suspicions confirmed and informed [illegible] Kennedy, much to the [illegible] of the C.I.A. com-[illegible]

[illegible] was not merely furious, [illegible] [illegible] the operation had taken place on American territory, because it would, if discovered, provide the Soviet Union with a propaganda field day, and because it could set a terrible precedent for chemical sabotage in the undeclared "back-alley" struggle that rages constantly between the West and the Communist countries.

Mr. Kennedy directed that the doctored sugar not leave Puerto Rico. This was more easily ordered than done, and it finally required the combined efforts of the C.I.A., the Justice Department, the Federal Bureau of Investigation, the State Department, customs agents and harbor authorities to dis-intrigue the intrigue.

The Soviet Union never got its 14,135 sacks of sugar; whether it was compensated for them has not been disclosed.

It would be unfair to conclude that this was a typical C.I.A. operation. On the other hand, it cannot be dismissed as merely the unwise invention of some agent who let his anti-Communist fervor get out of control.

There is good reason to believe that a high-level political decision had been taken to sabotage, where feasible, the Cuban economy. The sugar project, harum-scarum as it was, developed from a general policy determination in the Plans Division of the C.I.A., and the general policy, if not the specific [illegible], presumably had the approval of the interagency, sub-Cabinet group responsible for reviewing all operations that could have political consequences.

This was not, then, a well-laid plan that went sour in the operation; it was a badly laid plan that was bound to cause trouble.

It is instructive because it illustrates many of the control problems in C.I.A. operations and makes plain why, from the outset, so many questions have been so persistently raised by so many critics about the adequacy of these controls.

A Major Concern

First, there is the pre-eminent concern whether the C.I.A., despite its disclaimers to the contrary, does on occasion make policy—not willfully, perhaps, but simply because of its capacity to mount an operation and pursue it wherever it may lead without day-by-day guidance or restriction from the political departments of the Government.

Operations like that of sabotaging the Cuban economy can lead to such dangerous episodes as the sugar doctoring; they can acquire a momentum and life of their own, the consequences of which cannot be anticipated by political officers who may have given them original approval.

Thus, it should be noted that, in the sugar tampering, the C.I.A. and its agents unquestionably believed they were operating within approved instructions, and consequently resented what they regarded as "interference" by the White House officer who reported it to the President.

Another example of operations assuming a life of their own occurred in 1954 during the C.I.A.-engineered revolution against the Communist-oriented President of Guatemala, Jacobo Arbenz Guzman.

A P-38 fighter, piloted by an American, bombed a British ship, the Spring-Fjord, which was lying off-shore and was believed to be carrying aircraft to the Arbenz Government. Only one of the three bombs exploded, and no crew members were injured. The ship, which was actually carrying coffee and cotton, was beached.

Richard M. Bissell, a former C.I.A. deputy director for plans, has admitted that the bombing was a "sub-incident" that "went beyond the established limits of policy."

An outstanding example of an operation with political consequences was the dispatch of Francis Gary Powers on the U-2 flight from Pakistan to Norway across the Soviet Union on May 1, 1960, just before the Paris summit meeting and the scheduled visit of President Eisenhower to Moscow.

Unresolved Question

The U-2 photo-reconnaissance flights had been going on for nearly five years, with fabulously profitable results. It was established practice for the President to approve in advance a set of flights within a given time span, and there was also established machinery for the approval of each flight by the Secretary of Defense. Yet, to this day, no one then in the top councils of the Government is able to say with certainty whether the Powers flight, the last in a series of six, was specifically approved by Thomas S. Gates Jr., then the Secretary of Defense.

One Senator has said that the U-2 flight was a perfectly legitimate operation of great value, and that the embarrassment to the President was not inherent in the project but was the result of a lack of coordination and controls.

"The operation," he said, "just went along regardless of the political circumstances."

A second serious control question derives from the special position of the C.I.A. as the Government's fountain of necessary information. This appears to be at once the major advantage and a principal hazard of the C.I.A. operation today.

"Policy," Allen W. Dulles, the former C.I.A. chief, once said, "must be based on the best estimates of the facts which can be put together. That estimate in turn should be given by some agency which has no axes to grind and which itself is not wedded to any particular policy."

This point is often made by the C.I.A. and its defenders. They cite, for instance, the agency's accurate estimate on Soviet missile strength, as a contrast to the inflated estimates that came from the Pentagon in the late Fifties. The latter, they say, were surely influenced by service rivalries and budgetary battles—such as the Air Force's desire for more missiles of its own. The C.I.A. has no such vested interest and little to gain by distorting or coloring its reports and estimates.

Mr. Dulles—like Secretary of State Dean Rusk—insists that no C.I.A. operation "of a political nature" has ever been undertaken "without appropriate approval at a high political level in our Government" outside the C.I.A.

The problem is that the facts presented to the Government by the C.I.A. are sometimes dramatic and inevitably tend to inspire dramatic proposals for clandestine operations that the agency's men are eager to carry out, and that they believe can—or might—succeed.

Long Odds Can Help

Even long odds sometimes work to the agency's advantage. General Eisenhower, for instance, has written that he undertook to aid pro-Western rebels in Guatemala in 1954 because Mr. Dulles told him the operation had only a 20 per cent chance to succeed. If the C.I.A. director had estimated a better chance than that, General Eisenhower wrote in his memoirs, he would have been unrealistic, unconvincing and overruled.

Command of the facts—at least the best facts available—plus zeal to do something about them, many critics fear, can make the C.I.A. an unanswerable advocate, not for a vested budgetary or policy interest, but for its own sincere notions of how to proceed. And its advantage of providing the facts on which decision must be made, these critics feel, can enable it to prevail over the advice or fears of political officers.

Thus, in 1958, Ambassador John Allison strongly opposed the plan of Allen Dulles to aid the rebel movement in Sumatra against President Sukarno of Indonesia. But Mr. Dulles had won the powerful support of his brother, Secretary of State John Foster Dulles.

Ultimately, the plan went forward—with the result that an American pilot was shot down and captured by the Sukarno forces, causing a conspicuous deterioration of relations between Indonesia and the United States. The plan was not unapproved; it was just unwise.

A third problem of control arises from the necessary secrecy that surrounds the agency. To protect its sources of information, to permit it to proceed with any form of clandestine operations, to guard the nation's political relations with most other countries, it is necessary for the C.I.A. to be shielded—and Congress has so shielded it, by law—from the ordinary scrutiny, investigation and public disclosure of activities that other Government agencies must undergo.

Within the agency, until the Bay of Pigs disaster of 1961 in Cuba, even the Intelligence Division was not allowed to know about the "dirty tricks" being planned and carried out by the Plans Division.

Stevenson in the Dark

Many of the highest Government officials are told nothing of some of the agency's activities because, in the course of their own duties, they do not "need to know."

It is now well established, for instance, that until the disaster unfolded, Adlai E. Stevenson, the United States representative to the United Nations, knew nothing of the Bay of Pigs plan. As a result, he and his Government suffered grievous humiliation after he publicly misstated the facts.

In years past, C.I.A. secrecy reached some absurd proportions—with high-level employes identifying themselves solemnly at cocktail parties as "librarians" and "clerks." In its early days, for instance, C.I.A. employes who in their private lives needed to apply for credit were instructed by the agency to say, when asked for an employer's reference: "Call Miss Bertha Potts" at a certain number.

It was not long, of course, before the lenders who were told to call Miss Potts would say gleefully: "Oh, you work for the C.I.A."

For many years prior to 1961, a good many critics had been aware of the control dangers inherent in the C.I.A.'s peculiar position. In 1954, Senator Mike Mansfield, Democrat of Montana, obtained 34 cosponsors for a bill to create a 12-member joint committee on intelligence to keep watch over the C.I.A., much as the Congressional Joint Committee on Atomic Energy does over the Atomic Energy Commission.

Allen Dulles, who was completely satisfied with the scrutiny provided by four carefully selected subcommittees of the Senate and House Armed Services and Appropriations Committees, went to work. He succeeded in cutting away 14 of Mr. Mansfield's cosponsors, and the bill was defeated, 59 to 27.

Board Headed by Killian

A year later the second Hoover Commission also recommended a Congressional joint committee, as well as a Presidentially appointed board of consultants on intelligence activities.

To forestall the first, Mr. Dulles acquiesced in the second, and in January, 1956, President Eisenhower named a board of consultants on foreign intelligence activities, with James R. Killian Jr., president of the Massachusetts Institute of Technology, as chairman.

Those familiar with the board's work in the Eisenhower years say it performed a useful function on the technical side, where Dr. Killian, for instance, was a powerful advocate in the development of the U-2. However, it is generally agreed that the board did not give very critical attention to "black" operations, and then only after the fact.

In 1954 there was also established by the National Security Council — which advises the President on defense and foreign policy matters—what came to be known as "the special group," or the "54-12 group," after the date (December, 1954) of the secret directive ordering its formation.

This directive also provided the basic charter for the agency's countersubversive and counter-Communist activity. Until that time, these activities had been undertaken under authority of a secret memorandum from President Truman issued in 1947 and inspired principally by the Italian, Czechoslovak and Berlin situations, then acute cold-war issues.

The 54-12 group was—and still is—composed of the President's special assistants for national security affairs, the director of the C.I.A., the Deputy Secretary of Defense and the Under Secretary (or Deputy Under Secretary) of State for Political Affairs, plus other officers consulted occasionally on particular proposals.

The group seems to have been created, partly at least, in response to public concern [illegible] the problem of control. [illegible] was given responsibility [illegible] passing on intelligence [illegible] tions beforehand, however, [illegible] cause of the [illegible]

[illegible] of Allen Dulles and John Foster Dulles, because of their close relations with President Eisenhower and because Allen Dulles had the power to give it the facts on which it had to base its decisions, the 54-12 group during the Eisenhower Administration is believed by knowledgeable sources to have exercised little real control.

The Classic Disaster

At the Bay of Pigs, just after President Kennedy took office in 1961, the worst finally happened; all the fears expressed through the years came true.

The Bay of Pigs must take its place in history as a classic example of the disaster that can occur when a major international operation is undertaken in deepest secrecy, is politically approved on the basis of "facts" provided by those who most fervently advocated it, is carried out by the same advocates, and ultimately acquires a momentum of its own beyond anything contemplated either by the advocates or those who supposedly "controlled" them.

Responsible officials of the Eisenhower Administration report, for instance, that the invasion plan was not even in existence, as such, when they went out of office on Jan. 19, 1961; there was nothing but a Cuban refugee force, available for whatever the incoming Administration might ultimately decide to do with it.

Yet the testimony of Kennedy Administration officials—Theodore C. Sorensen and Arthur M. Schlesinger Jr., for instance—is that the matter was presented to Mr. Kennedy by the C.I.A. advocates as if he were already committed to it and would have to cancel it rather than approve it. Mr. Sorensen even wrote in his book, "Kennedy," that Mr. Kennedy had been subtly pushed to be no less "hard" in his anti-Castroism than President Eisenhower supposedly had been.

The ultimate disaster and its various causes need no retelling. Their effect was graphically described by an official who saw the shaken Mr. Kennedy immediately afterward. The President, he said, "wanted to splinter the C.I.A. in a thousand pieces and scatter it to the winds."

At the same time, to Clark M. Clifford, a Washington lawyer and close friend, who had written the legislation setting up the C.I.A. during the Truman Administration, Mr. Kennedy said flatly and poignantly:

"I could not survive another one of these."

An Inquiry Ordered

But because he could not simply abolish the agency, much less its function, the President decided he would "get it under control."

First, he ordered a thorough investigation by a group headed by Gen. Maxwell D. Taylor and composed also of Allen Dulles, Admiral Arleigh Burke, Chief of Naval Operations, and Attorney General Robert F. Kennedy.

Second, on Mr. Clifford's advice, the President recreated the old board of consultants under the title of the Foreign Intelligence Committee and asked Dr. Killian to resume the chairmanship. (Mr. Clifford became a member and later succeeded Dr. Killian as chairman.) The President directed the committee to investigate the whole intelligence community from "stem to stern," recommend changes and see that they were carried out.

Third, after a decent interval, the President replaced Allen Dulles with John A. McCone, a former chairman of the Atomic Energy Commission. He told the new director that he was not to be simply the director of the C.I.A. but should regard his primary task as "the coordination and effective guidance of the total United States intelligence effort." Mr. Dulles's key assistants were also removed.

Fourth, the President sent a letter to every Ambassador telling him he was "in charge of the entire diplomatic mission" at his post, including not only foreign service personnel but "also the representatives of all [illegible]."

These representatives of other agencies were to keep the Ambassador "fully informed of their views and activities" and would abide by the Ambassador's decisions "unless in some particular instance you and they are notified to the contrary."

The President followed this letter, which was made public, with a secret communication, saying he meant it and specifically including C.I.A. men among those responsible to the Ambassador.

A Blow to Bundy

Perhaps the most important change in control procedures, however, involved the 54-12 group within the political ranks of the Administration, and it came without any Presidential initiative.

The Bay of Pigs had dealt a severe psychological blow to McGeorge Bundy, who as the President's assistant for national security affairs was a member of the group, and perhaps also to his self-esteem. Thereafter he set about tightening up the surveillance of C.I.A. operations, subjecting them to searching analysis before and not after the event. The hard-eyed Mr. Bundy was notably relentless at that kind of administration.

The President accepted the advice of the Taylor and Killian investigations on two important questions.

First, he decided not to limit the C.I.A. to intelligence gathering and not to shift clandestine operations to the Pentagon, or to a special agency created for the purpose.

These ideas had found favor among some sections of the State Department, among many public critics and even among some members and the staff of the advisory committee. But it was stoutly opposed by Allen Dulles, who argued that this would result in duplication and rivalry, and that the two functions were interdependent, though he admitted that they had not been working in harness on the Bay of Pigs operation.

The two committees of inquiry agreed with Mr. Dulles, and so, finally, did the President.

Second, the committees recommended, and the President enthusiastically agreed, that the C.I.A. should leave sizable military operations to the Pentagon and henceforth limit itself to operations of a kind in which United States involvement would be "plausibly deniable." This, however, has proved to be a rule of thumb in which it is often difficult to hide the thumb.

Something Like Secrecy

For instance, the later creation of an air force of anti-Castro Cubans to fly for the Congolese Government was carried out and managed by the C.I.A., not by the Pentagon, despite the recommendation.

The obvious reason was that the agency could do the job in something like secrecy, while Defense Department involvement would have been necessarily more open, advertising the backing of the United States for the "instant air force."

It is beyond dispute, however, that the Bay of Pigs was a watershed in the life of the C.I.A. and its influence on policy-making. Before that, no matter how much administrative control and political approval there may have been, Mr. Dulles ran the agency largely as he saw fit.

He was able to do so because he could almost always get "approval"—and thus adhere to the forms of control — from his brother in the State Department or from President Eisenhower, with both of whom he had the closest relations of trust and liking.

The effect of the Kennedy shake-up was immediately apparent—on policy in Laos, for instance. W. Averell Harriman, then the Assistant Secretary of State for Far Eastern Affairs, was given a free hand in getting rid of the American puppet, Premier Phoumi Nosavan — whose backing by the C.I.A. President Eisenhower had specifically approved — and reinstating Souvanna Phouma at the head of a neutralist government.

By general agreement of virtually every official interviewed, the C.I.A. does not now directly make policy, and its operations are under much more rigorous surveillance and control than before. Nevertheless, there continue to be—and probably always will be—instances where the controls simply do not work.

Uncertain Boundaries

Richard Bissell, who as deputy director for plans was largely responsible for the U-2 reconnaissance triumph and for the Bay of Pigs disaster, has explained why this must be.

"You can't take on operations of this scope," he has said, "draw narrow boundaries of policy around them and be absolutely sure that those boundaries will never be overstepped."

Recently, for instance, the C.I.A. was accused of supporting Cambodian rebels who oppose Prince Norodom Sihanouk, the head of state. Even some senior United States Foreign Service officers said they were not sure that the agency's firm denials meant no agent in the field, no obscure planner in the huge C.I.A. building in Virginia, had strayed from the strict boundaries of policy.

A high degree of control of C.I.A. activities exists, however, and inquiry produced this picture of the controlling agencies and how well the control works:

The 54-12 Group

The 54-12 group is the heart of the control system. Its mem- members now are Admiral William F. Raborn, the C.I.A. director; U. Alexis Johnson, Deputy Under Secretary of State for Political Affairs; Cyrus R. Vance, Deputy Secretary of Defense, and two Presidential assistants, Bill D. Moyers and Walt W. Rostow, who have replaced McGeorge Bundy in representing the White House.

This group meets once a week with a detailed agenda. It concentrates almost exclusively on operations. It approves all proposed operations and it passes in great detail on expenditures as small as $10,000 that have political implications or could prove embarrassing if discovered. Any differences are referred first to the Cabinet level and then, if necessary, to the President.

While the group approves every "black" operation, it does not necessarily clear all the routine intelligence-gathering activities of the agency. Nor, once approval has been given for a "black" operation, does it maintain a running supervision over every detail of its execution.

Under a given policy decision approving a guerrilla operation in a certain country, for instance, the 54-12 group might also have to approve something as specific and important as a bridge-blowing. But the over-all program would go on by itself under the direction of agents in the field.

Bureau of the Budget

Another form of control is that of the pursestring.

The C.I.A.'s annual request for funds, which is hidden largely in the Defense Department budget, is the responsibility of the head of the Budget Bureau's International Division. The request has usually fared well, but in the fiscal year 1965, for the first time in several years, it was cut back sharply by the bureau.

Another form of budgetary control centers on the agency's "slush fund," which used to be about $100-million a year and is now in "the tens of millions." One official has said that "the C.I.A. can't spend a dollar without Bureau of Budget approval." But another official put a somewhat different light on how the "slush fund" is handled.

Suppose, he said, that Country X is having an election and the candidates backed by the United States Government seem headed for defeat. The Ambassador and the C.I.A. station chief—the agency's chief in that country—may forward a request for some fast money to spread around.

The request, when reviewed and cleared by the middle levels of the State Department and the C.I.A., goes to the 54-12 group for review.

This group will first decide whether the money should be spent, how the C.I.A. should spend it and how much should be made available. Then the request goes to the Budget Bureau to be justified in budget terms against other needs.

A Call Brings the Money

For example, this official said, one such project was recently trimmed by the Budget Bureau from $3-million to $1.7-million. But in the last week of the election, the C.I.A. ran out of funds just as it needed some more billboards plastered, and it was able to get the money simply by a phone call to the Budget Bureau. This official explained that there had to be some way of providing "quick-turn money" under tight controls and audit.

It should also be noted that this form of control is purely budgetary and not substantive. The Bureau of the Budget does not interpose any policy judgment but simply weighs a proposed operation against total money available and the outlays for other projects.

Foreign Intelligence Advisory Board

Another control agency is the Foreign Intelligence Advisory Board. This group has nine members. Four have had extensive government experience.

The chairman, Clark Clifford, was special counsel to President Truman from 1946 to 1950. Among the other members, Robert D. Murphy, former career Ambassador and former Under Secretary of State for Political Affairs, has had personal experience in clandestine operations, for he prepared the way for the American landing in North Africa in 1942. He is now a director of Corning Glass.

Gordon Gray, a director of the R. J. Reynolds Company and a newspaper owner, was Secretary of the Army under President Truman and later was President Eisenhower's special assistant for national security affairs. Frank Pace Jr., chairman of the Special Advisory Board, Air Force Systems Command, was director of the Bureau of the Budget in 1949-50 and Secretary of the Army from 1950 to 1953.

Two members are scientists connected with industry — William O. Baker, vice president in charge of research for the Bell Telephone Laboratories, a member for many years of the Science Advisory Board of the Air Force, and Edwin H. Land, chairman and president of the Polaroid Corporation, a former adviser to the Navy on guided missiles and an expert on photography.

There are two military representatives—General Taylor, former chairman of the Joint Chiefs of Staff and former Ambassador to South Vietnam, and Admiral John H. Sides, commander in chief of the Pacific Fleet from 1960 to 1963. Dr. William L. Langer, the ninth member, is Professor of History at Harvard and a frequent government consultant.

The board meets an average of one or one and one-half days a month. It is subdivided into two-man panels specializing in various fields, which meet more frequently. Individual members also take field inspection trips. Mr. Clifford went recently to South Vietnam; Mr. Gray has been on extensive trips to the Middle East and Southeast Asia.

There is divergent opinion on the control value of this board. Some of its members are highly pleased with their own work. They point out that over the last four and one-half years they have made some 200 recommendations, of which the President accepted 95 per cent.

They take credit for persuading President Kennedy and Secretary of Defense Robert S. McNamara to create the Defense Intelligence Agency, combining the separate service intelligence divisions. This had been recommended by Secretary of Defense Gates and by Lyman Kirkpatrick, Inspector general of the C.I.A., as a result of the widely differing estimates of the so-called "missile gap" in the late nineteen-fifties made by the intelligence arms of the services.

Another official in a position of authority, however, believes that the board does little more than provide a "nice audit" of C.I.A. operations and that any "control" it exercises is largely ex post facto. He asked what could be expected from a board that met only a few days a month.

"By 5 in the afternoon," he said, "the guys can't remember what they were told in the morning."

Even the members concede that their work has been aimed primarily at improving the efficiency and methods of the C.I.A., rather than at control of individual operations. Thus, if the board does investigate some "black" operations, its emphasis is placed on whether it was done well or could have been more successful, rather than on the political question of whether it should have been done at all.

One member reported, however, that the C.I.A. now brought some of its proposals to the committee for prior discussion, if not specific approval. This is not an unmixed blessing.

While the board might advise against some risky scheme, it also might not; in the latter case its weight added to that of the C.I.A., would present the responsible political officials in the 54-12 group with an even more powerful advocacy than usual.

An advantage of the board is its direct link to the President. Since this is augmented, at present, by Mr. Clifford's close personal and political ties to President Johnson, any recommendations the committee makes carry great weight with the bureaucrats of the C.I.A., even before they appear in a Presidential order.

State Department and Ambassadors

Also exercising some control over the C.I.A. are the State Department and Ambassadors. Secretary of State Rusk has confided to his associates that he is now quite certain the C.I.A. is doing nothing affecting official policy he does not know about. But he added that he was also sure he was the only one in the State Department informed about some of the things being done.

Despite this information gap as high as the Under Secretary and Assistant Secretary levels, State Department officers with a need to know are far better informed about operations than before the Bay of Pigs.

Moreover, in the 54-12 group and in interagency intelligence meetings, State Department officers are now more ready to speak out and more likely to be heeded on proposed intelligence operations that they believe would compromise larger policy interests.

President Kennedy's secret letter to the Ambassadors also had some effect in changing a dangerous situation.

In 1954, William J. Sebald resigned as Ambassador to Burma because of continued C.I.A. support to Chinese Nationalists in northern Burma despite all his protests. In 1956, James B. Conant, Ambassador to West Germany, was not told about the tunnel under East Berlin. In 1960, in Laos, Ambassador Winthrop G. Brown was often bypassed as the C.I.A. helped prop up the American-backed Premier Phoumi Nosavan, against his advice. The same year, the Ambassador in Malaysia knew nothing of the Singapore operation that ultimately was to embarrass the State Department in 1965.

It is doubtful whether such things could happen today if an Ambassador is forceful enough in establishing his authority.

In the last four years the Ambassadors have been kept much better informed, and their relations with C.I.A. chiefs of station have been consequently more cordial. Ambassadors Clare Timberlake and Edward Gullion were completely posted on C.I.A. operations during the Congo crisis and worked closely with the agency. So, apparently, was Henry Cabot Lodge after he took over the embassy in Saigon in 1963.

While the Ambassador may not always be completely master in his own house, neither does it seem to be true—as a staff report of Senator Henry M. Jackson's subcommittee on national security staffing and operations said in 1962 — that the primacy of the Ambassador, supposedly established by the Kennedy letter, was largely "a polite fiction.".

For example, Robert F. Woodward, Ambassador to Spain, vetoed a man chosen to be the C.I.A.'s Spanish station chief. And the State Department, while still complaining about the size of some C.I.A. stations, is now supposed to approve the number of agents in each diplomatic mission.

In secret testimony before the Senate Foreign Relations Committee in the summer of 1965, Under Secretary of State Thomas C. Mann made plain that the creation of the Imbert military junta in the Dominican Republic in May was a State Department, and not a C.I.A., idea.

Asked whether the C.I.A. would have set up the junta without orders from State, Mr. Mann replied:

"I will say that in the past this may have been; I do not know. But since I arrived in January, 1964, I have had an understanding first with Mr. McCone and now with Admiral Raborn, and I am sure the department has, even more importantly, that the policy is made here [at State] and that nothing is done without our consent.".

This "nothing" probably goes too far, since there remain areas of ambassadorial ignorance. An Ambassador is not always informed of "third-party" spying in his country — for example, spying in France on the Chinese Communists there. Nor is he given specific details on counterespionage and information gathering about which he may be generally informed.

If the C.I.A. has "bought the madam," as one official put it, of a house of ill fame patronized by influential citizens or officials of a host country, the Ambassador does not know it and probably doesn't want to. He would, however, have the dubious benefit of any information the madam might disclose.

These are the four institutional forms of "control" of the C.I.A. that now exist—save for Congressional oversight and the all-important role of the agency's director. And The New York Times's survey for these articles left little doubt that the newly vigorous functioning of these four groups has greatly improved coordination, more nearly assured political approval and substantially reduced the hazards implicit in C.I.A. operations.

Nevertheless, the agency still remains the fount of information on which many policy decisions rest, and the source of facts, selected or otherwise, on which to justify its own projects.

Nevertheless, the C.I.A. enjoys an inherent advantage in any conflict with the State or Defense Departments because of its undeniable expertise—especially in economics and science—and because it is free from such political entanglements as trying to build up a missile budget (as in the case of the Air Force) or of having to justify the recognition of a foreign leader (as in the case of State).

And nevertheless, in its legitimate need for secrecy, the C.I.A. simply cannot be subjected to as much public or even official scrutiny as all other agencies undergo.

A Call for More Control

For all these reasons, and because of occasional blunders, there has been no abatement in the demand of critics for more and stronger control. Inevitably, their call is for some form of increased supervision by the people's representatives in Congress, usually by a joint committee of the two houses.

The Times survey indicated a widespread feeling that such a committee would do the agency's vital functions more harm than good, and that it would provide little if any solution to the central problem of control.

The history of the Central Intelligence Agency since 1947 makes one thing painfully clear — that the control question, while real and of the utmost importance, is one of "not measures but men." The forms of control mean nothing if there is no will to control, and if there is a will to control, then the form of it is more or less irrelevant.

Such a will can only come from the high political officials of the Administration, and it can best be inspired in them by the direct example of the President.

But even the President probably could not impose his will on the agency in every case without the understanding, the concurrence and the vigorous and efficient cooperation of the second most important man in the matter of control—the director of the C.I.A.

Tomorrow: Not measures but men.

The C.I.A.: Qualities of Director Viewed as Chief Rein on Agency

4-29-66

Following is the last of five articles on the Central Intelligence Agency. The articles are by a team of New York Times correspondents consisting of Tom Wicker, John W. Finney, Max Frankel, E. W. Kenworthy and others.

Special to The New York Times,

WASHINGTON, April 25 — As copious evidence of a Soviet military build-up in Cuba, including the installation of anti-aircraft missiles, poured into Washington in the summer of 1962, the director of the Central Intelligence Agency, John A. McCone, had a strong hunch about its meaning.

He believed such an arsenal half-way around the world from Moscow had to be designed ultimately to protect even more important installations — long-range offensive missiles and nuclear weapons yet to be provided.

Mr. McCone told President Kennedy about his hunch but specified that it was a personal guess entirely lacking in concrete supporting evidence. He scrupulously refused to impose his hunch on the contradictory documentary and photoanalysis evidence being provided by the intelligence community over which he presided. He continued to pass to the President and his advisers reports and estimates—based on all available evidence—that the Soviet Union was not likely to do what he believed in his heart it was doing.

When the evidence that the Russians had implanted offensive missiles in Cuba did come in, Mr. McCone was among those around the President who argued for quick, decisive air action before the missiles could become operative. But when the President decided on his blockade-and-ultimatum policy, Mr. McCone loyally supported it and helped carry it out.

In 1963, Mr. McCone was personally in favor of the proposed limited nuclear test-ban treaty. He had backed such proposals since his years as chairman of the Atomic Energy Commission in the Eisenhower Administration.

Nevertheless, because of his desire that the facts should be known as fully as possible, he furnished a C.I.A. staff expert to assist Senator John Stennis, Democrat of Mississippi, chairman of an Armed Services subcommittee and an opponent of the treaty. This angered the White House and the State Department, but it was consistent with Mr. McCone's view of the C.I.A.'s role in informing the Government as fully as possible.

It is in this kind of intellectual effort to separate fact from fancy, evidence from suspicion, decision from preference, opinion from policy and consequence from guess that effective control of the C.I.A. must begin, in the opinion of most of those who have been surveyed by The New York Times.

And it is when these qualities have been lacking, the same officials and experts believe, that the C.I.A. most often has become involved in those activities that have led to widespread charges that it is not controlled, makes its own policy and undermines that of its political masters.

Inevitably, the contrast is drawn between John McCone and Allen W. Dulles, one of the most charming and imaginative men in Washington, under whose direction the C.I.A. grew to its present proportions and importance.

A Gambling Man

Digging a wiretap tunnel from West to East Berlin, flying spy planes beyond the reach of antiaircraft weapons over the Soviet Union and finding a Laotian ruler in the cafes of Paris were romantic projects that kindled Mr. Dulles's enthusiasm. Sometimes the profits were great; sometimes the losses were greater.

To Allen Dulles, a gambling man, the possibility of the losses were real but the chance of success was more important.

A 20 per cent chance to overthrow a leftist regime in Guatemala through a C.I.A.-sponsored invasion was all he wanted to give it a try. He charmed President Eisenhower with tales of extraordinary snooping on such rulers as President Gamal Abdel Nasser of the United Arab Republic and with accounts of the romantic derring-do of Kermit Roosevelt in arousing Iranian mobs against Mohammed Mossadegh to restore the Shah to his throne.

As long as his brother, John Foster Dulles, was Secretary of State, Allen Dulles had no need to chafe under political "control." The Secretary had an almost equal fascination for devious, back-alley adventure in what he saw as a worldwide crusade.

Personal Judgments

Neither brother earned his high reputation by taut and businesslike administration. Both placed supreme confidence in their personal judgments.

Colleagues recall many occasions on which Allen Dulles would cut off debate about, say, the intentions of a foreign head of state with the remark: "Oh, I know him personally. He would never do that sort of thing."

Allen Dulles was also an accomplished politician. Throughout his regime he maintained the best of relations with the late Clarence Cannon of Missouri, who as chairman of the House Appropriations Committee was the key figure in providing C.I.A. funds.

Mr. Dulles kept personal control of the selection of other members of Congress with responsibility for overseeing the C.I.A., with the result that he invariably had on his side those members of the Congressional establishment who could carry the rest of Congress with them.

Thus, in the Dulles period at the C.I.A., there was a peculiar set of circumstances. An adventurous director, inclined to rely on his own often extremely good and informed intuition, widely traveled, read and experienced, with great prestige and the best connections in Congress, whose brother held the second-highest office in the Administration, and whose President completely trusted and relied upon both, was able to act almost at will and was shielded from any unpleasant consequences.

Kennedy Kept Him in Office

When the Eisenhower Administration came to an end in 1961, Allen Dulles's reappointment was one of President Kennedy's first acts. Mr. Dulles, like J. Edgar Hoover, who was reappointed head of the Federal Bureau of Investigation at the same time, had great prestige and was thought to lend continuity and stability to the new Administration.

In fact, Mr. Dulles's continuance in office set the stage for the Bay of Pigs and the great crisis of the C.I.A.

In that incredible drama of 1961, it was Mr. Dulles's weaknesses as C.I.A. director — rather than, as so often before, his strengths—that came to the fore. He was committed to the Cuba invasion plan, at all costs, against whatever objections. The advocate overcame the planner.

As President Kennedy and others interposed reservations and qualifications, Mr. Dulles and his chief lieutenant, Richard M. Bissell, made whatever changes were required in order to keep the plan alive. For instance, they switched the landing site from the Trinidad area to the Bay of Pigs, to achieve more secrecy, thereby accepting an inferior beachhead site and separating the refugee force of invaders from the Escambray Mountains, where they were supposed to operate as guerrillas, by 80 miles of swamp.

Above all, lacking his old rapport with President Eisenhower and his brother, lacking a coldly objective approach to his plan, Mr. Dulles never realized that President Kennedy suffered from more than tactical reservations.

These misgivings—in reality a reluctance to approve the invasion — forced the frequent changes in plans, each weakening the whole, until whatever chance of success there might have been was gone.

At a Critical Hour

It was John McCone who replaced Allen Dulles at the C.I.A.'s most critical hour. After the Bay of Pigs fiasco, it had barely escaped dismemberment, or at least the divorce of its Intelligence and Operations Divisions. There were also new cries for greater control, and the men around President Kennedy were suspicious of, if not hostile to, the agency.

Like Mr. Dulles, Mr. McCone devoted much energy to resisting a formal Congressional watchdog committee, to courting the senior members of the Armed Services and Appropriations Committees on Capitol Hill and to converting the members of a resuscitated Presidential advisory board to his view of intelligence policies.

But those who observed him work believe he also brought a keen intelligence and energy to a tough-minded administration of the agency itself and to careful, challenging study of its intelligence estimates and recommendations.

He broke down the rigid division between operations and analysis that had kept the C.I.A.'s analysts—incredible as it seems—ignorant of the Operations Division's specific plan to invade Cuba. And he began to subject the C.I.A.'s own action programs to vigorous review and criticism by the agency's own experts.

Incisive Questions

The intellectual level of meetings among intelligence officials at the C.I.A. and other agencies improved greatly under Mr. McCone, primarily because he put difficult and incisive questions to those preparing formal analyses and plans, forcing them to challenge and defend their own judgments.

Above all, he set the hard example himself of putting aside personal preference, informed guesses and long gambles in favor of realistic weighing of available evidence and close adherence to administration policy.

He brought specialists and experts into conferences and decision-making at a much higher level of policy than before. Often he took such men with him to meetings at the Cabinet level. This exposed them to policy considerations as never before, and put policy-makers more closely in touch with the experts on whose "facts" they were acting.

As chairman of the United States Intelligence Board — a group that brings together representatives from the Defense Intelligence Agency, the State Department's intelligence unit and others—Mr. McCone won a reputation for objectivity by frequently overruling the proposals of his own agency, the C.I.A.

Some Criticism, Too

His regime was not without its critics. Many officials believe he narrowed the C.I.A.'s range of interests, which was as wide as the horizons under the imaginative Allen Dulles. For instance, they say, he was slow to mobilize the C.I.A. to obtain information about nuclear programs in India, Israel and other nations.

Mr. McCone also tried, but failed, to end interagency rivalries. He spent much time in bitter dispute with Secretary of Defense Robert S. McNamara about divisions of labor and costs in technological programs and about chains of command in Vietnam. He is reported to have feared the growth of the Defense Intelligence Agency as an invasion of C.I.A. territory.

With the State Department, too, rivalry continued—and still does. Much of this can be attributed, on the diplomats' side, to the C.I.A.'s readier access to the upper levels of government and to its financial ability to underwrite the kind of research and field operations that State would like to do for itself.

On the agency's side, there is undoubtedly some resentment at the State Department's recently increased political control of C.I.A. operations. For instance, until April 28, 1965, the day President Johnson ordered the Marines into Santo Domingo, the C.I.A. had reported the possibility of a rebellion and it knew of three Communist-controlled groups functioning in the Dominican Republic, but the agency had not suggested an imminent threat of a Communist take-over.

When the President and his advisers became persuaded that there was such a threat, however, C.I.A. agents supplied confirming intelligence — some of it open to challenge by an alert reader. C.I.A. officials seem a little red-faced about this compliance, and the intimation is that the C.I.A. may have gone overboard in trying not to undermine but to substantiate a political policy decision.

Within the Bounds of Policy

Mr. McCone's pride and the fierce loyalty to the agency that he developed made him resentful of Congressional and public criticism, not always to his own advantage. Nevertheless, as a result of his single-minded efforts to control himself and his agency, other former members of the Kennedy Administration—many of whom opposed his appointment—now find it hard to recall any time when Mr. McCone or the C.I.A. in his time overstepped the bounds of policy deliberately.

Thus, they are inclined to cite him as proof of the theory

that in the process of government men are more important than mechanics—and in support of the widespread opinion among present and former officials that the problem of controlling the C.I.A. must begin with men inside the agency itself.

The far more general belief is that Congress ought to have a much larger voice in the control of the agency. This belief is reinforced by the fact that the Congressional control that now exists is ill-informed, in the hands of a chosen few, subject to what the agency wishes to tell even these few, and occasionally apathetic.

There are four subcommittees of the Senate and House Armed Services and Appropriations Committees to which the director reports.

Mr. McCone met about once a month with the subcommittees. The present director, Adm. William F. Raborn, meets with them somewhat more often.

Conflicting Views

There are conflicting opinions on the value of these sessions. Some who participate say that they are "comprehensive," that the director holds back nothing in response to questions, that he goes into "great detail on budget and operations" and is "brutally frank." Others say that "we are pretty well filled in" but that the subcommittees get no precise information on the budget or the number of employes and that the director reveals only as much as he wants to.

These conflicting views probably reflect the composition and interests of the subcommittees. Those on the Senate side are said to be "lackadaisical" and "apathetic," with some Senators not wanting to know too much. The House subcommittees are said to be "alert, interested and efficient," with members insisting on answers to questions.

Representative George H. Mahon, Democrat of Texas, chairman of the House Appropriations Committee, has warned the Administration it must itself police the C.I.A. budget more stringently than that of any other agency because he and other Congressmen believe they should protect the sensitive C.I.A. budget, as it comes to them, from the Congressional economy bloc and the agency's more determined critics.

As a result of this and other Congressional representations, the C.I.A. "slush fund" for emergencies has been reduced below $100-million. And—much to Mr. McCone's annoyance—President Johnson's economy drives resulted in an Administration reduction in the agency's general budget.

Three things, however, are clear about this Congressional oversight.

No Real Control

One is that the subcommittee members exercise no real control because they are not informed of all covert operations, either before or after they take place.

The second point regarding Congressional oversight is that a handful of men like Mr. Cannon and Senator Russell, with their great prestige, do not so much control the C.I.A. as shield it from its critics.

Finally, even these establishment watchdogs can be told just as much as the C.I.A. director thinks they should know. In fact, one or two of the subcommittee members are known to shy away from too much secret information, on the ground that they do not want either to know about "black" operations or take the chance of unwittingly disclosing them.

For all these reasons, there is a large body of substantial opinion—in and out of Congress—that favors more specific monitoring of intelligence activity.

The critics insist that Congress has a duty periodically to investigate the activities of the C.I.A. and other intelligence arms; to check on the C.I.A.'s relations with other executive departments, study its budget and exercise greater and more intelligent oversight than the present diffused subcommittees, which operate without staff and with little or no representation from members most concerned with foreign affairs.

A Fountain of Leaks

But the overwhelming consensus of those most knowledgeable about the C.I.A, now and in the past, does not support the idea that Congress should "control" the C.I.A. A number of reasons are adduced:

¶Security. Congress is the well-known fountain of more leaks than any other body in Washington. The political aspirations of and pressures on members make them eager to appear in print; they do not have the executive responsibility weighing on them, and many C.I.A. operations could provide dramatic passages in campaign speeches.

¶Politics. Any standing committee would have to be bipartisan. This would give minority party members — as well as dissidents in the majority — unparalleled opportunities to learn the secrets of the executive branch and of foreign policy, and to make political capital of mistakes or controversial policies. Republicans, for instance, armed with all the facts and testimony that investigation could have disclosed, might well have wrecked the Kennedy Administration after the Bay of Pigs.

¶The Constitution. The C.I.A. acts at the direction of the President and the National Security Council. If a Congressional committee had to be informed in advance of C.I.A. activities, covert and overt, there might well be a direct Congressional breach of the constitutional freedom of the executive branch and of the President's right to conduct foreign policy.

¶Control. If a carefully chosen committee conscientiously tried to avoid all these dangers, it could probably exercise little real "control" of the kind critics desire. At best, for instance, it could probably do little more than investigate some questionable operations in secrecy and after they had taken place, and then report privately to the President, who might or might not respond.

¶Ideology. Congress is full of "professional anti-Communists" and has not a few "professional liberals." In its worldwide activities, the C.I.A. regularly takes covert actions that would profoundly offend either or both—for instance, supporting some non-Communist leftist against a military regime, or vice versa. To report this kind of activity to Congress would be certain to set off public debate and recriminations and lay a whole new set of domestic political pressures on the agency.

¶Policy. Knowledgeable men in Washington do not accept the Joint Committee on Atomic Energy as a desirable model for oversight of the C.I.A. They point out that the Atomic Energy Committee has developed its own staff of experts in its field, in some cases abler men than those in the Atomic Energy Commission, and these Congressional experts now have a vested interest in their own ideas of atomic policy and projects.

An Empire Foreseen

This, these sources fear, would be the outcome of a joint committee on intelligence —a new intelligence empire on Capitol Hill that could in time exert a direct policy influence on the C.I.A., separate from and challenging the President's policy decisions. This would diffuse rather than focus power over the agency and confuse rather than clarify the problem of control.

Other recommendations for a Congressional intervention have been advanced. The most drastic—and in some ways the most interesting—would be to legislate the separation of the C.I.A.'s intelligence and analysis function from the operations or "dirty tricks" function.

President Kennedy, after the Bay of Pigs, rejected a proposal to create a new and autonomous intelligence and analysis agency. This plan would have covert political operations under a small and largely anonymous section of the State Department.

Efficiency Drop Feared

If accepted, this plan would have had the great advantage, in terms of control, of divorcing "black" operators and their schemes from the source of information on which the decision to act must be made. Thus, the covert operators would have no more information than anyone else in government, no power to shape, color, withhold or manufacture information, and could, in effect, do only what they were told to do by political authorities.

It would also reduce the sheer size and power of the C.I.A. within the Government, much of which is based on its combination of functions—providing information, proposing action and having the ability to carry it out.

On the other hand, as Mr. Kennedy concluded, such a divorce might well lower the total overt and covert efficiency of the intelligence effort. Those who favor the present combined agency insist that intelligence and action officers must be close enough to advise one another—with analysts checking operators, but also profiting from the operators' experiences in the field.

Moreover, they point out that so-called paramilitary operations are more easily transferred on paper than in fact to the Defense Department. They note that the department, for instance, can by law ship arms only to recognized governments that undertake certain obligations in return, and cannot legally arm or assist, say, rebel groups or mercenaries, even for laudable purposes.

Nor could the Defense Department easily acquire the skill, the convenient "covers," the political talents and bureaucratic flexibility required for quick, improvised action in time of crisis.

As evidence of that, there is the case of the successful political and military organization of hill tribesmen in Vietnam carried out by the C.I.A. some years ago. When the Army won control of the operation in a bureaucratic in-fight, the good beginning was lost in a classic bit of military mismanagement, and the tribal project collapsed.

As for the State Department's taking over covert operations, the opponents ask, how could the department survive the inevitable exposure of some bit of political skulduggery in some other country, when it is supposed to be the simon-pure vessel of the United States' proper diplomatic relations?

A Less Drastic Plan

A far less drastic but perhaps more feasible approach would be to add knowledgeable Congressional experts in foreign affairs to the military and appropriations subcommittees that now check on the C.I.A.

Along this line is the idea backed by Senator McCarthy—that a subcommittee of the Senate Foreign Relations Committee should be added to the existing watchdogs.

Such men as J. W. Fulbright, Democrat of Arkansas, chairman of the Senate Foreign Relations Committee, Mike Mansfield of Montana, the Senate Democratic leader, and George D. Aiken of Vermont, a Republican member of the Foreign Relations Committee, might bring greater balance and sensitivity to the present group of watchdog subcommittees.

Most of those interviewed in the New York Times survey for these articles also believed that the C.I.A. should have no influence on the selection of members of the subcommittees.

While the excuse for giving the agency a voice is to make sure that only "secure" and "responsible" members of Congress are chosen, the net effect is that the agency usually manages to have itself checked by its best friends in Congress and by those who can best shield it from more critical members like Senator McCarthy and Senator Mansfield.

Fund Slash Proposed

Finally, many observers consider that it might be useful for some select, nonpermanent committee of independent-minded members of Congress to make a thorough, responsible study of the whole intelligence community. Such a group might set out to determine how much of the community's activity is actually needed or useful, and how much of the whole apparatus might be reduced in size and expense—and thus in the kind of visibility that brings the C.I.A. into disrepute overseas and at home.

One former offical said quite seriously that he was not sure how much the nation would lose in vital services if all the activities of the C.I.A apart from those dealing with technological espionage—satellites and the like—had their budgets arbitrarily reduced by half.

A number of others suggested that it was possible for a great many of the C.I.A.'s information-gathering functions and study projects to be handled openly by the State Department, if only Congress would appropriate the money for it.

But the State Department is traditionally starved for funds by members of Congress who scoff at the "cookie-pushers" and the "striped-pants boys." The same members are often quite willing to appropriate big sums, almost blindly, for the secret, "tough" and occasionally glamorous activities of the spies, saboteurs and mysterious experts of the C.I.A.

As another example of what a specially organized, responsible Congressional investigation might discover, some officials expressed their doubts about the National Security Agency. This Defense Department arm specializes in making and breaking codes, spends about $1-billion a year—twice as much as the C.I.A.—and, in the opinion of many who know its work, hardly earns its keep.

But to most of those interviewed, the question of control ultimately came down to the caliber and attitude of the men who run the C.I.A., and particularly its director.

The present director, Admiral Raborn, is a man who earned a high reputation as the developer of the Navy's Polaris missile but who had no previous experience in intelligence work. Nor is he particularly close to President Johnson or to other high Administration officials.

Inauspicious Start

The admiral took office on a bad day—the one on which Mr. Johnson dispatched the Marines to Santo Domingo last April.

Admiral Raborn and his predecessor, Mr. McCone, lunched together in downtown Washington that afternoon, unaware of the imminent intervention. As they parted, Admiral Raborn offered Mr. McCone a ride to the Langley, Va., headquarters of the C.I.A But Mr. McCone said he was going home to pack his clothes.

Those who know of this exchange have a hunch that if Mr. McCone had accepted the invitation and returned to the turmoil that quickly developed in his old office, the history of the intervention might have been different. Many are in-

clined to blame Admiral Raborn, in any event, for the mishmash, of hasty evidence the C.I.A. contrived to justify the State Department's claim that there was a threat of a Communist uprising.

One reason the admiral was chosen, after President Johnson had searched for six months for a successor to Mr. McCone, was that as head of the Polaris project he had shown great ability to work with and mollify inquisitive Congressmen.

Another was that his military background made him an unlikely target for charges of being too "soft" or too liberal for his post. The same consideration influenced President Kennedy in choosing the conservative Republican John McCone, and it is notable that no leading figure of the Democratic party, much less one of its liberals, has ever been the agency's director.

Because of his lack of experience in intelligence and international affairs, it is widely believed among present and former officials that Admiral Raborn was chosen primarily as a "front man." Ironically, the Congress that he was supposed to impress is actually concerned—interviews disclosed—because he has not seemed to have the sure grasp of the agency's needs and activities that would most inspire confidence in it.

Raborn Defended

Knowledgeable sources say the C.I.A. itself, in its day-to-day business, is a bureaucracy like any other, functioning routinely whatever the quality of its leadership. These sources argue that the experience and professionalism of its staff are so great that any lack of these qualities in Admiral Raborn is scarcely felt.

But they do not agree that "Red" Raborn is just a front man. He is different—as would be expected—from any director who preceded him, but there is evidence available to suggest that he may not be such an unfortunate choice as has been suggested in a number of critical articles in the press.

The admiral is said to have President Johnson's confidence, although in a different way from the confidence President Kennedy placed in Mr. McCone. The latter was a valued member of the group that argued out high policy and influenced the President's decisions, not with facts but also with opinions and recommendations.

Admiral Raborn is said to to make little effort to exert such an influence on policy. Partly, this is because Mr. Johnson apparently does not want the C.I.A. director in such a role—and among those interviewed by The New York Times there was a belief that one reason John McCone left the post was that he could not play as influential a role as he had in the Kennedy Administration.

The main reason for the admiral's approach, however, is his Navy background. He regards himself as having more of a service and staff mission than a policy-making job.

He believes it is his duty to lay the best available facts before the President and those other high officials who make or influence policy, so that their judgments may be as informed as possible. To enter into policy discussions as an advocate, in his view, would inevitably compromise his role as an impartial and objective source of information.

Among knowledgeable officials, moreover, Admiral Raborn is credited with at least two administrative developments within the agency—both stemming, again, from his Navy background.

Long-Range Planning

He has installed an operations center, not unlike a military command post or a Navy ship's "combat information center." In it, round-the-clock duty officers constantly monitor communications of every sort. They can instantly communicate with the White House, State Department, Pentagon and agents in the field, by means of the agency's wizardry with machines and electronics.

This represents primarily a drawing together and streamlining of capabilities the agency already had, but it is rated as a positive advance in C.I.A. efficiency.

The other Raborn innovation is a Navy-like system of long-range management planning. He has assigned a group of officials to "look ahead" for decades at the shape of the world to come.

Out of this continuing study, the admiral hopes to be able to make more precise plans for the agency's needs in manpower, money, equipment and organization in, say, 1975, so that it can be planned for right now.

There persists among many interested in the C.I.A., however, a reluctance to accept the idea that the agency should be headed by anyone other than an experienced, strong executive with a wide grasp of international affairs and intelligence work, strong ties to the Administration and the knowledge and determination to keep the agency's work within the limits of policy and propriety.

This concern has been heightened by the departure from the White House of McGeorge Bundy, now president of the Ford Foundation. As Mr. Johnson's representative on the 54-12 group, he was probably second only to the director of the C.I.A. in maintaining "control" and took an intense interest in this duty.

Thus, if the White House replacements, Bill D. Moyers and Walt W. Rostow, prove either less interested or less forceful in representing the White House interest in C.I.A. operations, and if Admiral Raborn's alleged lack of experience in intelligence and foreign affairs handicaps him, effective control of the agency could be weakened without any change at all in the official processes of control.

Promotion Debate

Some people concluded even before the end of the admiral's first year that the difficulties of finding a succession of suitable C.I.A. directors made it advisable to promote impressive professionals from within the agency.

The most widely respected of these is the deputy director, Richard Helms, who was said to have been Mr. McCone's choice to succeed him.

Others argue, however, that intelligence is too dangerous a thing to be left to professional spies and that a loyal associate of the President's with the political qualifications for a senior Cabinet position should hold the post.

Whatever his identity, however, the prime conclusion of The New York Times survey of the Central Intelligence Agency is that its director is or should be the central figure in establishing and maintaining the actual substance of control, whatever its forms may take. For if the director insists, and bends all his efforts to make sure, that the agency serve the political administration of the Government, only blind chance or ineptitude in the field is likely to take the C.I.A. out of political control.

Conclusions of Study

A number of other conclusions also emerge from the study:

¶Whatever may have been the situation in the past, and whatever misgivings are felt about Admiral Raborn, there is now little concern in the Johnson Administration or among former high officials, and there is even less evidence, that the C.I.A. is making or sabotaging foreign policy or otherwise acting on its own.

¶When C.I.A. operations acquire a life of their own and outrun approved policy, they often follow a pattern well known also in less secret arms of government. Diplomats frequently say more than they are told to say to other governments or otherwise exceed their instructions. Foreign aid and propaganda operations, though "public," can commit the United States to practices and men in ways not envisioned by Washington. Military operations can escalate by their own logic, and when things go wrong the Pentagon has at times been more reluctant than the C.I.A. in producing the facts.

¶Nonetheless, while the C.I.A. acts as the Government's fountain of information as well as its "black" operating arm, while it is the C.I.A. that both proposes operations and supplies the facts to justify them, the danger of its getting out of control of the Administration exists and ought to be taken seriously within and without the Government. The Bay of Pigs stands as enduring testimony to that fact.

¶The task of coping with this danger is essentially that of the President, his highest officials and the director of the C.I.A. It can only be met peripherally by Congressional oversight, and then with increased danger of security leaks and domestic political pressures on the agency.

¶The charges against the C.I.A. at home and abroad are so widespread and in many ways so exaggerated that the effectiveness and morale of the agency may be seriously impaired. In particular, there could ultimately be a problem in recruiting and keeping the high caliber of personnel upon whom the agency must rely both for doing useful work and for keeping that work within proper bounds.

Crucial Questions

Thus, there must be in this and in any Administration a tight, relentless, searching review and analysis of the C.I.A. and its activities, meeting squarely and answering honestly at least these questions:

Is any proposed operation or activity likely, on balance, to make a genuine and necessary contribution, in the long view as well as the short, to legitimate American interests and aspirations in the world, or is it merely convenient, expedient and possible without regard to its wider implications or to the real necessity for it?

In sum, is the government of a proud and honorable people relying too much on "black" operations, "dirty tricks," harsh and illicit acts in the "back alleys" of the world? Is there some point at which meeting fire with fire, force with force, subversion with subversion, crime with crime, becomes so prevalent and accepted that there no longer remains any distinction of honor and pride between grim and implacable adversaries?

These questions are a proper and necessary concern for the people of the United States. They are a proper and necessary concern for Congress. But in the nature of the case, neither the people nor Congress can easily learn the answers, much less insure that the answers are always the right ones.

The President's Task

That can only be done within the executive branch, by the highest authorities of the Government. Controlling the C.I.A. is a job that rests squarely upon the President of the United States, the director of the agency and the officials appointed by the President to check its work. And if these men are to insist that they do control the agency, then they are the ones who must be blamed if control fails.

"Those who believe that the United States Government on occasion resorts to force when it shouldn't," Richard Bissell, the C.I.A.'s former deputy director, once said, "should in all fairness and justice direct their views to the question of national policy and not hide behind the criticism that whereas the President and Cabinet generally are enlightened people, there is an evil and ill-controlled agency which imports this sinister element."

The New York Times study of the C.I.A. suggests that it is not an invisible government but the real government of the United States upon which the responsibility must lie whenever the agency may be found "out of control." For if that responsibility is accepted, there can be no invisible government.

Michael Wood, Ramparts
A Short Account of International
Student Politics and the Cold War
with particular reference to the
NSA, CIA, etc., 1967

A Short Account of
International Student Politics & the Cold War
with Particular Reference to the NSA, CIA, Etc.

[I. SOME NECESSARY BACKGROUND]

THE CHILL OF THE COLD WAR was already in the air in August of 1946, when some 300 students from 38 countries assembled in the flag-bedecked Artists' Hall in Prague for the first World Student Congress. Among the delegates were 24 American students, many of them World War II veterans, representing various youth and student organizations and ten prominent universities. The communists were in the majority at the Congress, and disputes arose as to the proper role of international student organizations. Still, the Congress ended on an amicable note, with a call for further cooperation and the building of a truly representative international student organization—which came into existence shortly afterwards, and was named the International Union of Students (IUS). The American delegates, who came to be known as the Prague 25, returned home, fully convinced that a new, truly representative *national* organization had to be created which could fittingly represent the U.S. student community in the international student world.

Establishing themselves as an organizing committee, the Prague 25 issued a call for a national conference of student leaders to organize a new national union of students. They were remarkably successful. In the summer of 1947, a new body known as the United States National Student Association (NSA) held its Constitutional Convention in Madison, Wisconsin. By the time of this convention, the atmosphere of the IUS had become even more openly pro-communist than it had been in Prague. However, it was not until the communist coup had taken place in Czecho-

slovakia in 1948 and the IUS had failed to condemn the communists' mishandling of Czech students that the break between NSA and IUS became official.

Finally, in 1950, NSA met in Stockholm with 18 other national student groups to form a new international student body which was ultimately called the International Student Conference (ISC). During the first meetings, the overwhelming majority of the delegates were opposed to the conception of the ISC as a "rival," set up to fight the IUS and international communism. The delegates to the first ISC wanted to avoid controversial political questions and any further schism of the international student world.

The new international organization grew quickly and impressively. By the middle '50s, over 55 national student unions were participating, more than half of which were from the underdeveloped "Third World," and the ISC had a huge budget providing for many programs of technical assistance, education and student exchanges. The ISC became the pacesetter for international student politics and NSA was on its way to becoming the most powerful force within the new international organization.

AS THE ISC GREW, the students of the underdeveloped world pressed the hardest for it to take political stands on controversial issues such as colonialism and racism. And as the "Third World" student unions started to press political issues in the ISC, it was usually the NSA delegation that played the moderating role, trying to keep the ISC focused on the problems of "students as students."

In a sense, the very growth of the ISC engendered its problems. Most student unions, originally attracted to the organization out of resentment against the strictures imposed by the IUS, became alienated from it when, partly under NSA's prodding, the ISC began to set forth its own tight Cold War positions. By the 1960's, the situation had begun to reverse itself: the IUS was making gestures for consultations that might lead to a reunification of the world student movement, while the ISC—with NSA in the lead—kept to a rigid Cold War line and put off most of these overtures.

At its peak in 1960, over 400 schools were affiliated with NSA. Its staff operations and budget grew every year. Though there was little income from the dues of its constituent members, NSA picked up financial support for its operations from a number of foundations. Most of this went entirely to NSA's international operations. NSA was able to sponsor yearly international relations seminars, foreign student leadership training projects, scholarships for foreign students, and still maintain a large travel budget for its international commission staff and its overseas representatives.

Despite the formal democracy in NSA, there was little relationship between its overseas operations and its on-campus base. NSA Congresses were massive affairs attended mostly by students sent as delegates from the student governments of NSA's member schools. They had little knowledge of NSA's year-round staff operations. International affairs and the operations of NSA's international staff were debated by a select few who could usually move the rest of the Congress on the basis of their esoteric expertise. Overseas representatives of NSA and delegates to the ISC were never elected by the NSA Congress.

NSA has always shown two faces. Its domestic programs, its Congresses and its regional meetings have always been open and spontaneous. If NSA national leaders were occasionally over-cautious, they still moved with the liberal currents of opinion among American students. In the '50s, NSA took even more liberal stands than the prevailing apathy among students might have suggested. And in the '60s, NSA responded to the new militant protest mood on the campuses. It supported students against the draft, opposed the war in Vietnam, and participated in civil rights struggles. It played a crucial role in the formation of the Student Nonviolent Coordinating Committee and was one of its staunchest supporters, a position which cost it the affiliation of many schools in 1961.

Yet NSA's overseas image has been very different. Despite its liberal rhetoric, NSA-ers abroad seemed more like professional diplomats than students; there was something tough and secretive about them that was out of keeping with their openness and spontaneity back home.

In the light of all this, it is not surprising that a number of NSA's critics have pointed a suspicious finger at its international operations. Nor is it a shock to discover that some people in the left wing of NSA, like Paul Potter, who was elected national affairs vice president in 1961 and went on to become president of Students for a Democratic Society, revealed that they had always suspected NSA's international operations of being tightly tied in with the State Department. Very few ever seriously raised the more sinister spectre of CIA involvement.

[II. SOME FANCY FINANCING]

It is widely known that the CIA has a number of foundations which serve as direct fronts or as secret "conduits" that channel money from the CIA to preferred organizations. An intimation of the scope of this financial web was afforded the public on August 31, 1964, when Texas Congressman Wright Patman, in the course of an investigation into the use of foundations for tax dodges, announced that the J. M. Kaplan Fund of New York was serving as a secret conduit for CIA funds. As soon as Patman made his announcement, representatives of the

CIA and Internal Revenue came scurrying to his office for a hasty conference. Patman apparently was satisfied with the results. Without retracting his allegations about the Kaplan Fund he announced: ". . . The CIA does not belong in this foundation investigation."

Before bringing down the curtain of secrecy, he did, at least, reveal one fact of substance. It turned out that a number of other foundations had contributed to the Kaplan Fund during the crucial years of 1961-63 when the Fund had been serving the CIA. Five of these foundations were not even on the Internal Revenue Service's list of tax-exempt foundations. They were the Borden Trust, the Price Fund, the Edsel Fund, the Beacon Fund and the Kentfield Fund. The implication was clear that some or all of these were the channel through which the CIA money passed into the Kaplan foundation coffers.

Ramparts was provided with an unusual insight into the manner in which the CIA uses legitimate foundations with liberal interests, such as the Kaplan Fund, in a recent conversation with the president of a prominent New England foundation who asked to remain anonymous: "I didn't want my foundation dragged through the CIA mud." In 1965 he was approached by what he described as "two nice middle-aged Irish cop types who flashed CIA cards at me." The men asked the foundation president if they could look over the list of organizations that his foundation supports. He volunteered the list to them and after looking it over, the agents said that there were organizations on the list that they would also be willing to support. The CIA men explained, "We are trying to pose an alternative to communism and want to back third-force programs, which we could not do if it was known that this support comes from a government source."

The agents then proposed to support some of the organizations already on the foundation's list as well as suggesting new prospective recipients. The agents promised that if this arrangement was accepted, they would be able to channel CIA money into the foundation without it ever being traced back to the CIA. They said that they were very skilled at these manipulations.

The president, however, took the proposal directly to the board which rejected it by a vote of four to one, out of what the foundation president called "a 19th century sense of morality. We just did not like the secrecy of it."

THE CIA-SUSPECT Funds mentioned in the Patman investigation are a key to understanding part of NSA's finances. Conveniently, they are spread all over the country (Borden in Philadelphia, Price in New York, Beacon in Boston, Kentfield in Dallas and Edsel, whose last known address was in San Francisco). When a Ramparts reporter checked out the addresses officially listed by the foundations, he usually found himself in a law office where no one was willing to talk about the Funds.

Two foundations that have supported the international programs of NSA—the J. Frederick Brown Foundation and the Independence Foundation—have received regular contributions from four of these CIA-linked Funds: Price, Borden, Kentfield, and Edsel. Both the J. Frederick Brown and the Independence Foundations list the same address, 60 State Street, Boston, which is also the address of the prestigious law firm of Hale and Dorr. Paul F. Hellmuth, a well-known Boston attorney and a member of Hale and Dorr, and David B. Stone, a Boston businessman and philanthropist, are the trustees of the Independence Foundation. Hellmuth alone is the trustee of the J. Frederick Brown Foundation.

Of the two, J. Frederick Brown is less important as a source of NSA funds. It made only $3300 in contributions to NSA, in 1963. It also made contributions to the American Friends of the Middle East, among other organizations with overseas interests. In an article in the May 9, 1966 issue of The Nation, Robert G. Sherrill implied that the American Friends had CIA ties. No official of the organization denied the allegations.

As far as NSA is concerned, the Independence Foundation is the more important of Mr. Hellmuth's two interests. Independence got its tax-exempt status in 1960. Since then, most of its funds have come from other trusts and foundations. In 1962, for example, the Independence Foundation received a total of $247,000, of which only $18,500 came from individuals or corporations; all the rest came from other foundations. Of the total, the four Funds cited in the Patman investigation gave $100,000.

Between 1962 and 1965, NSA received $256,483.33 in grants for its international programs from Independence. Much of that sum went to pay for NSA's International Student Relations Seminars, yearly extravaganzas which served as effective training grounds for future NSA international leaders.

NSA is still coasting on Independence's largesse. The building which houses NSA's present headquarters is occupied under a 15-year rent-free agreement with the Independence Foundation. Originally, NSA purchased the building with a down payment and a yearly mortgage payment to be secured from Independence. But Independence suddenly changed its mind and bought the property back from NSA. Deeds on file with the clerk of the District of Columbia reveal that NSA sold the property on October 20th, 1965, to the First National Bank, but that the bank was acting as a "trustee under an undisclosed trust." The undisclosed party is Paul Hellmuth, who secured the property, and leased it to the Independ-

ence Foundation which turned it over to NSA for the 15-year free rent agreement.

Shortly after NSA moved into its new, plush Washington offices in the fall of 1965, a reporter from the Washington Post, who was doing a feature article on NSA, asked NSA President Phil Sherburne who was paying the rent on the building. Sherburne refused to divulge this information. This secrecy in protecting the names of NSA's benefactors was not unusual. In fact, NSA has never made a full financial accounting to its own Congresses.

THE INDEPENDENCE FOUNDATION has served NSA's overseas operations in other indirect ways. It has provided a number of scholarships for former NSA officers, usually in the neighborhood of $3000 per year. The purpose of these scholarships was to enable former NSA officers to function as overseas representatives where they were free to make contacts with foreign student unions and roam as free operatives for NSA, sending back periodic reports. Ostensibly, the overseas representatives were supposed to be in overseas universities, but this was entirely pro forma.

Independence has not restricted its largesse exclusively to NSA. In the period between 1961 and 1965 it spent $180,000 in financing an interesting operation known as the Independent Research Service (IRS). This was the organization that made life so miserable for the organizers of the communist-leaning world youth festivals in Vienna in 1959, and in Helsinki in 1962. The Independent Research Service actively recruited a delegation of hundreds of young Americans to attend the festivals in order to actively oppose the communists. The travel expenses of all the delegates were fully paid for and the bill was footed as well for a jazz group, an exhibition of famous American painters and a daily newspaper printed in five languages, all of which accompanied the delegates.

Although the official position of the NSA Congress was not to participate in the youth festivals, important NSA officers and ex-officers were very active in the Independent Research Service activities in Vienna and Helsinki. The director of the IRS during the Helsinki Youth Festival was Dennis Shaul, who was elected NSA president shortly thereafter. Shaul has also been the recipient of one of the Independence Foundation's "scholarships" in 1964.

When questioned by a Ramparts reporter about some of the activities and sources of funds for his Independence Foundation, Mr. Hellmuth, a normally outgoing man, became guarded and curt. He refused to divulge the addresses or any other information about the money which had been donated to both of his foundations. However, he was quite voluble about his close friendship with the officers of NSA.

Still another foundation which has given to NSA is the Sidney and Esther Rabb Charitable Foundation of Boston. The similarities between the Rabb Foundation and the J. M. Kaplan Fund are striking. Rabb, like Kaplan, is a Jewish businessman, prominent in liberal democratic circles. The records show that up until 1963 the Rabb Foundation's only source of income was from Rabb himself. And up to that year, the Rabb Foundation's contributions were minimal and only to local charities.

Then, in 1963, two contributions to the Rabb Foundation flowed in from the Price Fund of New York—one of the Funds named in the Patman investigation, and a contributor to the J. Frederick Brown and Independence Foundations. The contributions were for $25,000 and $15,000 respectively. Strikingly, in the same year, the Rabb Foundation itself made two unusual and large contributions in precisely the same amounts—one for $25,000 to Operations and Policy Research Incorporated, a Cold War-oriented strategy organization; and $15,000 to the Fairfield Foundation. Fairfield, in its turn, has been a frequent contributor to the Congress for Cultural Freedom, previously identified in The New York Times as having received CIA funds.

During 1964, the Rabb Foundation again received unusual contributions, from three Funds, and also made three matching disbursements. It received $25,000 from the Tower Fund, and turned over the exact sum of $25,000 as a grant to the International Development Foundation which has been engaged in organizing anti-communist peasant unions in Latin America. It was particularly active in the Dominican Republic during that country's period of revolution and American intervention. The Rabb Foundation also received a $20,000 contribution from the Appalachian Fund, and during that year made a disbursement of $20,000 to the American Society of African Culture. Finally, the Rabb Foundation received $6000 from the ubiquitous Price Fund, and during the same year it turned over—would you believe—$6000 to the United States National Student Association to help retire an NSA deficit. Rabb made at least one other contribution to NSA in 1965 in the amount of $5000.

IT IS NOT ALWAYS EASY to obtain information on the foundations which have sustained NSA's international operations. Take the San Jacinto Foundation, for example. In the past, San Jacinto has not only funded important portions of NSA's international program, but it has also given huge sums of money to the program budget of the ISC. In particular, it has been overly generous in supporting The Student, an ISC publication printed in five languages and distributed all over the world as an anti-communist weapon.

One other interesting fact about the San Jacinto Foundation is that, like the J. Frederick Brown Foundation, it has contributed to the CIA-suspect American Friends of the Middle East. No one at NSA, or ISC for that matter, appears to have the vaguest notion of what the San Jacinto Foundation is, who is on its board of directors or where its money comes from. San Jacinto has also apparently managed to avoid the reporting procedures required by law of all tax-exempt foundations. No records for it have been entered at the district office of the Internal Revenue Service in Austin, or with the secretary of the State of Texas, or with the county clerk.

San Jacinto's mailing address is the offices of F. G. O'Conner in the San Jacinto Building in downtown Houston. Mr. O'Conner is the secretary of the foundation. When asked by Ramparts' peripatetic reporter for some information about the foundation, Mr. O'Conner, a graying, distinguished-looking man in his sixties replied, "It is a private, closed foundation, never had any publicity and doesn't want any."

As far back as anyone can remember, the mainstay of NSA's overseas operations has been the Foundation for Youth and Student Affairs of New York City, founded in 1952. In contrast to the likes of Independence and San Jacinto, FYSA has a for-real office, a full-time staff and an eminently respectable board of directors.

In recent years, FYSA annually pumped hundreds of thousands of dollars per year into NSA's treasury. The figure for October 1965 to October 1966 was $292,753.60. It provided a general administrative grant of up to $120,000 per year and funded projects such as NSA's magazine, The American Student, foreign student participation at NSA Congresses, technical assistance projects; and its funds paid NSA's dues to the ISC. In addition, FYSA could be relied upon to pick up any operating deficit that NSA incurred during the year, and FYSA gives "scholarships" to ex-NSA officers for overseas study.

FYSA has also been the chief U.S. source for channeling money overseas to national unions of students favored by the NSA leadership. And FYSA has been practically the only external source of support, except for the mysterious San Jacinto Foundation, of the programs of the ISC. Between 1962-1964, ISC records show that these two foundations provided over 90 per cent of ISC's program budget (most of it from FYSA)—a gargantuan total of $1,826,000 in grants completed or in progress. The ISC would be literally impotent as an international organization without the support of FYSA, having been unable to establish any sizable alternative sources of funding.

The executive secretary of FYSA is Harry Lunn, a tall, ruddy-faced, balding man in his middle thirties, himself a past president of NSA, who used to make applications for grants to the foundation which he now directs. Lunn vehemently denied the suggestion that his foundation might be channeling CIA money for NSA, although he would not release a financial statement to this magazine.

After his presidency of NSA (1954-55) had terminated, Lunn became a member of an ISC delegation to Southeast Asia. Then, following a short stint in the Army, he went to the Department of Defense as a research analyst. From there he went on up the ladder to the political desk of the American embassy in Paris and then on up to the Agency for International Development, where he worked on the Alliance for Progress. It was from this last position that Lunn came to FYSA in 1965. Lunn also took part in the activities of the militantly anti-communist Independent Research Service at the Vienna Youth Festival in 1959, while he was attached to the Department of Defense.

Lunn's career is a case study in the intimate relationship between NSA, international student politics and the Cold War. It is living documentation of a slogan that used to hang in NSA's old Philadelphia headquarters: "The student leader of today is the student leader of tomorrow."

[III. AN EXTRAORDINARY CONVERSATION]

THE SCENE WAS the Sirloin and Saddle, a plush, dimly-lit, continental style restaurant on Washington, D.C.'s Connecticut Avenue. It was lunchtime, the third week of March 1966, and over a table an earnest conversation was taking place that eventually resulted in the exposure of the CIA's 15-year infiltration of the National Student Association.

There were two people there that day. One of them was Phil Sherburne, NSA president for 1965-1966. Athletic-looking, blonde, self-possessed, his NSA post was his latest stop in a meteoric career in student politics.

Sherburne's luncheon companion that eventful day was 23-year-old Michael Wood, NSA's director of development, or fund raising chief. Wood, too, had risen rapidly in student politics. He left Pomona College during his senior year to become a civil rights worker in Watts, where one of his projects had caught the eye of an NSA officer. He became an NSA consultant in the spring of 1965, and was soon promoted to the post of director of development. Besides raising money for NSA, he helped Sherburne work out new programs, and had even been consulted by the White House staff on possible Presidential proposals about the draft and the lowering of the voting age. He had received a letter from Douglass Cater, special assistant to the President, commending him for his excellent reports.

Wood was talking to Sherburne because he was troubled. He had been running into irritating roadblocks in trying to raise money for NSA. He had encountered a curious lack of concern among other members of the

Association's international staff about the rigorous prep-aration usually required for foundation fund raising. The amount of money needed often ran into hundreds of thou-sands of dollars, yet the proposals being submitted to the foundations funding the international program were ill-prepared, perfunctory and brief. Furthermore, President Sherburne was negotiating with the foundations without Wood's participation.

After six months of this confusion, Wood told Sher-burne, with whom he had grown quite close, that he either had to be given full responsibility for the fund raising program or he would have to resign. It was at this time that Sherburne invited him to a heart-to-heart lunch con-ference. The following is Wood's account of what trans-pired during this and subsequent conversations:

Sherburne began by telling Wood that NSA had "cer-tain relationships with certain government agencies en-gaged in international relations" which Wood didn't know about. This, explained Sherburne, was why Wood couldn't have full responsibility for NSA's fund raising. Wood was astonished. "You mean the CIA?" he asked. Sher-burne nodded yes. Sherburne then told Wood that he was supposed to have been informed of the CIA relationship after he was appointed director of development, but that other NSA staff members and CIA contacts had decided he was politically unreliable. As well as having been a civil rights worker, Wood had gained a reputation as some-thing of a radical. Because he couldn't be told of the CIA relationship, it was necessary to keep him in the dark about certain aspects of NSA funding.

Sherburne told Wood he hoped that everything said over lunch that day would be kept secret. He was divulg-ing the information only because he did not want Wood to leave NSA. Later he explained that he wanted a friend he could trust with whom to discuss the CIA relationship, other than staffers who were already involved.

The CIA, said Sherburne, had managed to inject itself into the Association's international operations in the early 1950's. Since that time, virtually every president and inter-national affairs vice president of the organization had been aware of the CIA relationship and had cooperated.

Sherburne went on to say that most of the foundations that had funded NSA's international operations were merely passing along CIA money. Moreover, some of them had made up NSA's yearly deficits, and had financed the purchase and renovation of NSA's new offices in Washington. This explained the mystery surrounding the acquisition and the rent for NSA's new national offices.

Among the CIA-front foundations specifically mentioned, according to Wood, were the Independence Foundation, the San Jacinto Foundation, the Foundation for Youth and Student Affairs, the Sidney and Esther Rabb Founda-tion, and the J. Frederick Brown Foundation. To the best of Sherburne's knowledge, CIA money did not pass through the Ford Foundation, the Rockefeller Founda-tion, the Asia Foundation, and other groups which had also funded NSA international programs in the past.

Sherburne presented the Agency's involvement in inter-national student politics as a *fait accompli*; he argued that the CIA's vast supply of money was absolutely essential. Although he had serious doubts about the desirability of the relationship, he felt that NSA could not get as much money from any other source; moreover, the Agency had supported many worthwhile and liberal overseas pro-grams. In any event, Sherburne felt that a sudden termina-tion of the relationship would leave NSA in disastrous financial straits.

The CIA was interested almost exclusively in NSA's international programs. Over the years no staff member who worked exclusively on NSA's national program was involved in a CIA relationship, and few, if any, even knew about it. Keeping the CIA connection secret was made easier by the fact that NSA's national and international departments were in different cities from 1947-1960.

During their frequent conversations, Sherburne gave Wood a partial glossary of "black" language that was used by NSA's CIA operatives whenever they discussed the relationship in a semi-public place. They referred to the CIA as the "firm" and not the Agency; people were not described as operatives or agents but as being "witty"; those who worked inside the Agency bureaucracy were referred to as the "fellas" or the "boys." Frequently, im-portant NSA-ers were given code names for their contacts with the Agency. Sherburne's code name was "Mr. Grants" (based on his facility for fund raising).

Sherburne told Wood that normal procedure involved a careful evaluation by former NSA international officers of international staff members for their reliability—as well as a full national security check by the CIA. If a member passed the test, he was made "witty."

The prospective "witty" staff member would usually be taken out to lunch by another already "witty" staff member, and a representative of the CIA. NSA's dealings were with Covert Action Division No. Five of the CIA's Plans Division, and the personnel they dealt with there were themselves former NSA officers. Thus, when the new officer was taken to lunch, he at first assumed that he was merely going out with another staff member and an NSA alumnus. The prospective "witty" staff member was told at lunch that there was information relating to work on the international staff which affected national security and which he should know about, but which required him to sign a national security oath. If he signed the oath, which pledged him to keep secret any information that

was then divulged, he was then told about the CIA relationship and asked to cooperate.

The implication was clear that if the international staff member ever divulged any of the information about the relationship, there could be severe legal penalties. Thus the international officers were placed in a position in which they could not acknowledge the existence of the relationship, even to other "non-witty" NSA-ers. Sherburne made the first breach in a 15-year wall of secrecy.

The typical "witty" international staff member would first consult with an Agency representative about his overseas programs. Grants for international programs, travel allowances and expense accounts for NSA members going to overseas student conferences, would then all be supplied by CIA-front foundations.

SO INTIMATELY was the CIA involved in NSA's international program, that it treated NSA as an arm of U.S. foreign policy. The point is illustrated by a story that Sherburne told Wood. At one point during his tenure in office, Sherburne was to attend the International Student Travel Conference in Istanbul. There had already been much talk in NSA circles of opening up some bilateral contact with student unions in Soviet-bloc countries. Sherburne felt his trip to Turkey would provide a good opportunity to meet with Soviet students and discuss possible student exchanges. Sherburne sent off a cable to the Soviet National Union of Students saying that he would be in Istanbul and requesting permission to travel on to Moscow for a meeting with the Soviet student organization. But the CIA got wind of Sherburne's cable and admonished him for doing such things without first consulting the Agency. A CIA agent explained to Sherburne that since KGB (the Soviet "CIA") assumed that NSA took its cues from the U.S. government, Sherburne's gesture might be interpreted as an official change in CIA policy on bilateral student contacts. Sherburne, even though he was president of the United States National Student Association, was enjoined against making such diplomatic overtures without first requesting permission from the Agency.

The Soviet Union has always spent a good deal of money working with student and youth groups, especially in underdeveloped countries. The CIA's instrument for countering Soviet efforts was NSA, working through the International Student Conference. Former "witty" NSA staffers were always in the Secretariat of the ISC.

And NSA, with the CIA's aid, was able to play a major role in cooperating with favored national unions of students all over the world. No other union of students in the Western world has the kind of financial backing as NSA. The Canadian Union of Students, for example, operates

on a budget of about $14,000 a year for its international programs, all of which comes from the dues of member schools. NSA, with its almost unlimited funds, was able to conduct a full program of foreign diplomacy.

Of course, the CIA was also interested in intelligence. "Witty" NSA international staff members would pass along reports on foreign student leaders directly to the Agency. This information helped the CIA in evaluating the political tendencies of prospective political leaders in critical areas of the world.

One of the lures the CIA dangled before NSA was the assurance that this intelligence gathering role did not seem to require NSA to violate its foreign policy principles. The CIA is interested in alternatives to communism in the underdeveloped world, even if the only alternative is a moderate left. "Witty" staff members were told that, in working with the CIA, they would be providing the information that would help get a more enlightened foreign policy presented in high Washington circles.

Thus an NSA international staffer, while on an overseas assignment cleared with the CIA, visited student groups in Spain that were militantly protesting against the Franco dictatorship's suppression of free student unions. This NSA-er, a genuine supporter of the Spanish students, joined a protest meeting and was roughed up by the Spanish police, jailed, and held incommunicado for three days. The same staff member had previously gone to the Dominican Republic shortly after the American intervention there. He brought back a report on his contacts with university students who had participated in the civil war on the side of the constitutionalists.

To NSA the CIA relationship was a comfortable one. It meant lots of money, a sense of doing important work, overseas travel, and, perhaps most important of all, very little feeling of having sold out one's political convictions. The CIA relationship meant something more personal, too. For years elected (and appointed) officials and staffers of NSA have been getting draft deferments. The deferment given for having an "occupation vital to the national interest" would last as long as the member worked for NSA; it was then possible for him to go on to graduate school and receive a student deferment again.

The standard practice was for the president of NSA to send a letter to the local draft board stating that the staff member's services were required in an area that affected the national interest. Always included was a Cold War paragraph about how NSA was combatting communism. In what had become almost a form letter, the NSA president, asking for an occupational deferment for his staff member, wrote: "NSA is largely responsible for the creation and maintenance of the International Student Conference, which was established in 1950 to combat the

communist-controlled International Union of Students. More than 50 countries—almost every state with a national union this side of the Iron Curtain—now participate in the International Student Conference."

During 1965-66 the war in Vietnam escalated, and a panic developed in the NSA office when staff members suddenly found themselves re-classified I-A under the impact of the increased draft quotas. Sherburne took the matter of the office staff's status to the Selective Service Presidential Review Board, and also went directly to General Hershey. No NSA staff members, "witty" or "nonwitty," were drafted. The Agency looks after its own.

[IV. THE PRESIDENT REBELS]

WHEN THE CIA made Phil Sherburne "witty" it got more than it bargained for. Sherburne has a tough-minded, gritty independence that soon led him into conflict with those who were paying NSA's bills. Not only did Sherburne break the CIA cult of secrecy, but he also began fighting for NSA autonomy in international programming.

Sherburne's initial attitude to the Agency was friendly but reserved. He was willing to take CIA money for NSA projects and to consult with the Agency on matters of common interest, but he was the first NSA president who demanded full control of international programs. Previously, international programs—scholarships, student exchanges, conferences and the like—had all been worked out by NSA staff members and their CIA contacts.

But the Agency resisted Sherburne's reforms and applied pressure through their foundations. For the first time in years there were delays in the granting of funds from foundations such as FYSA and San Jacinto. But Sherburne fought back. He refused to release the funds (paid for by FYSA) that would have paid the dues of NSA to the International Student Conference. Finally, most of the money was released to NSA and a *modus vivendi* of sorts was reached. Eventually, Sherburne told Wood, Covert Action Division No. Five became so upset at its errant child, it considered severing ties with the NSA altogether.

Sherburne's effort at establishing some independence left its financial marks. Previously, any year-end operating deficits were quickly picked up by FYSA or some other foundation. In 1962-63 NSA had blundered into a disastrous financial venture with a book cooperative and wound up with approximately a $70,000 deficit. After NSA made a pro forma appeal to alumni that brought in practically nil, several key CIA foundations and indi
\u... came through with the cash and the debt was miraculously retired in two years. The cost of NSA's move f--m Philadelphia and at least $35,000 worth of furniture a.... renovations for the new Washington offices were just as easily absorbed. Among others, FYSA put up $15,000 and two men, Thomas Millbank and George Baker, put up $10,000 and $5000 respectively. Millbank and Baker are both well-established New York corporate executives and fellow members of the Racquet and Tennis Club. These two men once joined with FYSA in making an $18,000 grant to the ISC for a Latin American student conference. When asked about his interest in NSA and international student politics by this magazine, Mr. Millbank, once an assistant naval attache in Cairo, said: "It is none of your business," and promptly hung up the phone.

At the end of a year of relative independence, Sherburne was faced with approximately a $35,000 deficit that no one picked up. The deficit has remained, despite staff cutbacks. The "firm" doesn't like rebellious children.

By the end of a year of wrangling with the CIA, Sherburne was convinced that it was impossible to maintain an independent but friendly relationship. In an attempt to find new funds that would free NSA of its financial dependence on the CIA, Sherburne went to see Vice President Humphrey in July of 1966. Humphrey had been friendly to NSA, had addressed its National Congress in 1965, and had met Sherburne once previously.

Sherburne told the Vice President about the CIA ties and NSA's financial predicament. Humphrey promised to help NSA get other, independent sources of financing.

Humphrey kept his word and wrote to Roger Blough, Chairman of the Board of U.S. Steel, David Rockefeller of the Chase Manhattan Bank, and Henry Ford, among others. In a typical letter (the one to Roger Blough), Humphrey said:

> I have been very much impressed by the work done over the past few years by the National Student Association. I know the officers of the Association well.
>
> As with other such groups the NSA has had a continuing financial difficulty.
>
> I believe that this organization should be able to find support in the private sector, which will enable it to continue its work independently and in the best spirit of private initiative.

Despite Humphrey's entreaties, only a few hundred dollars rolled in from "the private sector." Thus NSA went to its 1966 Congress, the deficit still on its back, and its relationship with the CIA badly damaged. Sherburne continued to resist Wood's suggestions that he make a thoughtful public statement about the relationship and have it openly discussed as a public issue.

Yet what Sherburne had accomplished was considerable. For the first time in years, new national officers were elected without apparent commitments to the CIA relationship. The only problems bothering the new officers were their knowledge of the past, and the large financial

deficit—for it appeared that Humphrey's friends in the "private sector" were not as interested in supporting NSA as a rather un-public part of the "public sector" had been.

PHIL SHERBURNE FINALLY went to Harvard Law School after his year of escapades with the CIA. He was in Cambridge when Ramparts called him early last month to get his reaction to Mike Wood's revelations. In a subdued voice he said: "I think I would prefer not to say anything until I have had a chance to look at the article pretty carefully. . . . I think the article should be discussed by the current administration of NSA, and that anything that I would say would be resolved in discussions with them."

Then he was asked, "Did you sign a national security oath?" Sherburne paused a few moments and said, "At this point I don't want to make any comment."

Sherburne was under enormous pressure, not only out of a remaining loyalty to NSA, but also from the CIA. That "enlightened" organization had viciously turned on him for talking to Wood, and was trying hard to intimidate him into publicly denying Wood's story.

Sometime in the middle of January, the NSA officers and Sherburne heard that Michael Wood had passed his information along to Ramparts. Sherburne called Wood and asked him to fly to Boston, where Sherburne pleaded with him for an entire day to retract his story. Then they both flew to Washington for four more days of intense and harrowing discussion with two of the current NSA national officers, an NSA staff member, and a former national affairs vice president.

In the Washington conversations with Wood, the officers of NSA desperately tried to dissuade him from giving the information to this magazine. Wood refused and instead urged the officers to affirm the story publicly, which would be the only way of salvaging NSA's dignity. The officers would not commit themselves.

There followed two weeks of hectic caucusing and emergency meetings at NSA headquarters. NSA officers visited a number of well-known NSA alumni, including Douglass Cater of the White House staff, to ask their advice. At least one of the officers also went straight to the Agency. The current CIA operative whom he contacted is a former NSA president. He is officially employed by the Agency for International Development in Washington.

At one point the officers assembled the staff, told them of the impending story and flatly denied that it was true. They suggested that Wood was making up the story to revenge NSA for having lost his job as director of development. Finally, another staff meeting was called and it was admitted that the story was true.

Meanwhile, on the west coast, two Ramparts editors were talking to Ed Schwartz, NSA's current national affairs vice president. Schwartz, talkative and quick-witted, had been the leader of the liberal caucus in NSA. He was in Berkeley, working as a behind-the-scenes student political advisor-negotiator during the University of California campus crisis precipitated by the firing of Clark Kerr.

It seems a direct, ironic result of Cold War politics that Schwartz had to drop his liberal Berkeley activities and cross the Bay to discuss his organization's cooperation with the CIA. Through a long and tiring discussion that lasted most of one night, Schwartz did not deny NSA's relationship to the CIA. Instead, he pleaded that great damage would be done to the good works of NSA by the revelation of this relationship. As the discussion ended, he muttered something about losing his draft deferment.

A few days later, in Washington, D.C., a Ramparts editor had an almost identical conversation with two other NSA officers. The talk began in NSA's national headquarters, a four-story colonial-style brick building in a quiet residential section. On the desk in President Gene Groves' office there was an autographed picture of Hubert Humphrey. With Groves was Rick Stearns, the international affairs vice president.

During the conversation neither Stearns nor Groves denied NSA's CIA connections in the past but stated that "all of our current financing comes from legitimate sources which observe the normal legitimate reporting procedures." And yet NSA's current budget records grants totaling $56,673.30 from FYSA. Stearns was asked, "Will you flatly say you have had no contact with the CIA during your time in office?" He shook his head.

Stearns and Groves pleaded that disclosure of the CIA relationship would be disastrous for NSA. It would put them in an awful political predicament. If they publicly admitted past CIA connections, it would tarnish NSA's image badly at home and abroad, and hurt its chances of receiving grants from other government agencies. NSA staff members also feared CIA retaliation, especially the loss of their draft deferments.

Having kept quiet about the CIA since their election, the officers now went into action to minimize the effects of the forthcoming disclosures. NSA President Gene Groves flew off to Leiden, Holland for an emergency Summit meeting with the leaders of the ISC. Groves came back convinced that NSA must make some acknowledgment of the CIA relationship—but at the urging of his colleagues in Leiden there would be as few details as possible admitted.

If older Americans have been a little put off by the style of the draft card burners or the Mario Savios, there has always been somewhat of a consensus about the good

works of the young men and women of the United States National Student Association. The NSA seemed to mix the idealism of the community organizers, the FSM activists and the Peace Corps with the buttoned-down practicality of young junior executives.

The quality which rank and file NSA-ers have cherished most about themselves is independence, especially independence from government controls. It was this quality that was supposed to distinguish their organization from national unions of students in the communist world. The quality for the most part was genuine, for the rank and file never knew of the CIA connection.

There were many arguments put forward by NSA's current officers as to why the CIA-NSA relationship should be kept secret, and many similar arguments desperately made to Mike Wood as to why he should not have given the information to anyone. Of all the reasons given—by Stearns and Groves to Ramparts' editor in Washington, and by others who pleaded with Wood—the most pathetic, which appeared again and again, was this: exposing the story would not only hurt NSA, it would hurt the CIA. Covert Action Division No. Five, after all, was not in the business of assassinating Latin American leftists, it was supporting liberal groups like NSA, groups with international programs in the best tradition of cultural exchanges between countries. NSA might be anti-communist, but certainly no one could ever argue that its anti-communism was more militant or more narrow-minded than that of the average American. Rather, it was less so. Thus the exposure of the NSA-CIA tie would deeply hurt the enlightened, liberal, internationalist wing of the CIA. Conservative congressmen, such as L. Mendel Rivers of the House Armed Services Committee, would cut off Agency funds for these purposes, and the hard-liners in CIA's "core" would be proven right in their contentions that the Agency shouldn't give large sums of money to support liberal students, no matter what intelligence it was getting in return.

The twisted sickness of this Orwellian argument should speak for itself. Yet it is extraordinary, and frightening, that it could be so easily made by the talented young liberals at the head of NSA. One would think the idea of "an enlightened wing of the CIA" would be an obvious contradiction in terms. But the idea's acceptance and support by a generation of student leaders indicates how deeply the corruption of means for ends has become ingrained in our society, and how much dishonesty is tolerated in the name of the Cold War.

By Sol Stern
With the special assistance of Lee Webb, Michael Ansara and Michael Wood.

An Epilogue...

THE DECISION to tell this story was the most agonizing of my life. Phil Sherburne, whose personal trust I have betrayed, was a close friend. Though we disagreed on many subjects (especially on how to handle the CIA), in seeking to terminate NSA's relationship he acted with a dignity rare among those who knew the facts.

Moreover, I still believe in NSA, and deeply respect the progressive stance it has taken among American students for 20 years. Yet the issues involved are larger, and my public trust as a citizen of the United States must transcend my private trust.

For years the United States National Student Association has stood for "a free university in a free society." Its resolutions on academic, political and social freedoms are clear. Its constitutional commitment to free and open democracy is of long standing. Its defense of civil liberties has been staunch and consistent. Yet because of NSA's ationship to the CIA, its leaders have for 15 years undermined those principles.

This story is only a case study in CIA corruption. when I was told of Covert Action No. Five's infiltration of NSA, I was also told of numerous other organizations similarly infiltrated. A few have been named in this article; many others have had to be omitted. In an age when the average man's only access to the centers of decision is through private institutions, the responsiveness of those institutions to his wishes is critical to the healthy workings of a democracy. The spectre of CIA infiltration of domestic institutions—and the covert creation of coordinated leadership among them—must horrify those who regard unfettered debate as vital to representative democracy.

Those of us who worked for NSA during 1965-66, experienced an unusual sense of personal liberation. While actively involved in many of the insurgent campus and political movements of the day, we were also able to move freely through the highest echelons of established power. If those who occupied the command posts didn't always sympathize with our goals, they listened nonetheless and were sometimes affected. We felt like full citizens, able to move freely without compromising our principles. It gave us a heady feeling and a sense of power beyond our years.

The mobility and influence was as it should be for a national union of students; to learn that it had been bought with so terrible a compromise made me realize how impotent we really were.

Because of the pain involved in public discussion of so sensitive an issue, I have often wished that I had never learned the truth. Yet to avoid the truth, however painful, would be irresponsible.

There have always been staff members of the international commission who were entirely unaware of the relationship. It is unfortunate that all of them could not be protected, and that many of them may suffer the onus of NSA's guilt. I should like to note, however, that Gregory Delin, Gilbert Kulick, and Marcia Casey were in no way aware of the relationship. I am similarly sure that Mrs. Isabel Marcus Welsh, international affairs vice president in 1959-60 had no knowledge of the CIA's presence in NSA.

For those individuals in NSA who—like myself for a time—knowingly allowed themselves to be part of the relationship with the CIA, the worst consequences are internal. Very few staff members so involved were callous Cold Warriors who cynically appreciated their work with the CIA. Most of them, rather, were deeply committed liberals, whose consciences had no rest while they served two masters. All of them, I am sure, have at times felt horribly trapped in the conflict between their actions and their liberal principles.

Perhaps worst of all is the everyday dishonesty, the need to clam up when in the presence of "non-witty" staff members, to fudge, to make excuses and deflect embarrassing questions. Perhaps a professional intelligence operative, who sincerely believes in anti-communism at any price, can learn to suppress with not too much damage that most basic instinct of youth—to be open, frank, questioning of all things, in communion with his friends. But for the typical NSA staff member, part of a generation whose instinct is to unmask hypocrisy, the compromise comes very hard indeed. Many of them have suffered as a consequence the most agonizing sort of emotional schizophrenia—part of the human toll in an otherwise impersonal and cynical international intelligence operation.

MICHAEL WOOD
San Francisco, February 1967

...and a Judgment

IN SIMONE DE BEAUVOIR'S roman à clef, *The Mandarins*, there is a passage where the State Department tries to "help" Henri Perron (supposedly Camus) by offering him newsprint if his journal holds to an independent, neutralist line. Perron construes the offer to mean that the magazine should not criticize the fundamental methods of American foreign policy, and turns down the "aid." To protect the magazine's independence he also turns down aid from communist sources. But the gods play with men and their ideals. For a period of time the magazine receives its funds from a man who took gold from dentists who collaborated with the Nazis. Living in the world makes it hard to avoid dirty hands, perhaps because we are egocentric and overvalue the work we do. When we try to bring our projects into being they become more important to us than the reason we initiated them.

For example, it is not written in the Torah or the Constitution that educational institutions had to become fronts for the government, places where the rhetoric for the Cold War is supplied and the equations and technology for hydrogen bombs are manufactured. Nobody forced them into this position. Nor did the small, cliquish groups who ran the National Student Association have to take money from the CIA. Perhaps 15 years ago it was easier that way. For the young college graduate who was a "student leader" there was nothing quite as flattering as being approached by the CIA to help in the National Effort. Furthermore, it was the way up the status ladder, to success, travel, excitement, money, and government or foundation jobs. By following that road the student leaders of my generation—a decade ago—played it safe. As a result, they became instruments of the Cold War.

I have tried to figure out why the CIA would bother attempting to get to American students. After all, it takes a good deal of trouble and expense to set up front organizations and all the other tools that used to be the monopoly of the communists. The best way to understand the CIA's motives is to see it as primarily a commercial institution which deals in buying, renting and selling people.

Yet after we examine the CIA's motives and purposes, we are left with Cold War wreckage as serious and immoral as the Bay of Pigs operation, the U-2 overflights, or the Guatemalan caper. We are left with the fact that one generation attempted to corrupt the young by paying them off, buying and renting them on the installment plan. (Now that there is a crack in the door isn't it about time that we have a public accounting of CIA funds? How much of that loot sticks in the pockets of the CIA operatives themselves?) We are left with the fact that the CIA made patsies out of thousands of young Americans who went abroad to conferences or who studied under NSA auspices, but who unknowingly were being paid for, and were used by the CIA as contacts, covers and mail drops. Furthermore, how do we now face other nations who took us at our word that our students were "free" and therefore different from the communist-run youth groups? The CIA owes an apology to the innocent college students of this last generation.

MARCUS RASKIN
Co-Director, Institute for Policy Studies
Washington, D.C.

Chalmers M. Roberts
Washington Post Series 1970
on the Salt talks

SALT Tests Soviet Attitude

By Chalmers M. Roberts
Washington Post Staff Writer

Round three of the Soviet-American strategic arms limitation talks, opening in Helsinki on Monday, is widely regarded in Washington as a test of the true state of Moscow's attitude toward Washington.

Since round two in Vienna ended on good terms last Aug. 14, a spate of issues appears to have raised suspicions by each superpower of the other's intentions, if one goes by what is said both publicly and privately. These have included the Middle East cease-fire cheating issue, the putative Soviet missile submarine base in Cuba, an incident over the Berlin air corridors plus changes in the Soviet position on the Berlin negotiations and the case of American generals whose plane strayed into the Soviet Union.

All this has produced a second look in Washington at American policy toward, and proposals on, both the SALT talks and the Soviet-American-British-French negotiations over Berlin. The next Berlin meeting is Wednesday.

The dominant belief here is that, despite the rise in the propaganda decibel level in both Moscow and Washington, the two nations have more than sufficient reasons to keep SALT moving toward agreement.

As Washington sees it, the test will come in Helsinki, probably in the first two weeks of what is expected to be a six- or seven-week round, when the Soviets lay down what is expected to be their counter-proposal to that of the United States, which was tabled last July 24.

The core of that proposal, which Washington views as vital to any agreement, is this: A numerical ceiling on each nation's land- and sea-based ballistic missiles able to reach the territory of the other, with a sub-ceiling on missiles over a specified cubic volume (which would be a limit on the number of the huge Soviet SS-9 missiles) plus either a total ban on rival anti-missile (ABM) systems or, more likely, a limitation of ABMs to the protection of command and control centers in the two national capital areas, Washington and Moscow.

Moscow is on notice that it is expected to come up with its own proposal in Helsinki, since no one expects outright acceptance of the U.S. plan.

Since Vienna, the American plan has been re-examined here with no changes. Thus, there have been no National Security Council meetings or decisions by President Nixon in the interim, although there have been two sessions of the NSC's verification panel to refine and reaffirm details of the U.S. proposal.

There has been no word from Moscow as to what it may do. But Soviet diplomatic sources have stressed that the Soviet delegation, ever since the opening round last year, has contended that any strategic arms agreement must cover all nuclear weapons of one nation that can reach the territory of the other.

This means, as Moscow argues it, that U.S. tactical aircraft, both based on land in Western Europe and carrier based with the Sixth Fleet in the Mediterranean, that can deliver nuclear weapons to Soviet soil must be covered. The United States from the outset rejected this concept arguing that these aircraft are a counter to the 700 Soviet medium- and intermediate-range missiles located on Western Europe.

Since the Vienna round, this problem has been exacerbated, it is conceded here, by the assignment of U.S. F-111 fighter-bombers to Britain, capable of carrying nuclear weapons to Soviet territory. A dozen already are there, 12 more are due by the end of the year with a total of 75 by next spring now scheduled.

During the Vienna phase, the U.S. delegates made it clear, it is reported, that if the Soviets insist on including the tactical aircraft there will be no treaty. This is not to exclude, however, that some device such as unilateral statements pledging not to increase numbers of either these aircraft or the Soviet I/MRBMs might not be employed to skirt the issue.

In sum, then, the question is whether Moscow's expected counter proposal and the American proposal turn out to be in the same ballpark by the end of the Helsinki round; that is, whether the basis is found for writing a treaty.

If that turns out to be the case, then 1971 will be the critical year, probably the first six months, for SALT.

In the recent meetings between Secretary of State William P. Rogers and Soviet Foreign Minister Andrei Gromyko, as well as in Gromyko's meeting with the President, both sides were reported as agreeing that SALT should go ahead. It was not until later that The Washington Post reported that Frank Shakespeare, director of the U.S. Information Agency, had proposed breaking off the SALT talks because of Soviet behavior. Shakespeare and the White House both denied he made any such recommendation to Mr. Nixon, but administration sources insist he did.

At any rate, Gromyko in his United Nations speech, despite castigation of the United States on several issues, expressed Soviet "hope that eventually" the talks "will lead to positive results." Some in Washington read "eventually" to mean: If you Americans are in a hurry, you will have to give more; we can take our time.

Some also relate this and other Soviet remarks to Defense Secretary Melvin R. Laird's talk of "a tremendous increase" in military expenditures as being likely if there is no SALT agreement and that major decisions cannot be put off for more than another 12 months.

One effect of the Soviet-American tensions the past two months has been a closer look at the enforcement provisions of the proposed SALT treaty, as well as of the Berlin proposals.

In the case of SALT it always has been the U.S. intention to include a clause used in both the nuclear test ban treaty and the non-proliferation treaty. This escape clause would give each nation "the right to withdraw from the treaty if it decides that extraordinary events, related to the subject matter of his treaty, has jeopardized the supreme interests of its country." Notice of withdrawal would be required.

In addition, for SALT the United States wants a statement that each nation agrees not to interfere with the national means of detection on which both would depend to police adherence to the agreement. This amounts, without directly saying so, to legitimizing the current practice of each nation using observation or spy-in-the-sky satellites plus numerous electronic devices to check up on the other's strategic nuclear weapons systems. So far, there has been no sign of Soviet disagreement.

What the United States has proposed and what seems possible that the U.S.S.R. will propose are quantitative controls for the nuclear arms race. What is missing are qualitative controls, essentially some way to halt the deployment of multiple warheads known as MIRVs.

The Soviets have said both MIRV testing and deployment should be included but without any on-site inspection to verify. The Americans are adamantly opposed to including MIRVs except with on-site inspection. The issue is at impasse, and many observers feel the time in which MIRV control or prohibition was possible has passed.

Nor does the U.S. proposal prevent upgrading of rival missile systems. Under the proposal a one-for-one substitution would be permitted. This means that a Poseidon missile could replace a smaller Polaris missile, for example, or eventually that the new submarine system known as ULMS could replace the Poseidon-Polaris systems provided the same number of missiles were involved.

The ABM issue seems likely to end up with agreement to limit rival systems to the Washington and Moscow areas. However, there are many technical problems in prescribing what could and could not be done that remain to be worked out, one of several issues likely to call for an annex to a SALT treaty.

Such a resolution of the ABM issue would mean abandonment of the work already done on the United States in Montana and North Dakota and authorized this year for Wyoming as well. Congress has yet to authorize even site preparation for the Washington area though the Pentagon tried to have such a right agreed upon during the House-Senate conference on the 1971 military procurement bill. The conferees refused to do so.

Thus SALT round three in Helsinki should determine whether the two suspicious superpowers can do business on a critical issue despite their differences on a host of other matters; and if so how long it may take to produce a SALT treaty.

Conference Helsinki

DISARM.

Kremlin Split on SALT Talks

By Chalmers M. Roberts
Washington Post Staff Writers

American officials have now concluded that the Kremlin leaders have failed to agree on a Soviet proposal for the strategic arms limitation talks and that no plan will be forthcoming from Moscow until after the Communist Party Congress that begins next March 30.

This disappointing conclusion is based on the slow Soviet pace at the current Helsinki phase of the SALT talks and on Soviet hints that Moscow wants a recess until after the party congress.

The lack of progress at Helsinki was indirectly confirmed last night by President Nixon at his press conference. He said that "we're very far apart" at SALT but he took hope from the continuation of these and other negotiations involving the Soviet Union.

Hence the current talks are expected to wind up next week, probably a week from today, hardly any closer to agreement than when this phase began on Nov. 2. The two sides yesterday held their 12th session, lasting 45 minutes followed by a luncheon given by the U.S. delegation. The next session will be Dec. 16.

Disappointment Showing

Hints of the American disappointment already have shown in public. Officials now are saying they expect increased pressure within the administration to press forward with such new weapons systems as ULMS, a new generation of submarine missilry, and the long range B-1 bomber as well as to go forward with the Safeguard antimissile (ABM) system.

To some here the indecision in Moscow indicates Kremlin infighting in advance of the party congress. How much this relates to the generally deteriorating Soviet-American relationship over the past several months can only be guessed. The Middle East, Cuba and Berlin are all involved in the total picture.

The U.S. would like a short holiday recess in the SALT talks in the hope that another round at Vienna would lead to a treaty by mid-1971. That hope, however, now seems likely to be unfulfilled. Any sessions between Jan. 1 and the end of the party congress in early April are likely to be futile, it is felt here.

Secretary of State William P. Rogers said at the recent NATO meeting in Brussels that the SALT talks had gone more slowly than expected. The chief U.S. delegate at SALT, Gerard C. Smith, broke his two-year-old rule of no on-the-record interviews by telling U.S. News & World Report last week that "tensions with the U.S.S.R. in other areas cannot fail to have a negative influence on SALT"

Smith added that while it would not be "surprising or discouraging" if there were no agreement at Helsinki, the talks there should give "a clearer indication as to whether an agreement is possible." Even that latter hope is now uncertain.

The chief Soviet delegate, Vladimir S. Semyonov, is not personally faulted. He has been reading, at the twice-a-week sessions, papers on general concepts of an arms agreement but has steered away from all efforts to get him to be specific.

He has indicated a Soviet willingness to settle for ABM systems limited to the rival national capital areas but that was no real surprise as Soviet sources had indicated that preference some time ago.

But Semyonov has failed to answer the crucial American question: will the Soviet Union agree to put a gross numerical ceiling on rival land- and sea-based missiles and long-range bombers plus a sub-ceiling on the numbers of the huge Soviet SS-9 missiles?

Qualifications Discussed

Additionally, there has been at Helsinki considerable discussion of what are termed the qualifications for an agreement. This involves detailed definition of just what would be permitted or barred; for example, the U.S. wants a ban on new missile silos but agreement that existing silos can be "hardened" by additional steel and concrete.

Another such problem relates to defining the kind, size, numbers and locations of radars, the critical eyes for both offensive and defensive weapons systems.

SALT began Nov. 17, 1969, in Helsinki for five weeks of exploration. This was followed by four months at Vienna during which the U.S. on July 24 laid down a formal proposal. When the current Helsinki round opened on Nov. 2 the U.S. expected a Soviet counter-proposal before the holiday recess.

While it is widely believed that the Soviets are keenly interested in a possible agreement and that Semyonov and his fellow delegates have proved to be highly serious at the talks, the long delay is raising questions in Washington. Is it simply that the Kremlin leadership is divided on how, or even whether, to proceed or is there some more serious or even dangerous Soviet design involved?

The result is that persons on all sides of the internal Washington arguments over details of a SALT treaty now are in general agreement that the time to fish or cut bait, as it is put, is coming soon. The general view is that if there is to be a treaty it will have to be wrapped up by mid-1971 or else the nuclear arms race will accelerate even more than it already is.

Now, as Washington sees it, SALT is one of many issues the Kremlin will have to decide in closed-door sessions prior to the party congress, some of which will be made public there. Publicly, Moscow has been totally silent since SALT began on the substantive issues, limiting comments to accusations that the American military-industrial complex, as the Communists see it, is trying to prevent agreement.

N. Vietnam Warns Of American Attack

Reuter

HONG KONG, Dec. 10—North Vietnam's high command today called on the armed forces and militia to be fully prepared to repulse any American attack on the country, the North Vietnam news agency reported.

Third Round of SALT Winds Up in Helsinki

DEC. 19 1970

CONFERENCE

By Chalmers M. Roberts
Washington Post Staff Writer

The third round of the strategic arms limitation talks ended in Helsinki yesterday with a modest joint statement masking American disappointment at the Soviet failure to offer hard proposals for a treaty. DISARMAMENT

A fourth round in the SALT talks will open in Vienna on March 15. The SALT talks are now 13 months old.

With the third round thus ending with a whimper rather than a bang, American officials yesterday were trying to put the best face possible on the outcome.

Some contended that the net result is that negotiations can really begin in Vienna with a Kremlin decision to go ahead, now that so much detailed discussion has taken place.

But others feel that time is running out, that the nuclear arms race is continuing to spiral creating new problems and that the deteriorating over-all Soviet-American relationship is having its effect on SALT both in Moscow and Washington.

The Helsinki joint communique had this operative paragraph:

"In the continuing course of the negotiations a wide range of questions dealing with the problem of limiting strategic offensive and defensive armaments was considered. The exchange further clarified a number of aspects of the matters discussed. Both delegations expressed their determination to pursue the negotiations with the aim of limiting strategic offensive and defensive armaments."

The chief Soviet delegate, Vladimir V. Semyonov, said at the closing ceremony that what he termed "this discussion" had been "useful." His American counterpart, Gerard C. Smith, said at the same ceremony that during the seven-week session "both delegations have continued to set forth their views."

He made no reference to what he had said on arriving in Helsinki, that he looked forward to "significant progress."

Before leaving by plane for Washington, Smith added that an agreement is "possible" and that he felt "there has developed a greater understanding of the areas under discussion."

Soviet Counter-Proposal

What the U.S. had hoped for was a Soviet counter-proposal to the American plan laid down at the Vienna session last July 24. Most of all, the U.S. wanted Soviet agreement to put a numerical ceiling on rival missiles, both land and sea based, and on bombers, including a sub-ceiling on the massive Soviet SS-9 missiles.

No such figures were forthcoming. Instead, Semyonov concentrated on the need to curb rival anti-missile (ABM) systems. The U.S. offered either a complete ABM ban or ABM limited to what would be phase one of the American Safeguard system. The Soviets said they preferred to limit ABMs to protection of the two national capitals.

It is not yet clear whether the ABM issue has been affected by Pentagon talk of switching the U.S. ABM, given a limited agreement, from the Washington area to the Rocky Mountain area where the North American Air Command is located. No such proposal has been made to the Soviets, however.

On Wednesday the Pentagon announced that the Soviets had slowed SS-9 activity and that the total number of missiles operational or under construction was less than had previously been estimated.

This came after word by the diplomatic grapevine from the Soviets, though it was not said in Helsinki, that the U.S. should watch what was being done about SS-9s.

But it is now known that the Pentagon statement was not meant to be a signal to Moscow that this, indeed, had been noted. It is conceded here, however, that the Pentagon statement may be taken as just such a signal.

Divided Leadership

The basic judgment here is that Semyonov was unable to put forward a Soviet proposal because the Kremlin leadership is divided.

Since Moscow asked for the March 15 date to reconvene the talks, a date he referred to yesterday as "soon," it is assumed he must await decisions being made in preparation for the 24th Communist Party Congress. That Congress opens on March 30.

Since SALT opened Nov. 17, 1969, there have been 55 formal sessions totaling some 140 hours plus at least that much time devoted to informal and private talks.

But in the same period the U.S. completed a series of tests for multiple warheads (MIRVs) and began deploying them on Minuteman III missiles. Similar tests on the new Poseidon submarine MIRVed missile have continued and the first of these new subs with a longer missile range than the Polaris series is due to become operational next month.

On the other side, Wednesday's Pentagon statement said there has been "an accelerated test program of multiple re-entry vehicles" both for the giant SS-9 and for the SS-11, a missile comparable to Minuteman. Construction of missile-carrying nuclear submarines also has continued.

No effort was made at Helsinki to ban MIRVs because the U.S. demands on-site inspection for such a ban and the Soviet Union rejects the idea.

CONFERENCE

SALT Pause Sparks Alternatives

JAN 3 1971

By Chalmers M. Roberts

DISARMAMENT

News Analysis

When ongoing negotiations fall into a period of doldrums a sort of centrifugal force comes into play. This is the current case with the Soviet-American Strategic Arms Limitation Talks DISARMAMENT

The current U.S. line is that SALT is now hung up pending a political decision in Moscow to try for a treaty, meaning to put forward a full proposal on which bargaining can begin along with the U.S. plan already on the table. This is not expected until the decision-making for the forthcoming 24th Communist Party Congress is con-

cluded, probably in late March.

But science waits not for politics. Both nations are continuing work on schemes that will further destabilize the nuclear arms race, especially the anti-missile (ABM) systems and multiple warheads (MIRVs).

Both are destabilizing in that they alter the balance of terror. The United States, ahead in MIRVs, is emplacing them on Minuteman missiles and on submarine missiles. Moscow is perfecting its own MIRV system. The Soviets already have a partial ABM system and President Nixon in his new

budget will ask for a further go-ahead on the four sites already under way in the Safeguard ABM system.

The three SALT rounds so far have disclosed some difficult problems. Moscow wants to include the American forward-based aircraft and, at Vienna last summer, suggested that provision be made to permit mobile land missiles, among other problems.

A few days ago the Federation of American Scientists called for a SALT agreement on ABMs only, one "precluding missile defenses or limiting them drastically." Either a limited or zero ABM agreement would break the action-reaction weapons cycle, the FAS

argues, and eliminate rival fears of a first-strike potential.

But on the other hand there are rumbles that the Joint Chiefs of Staff are increasingly opposed to any ABM agreement on the grounds of what Defense Secretary Melvin R. Laird constantly calls the "momentum" of Soviet rocket construction and deployment. Some think that the JCS ploy, if that is what it turns out to be, has been undercut, deliberately or not, by Laird's recent statement that Moscow has begun to slow "the level of activity associated with SS-9 construction."

Ironically, the U.S. initially proposed the SALT talks to limit ABMs alone but the U.S.S.R. insisted that the talks also should cover offensive weapons. But the U.S. is now in the position of opposing an ABM agreement alone, having insisted to the Senate last fall that Safeguard was the best bargaining chip in the effort to win Soviet agreement to limit SS-9s, the giant Russian missile doubtless soon to be MIRVed.

Internal Discussion

Thus it is probable that the idea of a separate ABM agreement, leaving a curb on offensive weapons until later, will not become a major issue in Washington, if it ever does, until we know the outcome of the current internal Soviet discussion of what to do at SALT.

The complexity of constructing a meaningful curb on offensive as well as de-

fensive weaponry is well illustrated in a lengthy article in the January issue of Scientific American. There Herbert Scoville Jr., long an insider (first at the Central Intelligence Agency and then at the Arms Control and Disarmament Agency) who had a hand in the FAS statement, examines four types and seven sub-types of possible agreements.

Scoville rates the Nixon proposals as far from satisfactory, even if acepted in Moscow, on the grounds that they would do little to halt the arms race and might very well "provide strong incentives for accelerating it along new directions."

Quantitative Control

This is not denied by the administration since the plan is for quantitative rather than qualitative control. Any real qualitative control would include MIRVs but they are now so far advanced on both sides that only through rigid on-site inspection would either side likely have trust in an agreement. And neither Washington nor Moscow is prepared to have agents of the other poking into the vitals of such critical weapons as missiles to see how many warheads they have.

The fact is that the bureaucratic investment in the current American plan has been so great that a major change in policy would be a major wrench. This may be a good time to talk about such ideas but probably only a Moscow offer containing some attractive and negotiable ideas will change the U.S. proposals.

JAN. 9 1971

Soviets Propose ABM Limit

CONFERENCE

By Chalmers M. Roberts
Washington Post Staff Writer

The Soviet Union has proposed a limited, first-step strategic arms agreement that would bar rival antimissile (ABM) systems other than for the protection of Washington and Moscow.

This would leave until later an agreement on limiting rival land and sea-based missiles.

The Soviet proposal came toward the end of round three of the SALT talks that wound up in Helsinki last Dec. 18, it has now been learned.

But the Nixon administration opposes an ABM-only DISARMAMENT

agreement despite the fact that the United States, under President Johnson, originally sought the SALT talks in order to curb ABMs. It was the Soviet Union that insisted on including offensive nuclear weapons as well as defensive systems before Moscow would agree to SALT.

The reversal of position on Moscow's part came about this way:

During the Helsinki round, from Nov. 2 to Dec. 18, the Soviet delegation placed major emphasis on a demand that in any overall agreement covering both offensive and defen-

sive weapons, the United States must include its aircraft in Western Europe and aboard carriers in both the Atlantic-Mediterranean area and in the Pacific, since such planes can deliver nuclear weapons to Soviet soil.

But the American delegation was under presidential instruction to reject the inclusion of what are known as FBS, forward based systems. In essence, the United States stood pat on its proposal put forward at the Vienna round last July 24.

See SALT, A6, Col. 1

Russia Proposes Limiting ABMs To Washington and Moscow Only

SALT, From A1

In turn, the Soviets refused to put forward a counterproposal covering both offensive and defensive weapons until the United States agreed in principle to include FBS. But finally, in December, in the face of this deadlock the Soviets suggested breaking out the ABM issue from the larger package.

Gerard C. Smith, the chief American negotiator, was forbidden by Washington to consider this proposal. Hence the Helsinki session ended in disappointment with the next round due to open in Vienna on March 15.

It is now conceded within the administration that pressure can be expected from the new Congress, especially in the Senate, to accept the idea of an ABM-only agreement as a first SALT step. The Federation of American Scientists recently called for just such a step.

The argument here is that

the two destabilizing steps in the arms race are the creation of rival ABM systems and the development and deployment of multiple warheads, MIRVs. It is generally agreed that control of MIRVs is now impossible, given their deployment by the United States and testing with a view to deployment by the Soviet Union.

The Pentagon said yesterday that the Air Force has completed installation of the first 50 Minuteman III intercontinental missiles with MIRV warheads. The installation began last June at Minot Air Force Base, S.D.

The unit is designated as the 741st Strategic Missile Squadron, part of the 91st Strategic Missile Wing. Each of the 50 missiles carries three warheads, and each of these a nuclear punch of around 170 kilotons compared to the 20-kiloton warhead of the Hiroshima bomb. About half the 1,000 Minutemen are due to be converted to MIRV warheads.

In addition, the first American Poseidon submarine with up to 14 missiles, each with an 18-kiloton punch, is due to become operational in a few days. The Soviet MIRV program is thought to be about a year and a half behind the American development.

Thus with MIRVs so far developed and deployed that control is rated next to impossible, there is bound to be increased pressure in Washington to control the other destabilizing development, the ABMs.

But thus far the Nixon administration flatly opposes an AMB-only agreement. The desire, and still the hope, is that a way can be found around the FBS issue so that an ABM limitation can be linked in a SALT treaty to a numerical limitation on rival missile systems, including a sub-ceiling on the giant Soviet SS-9s.

In proposing an ABM-only agreement, the Soviets offered to give details on how it might be done if the United States would accept the principle. But since Smith was foreclosed on that, the details were not forthcoming at Helsinki.

Defense Secretary Melvin R. Laird on Dec. 16 announced that Moscow had begun to slow its SS-9 program, an announcement that followed Soviet hints that this somewhat was related to SALT. The Soviets also have complained that the United States missed their "signal" in late 1969, at the start of SALT, when they first halted SS-9 construction.

However, in order to win Senate approval for phase two of the Safeguard ABM system last August, the administration argued that continuation of the program would be a "bargaining chip" in winning Soviet agreement to an SS-9 limitation by treaty.

Between now and March 15 the administration will have to decide whether to go back to the Johnson administration position, which was an ABM-only agreement, or to find some solution to the FBS issue in order to get a formal SS-9 limitation agreement.

David Kraslow and Stuart H. Loory
Los Angeles Times Series 1968

SEARCH FOR PEACE

Continued from 20th Page

diaries. It is, at best, a chancy undertaking. There can be and have been serious misunderstandings.

Washington and Hanoi can communicate directly—through speeches and statements and press conferences as they did Wednesday. But peace is not usually found in broad daylight.

Intermediaries do have one distinct advantage. As a senior State Department official put it: "Foreign diplomats, newsmen, private travelers can move around without attracting attention. And they can say things that are deniable later by either side if problems arise."

Some Drawbacks

"Some intermediaries we are quite happy with," he continued. "Some we encourage and push along, but some are a cross to bear and we just have to deal with them. The people who are encouraged are given a good briefing. You tell them what to look for, but you never know whether they know enough to report accurately."

Kissinger and his Frenchmen were no cross to bear. They reported accurately.

The message to Hanoi through Kissinger and the Frenchmen, it now appears, was sent in the hope that if an opportunity for peace talks had been lost in London and Moscow the previous February, it could be recovered. It seemed for a long while that it couldn't.

One informed critic of the Administration's Vietnam policy said of the August message: "It was too late. Hanoi just didn't believe us."

That source felt Hanoi didn't believe the Johnson Administration because of what occurred behind the scenes in London and Moscow the previous February.

Friday: What happened in London and Moscow?

This series for the Los Angeles Times will be expanded into a book, "The Secret Search for Peace in Vietnam," to be published this spring by Random House.

Copyright 1968 Los Angeles Times. World rights reserved.

Slow, Careful Effort Opened Way to Hanoi

APR 24

BY DAVID KRASLOW and STUART H. LOORY
Times Staff Writers
Copyright 1968 Los Angeles Times. World rights reserved.

WASHINGTON—Two unheralded Frenchmen—one a microbiologist, the other an old friend of Ho Chi Minh—arrived last July 21 in Hanoi in the unusual and secret role of emissaries of the U.S. government.

Their presence in the capital of North Vietnam was unknown to the world at that time, and has been unreported until this moment.

Yet it was their mission that initiated a new phase of diplomacy in the Johnson Administration's secret search for peace in Vietnam over the last three years. The culmination came in Hanoi's dramatic announcement Wednesday that it is willing to talk with American negotiators.

A month after their visit to Hanoi, the Frenchmen—working with Prof. Henry A. Kissinger of Harvard University — delivered to North Vietnam the first version of an American peace proposal more conciliatory than any made before.

Johnson's Vague Allusion

President Johnson, announcing a partial halt in the bombing of North Vietnam Sunday, alluded vaguely to the proposal they carried when he said:

"Tonight, I renew the offer I made last August."

Behind that little noticed sentence was the secret work of Kissinger, a mystery man in Vietnam diplomacy; Dr. Herbert Marcovich, 47, a University of Paris microbiologist, and Raymond Aubrac, 53, a director of the Food and Agricultural Organization, a UN agency based in Rome.

Their channel, which involved a meeting with North Vietnam's President Ho, functioned in this fashion:

1—Kissinger, 44, a government consultant on national security matters for the last 17 years, was the Administration's link to the Frenchmen.

2—Marcovich linked Kissinger to Aubrac.

3—Aubrac, who had befriended Ho in Paris more than 20 years ago, completed the chain from the White House to the presidential palace in Hanoi.

It was more out of necessity than choice that the United States resorted to these intermediaries to transmit a major peace offer.

The channel was used because, contrary to what Administration officials have often said, direct communication with Hanoi has been —more often than not—a problem.

In fact, the Kissinger-Frenchmen channel came into being because direct contact with Hanoi on the subject of peace negotiations was not then possible. Such contact between U.S. and North Vietnamese diplomats was ended in Moscow on Feb. 15, 1967, after a series of seven secret meetings in 36 days.

Le Trang, deputy chief of the North Vietnamese mission in Moscow told John C. Guthrie, his American counterpart, on that day that no more direct contacts would be permitted until the United States unconditionally halted the bombing of North Vietnam. American

Against the background of the dramatic news about Hanoi's willingness to talk to the United States, The Times herewith begins a series of articles on the secret search for peace in Vietnam over the last three years, which led to Wednesday's developments.

The authors, David Kraslow and Stuart H. Loory of The Times Washington Bureau, have been investigating the subject for more than seven months in the United States and abroad. Their inquiries took them to Rome, London, Paris, Florence, Prague, Warsaw, Ottawa, Vatican City and U.N. headquarters in New York. They interviewed scores of foreign diplomats and high-ranking U.S. officials in the White House, State Department, Department of Defense and other agencies.

Please Turn to Page 20, Col. 1

[...] left, no[...] to one in[...] formal circuit, that the [...] might be a so[...] to do a more convincing selling job if he thought he had something new.

It may be, however, that the January message contained even further concessions by the United States than the terms of the message delivered in August.

Neither message has been made public, but both are within the framework of a flexible American plan for achieving negotiations. The plan, developed in the fall of 1966, is known to only a few men within Washington's national security bureaucracy as "Phase A-Phase B."

Under Phase A the United States would halt the bombing of North Vietnam. To all the world it would appear that the United States had done this unilaterally. Actually, Phase A would not take effect until there had been secret agreement on Phase B—a mutual de-escalation of the ground war, with the United States again making the first move.

The Phase A-Phase B plan, in some variations, even contemplated agreement on public statements to be made by each government.

Modification Seen

A limited bombing halt announced as a unilateral gesture by the President Sunday suggests a modification of the Phase A-Phase B plan.

The August message sent through the Frenchmen represented a sharp pullback from a position the President had taken in a letter to Ho the previous February, which may have resulted in Hanoi's closing of the Moscow channel.

The President told Ho he would stop the bombing of North Vietnam after Ho stopped infiltration into South Vietnam. In short, he demanded that Ho make the first de-escalatory move. Privately, American officials later conceded the letter could have been taken as an ultimatum.

Stage Set

During the spring and early summer of 1967, the Administration searched for ways to renew the secret dialog with the enemy. This set the stage for the channel that ran from Washington through Cambridge, Mass., Paris, and Rome to Hanoi.

Kissinger and the Frenchmen became a high-priority channel to Hanoi when American officials were belatedly realizing the Johnson Administration might have misread the military and diplomatic situation the previous winter. Efforts that winter to get negotiations started in London and Warsaw, as well as Moscow, all collapsed.

American officials began to wonder later if a moderate proposal—such as the San Antonio formula — would have made any difference if it had been offered to Hanoi.

"We began to think that Hanoi really wanted to talk in February," one official said.

How the Frenchmen channel originated is unclear. In any case, Kissinger discussed it with Ambassador-at-large W. Averell Harriman, whom the President asked in 1966 to take charge of the search

[...] and Marcovich [...] not previously, but they became well acquainted at the September, 1966, Pugwash conference at Sopot, Poland. They talked about Vietnam.

It was at Sopot, perhaps, that Kissinger learned of the connection Marcovich's friend Aubrac had with Ho. He probably learned, too, that Aubrac was deeply troubled by the Vietnam war.

Aubrac is an engineer and administrator who was an underground leader in France during World War II and who twice escaped from the Nazis. He met Ho in Paris in 1946 when Ho came to negotiate his country's independence from France.

Close Ties

Ho stayed at Aubrac's suburban villa. He took his meals with the Aubrac family and had long talks with Aubrac. When Mrs. Aubrac gave birth to a daughter, Elizabeth, during that period, Ho went to her hospital bedside bearing toys and flowers. Ho became known as Elizabeth Aubrac's godfather.

Aubrac and Ho lost touch when France and the Viet Minh went to war. Kissinger and Marcovich learned that if his old, interrupted friendship could help in bringing peace, Aubrac was willing to try.

In July, the Frenchmen were briefed on the American position by Kissinger, who also instructed them on what to look for in replies.

Little Noted

Aubrac and Marcovich attracted no public notice as they flew to Phnom Penh, Cambodia, on July 21 and then, aboard the International Control Commission plane, to Hanoi.

They spent four days in Hanoi. Aubrac went to the presidential palace for a talk with his old house guest. He carefully noted Ho's views on restoring peace in Vietnam.

On July 25, the two Frenchmen went out to Hanoi's Gia Lam Airport, a MIG base as well as a commercial field that has been spared American bombing so that missions like theirs would not be impeded, and caught the ICC flight to Cambodia. They returned to their homes.

Early in August, Kissinger went to France to see Marcovich, and then made his report to the State Department.

Worth Exploring

"Aubrac and Marcovich brought back something that sounded interesting," one official said. "It was worth following up."

Precisely what they brought back is not known, but the Administration decided it wanted the Frenchmen to return to Hanoi with a formal American proposal. The two were willing, but this time Hanoi inexplicably turned down their visa. The suggestion apparently was made that if they simply wanted to deliver a message, it could be done through the North Vietnamese mission in Paris.

Kissinger returned to France with a message dated Aug. 25, apparently to conform with an appointment Marcovich had arranged with Mai Van Bo, Hanoi's senior representative in the non-Com-

[...] delivered in Hanoi on Aug. [...].

The [...] France hinted that the United States had scrapped its hardline demand of the previous winter came at the United Nations Sept. 21 when U.S. Ambassador Arthur J. Goldberg, opening the annual General Assembly debate, said, "The United States would be glad to consider and discuss any proposal that would lead promptly to productive discussions that might bring peace to the area."

His speech, drafted with the help of the White House and the State Department, did little to still the chorus of criticism against the United States bombing policy.

In the debate, only four countries—Australia, New Zealand, Thailand and Nationalist China—approved the bombing of North Vietnam. In contrast, 45 countries, including such allies as Canada, Denmark, the Netherlands and Norway, called for an end to the bombing.

Hints at Proposal

Goldberg only hinted at an American proposal. President Johnson stated the basic principle of the August offer in a speech at San Antonio on Sept. 29. He said:

"The United States is willing to stop all aerial and naval bombardment of North Vietnam when this will lead promptly to productive discussions. We, of course, assume that while discussions proceed, North Vietnam would not take advantage of the bombing cessation or limitation."

Though more conciliatory than any offer thus far, the San Antonio formula reserved Mr. Johnson's right to determine what might be productive and whether the North Vietnamese might be taking advantage of the bombing cessation.

The President's plan was denounced in Hanoi on Oct. 3 and Oct. 19 as a "faked desire for peace" and "sheer deception." On Oct. 20, Wilfred Burchett, the Australian leftist journalist who specializes in covering stories in Communist countries normally off limits to other Western correspondents, wrote that Hanoi would not negotiate the terms of a bombing halt.

'In No Mood . . .'

"Hanoi is in no mood for concessions or bargaining," he wrote in an article for the Associated Press.

Burchett's article, based on interviews with North Vietnam's Premier Pham Van Dong and Foreign Minister Nguyen Duy Trinh, was taken as a rejection of the San Antonio formula.

He also noted that North Vietnam's leaders simply did not trust President Johnson, saying:

"Because of experiences in certain earlier private and secret moves . . . there has been deep skepticism about any public statements or private feelers coming through diplomatic and other channels . . . I know of no leader who believes President Johnson is sincere in stating that he really wants to end the war on terms that would leave the Vietnamese free to settle their own affairs or that he does not intend to keep a permanent U.S. military presence in South Vietnam."

On Nov. 27, Harriman,

Some Answers

As well as representing the August offer made through Aubrac and Marcovich, the Romanian perennially sought answers for Hanoi's questions.

In his State of the Union message on Jan. 17, the President eased the San Antonio formula a bit when he changed the word "productive" to "serious" and Administration officials explained that meant the North Vietnamese only had to be sincere in seeking peace.

On Jan. 25, after the Romanian delivered the message to Hanoi, Secretary of Defense Clark M. Clifford testified before the Senate Armed Services Committee. He revealed a more precise definition of the San Antonio formula, saying the North Vietnamese could continue "normal" infiltration of men and supplies into the south after a bombing halt takes place.

Not Defined

Neither Clifford nor anyone else in the Administration defined "normal" infiltration—but that definition certainly could not be stretched to include the effort mounted by the Viet Cong and the North Vietnamese during the explosive Tet offensive which started Jan. 31.

While enemy troops wreaked havoc in the big cities of South Vietnam, there were indications of a willingness to talk. The enemy appeared to be whipsawing the Johnson Administration with the allurement of peace and an escalated war at once—a tactic that had been used in the past by Mr. Johnson.

Despite the denunciatory blasts both sides leveled at each other, they continued to give ground grudgingly as the Kissinger-Aubrac-Marcovich intermediary channel gave way to the climactic announcements by Hanoi and Mr. Johnson Wednesday. Once again the stage was set for direct contacts. They have been rare in the past and, like that between Trang and Guthrie in Moscow last year, they all failed.

Rangoon Sessions

Ambassador Henry A. Byroade and Vu Huu Binh, the North Vietnamese consul general in Burma, had beer-and-peace talk sessions in Rangoon during the 37-day bombing pause that ended Jan. 31, 1966. The United States and North Vietnam exchanged secret messages through Byroade and Binh during that period.

Also in 1966, Ambassador Foy D. Kohler in Moscow, after much effort, finally arranged a meeting with Le Trang at the North Vietnamese Embassy. It was a stiffly formal and fruitless three-hour conference. Kohler was rebuffed in his attempt to follow up that meeting.

(American and North Vietnamese diplomats met in Vientiane, Laos, last month, but only to arrange the release of three North Vietnamese sailors held by the United States. This was in return for the release of three American pilots by Hanoi in February.)

The United States would prefer to deal directly with the enemy, but it has found itself compelled to seek an end to the ever-enlarging war through one or more layers of intermediaries.

Please Turn to Pg. 21, Col. 1

SECRET SEARCH FOR VIET PEACE

Continued from First Page

officials have since tried many times, without success, to re-establish direct contact.

That is why Hanoi's statement Wednesday is so significant. It marks the end of a 14-month freeze on face-to-face peace talks.

The new peace offer—which came to be known as the San Antonio formula—transmitted to North Vietnam via Kissinger and the Frenchmen last summer was delivered again to Hanoi last January by a ranking Romanian official.

Sources, who asked that the Romanian's identity not be disclosed, said he agreed to carry the message for the United States not knowing what had transpired last summer.

U.S. Feeling

The State Department felt, according to one informed official, that the Romanian might be able to do a more convincing selling job if he thought he had something new.

It may be, however, that the January message contained even further concessions by the United States than the terms of the message delivered in August.

Neither message has been made public, but both are within the framework of a flexible American plan for achieving negotiations. The plan, developed in the fall of 1966, is known to only a few men within Washington's national security bureaucracy as "Phase A-Phase B."

Under Phase A the United States would halt the bombing of North Vietnam. To all the world it would appear that the United States had done this unilaterally. Actually, Phase A would not take effect until there had been secret agreement on Phase B—a mutual de-escalation of the ground war, with the United States again making the first move.

The Phase A-Phase B plan, in some variations, even contemplated agreement on public statements to be made by each government.

Modification Seen

A limited bombing halt announced as a unilateral gesture by the President Sunday suggests a modification of the Phase A-Phase B plan.

The August message sent through the Frenchmen represented a sharp pullback from a position the President had taken in a letter to Ho the previous February, which may have resulted in Hanoi's closing of the Moscow channel.

The President told Ho he would stop the bombing of North Vietnam after Ho stopped infiltration into South Vietnam. In short, he demanded that Ho make the first de-escalatory move. Privately, American officials later conceded the letter could have been taken as an ultimatum.

Stage Set

During the spring and early summer of 1967, the administration searched for ways to renew the [illegible] ...

for peace, and other officials.

Kissinger is an expert on nuclear strategy and foreign policy and head of Harvard's defense studies program. It has been hardly noticed, but since 1965 he has been intimately involved in Vietnam policy, advising on internal political matters in South Vietnam and the American pacification effort there.

He also has been secretly immersed in the search for peace, largely as an adviser. He has access to the sensitive peace file in Secretary of State Dean Rusk's office.

Peace Group

Marcovich is a member of the governing board of the Pugwash conferences, the meetings begun during the height of the cold war by Cleveland industrialist Cyrus Eaton to foster better East-West relations.

Kissinger and Marcovich had met previously, but they became well acquainted at the September, 1966, Pugwash conference at Sopot, Poland. They talked about Vietnam.

It was at Sopot, perhaps, that Kissinger learned of the connections Marcovich's friend Aubrac had with Ho. He probably learned, too, that Aubrac was deeply troubled by the Vietnam war.

Aubrac is an engineer and administrator who was an underground leader in France during World War II and who twice escaped from the Nazis. He met Ho in Paris in 1946 when Ho came to negotiate his country's independence from France.

Close Ties

Ho stayed at Aubrac's suburban villa. He took his meals with the Aubrac family and had long talks with Aubrac. When Mrs. Aubrac gave birth to a daughter, Elizabeth, during that period, Ho went to her hospital bedside bearing toys and flowers. Ho became known as Elizabeth Aubrac's godfather.

Aubrac and Ho lost touch when France and the Viet Minh went to war. Kissinger and Marcovich learned that if his old, interrupted friendship could help in bringing peace, Aubrac was willing to try.

In July, the Frenchmen were briefed on the American position by Kissinger, who also instructed them on what to look for in replies.

Little Noted

Aubrac and Marcovich attracted no public notice as they flew to Phnom Penh, Cambodia, on July 21 and then, aboard the International Control Commission plane, to Hanoi.

They spent four days in Hanoi. Aubrac went to the presidential palace for a talk with his old house guest. He carefully noted Ho's views on restoring peace in Vietnam.

On July 25, the two Frenchmen went out to Hanoi's airport, [illegible] a MIG base as well as a commercial field that has been spared American bombing [illegible] ...

munist world and head of the Paris mission.

Aubrac flew up from Rome. On Aug. 25, he and Marcovich handed the American proposal to Bo. It is believed the cabled relay from Bo arrived in Hanoi on Aug. 26.

The first public hint that the United States had scrapped its hard-line demand of the previous winter came at the United Nations Sept. 21 when U.S. Ambassador Arthur J. Goldberg, opening the annual General Assembly debate, said, "The United States would be glad to consider and discuss any proposal that would lead promptly to productive discussions that might bring peace to the area."

His speech, drafted with the help of the White House and the State Department, did little to still the chorus of criticism against the United States bombing policy.

In the debate, only four countries—Australia, New Zealand, Thailand and Nationalist China—approved the bombing of North Vietnam. In contrast, 45 countries, including such allies as Canada, Denmark, the Netherlands and Norway, called for an end to the bombing.

Hints at Proposal

Goldberg only hinted at an American proposal. President Johnson stated the basic principle of the August offer in a speech at San Antonio on Sept. 29. He said:

"The United States is willing to stop all aerial and naval bombardment of North Vietnam when this will lead promptly to productive discussions. We, of course, assume that while discussions proceed, North Vietnam would not take advantage of the bombing cessation or limitation."

Though more conciliatory than any offer thus far, the San Antonio formula reserved Mr. Johnson's right to determine what might be productive and whether the North Vietnamese might be taking advantage of the bombing cessation.

The President's stand was denounced at Hanoi on Oct. 3 and Oct. 19 as a "faked desire for peace" and "sheer deception." On Oct. 20, Wilfred Burchett, the Australian leftist journalist who [illegible] has good contacts at Communist councils in [illegible] ...

on one of his many wide-ranging trips around the world, stopped in Bucharest to confer with Romanian officials who had recently returned from Hanoi. Publicly, little resulted from Harriman's talks. They could have, however, set the stage for the Romanian involvement in January.

On Dec. 29, Trinh made the second of his one-word concessions that have marked changes in North Vietnamese policy.

On Jan. 28, 1967, he had said talks "could" result from an unconditional halt in the bombing. In the December statement he said they "will" result.

Rusk took it as a "new formulation" but put stress on unanswered questions still remaining such as: How soon after the bombing halt would talks begin? What would Hanoi agree to talk about? Would Hanoi stall at the conference table while taking military advantage of a bombing cessation?

After the Trinh statement, the United States put a ban on the bombing of Hanoi that lasted throughout most of January.

Some Answers

As well as repeating the August offer made through Aubrac and Marcovich, the Romanian presumably sought answers for Rusk's questions.

In his State of the Union message on Jan. 17, the President eased the San Antonio formula a bit when he changed the word "productive" to "serious" and Administration officials explained that meant the North Vietnamese only had to be sincere in seeking peace.

On Jan. 25, after the Romanian delivered the message to Hanoi, Secretary of Defense Clark H. Clifford testified before the Senate Armed Services Committee. He revealed a more precise definition of the San Antonio formula, saying the North Vietnamese could continue "normal" infiltration of men and supplies into the south after a bombing halt takes place.

Not Defined

Neither Clifford nor anyone else in the Administration defined "normal" infiltration—but that definition certainly could not be stretched to include the effort mounted by the Viet Cong and the North Vietnamese during the explosive Tet offensive which started Jan. 31.

While enemy troops wreaked havoc in the big cities of South Vietnam, there were indications of a willingness to talk. The enemy appeared to be whipsawing the Johnson Administration with the allurement of peace and an escalated war at once—a tactic that had been used in the past by Mr. Johnson.

Despite the denunciatory blasts both sides leveled at each other, they continued to give ground grudgingly as the Kissinger-Aubrac-Marcovich intermediary channel gave way to the climactic announcements by Hanoi and Mr. Johnson Wednesday. Once again the stage was set for direct contacts. They have been rare in the past and, like that between Trinh and Guthrie in Moscow last year, they all failed.

Rangoon Sessions

Ambassador Henry A. Byroade and Vu Huu Binh, the North Vietnamese consul general in [illegible] ...

Italian, Pole Developed 'Marigold' Initiative

BY DAVID KRASLOW and
STUART H. LOORY
Times Staff Writers

WASHINGTON — In the huge American national security bureaucracy, Saturday, Dec. 3, 1966, was a quiet time in the secret search for peace in Vietnam.

Behind the scenes at the State Department, functionaries were making important preparations for the possible opening three days hence of a meeting between North Vietnamese and American negotiators in Warsaw, but the activity was all technical.

Would anything come of it? No one knew.

Either way, it was exciting. Five months of arduous negotiations in Saigon were coming to fruition.

But there was nothing a policy-maker could do that Saturday to help things along. That morning, a senior national security officer picked up his daily newspaper and read:

U.S. Bombs
Site 5 Miles
From Hanoi
 Raids Are Closest
 to Reds' Capital
 Since Last June

"Oh, my God," the official muttered. "We lost control."

He read the story, which told of raids by carrier-based fighter-bombers the day before on a truck depot five miles south of Hanoi and of North Vietnamese charges that the planes had attacked a populated area inside the capital city itself.

He was one of a handful of men in Washington who knew of a peace initiative named "Marigold" containing:

A cable on the forthcoming meeting in Warsaw . . . others from Ambassador Henry Cabot Lodge on just-completed secret negotiations in Saigon . . . information on Giovanni d'Orlandi and Janusz Lewandowski . . . a memorandum on an elegant luncheon in Rome . . . Reports on trips to Hanoi.

How might the bombing reported to the American people that morning affect all this?

"Oh my God, we lost control."

The official's shock stemmed from knowledge that a foreign capital had

Please Turn to Page 6, Sec. B

Italian, Pole Sparked Secret Peace Initiative

Continued from First Page

been bombed, and President Johnson and his top civilian lieutenants had forgotten the raids had been authorized several weeks earlier.

The idea for Marigold had been developed by d'Orlandi, the 50-year-old Italian ambassador to Saigon, and Lewandowski, who, at 35, had just arrived in Vietnam in the spring of 1966 to head the Polish mission to the International Control Commission.

The Italian and the Pole decided that all attempts thus far to settle the war had been erroneously based on schemes to scale down the fighting slowly. They thought this could not work as long as neither side had presented any detailed picture of just what they would gain from the war.

They wanted to conduct a "diplomatic exercise in style" in which the combatants, through intermediaries, could express their views on the "least unacceptable" permanent settlement in Vietnam. In short, they were thinking of a text-book approach to the problem—the kind the suave, soft-speaking d'Orlandi might discuss with his classes of American graduate students at the University of Bologna, where he taught part-time before he went to Saigon.

Went to Lodge

After d'Orlandi and Lewandowski worked out the idea between themselves, the Italian diplomat went to Lodge with the proposal. They met on June 29, 1966. Ironically, it was the day the United States bombed the Hanoi area for the first time. The raids were so sensitive that President Johnson, back in Washington, stayed up all night awaiting results, and even went to pray for their success in a Catholic church.

Lodge relayed the d'Orlandi proposal to Washington and was given permission to participate. On July 9 he went to d'Orlandi's apartment on the fifth floor at 135 Duong Pasteur in Saigon for the first meeting with the Italian and Lewandowski.

D'Orlandi's apartment was admirably suited for a secret meeting. It was next door to the headquarters of Gen. William C. Westmoreland, U.S. commander in Vietnam, and in a building where other Americans lived. Lodge could go to the area and into the building without attracting attention. The apartment had become known as a haven for deposed Saigon government officials escaping retribution in successive coups, and was thus, by it agreement of those might need it next, not free of eavesdropping devices.

The meetings of the three diplomats developed a "drink-in-hand, football sessions," an official said. At the first session, the European diplomats asked Lodge only two questions:

1. Did the Johnson Ad-

This is another in a series of articles on the secret, three-year search for peace in Vietnam which led to the current movement toward negotiations between the United States and North Vietnam.

The authors, David Kraslow and Stuart H. Loory of The Times Washington Bureau, have been investigating the subject for more than seven months in the United States and abroad. Their inquiries took them to Rome, London, Paris, Florence, Prague, Warsaw, Ottawa, Vatican City and U.N. headquarters in New York. They interviewed scores of foreign diplomats and high-ranking U.S. officials in the White House, State Department, Department of Defense and other agencies.

---

side withdraws its forces to the north, ceases infiltration and the level of violence thus subsides."

Though tough in substance, the Manila proposal contained visions of the prosperity that could come to Southeast Asia after the fighting stopped and was widely greeted as conciliatory.

Mr. Johnson sent his roving peace ambassador, W. Averell Harriman, around the world to explain the Manila declaration to leaders of neutral and friendly nations. Harriman stopped in Rome and was feted Nov. 2 at a lavish luncheon in a villa on a hillside overlooking the Tiber River.

D'Orlandi, home for consultations with Foreign Minister Amintore Fanfani and for medical treatment, spoke to Harriman and Harriman's deputy, Chester L. Cooper, about the promise of the Saigon meetings.

The Italian told them peace possibilities in Saigon were more alive than anyone in the Johnson Administration realized.

At one point, d'Orlandi and Harriman went to a corner of the room and huddled intently. Fanfani, noting the tete-a-tete, turned to a colleague, smiled and said:

"I don't know what they're talking about and I don't want to know. But I hope it works out."

D'Orlandi had told the Americans that his colleague Lewandowski would soon be making another of his regular trips to Hanoi as a member of the ICC. That organization, by then moribund, had originally been established to police the 1954 Geneva Conference peace arrangement. Now it was only an empty shell.

The Italian urged the Americans to supply Lewandowski with a detailed rundown of the American position that he could present in Hanoi.

From the time Harriman and Cooper arrived back in Washington after hearing d'Orlandi's presentation, Marigold became an active peace initiative of

---

well-tested rule of thumb: The more serious any undertaking, the fewer the people who should know about it. Before the mid-November meetings in Saigon, there were perhaps 40 officials in Washington who knew of Marigold.

According to one official, this is what happened when Marigold's new promise developed in mid-November:

"The President woke up one morning, picked up the telephone and put the Lodge-Lewandowski business on a 'nodis Marigold' basis with an order to cut the squad. He said he wanted to know the names of everyone who knew about it."

In an era when secret-keeping has become an important tool of government, the President's order meant work for Benjamin H. Read, 42, the executive secretary of the State Department and its chief secret-keeper.

Read's tools are a little-known hierarchy of security classifications — "no distribution" (nodis), "exclusive distribution" (exdis) and "limited distribution" (limdis) — that go above the statutory "top secret" classification. Items marked "nodis" or "exdis" are handled in the State Department only by Read or one assistant and the men cleared to read them.

More Secrecy

Within "nodis" there can be even a more sensitive and exclusive category marked by a code name for each individual operation. Thus Marigold was the code of a peace initiative that could be seen only by specific men on the Marigold list in Read's office.

It was William P. Bundy, assistant secretary of state for East Asian and Pacific affairs, who picked the names of flowers as the codes for peace initiatives. Considering the symbolic meaning of flowers for the peace movement, the irony was exquisite.

After he "cut the squad," no more than 10 men out of the thousands in the Department of State saw Marigold information. That fact would, in a few weeks, become critical.

On the day Lewandowski left for Hanoi, the President, Secretary of Defense Robert S. McNamara, Secretary of State Dean Rusk and Walt W. Rostow, the President's special assistant for national security affairs, approved, for the first time in almost five months, the bombing of targets in the

---

of command, meant the targets could be struck on the first day with favorable weather conditions. At this point, there was no reason to believe they would interfere with the still tentative Marigold initiative. No serious negotiating sessions were yet in the offing.

In Hanoi, Lewandowski was repeating Lodge's presentation to North Vietnamese leaders. He had reduced the American position to what would come to be known as the Ten Points and reportedly received a favorable reaction.

Lewandowski returned to Saigon Nov. 29. A meeting with Lodge and d'Orlandi was arranged for Dec. 1, at which the Pole presented the Ten Points. They covered the American position on North Vietnam's famous "Four Points," the meaning of the Manila declaration, withdrawal of North Vietnamese troops from the south, a bombing cessation and cease-fire, principles of governmental organization after peace

---

comes to the south, holding of free elections and the problem of troop resupply by both sides between a cease-fire and final settlement.

Although this was the American position, the actual wording was Lewandowski's. Lodge said he would have to cable the Ten Points to Washington for study. American officials later labeled the document a hopeless mishmash of language. Polish sources say the document used American wording to a great extent.

On Friday, Dec. 2, Lodge, who had received instructions from Washington, met Lewandowski and d'Orlandi again to say that, despite needed clarification in the points, the United States would accept them as the basis for

---

further discussion. Lewandowski suggested the United States appoint a negotiator to meet a North Vietnamese representative in Warsaw as early as Tuesday, Dec. 6.

At about the same time, the monsoon weather broke over North Vietnam. Through breaks in the thunderstorms, mist, fog and low-hanging clouds, American bombers struck the Hanoi area for the first time since June 29.

Once again Lodge said he would have to consult Washington. Once again the meeting adjourned.

On Saturday, Dec. 3, the day after the raids, Lodge met Lewandowski and d'Orlandi to deliver an answer. Warsaw on Dec. 6 would be just fine, he said.

Lewandowski com-

---

plained that a repetition of the Dec. 2 raid on Hanoi might hurt. Lodge replied that the raids had been long-planned, that they could not be canceled without compromising the secrecy that was so important to the initiative and that there had been no coordination between the diplomacy and the raids. He asked Lewandowski to make that clear to Hanoi.

D'Orlandi appeared to understand.

D'Orlandi poured a round of Scotch for each

It [illegible]

They wanted [illegible] of a "diplomatic exercise" in which the two antagonists, through intermediaries, could express their views on the "most uncontestable" permanent settlement in Vietnam. In short, they were thinking of a text-book approach to the problem—the kind the suave, soft-speaking d'Orlandi might discuss with his classes of American graduate students at the University of Bologna, where he taught part-time before he went to Saigon.

Went to Lodge

After d'Orlandi and Lewandowski worked out the idea between themselves, the Italian diplomat went to Lodge with the proposal. They met on June 29, 1966. Ironically, it was the day the United States bombed the Hanoi area for the first time. The raids were so sensitive that President Johnson, back in Washington, stayed up all night awaiting results, and even went to pray for their success in a Catholic church.

Lodge relayed the d'Orlandi proposal to Washington and was given permission to participate. On July 9 he went to d'Orlandi's apartment on the fifth floor at 135 Durong Pasteur in Saigon for the first meeting with the Italian and Lewandowski.

D'Orlandi's apartment was admirably suited for a secret meeting. It was next door to the headquarters of Gen. William C. Westmoreland, U.S. commander in Vietnam, and in a building where other Americans lived. Lodge could go to the area and into the building without attracting attention. The apartment had become known as a haven for deposed Saigon government officials escaping retribution in successive coups, and was thus, by tacit agreement of those who might need it next, left free of eavesdropping devices.

The meetings of the three diplomats developed into "drink-in-hand, feet-up bull sessions," an official said. At the first session, the European diplomats asked Lodge only two questions:

1—Did the Johnson Administration view the war as part of a wider conflict or as one limited to Vietnam?

2—Would the Americans dismantle their bases and leave Vietnam after a settlement?

Rather than answer casually, Lodge decided to consult Washington. At a second meeting on July 24, he reported to his colleagues in Saigon that the United States truly saw the conflict as one limited to protecting South Vietnam and that American military forces would certainly be withdrawn after the war was over.

After that, Lodge dropped out of the discussions. D'Orlandi and the young, ambitious Lewandowski continued to meet. Meanwhile, the war grew hotter. South Vietnamese Premier Nguyen Cao Ky even talked of invading North Vietnam—talk the State Department disavowed.

Manila Conference

In October, Mr. Johnson brought all of South Vietnam's allies together for a conference at Manila. A declaration resulted stating the allies would withdraw their forces from South Vietnam six months after "the other

side withdrew its forces to the north, ceases infiltration and the level of violence thus subsides."

Though fourth in substance, the Manila proposal contained visions of the prosperity that could come to Southeast Asia after the fighting stopped and was widely greeted as conciliatory.

Mr. Johnson sent his roving peace ambassador, W. Averell Harriman, around the world to explain the Manila declaration to leaders of neutral and friendly nations. Harriman stopped in Rome and was feted Nov. 2 at a lavish luncheon in a villa on a hillside overlooking the Tiber River.

D'Orlandi, home for consultations with Foreign Minister Amintore Fanfani and for medical treatment, spoke to Harriman and Harriman's deputy, Chester L. Cooper, about the promise of the Saigon meetings.

The Italian told them peace possibilities in Saigon were more alive than anyone in the Johnson Administration realized.

At one point, d'Orlandi and Harriman went to a corner of the room and huddled intently. Fanfani, noting the tete-a-tete, turned to a colleague, smiled and said:

"I don't know what they're talking about and I don't want to know. But I hope it works out."

D'Orlandi had told the Americans that his colleague Lewandowski would soon be making another of his regular trips to Hanoi as a member of the ICC. That organization, by then moribund, had originally been established to police the 1954 Geneva Conference peace arrangement. Now it was only an empty shell.

The Italian urged the Americans to supply Lewandowski with a detailed rundown of the American position that he could present in Hanoi.

From the time Harriman and Cooper arrived back in Washington after hearing d'Orlandi's presentation, Marigold became an active peace initiative of the United States government and no longer just a "diplomatic exercise."

Lodge met in Saigon with Lewandowski and d'Orlandi learned the Pole would leave the next day for Hanoi and wanted an indication of American thinking. Lodge cabled Washington. By return cable he was given a "talking paper" outlining the American long range aims in South Vietnam.

Washington Reaction

There was another meeting in d'Orlandi's apartment the day Lewandowski left. Lodge spoke for a long time. Lewandowski took careful notes and then departed.

Meanwhile, back in Washington, where information is power, the national security bureaucracy reacted according to a

[illegible]

"The President woke up one morning [illegible] picked up the telephone and told the Lodge Lewandowski business was a hoax. Marigold [illegible] with an order to cut the squad. He said he wanted to know the names of everyone who knew about it."

In an era when secret-keeping has become an important tool of government, the President's order meant work for Benjamin H. Read, 42, the executive secretary of the State Department and its chief secret-keeper.

Read's tools are a little-known hierarchy of security classifications — "no distribution" (nodis), "exclusive distribution" (exdis) and "limited distribution" (limdis) — that go above the statutory "top secret" classification. Items marked "nodis" or "exdis" are handled in the State Department only by Read or one assistant and the men cleared to read them.

More Secrecy

Within "nodis" there can be even a more sensitive and exclusive category marked by a code name for each individual operation. Thus Marigold was the code of a peace initiative that could be seen only by specific men on the Marigold list in Read's office.

It was William P. Bundy, assistant secretary of state for East Asian and Pacific affairs, who picked the names of flowers as the codes for peace initiatives. Considering the symbolic meaning of flowers for the peace movement, the irony was exquisite.

After he "cut the squad," no more than 10 men out of the thousands in the Department of State saw Marigold information. That fact would, in a few weeks, become critical.

On the day Lewandowski left for Hanoi, the President, Secretary of Defense Robert S. McNamara, Secretary of State Dean Rusk and Walt W. Rostow, the President's special assistant for national security affairs, approved, for the first time in almost five months, the bombing of targets in the Hanoi area requested by the military.

Their approval, transmitted through the chain

[illegible]

[illegible] had reduced the American position to what would come to be known as the Ten Points and reportedly received a favorable reaction.

Lewandowski returned to Saigon Nov. 29. A meeting with Lodge and d'Orlandi was arranged for Dec. 1, at which the Pole presented the Ten Points. They covered the American position on North Vietnam's famous "Four Points," the meaning of the Manila declaration, withdrawal of North Vietnamese troops from the south, a bombing cessation and cease-fire, principles of governmental organization after peace

, Pole Sparked
Peace Initiative

n First Page

and Pre-
and his to
tnants had
raids had
ed several

r Marigold
veloped by
50-year-old
dor to Sai-
andowski,
d just ar-
m in the
head the
to the In-
trol Com-

d the Pole
l attempts
e the war
rroneously
s to scale
ng slowly.
his could
as neith-
ented any
of just
ld gain

o conduct
ercise in
e comba-
termedia-
ss their
st unac-
ent set-
am. In
thinking
roach to
kind the
ng d'Or-
ss with
merican
at the
Bologna,
art-time
Saigon.

d l and
ked out
them-
diplo-
e with
met on
ally, it
United
Hanoi
e. For
sitive
hnson,
ton,
await-
went
cess in

d'Or-
Wash-
per-
e. On
rtan-
fifth
Pas-
the
Ital-
i,
ment
for a
was
uar-
C.
com-
d in
ther
dge
and
out
The
m e
for
rn-
ing
ive
by
se
t,
ng

he
ed
-
fi-
-
y
.

This is another in a
ries of articles on the
ecret, three-year search
for peace in Vietnam
which led to the current
movement toward nego-
tiations between the United States and North Viet-
nam.

The authors, David
Kraslow and Stuart H.
Loory of The Times Wash-
ington Bureau, have been
investigating the subject
for more than seven
months in the United
States and abroad. Their
inquiries took them to
Rome, London, Paris,
Florence, Prague, War-
saw, Ottawa, Vatican City
and U.N. headquarters in
New York. They inter-
viewed scores of foreign
diplomats and high-rank-
ing U.S. officials in the
White House, State De-
partment, Department of
Defense and other agen-
cies.

side withdraws its forces
to the north, ceases infiltration and the level of
violence thus subsides."

Though tough in sub-
stance, the Manila propo-
sal contained visions of
the prosperity that could
come to Southeast Asia
after the fighting stopped
and was widely greeted as
conciliatory.

Mr. Johnson sent his
roving peace ambassador,
W. Averell Harriman,
around the world to ex-
plain the Manila declara-
tion to leaders of neutral
and friendly nations. Harriman stopped in Rome
and was feted Nov. 2 at a
lavish luncheon in a villa
on a hillside overlooking
the Tiber River.

D'Orlandi, home for con-
sultations with Foreign
Minister Amintore Fanfa-
ni and for medical treat-
ment, spoke to Harriman
and Harriman's deputy,
Chester L. Cooper, about
the promise of the Saigon
meetings.

The Italian told them
peace possibilities in Saigon were more alive than
anyone in the Johnson
Administration realized.

At one point, d'Orlandi
and Harriman went to a
corner of the room and
huddled intently. Fanfani,
noting the tete-a-tete,
turned to a colleague,
smiled and said:

"I don't know what
they're talking about and I
don't want to know. But I
hope it works out."

D'Orlandi had told the
Americans that his col-
league Lewandowski
would soon be making
another of his regular
trips to Hanoi as a mem-
ber of the ICC. That
organization, by then moribund, had originally been
established to police the
1954 Geneva Conference
peace arrangement. Now
it was only an empty shell.

The Italian urged the
Ame... to supply Lew-
andowski with a detailed
rundown of the American
position that he could
present in Hanoi.

Fr... time Harriman
and ... arrived back
in Washington after he re-
ing d'Orlandi's presenta-
tion, Marigold became an
active peace initiative of
the United States govern-

well-tested rule of thumb:
The more serious any
undertaking, the fewer the
people who should know
about it. Before the mid-
November meetings in
Saigon, there were per-
haps 40 officials in Washington who knew of Mari-
gold.

According to one official,
this is what happened
when Marigold's new
promise developed in mid-
November:

"The President woke up
one morning, picked up
the telephone and put the
Lodge-Lewandowski busi-
ness on a 'nodis-Marigold'
basis with an order to cut
the squad. He said he
wanted to know the names
of everyone who knew
about it."

In an era when secret-
keeping has become an
important tool of govern-
ment, the President's or-
der meant work for Benja-
min H. Read, 42, the
executive secretary of the
State Department and its
chief secret-keeper.

Read's tools are a little-
known hierarchy of secur-
ity classifications — "no
distribution" (nodis), "exclusive distribution" (exdis) and "limited distribution" (limdis) — that go
above the statutory "top
secret" classification.
Items marked "nodis" or
"exdis" are handled in the
State Department only by
Read or one assistant and
the men cleared to read
them.

More Secrecy

Within "nodis" there
can be even a more sensi-
tive and exclusive cate-
gory marked by a code
name for each individual
operation. Thus Marigold
was the code of a peace
initiative that could be
seen only by specific men
on the Marigold list in
Read's office.

It was William P. Bun-
dy, assistant secretary of
state for East Asian and
Pacific affairs, who picked
the names of flowers as
the codes for peace initiatives. Considering the
symbolic meaning of flow-
ers for the peace move-
ment, the irony was exquisite.

After he "cut the squad,"
no more than 10 men out
of the thousands in the
Department of State saw
Marigold information.
That fact would, in a few
weeks, become critical.

On the day Lewandow-
ski left for Hanoi, the
President, Secretary of
Defense Robert S. McNa-
mara, Secretary of State
Dean Rusk and Walt W.
Rostow, the President's
special assistant for na-
tional security affairs, approved, for the first time
in almost five months, the
bombing of targets in the
Hanoi area requested by

of command, meant the
targets could be struck on
the first day with favorable weather conditions. At
this point, there was no
reason to believe they
would interfere with the
still tentative Marigold
initiative. No serious negotiating sessions were
yet in the offing.

In Hanoi, Lewandowski
was repeating Lodge's
presentation to North
Vietnamese leaders. He
had reduced the American
position to what would
come to be known as the
Ten Points and reportedly
received a favorable reaction.

Lewandowski returned
to Saigon Nov. 29. A
meeting with Lodge and
d'Orlandi was arranged
for Dec. 1, at which the
Pole presented the Ten
Points. They covered the
American position on
North Vietnam's famous
"Four Points," the mean-
ing of the Manila declaration, withdrawal of North
Vietnamese troops from
the south, a bombing ces-
sation and cease-fire, principles of governmental organization after peace

comes to the south, hold-
ing of free elections and
the problem of troop re-
supply by both sides be-
tween a cease-fire and final settlement.

Although this was the
American position, the actual wording was Lewan-
dowski's. Lodge said he
would have to cable the
Ten Points to Washington
for study. American officials later labeled the document a hopeless mish-
mash of language. Polish
sources say the document
used American wording to
a great extent.

On Friday, Dec. 2,
Lodge, who had received
instructions from Wash-
ington, met Lewandowski
and d'Orlandi again to say
that, despite needed clarification in the points, the
United States would ac-
cept them as the basis for

further discussion. Lewandowski suggested the
United States appoint a
negotiator to meet a North
Vietnamese representa-
tive in Warsaw as early as
Tuesday, Dec. 6.

At about the same time,
the monsoon weather
broke over North Vietnam.
Through breaks in the
thunderstorms, mist, fog
and low-hanging clouds,
American bombers struck
the Hanoi area for the
first time since June 29.
Once again Lodge said
he would have to consult
Washington. Once again
the meeting adjourned.

On Saturday, Dec. 3, the
day after the raids, Lodge
met Lewandowski and
d'Orlandi to deliver an
answer. Warsaw on Dec. 6
would be just fine, he said.
Lewandowski com-

plained that a repetition of
the Dec. 2 raid on Hanoi
might hurt. Lodge replied
that the raids had been
long-planned, that they
could not be canceled
without compromising the
secrecy that was so important to the initiative and
that there had been no
coordination between the
diplomacy and the raids.
He asked Lewandowski to
make that clear to Hanoi.
The Pole appeared to
understand.

D'Orlandi poured a
round of Scotch for each

man, and they drank a
toast to their work.

"I thought I had done
something worthwhile in
my life," Lodge told an
associate several months
later.

Monday: The problems
involved in fighting a war
and seeking the peace by
the Tuesday lunch group
at the White House and
how they affected Mari-
gold.

*This series for The Los Angeles Times will be expanded into a book, "The Secret Search for Peace in Vietnam," to be published this spring by Random House.

Copyright 1969, Los Angeles Times. World rights reserved.

THE SECRET SEARCH FOR PEACE

Wilson Switch at U.S. Behest
Blamed for Lost Opportunity

BY DAVID KRASLOW and STUART H. LOORY

Times Staff Writers

APR 5 1968

Copyright, 1968, Los Angeles Times. World rights reserved.

WASHINGTON—With the White House dictating the moves on the transatlantic cable, British Prime Minister Harold Wilson switched and toughened a Vietnam peace proposal he had given, just hours before, to Soviet Premier Alexei N. Kosygin last year.

The switch forced by President Johnson occurred in London during the evening hours of Feb. 10, 1967. It deeply embarrassed Wilson and may have confused Kosygin and President Ho Chi Minh of North Vietnam.

Some informed critics of Mr. Johnson's Vietnam policies feel the London switch, along with a personal letter the President had sent to Ho two days before, may have ruined a promising opportunity for negotiations 14 months before this week's breakthrough.

The switching in peace terms came at the climax of a weeklong effort by Wilson and Kosygin to end the war in Vietnam.

While their talks were under way, the United States was secretly dealing with the North Vietnamese in face-to-face contacts in Moscow.

Shortly before the White House dictated the peace message change to Wilson, a draft of the President's letter to Ho was toughened and delivered through the Moscow channel. American officials later conceded privately that the substituted terms in the letter could be read as an ultimatum.

Wilson, who thought he was being kept fully informed by Washington during his talks with Kosygin, was not given the text of the letter.

Please Turn to Page 10, Col. 1

Late Switch Blamed for Lost Opportunity

Continued from First Page

To guard against any misunderstandings in the London meetings, which began Feb. 6, the Johnson Administration dispatched Chester L. Cooper, an expert in Vietnam diplomacy, to brief Wilson on the American position and to monitor the talks with Kosygin.

Since Great Britain and the Soviet Union were cochairmen of the 1954 Geneva Conference, which partitioned Vietnam originally, any talks they might have on the war were considered of extreme importance by the Johnson Administration.

Unnoticed, Cooper left Washington on Feb. 2, the day the President told the world at a press conference that "just almost any step" by North Vietnam could bring surcease from American bombing.

Cooper had seen the Feb. 2 draft of the President's letter and knew what had been happening in Moscow in the secret talks between John Guthrie, deputy chief of the American Embassy, and Le Trang, his North Vietnamese counterpart.

Latest Version

Cooper took with him to London the latest version of an American negotiating scenario secretly designated Phase A-Phase B, which conformed to the draft he had seen of the President's letter. It was a flexible plan for de-escalating the war in such a manner that neither the United States nor North Vietnam would lose either face or military advantage.

Phase A-Phase B was no peace plan as such. It was more a plan to cool off the war in the hope that once that was accomplished serious negotiations involving the interests of all combatants — the Saigon regime and the National Liberation Front as well as the United States and North Vietnam—would result.

Phase A involved the cessation of American bombing of North Vietnam. It would only take effect, however, after Washington and Hanoi had secretly agreed on Phase B—an act of de-escalation of the ground war by both sides. The United States would move first in Phase B as well.

Resupply Continuance

The indication is that under the plan Cooper took to London, North Vietnam would be permitted to continue resupplying its forces in the south.

Most important, however, was the time lag between the two phases. One source said the plan Cooper presented to Wilson provided for a time spread of about three weeks between A and B. Another said the spread was several days, perhaps a week.

Wilson and Kosygin began their Vietnam talks on the day of the Soviet premier's arrival—Feb. 6, two days before the truce in Vietnam for Tet (the lunar new year) was to begin.

Wilson laid out the A-B scheme, with Kosygin understanding that Wilson was fully authorized to speak for Mr. Johnson. Kosygin reiterated the line North Vietnam had taken Jan. 28 when Foreign Minister Nguyen Duy Trinh said peace talks "could" begin once the U.S. unconditionally stopped its bombing.

But, whereas Trinh had been conditional on this point. Kosygin reportedly told Wilson in private that talks "would" follow a bombing halt.

Kosygin insisted Trinh's public gesture was enough to get talks started. Once they began, he said, all else would fall into place.

Both Wilson and Kosygin knew that U.S.-North Vietnamese contacts had begun in Moscow on Jan. 10, but how much they knew of the substance of those talks is unclear.

Seek Quick Halt

Wilson and Kosygin were seeking to arrange a quick halt to the fighting. Guthrie, however, in a series of meetings, was spreading what one official described as a "whole smorgasbord" of possible approaches to a long-range settlement.

Wilson, speaking for the U.S. and Kosygin, presumably speaking for North Vietnam, held fast to their positions through the week. Kosygin, nevertheless, impressed both the Americans and the British privy to the talks with his forthrightness and his apparently sincere efforts to find peace.

Thursday, Feb. 9, Kosygin again echoed the Trinh statement in an internationally televised press conference which the President watched at the White House.

Quick Reaction

The White House reacted quickly: "Mr. Kosygin commented on the military action the United States should take but made no mention of the military action the other side should take."

At a press conference that afternoon, Secretary of State Dean Rusk deplored the "systematic campaign by the Communist side" to bring about an American bombing halt without corresponding military action by Hanoi.

Rusk called on North Vietnam to recognize the need for "elementary reciprocity."

What Rusk termed "elementary reciprocity" on Feb. 9 and what the President had termed "just almost any step" on Feb. 2 was put somewhat differently in the secret letter from Mr. Johnson to be delivered in Moscow on Feb. 8.

The President's letter said: "I am prepared to order a cessation of bombing against your country and the stopping of further augmentation of U.S. forces in South Vietnam as soon as I am assured that infiltration into South Vietnam by land and by sea has stopped."

America First

Under the Phase A-Phase B plan that Wilson had, on America's behalf, been presenting to Kosygin, the United States would make the first act of de-escalation. The Johnson letter turned this around and demanded North Vietnam move first to end all infiltration before the bombing ended.

Wilson did not learn of the change in the President's letter to Ho making the turnaround. On Friday, Feb. 10, Kosygin asked for the first time in the week that Wilson put into writing the American proposal he had been giving orally.

The Soviet leader was leaving shortly after 11 a.m. for a train tour of Scotland. He appeared eager to transmit the proposal to Moscow before departure.

After Kosygin had left 10 Downing St., where he had lunched, Wilson and Cooper, according to London sources, drafted a memorandum.

A copy was cabled to Washington, where it was received simultaneously in the White House Situation Room and the State Department Operations Center.

Wilson put the message in his inside coat pocket and went off to a 5:30 reception at the Soviet Embassy, where he spent 90 minutes. During the reception, Kosygin took Wilson into an anteroom and asked him if he had the message.

Delivered Message

If there was anything wrong with the message, Wilson thought, he would have heard from Washington by then. He hadn't. He gave Kosygin the message and returned to 10 Downing St.

At about 10:15 p.m., London time (4:15 p.m. in Washington), when Kosygin left the embassy for the 10- to 20-minute ride to Euston Railroad Station, transatlantic chaos set in. The President and others, having read the cabled memo from Downing St., became alarmed when they realized the inconsistency between it and the letter to Ho Chi Minh.

Rusk and presidential assistant Walt W. Rostow were summoned to the Situation Room. While Rostow contacted Wilson, the men in the room were drafting a new paragraph to substitute for the unacceptable section in the Wilson message to Kosygin.

Too Much Time

Wilson, the men in the White House decided, allowed too much time between the Phase A bombing halt and the Phase B de-escalation by North Vietnam. Their substitute telescoped the phases, according to one source, to make their proposed implementation virtually simultaneous and thus placing the memo to Kosygin more in accord with the letter to Ho.

The substitute paragraph was dictated to 10 Downing St. It was now approaching 11 p.m. in London. Wilson dispatched one of his aides with orders to hand it personally to Kosygin at Euston Station.

The aide raced through London in his car. He dashed through the doorway of Euston Station, down the stairs, through the crowds and finally, out of breath, to Platform No. 1. He just made it.

If Kosygin was startled or irritated—or amused—when the aide to the prime minister gave his explanations, there is no record of it.

But at 10 Downing St. it was said, "The British were embarrassed." Wilson had dealt with Kosygin in good faith. Now he found himself in a predicament. He was being forced to admit, in effect, that he had misrepresented the American position to Kosygin.

The British were not alone in their feelings. Americans were shamed as well. "Everybody who knew was embarrassed. It shouldn't have happened," according to one source.

How had Wilson taken the embarrassment?

"He took it like a man," one who knew reported. The prime minister never revealed his hurt publicly.

A combination of explanations has been offered by officials for the hardening of the U.S. position in February, 1967.

Becoming Concerned

The President, the officials explained, was becoming increasingly concerned with intelligence reports from American pilots suggesting a large resupply effort by North Vietnamese forces during Tet.

Three times during the London meeting, Wilson was asked by Washington to caution Kosygin that the North Vietnamese buildup would impede efforts to begin talks. The third time Wilson was asked to urge Kosygin to try to put a "damper on the flow."

The President was also understood to have been distressed by the massive publicity given the London talks and feared that Wilson, by nature an optimist, might somehow soften the American terms.

Under Wilson's urgings, the Johnson Administration did agree to extend the pause in the bombing of North Vietnam from the end of the Tet truce Feb. 11. As the hours beyond the ending of the truce in the ground war

Please Turn to Pg. 11, Col. 1!

This is another in a series of articles on the secret, three-year search for peace in Vietnam which led to the current movement toward negotiations between the United States and North Vietnam.

The authors, David Kraslow and Stuart H. Loory of The Times Washington Bureau, have been investigating the subject for more than seven months in the United States and abroad. Their inquiries took them to Rome, London, Paris, Florence, Prague, Warsaw, Ottawa, Vatican City and U.N. headquarters in New York. They interviewed scores of foreign diplomats and high-ranking U.S. officials in the White House, State Department, Department of Defense and other agencies.

Late Switch Complicates Peace Search

Continued from 10th Page

went on and the bombing did not resume, hopes were raised.

Wilson kept trying for an agreement despite his embarrassment of two days before. He met Kosygin Feb. 12, the day after the truce ended, and then he rushed off to Kosygin's hotel suite at 1 a.m., Feb. 13, apparently after a post-midnight conversation with the White House.

At that meeting Wilson reportedly informed Kosygin the American bombing would be resumed later in the day. One source suggested he also presented, with White House approval, a modification of the offer contained in the switched message.

Later in the day, Kosygin left London. Washington had received no reply to the President's letter from Ho but the North Vietnamese leader had written a bitter letter to the Pope that was taken as an answer. Shortly after Kosygin's plane touched down in Moscow, the bombing resumed. Wilson's efforts collapsed.

Handed Reply

On Feb. 15, Le Trang, the North Vietnamese deputy, handed Guthrie Ho's vitriolic reply and told him North Vietnam was shutting off any further direct contact. A long period of a diplomatic freeze and an enlarging war set in.

Wilson publicly blamed the failure of the London talks on North Vietnam, but privately most British officials—and some American officials—felt the resumption of bombing had been precipitous. Other sources suggest that the President's tough demand to Ho and the sudden changing of a peace proposal in London were not conducive to good bargaining, and might have been more basic causes for the failure.

Seven months later, on Sept. 21, George Brown went to a private luncheon while in New York for the U.N. General Assembly. The luncheon at the prestigious Council on Foreign Relations was attended by some 15 persons, including U.N. Ambassador Arthur Goldberg.

Brown's Statement

It was a relaxed affair. Brown had a few drinks. The talked turned to Vietnam and then to the Wilson-Kosygin meetings of the previous February.

Suddenly Brown was saying the problem in London had been a switch in the American position. (One guest at the luncheon thought Brown used the term "hardening" rather than "switch.")

Then Brown caught himself. He shouldn't have said that, he remarked. He asked the guests please not to repeat it.

In the months after the collapse of the Wilson-Kosygin attempt and Hanoi's closing of the Moscow channel, some American officials began to wonder whether the Administration had not miscalculated in February.

Sunday: The intricate history of a 1966 peace initiative code-named "Marigold" that, many charge, was punctuated by American bombs.

Poorly Timed Bombing Hurt Good Chance for Talks in '66

BY DAVID KRASLOW and STUART H. LOORY
Times Staff Writers

APR 8 1968

WASHINGTON — The Johnson Administration's penchant for secrecy caused a breakdown in coordination that damaged, in December, 1966, what many regarded as one of the most promising of the Vietnam peace initiatives.

President Johnson and his closest advisers overlooked the scheduling of bombing raids at a critical time. The information necessary to prevent a breakdown was kept from those officials in a better position than their preoccupied superiors to coordinate diplomacy with military action.

As a result, Hanoi was bombed just a day before American Ambassador Henry Cabot Lodge agreed with a Polish diplomat, Jausz Lewandowski, to arrange a North Vietnamese-U.S. meeting in Warsaw only three days hence, on Tuesday, Dec. 6, 1966.

On Dec. 4. 1966, a day after Lewandowski warned Lodge about the possible harmful effects of the bombing and Lodge explained the raid away, the bombers struck Hanoi again.

This breakdown may be explained by examining the organization of the national security bureaucracy in Washington. Just who selects each of those bomb targets—each truck depot, rail yard, antiaircraft emplacement, road junction, power

Please Turn to Page 8, Col. 1

PEACE SEARCH

Continued from First Page

plant, airfield, shipyard or dock in the northern part of North Vietnam? Who decides what marching orders to give the diplomats?

Who decides which men in government should know what the generals and admirals are doing or what the diplomats are doing or both?

The answer to all those questions is the President of the United States.

"The only place important decisions are made here in Washington is in the mind of Lyndon Johnson," one official said. "And that could happen anytime—at 4 o'clock in the morning, at lunch, in the bathtub."

To understand the meaning of this for the Marigold peace initiative to establish talks in Warsaw, consider that the "Vietnam working group" in the State Department, the organization originally established as a special task force to oversee the growing American involvement in the war, has grown virtually powerless.

"County Desk"

The 10-man group, which was conceived as a kind of "country desk" staffed by experts with all the facts and figures at their command, has become in large part a speaker's bureau and public relations agency for the Johnson Administration. In addition, the group functions as a service organization, preparing the memoranda and analyses requested by superiors.

Its members say they are well informed about the war. "We are kept ignorant of a very small amount of information—an infinitesimal amount of the total flow of traffic," one group member said.

The infinitesimal amount missing was precisely the information that counted in Marigold. It related to the serious peace moves and it prevented the group from coordinating — or even suggesting coordination of— the military effort with the peace effort.

When Marigold reached a critical stage, the Vietnam working group — those involved full time in the day-to-day problems of the war and the efforts to settle it—were cut from the list of officials entitled to Marigold information.

That act prevented the working group from raising a danger flag on bomb targeting in the Hanoi area late in 1966.

On top of the experts in the working group, the State Department has superimposed layers of supervisors and has buttressed the structure with organizations outside the normal chain of command.

Organization Hit

As a result, one official observed:

"The State Department is organized atrociously to handle the Vietnam war. The difficulty arises from the fact that in the last two or three years the Vietnam desk has been moving successively further and further to the top of the government. Now the chief of the desk is Lyndon B. Johnson, the chief of the desk in the Defense Department is Robert S. McNamara and the chief of the desk in the State Department is Dean Rusk. (Since that official spoke, Clark Clifford has succeeded McNamara.)

"The problem with this is that each one of these men has much more to do than worry only about Vietnam. Despite the fact that they are running the war and seeking the peace, you have to go all the way down to the deputy assistant secretary level until you find someone working only on Vietnam."

Other Crises

At the same time the President and his lieutenants operate the Vietnam desk, this official noted, they must also worry about such things as riots in urban ghettos, Middle East war, a North Korean ship seizure or a gold crisis. Such matters have at times rendered the Vietnam war a secondary problem for them.

The device the Johnson Administration worked out for coordinating the Vietnam war efforts is the "Tuesday lunch," named because it convenes usually—but not always—every Tuesday at 1 p.m. in the White House family dining room.

To the extent that the President shares decision-making at all, he does much of it at the Tuesday lunch with the secretaries of defense and state, Walt W. Rostow, his special assistant for national security affairs, and Press Secretary George Christian. Occasionally, Gen. Earle G. Wheeler, chairman of the Joint Chiefs of Staff; CIA Director Richard Helms and others sit in.

Targets Checked

The Tuesday lunch group, using a four-part check list, approved, before the bombing cutback announced by the President on March 31, all strategic targets in North Vietnam. In doing so, they weighed the possible military gain from an attack against three factors: the danger of American airplane and pilot loss, the risk of North Vietnamese civilian casualties and the risk of widening the war by bringing in Red China or the Soviet Union.

At the Tuesday lunch, Mr. Johnson and his advisers worked over the targets, each listed on a separate sheet of paper, like teachers grading examination papers.

In grading those papers and approving targets, they accounted for every apparent contingency. Except one. Once the targets were put on the strike list, none of the officials who selected them — that is, none of the Tuesday lunch group members—took responsibility for watching the exact time when a particular target was to be struck.

Depending on the weather and operational capabilities of squadrons on Navy aircraft carriers and air bases in the Thailand jungles, that could be anywhere from a few

Please Turn to Pg. 9, Col. 1

PEACE SEARCH

Continued from 8th Page

hours to days or even weeks after the authorization.

There was a fail-safe mechanism to allow for coordination of military actions with diplomacy. But, in December, 1966, it had fallen into disuse.

The Hanoi targets struck Dec. 2 and 4 were authorized at a Nov. 15 Tuesday lunch, when there was no immediate prospect of a direct peace negotiation. A day before each of the bombings, the field commanders sent cables through the chain of command from Saigon to Pacific military headquarters in Honolulu to Washington advising of air raids upcoming in the next 24 hours.

Knew Nothing

State Department liason men in Honolulu and at the Pentagon as well as military liason men in the State Department, who studied those cables, knew nothing of the Marigold initiative. Thus they raised no red flags.

The only man who would have known of the delicate diplomacy under way and also had regular access to the target information was Benjamin H. Read, the executive secretary of the State Department. All sensitive cable traffic going into or leaving the building in Foggy Bottom crosses his desk.

He cannot possibly read it all, however, and the target cables had become routine matter over a two-year period. Hardly anyone paid attention to them.

The men in the Vietnam working group would have spotted the possible harmful effects of an unusual raid on Hanoi at the same time a meeting was being arranged, but they no longer knew what was happening with Marigold.

Some high officials realize the problems inherent in this organization. One said:

"The Tuesday lunch is a terrible way to achieve effective coordination. The problem is that all the people making the decisions at the lunch know the least about Vietnam. Wheeler knows most, McNamara is next and Helms is third. I'm a believer in bureaucracy, in adequately staffing a decision. The people who have the information should participate in the decisions."

Because of all the other duties of the Tuesday lunch group members, they could not devote a lot of time to the mechanics and techniques of developing peace initiatives. That was handled, under order from President Johnson, by Ambassador W. Averell Harriman and his small staff.

"They were in charge of dreaming up scenarios, dreaming up ideas, chasing will-of-the-wisps, pushing, cajoling," one official said.

Imbalance Seen

Though grand in concept, Harriman's office had almost no power. "On the one hand you had a carefully organized military machine," one official said. "On the other, there was Harriman with no real mandate. I'd say there was a slight imbalance there."

"Realistically," another official said, "the secretary of state just has to be in charge of all diplomacy. That responsibility can't be transferred to someone like Harriman."

The imbalance and the coordination breakdown resulting in the Dec. 2 and 4 raids inspired a greater degree of alertness in the State Department. Officials began checking the daily bombing lists.

On the weekend of Dec. 3-4, however, their more immediate concern was getting ready for the impending Warsaw Marigold meeting.

Tuesday: The Long Marigold telegram to Warsaw and the collapse of the peace probe.

This series for the Los Angeles Times will be expanded into a book, "The Secret Search for Peace in Vietnam," to be published this spring by Random House.

THE SECRET SEARCH FOR PEACE

Flash Telegram Set '66 Scene for Talks That Never Came

APR 9 1968   BY DAVID KRASLOW and STEWART H. LOORY

Times Staff Writers

WASHINGTON—Near midnight on Saturday, Dec. 3, 1966, the United States marine guard at the American Embassy in Warsaw picked up the telephone and called Ambassador John A. Gronouski at home. There was a flash telegram coming in marked "Nodis" (no distribution).

That meant only the ambassador himself could read it.

Gronouski, who had been asleep, dressed and hurried to the embassy. The telegram was still running when he arrived. It spilled relentlessly out of the teletype machine. The message ran all night and through much of Sunday. Gronouski worked all weekend reading it.

The seemingly endless telegram was a verbatim record of the Marigold peace initiative undertaken by Ambassador Henry Cabot Lodge in Saigon with Italian Ambassador Giovanni D'Orlandi and Janusz Lewandoski, chief of the Polish Mission to the International Control Commission. Those three had agreed the time was right for a face-to-face U.S.-North Vietnamese meeting. Lewandoski, on Dec. 3, suggested they could start as early as Dec. 6 in Warsaw. The United States had agreed.

Gronouski, Washington decided, would do the talking. Now the telegram was instructing him to make preliminary arrangements with Polish Foreign Minister Adam Rapacki. The long telegram would familiarize Gronouski with every detail of the five-month-long negotiation involving Lodge, Lewandoski and D'Orlandi on the complicated

Please Turn to Page 16, Col. 1

Telegram Set '66 Scene but Talks Never Came

Continued from First Page

Marigold plan, so that he could talk intelligently with the North Vietnamese.

The whole prospect excited Gronouski. He was eager about playing a role in settlement of the war.

On Monday, Dec. 5, Gronouski, having studied the Marigold record for 30 hours in his office with only an occasional catnap and snack, went to see Rapacki for the first time. He had gone to make arrangements for what he thought would be the next day's meeting with the North Vietnamese.

Rapacki told him there would be no meeting. He was vague on the reasons but did mention, in a low-keyed "fatherly" sort of way, that the bombings around Hanoi on Dec. 2 and 4 could damage the initiative. Gronouski knew not only of the bombings but also of some enemy mortar raids on Saigon's Tan Son Nhut Airport over the weekend. He replied that those attacks could hurt as well.

'10 Points'

Gronouski also mentioned that the status of the "10 Points," which Lodge had agreed could be the basis for direct discussions, needed clarification.

The United States considered the points only "topic headings" and not "agenda items." As one official said, "We still don't know to what degree we had to subscribe to the language of the 10 Points . . . we had to make certain that our attendance at a meeting did not create the misunderstanding that we accepted their language."

From various accounts of the Gronouski-Rapacki meeting, it appears that some misunderstanding did develop over the type of clarification the United States wanted. Gronouski wanted only clarification of the status of the points from the Poles. He wanted to clarify the meaning of each point—that is discuss them — with the North Vietnamese directly.

From Dec. 5 to Dec. 13, Gronouski and Rapacki met daily. Each time Gronouski pleaded for a meeting with the North Vietnamese. Each time there was a confused discussion involving the harmful effects of bombing Hanoi and the nature of the clarification the United States sought.

Gronouski's frustration rose. He was hopeful the meeting could be arranged. In fact, he later admitted to associates in Washington he may have been guilty of "wishful thinking." At one point he made a special trip to the Foreign Ministry to urge Rapacki that talks begin "that afternoon, that night, at 3 in the morning." The talks with the North Vietnamese always seemed imminent but they never materialized.

Raids Reconsidered

Meanwhile, back in the United States, the continued bombing of Hanoi was reconsidered. Several persons in the State Department thought the raids should be discontinued.

Some felt it would harm the initiative. Others felt the initiative might not succeed anyhow but felt that when it failed the enemy could blame the raids for the failure.

What one official described as "grumblings and murmurings" about the raids developed into a secret debate among President Johnson's advisers.

Nicholas D. Katzenbach, undersecretary of state; Benjamin H. Read, executive secretary of the State Department; Ambassador W. Averell Harriman, the man in charge of peace seeking, and Chester L. Cooper, his deputy, all opposed continued bombing of Hanoi while Marigold was alive.

The President decided in favor of continuing the raids. Secretary of State Dean Rusk, who was then touring the Far East, agreed. So did Walt W. Rostow, the President's special assistant for national security affairs. So also did the Joint Chiefs of Staff and civilian officials in the Defense Department

even though D'Orlandi warned him about the bad effects the bombings might have on Marigold during a talk in Saigon on Dec. 9. Rusk replied to the Italian that Rapacki seemed to be doing some foot-dragging in arranging the meetings. D'Orlandi reportedly agreed that the Poles were acting in an inexplicable way.

On Dec. 13 American bombers struck the Hanoi area for the third time since the beginning of the month and on the following day they struck again. Gronouski's immediate reaction was despair. He felt the raids should not have happened.

Hanoi Withdraws

He was not surprised when Rapacki called him in on Dec. 15 and told him that, because of the raids the previous two days, the North Vietnamese had withdrawn from the initiative. Rapacki was clearly angry at the United States.

Gronouski cabled news of the collapse—and the reasons given for it—to Washington. He then set about trying to revive Marigold. Despite what Rapacki said, Gronouski thought it could be revived.

On Dec. 21 Gronouski

and the State Department agreed that he should return to Washington for a quick consultation on Marigold. The embassy put out a cover story saying that the ambassador was returning home to discuss the final stages of a financial agreement.

Gronouski flew all night, arriving in Washington at 6 p.m. on Dec. 22. He spent 24 hours in conferences and finally, on Dec. 23, President Johnson decided to create a bomb-free zone with a 10-mile radius around the center of Hanoi to show American sincerity in wanting to talk.

Once again Gronouski flew all night to get back to Warsaw. He arrived after dark on Christmas Eve and met Rapacki at 7 p.m. in the Foreign Ministry. Rapacki appeared pleased with the American gesture.

On Dec. 27 Gronouski

epartment
e should
gton for a
on on Ma-
nassy put
ry saying
sador was
to discuss
of a finan-

all ni_ ,
nington at
He spent
onferences
Dec. 23,
n decided
=free zone
e radius
:r of Han-
rican sin-
g to talk.
Gronouski
get back
: arrived
Christmas
packi at 7
gn Minis-
appeared
e Ameri-

Gronouski

received a call from the
Polish Foreign Ministry.
"Was that statute miles or
nautical miles?" He
checked with Washington
and learned it was nauti-
cal miles. The call gave
him hope.

Will Not Talk

On Dec. 30, Rapacki
summoned the American
to the Foreign Ministry
and told him once again
the North Vietnamese de-
finitely would not talk and
that the Polish govern-
ment was withdrawing
completely from the initiative. Gronouski thought
he heard a note of sym-
pathy for the United
States in Rapacki's voice.

In the months that fol-
lowed, the State Depart-
ment conducted a post-
mortem on its conduct of
the Marigold initiative
and decided it had done
nothing wrong. The only
dissent came from some
officials who felt the

bombings of Hanoi should
not have occurred.

Disagreement on this
major point, of course,
meant disagreement on
whether any blame for
collapse of Marigold could
be ascribed to the United
States.

Some high officials con-
cluded that the Poles had
exteeded their authority
and had promised a face-
to-face meeting when the
North Vietnamese really
had not given them au-
thorization to make such a
promise.

Still later, two high
officials privately placed
the blame for the collapse
on articles by Harrison
Salisbury, assistant man-
aging editor of the New
York Times. He became
the first correspondent for
a large, respectable American newspaper to visit
Hanoi. His stories created
a furore in the United
States.

They documented, for

the first time by an American, charges that civilian
areas had been bombed by
U.S. planes, however accidentally that might have
occurred.

"After Harrison Salis-
bury's copy, they (the
North Vietnamese)
copped out," one official
said. "They realized they
had a pretty good thing
going and could use Amer-
ican public opinion to get
a better deal. We never
did for Hitler's Germany
what we did for Hanoi."

The official did not men-
tion that Salisbury's first
report, on Christmas Day,
1966, did not appear until
10 days after Rapacki told
Gronouski that American
bombings had destroyed

the peace initiative.

Conclusion Wednesday:
The "three-months air
war" and the complex
search for peace.

This series for the Los Angeles
Times will be expanded into a book,
"The Secret Search for Peace in Viet-
nam," to be published this spring by
Random House.

Polish Envoy Runs Into Great Wall of China

BY DAVID KRASLOW and STUART H. LOORY
Times Staff Writers

WASHINGTON—On Jan. 16, 1966, Jerzy Michalowski, a high official in the Polish Foreign Ministry, returned to Warsaw from a secret 18-day visit to Hanoi.

He had been on a peace mission at the urging of the U.S. government.

One of the first foreigners to see him after his return was George Clutton, the British ambassador. Clutton casually asked the Pole how the trip had gone.

Michalowski, in a manner that was at once cryptic and revealing, answered:

"Goddam those Chinese."

The Pole was one of the actors in a gala peace-seeking production mounted in December, 1965, by President Johnson that was intended as much to show the world the President wanted peace as it was to obtain it. The gala went into the Vietnam war records under the name, "37-Day Bombing Pause."

In it, American diplomats skittered hither and yon around the globe, urging leaders in friendly and not-so-friendly capitals to urge Hanoi to negotiate. Michalowski's trip had been an outgrowth of a plea made in Warsaw by Ambassador W. Averell Harriman, the United States' old soldier of diplomacy.

Hanoi's rejection of the Michalowski overture and the Pole's stated reason for it illustrate the complexities involved in peace-seeking. Not only does Ho Chi Minh's attitudes and those of the other North Vietnamese leaders have to be considered but so do those of the South Vietnam National Liberation Front, Peking, Moscow and, on the allied side, the Saigon government and the other governments which sent troops into South Vietnam.

If the Chinese were a complicating factor in the search for peace in 1966, a miscalculation by the Johnson Administration was the complication a year earlier—before the bombing of North Vietnam even began.

U.N. Secretary General U Thant had received North Vietnamese agreement to attend a meeting with American negotiators. With Adlai Stevenson's encouragement, Thant in January, 1965, had even arranged

Please Turn to Page 8, Col. 1

SEARCH FOR PEACE

Continued from First Page

a site for the talks—Rangoon. On Jan. 30, Stevenson was compelled to tell Thant the United States would not attend the meeting.

As a few officials in the White House and State Department then knew and now acknowledge, the very idea of negotiations was "anathema" to the President and his top advisers during that period.

The Administration felt that a settlement satisfactory to the United States could not then be achieved. The Saigon government was in a shambles. The military situation was worsening. The President and his chief advisers concluded that the United States would have to correct the military imbalance before it could consider talks. To bargain with Hanoi in January, 1965, would mean bargaining from a position of weakness.

With the Thant initiative rebuffed, plans for the bombing of North Vietnam were advanced.

Bombing Begins

The United States began bombing the north on Feb. 7, 1965, ignoring Soviet Premier Alexei N. Kosygin's presence in Hanoi. Kosygin and the Soviet government made its anger at the embarrassment plain.

Those first raids were said to be in retaliation for Viet Cong attacks on American installations in South Vietnam. But already the President had all but decided on a regular program of bombing in the north.

McGeorge Bundy, then the President's special assistant for national security affairs, among others, advised the President that a relatively short period of steady bombing would not only arrest the deteriorating situation but also would avoid the need for sending American combat troops to South Vietnam.

Of the two choices— American troops to fight in Asia or American

bombing of North Vietnam — bombing was far more palatable to the American public.

Sources then on the White House staff now talk of Bundy's "three-month plan." Bundy, it is said, felt that after three months of sustained bombing Hanoi would be ready to make significant concessions.

The bombing, it was felt, would be something the United States could agree to stop doing in return for concessions by North Vietnam.

It didn't work.

In May, 1965, the United States did stop the bombing for five days in an effort to test the three-month thesis. Secretary of State Dean Rusk asked North Vietnam for significant reductions in the fighting if it wished the bombing pause to continue. Hanoi, receiving aid from Peking and Moscow, wasn't interested. It contemptuously returned American messages in Moscow and, through the British, in Hanoi.

No Improvement

"We miscalculated," one former White House official said. "The bombing did not improve our postion."

Proven right were those few in the Administration who feared the bombing would lead quickly to an escalation of the war by both sides and the very result the President had sought to avoid—the sending of combat troops to South Vietnam.

They felt this would

inevitably occur unless talks could be arranged quickly in the early stages of American bombing. Their advice was not followed.

With the failure of the short air war theory, third parties—professional and amateur diplomats—intervened to help in finding a settlement.

One of them was Prof. Giorgio LaPira, the former mayor of Florence, Italy.

LaPira is a modern-day Savonarola, a Catholic aesthete whose political philosophy is based on making the Sermon on the Mount come true. He lives in cell-like quarters at the monastery of San Marco in downtown Florence, the same monastery Savonarola headed and lived in when, during eight years of the Renaissance, he railed against the moral degradation of Italy and the simony of the "false popes" in Rome.

Burned at Stake

Savonarola was burned at the stake in 1498. LaPira, after long service as mayor of Florence after World War II and working an anti-Communist economic and social miracle, was defeated at the ballot box in 1965.

As LaPira had tried unsuccessfully to help settle the Arab-Israeli dispute and the French-Algerian war, he attempted to mediate the Vietnam war. He went to visit Ho Chi Minh in November, 1965, thinking he had, through Italian Foreign Minister Amintore Fanfani, a mandate from President Johnson. He brought back a message that Ho would talk without first demanding the withdra-

Please Turn to Pg. 9, Col. 1

PEACE SEARCH

Continued from 8th Page

wal of American troops. There also was a suggestion that any bombing of Hanoi and Haiphong would destroy the possibility for talks.

If there was ever anything important about the initiative, it was negated after (1) Secretary of State Dean Rusk proposed complicating terms to Fanfani; (2) the initiative became public knowledge through no fault of the Administration, and (3) the United States bombed the Haiphong area for the first time.

Efforts of Others

The failure of the Italian initiative was followed by the efforts of others to mediate the war. Most notably, after the 37-day pause, the Canadians summoned out of retirement one of their ablest Asian hands, 71-year-old Chester Ronning. With Washington's approval, Canada dispatched Ronning on two peace missions to Hanoi.

A week after Ronning returned from his second trip to Hanoi in June, 1966, the United States bombed the Hanoi area for the first time. This was done despite a Canadian plea that escalation of the air war would not only embarrass the Canadian government but also would destroy the new and potentially useful channel Ronning had opened to Hanoi. Ronning hasn't been back to Hanoi since that bombing.

Ironically, the Marigold peace initiative was born in Saigon on the day Hanoi was bombed. It was to die a controversial death in Warsaw six months later while bombs were dropped once more in the Hanoi area. The area had been untouched in the interim.

The death of Marigold was soon followed, in early 1967, by the episodes of the switched secret peace message in London during the talks between British Prime Minister Harold Wilson and Soviet Premier Alexei N. Kosygin, and the secret toughening of a letter from President Johnson to Ho Chi Minh.

Some present and former officials feel that the Thant initiative of 1964-65 was the most important missed opportunity for a compromise political settlement.

"When you think of what came later," one former official said, "you realize how important that opportunity was."

His point was: not any certainty that a satisfactory settlement would have resulted then from talks, but that the effort to find out wasn't made.

Other informed sources feel there were other opportunities at various stages of the burgeoning war.

The stories of the Marigold initiative and the Wilson-Kosygin talks, for instance, suggest carelessness by the Johnson Administration about possible negotiating opportunities. Certainly, according to officials deeply involved in both instances, the coordination within the Administration was something less than outstanding.

Diplomatic Record

The record—private and public—of Vietnam diplomacy in the past three years suggests missed opportunities by the Johnson Administration to secure, if not peace, at least negotiations; if not negotiations, at least talks; if not talks, at least a propaganda advantage over the enemy which would have improved this nation's standing in the world community.

Now the United States and North Vietnam are on the threshold of direct talks that show more promise than anything that has happened so far in the three-year search for peace. One who studies the record may feel compelled to ask: Can the United States achieve a more satisfactory settlement in Vietnam today than might have been obtainable a year or more ago?

This article concludes a six-part series for The Los Angeles Times. The series will be expanded into a book, "The Secret Search for Peace in Vietnam," to be published this spring by Random House.

Philip Geyelin
The Wall Street Journal 1965
"Dominican Flashback: Behind the Scenes"

Dominican Flashbac

* * *   * * *

By Philip Geyelin

WASHINGTON — For lean, bespectacled John Bushnell, U.S. officer in charge of the rescue efforts at the Hotel Embajador in Santo Domingo, Wednesday, April 28, was one long blur of buses bringing distraught refugees to the nearby polo grounds from the American embassy, and one long, noisy clatter of hovering helicopters, hauling them out to the U.S. aircraft carrier Boxer offshore.

By 5:30 or so, he was almost too tired to be taken aback when the familiar flight of copters came whirling in, the doors burst open and out jumped a platoon of grim-faced, combat-clad Marines. With drill-field precision, they darted forward 50 paces or so, then flung themselves prone, weapons at the ready.

Mr. Bushnell, a bright, brisk, young embassy economist, remembers watching numbly, then walking over to the nearest Leatherneck, bending down to tap him on the shoulder, and inquiring politely if he could be of any help. "How do you get to the embassy?" he was asked. "It's over that way," he indicated, adding: "But it's several miles." So the Marines scrambled to their feet and hitchhiked to war in the empty buses that were already headed back for another load of evacuees.

Thus was the power, as well as the prestige, of the U.S. Government and the Johnson Administration hooked irretrievably to the outcome of the bloody and unbelievably complicated political imbroglio that had begun five days earlier to tear the Dominican Republic to bits.

The Fateful Decision

The initial plunge, on less than one hour's notice, was relatively easy, given that handy helicopter-and-bus shuttle service—once the fateful decision was made. But the story of the decision-making itself is infinitely more intriguing and considerably more complex. As U.S. diplomats struggle to get out of the Dominican mess, and a Senate committee prepares a quiet investigation of how the U.S. got in, those first five frantic days of Dominican upheaval deserve a careful look --in part for what they tell about the likely course of future events.

As revealed in official records and in conversations here and in Santo Domingo with most of the key men involved, the story suggests that even the President of the world's most powerful nation is remarkably at the mercy of events and his own subordinates' advice; that getting hooked in a foreign trouble spot is a lot easier in this hemisphere than elsewhere, because of the ominous shadow cast over all U.S. policy deliberations by the presence of Fidel Castro at the helm in Cuba; and that for this and other reasons, President Johnson was hooked, to a considerable extent, almost the moment the rebellion began.

In short, whatever else may be said for what eventually happened, the U.S. action clearly didn't even begin as the Administration says it did, as an even-handed, emergency humanitarian effort. U.S. Marines

phrased. If the policy-makers preferred, the embassy said in effect, the troops could be sent in with a mission of covering the evacuation; the clear implication was that the embassy had some other real mission in mind, such as a show of force to hearten the anti-rebel junta.

ITEM: Though Ambassador Bennett, early on the morning of April 29, was arguing against actual U.S. military intervention on behalf of the loyalists, or even against too overt U.S. association with the San Isidro camp, he told Washington he saw no harm in the fact that the junta radio was reading U.S. backing for its side into the Marine landings, if doing so would buck up the loyalists. Physical intervention, he warned Washington officials, would "take us down a tortuous path." But quite specifically, he added he was entirely ready to recommend it, if a further survey later in the morning showed the situation continuing to fall apart.

The clear conclusion from all this is that, at the very least, the embassy's concern for American lives and its yen to stop the rebel movement were inextricably interlocked. And while this is partly because the widening rebel rampage posed the main threat to life and property, the record strongly suggests that the embassy's major preoccupation, and the decisive factor in much of its counsel at almost every step of the way, was the ebb and flow of rebel fortunes, rather than the degree of danger to U.S. or other foreign nationals.

All this does not mean, of course, that Ambassador Bennett did not have life-saving much in mind, when he dashed off his urgent cable calling for the Marines. Nor does it mean that President Johnson would not have acted, as he himself privately insists, exactly as he did even if there had been no hint of Reds in the rebel woodwork. Aides insist he could not have done otherwise, once the Bennett cable was received. "It works both ways," says one official. "If you can argue that it provided the President with a handy excuse, you can also argue that it left him no alternative."

What the record also strongly suggests, however, is that the President would have been under an almost irresistible compulsion to order some sort of military intervention, even if there had been no U.S. lives at stake. The reason for thinking so can be traced almost directly to the impact on U.S. public opinion and politics of the nearby existence of a Communist Cuba. "If there hadn't already been one Cuba," says a Presidential aide, "the response might have been entirely different. But no President could accept a second Communist country in this hemisphere."

How Strong Were the Reds?

The crucial question naturally is whether a Communist government in Santo Domingo was necessarily going to develop out of the initial Dominican revolt, and here the theory of the "Cuban reflex" must be applied to the diplomats and intelligence experts on the spot. Clearly, in Santo Domingo, few of the men who were likely to be held ultimately responsible were prepared to take that chance, if it is correct to the home office by any gauge. One fact is that a full

with no more motive than that of saving lives. What the record reveals, in fact, is that from the very outset of the upheaval, there was a concerted U.S. Government effort, if not actually a formal decision, to checkmate the rebel movement by whatever means and at whatever cost. Consider these facts:

ITEM: By Sunday, April 25, just one day after the uprising got under way, while Washington remained openly confused and non-committal, the Santo Domingo embassy had clearly cast its lot with the "loyalist" military cabal and against the rebellion's original aim: The return of Juan Bosch, who had been deposed by the generals in 1963 after winning the first free election in the republic in 40 years. Restoration of the Bosch regime would be "against U.S. interests," the embassy counseled. Blocking Bosch could mean further bloodshed, the embassy conceded. Nonetheless, Washington was advised, the embassy military attaches had given "loyalist" leaders a go-ahead to do "everything possible" to prevent what was described as the danger of a "Communist take-over."

ITEM: While Washington continued to proclaim impartiality and to decry continued bloodshed, the Santo Domingo embassy, by Wednesday, was even more actively laboring in the "loyalist" cause. Communications gear was urgently requested, to help the isolated anti-rebel units maintain closer contact.

Embassy's Warning

Though regretting the necessity for a "military solution for a political crisis," the embassy went on to warn, in the afternoon of the day the Marines finally landed, that denial of communications help could so dishearten the junta forces that U.S. military intervention might well be recommended 'in the near future" to protect citizens and "possibly for other purposes." Pointedly, Washington was asked to make a choice.

ITEM: By mid-afternoon, that same decisive Wednesday, embassy officials were still against a troop landing, despite a formal request from the military junta chief, Col. Pedro Bartolome Benoit, for "unlimited" U.S. assistance, including the immediate landing of 1,200 U.S. Marines. That request, which said the revolt was of "authentic Communist stamp" and warned quite specifically of "another Cuba," was turned down. Curiously, U.S. Ambassador W. Tapley Bennett, Jr., reportedly on Washington's instructions, sent a U.S. helicopter 16 miles that evening to fetch from Col. Benoit a slimmed-down version of his original request; the new version talked only of preserving order and saving lives and was carefully stripped of any political motive or characterization of the rebels which might have invited controversy.

ITEM: Though Mr. Johnson, with the poetic license to which a politician may be entitled, was later to report that he received at 5:16 p.m. on Wednesday a cable from Ambassador Bennett, warning that "you must land troops immediately or blood will run in the streets, American blood will run in the streets," the actual message was considerably more low-key.

It did recommend the landing of Marines and did state, in one short sentence, that the lives of U.S. citizens were endangered. But it dwelt at far greater length on the rapid collapse of the anti-rebel drive and on the pathos of the weary, weeping generals in the "loyalist" headquarters at San Isidro air base. And it contained a revealing passage which for security reasons must be paraphrased:

four days before the Central Intelligence Agency in Washington was able to give the President the names of more than three Communists identified as engaged in the rebel movement, the embassy was warning darkly of "extremists" in the rebel coup and of "Communist advocacy" of Mr. Bosch's return, and framing its recommendations accordingly.

Not until his TV address on the night of May 2 did President Johnson apparently feel a case had been sufficiently documented to justify a declaration that the rebellion had been taken over by a "band of Communist conspirators." But five days earlier, Ambassador Bennett had told Washington "the issue here now is a fight between Castro-type elements and those who oppose. I do not wish to be over-dramatic but we should be clear as to the situation."

A President can ignore such counsel, but only at his political peril. For if a plea for help to save U.S. lives can be said to force a President's hand, so can an official judgment, from authorities on the spot, that a Communist take-over impends. The authorities may well be overly alarmed or simply wrong, but their opinion on the record makes it practically imperative for a U.S. President to assess the risk in a somewhat different way, on the chance that the warning may be right.

The Opera

Met, 1; New York, 0

New York City

Kurt Adler outlasted Whitey Ford the other evening. The famed Yankee southpaw, although he managed to gain a win over Kansas City, succumbed to the near-90-degree heat and gave way to a relief pitcher in the seventh inning. But over at Lewisohn Stadium, Mr. Adler, who we suspect outweighs Mr. Ford by a considerable number of pounds, doggedly went the route, conducting the second of the Metropolitan Opera's new summer concerts. Beads of sweat rolling off his forehead, his white dinner jacket understandably unbuttoned, the large conductor guided the assembled artists through a delightful potpourri packaged under the title "Great Moments From Opera."

It was a great moment for the Met. The opera company somehow emerged triumphant over the multifarious hostile forces this city conspired to throw against it. Not only was the night hot. That unwelcome newcomer to our weather reports, the air pollution index, was high and what breeze there was produced more dust than comfort in the dirt-floored stadium.

Still, the Met triumphed. Even a nearby cricket was heard to applaud when Jean Fenn, a blond and beautiful soprano, concluded Puccini's "Vissi D'arte" from "Tosca." The other singers were the dark and handsome bass, Justino Diaz, who looks like a tenor, and the dark and handsome tenor, Bruno Prevedi, who also looks like a tenor.

The enthusiastic turnout of 9,500 fans, almost as many as were watching Mr. Ford over in the Bronx, is a testament to the pulling power of the great old opera company and appliance dealers among our readers please take note also an indication that not everyone in New York yet has an air conditioner.

—A.L.M.

This "Cuban reflex," as strong in the President's office as it was in Santo Domingo, probably did more to shape U.S. official thinking and actions in the pre-landing days, in the opinion of many officials in a position to judge, than the advice of alleged "hard-liners" among his closest counselors. It's true that Under Secretary of State Thomas Mann, for one, was quicker to read a Red threat into the Dominican conflict than others in the President's high command; but there's also scant evidence of serious official dissent from the actions taken in the crisis' early days.

This doesn't mean, of course, that the Johnson Administration will be moved to ship in Marines at every sign of a Red threat. What the record of the Dominican affair does suggest to a good many diplomats, however, is the Johnsonian response to any Latin leftist political movement is likely to be quicker and sharper than that of his predecessor, even at the risk of offending Latin sensibilities. What the record also suggests is a sometimes-carefree, sometimes-clumsy tendency toward inconsistency, contradiction and even outright misrepresentation for the sake of expediency.

None of this is likely to matter much, to be sure, if the U.S. can achieve its admittedly ambitious Dominican aims: The quashing of any serious Communist take-over threat; the barring of another Dominican dictatorship; a popular, "broadly-based" government, installed by decree on a provisional basis at first, perhaps, but then by honest vote. If, in the process, there emerges a strengthened, more effective Organization of American States, capable of moving against Communist conspiracies and uprisings, the whole affair could become a resounding plus.

But let the situation crumble, as it could on short notice in that fragile nation, and history, not to mention the Congressional probers, will almost certainly subject the whole affair to more penetrating assault. In that case, the Administration may find less safety behind the earthworks of public statements and private "background" briefings, hastily and often belatedly thrown up to defend successive intervention moves.

Impossible to Prove

One reason is that the central point in the Administration argument—that the rebel movement had fallen under Communist control—is, by the nature of things, impossible to prove. Most experts agree that nobody will probably ever know just how great was the Communist threat. Ironically, it was probably at its worst when the Administration was talking solely of saving lives; U.S. Intelligence reports now concede that it began to diminish a day or so after the President, in his May 2 television speech, pronounced the U.S. purpose to be "to help prevent another Communist state in this hemisphere."

Administration officials argue, naturally, that this easing of the threat was only to be expected with U.S. troops foreclosing total rebel victory, and therefore shows that the landing of American forces had precisely the desired effect. But a look at the chronology still leaves open the question of whether, well before the troops got orders to go,

conviction that if they didn't something drastic would have to be done.

Events on Tuesday, April 27, throw more light on the U.S. attitude. Law and order had almost completely broken down; evacuation of civilians had begun; in the morning, shooting erupted in the midst of a group of U.S. citizens swarming in front of the Hotel Embajador. Though U.S. officials quickly laid the blame on rebel ruffians, later accounts indicate that the firing was started by anti-rebel sympathizers, as one of their number was being hauled away by the rebel gang.

In any event, this was, as far as can be discovered, the closest U.S. citizens came to the sort of mass slaughter the Administration later pictured as their likely fate if the Marines did not intervene. Yet on Tuesday there was no appeal to Washington to intervene—which might be accounted for by the hardening conviction that the crisis was easing and that the rebel movement, together with the Red takeover threat, was in the process of defeat. U.S. officials in Santo Domingo won't concede this was the case. But they did have good reason to anticipate a rebel collapse.

The first hint of collapse came at 3:00 p.m. that day, when Col. Francisco Caamano Denó, Col. Miguel Angel Hernando Ramirez and six associates showed up at the embassy and were shown into the office of Benjamin J. Ruyle, embassy first secretary. Unanimously they asked for U.S. help in arranging a cease-fire; when the point was made that rebel "President" Molina ought to be in on the discussion, Mr. Ruyle suggested they seek him out together at the palace; when the rebels said that was too dangerous, because of the junta strafing, the embassy official boldly set out without them.

As Mr. Ruyle describes it, "President" Molina was ultimately found "huddled in a tiny corridor deep inside the palace" surrounded by a handful of men. Defeated but defiant, he first resisted, then agreed to try to seek a cease-fire under strong urging from Mr. Ruyle—urging which throws sharply into question rebel charges that Ambassador Bennett rudely rebuffed the rebels in a second, better-publicized encounter later in the day, and refused to cooperate in promoting a cease-fire.

Ambassador Bennett did indeed decline to sit in on cease-fire talks, on the ground that he had no authority for that. He also read the rebels a stern lecture for allowing Communists to "take advantage of their legitimate movement" and charged that Red infiltration and influence were undeniable. But most important, he got the impression, reinforced by Mr. Molina's plunge into asylum that Tuesday night, that there was little chance of rebel victory.

"Started Up Again"

"I went to bed that night thinking it was all over," recalls Mr. Ruyle. "The next day I woke up and it had started up again."

What started it up, most analysts think, was nothing more than the result of General Wessin to risk his depleted force of tanks across the Duarte bridge, in a real drive to mop up the rebel troops. When the tanks were advancing toward the city, the rebel Col. Caamano was the loud- [illegible]

meat ... not ... ... the ... of serious Communist taint, especially if it had received timely U.S. support.

On Saturday, April 24, when the first uprising began, everybody, including most of the important Dominican figures, was confused. In fact, the first move came from pro-Bosch members of his Popular Democratic Party (whose initials, in Spanish, come out PRD), which had been busily recruiting cohorts from the army and was, reportedly, originally aiming at a D-Day in early June. But President Donald Reid Cabral got wind of their activities, and when he tried to nip the coup by arresting suspect officers, the rebels struck.

What made it especially confusing, however, is that there was one and possibly two other coups working at the time. Brig. Gen. Antonio Imbert, who is now head of the anti-rebel junta, even dropped in on one of the military camps seized by the rebels, just to see if it was his kind of coup. Gen. Elias Wessin y Wessin is said to have thought, at first, that the outbreak was part of a revolt he was currently working up—such is the secrecy involved in such endeavors—and only got around to leading the fight against it when he discovered it was pro-Bosch, the man he had helped throw out in 1963.

Another Group at Work

Still another group of politicians and military men, it's said, was working quietly to topple President Reid in favor of the return of Joaquin Balaguer, exiled one-time figurehead president under dictator Rafael Trujillo.

This fragmentation probably saved the rebellion from a quick demise. By the end of Saturday, Reid forces had actually recaptured Radio Santo Domingo, which had fallen to the pro-Bosch faction, and the rebellion seemed to be sputtering out. But, on Sunday, a second rebellion flared as disgruntled right-wing generals saw a chance to dispose of President Reid, who promptly resigned. The initial upshot was no government, and a new lease on life for the rebels: arms stocks were broken into, weapons handed out to civilians, and according to an official U.S. record of events, known Communists began actively to exploit the anarchy that was setting in.

However, not even this Government "white paper," parts of which have been circulated to newsmen, claims the Reds were in the driver's seat. Moreover, its detailed and impressive documentation of Communist activity suffers from a serious flaw as a chronology of events: Most of its findings were collected as much as 48 hours after the fact; indeed, the record begins by declaring that "much of the information concerning the first few days was obtained only after the landing of U.S. forces, April 28." So, however right U.S. embassy experts may subsequently have been proven to be in their initial hostility to the rebel forces, they had little if any current and convincing evidence.

By Monday a rebel government of sorts, under Bosch supporter and PRD leader Rafael Molina Urena, had been installed in the palace, but the embassy obviously did not consider it either Communist-proof or in control. The local U.S. sympathies, by that time, were plainly with the military junta and the forces under Gen. Wessin's command, which were beginning to shell and strafe rebel strong-points, including the national palace. U.S. policy, officially, was promotion of a cease-fire. Unofficially, the embassy's attitude seemed to consist of a hope that the Wessin forces would prevail, and a

when the talks stopped, ... who was to become boss of the rebel forces popped up again.

For most of Wednesday, April 28, the Santo Domingo war-watchers clung to the hope that the San Isidro generals would turn the tide. But the trend was all toward increased chaos, with stepped-up sniping at U.S. and other embassies. "Power," as one official puts it, "was in the streets," and in such circumstances there's little doubt that the disciplined Red agitators, no matter how large their number, were in the best position to gain.

By the time the urgent Bennett cable finally crackled into the White House "situation room" on Wednesday afternoon and was rushed to the President, the final decision-making was almost a formality. The Boxer had been moved into position on Sunday; a raft of "contingency" plans had been prepared. The President was meeting, on Southeast Asia, with Secretary of State Rusk, Under Secretary of State Ball, Secretary of Defense McNamara and special White House Assistant McGeorge Bundy, and a call was quickly made to Tom Mann, who was meeting with his staff; but even before Mr. Mann telephoned back his recommendations in favor of a troop landing, the men in the White House had concluded there was no other course.

Efforts were made, belatedly, to notify the OAS. But even if the hemisphere group had been in session, it's unlikely Mr. Johnson would have asked it to approve the landings of Marines; he felt there wasn't time, and he feared a refusal would force him to defy the group. He decided instead to work to bring an OAS "presence" as quickly as possible into the act.

Aides estimate Mr. Johnson made 35 telephone calls in five days on the Dominican situation, and met formally with his advisers a half-dozen times. In the last analysis, he was certainly moved by the threat to U.S. citizens; but other events and other pressures had done a lot to force his Hand.

THE WALL STREET JOURNAL.

DOW JONES & COMPANY, INC.

Publisher — Founded 1882

11501 COLUMBIA PIKE, SILVER SPRING, MD
Zip Code 20910 — Telephone: (301) 622-2000
WASHINGTON NEWS AND SALES OFFICES
1015 14th St., N.W. 20005 — (202) 783-0164

BERNARD KILGORE
PRESIDENT

WILLIAM F. KERBY
VICE PRESIDENT AND EDITORIAL DIRECTOR

BUREN H. McCORMACK
VICE PRESIDENT AND EDITORIAL DIRECTOR

ROBERT BOTTORFF   VERMONT ROYSTER
EXECUTIVE EDITOR   EDITOR

SUBSCRIPTION RATES (Mail) — United States, territories and possessions, and Canada: $26 yearly, six months $14, three months $7.50; less than three months 15 cents a copy but not more than $7.50. Other countries: $36 yearly, six months $19, three months $10; less than three months 20 cents a copy but not more than $10. Postage paid.

Subscriptions and Changes of Address should be sent to The Wall Street Journal, 11501 Columbia Pike, Silver Spring, Md. 20910, giving old and new addresses in requesting changes.

NEWS OFFICES: ATLANTA, BOSTON, CHICAGO, CHICOPEE, Mass., CLEVELAND, DALLAS, DETROIT, HONG KONG, LONDON, LOS ANGELES, MONTREAL, NEW YORK, OTTAWA, PARIS, PHILADELPHIA, PITTSBURGH, SAN FRANCISCO, St. LOUIS, TOKYO, TORONTO, WASHINGTON, D.C., WHITE OAK, Md.

The Associated Press is exclusively entitled to republish news dispatches originated by The Wall Street Journal. All other republication rights are reserved.

Max Frankel

New Master Strategy Plan Under White House Study

Policy-Makers' Guide to Replace Eisenhower's —Rostow in Charge

WASHINGTON, April 15—A new master plan of the nation's objectives, strategies and tactics has been written in the Administration and is moving toward more formal review.

President Kennedy and the National Security Council are expected soon to look over the plan before it is officially adopted as a replacement for the national policy paper left over from the Eisenhower Administration.

The White House, State Department, Pentagon and Treasury are known to be some of the departments that contributed to the writing of the report, now in its third draft. Walt W. Rostow, counselor and chairman of the Policy Planning Council of the State Department, has shepherded the plan around the Government.

The document of nearly 300 pages is to remain secret and for the guidance of policy makers only. Persons familiar with it say it offers no sweeping

Associated Press
Walt W. Rostow

new policies, but does point to a number of ambiguities that require prompt attention by many departments of the Government.

The most notable feature of the plan is that it does not gloss over disagreements with-

Continued on Page 14, Column 3

NEW MASTER PLAN ON STRATEGY DUE

Continued From Page 1, Col. 3

in the Administration. It contains a list of disputed policies and concepts and commentary on the difficulties these differences have posed.

In the past, officials point out, there has been a tendency here to "negotiate the language" on disputed points so that partisans of different concepts can accept the wording and interpret it to suit their own ideas. The practice often left only the illusion of an agreed policy.

Some of the differences in the new plan are said to be in the areas of strategic military planning and in sections dealing with the objectives of foreign aid. But since the plan also covers foreign policy, fiscal policy and national goals, there are probably other differences as well.

Completion Deferred

Completion of the master plan was deferred until the second year of the Kennedy Administration to give various agencies and officials time to learn their functions and to test their policy ideas.

According to an article by the Washington correspondent of The Chicago Sun-Times, Thomas B. Ross, the plan is said to include recommenda-

Good Use of Time

Most of the young men on active duty in the armed forces are not professional soldiers. Most plan to return to schools, factories or offices. Consequently, many looked upon the two, three, or four years on military duty as time lost. It could be if an individual made no effort to continue his education or acquire training and experience in his chosen field.

Realizing this, the U. S. O. has developed programs directed at helping young men take advantage of the many opportunities available in the armed forces. In New York, for example, a committee made up of retired senior business executives was organized a few years ago to counsel young G. I.'s.

Your contribution can help the U. S. O. continue to help young service men. Why not send a check today to the New York City U. S. O., 150 Fifth Avenue?

tions for a still greater build-up of the nation's capacity to wage conventional warfare.

In this it is said to follow some public declarations by Administration members who argue that even in the event of war the nuclear bombardment of major civilian targets should be avoided with an enemy. Mr. Ross also reports a provision in the plan that the

United States would never strike the first nuclear blow unless it were faced with a massive conventional assault, such as a full-scale invasion of Western Europe.

Administration sources refused to comment on this and other partial reports of the plan's content.

...sometimes, the big [...] of forces here do not accept the judgment of some analysts and journalists that the operation was ill conceived or that the military results failed to justify the costs.

They are asking the President to keep in view its essential purpose: the disruption of North Vietnamese supply operations so that South Vietnam could be spared major military challenges through another period of American troop reductions.

Emboldened by the disruption of Hanoi's supply routes and bases in Cambodia last year, which brought relative tranquillity to the southern regions of South Vietnam, the Nixon Administration had hoped to win a similar respite for Cambodia and the northern parts of South Vietnam for a period stretching well into 1972.

The largest gain claimed for the operation, therefore, is the pre-emption of enemy supplies and energies to ward off big attacks that would have been mounted over the coming year.

Heavy Toll of Enemy

The North Vietnamese are believed to have suffered at least as many casualties as the South Vietnamese and probably many more, from saturation United States bombing if not from engagements on the ground. They have been forced to use the better part of the dry season and their best reserves to repel the invasion. They will probably need a good part of the coming year to recuperate and to re-establish supply lines.

"When you ask whether it was worthwhile," a senior official remarked. "you have to ask whether you are better off than we would have been if we had not gone into Laos. Obviously, we are."

By that the President's men mean in a better position to continue the withdrawal of American forces without risking major North Vietnamese challenges. They think the South Vietnamese fought well under trying circumstances. They believe in any case that by buying time they have given the Saigon Government an even longer period in which to prepare to assume the total defense of its territory.

They had expected Hanoi to build up its forces for an effort to strike hard against the South Vietnamese Army some time before the presidential election in South Vietnam this fall, and they had expected major assaults against American forces next winter and spring to influence the course of political debate in the United States.

Revival of Opposition

What the officials are asking themselves—if not the President—is whether the high military costs inflicted so much political damage on President Nixon, and perhaps also on President Nguyen Van Thieu, as to negate the benefits they had wanted to achieve.

It is acknowledged around the White House that opposition to Mr. Nixon's tactics of gradual withdrawal has been reignited by the invasion. He has lost ground in his bid for public support, they say, and cannot afford to lose much more without also losing flexibility in working for the survival of a non-Communist regime in Saigon.

They can only hope that Mr. Nixon will use the coming months to repair his standing and that Mr. Thieu can ward off challenges to his leadership.

At the middle levels of Government here, the re-examination of the Laos venture has provoked quarrels about responsibility for the poor intelligence. There is also a continuing debate about the accuracy and value of the calculations being made to assess the degree of disruption or diversion of North Vietnamese supplies.

Nixon's Aides Insist Drive In Laos Was Worth Price

MAR 30 1971

By MAX FRANKEL

Special to The New York Times

WASHINGTON, March 29—President Nixon has begun to review the post-mortem studies of the South Vietnamese invasion of Laos, which cover some serious military misjudgments as well as claims of strategic benefit.

The President is being advised that the allies badly underestimated North Vietnam's battlefield strength while overestimating their own. Yet, despite the high costs and the failure to realize maximum objectives, he is being asked to take comfort from the fact that more time was gained for the defense of South Vietnam and the continuing withdrawal of American forces.

Mr. Nixon is starting to look through the materials and analyses at his seaside retreat in San Clemente, Calif., to determine how to give the nation a further explanation of the Laotian venture, and how to profit from the experience in policy planning.

Some of the officials who helped assemble the materials doubt that the President, even in his own mind, will alter the judgment that the invasion was worthwhile. But they think that the presumed advantages, bought at such high cost in battle, must be weighed against political losses at home, and, possibly, in Saigon. They expect that no one here will feel comfortable about the outcome for many months, at best.

The most conspicuous tactical setbacks are being attributed to intelligence failures. Mr. Nixon is being told that no one expected the North Vietnamese to be able to reinforce their units in Laos as quickly as they did or to supply them with 150 tanks and other heavy equipment in time to stage a massive counterattack.

Moreover, American air cover for the invading South Vietnamese is judged to have been much less effective than planned at early but critical stages of the six-week operation. Flights by helicopters and tactical support aircraft were hampered not only by poor weather but also by poor co-ordination with South Vietnamese guides and controllers on the ground.

Together those misjudgments are believed to have virtually eliminated the advantages in firepower and mobility contemplated for the 20,000-man invasion force. As they became

Continued on Page 9, Column 1

DRIVE WORTH COST, NIXON'S AIDES SAY

Continued From Page 1, Col. 7

apparent, American military commanders wanted to rush reinforcements into the region, but their request was rejected by the Saigon Government and perhaps also by Washington.

The surprising enemy resistance, it is acknowledged, cut short both the reach and the duration of the invasion. It resulted in a casualty rate of at least 25 per cent, and perhaps as much as 50 per cent, for the South Vietnamese, with as yet incalculable effects on their morale. And it left the North Vietnamese with at least a month more of relatively good weather to resume the shipment of men and supplies through the Laotian trails toward Cambodia and South Vietnam.

Nonetheless, the highest officials here do not accept the judgment of some analysts and journalists that the operation was ill-conceived or that the military results failed to justify the costs.

They are asking the President to keep in view its essential purpose: the disruption of North Vietnamese supply operations so that South Vietnam could be spared major military challenges through another period of American troop reductions.

Emboldened by the disruption of Hanoi's supply routes and bases in Cambodia last year, which brought relative tranquillity to the southern regions of South Vietnam, the Nixon Administration had hoped to win a similar respite for Cambodia and the northern parts of South Vietnam for a period stretching well into 1972.

The largest gain claimed for the operation, therefore, is the pre-emption of enemy supplies and energies to ward off big attacks that would have been mounted over the coming year.

Heavy Toll of Enemy

The North Vietnamese are believed to have suffered at least as many casualties as the South Vietnamese and probably many more, from saturation United States bombing if not from engagements on the ground. They have been forced to use the better part of the dry season and their best reserves to repel the invasion. They will probably need a good part of the coming year to recuperate and to re-establish supply lines.

"When you ask whether it was worthwhile," a senior official remarked, "you have to ask whether you are better off than we would have been if we had not gone into Laos. Obviously, we are."

By that the President's men mean in a better position to continue the withdrawal of American forces without risking major North Vietnamese challenges. They think the South Vietnamese fought well under trying circumstances. They believe in any case that by buying time they have given the Saigon Government an even longer period in which to prepare to assume the total defense of its territory.

They had expected Hanoi to build up its forces for an effort to strike hard against the South Vietnamese Army some time before the presidential election in South Vietnam this fall, and they had expected major assaults against American forces next winter and spring to influence the course of political debate in the United States.

Revival of Opposition

What the officials are asking themselves—and not the President—is whether the high military costs offset or not a political danger to President Nixon and, perhaps, to President Nguyen Van Thieu as to restore the hopes of the Democrats...

It is a sensitive account that the White House does not...

Nixon Aides Reported to Debate Setting Of a Definite Date for Ending War Role

By MAX FRANKEL
Special to The New York Times

WASHINGTON, Feb. 28— There is said to be a subtle but intensive debate in the upper ranks of the Government about whether President Nixon should now commit himself to the definite termination of American involvement in the Indochina war.

It is not, so far as can be determined, one of those flaring controversies about ultimate aims. President Nixon and his advisers are unanimous in wishing to disengage. He is committed to a continuing and irreversible withdrawal of American ground troops until the "bulk" of them are gone.

But there is reported to be a significant difference of opinion whether the United States should move toward disengagement with some ambiguity about its future participation in the war or with firm notice now—to the Saigon Government and American military planners—that the President intends to let the South Vietnamese fend for themselves by a certain and relatively early date.

Nixon Remains Flexible

According to officials, the case for scheduling the end of American participation is being pressed by Secretary of Defense Melvin R. Laird. He is believed to have the close support of Secretary of State William P. Rogers, who has been heard to say that the problem was something like teaching a child to ride a bike—at some point the instructor must decide simply "to let go."

Judging by his State of the World message and other recent policy declarations, President Nixon has not yet reached that point. Apparently preferring the advice of his national security adviser, Henry A. Kissinger, some of the members of the Joint Chiefs of Staff and leading American officials in Saigon, the President is trying, throughout the period of withdrawal, to retain some flexibility.

Without doubting Mr. Nixon's intention to keep reducing the American involvement, Mr. Laird and others appear to believe that neither the Saigon Government nor American military commanders clearly understand their responsibilities in this ambiguous situation. Moreover, they contend that the availability of American combat support will continue to stimulate reliance upon it.

Mr. Nixon, however, seems to believe that if political or diplomatic considerations ever require it, he can always fix a final withdrawal date—but not now.

Meanwhile, he has served notice that some American troops will remain in South Vietnam until Hanoi agrees to release all American prisoners. He has promised—if needed—"high levels of American assistance in air operations" to the South Vietnamese not only in their own country but also in Cambodia, Laos and—if they were ever to deem it wise—in North Vietnam. He has threatened increased bombing of North Vietnam if allied forces feel menaced in the south and has offered total withdrawal only as part of an over-all Indochina peace settlement.

Diplomatic Considerations

The case for such flexibility and "open options" seems to rest on both diplomatic and military considerations.

It is argued that a commitment to disengagement from all ground and air combat by a specified date would destroy whatever slim chance still remains of persuading North Vietnam to negotiate in over-all settlement.

It is argued even more strongly that Saigon's forces are not yet able to handle every possible military challenge and that their confidence will develop faster if they can rely on some degree of American help in battle.

It is argued that as long as troop withdrawals continue and American casualty rates decline the American people can be persuaded to support a relatively flexible battlefield posture.

The case for a decision to terminate appears to come from concern about both the risks and costs of a drawn-out involvement. It is argued that the American field commanders, so long as they are charged with some responsibility for the course of battle, will continue to be tempted to move against enemy supply lines and concentrations in ways that may be militarily sound but may also heighten Saigon's reliance on American support.

It is also argued that the Saigon Government will not fully face up to both the military and economic consequences of total American disengagement until it is clearly ordered, with corollary schedules for the withdrawal from ground combat, for the total turnover of air support and equipment transfers and other related activities.

Those favoring a deadline for withdrawal also contend that further delay can no longer bring the kind of military results in Southeast Asia that would offset the drain on defense energies and the deferral of other military projects needed to match the more worrisome Soviet advances in both strategic and naval power.

Mr. Laird is said to be trying to introduce the word "terminate" into the official vocabulary describing American intentions in Vietnam—with or without a private timetable. He has tried to speak publicly of "accelerated" withdrawals of troops, to fix a date this spring for the end of American participation in ground combat and to suggest that Saigon will be ready to assume air combat duties much sooner than previously expected.

Americans in Saigon are reported to have complained against such rhetorical pressure, contending that too much has been invested and too much achieved to arouse anxiety and fear among the South Vietnamese at this stage.

Troop Withdrawals

The White House has pulled back from some statements by Mr. Laird and Mr. Rogers that American combat duties in Vietnam would be ended next May. But the President has promised "an announcement" on that subject later this year. He has also promised another target for troop withdrawals in April, by which time the American forces in Vietnam are scheduled to number 284,000.

At least half of these, and probably more, are to be pulled out over the next 12 months, and there has been discussion of maintaining a residual force of 60,000 men or less by the start of the Presidential election campaign in 1972. It is not so much the size as the mission of this constantly dwindling force that is being debated now.

... could not be determined over the
last 10 days whether Israeli
planes heading for the canal
region have approached
Egyptian air space. MIG-21's
in pairs and fours with Russian-speaking pilots at the controls are reported to have
scrambled from three different
bases in pursuit patterns. According to the Israelis, they
have made ready to attack any
intruder of the interior regions.

The planes are believed to
bear Egyptian markings, but
they have not been observed
by Israeli pilots. At least 50
different Soviet fliers are
said to have been overheard
on many more sorties.

The anxiety prompted by the
Soviet operations in Egypt ex-
tends in several directions.
These include the following:

¶President Nixon has repeatedly cautioned the Soviet Union
against "steps which could have
the effect of drawing the major
powers more deeply into the
Arab-Israeli conflict." He said
in his state-of-the-world message that he would view any
effort by the Soviet Union "to
seek predominance in the
Middle East as a matter of
grave concern."

¶The still developing involvement of Soviet fliers and soldiers in Egypt is seen here as
an extension of Moscow's bid
for "predominance." It is also
seen as a commitment to the
United Arab Republic from
which the Soviet Union could
not easily withdraw in case of
still more intense fighting there.

Moreover, through the
United States has no treaty
commitments for the defense of
Israel, it is pledged to supply
her with enough arms to preserve "the military balance" in
the area—meaning Israels ca-
cacity to defend herself. In
postponing action on Israel's
latest request for additional
Phantom and Skyhawk planes
last month, Secretary of State
William P. Rogers said that "if
steps are taken which might
upset the current balance or
if in our judgement political
developments warrant, the
President will not hesitate to
reconsider this matter."

¶The Nixon Administration
interpreted this delay as an act
of "restraint" and pleaded with
Moscow to follow its example,
despite earlier threats.

Premier Aleksei N. Kosygin
had written to President Nixon
early in February that if Israel
continued her raids into central
Egypt then the Soviet Union
"will be forced to see to it
that the Arab states have
means at their disposal with
the help of which a due rebuff
to the arrogant aggressor could
be made."

American officials now believe this message may have
been misleading and that arrangements for Egypt's air defense were actually concluded
late in January, during President Gamal Abdel Nasser's visit to Moscow. Israeli officials
tend to believe that Moscow
has been testing American responses one step at a time and
that the now evident flight operations were determined only
after Washington postponed
any further commitments on
the sale of aircraft to the Israelis.

¶Either way, at least some
officials here are seriously concerned that Moscow chose to
act more boldly in the Middle
East in the belief that the Nixon
Administration was mired down
in Southeastern Asia and was
prevented by public opinion
from any decisive defense of
American interests abroad.

Israeli Army Declines Comment
Special to The New York Times

Jerusalem, April 28—An Israeli Army spokesman declined
tonight to confirm a report
from Washington that Israeli
sources had said Russian pilots
were flying air cover in Egyptian aircraft over the United
Arab Republic.

He said that it had been
known for some time that Russian pilots were flying recon-
naisance missions in Egyptian
aircraft over the Mediterranean,
but he could add nothing about
flying air cover over Egyptian
territory.

Reports to this effect began
circulating abroad some weeks
ago. Israeli military officials
said at the time that they had
no independent information to
support this speculation and
have not confirmed it since
then, officially or unofficially.

RUSSIAN AIRMEN BELIEVED FLYING MISSIONS IN U.A.R.

APR 29 '70

But Evidence in Washington Indicates Role Is Defense of Egyptian Interior

---

U.S. CONCERN MOUNTING

No Direct Clashes Reported —Israelis Limiting Their Targets to Canal Area

By MAX FRANKEL
Special to The New York Times

WASHINGTON, April 28 — There is growing evidence that Soviet pilots are now participating in the defense of central Egypt against penetration raids by the Israeli Air Force. But no direct clashes have been reported so far.

Israeli diplomats say that their Government has become convinced over the last 10 days that Russian-speaking pilots flying MIG-21's are scrambling into attack formations at almost every potential approach by an Israeli plane, with orders to intercept.

United States officials are still studying their own intelligence reports, but in what is visibly an atmosphere of mounting concern. An intensified Soviet involvement in the Middle East fighting would be expected to have a serious effect on the balance of forces there.

Jets Reported Pursued

While Soviet and Israeli fliers have not made direct contact or exchanged any fire, the Israelis report that two of their planes were pursued by eight Soviet-flown MIG fighters on April 18, the day that a new pattern of Soviet operations was first detected.

The Israelis say that they have been careful since then to avoid provocative flights beyond the Suez Canal region, in which they have concentrated most of their recent bombing attacks. The Soviet pilots, in turn, are said to have been careful so far to avoid the canal region, as if to signal a primary interest at this time in the defense of Cairo and other population centers around which they have been emplacing modern SAM-3 antiaircraft missiles since early March.

Considerable Effect Seen

If the Russians' purpose is to deter Israeli attacks on Cairo and Alexandria and on the Soviet missile sites, their action has already had a considerable effect. The last announced Israeli raid on targets in the Egyptian interior was on April 13. The two planes that turned tail at the approach of Soviet-flown MIG's on April 18 are said to have been on a reconnaissance mission. The Israelis say that none of their planes have penetrated so deeply since.

Neither American nor Israeli officials would discuss the detailed intelligence information on which they must base their judgments.

It had been established for some time that Russian-speaking pilots were flying reconnaissance missions in Soviet

Continued on Page 8, Column 1

RUSSIAN AIRMEN SAID TO AID U.A.R.

Continued From Page 1, Col. 8

planes with Egyptian markings over the Mediterranean, close to the vessels of the United States Sixth Fleet. Soviet pilots have also flown training missions in Egypt, presumably for the benefit of Egyptian fliers and ground controllers.

But this pattern of activity is said to have changed drastically earlier this month. The Israelis believe that the Russians are assuming responsibility — with missiles and planes — for the defense of most of the United Arab Republic, thus freeing the best Egyptian pilots for more combat duty near the Suez Canal and beyond it in the Israeli-occupied Sinai Peninsula. They also fear that Soviet pilots will eventually be ordered to join in the defense of the canal region, making a direct clash inevitable.

Even the most cautious analysts here appear to believe that the new flight operations by Russian-speaking pilots are designed, at the least, to train Soviet fliers for the active air defense of Egypt under combat conditions and to lead the Israelis to believe that they are in fact performing that mission.

At supersonic speeds, however, the destination of an oncoming Israeli fighter-bomber cannot be determined. Over the last 10 days, whenever Israeli planes heading for the canal region have approached Egyptian air space, MIG-21's in pairs and fours with Russian-speaking pilots at the controls are reported to have scrambled from three different bases in pursuit patterns. According to the Israelis, they have made ready to attack any intruder of the interior regions.

The planes are believed to bear Egyptian markings, but they have not been observed by Israeli pilots. At least 50 different Soviet fliers are said to have been overheard on many more sorties.

The anxiety prompted by the Soviet operations in Egypt extends in several directions. These include the following:

¶President Nixon has repeatedly cautioned the Soviet Union against "steps which could have the effect of drawing the major powers more deeply into the Arab-Israeli conflict." He said in his state-of-the-world message that he would view any effort by the Soviet Union "to seek predominance in the Middle East as a matter of grave concern."

¶The still developing involvement of Soviet fliers and soldiers in Egypt is seen here as an extension of Moscow's bid for "predominance." It is also seen as a commitment to the United Arab Republic from which the Soviet Union could not easily withdraw in case of still more intense fighting there.

Moreover, through the United States has no treaty commitments for the defense of Israel, it is pledged to supply her with enough arms to preserve "the military balance" in the area—meaning Israel's capacity to defend herself. In postponing action on Israel's latest request for additional Phantom and Skyhawk planes last month, Secretary of State William P. Rogers said that "if steps are taken which might upset the current balance or if in our judgment political developments warrant, the President will not hesitate to reconsider this matter."

¶The Nixon Administration interpreted this delay as an act of "restraint" and pleaded with Moscow to follow its example, despite earlier threats.

Premier Aleksei N. Kosygin had written to President Nixon early in February that if Israel continued her raids into central Egypt then the Soviet Union "will be forced to see to it that the Arab states have means at their disposal with the help of which a due rebuff to the arrogant aggressor could be made."

American officials now believe this message may have been misleading and that arrangements for Egypt's air defense were actually concluded late in January, during President Gamal Abdel Nasser's visit to Moscow. Israeli officials tend to believe that Moscow has been testing American reactions one step at a time and that the new missiles flights can proceed because little, if any, adverse Washington reaction has been forthcoming.

Johnson's Council of War Advises Him Not to Undertake Any Basic Change of Course

Continued From Page 1, Col. 7

he wisdom of a quick thrust by ground troops into and out of the southern sectors of North Vietnam to break up major troop concentrations. But even they, it is said, are not advocating an invasion of the North.

Neither does there appear to be any advice to end the bombing of the North permanently, to retreat to enclaves in South Vietnam or otherwise to reduce the scale of the fighting in any major way.

It is impossible to tell whether this relative unanimity of counsel reflects Mr. Johnson's choice of intimates in the first place or their rather uniform accommodation to his views and predicament. It appears, however, that while he suffers abuse and dissent in public, the President can now usually find relative comfort and support in his most relaxed private moments.

Who advises what, and which advice counts for most in the White House these days, is beyond the ken even of some of the closest advisers. On any important problem, Mr. Johnson reaches far and wide for ideas and for a discreet and familiar audience of friends before whom he can talk out his own. How and when his judgment is finally made on a matter remains a mystery even to most White House staff members.

No one around him, therefore, doubted the accuracy of President's admonition to reporters last Wednesday when he was asked to discuss the arguments for and against a bombing pause.

"I would admonish and caution all of you," he said, "to avoid irresponsibility and quit grabbing out of the air these speculative future 'ventures about which we [meaning Mr. Johnson himself] know very little and about which the folks that apparently are guessing for you know nothing."

It is generally known, however, to whom the President turns relatively often for special counsel.

Unofficial Advisers

Highest in his regard among unofficial Washington advisers are Clark M. Clifford, a lawyer, and Supreme Court Justice Abe Fortas. Both are old friends to whom Mr. Johnson has entrusted the most sensitive political missions and whose views he solicits on many public issues.

Their judgment on Vietnam issues ranks particularly high because they opposed the 37-day bombing pause in 1965-'66 against all of Mr. Johnson's official advisers and because he came to believe that they had been right. They argued that the doveish critics of the war would not be appeased by the gesture and that Hanoi's predictable rejection of negotiations would only agitate the hawks who believe Mr. Johnson is not fighting hard enough.

A similar debate is again shaping up around the President, and there is reason to believe that these friends have changed their views. Nonetheless some advisers, probably including Arthur J. Goldberg, the chief United States delegate to the United Nations, are said to be urging at least a partial pause of some kind so as to prove to the critics that their hope of early negotiations is illusory.

Mr. Clifford has done more than advise. He traveled to Asia as a full member of the President's delegation a year and again last summer.

Gen. Maxwell D. Taylor to assess the situation in Saigon and the mood of Asian allies involved in the fighting. General Taylor and Henry Cabot Lodge, former Ambassador to South Vietnam, are also special consultants to the President.

General Taylor had volunteered to help Mr. Johnson during the 37-day pause. He appears to have a particular affection and respect for the President has tried to against critics who might charge that the maneuver was costing lives on the battlefield. Recently, however, he reported the feeling of military men in Vietnam that a pause would indeed be costly, reports that raised the possibility of a damaging challenge by senior officers in an election year if the President attempts another pause.

Mr. Johnson seeks the political as well as policy judgment of many members of Congress. Governors and party chairmen, that permit cooperation in other spheres.

The President has tried to placate the interest of Senator Mike Mansfield of Montana, Senator Wayne Morse, Democrat of Oregon, in some new initiative on Vietnam at the United Nations. But they are though much affection remains between Mr. Johnson and Mr.

The President's Senate critics on Vietnam, some of whom once had close ties with Mr. Johnson, have largely been reduced to correct relationships.

Day in and day out, the most influential policy advisers, of course, are Secretary of State Dean Rusk and Defense Secretary Robert S. McNamara. And the interest of Senator Richard B. Russell, Democrat of Georgia, Senator Everett McKinley Dirksen of Illinois, the minority leader, and Senator Richard B. Russell has been ill for long periods in the last year but Mr. Dirksen is a regular social guest at the White House.

their active collaboration on education and labor matters.

Day in and day out, the most strictly military action as over-all intimate advisers, even that all three men leave the table agreed on every significant matter. Contrary to public impression, officials say, Mr. Rusk often shows as much or more concern for inhibiting military involvement, and the Secretary of State. Just behind them in access Komer, who is in charge of the pacification program in the countryside, and Gen. William C. Westmoreland, the military commander.

Vietnam — Ambassador Ellsworth Bunker, who manages interests in the politics of Saigon, are Walt W. Rostow, Mr. Johnson's special program for extending stability in Vietnam at the White House.

Vice President Humphrey is a vigorous supporter of the President's Asian policies and was an early advocate of intervention in that country; the President's Joint Chiefs of Staff, whose influence appears to have grown with the nation's military involvement, and to sit regularly among the official policy planners.

Johnson's Council of War

NOV 5 - '67 By MAX FRANKEL

Special to The New York Times

WASHINGTON, Nov. 4—The indications around the White House are that the most intimate advice on Vietnam now reaching President Johnson includes some proposals for tactical policy adjustments but none for any basic change in course.

Some of Mr. Johnson's most trusted counselors, in and out of Government, are said to be urging changes that range from a pause in the bombing of North Vietnam to the mining of Haiphong harbor. And Mr. Johnson is weighing these ideas with varying degrees of interest, officials say.

But in his talks with the highest and closest officials, with New Deal friends, Texas companions and old Senate colleagues—most of whom think of Mr. Johnson's political problems at home as well as the battlefield realities—the President is said to be hearing no profound dissent of either a hawkish or dovish nature.

Some military men have occasionally speculated about

Continued on Page 7, Column 1

Seven-Hour Meeting

Mr. Schwebel is a former State Department legal adviser on United Nations affairs, a student of the organization and author of a study of the Secretary General's powers and practices.

The issue carrying the Hammarskjold memorandum is to be sent to subscribers this week.

The memorandum states that the matter of how and when the United Nations forces could be asked to leave Egyptian soil was virtually the only issue discussed by Mr. Hammarskjold and Mr. Nasser in a seven-hour meeting in Cairo on Nov. 17, 1956.

Public agreements bearing on this question were ambiguous, the document concedes. But it also contends that Mr. Hammarskjold obtained Mr. Nasser's agreement to a circuitous formula limiting Mr. Nasser's use of the right to expel the troops.

It also contends that Mr. Nasser "showed that he very fully understood that, by limiting their freedom of action in the way I proposed, they would take a very serious step."

As proof that Mr. Nasser understood, Mr. Hammarskjold pointed out that the Egyptian leader had strongly resisted the formula, and had yielded only after the Secretary General threatened three times "that unless an agreement of this type was made I would have to propose the immediate withdrawal of the troops."

The Egyptian Government was eager at that time to have the peace force stationed on its territory to force a withdrawal of Israeli troops from the territory they had seized in the Sinai Peninsula.

Strength Reached 6,000

The force, numbering about 600 men at the outset, was finally admitted to Egypt, moving first into the Suez Canal region and gradually up to the demarcation line—that is, to Israel's prewar frontiers.

Within months the force grew to 6,000 men from seven nations, but it still took energetic bargaining to persuade Israel to yield the Gaza Strip and Sharm el Sheik, commanding the entrance to the Gulf of Aqaba.

Israel refused to admit the force to her own territory, being somewhat mistrustful of Mr. Hammarskjold and contending that she had done nothing to warrant any infringement of her sovereignty by United Nations troops.

The force remained in Egypt until last May 16, when Cairo requested its redeployment. This original request appeared to demand only that it vacate the frontier region to let Egyptian forces move up.

Secretary General Thant took the position that the force could not be redeployed but would have to be withdrawn if Cairo so requested, and he ordered it to pull out when he received the request on May 18. That was 17 days before the start of the war that has again resulted in Israel's occupation of Sinai.

Mr. Hammarskjold wrote that under the formula he had devised, any Egyptian request for withdrawal of the forces would at once be brought before the General Assembly.

"If the General Assembly found that the task was completed, everything would be all right," the memorandum states. "If they found that the task was not completed and Egypt, all the same, maintained its stand and enforced the withdrawal, Egypt would break the agreement with the United Nations."

"There was no question of Egypt's sovereign right to expel the force from her soil any time," Mr. Hammarskjold said. But he insisted that his formula obliged Egypt, if she wished to act in good faith under her agreement with him—not to exercise that sovereign right until she had persuaded the United Nations

to this ... give warning ... under which ... Egypt would propose to exercise ... its right ... on the basis of a good faith interpretation of the task of the force, that is, the General Assembly's conclusion that the mission of the troops had been fulfilled.

An added reason for President Nasser's resistance to this formula, Mr. Hammarskjold recalled, was that "he felt, not without justification, that the definition given of the task in the U.N. texts was very loose," and that tying Egypt's freedom of action to the concept of "the task" in a written agreement was a far-reaching and unpredictable restriction.

Mr. Hammarskjold acknowledged the point, because the General Assembly resolution creating the force had defined its task with only a single phrase—"to secure and supervise the cessation of hostilities." It was to force Mr. Nasser to tolerate this vagueness, the memorandum suggests, that Mr. Hammarskjold then threatened immediate withdrawal of the force.

The public version of the agreement is expressed in Mr. Hammarskjold's report to the General Assembly "on the basic points for the presence and functioning in Egypt of the United Nations emergency force." It is dated Nov. 20, 1956 —three days later than the Cairo conference—and was approved by the General Assembly with Egypt's concurrence.

It committed Egypt, when exercising her rights on any matter concerning the presence and functioning of force, to be guided "in good faith" by her original acceptance of the Assembly resolution that established the force and defined its task. And it committed the United Nations, in directing the force, to be guided "in good faith" by the definition of the mission had been decided upon.

place until the task was completed.

Thus the public version was left more vague than the private agreement, apparently to spare Mr. Nasser's feelings on sovereignty and because Mr. Hammarskjold assumed that he would himself be dealing with any dispute about the issue.

Mr. Hammarskjold was Secretary General from 1953 until 1961, when he was killed in an airplane crash in Rhodesia.

Even the public version of the Hammarskjold-Nasser accord has since been interpreted as a gentlemen's agreement that neither Egypt nor the United Nations would decide alone to expel or withdraw the troops until the completion of their mission had been decided upon. Representatives of Canada,

Brazil and Denmark, among others, so argued to Mr. Thant last month, and urged him to raise the issue with Cairo and perhaps to bring it before the General Assembly.

But India and Yugoslavia, which had also contributed troops to the force, upheld Mr. Thant's view that the General Assembly had no rights in the matter.

Mr. Thant maintained that the force it was the Secretary General and the Egyptian Government who had negotiated its admission to Egypt. No matter how unfortunate the decision, in his view, the Cairo Government had a sovereign right to order the troops off its territory.

The first part of Mr. Ham-

marskjold's memoran calls that he sought start of the peace-keeping action to find some formula Egypt's ability

the troops—a form would nonetheless respect nation's sovereign right. Mr. Hammarskjold that he had tried to issue ambiguous, hoping would never arise, the Egyptian Government free to withdraw at any time. The whole exchange he wrote in conclusion, a formal explicit recognition by the stand I had through," thus nullifying earlier exchanges of

PRESIDENT ALOOF IN BUGGING FEUD

Implies He Will Let Hoover Handle Kennedy Fight

By MAX FRANKEL

Special to The New York Times

WASHINGTON, Dec. 12 — President Johnson remained aloof today from the electronic eavesdropping controversy between Senator Robert F. Kennedy and J. Edgar Hoover, director of the Federal Bureau of Investigation.

In effect, therefore, the President left the impression that he was satisfied to let Mr. Hoover, his subordinate, handle the matter in his own way.

Mr. Johnson authorized a spokesman to say in response to questions that the President was not investigating the dispute to determine who had really authorized the electronic bugging that is threatening to upset several important Government prosecutions for tax evasion and other crimes.

The President also let it be known that the White House would have nothing further to say about the issue beyond recalling its 18-month-old order that the tapping of telephones and other forms of electronic eavesdropping be limited to cases involving national security. The Kennedy-Hoover argument is not about direct wiretaps of telephone lines but about F.B.I. eavesdropping through hidden electronic devices.

His Own Observation

George Christian, the White House spokesman who relayed Mr. Johnson's views, added what he described as his own observation that the incidents leading to the current controversy occurred before Mr. Johnson became President on Nov. 22, 1963.

The dispute arose from recent Justice Department admissions that the F.B.I. had electronically bugged the Washington hotel rooms of Fred R. Black Jr., a public relations man and former business associate of Robert G. Baker, former secretary to Senate Democrats and thus a lieutenant of President Johnson in his years as majority leader.

Mr. Black's conviction for income tax evasion has been nullified as a result. Charges of tax evasion and fraud against Mr. Baker are before a Federal Court here.

In confessing to the eavesdropping, the Justice Department implied that the practice had been approved by Mr. Hoover but not by the Attorney General at the time, Mr. Kennedy. The department also said it was looking over its files to see what other cases were affected by the use of bugs in investigations of crime and other cases not normally regarded as involving national security.

Documents Released

Last week, in an effort to explain his own role, Mr. Hoover released documents charging that Mr. Kennedy had approved all wiretapping and eavesdropping conducted during his years as Attorney General, 1961 to 1964. The Senator denied any knowledge of such practices. Both men then characterized the other's statements as hard to believe.

Legally, the F.B.I. director is a subordinate of the Attorney General, a vacant position now filled on an acting basis by Ramsey Clark. But in most recent Administrations, Mr. Hoover has conducted himself most like the head of an independent agency directly responsible to the President. His relations with Mr. Johnson are reported to be close, and markedly better than they were with President Kennedy and his brother, Robert, then Attorney General.

Since Senator Kennedy has tried on several other issues to take positions more to the left than those of the President, the impression has spread that Mr.

In Own Observation

George Christian, the White House spokesman, was relaying Mr. Johnson's view, added what he described as his own observation that the incidents leading to the current controversy occurred before Mr. Johnson became President on Nov. 22, 1963.

The dispute arose from recent Justice Department admissions that the F.B.I. had electronically bugged the Washington hotel rooms of Fred B. Black Jr., a public relations man and former business associate of Robert G. Baker, former secretary to Senate Democrats and thus a lieutenant of President Johnson in his years as majority leader.

Mr. Black's conviction for income tax evasion has been nullified as a result. Charges of tax evasion and fraud against Mr. Baker are before a Federal Court here.

In confessing to the eavesdropping, the Justice Department implied that the practice had been approved by Mr. Hoover but not by the Attorney General at the time, Mr. Kennedy. The department also said it was looking over its files to see what other cases were affected by the use of bugs in investigations of crime and other cases not normally regarded as involving national security.

Documents Released

Last week, in an effort to explain his own role, Mr. Hoover released documents charging that Mr. Kennedy had approved all wiretapping and eavesdropping conducted during his years as Attorney General, 1961 to 1964. The Senator denied any knowledge of such practices. Both men then characterized the other's statements as hard to believe.

Legally, the F.B.I. director is a subordinate of the Attorney General, a vacant position now filled on an acting basis by Ramsey Clark. But in most recent Administrations, Mr. Hoover has conducted himself almost like the head of an independent agency directly responsible to the President. His relations with Mr. Johnson are reported to be close, and markedly better than they were with President Kennedy and his brother, Robert, then Attorney General.

Since Senator Kennedy has tried on several other issues to take positions more "liberal" than those of the President, the impression has spread that Mr. Johnson did not mind some difficulty for Mr. Kennedy in liberal circles.

One possible way out of the controversy was suggested here last night by a man close to both the President and the Senator, but Mr. Johnson did not pick up the cue. It was offered by Nicholas deB. Katzenbach, Under Secretary of State, who was Deputy Attorney General under Mr. Kennedy and then succeeded him as Attorney General under President Johnson.

In a statement distributed to newsmen, Mr. Katzenbach implied that the dispute resulted from an honest misunderstanding.

"I do not believe Senator Kennedy was in fact aware of the practices of the F.B.I. with respect to electronic surveillance other than those involving wiretapping, which he, like his predecessors, specifically authorized," Mr. Katzenbach said.

"I do not believe that Mr. Hoover would have used such techniques unless he had thought that the Attorney General in fact sanctioned them. Neither Mr. Hoover nor Senator Kennedy, to the best of my knowledge, ever specifically discussed with each other any such practice other than wiretapping."

Senate Inquiry Due

Senator Edward V. Long, head of a subcommittee investigating wiretapping, said last night he would invite J. Edgar Hoover and Senator Robert F. Kennedy to a public hearing on the "furor" over the use of listening devices by the Justice Department.

Mr. Long made the statement at Kennedy International Airport after his arrival from Greece.

REMEMBER THE NEEDIEST!

Johnson Aides Said to Feel War May Last 6 or 7 Years

By MAX FRANKEL
Special to The New York Times

WASHINGTON, Jan. 29—President Johnson is said to have been told by his senior advisers that it would take at least six or seven years of military action to bring about a satisfactory situation in South Vietnam.

Even this estimate of protracted conflict depends upon the gradual commitment of many more American troops, it is said—perhaps half a million more.

It also depends upon reasonable success in the establishment of a working political structure in the areas that must be brought under the control of the South Vietnamese Government.

Many other variables will influence the course of the war, officials predict, including the degree of intervention by the army of North Vietnam, the stability of the military Government in Saigon and the possibility that some diplomatic break may produce negotiations.

Some Favor Speedy Build-up

Some military men are also said to have seen an advantage in speeding the contemplated build-up of American forces.

But the essence of the judgments placed before the President by Secretary of Defense Robert S. McNamara, officials report, is that no military short cut could produce significant results in the next year or two.

They say that behind the brooding predictions all over Washington, that the war promises to be very long, is a private estimate of six or seven years at least.

Estimates of the duration of even a successful military campaign, and of the number of American troops needed under

Continued on Page 2, Column 3

Postage Paid at nal mailing offices.

THE NEW YORK TIMES, S

U.S. Aides Said to Feel Vi

Continued From Page 1, Col. 6

various circumstances, are believed to be under consideration in the current White House discussions of when to resume the bombing of North Vietnam and with what intensity.

Although public attention has been drawn to the immediate decision about the bombings, the Administration is said to be reviewing its total war effort. The review is prompted by a belief that new attacks upon North Vietnam will confirm the failure of diplomatic appeals for peace and will leave no alternative to the quest for a military decision.

Mike Mansfield of Montana, the Senate majority leader, and Senator J. W. Fulbright of Arkansas, chairman of the Foreign Relations Committee, are among the influential Senators pleading with the President to defer the bombings of North Vietnam. They are also urging him to give the public his best estimates of the cost in men and money, and of the duration of the conflict.

'Astronomical' Build-up

If the legislators have received such estimates, they have not disclosed them. But some are predicting a very long war and a build-up of American forces to "astronomical" proportions.

Fighting now beside the 600,-000-man army of South Vietnam are 197,000 American troops, 21,000 South Koreans, 1,200 Australians and about 200 New Zealanders.

In addition, 40,000 to 50,000 servicemen of the Seventh Fleet in the Western Pacific are said to be engaged in the Vietnam war.

In its formal statements, the Administration has not gone beyond President Johnson's assertion, in the State of the Union Message, that 'we just cannot know what the future may require."

"We may have to face long, hard combat or a long, hard conference or even both at once," he told Congress on Jan. 12.

Virtually no one in Washington now expects the United States and North Vietnam to define their objectives in such a way as to make possible negotiations in the foreseeable future. Those who are arguing against a resumption of bombing are pleading only that the President must not slam the door on further diplomatic maneuvering and that he must delay an all-out commitment to the military contest.

Intelligence estimates under scrutiny by Administration officials indicate that the Vietcong and the North Vietnamese are reinforcing and regrouping their units and possibly preparing to stage some large attacks. Officials suggest that the

Vietcong may be following their past pattern in the wake of the Lunar New Year truce, which ended Sunday. Officials say this pattern has been to take days or even weeks to build up to major actions involving large numbers of men.

The top advisers included Secretary of State Dean Rusk, Secretary of Defense McNamara, Arthur J. Goldberg, United States representative at the United Nations; McGeorge Bundy, special assistant to Mr. Johnson for national security; Gen. Earle G. Wheeler, Chairman of the Joint Chiefs of Staff; Adm. William F. Raborn, Director of Central Intelligence, and William P. Bundy, Assistant Secretary of State for Far Eastern Affairs.

THE NEW YORK TIMES, SUNDAY, MAY 23, 1965.

WIDER SOVIET AID TO HANOI SIGHTED

U.S. Watching Missile Areas Amid Signs of Expansion

By MAX FRANKEL
Special to The New York Times

WASHINGTON, May 22 — The United States has been closely watching the preparation of several sites for Soviet antiaircraft missiles in and around Hanoi. The construction efforts suggest a considerably larger Soviet commitment to North Vietnam's defense effort than officials expected some weeks ago.

It is believed that some missiles for the installations — known here as SAM sites — have arrived in North Vietnam, but that none have been placed in firing position.

Officials here believe it will take a sizable contingent of Soviet technicians to man the site, some of which are 40 to 50 miles north of targets now being attacked by United States aircraft. One report, which could not be confirmed here, said that Soviet personnel were already at work on the projects.

Administration sources said that there had been no decision here to strike at the missile sites or otherwise to risk injury to Soviet citizens.

As the United States air attacks continue to creep northward, there is again some concern about the likelihood of renewed contact with Communist MIG fighters.

Two Air Force jets were shot down by MIG's April 4, in the only air engagement over North Vietnam. The Communist jet fighters appeared during an attack on a bridge at Thanhhoa, 75 miles south of Hanoi.

The officials here said there had been no major change in the types of targets selected for air attack since the bombings were renewed last week after a six-day pause.

United States planes are still striking at military installations and at roads and bridges used for military supply. Several recent raids have been within 60 miles of Hanoi.

Renewed contact with the MIG's would revive the question whether the United States should strike at their bases within 10 miles of North Vietname's capital. Those bases apparently will be defended by Soviet antiaircraft missiles.

A month ago intelligence reports indicated work on only one missile site. At the same time there were indications that the Soviet Union was having trouble shipping the weapons and other materials through Communist China—either because Peking wished to slow the Soviet aid effort or because Moscow deliberately arranged the shipments to incur delays.

Officials here had suspected at the time that the Soviet Union was reluctant to commit a great number of weapons or men to North Vietnam, especially as long as it appeared to be aligned politically with China. More recently, the North Vietnamese have shown somewhat greater sympathy for Soviet views, and this may have brought them promises of greater support.

East German Communists have said Moscow was sending more jet planes as well as antiaircraft missiles to Vietnam. If more air engagements are planned, it is thought that Hanoi will also soon need Chinese or Soviet fighter pilots.

The construction of the missile sites can lead to more intensified air combat in North Vietnam in the months ahead, officials warned, but their immediate concern was with prospects in the South.

The season of heavy rains has begun and will continue to plague the more mechanized and extended United States forces until mid-September. Air and ground supply to remote jungle positions will be threatened and tactical air strikes against the Vietcong rebels will be possible only during afternoon breaks in the weather.

To prevent some major Vietcong assaults and to protect major United States installations, officials expect that they will have to increase the number of combat troops, perhaps by 20,000 or more men.

The last official count of United States forces put the total at 42,200, but the build-up has continued since toward 50,000.

Officials also expect increasing commitments of United States forces to direct combat and a corresponding increase in American casualties.

Political assessments of these developments vary. Some officials fear that a greater involvement will make it ever more difficult for the United States to reach the conference table with honor. Others contend that the Communists will not display any interest in negotiations until their expected ground attacks during the rainy season have been effectively repulsed.

Duck Hatches 5 Eggs Off Lobby of School

Special to The New York Times

NORWALK, Conn., May 22 —Daphne Duck hatched five ducklings yesterday. Daphne, a wild duck, was discovered on April 20 in shrubbery just off the main lobby of the Norwalk State Technical Institute on Richards Avenue, sitting on a nest of six eggs.

For a month she had jealously guarded the eggs. To keep her from becoming frightened by the traffic to and from the lobby, institute authorities had a blind erected to give her privacy. Both the staff and student body watched her daily through peepholes in the blind.

Officials believe that Daphne will take off with her young ones within a few days. Last year, they say, Daphne or her twin mothered four ducklings at approximately the same place.

U.S. Lists

WASHINGTON CITES 3 LEFTIST GROUPS

Many Cuba-Trained Agents Reported to Have Seized Control of Uprising

Continued From Page 1, Col. 7

accounts must not be identified or quoted directly.

The materials circulated within the Government listed 58 names, and Administration officials had come to speak of "the 58." But four names were discovered today to have been duplicated on the Government lists.

The accounts made available here were drawn from material supplied to the President last Friday and Saturday.

On Friday, the Administration was said to have reached the following conclusions:

¶That 54 prominent Communist and Castroist leaders were playing an important role in organizing mobs among the much of the paramilitary action. Of these, 18 were known or reliably reported to have been trained in subversive tactics by Cuban organizations and 36 had been clearly identified in recent years as Communist and Castroist subversives. Playing a key role in the tactical direction of the rebel forces was Manuel Gonzalez Gonzalez, a Spanish Communist.

¶That three Communist political organizations were involved: the Dominican Popular Socialist party, which follows Moscow's direction; the Dominican Popular Movement, a small but aggressive group that follows the Chinese Communist line, and the 14th of June political group, the largest of the three, which is known to have connections with the Soviet, Cuban and Chinese Governments. The movement takes its name from the date on which a 1959 invasion attempt failed.

¶That a number of the 14th of June and Popular Movement leaders traveled through Communist countries during a period of exile in 1964 and rejoined their Dominican organizations, some secretly, beginning late last year.

¶That 14th of June members were in the streets in the first hours of the revolt on April 24, calling for popular demonstrations for the restoration of the constitutional Government of former President Juan Bosch.

¶That shortly afterward Communist and Castroist leaders obtained arms and ammunition from arsenals of the army camp known as 27th of February, outside Santo Domingo. A sizable number of these fell into the hands of leaders of the Moscow-oriented Popular Socialists. Party members were formed into armed teams, which fanned out in the downtown and slum sections under the conspicuous direction of the party leaders Buenaventura Johnson and Fidelio Despradel.

¶That a party military headquarters was established at the same time to collect arms from the police and the armed forces and that other strong points were organized. Jaime Duran and Juan Ducoudray, both linked to Cuba, were among the leaders.

¶That all three extreme leftist groups were soon providing a significant portion of the rebel forces and decisively influencing the political leadership of the rebellion that had been in the hands of Bosch followers. They took control of the Santo Domingo radio and operated in [illegible] parading captured loyalists before television [illegible] [several lines illegible]

[lower section illegible] of the Bosch movement were said to have conceded privately that the revolt had been captured by the extreme left. Most of the non-Communist took [illegible] factory by Saturday [illegible] [several lines illegible]

Washington
Of Three L

Training in Cuba Cited

By MAX FRANKEL
Special to the New York Times

WASHINGTON, May 5—Government sources made available today a list of 54 "Communist and Castroist" leaders whom President Johnson has accused of having seized control of the rebellion in the Dominican Republic.

Also made available here, in response to inquiries about the evidence for the President's contention, were accounts of some intelligence information about activities in the early days of the revolt.

The information was said to demonstrate that Communists were conspicuously active among the rebels and that they had successfully infiltrated the rebel leadership.

Officials said that other evidence had been gathered but could not be made available without compromising sources of information. They also stipulated that the sources of the

Continued on Page 15, Column 1

...ical organizations were involved, the Dominican Popular Socialist party, which follows Moscow's direction; the Dominican Popular Movement, a small but active group that follows the Chinese Communist line, and the 14th of June political group, the largest of the three, which is known to have connections with the Soviet, Cuban and Chinese Governments. The movement takes its name from the date on which a 1959 invasion attempt failed.

¶That a number of the 14th of June and Popular Movement leaders traveled through Communist countries during a period of exile in 1961 and rejoined their Dominican organizations, some secretly, beginning late last year.

¶That 14th of June members were in the streets in the first hours of the revolt on April .24, calling for popular demonstrations for the restoration of the constitutional Government of former President Juan Bosch.

¶That shortly afterward Communist and Castroist leaders obtained arms and ammunition from arsenals of the army camp known as 27th of February, outside Santo Domingo. A sizable number of these fell into the hands of leaders of the Moscow-oriented Popular Socialists. Party members were formed into armed teams, which fanned out in the downtown and slum sections under the conspicuous direction of the party leaders Buenaventura Johnson and Fidelio Despradel.

¶That a party military headquarters was established at the same time to collect arms from the police and the armed forces and that other strong points were organized. Jaime Durán and Juan Ducoudray, both linked to Cuba, were among the leaders.

¶That all three extreme leftist groups were soon providing a significant portion of the rebel forces and decisively influencing the political leadership of the rebellion that had been in the hands of Bosch followers. They took control of the Santo Domingo radio and operated in typical Castro style, parading captured loyalists before television cameras and using slogans and denunciations of "bourgeois reactionaries" and "imperialists."

¶That by April 27, the day before United States troops landed in Santo Domingo, the provisional Government formed by Rafael Molina Ureña comprised members and officials who either were known Communists or Castroists or had histories of association with the extreme left. They included Alfredo Cond Pausa, a Popular Socialist sympathizer, and Luis H. Lajara Gonzales, a follower of the late dictator Rafael Leonidas Trujillo Molina who switched to the Castroist camp.

Further Reports Arrive

On Saturday, intelligence reports were said to include the following additional details on Communist and Castroist activities:

¶A number of party leaders were seen with weapons and gasoline bombs as early as April 25. Last Wednesday, they were suspected of complicity in the execution of captured policemen, the sacking of local banks and the looting of private institutions and businesses.

¶Mobs described as subversive-directed sacked the offices of anti-Communist political parties and publications. Party leaders used the sacked plant of the newspaper Prensa Libre to produce propaganda leaflets. Popular Socialist leaflets included one accusing the United States Embassy of interference in the country's internal political affairs and one calling for Mr. Bosch's return to power.

¶By the third day of the revolt, the extreme leftists, acting both independently and together, had established strong points and temporary headquarters at several places, including the home of Buenaventura Johnson, where they stored arms and issued orders to parliamentary units.

¶Joint meetings of Popular Socialist members and followers of Mr. Bosch were held at the home of Communists to coordinate military and political action.

Non-Communist civilian leaders of the Bosch movement were said to have conceded privately that the revolt had been captured by the extreme left. Most of the non-Communists took sanctuary by Saturday in embassies and private homes. After withdrawing from the revolt, one of them, Jose Francisco Peña Gómez, told a United States Embassy officer that Communists had infiltrated positions of importance and that it was very difficult to stop them.

The Bosch party's secretary general, Martinez Francisco, was believed to have implied the same contention in a radio appeal for a cease-fire last Wednesday. He said the revolt was "no longer a fight between political parties."

Government sources said the following Dominican rebels were known to have had Cuban training:

Luis Felipe Valentino Giro Alcantara—Popular Socialist member, fanatic who "loves" using gasoline bombs, received guerrilla warfare training in Cuba in 1963.

Manuel Gonzalez Gonzalez—Spanish Communist who has been in the Dominican Republic since 1940 and is a Popular Socialist member; probable military leader in current insurrection; has knowledge of military tactics. Reported Cuban intelligence agent.

Miguel Angel Deschamps Erickson—Popular Movement member; received guerrilla warfare training and explosives course in Cuba in 1962. Carried instructions from Cuba to Dominican Republic for movement in 1963.

Lisandro Macarrulla Reyes—Popular Socialist leader; six-month course in Marxism-Leninism in Cuba.

Hector Florentino Olivares—Actively recruits among Communists and leftists for insurrection. Highly skilled and indoctrinated for this role. Visited to China and ardent admirer of Mao Tse-tung, Chinese Communist leader.

Juan Miguel Roman Diaz—High-level member of 14th of June group; was key man in guerrilla activities in Dominican Republic; late in 1963 conferred and went to Cuba June, 1964; appeared in a series November, 1964, on party missions.

Manuel Escobar...—Popular Socialist...in 1963.

Jose Rodriguez Acosta—High-level Popular Socialist member; received guerrilla warfare training in Cuba in 1962; has also been in Czechoslovakia and in the Soviet Union.

Fidelio Despradel Roques—14th of June leader; received guerrilla training in Cuba in 1963; trained in one of a rebel garrisons.

Cayetano Rodriguez del Prado—Popular Movement (leftist) Communist revolutionary; received training in Cuba, has trained in Soviet bloc and Communist China. Involved in Cuban intelligence operations in 1963 to infiltrate himself, two others, arms and communications equipment into the country.

Nestor Quirico Valdez Conde—High-level popular socialist member; has lived in Moscow and speaks Russian fluently; was Russian interpreter for Premier Fidel Castro.

Ramon Agustin Pinedo Mejia—Popular Movement leader; was involved in 1963 guerrilla movement.

Jaime Castell Bello—14th of June leader; associated with Popular Movement. Traveled to Cuba, Soviet Union and Czechoslovakia; arrested April, 1961.

Josefina (Pinyo) Lora Iglesias—Female with vertical training, 14th of June leader; involved in 14th of June guerrilla movement in 1963; had political indoctrination course in Cuba late in 1964.

Rafael de la Altagracia (Baby) Mella Lluberes—14th of June leader, long-time Communist revolutionary; involved in 1963 attempt to overthrow President Romulo Betancourt of Venezuela; had guerrilla training and political-indoctrination course in Cuba in 1963.

Norge Williams Botello Fernandez—14th of June militant activist, had intensive military training in Cuba 1963-64.

Hector Homero Hernandez Vargas—14th of June leader, took part in student riots in 1961, had training in Cuba in 1964, visited Communist China same year.

Luis Bernardo Genao—14th of June leader, involved in 1963 guerrilla activities, was in Cuba in 1962.

The following were described as rebels of known leftist affiliation:

Carlos Dore—Popular Socialist member, official of pro-Communist Student Federation. Preparing Molotov cocktails.

Asdrubal Dominguez Guerrero—Popular Socialist leader and a student leader armed for action.

Emma Tavare Justo—14th of June leader agitating for Dominicans to join in the insurrection.

Pedro Julio Evangelista—Pro-Popular Socialist labor leader exhorting workers to support rebel government.

Edmundo Garcia Castillo—Popular Socialist member distributing leaflets.

Porfirio Nabor...Garcia—Popular Socialist member making Molotov cocktails.

Facundo Gomez—Popular Socialist member. Part owner of boat that landed arms, ammunition and three top Popular movement leaders in Dominican Republic from Cuba late in 1963 during guerrilla activities.

Eduardo (Pitt) Heullemant—Popular Socialist member or sympathizer fighting in streets with arms.

Antonio Isa Conde—Popular Socialist member distributing flysheets calling on people to fight.

Narcisco Isa Conde—Popular Socialist member or sympathizer fighting in the streets with firearms.

Alejandro Lajara — 14th of June member; named deputy chief of intelligence under his father. Record of arson.

Juan Ducoudray Mansfield — A long-time leader of the Dominican Communist party, who has extensive contact with foreign Communists, Now in hiding, he has been involved in the direction of the insurrection.

Felix Servio Ducoudray Mansfield Jr.— Probable a leader of Dominican Communist party. Has lived in Soviet Union and in Cuba, and has received indoctrination. Has made numerous trips between the Dominican Republic and Cuba. Prensa Latina representative in the Dominican Republic.

Buenaventura Johnson Pimentel—Popular Socialist member with machine guns.

Marcos de Vargas—Pro-Communist labor leader armed or sympathizer to support rebels.

Arnesto Sosa Valerio—Popular socialist member preparing Molotov cocktails.

Ubaldo Roa del Rosario—Popular Socialist sympathizer, armed for action.

Luis Reyes—Pro Castro student leader.

Milvio Perez Perez—Popular Socialist leader agitating arms.

Ignacio Peret Mencia—Popular Socialist member preparing Molotov cocktails.

Manuel Ortiz Dimontet—Popular Socialist member preparing Molotov cocktails.

Luis Montas Corrales—14th of June leader and federal representative to central committee carrying firearms.

Diomedes Mercedes Batista—Popular Socialist...

Arseno Ortiz de Ferran—French-born Dominican; in 1962 was in contact with Cuban Ambassador at Paris.

Silvano Lora Vicente—Popular Socialist member, pro-Communist Castroist, had training in Cuba in 1943-44; in 1944 traveled to Africa and Mexico.

Franklin Franco Pichardo—Popular Socialist member; training in Soviet Union and Cuba; recent trip to Moscow and Prague.

Ramon Andres Avelino Garcia—Was in Cuba in 1963.

Delta Bohemia Soto Grullon—Popular Socialist member, wife of Rafael Villalona who is in Soviet Union.

Eduardo Houellamont Roces—Was in Cuba in 1963. Activities as a pro Castro student agitator back in 1961.

Dato Pasan Perdumo—Thoroughly schooled Communist agitator; was in area in Dominican Republic from Cuba in 1959.

Wilson del Orbe—Popular Socialist member, trained in Cuba in 1963.

Abelardo Vicioso Gonzalez—Popular Socialist member who has lived in Cuba, has been in Moscow and Prague, has had indoctrination in both cities.

Pedro Julio Mir Valentin—Important Popular Socialist member; reputed to be the close friend of Fidel Castro; Communist activities, including travel to Communist countries; was in Cuba in 1962, has traveled to Dominican Republic on the Havana run.

Juan Jose Matos Rivera—14th of June party secretary; was born in Cuba, returned to join clandestine party early in 1965. Political Communist intelligence agent.

Tomas Parmenio Erickson Alvarez—14th of June Communist; reputed Popular Movement member; ardently anti-United States; had training in Cuba in early nineteen sixties.

Origins of Foreign Policy: Secrets, Crises and Vision

By MAX FRANKEL
Special to The New York Times.

WASHINGTON, June 28—Out of the State Department last week there came a secret, a phone call, a book and a murmur of complaint—little symptoms of a big problem: the unordered process by which United States foreign policy is determined.

The secret, plucked out of the Washington air by a columnist, was that Secretary of State Dean Rusk was the unmentioned author of an unwritten talk at an unmentioned press luncheon that made headlines around the world about the possibility of war in Southeast Asia.

It was a familiar but still startling way for the Government to communicate some of its most carefully weighed words to a potential enemy.

The phone call, by a high official to a newspaper, sought some information originally obtained from the official's own subordinates. It was a vivid demonstration of how the Government does not dare to rely upon its own resources and how its different layers often communicate through the most unorthodox channels.

Definitions of Policy

The book, by the Administration's principal policy planner, Walt W. Rostow, was meant to satisfy the public clamor for a concise definition of American foreign policy. But many of his colleagues found it so general as to be almost irrelevant to their daily tasks, while others cited a great dispute within the Government even about the generalities.

And the murmur of complaint from many sections of Foggy Bottom was about the assignment of U. Alexis Johnson, Deputy Under Secretary, as Deputy Ambassador to South Vietnam, depriving the State Department of its firmest foe of administrative chaos and principal link to the military and intelligence agencies that can row with or against the established policy course.

It was not an unusual week. The symptoms changed, but the problem remains. Decisions relating to war and peace, stability and revolution, friends and

Continued on Page 8, Column 3

Foreign Policy: Crises and Vision

Continued From Page 1, Col. 6

enemies are made and unmade daily, now here, now there, by a conspicuous official or by an unseen, informal group of subordinates.

These decisions are applied, altered, conveyed, compounded and opposed by others, sometimes in the way that the textbooks prescribe, but usually in ways that the men in government themselves cannot describe, no less control.

The problem has troubled presidents and legislators, scholars, diplomats and observers. They know they cannot "solve" it and would be happy for the time being to understand it.

Simultaneously, out of the Congress last week, there came the latest of a series of studies of the management of national security operations. It found that an American ambassador abroad, like the Secretary of State at home, was not really the master of his organization, nor, as intended, of the many arms of government that wittingly and otherwise "make" foreign policy.

It also found that the connection between policy planning and policy decision was often merely a "dreamlike logic."

But the reports of the Senate subcommittee, headed by Senator Henry M. Jackson, Democrat, of Washington, have also been careful to note that the disorder was chronic and common to all recent Administrations.

Flexibility vs. Stability

The trouble it found, begins at the very top because a President needs flexibility, that is, freedom to improve, while officialdom needs stability, assurance of regularity.

"It is not surprising that the departments often find a President's way of doing business unsettling—or that Presidents sometimes view the departments almost as adversaries," the committee said in defining one of the central dilemmas of foreign policy administration.

And out of the White House last week there came a fair amount of evidence of a President's customary style of operations: tough and personal conversation about Cyprus with the urgently summoned leaders of Turkey and Greece; sanction for the Attorney General to move into the sensitive capitals of West Germany and Poland; a eager minuet with a prominent Republican resigning as Ambassador to South Vietnam; some guarded public dialogue with the Chinese Communists; and a desalination agreement with Moscow after some more secret correspondence with Premier Khrushchev.

No one regards a President's maneuvering as improper or unwise. Some of it is planned. Some is highly personal. The point is that the mechanics of government, the distribution of power, the pressure felt at different points and the great influence of individual personality and talent render almost meaningless the oft-heard question, "How is foreign policy made?"

Policy Managed, Not Made

The testimony of thoughtful officials and observers suggests that foreign policy is not really made at all, only managed, on an ad hoc basis at best. It is buffeted by the colliding visions, gripes, talents, fights, fears, errors, powers and pressures of hundreds of people and dozens of institutions, of politicians and scholars, businessmen and newspapermen, foreign and domestic.

As the Jackson subcommittee put it, "The nature of concrete policy issues and the character of governmental action processes push for a pragmatic one-thing-at-a-time, on-its-own-terms approach."

Or, as Prof. Richard E. Neustadt of Columbia University has found in his extensive studies of recent Administrations, "Information is not only a key to action, it is a key to power in this Government," and "the right to information about important things is hardly guaranteed to anybody."

Even less secure is an official's claim to status or influence according to the real boxes of Washington's organization charts.

By these charts foreign policy is determined by the President...

bassies, missions and offices abroad.

Only 15 years ago, the Secretary of Defense could forbid contacts with the State Department at any level lower than his own. But today the officials of all these enterprises are forever gathering in committees, boards, commissions and task forces that are permanent, ad hoc, large, small, formal, informal, high-level, working level, intra-agency, interagency, and now intergovernmental.

When not in meetings they are sending or carrying papers around town seeking clearances and concurrences to avoid losing a problem to arbitration at the next highest level.

The grist for this mill at the State Department, in telegraphic traffic alone, is a daily flow of 1,300 incoming and 1,500 outgoing cablegrams, carrying more than 400,000 words. Secretary Rusk receives only a handful of these, but he has told much of the story of political management in this simple illustration:

"When I read a telegram coming in in the morning, it poses a very specific question, and the moment I read it I know myself what the answer must be. But that telegram goes on its appointed course into the bureau, and through the office and down to the desk. If it doesn't go down there, somebody feels that he is being deprived of his participation in a matter of his responsibility.

"Then it goes from the action officer back up through the department to me a week or 10 days later, and if it isn't the answer that I knew had to be the answer, then I change it at, that point, having taken into account the advice that came from below. But usually it is the answer that everybody would know has to be the answer."

Crises Disrupt Bureaucracy

When the Government must deal with the routine visit of a foreign dignitary or instruct an ambassador to deliver a routine message, this system functions reasonably well. But at the first sign of trouble—precisely because foreign policy cannot be planned or codified for even predictable contingencies because an issue cannot be decided until the concrete circumstances and potential ramifications are evident—the fuses pop and the normal flow of bureaucratic energy is disrupted. No two emergencies or crises are ever handled in the same way.

After much hauling and pulling and crystal-ball gazing, energetic men like Mr. Rostow, the policy planning chief, can forge a consensus of an expected problem, such as the possible detonation by Communist China of a nuclear device. They can obtain agreement on American aspirations and objectives when it happens—prevent panic, reassure the allies, resist diplomatic blackmail.

But no responsible official will ever write a blank check on his future decisions and actions. Even when the expected happens, officials all over town, from their separate perspectives, will weigh American power and interests against requirements near and far. They may then act on the predetermined priorities, but they may be guided by a momentary set of priorities, pressures and preferences.

When something like this...

Senator Henry M. Jackson, Washington Democrat. His subcommittee made report on policy making last week.

another crisis, this time, almost unaccountably, between the world's closest allies, the United States and Britain.

The two countries had been in constant touch at many levels. The British Ambassador was a personal friend of the President. The White House and 10 Downing Street were constantly in touch by telephone. But still the two sides woefully misjudged each other and their problems.

The United States treated the Skybolt as a costly and technologically difficult item of superfluous military equipment, whereas Britain pinned to the project all her plans for the preservation of an independent national nuclear force, her diplomatic sovereignty.

London had invested the fate of a government in the weapon. But Washington, almost routinely, left decisions and negotiations about it to the cost-conscious managers of the Defense Department.

In the end, the heads of government had to improvise a hasty way out of the bitterness at a meeting in Nassau. They did it in a way that gave President de Gaulle of France at least a pretext for barring Britain from the Common Market early in 1963 and they provoked an entirely new set of policy problems around the project of a mixed-manned nuclear-armed fleet under the Atlantic alliance.

This proposed fleet was at one time almost the purest example of promising policy planning. Sensing a desire in Europe for a greater voice in the management of Western nuclear defenses, but fearing the spread of national nuclear forces, the planners here evolved the idea of an allied navy with American Polaris missiles, to be jointly financed and serviced by mixed crews of the allies but to be used only with the consent of Washington and other major participants.

Military leaders thought it was unnecessary. Diplomats working toward arms control with the Soviet Union thought it was a step backward. But the fears of a sudden German desire for atomic weapons kept the project alive. It has remained alive because new situations seemed to give it new purposes.

How motives shift with time beneath the false front of consistency is probably best illustrated by the 10-year history of diplomacy toward a nuclear test ban treaty. That history also shows the gaps that develop between policies as they are planned, as they are declared and as they are pursued.

A decade ago, nuclear testing was only a minor item in the carefully prepared rival disarmament programs of Moscow and Washington.

Propaganda and Pressures

But propaganda and pressures from other countries and failure on other issues pushed the question forward until the two giant nuclear powers, making separate calculations of the military balance, alternately favored and resisted a test ban under different conditions at different times.

Each, of course, wanted to inhibit the other's weapons development. Each also sought different kinds of precedent for East-West agreements. President Dwight D. Eisenhower, although he favored a treaty, presided over a vacillating group of advisers whose meetings were long and diffuse and whose decisions were rarely clear. President Kennedy imposed greater enthusiasm on his principal aides, who therefore concentrated more on tactical advice than on debate of the basic question.

But the final treaty, signed in Moscow in 1963 and banning all but underground tests, came quickly, almost unexpectedly, after the Cuban crisis, after the military balance of 1957-58 that had so intrigued Moscow and Washington was shattered by nuclear tests in 1961-62. And the immediate motives, in the end, were dominated by Washington's wish to limit the club of nuclear powers and Moscow's desire to steer a new course of coexistence away from Communist China.

The mere declaration—too often called a "policy"—is impotent, of course, to set a tone and to educate as administration find at all as at source and foreign policies...

Flexibility vs. Stability

The trouble it found, begins at the very top because a President needs flexibility, that is the need... freedom to improve, while officialdom needs stability, a sense of regularity.

"It is not surprising that the departments often find a President's way of doing business unsettling—or that President sometimes view the department almost as adversaries," the committee said in defining one of the central dilemmas of foreign policy administration.

And out of the White House last week there came a fair account of evidence of a President's customary style of operations: tough and personal conversation about Cyprus with the urgently summoned leaders of Turkey and Greece; sanction for the Attorney General to move into the sensitive capitals of West Germany and Poland; a cagey minuet with a prominent Republican resigning as Ambassador to South Vietnam; some guarded public dialogue with the Chinese Communists; and a desalination agreement with Moscow after some more secret correspondence with Premier Khrushchev.

No one regards a President's maneuvering as improper or unwise. Some of it is planned. Some is highly personal. The point is that the mechanics of government, the distribution of power, the pressure felt at different points and the great influence of individual personality and talent render almost meaningless the oft-heard question, "How is foreign policy made?"

Policy Managed, Not Made

The testimony of thoughtful officials and observers suggests that foreign policy is not really made at all, only managed, on an ad hoc basis at best. It is buffeted by the colliding visions, gripes, talents, fears, errors, powers and pressures of hundreds of people and dozens of institutions, of politicians and scholars, businessmen and newspapermen, foreign and domestic.

As the Jackson subcommittee put it, "The nature of concrete policy issues and the character of governmental action processes push for a pragmatic one-thing-at-a-time, on-its-own-terms approach."

Or, as Prof. Richard E. Neustadt of Columbia University has found in his extensive studies of recent Administrations, "Information is not only a key to action; it is a key to power in this Government" and "the right to information" about important things "is hardly guaranteed to anybody."

Even less secure is an official's claim to status or influence according to the neat boxes of Washington's organization charts.

By these charts, foreign policy is determined by the President with the occasional advice and financial support of Congress and with the more regular Counsel of key Cabinet members, notably the Secretary of State.

The Secretary, his deputies and the ambassadors overseas are supposed to be, in their separate realms, the overseers and coordinators of the work of all other interested agencies, especially those dealing with military affairs, intelligence, finance, commerce, foreign aid and propaganda.

Structure Is Complex

And inside the State Department, the work of the coordinators is supposed to be structured neatly beneath the Secretary, through his personal staff and deputies, through bureaus of broad geographical responsibility that supervise offices for smaller regions, which, in turn, supervise "desks" for individual countries.

There are also collateral bureaus, offices and desks that specialize in planning, research, economics, international organizations, cultural affairs, law, public and Congressional relations, administration and other distinctive services.

This structure is duplicated in the foreign aid, information and Central Intelligence agencies, in smaller versions at the Pentagon and some other departments and, in most compact form, on the President's personal staff. Many of these separate bureaucracies have their representatives at many of the 274 United States embassies...

...how interests... When not in meetings they are working around for a week to handle... The grief for this at the State Department, in telegraph traffic alone, is a daily flow of 1,300 incoming and 1,000 outgoing cables... Dean Rusk receives only a handful of these, but he has told much of the story of public management in this simple illustration:

"When I read a telegram coming in in the morning, it poses a very specific question, and the moment I read it I know myself what the answer must be. But that telegram goes on its appointed course into the bureau, and through the office and down to the desk. If it doesn't go down there, somebody feels that he is being deprived of his participation in a matter of his responsibility.

"Then it goes from the action officer back up through the department to me a week or 10 days later, and if it isn't the answer that I know had to be the answer, then I change it at that point, having taken into account the advice that came from below. But usually it is the answer that everybody would know has to be the answer."

Crises Disrupt Bureaucracy

When the Government must deal with the routine visit of a foreign dignitary or instruct an ambassador to deliver a routine message, this system functions reasonably well. But at the first sign of trouble—precisely because foreign policy cannot be planned or codified for even predictable contingencies because an issue cannot be decided until the concrete circumstances and potential ramifications are evident—the fuses pop and the normal flow of bureaucratic energy is disrupted. No two emergencies or crises are ever handled in the same way.

After much hauling and pulling and crystal-ball gazing, energetic men like Mr. Rostow, the policy planning chief, can forge a consensus of an expected problem, such as the possible detonation by Communist China of a nuclear device. They can obtain agreement on American aspirations and objectives when it happens—prevent panic, reassure the allies, resist diplomatic blackmail.

But no responsible official will ever write a blank check on his future decisions and concerns. Even when the expected happens, officials all over town, from their separate perspectives, will weigh American power and interests against reactions near and far. They may then act on the predetermined aspirations, but they will be guided by a momentary set of priorities, pressures and preferences.

"When something like this happens," said Secretary Rusk after the Cuban missile crisis of 1962, "and you haven't read or learned from the basic papers, it's too late. You just have to deal with things as they happen."

Most Actions Are Reactions

Even in its most imaginative acts, government reacts. Decisions to act, or not to act, are forced upon it by events and schedules, by the need to compose a budget, make a speech, answer a diplomatic note, recognize a new government, respond to a threat or resist an attack.

As the Jackson studies point out, the Marshall Plan for European recovery "was not dreamed up on a campus." It was the product of the interplay of minds of men like General of the Army George C. Marshall, Robert A. Lovett, Dean Acheson and President Harry S. Truman, who were searching for ways to reverse the trend toward collapse and Communism.

And as the whole country now knows, the brilliantly conceived and controlled diplomatic and military effort to force Premier Khrushchev to withdraw his missiles from Cuba was developed on an hour-to-hour basis in extraordinary consultation among a few Administration leaders and experts who turned their backs on every other problem.

Shortly after the Cuban crisis, the Pentagon's cancellation of the project for the Skybolt airborne missile caused still...

...charge, sensing a desire in Europe... government of Western nuclear defenses but fearing the spread of national nuclear forces, the planners here evolved the idea of an allied navy with American Polaris missiles to be jointly financed and serviced by crews of the allies but to be used only with the consent of Washington and other major participants.

Military leaders thought it was necessary. Diplomats working toward arms control with the Soviet Union thought it was a step backward. But the fears of a sudden German desire for atomic weapons kept the project alive. It has remained alive because new situations seemed to give it new purposes.

How motives shift with time beneath the false front of consistency is probably best illustrated by the 10-year history of diplomacy toward a nuclear test ban treaty. That history also shows the gaps that develop between policies as they are planned, as they are declared and as they are pursued.

A decade ago, nuclear testing was only a minor item in the carefully prepared rival disarmament programs of Moscow and Washington.

Propaganda and Pressures

But propaganda and pressures from other countries and failure on other issues pushed the question forward until the two giant nuclear powers, making separate calculations of balance, alternately favored and resisted a test ban under different conditions at different times.

Each, of course, wanted to inhibit the other's weapons development. Each also sought different kinds of precedent for East-West agreements. President Dwight D. Eisenhower, though he favored a treaty, presided over a vacillating group of advisers whose meetings were long and diffuse and whose decisions were rarely clear. President Kennedy imposed greater enthusiasm on his principal aides, who therefore concentrated more on tactical advice than on debate of the basic question.

But the final treaty, signed in Moscow in 1963 and banning all but underground tests, came quickly, almost unexpectedly, after the Cuban crisis, after the military balance of 1957-58 that had to intrigue Moscow and Washington was shattered by nuclear tests in 1961-62. And the immediate motives, in the end, were dominated by Washington's wish to limit the club of nuclear powers and Moscow's desire to steer a new course of coexistence away from Communist China.

The mere declaration—too often called a "policy"—is important, of course, to set a tone and to educate an administration as well as domestic and foreign publics. But frequently, as in the case of the "grand design" of a united Europe and an Atlantic partnership, that aspiration is barely relevant to daily decision-making.

Similarly, preparation of "contingency" policies is useful to prepare a government and an alliance for the subtleties and possible consequences of future events and to train military, intelligence and diplomatic officers to think in each other's terms.

But the way in which a particular convoy to Berlin is stopped and the state of the world at that moment will determine the response much more than any plan.

Finally, in this endlessly complicated business, there is the unspoken policy that develops in fact but is not yet discussed or formulated or built upon. For many years, Washington has treated Communist China and Taiwan as if they were two separate nations.

But there is still great bureaucratic intrigue here when one group of officials seeks approval of a speech that would begin to make the Government's words match its deeds. The Administration's unwillingness to run the risk of trying to overthrow the Castro Government in Cuba is another "policy" that is rarely acknowledged and sometimes even denied.

It is impossible, therefore, to speak of foreign policy as a single will or purpose, or even as a series of fixed and identifiable objectives. There are aspirations and there are actions, intents and events, and thousands of decisions and non-decisions the account of any one of which would be a history unto itself.

UNITED STATES DISTRICT COURT

SOUTHERN DISTRICT NEW YORK

--X
                                        :

UNITED STATES OF AMERICA,   :

      Plaintiff   :

                              :

         v.   :   71 Civ. 2662

                              :

THE NEW YORK TIMES COMPANY et al, :

      Defendants.   :

--X

          AFFIDAVIT of NEIL SHEEHAN

STATE OF NEW YORK   )
                     : ss.:
COUNTY OF NEW YORK)

        NEIL SHEEHAN, being duly sworn, deposes
and says:

        1. I am a reporter employed by The New York Times
regularly engaged in writing articles on matters of military,
national or international affairs that are published in The
Times.

        2. Annexed to this affidavit are a number of
such articles. In writing each article I obtained information from governmental sources either in the form of
oral information that I understood to be classified or
from classified documents. Such articles indicate
expressly or by clear implication the nature of their
confidential or restricted source. I made no inquiry
whether such information was lawfully authorized to be
disclosed to me. The articles were published without

interference, objection or resulting action by the government, notwithstanding the information disclosed thereby.

Neil Sheehan (signature)

Sworn to before
me this _7th_ day
of June 1971

(notary signature)

Notary Public

[The following pages contain copies of exhibits submitted with Mr. Sheehan's affidavit. articles copied from The New York Times.]

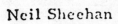
Neil Sheehan

HANOI BOLSTERING AIR RAID DEFENSES

System Is Called Toughest Ever Faced by U.S. Pilots

By NEIL SHEEHAN

Special to The New York Times

WASHINGTON, Sept. 27—North Vietnam, with Soviet aid, is responding to an increase in United States bombing raids by developing a formidable antiaircraft defense system, American military analysts say.

The antiaircraft defense, according to one highly placed source, is already the most advanced that American pilots have ever faced. Indications are that the system will be further elaborated and strengthened.

Since last fall, the number of conventional antiaircraft guns in the north has increased from 1,500 to 5,000. One unofficial estimate put the current number of guns at 7,000. Some analyst said that they believed this was too high.

The North Vietnamese deployed four firing batteries for Soviet-made antiaircraft missiles last fall, but they now have 25 to 30.

There are said to be more radar sets per square mile in operation in North Vietnam than in Eastern Europe. Over recent months there has been a particularly significant increase in the type of radar designed to track American planes at the relatively low altitudes they often use.

Analysts believe that the bulk of this antiaircraft equipment is being supplied by the Soviet Union, rather than Communist China. United States reconnaissance planes have repeatedly photographed conven-

Continued on Page 3, Column 4

HANOI BOLSTERING AIR RAID DEFENSES

Continued From Page 1, Col. 1

tional antiaircraft guns, missiles and launching equipment being unloaded from Soviet ships in Haiphong.

The advanced technology of the antiaircraft defenses gives rise to a suspicion that Soviet Air Force personnel are to some extent involved in running the network, instead of merely giving training and advice. In the summer of last year the antiaircraft defenses were put under a central control apparatus, and since then North Vietnam has displayed an increasing ability to operate the system as a whole in response to American attack patterns.

The Soviet-built missiles, for example, have not proved successful in destroying aircraft by themselves because of

American evasion tactics. Although more than 500 missiles have been fired, they have brought down only 14 of the 384 American aircraft lost over the North and over Communist-held areas of Laos since regular bombing raids began on Feb. 7, 1965.

Used in combination with the conventional antiaircraft guns, however, the missiles drive American planes down from high altitudes where the missiles are dangerous into the flak canopies thrown up by the radar-controlled 37-mm., 57-mm., 85-mm., and 100-mm. cannon.

Effectiveness Impeded

Besides the elaboration of the antiaircraft defenses, the North Vietnamese have developed simple but ingenious methods to meet the problems caused by the American bombing.

The chief technique is simply the employment of tens of thousands of manual laborers, posted as many as 250,000 trees to simulate truck headlights, at times on hillsides in the hope that an over-eager pilot will crash his plane into it. The sources declined to disclose whether this technique had ever succeeded.

throughout the country, to repair damaged roads, bridges and rail lines.

Roads and railroads are often repaired overnight. If a railroad bridge is destroyed, a fully loaded train is brought to one side of the river or gorge, the cargo is unloaded and pushed across over a pontoon bridge in carts and then reloaded into an empty train on the other side.

Trucks are elaborately camouflaged and the camouflage is constantly changed to conform to whatever terrain the trucks happen to be passing through at the moment.

Motorized junks are hidden under the foliage of river banks a few miles above the point where a road bridge has been knocked out. At night the junks are brought down the river, planks are laid across the decks and trucks run over. Before dawn the planks are removed and the junks hidden once more.

Despite the increasing effectiveness of the antiaircraft defenses, American military analysts do not believe North Vietnam will ever be able to bring the system to the point where it will make the United States bombing raids too expensive to continue.

Analysts feel confident that United States countermeasures such as evasive tactics by pilots, electronic jamming of radar and the extensive use of antipersonnel bombs to kill or disable crews of antiaircraft guns, will continue to develop in proportion to the strengthening of the North Vietnamese defenses.

U.S. MAY SOON END ITS THAI BUILD-UP

Stabilization of Strength at 35,000 Servicemen Seen

By NEIL SHEEHAN
Special to The New York Times

WASHINGTON, Nov. 17—The United States plans to halt its military build-up in Thailand in the near future and to stabilize the number of American servicemen there at a level of about 35,000, informed sources said today.

There are now about 33,000 American servicemen in Thailand, most of whom are in the Air Force, the sources said. The 2,000 additional men—specialists on administration, planning, supply and transportation, as well as technicians — will gradually be added over the next few months. They will man a countrywide communications network that is nearing completion.

The major portion of the planned build-up—the deployment of fighter-bomber, reconnaissance and air refueling tanker squadrons to pursue the air war against North Vietnam —has virtually been accomplished, the sources said.

The United States has about 400 planes stationed in Thailand. These planes fly more than 50 per cent of the missions against North Vietnam.

Seven Airfields Used

The aircraft, which include 14 squadrons of F-105 Thunderchief and F-4 Phantom fighter-bombers as well as KC-135 jet tankers, operate from seven airfields in the country.

The fighter-bombers are at bases in central and northeastern Thailand, while most of the tankers are reported to operate from the new U-Tapao airfield adjacent to the American logistics center at Sattahip on the Gulf of Siam south of Bangkok.

The construction of the U-Tapao field, officially opened last August, aroused considerable controversy in the United States because its 11,500-foot runway is capable of handling B-52 bombers and there were persistent reports last summer that Washington was planning to station Stratofortresses there.

Informed sources said, however, that while the relatively long runway at U-Tapao was obviously built with the idea that the United States might some day decide to station B-52's there, no decision about such use has yet been made.

The sources said they expect o see most of the $200-million American program of road-building and base construction in Thailand completed by next June.

Unloading fuel at Sattahip will allow tankers to save time by avoiding the busy port of Bangkok and will ease some of the strain on the capital's port. The fuel will then be transported to the airfields by truck or pipe.

The second major logistics

center is located at Korat, northeast of Bangkok. Road-building and other engineering equipment has been stored there along with enough vehicles and other supplies to equip at least one American infantry brigade.

Washington has consistently been reluctant to disclose details of the build-up in view of Thailand's unwillingness to become openly and officially identified with the American air war against North Vietnam.

M'NAMARA VICTOR IN STAND ON THAIS

NOV 3 '66

U.S. Copter Units Barred in Fight on Insurgents, but Other Aid Is Increased

By NEIL SHEEHAN
Special to The New York Times

WASHINGTON, Nov. 2—Secretary of Defense Robert S. McNamara has won an argument over whether the United States should become physically involved in putting down a Communist rising in northeast Thailand.

The White House has upheld Mr. McNamara's contention that Washington should not dispatch United States Army helicopter companies to Thailand and should not assign American military advisers to battalion-level units of the Thai army.

He is understood to be reluctant to see the United States become physically involved in combating another Communist insurgency on the Asian mainland unless there is a vital need.

Graham A. Martin, United States Ambassador to Thailand, has contended for several months that helicopter companies should be sent to Thailand and military advisers assigned to Thai battalion-level units.

Mr. Martin has argued that the Thais need the mobility the

Continued on Page 15, Column 1

M'NAMARA VICTOR IN STAND ON THAIS

Continued From Page 1, Col. 4

helicopters would provide to deal adequately with the insurgents. The Thais have only a limited number of helicopters and military observers estimate it would take a year to 15 months to organize and equip enough Thai helicopter units.

The assignment of United States Army officers as advisers to battalion-level units of the Thai Army, the Ambassador has asserted, would allow the United States to monitor the results of training programs provided by the American Military Assistance and Advisory Group in Thailand. Thus, he has argued, the training programs could be changed or improved and the effectiveness of the Thai Army heightened.

American military advisers are not assigned below regimental level in the Thai Army and they normally do not accompany Thai units into the field on operations.

Mr. Martin has been supported in his arguments by Maj. Gen. Richard G. Stilwell, chief of the Military Assistance and Advisory Group in Thailand.

United States physical engagement in the Vietnam war began in the fall of 1961 with the dispatch of Army helicopter companies and the assignment of American advisers to battalion-level units of the Vietnamese Army.

While ferrying the Vietnamese into the field and advising the battalions, the Americans became engaged in the shooting themselves and the United States commitment to South Vietnam gradually deepened.

Although the United States is committed to the defense of Thailand by treaty and American Air Force bases are established there to prosecute the air war against North Vietnam, Mr. McNamara is reported to believe that the United States should not become any more involved in Thailand than is necessary.

He is also understood to feel that the insurgency is small enough for the Thais to handle themselves and there is no need for Americans to become directly engaged. Military sources estimate that 600 to 1,000 Communist insurgents are active in northeast Thailand.

While recognizing the need for helicopter companies, Mr. McNamara is reported to believe that the Thais can wait until their own helicopter companies have been equipped and organized.

Arms Aid Increased

The announcement Sunday of a 30 per cent increase in American military aid to Thailand during the current fiscal year formed something of a compromise between the position of Mr. McNamara and that of Ambassador Martin and General Stilwell.

Military aid to Thailand for the 1967 fiscal year had previously been scheduled at about $40-million. The level has now been raised to about $60-million.

Along with the dispatch of helicopter companies and the assignment of advisers to battalion-level, Mr. Martin and General Stilwell had urged an increase in military aid of about 40 per cent. Mr. McNamara was reported to have favored a simple increase in military aid of about 15 per cent.

Mr. Martin and General Stilwell obtained an increase in aid close to their requests, while Mr. McNamara won his major point by successfully arguing for the present at least, against sending helicopter companies to Thailand or assigning American advisers to Thai army battalions.

The increase in aid will consist largely of equipment for use in fighting the insurgents. It will include small arms, communications equipment, vehicles and helicopters to form new Thai helicopter units.

The United States will also provide river patrol boats for the Thai police and navy for patrolling the Mekong River frontier between Thailand and Laos, across which Communist guerrillas have been infiltrating.

U. S. EASES CURBS ON PILOTS IN NORTH

DEC 20 '67

Restrictions on Flying Near Hanoi and China Relaxed —2 MIG's Are Downed

By NEIL SHEEHAN
Special to The New York Times

WASHINGTON, Dec. 19—The White House has relaxed restrictions governing the air war against North Vietnam to permit American pilots to fly with relative freedom through the so-called buffer strip along the Chinese border and the outer 20-mile circle around Hanoi.

Well-placed informants said the relaxation, granted in recent weeks, was one of a number of White House moves that allowed a sharp escalation of the bombing raids since hearings on the air war before the Senate's Subcommittee on Preparedness Investigation last August.

[The United States command announced the downing of two MIG-17 interceptors and the probable downing of a third on Tuesday over the Hanoi area, The Associated Press reported. Page 9.]

The recent bombing escalation, the informants noted, has wrought a significant change in the strategy behind the attacks against targets in the Tonkin delta, and particularly the

Continued on Page 10, Column 1

U.S. Relaxes Curbs on Fliers On Missions in North Vietnam

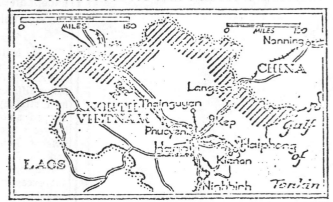

The New York Times   Dec. 20, 1967

Shading shows former buffer zone along Chinese border

Continued From Page 1, Col. 2

Hanoi-Haiphong areas — the heartland of North Vietnam.

Where previously the strategy governing the air war against the North was the interdiction of supplies flowing to Communist forces in South Vietnam, the concentrated bombing in the delta is now aimed directly at breaking the will of North Vietnam to continue the war and forcing Hanoi to the negotiating table.

Senior military officials hope to accomplish this objective, informants said, by gradually reducing the flow of imported food, petroleum and manufactured goods required for the functioning of North Vietnam itself.

Thus the raids are being directed with as much ferocity as possible against the northwest and northeast rail lines from Communist China and transportation links, such as bridges, in the immediate vicinity of Hanoi.

Military commanders are still forbidden to bomb the docks in Haiphong, the main port, for fear of hitting Soviet or Chinese ships. But they have been attempting to cut the road and rail links leading out of the city.

McNamara Advice Rejected

The change in strategy amounts, in effect, to the basic acceptance by President Johnson of the advice of the Joint Chiefs of Staff and the rejection of that of outgoing Secretary of Defense Robert S. McNamara.

Under the latest relaxation in the so-called rules of engagement, White House permission is still required to attack targets in the 25-mile buffer strip just below the China border and in the outer 20-mile circle around Hanoi, which extends from an inner 10-mile circle immediately around Hanoi and has a radius of 30 miles.

But American pilots are now authorized to fly through both areas on their way to attack targets outside these restricted zones. This relaxation, informants said, has permitted Air Force and Navy air commanders to adopt more flexible tactics and to better avoid concentrations of North Vietnamese antiaircraft batteries and ground-to-air missiles.

New Limits Not Disclosed

It is unknown exactly how close pilots may now fly to the Chinese border without specific approval. Advance White House permission is still required for flights within the inner 10-mile circle around Hanoi.

One relaxation that senior officials have welcomed is the permission now being given for restrikes on sensitive targets that the North Vietnamese have managed to repair after the initial raids. The Longbien Bridge, across the Red River on the edge of downtown Hanoi, for example, has been bombed four times, the latest yesterday, since it was first attacked on Aug. 11.

Rail bridges within the 25-mile buffer strip along the Chinese border are also being repeatedly attacked. "Now, when the North Vietnamese repair the bridge we can go in and knock it right down again," one informant said.

THE NEW YORK TIMES, T[

M'NAMARA SPLIT WITH JOINT CHIEFS

Except on Bombing Step-up, He Won Johnson's Support

By NEIL SHEEHAN
Special to The New York Times

WASHINGTON, Nov. 27 — Major differences on three Vietnam strategy issues have developed since the summer of last year between Secretary of Defense Robert S. McNamara and the Joint Chiefs of Staff.

With one partial but important exception, however, Presidental Johnson has taken the same view as Mr. McNamara on the three matters which were:

1. The nature of the bombing campaign against North Vietnam.

2. The number of American troops needed to fight the ground war in the south.

3. The erection of an anti-infiltration barrier along the 17th parallel, which divides North and South Vietnam.

The partial exception has been the bombing campaign against the north, where the President granted the Joint Chiefs a significant step-up this summer and fall against the strong advice of Mr. McNamara.

Bombing Appeal Rejected

But Mr. Johnson has so far continued to deny military leaders their major objective in bombing strategy — permission to intensify the raids significantly beyond their present level, including the mining and aerial destruction of the port of Haiphong. The military men advocate this as necessary to break the will of North Vietnam to support and carry on the war in the south.

The disagreement between Mr. McNamara and military leaders over the bombing campaign first came into public prominence during hearings before the Senate Preparedness subcommittee last August. Its Investigation chairman is Senator John Stennis, Democrat of Mississippi.

The hearings showed that, in contrast to the military leaders' conception of the air war as a will-breaking campaign, Mr. McNamara saw the bombing raids as simply an effort to interdict the flow of men and supplies into South Vietnam and to exact a political "price" from North Vietnam for its prosecution of the war there.

He argued that the raids had not seriously affected the "war-making capability" of North Vietnam and had not been able and would probably not be able in the future to limit the Communist military activity in the south below the present level."

1. The nature of the bombing campaign against North Vietnam.
2. The number of American troops needed to fight the ground war in the south.
3. The erection of an anti-infiltration barrier along the 17th parallel, which divides North and South Vietnam.

The partial exception has been the bombing campaign against the north, where the President granted the Joint Chiefs a significant step-up this summer and fall against the strong advice of Mr. McNamara.

Bombing Appeal Rejected

But Mr. Johnson has so far continued to deny military leaders their major objective in bombing strategy — permission to intensify the raids significantly beyond their present level, including the mining and aerial destruction of the port of Haiphong. The military men advocate this as necessary to break the will of North Vietnam to support and carry on the war in the south.

The disagreement between Mr. McNamara and military leaders over the bombing campaign first came into public prominence during hearings before the Senate Preparedness subcommittee last August. Its Investigation chairman is Senator John Stennis, Democrat of Mississippi.

The hearings showed that, in contrast to the military leaders' conception of the air war as a will-breaking campaign, Mr. McNamara saw the bombing raids as simply an effort to interdict the flow of men and supplies into South Vietnam and to exact a political "price" from North Vietnam for its prosecution of the war there.

He argued that the raids had not seriously affected the "war-making capability" of North Vietnam and had not been able and would probably not be able in the future 'to limit the [Communist military] activity in the south below the present level."

Mr. McNamara argued that a significant intensification, including the destruction of Haiphong, would not alter this situation and that the level of bombing had no direct relationship" to the number of American troops required in the south and to American casualties there.

The testimony of military leaders directly contradicted these arguments. For instance, Gen. Earle G. Wheeler, chairman of the Joint Chiefs, asserted that the closing of Haiphong would materially shorten the war.

In a news conference shortly after the testimony, Mr. Johnson did not come to the support of Mr. McNamara on this issue, and it soon seemed clear to observers that he was accepting the military advice to a significant degree.

There have been repeated differences between Mr. McNamara and the Joint Chiefs over how many United States troops are needed to fight the war in the South. These differences have been cropping up since the American military buildup began in the South in June of 1965. In this area, however, it is believed that there has not been any disagreement between Mr. McNamara and the President.

The differences last came to the forefront in the spring of this year when the Joint Chiefs supported a request from Gen. William C. Westmoreland, American military commander in Vietnam, for 75,000 more troops beyond the 450,000 the Administration planned to have there by mid-1968.

The chiefs also recommended a partial mobilization of the reserves to provide the troops General Westmoreland desired and to refurbish the Army's frayed training manpower base. This was the third occasion on which the chiefs had recommended mobilizing reserves. Previously, they did this in the summer of 1965 and in February of 1966.

Joint Chiefs Said to Oppose Any Bombing Pause

By NEIL SHEEHAN
Special to The New York Times

WASHINGTON, Nov. 13 — The Joint Chiefs of Staff have conveyed in detail to President Johnson their contention that another pause in the bombing of North Vietnam would be harmful to the American war effort, well-placed informants said today.

The military leaders' case against a suspension of the bombing was presented to the President in recent weeks by Gen. Earle WGheeler, Chairman of the Joint Chiefs of Staff.

There has been widespread speculation that the President might offer a significant pause or reduction in the bombing this winter or next spring in an effort to persuade North Vietnam to enter peace negotiations.

General Wheeler, the informants said, told the President that the Joint Chiefs were unanimously opposed to any bombing pause, even for 24 hours, if it could be avoided.

3 Cease-Fires Probable

President Nguygen Van Thieu of South Vietnam said Saturday that the allied forces probably would observe 24-hour cease-fires at the Christmas and New Year's holidays and a third 48-hour cease-fire at Tet, the Vietnamese lunak New Year in February. Bombing raids against the North are normally suspended during such cease-fires.

But while the Joint Chiefs are understood to oppose a pause even for periods as short as these, informants said that their argument was principally directed at a longer suspension of bombing, such as the 37-day pause in 1965-1966.

Some senior military leaders are said to feel that short cease-fires and bombing pauses for the Christmas and New Year's holidays and for Tet will probably be unavoidable for political reasons.

Wheeler Reported to Have Presented Arguments of Leaders to President

The first reason cited by the Joint Chiefs against a bombing pause, the sources said, was that it would have a detrimental effect on the morale of the American troops in South Vietnam.

To suspend the bombing of North Vietnam while these men are still under fire from the Vietcong and North Vietnamese in the South could create an adverse change in the attitude of the American troops, the Joint Chiefs are said to believe.

A second argument, the sources said, was that a pause would result in increased American casualties in South Vietnam.

This contention has been frequently put forward by military leaders arguing against past pauses in the bombing. It was challenged last August by Secretary of Defense Robert S. McNamara in testimony before the Senate Preparedness Subcommittee.

Political Impact Cited

Mr. McNamara argued that the bombing had the political impact of exacting a price from North Vietnam for its military activity in the South but had a negligible effect on reducing enemy military pressure there.

The Joint Chiefs argue that the bombing does limit the scale of enemy military activity in the South. In their presentation to the President, they are understood to have pointed to the 23,000 tons of supplies they say the North Vietnamese moved into South Vietnam or into staging areas adjacent to the demilitarized zone straddling the border between North and South Vietnam during the four-day jet bombing suspension early this year.

The Joint Chiefs contended that the United States paid for these supplies with American lives and that another bombing pause would have similar consequences, informants said.

A third assertion made by the Joint Chiefs to the President, the sources said, was that earlier pauses in the bombing had shown that the North Vietnamese would not be enticed into serious peace negotiations by such gestures.

The Joint Chiefs are said to have argued that Noth Vietnam had made clear that it would settle for nothing less than a permanent halt in the bombing and the withdrawal of American troops from South Vietnam.

Dissension in the United States over the war

States over the war has led the North Vietnamese to believe that they may eventually achieve these aims, the Joint Chiefs are understood to have argued, and another pause in the bombing will be interpreted by Hanoi as evidence that domestic dissension is eroding the will of the Administration to continue the conflict.

Thus, the Joint Chiefs asserted, according to the informants, that a suspension would prolong, rather than shorten, the war.

The fourth argument against a bombing suspension, informants said, was that the North Vietnamese might react to a pause by opening talks intended to continue the pause rather than achieving a peaceful settlement acceptable to the United States.

STUDENT IS SEIZED

Clashes Break Out

Success Sto

Soviet Arms Aid to Non-Red Lands Nearing $500-M

Continued From Page 1, Col. 7

leaders to deal with the so-called bourgeois-nationalist governments in the developing nations. Previously, Soviet foreign policy had concentrated on attempting to further the interests of the Communist parties in these countries. The Soviet Union has sought to replace the Western presence, which formerly held sway in these countries, with its own.

Aid Is Widespread

Soviet arms diplomacy has been directed mainly at an arc of countries ranging from India through the Middle East to North Africa, but the effort has not been limited to this area. It has extended to Southeast Asia, to sub-Saharan Africa and to Latin America in the case of Cuba, a Communist underdeveloped country. Cuba has received $750-million in Soviet arms.

The Soviet Union moved cautiously in its first experiment, the 1955 Egyptian deal, using Czechoslovakia as the intermediary and ostensible source of $80-million worth of MIG's, tanks, artillery, small arms and naval vessels.

The arrangement worked well in terms of increased Soviet influence with President Gamal Abdel Nasser, and a second arms deal followed in November, 1956.

Apparently encouraged by the Egyptian experience, the Soviet Union provided Afghanistan with $25-million worth of MIG-15's, tanks and infantry weapons. A small-scale arms arrangement was made with the anti-Western regime in Syria, and Yemen received some Soviet infantry weapons.

In 1958, another major opportunity opened in the Middle East with the fall of a pro-Western Government in Iraq. Moscow moved quickly, and Iraq became the fourth Middle Eastern country to obtain Soviet military equipment.

The first instance of Soviet arms diplomacy in Southeast Asia also occurred in 1958. Angered by American support for rebels in Sumatra who demanded that the Jakarta regime resign and form a new Cabinet without pro-Communist members, President Sukarno obtained $250-million worth of Soviet arms. Western countries had refused to sell him advanced weapons.

The following year the first transaction in sub-Saharan Africa took place when Guinea received Soviet armored cars, artillery and small arms.

During the next two years India, Ghana, Morocco, Mali, the Sudan and the Algerian rebels, who were fighting for independence from France, joined the list.

Sukarno Gets 2d Shipment

In 1961, President Sukarno again sought arms for his campaign to force the Netherlands to relinquish West Irian, the former Dutch New Guinea. The Soviet Union agreed to supply Indonesia with $1-billion worth of weaponry.

By 1965, six other countries, four of them in sub-Saharan Africa, had become Soviet arms recipients. They were the Congo Republic, Tanzania, Uganda, Somalia, Cyprus and Cambodia.

Soviet weapons were also shipped to rebels in the former Belgian Congo in 1964 and 1965.

The Soviet arms shipments to some of these sub-Saharan countries have been aimed as much at offsetting Chinese activity as at competing for influence with the West. Because the capacity of these nations to absorb arms is limited, the Chinese have been able to afford to compete with the Russians to some extent.

The desire to offset Chinese influence is also believed to be a major reason for a 1966 agreement under which Pakistan acquired about $10-million worth of Soviet military trucks and helicopters. A year earlier, Pakistan signed an agreement with China for $30-million to $40-million worth of Chinese-owned MIG-19 fighters, light bombers, tanks and other ground equipment.

In all of its arms arrangements, Moscow has followed the principle that it is better from a psychological as well as a financial viewpoint to sell the weapons than to give them away.

The Soviet sales have almost always been barter arrangements, with repayments spread over eight to ten years or more at nominal interest rates.

In practice, however, most of the sales have developed into virtual gifts because the recipients are either unable or unwilling to pay their debts.

The huge Indonesian arms debt continues to be a sore point in Soviet-Indonesian relations. It has been estimated that the Indonesians have paid for only about $100-million to $200-million of the $1.2-billion in weapons they received from the Soviet Union after 1958.

Indonesia has also been the most conspicuous failure in Soviet arms diplomacy. After accepting the weapons, President Sukarno betrayed Soviet interests by adopting a pro-Chinese foreign policy. The Indoesian Army then deposed Mr. Sukarno after a Communist coup attempt in 1965 and used its Soviet arms to massacre members of the Indonesian Comunist party.

Outcome Is in Doubt

The outcome of the Soviet arms diplomacy in United Arab Republic is also in doubt.

The arms increased President Nasser's confidence and undoubtedly helped provoke the latest Arab-Israeli war. Mr. Nasser then lost most of his $1-billion worth of Soviet arms in the Sinai Desert and the Soviet Union's prestige with the Arabs suffered when it refused to intervene militarily to prevent the debacle.

Since the end of the fighting Moscow has shipped about $150-million in MIG's, tanks and other equipment to Cairo. Soviet arms shipments to the Arab nations have increased 50 per cent, from an average of six to nine shiploads a month, since the war.

The Soviet experiences in Afghanistan and India have been less turbulent so far. In both instances the Soviet Union has succeeded in replacing the West as the major source of arms.

The growing desire of some underdeveloped countries to avoid complete dependence on one source of arms has apparently been responsible for the most recent instance of Soviet arms diplomacy in the Middle East: the barter sale late this

t Arms Aid to Non-Red Lands Nearing $500-Million a Year

m Page 1, Col. 7

al wit... the so- is-nationalist gov- the developing ously. Soviet for- iad concentrated to further the in- Communist par- ountries. The So- has sought to Vestern presence, y held sway in s, with its own.

Videspread

; diplomacy has mainly at an are nging from India Middle East to but the effort limited to this tended to South- ub-Saharan Afri- n America in the a Communist un- country. Cuba $750-million in

Inion moved cau- first experiment, tian deal, using . as the inter-

mediary and ostensible source of $80-million worth of MIG's, tanks, artillery, small arms and naval vessels.

The arrangement worked well in terms of increased Soviet influence with President Gamal Abdel Nasser, and a second arms deal followed in November, 1956.

Apparently encouraged by the Egyptian experience, the Soviet Union provided Afghanistan with $25-million worth of MIG-15's, tanks and infantry weapons. A small-scale arms arrangement was made with the anti-Western regime in Syria, and Yemen received some Soviet infantry weapons.

In 1958, another major opportunity opened in the Middle East with the fall of a pro-Western Government in Iraq. Moscow moved quickly, and Iraq became the fourth Middle Eastern country to obtain Soviet military equipment.

The first instance of Soviet arms diplomacy in Southeast Asia also occurred in 1958. Angered by American support for rebels in Sumatra who demanded that the Jakarta regime re-

sign and form a new Cabinet without pro-Communist members, President Sukarno obtained $250-million worth of Soviet arms. Western countries had refused to sell him advanced weapons.

The following year the first transaction in sub-Saharan Africa took place when Guinea received Soviet armored cars, artillery and small arms.

During the next two years India, Ghana, Morocco, Mali, the Sudan and the Algerian rebels, who were fighting for independence from France, joined the list.

Sukarno Gets 2d Shipment

In 1961, President Sukarno again sought arms for his campaign to force the Netherlands to relinquish West Irian, the former Dutch New Guinea. The Soviet Union agreed to supply Indonesia with $1-billion worth of weaponry.

By 1965, six other countries, four of them in sub-Saharan Africa, had become Soviet arms recipients. They were the Congo Republic, Tanzania, Uganda, Somalia, Cyprus and Cambodia.

Soviet weapons were also shipped to rebels in the former Belgian Congo in 1964 and 1965.

The Soviet arms shipments to some of these sub-Saharan countries have been aimed as much at offsetting Chinese activity as at competing for influence with the West. Because the capacity of these nations to absorb arms is limited, the Chinese have been able to afford to compete with the Russians to some extent.

The desire to offset Chinese influence is also believed to be a major reason for a 1966 agreement under which Pakistan acquired about $10-million worth of Soviet military trucks and helicopters. A year earlier, Pakistan signed an agreement with China for $30-million to $40-million worth of Chinese-owned MIG-19 fighters, light bombers, tanks and other ground equipment.

In all of its arms arrangements, Moscow has followed the principle that it is better from a psychological as well as a financial viewpoint to sell the weapons than to give them away.

The Soviet sales have almost

always been barter arrangements, with repayments spread over eight to ten years or more at nominal interest rates.

In practice, however, most of the sales have developed into virtual gifts because the recipients are either unable or unwilling to pay their debts.

The huge Indonesian arms debt continues to be a sore point in Soviet-Indonesian relations. It has been estimated that the Indonesians have paid for only about $100-million to $200-million of the $1.2-billion in weapons they received from the Soviet Union after 1958.

Indonesia has also been the most conspicuous failure in Soviet arms diplomacy. After accepting the weapons, president Sukarno betrayed Soviet interests by adopting a pro-Chinese foreign policy. The Indonesian Army then deposed Mr. Sukarno after a Communist coup attempt in 1965 and used its Soviet arms to massacre members of the Indonesian Communist party.

Outcome Is in Doubt

The outcome of the Soviet arms diplomacy in United Arab Republic is also in doubt.

The arms increased President Nasser's confidence and undoubtedly helped provoke the latest Arab-Israeli war. Mr. Nasser then lost most of his $1-billion worth of Soviet arms in the Sinai Desert and the Soviet Union's prestige with the Arabs suffered when it refused to intervene militarily to prevent the debacle.

Since the end of the fighting Moscow has shipped about $150-million in MIG's, tanks and other equipment to Cairo. Soviet arms shipments to the Arab nations have increased 50 per cent, from an average of six to nine shiploads a month, since the war.

The Soviet experiences in Afghanistan and India have been less turbulent so far. In both instances the Soviet Union has succeeded in replacing the West as the major source of arms.

The growing desire of some underdeveloped countries to avoid complete dependence on one source of arms has apparently been responsible for the most recent instance of Soviet arms diplomacy in the Middle East: the barter sale late this

year of $110-million in weapons to Iran.

Iran has been a major beneficiary of American military assistance, with grants of about $850-million and long-term sales credits of $210-million.

Despite this aid, Iran has broadened her source of supply by trading natural gas for Soviet arms. Shah Mohammed Riza Pahlevi has told American officials that he will receive only such ground equipment as armored personnel carriers, antiaircraft guns, artillery and trucks.

There is a suspicion that more advanced items, possibly aircraft or missiles, were included in the agreement.

Morocco, another beneficiary of long-term American arms sales credits this year, has since revived her arms arrangement with the Soviet Union to obtain spare parts for the dozen MIG-17 fighters and 70 Soviet tanks she received in 1961 and 1962.

MOSCOW STEPS UP ARMS DIPLOMACY.

SEP 5 67

Its Military Aid to Non-Red Nations Seems to Be Near $500-Million Annually

N. Sheehan

Special to The New York Times

WASHINGTON, Sept. 4—In mid-August the airfield at Kano, in northern Nigeria, was suddenly closed to commercial flights by the Nigerian federal authorities. The reason became clear during the next several days when 15 Soviet Antonov-12 transports landed there and ground crews unloaded crates from the four-engine cargo planes.

In the crates were 10 disassembled MIG jet fighter-bombers. Two were MIG-15's of Korean war vintage and eight were more modern MIG-17's. About 50 Soviet technicians and instructors arrived with the crates. Apparently, their mission was to assemble and maintain the MIG's and to teach Nigerians, or European mercenaries the Nigerians were attempting to hire, how to fly the planes against rebels from the Eastern Region.

Total Exceeds $4-Billion

Nigeria was the 22d and latest example of Soviet arms diplomacy in the non-Communist, underdeveloped world.

According to information available here, the Soviet Union has provided $4-billion to $5-billion worth of weaponry to non-Communist developing nations since 1955, when its first arms deal with the United Arab Republic was closed. The aid has included about 2,500 military planes and helicopters and more than 3,000 tanks. By 1965, exports were running at about $400-million a year. They are believed to have risen since then to an annual average of more than $500-million.

American arms exports to the underdeveloped nations have also increased in recent years, and sales alone totaled $534-million for the fiscal year that ended June 30.

3,000 Russians Abroad

The arms export program has become a major element in foreign policy for the Soviet Union as well as the United States. About 3,000 Soviet military personnel and civilian technicians are permanently stationed overseas in military assistance and advisory groups.

Between 15,000 and 20,000 military personnel from the developing nations, ranging from privates first class to generals, have gone to the Soviet Union for six months or more of training.

Arms diplomacy has been a post-Stalin development in Soviet foreign policy, reflecting the willingness of the Soviet

Continued on Page 24, Column 2

PENTAGON LOANS FINANCING ARMS

Continued From Page 1, Col. 8

held up action on legislation to extend the life of the Government-owned institution for five more years and expand its lending authority.

In closed hearings before the House Banking and Currency Committee last Monday, Harold Linder, the bank president, asserted that until that day he had not known nor wanted to know the names of the countries that had received the loans.

Five of the countries are in Latin America—Brazil, Argentina, Peru, Chile and Venezuela. Four are Middle Eastern countries—Iran, Saudi Arabia, Jordan and Israel. Three are in South and Southeast Asia—Pakistan, India and Malaysia. The North African country is Morocco. Taiwan is the 14th recipient.

In addition to the country-X loans since mid-1965, the Defense Department is believed to have outstanding about $60-million in loans to underdeveloped countries that the Pentagon made directly from the revolving credit account or obtained from commercial banks.

The Export-Import Bank has also directly lent at Defense Department request since the fiscal year 1963, $1.1-billion more to a number of developed countries, including Austria, Italy, Britain and Australia, for arms purchases from Mr. Kuss.

Over the last two fiscal years, arms loans have constituted more than 39 per cent of the bank's lending business, and senior administration officials have testified that the bank has made further commitments to lend $1-billion more for weapons during the current and future fiscal years.

The exact amounts of the country-x loans to each of 14 aforementioned nations are unknown. It is also believed that some of the loans as of last June 30 were increments of large arms purchases that will require future loans to complete financing of the sales.

The informants, however, supplied some regional and local breakdown.

About 75 per cent of the country-x loans, they said, approximately $450-million, went to the four Middle Eastern countries and Morocco.

The five Latin-American countries reportedly obtained about $100-million. Brazil is understood to have received about $43-million — Argentina about $21-million and Venezuela approximately $29-million, with the remaining 57-million divided between Peru and Chile.

Approximately $24-million, about 4 per cent, was lent to India and Pakistan, and the remainder of the $591-million went to Malaysia and Taiwan.

Iran apparently obtained a loan as at least partial credit toward a $200-million purchase in 1966 of F-4 Phantom jets, the most advanced of American operational fighter-bombers, and ground equipment. The loan to Saudi Arabia was ap-

Anonymous Loans by Pentagon Financing Arms to 14 Countries

By NEIL SHEEHAN
Special to The New York Times

JUL 24 '67

WASHINGTON, July 23—The Defense Department has been using anonymous loans from the Export-Import Bank to finance arms sales in Latin America, the Middle East, North Africa and Southeast Asia.

Informants have disclosed that the $591-million the Pentagon obtained from the bank between mid-1965 and last June 30 through so-called "country-X accounts" was lent to 14 countries for purchases of American armaments.

Under the country-X device, the bank opens a line of credit to the Defense Department arms salesman, Henry J. Kuss Jr., which Mr. Kuss lends to the country involved for the arms purchase.

The loans are guaranteed by

the Defense Department through its $983-million revolving arms sales credit fund under a law that requires that only 25 per cent of the loan must be covered by the fund.

The extent of the bank's involvement in the arms traffic brought vigorous protests in Congress last week and has

Continued on Page 8, Column 1

parently financed toward a purchase of $120-million in Hawk antiaircraft missiles and assorted other hardware.

Israel is believed to have obtained its loan for Hawk antiaircraft missiles and tanks that Mr. Kuss sold the Israelis in 1965 and 1966. Jordan was apparently lent the money for the tanks and armored personnel carriers it obtained last year from the United States.

Argentina purchased 25 A-4 Skyhawk fighter-bombers from the United States in 1966 and Venezuela has reportedly been sold helicopters for use against the pro-Communist guerrillas there.

Morocco has been sold a squadron of F-5 Freedom fighters and Malaysia reportedly obtained a loan of about $15-million for jet trainers and other equipment.

The loan to India is somewhat mystifying because until last May the Administration officially imposed an embargo on the shipment of so-called lethal military equipment to India and Pakistan. Shipments of what the Administration calls nonlethal equipment, such as radar and trucks, had been allowed.

Some military specialists consider the distinction specious because an armed force needs support equipment as well as guns and tanks to be effective.

A sizable number of Democrats and Republicans on the House and Senate Banking Committees are angry about the use of the bank to finance arms business, but they are even more disturbed by the fact that its funds have been employed to sell arms to countries involved in disputes with their neighbors.

They point out that the major portion of the loans within the last two fiscal years, about $450-million, went to the Middle East and North Africa, the most explosive areas.

Hanoi's Air Force Being Trained at Chinese Bases

BY NEIL SHEEHAN
Special to The New York Times

WASHINGTON, March 13—Some members of the North Vietnamese air force are training in southern China, well-placed military sources said today.

The sources said that, according to intelligence reports, 32 North Vietnamese MIG-15 and MIG-17 jet fighters and two Ilyushin-28 twin-jet bombers are based in southern China. One base mentioned is at Mengtsz in Yunnan Province, about 40 miles north of the Vietnam-China border.

As far as they can determine, the sources said, the North Vietnamese planes conduct training flights but are not using the Chinese fields as bases from which to attack American aircraft. Some of the North Vietnamese planes may also have been rotated to China for maintenance, the sources said. It is believed that the North Vietnamese planes have been based in China for several months.

Including the aircraft in China, North Vietnam is believed to possess 122 jets—18 MIG-21 jets, the most advanced of the Soviet-made operational fighters, 96 older model MIG-15 and MIG-17 jets and eight IL-28 bombers.

The force may have been reduced to 120 jets as a result of the attack on the large Thainguyen iron and steel complex 38 miles south of Hanoi on Friday. During the raid, American officials said, one North Vietnamese MIG was shot down and another "probably destroyed."

The fuel capacity of the MIG-15's and 17's would limit the time in which they could attack American planes over the central Tonkin Delta, the heart of North Vietnam, to about 10 or 15 minutes if China permitted the MIG's to use its bases for attacks on American planes, one senior source said.

American planes have maintained a clear superiority over

But U.S. Sources Report That Fields Aren't Being Used to Attack American Planes

the North Vietnamese in aerial combat and the ratio of North Vietnamese planes downed to American losses from MIG's is about 3.5 to 1. Since regular raids against the north began in February of 1965, the United States has lost 10 aircraft in aerial combat while at least 37 North Vietnamese MIG's have been destroyed.

Two 'Nuisance Factors'

The sources said the North Vietnamese Air Force has been sufficiently irritating for senior Air Force and Naval air commanders to urge the bombing of airfields in the Hanoi-Haiphong area where the MIG's are based. The White House has so far refused permission.

The North Vietnamese Air Force creates two principal nuisance factors, the sources said.

One is that American aircraft are sometimes forced to jettison their bombs and divert from assigned targets when attacked by MIG's. The F-105 Thunderchief Jets, the workhorses of the American air war against the north, are unable to evade the MIG's or engage them in combat when loaded with bombs.

The second is that because of the MIG's, American F-4 Phantoms must be regularly assigned to escort duty to protect the F-105's and other F-4's carrying out the bombing missions.

If the North Vietnamese Air Force were severely crippled, the sources contend, Phantoms employed on escort duty could be assigned to bombing missions and the number of planes available for bombing runs thus increased.

New Airfields Built

The three principal airfields used by the North Vietnamese Air Force are Phucyen, about 18 miles north of Hanoi; Kep, about 40 miles northeast of the capital, and Gialam, in the suburbs of Hanoi.

Two new airfields at Hoaloi and Baithuong, south of Hanoi, have recently been constructed and the old French airfield of Catbi near Haiphong is also being improved to handle jets.

FOE IS SAID TO USE HAVEN NEAR CHINA

MAR 8 '67

Area U.S. Will Not Attack Is Reported a Sanctuary for Convoys by Day

Special to The New York Times

WASHINGTON, March 7— North Vietnam is using a restricted zone about 25 miles deep along the Chinese border as a daytime sanctuary for truck convoys, informed military sources said today.

American aircraft are prohibited from bombing within the zone without special permission from Washington. The restriction is intended to avoid the diplomatic and political consequences of intrusions into Chinese airspace.

The zone runs along the length of North Vietnam's border with China. The depth varies, but it is usually about 25 to 30 miles.

U.S. Cautions Pilots

Except for reconnaissance aircraft on assigned surveillance missions, American pilots are normally cautioned against flying within the zone unless there is a necessity to do so.

[In the fighting Tuesday, North Vietnamese gunners continued their mortar attacks on an American artillery position near the demilitarized zone, killing six marines. Page 3]

The informed Washington military sources discussing enemy convoys said trucks also were being sheltered in North Vietnamese cities during the day, apparently because American

---

THE NEW YORK TIMES, WEDNESDAY, MARCH 8, 1967

Enemy Is Said to Exploit Sanctuary Near China

Continued From Page 1, Col. 2

pilots are restricted in any attacks on populous areas.

Two cities mentioned by the military sources are Thanhhoa, 80 miles south of Hanoi, and Vinh, about 165 miles south of the North Vietnamese capital.

It could not be determined whether the Joint Chiefs of Staff have begun to put pressure on Secretary of Defense Robert S. McNamara and President Johnson for permission to attack truck convoys in the restricted zone along the Chinese border and in population centers to the south.

Aerial reconnaissance photographs, the sources said, show hundreds of trucks loaded with supplies lined up along the roads within a zone along the Chinese border during the daytime.

The sources said the trucks bring supplies from China into North Vietnam.

At night, the trucks move south in small convoys and the roads within the restricted zone are emptied, the sources said.

Repeated reconnaissance photography of a number of North Vietnamese cities show a similar pattern. During the day, the centers of the cities are filled with trucks. At night, the trucks move out in small convoys.

The North Vietnamese are also using population centers to shelter many small supply dumps. The military sources said the enemy often stacked 55-gallon drums of gasoline and other petroleum supplies in the towns.

"You can hardly blame them for doing this," one source said. "It makes sense from their point of view. They know we're restricted in these areas so they take advantage of it."

A number of roads run from China through the restricted zone into the heart of North Vietnam. Some of the principal ones pass through the towns of Langson and Caobang, on the eastern half of the border.

American pilots have, with advance permission, occasionally attacked specific, fixed targets within the restricted zone, such as railroad bridges and marshaling yards along the two rail lines that run northwest and northeast from Hanoi to China.

It is also believed that pilots may, when necessary, attack Soviet-made surface-to-air missile batteries in the zone when the missiles are endangering planes bombing a target south of the prohibited strip.

Except for the restricted areas around Hanoi and Haiphong, which pilots may bomb only with advance permission, Air Force and Navy commanders are relatively free to order strikes against specific military

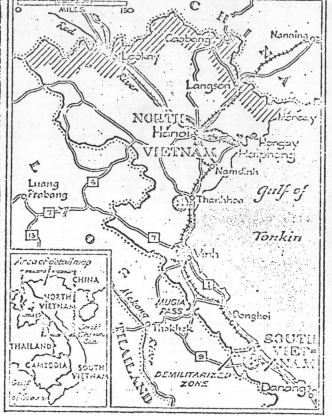

The New York Times   March 8, 1967

North Vietnamese are reported to be protecting truck convoys in zone (shown by shading) that is off-limits as well as in Thanhhoa (1) and Vinh (2). American artillery base near neutral zone (3) came under enemy fire again.

targets within the smaller population centers.

These include bridges, major supply depots, barracks, rail yards and truck parks. Pilots also have considerable discretion in deciding whether to strike conventional antiaircraft guns or missile batteries within towns that are endangering their own or accompanying aircraft.

But the pilots are restricted from freely bombing groups of trucks or small supply dumps they happen to sight within the towns.

It is known that senior military officials are pleased by President Johnson's recent decision to remove some of the restrictions on the war against North Vietnam by allowing attacks on more thermal power stations, aerial mining of rivers and naval shelling of coastal installations.

One senior military source, however, expressed some reluctance when asked whether he favored bombing truck convoys parked within the towns during the day. "We'd kill a lot of civilians if we did that," he said.

Less senior military sources cited the inevitable political complications that would result from a relatively free bombing policy within the restricted zone along the Chinese border. They pointed out that American aircraft would inevitably stray across the border during attacks and incidents would result.

Blunting of Intelligence Weapons Feared Since Disclosure

RED BLOC OUTLAYS ON STUDENTS CITED

U.S. Aides Say That Small, Covert Efforts Avoid Large, Costly Clashes

Continued From Page 1, Col. 6

dollar payments to a South American labor union threatened by Communist takeover or Communist rifles smuggled to rebellious Kurdish tribesmen in cases marked "sewing machines," this is a battle to influence and penetrate foreign countries, the sources said.

¶United States aid to student and youth groups around the world has been effectively halted by the disclosures. No delegation of non-Communist American youths is expected to attend the next World Youth Festival in Sofia, Bulgaria, next year. At previous festivals, in Vienna and Helsinki, American students, secretly financed by the C.I.A., prevented Communist delegations from speaking unchallenged.

¶American intelligence officials are dismayed at what they consider unjustified criticism of covert political activities and frustrated over security requirements that prevent them from replying openly. They see a sense of false security in this country — what one official called "a misunderstanding of the arena of conflict."

Hungarian Defector Speaks

One man who could speak out was Laszlo Szabo, a former major in the Hungarian intelligence service who defected to the United States in 1955. He expressed amazement at the "naive attitude of Americans about propaganda."

"It is the big front in the secret war," he said.

Some American intelligence officials were willing to be quoted directly on their views and on their information supporting these conclusions, although their names and positions cannot be given.

One of these sources summed up the American intelligence community's feeling about covert political action this way:

"If a little money was put into a free labor union or other institution in a proper country to keep it alive under adverse circumstances, it was worth it.

"The big purpose is, and was, pre-emptive — to prevent the Communists from taking over. In this way we have succeeded in many cases in avoiding confrontations that might have been far more costly and difficult if the Communist-bloc efforts had prevailed."

All the intelligence officers interviewed said they strongly believed that clandestine financial support for certain private organizations should continue, except in fields where the support has been exposed.

This view has run into strong opposition in the United States Government. Vice President Hubert Humphrey said the students financing program represented "one of the saddest times," in reference to public policy.

Some observers have pointed out that much of the support for international activities could have been given overtly, by Government agencies other than the C.I.A. Suspicion of espionage motivations, these people believe, could thus have been avoided.

Defenders of the C.I.A. view say such opinions reflect a poor grasp of the nature of modern intelligence.

"There are not that many secrets," one American official said. "The major thrust of Soviet officials is not collecting information — though they certainly do that as well—but in exerting influence.

"So we, too, are in the influence business."

Recent defectors from Communist intelligence services don't want Communists. They want citizens with money and influence. They want aristocrats and opinion-makers.

"They flatter the intellectuals and the non-Communist left and they get them to do the work. They don't want them as Communist party members but as stooges who have entree in society.

"To prove to the world that you are saving the world and that you are the wave of the future, you need respectable people—not workers, but students, churchmen, professors and doctors."

The Battle for Influence

This is the battle for influence that the intelligence officers say the general public does not understand.

Officials point to world press reaction as an indication of the crippling of United States covert political activities.

The Cairo newspaper Al Ahram said: "It is the right of people of liberated countries to be more vigilant in dealing with the organizations and groupings whose connections with the C.I.A. have been revealed."

Radio listeners in Rumania heard Government reports that "a number of young people, both from the United States and other countries, came under police attention for their progressive and democratic opinions or activities."

A Havana radio station commented that the C.I.A. money "is nothing less than a bribe, a bribe to a small minority of student and youth leaders at the top who are prepared to betray the interests of the members that they are supposed to represent."

An American intelligence official said: "We are, in effect, disarmed in this area. Now the question is whether the international youth movement is going to be taken over completely by the Communists without a fight."

Western intelligence services estimate that the Communist bloc has spent $10-million annually since the end of World War II to maintain Communist-dominated international youth organizations.

This figure includes parts of the costs of the eight World Youth Festivals held since the nineteen-forties. The festival in Helsinki in 1952 was estimated to have cost $25-million to $30-million. The 1957 festival, held in Moscow, cost well over $50-million, according to the Western estimates.

"Tried to Sow Doubts"

The Central Intelligence Agency's financial support to the National Student Association, which sent delegates to several of these festivals, totaled $3-million over 15 years, according to published statements.

At the festivals in Helsinki and in Vienna, in 1959, there was conspicuous anti-Communist activity by the Americans, and Soviet spokesmen still voice their annoyance.

Sergei P. Pavlov, head of the young Communist League—wrote in November that Americans in Helsinki tried to "sow doubts, blacken the Soviet Union's history and discredit Marxism-Leninism."

Besides the festivals, Communist youth organizations sponsor summer camps to which young people from many countries can go cheaply and receive training and indoctrination in Communism.

For students from developing countries, Patrice Lumumba Friendship University in Moscow offers the promise of education. Lumumba University graduated its first four-year class last June.

According to Western intelligence sources, the university is operated directly by the senior staff officers of the main Soviet intelligence organization. Western sources identified a former rector of the university, Pavel D. Yerzin, as a general on the intelligence agency staff.

Graduates in Governments

Former students at Lumumba University are now to be found in Government positions in several African countries, and Western intelligence officers believe them to be in active collaboration with their mentors in Moscow.

Further description of the Communist bloc's activity with students in the West came from Mr. Szabo, who was interviewed in the United States. He had been chief of the British section of the Hungarian intelligence service.

He said he had sent a Hungarian professor to study at the University of London. The professor was told not to waste time with Communists or with the far left, he said, but to get to know influential people who might be sympathetic and helpful later. Mr. Szabo said that the target of first importance was students who might later hold positions of power.

U.S. YOUTHS AT WORLD FESTIVAL: American delegates parading at Communist-sponsored World Youth Festival in Vienna in 1959. C.I.A.-supported Americans were in delegation and carried out conspicuous anti-Communist activity that annoyed Russians.

Blunting of C.I.A. Drive By Disclosures Is Feared

MAR 6 '57

Officials active in United States intelligence operations have expressed the fear that some of their most effective weapons have been blunted by disclosures of the secret financial support provided by the Central Intelligence Agency to other groups.

These officials, in this country and abroad, argued in defense of the controversial C.I.A. programs, saying the funds involved amounted to "only a fraction" of investments by Communist nations in covert attempts to penetrate Western and neutralist governments.

An intricate web of undercover political activities and propaganda by American intelligence has been exposed to public view since disclosure last month of the agency's financial support for the National Student Association.

Can't Respond Publicly

While the American intelligence community has been unable to respond publicly to the resulting criticism, New York Times correspondents in various capitals interviewed United States officials and other qualified people who are not normally available to be questioned. The following main points emerged:

¶A struggle through subversion and influence-seeking continues unabated—particularly in Africa, Asia and Latin America—although East-West tensions on the high political level have subsided. And in Europe, the only actual cold war battle ground has stabilized.

Whether the tactics involve

Continued on Page 13, Column 1.

...nce Weapons Feared Since Disclosure of C.I.A. Financing

FESTIVAL: American delegates parading at Communist festival in Vienna in 1959. C.I.A.-supported Americans were in conspicuous anti-Communist activity that annoyed Russians.

have confirmed that the basic motivation of covert Communist activity in the West is not to steal documents but to disseminate propaganda and carry on "relentlessly political" activity.

"You Americans simply do not understand that," said Wladyslaw Tykocinski, former chief of the Polish military mission in West Berlin. Mr. Tykocinski, 43 years old, was interviewed in Washington, where he now lives after defecting in May, 1965. He said he was "angry" that the covert subsidy programs were "so stupidly managed."

"In the East we have no such problems," he said. "The orders are given in Moscow and the money is there. Moscow says, 'Pay for this', and it is paid."

He discussed the strategy of Communist intelligence services in the West.

"It is not the recruiting of spies—that is quite easy," he said. "The whole thing is political—everything should show that world opinion is supporting Communism.

"You are always looking here at home for Communists. But they—the real Communists of the intelligence apparatus—don't want Communists. They

want citizens with money and influence. They want aristocrats and opinion-makers.

"They flatter the intellectuals and the non-Communist left and they get them to do the work. They don't want them as Communist party members but as stooges who have entree in society.

"To prove to the world that you are saving the world and that you are the wave of the future, you need respectable people—not workers, but students, churchmen, professors and doctors."

The Battle for Influence

This is the battle for influence that the intelligence officers say the general public does not understand.

Officials point to world press reaction as an indication of the crippling of United States covert political activities.

The Cairo newspaper Al Ahram said: "It is the right of people of liberated countries to be more vigilant in dealing with the organizations and groupings whose connections with the C.I.A. have been revealed."

Radio listeners in Rumania heard Government reports that "a number of young people, both from the United States and other countries, came under po-

lice attention for their progressive and democratic opinions or activities."

A Havana radio station commented that the C.I.A. money "is nothing less than a bribe, a bribe to a small minority of student and youth leaders at the top who are prepared to betray the interests of the members that they are supposed to represent."

An American intelligence official said: "We are, in effect, disarmed in this area. Now the question is whether the international youth movement is going to be taken over completely by the Communists without a fight."

Western intelligence services estimate that the Communist bloc has spent $10-million annually since the end of World War II to maintain Communist-dominated international youth organizations.

This figure includes parts of the costs of the eight World Youth Festivals held since the nineteen-forties. The festival in Helsinki in 1962 was estimated to have cost $20-million to $30-million. The 1957 festival, held in Moscow, cost well over $50-million, according to the Western estimates.

'Tried to Sow Doubts'

The Central Intelligence Agency's financial support to the National Student Association, which sent delegates to several of these festivals, totaled $3-million over 15 years, according to published statements.

At the festivals in Helsinki and in Vienna, in 1959, there was conspicuous anti-Communist activity by the Americans, and Soviet spokesmen still voice their annoyance.

Sergei P. Pavlov, head of the Communist League—wrote in November that Americans in Hel-

sinki tried to "sow doubts, blacken the Soviet Union's history and discredit Marxism-Leninism."

Besides the festivals, Communist youth organizations sponsor summer camps to which young people from many countries can go cheaply and receive training and indoctrination in Communism.

For students from developing countries, Patrice Lumumba Friendship University in Moscow offers the promise of cheap, even free, university education. Lumumba University graduated its first four-year class last June.

According to Western intelligence sources, the university is operated directly by senior staff officers of the main Soviet intelligence organization. Western sources identified a former rector of the university, Pavel D. Yerzin, as a general on the intelligence agency staff.

Graduates in Governments

Former students at Lumumba University are now to be found in Government positions in several African countries, and Western intelligence officers believe them to be in active collaboration with their mentors in Moscow.

Further description of the Communist bloc's activity with students in the West came from Mr. Szabo, who was interviewed in the United States. He had been chief of the British section of the Hungarian intelligence service.

He said he had sent a Hungarian professor to study at the University of London. The professor was told not to waste time with Communists or with the far left, he said, but to get to know influential people whose help might be sympathetic and helpful later. Mr. Szabo said that the target of first importance was students who might later

work for the British Foreign Office.

According to Mr. Szabo, the Hungarian intelligence system sought every opportunity to plant agents in British universities. In 1961, he said, the British Broadcasting Corporation offered two-week visits to Britain for writers of the best essays on Shakespeare.

"A number of intelligence officers in the universities were ordered to write essays that would win the contest," he said. Apparently the agents were unable to brush up their Shakespeare fast enough, Mr. Szabo went on, for the contest was won by two legitimate students. "We could not recruit and train them in time," Mr. Szabo said.

Covert political activity extends beyond youth movements. C.I.A. financing for labor unions, research organizations and other public institutions has been disclosed.

Here, the American intelligence officials also argued in terms of what the other side was doing.

The Communists smuggle arms, bribe officials and nurture subversive organizations, the officials said, and must be countered by someone.

Activity in Uruguay Charged

Western intelligence sources said that boxes labelled "sewing machines" were unloaded from a Bulgarian freighter in Beirut, Lebanon, in January of 1956. They were found to contain 1,500 rifles and a million rounds of ammunition believed to be consigned to Kurdish rebels in Iraq, the intelligence sources continued.

In Uruguay the Soviet bloc was said to have pumped nearly a million dollars into the last Communist party's campaign for the national elections in November.

Intelligence sources said the money came from local bank accounts, money deposited by

Uruguayan companies that did business with the Soviet Union. By contract, part of the payment was to be deposited into secret accounts.

The Uruguayan Government charges that Communist diplomatic missions are being used as covers for political operations. The Government has tried to expel the East German trade mission, noting that it has not drummed up any trade in three years.

At a meeting of the Afro-Asian Peoples' Solidarity Organization in Nicosia, Cyprus, last month, a Kenya delegation friendly to the Soviet Union was seated in place of the Government delegation. Western intelligence sources said organizing officials of the meeting had received $23,000 from the Soviet Embassy.

Agents Seen in Embassies

According to official Western estimates, over 40 per cent of Soviet ambassadors now serving in embassies have prior intelligence connections and many of them are known to Western officials as intelligence agents.

In December, 1966, there were 776 Soviet officers serving in various official positions in 29 African countries. Western sources said, and 420 of them were said to have been identified as intelligence officers.

"What we see is a Soviet diplomatic establishment far larger than it needs to be," said one American official. "There are 24 Soviet diplomats in Argentina, for example. Italy, which has much more commerce with Argentina, has 16 diplomats there; West Germany, with even closer trade relations, has only 14 diplomats in Argentina. "We have to ask ourselves what these Soviets are doing there," this intelligence source said, "and, when we find out, we are out to take over."

C. I. A. MEN AIDED STRIKES IN GUIANA AGAINST DR. JAGAN

FEB 22 '67

Worked Under the Cover of U.S. Union in 1962 Drive on Marxist Premier

AGENTS PROVIDED FUND

Public Employes Group in Washington Got Agency Money for 4½ Years

By NEIL SHEEHAN

WASHINGTON, Feb. 21 — Operatives of the Central Intelligence Agency, working under cover of an American labor union, helped organize strikes in British Guiana in 1962 and 1963 against Dr. Cheddi Jagan, a marxist who was Prime Minister there, an informed labor source said today.

The sources said the international affairs department of the American Federation of State, County and Municipal Employees was actually run by two intelligence agency aides who operated out of the union's former headquarters in Washington with the knowledge of the union leadership.

The union used agency funds for four and a half years—from 1959 until May, 1964—to finance its overseas activities, mainly in Latin America, the sources said.

The international affairs department was officially known as the Public Service International Inter-American Affairs Branch because of the American union's affiliation with the Public Service International in London, an international confederation of public employees.

American Funds Used

The section was situated in the American union's former headquarters here in Washington, however and, supported itself entirely with American funds. Most of the funds were supplied by the intelligence agency. A small portion came from the unions own treasury.

The relationship with the intelligence agency was completely severed in 1964 by Jerry Wurf, the current president of the federation who defeated Arnold Zander, the former president, at the union's conference in 1964.

Mr. Wurf disbanded the international section. One of the two intelligence agents who ran it is now a provincial adviser for the Agency for International Development in Vietnam. The other worked for a time in a Washington law firm and then left the city. His present whereabouts is unknown.

Mr. Zander, who is now

Continued on Page 17, Column 2

C.I.A. MEN AIDED STRIKES IN GUIANA

Continued From Page 1, Col. 1

president of the United World Federalists in Washington, had no comment.

Dr. Jagan, who was considered pro-Communist by the Kennedy Administration, was later ousted by Forbes S. Burnham, the current and pro-American Premier of the former British colony, in elections in December, 1964.

British Guiana adopted the name of Guyana when it gained its full independence from London in May of last year.

The Kennedy Administration had feared that Dr. Jagan would transform Guyana into another Cuba if he retained power. The riots, racial strife and strikes, some of which were reportedly instigated by Mr. Burnham's faction, undoubtedly played a major part in bringing about Dr. Jagan's downfall.

Mr. Burnham was favored by the United States throughout the struggle.

The sources said the intelligence agency aids operating under cover of the American union helped pro-Burnham dike and public employees unions organize strikes against Dr. Jagan in 1962 and 1963.

The agents gave advice to local union leaders on how to organize and sustain the strikes. They also provided funds and food supplies to keep the strikes going and medical supplies for pro-Burnham workers injured during the turmoil.

At one point, one of the agents even served as a member of a bargaining committee from a Guiana dike workers union that was negotiating with Dr. Jagan.

This agent was later denounced by Dr. Jagan and forbidden to enter the country, but he continued to do so by clandestine means, the sources said.

The sources said the American union's relationship with the intelligence agency began in 1959 when the federation's leadership sought funds from private sources to finance training programs in organizing unions, cooperatives and other similar societies in Africa.

At that time, the African labor nd cooperative movement was in a primitive state, and the American union was attempting to finance some training programs in Africa for unions affiliated with the Public Service International in London.

The union leadership was unable to obtain money from some of the more prominent American foundations, but finally obtained a small grant through the Gotham Foundation of New York, which served as a conduit for money from the intelli-

At first, the union leadership was unaware that the funds had come from the intelligence agency, but when the source of the money was learned shortly afterward, the union leadership decided to maintain the relationship because funds were not available elsewhere.

Although the initial grant was

a small one—$7,500—the funds were steadily expanded until by 1961 the agency was supplying about $60,000 a year through the Gotham Foundation.

In 1960, the first intelligence agency aide was also accepted by the union leadership to set up and run the small international affairs section. Later, he was joined by the second agent, and the branch added two translators and two clerical aides.

The international section never expanded beyond six persons, but the funds continued to flow in at the rate of about $60,000 annually until Mr. Wurf severed the relationship in May, 1964.

Between 1960 and the present, the American Newspaper Guild has received about $1-million from foundations believed to be conduits for the intelligence agency. The Guild used the money for its activities overseas, mainly in Latin America.

The Retail Clerks International Association also received a grant of $53,000 in 1965 from the Granary Fund of Boston, which has been identified as a fund channel for the intelligence agency.

Units Linked With C.I.A.

FEB 19 67

Special to The New York Times

WASHINGTON, Feb. 18 — *Following is a partial total of foundations that are cooperating with the Central Intelligence Agency and some of the organizations to which they have contributed. It has been compiled by The New York Times through a perusal of tax returns, financial statements and other documents, as well as public and private declarations by officers of groups involved. Conduits are listed in bold face.*

Foundation for Youth and Students Affairs, 1 East 54th Street, New York City:

Asian Student Press Bureau.
Council for International Programs for Youth Leaders and Social Workers.
Conference on the Atlantic Community.
Council of European National Youth Committees.
Crossroads Africa.
Gambia National Youth Council.
Guyana Assembly of Youth.
International Confederation of Free Trade Unions.
International Student Conference.
International Union of Young Christian Democrats.
International Union of Socialist Youth.
International Youth Center, New Delhi.
National Federation of Canadian University Students.
National Newman Club Federation.
National Student Press Council of India.
North American Secretariat of Pax Romana.
Oficina Relacionadora Movimientos Estudiantiles Univeraitarios.
Pax Romana, International Secretariat.
United States National Student Association.
United States Student Press Association.
United States Youth Council.
World Assembly of Youth.
World University Service.
Young Christian Workers.
Young Women's Christian Association.

The Independence Foundation, 60 State Street, Boston.

The National Student Association.
The Independent Research Service.
The International Market Institute.

The J. Frederick Brown Foundation, 60 State Street, Boston (trustee and address of Brown and Independence Foundation are the same):

Pan American Foundation.
International Development Foundation.
Institute of Public Administration.
American Society of African Culture.
American Fund for Free Jurists.
Fund for International and Economic Education.
Committee of Correspondence, Inc.
American Friends of the Middle East.
Foreign Policy Research Institute of the University of Penn.
National Education Association.
Freedom Fund, Inc.

The Sidney and Esther Rabb Foundation of Boston:

The National Student Association.
Operations and Policy Research, Inc.
The International Development Foundation.

The San Jacinto Foundation of Houston:

The National Student Association.
The International Student Conference.
The United States Council of New York.

The Catherwood Foundation:

The National Student Association.

The Granary Fund, 73 Tremont Street Boston:

The American Newspaper Guild.
American Friends of the Middle East.
Operations and Policy Research, Inc.
The International Development Foundation.
The Pan American Foundation.
The Retail Clerks International Association.
The Institute d' Histoire Sociale.
The fund for International Cooperative Development.
The American Fund for Free Jurists.
The Friends of India Committee Trust.

The Andrew Hamilton Fund of Philadelphia:

The American Newspaper Guild.

The following funds contributing heavily to the Newspaper Guild refuse to disclose their source of income and contributions to other organizations:

The Warden Trust of Cleveland.
The Chesapeake Foundation of Baltimore.
The Freed High Foundation of Columbus, Ohio.

Other organizations reported to have received agency contributions could not be reached for comment.

FUNDS IDENTIFIED AS GO-BETWEENS

FEB 1-6 '67

One Student Group, a Rival of Soviet-Controlled Body, Was Established in 1950

By NEIL SHEEHAN
Special to The New York Times

WASHINGTON, Feb. 15 — Foundations that have been channeling Central Intelligence Agency funds to the National Student Association have also been helping to subsidize at least four other youth organizations.

It seemed clear that some portion of the subsidies came from the C.I.A., but inquiries here failed to determine exactly how much, if any, was given to each group by the intelligence agency and how much was given by private sources, either independently or at the request of the agency.

The four other youth organizations are the International Student Conference of Leyden, the Netherlands; the Independent Research Service of New York; the United States Youth Council of New York, and the World Assembly of Youth of Brussels.

Officers of the two foreign-based organizations could not be reached for comment.

Eugene A. Theroux, a graduate of the Pratt Institute and director of the Independent Research Service, said in a telephone conversation that his group had received funds from the Independence Foundation. He said, however, that he had not been able to talk to officers of the foundation to ask whether the funds came from the C.I.A.

James D. Fowler, president of the United States Youth and Student Council, acknowledged in a telephone interview that his organization had obtained money from the Foundation for Youth and Student Affairs, but he said he had no reason to believe that his group had been "covertly funded." Neither he nor the other officers have a "relationship with the C.I.A." he said.

Mr. Fowler said he had called the foundation and had been told that the funds his group received did not come from the C.I.A.

According to record uncovered today, all of the organization have been receiving funds from the Foundation for Youth and Student Affairs of New York, the Independence Foundation of Boston and the San Jacinto Foundation of Houston.

The three foundations have been identified by officers of the National Student Association as conduits for the funds given by the C.I.A. to their organization.

Funds to Women's Group

A fourth foundation with ap-

J. Frederick Brown Foundation of Boston, Mass., has been making contributions to a New York-based women's group called the Committee of Correspondence. The committee works with women's groups in foreign countries.

The most important of the four organizations is the International Student Conference, a confederation of student unions from 80 non-Communist countries. It has served as a counter-poise in international student affairs to the Soviet-controlled International Union of Students.

The organization was founded in 1950, shortly after the outbreak of the cold war when it became apparent that without an effective rival, the Communist organization would dominate international student politics.

It finances international student conferences and such publications as the multi-lingual magazine, The Student, as well as holding student seminars and financing student exchange and scholarship programs.

It has taken a liberal but almost always pro-Western position on world issues.

Analysis of Support

According to a study of the International Student Conference's financial statements for 1964-66 made by the Canadian Union of Students, the organization received most its support during this time from the Foundation for Youth and Student Affairs and the San Jacinto fund.

In this period, only about $45,000 of the conference's yearly income came from dues and contributions of member student unions, while about $650,000 a year was supplied by foundations, most of the funds by the two C.I.A.-connected foundations.

The San Jacinto fund for example, paid the $125,000 yearly costs of the magazine, The Student, and half of the expenses of the organization's conferences in 1964 and 1966, which cost about $270,000 each.

The Canadian Student Union estimated that between 80 and 90 per cent of the total conference programs were financed by funds from American foundations.

Officers of the International Student Conference could not be reached today for comment.

Arthur Houghton Jr., president of Steuben Glass of New York and also president of the Foundation for Youth and Student Affairs, obliquely acknowledged in a statement issued today by his office that the foundation had cooperated with the "Government," but he refused to elaborate.

"If at any time I have cooperated with our Government on matters affecting the national interest, that is my own affair," the statement said.

Mr. Houghton asserted that the foundation had "never placed conditions on the grants that it has made."

Harry H. Lunn, executive director of the foundation and a president of the National Student Association in the mid-fifties, denied today that he was an employe of the C.I.A. but declined to say whether he had served as an intermediary between the intelligence organization and student groups.

Mr. Lunn has been identified by student association officers as one of the principal contacts with the C.I.A.

He also denied that the foundation's funds came from the C.I.A. and said that "all the money has come from the Houghton family and members of the board."

Mr. Lunn acknowledged that the foundation had made "substantial" contributions "for many years" to the four youth and student organizations.

The World Assembly of Youth, the other foreign-based organization that has been receiving funds from the Foundation for Youth and Student Affairs, is a confederation of 51 youth groups from Western and non-Communist countries.

It publishes pamphlets and a monthly magazine called Way, finances youth seminars and youth leadership conferences and international youth meetings.

While the International Student Conference competes in international student affairs with the Communist-controlled International Union of Students, the World Assembly of Youth counters the World Federation of Democratic Youth, which has its headquarters in Warsaw.

The World Assembly of Youth was also founded at the outbreak of the cold war, in 1948.

The United States Youth Council of New York, a coordinating body for 37 American youth and student groups ranging from the leftwing Students for a Democratic Society to the Young Democrats and major religious youth organizations, has reportedly sent delegates to World Assembly of Youth meetings.

The Independent Research Service, the other New York-based organization that received funds from the C.I.A.-connected Independence Foundation of Boston, has existed almost solely to finance the sending of delegations of American students and intellectuals to Communist-sponsored international youth festivals.

The organization was founded in 1958 by Paul Sigmund, now a professor at Princeton, and Gloria Steinem, a New York journalist, just before the Vienna youth festival of 1959.

In 1962, the Independent Research Service sent a delegation of more than 100 students, teachers and intellectuals to the Communist you festival in Helsinki.

A report filed by the Independence Foundation with the Massachusetts State Attorney General's Office in Boston shows a grant of $125,000 to the Independent Research Service that year.

National Student Association officers have said that the foundation was one of their sources of C.I.A. funds and that its trustee, Paul Helmuth, was one of their contacts with the intelligence agency.

Mr. Helmuth, a member of the prestigious Boston law firm of Hale & Dorr, has, according to his secretary, been at meetings for the last several days and unavailable for comment.

Disruptive Element

The delegation sent to the Helsinki festival was liberal and did not reflect official United States policy at the time, but the delegation did serve as a disruptive element in the festival.

It published a newspaper, ran an information bureau and participated in a number of the forums and seminars.

As a result of its efforts, delegations from a number of countries, including Ceylon, Uganda and Nigeria, left the festival to protest the attitude of the Communist youth groups and the festival's sponsoring committee.

W. Dennis Shaul, a former Rhodes scholar who was head of the Independent Research Service in 1962 and president of the National Student Association during the same period, said in a telephone interview today that he was uncertain whether the C.I.A. had indirectly financed the research service, but that he was certain most of its funds had come from legitimate foundations.

As a president of the National Student Association, Mr. Shaul would presumably have known that the Independence Foundation was a conduit for C.I.A. funds.

Both current association officers and State Department officials have said that two to three senior members of the student association knew each year of the C.I.A. subsidy.

U.S. PUTS OFF RAID ON RAILROAD YARD IN THE HANOI AREA

JAN 11 '67

Temporary Step Apparently Tied to Controversy Over Previous Air Attacks

By NEIL SHEEHAN
Special to The New York Times

WASHINGTON, Jan. 17 — The Administration has temporarily rescinded permission for a raid on a railroad yard near Hanoi.

The action apparently was taken because of the controversy over whether American bombs had fallen on the North Vietnamese capital during previous attacks, Defense Department sources said today.

Air Force planes struck the Yenvien railroad yards five miles northeast of Hanoi three times, on Dec. 4, 13 and 14.

The Air Force intended, the sources said, to attack the rail yards a fourth time at the first good opportunity after the Dec. 14 raid, and received permission from Washington to do so.

Effect Questioned

It is understood that while the first three raids seriously damaged the rail yard, they had not been sufficiently effective to satisfy Air Force commanders in Vietnam.

Around Christmas, however, the Administration rescinded permission for the intended raid, the sources said, apparently because of the international controversy provoked by North Vietnamese charges that American planes had bombed populated areas in the capital during the Dec. 13 and 14 attacks.

It could not be learned exactly when the Air Force had planned to bomb the railroad yard a fourth time, but the Defense Department sources said the strike would have taken place by now if permission had not been rescinded.

The sources added that while the weather has frequently been bad over North Vietnam this month, it has not been bad enough to prevent a raid.

After the Dec. 13 and 14 attacks, North Vietnam accused the United States of having bombed workers' quarters in metropolitan Hanoi near the Paul Doumer Bridge across the Red River. Hanoi said 100 persons had been killed or wounded.

On Dec. 13 and 14, Naval fighter-bombers from the Seventh Fleet also attacked the Vandien truck park five miles south of Hanoi.

Administration spokesmen did not deny the possibility that some bombs had been dropped on the city by Navy or Air Force planes, but said that to the best of their knowledge the bombs had fallen on the targets or adjacent to them.

The spokesmen said the most likely cause of the damage in

Continued on Page 6, Column 7

f American Bombing

U.S. Cancels Permission to Raid Railroad Yard in Hanoi Region

Continued From Page 1, Col. 1

Hanoi itself were North Vietnamese antiaircraft shells or Soviet-made SAM antiaircraft missiles that had fallen back into the city after having been fired at the American planes.

Despite Administration attempts to counter the North Vietnamese accusations, Hanoi's charges were given wide credence in Europe and the Administration came under severe criticism for having staged the raids.

The Defense Department sources said today that while they could not say for certain that the withdrawal of permission had been a direct result of the adverse political repercussions of the Dec. 13 and 14 raids, they believed this was so.

They noted that the withdrawal of permission had occurred while the controversy was still on and that there had been no other apparent reason to call off the attack.

An official Defense Department spokesman declined all comment on the report today.

The sources in the department said they did not believe that permission for the raid had been withdrawn as a result of a series of dispatches from Hanoi by Harrison E. Salisbury, an assistant managing editor of The New York Times.

Mr. Salisbury's first dispatch was printed in a late edition of The Times of Dec. 25. The subsequent dispatches, which appeared in the issue of Dec. 27, attracted widespread attention.

Permission for a fourth raid on the railroad yards had already been rescinded by then, the sources said.

It was considered possible, however, that Mr. Salisbury's dispatches might have contributed to the fact that the Administration did not renew permission for the raid on the rail yard, and to the fact that no attacks have taken place within a 10-mile radius of Hanoi since Dec. 14.

Targets within 10 miles of the center of Hanoi can be attacked only with the permission of the Joint Chiefs of Staff. This, in effect, means that Secretary of Defense Robert S. McNamara and President Johnson must give the final approval.

Lists of targets approved by the Chiefs of Staff are submitted to Secretary McNamara and the White House before they are transmitted to commanders in the field.

It could not be learned today at what level of the Administration the decision had been taken to withdraw permission for a fourth raid. But the sources speculated that the final decision came from the White House.

PENTAGON TO SELL $4.5-BILLION ARMS ABROAD IN 3 YEARS

JAN 5—'68

Continued Exports, Mainly to NATO Allies, Will Help Curb Payments Deficit

By NEIL SHEEHAN
Special to The New York Times

WASHINGTON, Jan. 4—Defense Department arms sales will reach a combined total of at least $4.5-billion to $4.6-billion over this and the next two fiscal years, Pentagon sources said today.

The Pentagon sales to foreign countries, largely to the North Atlantic Treaty Organization allies, will thus continue to make a major contribution to efforts to solve the United States' balance-of-payments problem.

Defense officials have estimated that past arms sales met the bulk of the foreign exchange costs of United States overseas troop commitments outside of Southeast Asia.

According to the latest and most accurate statistics, United States arms sales totaled $10.14-billion over the six-year period that ended last June 30.

The Defense Department had estimated earlier that arms sales would decline during the fiscal year 1968, and possibly in the fiscal year 1969 as well, because of the extensive arms modernization programs undertaken by the NATO countries in the last few years.

Estimate Called High

However, because of developments since last fall—principally a new West German desire to purchase a large number of F-4 Phantom jets—this estimate has proved conservative.

Pentagon officials are now reasonably certain, the sources said, that arms sales will average at least $1.5-billion this fiscal year and in each of the next two fiscal years.

Some officials say that sales could average $2-billion for each of the three fiscal years, but this is considered too high by others experienced in the arms trade.

The German purchase of F-4 Phantom jets could run as high as $700-million to $800-million. The sources declined to specify the number of aircraft involved, but Germany is believed to want more than 200.

The Defense Department is understood to have quoted a $700-million to $800-million total price to West Germany in its latest offer this winter, and the Bonn Government has promised a decision by April.

The Phantoms, the most sophisticated of operational American jets, would be used to replace the more than 70 American-designed F-104 Star-

Continued on Page 14, Column 3

PENTAGON TO SELL $4.5-BILLION ARMS

Continued From Page 1, Col. 4

fighters lost in crashes by the West German Air Force and to provide a modern reconnaissance plane and naval fighter-bomber until Germany acquires a more advanced plane in the mid-nineteen-seventies.

Trade With Italy

The Starfighter is now the main West German combat aircraft.

If Germany decides to buy the Phantom, deliveries of the plane would possibly begin late this year or in 1969.

Sales to and co-production arms agreements with Italy are also expected to provide about

$300-million in weapons business for the Defense Department over the three fiscal years.

The Italians have already spent $40-million in the United States for co-production of an advanced version of the F-104 and will probably spend another $120-million here on this program by mid-1970. The Italians may also buy a substantial number of CH-47 Chinook transport helicopters.

Norway and Denmark

Italy plans to modernize her 2,000 old model M-47 tanks with new American engines, and an advanced fire control system and may possibly replace the old 90-mm. guns on these tanks with more powerful 105-mm. models.

The Italian Navy intends to buy new American standard model antiaircraft missiles to replace the United States-made Tartar-Terrier series it now uses, and the Italians are also

involved in a self-propelled howitzer co-production program.

Norway and Denmark are planning sizable modernization programs over the next two to three years, which could also bring the United States more than $100-million in arms business by mid-1970.

Both countries need new jet fighter-bombers and may decide to buy Northrop F-5 Freedom Fighters. Norway has already agreed to purchase American P-3 anti-submarine patrol aircraft, and Denmark also wants a more modern antisubmarine patrol plane.

The Netherlands, too, is considering a purchase of P-3 planes from the United States.

In Asia, Japan has announced plans to undertake a five-year arms modernization program that may also result in substantial American weapons purchases.

The Japanese want new naval craft for their self-defense forces, a modern jet

trainer and an advanced fighter-bomber to replace the American designed F-104 Starfighter they now use.

Both planes may actually be built in Japan, but the United States hopes to sell the Japanese a good many of the components, particularly the advanced navigation, radar and fire control electronics equipment that Japan could not produce herself without prohibitive research and development costs.

VOL. CXVII....No. 40

U.S. UNDERVALUED ENEMY'S STRENGTH BEFORE OFFENSIVE

MAR-1-9-'68

C.I.A. Reports Forces Were Significantly Larger Than Intelligence Estimates

GAP IS 50,000 TO 100,000

New Assessment of Foe's Manpower Is Awaited— Losses Are in Dispute

By NEIL SHEEHAN
Special to The New York Times

WASHINGTON, March 18— The Central Intelligence Agency has concluded that the enemy's strength in South Vietnam at the beginning of its winter-spring offensive was significantly greater than United States officials thought at the time.

The new assessment was sent to the White House and the State and Defense Departments early this month, well-placed informants said today.

It puts at 515,000 to 600,000 men the force available to the enemy when the offensive against South Vietnamese cities and major towns was launched on Jan. 30, at the time of the Lunar New Year.

The so-called national intelligence estimate of enemy military and political manpower in South Vietnam current at the time put the range at 443,000 to 453,000 men.

Estimate Was Augmented

The national intelligence estimate is a compromise reached after discussion in the American intelligence community — the C.I.A., the Defense Intelligence Agency, the National Security Agency, the State Department's Bureau of Intelligence and Research, the intelligence branch of the Atomic Energy Commission and the Federal Bureau of Investigation.

The estimate was arrived at last November, but it was still being used in January, though it was modified by the addition of approximately 15,000 North Vietnamese troops that had begun infiltrating in December. With the addition it was 52,000 to 102,000 men below the estimate the C.I.A. has now propounded.

Toll Is Put at 50,000

A new national intelligence estimate on enemy strength in South Vietnam in the light of the offensive has apparently not yet been completed.

American military officials in Saigon have reported that 50,000 North Vietnamese soldiers and Vietcong guerrillas were killed between Jan. 30 and the end of last week.

This figure is disputed. Some intelligence officials here are understood to believe that the enemy forces have probably replaced the majority of their casualties with recruits. Reports from the scene support this view.

During his visit to Washing-

Continued on Page 3, Column 1

U.S. UNDERVALUED ENEMY'S STRENGTH

Continued From Page 1, Col. 1

ton last November, Gen. William C. Westmoreland, United States commander in Saigon, cited as evidence of "remarkable progress" in Vietnam a decline in enemy armed strength from 285,000 in the fall of 1966 to 242,000 as of November.

Last week American military officials in Saigon said they estimated that armed enemy manpower had further declined to a range of 207,000 to 220,000 men. No explanation was available here on how this estimate had been reached.

Officials later acknowledged that General Westmoreland's comparison had been achieved by deleting two categories of manpower—the political apparatus and the part-time irregulars—that had been included in the figure of 285,000.

If these categories were included, they said, the comparison would be between the 1966 figure of 285,000 and the 443,000 - to - 453,000 - man range reached in the national intelligence estimate.

General Westmoreland's total included the three other categories of main North Vietnamese and Vietcong divisions, regiments and battalions; the Vietcong guerrilla platoons and squads on the village level, and the Vietcong administrative and logistic structure.

Discrepancy Unexplained

These were placed at 223,000 to 243,000 men in the national intelligence estimate, the officials said. Why General Westmoreland used the 242,000 figure has never been explained.

Even if his calculations were applied to the new C.I.A. estimate, there would still be a significant increase.

The two categories excluded by General Westmoreland, the political cadres and the hamlet-level irregulars—loosely organized lightly armed and including some women and old men — played a major role in the assault on the cities, military and civilian sources say.

It is believed that the larger part of the higher estimate of enemy strength reached by the C.I.A. has resulted from improved intelligence and the surfacing of more of the Vietcong apparatus during the offensive. The rest of the increase is attributed to actual growth between November and January.

United States intelligence, perhaps because of its heavy military emphasis, has consistently underestimated the extent of the enemy's political, administrative and logistic network.

Comparisons of Results

Following is a comparison of the five categories of enemy military and political manpower as given in the national intelligence estimate and the new C.I.A. estimate:

North Vietnamese and Vietcong units — the national intelligence estimate gives a [figure] of 115,000 men with 5,000 North Vietnamese and 6,000 Vietcong; the C.I.A. estimate is 160,000, about equally divided.

Village guerrilla platoons and squads — the national intelligence estimate was 70,000 to 90,000 men; the C.I.A. figure is 100,000 to 120,000.

Administrative and logistic apparatus — the national intelligence estimate was 35,000 to 40,000 men; the C.I.A. calculated 75,000 to 85,000.

Political cadres — the national intelligence estimate was 75,000 to 85,000 men; the C.I.A. figure is 80,000 to 120,000.

Irregulars (also referred to as self-defense militia) — the national estimate was 100,000 to 120,000; C.I.A. calculates 120,000.

The C.I.A. appraisal is also that North Vietnam will counter the advantage of any American reinforcements sent to Vietnam by moving more infantry battalions into the South. The conclusion has been cited by a number of senior civilian officials in the State and Defense Departments in their argument against giving more troops to General Westmoreland.

Army Accused of Rushing Work On Tanks to Avoid Budget Study

By NEIL SHEEHAN
Special to the New York Times

WASHINGTON, May 14—A confidential report by the Government Accounting Office accuses the Army of rushing ahead in May, 1966, with the $1.3-billion Sheridan armored vehicle program to avoid "adverse political and budgetary impacts," even though it was uncertain the ammunition for the vehicle's gun would work.

The report says that for the same reason—to escape a review by the Bureau of the Budget and civilian Defense Department analysts—the Army also spent $250-million producing a new version of the M-60 heavy tank that is still not usable because of technical failures. Such a review might have resulted in a reduction of funds.

The report by the Congressional watchdog agency is still confidential because it contains military information that only the Defense Department has the authority to release. Details of the report were obtained from knowledgeable sources.

An official of the accounting office said that the agency sent a letter to the Defense Department last Feb. 7 requesting release of the report and asking for an answer within 60 days. It has not received a reply.

General Is Queried

Maj. Gen. Roland B. Anderson, director of matériel acquisition for the Department of the Army, was questioned about the report today by Representative William S. Moorhead, Democrat of Pennsylvania, in testimony before the Subcommittee on Military Operations of the House Government Operations Committee.

General Roland acknowledged that it would not have been "illogical" to have delayed mass production on the Sheridan until the ammunition for the vehicle's 152-mm. gun had been made workable, as the accounting office contends the Army should have done. But General Roland said that the ammunition problem has now been solved.

He said that the army is still experiencing "turret stabilization" problems with the new version of the M-60 heavy tank.

The reports says the Army now has 300 of the new version of the M-60 tank in storage until the technical failures can be rectified. They were produced under a 1966 contract. In addition, 243 separate turrets of a new type for the advanced M-60 are also in storage.

Despite the technical problems, the report says, the army has continued with the M-60 production and awarded another contract for 243 more tank chassis last September, long after deficiencies were known.

The new version of the 52-ton M-60 incorporates the same weapons system as the 16-ton Sheridan, an assault vehicle with light aluminum armor. The system consists of a 152-mm. gun that fires an advanced type of ammunition with a combustible cartridge casing. The gun can also be used to launch an electronically guided Shillelagh missile against tanks or bunkers.

Conventional shells have a brass casing that the gunner must remove after each round is fired. The combustible cartridge is consumed by the detonation of the shell in the gun breech and eliminates the necessity of removing a casing.

Problem Reported Solved

The problem was that the combustible cartridge left in the breech burning residue that prematurely detonated shells that were subsequently loaded.

Army officials say they have now satisfactorily solved this problem by installing a so-called scavenger device on the breech. The device blows the burning residue out of the gun barrel with forced air, the Army says.

They say that two squadrons of Sheridans, about 54 in all, have been operating successfully in Vietnam since February and have had no difficulty with the combustible cartridge because of the scavenger device. These two squadrons were sent on an experimental basis, but the results have been so favorable that the Army has now decided to begin deploying hundreds of Sheridans in Vietnam.

The decision to go into mass-production before the ammunition problem was solved was a gamble, officers acknowledge. But they contend that it was justified by an urgent need for the Sheridan in Vietnam because of its ability to move cross-country through wet rice paddies, which cannot be done by the medium M-48 tank that the Army now has in quantity in Vietnam.

Influence of the Joint Chiefs Is Reported Rising Under Nixon

Continued From Page 1, Col. 7

ning involved. Gen. Creighton W. Abrams, the American military commander in Vietnam, is being allowed, after review and concurrence by the chiefs, to determine more or less the rate at which South Vietnamese forces can take over responsibilities from the Americans and thus free United States troops for withdrawal.

Another example is the reversal of the civilian defense position on the Spanish base issue after Mr. Laird took over. Under Paul C. Warnke, the former head of the Office of International Security Affairs, the office had adopted a position paper that expressed considerable skepticism about the military value of the air bases in Spain and recommended that no further commitments be made to retain them.

This position was subsequently reversed at the request of the Joint Chiefs. The old agreement and its commitment was extended until September, 1970, and Spain was given a $50-million arms aid grant and a $35-million credit from the Government's Export-Import Bank to purchase weapons here.

The commitment to Spain is unclear, but the prolonged agreement contains a provision that "a threat to either country, and to the joint facilities that each provides for the common defense, would be a matter of concern to both countries and each country would take such action as it may consider appropriate."

The extent to which the newfound influence of the chiefs will affect politico-military policy and defense spending is still unclear, however. The organizational check on their power within the Pentagon has been replaced to some degree by the growing antimilitary mood in Congress and the country.

This climate is exerting pressure on President Nixon to hold down military spending and is strengthening the ability of outside agencies like the Bureau of the Budget to do the cutting.

Laird Economy Move

And despite the public compatibility with military views that Mr. Laird has displayed on such issues as the antiballistic missile controversy, he is said to be very conscious of the need for economy.

The Defense Secretary is understood to have quietly warned the chiefs that Congress simply will not accept any major increases in the current $80-billion defense budget and that for the first time since Dwight D. Eisenhower was President, the Defense Department will have to do its planning for the 1971 fiscal year budget with a preconceived ceiling in mind.

Informed observers do not believe that Mr. Laird intends to relinquish civilian control over the Pentagon to the military.

They think that as a professional politician he means to retain control by establishing cordial working relationships with the military and thus to be able to work out mutually acceptable compromises on key problems.

Mr. McNamara, the professional manager, believed that only a hard-nosed civilian staff responsive to his direction could achieve real civilian control.

Conversations with senior and working level officials in and outside the Pentagon disclose several reasons for the increased weight of the Joint Chiefs in the bureaucratic [illegible]on.

[illegible] two principal reasons are:

1. A personal inclination by Mr Laird and his chief civilian [illegible] to seek and carefully [illegible] to military judgment in [illegible]on-making.

2. The new National Security Council machinery that provides a clearly defined channel for the Joint Chiefs to express their views.

Defense Secretary Melvin R. Laird has enhanced Joint Chiefs of Staff's status.

and to the loss of the maverick independence on foreign policy matters that the International Security Office preserved under former Secretaries McNamara and Clark M. Clifford.

The office then played a key role in turning around the Johnson Administration's Vietnam war policy and often outweighed the State Department in formulating foreign policy.

Now, under the new Assistant Secretary for International Security Affairs, Warren Nutter, a former foreign policy adviser to Barry Goldwater, and men of like political views he has brought in to assist him, the office inclines to positions similar to those of the Joint Chiefs on foreign policy questions.

Systems Analysis Decline

As a result, the State Department pays much less attention to it in the interagency bargaining through which policy documents are drawn up for eventual submission to the National Security Council.

A third major development has been the very noticeable weakening in bureaucratic muscle of the Office of Systems Analysis, which held a pivotal position under Mr. McNamara and Mr. Clifford.

Like the international security office, the systems' analysis office has a combined civilian-military staff but is run by civilians and is an operating arm of the Secretary of Defense.

The cost effectiveness and strategic analysts in the systems analysis office, irritably dubbed "the whiz kids" by the military, review all weapons proposals by the military.

Very frequently under Secretaries Clifford and McNamara, the reviews were so different in content from the original proposals that they constituted independent weapons programs, and the systems analysis office also often instituted its own strategic studies on both conventional and nuclear war.

The systems analysis technique compares alternative weapons systems and strategies in terms of their cost in money and manpower and their military effectiveness in meeting potential enemy threats and the nation's foreign policy commitments. The comparisons are made primarily through the use of statistical and mathematical data.

Secretary McNamara put great faith in this quantitative approach to such problems and had deep confidence in the work of the former Assistant Secretary for Systems Analysis, Alain C. Enthoven.

Reversal of Roles

The Joint Staff, the chiefs' operating arm, and the individual armed services, which each of the chiefs except the chairman heads in a separate capacity, found themselves continually reacting to papers initiated by systems analysis personnel.

"The whole system was designed to keep the chiefs off balance," one well-informed source said.

Now the roles have been reversed. The Joint Staff and the services are initiating most of the position papers and the systems analysis office has been largely reduced to commenting on the papers.

"If you can initiate the paper, that gives you one leg up in the bureaucracy," the source commented.

Secretary Laird and his Deputy Secretary, David Packard, have indicated some skepticism about the value of the systems analysis approach by paying considerably less attention to its reviews than Mr. McNamara did, knowledgeable officials say.

Significantly, they have also continued to delay nominating a permanent Assistant Secretary to head the office and have reduced its work load. Where systems analysis formerly did a sizable number of major studies each year, it is scheduled to do only two this year—one on nuclear forces and the other on general purpose (conventional warfare) forces.

"Hopefully we can do it right the first time and save some money," Mr. Packard was quoted as saying in a recent interview to explain the reversal of roles between systems analysis and the Joint Staff. "Now an awful lot of people are going over the same thing time after time," he added.

Some informed observers speculate, however, that the downgrading of the systems analysis office may prove somewhat temporary, a kind of internal public relations effort by Mr. Packard and Mr. Laird to mollify the Joint Chiefs and to establish cordial working relations, and that they may later come to rely on it more as a tool to exert civilian control.

But the McNamara era also

Former Secretary Robert S. McNamara put civilian control above the military.

taught the military to establish its own capability in this field by educating officers in this quantitative analytical technique. The Joint Staff and the individual services are now much better equipped to counter systems analysis arguments.

Mr. Laird and Mr. Packard have clearly created an atmosphere within the department in which the chiefs feel much more comfortable and efficacious, knowledgable sources say.

The civilian staffs at the working level are under implicit instructions to try to work out compromise solutions with the military and to arrive at what Mr. Laird refers to as common "defense positions."

Under Mr. McNamara, "the marching orders were to be tough and skeptical," one informed observer noted.

Consequently, the chiefs are understood to feel a lessening of over-all bureaucratic pressure. They were glad to see the departure of Mr. Warnke, the former Assistant Secretary for International Security Affairs, whom some are said to have regarded as "a unilateral disarmer," and of Mr. Enthoven, who one source said "was always coming up with his own strategies."

Now senior civilian officials in international security, before arriving at their own positions, will sometimes telephone their counterparts on the Joint Staff and ask for advice on foreign policy questions.

Where there is disagreement with the chiefs on a specific issue, the dissenting views are now included in the basic document, instead of being footnoted, as they often were under Mr. McNamara—an important bureaucratic distinction. "It's easy to overlook footnotes," one officer said.

The National Security Council system also has precise machinery for the chiefs to present a formal, separate view to the President. They do not have to hope that the chairman, General Wheeler, will manage to work it in at the Tuesday lunches that constituted President Johnson's policy-making group.

Mr. Laird has also expanded the Secretary's regular Monday morning meeting with his Assistant Secretaries, the service secretaries and the chiefs. Under Mr. McNamara these meetings tended to be formal, half-hour sessions that dealt with technical items, like 500-pound bomb production, and the civilians did most of the talking.

Now the meetings last an hour to an hour and a half and range over all issues facing the department that week, such as the strategy to be adopted at committee hearings on Capitol Hill, major weapons programs, manpower, training or the latest analysis of the situation in Vietnam. "There's no end to what's discussed," one source said.

The chiefs have been encouraged and do join freely in the discussion, offering their advice.

Mr. Laird meets again separately with them each Monday afternoon, and he frequently spends other long hours with them in the chief's council chamber in the bowels of the Pentagon, colloquially referred to as "the tank," talking over such matters as the nuclear threat posed by the Soviet SS-9 missile, the condition's under which Okinawa should revert to Japan and other matters of current concern.

Informed sources say that the chiefs, as separate heads of their services, also now have direct access to Deputy Secretary Packard on major budget and weapons program management questions, the details of which he usually handles. They normally see him accompanied by their civilian service secretary.

Mr. Laird and Mr. Packard have coined a term for their approach to relations with the military. They call it "participatory management."

But the question remains: Which side will participate most?

NEW YORK, MONDAY, JUNE 30, 1969

Influence of Joint Chiefs Is Reported Rising

Members of the Joint Chiefs of Staff, from left: Gen. William C. Westmoreland, Army; Gen. John P. McConnell, Air Force; Gen. Earle G. Wheeler, Chairman; Adm. Thomas H. Moorer, of the Navy; and Gen. Leonard C. Chapman, Marine Corps.

By NEIL SHEEHAN

WASHINGTON, June 29—Although the lines of power within the Nixon Administration's Defense Department have not yet been definitively drawn, the influence of the Joint Chiefs of Staff appears to have grown appreciably.

The new Secretary of Defense, Melvin R. Laird, has substantially vitiated the effect of the elaborate machinery constructed by former Defense Secretary Robert S. McNamara to impose aggressive civilian management and control over the military from the top, knowledgeable sources say.

Mr. Laird is not dismantling the machinery, but he has weakened its impact by changing the character and role of two of its major components, the sources say.

The changed components are the Office of International Security Affairs, which is the Pentagon's foreign policy section; and the Office of Systems Analysis, created to oversee all weapons programs and strategic planning.

The counsel of the Joint Chiefs is being heard and considered as it has not been since the end of the Eisenhower era, well informed sources say. The chiefs are initiating proposals instead of reacting to those initiated by the civilian staffs of the Secretary of Defense.

In general, military leaders are pleased with the way things are going under the Republican Administration.

One example of the increased influence of the chiefs cited by military sources is the rate at which American troops are being withdrawn from Vietnam. Although Mr. Laird is pushing for disengagement as quickly as possible, the Joint Staff, the operating agency of the chiefs, is understood to be controlling the detailed plan-

Continued on Page 23, Column 1

agreement contains a provision that "a threat to either country, and to the joint facilities that each provides for the common defense, would be a matter of concern to both countries and each country would take such action as it may consider appropriate."

The extent to which the newfound influence of the chiefs will affect political, military policy and defense spending is still unclear, however. The organizational check on their power within the Pentagon has been replaced to some degree by the growing antimilitary mood in Congress and the country.

This climate is exerting pressure on President Nixon to hold down military spending and is strengthening the ability of outside agencies like the Bureau of the Budget to do the cutting.

Laird Economy Move

And despite the public compatibility with military views that Mr. Laird has displayed on such issues as the antiballistic missile controversy, he is said to be very conscious of the need for economy.

The Defense Secretary is understood to have quietly warned the chiefs that Congress simply will not accept any major increases in the current $80-billion defense budget and that for the first time since Dwight D. Eisenhower was President, the Defense Department will have to do its planning for the 1971 fiscal year budget with a preconceived ceiling in mind.

Informed observers do not believe that Mr. Laird intends to relinquish civilian control over the Pentagon to the military.

They think that as a professional politician he means to retain control by establishing cordial working relationships with the military and thus to be able to work out mutually acceptable compromises on key problems.

Mr. McNamara, the professional manager, believed that only a hard-nosed civilian staff responsive to his direction could achieve real civilian control.

Conversations with senior and working level officials in and outside the Pentagon disclose several reasons for the increased weight of the Joint Chiefs in the bureaucratic equation.

The two principal reasons are:

1. A personal inclination by Mr. Laird and his chief civilian aides to seek and carefully listen to military judgment in decision-making.

2. The new National Security Council machinery that provides a clearly defined channel for the Joint Chiefs to express their views.

Five Service Leaders

The Joint Chiefs of Staff consist of five armed forces leaders, including the chairman. They are Gen. Earle G. Wheeler, chairman; Gen. William C. Westmoreland, Army Chief of Staff; Admiral Thomas H. Moorer, Chief of Naval Operations; Gen. John P. McConnell, Air Force Chief of Staff, and Gen. Leonard C. Chapman, Commandant of the Marine Corps.

The conversations with Pentagon officials reveal that while the power of the Joint Chiefs has increased, the influence of the Pentagon's civilian-run Office of International Security Affairs has declined both within and outside the Defense Department.

Its decline is attributed to the fact that Mr. Laird, unlike his predecessors, has not actively sought a foreign policy role

Administration's Vietnam war policy and often outweighed the State Department in formulating foreign policy.

Now, under the new Assistant Secretary for International Security Affairs, Warren Nutter, a former foreign policy adviser to Barry Goldwater, and men of like political views he has brought in to assist him, the office inclines to positions similar to those of the Joint Chiefs on foreign policy questions.

Systems Analysis Decline

As a result, the State Department pays much less attention to it in the interagency bargaining through which policy documents are drawn up for eventual submission to the National Security Council.

A third major development has been the very noticeable weakening in bureaucratic muscle of the Office of Systems Analysis, which held a pivotal position under Mr. McNamara and Mr. Clifford.

Like the international security office, the systems' analysis office has a combined civilian-military staff but is run by civilians and is an operating arm of the Secretary of Defense.

The cost effectiveness and strategic analysts in the systems analysis office, irritably dubbed "the whiz kids" by the military, review all weapons proposals by the military.

Very frequently under Secretaries Clifford and McNamara, the reviews were so different in content from the original proposals that they constituted independent weapons programs, and the systems analysis office

C.I.A. Report Says Enemy Has Put 30,000 Agents Into

Continued From Page 1, Col. 4

American men in South Vietnam to 284,000 by next May. He has indicated, however, that he hopes to make further withdrawals as his Vietnamization program continues. The President has also repeatedly stated, as did high White House officials in commenting on the C.I.A. analysis, that the Vietnamization program is going well.

Details of the top-secret study were made available to The New York Times by the Government officials who read it. The study was made last May, the officials said, and has been circulated in the White House, the Pentagon and the State Department. Information received since May—especially after the two-month attack on Communist sanctuaries in Cambodia that ended June 30—has continued to confirm the C.I.A.'s findings, the officials said.

The study was apparently based on new information about the nature and size of the Communist spy organization in South Vietnam as well as on a fresh analysis of captured documents and interrogations of prisoners and defectors during the last two to three years.

In its analysis, the Central Intelligence Agency says that early last year, after a number of setbacks on the battlefield, the Communists decided to shift their long-range strategy from intense military activity to political erosion, against the day when American troop strength would no longer be a serious threat because of withdrawals.

The enemy is confident that this strategy will succeed, the analysis pointed out. It offered no contradiction.

To carry out the new strategy, the report asserts, the Communists stepped up their infiltration of secret agents into various branches of the South Vietnamese Government.

Most Natives of South

The study estimates that the enemy has infiltrated more than 30,000 agents—most of them natives of the southern part of divided Vietnam—into the armed forces, the police force and the South Vietnamese intelligence organizations charged with eradicating the Vietcong guerrillas and their North Vietnamese allies. (High White House officials said that the study gave a total of about 20,000 agents, but the officials who had read it said they were certain the figure was 30,000.)

The number of such agents is said to be growing, with a goal of 50,000. If this goal is reached, the spy organization would be 5 per cent of the South Vietnamese military and police forces. The C.I.A. study doubts, however, that the Communists achieved their goal by the end of 1969, the target date.

While the enemy operatives range from very effective to very poor, the study says, the network derives its power from the fact that the United States and the South Vietnamese Government have nothing remotely comparable.

The study describes the workings of three Communist political-action and intelligence organizations, one of which has proven so impervious to Government countermeasures that none of its important agents have been arrested. The C.I.A. refers to the relatively few arrests to tell how Communist agents have reached into army headquarters, into President Thieu's office and even into the negotiating team at the Paris peace talks.

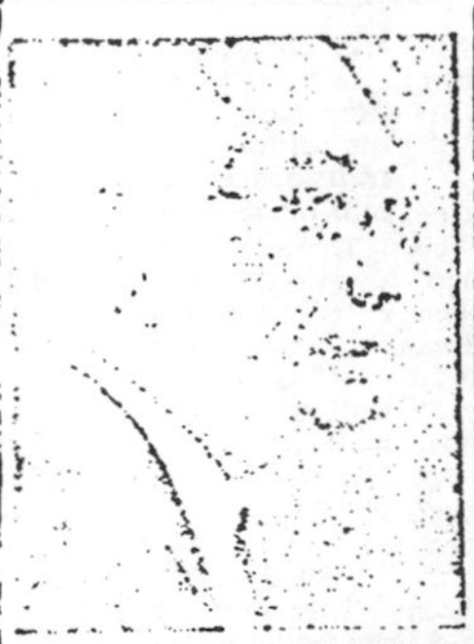

Associated Press

Huynh Van Trong, a special aide to President Thieu, during his trial for treason held in Saigon last year.

Apathy a Possible Reason

In addition, the Central Intelligence Agency reports the failure of hundreds of thousands of South Vietnamese policemen and soldiers to report contacts by Vietcong agents. The report adds that the enemy network could not exist without the tacit complicity—whether from fear, sympathy or apathy—of the majority of South Vietnamese soldiers and policemen.

The C.I.A. cited such feelings as evidence that the Saigon Government could not command the deep loyalty of the men on whom it depends to defend itself.

Although the South Vietnamese Government is infiltrated from bottom to top, the study says, the United States and Saigon have had little success not only in penetrating the Communist organization but also in keeping agents alive in areas the Communists control.

The study offers the following assessment of the advantages of the enemy's virtual monopoly on subversion:

¶There is a permanent imbalance in tactical military intelligence. The enemy is usually forewarned of allied moves and the United States and South Vietnam are usually ignorant of Communist ones.

¶Because most Government-held areas are nominally, rather than firmly, controlled, the enemy is able to recruit selectively and to decide freely who should be assassinated for maximum political effect.

¶The enemy has excellent security and can thwart Government efforts to infiltrate its organization and territory. Government agents are exposed in advance and programs such as Phoenix—an effort begun in 1967 to uncover and destroy the Vietcong apparatus in the countryside—are undermined. Officials noted that the study provided the most plausible explanation yet for the continuing failure of Phoenix, a program considered vital to Vietnamization.

¶Penetration of non-Communist political parties and religious groups allows the Communists to take advantage of, and worsen, the chronic political weakness of the South Vietnamese Government.

¶The Communists can survive despite great allied military pressure. Thus, as American troop withdrawals proceed, a resurgence of Communist strength can be expected. In cutting toward its goal of 284,000 men, the United States expects to have 344,000 soldiers in Vietnam by the end of 1970—a reduction of 205,000 in two years.

Discussing the make-up of the enemy apparatus, the C.I.A. report says that the three Communist organizations that control the estimated total of 30,000 agents receive their orders from Hanoi, through the Central Office for South Vietnam, the Communist command for the South. The destruction of its headquarters was a goal of the American drive into Cambodia, but it is still operating in the jungles.

According to the C.I.A., the full-time operatives are to be distinguished from the many more tens of thousands of part-time agents and Vietcong sympathizers in South Vietnam.

The largest segment of about 20,000 full-time operatives is run by the Military Proselyting Section, whose primary aim is to undermine the morale and effectiveness of the South Vietnamese armed froces and police, according to the study.

Many of these operatives are South Vietnamese officers and noncommissioned officers. They try to recruit other soldiers to the Communist cause, foment dissent within units, perform covert assassinations, encourage desertions and defections and arrange accommodations in which Government military units, to avoid casualties, tacitly agree not to attack Communist forces. Such accommodations are a widespread practice that American military advisers have not been able to end.

Network of Couriers

This group of 20,000 agents is supported by a large network of couriers and keepers of safe-houses, where agents can take refuge. Most keepers of these refuges are the wives or relatives of South Vietnamese soldiers and policemen, the study continues.

A second group—about 7,000 agents—is run by the Vietcong Military Intelligence Section, the study says. These agents are said to be spotted throughout all levels of the police, armed forces and civilian administration, principally for espionage. The study notes that the mission of some of the high-level agents is to try to manipulate Government policy. The Military Intelligence Section also intercepts South Vietnamese Army and police radio communications.

South Vietnamese counterintelligence has had its greatest success against these military intelligence agents, but the study cautions that the success has been a limited one. A widely publicized roundup last year probably apprehended less than half of the high-level agents working solely in the Saigon area, the study says.

The third and possibly most dangerous network of agents reported by the Central Intelligence Agency is an estimated total of 3,000 members of the Vietcong security service who permeate the South Vietnamese police intelligence service, the army intelligence and military security service, and the Central Intelligence Office, the South Vietnamese counterpart of the C.I.A. Other agents from the secret service are reported to be active throughout the non-Communist political parties and religious groups.

The Vietcong security service is reportedly a type of political and secret police with the main mission of combating infiltration or disloyalty in the Communist party, the armed forces and the population in Communist-dominated regions in the South.

The service also reportedly operates large networks of civilian informants in Government areas, draws up blacklists in the event a Communist-influenced government takes power in South Vietnam, and selects and kills those people on the blacklists whose deaths might have an immediate psychological and political impact.

The chief mission of its 3,000 agents in the South Vietnamese structure is to keep the Communists informed of how much the Government knows about them and to block any penetration by Government.

The Vietcong security service is so efficient that none of its important agents have been apprehended, the study says.

The analysis makes the point that although sufficient data are available to estimate the size of the clandestine apparatus and how it works, both the United States and the South Vietnamese Government have not been able to obtain the kind of precise information needed to identify and arrest thousands of individual agents and destroy the network.

The South Vietnamese Government has been making greater efforts in recent months to apprehend agents, the officials who read the report said, but has not achieved meaningful progress because the penetration by the enemy is already so great.

To illustrate the omniscience of the subversive apparatus, the study gives some examples from among the relatively small number of agents who have been apprehended.

One was Huynh Van Trong, President Thieu's special assistant for political affairs. As such he was privy to the innermost workings of the South Vietnamese Government as well as to secret communications between Mr. Thieu and President Nixon. He had also participated in the Paris peace talks and had been sent on a sensitive political mission to the United States.

Another agent was a National Assembly deputy and two more were army majors who had served in the section of the police force whose mission is to prevent Communist infiltration. A fourth agent was the former assistant chief of the counterintelligence branch of the army security service. One agent was the chief medical officer of the national police, another was a former province chief and another was the former deputy police chief of Hue, the old imperial capital. The chief of the [illegible] army communicat[illegible] Dalat was also rep[illegible] covered to be acting [illegible] Vietcong.

Some agents at the [illegible] have turned up in [illegible] useful posts. One was [illegible] fear for the comm[illegible] eral of the army corps [illegible] compasses the [illegible] provinces of the country [illegible] ond agent was the [illegible] in another general's [illegible]

In tracing the enemy's [illegible] sion to shift to a strat[illegible] phasizing political ero[illegible] study said that it had [illegible] made by the North [illegible] Politburo. In addition [illegible] ing a reduction in [illegible] Politburo called for [illegible] infiltration from North [illegible] nam, the Central Intel[illegible] Agency said. Infiltr[illegible] clined from about [illegible] in 1968 to approxim[illegible] 000 in 1969, with the [illegible] year reportedly running [illegible] half the 1969 total.

Amnesty Program [illegible]

The Communists also [illegible] thousands of trained [illegible] from their military [illegible] the three political [illegible] cies that penetrate the [illegible] Vietnamese Government [illegible] sent large numbers of [illegible] leaders into government [illegible] tory, the study says.

These new agents [illegible] South Vietnamese struc[illegible] several routes, one of the [illegible] common of which is the [illegible]

C.I.A. Says Enemy Spies Hold Vital Posts in Saigon

OCT 19 1970

By NEIL SHEEHAN

Special to The New York Times

WASHINGTON, Oct. 18—The Central Intelligence Agency has told President Nixon that the Vietnamese Communists have infiltrated more than 30,000 agents into the South Vietnamese Government in an apparatus that has been virtually impossible to destroy.

Because of this, the C.I.A. reported, as United States troop withdrawals proceed, a resurgence of Communist strength in South Vietnam can be expected.

The report to Mr. Nixon said that the secret Communist agents had included an aide to President Nguyen Van Thieu of South Vietnam, a former province chief and high officials of the police and of military intelligence.

Confirmation by Officials

While the study is not addressed specifically to the question of the President's war policy, officials of the United States Government who have read it say that it does raise questions about a key aspect of this policy—Vietnamization, or gradually giving the South Vietnamese the main burden of defending themselves against the Vietcong and North Vietnamese and thus allowing American troop withdrawals.

High White House officials confirmed the existence of the report. They contended, however, that it exaggerated the extent of infiltration and they rejected the analysis as inaccurate and "overly pessimistic."

They said that the President had read a summary of its contents and that he is understood to believe that the analysis is unwarranted because of the generally optimistic reports he has been receiving from other sources about the progress of pacification, the improved military performance of the South Vietnamese and the effects of the Cambodian incursion.

No Implication of Fall

The Central Intelligence Agency's analysis does not assert or imply that the South Vietnamese Government is likely to fall in the next few months, the officials who have read it said. Nor does the study discount the likelihood that the South Vietnamese Army will perform well in battle for some time to come, as occurred in Cambodia.

What the study does imply, the officials said, is that the South Vietnamese Government has little chance of enduring over the long run because of the great extent of Communist penetration.

In terms of troop withdrawals the President has so far committed himself only to reducing

Continued on Page 14, Column 1

Enemy Has Put 30,000 Agents Into Saigon Governmen

tary pressure. Thus, as American troop withdrawals proceed, a resurgence of Communist strength can be expected. In cutting toward its goal of 234,000 men, the United States expects to have 344,000 soldiers in Vietnam by the end of 1970 — reduction of 205,000 in ears.

Discussing the make-up of the enemy apparatus, the C.I.A. report says that the three Communist organizations that control the estimated total of 30,000 agents receive their orders from Hanoi, through the Central Office for South Vietnam, the Communist command for the South. The destruction of its headquarters was a goal of the American drive into Cambodia, but it is still operating in the jungles.

According to the C.I.A., the full-time operatives are to be distinguished from the many more tens of thousands of part-time agents and Vietcong sympathizers in South Vietnam.

The largest segment of about 20,000 full-time operatives is run by the Military Proselyting Section, whose primary aim is to undermine the morale and effectiveness of the South Vietnamese armed forces and police, according to the study.

Many of these operatives are South Vietnamese officers and noncommissioned officers. They try to recruit other soldiers to the Communist cause, foment dissent within units, perform covert assassinations, encourage desertions and defections and arrange accommodations in which Government military units, to avoid casualties, tacitly agree not to attack Communist forces. Such accommodations are a widespread practice that American military advisers have not been able to end.

Network of Couriers

This group of 20,000 agents is supported by a large network of couriers and keepers of safe-houses, where agents can take refuge. Most keepers of these refuges are the wives or relatives of South Vietnamese soldiers and policemen, the study continues.

A second group—about 7,000 agents—is run by the Vietcong Military Intelligence Section, the study says. These agents are said to be spotted throughout all levels of the police, armed forces and civilian administration, principally for espionage. The study notes that the mission of some of the high-level agents is to try to manipulate Government policy. The Military Intelligence Section also intercepts South Vietnamese Army and police radio communications.

South Vietnamese counterintelligence has had its greatest success against these military intelligence agents, but the study cautions that the success has been a limited one. A widely publicized roundup last year probably apprehended less than half of the high-level agents working solely in the Saigon area, the study says.

T hird and possibly most la s network of agents eported by the Central Intelli. ence Agency is an estimated otal of 3,000 members of the Vic security service who er the South Vietnamese police intelligence service, the rmy intelligence and military security service, and the Central Intelligence Office, the South Vietnamese counterpart of the C.I.A. Other agents from

the secret service are reported to be active throughout the non-Communist political parties and religious groups.

The Vietcong security service is reportedly a type of political and secret police with the main mission of combating infiltration or disloyalty in the Communist party, the armed forces and the population in Communist-dominated regions in the South.

The service also reportedly operates large networks of civilian informants in Government areas, draws up blacklists in the event a Communist-influenced government takes power in South Vietnam, and selects and kills those people on the blacklists whose deaths might have an immediate psychological and political impact.

The chief mission of its 3,000 agents in the South Vietnamese structure is to keep the Communists informed of how much the Government knows about them and to block any penetration by Government The Vietcong security service is so efficient that none of its important agents have been apprehended, the study says.

The analysis makes the point that although sufficient data are available to estimate the size of the clandestine apparatus and how it works, both the United States and the South Vietnamese Government have not been able to obtain the kind of precise information needed to identify and arrest

thousands of individual agents and destroy the network.

The South Vietnamese Government has been making greater efforts in recent months to apprehend agents, the officials who read the report said, but has not achieved meaningful progress because the penetration by the enemy is already so great.

To illustrate the omniscience of the subversive apparatus, the study gives some examples of how among the relatively small number of agents who have been apprehended.

One was Huynh Van Trong, President Thieu's special assistant for political affairs. As such he was privy to the innermost workings of the South Vietnamese Government as well as to secret communications between Mr. Thieu and President Nixon. He had also participated in the Paris peace talks and had been sent on a sensitive political mission to the United States. Another agent was a National Assembly deputy and two more were army majors who had served in the section of the police force whose mission is to prevent Communist infiltration. A fourth agent was the former assistant chief of the counterintelligence branch of the army security service. One agent was the chief medical officer of the national police, another was a former province chief and another was the former deputy police chief of Hue, the old imperial capi-

tal. The chief of the principal army communications center in Dalat was also reportedly discovered to be acting for the Vietcong.

Some agents at the bottom have turned up in deceptively useful posts. One was the chauffeur for the commanding general of the army corps that encompasses the northernmost provinces of the country. A second agent was the main servant in another general's house.

In tracing the enemy's decision to shift to a strategy emphasizing political erosion, the study said that it had been made by the North Vietnamese Politburo. In addition to ordering a reduction in fighting, the Politburo called for a cut in infiltration from North Vietnam, the Central Intelligence Agency said. Infiltration declined from about 250,000 men in 1968 to approximately 120,000 in 1969, with the rate this year reportedly running toward half the 1969 total.

Amnesty Program Used

The Communists also shifted thousands of trained personnel from their military forces into the three political bureaucracies that penetrate the South Vietnamese Government and sent large numbers of political leaders into government territory, the study says.

These new agents enter the South Vietnamese structure by several routes, one of the most common of which is the Gov-

ernment's amnesty program for Communist defectors. Some Communist documents refer to the infiltration process as "the transformation of party cadres into innocent people."

There is evidence that at least several thousand false defectors entered through more than half the provinces of South Vietnam in 1969, the study says. Officials said they could not estimate what percentage of the 47,203 Vietcong defectors reported by the Saigon Government last year were actually Vietcong agents.

The study asserts that large numbers of what the Communists call "legalized cadres" are now quietly living and working in supposedly pacified districts. A legalized cadre is an agent who has acquired legitimate status in South Vietnamese society.

As an example of such cover activities, all members of a village council in an ostensibly pacified district recently were discovered to be Vietcong agents.

Although the study does not do so directly, it raises questions about the optimistic reports on pacification that Mr. Nixon has been receiving. Its implication, some officials who have read it said, is that the Communists have decided—to a some extent at least—not to oppose allied pacification efforts frontally but to concentrate on infiltrating the pacifiers. Concluding by discussing the

lack of meaningful poli commitment to the Saigon G ernment by the majority South Vietnamese soldiers, study remarks that during 18-month period only soldiers reported that they been approached by the V cong. During this time, Central Intelligence Ag says, it is known that the cong made hundreds of approaches to m tary personnel.

Comment by Officials

When first asked about study yesterday, the House declined to acknowl its existence. Today high W House officials did so but tended that the study had a "essentially a one-man that it did "not repre the formal position of C.I.A." and that it had n volved a combined anal effort by all American i gence services.

Under questioning, they plained that what they done "on a narrow basis" the Central Intelligence Ag but with raw material furn by all the intelligence ag They also said that the an had been coordinated w the C.I.A., then with the of the intelligence agencies a limited basis" and last gence Agency stamp as an stitutional report.

A spokesman for the ag had no comment on the s

THE NEW YORK TIMES, TUESDAY, JUNE 30, 1970

Ouster of Sihanouk Depicted as Almost an Accident

By NEIL SHEEHAN
Special to The New York Times

WASHINGTON, June 29 — The overthrow of Prince Norodom Sihanouk of Cambodia, the event that thrust another Asian country into the Indochina war, appears to have been almost an accident for everyone concerned.

The full account of how and why Prince Sihanouk fell as Chief of State is still unknown. However, the United States Government and diplomatic sources here have pieced the fragments together and have produced an account of a Cambodian élite that wandered into a coup d'état and of competing outside powers maneuvering toward a climax that none expected.

Apparently Premier Lon Nol and his colleagues did not decide to oust the Prince until one or two days before they formally announced his overthrow on March 13.

While there is a suspicion that some South Vietnamese leaders encouraged the coup, there is no evidence that they knew it was coming. Both the United States and North Vietnam, the two other foreign countries most vitally affected, were apparently surprised and unprepared.

The Soviet Union is said to have offered to fly the Prince back to Pnompenh on the day of the coup in the hope that his presence would reverse events. When he declined, Moscow set about quietly to try to do business with his anti-Communist successors.

Peking Backs Sihanouk

Communist China is thought to have tried to persuade North Vietnam to come to terms with the new Cambodian regime. When it failed, it wound up supporting Prince Sihanouk's government in exile.

Here is the account as it is being recounted by informed sources here:

The Vietnamese are the Cambodians' traditional enemies. Prince Sihanouk decided late in 1963, however, that it would be useful to gain some credit with Hanoi, whose side he believed would win the Vietnam war. Over several years he permitted the Vietnamese Communists to construct a complex of bases along the Cambodian border with South Vietnam and to open a sea supply route through the port of Sihanoukville, now Kompong Som. By 1968, these Vietnamese guests were behaving in a fashion the Cambodians had not bargained for. They reorganized and armed the dissident Cambodian Communist movement, the Khmer Rouge, and began using the bases as staging points for assaults on American and South Vietnamese outposts just across the border.

The Cambodian casualties caused by retaliatory allied bombing and shelling and the incitement of the Khmer Rouge so disturbed the Prince and his army that he shut off the Sihanoukville supply route in the spring of 1969.

Last August, economic troubles resulting from the Prince's nationalization policies and unrest over North Vietnamese encroachment forced him to form another government. He named a Cabinet led by an old associate, Lieut. Gen. Lon Nol. It had a basically rightist complexion and was designed to liberalize and stimulate the economy.

In September, Prince Sihanouk went to Hanoi for the funeral of President Ho Chi Minh and extracted a promise of better behavior from the North Vietnamese.

But the North Vietnamese did not change their ways. The Cambodian Army engaged them as well as Khmer Rouge bands in scattered clashes. Shortly before he arrived in France in January for a lengthy visit, the Prince warned that he might have to break off relations with Hanoi and with the provisional revolutionary government of the Vietcong guerrillas.

Sihanoukville Cut Off

Premier Lon Nol once more cut off Sihanoukville to the Vietnamese at the beginning of this year, apparently with the Prince's acquiescence. In February, the provincial governors met with the central Government in Pnompenh and delivered a detailed and alarming account of the extent of Vietnamese penetration throughout the country.

Trying to compel Hanoi to restrict its activities, the Lon Nol Cabinet arranged anti-Vietnamese demonstrations early in March. The Cambodian authorities appear to have lost control over the demonstration in Pnompenh on March 11 and a mob sacked the North Vietnamese and Vietcong Embassies.

Premier Lon Nol and his colleagues are said to have expected the Prince to criticize this violence but to back their underlying aims. Instead, in statements from Paris, he shocked them by denouncing General Lon Nol for alleged pro-American sympathies.

The Prince did not appear to associates to be really expecting a coup. He did, however, make clear that he would dismiss Premier Lon Nol on his return.

Premier Lon Nol began negotiations with the North Vietnamese on March 13, two days after the sacking of the embassies. He opened with a public demand that he apparently regarded as little more than a high bid to start the bargaining —the withdrawal of all of the estimated 60,000 Vietnamese troops from Cambodia within 72 hours. Privately, he indicated a readiness to settle for much less.

The Vietnamese refused to have their activities thus curtailed. They appeared to be stalling on the assumption that Prince Sihanouk's return would restore the old arrangements.

The North Vietnamese representatives reiterated a hard line in a three-hour confrontation with the Cambodians on March 16, demanding reparations and an apology.

It was after this meeting, or the next day, that Premier Lon Nol and his colleagues are said to have decided to depose Prince Sihanouk.

Although there has been speculation that individual United States intelligence agents in Pnompenh may have encouraged the coup, there is no evidence here of a United States Government involvement.

Several days after the March 18 announcement of the Prince's ouster, high officials in Washington were still conjecturing that he had arranged the whole thing as an elaborate sham, another of the maneuvers that the Prince had pursued through 15 years of rule to preserve a precarious neutrality for his country. When they finally recognized his fall, they saw too that the United States as well as Cambodia faced an entirely new situation.

Gen. Lon Nol, left, took control of the Cambodian Government when a coup deposed Prince Norodom Sihanouk.

United Press International

Camera Press-Pix

U.S. SAID TO KEEP NERVE GAS ABROAD AT MAJOR BASES

JUL 19 '69

Report of Okinawa Accident Sets Off Furor in Japan— Tokyo Asks Explanation

By NEIL SHEEHAN
Special to The New York Times

WASHINGTON, July 18 — Artillery shells and bombs loaded with lethal nerve gas have been shipped to major United States military bases overseas on a worldwide basis for years, knowledgeable sources said today.

The exact number of countries where such deadly chemical munitions are stored was not disclosed, but the sources said artillery shells and bombs filled with nerve gas were being kept in American depots in West Germany as well as Okinawa. They may also be stored in United States depots in South Korea, where two American infantry divisions are stationed.

Knowledge of this secret storage of nerve gas munitions abroad came to light as a result of inquiries spurred by an article in today's issue of The Wall Street Journal reporting that 25 Americans were hospitalized last week after an accidental discharge of highly toxic nerve gas at a depot on Okinawa.

Policy Since 1950's

The news that nerve gas is being stored on the island has set off a public furor in Japan and among the Japanese inhabitants of the large American Pacific island base, which is controlled by the United States military but is under residual Japanese sovereignty.

The secret issuing of limited stocks of nerve gas munitions to forces deployed overseas has been standard United States policy since the nineteen-fifties, he said. The shells and bombs are kept in potential trouble areas to be available quickly for retaliatory use if an enemy resorted to chemical warfare. The direct permission of the President is required before they can be used in combat.

It is understood that the State Department, in response to Japanese inquiries about last week's accident, has not denied that nerve gas was included.

The Japanese Government today summoned David Osborn, a United States Embassy official in Tokyo, to the Foreign Ministry and demanded a full explanation of the incident.

Effect on Talks Feared

At a news conference in Tokyo Kiichi Aichi, the Japanese Foreign Minister, was quoted as having said that he had requested the United States "not to cause uneasiness among the people of Okinawa" by storing nerve gas there.

The incident is expected to complicate Japanese-American negotiations for the return of the island to Japanese control. Diplomatic observers here expressed concern that it might set off a wave of leftist demonstrations in Japan during the scheduled visit there of Secretary of State William P. Rogers early next month. He will discuss the status of

Continued on Page 2, Column 7

U.S. SAID TO KEEP NERVE GAS ABROAD

Continued From Page 1, Col. 5

American bases on Okinawa after the island reverts to Japan.

The giant complex of airfields, storage depots and troop training centers on Okinawa is a keystone of the American military presence in Asia.

The Defense Department issue a brief statement here today describing the incident as a mishap involving 24 Americans, but refused to say whether gas of any kind had caused their brief hospitalization.

The carefully prepared statement was read to reporters by Jerry W. Friedheim, deputy assistant Secretary of State for Public Affairs. It said: "As a result of a mishap on Okinawa, which occurred July 8 while they were working on a maintenance operation, 23 United States military personnel and one United States civilian employe were placed under medical observation. All were released and returned to full duty within about six hours. No other persons were involved."

Refuses to Elaborate

Mr. Friedheim then refused to elaborate when asked to describe the "maintenance operation" or to say if nerve gas or any other kind was involved or even what branch of the service the 23 military personnel belonged to.

When the Pentagon was subsequently asked to disclose at exactly which bases overseas chemical munitions were stored and to give an official explanation, a spokesman replied: "We are not going to discuss it."

Reports from Okinawa said the accident occurred in a chemical unit of the Army's Second Logistical Command there. Sources familiar with the handling of chemical munitions speculated that a faulty shell, bomb or some other kind of container of nerve gas might have leaked or cracked open when dropped.

Nerve gas munitions being stored overseas are periodically checked for deterioration by depot personnel, the sources said, and are also periodically shipped from central area logistics bases such as Okinawa, to depots closer to potential trouble areas, such as those in South Korea.

VOL.CXVIII....No.40.

U.S. WILL REMOVE NERVE-GAS ARMS AT OKINAWA BASE

JUL 23 '69

The Pentagon Admits Lethal Chemical Munitions Were Sent to Forces Abroad

OTHER SITES UNCERTAIN

Official Declines to Discuss Possible Storage Areas but Germany Is Mentioned

By NEIL SHEEHAN
Special to The New York Times

WASHINGTON, July 22 — The Department of Defense acknowledged today for the first time today that the United States had shipped lethal nerve-gas munitions to American forces overseas. It said it was removing all such munitions from Okinawa.

Daniel Z. Henkin, Assistant Secretary of Defense for Public Affairs, announced the removal of nerve-gas munitions from the key American-held Pacific island base in a statement read to reporters at the Pentagon this afternoon.

Mr. Henkin refused to say whether nerve-gas munitions were stored at other foreign sites besides Okinawa. His prepared statement said that "no toxic chemical agents have been deployed overseas" since the Republican Secretary of Defense, Melvin R. Laird, took office last January.

Other Sites Reported

Knowledgeable sources said last week that artillery shells and bombs loaded with deadly nerve gas had been issued to major United States forces overseas on a worldwide basis since the nineteen-fifties. The gas is also loaded into missile warheads.

The sources said they did not know the exact number of countries where such munitions were currently stored. But they said that in addition to the stores in Okinawa, nerve gas was definitely being stocked at American depots in West Germany and might also be stored under United States control in South Korea.

Mr. Henkin asserted this afternoon, however, that the United States had not shipped any germ-warfare agents abroad. "I can state unequivocably that there are United States biological weapons stored overseas," he said.

His statement said that the nerve gas in Okinawa had been sent there, "several years ago, as a result of decisions made in 1961 and 1963" during the Administration of John F. Kennedy.

Continued on Page 4, Column 3

Pentagon Says Nerve Gas Is Being Removed From Okinawa

Continued From Page 1, Col. 1

nedy. While Robert S. Mc-Namara, now president of the World Bank, was Secretary of Defense.

The Defense Department announcement came a few hours after the Okinawan legislature adopted a resolution in special session demanding the removal of nerve-gas stocks from the island.

News last week that the lethal gas was secretly stored in Okinawa set off an outcry among the Japanese inhabitants of the island and in Japan itself. The disclosure resulted from an accidental leakage of the gas at a United States munitions storage depot.

Okinawa is controlled by the United States military, but remains under residual Japanese sovereignty. The timing and conditions for its return to Japanese rule are a subject of delicate negotiation between Washington and Tokyo.

Last week the Defense Department would say only that a "mishap" had occurred as a result of which 24 Americans—24 military personnel and one civilian employe—"were placed under medical observation" for about six hours. The Pentagon would not say whether gas of any kind was responsible.

Mr. Henkin's statement today said the accident had occurred at a depot of the 267th Chemical Company, one of two chemical companies under the Army's Second Logistical Command on Okinawa, and that the nerve gas that had leaked was a type of nerve agent called GB.

This is the original form of nerve as developed by Nazi Germany during World War II and further developed and produced in the United States after the war from analysis of captured German stocks.

"During a paint removal procedure, a small leak developed in one weapon adjacent to the fill plug," the statement said. "The 24 personnel experienced minor symptons of toxi expo-

sure, and standard safety procedures, including the use of protective masks, were immediately instituted."

Mr. Henkin declined to describe the weapon involved, other than to say that it was "ordnance." Chemical shells, bombs and missile warheads are commonly painted gray, and toxic munitions are code-marked with three concentric red stripes to signify their lethal nature. Nonlethal munitions, such as tear gas, are marked with only one stripe.

None of the 24 Americans was "seriously affected," the statement said, and "after precautionary medical observation, including brief hospitalization of four military personnel, all 24 persons were returned to full duty within six hours. There were no ryukyuans [Okinawans] or other non-U.S. nationals involved."

Destination Uncertain

"Ordnance teams entered the building involved and rapidly eliminated the unsafe conditions," the statement continued. "The building was cleared and decontamination process was completed without incident. A team of experts from the Army's Edgewood Arsenal, Maryland, has been sent to Okinawa to assist in detoxifying and disposing of the weapon."

The statement maintained that "strict safety precautions had always been observed in the storage of nerve gas on Okinawa and that there had never been "any serious injury to a single individual" as a result.

Mr. Henkin did not say when the nerve-gas stocks would be removed from Okinawa or how they would be shipped. The statement did not indicate whether the gas would be returned to the United States or sent to another major military base overseas. It asserted that "military officials have been working on plans" to take the nerve gas out of Okinawa "for some time."

The removal is being accelerated, it said, because of the accident and because of an over-all review of United States chemical and biological warfare activity now being coordinated by the National Security Council staff.

In a separate statement today, Secretary Laird said he felt it essential to review the nerve gas developed during the nineteen-fifties called by the code name VX. The exact formula is highly secret.

Although a number of Government agencies, including the Arms Control and Disarmament Agency, are participating in the review, it was learned that some senior military officials occurred. The Pentagon gave no quest the study because they asked if VX munitions were thought the United States was not doing enough in the field edgeable sources said they believe such weapons were fare to counter Soviet activities there.

United States work in chemical and biological warfare is now costing $350-million a year, according to official estimates, and about $500-million, according to some unofficial ones.

VX is an oily substance that covers the ground, vegetation and buildings where it has been dispersed and can linger for months under certain climatic conditions. It is more lethal than GB and a few inhaled milligrams can be fatal within seconds if inhaled in amount on the skin kills within

sufficient quantity. It is a volatile substance that lingers less in an area where it has been dispersed for 10 minutes to 12 hours, depending on weather conditions.

The United States has also produced and employed overseas in bombs, shells and rocket warheads an improved type of nerve gas developed during the nineteen-fifties called by the code name VX. The exact formula is highly secret.

The initial report of the Okinawa accident published in the Wall Street Journal last week had encouraged Mr. Laird to reimmediate reply today when edgeable sources said they believe the United States was stored on Okinawa, but know-ledgeable sources said they believe such weapons were fare to counter Soviet activities there.

GB, also called tabun, kills seconds. A slightly larger amount on the skin kills within minutes unless antidotes are administered immediately.

U.S. Policy at Geneva Delayed
Special to The New York Times

GENEVA, July 22—James E. Leonard, the United States representative at the disarmament conference here, said today that the Nixon Administration had not decided whether to join a British draft convention to prohibit the acquisition or use of biological weapons.

Mr. Leonard told the conference delegates that the British proposal warranted serious discussion. He said, however, that "we are not clear in our own minds whether it would be desirable to conclude a separate measure relating only to biological weapons," which would thus not prohibit chemical weapons.

The United States representative added, that the British draft convention July 10, had never been used and that their characteristics and effects are different from those of chemical weapons.

UNITED STATES DISTRICT COURT

SOUTHERN DISTRICT NEW YORK

---X
                                         :
UNITED STATES OF AMERICA,   :
                                         :
        Plaintiff   :
                                         :
                                         :
        v.   :   71 Civ. 2662
                                         :
                                         :
THE NEW YORK TIMES COMPANY et al,   :
                                         :
        Defendants.   :
                                         :
---X

                AFFIDAVIT of HEDRICK SMITH

STATE OF NEW YORK   )
                       :   ss.:
COUNTY OF NEW YORK   )

        HEDRICK SMITH, being duly sworn, deposes
and says:

        1. I am a reporter employed by The New York Times
regularly engaged in writing articles on matters of military,
national or international affairs that are published in The
Times.

        2. Annexed to this affidavit are a number of
such articles. In writing each article I obtained information from governmental sources either in the form of
oral information that I understood to be classified or
from classified documents. Such articles indicate
expressly or by clear implication the nature of their
confidential or restricted source. I made no inquiry
whether such information was lawfully authorized to be
disclosed to me. The articles were published without

interference, objection or resulting action by the government, notwithstanding the information disclosed thereby.

Hedrick L. Smith

Sworn to before
me this 17th day
of June 1971

[notary signature]

Notary Public

TRUMAN W. EUSTIS, III
Notary Public, State of New York
No. 31-6210650
Qualified in New York County
Commission Expires March 30, 1972

[The following pages contain copies of exhibits submitted with Mr. Smith's affidavit, articles by him copied from The New York Times.]

Hedrick Smith

NEW HANOI STAND VIEWED AS A SHIFT

U.S. Is Exploring Statement That North 'Will' Confer if War Against It Ceases

Excerpts from statement by foreign minister, Page 2.

By HEDRICK SMITH

WASHINGTON, Jan. 2—The United States is using diplomatic channels to try to determine Hanoi's intentions in issuing a statement promising peace talks once American bombing raids and other acts of war against North Vietnam were unconditionally halted.

A statement to this effect by the North Vietnamese Foreign Minister, Nguyen Duy Trinh, broadcast in English yesterday by the Hanoi radio, has stirred considerable interest here and at the Texas White House.

For the first time, it appeared, the North Vietnamese Government has stated explicitly that it "will" hold talks with the United States on relevant, but unspecified, questions once American bombing and all other acts of war against North Vietnam have ended. Previously, Hanoi's position was more vague — that there "could" be talks if the acts of war ceased.

Gap Said to Narrow

The White House and State Department avoided any official reaction to the statement, enunciated at a Hanoi reception for a delegation from Mongolia.

Privately, both Administration sources and sympathetic Western diplomats voice the view that the statement marked a definite shift in North Vietnam's position. They said that it narrowed the gap between Washington and Hanoi on terms for holding peace talks but that there still were important differences.

United States officials noted that the statement, in addition to reiterating that "the basis for settlement" was the hitherto unacceptable formulas of North Vietnam and the National Liberation Front in South Vietnam, left a number of questions unanswered.

How soon, for example, would talks start after the bombing halted? What assur-

Continued on Page 2, Column 4

NEW HANOI STAND VIEWED AS A SHIFT

Continued From Page 1, Col. 7

ances are there that the talks would be productive and not stalled indefinitely? What would be discussed? And what about President Johnson's implied requirement for reciprocal military de-escalation by Hanoi in return for the bombing halt?

In a related development, the State Department disclosed that the United States was urging Poland, Canada and India, as members of the International Control Commission, to take steps to improve supervision of Cambodia's frontiers and thereby reduce the danger of military clashes in Cambodia.

The questions raised by the North Vietnamese statement are apparently being explored through the diplomatic channels, Carl Bartch, a State Department press officer, said that the Government was seeking clarification of the North Vietnamese statement and that it was Administration policy to "explore every possible lead." He declined to go into details.

A number of the questions, other officials said, were implicit in President Johnson's remarks on Sept. 29 at San Antonio, Tex. He said then that the United States "is willing to stop all aerial and naval bombardment of North Vietnam when this will lead promptly to productive discussion."

Statement Was Mild

The President, in a mild statement of American requirements, added:

"We, of course, assume that while discussions proceed, North Vietnam would not take advantage of the bombing cessation or limitation."

This phrasing was used, it was explained, to make it easier for Hanoi to enter into talks without having to promise publicly to step down its war effort, as the Administration has demanded.

With regard to the International Control Commission, Washington would like to see it made more effective to reduce North Vietnamese and Vietcong use of Cambodia as a sanctuary.

Activities Are Limited

The commission, established in 1954 by the Geneva agreements that ended the first Indochina war, has confined its activities in Cambodia to investigating complaints by the Government that allied forces have intruded into or attacked Cambodian territory. Recently, Prince Norodom Sihanouk has indicated willingness to have the commission check into charges that Communist forces have set up base camps in Cambodia.

Meanwhile, Gen. Earle G. Wheeler, Chairman of the Joint Chiefs of Staff, issued a statement warning against "unilateral cessations" of allied military operations. He noted that the Third Brigade of the United States 25th Infantry Division was "subjected to a sustained ground attack and deliberate mortar bombardment" in violation of the New Year's holiday cease-fire last night and early this morning.

"That our troops beat off this attack with heavy and disproportionate losses [to the enemy] should never disguise two harsh facts," General Wheeler asserted. "The enemy cynically disregarded his own cease-fire announcement.

"The enemy flagrantly violated the 12-hour truce extension put forward by His Holiness Pope Paul VI."

Do Discerns a Change

TUNIS, Jan. 2 (AP) — The South Vietnamese Foreign Minister, Tran Van Do, said today that North Vietnam's latest statement on conditions for starting peace talks could represent an important change in position.

"I believe that if Hanoi accepted negotiations if we stopped the bombings permanently and unconditionally, this would constitute a very appreciable change in attitude on the part of Hanoi," he said.

He spoke with newsmen when he arrived from Geneva.

Johnson Said to Have Promised To Sell Israel More Jet Planes

Continued From Page 1, Col. 6

negotiations on Jordan's arms requests.

Diplomatic sources said that no timetable had yet been established for deliveries of the arms.

When the United States relaxed its over-all embargo on arms shipments to the Middle East last Oct. 24, it omitted Jordan from the five Arab countries that would be receiving arms along with Israel. It was disclosed that a previous American agreement to sell Jordan 36 F-104 jet fighters had been canceled.

Eshkol Leaves U. S.

Premier Eshkol, ending his nine-day visit to the United States yesterday, emphasized that he was leaving "deeply convinced" of President Johnson's friendship and understanding of Israel's problems.

In a statement before boarding an Air Canada charter flight for Toronto, Premier Eshkol, accompanied by his wife, Miriam, said he had been "moved and uplifted by the demonstrations of amity shown to me at every side," particu-

larly by the "great Jewish community."

Premier Eshkol also is scheduled to visit Montreal and Ottawa, where he will confer with Prime Minister Lester B. Pearson. He is due to return to Israel next Thursday.

Deeds, Not Words, Asked
Special to The New York Times

TORONTO, Jan. 12—Premier Eshkol said today he would rather have deeds, such as delivery of jet warplanes, than kind words from President de Gaulle of France.

When he arrived here from the United States he was asked whether he was satisfied with the explanation President de Gaulle gave recently of his Nov. 27 characterization of Jews as "an elite people, sure of itself and domineering." The President later said he meant that as a compliment.

Premier Eshkol replied: "Words are words and I would like to see deeds."

When pressed, he said General de Gaulle should permit delivery of 50 Mirage planes ordered by Israel, which he said were already two-thirds paid for.

By HEDRICK SMITH

ISRAEL SAID TO GET JOHNSON'S PLEDGE OF MORE A-4 JETS
—JAN 13 '68

Total Probably About 20— No Commitment Reported to Eshkol on F-4's

WASHINGTON, Jan. 12 — Informed sources reported today that President Johnson had promised Premier Levi Eshkol of Israel more American Skyhawk A-4 fighter-bombers to help Israel maintain her military superiority over the Arab states.

These sources said that no specific number of planes had been set, but, subject to further negotiations at the working level, it would probably be about 20 planes, or roughly a squadron.

These sources said, however, that the President had made no commitment to Mr. Eshkol on an Israeli request for 50 F-4 Phantom jets, the most advanced operational plane in the American arsenal.

'Sympathetic' Consideration

The two leaders conferred last Sunday and Monday at President Johnson's LBJ Ranch at Johnson City, Tex. A communiqué issued after their meetings said that the United States would give "active and sympathetic" consideration to Israel's requests for arms, but disclosed no details.

Before the talks, Israel had been pressing vigorously for an American agreement to supply the Phantoms as well as more Skyhawks in order to offset Soviet military shipments to the Arab states defeated by Israel in the six-day war last June.

The United States has already begun shipment of three squadrons of 48 Skyhawks under a sales agreement concluded in 1966. Delivery of these planes is expected to be completed late this year.

Informed sources said that shipment of additional Skyhawks would follow that, but they gave no schedule for delivery. American officials do not rule out the possibility of further agreements of this kind, depending on the scale of Soviet arms shipments to the Arab states.

Communiqué Recalled

In the joint communiqué last Monday, the President indicated that deliveries of Soviet arms to the Middle East would be a key factor in future consideration of Israeli requests.

Western diplomats also disclosed that the French Foreign Minister, Maurice Couve de Murville, had recently indicated to the Israelis that they should not give up on France as a future source of arms.

Israel has been concerned by President de Gaulle's embargo on arms shipments to combatants in the Arab-Israeli war. This has delayed scheduled delivery of 50 Mirage jets ordered by Israel before the war.

In regard to arms sales to other countries involved in the war, the United States has privately informed Jordan that Washington is prepared to resume negotiations on an agreement to sell jets to the Jordanians.

The Events Aboard Pueblo

FEB 4 -'68

By HEDRICK SMITH

Special to The New York Times

Efforts to Destroy Secret Devices on Ship Described

WASHINGTON, Feb. 3—The commander of the intelligence ship Pueblo and part of his crew are reported to have locked themselves in a compartment and worked furiously for 45 minutes or longer to destroy secret documents and sensitive equipment after North Korean sailors boarded the ship 11 days ago.

Comdr. Lloyd M. Bucher, the Pueblo's skipper, and his men apparently managed to fend off North Korean sailors long enough to destroy some code books and equipment, throwing pieces of documents through portholes.

They are also believed to have used explosives to destroy secret electronic equipment.

Government officials believe that not all the electronic equipment was destroyed. As a precaution, the Government immediately changed some codes of the United States Navy and other agencies.

The dramatic story of the Pueblo's final resistance before capture on Jan. 23 has been pieced together from reports of well-placed sources, including members of Congress who have been briefed at the highest levels of government.

The Administration's information is based largely on the Pueblo's final series of messages and an interpretation of these messages, but the sources said that not even the Government knew the full story.

The picture that has emerged indicates, more so than the Administration's first reports did, that Commander Bucher and his crew acted with dispatch and heroism once they realized that their ship was going to be captured.

Government officials report that until then Commander Bucher apparently assumed that the Pueblo was being given the same type of Communist harassment that other electronic intelligence ships have experienced.

According to the Administration's first reports, the Pueblo was encircled by four North Korean patrol boats and taken into the port of Wonsan. Administration officials have since told members of Congress that at the time of boarding there were also eight MIG jet fighters overhead.

As the North Koreans scrambled aboard, the Pueblo sent a message to the effect that she was being seized and that her crew was proceeding to destroy codes, classified papers, and highly sensitive electronic gear to prevent them from falling into enemy hands.

Like all such intelligence ships, the Pueblo had rigid standing orders to destroy such materials and equipment when in serious trouble. But informed officials reported that the ship had not been fully equipped with built-in destructive mechanisms for all of her highly secret electronic gear.

Intelligence ships are supposed to have some type of incendiary detonating device so that if the vessel is about to fall into enemy hands, "you push two buttons and all they get is a mass of melted metal," as one source put it. But this source and others indicated

Continued on Page 7, Column 1

The Events Aboard the Pueblo After Her Capture at Sea by North Koreans

Continued From Page 1, Col. 4

that since there were not enough automatic destruction devices, the crew had to use its ingenuity.

Some sources said that the crew apparently had to use a makeshift explosive to destroy or damage some of their equipment. Several sources speculated that hand grenades and possibly incendiary devices or even sledge hammers might have been used.

At one point after the North Koreans boarded the vessel, the Pueblo messaged that one man had been severely injured. Officials here have surmised that this was either the crewman later reported by diplomatic channels to have died or the one, mentioned in the Pueblo's own message, whose leg was blown off.

Government officials have guessed that this injury came in the process of destroying equipment.

A later message from the Pueblo said that three men were "wounded." Gen. Earle G. Wheeler, Chairman of the Joint Chiefs of Staff, was reported to have suggested in briefings to members of Congress that this description apparently was military parlance, meaning wounded in enemy action. General Wheeler was said to have contrasted this with the word "injured" used for the earlier incident.

There are differing versions of the Pueblo's final message, which was sent, according to the Pentagon, at 12:32 A.M. Eastern standard time, Jan. 23—47 minutes after the Pueblo radioed that she was being boarded.

The Government's initial statements on the incident said simply that the Pueblo had radioed finally that she was "going off the air." According to some sources, however, Government officials later said that the final message was: "Send help. These guys mean business."

Still a third version was that the final call was: "I got to go off the air, good-by."

In reports to members of Congress, Secretary of Defense Robert S. McNamara was said to have expressed complete confidence in Commander Bucher. But some members of Congress got the impression that the State Department did not concur wholeheartedly.

Top Administration officials were said to have explained that the reason the Pueblo had not been given escort ships or air cover for protection was the fear that this would provoke an incident.

This was the gist of Secretary McNamara's comments to newsmen last Thursday in response to criticism from Richard M. Nixon, the former Vice President.

Mr. Nixon, endorsing President Johnson's efforts to obtain the release of the Pueblo's 83-man crew, said at a news conference at Manchester, N.H., that it was "simply unthinkable" that a ship like the Pueblo, carrying only two .50-caliber machine guns as armament, had been sent so close to the North Korean coast without protective escorts.

Mr. McNamara said that it would have been unthinkable to provide escorts because this would have amounted to provocative action that might have led to "fired shots."

Although the Administration has held extensive briefings for a considerable number of members of Congress, some senators are reported to have pressed for still further details.

"This was a national disaster," one Congressional source said, "and we want to know what the heck took place."

During secret testimony on the defense budget last week, Secretary McNamara and General Wheeler were reported to have provided the Senate Armed Services Committee with the complete file of the Pueblo's outgoing messages during her seizure, but not the messages being sent at that time to the Pueblo from American naval headquarters.

Some senators were said to be eager to get these messages as well, in order to investigate further the question of why the Pueblo was not sent assistance by other American or allied forces in the region.

There was no firm indication whether there would be a full investigation by the Senate committee or its Preparedness Subcommittee, headed by Senator John C. Stennis, Democrat of Mississippi.

Since the incident, the Administration has sought to [illegible]per passions to allow time for diplomatic efforts to free the American crew, which originally consisted of 6 officers, 75 enlisted men and 2 civilians.

But the intense interest of members of Congress indicated that the matter will not be allowed to rest.

Some Government officials with knowledge of the events surrounding the Pueblo's capture have told newsmen that they are under instructions not to discuss details that not yet have been made public.

'Some Assurance' Needed

"The emissary's mission was to explain that San Antonio formula and to make clear that we needed some assurance that Hanoi would not pour six or eight or ten divisions into South Vietnam during the pause in bombing," said Mr. Pucinski.

"If we could have gotten some assurance that the North Vietnamese would not accelerate the movement of troops during the pause," he added, "my judgment is that we would now be negotiating."

This explanation is consistent with terms first publicly detailed by the Secretary of Defense-designate, Clark M. Clifford, in testimony before Congress on Jan. 23. Officials later indicated that this position had been indirectly relayed to the North Vietnamese Government.

Nine days ago Secretary of State Dean Rusk disclosed that the United States had suspended its air attacks on the Hanoi and Haiphong regions during January to promote explorations of North Vietnam's offer on Dec. 29 to hold talks if the bombing and other acts of war were halted unconditionally.

The raids in the Hanoi region were suspended on Jan. 15 and resumed last Saturday; those on the Haiphong region were suspended around Jan. 18 and resumed last Friday.

"Without Any Hazard"

"We actually suspended bombing of Hanoi in order to get this emissary of ours a chance to get in without any hazard," Mr. Pucinski reported. He added that he did not know the date that the intermediary arrived in Hanoi but that he presumed that it was in the latter half of January.

The 'primary point,' Mr. Pucinski said, was to obtain "some assurance" from Hanoi that it would "not accelerate the movement of troops" into South Vietnam once the bombing stopped.

"There were a lot of other questions that had to be answered," Mr. Pucinski said, ranging "like the question: To what extent can North Vietnam commit the Vietcong to any cease-fire. Secondly, who are going to be the people that would engage in the negotiations? Thirdly, would the agreement to negotiate call for a total ban on shipments into South Vietnam or would it merely freeze at the present level such shipments and insure no increase? Fourth, the timing of when the talks would start."

Mr. Pucinski said President Johnson "wants the talks to begin almost immediately" after any stop in bombing raids.

"Our people are concerned that we don't get into another Korea thing," he went on on "they are concerned that we're still negotiating 15 years later in Korea."

In his San Antonio speech, the President said he would stop the bombing if this would lead "promptly to productive" talks, and assuming Hanoi would not take military advantage of the cessation.

Since then, the North Vietnamese have said that talks would start "a suitable time" after the bombing was stopped "unconditionally" and "as soon as the United States has proved that it has really stopped unconditionally the bombings and all other acts of war" against North Vietnam.

Nguyen Duy Trinh, the North Vietnamese Foreign Minister, said in an interview last Thursday that the talks could take up questions "raised by either side" as well as "questions related to a settlement of the Vietnam problem on the basis of the 1954 Geneva agreements on Vietnam.

But American officials noted that he accused Washington of imposing conditions on a bombing halt, thereby spurning the President's terms for entering talks. They have interpreted the recent offensive as an indication that Hanoi does not want to talk at this juncture.

Johnson Talks With Students

WASHINGTON, Feb. 12 (AP) —President Johnson said tonight that despite the offensive in Vietnam, his San Antonio formula offer for peace talks still stood. "We would meet them tomorrow," he added.

Mr. Johnson discussed Vietnam, dissent at home and unrest in the cities in a wide-ranging 75-minute question-and-answer session with 11 college students.

The President said that in seeking peace in Vietnam, "we have gone just as far as decent and honorable people can go."

He said he stood behind his offer to halt the bombing and talk promptly if North Vietnam indicated that this would be productive.

But addressing the enemy in effect, he added: "We don't want you to take advantage if Hanoi is interested," he said, "it wouldn't have to change a 'could' to a 'will' or indulge in any other semantic niceties."

"As an example," he went on, all it would have to do "is drop a line and say Geneva is the place and tomorrow is the day."

Mr. Johnson said Hanoi's answer to his earlier offer of the San Antonio formula was the assault on 44 South Vietnamese cities and 24 United States bases "on a sacred day"—the Lunar New Year.

"Yet we would meet them tomorrow," he added, "but we're not going to surrender."

The college students were members of the National Board of Choice 68, a collegiate presidential preference primary to be held on more than 100 campuses April 24.

AN ENVOY SOUNDED HANOI FOR THE U.S.

Continued From Page 1, Col. 5

the emissary had left Hanoi without receiving an acceptable response from the North Vietnamese Government.

Representative Pucinski, reached by telephone at his Chicago office, said he was making the disclosure to let "the American people know the extent to which the President is trying to find some basis for negotiation."

The Illinois Congressman, a supporter of the President's policies, said he understood that as of last Wednesday the Johnson Administration had received no report from the envoy, whom he declined to identify on the ground that it would jeopardize further efforts.

"This a continuing process so it would be a mistake to surface his identity," Mr. Pucinski, who is serving his fifth term, explained. "Obviously we have enough confidence to send him there."

According to Mr. Pucinski, the emissary was instructed to explain the United States' terms for halting the bombing and entering talks, as outlined by Mr. Johnson in a speech at San Antonio, Tex., last Sept. 29, and was asked to persuade Hanoi to give assurances that it would not use a bombing halt to step up infiltration into South Vietnam.

Continued on Page 5, Col.

Johnson Sent a Foreign Envoy To Query Hanoi in Raid Let-U

By HEDRICK SMITH

WASHINGTON, Feb. 12 — A foreign emissary went to Hanoi last month at President Johnson's request to explore North Vietnam's terms for entering peace talks, and the United States suspended bombing around Hanoi to promote and protect his mission.

These moves came to light today as a result of disclosures by Representative Roman C. Pucinski, Democrat of Illinois, who said his information had come from "the highest sources in the Administration." It was later confirmed by Government officials.

[President Johnson said that his San Antonio formula for peace talks was still in effect despite the enemy offensive in South Vietnam, The Associated Press reported. "We would meet them tomorrow," he said, adding that the Government had gone "just as far as decent and honorable people can go." Page 5.]

Mr. Pucinski said he believed that "we would now be negotiating" if Hanoi had given the intermediary some assurance that it would not accelerate the movement of its troops

Representative Roman Pucinski told about miss

into South Vietnam during halt in American bombing the North.

He did not write off the sion as a failure, but the ernment officials said it not produced any diplo breakthrough.

The State Department clined to comment on Mr cinski's report. The of who confirmed the genera line of his disclosure said

Continued on Page 5, Col.

FEB 13 68

Fear in Hamlets Is Still Hampering Pacification

By HEDRICK SMITH

Special to The New York Times

Officials Term Psychological Blows a Greater Setback Than Physical Damage

WASHINGTON, March 28 — Government reports from Saigon indicate that the psychological blows of the enemy's Lunar New Year offensive were worse than the physical disruption to the program of pacifying the South Vietnamese countryside.

Officials engaged in the program are reported to be telling Washington that "insecurity and fear of further Vietcong and North Vietnamese attacks remain key problems in many cities and even more so in the countryside."

The official reports explain that North Vietnam and the National Liberation Front have cleverly played on these fears among the South Vietnamese by warning repeatedly that a "second wave" of assaults was imminent.

"Our biggest concern," said one senior official, "lies in the greater fear and apathy among the rural population, some loss of confidence in the Government's ability to protect them, and a greater defensive-mindedness among Government security forces worried over renewed Vietcong attacks."

Reports from Komer Office

The officials explained that the comments were based on the latest findings of the office of Robert W. Komer, who is in charge of the pacification program. In the past he has been one of its most enthusiastic exponents.

The most optimistic officials now contend that there already is a change for the better in the psychological situation and that a large portion of the South Vietnamese troops and pacification teams are back in the rural areas. These officials maintain that the pacification program, though severely set back by the Lunar New Year offensive, is "still alive and kicking."

Nationwide, officials managing the program contend, the setback was physically less severe than originally thought. "The pessimists were overreacting," said one advocate of pacification.

Nonetheless, he acknowledged that if the enemy was determined to press his campaign of large-scale fighting and widely coordinated offensives, the program would move too slowly to affect the outcome of the war.

Other officials well acquainted with the program are even more pessimistic, fearing that the offensive and the allied reaction have undercut the basic rationale of the program: trying to win the sympathy and support of the villagers through offers of protection and of economic and social improvements.

The pessimists contend that the program was left "in shambles" because the Vietcong concentrated their attacks against the very best pacified hamlets and then moved in to occupy them.

The allied forces used air attacks and artillery barrages to try to dislodge the Vietcong. As a result, the officials explained, the Saigon Government is now in a poor position to return and try to win support with offers of safety and protection.

With somewhat improved access to the countryside, Mr. Komer's office is said to be providing Washington with statistical breakdowns on the damage left by the enemy offensive and on the Saigon regime's recovery efforts.

The latest reports, the officials here disclose, estimate that the offensive left 650,000 new refugees, now reduced to under 400,000, and 95,000 homes destroyed or damaged in addition to 7,500 civilians killed and 15,500 wounded. The damage to business facilities and transportation networks was extensive, the reports indicate.

No Precise Breakdown

The officials still offer no precise breakdown on the Government's control of the rural hamlets — information previously provided by an elaborate reporting system. But the reports indicate that about 200 of the 8,500 hamlets that had some degree of governmental presence before the offensive have reverted to Vietcong control. The officials said many more had been downgraded to the status of being contested.

Mr. Komer is reported to have been encouraged by the fact that 454 of the 595 Revolutionary Development teams have returned to their assigned hamlets. These teams, protected by South Vietnamese military units, are the backbone of the pacification program.

The reports indicate that recovery has occurred primarily in the II and III Corps areas, north of Saigon.

Recovery is described as slow in the heavily populated, rice-rich Mekong Delta, south of the capital, and in the northern portion of the I Corps region, the northernmost tip of South Vietnam, which has been exposed to large scale North Vietnamese military action.

Westmoreland Seeks 206,000 More Troops, Stirring Debate in Administration

FORCES IN VIETNAM NOW TOTAL 510,000

Some Officials in State and Defense Departments Feel Foe Would Match Rise

Continued From Page 1, Col. 8

Seeking Initiative

Only First Request

The White House, however

'A Lot More Killing'

The Argument

Strategy Is Doubted

Compromise Envisaged

Some in Defense and State Departments Oppose Increase

MAR 10 '68

The following dispatch was written by Hedrick Smith and Neil Sheehan, assisted by Max Frankel and Edwin L. Dale Jr.

Special to The New York Times

WASHINGTON, March 9 — Gen. William C. Westmoreland has asked for 206,000 more American troops for Vietnam, and the request has touched off a divisive internal debate within high levels of the Johnson Administration.

A number of sub-Cabinet civilian officials in the Defense Department, supported by some senior officials in the State Department, have argued against General Westmoreland's plea for a 40 per cent increase in his forces "to regain the initiative" from the enemy.

There are now about 510,000 American troops in Vietnam, and the President has authorized a level of 525,000 by next fall. Many of the civilian officials are arguing that there should be no increase beyond the movement of troops now under way.

Fear Matching Rise

The contention of these high ranking officials is that an American increase will bring a matching increase by North Vietnam, thereby raising the level of violence without giving the allies the upper hand.

Senior Pentagon civilians have put forward a written counter-proposal to President Johnson, calling for a shift in American strategy to a concept of close-in defense of populated areas with more limited offensive thrusts than at present. Much of the military hierarchy is reported to oppose this approach.

General Westmoreland, the American commander in Vietnam, has been seeking to persuade the President to approve bolder strategy. Officials report that he has been proposing ground actions into Laos and Cambodia to disrupt the enemy's base areas and infiltration routes.

Compromise Suggested

But the enemy's winter offensive has had such stunning impact on some high civilian officials here that they question privately whether the Government should not [. . . . . i] war objectives. Some ha [. . .] gested that the ground be prepared for a political compromise with the Vietcong. But this is a position that President Johnson and his inner circle of advisers firmly reject at this point.

The President has not yet decided on the question of substantial increases in American forces in Vietnam.

"He is keeping an open mind," said one senior adviser.

For the time being Mr. Johnson is reported to be holding to current strategy and urging General Westmoreland to wring the utmost combat capacity out of the 510,000 American troops already in Vietnam. The White House maintains officially that the question of more troops is "not a matter of decision at this point."

Offensive Causes Doubts

Nonetheless, the scope and depth of the internal debate within the Government reflect the wrenching uncertainty and doubt in this capital about every facet of the war left by the enemy's dramatic wave of attacks at Tet, the Lunar New Year holiday, six weeks ago. More than ever this has left a sense of weariness and irritation over the war.

Officials themselves comment in private about widespread and deep changes in attitudes, a sense that a watershed has been reached and that

Continued on Page 6, Column 1

refueling planes:

The United States arsenal includes 2,260 missile launchers — 1,054 intercontinental missiles, 656 submarine-based missiles and about 550 B-52 strategic bombers.

An Administration official repeated earlier White House assertions that the American antiballistic missile program provided the one real inducement for the Russians to agree to a limit on SS-9's.

After an intensive debate, the Administration won a major legislative victory last Wednesday when the Senate, by a vote of 52 to 47, rejected an amendment that would have blocked expansion of the Safeguard antiballistic missile system to include two new bases.

This week the Senate will vote on an amendment offered by Senator Edward W. Brooke, Republican of Massachusetts, that also would prevent geographical expansion of the Safeguard system but would allow the full $1.3-billion authorization to permit expansion of the two original antiballistic missile sites.

U.S. Would Scrap ABM's

American negotiators, an Administration source said, have indicated Washington's willingness to reduce the American antiballistic missile system to very small proportions; indeed, to abandon it, if the Russians were willing to abandon their 64-site antimissile system now installed around Moscow and to limit their inventory of SS-9's.

The basic American proposal had already been reported, but last week's briefing with newsmen was the first time it had been stated for publication by such high officials.

There has been no conclusive response from the Russians on whether they considered the July 24 proposal as an acceptable offer. But for three weeks, until the arms talks adjourned last Friday, Soviet negotiators intensively questioned the Americans about all facets of the proposal.

Their active interest has been interpreted by some American officials as an indication that the Russians consider the American offer a reasonable possibility, although American officials expect months of hard bargaining — and possibly a Soviet counter offer — when the talks resume in Helsinki.

Russian Questions U.S. Strategy

MOSCOW, Aug. 16 (Reuters) —A Soviet commentator suggested today that President Nixon regarded negotiations with Russia on limiting strategic arms as "some kind of market dealing."

Writing in Pravda, the Communist party daily, Georgi Ratiani hinted that it was misleading to believe that the United States would retain a bargaining advantage by continuing its Safeguard antiballistic missile system.

U.S. MAKES OFFER TO GIVE UP ABM'S IF SOVIET DOES SO

AUG 1 7 '70

Calls on Russians to Limit SS-9's and to Dismantle Own Missile Defenses

OFFICIALS BRIEF EDITORS

Vienna Proposal Outlined— Territorial Compromise Termed Aim in Mideast

By HEDRICK SMITH

WASHINGTON, Aug. 16 — The United States has offered to give up its antiballistic missile defense system entirely if the Soviet Union would agree to limit the number of its huge SS-9 offensive missiles and abandon its own missile defenses, a Nixon Administration source reports.

The official said that, at the conclusion of four months of negotiations with the Soviet Union in Vienna last week, the United States was extremely optimistic about the progress made and fairly hopeful about reaching an agreement on limiting missile systems.

His comments were made at a background briefing organized by the White House for news editors at New Orleans last Friday and made available for publication tonight. New Orleans newspapers have reported that the editors met with President Nixon and were briefed by Henry A. Kissinger, his special assistant for national security affairs, and other Administration officials.

Compromise Sought

At the briefing, the editors were told by one official that the United States would try to encourage Israel and the Arab states to reach some territorial compromise in their expected negotiations through Dr. Gunnar V. Jarring, the United Nations representative.

An Administration official said that no political solution to the Arab-Israeli dispute could be achieved if the Arabs continued to insist that Israel must withdraw completely to her borders before the six-day war of June, 1967, or if Israel insisted on "substantial acquisition" of territory.

This official explained that Israel, Egypt and Jordan had accepted the American proposal for a standstill cease-fire and resumption of negotiations on a political settlement with the understanding that one of the principal items for negotiation would be Israel's final borders.

Arabs Firm on Withdrawal

Nonetheless, Egyptian and Jordanian officials have already said that they would stand firm on demands that Israel should withdraw to her 1967 lines and that what remained to be negotiated was the timetable and mechanics of the withdrawal.

The news editors were also told that the Administration saw no chance for a settlement if the Arab states maintained their demand for the return of 1.3 million [illegible] to their [illegible]

[illegible]

U.S. MAKES OFFER TO GIVE UP ABM'S

Continued From Page 1, Col. 8

ing Israel assurance that she was not expected to take them all back at the risk of altering the fundamental Jewish character of the state of Israel.

In the coming weeks and months, an Administration source said, the United States will have the task of encouraging both sides to move away from their stated positions on territories and refugees, to strike a compromise.

An official said that the United States should reach a judgment by tomorrow on Israeli complaints that the United Arab Republic had violated the cease-fire by moving new missiles into forward positions near the Suez Canal.

In discussing the negotiations with the Soviet Union on limiting strategic arms, now in recess until the next round begins in Helsinki on Nov. 2, Administration officials defended the White House contention that the continuation of construction of the Safeguard missile defense system provides the United States with the best leverage for achieving an ultimate agreement.

One Administration official said that, during the negotiations thus far, the one American development in the missile field that the Russians seemed most interested in stopping was the antiballistic missile, or ABM, program.

This official said that it would be very easy for Moscow to stop this program by agreeing to limits on deploying of Soviet SS-9 missiles, which worry Washington. In a package proposal submitted to the Soviet negotiators on July 24, the United States suggested numerical limitations on nuclear delivery systems of all types, with a special quota on huge missiles such as the SS-9.

The Russians now have about 300 SS-9's in operation or in some stage of deployment. The Nixon Administration, fearful of the potential threat to American missiles from these weapons if their numbers are increased, wants to limit the Russians to no more than their present inventory of SS-9's.

Arsenals Compared

The Soviet Union currently is known to have about 1,550 offensive missile launchers and bombers — about 1,050 land-based intercontinental missiles such as the SS-9's and the smaller SS-11's and SS-13's, 200 submarine-based missiles and 200 strategic bombers and refueling planes.

The United States arsenal includes 2,200 missile launchers — 1,054 intercontinental missiles, 656 submarine-based missiles and about 550 B-52 strategic bombers.

An Administration official repeated earlier White House assertions that the American antiballistic missile program provided the one real inducement for the Russians to agree to a limit on SS-9's.

After an intensive debate, the Administration won a major legislative victory last Wednesday when the Senate, by a vote of 52 to 47, [illegible] an amendment that would have blocked expansion of the Safeguard antiballistic missile system to include two new bases.

This week the Senate will vote on an amendment offered by Senator Edward W. Brooke, Republican of Massachusetts, that also would prevent [illegible]

U.S. AIDES IN PARIS SAID TO URGE HALT

OCT 6 '68

Negotiators Are Reported Asking Johnson to Consider Stopping Bombing Now

By HEDRICK SMITH
Special to The New York Times

PARIS, Oct. 5—The United States negotiators are apparently urging President Johnson to consider halting the bombing of North Vietnam to get the negotiations here moving before he leaves office.

There are indications that Ambassador at Large W. Averell Harriman and Cyrus R. Vance, the two chief negotiators, would favor such a move at this time, when there is a slight reduction in combat activities, when American casualties are running at a lower rate than recently and when some statistics point toward a recent reduction in North Vietnam infiltration into South Vietnam.

Once before the American negotiators urged the President to stop the bombing, keeping the option to resume it if the North Vietnamese significantly improved their military position as a result.

[In Saigon, the Government eased the curfew on the ground that the threat to the capital had diminished. Page 15]

Vance Left Hurriedly

Mr. Vance left hurriedly for Washington on Wednesday, apparently to put the case for a bombing halt to President Johnson. He is reported to have met the President yesterday for breakfast.

American officials here have refused to discuss Mr. Vance's mission, which was decided on only the night before, or to discuss the negotiating delegation's possible recommendations to the President.

It is reported nonetheless, that Ambassador Harriman and Mr. Vance believe that the Viet-

Continued on Page 20, Column 3

U.S. Aides in Paris Said to Urge Johnson to Weigh Bombing Halt

Continued From Page 1, Col. 2

nam talks have reached the point of no return for President Johnson. They are understood to believe that if the President wants to see real results during his term of office, he must make his move in the next few days.

To wait until late this month would look like a political move to help Vice President Humphrey, American diplomats reason. After the election, President Johnson will be a lame duck and the American negotiators apparently think it will be too late then for Mr. Johnson to get anything new under way with the North Vietnamese.

The delegation is understood to believe that the North Vietnamese intend to stand firm on their demand for an unconditional halt of the bombing. The Americans also apparently consider it likely that Hanoi will let the talks proceed to substantive issues once the bombing stops.

Earlier this summer, Ambassador Harriman and Mr. Vance are reliably reported to have recommended a bombing halt.

Their suggestion, it is understood, was that the President stop the bombing and reserve the right to resume it if the North Vietnamese took advantage of the cessation to mount a new offensive, particularly in the area of the demilitarized zone.

At that time, North Vietnamese officials were drawing attention to the end of rocket attacks on Saigon and to the fact of a battlefield lull. In view of Hanoi's aversion to American demands for reciprocal restraint, some American officials thought at the time it was unlikely that Hanoi would go any further than hinting that the combat situation had political significance.

But President Johnson re-jected the negotiating team's recommendations on the basis of estimates from the American military command in Saigon that the enemy was simply recuperating from earlier combat and was preparing for a new offensive.

Fighting did eventually accelerate about Aug. 18, but some Western diplomats contend that this was only after the North Vietnamese saw that President Johnson would not stop the bombing on the basis of what one termed a "face-saving lull."

There has been some diplomatic speculation in the last few days that the North Vietnamese might have secretly hinted to the Americans that there was some moderation on the bombing issue and that this, it was said, might lie behind Mr. Vance's mission in the United States.

But there is no public evidence of this, and American officials deny it, as indeed they would have to, even if it were true, to protect the secret.

Paris Talks' New Phase

Focus Seems to Shift to Role of Saigon And Liberation Front in Negotiations

By HEDRICK SMITH
Special to The New York Times

PARIS, Oct. 13—Despite the public picture of unrelieved deadlock, the Vietnam talks here are reliably reported to be going through a delicate and important phase.

Much of the attention of the negotiators in the last month or so has shifted away from the seemingly sterile argument over a bombing halt to a vital political issue at the core of the talks — the relative strength and political legitimacy of the Saigon Government and of the National Liberation Front, the political arm of the Vietcong.

News Analysis

This has been true of the publicized statements of the two chief negotiators—Ambassador W. Averell Harriman of the United States and Minister ofSt ate Xuan Thuy of North Vietnam—and, apparently, of the private dialogues between the two sides.

It seems clear that the two sides have also been engaged for some time in exploring privately the possible terms under which the South Vietnamese Government and the National Liberation Front could be admitted into next stage of the talks, possibly as part of an over-all arrangement that would bring an end to the American bombing of the North.

This process took on importance at about the time that Pham Van Dong, North Vietnam's Premier, demanded Sept. 2 that the United States halt the bombing of North Vietnam, withdraw its troops and other allied troops from South Vietnam, and "recognize the N.L.F. and talk with the Front on problems of concern to the two sides in South Vietnam."

That was Hanoi's most explicit and authoritative call so far for full participation by the Front in the next phase of negotiations. The American response was to say that if North Vietnam wanted to "bring its friends" to the next stage, it would have to accept "America's friends in South Vietnam as well."

Hanoi has rebuffed the idea of any talks with Saigon. But recently, and apparently for the first time, there have been some hints that Hanoi might regard this as a negotiable issue.

In essence, the position of the North Vietnamese Government is that it cannot agree to talks with the South Vietnamese as long as they refuse to talk with the Front, refuse to recognize the Front, reject the idea of a coalition government and continue to support American bombing of North Vietnam.

In some quarters, that language is felt to imply new willingness by Hanoi to bargain over the question of who will take part in the next phase of talks and how.

The American approach, as it is understood here, has been marked deliberately ambiguous, leaving unclear what status Washington envisages for the Saigon re-gime and the Front in future negotiations.

Independent diplomats observe that it would be a major gain for Hanoi if the Front and Saigon were admitted on an equal footing. The United States would probably oppose parity strongly. Saigon would presumably insist in any case on being recognized by all as the sovereign government of South Vietnam, with the Front treated only as a political party.

Nonetheless, some knowledgeable analysts envisage the possible emergence of a package. They believe American bombing could be stopped if the hard political question of the future negotiating roles of Saigon and the Front were resolved. Part of any such package apparently would be some sort of lull, declared or not, in enemy activity on the battlefield.

Some diplomats suspect that when Cyrus R. Vance, the second-ranking American negotiator, flew to Washington Oct. 2, it was to sound out President Johnson on whether he would be willing to declare a bombing halt in such a situation. It was reported at the time that Mr. Vance was seeking greater flexibility in American terms and was urging renewed consideration of the bombing issue. There was no public indication of President Johnson's reaction.

Although both North Vietnam and the United States reported no progress in the talks Wednesday, the day after Mr. Vance's return from Washington, there were indications that the session might not have been wholly negative.

Some Western analysts concluded that, at a minimum, the North Vietnamese did not hear anything at the Wednesday meeting to suggest that previous explorations of political questions had been undercut by Mr. Vance's trip home.

It could not be learned whether the American negotiators had presented a new or more specific proposal to the North Vietnamese in private.

Since there are only three more negotiating sessions scheduled before the Presidential election Nov. 5, the Johnson Administration is under time pressure.

For that reason, some American officials and allied diplomats were encouraged when Mr. Thuy, in his latest formal statement, asserted that President Johnson still had "enough time and power" to resolve the Vietnamese problem.

Some independent diplomats doubt that there is enough time before the election, or before a new President takes office Jan. 20, to resolve so difficult and central an issue as the roles of Saigon and the National Liberation Front in the next stage of negotiations. The diplomats reason that the solution will foreshadow the ultimate political settlement of the war, and both sides will move most cautiously.

An American spokesman remarked the other day that there was "no basis for speculation that a breakthrough in the negotiations is imminent."

DELIBERATE DELAY ASCRIBED TO HANOI

Continued From Page 1, Col. 7

They theorize that Hanoi's objective has been either to win concessions from President Johnson or to press the United States into getting the South Vietnamese Government to ease its terms for a bombing halt.

At the same time, some allied diplomats suggest, Hanoi has been trying to capitalize upon Saigon's fears that Washington will make an unfavorable agreement at a time when American political pressures for negotiating a breakthrough are at a peak.

Neither the United States nor North Vietnam has acknowledged that concrete proposals are under secret discussion.

Publicly the North Vietnamese have rebuked the Western press for having reported that Hanoi had been bargaining secretly over United States terms for a bombing halt. Hanoi has repeated its standard demand for an unconditional cessation of the bombing.

North Vietnamese sources said tonight that Hanoi's negotiators would repeat this demand at tomorrow's meeting with United States representatives.

Last Session Before Election

Tomorrow the two delegations will hold their last formal session before the United States election. This has apparently put pressures on the United States to resolve its differences with Saigon on terms for a halt in the bombing.

But American and North Vietnamese negotiators are also known to have held clandestine meetings in addition to their formal once-a-week sessions on Wednesday. If more such sessions are held, it would allow nearly a week before the election to make a bargain.

In secret, the American efforts are reported to have concentrated on winning agreement from Hanoi—and from Saigon—for broadening the next phase of talks to include South Vietnamese representatives, as part of an overall package to end the bombing of the North.

The United States has also sought evidence of military restraint from Hanoi so that it could be assured that North Vietnam would not gain military advantage from a bombing cessation.

Formula a Problem

But the critical problem, well-informed diplomats report, has been finding a formula for admitting both the Saigon regime and the National Liberation Front, or Vietcong, and its allies to talks on terms that would allow all sides to maintain they had not made vital concessions.

North Vietnam has been demanding recognition of the Front or Vietcong, and its acceptance as a full negotiating partner. Saigon has refused to recognize the Front or to agree to its admission except as part of Hanoi's delegation.

The United States wants Hanoi to accept the South Vietnamese Government as a full participant in the next phase of talks. The well-placed diplomats say that Hanoi has not accepted this, though it has indicated a willingness to negotiate on the issue.

Reports from Saigon tonight Western analysts suggested indicate that a new proposal by Hanoi is being planned, based on a complex formula.

Thieu Said to Agree

Authoritative sources were quoted as having said that President Nguyen Van Thieu had agreed to a plan that would admit Saigon and the Front to the talks, leaving all sides free to disagree on their comparative status.

Saigon's negotiators would talk to the Americans and the Front's officials would talk to the North Vietnamese. Each would claim full status for itself and deny it to the other.

Until now, South Vietnamese officials have objected to such a plan because it would, in their interpretation, be interpretation and public that Saigon and Front were being admitted to the talks on equal terms.

Today, Paris [illegible]. South Vietnam's [illegible] the preliminary talks [illegible] asserted that [illegible] to sit as part of the [illegible] delegation. This [illegible] conference has [illegible] the Republic of V[ietnam] [illegible] reports on [illegible] had joined the [illegible] the three talks [illegible]

In Secretly,
n on Vietnam
OCT-30 '68

Hanoi Delay in Replying Seen as Bid for Gains as Election Nears

By HEDRICK SMITH

PARIS, Oct. 29—Usually informed diplomats said today that North Vietnam had been seeking an advantage by pressing President Johnson as close as possible to the Presidential elections before giving a final answer to American proposals for a bombing halt.

The diplomats reported that the United States had secretly presented several variations of its package proposal in the last month.

They said that in secret exchanges with the Americans, North Vietnam had shown interest, but had not given a satisfactory response to any of the American initiatives.

Some diplomats have concluded that Hanoi has been delaying deliberately without cut-

The Vietnam Policy Reversal of 1968

(Smith)

Special to The New York Times

WASHINGTON, March 5— On the cold and cheerless early morning of Feb. 28, 1968, the Chairman of the Joint Chiefs of Staff, Gen. Earle G. Wheeler, landed at Andrews Air Force Base after an urgent mission to Saigon. Pausing only to change into a fresh uniform, he hurried through the rain to the White House to deliver a report and make a request.

The report was designed to encourage an anxious President and his beleaguered advisers, but it served only to

This is ⒍'69 of two articles written by Hedrick Smith in collaboration with William Beecher, and incorporating reports by Peter Grose, John W. Finney, E. W. Kenworthy, Roy Reed, Benjamin Welles, Edwin L. Dale Jr. and Max Frankel.

shock them into extended debate.

The request — for more troops—was designed to bring military victory at last in the eight-year American military effort, but it led instead to a fateful series of decisions that

stand in retrospect as one of the most remarkable turnabouts in United States foreign policy.

The month of March, 1968, became a watershed for a nation and a Government in turmoil. The Johnson Administration, by pulling back from the brink of deeper commitments and moving toward disengagement, set a course that affects the daily decisions of the Nixon Administration.

Many of the ingredients of

Continued on Page 14, Column 1

Continued From Page 1, Col. 7

Led Way to a Less Militant Line

Clifford Under Pressure

Spreading Doubts About War

Clark M. Clifford conferring with President Johnson at ... of Defence. It was Mr. Clifford who was to play the ... the White House on Jan. 19, 1967, the day the President ... pivotal role in the governmental infighting that led to the ... named him to succeed Robert S. McNamara as Secretary ... United States military policy in Vietnam.

Confidence Is Shattered

Questions Others Avoided

'Hidden Doves' Discovered

His Words Carried Weight

The March of Events

Confidence Is Shattered

A Big Shopping List'

Gen. Earle G. Wheeler, chairman of the Joint Chiefs of Staff, at his White House briefing for the President and the Cabinet on Feb. 28, 1963, after returning from his inspection tour of Vietnam. It was his request for 206,000 additional troops that brought about the reappraisal of Vietnam policy.

From Divergent Points of View

'Hidden Doves' Discovered

Questions Others Avoided

The March of Events

Tomorrow: President Johnson's conversion on the war.

'68 Shift on Vietnam—II

MAY 7 '69

Special to The New York Times

WASHINGTON, March 6— If ever there was a demonstration that no decision in Washington is final and that the struggle for a President's mind never really ends while he remains in office, it came a year ago this month.

"Let's get one thing clear!" President Johnson said forcefully to his Vietnam advisers on March 16, 1968. "I'm telling you now I am not going to stop the bombing. Now is there anybody here who doesn't understand that?"

No one misunderstood. The gathering in the gold and white Cabinet Room of the White House fell silent—but only temporarily. The dissenters from existing policy on Vietnam, who for two weeks had been battling against a request for massive troop reinforcements, chose to understand the President's pronouncement quite literally. They shifted tactics, and the argument flared up again.

In the Administration, Secretary of Defense Clark M. Clifford, who had entered the Government March 1 as a moderate hawk but was now an active dissident, took the initiative. He proposed that the bombing be restricted to the Panhandle region of North Vietnam south of the 20th Parallel.

This is the second of two articles written by Hedrick Smith in collaboration with William Beecher, and incorporating reports by Peter Grose, John W. Finney, E. W. Kenworthy, Roy Reed, Benjamin Welles, Edwin L. Dale Jr. and Max Frankel.

No one knew where Mr. Johnson stood on that issue. It was still two weeks before he would announce a major shift in the direction of his Vietnam policy—a shift toward de-escalation that is still having its impact on the daily decisions of the Nixon Administration.

At that time the pressures for change—political and economic—were mounting. The public was increasingly impatient with the war.

"Something had to be done to extend the lease on public support for the war," a high State Department official remarked. "We were focused on what we could do without significant military drawbacks to make clear to people we were serious about peace."

Secretary Clifford pleaded skillfully for the proposal that the bombing be restricted to the region south of the 20th Parallel. A cutback, he said, would not violate the

Continued on Page 14, Column 1

1968 Curb on Bombing of North Was Hammered Out by Johnson's Close Advisers

Dissenting Line Won at Parley Late in March

Continued From Page 1, Col. 3

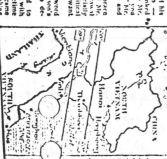

President Decides Critics

With Senator Robert F. Kennedy now

General Wheeler flew back to report to the President, General Westmoreland sent a follow-up summary of his needs on March 29, three days before the President was to address the nation. No one was informed of the President's change of...

Goldberg Calls at White House

Doves Still Trying

'Wise Men' Have New Thoughts

The Primary Was Secondary

Some President Is Voiced

Rusk Swayed by the Debate

'I May Have One of My Own'

Five More Drafts of Speech

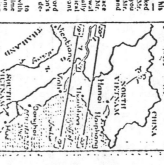

President Johnson during his televised address to the nation on March 31, 1968, as he disclosed that he would not seek re-election and announced that the U.S. had halted air and naval bombardments over most of North Vietnam.

U.S. SEES OPENING IN VIETCONG PLAN

MAY 9 - '69

Paris Proposal Seems to Be First Offer to Collaborate With Saigon Leaders

By HEDRICK SMITH

WASHINGTON, May 8—There is intense official interest here in the 10-point Vietcong proposal for an "over-all solution" of the war because it appears to be the first offer to collaborate with the current Saigon leaders in a coalition government.

White House and State Department officials would not comment on the substance of the proposals, which appeared to contain significant departures from previous formulations of the Vietcong, the National Liberation Front.

But the silence of the Nixon Administration and the activity at the State Department and at the White House, both here and in Key Biscayne, were signs of acute interest. Officials emphasized that they wanted to study the proposals before commenting.

President Nixon, on a long weekend in Florida, got a quick analysis of the proposal in a telephone talk with Henry A. Kissinger, his adviser on national security affairs. Mr. Nixon's press spokesman, Ron-

Continued on Page 6, Column 4

U.S. SEES OPENING IN VIETCONG PLAN

Continued From Page 1, Col. 1

ald L. Ziegler, said they would discuss it further face to face.

The most dramatic change, it appeared to some analysts here, was the absence of a customary call for the overthrow of the Saigon Government and a willingness to envision a postwar coalition including all social strata and political forces "no matter what their political beliefs and their past may be." The only qualification was that they stand for peace, independence and neutrality.

This was seen here as a response to Saigon's offer late in March to allow the Vietcong to take part in elections. This move put Hanoi and the National Liberation Front on the diplomatic and propaganda defensive.

The new language was seen as far more flexible than previous Vietcong proposals for a national union government of the most representative and patriotic elements — language presumed to exclude President Nguyen Van Thieu and other leaders in the present Government.

But the heavy emphasis on coalition — both a provisional coalition government to oversee American troop withdrawals and an ultimate postwar coalition—was seen here as a device to increase pressures on the Nixon Administration to accept such a compromise and at the same time to frighten the Saigon leadership.

New Ingredient Seen

Although it was noted that the proposals would require detailed examination in negotiation, the first assessment was that one new ingredient was the demand for a provisional coalition government that would allow participation by Saigon, the Front and others in unspecified proportions.

The proposals suggested that political exiles, presumably including some active leftists and neutralists in Paris, be included in talks on the formation of the coalition.

This would evidently pose difficulties for the Saigon regime by diluting its status as the Government in power with claims to a special negotiating role. Saigon was reluctant to negotiate with potential opposition and exile elements, let alone on an equal footing with the Vietcong.

There were also several important obstacles for the Nixon Administration, which has been emphasizing free elections as the means to South Vietnam's self-determination. The Vietcong plan seemed to indicate that the make-up of both the provisional and the final coalition governments would be a subject of negotiations. The final coalition, it said, would be "installed" — not necessarily elected.

In effect, in this view, the National Liberation Front seemed to be insisting on inclusion in the provisional coalition while refusing to risk being excluded from the final coalition if the Front fared badly in an open election.

The ultimate coalition, according to the new proposal, should reflect "the national concord and the broad union of all social strata—a formulation that would allow the present Saigon leaders, the Front and others to participate to varying degrees.

Other Aspects Studied

The following other points attracted attention here:

¶For the first time, the Vietcong proposed negotiations on the release of prisoners—"the army men captured in war."

¶They demanded international supervision of the withdrawal of military forces and matériel of "the United States and other foreign countries of the American camp" while leaving the question of "the named armed forces in South Vietnam" to be resolved by negotiations among Vietnamese.

¶American troop withdrawal would be unconditional but nothing in the document's wording appeared to establish a secret understanding on withdrawal of North Vietnamese forces, along the lines of the secret arrangements that led to an end of the bombing of North Vietnam on Nov. 1 last year.

¶The Vietcong apparently demanded that the United States pay reparations—or "be responsible for the losses and devastations it has caused to the Vietnam people in both zones."

U.S. Said to Be Sounding Hanoi on War Lull and De-escalation

By HEDRICK SMITH
Special to The New York Times

WASHINGTON, July 8—The United States was understood today to have begun probing through diplomatic channels to learn if North Vietnam has been using battlefield pullbacks to signal a desire to reduce the scale of the war in Vietnam.

It was not immediately clear whether the American soundings were being undertaken through new, secret contacts with North Vietnamese negotiators in Paris or through such intermediaries as the Soviet Union, France or Rumania, all of which have been useful in the past.

Administration officials refused to discuss the Government's efforts to sound out Hanoi on the meaning of the reported drop in enemy infiltration toward South Vietnam and the pullback of three enemy regiments—or 7,500 soldiers—from the northern region of South Vietnam.

Officials would say only that there had been no positive word from Hanoi so far on whether the enemy cutbacks were in response to the American decision to withdraw 25,000 United States servicemen by the end of next month or a signal that Hanoi wanted to start a process of mutual withdrawals.

Robert J. McCloskey the State Department spokesman, also discounted a French report, printed by the left-wing Paris newspaper Combat, that an unwritten agreement on the gradual withdrawal of American and North Vietnamese forces had been "virtually agreed upon, if not already achieved."

Asked about the Combat report, Mr. McCloskey replied: "I certainly wouldn't give it any credibility." Other officials said that there was no agreement yet and none now in the offing.

But the State Deprtment said that, despite an increase in enemy shelling and ground action in the last three days, Washington considered that the lull in enemy activity noted by Secretary of State William P. Rogers last Wednesday still persisted.

"As an over-all characterization of the situation, what the Secretary said in his press conference stands," Mr. McCloskey said today.

Meeting with newsmen last Wednesday, Secretary Rogers declared that the level of enemy combat activity was the "lowest in a long while" and reported that North Vietnamese infiltration into South Vietnam had been "at a fairly low level in the last two or three months."

Subsequently, officials in Saigon and Washington also reported the pullback into North Vietnam of the 27th, 36th, and 138th North Vietnamese regiments.

American officials emphasized today that they were still as uncertain as Mr. Rogers was last Wednesday whether the enemy moves were determined primarily by weather and the need to resupply and replenish some battle-scarred units, or by a desire to begin serious disengagement and de-escalation.

American officials said that Secretary Rogers had been deliberately conciliatory in his comments and noncommital in his interpretation of the enemy moves in order to invite and encourage the enemy to enter into the process of de-escalation, even if that had not been Hanoi's original intention.

They also recalled President Nixon's statement on May 14 that if North Vietnam wanted to insist that it had no troops in South Vietnam, "we will no longer debate the point—provided that its forces cease to be there, and that we have a reliable assurance that they will not return."

Last Wednesay, Mr. Rogers said Washington would talk to north Hanoi about its troop movements "when the right time comes." Previously, when newsmen asked if the time had come, American officials said the queries were premature.

But today, Mr. McCloskey simply refused to make any comment, and some well-placed informants indicated that American consideration of the enemy moves had reached a sensitive phase.

Saigon Hit by Rockets

SAIGON, South Vietnam, July 8 (AP) — At least five enemy rockets were fired into a Saigon riverfront district tonight and touched off a large blaze, officials said.

Reports said the rockets had landed near one of the capital's principal military and civilian cargo unloading areas.

It was the second enemy rocket attack in three days. Two missiles hit in and near the Saigon River Sunday but caused no damage or casualties.

The enemy command launched 27 rocket and mortar attacks during the night, but United States and South Vietnamese headquarters said that only nine had caused any casualties or damage. Otherwise there was little war action.

The targets of the enemy firing included the headquarters of the Ninth Marine Regiment at the Vandergrift combat base. The regiment is one of the units to be pulled out of Vietnam soon under President Nixon's withdrawal order and will be redeployed to Okinawa. Spokesmen said some Marines had been wounded by the 10 enemy rounds.

Also hit were a bivouac of the 25th Infantry Division, 27 miles northwest of Saigon, and two base camps near the demilitarized zone, which straddles the border with North Vietnam. South Vietnamese headquarters said a civilian bus had run over an enemy mine on Highway 1 southeast of Danang, killing eight passengers and wounding eight.

U.S. SAID TO PLAN AN OKINAWA DEAL BARRING A-BOMBS

Nixon Decision Reported—Timing Hinges on Terms for Isle's Return to Japan

By HEDRICK SMITH
Special to The New York Times

WASHINGTON, June 2—President Nixon has made a decision to remove American nuclear weapons from Okinawa once an over-all plan for turning the island back to Japanese rule has been agreed upon, well-placed informants disclosed today.

The actual timing of the removal of the weapons to other sites in the Pacific area will depend on the terms of the reversion agreement, the sources indicated. Japan wants the weapons removed and the island returned, with the rest of the Ryukyu chain, by 1972.

Mr. Nixon's decision, reportedly taken after a National Security Council meeting in late April on the Okinawan question and related issues, is an important one. It is understood to reflect the judgment of the President's civilian advisers that maintenance of sound, long-term relations with Japan is more important than the military advantage of retaining complete freedom of operation on Okinawa.

Negotiations to Continue

Informed sources said Mr. Nixon's decision had not yet been communicated formally to the Japanese Government. But presumably it will be made known in the course of negotiations with Tokyo on the Okinawa issue this summer and fall.

The Japanese Foreign Minister, Kiichi Aichi, met with President Nixon for 40 minutes this morning at the White House to present his Government's request that the Ryukyu Islands, held by the United States since 1945, be returned to Japanese rule by 1972.

Mr. Aichi's call on the President marked the formal beginning of negotiations on the Okinawa issue, though there have been months of preliminary discussions at lower levels. The negotiations are expected to culminate in November with a visit to Washington by Japan's Premier, Eisaku Sato.

Now Under Military Rule

Mr. Aichi told the President today that Japan would like American bases in Okinawa to function after reversion on the same basis as United States installations in Japan's four home islands.

Under present conditions, with the Ryukyus governed by a United States administration headed by a military High Com-

Continued on Page 14, Column 1

U.S. SAID TO PLAN AN OKINAWA DEAL

Continued From Page 1, Col. 6

missioner, the United States has complete freedom to move nuclear weapons to and from the islands and store them there. It can also mount offensive operations against other parts of Asia, such as B-52 bombing raids in Vietnam.

Nuclear weapons are barred from United States bases in Japan proper, and under terms of the two countries' security treaty, the United States must obtain Japan's approval in "prior consultations" before using her bases in Japan for combat operations in other Asian areas.

The Ryukyus were captured by American forces in a bloody battle in the late stages of World War II. The peace treaty provided for United States administration of the islands, but Washington has acknowledged that Japan retained nominal sovereignty over them and gave a pledge that the islands would eventually revert to Japanese rule.

A Defense 'Keystone'

In the intervening years, the United States has built a multibillion-dollar complex of bases that Defense Department officials describe as the "keystone" of the American defense network in the Pacific.

After years of hearing American commitments in principle to return the islands to Japan, Japanese public opinion has become insistent on obtaining a specific timetable from Washington. The status of the American bases and terms governing their operation after reversion have become the central problem in relations between Tokyo and Washington.

American and Japanese sources reported that President Nixon did not spell out in detail to Mr. Aichi today the American position on nuclear weapons and term for the use of the "keystone" Okinawa bases. It is not yet clear whether Washington will try to retain some special rights, while giving ground on the nuclear issue.

Foreign Minister Aichi is expected to go into greater detail on these issues later this week with Secretary of State William P. Rogers and Secretary of Defense Melvin R. Laird.

Today, the Foreign Minister underscored his country's sensitivity on the question of nuclear weapons on the soil of Japan, the only nation to have been subjected to nuclear attack.

"Mr. Aichi stressed that the Japanese people have unique feelings toward anything nuclear," a Japanese Embassy spokesman said. "He stressed that, in considering the Okinawa question, President Nixon should also consider the importance of the stability of Japanese politics and future cooperation between Japan and the United States."

Many American officials believe that the pro-American Government of Premier Sato could fall if the Okinawa issue—and the issue of nuclear weapons—is not satisfactorily resolved this year.

U.S.-THAI ACCORD ON TROOPS ALLOWS LAOS OPERATIONS

AUG 16 '59

Provision of 1965 Pact for Use of American Forces Are Also Disclosed

By HEDRICK SMITH

Special to The New York Times

WASHINGTON, Aug. 15—Sources in the Nixon Administration disclosed today that a secret contingency plan drawn up with Thailand in 1965 contains provisions for using American troops to help the Thai Army oppose Communist forces in Laos before any such troops cross the Thai borders.

The sources also disclosed that if the plan were put into operation, some American troops would be placed at least nominally under Thai command.

But the State Department, responding to current criticism from the Senate that this plan goes beyond American treaty commitments to Thailand, emphasized that the contingency plan cannot be carried out without the approval of the American President.

"The plan specifically states that it cannot be carried into effect without the specific agreement of both the United States and Thai Governments," Robert J. McCloskey, the State Department spokesman, said today. State Department officials said this meant it would require a decision by the President.

Approval Unneeded

But Mr. McCloskey indicated that action would not require advance Congressional approval. "It is not a treaty so that it is not one on which the Senate would be required to provide advice and consent," he said.

Despite the controversy surrounding the plan, Defense Department officials said that it was still valid—"still on the shelf," one official said—and available for use if both Governments approved it.

The Nixon Administration, under fire from liberals in the Senate, has taken the position, reaffirmed today by Mr. McCloskey, that the contingency plan "has not expanded our defense commitment to Thailand beyond that already contained in the Senate treaty."

Senator J. W. Fulbright of Arkansas and Senator Frank Church of Idaho have questioned whether the plan might be used to draw American forces into Thailand to help combat a domestic insurgency, opening the way for the United States to be "inched into another Vietnam," as Mr. Church put it.

The treaty of the Southeast Asia Treaty Organization calls for members to come to one

Continued on Page 8, Column 3

U.S.-THAI ACCORD AROUSES DISPUTE

Continued From Page 1, Col. 3

another's aid in the event of "aggression by armed attack" and today Mr. McCloskey asserted that the secret papers, signed by American and Thai military officials, "involve the defense of Thailand against an external threat."

The State Department spokesman was repeatedly pressed for details but refused to disclose them. State Department officials said later that they believed the language of the plan was "unequivocally clear" and that it was directed not at combatting internal subversion supported from outside, as in Vietnam, but a more conventional threat from outside Thailand.

The plan was developed at a time when the Thai Government was particularly concerned about advances by pro-Communist Pathet Lao and North Vietnamese forces in Laos, menacing the Mekong River Valley.

Both American and Thai officials have long considered a move by Communist forces into the river valley as a potential threat to Thailand's security. The river itself forms much of the Thai-Laotian border.

Much more than the contents of the contingency plan is now at issue between the Senate, especially the Senate Committee on Foreign Relations, and the Executive Branch of the Government. The committee is attempting to assert what its members believe to be the Senate's Constitutional prerogative to pass judgment on the contingency plan.

Mr. Fulbright, as the committee chairman and backed by other members, has asked the state and defense departments to provide the committee with a text of the contingency plan.

Secretary of Defense Melvin R. Laird has offered to show it to members of the Senate at the Pentagon but has so far not yielded to the request to send a copy to Capitol Hill. Pentagon officials explain that such top-secret contingency plans "are not normally passed around up on the Hill."

But this fencing over where the document should be seen touches on the Senate's claim that it has a Constitutional right to review such contingency plans and the contention of the Administration that this is not a treaty subject to a senatorial advice and consent.

Thus, for the moment, the Administration appears to regard its willingness to show the document to Senators at the Pentagon as a courtesy rather than an acknowledgment of senatorial prerogatives.

Some officials also believe that senatorial pride has also become involved. Yesterday Senator Church asserted that it would be "demeaning" for Senators to go to the Pentagon "hat in hand" to try to "take a peek" at the document.

NIXON-THIEU TALK MAY BRING ACCORD ON U.S. TROOP CUT

JUN—4-'69

Washington Aides Prepare for a Joint Announcement at Meeting on Midway

---

TIMING A MAJOR FACTOR

Officials Feel Statement on Sunday Would Illustrate a Unanimity of Views

---

By HEDRICK SMITH
Special to The New York Times

WASHINGTON, June 3 — United States officials said today that preparations were being made for a joint announcement at Midway by President Nixon and the South Vietnamese President, Nguyen Van Thieu, of the first unilateral reductions in American forces in Vietnam.

Informants said the announcement was considered likely but that final decision to go ahead with the cutback in American forces awaited agreement by the two men at their one-day meeting on the Pacific island Sunday.

Informants said several senior officials of the Nixon Administration believe the Midway meeting would afford a proper, positive occasion for such an announcement. Their reasoning is that a joint announcement would demonstrate solidarity on the troop issue and undercut in advance any speculation that either Washington or Saigon was trying to set a timetable for troop reductions.

Thieu Gives His View

In a news conference at Taipei today, President Thieu indicated the agenda for the Midway talks would include "replacement of U.S. troops by South Vietnamese troops" paving the way for withdrawal of some of the 540,000 Americans in Vietnam.

Military and civilian sources said that the Administration was thinking of pulling out about 50,000 troops this year, starting about Sept. 1.

One possibility, Vietnam planners said, was to withdraw part of the United States Ninth Infantry Division, operating in the Mekong Delta south of Saigon, and part of one other combat division.

Differences Are Denied

Some informants cautioned that the announcement of a withdrawal might include a provision that the rate of withdrawal would be affected by the response of enemy forces. If they launched large attacks against the South Vietnamese forces that replaced American troops, officials said, Saigon and Washington could decide to suspend withdrawals.

Both South Vietnamese and American officials continue to insist there are no basic differences between the two Governments as the Midway talks approach.

But privately, some American officials concede that the Administration is backing off from some of the [illegible] in Wash[...]

Continued [illegible], Col[...]

NIXON-THIEU PACT ON TROOP CUT SEEN

Continued From Page 1, Col. 1

[Wash]ington's negotiating posture made by Secretary of State William P. Rogers when he visited Saigon in mid-May.

Mr. Rogers was reported to have indicated that the United States considered an interim coalition Government—as demanded by the Vietcong—special elections in Vietnam under international supervision, and amendments to the South Vietnamese Constitution as items open for negotiation in the Paris talks.

Although no one has disavowed these positions, some officials have suggested privately that Mr. Rogers may have overstepped in the interest of demonstrating American flexibility. But they also assert that Washington's acceptance of these ideas has always been clearly made contingent upon Saigon's concurrence.

Some high American officials are reported to be thinking of a mixed commission of Communist and anti-Communist elements to oversee elections in South Vietnam, but it is not clear whether Washington will put forward this plan at Midway.

The reasoning of some Americans is that this would strike a balance between the Vietcong demand for a provisional coalition to oversee the elections and Mr. Thieu's rejection of the coalition idea.

Independent diplomats have suggested that Mr. Thieu's rejection of a coalition, in public appearances in South Korea and Taiwan in the last week, was intended to quiet any private discussion of coalition schemes by United States officials.

Even before he spoke out, there was no American effort to persuade Mr. Thieu to accept a coalition. But since he has spoken out, American officials have been at pains to point this out and generally avoid discussion of the idea of coalition.

Officials also insist that President Nixon's Vietnam speech of May 14, outlining Washington's peace program, was checked out line by line with President Thieu. The South Vietnamese leader, officials say, gave the speech detailed approval after having suggested several changes in language.

The speech contained a proposal for international supervision of South Vietnamese elections, which would come "as soon as possible" after the commission is named. South Vietnamese politicians have objected to both procedures on the ground that these proposals [in]fringe on the South [Viet]namese constitution and [natio]nal sovereignty. But [Wash]ington is holding firm [on these] points and expects to [discuss] them at Midway.

Thieu Again Bars Coal[ition]

SAIGON, South Vietnam, June 3 (Reuters) — President Nguyen Van Thieu [returns] home tonight after stops to Taiwan and South [Korea] and again said he rejected a coalition government with the Vietcong.

President Thieu, now preparing to meet with President [Nixon] on Sunday on the island [of] Midway in the Pacific, said in a televised address today that he and the leaders of South Korea and Taiwan had agreed that a coalition with Communists should be ruled out.

Of his meeting with Nixon, the South Vietnamese leader said only, "I will talk to you after I see Mr. Nixon."

Before leaving Taiwan earlier today, Mr. Thieu joined with Chiang Kai-shek in a communiqué calling the formation of a coalition government an "absurd demand."

The communiqué said the two men "maintain [that] the existing and popularly elected and legitimate Government of the Republic of Vietnam must be respected and that the absurd demand by the Communists for organization of a coalition government must be resolutely rejected."

Although officials in Saigon and Washington deny any major disagreements between Mr. Nixon and Mr. Thieu, the future role of the Vietcong appears to be a major difference between the two leaders. President Nixon has called for prompt elections in South Vietnam to include the Vietcong. Mr. Thieu appears to want to postpone any such election until the South Vietnamese presidential elections in 1971.

Continued From Page 1, Col. 3

coalition government. Washington and Saigon are not ready to go along with these proposals at this time. The assumption here is that Hanoi and the Front are stalling in Paris, in the hope of finding a split between Washington and Saigon on the coalition issue and of playing on American public impatience with the war.

Administrative sources have indicated that one task of the Midway meeting will be to develop some techniques to prod the other side to enter into private talks with Saigon, as proposed by President Thieu on March 25.

President Nixon has taken the unusual step of summoning Ambassador Henry Cabot Lodge, the chief American negotiator, home from Paris to take part in the Midway session.

Some American officials believe that announcement of a reduction in American forces, expected at Midway, could put pressure on the enemy by demonstrating allied confidence in the growing strength of the Saigon regime.

Other officials are weighing the idea of a mixed election commission to supervise South Vietnam's elections, as a compromise between the Vietcong's demand for a provisional coalition government and Saigon's rejection of this proposal.

But there is no confidence here that either move will give fresh impetus to the Paris negotiations. The only positive sign reported recently in Paris is the fact that North Vietnamese negotiators have been inquiring privately, mainly through such

intermediaries as the French, about elements of President Nixon's eight-point peace proposal of May 14.

Despite the sparseness of movement, allied diplomats suggest that the pace of the Vietnam talks does not compare unfavorably with the experience of such prolonged negotiations with Asian Communists as the two-year talks on the Korean war.

They cite three major moves this spring — President Thieu's offer to talk secretly with the Vietcong and to allow them to participate as a party in national elections, abandoning his previous refusal to consider either step; the Vietcong announcement of the peace plan of May 8; and President Nixon's speech outlining the peace program of May 14.

The Vietcong plan, allied diplomats observe, accepted for the first time the principle of international supervision of the withdrawal of outside forces and left an opening for South Vietnamese political figures, if not Americans, to bargain over withdrawal of North Vietnamese forces.

The program also appeared to allow for collaboration with some elements of the Saigon regime in future South Vietnamese governments by loosening the previously atringent Vietcong restrictions on who could participate.

The latest plan permits participation of individuals "no matter what their political beliefs and their past may be, provided they stand for peace, independence and neutrality."

President Nixon's program was somewhat more flexible than previous American statements. It called not only for international supervision of troop withdrawals but also of national elections, a concession to the enemy.

Mr. Nixon also implied that there could be special elections, as the Vietcong have demanded, by suggesting that they take place "as soon as possible" after the international

supervisory body starts functioning.

Although President Thieu has avoided a firm public commitment to these proposals, American officials insist that he has privately approved them.

But the crucial point, independent observers note, is that they still fall short of the implied Vietcong demand that it be guaranteed a share of power no matter what the outcome of the elections. And that is the basis for the fundamental deadlock at present.

Hanoi's View Given

HANOI, North Vietnam, June 4 (Agence France-Presse)—The formation of a provisional coalition government in South Vietnam and the withdrawal of American forces appeared more clearly than ever today to be the chief North Vietnamese aims in Paris.

An editorial in the Communist party newspaper Nhan Dan, giving details of Hanoi's idea of self-determination for the South, was considered particularly significant on the eve of the 21st session of the Paris talks and five days before President Nixon's meeting with President Thieu.

The editorial said that the role of a provisional coalition government should be to organize general elections.

However, the editorial said, the elections themselves could be held only in the absence of the "American war of aggression" and after the withdrawal of American troops.

Vietnam Casualties

WASHINGTON, June 4 (AP) —The following servicemen from the New York area were identified by the Defense Department today as having been killed in Vietnam:

Army

NEWSOME, Roy C., Specialist 4,

Vietcong Reported to Bar Secret Talks With Saigon

But Gap Between Negotiating Positions of Allies and the Enemy Appears to Have Narrowed in Recent Months

By HEDRICK SMITH
Special to The New York Times

WASHINGTON, June 4 — Informed sources said today that the National Liberation Front, or Vietcong, refused to accept South Vietnam's 10-week old offer of secret negotiations in Paris.

Nonetheless, in the seven months since President Johnson halted American bombing of North Vietnam, the gap between allied and enemy negotiating positions was narrowed somewhat. Some American officials say they have detected what may be the first indication of a

coalition rule in Saigon — both now and after a new national election—and the allied insist once that the Vietcong take the gamble of seeking power in free elections and thus running the risk of exclusion from a post war government.

President Nixon and President Nguyen Van Thieu of South Vietnam, who will meet Sunday at Midway Island for a strategy session, are said to consider somewhat. Some American officials believe that the Vietcong will try to gain control through the

ambodia Decision: Nixon Sought to Save Anti-Red Regime

On April 30, announcing U.S. troops would be sent into Cambodia, President Nixon compared distance from Fishhook area to Saigon to that from Baltimore to Washington.

Cambodian Decision: Why President Acted

By HEDRICK SMITH

WASHINGTON, June — President Nixon's venture into Cambodia is ending with proclamations of undreamed military gain, but it was launched for the broader purpose of rescuing Cambodia from sudden Communist domination and that purpose is still unrealized.

Reconstruction of Cambodia Decision: Nixon Sought to

Continued From Page 1, Col. 7

can troops in Cambodia from Secretary of State William P. Rogers, stressing the risks of this — if not on Vietnam alone domestic discontent, caused Mr. Nixon to delay the operation 24 hours.

Once decided, Mr. Nixon also ordered four heavy bombing raids against North Vietnam despite the year-and-a-half-old cessation of United States raids on the North—with the purpose, officials now acknowledge, of warning Hanoi against counterattacking across the demilitarized zone into South Vietnam. The four attacks appeared to be a violation of the private understandings with Hanoi prohibiting bombing of the North.

Like Predecessors, Uneasy

Formally, the Cambodian operations began with a Presidential announcement on April 30. But for Mr. Nixon, the beginning was well before that.

Like President Kennedy in the Cuban crisis and President Johnson in Vietnam, he felt Communist forces crowding and testing him. He had contained the frustration of not retaliating when the North Vietnamese shelled Saigon early in his term, when North Korea shot down an American intelligence plane, when the Paris peace talks bogged down. Now the Soviet Union was moving combat pilots into the United Arab Republic and Communist forces were threatening another nation in Indochina.

Of all these situations, Mr. Nixon felt, Cambodia offered the first opening for effective military reaction that would carry his larger political message. As the President confided to a senior adviser: This is a risk, but this is the kind of thing he had been waiting for.

Mr. Nixon's objectives in Cambodia centered on staving off Communist domination. Survival of Premier Lon Nol's Government, for a time, at least, appeared essential. Its survival was needed to assure the defense of South Vietnam and the process of American withdrawal, to spare Saigon the blow of seeing a neighbor collapse while the United States did nothing and to deny Hanoi a gain that would tempt it, in the words of one senior adviser, to "go for all the marbles" in Indochina and forever spurn negotiation.

Lift for the Premier

An American attack from the rear, Mr. Nixon thought, would divert and disrupt the enemy forces threatening General Lon Nol and also give the Cambodian Premier a badly needed political lift. But it required no open commitment.

Despite his preference for orderly procedure, President Nixon, like his predecessors, reacted in crisis with rump group meetings, late phone calls, an out-of-channel message to the field and other activities that bypassed the members at the State and Defense Departments.

The White House became so worried about security leaks that even members of the Joint Chiefs of Staff were late to learn of some critical discussions. State Department lawyers were not told to prepare the legal case for invasion until four days after it began.

The gestation process for Mr. Nixon's decision was much longer than Administration accounts suggest. It began almost immediately after General Lon Nol and others deposed Prince Norodom Sihanouk on March 18.

Twilight Zone of War

For years, Cambodia was a twilight zone of the Vietnam war. Prince Sihanouk, balancing between the belligerents, had let the North Vietnamese create a deep but porous sanctuary on grant, improvised shelter along South Vietnam's secretary level. The province of South Vietnamese generals bid of lower casualties...

---

haps Hanoi, with its forces now less secure in Cambodia, would show interest in negotiation in the context of an international conference on all Indochina, which France proposed on April 1.

General Lon Nol tried to work out live-and-let-live arrangements with the North Vietnamese, first in direct talks and then through Chinese and other Communist intermediaries. He asked North Vietnam to reduce its military presence in Cambodia and its reliance on shipments through Sihanoukville. Hanoi refused. Washington made no direct approach to Hanoi, but passed word to Asian intermediaries that it would respect any deal General Lon Nol made, it got no diplomatic reply.

One Diplomat Unsure

One diplomat said the American approach was so feeble and casual that he was not sure the intermediaries understood that the messages were meant for Hanoi. American officials, moreover, were sure that Hanoi suspected the United States of having ousted Prince Sihanouk and could not, therefore, credit Washington with good faith.

South Vietnamese forces, meanwhile, were staging sporadic raids across the Cambodian border, against the advice of American officials in Saigon. The United States increased bombing raids against enemy concentrations in Cambodia, but General Abrams's contingency plans, now sent by the Joint Chiefs of Staff to the White House, were in limbo. Secretary Laird, talking with President Nixon in the second week of April, opposed an American assault because he feared heavy casualties — as high as 400 to 500 dead in the first week alone — and a public outcry.

Movements Westward

In mid-April the combat situation changed. Starting April 13, enemy forces were detected moving westward into Cambodia from the border areas, cutting roads, blowing up bridges, harassing military posts and towns. The White House interpreted the reports "elementary" — as relative only to the location of enemy actions, but not on their size, seriousness or intent.

In Saigon, however, General Abrams was particularly struck by the thinning out of enemy forces in the Fishhook, a Cambodian salient that juts into South Vietnam 75 miles northwest of Saigon. The Fishhook was considered the most important enemy refuge area.

General Abrams and Ellsworth Bunker, the American Ambassador, met privately for several nights and about April 15, sent parallel recommendations to the Departments of State and Defense. They urged an American attack into the Fishhook and joint attacks with the South Vietnamese against other bases.

Arguments Summarized

High military sources summed up General Abrams's arguments as follows:

One of the two American divisions stand as guard against attacks from the enemy bases in Cambodia. With going home soon under President Nixon's withdrawal program, shifting a major burden on to Saigon's forces. With so many serious apprehensions and the Lon Nol Government unlikely to survive would fall, the time was right. An attack would give any secret calculations the South Vietnamese could make unless before the fall of Saigon...

On April 30, announcing U.S. troops would be sent into Cambodia, President Nixon compared distance from Fishhook area to Saigon to that from Baltimore to Washington.

By April 17, the President got daily briefings from attack on April 29, which had also approved a secret shipment of 6,000 captured AK-47 rifles of Soviet design to the Cambodian Army. The United States first tried to use Indonesia as a cover for this aid, but for reasons of diplomacy, shifted to South Vietnam.

Plans were also made to assemble a force of 2,000 Khmer Krom troops to stiffen the Cambodian army. These mercenaries fighting in South Vietnam for the American special forces were later flown secretly to Pnompenh.

President Distracted

President Nixon evidently hoped that these measures would win time. He was, in any case, distracted by the battle over his Supreme Court nomination, the April 13 astronauts and the need to announce an American troop withdrawal.

General Abrams was pressing for a 60-day delay on withdrawals. Secretary Laird wanted a cutback of 50,000 by Aug. 15. With the issue unresolved, Mr. Nixon went to greet the returning astronauts in Honolulu.

He finally hit on a compromise, surprising even some of his senior advisers to delay withdrawals for 60 days but to hide that fact in an announcement on April 20 of a full year's pullout—150,000 men by May, 1971. Mr. Nixon flew back to San Clemente, Calif., to make the announcement April 20—a long one, and as it turned out, fateful day in his perception of the situation in Indochina.

He Reiterates Warnings

He did point with concern to "the enemy's escalation in Laos and Cambodia" and repeated warnings that if that created enemy action jeopardizes our remaining forces in Vietnam, I shall not hesitate to take strong and effective measures to deal with that situation.

There was no real hint of the internal discussions about Cambodia.

Officials insist that Mr. Nixon's intimation did not disclose any secret calculations...

---

data gone, was dawn, April 30. Saturday...

The President flew to Camp David, Md., Friday afternoon, Mr. Kissinger brought the plans and met Saturday and the two men studied them. In Washington that evening, they conferred with Secretary Laird and Attorney General John N. Mitchell aboard the Government yacht Sequoia on the Potomac. They then attended a private showing of "Patton," the film biography of the defiant general, which Mr. Nixon was eager to see for a second time.

Two Members Absent

Secretary of State Rogers returned from New York on Sunday morning and, with Secretary Laird, heard a Pentagon briefing on the Fishhook plans. He feared that it might.

Thus all participants in the afternoon meeting of the Security Council were prepared for a major North Vietnamese attack across the DMZ.

Crisis Schedule Enforced

The next morning, the President, the Attorney General, General Wheeler, Mr. Rogers and Mr. Kissinger in the Executive Office Building broke their own dead—next to the White House. Two called meetings—Monday morning, April 27, Mr. Rogers, Mr. Laird...

military or not, came to decided "to do something." The Mr. Rogers—indicated his military priority, he or the President on a possible...

Nixon Is Irritated

fided to a senior adviser: This is a risk, but this is the kind of thing he had been waiting for.

Mr. Nixon's objectives in Cambodia centered on staving off Communist domination. Survival of Premier Lon Nol's Government, for a time, at least, appeared essential. Its survival was needed to assure the defense of South Vietnam and the process of American withdrawal, to spare Saigon the blow of seeing a neighbor collapse while the United States did nothing and to deny Hanoi a gain that would tempt it, in the words of one senior adviser, to "go for all the marbles" in Indochina and forever spurn negotiation.

Lift for the Premier

An American attack from the rear, Mr. Nixon thought, would divert and disrupt the enemy forces threatening General Lon Nol and also give the Cambodian Premier a badly needed political lift. But it required no open commitment.

Despite his preference for orderly procedure, President Nixon, like his predecessors, reacted in crisis with rump-group meetings, late phone calls, an out-of-channel message to the field and other activities that bypassed planners at the State and Defense Departments.

The White House became so worried about security leaks that even members of the Joint Chiefs of Staff were late to learn of some critical discussions. State Department lawyers were not told to prepare the legal case for invasion until four days after it began.

The gestation process for Mr. Nixon's decision was much longer than Administration accounts suggested. It began almost immediately after General Lon Nol and others deposed Prince Norodom Sihanouk on March 18.

Twilight Zone of War

For years, Cambodia was a twilight zone of the Vietnam war. Prince Sihanouk, balancing between the belligerents, had let the North Vietnamese create a dozen base areas to shelter 40,000 to 60,000 troops for use against South Vietnam.

American generals had periodically pressed the Johnson Administration for permission to attack these sanctuaries, but President Johnson had refused. The Nixon Administration grudgingly tolerated the situation. Its plans for a gradual troop withdrawal from Vietnam assumed that the enemy bases in Cambodia would remain intact.

Within the last year, however, even Prince Sihanouk began to worry about the expanding enemy activity on his soil. He allowed American B-52's to bomb the base areas. For a time, he curtailed the enemy supply shipments to the bases through the port, then Sihanoukville, now Kompong Som.

Prince Sihanouk's ouster, described as a surprise in Washington, posed an opportunity. All foreign-policy agencies quickly drafted proposals for dealing with the new situation. In this process, Secretary of Defense Melvin R. Laird invited the generals in Saigon to submit contingency plans.

Abrams's Options

By April 1, Gen. Creighton W. Abrams, the United States commander in Vietnam had offered the Pentagon several options:

First, to let South Vietnamese troops harrass the enemy across the border.

Second, to help the South Vietnamese Army conduct larger attacks over a period of months to disrupt the enemy bases.

Or third, to let American forces join the South Vietnamese in a swift full-scale assault on the bases.

Using the American forces was the "top option" but General Abrams did not formally recommend any course.

Washington was still looking for diplomatic ways to contain Cambodia.

week of April, opposed an American assault because he feared heavy casualties — as high as [illegible] to 500 dead in the first week alone — and a public outcry.

Movements Westward

In mid-April the combat situation changed. Starting April 13, enemy forces were detected moving westward into Cambodia from the border areas, cutting roads, blowing up bridges, harassing military posts and towns. The White House interpreted the reports "leniently" — as reliable on the location of enemy actions, but not on their size, seriousness or intent.

In Saigon, however, General Abrams was particularly struck by the thinning out of enemy forces in the Fishhook, a Cambodian salient that juts into South Vietnam 75 miles northwest of Saigon. The Fishhook was considered the most important enemy refuge area.

General Abrams and Ellsworth Bunker, the American Ambassador, met privately for several nights and about April 15, sent parallel recommendations to the Departments of State and Defense. They urged an American attack into the Fishhook and joint attacks with the South Vietnamese against other bases.

Arguments Summarized

High military sources summed up General Abrams's arguments as follows:

One of the two American divisions standing guard against attacks from the enemy bases in Cambodia was going home soon under President Nixon's withdrawal program, shifting a major burden to Saigon's forces. With the rainy season approaching and the Lon Nol Government unlikely to survive until fall, the time was right. An attack would help the South Vietnamese and assure further American withdrawals. With a third of the enemy forces moved west, the risks of American casualties were reduced.

The general's argument, envisioning benefits for the Vietnamization program, impressed Secretary Laird. The promise of lower casualties convinced him, and he endorsed the proposal.

But at the White House, the military possibilities were still offset by the fear of pushing the war deeper into Cambodia and the fear of spoiling the chances for negotiation.

The prospects for diplomacy had unexpectedly improved when the Soviet Union said that it, too, was interested in an Indochina conference. "Only a new Geneva conference could bring a new solution and relax tension," Yakov A. Malik, the Soviet representative at the United Nations, said on April 16. The Americans got private indications that this as a deliberate initiative and assumed that the Russians had cleared it with Hanoi.

Pressures Still Rise

Still, the pressures in Cambodia were building up. Premier Lon Nol pleaded with greater urgency each day. Mr. Nixon did not want another state in Southeast Asia dependent on the United States, but neither did he want to stand idly by. High officials felt the whole rationale for defending South Vietnam would collapse if they acquiesced in a Communist take-over of Laos and Cambodia. Also, the President feared Prince Sihanouk, with Hanoi's aid, might be returned to power.

So Mr. Nixon set out to help Premier Lon Nol clandestinely. He let Saigon's forces increase the scope and frequency of their attacks into Cambodia. The purpose, one high official said later, was "to put pressure on the enemy forces so they wouldn't turn toward Phnom penh."

American advisers were told to help plan the enlarged raids, but not get into combat inside Cambodia.

[illegible] troops to stiffen the [illegible] Cambodian army. These mercenaries fighting in South Vietnam for the American Special Forces were later flown secretly to Phnompenh.

President Distracted

President Nixon evidently hoped that these measures would win time. He was, in any case, distracted by the battle over his Supreme Court nominees, the Apollo 13 astronauts and the need to announce another troop withdrawal.

General Abrams was pleading for a 60-day delay in withdrawals. Secretary Laird wanted a cutback of 50,000 by Aug 15. With the issue unresolved, Mr. Nixon went to greet the returning astronauts in Honolulu.

He finally hit on a compromise, surprising even some senior advisers: to delay withdrawals for 60 days but to hide that fact in an announcement of a full year's pullouts—150,000 men by May, 1971. Mr. Nixon flew back to San Clemente, Calif., to make the announcement April 20—a long and, as it turned out, fateful day in his perception of the situation in Indochina.

The speech emphasized his terms for a political settlement in more flexible terms than ever before.

He Reiterates Warnings

He did point with concern to "the enemy's escalation in Laos and Cambodia" and repeated warnings that if "increased enemy action jeopardizes our remaining forces in Vietnam, I shall not hesitate to take strong and effective measures to deal with that situation."

There was no real hint of the internal discussions about Cambodia.

Officials insist that Mr. Nixon's optimism did not disguise any secret calculations. Press dispatches had already reported the fall of Saang, a district capital 13 miles from Phnompenh, but official confirmation did not reach the traveling White House until late on April 20.

On that day, too—although it was probably unknown to Mr. Nixon as he spoke—Hanoi's spokesman in Peking indicated that Prince Sihanouk was joining a new united military front for the "liberation" of all Indochina; the Russians backed off their interest in a Geneva conference, and the Lon Nol regime submitted a request for more than $500-million in military aid.

Mr. Nixon was restless that night—"wound up," his wife said—and after his speech, abruptly flew back to Washington. One aide said afterward that the President might have sensed "something was up."

Confirmed by Intelligence

By morning, intelligence reports had built up a picture of steady deterioration in Cambodia, but the problem hit Mr. Nixon with sudden force.

From that day on, Mr. Nix-

[illegible] maneuvers to create an impression of civil war. The Pentagon view, more persuasive to the White House, was that the North Vietnamese had decided to overthrow Lon Nol by isolating his capital, or taking it.

Mr. Nixon summoned the National Security Council to meet on April 22, the group's first consideration of the contingency plans. The talk centered largely on a proposed South Vietnamese offensive into the Parrot's Beak, an enemy position jutting into Vietnam 33 miles from Saigon. There was some discussion of an American attack into the Fishhook.

Crisis Schedule Enforced

The next morning, the President seemed bent on some kind of action. He called for operational plans for the Parrot's Beak, forcing a crisis schedule upon the Washington Special Action Group — a body headed by Henry A. Kissinger, his special assistant for security affairs.

The group, which is called WASAG, was created in April, 1969, when North Korea shot down an American intelligence plane. It played a central role in the Cambodian venture from late March onward by assembling and refining all contingency plans, assessing their consequence, and managing the execution of Presidential orders.

At the peak of crisis, the group's members were Mr. Kissinger, David Packard, Deputy Secretary of Defense; U. Alexis Johnson, Under Secretary of State for Political Affairs; Mr. Helms; Gen. Earle G. Wheeler, then Chairman of the Joint Chiefs; Adm. Thomas H. Moorer, his successor, and Marshall Green, Assistant Secretary of State for East Asian Affairs.

The group met twice on April 23, again on April 24. In Saigon, the South Vietnamese generals were hesitant about a major strike without the Americans. General Abrams and Ambassador Bunker met with President Nguyen Van Thieu, after which Saigon finally geared for action while General Abrams pressed Washington to use American advisers in the Parrot's Beak operation.

Nixon Is Irritated

Mr. Nixon was now pushing the process of making decisions, irritated that the enemy appeared complacent. American intelligence confirmed anew that the enemy command was telling its troops to push west without fear of an American attack from the rear. The White House denounced the enemy moves as a "foreign invasion."

On Friday morning, April 24, the President called for operational plans for the Fishhook operation to be delivered from Saigon within 24 hours. He called a secret meeting of the National Security Council for Sunday, pointing toward a final decision Sunday night. This would give the generals the 72 hours they said they needed to

[illegible] General John Mitchell aboard the Government yacht Sequoia on the Potomac. They then attended a private showing of "Patton," the film biography of the defiant general, which Mr. Nixon was eager to see for a second time.

Two Members Absent

Secretary of State Rogers returned from New York on Sunday morning and, with Secretary Laird, heard a Pentagon briefing on the Fishhook plans. Thus all participants in the afternoon meeting of the Security Council were prepared for the main topic of debate.

The two Secretaries joined the President, the Attorney General, General Wheeler, Mr. Helms and Mr. Kissinger at the Executive Office Building next to the White House. Two statutory members of the Council, Vice President Agnew and George A. Lincoln, director of the Office of Emergency Preparedness, were not present.

Mr. Nixon said that he had decided "to do something." The Parrot's Beak operation had his tentative approval, with American air support but not American ground advisers. The Fishhook was the problem at hand.

The Pentagon representatives argued that a full assault, with American troops, was essential. Military analysis showed the enemy seeking either to topple the Lon Nol regime or to clear a supply corridor to the sea in eastern Cambodia. Either prospect jeopardized the defense of South Vietnam and American withdrawal. The Parrot's Beak alone would serve only as a warning. Using the South Vietnamese in the Fishhook would require a major reshuffle of armies, and might prove too difficult for them. With the heavy rains due in a month, and Lon Nol unlikely to survive until fall, it was now or never.

Secretary Rogers carried the principal burden of opposition. The use of American troops in Cambodia meant widening the war. The risk was grave of

[illegible] entry saying that [illegible] by both sides would [illegible] "ambiguous situation" [illegible] time favoring the C[illegible]

Liabilities Listed

The President then [illegible] pros and cons for A[illegible] action in the Fishhook a[illegible] a South Vietnamese [illegible] alone in the Parrot's [illegible] recognized that the F[illegible] move would bring a "[illegible] vision" of the A[illegible] He feared that it m[illegible] voke a collapse of the P[illegible] talks, an attack on P[illegible] or a major North V[illegible] attack across the DMZ.

Mr. Nixon seemed de[illegible] mined to attack, but the [illegible] ing arguments of S[illegible] Rogers evidently led [illegible] break his own dead[illegible] called another meeting [illegible] Monday morning, April 27, [illegible] Mr. Rogers, Mr. Laird, Mr. [illegible] singer and H. R. H[illegible] chief of staff, but with[illegible] military or intelligence [illegible]

Someone—apparent[illegible] Mr. Rogers—suggested that [illegible] military might be [illegible] President only what [illegible] he wanted to hear. The s[illegible] tion haunted Mr. Nixon [illegible] that meeting came his [illegible] out-of-channels message [illegible] General Abrams [illegible] "the unvarnished truth," [illegible] to man.

Abrams Sees Necessity

That afternoon, Mr. Rog[illegible] testified at a closed ses[illegible] the Senate Foreign Re[illegible] Committee and ran into a [illegible] of opposition to possible A[illegible] ican involvement in Camb[illegible] Without directly dis[illegible] contemplated use of U[illegible] States troops, he tried [illegible] at the imminence of a [illegible] decision. Mr. Rogers re[illegible] the Senators' objections [illegible] long telephone report to [illegible] President that evening.

From Saigon, General Abra[illegible] replied that an Ameri[illegible] sault was necessary. [illegible] message and new memos [illegible] other advisers, and a[illegible] more call to Mr. L[illegible] Nixon withdrew to make [illegible]

UNITED STATES DISTRICT COURT

SOUTHERN DISTRICT NEW YORK

--x
                                     :

UNITED STATES OF AMERICA,   :

       Plaintiff   :

                                       :

            v.   :   71 Civ. 2662

                                         :

THE NEW YORK TIMES COMPANY, et al,   :

       Defendants.   :

                                         :
--x

                   AFFIDAVIT of TAD SZULC

STATE OF NEW YORK   )
                   :   ss.:
COUNTY OF NEW YORK)

            I, TAD SZULC   , being duly sworn, deposes and says:

        1. I am a reporter employed by The New York Times regularly engaged in writing articles on matters of military, national or international affairs that are published in The Times.

        2. Annexed to this affidavit are a number of such articles. In writing each article I obtained information from classified documents made available to me by governmental sources or oral information from such sources that I understood may be classified. Such articles indicate expressly or by clear implication the nature of their confidential or restricted source. I made no inquiry whether such information was lawfully authorized to be disclosed to me. The articles were published without

418

interference, objection or resulting action by the government, notwithstanding the information disclosed thereby.

[signature]

Sworn to before

me this '7ᵗʰ day

of June 1971

[signature]

Notary Public

TRUMAN W. EUSTIS, III
Notary Public, State of New York
No. 31-6210650
Qualified in New York County
Commission Expires March 30, 19___

[The following pages contain copies of exhibits submitted with Mr. Szulc's affidavit, articles by him copied from The New York Times.]

Tad Szulc

CASTRO FOES TRAIN TROOPS IN FLORIDA

Continued From Page 1, Col. 1

mer, groups were instructed in drill and the use of arms by individual Cuban organizations Since last fall the training has been centralized under the direction of a united Cuban political command.

This command was the Democratic Revolutionary Front originally formed by five anti-Castro groups. It has enjoyed the tolerance and the active co-operation of United States officials.

Opponents United

The front was organized in Miami late in the spring of 1960 as the principal anti-Castro organization. Last month it was absorbed into the Revolutionary Council formed to unite all the factions opposed to the Castro regime and to any resurgence of a Batista-type dictatorship.

Until the signing of the unity pact last month and the establishment of the Revolutionary Council under Dr. José Miro Cardona, the military units of the Democratic Front operated separately from the groups of the Peoples' Revolutionary Movement headed by Manuel Ray, Dr. Castro's former Minister of Public Works.

The Ray movement is the foremost underground organization in Cuba, but it also has small military groups in the United States.

After the unity pact brought together the Democratic Front and the Peoples' Revolutionary Movement under the leadership of Dr. Miró Cardona, the Ray organization instructed its members to report to the training camps and staging areas in Guatemala where the Democratic Front officers remain in command.

This was done to maintain the unity of the exile groups although there are deep differences in political views between Señor Ray and the leaders of the Democratic Front.

Quick Action Opposed

Señor Ray, a soft-spoken engineer who studied in Utah, is opposed to any early military operation from abroad against Dr. Castro.

He thinks that it may open the United States to charges of collusion. He takes the view it would be better to strike through an internal uprising aided from abroad.

Some of Señor Ray's military associates even question whether a force of 5,000 or 6,000 men, no matter how well trained and equipped, could actually succeed in establishing a substantial beachhead on Cuban territory against the powerful militia regiments armed with Soviet-bloc weapons.

Although some other members of the council have different views Señor Ray has agreed to serve on it in the interest of unity. Dr. Miro Cardona, acting as Cuba's provisional President-in-Exile, formally announced the formation of the council Tuesday night.

In addition to Dr. Miro Cardona, [...]

the Democratic Front investigates the volunteers to eliminate suspected Castro agents or persons connected with the former Batista regime.

This is a twin problem facing the council inasmuch as both groups are seeking to infiltrate its army.

Because of charges by Señor Ray's movement that Batista supporters had infiltrated, a new effort is now under way to oust them, especially from positions of influence. United States officials are equally eager to see this completed rapidly and successfully.

The Castro agents—and hundreds of them are believed to be operating rather freely here—pose a more difficult problem. Although the Florida police and Federal authorities are aware of the presence of at least 100 of them little has been accomplished in efforts to deport them.

Occasionally, some are briefly detained on such charges as vagrancy and sometimes are brought into court on what a local police official described as "effective law enforcement."

Officials here who read today of the charges made yesterday by Cuba's Foreign Minister, Raúl Roa, in New York that an attack was being prepared here and that the Castro regime anticipated that most of it, presumably would come from the approaching assault.

ers who are in the army camps, but the letters are often censored. It is impossible to determine from what precise spot they have been mailed.

The traffic of couriers between Florida and the island, serving the underground, goes on constantly, sometimes using the remaining passenger flights between Havana and Miami. More often the couriers travel by boats that run a virtual shuttle between the Florida coast and Cuba carrying instructions, weapons and explosives.

Some of the fast, patrol-type boats are built to specifications in the Miami area. Many of them are tied in the Miami River and navigate freely to and from the Caribbean on their missions.

Special boats equipped with powerful radio transmitters make daily runs to the Cuban coast and relay anti-Castro broadcasts originating here.

A few weeks ago a patrol boat of the United States Wild Life Service captured a vessel carrying explosives for Señor Ray's underground. Subsequently, the boat was released and the inspectors were told to be less observant next time.

Young Democrats to Meet

MIDDLETOWN, Conn., April [...] (UPI) Young Democrats from throughout the Northeast [...]

Force There and in Central America Is Reported to Total 5,000 to 6,000

By TAD SZULC
Special to The New York Times.

MIAMI, Fla., April 6—For nearly nine months Cuban exile military forces dedicated to the overthrow of Premier Fidel Castro have been training in the United States as well as in Central America.

An army of 5,000 to 6,000 men constitutes the external fighting arm of the anti-Castro Revolutionary Council, which was formed in the United States last month. Its purpose is the liberation of Cuba from what it describes as the Communist rule of the Castro regime.

Many of those in the exile forces were companions of Dr. Castro in his revolution against the Batista regime.

Within Cuba, the Revolutionary Council counts on an ever-growing underground network engaged in organizing guerrillas, carrying out sabotage and gathering intelligence.

Cuban leaders here expect that it will be possible to coordinate the activities of the external forces—those trained outside Cuba—and the internal forces when the time comes for a major move against the Castro fortress in Cuba.

Recruiting Ended

The recruiting of Cubans, which has been proceeding since last summer, is being discontinued as the anti-Castro leaders believe that their external forces have reached the stage of adequate preparation.

The external forces, many of them highly trained in landing, infiltration and sabotage operations, are now concentrated at two major camps in Guatemala and at a base in Louisiana, not far from New Orleans.

This latest Cuban revolutionary army is reported by its leaders to include an air force, a navy and paratrooper units.

It is supported by commando-type groups of infiltrators, saboteurs and guerrilla specialists who have been landing in Cuba for months from hidden bases in the Florida Keys in cooperation with the growing underground on the island.

Most of the instruction given to the anti-Castro forces was reported to have been centered in the Guatemalan camps where infantry and artillery units are being trained by United States experts.

But special instruction has been available in small camps in Florida.

Reports said that some of the air and paratroop units have their bases in those camps.

In the patrol bases of training that [...]

bers to report to the training camps and staging areas in Guatemala where the Democratic Front officers remain in command.

This was done to maintain the unity of the exile groups although there are deep differences in political views between Señor Ray and the leaders of the Democratic Front.

Quick Action Opposed

Señor Ray, a soft-spoken engineer who studied in Utah, is opposed to any early military operation from abroad against Dr. Castro.

He thinks that it may open the United States to charges of collusion. He takes the view that it would be better to strike through an internal uprising aided from abroad.

Some of Señor Ray's military associates even question whether a force of 5,000 or 6,000 men, no matter how well trained and equipped, could actually succeed in establishing a substantial beachhead on Cuban territory against the powerful militia regiments armed with Soviet-bloc weapons.

Although some other members of the council have different views Señor Ray has agreed to serve on it in the interest of unity. Dr. Miro Cardona, acting as Cuba's provisional President-in-Exile, formally announced the formation of the Council Tuesday night.

In addition to Dr. Miro Cardona and Señor Ray, the Council includes Dr. Manuel Antonio Varona, who heads the Democratic Revolutionary Front; Manuel Artime, the Front's military commander; Dr. Carlos Hevia, a former President of Cuba; Dr. Justo Carrillo and Dr. Antonio Maceo.

Dr. Miro Cardona, who toured the Guatemalan camps late last week, went to Washington yesterday. This week-end, Dr. Miro Cardona and Dr. Varona plan to meet in New York for a conference. Captain Artime is in Guatemala, acting as Dr. Miro Cardona's personal representative.

Both the Front and the people's Revolutionary Movement are closing their training facilities in Florida.

Members of other groups are still arriving from New York, where recruitment has been under way for months.

Doctors Join Movement

Numerous Cuban doctors in exile in Florida have recently joined the revolutionary forces. Among them there were two of Cuba's most famous surgeons.

According to reports here, a hospital vessel — a converted yacht — has been equipped and is moored somewhere in the Florida keys. Surgical supply concerns here have reported that Cuban doctors have been making heavy purchases of blood plasma and other medical items.

The Cubans here — some of them with military training acquired in fighting with Dr. Castro — are being organized through a system of calls based on applications submitted by the volunteers.

A special intelligence unit of the Democratic Front investigates the volunteers to eliminate suspected Castro agents or persons connected with the former Batista regime.

This is a twin problem facing the council inasmuch as both groups are seeking to infiltrate its army.

Because of charges by Señor Ray's movement that Batista supporters had infiltrated, a new effort is now under way to oust them, especially from positions of influence. United States officials are equally eager to see this completed rapidly and successfully.

The Castro agents—and hundreds of them are believed to be operating rather freely here—pose a more difficult problem. Although the Florida police and Federal authorities are aware of the presence of at least 100 of them little has been accomplished in efforts to deport them.

Occasionally, some are briefly detained on such charges as vagrancy and sometimes are brought into court on what a local police official describes as "selective law enforcement."

Officials here who read today of the charges made yesterday by Cuba's Foreign Minister, Raul Roa, in New York that an attack was being prepared here against the Castro regime are convinced that most of his information came from these intelligence agents.

But they said, many of the detailed charges were completely inaccurate.

They said there appears to be no evidence to support Dr. Roa's accusation that the anti-Castro army is made up of "mercenaries and adventurers.." It was ointed out that the vast majority of the Council's soldiers are Cubans and not what the Cuban Foreign Minister described as "Americans, Puerto Ricans, Spaniards, Nicaraguans, Guatamalans and former Nazis."

Flights to Guatamala

After the front's intelligence unit is satisfied that the volunteers are "clean," they are being advised to report to a assembly point in the Miami area where they are taken by trucks to one or more deactivated air bases. There they are issued khaki uniforms and board unmarked aircraft for flights to Guatamala.

In the strange atmosphere of Miami, bulging with refugees and revolutionaries, the preparations against Dr. Castro are an open secret. They are discussed in the streets, Cuban cafes and restaurants and almost everywhere that two or more Cubans congregate. Local newspapers openly refer to incidents in camps.

The families of the men in camp are reported to receive monthly checks from the Front. In the past, many of the Cubans were training at night or during week-ends while holding regular jobs here.

Even those commando specialists who engage in deliveries of weapons and sabotage material to the Cuban underground try to hold jobs.

Families receive letters from their husbands, sons and broth-

ers who are in the army camps but the letters are often censored. It is impossible to determine from what precise spot they have been mailed.

The traffic of couriers between Florida and the island, serving the underground, goes on constantly, sometimes using the remaining passenger flights between Havana and Miami. More often the couriers travel by boats that run a virtual shuttle between the Florida coast and Cuba carrying instructions, weapons and explosives.

Some of the fast, patrol-type boats are built to specifications in the Miami area. Many of them are tied in the Miami River and navigate freely to and from the Caribbean on their missions.

Special boats equipped with powerful radio transmitters make daily runs to the Cuban coast and relay anti-Castro broadcasts originating here.

A few weeks ago a patrol boat of the United States Wild Life Service captured a vessel carrying explosives for Señor Ray's underground. Subsequently, the boat was released and the inspectors were told to be less observant next time.

Young Democrats to Meet

MIDDLETOWN, Conn., April 6 (UPI)—Young Democrats from throughout the Northeast will discuss "Political Ideals and Goals" at a three-day conference at Wesleyan University here starting tomorrow. The speakers will include John W. Macy Jr., chairman of the United States Civil Service Commission, and Mark Lane, New York State Assemblyman from Manhattan.

Educators Name President

OMAHA, April 6 (AP)—Dr. Lucile Lindberg of Queens College, New York City, was named president today of the Association for Childhood Education International. The association, which is concerned with children 2 to 12 years old, opened a six-day study conference on Sunday.

ACCORD REPORTED IN SANTO DOMINGO

Continued From Page 1, Col. 8

between the United States and the Caamaño movement.

This situation raised the question of whether United States forces would be employed to control the junta troops.

Earlier, General Palmer expressed concern that the heavy fighting uptown might endanger the international zone in Santo Domingo's southwestern section.

With the knowledge and approval of both Colonel Caamaño and Mr. Bosch, the Administration arranged for Mr. Guzmán to be flown secretly to Washington last Friday aboard a United States military aircraft for conferences with White House and State Department officials.

Mr. Guzmán returned here about the time that Mr. Bundy and three other high Administration officials landed in Santo Domingo.

In addition to Mr. Bundy the mission comprises Thomas C. Mann, Under Secretary of State for Economic Affairs; Cyrus R. Vance, Deputy Secretary of Defense, and Jack Hood Vaughn, Assistant Secretary of State for Inter-American Affairs.

According to reliable informants, the coalition plan for a government under Mr. Guzmán was presented to General Imbert last night at his residence by Mr. Bundy, Mr. Mann and Mr. Vaugh. General Imbert, according to this informant, was not specifically asked to resign, but the White House team left no doubt of its intentions.

Imbert Tells of Rebuff

The Administration was understood to have decided to move into quiet negotiations with Mr. Bosch, who lives in San Juan, P. R. and with the Caamaño group after the rebels had made it clear that they would not deal with the Imbert junta but were eager to deal with Washington.

It was also understood that Washington had become impressed with the extent of popular support enjoyed in the Dominican Republic by the constitutionalists, Colonel Caamaño's faction, which takes its name from its support of the 1962 Constitution. Mr. Bosch governed under that Constitution until 1963, when he was ousted by a junta that was a predecessor of the Imbert group.

While United States officials refused to discuss their meeting with General Imbert, the junta chief himself reported having turned down the Guzmán coalition plan.

"I told them," he said, "that if they wanted to turn the country over to Communism, we would have no part of it."

General Imbert then said that Mr. Guzmán, a member of Mr. Bosch's Dominican Revolutionary party, was "a Bosch puppet."

He told the White House team that President Johnson had said that the mission of United States forces in the Dominican

Republic was to prevent a Communist takeover.

"I made it clear that we would continue fighting for the same objective, even if it meant that the American troops would have to be turned against us," he went on. "It was because of such calculations that Cuba fell under Communism. But we are determined that it will not happen here."

United States Embassy sources indicated that the Administration team, which initially planned to spend only a day here, might stay three days in efforts to settle matters with the recalcitrant junta and to seek a cease-fire.

The group was also expected to establish direct contact with the Caamaño movement.

At a news conference in his headquarters, Colonel Caamaño said he had had no dealings yet with the White House team. But some rebel sources said Colonel Caamaño had been visited by one or more of President Johnson's envoys. The embassy refused to confirm or deny this report.

Air Raids Disturbed U. S.

According to qualified sources here, United States attitudes began to shift last Thursday after the junta's aircraft strafed the rebels' downtown radio station and, apparently accidentally, sprayed machine-gun bullets into the security corridor, near the United States Embassy.

The United States formally protested this action as a violation of the cease-fire that had been signed May 5 under the auspices of the Peace Committee of the Organization of American States.

Official United States spokesmen here also made a point of declaring that the air raids, in which a number of civilians were killed and injured, ran against Washington's policy of seeking Dominican peace.

The junta later maintained that its P-51 fighter planes

had attacked the radio station because rebel propaganda was an incitement to violence and thus represented a rebel violation of the cease-fire.

On Friday, after the rebels radio returned to the air, junta commandos struck it again, in a bazooka raid. Again United States spokesmen expressed dismay. Privately, American officials began expressing concern that the United States was becoming too identified with the junta's military group.

At the same time the United States command assigned a unit of the 82d Airborne Division to the runway area of San Isidro Air Force Base, where the junta's planes are parked, to prevent them forcibly, if necessary, from making new strikes.

San Isidro is the junta's military center, but it is also used by the United States as a major army staging area.

Washington's annoyance with the junta, which was created on May 7 to replace an earlier military junta, grew when General Imbert and his commanders ordered an offensive last Saturday against the rebel stronghold north of the security corridor that bisects the rebel territory.

While the Caamaño forces maintained restraint and fought the junta forces only when attacked, General Imbert's command repeatedly ignored written and oral appeals from the O.A.S. to halt the fighting.

There have been many instances of rebel sniping at American positions, but Colonel Caamaño has insisted that these attacks were not carried out by his troops or by the armed civilians under his command.

JUNTA IS DEFIANT

Street Battle Mounts as Imbert Refuses to Give Up Post

By TAD SZULC

SANTO DOMINGO, Dominican Republic, May 17 — The United States was reported today, on the highest authority, to have reached a secret agreement in principle with the rebel movement of Col. Francisco Caamaño Deño to settle the Dominican civil war.

But hostilities went on throughout the day with mounting fury and rapidly rising casualties.

Under the reported agreement, Antonio Guzmán, a 54-year-old farm owner and businessman who served as Minister of Agriculture before the ouster of President Juan Bosch, would serve as President of the Dominican Republic until December, 1966. A successor would then be chosen in a regularly scheduled election.

Mr. Guzmán, who returned yesterday from a secret trip to Washington, was busy today organizing a government.

Bosch Backing Reported

According to information from highly reliable quarters, the tentative agreement with the rebels was reached over the weekend with the support of Dr. Bosch, in whose behalf the Caamaño movement began its revolt on April 24.

Meanwhile a peace - making team from the Organization of American States left for Washington suddenly and without explaining its reasons after a meeting with Colonel Caamaño and his aides.

The decision to back Mr. Guzmán signified a major victory , for Colonel Caamaño's movement, which had steadfastly denied Communist influence. The Johnson Administration had taken the position that his movement was dominated by Communists.

The charges of Communism against the rebels had led the United States to land 22,000 troops here nearly three weeks ago, a move that resulted in a surge of anti-American sentiment here.

Imbert Faction Adamant

The apparent decision to back Mr. Guzmán has run into head-on opposition from the civilian-military junta of Brig. Gen. Antonio Imbert Barreras, which the United States helped to create nine days ago to oppose the rebels.

General Imbert refused last night to resign in favor of a Guzmán coalition when this solution was suggested to him by McGeorge Bundy, President Johnson's special assistant for national security, and two high State Department officials who arrived yesterday on a confidential mission.

Tanks and troops of the Imbert junta continued their offensive against the rebels in the northern part of the city in the heaviest fighting of the three-week-old war.

In the house-to-house battle, casualties were rising rapidly.

Lieut. Gen. Bruce Palmer, commander of the United States forces here, estimated that each side had suffered 80 to 100 dead in the last few days.

Because of the intensity of the fighting, the Dominican Red Cross appealed to both sides to order a 24-hour truce, to begin at 7 A M tomorrow, so the dead and the wounded could be evacuated.

The junta, whose troops apparently broke into rebel territory from the north, seemed determined to win a military victory before a final political settlement could be reached

Continued on Page 14 Column 3

NEWS INDEX

VOL. CXIV....No.

IMPASSE REACHED IN SANTO DOMINGO; BUNDY RETURNING

Some Administration Aides Are Said to Hamper His Dominican Peace Efforts

GUZMAN ROLE AT ISSUE

Bank Case Reported Leaked to Block Presidency—U.S. Looks to O.A.S. in Crisis

By TAD SZULC
Special to The New York Times

SANTO DOMINGO, Dominican Republic, May 25—McGeorge Bundy, President Johnson's special assistant for national security affairs, prepared today to end, at least temporarily, his mission here and to return to Washington tomorrow.

The Dominican peace negotiations had become deadlocked within the last 48 hours, with no prospects of immediate settlement.

Authoritative sources reported that Mr. Bundy's efforts at negotiating a solution of the Dominican crisis to install a constitutional regime headed by Antonio Guzmán Silvestre were being seriously hampered by opposition in many Johnson Administration quarters.

The latest in these acts of opposition, according to informants here, was the reported leak in Washington yesterday, supposedly by sources within the Administration, of allegations that serious irregularities had occurred in the Dominican Agricultural Bank while Mr. Guzmán was a director.

10 Days of Negotiations

This reported leak of charges may be a principal reason for Mr. Bundy's departure, after 10 days of negotiating with Mr. Guzmán, particularly in the light of evidence here indicating that the allegations are unfounded.

[In Washington, the deadlock in Santo Domingo was ascribed partly to disagreements over the proposed candidates for a Dominican coalition. There was no confirmation of reports that Administration officials were in effect sabotaging Mr. Bundy's efforts. The ending of his negotiations left the Administration hoping that the cease-fire would continue and that the Organization of American States would take a more prominent mediation role.]

The charges involving Mr. Guzmán, as published yesterday in The Washington Daily News, suggested that an audit of the books of the Agricultural Bank showed it had over $15 million in assets by $13 million and that those and several of notes and $1 mil-

Continued From Page 1, Col. 1

lion in mortgage collateral were missing.

However, the allegations were denied in a three-page written statement by Mr. Guzmán, and the administrator of the Agricultural Bank and the local manager of the New York accounting firm that prepared the audit said in separate interviews that the charges were without foundation.

According to the impression here, the accusations were designed to embarrass Mr. Guzmán, if not to eliminate him from the Dominican political scene, by associating him with alleged scandals.

Formula Opposed by Junta

The formula for a regime centering on Dr. Guzmán had been opposed from the start by the civilian-military junta that the United States Embassy here helped create last month with Brig. Gen. Antonio Imbert Barreras as its head. Subsequently several factions in the Johnson Administration were reported to have marshaled their forces against the proposed Guzmán regime.

It was former President Juan Bosch, whose Government was overthrown by the military in September, 1963, who advanced the name of Mr. Guzmán for the Presidency. Mr. Guzmán was Minister of Agriculture in the Bosch Cabinet.

The current revolt, led by Col. Francisco Caamaño Deñó, began April 24 with the aim of returning Mr. Bosch to power or of restoring constitutional government in some other form here.

The Bosch suggestion of Mr. Guzmán for the Presidency of a compromise regime was accepted by the Johnson Administration in an apparent policy switch 12 days ago.

Rafael David Castillo, administrator of the Agricultural Bank, a post equivalent to bank president, said today that the audit by the New York firm of Ernst & Ernst covered the period between Feb. 12, 1962, and March 1, 1964.

Both Mr. Guzmán in his statement and Mr. Castillo in the interview stressed that Mr. Guzmán was named a member of the four-man executive board of the Bank April 6, 1964, or seven months after the Bosch regime was ousted. This was subsequent to the period covered by the Ernst & Ernst audit.

Guardsman Named by Cabral

Mr. Guzmán was named to the bank by the civilian junta of Donald Reid Cabral, who succeeded Mr. Bosch and was, in turn, ousted at the start of the current revolt.

Both Mr. Castillo and officials of the United States Agency for International Development said

regime was ousted. This was subsequent to the period covered by the Ernst & Ernst audit.

Guzmán Named by Cabral

Mr. Guzmán was named to the bank by the civilian junta of Donald Reid Cabral, who succeeded Mr. Bosch and was, in turn, ousted at the start of the current revolt.

Both Mr. Castillo and officials of the United States Agency for International Development said today that the audit was ordered by Rafael Jorge, a former bank administrator, to clarify the procedures used in the processing of United States loans of excess farm commodities under Public Law 480.

Mr. Castillo, a career bank official who was appointed administrator 10 days ago by the anti-Guzmán junta of General Imbert, declared that "under no circumstances can Guzmán be associated with any irregularities in the bank, and besides there were none."

In his statement, Mr. Guzmán stressed that the charge that the bank had overstated its assets by 75 million was inaccurate.

"As a result of the economic prostitution to which the bank was submitted during the tyranny of Trujillo, the bank's capital was fictitiously augmented from $5 million to $100 million, through the transfer of ill-planned and overvalued enterprises."

Subsequently, Mr. Guzmán said, the Government that succeeded the regime of Generalissimo Rafael Leonidas Trujillo Molina was forced in 1962 to issue a law increasing the bank's capital from the legal limit of $50 million to $85,512,150. This was done on the advice of the Inter-American Development Bank, he added.

Auditor Denies Allegations

Benjamin Berezovsky, the Santo Domingo manager of Ernst & Ernst, who directed 40 accountants in studying the bank's operations, said the audit had showed "no irregularities of any kind," except for chaos caused by operations conducted by the Trujillo dictatorship.

He said the firm of Ernst & Ernst had recommended that the bank's working capital be increased to $75 million for balance-sheet purposes to make it more attractive to investors or lenders on the New York money market.

Mr. Berezovsky said the proposal was accepted both by the Inter-American Development Bank and by the Dominican Government. The figure of $75 million was reached by consolidating the bank's assets, liabilities and reserves, he asserted, calling it a routine book-keeping operation, not an overstatement of the capital.

Bundy Visits Guzmán

Concerning the allegedly missing mortgage notes, both Mr. Castillo and Mr. Berezovsky said that the copies were indeed missing but that the originals remained at the government's registration office and that copies could be obtained at $3 each.

Therefore, both officials said, it was inaccurate to contend that the titles were actually missing.

Mr. Bundy, who apparently had no advance knowledge of the Washington allegations, visited Mr. Guzmán this morning to give him the full text of the article in question.

Deputy Secretary of Defense Cyrus R. Vance, who arrived with Mr. Bundy and other ranking officials, is to remain in Santo Domingo partly to coordinate the establishment of the inter-American armed force, which is responsible for peace-keeping in this war-torn city.

Whatever political negotiations are to be pursued here in the meantime, will be handled by Dr. José A. Mora, Secretary General of the Organization of American States.

In the light of the controversy over Mr. Guzmán, some political sources here raised the possibility that Joaquín Balaguer, who served as President for seven months after Generalissimo Trujillo was assassinated in 1961, may become the next candidate for head of a coalition as a compromise in the crisis.

Mr. Balaguer, who lives in New York, arrived in San Juan, Puerto Rico, several days ago and has been making radio and television talks.

Tonight, Mr. Bundy and Mr. Vance held what was described as a cordial meeting with Colonel Caamaño, the rebel chief, and his aides. This was Mr. Bundy's first meeting with the colonel since his arrival here 10 days ago.

At about the same time, a brief but furious exchange of fire erupted along the border of the International Security Zone, right above the United States Embassy compound.

According to United States officials, rebel rifle fire hit the embassy area. The fire was returned, but it was not immediately known if there were any casualties.

In general, the cease-fire which has been in effect since last Friday, was being observed, with the exception of isolated incidents.

Crisis in Santo Domingo: Anti-U.S. Feeling Surges

By TAD SZULC
Special to The New York Times

SANTO DOMINGO, Dominican Republic, May 14—Two weeks after the first American troop landings in Santo Domingo, the United States is facing a surge of anti-American sentiment here. Virtually no such hostility existed before the landings.

Communist elements in the rebel movement of Col. Francisco Caamaño Deñó have withdrawn from conspicuous positions, apparently on the theory that the United States is effectively doing their work for them.

This sentiment is powerfully expressed in broadcasts of the "constitutionalist" rebels, and it is strongly felt in the streets of the rebel zone. Hopes for American understanding are giving way to anger over United States support for the new military-civilian junta of Brig. Gen. Antonio Imbert Barreras.

Troops an Irritant

The deepening anti-Americanism is a result of the presence of 22,000 troops who regularly come into conflict with the rebels as they guard the international safety zone and the corridor across the city.

Evidence available here strongly indicates that the United States decision to intervene in the Dominican Republic was motivated largely by fear of a Communist takeover. Marines landed April 28, but it was at least three days before President Johnson acknowledged publicly that this was a purpose of the military operation.

As a result of the decision, the United States finds itself identified with a military junta that is widely hated, and it may be standing on the threshold of a violent showdown with the highly popular rebel movement.

Since April 24, when the revolution erupted here, the United States has in effect closed all options even to non-Communist members of the rebellion.

A growing consensus among Dominicans and Americans here is that the United States may now be forced to keep occupation troops here for long months, if not for years, amid the rising hatred of the Dominicans, who greatly admired the United States until recently.

U.S. Moves Recalled

A reconstruction of events since the start of the revolt shows that almost as soon as the rebels appeared to be winning, Washington prepared to act militarily against what it believed to be a Communist danger.

The pattern of United States troop movements preparing for landings here, the information supplied to the White House and the State Department by the embassy in Santo Domingo, and other available evidence, made it clear that the United

Continued on Page 10, Column 2

Crisis in Santo Domingo: Anti-U.S. Feeling Surges in the Wake of Military Intervention

Continued From Page 1, Col. 4

States was embarking on a large political and military enterprise.

At the same time, it was insisting that its goal was limited to the protection of the lives and property of Americans and other foreigners in the path of the Dominican fighting.

Guerrilla warfare in the capital has already cost the lives of 16 United States servicemen, and the list of those wounded in action stands at 86.

The toll among Dominicans in three weeks of carnage in the capital is staggering. The estimate of the rebels is that 1,500 persons have been killed and 3,500 wounded. But no one seems sure, and more people are killed every day.

The revolt began as an attempt to restore the presidency to Juan Bosch, who was governing under a year-old constitution when he was ousted and exiled to Puerto Rico in 1963 by a junta under Donald Reid Cabral. The Reid junta had labeled Mr. Bosch soft on Communism.

After the United States intervention last month, Mr. Bosch told his supporters, now led by Colonel Caamaño, that he no longer wished to return to power. Colonel Caamaño was named president by legislators loyal to the rebel movement, acting under the 1962 constitution.

Meanwhile the Reid junta dissolved, and the constitutionalist rebels were opposed chiefly by right-wing forces under Brig. Gen. Elias Wessin y Wessin. It was with the support of these forces that the Imbert junta was formed last week.

Setbacks for U.S.

For the United States several setbacks have afflicted the complicated diplomatic efforts to back the Imbert junta while maintaining publicly that it remains neutral and seeks only peace and democracy for the Dominicans.

Thus far the United States command has refused to "unleash" General Imbert against the rebels. Yesterday, therefore, the junta took matters into its own hands, sending five aircraft to strafe the city and fire rockets. The planes, taking off from the American-controlled base at San Isidro, knocked out the main transmitter of the rebels' radio station, killing at least a woman and a child.

General Imbert's pilots also strafed so close to the United States Embassy that American officials had to dive under their desks for safety. American marines shot down one of the Imbert aircraft, and the embassy sent an angry protest to the Organization of American States, charging that the junta had violated the O.A.S. cease-fire agreement.

Resignation Rescinded

United States diplomacy had already suffered a setback at the hands of the Imbert junta. On Monday General Wessin, principal object of the rebels' ire, promised Ambassador W. Tapley Bennett Jr. that he would resign, then went back on his word after a meeting with General Imbert.

The embassy had hoped General Wessin's removal would improve the political atmosphere and help the inter-American Organization to negotiate a settlement. The move to drop

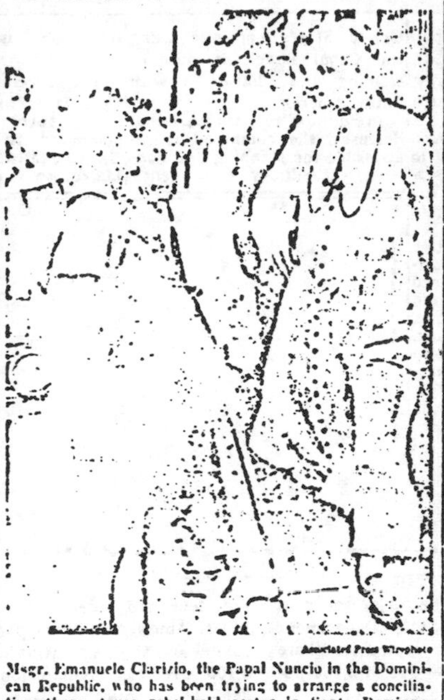

Associated Press Wirephoto

Msgr. Emanuele Clarizio, the Papal Nuncio in the Dominican Republic, who has been trying to arrange a conciliation there, tours rebel-held sector in Santo Domingo.

General Wessin coincided with a United States offer to make $750,000 available to the Imbert junta to pay the salaries of government employes. But General Imbert kept both the money and General Wessin.

As matters are now developing, the United States not only is sporadically fighting the rebels, whom it sees as the enemy, but also is increasingly at odds with the Imbert junta, which it supports and finances.

Caamaño Widely Backed

Although the Caamaño movement physically controls only the downtown and northern sections of Santo Domingo, it enjoys considerable support in the provinces.

Some officials question whether the Caamaño election — by members of the Dominican congress last week — was legal from a constitutional viewpoint, but the legality of the two military juntas that the United States has successively sponsored in the last 15 days is also in doubt.

The Imbert junta stands primarily for elections as soon as possible, according to its chairman. But not even United States Embassy officials, who helped the general rise to the presidency of his faction, maintain that he represents a long-term solution for a breakdown of authority and political life in the Dominican Republic.

Contrary to views expressed by United States spokesmen, General Imbert is not a popular national figure in this country, despite his role in the assassination of the former dictator Rafael Leonidas Trujillo Molina in 1961.

Imbert Called a Symbol

General Imbert is becoming the symbol of a new military dictatorship as General Wessin symbolized it earlier.

Few officials of the United States or the Organization of American States take seriously the recent Washington announcement that the Johnson Administration hopes for a coalition of elements from the Caamaño and Imbert factions.

It is felt that neither faction will budge from its basic [illegible] unless the United States [illegible] to come to terms with the [illegible]

rebels. But Washington seems firmly committed to the Imbert junta and to its belief that either the return of Mr. Bosch or the retention of the Caamaño group will mean the triumph of Communism in the Cuban mold.

New Outbreak Feared

Both Americans and O.A.S. diplomats voice hope that a political solution can be reached. But the truce is so tenuous and the tensions are so high that from moment to moment there is a danger that the situation may get out of hand.

American officials say that a "military solution" — an attempt to dislodge the rebels from the city area they hold — can be discussed only "in hypothetical terms."

But as more Americans are killed by Dominicans and as more Dominicans are killed by Americans, the dangers of a large explosion seem to be growing hourly.

The rebels regard the United States forces here as enemy occupation troops and the rebel radio whips up anti-American sentiment to an angry pitch. The Americans counter by jamming the station.

Broadcasts Resume

This morning, in the aftermath of the attack by the junta's aircraft, the rebel station was back on the air. The anti-American and anti-Imbert attacks had been stilled for a time, but the rebels were further embittered by the feeling that the United States had authorized the air strikes. Both the Communists and the agents of the Imbert junta seemed eager to perpetuate this impression while American officials winced.

In the narrow streets of downtown Santo Domingo groups of Dominicans shouted yesterday that "the Yankees are the killers." In a chilling episode, an American television crew was forced at gunpoint to look at the mangled body of the child killed in the air attack.

The greatest danger here appears to be in the rebel charges that United States forces are constantly violating the cease-fire signed last week between the factions. The rebels say that United States marines and

paratroops of the 82d Airborne Division are intentionally moving, a bit each day, into the constitutionalist zone.

United States officials reply that to assure the security of the international safety zone and of the corridor running through rebel territory from the international zone to the other side of Ozama River, it is sometimes necessary to move a block or two into the Caamaño area.

Besides, Lieut. Gen. Bruce Palmer, commander in chief of the American forces, has made a point of saying that the United States is not a party to the truce arranged by the O.A.S.

U.S. Forays Frequent

American patrols have often been seen plunging into the rebel zone, sometimes in pursuit of snipers and sometimes for reasons that United States briefing officers have not fully explained.

On the rebel side, there are continual sniper attacks on American positions as well as on American-controlled hotels deep in the international zone.

In the last 24 hours, a typical period, 16 such violations were reported by American forces. They included the fatal shooting of a marine lieutenant a block from the Embajador Hotel.

The question of who is responsible for this continual and highly skillful sniping is a key issue of debate here.

Colonel Caamaño and his aides have publicly insisted from the beginning that their interests cannot be served by such sniping, as they are eager to earn the reputation of a responsible government deserving international recognition.

But Colonel Caamaño has acknowledged that he does not control all the armed men in this wartorn city. He has told Latin-American diplomats that as many as 30 per cent of the rebel zone's 10,000 armed men are operating on their own.

Some suggest that an important number of the snipers are Communists eager to widen the gap between the Caamaño group and the United States. They say that other snipers may be agents from the Wessin forces who are interested, for their own reasons, in keeping the Americans and the constitutionalists apart.

Finally there are said to be unruly bands without political motives.

Rebels Set to Resist

The 105-mm. howitzers of the Marines and of the Army's 82d Airborne Division, pointing at the rebel area from both sides of the city, are a constant reminder that the United States may find itself pushed into an all-out attack on the rebel zone.

The rebels are prepared to resist. They have weapons and gasoline bombs stored in houses in the maze of narrow streets that make up the rebel zone. They have a complete plan for the area's defense, and from all visible indications they are determined to fight to the end.

When the first American troops landed in Santo Domingo the soldiers often asked strangers, "What is all this about, anyway?" or, "Can anybody tell us who are the good guys and who are the bad guys?"

One answer is that from the outset the Johnson Administration, advised by its embassy and by such Washington officials as Thomas C. Mann, Under Secretary of State for Economic Affairs, appeared to have made up its mind that the pro-Bosch movement and then the Caamaño group were Communist-dominated — though no

proof of this charge is apparent here — and that they had to be destroyed.

Though a revolt against the Reid junta had been impending for some time, the April 24 uprising clearly caught the United States by surprise. Ambassador Bennett was in Washington. He says he went for consultations because he thought it was his last chance to do so before major trouble developed here. But 11 out of 13 officers of the Military Advisory and Assistance Mission were in Panama, attending a routine conference. The local mission chief of the Agency for International Development was in Washington, at another routine conference.

State Department Calm

The evening of April 24 the State Department assured callers in Washington that the situation was under control.

But on Sunday, April 25, when it became clear that the revolt had triumphed and that Mr. Bosch was on the verge of returning from Puerto Rico, the State Department was said to have decided that such an event would pose a threat of Communism in the Dominican Republic "within six months."

This judgment, according to American sources here, was made by Mr. Mann, who stepped into the State Department's operations center on Sunday to coordinate United States actions. Mr. Mann was formerly Assistant Secretary of State for Inter-American Affairs.

Embassy Plan Vetoed

On April 25 and April 26, the United States made no move to express interest in the pro-Bosch movement or sympathy for it. When the embassy, still in Ambassador Bennett's absence, recommended that American officials establish a contact with Mr. Bosch in Puerto Rico, the State Department vetoed the idea.

Bosch followers here were surprised. In the wake of Mr. Bosch's election in December, 1962, as the first freely chosen Dominican President in 38 years, President Kennedy's Administration bent its efforts to make this country "the showplace of democracy" under the Alliance for Progress.

When military men, led by General Wessin, ousted Mr. Bosch seven months later, the Kennedy Administration suspended diplomatic ties and halted economic aid.

It was under the Johnson Administration that Dominican ties were restored.

Late on April 26, military and civilian leaders of the Caamaño movement began distributing weapons to civilians in Santo Domingo. Several truckloads were brought to Independence Park, in the heart of the city, to be passed out to all comers. Army arsenals controlled by the rebels also threw their doors open to civilians.

Step Linked to Reds

It is still unknown who ordered the distribution of arms to the population. There are reasons to believe that some Communist leaders encouraged the step. But the rebels were being bombed and attacked by General Wessin's forces and they evidently needed reinforcements.

But the United States took this move as a sign that, in the State Department's words, a revolution started by democratic elements had fallen into the hands of Communists.

By nightfall on April 28, concern developed over the safety of some 3,000 United States citizens. There had been no attacks on them, but the fighting was heavy and the situation was out of hand. The United States Navy's Amphibious Squadron, standing offshore

with 1,500 marines aboard, was ordered to prepare for a landing in Santo Domingo to evacuate the Americans.

No one here — not even the rebels — has seriously questioned the wisdom of that move on the part of the Johnson Administration. There was no other authority here to protect the foreigners, and unruly armed mobs were roaming the streets.

But at that point the Administration was thinking ahead to large-scale intervention.

At 4 P.M. on April 27, about 18 rebel officers arrived at the embassy to request a meeting with Ambassador Bennett, now back at his post. They were led by Col. Miguel Angel Hernando Ramirez, military chief of the rebellion. Colonel Caamaño was in the group, but his role in the meeting was secondary.

The other officers said there had already been enough bloodshed. They asked Mr. Bennett to negotiate a settlement with the Wessin forces. General Wessin's aircraft had been bombing the National Palace, and that afternoon they were threatening to break into the rebel zone over the Ozama River bridge.

Mr. Bennett says that while he told the rebels he had no authority to mediate, he would urge all parties to seek a settlement. He said he understood that General Wessin was willing to talk peace.

Accord Is Reached

Mr. Bennett agreed to send a representative to the palace to convey the rebel officers' desire for peace to their acting president, José Rafael Molina Ureña. Mr. Molina, who had served as president of the Chamber of Deputies under the Bosch Government, had been sworn in on Sunday as acting president while Mr. Bosch, in Puerto Rico, contemplated his course.

A second conference was held at the embassy that afternoon, with Mr. Molina. The whole rebel group now appeared ready to abandon the fight. The acting president drove to the Colombian Embassy to seek asylum, and several officers lingered around Ambassador Bennett's office, apparently hoping they could remain there for safety.

But, as Mr. Bennett recalls, Colonel Caamaño had a parting remark. As he left the Ambassador's office, he said, "We shall go on fighting." Colonel Caamaño's version is that Mr. Bennett "insultingly" demanded that the rebels surrender at once.

Mr. Bennett denies this charge, but the incident colored Colonel Caamaño's attitude toward the Ambassador for the days and weeks to come.

That night, the embassy and most other here, assumed the rebellion had ended. Instead, it was entering a new phase.

Forces Rallied Anew

It is still not clear how Colonel Caamaño, suddenly chief of the movement, succeeded in rallying his troops and his civilian irregulars.

The embassy maintains that at this point Communist professionals moved in to keep the revolution from collapsing. But there is evidence that the decision to keep fighting also came from [illegible] civilians, notably Héctor Aristy, now Colonel Caamaño's chief minister, and from several European veterans of the [illegible] who had acted as military advisers to the movement.

Colonel Caamaño and Mr. Aristy had the rebellion going again by the morning of April 28. By then, both the embassy and the State Department were

convinced that the rebellion was dominated by Communists.

Before noon, an antirebel military junta was created at San Isidro under Col. Pedro B. Benoit, a little-known air force officer. General Wessin and other key commanders of the antirebel struggle were kept out of the junta, apparently on American advice, to avoid antagonizing the rebels.

But the junta's control over the city [illegible] slipping. After lunch on April 28, Colonel Benoit notified Ambassador Bennett that he could no longer assure the safety of foreigners in the city. Mr. Bennett passed this information to Washington at 3:14 P.M., and the die was cast for United States military intervention.

At 6:55 P.M. the fleet received the Presidential order "Prepare to land" and within minutes the first helicopters from the carrier Boxer began to ferry marines to the polo field at the Embajador Hotel.

By the morning of April 29, 520 marines had come ashore, taken control of the hotel area and established a platoon at the embassy, about two miles away.

Aboard the Boxer that morning, Capt. James A. Dare, commodore of the amphibious task force, said the marines would stay in the Dominican Republic as long as it was necessary "to keep a non-Communist government there."

Also that morning, United States officials quietly flew General Imbert from the Embajador to the Boxer in the first step intended to elevate him to power under American auspices.

More Marines Arrive

On the night of April 29 as more marines were coming ashore and as the entire 82d Airborne Division was being airlifted to San Isidro, the embassy made new efforts to present its case against the rebellion as Communist-dominated.

On May 1, President Johnson's personal representative, John Bartlow Martin, arrived to work with Mr. Bennett. Mr. Martin had been the Ambassador here during Mr. Bosch's presidency, and had many political ties.

After a meeting with Colonel Caamaño that afternoon, Mr. Martin concluded that "the Communists have taken over" and that "all is lost" as democratic elements [illegible] from the pro-Bosch [illegible].

Mr. Martin reported this to President Johnson and the Administration became more convinced that its initial judgment had been right.

Yet Mr. Martin's assessments were not shared by many embassy officials or by most American and foreign [illegible] here.

Over the weekend the United States doubled its forces to 12,000 men and by the middle of the week of May 3 it [illegible] 20,000 troops ashore and [illegible] Navy vessels offshore. Air Force troop carriers, [illegible] the clock, were landing at San Isidro every two or three minutes in one of the biggest peacetime airlift operations.

Defense Department Avoiding Cuts in Some Intelligence Units

Continued From Page 1, Col. 6

eigners abroad by all the Government agencies is 351,691.

Strictly speaking, the Defense Department is making a 10 per cent cut in both its military and civilian personnel abroad. But the distribution of the cuts, left to the department's discretion, maintained abroad intelligence and psychological-warfare personnel in numbers that the Richardson report considered as highly excessive.

On the other hand, the Central Intelligence Agency was reported to have reduced its American personnel abroad by between 10 and 12 per cent. It is believed that the agency employs 30,000 foreigners abroad, directly or indirectly.

The Richardson report said that 28,000 Americans, mainly Defense Department personnel, are engaged in intelligence activities in East Asia.

Under its interpretation of a July 21 directive to Mr. Richardson from Henry A. Kissinger, the President's Special Assistant for National Security, the Pentagon was able to exempt 12,000 of the 28,000 intelligence personnel in East Asia from the cuts. This meant that only 1,600 instead of 2,800 were sent home. Statistically, the reduction in the intelligence staffs in East Asia were only 6.4 per cent instead of 10 per cent.

Mr. Richardson's report commented that although the intelligence community as a whole had complied with the 10 per cent cut, he believed there were "intelligence activities which can probably stand further reductions without a real detriment."

The report discussed the feasibility of alternative systems of collecting intelligence following the closure or consolidation of some activities, including the establishement of mobile operations in the United States and "closely allied countries."

A joint C.I.A.-State Department subcommittee was charged with the "reconsideration of the role of intelligence collection organizations overseas" operating under Washington's direct guidance or under foreign control points.

It was in this context that Mr. Richardson proposed the independent study of intelligence operations under "the aegis of the national policy level"—meaning the National Security Council.

U. S. I. A. Is Involved

The Richardson report further found fault with the Pentagon's insistence on maintaining the level of its psychological warfare operations in Asia. These are coordinated with the C.I.A. and receive "general policy guidance" from the United States Information Agency. The information agency's legal mandate, incidentally, does not provide for involvement in psychological warfare in war theaters.

These operations are chiefly aimed at Communist China, North Vietnam and North Korea and include radio broadcasts, leaflet drops and the dissemination of written pamphlets "through other means."

The Richardson report said, "In Southeast Asia and Korea, civilian agencies are reducing the level of operations, but the Department of Defense does not plan to reduce the level of psychological warfare operations.

"Since the policy trend is in the direction of reducing the level of psychological warfare operations in the area, it does not appear fully consistent with that trend for the Department of Defense to exclude its units from any reduction on the technicality of the White House directive."

"As a consequence of exemptions, the military psycho-

logical warfare units will assume a disproportionate rule in comparison to civilians," it said.

Mr. Richardson then cited a number of examples of military and intelligence operations abroad that may be eliminated or reduced.

He urged the elimination of the Voice of the United Nations Command, a radio station in South Korea run by the United States military.

Its liquidation has been recommended by the American Embassy in Seoul.

Mr. Richardson noted that 1,950 American employes, mainly military, operate a highly secret intelligence operation in

Ethiopia and that the Pentagon has exempted the entire staff, although "it is in our interest to reduce our profile as much as we can."

He said that there had been only 4 per cent reduction in two military intelligence stations in Morocco, where 1,700 Americans, chiefly military, are employed.

The Richardson committee also asked the Defense Department to re-examine the need for a separate unified command in the Panama Canal Zone, which has 12,000 Americans.

The report remarked that in 1967, the Panamanian Government only "with the greatest reluctance" agreed to let the

United States continue using the Canal Zone for military training and "liaison" with Latin America.

In addition to Panama Canal defenses, the command is responsible for planning and controlling "military contingency"

operations" in Central America and South America.

The special report due on Dec. 31 is to suggest alternatives, such as moving the command to the continental United States, presumably Florida, or to Puerto Rico.

DEC 14 '69

By TAD SZULC
Special to The New York Times

WASHINGTON, Dec. 13— United States intelligence services—notably the Defense Department's agencies—have won exemptions for thousands of their personnel from an order by President Nixon to reduce by 10 per cent the number of American officials serving abroad.

Most of these exemptions over the Pentagon's intelligence and psychological-warfare operations in East Asia, which a total of 28,000 Americans are engaged.

The military intelligence exemptions, along with smaller ones for other Government agencies represented overseas, were granted by the White House.

Approval came despite State Department recommendations at a study of further cuts intelligence operations abroad be undertaken "by leaders independent of the intelligence community under the aegis of the national policy level."

Among the major agencies, only the State Department has fully accepted its share of the cuts—517 of 5,166 positions abroad.

Under Secretary of State Elliot L. Richardson served as as chairman of the National Security Council's permanent committee of under secretaries, which was charged with carrying out the President's "Operation Reduction."

He noted in a report to Mr. Nixon that under the Defense Department exemptions "the military psychological-warfare units" would assume "a disproportionate role in comparison to civilians."

The Richardson report, which has not been made public, was obtained from high Administration quarters. President Nixon ordered "Operation Reduction," known in Federal jargon as OPRED, on July 9.

Mr. Richardson's report was sent to the White House on Oct. 3.

On Nov. 26, the White House announced that the

President had ordered home 14,937 American military personnel and the elimination of 5,100 overseas civilian jobs held by Americans, 10 per cent of whom are Foreign Service officers.

This is to be effective on June 30, 1970 with a saving of $50-million a year.

The White House said that the order excluded troops in Southeast Asia, South Korea and Berlin and those in Europe under the North Atlantic Treaty Organization.

Subject to the cut in the military field, therefore, were the 144,889 Defense Department personnel, of whom 39,281 were civilians.

The total military strength of the United States abroad is about 1.7 million.

In addition, the Defense Department employs 324,682 foreign citizens abroad. The Richardson group is to make recommendations by Dec. 31 on reducing foreign employes. Total employment of for-

Continued on Page 24, Column 1

THE NEW YORK TIMES, THURSDAY, DECEMBER 18, 1969

Nixon's Budget Cuts Will Spare Global Net of F.B.I. and Narcotics Agents

By TAD SZULC
Special to The New York Times

WASHINGTON, Dec. 17—The Nixon Administration has decided to maintain intact the limited worldwide network of Justice Department of undercover Federal agents because of the international ramifications of organized crime and the growing contacts of black militants abroad.

The recommendation by the permanent committee of under President Nixon as-National Security Council, secretaries, presided over by Under Secretary of State Elliot L. Richardson, to exempt the Department of Justice, nor did it mention exclusions of thou-Justice was approved by the White House.

The committee's report, sub-logical-warfare operatives mitted to the White House on Dec. 173

agents of the Federal Bureau of Investigation and the Bureau of Narcotics and Dangerous Drugs be exempted.

With regard to the black militants, the Department of Justice contended that foreign contacts by representatives of the Black Panthers "pose a serious threat to our Government and demand close attention."

The recommendation by the permanent committee of under 1970.

The announcement made no reference to exemptions for the foreign nationals—representing 18 departments and agencies ranging from the State and Defense Departments and the sands of the Defense Department's intelligence and psycho-Central Intelligence Agency to logical-warfare operatives in the Interior Department's Fish and about 250 American and Wildlife Service and the tions.

Oct. 3, has not been published, but its text was made available to The New York Times.

On Nov. 26 the White House announced that 14,937 military men not in troop units and civilian employes of the military would be brought home and that 5,100 civilian overseas jobs would be abolished by June 30, 1970.

Apart from troops, the Government maintains nearly 550,000 people overseas—145,000 military men not in troop units, 52,500 civilians and 351,700 men.

When the committee began studying the reduction ordering the reduction with foreign based on a directive from President Nixon July 9, a number of departments and agencies appealed for partial or full exemp-

employes of the Commerce, Agriculture and Treasury Departments.

The Peace Corps, with 473 staff officials and about 11,000 volunteers throughout in Germany to air and naval world, also was exempted from combat commands in Japan, Okinawa, Thailand, South Korea, Taiwan, Laos and the Philippines, and the Atlantic, Pacific and Mediterranean fleets. The feets account for 643,000 men.

When the committee began studying the reduction with foreign police forces tracked down James Earl Ray in Britain after his trip to Canada and Portugal.

Library of Congress.

In addition, the United States has 1.7 million men abroad in military units—from the armies in South Vietnam and West bases of nine positions, or roughly 5 per cent.

in Spain, Turkey and Canada, what is known as Operation Reduction, or OPRED.

"adequate coverage of major cases such as the identification and extradition of King would have been jeopardized" by reductions in F.B.I. Agents work.

When the Department of Justice asked Sept. 5 that all F.B.I. and Narcotics Bureau agents be kept abroad, the committee had planned a cut of the department said that "adequate coverage of major cases such as the identification and extradition of Martin Luther King's assassin of Martin Luther King would have been jeopardized" by reductions in F.B.I. Agents work.

Pentagon Doubles Arms Aid to Athens Despite Restriction

By TAD SZULC

Special to The New York Times

WASHINGTON, April 16—Despite United States restrictions on arms shipments to the Greek junta, the Defense Department is reported to have secretly supplied this year nearly twice as much military aid to Greece as authorized by Congress.

APR 17 70

The United States imposed the curb on deliveries of "major" military items to Greece in 1967 to show its displeasure over the overthrow of the government by the army.

However, the nature of this curb has never been publicly defined and the flow of equipment has continued at levels considerably above those approved by Congress under the military assistance program.

At the same time, the Administration is considering lifting altogether the embargo on military deliveries to Greece, reportedly under the pressure of the Defense Department, which is concerned over the situation in the Eastern Mediterranean, where the Soviet Union has been building up its fleet.

Figures made available in Congressional quarters showed that while Congress had authorized $24,498,000 in military aid

Continued on Page 5, Column 1

'SECRET ARMS AID' GIVEN TO ATHENS

Continued From Page 1, Col. 3

to Greece in the 1970 fiscal year, the Pentagon plans to deliver additional equipment worth $20-million from stocks described as surplus.

Figures obtained here also showed that in the 1969 fiscal year the Pentagon quietly gave $470-million in surplus armaments to the four "forward defense countries" — Nationalist China, South Korea, Turkey and Greece—in addition to the total of $350-million in military aid approved by Congress.

The principal beneficiary was Nationalist China, which received about $157-million from this total, while Greece received nearly $26-million in 1969 on top of the authorized deliveries of $37,501,000.

Congressional sources said that the Pentagon set a "utility value" on the material of 25 per cent to 30 per cent of the cost, even if the equipment was new. Congressional experts have adopted the method of multiplying the utility figures by four to arrive at the cost of the surplus shipments.

The Pentagon's actions have raised indignation among many members of Congress, who consider their authority disregarded by the department. But the Greek situation has international implications as well because of the strong sentiment in Western Europe against the authoritarian practices of the Athens junta.

Today, Senator Stephen M. Young introduced legislation requiring the Pentagon to make "complete and prior disclosure of all proposed disposals of surplus weapons."

The Ohio Democrat cited Nationalist China and Greece as the countries where, "through the surplus disposal program, Pentagon officials have been secretly subsidizing at least two tyrannical dictatorships without any advance information given to Congress nor any authorization sought nor secured."

The restriction on arms to Greece was imposed by the Johnson Administration after the colonels overthrew the constitutional regime on April 21, 1967, and it has thus far been maintained by the Nixon Administration.

Under this ban, Greece is denied so-called "heavy" items, such as tanks and combat aircraft. But neither Administration has defined what items are considered "heavy."

In 1966, before the restrictions were applied, the total military aid to Greece was about $90-million.

$55-Million in Minor Items

Although the government said that only spare parts, trucks and minor items were being provided after the coup, Greece received $44-million in 1967 and $55-million in 1968.

Officials here were unable to explain at the time how this "marginal" aid could amount to such high figures.

Following the invasion of Czechoslovakia by Soviet-bloc armies in August, 1968, the United States temporarily lifted the Greek embargo as it sought to encourage the allied countries to build up their defenses. As a result, Greece received in 1969 about $26-million in military aid, of which the subsidized surplus shipments made up...

Many U.S. Civilian Roles In Asia May Go to Military

By TAD SZULC
Special to The New York Times

WASHINGTON, June 9—The Nixon Administration is drawing up plans for the shift of numerous American economic and social programs in South Vietnam and Laos from civilian to military control.

Under the plans, the United States Defense Department would gradually take over, wholly or in part, the financing and operation of such programs as the balancing of the South Vietnamese defense budget, pacification of rural areas, public health, the training of the police and the care of refugees.

Those programs are financed and administered alone or in cooperation with the Defense Department by the Agency for International Development. In many instances the Central Intelligence Agency and the United States Information Agency also participate.

During the fiscal year ending on June 30, the aid agency, it is estimated, will have spent $365-million in Vietnam.

The Administration plans to incorporate some of the changes in its revision of the foreign-aid program, which is expected soon. Part of the program will require Congressional approval.

The plans are expected to generate considerable controversy in and out of Congress because they deal with the subject of civilian vs. military control of policy. The contemplated shift could transfer the responsibility of Senate review from the Foreign Relations Committee, which has generally been critical of American operations in Southeast Asia, to the Armed Services Committee, which has generally been sympathetic.

Civilian officials have been citing private remarks by high-ranking officers involved in policy planning for Vietnam to the effect that civilian leadership is failing and that well-

Continued on Page 5, Column 1

Pentagon May Get a Wider Role in Asi

Continued From Page 1, Col. 3

trained Army men should be increasingly assigned to positions of responsibility in the administration of wartime and postwar programs.

A major argument among Administration officials favoring an increase in the military role in Asian and other support-assistance programs is said to be that the Defense Department is expected to have an easier time getting funds from Congress, where opposition to foreign-aid appropriations has been growing in recent years.

Support at White House

Indications are that the new approach has support in the White House staff as well as among many though not all civilian and military officials in the Defense Department. Top officials in the aid agency are described as resigned to the change, partly because A.I.D. as an entity would disappear under the projected reorganization of the foreign-aid program.

Secretary of State William P. Rogers has participated in the discussions only to a limited extent. The whole question is expected to be reviewed by the National Security Council.

Dr. John A. Hannah, the aid administrator, discussed the problem with President Nixon at the White House on May 25 in one of their rare meetings.

In recent public statements Dr. Hannah has made it clear that the "supporting assistance" programs would be divested from the agency that would be set up to handle overseas economic development under the reorganization, expected to take effect in about a year. He has recognized that some of the support functions would be turned over to the Defense Department.

Other aid officials foresaw a tug-of-war between the Pentagon and civilian agencies over the extent to which the military establishment would assume responsibility for the activities now performed by the aid agency.

They said that the State Department, which is to coordinate the support assistance under the reorganization blueprint, does not have "enough clout," funds or experienced personnel to run the programs.

Larger C.I.A. Role Foreseen

The officials also foresaw that the C.I.A. would seek to increase its role in the support programs. They noted that in a radio interview last Sunday Dr. Hannah conceded that the intelligence agency had been using A.I.D. as a cover for its activities in Laos since 1962. In Vietnam, the C.I.A. is an active partner in the pacification program, which it created eight years ago, and is engaged in many other operations.

While there is resistance among civilian officials to what is viewed as military encroachment, A.I.D. recognizes its inability to obtain sufficient funds and personnel to finance and operate some programs in Vietnam.

Early this year, for example, the United States Ambassador to South Vietnam, Ellsworth Bunker, turned down insistent proposals by the United States Military Assistance Command in Saigon that he accept 135 Army officers as advisers to the aid agency's public-safety program, which seeks to build up the South Vietnamese civilian police.

The Defense Department plans to finance several projects that have been administered and funded by the aid agency, among them the supply of high-protein food to the South Vietnamese Army. Tentative estimates are that in fiscal 1971 the Defense Department will finance up to $30-million in programs that previously were paid for from aid funds.

In many recent situations, officials said, A.I.D. had to turn to the military for administrators and physicians to run refugee and public health projects because of a shortage of civilians willing to serve in Vietnam.

a law covering both military assistance and support assistance, if, in theory, the State Department retained overall national security cooperation in direction.

The State Department that would supersede the present one are convinced that the aid agency. The law would vest Pentagon financing in the State Department that direction and coordination of efforts be increasingly administered by the military.

While the Defense Department would control military assistance, the State Department, main in Vietnam and Laos under the Peterson recommendations, would be responsible that they will be replaced for support-assistance and public-safety programs.

Senior Administration officials said that it appeared inevitable that considerable responsibility for the support programs would shift to the military.

Larger C.I.A. Role Foreseen

The officials also foresaw that the C.I.A. would seek to increase its role in the support programs. They noted that in a radio interview last Sunday Dr. Hannah conceded that the intelligence agency had been using A.I.D. as a cover for its activities in Laos since 1962. In Vietnam, the C.I.A. is an active partner in the pacification program, which it created eight years ago, and is engaged in many other operations.

While there is resistance among civilian officials to what is viewed as military encroachment, A.I.D. recognizes its inability to obtain sufficient funds and personnel to finance and operate some programs in Vietnam.

Early this year, for example, the United States Ambassador to South Vietnam, Ellsworth Bunker, turned down insistent proposals by the United States Military Assistance Command in Saigon that he accept 135 Army officers as advisers to the aid agency's public-safety program, which seeks to build up the South Vietnamese civilian police.

The Defense Department plans to finance several projects that have been administered and funded by the aid agency, among them the supply of high-protein food to the South Vietnamese Army. Tentative estimates are that in fiscal 1971 the Defense Department will finance up to $50-million in programs that previously were paid for from aid funds.

In many recent situations, officials said, A.I.D. had to turn to the military for administrators and physicians to run refugee and public-health projects because of a shortage of civilians willing to serve in Vietnam.

Rapidly Growing Ability

Such developments indicate the rapidly growing capability of the military, especially the Army, to administer typically civilian programs.

This month the newly reorganized John F. Kennedy Center for Military Assistance at Fort Bragg, N. C.—originally established by the Army to teach antiguerrilla warfare—will graduate the first class of Army officers trained in the political, social, economic, cultural and linguistic aspects of overseas military activities.

Commenting on the trend, a civilian official said that "the realities of the situation" would increasingly force the Administration to turn to the military for the financing and management of certain programs because of the inability of civilian agencies to muster adequate funds and personnel.

The major institutional changes are expected to come in the message that President Nixon will send to Congress later this month.

Deriving from the report of the task force on international development headed by Rudolph A. Peterson, retired president of the Bank of America, the Presidential message is expected to recommend a clear separation of international economic-development assistance from military and support aid. It is the latter that, in situations like Vietnam, has been administered by A.I.D. while the Pentagon has handled military sales and grants.

The Peterson report call for

Briton to Go to Saigon for U.S. Again

By TAD SZULC

Special to The New York Times

WASHINGTON, Jan. 15 — President Nixon is sending Sir Robert Thompson, the British expert on guerrilla warfare, back to South Vietnam next month for an urgent evaluation of the Saigon Government's police and public-safety programs, State Department officials said today.

Other Administration informants said that the British expert would also look into the joint American-South Vietnamese police and pacification activities, which range from efforts to wipe out the Communist political organization in the South to operation of South Vietnamese prisons with United States assistance.

State Department officials said that the proposal for Sir Robert to accept another mission in South Vietnam was made by the Saigon Government with the concurrence of the United States.

They said the request was forwarded by Ellsworth T. Bunker, the American Ambassador in Saigon, in a message to President Nixon earlier this month.

Sir Robert undertook a five-week secret mission for President Nixon last autumn — his second visit to South Vietnam in a year—but it was not clear for what specific reasons he and his group of British police specialists had been asked to go back after so short an interval.

There was strict secrecy here surrounding Sir Robert's trip. But the speculation in informed quarters is that both Mr. Bunker and the Administration were eager to have an up-to-date independent evaluation of the progress of pacification and related public safety efforts. It is felt such an evaluation is needed before decisions are made on additional withdrawals of American troops from South Vietnam.

Another possible reason for the mission is that the Civil Operations and Rural Development Support Program, which is in over-all charge of pacification, is to be reorganized, effective March 1, as the Community Defense and Local Development Program.

Other informed sources said that both the Administration and Ambassador Bunker still appeared to be troubled by the relative lack of success in the destruction of the secret Communist network in South Vietnam.

Secret Reports Keep Air Force Informed on Radicals

Bimonthly Bulletin Being Sent to Base Commanders

By TAD SZULC
Special to The New York Times

WASHINGTON, Jan. 28—Commanding officers at hundreds of Air Force bases in this country and abroad regularly receive secret reports on the activities of antiwar, dissident and radical groups, chiefly the Black Panther party.

This information, including comment and analysis of the current trends in what the Air Force calls "radical anti-Establishment groups" at home and overseas, is contained in a secret bimonthly bulletin, "Significant Counterintelligence Briefs." Known as SCIB, it is issued by the Air Force's Office of Special Investigations.

The Air Force believes that the reports are vital in acquainting its key officers with the background of political dissidence that increasingly faces them among black airmen and others in their commands.

The bulletin is now in its 20th year of secret publication. Only in recent years has it turned toward domestic political problems.

A copy of the bulletin was made available to The New York Times as controversy continued here over the role of Army counterintelligence, which has been shown to have spied on more than 18,000 American civilians from 1967 to 1969.

'Security Problem' Seen

A high-ranking Defense Department official said in an interview this week that the Air Force's Office of Special Investigations fulfilled its "specific responsibility of keeping commanders in the field fully informed" by supplying them with political information that might be related to the "security, mission or viability of United States Air Force bases and other installations."

But Defense Department officials have acknowledged, under questioning, that whether domestic political intelligence should be fed to field commanders raises an issue of propriety.

These officials said that an Air Force commander must be aware of the background and nature of dissidence to be able to deal "intelligently and constructively" with such phenomena as Black Panther memberships on his base.

They said that a "security problem" was involved inasmuch as black airmen were increasingly receiving mailed Panther literature, including leaflets urging them to desert, "destroy the Army from the inside," sabotage equipment and kill officers.

"If only one black airman responds to this sort of appeal and picks up a gun, we may have a tragedy on our hands," a Defense Department official said. "So it is the responsibility of our counterintelligence people to keep the commanders informed about what the black Panthers are doing and saying. We cannot ignore it."

The Air Force asserts that, unlike Army counterintelligence, its Office of Special Investigations has never engaged in collecting information on civilian groups and persons considered radical or subversive.

Uses Data From F.B.I.

The office, according to the Air Force, obtains its basic data from the Federal Bureau of Investigations, local police forces, various United States intelligence agencies and, on occasions involving potential security problems overseas, even from foreign police departments.

But the office, which is the investigative arm of the Air Force Directorate of Special Investigations, headed by Brig. Gen. Joseph J. Cappucci, is the agency that evaluates and analyzes all this data in preparing the secret SCIB reports.

The Air Force's counterintelligence effort in the field of domestic politics differs considerably, therefore, from the operations of the Army, which used its own covert agents to spy on Americans and built a computer bank of data resulting from these investigations.

In the wake of disclosures of the Army's operations, the Defense Department now authorizes only limited intelligence-gathering on incidents that might lead to a Presidential call for Federal troops.

Senate Hearings Slated

The controversy over the Army's activities, and Congressional skepticism over its statement that it has discontinued most of the spying, has led to the scheduling of hearings on Feb. 23 by the Senate Subcommittee on Constitutional Rights, headed by Senator Sam J. Ervin Jr., Democrat of North Carolina.

The House Committee on Government Operations may hold hearings earlier on the domestic counterintelligence activities of the Army, the Air Force and the Navy.

The Air Force's assigned role under the Federal Directorate for Civil Disturbance Planning and Operations, set up in 1968, and Operations, set up in 1968

is to provide airlift capability for troops ordered by the President in the event of major disorders.

A delimitations agreement was signed July 2, 1969, by the members of the United States Counterintelligence Investigative Agencies, as association, including the F.B.I. and Army, Navy and Air Force intelligence. Under the agreement, the Air Force's Office of Special Investigations is responsible for the investigation anywhere of "all activities falling under the categories of espionage, counterespionage, subversion and sabotage" involving "active and retired military personnel of the Air Force."

Restricted Jurisdiction

In all cases involving Air Force civilian employes in the Continental United States, Hawaii, Alaska, Puerto Rico and the Virgin Islands, it is charged with taking whatever actions are necessary as a result of any investigation, although it is not responsible for the inquiry itself. But it has the authority for both investigation and disposal of the cases of Air Force civilian employes abroad.

The Office of Special Investigations, which reports directly to the Inspector General of the Air Force, Lieut. Gen. S. W. Wells, interprets its counterintelligence mission as being essentially restricted to Air Force bases and installations and military and civilian personnel.

Established Requirements

An internal Defense Department document, dated Sept. 9, 1970, and signed by the department's controller, Robert S. Moot, says, "The O.S.I. has established requirements for collecting and reporting information relating to: demonstrations, agitation, propaganda and disruptive activities directed against the role of the United States in Vietnam, Selective Service, or the military establishment which affect the security, mission or viability of United States Air Force bases and other installations."

The office, according to Mr. Moot, is also responsible for information on "civil rights and racial agitations occurring on Air Force bases or involving Air Force personnel."

But the Air Force insists that this "collecting and reporting" is confined to its bases and installations and does not

Black Panther Party Major Subject of Intelligence Unit

include investigations among civilian groups.

Officials said, however, that it would be normal practice for an Air Force commander to be in touch with the F.B.I. and the local police if his base appeared to be threatened by demonstrations or similar activities.

They said that the Office of Special Investigations had no authority to assemble dossiers on Black Panthers in the Air Force because the party is not illegal. They said the office would act only if a Panther engaged in "illegal" activity.

Interviews with Defense Department officials and the contents of the secret intelligence bulletins suggested that the Air Force was principally concerned with the Black Panthers in its midst, along with general antiwar activities.

The officials said that Students for a Democratic Society and its Weatherman faction were not considered a serious security problem.

They said that an increase in Black Panther militancy in the Air Force dated to last autumn, a judgment reflected in the comments in the secret reports.

The SCIB reports, which carry a "secret" stamp on the cover and inside pages, provides Air Force commanders with a counterintelligence digest of "radical" activities at home as well as of Communist and other political or subversive organizations abroad.

The reports offer comment and analysis, such as the conclusion in the bulletin issued Jan. 6, that, while antiwar efforts in the United States diminished in the second half of last year, "this could easily be the calm before another storm."

Newton Activities Discussed

The issue devoted a long section to the activities of Huey P. Newton, minister of defense of the Black Panthers, contending that he was "reportedly discouraged over the poor reception of his speeches" since his release from prison.

However, the bulletin remarked, "The failure of Newton's speaking campaign does not in itself constitute a turning point in Black Panther party fortunes."

The bulletin reported that "the Black Panther party and several black extremist groups affiliated with them" had been "foremost" among those distributing a new "underground manual" throughout the United States.

It described the manual as a "46-page, profusely illustrated pamphlet [that] contains explicit instructions on production of all varieties of explosive and incendiary devices, and for this reason is considered very dangerous in the hands of extremists."

Recent Air Force brief refers to Huey Newton, leader of the Black Panthers, on cover

[image box: SECRET / CONTENTS / SIGNIFICANT COUNTERINTELLIGENCE BRIEFS / OFFICE OF SPECIAL INVESTIGATIONS]

SECRET

SIGNIFICANT COUNTERINTELLIGENCE BRIEFS

OFFICE OF SPECIAL INVESTIGATIONS

Vol. 20 No. 1   DATE 6 Jan 71

* * *

orth Ame .ca

PACIFICATION PUSH BEGUN IN VIETNAM

APR 7 1971

New Program, Most Costly Yet, Aimed at Vietcong's Political Apparatus

By TAD SZULC
Special to The New York Times

WASHINGTON, April 6—The most ambitious and costly pacification program yet planned for South Vietnam has been put into effect by Saigon and Washington.

Reportedly costing the United States considerably more than $1-billion and Saigon an undisclosed sum, the 1971 Community Defense and Local Development Plan would greatly expand pacification activities which are aimed at destroying Communist subversive forces and widening self-government and development.

The 304-page plan, a copy of which was made available to The New York Times, lists as the "top priority" for the year the "neutralization" of the entrenched Vietcong political apparatus.

Authenticity Confirmed

The authenticity of the document was confirmed by Administration sources, who declined to discuss the contents because of the plan's confidential character.

In operation since March 1, and endorsed by the American command in Saigon, the new plan is reportedly the subject of wide controversy among United States officials, some of whom term it unrealistic and artificial.

Administration officials were

Continued on Page 15, Column 1

Big New Pacification Program Started

Continued From Page 1, Col. 1

unable to provide cost figures to the United States for previous pacification programs, but they said that the current plan, financed almost entirely in its military, security and civilian aspects by the Defense Department and the Central Intelligence Agency, was much more costly because of its increased scope.

Acknowledging for the first time that the activities of the Vietcong apparatus remain a major problem in 8 of South Vietnam's 44 provinces, including four in the allegedly pacified Mekong River Delta, and that South Vietnamese forces often prefer to "accommodate, rather than resist, the enemy," the plan provides for:

¶Expansion of the People's Self-Defense Force—the civilian antiguerrilla combat organization in rural areas—from 500,000 to four million. Women would be enlisted in combat units and children of both sexes over the age of 7 in supporting units.

¶Establishment of an elaborate "people's intelligence network" to inform on the enemy.

¶Elimination in the year starting last month, through killing or capture, of 14,400 Vietcong agents under expansion of the three-year-old Operation Phoenix, an intelligence-gathering program that is supported by the United States military.

Wider Social Benefits

The new pacification plan also seeks to complete the program of holding elections in all villages and hamlets; spur land reform by setting a goal of distributing nearly a million acres of land to farmers, and widen social benefits. This would be done by providing new assistance to 216,000 war veterans, and increasing aid to 43,002 disabled soldiers, 33,743 parents of dead servicemen, 71,005 war widows and 284,000 war orphans. In addition, the plan hopes to resettle 430,000 war refugees in new homes.

Other innovations in the 1971 pacification plan include programs for ethnic minorities and for cities where crime is rising.

Elaborated upon by the South Vietnamese Government, approved by President Nguyen Van Thieu and his Cabinet and fully endorsed by Gen. Creighton W. Abrams, the United States commander in Vietnam, the plan is designed to dovetail with the Nixon Administration's policy of Vietnamization, under which combat responsibilities are being gradually assumed by the South Vietnamese forces.

In transmitting the plan to Washington in January, General Abrams wrote in a covering memorandum that "while it is a Government of Vietnam document, it has been thoroughly coordinated" with the United States command and "I strongly endorse the 1971 Community Defense and Local Development Plan and request your full support in its implementation."

"This document will be regarded as guidance, directive in nature, to advisory personnel at all echelons," he wrote.

While the Administration here and the Saigon Government report success for earlier pacification programs, some American experts question their effectiveness so far and are skeptical about the soundness of the new plan.

Their main criticism is that the whole pacification effort depends too much on the 8,000 United States officials and advisers in the Civil Operations and Rural Development Support program, an agency known as CORDS.

The agency, which supervises projects from Operation Phoenix to rural economic programs, is chiefly made up of Defense Department and Central Intelligence Agency employes, although it includes officials of the State Department, the Agency for International Development and the United States Information Agency.

Reports from the field indicate that CORDS officials are frequently not aware of the true state of affairs in districts and villages and that their colleagues in civilian government and the police fail to carry out their tasks.

Critics of the pacification program point to this statement in the 1971 plan:

"In some areas, the people are reluctant to associate with the Government of Vietnam for fear of retaliation by the enemy. Civil officials often become the target of enemy terrorism and assassination and thus are reluctant to perform their government tasks.

"Some police hesitate to conduct operations against the V.C. because they fear retaliation, and local security forces, under the threat of terrorism, often accommodate, rather than resist, the enemy."

The critics also raise the question of what will happen if CORDS is phased out and ask whether the agency may not have to be maintained in South Vietnam indefinitely.

Three Major Objectives

As expressed in the 1971 plan, the over-all concept of pacification consists of the three objectives of "local self-defense, local self government and local self-development."

The philosophy of the program is stated as follows in the plan:

"In his efforts to achieve political control of the Republic of Vietnam, the enemy attempts to demonstrate that the Government of Vietnam is not capable of governing the country or of providing credible security to the people. His offensive operations and the resultant reaction operations by friendly forces produce adverse effects on security of the people. The most effective way of assuring security of the Vietnamese people is to keep enemy forces away from them and by neutralizing the Vietcong infrastructure."

The plan emphasizes that the "strategic concept of national security" is not dependent on the presence of American forces and "paves the way for the transfer of the responsibility for security from military agencies to civilian ones."

To assist this proposed transfer and supervise the new police functions the South Vietnamese and United States Governments have turned to Sir Robert Thompson, the British counterinsurgency expert.

The pacification plan emphasized that among the 1971 targets is the reduction of "enemy terrorist incidents" to 6910. The document did not report how many such incidents occurred in 1970, but said that the current target was to reduce them by 75 per cent in "secure areas" and by 50 per cent in areas "still undergoing pacification."

Statistics included in the plan showed that the military region that includes 15 provinces south of Saigon and in the Mekong Delta poses the most serious security problems.

The delta has been declared by the Saigon Government to be virtually pacified, except for the U Minh Forest area, and all American troops left the area in 1969. But the plan reports serious problems with an entrenched Vietcong apparatus in the provinces of Vinhlong, Dinhtuong, Kienhoa and Anxuyen. Similar problems are reported in Binhdinh province in the central part of the country and in Quangnam, Quangtin and Quangtri Provinces in the northern part.

The plan urges that special police units be assigned to these eight provinces.

To deal with the Vietcong apparatus the plan provides for 700,000 weapons to be issued this year to the People's Self-Defense Forces and for the establishment of the intelligence operation reaching into all of South Vietnam's villages and hamlets.

While the plan offers no over-all cost figures, informed officials here estimated the expense to the United States at $1-billion from Defense Department Funds and an unknown amount from the C.I.A. In the phasing out of CORDS operations, the Agency for International Development has programed $32-million in the 1972 fiscal year for pacification.

No figures are available here for the previous pacification plans but the costs were reported to have been below the 1971 program.

UNITED STATES DISTRICT COURT

SOUTHERN DISTRICT OF NEW YORK

- - - - - - - - - - - - - - - - x

UNITED STATES OF AMERICA,   :

             Plaintiff,   :

             v.   :   AFFIDAVIT

NEW YORK TIMES, et al.,   :   71 Civ. 2662

            Defendants.   :

- - - - - - - - - - - - - - - - x

DISTRICT OF COLUMBIA ss.:

        ROBERT M. SMITH, being duly sworn, deposes and says:

        1. I am a reporter employed by The New York Times engaged in writing articles on matters of military, national or international affairs that are published in the Times.

        2. In such occupation, I have written articles which contained information, received from government sources, which I had reason to believe or suspect was classified.

        3. It is not an uncommon practice for government personnel to make such classified information available to reporters.

Robert M. Smith
                ROBERT M. SMITH

Sworn to before me this

   day of June, 1971.

         Notary Public

UNITED STATES DISTRICT COURT

SOUTHERN DISTRICT OF NEW YORK

- - - - - - - - - - - - - - - - - x

UNITED STATES OF AMERICA,   :

        Plaintiff,   :

        v.   :   AFFIDAVIT

NEW YORK TIMES, et al.   :   71 Civ. 2662

        Defendants.   :

- - - - - - - - - - - - - - - - - x

DISTRICT OF COLUMBIA   ss.:

        WALTER RUGABER, being duly sworn, deposes and says:

        1. I am a reporter employed by the New York Times engaged in writing articles on matters of military, national or international affairs that are published in the Times.

        2. In such occupation, I have written articles which contained information, received from government sources, which I had reason to believe or suspect was classified.

        3. It is not an uncommon practice for government personnel to make such classified information available to reporters.

                                       WALTER RUGABER

Sworn to before me this
    day of June, 1971.

    Notary Public

[The following pages contain copies of exhibits submitted with Mr. Rugaber's affidavit, articles by him copied from The New York Times.]

Walter Rugaber

PX System: One of Most Powerful and Least Visible Re

ARMED FORCES

BY WALTER RUGABER

Special to The New York Times

WASHINGTON, Feb. 26—A Government agency operating with an aggressive and largely unfettered management has built an obscure string of stores into one of the largest, most powerful and least visible retail enterprises in the world.

It enjoys a substantial Federal subsidy, an exclusive license to trade on American military installations throughout the world, and a firm hold on nearly 5 per cent of the nation's consumers.

But it labors under few of the controls imposed on most Government units. There are no anxious sessions with the Budget Bureau, no annual appearances before Congress and no sudden visits from auditors in the General Accounting Office.

There is from time to time a vague uneasiness about this curious institution, known broadly as the military exchange system and informally as "the PX," or post exchange.

7 Are Indicted

Yesterday, a Federal grand jury in New York indicted seven former and present employes of an exchange unit in Europe on charges that they had accepted kickbacks in return for placing large PX orders with an American sales representative.

There is no doubt that others among the more than 115,000 people who work for the exchange system not only have taken bribes but also have stolen money directly from cash registers and have pilfered merchandise from stores and warehouses.

Thefts and the like, along with innocent bookkeeping errors and shoplifting by patrons, cost the Army and Air Force exchange organization $22.3-million in one year. This amount included a $12-million shortage in Vietnam.

The $22.3-million is just over 1 per cent of sales, which compares favorably with the experience of many civilian outlets. Losses in many American stores have been increasing lately, and shortages of 3 per cent and more are said to be common.

Luxuries in Vietnam

Many of the exchange system's difficulties have been traced to Vietnam, where the PX has offered Americans an array of home-front luxuries unheard of in any other war, and has created tremendous business opportunities.

Specific abuses help attract attention. The Federal grand jury in New York is likely to continue its bribery investigation, and the staffs of at least two Congressional committees have been making inquiries about the exchanges.

The General Accounting Office has tried more than once to inspect the PX records and has been turned down each time. But it recently has made still another approach, and there is some prospect of an audit.

There are questions much broader and more intricate than kickbacks and black markets, however. About general operating policies, relatively little is known, and there is uneasiness about that fact alone.

"Off the record," remarked a source with broad knowledge of the exchanges, "I think it's bad, just as a matter of public policy, to have an operation that big without anybody keeping up with what's going on inside."

Civilian Retailers' View

Small civilian retailers are convinced that the exchanges are dangerous and unfair competitors that ought to be abolished entirely or at least reduced to the sale of a few very

consequential enough to those who think of a PX as the homely, out-of-the-way place where servicemen buy cigarettes and chocolate bars and nylon stockings at cut-rate prices.

A Venturesome Organization

The reality, however, is a venturesome merchandising organization that sells mutual funds, baby furniture, diamonds, automobiles and tape recorders; invests in sophisticated computers, and buys in huge volume to drive down prices.

More than $3.1-billion in annual sales rank the military exchange system above Montgomery Ward, F.W. Woolworth, S.S. Kresge, W.T. Grant, and every other chain in the United States except Sears, Roebuck and J.C. Penney.

While exchanges do business on a global basis and sell, according to one estimate, at an average of 35 per cent below list price, the profits rarely fall under 5.5 per cent of sales, and thus exceed those of any major competitor.

The most profitable civilian retailer, Sears, Roebuck, reported a net income of 5.1 per cent on sales. The exchanges have the advantage of a Federal tax exemption.

Their gains are divided between individual services, welfare and recreation funds and exchanges' reserves. The exchanges some $110-million donated to the funds is about equal to direct subsidies for items such as overseas shipping of merchandise.

theoretically responsible to the services and — much more ultimately and theoretically — to an Assistant Secretary of Defense.

The exchanges are an instrument of the Government only because of some indirect statutory reference and court decisions. There is no formal legislative authority; their only real charter is a collection of military regulations.

Relatively little of the money is appropriated by Congress, and it probably would be impossible to identify in the Federal budget. Most funds are generated by servicemen's purchases and therefore are considered beyond regular scrutiny.

Two of the military departments have formed the Army and Air Force Exchange Service, which dominate the service exchange field by making more than 70 per cent of the sales and establishing much greater centralization and control.

More than 98 per cent of the Army and Air Force Exchange Service's 80,000 employes are neither military men nor civil servants but workers with their own pay scales, insurance programs and retirement benefits.

Thin Military Layer

Many of these men and women have been running things for years. Above them is a thin layer of military officers, a single chief executive, a board of directors composed largely of widely separated generals, and two or three men in the Pentagon.

The military executives are regularly rotated. All the directors have other jobs and their strictly private meeting are said by several sources to mask a somewhat limited knowledge of exchange operations.

The Pentagon frequently is not consulted on policy, a recently obtained civilian study reports, and the tiny staff there is described as mainly "a problem solver rather than a problem preventer."

The most recent public hearings before a Congressional committee were held 13 years ago. The panel was concerned exclusively with one of the periodic battles over the items to be sold in domestic exchanges.

A 4-Page List

The House Armed Services

subjective and could be difficult to explain.

"Flexibility" is an article of faith with Brig. Gen. George C. McCord, the 52-year-old Air Force officer currently running the Army and Air Force Exchange Service from its new, six-story, well-appointed headquarters in Dallas.

"We operate essentially as a commercial corporation does,"

he said. "We're quite different from the Department of Interior. Does anybody from outside look at Sears, Roebuck or Montgomery Ward?"

Annual Audit

The exchange can react to special circumstances such as the build-up in Vietnam more smoothly than military commissaries (grocery stores). It is

widely agreed that the traditional restraints hobble it badly.

If the PX was subject to the appropriations process, General McCord argues, take six months if you ever get the money at all."

General McCord argues that he is hardly on his own. There is an audit each year by a civilian firm. The exchange service checks major issues with the Armed Services committee staff, much as business checks price increases with the White House.

More important, there is an extensive system of internal controls, and its civilian head, Robert K. Jamison, is not an auditor but a man with more than 25 years experience with PX operations in the field.

"The emphasis is not on getting two and two and getting four," Mr. Jamison says. There are shelves full of regulations and his staff is blunt and unforgiving about the most serious and most trivial transgressions. Some examples are:

¶Tailoring contracts in Vietnam were extended with no increase in the fees paid by concessionaires. Under pressure officials exacted an additional per cent "without much effort," but meanwhile the exchanges lost more than $103,000.

¶Officials in Vietnam taking their orders on sales, were considering items that had been unavailable, and helped reduce shortages. Twelve of 15 main stores were out of safety matches, and a main depot had seen none for eight months.

¶A food concessionaire at Fort Benning, Ga., was reprimanded of contract specializing-minded of contract specifications-after he had sold steak sandwiches

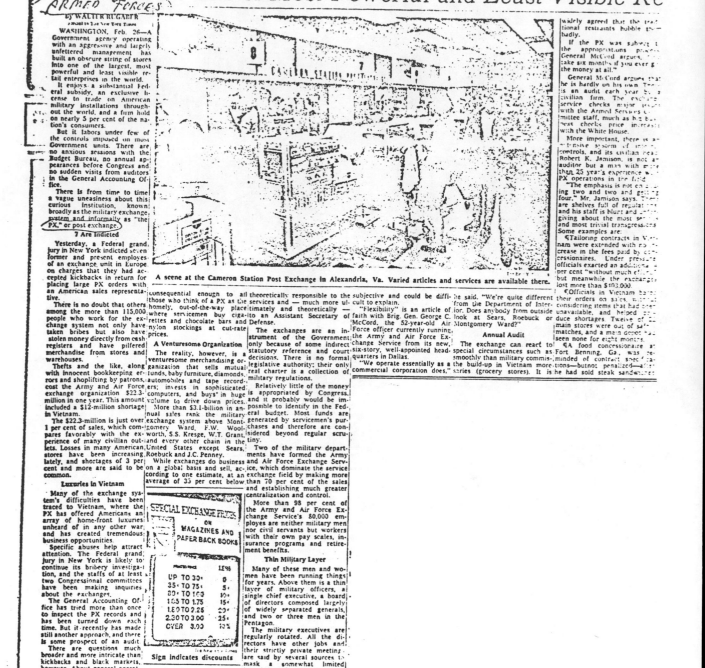

A scene at the Cameron Station Post Exchange in Alexandria, Va. Varied articles and services are available there.

SPECIAL EXCHANGE PRICES ON MAGAZINES AND PAPER BACK BOOKS

PRINTED PRICE	LESS
UP TO 30¢	0
35¢ TO 75¢	5¢
80¢ TO 100¢	10¢
105 TO 1.75	15¢
1.80 TO 2.25	20¢
2.30 TO 3.00	25¢
OVER 3.00	10%

Sign indicates discounts

million in one year. This amount included a $12-million shortage in Vietnam.

The $22.3-million is just over 1 per cent of sales, which compares favorably with the experience of many civilian outlets. Losses in many American stores have been increasing lately, and shortages of 3 per cent and more are said to be common.

Luxuries in Vietnam

Many of the exchange system's difficulties have been traced to Vietnam, where the PX has offered Americans an array of home-front luxuries unheard of in any other war and has created tremendous business opportunities.

Specific abuses help attract attention. The Federal grand jury in New York is likely to continue its bribery investigation, and the staffs of at least two Congressional committees have been making inquiries about the exchanges.

The General Accounting Office has tried more than once to inspect the PX records and has been turned down each time. But it recently has made still another approach, and there is some prospect of an audit.

There are questions much broader and more intricate than kickbacks and black markets, however. About general operating policies, relatively little is known, and there is uneasiness about that fact alone.

"Off the record," remarked a source with broad knowledge of the exchanges, "I think it's bad, just as a matter of public policy, to have an operation that big without anybody keeping up with what's going on inside."

Civilian Retailers' View

Small civilian retailers are convinced that the exchanges are dangerous and unfair competitors that ought to be abolished entirely or at least reduced to the sale of a few very basic necessities.

Big business, for its part, sees the military market not only as an important outlet for its products but also as a valuable promoter of sustained brand loyalties among a predominantly young and susceptible customer population.

Individual Senators and Representatives receive endless appeals from both forces and intervene for this side or that, always with discretion and generally with effect. Congressmen fire off dozens of letters to the exchanges each week.

The managers wield great power under pressure, the pressure applied by others and the pressure of their own aims. The process often makes them nervous and defensive, and serves to heighten the suspicions held by others.

'Cover-up' Alleged

"I feel more strongly than ever that there is a cover-up," a frustrated businessman said after losing a major contract under what he considered questionable circumstances, "because the reply is weak and evasive." He was referring to the exchange system's reply to his complaints.

Exchange officials decide which products to buy and place on the shelves — and which ones to ignore. Favored items can become "musts," which require every store in the world to keep them in stock at all times.

Pleasing the men on active duty, and their families, is important to the Pentagon. The exchanges are a major fringe benefit, so considered in pay arrangements, and they influence re-enlistment rates.

The consumers are indifferent to the established wishes of Congressmen and other outsiders who want a limited PX. The people who shop in them want a bigger and bigger exchange, and in that they have been well accommodated.

The business may seem in-

---

volume to drive down prices.

More than $3.1-billion in annual sales rank the military exchange system above Montgomery Ward, F.W. Woolworth, S.S. Kresge, W.T. Grant and every other chain in the United States except Sears, Roebuck and J.C. Penney.

While exchanges do business on a global basis and sell, according to one estimate, at an average of 35 per cent below

SPECIAL EXCHANGE PRICES ON MAGAZINES AND PAPER BACK BOOKS

UP TO 35¢	0
35¢ TO 75¢	5¢
80¢ TO 1.00	10¢
1.05 TO 1.75	15¢
1.80 TO 2.25	20¢
2.30 TO 3.00	25¢
OVER 3.00	10%

Sign indicates discounts

list price, the profits rarely fall under 5.5 per cent of sales, and thus exceed those of any major competitor.

The most profitable civilian retailer, Sears, Roebuck, reported a net income of 5.1 per cent on sales. The exchanges have the advantage of a Federal tax exemption.

Their gains are divided between individual services, welfare and recreation funds and the exchanges' reserves. The some $110-million donated to the funds is about equal to direct subsidies for items such as overseas shipping of merchandise.

Fuel For the Boom

The PX boom is fueled only in part by the higher troop levels brought about by the war in Vietnam. At least as important to its rise is the response by its consumers to the explosion of brands, advertising and display.

More and more of the outlets on military bases are simply modern department stores. More than 20,000 items often are laid out in an attractive, neon-lit, tiled and carpeted expanse that covers a half-acre or more.

"What a far cry from the old days of 20 or more years ago when I was on active duty," said a retired serviceman who had just strolled through one of the exchange system's elaborate emporiums.

Whatever the troop levels, the individual patron is buying more in the PX. Per capita sales in Army and Air Force exchanges have climbed dramatically from $536 in 1960 to $834 in 1969.

Outsiders interested in this increasingly successful system find even its most fundamental aspects, such as organization, a forbidding tangle of imbalance, contradiction, interrelation and exception.

The Army, Navy, Air Force, Marines and Coast Guard all have exchanges ultimately and

---

and it probably would be impossible to identify in the Federal budget. Most funds are generated by servicemen's purchases and therefore are considered beyond regular scrutiny.

Two of the military departments have formed the Army and Air Force Exchange Service, which dominate the service exchange field by making more than 70 per cent of the sales and establishing much greater centralization and control.

More than 98 per cent of the Army and Air Force Exchange Service's 80,000 employees are neither military men nor civil servants but workers with their own pay scales, insurance programs and retirement benefits.

Thin Military Layer

Many of these men and women have been running things for years. Above them is a thin layer of military officers, a single chief executive, a board of directors composed largely of widely separated generals, and two or three men in the Pentagon.

The military executives are regularly rotated. All the directors have other jobs and their strictly private meetings are said by several sources to mask a somewhat limited knowledge of exchange operations.

The Pentagon frequently is not consulted on policy, a recently obtained civilian study reports, and the tiny staff there is described as mainly "a problem solver rather than a problem preventer."

The most recent public hearings before a Congressional committee were held 13 years ago. The panel was concerned exclusively with one of the periodic battles over the items to be sold in domestic exchanges.

'A 4-Page List'

The House Armed Services Committee first drew up a list of "authorized" merchandise and maximum prices in 1948, and it has amended this document in private negotiations and public sessions several times since.

The accepted products march with precision and solemnity down four single-spaced pages. There are, for example, "bags, shoulder," "bags, garment and laundry," and "bags, sleeping, including mattress."

The Congressmen added electric blankets, coffeemakers and portable typewriters in 1957. They raised the cost limits on girdles and garter belts from $4.50 to $10 in 1965, and they approved sport coats and surfboards in 1967.

Certain goods are conspicuously missing. The committee always had made it a point to check exchange suggestions with lobbyists for the relevant retail association, and some never survive the process.

A serviceman may buy gasoline, oil, batteries, and auto accessories such as seat covers and luggage racks, but not tires. He may purchase radios, tape recorders and record players, but not television sets.

The exchange system defends its independence with much persistence and determination. Many of its judgments, like judgments generally, are

0.

Visible Retailing Enterprises

widely agreed that the traditional restraints hobble them badly.

If the PX was subject to the appropriations process. General McCord argues, "it'd take six months if you ever got the money at all."

General McCord argues that he is hardly on his own. There is an audit each year by a civilian firm. The exchange service checks major issues with the Armed Services Committee staff, much as big business checks price increases with the White House.

More important, there is an extensive system of internal controls, and its civilian head, Robert K. Jamison, is not an auditor but a man with more than 25 year's experience with PX operations in the field.

"The emphasis is not on adding two and two and getting four," Mr. Jamison says. There are shelves full of regulations, and his staff is blunt and unforgiving about the most serious and most trivial transgressions. Some examples are:

¶Tailoring contracts in Vietnam were extended with no increase in the fees paid by concessionaires. Under pressure, officials exacted an additional 4 per cent "without much effort," but meanwhile the exchanges lost more than $403,000.

¶Officials in Vietnam based their orders on sales, without considering items that had been unavailable, and helped produce shortages. Twelve of 22 main stores were out of safety matches, and a main depot had seen none for eight months.

¶A food concessionaire at Fort Benning, Ga., was reminded of contract specifications—butnot penalized—after he had sold steak sandwiches

for 45 cents instead of 40 cents and had served three ounces of meat instead of four.

¶The exchange headquarters leased office space from a prominent businessman, James S. Lee, and violated command regulations by paying the rent for a full year in advance and by paying more than the officially established ceiling.

Detailed Regulations

The regulations are systematic and handy and detailed enough to produce the complaints from auditors that a few documents were not "securely fastened" to their file folders. But sometimes things are not so pat.

There is considerable evidence that the exchanges lack enough really broad review, an independent skepticism that is aimed at entire ventures and policies and is difficult to mount from within. Some examples include the following:

¶Impatient with the Pentagon's pace in providing store facilities from appropriated funds, the exchanges simply started building their own and

spent $151-million before a startled Congress asked for a "clarification of procedures."

¶The Army and Air Force Exchange Service has poured its goods into Vietnam despite a notorious and thriving black market, allowing no more than 7 per cent of its total customers, in the midst of a war, to account for 15 per cent of its sales.

¶With scarcely a word to anyone, the exchanges began awarding single worldwide contracts to one or two large companies, thus abruptly dropping many smaller concerns though many customers like wider selections.

¶Concessionaires are loosely controlled, especially in Vietnam where many operate entirely on their own, and companies that supply shoddy goods or commit other infractions are rarely penalized or even named.

"We're almost forced to give a guy a second chance all over again," an official remarked, "because invariably you're called on to justify whatever you've done through political channels."

G.I.-Businessman Group Sells Millions in Goods to Army Clubs

SEP 26 '69

WALTER RUGABER

WASHINGTON, Sept. 25—A group of soldiers and former soldiers owns a company that has been selling millions of dollars worth of supplies to servicemen's clubs, including those around the world. They

The conduit for this operation is the Meredem Company, a highly profitable concern that lists among its stockholders Sgt. Maj. William O. Woolridge, who served for two years as the first Sergeant Major of the Army.

The operation has come to light at a time when Congress and the Defense Department are studying reports of widespread abuse in the club system. The Senate Permanent Subcommittee on Investigations is scheduled to begin

hearings on the subject next week.

The service clubs are part of an officially sanctioned enterprise at military installations servicemen's clubs. They took in more than $275-million last year from Army personnel alone.

While no Federal funds are

Continued on Page 24, Column 1

NEWS INDEX

G.I.'s and Ex-G.I.'s Are Owners of Company That Sells Mill.

Continued From Page 1, Col. 8

directly involved in the club operations, the clubs depend on more than $17-million in dues and the money that soldiers spend in them for food, drink and entertainment.

The Meredem Company's soldier-businessmen, long involved in the purchasing activities of such service clubs, have formally organized what one of them called a "buddy-buddy system."

Meredem has sales placed at from $3-million to $4-million annually and, according to a reliable financial source, returned a gross profit of $250,000 on the first $1-million it took in.

One of the men with a financial interest in the company placed sizable orders with it while he served as the custodian of about 32 service clubs within the First Infantry Division in Vietnam.

A second stockholder provided the corporation with substantial business while managing another series of clubs. He was replaced a few weeks ago in his most recent club job at the Redstone Arsenal near Huntsville, Ala.

A third soldier who invested in Meredem is Sergeant Woolridge, a veteran of three wars who became the Army's ranking enlisted man upon his selection in July, 1966, as Sergeant Major of the Army.

Although Sergeant Woolridge has not been in a position to trade with the company himself, he has been influential in the club system and has been counted a valuable ally by at least one of his business associates.

The company's dealings are particularly important in the context of a broader controversy that has brought intense official scrutiny to the esoteric but extensive financial operations on military bases in this country and abroad.

There have been persistent reports to officials in Washington that these activities include kickbacks in the arrangement of entertainment for the troops, mismanagement in post exchanges, and improper ties between military men and unsavory civilians.

There is concern in Washington that the reported abuses, should they go unchecked, may become more and more widespread, corrupting the climate of career Army life and the routine that makes it work.

Study by Senate Panel

Much of this concern, both in and out of the military, is focused on the service clubs.

Both the Senate Permanent Subcommittee on Investigations and the Army's Criminal Intelligence Division are engaged in an extensive study of club operations in the Far East, Europe and the United States.

Members of the subcommittee staff have spent about four months in Vietnam, and the panel is scheduled to open hearings next Tuesday. The sessions are expected to continue for about five weeks.

Senator Abraham A. Ribicoff, the Connecticut Democrat who is acting chairman of the subcommittee, said in an interview last week that he did not want to comment on specific issues or "prejudge the case."

But he said, "Even though the funds aren't appropriated [by Congress] they do involve the funds of military personnel, and I think they should be getting full value [with] no one skimming off funds for their own benefit."

Mr. Ribicoff called for "a reappraisal of the entire military practice in this field" and said that he would propose, among other safeguards, "more rigid auditing and supervision" in the administration of service clubs.

The Pentagon announced last month that it had about 40 agents working on the club inquiry and that "the contracts and purchases which are being reviewed have a total value in the millions of dollars."

At the same time, Defense

Building at edge of municipal airport in Fullerton, Calif., which houses Meredem Company

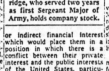

Sgt. Maj. William O. Wooldridge, who served two years as first Sergeant Major of Army, holds company stock.

or indirect financial interest which would place them in a position in which there is a conflict between their private interest and the public interests of the United States, particularly those related to their duties and responsibilities as Department of the Army personnel."

Details of the Meredem operations were obtained by The New York Times from a number of sources, and it was apparent that the subcommittee had collected additional privately held information for its projected hearings.

The Meredem stockholders, named in records filed with the California Department of Corporations in Los Angeles, are all sergeants or former sergeants with years of service in the army.

Seymour Lazar, the company president, spent 23 years on active duty, became a master sergeant and officially retired Jan. 1, 1968. Because of accumulated leave, he left the service a month or so earlier.

2 Remain In Service

Theodore D. Bass, the vice president, was honorably discharged June 22, 1966, before the apparent organization of the Meredem company. Narvaez Hatcher retired on Nov. 1, 1968, after the corporation was established.

Two other stockholders have remained on active duty. Sgt. William Higdon is based at the Redstone Arsenal, and Sergeant Wooldridge is at the White Sands Missile Range in New Mexico.

Mr. Hatcher, who now lives in Gulf Breeze, Fla., said in a telephone interview recently that the five men first met "many years" ago and that they often served together at various posts.

They were in Germany in

five men talked about organizing a business to supply the service clubs for several years before the Meredem concern was set up.

The date of its birth is vague but the concern placed its first orders with the Diamond Head Food Company of Los Angeles, a manufacturer of snack items, in December, 1967.

About this time, Mr. Lazar, then retired from the Army, appeared in Mr. Haar's offices in Stanton, Calif., and arranged to become the sales representative in Vietnam for the bar equipment that had brought the two together in Germany.

The equipment consists of tanks, hoses and a nozzle that dispenses soft drinks and mixers. In addition to outright sales at $1,895 a unit, Mr. Haar said he had $400,000 worth of equipment on lease to military clubs overseas.

In a signed statement provided to The New York Times, Mr. Haar said his business records showed that, at the direction of Meredem, he had shipped bar equipment to clubs in Vietnam managed by Sgt. Higdon and Mr. Hatcher.

Also, John Hosterman, sales manager of Diamond Head, referred to records in a recent interview in his office and said that Meredem had directed his company to ship goods to the same clubs.

Mr. Hatcher acknowledged that Meredem started in business "late in 1967" and said that all five of the present stockholders had been initial investors. They were, he remarked, "just a bunch of soldiers getting together."

Better Position Sought

"The purpose of the company was to better our own position and to give the soldier what he wanted," the former sergeant continued. "It's like a buddy-buddy system, that's all."

Mr. Hatcher explained that he was the custodian for some 32 clubs while serving with the First Infantry Division in Vietnam last year. He was questioned about placing orders with Meredem.

"You'd buy from anybody you could get it from," he said. Pressed as to whether that specifically included his own company, Mr. Hatcher replied, "I imagine."

When the retired soldier was asked whether he considered his purchases a conflict of interest, he said, "You could show that you could get a cheaper price from them [Meredem]."

In answer to another question, Mr. Hatcher said that Sergeant Wooldridge was an "old-time friend" who, it was believed, could help advance the company because of a "good personality" and an ease in meeting people.

Sergeant Wooldridge, reached at the White Sands Missile Range, declined to discuss his role in Meredem or anything

source familiar with the concern's activities noted, "nuts ain't 'peanuts'" manufacturer whose orders include peanuts said that Meredem's orders had run to figure sums.

While the company must do its manufacturing so promptly, there can be significant delays in collecting the military clubs, and Meredem's accounts receivable been placed as high as $300,000.

Such figures appear common in this field. One company halted direct dealings with the clubs because of difficulties in carrying the amount. But Meredem evidently retained the necessary financial

After operating for a time as Meredem, Ltd., the concern was incorporated in California as Marmed, Inc., on Sept. 1968, but filed notice that it would do business as the Meredem Company.

For reasons that are not entirely clear, the company decided to issue shares formally and, under a state securities law that went into effect this year, filed a notice listing five owners on Feb. 20.

Profit for Clubs

The clubs that Meredem and other concerns supply can operate with Federal funds, with dues and the money that members spend while in them. The Army earned a net profit of $5 million last year.

Their administrators appear to be heavily local. The clubs buy their supplies individually, the prices charged them are set separately, and auditing is carried out by various installation commanders.

focused on the service clubs.

Both the Senate Permanent Subcommittee on Investigations and the Army's Criminal Intelligence Division are engaged in an extensive study of club operations in the Far East, Europe and the United States.

Members of the subcommittee staff have spent about four months in Vietnam, and the panel is scheduled to open hearings next Tuesday. The sessions are expected to continue for about five weeks.

Senator Abraham A. Ribicoff, the Connecticut Democrat who is acting chairman of the subcommittee, said in an interview last week that he did not want to comment on specific issues or "prejudge the case."

But he said, "Even though the funds aren't appropriated [by Congress] they do involve the funds of military personnel, and I think they should be getting full value [with] no one skimming off funds for their own benefit."

Mr. Ribicoff called for "a reappraisal of the entire military practice in this field" and said that he would propose, among other safeguards, "more rigid auditing and supervision" in the administration of service clubs.

The Pentagon announced last month that it had about 40 agents working on the club inquiry and that "the contracts and purchases which are being reviewed have a total value in the millions of dollars."

At the same time, Defense Secretary Melvin R. Laird ordered the services to study "the procedures now employed in the handling of funds" for military clubs and to submit a report on the survey last week.

Medal Is Revoked

"This report should contain recommendations for any changes which may be necessary to make certain that these clubs function in the best interests of their members and in strengthening morale," the Secretary said.

Neither the report nor any of the Army's findings have been made public, but the Pentagon has supplied information to the Senate "in recognition of the potential serious ness of some of the matters under investigation."

Earlier this month, the Defense Department disclosed that it had revoked the Distinguished Service Medal held by Sergeant Wooldridge on the ground that he "did not deserve the award."

The department did not elaborate nor bring any charges against the sergeant, but both the Pentagon and the subcommittee are aware of his financial interest in Meredem.

Asked for specific comment on the company, the Pentagon declined on the ground that to comment "on any particular activity which may be under investigation at this time would be inappropriate."

In response to another inquiry, a spokesman cited an Army regulation that bars servicemen from "having any direct

ations were obtained by the New York Times from a number of sources, and it was apparent that the subcommittee had collected additional privately held information for its projected hearings.

The Meredem stockholders, named in records filed with the California Department of Corporations in Los Angeles, are all sergeants or former sergeants with years of service in the army.

Seymour Lazar, the company president, spent 23 years on active duty, became a master sergeant and officially retired Jan. 1, 1968. Because of accumulated leave, he left the service a month or so earlier.

2 Remain In Service

Theodore D. Bass, the vice president, was honorably discharged June 22, 1966, before the apparent organization of the Meredem company. Narvcaz Hatcher retired on Nov. 1, 1968, after the corporation was established.

Two other stockholders have remained on active duty. Sgt. William Higdon is based at the Redstone Arsenal, and Sergeant Wooldridge is at the White Sands Missile Range in New Mexico.

Mr. Hatcher, who now lives in Gulf Breeze, Fla., said in a telephone interview recently that the five men first met "many years" ago and that they often served together at various posts.

They were in Germany in 1964 and 1965, and Phillip M. Haar, a major distributor of bar equipment to military clubs, encountered each of them on a sales mission to Europe at that time.

Sergeant Higdon and Mr. Bass were then managers of separate service clubs. Mr. Hatcher was the custodian for 10 or 12 clubs in the Augsburg area, and Mr. Lazar served as his deputy.

Served In Same Areas

Mr. Haar said that, in arranging to place his equipment in the clubs under Mr. Hatcher's jurisdiction, four members of a supervisory board of governors met with him to negotiate on costs. One of them was Sergeant Wooldridge.

A striking characteristic of the Meredem group is the regularity with which its members turned up in subsequent years at the same Army installations and in the same kinds of jobs.

Mr. Lazar, Sergeant Higdon and Mr. Bass all went from Germany to Fort Riley, Kan. There was intermittent scattering, but several of the men were in Vietnam together and Mr. Hatcher replaced Mr. Lazar as a custodian there in 1967.

Sergeant Wooldridge served his two-year tour as Sergeant Major of the Army at the Pentagon and was the leading adviser there on enlisted men's affairs. Last year, he was transferred to the Vietnam command.

Mr. Hatcher said that the

that Meredem started in business "late in 1967" and said that all five of the present stockholders had been initial investors. They were, he remarked, "just a bunch of soldiers getting together."

Better Position Sought

"The purpose of the company was to better our own position and to give the soldier what he wanted," the former sergeant continued. "It's like a buddy-buddy system, that's all."

Mr. Hatcher explained that he was the custodian for some 32 clubs while serving with the First Infantry Division in Vietnam last year. He was questioned about placing orders with Meredem.

"You'd buy from anybody you could get it from," he said. Pressed as to whether that specifically included his own company, Mr. Hatcher replied, "I imagine."

When the retired soldier was asked whether he considered his purchases a conflict of interest, he said, "You could show that you could get a cheaper price from them [Meredem]."

In answer to another question, Mr. Hatcher said that Sergeant Wooldridge was an "old-time friend" who, it was believed, could help advance the company because of a "good personality" and an ease in meeting people.

Sergeant Wooldridge, reached at the White Sands Missile Range, declined to discuss his role in Meredem or anything else. Efforts to reach Sergeant Higdon were unsuccessful, and Mr. Bass was said to be out of the country.

Business Is "Substantial"

Mr. Lazar said that his attorney, Lawrance William Steinberg of Beverly Hills, had instructed him to make no statements. Mr. Steinberg explained that he had based this advice on the ground that no charges had been made against Mr. Lazar.

A source close to Mr. Lazar, the company president, said that Meredem was not organized before Mr. Lazar's release from the Army and that, while "it did do a fairly substantial business and did do it fairly soon," it charged competitive prices.

The source acknowledged that Mr. Lazar had worked in service clubs "in one function or another at least sometime" and that as a result "he felt there is an honest dollar to be made by serving their needs."

Mr. Lazar had observed, the source continued, "that the products in these clubs were not what they might be, that the prices were high, that the quality [of items] was often deteriorated."

The Meredem company's handsomely furnished offices are tucked away in a one-story concrete block building on the edge of the municipal airport in Fullerton, Calif., an Orange County suburb of Los Angeles.

The corporation reportedly has a work force of 13 people,

Owners of Company That Sells Millions in Supplies to Servicemen's Clubs

airport in Fullerton, Calif., which houses Meredem Company

five men talked about organizing a business to supply the service clubs for several years before the Meredem concern was set up.

The date of its birth is vague but the concern placed its first orders with the Diamond Head Food Company of Los Angeles, a manufacturer of snack items, in December, 1967.

About this time, Mr. Lazar, then retired from the Army, appeared in Mr. Haar's offices in Stanton, Calif., and arranged to become the sales representative in Vietnam for the bar equipment that had brought the two together in Germany.

The equipment consists of tanks, hoses and a nozzle that dispenses soft drinks and mixers. In addition to outright sales at $1,895 a unit, Mr. Haar said he had $400,000 worth of equipment on lease to military clubs overseas.

In a signed statement provided to The New York Times, Mr. Haar said his business records showed that, at the direction of Meredem, he had shipped bar equipment to clubs in Vietnam managed by Sgt. Higdon and Mr. Hatcher.

Also, John Hosterman, sales manager of Diamond Head, referred to records in his office and said that Meredem had directed his company to ship goods to the same clubs.

Mr. Hatcher acknowledged that Meredem started in

including six salesmen overseas who are said to work on a commission. None of the six could be identified.

There are no apparent manufacturing or warehousing facilities. Meredem acts as a middle man, lining up orders in service clubs for goods that it then obtains from other concerns.

Some of the supplies are literally peanuts, but, as one

source familiar with the concern's activities noted, "Peanuts ain't 'peanuts'." One manufacturer whose products include peanuts said that Meredem's orders had run to six-figure sums.

While the company must pay its manufacturing sources promptly, there can be significant delays in collecting from the military clubs, and Meredem's accounts receivable have been placed as high as $500,000.

Such figures apparently are common in this field. One company halted direct dealings with the clubs because of difficulties in carrying the amounts. But Meredem evidently obtained the necessary financing.

After operating for a time as Meredem, Ltd., the concern was incorporated in California as Marmed, Inc., on Sept. 3, 1968, but filed notice that it would do business as the Meredem Company.

For reasons that are not entirely clear, the company decided to issue shares formally and, under a state securities law that went into effect this year, filed a notice listing the five owners on Feb. 20.

Profit for Clubs

The clubs that Meredem and other concerns supply do not operate with Federal funds but with dues and the money their members spend while relaxing in them. The Army clubs earned a net profit of $15.8-million last year.

Their administration appears to be heavily local. The clubs buy their supplies individually, the prices charged members are set separately, and the auditing is carried out by the various installation commanders.

The General Accounting Office, the Congressional auditing agency, has been rebuffed in several efforts to study the handling of nonappropriated funds. The military has cited the absence of Federal money.

Some Government investigators believe that, behind the reported abuses, there is a wide pattern of kickbacks by salesmen to individual managers. The amounts are said to range from 5 to 10 per cent on purchases.

Such arrangements would bring in sums of five figures often enough to make traditional Army grafting seem insignificant. That possibility makes up part of the background for the more spectacular aspects of the current investigations.

UNITED STATES DISTRICT COURT

SOUTHERN DISTRICT OF NEW YORK

- - - - - - - - - - - - - - - - - x

UNITED STATES OF AMERICA,   :

                    Plaintiff,   :

          v.   :   AFFIDAVIT

NEW YORK TIMES, et al.,   :   71 Civ. 2662

                    Defendants.   :

- - - - - - - - - - - - - - - - - x

DISTRICT OF COLUMBIA ss.:

          JOHN W. FINNEY, being duly sworn, deposes and says:

          1. I am a reporter employed by The New York Times
engaged in writing articles on matters of military, national
or international affairs that are published in the Times.

          2. In such occupation, I have written articles which
contained information, received from government sources, which
I had reason to believe or suspect was classified.

          3. It is not an uncommon practice for government
personnel to make such classified information available to
reporters.

                                        John W. Finney
                                          JOHN W. FINNEY

Sworn to before me this

_____ day of June, 1971.

_____
      Notary Public

[The following pages contain copies of exhibits submitted with Mr. Finney's affidavit, articles by him
copied from The New York Times.]

                         422

John W. Finney

By JOHN W. FINNEY
Special to The New York Times

WASHINGTON, Dec. 21—The Defense Department has drafted long-term requirements for its nuclear arsenal that would call for a substantial cutback in the production of atomic weapons in the coming decade.

The Pentagon requirements presented to the White House are being studied by the Atomic Energy Commission, which has the legal and fiscal responsibility for building and paying for the weapons.

Some differences of opinion have developed between the Defense Department and the commission over the future requirements and how to scale down the production of fissionable materials for weapons.

General Agreement

But on all sides there is now general agreement that, with an arsenal filled with tens of thousands of warheads, the time is approaching when weapons production must be curtailed.

The only basic questions that remain to be resolved are how and when to begin the cutback. The answers to these questions involve economic and political considerations that in many ways are more complex than the military requirements.

The planned cutback would represent the first significant reversal in the upward trend of weapons production that has prevailed ever since World War II. The dramatic increases have come in the last decade as the commission expanded its production capability and the Pen-

Continued on Page 26, Column 4

2 Die 9 Hurt in

than a reduction in plutonium production.

Economic Impact

About 5,200 persons are employed at the three gaseous diffusion plants—less than half the number employed at the Hanford and Savannah River plutonium centers.

But more important is the indirect employment provided by the gaseous diffusion plants through their tremendous consumption of electricity. About 6 per cent of the nation's total electrical capacity goes to run the plants, and the energy for this electricity comes largely from coal mined in West Virginia, Ohio, Tennessee, Illinois and Kentucky.

Because of this combination of military, economic and political complications, it now appears unlikely that any substantial reduction in weapons production will be reflected in the budget that the Administration will present to Congress in January.

It is a decision, however, that the Johnson Administration will have to make before too long another year and studies aimed at making pete cuts.

U.S. WEIGHS CURB ON A-ARMS OUTPUT

Continued From Page 1, Col. 4

tagon developed warhead requirements for every weapon from a bazooka to an intercontinental missile.

A decade ago, for example, the commission spent $758 million for mining uranium, processing weapons materials and developing and producing atomic weapons. By 1962 the expenditures had risen to $1.9 billion, including funds for an extensive test series.

The first steps to reverse this trend came in 1962 when President Kennedy directed the military to cut back its requirements. The Kennedy move, in turn, set in motion the long-range studies that resulted in the current recommendations for far more substantial reductions in weapons production.

Within the commission there has been a growing realization in recent years that its capacity to produce fissionable materials was beginning to outstrip the military demand for weapons.

In 1960-61, the commission belatedly realized that a huge surplus of uranium was accumulating and began stretching out the deliveries of ore and scaling down its refinement.

This stretchout, however, was not reflected in any sizeable cutback in the production of weapons. Rather, the pressure from both the military and the Joint Congressional Committee on Atomic Energy was for increasing production, particularly of smaller weapons.

Pattern Changed

Now this pattern of gearing requirements to production capacity has been broken. In place of an annual determination, the Defense Department has outlined its long-term requirements until 1973. These requirements, particularly in the later years, fall far short of the commission's production capacity.

Translating these reduced requirements into production cutbacks, however, is not proving to be a simple, straightforward matter for the commission or the Administration.

Part of the difficulty is in establishing now what kind of weapons and warheads the Pentagon will be needing a decade hence. For example, a decision to develop an antimissile missile system would greatly increase the demand for weapons materials.

Further complicating the projections are economic considerations, such as how soon an atomic power industry will need the uranium that is now largely going into weapons.

There also are political complications, for any cutbacks will fall heavily on regions, some already economically depressed, that are highly dependent upon the atomic business and powerfully represented on Capitol Hill.

In 1959-60, for example, the Joint Chiefs of Staff, under prodding from the Congressional committee, drafted long-term requirements that called for production of large numbers of small weapons. These requirements were used as the initial justification for the large plutonium-producing reactor now being completed at Hanford, Wash.

In the last year, two interrelated developments, one policy, the other administrative, have served to check the upward trend in weapons production.

'Overkill' Questioned

At the White House level there has been a growing concern over the proliferation of small atomic weapons throughout military commands. Questions have also been raised as to whether the military was not acquiring an "overkill" capacity in its nuclear arsenal.

This changing attitude at the White House level was reflected in a significant change in the method of determining military requirements for atomic weapons.

Until now it has been the practice of the Pentagon to submit an annual "build order" for atomic weapons. This order, in turn, was based largely on the capacity of the commission to produce the weapons.

The disagreement between the Pentagon and the commission spring in part from differing approaches in projecting the future requirements for

weapons material. In its calculations, for example, the Defense Department makes little allowance for the materials that might be needed for such future weapons as the antimissile missile or the medium range ballistic missile.

Furthermore, the Defense Department projections are based largely on existing weapons technology and make little allowance for the fact that by using more plutonium, better warheads could be developed for existing weapons.

Even within the commission, however, it is acknowledged that in the reasonably near future, probably some time after 1965, the production of weapons materials will exceed military requirements.

Sources of Materials

There are now two sources of fissionable material: the plutonium that is turned out by eight reactors at Hanford, Wash., and the five reactors at Savannah River, S.C., and the enriched uranium that is produced by gaseous diffusion plants at Oak Ridge, Tenn.; Paducah, Ky., and Portsmouth, Ohio.

From a strictly technical standpoint, any cutback probably would fall most heavily on enriched uranium production.

While enriched uranium is cheaper pound for pound, plutonium has technical advantages for fabricating weapons, particularly in the smaller sizes. For example, it takes roughly three times as much enriched uranium as plutonium to make a critical or explosive mass.

Furthermore, plutonium is still in relatively tight supply. In contrast, a large surplus—some commission officials have estimated it will amount to about $1 billion by 1966—is building up of enriched uranium.

It is at this point, however, that the problem of how and where to cut back the production of weapons materials gets involved in economic and political considerations.

Enriched uranium can be used as a fuel for atomic power plants; the potentiality of plutonium as a fuel has not yet been developed.

A cutback in uranium production also could be expected to have a broader economic impact

---

secrecy for the last year.

The first indication that the Administration was re-examining the steadily increasing production of atomic weapons came at a secret White House meeting on May 4, 196. President Kennedy approved an order at that time directing the Pentagon to cut its orders for nuclear warheads, particularly small, battlefield-type weapons, by several thousands.

In terms of the cutbacks now being considered, the Presidential order was relatively small. But symbolically the decision marked the point at which the Government began serious consideration of the question whether the United States, after 17 years of ever-increasing production and billions of dollars of investment, had reached the point where it had built as many nuclear weapons as it really needed.

The impetus for the current re-examination was said to have come more from the Bureau of the Budget and White House advisers than from the Defense Department. In general, the Defense Department was reported to endorse the current rate of weapon's production.

Long-Term Guide Sought

The objective of the current study is to establish for the first time the long-term requirements of the military for atomic weapons. It would then try to determine if these requirements will permit a shutting down of some of the industrial complex built up by the commission in the last decade to refine or transmute uranium ore and fabricate the resulting enriched uranium or plutonium into weapons.

The establishment of long-term requirements for atomic weapons has always proved to be a peculiarly difficult problem, both from a military and a budgetary standpoint.

In a budgetary situation unique within the Government, the Defense Department has been in a position where it could order atomic weapons and have them paid for by another agency, the A.E.C.

Thus, the Pentagon was not under the normal budgetary restraints of balancing its atomic requirements against all its other needs. Only in recent months has the Administration attempted to correct this situation by requiring the Pentagon to submit a cost estimate along with orders for atomic weapons.

Despite repeated efforts and Congressional prodding, the Pentagon has never really been able to define its long-term requirements for atomic weapons. Instead, as a practical matter it has tended to fix these requirements on a year-by-year basis. The requirements, in turn, have generally been tailored to the commission's capability to produce atomic weapons.

Question of 'Overkill'

In the current efforts to establish long-term requirements, the underlying issue is whether the United States is now approaching a surfeit of atomic weapons or perhaps even has acquired an unnecessarily large "overkill" capability.

But into the discussions enter equally imponderable issues. Questions are raised as to atomic weapons would ever be used in limited wars, on the possibility of developing new weapons systems—such as an anti-missile missile missile — that might suddenly require large new amounts of weapons material and on the political and economic repercussions that could follow a sharp cutback in weapons production.

The "overkill" question is one that is being argued with increasing vehemence, particularly since there is no simple answer.

From a strictly numerical standpoint, if every weapon were used, there is general agreement that the United States has more than enough weapons to knock out the Soviet Union and to defend the United States. As one policy-making official in the weapons field put it:

"We have tens or hundreds of times more weapons than we would ever drop even in an all-out war, and we have had more than we needed for at least two years."

The counter-argument raised by the military is that a surplus of warheads is necessary because in a wartime situation it cannot be assumed that all the weapons will be available for use. In some ways, that situation is analogous to that during World War II, when the pipe... filled with million of...

U.S. WEIGHS SLASH IN A-ARMS OUTPUT

Continued From Page 1, Col. 1

gressional sources, has been treated as top secret by the Administration. It was apparently somewhat premature and a source of some embarrassment to disarmament planners.

According to Congressional sources, the Administration had been considering a proposal at the high-level disarmament talks opening in Moscow in mid-July that both sides shut down some of their weapons material plants. Now that it has been disclosed that the United States is planning unilaterally to shut down some of its plutonium production reactors, the proposals obviously has lost some of its bargaining and propaganda appeal.

No decision has been reached on cutting weapons production, but there is some hope that a choice can be reached by this fall between several plans now under consideration. Even among the strongest proponents of weapons production, it is now accepted that some of the 13 plutonium reactors—eight at Hanford, Wash., and five at Savannah River in Aiken S. C. will be shut down in the next two or three years.

Secrecy Dropped

The effect of the Pentagon official's statements was to bring out into the open a study that has been going on within the Administration in tightest secrecy for the last year.

The first indication that the Administration was re-examining the steadily increasing production of atomic weapons came at a secret White House meeting on May 4, 196. President Kennedy approved an order at that time directing the Pentagon to cut its orders for nuclear warheads, particularly small, battlefield-type weapons, by several thousands.

In terms of the cutbacks now being considered, the Presidential order was relatively small. But symbolically the decision marked the point at which the Government began serious consideration of the question whether the United States, after 17 years of ever-increasing production and billions of dollars of investment, had reached the point where it had built as many nuclear weapons as it really needed.

The impetus for the current re-examination was said to have come more from the Bureau of the Budget and White House advisers than from the Defense Department. In general, the Defense Department was reported to endorse the current rate of weapon's production.

Long-Term Guide Sought

The objective of the current study is to establish for the first time the long-term requirements of the military for atomic weapons. It would then try to determine if the requirements will permit a shutting down of some of the industrial complex built up by the commission in the last decade to refine or transmute uranium ore and fabricate the resulting enriched uranium or plutonium into weapons.

The establishment of long-term requirements for atomic weapons has always proved to be a peculiarly difficult problem, both from a military and a budgetary standpoint.

In a budgetary situation unique within the Government, the Defense Department has been in a position where it could order atomic weapons and have them paid for by another agency, the A.E.C.

Thus, the Pentagon was not under the normal budgetary restraints of balancing its atomic requirements against all its other needs. Only in recent months has U. S. Administration attempted to correct this situation by requiring the Pentagon to submit a cost estimate along with orders for atomic weapons.

Despite repeated efforts and Congressional prodding, the Pentagon has never really been able to define its long-term requirements for atomic weapons. Instead, as a practical matter it has tended to fix these requirements on a year-by-year basis. The requirements, in turn, have generally been tailored to the commission's capability to produce atomic weapons.

Question of 'Overkill'

to be certain that the ammunition was available where needed.

The question of whether the United States was developing an unnecessarily large "overkill" capability began to emerge only in the last couple of years as the atomic weapons suddenly multiplied.

Until the later part of the last decade, a year's production of atomic weapons was numbered in the hundreds. But then, starting about 19.8, there was a rapid increase in output.

The reason was a large expansion between 1951 and 1955 in the facilities for producing enriched uranium and plutonium for weapons. During this period the commission placed in operation three plutonium production reactors at Hanford and five at Savannah River.

In addition, gaseous diffusion plants to turn out enriched uranium were placed in operation at Paducah, Ky., and Portsmouth, Ohio, and three new units were added to the original diffusion plant at Oak Ridge, Tenn.

The expansion was also explained by still-secret advances made in the more economic use of fissionable materials, particularly in what had been considered "dirty" forms of plutonium, and in the emphasis placed upon the development of battlefield weapons.

Plutonium Output Unabated

From public and private actions taken by the A.E.C. in the last two years, it has become apparent that a surplus, particularly of enriched uranium, was developing. Publicly, the commission stretched out its purchases of uranium ore, 90 percent of which is going into weapons. With little public attention, the commission began

cutting the rate of enriched uranium production.

Thus far, however, the commission has not slowed the rate at which the reactors are turning out plutonium for weapons. One reason is that in the last two years there has been a decided shift in the research effort to the development and production of plutonium weapons.

Within both Congress and the Executive branch, it is recognized that any move to cut production of weapons materials would run into resistance from regional and political interests, powerfully represented on the Joint Congressional Atomic Energy Committee.

From the plants that refine the uranium ore to the centers and laboratories that fabricate the materials into atomic weapons, more than 100,000 persons are engaged in the development and production of atomic weapons. In addition, countless miners are digging the uranium ore.

To ease the economic and political impact, therefore, it is being urged by influential members of the Congressional Atomic Energy Committee that any cutback finally decided upon by the Administration should be gradual rather than abrupt and phased out over several years.

U. S. CONSIDERING CUT IN ITS OUTPUT OF ATOMIC ARMS

JUN 30 1963

Growing Number Assigned to Forces Raises Fear of Accidental Explosion

Weapons

PLANTS MAY BE CLOSED

Arsenal Believed Equal to Possible Military Needs, and Perhaps Excessive

By JOHN W. FINNEY
Special to The New York Times

WASHINGTON, June 29 — The Administration is giving serious consideration to ordering the first substantial cutback in the production of atomic weapons since the United States began building up its nuclear arsenal after World War II.

Behind the current study is a belief that the United States with an arsenal of tens of thousands of atomic weapons, has a sufficient and perhaps an excessive number of nuclear arms to meet its military needs.

There also is rising concern in high Administration circles over the multiplying number of warheads that have been assigned to the military forces in the last five years. The major fear is that a continuing production would only increase the chances of accidental explosion or unauthorized use of the weapons.

Cites 'Growing Concern'

The concern is also beginning to be shared in the Joint Congressional Committee on Atomic Energy, which in the past has been an influential force prodding the Administration to expand production, particularly of small atomic weapons.

In a recent draft version of a report on Atomic Energy Commission legislation, the committee for the first time publicly emphasized "its past and growing concern with the steady and high production rate of material for atomic weapons."

In the final version, in the interest of historical accuracy the report was changed to have the committee "strongly reiterate its past and continuing concern with the method of establishing requirements for weapons material."

Discussion Embarrassing

The language was somewhat milder but behind both statements was a suspicion of many committee members that the production of atomic weapons was coming to be based more on the capabilities of the Atomic Energy Commission to manufacture them than on the actual requirements of the military.

In a "background meeting" with Pentagon reporters this week, a highly placed Defense Department official raised the possibility that it might be possible to make a $1,000,000 cut in the commission's $1,000,000,000 annual budget for weapons production.

The official's discussion of a subject that, according to Con-

Continued on Page 9, Column 1

WARHEAD FOR ABM TERMED OBSOLETE

MAY 3 0 1971

Scientists Cast Doubt on Big H-Bomb Device Slated for Test Blast in Aleutians

By JOHN W. FINNEY

Special to The New York Times

WASHINGTON, May 29—The Atomic Energy Commission is spending $190-million to test-fire an antimissile warhead that it contends is vital for national defense but that some scientists allege is obsolete.

At that cost, the underground test, scheduled for this October on the Aleutian island of Amchitka, will be one of the most expensive ever conducted by the commission. It is also proving to be one of the most controversial.

The test will involve a thermonuclear warhead developed for the Spartan missile, the long-range interceptor in the Safeguard missile defense system. Designed to destroy attacking missiles with huge bursts of X-rays in the vacuum of space, the Spartan warhead would have an explosive force of nearly five megatons—the equivalent of five million tons

Continued on Page 40, Column 2

Continued From Page 1, Col. 5

of TNT. The commission has never publicly stated the specific purpose of the test but has argued that, in "the development of nuclear weapons technology," it is "of prime significance to our national security requirements."

Various scientific groups opposed to an antimissile system now contend that the warhead has become outmoded.

They contedn that the warhead was originally designed for an antimissile system that was supposed to provide a defense of heavily populated areas of the United States against a small attack, such as might be launched by Communist China. Now that the mission of the Safeguard system has been changed to one of providing defense for Minuteman offensive missile bases, they argue that such a large warhead is no longer needed.

In order to contain the radioactivity from the unusually large underground explosion, the warhead will be detonated at the bottom of a 6,000-foot well that has been drilled through the volcanic rock of the isolated island.

In response to inquiries, a commission spokesman said that the test was estimated to cost $190-million and that $160-million has already been spent.

High Cost of Drilling

Much of the cost of the test, code-named Cannikin, has resulted from the difficult engineering task of drilling the well, 120 inches in diameter at the top and 54 inches in diameter in the lower part. Also included in the cost were a one-megaton "calibration shot," which was conducted on the island in October, 1969, to test the effects of a large underground explosion, and extensive environmental studies.

Much of the opposition to the Cannikin test has centered on the contention that the explosion could have adverse environmental effects. Testifying this week before the Senate Appropriations Committee, for example, the United Nations Association, which was instrumental last year in Congress's deferment of funds for the test, complained that the commission was minimizing the environmental hazards and overstating the defense value of the test.

Testimony In Alaska

In a revised "environmental impact statement" issued last month, the commission said it was "highly unlikely" that the explosion would trigger a severe earthquake and "even more unlikely" that it would cause a damaging seismic tidal wave. The report also contended that radioactivity from the explosion would be "trapped deep underground."

The argument that the warhead, first conceived five years ago, is irrelevant to the changed mission of the Safeguard system, was made yesterday by Dr. Jeremy J. Stone, director of the Federation of American Scientists, in testifying before an A.E.C. board in Anchorage, Alaska.

"Basically," he said, "Cannikin is a bureaucratic oversight—an experiment that has been waiting to be canceled since, in early 1969, the President changed the rationale for the U.S. ABM away from the anti-Chinese system."

So long as the United States was proposing to build an anti-Chinese system, he conceded there was a need for multi-megaton warheads that could provide a curtain of X-rays over the nation against a small-scale attack.

But now that the Safeguard mission has been reoriented for protection of Minuteman bases, he said, there was no longer a "compelling necessity" for the large Spartan warhead.

For defense of Minuteman bases against a large-scale Soviet attack, he said, the primary reliance will be placed on short-range Sprint missiles, carrying relatively small warheads, with the Spartan at best playing a supplementary role in attempting to intercept some of attacking missiles before they enter the atmosphere.

The case for Cannikin, he said, has been "further undermined" by the Defense Department's announced intention to develop an "improved Spartan" with a warhead of "much lower yield." The "improved Spartan" is designed to give the Safeguard system a greater ability to intercept submarine-launched missiles as well as intercontinental missiles fired with a depressed trajectory so as to avoid detection.

"Many defense planners," Dr. Stone said, "believe that, in essence, there is nothing important which basic Spartan can do that improved Spartan cannot do better."

TONKIN SHIP CITED SONAR DIFFICULTY

FEB 4 - '68

Senate Unit Notes Message Sent Before '64 Attack

By JOHN W. FINNEY
Special to The New York Times

WASHINGTON, Feb. 3 — A Senate Foreign Relations Committee staff study has disclosed that the destroyer Maddox encountered technical difficulties with its sonar shortly before detecting a torpedo attack by North Vietnamese PT boats in the Gulf of Tonkin.

The disclosure was described by Senators on the committee as one of the most significant points developed in the still secret staff study of the Tonkin Gulf incidents in early August, 1964.

Committee members believe the disclosure raises further questions about the reliability of the evidence on which the Administration based its conclusion that the Maddox and another American destroyer, the Turner Joy, had come under North Vietnamese attack the night of Aug. 4.

In reprisal for the attack some 65 miles off the coast of North Vietnam, the Administration immediately ordered the first bombing raids against North Vietnam. It also obtained Congressional approval of a joint resolution that was later to be interpreted by the State Department as the "functional equivalent" of a declaration of war against North Vietnam.

The Pentagon's Explanation

On the basis of the evidence thus far made public by the Pentagon, it appears that the Administration's conclusion that an attack had occurred was based in large measure on reports from the Maddox that her sonar had detected numerous torpedoes fired by the North Vietnamese PT boats.

The Turner Joy detected no torpedoes, a fact that is now explained by the Defense Department on the ground that the Turner Joy had a more advanced, lower-frequency type of sonar not particularly adapted to picking up shallow-running torpedoes.

The Maddox alone had been attacked two days earlier.

In the course of its re-examination of the Tonkin incidents, the Senate committee staff discovered that, some six hours before the Aug. 4 attack began, the Maddox sent a message reporting a "matériel deficiency" in her sonar. "Matériel deficiency" is a term used by the Navy for technical difficulties in equipment.

In response to inquiries by The New York Times, the Defense Department declined to discuss the matériel deficiency message on the ground that "details of the maintenance record of the sonar of the Maddox are classified."

Reported Working Later

The Defense Department offered no explanation as to why it felt it necessary for security reasons to keep classified these records, now nearly four years old. But the Pentagon did feel free under its security regulations to say, "At the time of the attack, the sonar was working well."

If the Maddox's sonar had been repaired by the time of the attack, as suggested by the Pentagon statement, this fact apparently was unknown by higher military and civilian authorities who were assessing the Maddox's reports of a torpedo attack.

According to committee members, the committee staff, which had access to the messages sent and received by the Maddox, found no subsequent message from the Maddox reporting that the matériel deficiency had been corrected. Nor did the staff study show that during the attack higher authorities had sent any message to the Maddox inquiring about her sonar state of repair.

McNamara to Testify

As a result of the staff study, the Foreign Relations Committee decided this week to reopen the Tonkin inquiry with further testimony from Secretary of Defense Robert S. McNamara. Mr. McNamara has agreed to testify in closed session on Feb. 20.

In reopening its inquiry, the committee is not so much questioning whether the Aug. 4 attack took place, although some members have doubts on this point.

Rather, the committee is interested in exploring the command-and-control procedures followed by the Administration in gathering and assessing reports from the two destroyers and in reaching a determination to undertake military retaliation against North Vietnam. It is taking this view particularly in light of North Korea's recent seizure of the American intelligence ship Pueblo.

Committee members who were not inclined to reopen the inquiry acknowledged privately that they had been "swung around" by the staff study, ordered last fall by Senator J. W. Fulbright, Democrat of Arkansas, the committee chairman.

In the opinion of committee members, the study raised serious questions as to whether the Administration had conclusive proof of the Aug. 4 attack before it ordered the air strikes against North Vietnam eight hours later.

In addition, the study was reported to have turned up apparent discrepancies in the original accounts of the attacks as presented by Mr. McNamara and Secretary of State Dean Rusk in testimony before the Senate Foreign Relations and Armed Services Committees on Aug. 6, 1964.

One "gross disparity" was cited this week by Senator Wayne Morse, Democrat of Oregon, in a speech in Portland, Ore. Senator Morse disclosed that at the Aug. 6 hearing he asked a series of questions, subsequently censored from the published testimony by the State Department. He had questioned whether the two American destroyers were "party to or had any knowledge" of the raids undertaken a few days earlier by South Vietnamese boats against two North Vietnamese islands in the Gulf of Tonkin.

Mr. Morse said that Mr. McNamara's answer had been, "No, they were not party to them and had no knowledge of them."

But Senator Morse said that information uncovered by the staff study, in an examination of the destroyer logs and messages, was "entirely opposite" from the answers given by Mr. McNamara.

Two days before the Maddox first came under attack on Aug. 2, South Vietnamese PT boats shelled Hon Me and Hon Ngu, islands to the north in the Gulf of Tonkin. It has been Senator Morse's contention that the presence of the American destroyers in the neighborhood "could not help but lead North Vietnam to assume that our destroyers were in some way associated with the South Vietnamese raids."

Another question raised in the staff study, according to Foreign Relations Committee members, is how the destroyers, which were engaged in high-speed, evasive maneuvers, would have been able to detect torpedoes with their sonar in the Aug. 4 engagement. At speeds of about 18 knots, such turbulence builds up around the sonar dome beneath the hull of a destroyer that the sonar has only limited detection capabilities, particularly against such a small object as a torpedo.

The Defense Department, in response to inquiries by the New York Times, declined to give the speed of the destroyers at the time the torpedoes were detected by the Maddox. All the Pentagon would say was that "the destroyer speeds varied up to 31 knots and further details are classified."

It is possible that the detection limitations imposed by speed could have been overcome in part if the sonars were operating in the passive mode, listening for the whine given off by the torpedo screws, rather than in the active mode, attempting to bounce sound signals off the torpedoes. The Defense Department, however, declined to say whether the sonars were operating in the passive or active mode.

Position Is Modified

Since the Aug. 6 testimony, the Defense Department has modified several points in its original accounts of the Aug. 4 attack. For example, it is no longer contending that the destroyers came under automatic weapons fire, as was asserted at the time by Mr. McNamara. The Pentagon is also acknowledging that at most one or two torpedoes were fired, instead of the "many torpedoes" initially cited by Mr. McNamara.

The Pentagon introduced a new modification today by lowering the reported speed of the North Vietnamese PT boats. In his Aug. 6 testimony, Mr. McNamara stated that the PT boats had closed rapidly on the destroyers at "speeds in excess of 10 knots."

Former PT boat officers have raised doubts with the committee staff as to whether North Vietnamese craft could have maintained such speeds in the open seas, where the waves, according to the Pentagon, were running two to three feet high, and in warm tropical waters that reduce the efficiency of the boats' engines.

When presented with these doubts, the Pentagon, in response to inquiries, said the speeds of the North Vietnamese boats "varied but at times were in excess of 30 knots."

The modification on the speed of the PT boats raises questions, in turn, about the reliability of the original radar reports showing the boats to be first paralleling and then closing in on the destroyers. The Pentagon declined to discuss whether on the night of Aug. 4 there were peculiar atmospheric conditions, such as have been reported by some crew members on the two destroyers, that could have produced misleading radar reflections. The Defense Department said that "information about radar performance is classified."

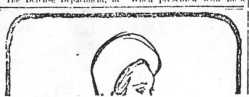

Move to Counter Fulbright's Tonkin Investigation Cites Secret Intelligence

JAN 21 '68

By JOHN W. FINNEY
Special to The New York Times

WASHINGTON, Jan. 20—The Administration has been seeking to dissuade Senator J. W. Fulbright from pursuing his inquiry into the 1964 Gulf of Tonkin incidents by suggesting it has secret intelligence information confirming that American destroyers were attacked by North Vietnamese PT boats.

Shortly before Christmas, it was learned, the Administration sent Paul H. Nitze, the Deputy Secretary of Defense, to Capitol Hill with the mission of persuading Senator Fulbright to call off the inquiry by the Senate Foreign Relations Committee staff into the Tonkin incidents.

In a private meeting with Mr. Fulbright, the committee chairman, Mr. Nitze was understood to have argued that the Administration had conclusive proof that North Vietnam had ordered a deliberate attack against the destroyers Maddox and Turner Joy on the night of Aug. 4, 1964, in the Gulf of Tonkin.

Radio Messages Cited

As part of the proof, Mr. Nitze was said to have cited "special intelligence" information, consisting of North Vietnamese radio messages monitored by United States electronic intelligence stations.

The incidents — an attack Aug. 2 on the Maddox and an attack Aug. 4 on the Maddox and Turner Joy—marked a decisive turning point in the American involvement in the Vietnam war. After the second incident, the Administration ordered the first bombing strikes against North Vietnam and obtained Congressional approval of a resolution endorsing "all necessary measures" taken by the Administration to prevent further aggression.

The Fulbright inquiry, quietly under way for nearly six months, will reach its own decisive turning point Wednesday at a meeting of the Foreign Relations Committee. At the meeting, Senator Fulbright will present the results of his inquiry thus far and ask for a decision by the committee on whether it wants to undertake a formal investigation of the incidents.

In response to inquiries, the Defense Department refused to confirm or deny the existence of such "special intelligence" information, saying only that the Administration had "verified evidence" that the destroyers had been attacked before ordering retaliatory air strikes against North Vietnam.

It was not immediately clear whether the electronics intelligence cited by Mr. Nitze included radio messages commanding the North Vietnamese PT boats to attack the destroyers or whether such intelligence information was available to the Administration prior to its decision to retaliate against North Vietnam.

Orders An Inquiry

In any event, it was apparent that Senator Fulbright did not find the intelligence information persuasive. A few days after the meeting with Mr. Nitze he publicly announced that he had ordered the committee staff to conduct an inquiry to "clear up uncertainties" about the Gulf of Tonkin incidents.

Within the committee, Mr. Fulbright is likely to find himself in a difficult political position. Personally, he is known to believe that a further investigation may be warranted, but he cannot advocate this step too forcefully without being accused of wanting to undertake a personal vendetta against the Administration on its Vietnam policy.

The committee's decision is likely to be influenced in large measure by a staff report to be submitted at the meeting. Based on ship logs, messages and other information made available by the Defense Department. The staff study is a detailed, chronological account of the two engagements with some analysis of the reliability of the evidence used by the Administration in reaching its decision.

The staff report is said not to question that the second attack took place, but it is believed to raise questions as to whether the Administration had conclusive proof of the attack before retaliating, some eight hours after the attack was concluded, in retaliation against North Vietnam.

In large part, the Defense Department ...

fast craft paralleling and then that the North Vietnamese craft closing in on the destroyers were engaging in harassing or sonar detection of "numerous" torpedoes fired at the destroyers. The basic question being raised, at least by implication, in the staff report, is a question whether this evidence was conclusive and reliable enough to warrant the Administration's small, fast object as a torpedo decision.

There is some evidence, uncovered in the staff study, that who have examined all the evidence are acknowledging that the sonar reports of "numerous" torpedoes undoubtedly were erroneous and that "at most two or more likely only one torpedo" was fired at the destroyers. The "special intelligence" in-

the destroyer radars were encountering atmospheric interference during the Aug. 4 engagement. Even assuming the radar was working correctly, however, the question remains whether the radar tracks were proof of attack or showed only "numerous" perhaps menacing maneuvers. The evidence of attack is thus largely reduced to the sonar detection of the torpedoes. But a question is being raised as to the reliability of the sonar, particularly in detecting such a small, fast object as a torpedo moving near the surface. Privately, some defense officials who have examined all the evidence are acknowledging that the sonar reports of "numerous" torpedoes undoubtedly were erroneous and that "at most two or more likely only one torpedo" was fired at the destroyers. The "special intelligence" in-

formation cited by Mr. Nitze, therefore, could become of crucial importance in buttressing the Administration's case. But it has not yet been presented to the committee staff, although the Defense Department reportedly had promised the staff it would turn over "all available evidence."

One possible explanation for the Administration's reluctance to provide the "special intelligence" information may be that it would raise a question as to whether the then monitoring the North Vietnamese PT boats were on "routine patrol" in the Gulf of Tonkin, as repeatedly asserted by the Administration.

Shortly before the Aug. 2 attack, the Maddox reportedly was in and out of the 12-mile territorial waters claimed by North Vietnam. On the day prior to the Aug. 4 attack, the Maddox and Turner Joy steamed for North Vietnamese territorial waters and then turned out to sea at dusk.

There are indications that the two destroyers had been alerted, presumably on the basis of electronic intelligence, to expect an attack and had been instructed to continue on their patrol after the task group commander had suggested the destroyers should leave the area.

Fulbright Says McNamara Deceives Public on Tonkin

Asserts Secretary Offered One-Sided Account of '64 Raids in Gulf—Morse Declares Destroyer Was Spy Ship

By JOHN W. FINNEY
Special to The New York Times

WASHINGTON, Feb. 21 — Senator J. W. Fulbright, chairman of the Senate Foreign Relations Committee, accused Secretary of Defense Robert S. McNamara today of deceiving the American public by presenting a one-sided story of the Gulf of Tonkin incidents.

The Senator suggested that the Defense Secretary was suppressing information that

Fulbright text, excerpts from Morse speech, Page 14.

cast doubt on whether two American destroyers came under North Vietnamese attack in August, 1964.

At the same time, Senator Wayne Morse, Democrat of Oregon, took issue on the Senate floor with the Secretary's assertion that one of the destroyers, the Maddox, was on routine patrol.

"The Maddox," Senator Morse said, "was a spy ship under instruction to stimulate the electronic instruments of North Vietnam to carry out a spying activity. That is not a routine patrol for a destroyer."

Senator Fulbright, an Arkansas Democrat, issued a statement challenging the reliability of what Mr. McNamara called "highly classified and unimpeachable" intelligence information demonstrating beyond doubt that the destroyers had been attacked.

Mr. McNamara told of the intelligence report yesterday as the Senate Foreign Relations Committee began hearings on the Administration's handling of the Tonkin incidents. The incidents, involving North Vietnamese attacks on Aug. 2 and Aug. 4 against American destroyers, marked a turning point in American involvement in Vietnam and led to the decision to carry the war to North Vietnam.

Now, three and a half years later, the Senate committee wants to know whether the Administration had sufficient proof of the second PT boat attack on the destroyers Maddox and Turner Joy to warrant its decision to bomb North Vietnam and get Congressional approval.

Continued on Page 15, Column 1

FULBRIGHT REBUTS M'NAMARA REPORT

Continued From Page 1, Col. 6

proval of "all necessary measures" to repel aggression.

Instead of resolving committee doubts with his testimony, Mr. McNamara has apparently precipitated what was expected to be a brief investigation into an angry political confrontation.

In their indignation, committee members began throwing angry personal charges at the outgoing Secretary of Defense and disclosing secret information about the Tonkin incidents that could prove politically embarrassing to the Administration in an election year.

In part, the indignation of the Senators was provoked by Mr. McNamara's action in making public his testimony without the approval of the committee. But beyond this point of protocol, some committee members were irate over what they regarded as the one-sided, self-serving nature of Mr. McNamara's testimony.

Mr. Fulbright charged that the Defense Secretary had presented "only one side of the story" and had suppressed information that did not serve his case. The Senator declared: "Secretary McNamara's statement is a classic example of selective declassification of security material. Everything related to the Tonkin incidents is 'secret' except that which the Pentagon dems should be made public. This, I believe, deceives the American public."

For example, the Senator said, the Defense Secretary has refused to release information that raises questions about the detection of torpedoes by sonar on the Maddox and task force messages that indicated doubts about the second attack.

But at the same time, Mr. Fulbright went on, the Defense Secretary saw fit to discuss secret intelligence information apparently obtained by monitoring North Vietnamese radio circuits.

In reply to Senator Fulbright, the Defense Department issued a statement tonight saying: "The charge the Defense Department has suppressed information suggesting no attacks were made on the destroyers Maddox and Turner Joy in the Gulf of Tonkin is totally without foundation."

In the course of a day of statements to reporters, Senator Fulbright had not made such a specific charge. Rather, he repeatedly suggested that the Administration was withholding information raising doubts about the reliability of the evidence available to the Administration when it decided upon retaliation against North Vietnam.

In his statement yesterday, Mr. McNamara based his case largely on this intelligence information, which he described as being of "a highly classified and unimpeachable nature."

This information, he said, showed that North Vietnamese naval forces had been ordered to attack the two destroyers and then that the North Vietnamese PT boats reported they were involved in an engagement and had lost two boats.

On the basis of their reading of the intelligence reports, both Senator Fulbright and Senator Albert Gore, Democrat of Tennessee, challenged whether the intelligence information provided "unimpeachable" proof of an a—

On—e different points, Sen—re said the intelli—

mentally sound, the Senator said, but such action represents "a threat to anyone who is willing to tell the truth about this or any other incidents."

Senator Fulbright said in his statement that he agreed with Mr. McNamara's assertion yesterday that it would be "monstrous" to suggest that the United States had induced the incidents as an excuse to carry the war to the North.

"But is is equally monstrous," the Senator continued, "to insinuate that any member of the committee holds such an opinion."

At the same time Senator Morse, a colleague on the committee, said he thought that the destroyers' mission "constituted picking a fight, that it constituted a hostile action, that it constituted an action on the part of the United States seeking to try to get the North Vietnamese to involve themselves in a dispute with us, entirely uncalled for, if peace was what he wanted."

At a late afternoon meeting called by Senator Fulbright, the committee decided to make public next week all the McNamara testimony — not just the prepared statement released by the Pentagon.

Morse Speaks in Senate
By E. W. KENWORTHY
Special to The New York Times

WASHINGTON, Feb. 21—A study prepared by the staff of the Senate Foreign Relations Committee asserts that the destroyer Maddox was under orders in 1964 to take provocative action in order to induce the Chinese Communists and North Vietnamese to turn on their radio and radar so the destroyer could monitor them. This finding led Senator Wayne Morse, Democrat of Oregon, to take issue today on the Senate floor with testimony by Secretary of Defense Robert S. McNamara on Aug. 6, 1964, and again yesterday, in which Mr. McNamara said the Maddox was "on routine patrol."

"He calls it a 'routine patrol,'" Mr. Morse said. "The Maddox was a spy ship under instruction to stimulate the

that raises questions about the detection of torpedoes by sonar on the Maddox and task force messages that indicated doubts about the second attack.

But at the same time, Mr. Fulbright went on, the Defense Secretary saw fit to discuss secret intelligence information apparently obtained by monitoring North Vietnamese radio circuits.

In reply to Senator Fulbright, the Defense Department issued a statement tonight saying: "The charge the Defense Department has suppressed information suggesting no attacks were made on the destroyers Maddox and Turner Joy in the Gulf of Tonkin is totally without foundation."

In the course of a day of statements to reporters, Senator Fulbright had not made such a specific charge. Rather, he repeatedly suggested that the Administration was withholding information raising doubts about the reliability of the evidence available to the Administration when it decided upon retaliation against North Vietnam.

In his statement yesterday, Mr. McNamara based his case largely on this intelligence information, which he described as being of "a highly classified and unimpeachable nature."

This information, he said, showed that North Vietnamese naval forces had been ordered to attack the two destroyers and then that the North Vietnamese PT boats reported they were involved in an engagement and had lost two boats.

On the basis of their reading of the intelligence reports, both Senator Fulbright and Senator Albert Gore, Democrat of Tennessee, challenged whether the intelligence information provided "unimpeachable" proof of an attack.

On three different points, Senator Gore said, the intelligence reports obtained from intercepted North Vietnamese radio messages contained information that "was completely in error." He said this fact was not disclosed by the Secretary of Defense.

Senator Gore declined to elaborate. But Senator Fulbright suggested that the North Vietnamese PT boat commanders might have engaged in "a little puffery" such as reporting they had inflicted damage on the destroyers.

As an example of what he said was the misleading nature of the McNamara testimony, Senator Gore noted how the Defense Secretary had testified that Lieut. Gen. David A. Burchinal, director of the Joint Staff, had analyzed the incoming messages and had given the evaluation: "The actuality of the attack is confirmed."

The Defense Secretary did not note, the Senator said, that this evaluation was given on Aug. 6—two days after the decision to retaliate against North Vietnam.

Nor, Senator Gore said, did the Defense Secretary point out that at the time the retaliatory strike order was issued at 6:30 P.M., Eastern daylight time on Aug. 4, further doubts were being raised by the destroyer task group and by the commander of the Pacific fleet as to whether the attack had actually taken place.

The Chief of Naval Operations, Adm. Thomas H. Moorer, said in a statement issued tonight: "I know of no report made by the Navy which casts any doubt on the fact that the destroyers were attacked on 2 August and 4 August, 1964."

Senator Fulbright also accused the Defense Department of engaging in "intimidating" practices against naval officers wishing to supply information to the committee.

He disclosed that a Navy commander was ordered to take a psychiatric examination after he conferred with the committee staff and raised questions as to whether there was evidence substantiating the Aug. 4 attack.

The Navy officer was found

strous" to suggest that the United States had induced the incidents as an excuse to carry the war to the North.

"But is is equally monstrous," the Senator continued, "to insinuate that any member of the committee holds such an opinion."

At the same time Senator Morse, a colleague on the committee, said he thought that the destroyers' mission "constituted picking a fight, that it constituted a hostile action, that it constituted an action on the part of the United States seeking to try to get the North Vietnamese to involve themselves in a dispute with us, entirely uncalled for, if peace was what he wanted."

At a late afternoon meeting called by Senator Fulbright, the committee decided to make public next week all the McNamara testimony — not just the prepared statement released by the Pentagon.

Morse Speaks in Senate

By E. W. KENWORTHY
Special to The New York Times

WASHINGTON, Feb. 21—A study prepared by the staff of the Senate Foreign Relations Committee asserts that the destroyer Maddox was under orders in 1964 to take provocative action in order to induce the Chinese Communists and North Vietnamese to turn on their radio and radar so the destroyer could monitor them.

This finding led Senator Wayne Morse, Democrat of Oregon, to take issue today on the Senate floor with testimony by Secretary of Defense Robert S. McNamara on Aug. 6, 1964, and again yesterday, in which Mr. McNamara said the Maddox was "on routine patrol."

"He calls it a 'routine patrol,'" Mr. Morse said. "The Maddox was a spy ship under instruction to stimulate the electronic instruments of North Vietnam to carry out a spying activity. That is not a routine patrol for a destroyer. The United States was a provocateur in the Gulf of Tonkin on Aug. 4, 1964, and history will so record."

The Maddox came under attack by North Vietnamese patrol craft on Aug. 2, and the Maddox and the Turner Joy were reported to have been attacked on Aug. 4.

In secret testimony on Aug. 6, 1964, Mr. McNamara did not tell the committee that the ships were on intelligence missions. Yesterday, he told the committee of their mission, but still insisted the patrols were "routine."

According to the staff study, the Maddox, which had gone on patrol on July 28, was under orders from the commander in chief of United States forces in the Pacific "to stimulate ChiCom/North Vietnamese electronic reaction."

The study also asserts that the ships, operating under the code name "De Soto," also spied along the coast of Communist China.

The study also disputes Mr. McNamara's testimony in 1964 that "our Navy played absolutely no part in, was not associated with, was not aware of, any South Vietnamese actions [against the islands of Hon Me and Hon Nieu], if there were any."

These two North Vietnamese islands were bombarded by South Vietnamese PT boats on the night of July 30-31 and again on the night of Aug. 3-4.

The staff study says that the United States Navy provided the advice. Crew training and the boats for these South Vietnamese raiding operations known as 34-A, which were set up in February, 1964, by South Vietnam and the United States Military Advisory Group.

Morse Declares Navy Messages Show Intent to Bait Hanoi in Gulf of Tonkin Incident of

By JOHN W. FINNEY
Special to The New York Times

WASHINGTON, Feb. 28— Senator Wayne Morse charged today that Navy messages prior to the incident in the Gulf of Tonkin on Aug. 4, 1964, demonstrated that the Navy was intent on "bloodying the nose" of North Vietnam.

On the basis of the messages, the Oregon Democrat said in a Senate speech, it is apparent that the United States Navy did not believe that two American destroyers were on a "routine patrol" in the Gulf of Tonkin, as has been repeatedly asserted by the administration.

Renewing his charge that the destroyers, the Maddox and Turner Joy, had engaged in "provocative" actions, Senator Morse made public a previously secret Navy message warning the two ships that North Vietnam had "thrown down the gauntlet and now considers itself at war with the United States." The message went on:

"It is felt that they will attack U. S. forces on sight and with no regard for cost. U. S. ships in the Gulf of Tonkin can no longer assume that they

will be considered neutrals exercising the right of free transit. They will be treated as belligerents from first detection and must consider themselves as such."

The message was sent by the commander of the destroyer task group, Capt. John J. Herrick, to the two destroyers.

It was sent following a North Vietnamese attack Aug. 2 on the Maddox, but, according to Senator Morse, "several hours before the commencement" of the patrol by the Maddox and the second incident on Aug. 4.

It was on the basis of the second incident, which the Administration has described

as an "unprovoked" North Vietnamese attack on the two destroyers, that the Administration ordered the first bombing raids against North Vietnam and obtained Congressional approval on the Tonkin resolution. The resolution was later interpreted by the State Department as a "functional equivalent" of a declaration of war.

In view of the message, Senator Morse questioned whether the Administration could "honestly" contend that the two were on "an innocent, routine patrol," asserting legitimate rights to travel on the high seas."

From the message, he said, it was apparent that "the assertion of rights of this kind was not viewed as routine by the Navy."

"We were out to bloody their nose," he declared. "We had the chip on our shoulder."

As another indication of the "Navy attitude toward the purpose of the patrol," Senator Morse cited a message sent on Aug. 4 by Adm. Thomas H. Morrer, then commander in chief of the Pacific fleet and now Chief of Naval Operations.

The Morrer message urged that the destroyer patrol be continued in order to "clearly demonstrate our determination

to continue these operations."

It went on to recommend, among other things, that the course of the destroyer patrol be changed to the northward so that it might possibly draw North Vietnamese patrol boats away from the area of South Vietnamese naval operations against North Vietnam.

In the Senate Foreign Relations Committee's inquiry into the Gulf of Tonkin incidents, the Morrer message has played a critical part because it indicates that contrary to Administration assertions there was a connection between the destroyer patrol and the South Vietnamese naval operations, known as "Op 34-A."

When the Moorer message was first disclosed last week by Senator Morse, the Defense Department, in rebuttal, said the message was not an order recommendation to higher command that eventually "died" without approval by the Joint Chiefs of Staff.

But the Pentagon did not disclose, according to Senate sources who have studied the messages, that on Aug. 3, a day before the Moorer "recommendation," Vice Adm. Roy L. Johnson, commander of the seventh fleet, had already ordered the destroyers to modify their course to the northward.

It was in response to an order that Captain Herrick's warning that North ... troyer patrol ... operations and was to treat the destroyer ... "enemies."

The Herrick message ... publication of ... fense Secretary Rob ... Foreign Relations C ...

The Morse speech ... first of two that the ... plans to ... Mr. McNamara

C.I.A. Said to Dispute Pentagon's View

Continued From Page 1, Col. 1

entirely new missile system. Much of the concern and speculation over the intended purpose for the new silos has sprung from their unusual size.

According to data obtained by the satellites, the holes were larger than those that had previously been dug for the SS-9, a large intercontinental missile that Defense Department officials have suggested the Soviet Union may be deploying as a "first strike" weapon against the United States's Minuteman force. This in turn gave rise to official speculation that the Soviet Union was planning to deploy an improved version of the SS-9 or perhaps an even larger, more powerful weapon.

Senator Henry M. Jackson, who first disclosed the detection of the new silo holes on a national television program March 7, said at the time that "the Russians are now in the process of deploying a new generation, an advanced generation of offensive systems." The Washington Democrat, a member of the Senate Armed Services Committee, described the development as "ominous indeed."

The Defense Department took a somewhat more cautious interpretation, saying that it had detected new ICBM construction but was not sure what the Soviet Union's intentions were.

Laird Confirms Finding

But in a television appearance on March 10, Melvin R. Laird, the Secretary of Defense, said that the silo construction "confirms the fact that the Soviet Union is going forward with construction of a large missile system.

"We cannot tell at this time whether it is a modified version of the SS-9 . . . or whether it is an entirely new missile system," he said.

Then, in a speech April 22 before the American Newspaper Publishers Association, Mr. Laird said the United States had fresh intelligence information "confirming the sobering fact that the Soviet Union is invoved in a new—and apparently extensive—ICBM construction program."

He warned that if this Soviet missile build-up continued, the Defense Department might find it necessary to seek a supplementary appropriation for more strategic weapons.

Last week, Administration officials were reported to have said that the Soviet Union was pressing ahead with its new missile program so rapidly that test firings of an improved SS-9 or an entirely new and larger missile were expected by this summer.

On the basis of new intelligence information, the C.I.A. was said today to have concluded that the larger holes could be explained not by a Soviet move to a larger missile but by an engineering step intended to protect the existing Soviet missile force.

According to the intelligence agency's analysis, the larger holes can be explained as an effort to "harden" the silos, by emplacement of a concrete shell around them, to protect the weapons against the blast effects of a nuclear explosion. The larger hole is required to accommodate the concrete liners, according to the C.I.A. analysis.

Old Missile Fields Utilized

It was said that the first evidence that the Soviet Union might be "hardening" its missile sites rather than developing a new missile system appeared in the fact that the new holes were detected primarily in existing SS-11 missile fields.

If the Soviet Union was deploying a new weapon, it presumably would not situate the new missile emplacements among older missiles, according to the C.I.A. view.

The conclusive piece of evidence was said to have been received early last week when reconnaissance satellite pictures were received showing silo liners arriving at the missile holes. The photographs were said to have indicated that the liners at neither the SS-11 nor the SS-9 sites were big enough to accommodate larger missiles, and those at the SS-9 sites did not seem intended for weapons of altered design.

The United States started hardening its Minuteman silos some years ago as it saw the Soviet Union expanding its ICBM forces, and then began "superhardening" them as the Soviet Union began deploying the SS-9 missile.

Some arms control specialists now maintain that the Soviet Union is turning to hardening its SS-11 and SS-9 missiles as it sees the United States deploying multiple independently targeted re-entry vehicles, or multiple warheads, known as MIRV's, which potentially could acquire the accuracy to strike precisely at Soviet missile sites.

This was a point made today before the Senate Appropriations Committee by Dr. Herbert Scoville Jr., a former official of the C.I.A. and the

Disarmament and Arms Control Agency, now chairman of the strategic weapons committee of the Federation of American Scientists.

A hardening of the Soviet missile sites, he observed "would not contribute to a first-strike capability and, if anything, would be an indication that a first strike was not a critical Soviet policy objective."

If it now turns out that the Soviet Union is only hardening the SS-9 and SS-11 missile silos, he said, "We must ask ourselves how many times we are going to allow the 'weaponeers' to come before the Congress and the people shouting 'missile gap,' when in reality they are only creating another 'credibility gap.'"

FRESH AIR FUND. PLEASE GIVE.

VOL. CXX .... No. 41,39

C.I.A. SAID TO DOUBT PENTAGON'S VIEW ON MISSILE THREAT

MAY 26 1971

Senate G.O.P. Sources Say Agency Thinks Soviet Silos Are for Existing Arms

PROTECTIVE STEP SEEN

Moscow Is Reported to Be Installing 'Hardened' Sites to Defend Its SS-11's

By JOHN W. FINNEY
Special to The New York Times

WASHINGTON, May 25 — Senate Republican sources reported today that the Central Intelligence Agency concluded that at least two-thirds of the large new silo holes recently detected in the Soviet Union were intended for the relatively small SS-11 intercontinental missile and not for a large new weapon as the Defense Department has suggested.

This assessment casts a different light on Moscow's strategic intentions at a crucial time in the negotiations with the Soviet Union to achieve some limitation on defensive and offensive strategic weapons.

It now appears to some arms control specialists that the Soviet Union, rather than seeking to achieve a first-strike capability against the United States with large new missiles, is following the American course of trying to protect its missiles against attack with "hardened" silos.

60 New Silos Detected

Some 60 large new missile silos in the Soviet Union have been detected in recent months by means of reconnaissance satellites. The C.I.A. was said to have concluded that at least two-thirds were intended for the SS-11 intercontinental missile, which is comparable to the Minuteman ICBM of the United States.

Some non-Governmental sources with access to Central Intelligence Agency information said that all but 15 of the new excavations were situated in existing SS-11 missile fields.

The Senate Republican sources said they had been informed of the C.I.A. assessment by non-Governmental arms control experts who earlier had been briefed by the intelligence agency. These sources declined to be identified by name.

The Defense Department declined today to comment on the reported C.I.A. assessment because, as a department spokesman put it, "We would not have any comment on a speculative report like that."

But the spokesman said the department still held to the interpretation that the Soviet Union was deploying a modified version of its large SS-9 intercontinental missile or an

Continued on Page 4, Column 3

THE NEW YORK TIMES, TUESDAY, JULY 28, 1970

Senate Unit Finds U.S. Has Secret Base In Morocco for Navy Communications

By JOHN W. FINNEY
Special to The New York Times

WASHINGTON, July 27—A Senate Foreign Relations subcommittee has discovered that when the United States withdrew its military forces from bases in Morocco in 1963 it entered into a private arrangement with the Moroccan Government to retain a large naval communications center.

Meanwhile, according to testimony received by the subcommittee, the Pentagon, anticipating loss of the Moroccan base, constructed duplicate communications facilities at Rota, in Spain. Both communications centers have remained in operation, although Senate testimony indicates that they are performing essentially the same mission.

The existence of a communications center at Rota, a large naval base for Polaris submarines, is openly acknowledged by the Pentagon. But the communications center in Morocco, at Sidi Yahya, some 50 miles northeast of Rabat, has been kept secret by the Pentagon and the State Department for seven years as part of an understanding with the Moroccan Government.

Defense Department spokesmen refused today to answer questions about the Sidi Yahya base or even to confirm its existence. The Pentagon referred inquiries to the State Department, which in turn refused to discuss the base because of what a spokesman described as the sensitivity of the arrangements with the Moroccan Government.

While neither the State nor the Defense Department would comment formally, officials who would agree to be identified only as "official sources" acknowledged that the Navy was operating a communications center

The New York Times   July 28, 1970
U.S. Naval communications center is at Sidi Yahya.

at Sidi Yahya. These sources said agreement to operate the communications station was reached by the two Governments in 1963 when the United States was closing its bases in Morocco.

Testimony Taken by Panel

The base arrangements were discussed in closed-door testimony taken last week by the Subcommittee on Foreign Commitments, headed by Senator Stuart Symington, Democrat of Missouri. The outlines of the testimony on the Moroccan base were provided by a subcommittee member in an interview.

Now that the United States has been compelled to leave Wheelus Air Force Base in Libya, the Sidi Yahya communications center is the last remaining American military base in North Africa. According to State Department officials, this contributes to the "sensitivity" of the issue.

If public attention is drawn to the American military presence at Sidi Yahya, these officials explained, it might embarrass King Hassan II of Morocco, who is regarded as a moderate in the Arab world. The Pentagon was said to be fearful that publicity might provoke the Moroccan Government to demand American withdrawal, just as the new military Government of Libya recently demanded that the Air Force shut its large base at Wheelus.

Fulbright Critical

Members of the Senate Foreign Relations Committee, including Senator J. W. Fulbright, the chairman, maintain that the Administration has made no attempt to inform Congress on the nature of the secret arrangements it may have entered into with the Moroccan Government. The voluminous State and Defense Department "justification" document for the military aid program, for example, contains no mention of the communications base in Morocco.

During the subcommittee investigation, it was established that the United States maintains major naval bases in three countries with which it has no military treaties. They are Morocco, Spain and Ethiopia, although it is a member

larger than the one in Morocco.

The maintenance of the communications base at Sidi Yahya apparently dates from an agreement reached between President John F. Kennedy and King Hassan in March, 1963. In a communiqué issued after a meeting with the Moroccan King, President Kennedy declared that evacuation of the American bases in Morocco "would take place" as provided for in a 1959 agreement between President Eisenhower and King Mohammed V, who was succeeded on his death in 1961 by Hassan, his son.

Big Base Complex Closed

The 1959 agreement provided for withdrawal of all American forces from Morocco by the end of 1963 and the closing down of the $400-million complex of bases that had been built to handle Air Force strategic bombers as well as Navy planes at a naval base at Kenitra.

At the time the 1963 communiqué was issued, there were suggestions by "informed sources" that some Americans might remain behind to train Moroccan forces in the use of the bases and equipment. According to Senate sources, this "training mission" was part of the "cover story" to conceal the continuing existence of an American base in Morocco.

Under the same Navy command as the Sidi Yahya station, the United States does maintain a training mission at Kenitra, about 20 miles away. Naval personnel assigned to the command total about 1,500 plus 1,500 dependents.

The sources said that the naval personnel were assigned to Kenitra "primarily to train Moroccan personnel in communications work but they also operate the communications facilities at Sidi Yahya."

The sources said that the communications station at Sidi Yahya was designed to "service the Sixth Fleet," stationed in the Mediterranean, while the communications facilities at Rota "provide support for ships operating near the base."

UNITED STATES DISTRICT COURT
SOUTHERN DISTRICT OF NEW YORK

-------------------------------x

UNITED STATES OF AMERICA,   : Index No. 71 Civ. 2662

          Plaintiff,   :

     -against-   :   __AFFIDAVIT__

NEW YORK TIMES COMPANY, et al.,:

         Defendants. :

-------------------------------x

STATE OF NEW YORK)
              : ss.:
COUNTY OF NEW YORK)

     SANFORD COBB, being duly sworn, deposes and says:

     1.   He is the president and principal executive officer of the Association of American Publishers, Inc.

     2.   On June 16, 1971, at a duly convened meeting of the Board of Directors in New York City on motion, duly made, seconded, and unanimously carried the following resolution was adopted:

> "The Board of Directors of the Association of American Publishers commends the New York Times for its courage and initiative in publishing the Pentagon documents concerning the history of our Vietnam involvement. We believe that freedom to publish without prior restraint is of vital importance in maintaining the checks and balances that are the only basis on which our democracy can survive."

_____
Sanford Cobb

SWORN to before me this
17th day of June, 1971.

_____
    Notary Public

MARY ANN C. SIMPSON
Notary Public, State of New York
No. 41-3602775
Qualified in Queens County
Commission Expires March 30, 1973

423

IN THE UNITED STATES DISTRICT COURT
SOUTHERN DISTRICT OF NEW YORK

---------------------------------------X

UNITED STATES OF AMERICA,   :

                          Plaintiff,   :

                    v.   :   Civil Action

THE NEW YORK TIMES COMPANY, et al.,   :   71-2662

                          Defendants.   :

---------------------------------------X

STATE OF NEW YORK   :
                         : ss.
COUNTY OF NEW YORK   :

        THEODORE C. SORENSEN, being duly sworn, deposes and
says:

        1. I am a member of the law firm of Paul, Weiss,
Goldberg, Rifkind, Wharton & Garrison, 345 Park Avenue, New
York, New York.

        2. Having served as a lawyer in both the Executive
and Legislative branches of the Federal Government from 1951
to 1964, including more than three years as Special Counsel
to the President, at which time I held a top security
clearance, read classified documents daily, and drafted many
such documents to or for the President, I am very familiar with
the United States Government's practices regarding the classification of various papers in the name of national security.

        3. Having read the materials appearing in the New York
Times on June 13, 14 and 15, 1971, I am familiar in a general
way with the Times' publication of summaries of, excerpts from
and documents attached to a historical study of this nation's

424

deepening involvement in the Vietnam War conducted by the Department of Defense.

4. A determination by the Government or anyone else as to whether our nation's security requires the withholding from public view of any particular document or documents is not a matter requiring military or other highly specialized expertise. The highly individual and frequently arbitrary opinion of the classifying officer is thus entitled to no or little more weight than the opinion of any other informed and concerned citizen. "Top secret" stamps are frequently and routinely applied with only the briefest and loosest consideration of what, if any, direct and concrete injury to the nation's security interests would result if the general public were to be granted access to the information; and, once applied, the tenure of such classifications rarely if ever reflects a thoughtful reconsideration of whether the passage of time and events has altered the original grounds. The public's right to be informed, and the Congress' right to be informed, have not to my knowledge been regarded as important criteria by those determining classifications.

5. The nation's security does legitimately require the withholding from public view for an appropriate period and no longer certain documents, including those which if revealed could endanger or otherwise adversely affect the lives or movements of American military personnel. In addition, foreign governments are ordinarily entitled to expect that their confidential communications to our government will be treated with the same regard for their wishes as they provide for our confidential communications to them; and the President is ordinarily entitled to receive the kind of candid advice and reports from

his top civilian and military subordinates which is possible only if they can be certain that words intended for his eyes alone are not shortly thereafter transmitted to the general public.

6. The question of whether any particular document or documents should remain secret today is thus one of balancing these interests, and the New York Times, a Federal Judge, a Senator or a citizen may be as capable of making that judgment as anyone in the Executive Branch. My own judgment is that, on balance, publication by the New York Times of the documents in question is that case is not injurious to the national security. No current or future military operations or present top government officials appear to be involved in any way. No serious embarrassment to any foreign government appears to be involved. None of the information and opinions revealed appear to have any current facets requiring continued secrecy.

7. On the contrary I believe the national security interests of the United States will be irreparably injured if these documents are suppressed from public and Congressional view; if the United States, on the verge of several fateful decisions in the Middle East, Latin America and Asia, is thereby prevented as a nation from learning the true history of what went wrong in Vietnam; if the same policies of concealment and deception which prevented debate and produced mistakes in this nation's approach to Vietnam are thereby judicially encouraged to continue; if the very purpose of this objective historical study is thereby frustrated, and the cost in time and talent invested in its

evolution wasted, by confining its circulation to a handful of
high officials who largely supported the original policy; and
if the courts of this country, by enjoining a free press and
permitting the concealment of official error, thereby erase
still one more important distinction between ourselves and our
adversaries.

8. I understand that this affidavit will be submitted
in opposition to the motion made on behalf of the Plaintiff
for an order enjoining the further publication by the New York
Times of this material.

/s/ Theodore C. Sorensen
Theodore C. Sorensen

New York, N.Y.
June 17, 1971

Sworn to before me this 17th day
of June, 1971.

```
* * * * * * * * * * * * * * * * * * * * * * * * * * *
                                              *
UNITED STATES OF AMERICA,                     *
                                              *
                 Plaintiff                    *
                                              *       71 Civil 2662
      - AGAINST -                             *
                                              *
NEW YORK TIMES COMPANY, ET AL.,               *
                                              *
                 Defendants                   *
* * * * * * * * * * * * * * * * * * * * * * * * * * *
```

COMMONWEALTH OF MASSACHUSETTS)
                                ): SS.:
COUNTY OF BERKSHIRE   )

JAMES MAC GREGOR BURNS, being duly sworn, deposes and says:

1.   I am Woodrow Wilson Professor of Government at Williams College and the author of, among other works, "Roosevelt, The Soldier of Freedom" and "Roosevelt, The Lion and the Fox", studies of the Roosevelt administrations.

2.   During World War II, I served at several levels of Army Intelligence as well as a military historian. As such I had access to classified documents at all levels of security classifications.

3.   As a result of my military experience and my work as a professional historian specializing in the study of government, I have had extensive experience with classified government documents. I have had on numerous occasions the opportunity to deal with material in its classified state and later as unclassified. My experience has not been limited to the handling of documents by the United States government alone, but has also included experience with the policies in such matters of foreign governments.

4.   I have come to the firm, and I believe informed,

conviction that it is the invariable attitudes of governments to exaggerate

grossly the security aspects of their documents. Government officials

tend to take a parochial and excessively cautious and self-protective

view of the security problem. They tend also to fail to assess correctly

the true public interest in full, frank and early disclosure of historical

events and hence they minimize the opportunity for history to teach and

the public and the government to learn from the mistakes of the past.

5.   In my judgment, these unfortunate tendencies are

increasing. The declassification of supposedly sensitive documents,

always too slow, has in recent years been occurring at an even slower

rate. In contrast, history is speeding up. I believe it to be desparately

important that we understand the circumstances surrounding our inter-

ventions in so-called limited wars such as Korea and Viet Nam. I say

this entirely divorced from my opinions with respect to our present and

future Viet Nam policy.

6.   It is Based upon this experience and for these reasons

that I wish to submit this affidavit in opposition to the application made

on behalf of the United States government for an injunction restraining

publication by the New York Times of any further articles based upon

the study commissioned by Defense Secretary McNamara of the historical

events of our intervention in Viet Nam. I have read with care the

articles which appeared in the New York Times' issues of June 13, 14

and 15, 1971. I fail to see any injury to the national defense or any

other national interest presently deserving protection. To the contrary,

I firmly believe that publication of materials such as those I have read

has served the national interest. In my judgment, the New York Times

has earned the protection which the First Amendment creates by performing

the correlative obligation of publishing such materials.

James Mac Gregor Burns

429   James Mac Gregor Burns

COMMONWEALTH OF MASSACHUSETTS

BERKSHIRE, ss.   June 17, 1971

Then personally appeared the above-named, JAMES MAC GREGOR

BURNS, and acknowledged the foregoing instrument to be his free act and deed, before

me,

Lawrence B. Urbano
Notary Public

My commission expires: October 27, 1977

430

STATE OF NEW YORK)
                   : ss.:
COUNTY OF NEW YORK)

- - - - - - - - - - - - - - - - - - X

UNITED STATES OF AMERICA,   :

                    Plaintiff,   :

            v.   :   AFFIDAVIT

NEW YORK TIMES COMPANY, ET AL.,   :

                    Defendants.   :

- - - - - - - - - - - - - - - - - - X

   FRANCIS T. P. PLIMPTON, being first duly sworn, deposes and says:

   1. I make this Affidavit in opposition to the motion of the Government, plaintiff herein, for a preliminary injunction in the above-captioned matter.

   2. I am a member of the Bar of the State of New York, having been admitted to practice in the Appellate Division, First Department, on February 8, 1926 and a member of the firm of Debevoise, Plimpton, Lyons & Gates. I am a member of the Bars of the United States District Court for the Southern District of New York, the United States Court of Appeals for the Second Circuit and the Supreme Court of the United States. I am a resident of 131 East 66th Street, New York, New York 10021.

   3. From 1961 to 1965 I was Ambassador and Deputy United States Permanent Representative to the United Nations by appointment of President Kennedy, and was a delegate to the 15th (resumed) to 19th General Assemblies of the United Nations by appointment of Presidents Kennedy and Johnson.

From 1932 to 1933 I was General Solicitor of the Reconstruction Finance Corporation in Washington. Except for the periods aforesaid, I have been actively engaged in the private practice of the law.

4. I was President of The Association of the Bar of the City of New York from 1968 to 1970.

5. I have carefully read the articles in The New York Times which are the subject of this action. In my opinion, the publication of these articles, covering the period 1945-1967, in no way jeopardizes the national security of the United States or harms any United States interests. On the contrary, it is my opinion that the publication of these historical materials, relating solely to past periods, far from being deleterious to the interests of this country, is in the public interest, for surely the American people are entitled to know the truth about the past conduct of their foreign affairs by their Government.

6. It is also my opinion that the classifications "Top Secret" and "Secret", as applied to the more than four year old material quoted in those articles, if at the time proper, can no longer, years later, be justified. The present disclosure of the information contained therein cannot, to quote the wording of Executive Order 10501, result in "exceptionally grave damage to the nation" or "serious damage to the nation"; paraphrasing the examples given in the Executive Order, international relations are not jeopardized by that aging information, the effectiveness of any program or policy of vital importance to the national defense is not endangered, and there is no compromise of important military

-2-

432

or defense plans, scientific or technological developments important to national defense, or information revealing important intelligence operations.

Francis T. P. Plimpton

Subscribed and sworn to before me
this 17th day of June 1971.

Notary Public

BARBARA J. RUBY
Notary Public, State of New York
No. 31-8696385
Qualified in New York County
Term Expires March 30, 1972

-3-

UNITED STATES DISTRICT COURT

SOUTHERN DISTRICT OF NEW YORK

--x
                                          :
UNITED STATES OF AMERICA,   :
                                          :
                          Plaintiff,   :
                                          :
              -against-   :   71 Civil 2662
                                          :
THE NEW YORK TIMES COMPANY, ET AL.,   :
                                          :
                          Defendants.   :
                                          :
--x

STATE OF NEW JERSEY   )
                       : SS.:
COUNTY OF MERCER   )

          ERIC F. GOLDMAN, being duly sworn, deposes and
says:

          1. I am Rollins Professor of History at Princeton
University and am the author of, among other works, "Rendezvous
With Destiny," "The Crucial Decade," and "The Tragedy of
Lyndon Johnson." I served from 1964 to 1966 as Special
Consultant to President Johnson.

          2. I have read with great interest the articles
and published texts drawn from the historical collection
commissioned by Secretary McNamara which appeared in The
New York Times for June 13, 14 and 15.

          3. In my judgment as a historian and as a
citizen:

          (a) The published material constitutes

an important source for historical study.

(b) The historical documents thus made available to the citizens of this country and to all branches of their Government are the kind,of history which helps us, hopefully, to learn from mistakes of the past.

(c) The national interest has not been harmed. On the contrary, this publication could be distinctly helpful to the best interests of the American people.

4. I understand that this affidavit will be submitted in opposition to the Government's demand that The New York Times be enjoined from further publication of this material.

Eric F. Goldman

Sworn to before me this
17th day of June, 1971.

Edith Quaresima

EDITH QUARESIMA
NOTARY PUBLIC OF NEW JERSEY
My Commission Expires September 18, 1975

UNITED STATES DISTRICT COURT

SOUTHERN DISTRICT OF NEW YORK

- - - - - - - - - - - - - - - - -)
)
UNITED STATES OF AMERICA,   )
)
                    Plaintiff,   )
)
        - - against - -   ) 71 Civ. 2662
)
THE NEW YORK TIMES COMPANY, et al.,)
)
                    Defendants.   )
)
- - - - - - - - - - - - - - - - -)

STATE OF CONNECTICUT)
) ss.   *Greenwich*
COUNTY OF FAIRFIELD   )

        BARBARA W. TUCHMAN, being duly sworn, deposes and
says:

        1. I am an independent writer and historian.
Among my works are "The Guns of August" which was awarded
the Pulitzer Prize , and most recently "Stillwell and the
American Experience in China", 1911-45. I am President of
the Society of American Historians and Executive Officer
of both the Authors Guild and the Authors Fund. I am Trustee
of Radcliffe College.

        2. I have read the articles and published docu-
ments contained in the Pentagon collection of historical
documents relating to our intravention in the Vietnam War
which appeared in the New York Times on June 13-14-15.

        3. It is my judgment that the publication of this
material far from harming the national interest serves the
national interest. It illustrates the need, indeed the
necessity, of public information on the processes of policy
making. I strongly feel that the disclosure that war

making policy was formed and thereafter extended into the ultimate and extreme form of national action - active beligerency - by those who did not themselves believe in it is of crucial importance. When the public is asked to serve in carrying out policy it surely should have confidence that the policy makers who demand this duty believe in the correctness and ultimate success of the endeavor.

4. I oppose the Government's demand that The New York Times be prohibited from further publication of this material.

Sworn to before me this 17th day of June, 1971.

CHARLES W. PETTENGILL
Notary Public
My Commission Expires April 1, 1972.

UNITED STATES DISTRICT COURT
FOR THE SOUTHERN DISTRICT OF
NEW YORK

United States of America,
             Plaintiff
             v.   71-Civ. 2662
New York Times, et al   State of North Carolina
                                               County of Mecklenburg:

Colbert Augustus McKnight, being first duly sworn, deposes
and says:

1. I am President of the American Society of Newspaper Editors
and have been since April of 1971. ASNE's membership includes
more than 700 directing editors of leading U. S. daily newspapers.

2. I submit this affidavit on behalf of the Board of Directors
of the American Society of Newspaper Editors in opposition to
the action by the Government of the United States to prohibit
the New York Times from continuing to publish articles with
respect to the Vietnam war such as those contained in the issues
of June 13, 14 and 15, 1971 which are the subject of this litigation.

3. In my view and the view of the Board of ASNE, the freedom
to publish without prior restraint is a cornerstone of the
American people's right to know and any order to the contrary
destroys a basic constitutional right of the people under a
democratic government.

                          _C. A. McKnight_____
                          C. A. McKnight, President
                          American Society of Newspaper Editors

Before me this 17th day of June, 1971, appeared C. A. McKnight,
who upon his oath did acknowledge that he is the President of
the American Society of Newspaper Editors and that the facts
contained in this affidavit are true to the best of his
knowledge and belief.

_Dorothy H. Fleck_____
   Notary Public

My commission expires: My Commission Expires August 7, 1975

UNITED STATES DISTRICT COURT

SOUTHERN DISTRICT OF NEW YORK

------------------------------- x

UNITED STATES OF AMERICA,

             Plaintiff,   :

    -against-   :   AFFIDAVIT

NEW YORK TIMES, et al.,   :   71 Civ. 2662

           Defendants. :

----

      1. I am Dean of the Georgetown University Law Center, a position I have held since June, 1969. I have held two Government positions relevant to the circumstances of this affidavit. From June 1949 to February 1953 I was the Legal Adviser to the Department of State. During this period I had occasion to serve as one of the security advisers to the Department of Defense in "screening" the Forrestal Diaries for publication. From mid-1961 to early 1969, I was the Deputy Director of the U.S. Arms Control and Disarmament Agency. In this connection I served on numerous occasions as the U.S. Representative to the Eighteen Nation Committee on Disarmament in Geneva and conducted numerous bilateral negotiations with the Soviet Union.

      2. I have read the articles and accompanying documents dealing with U.S. involvement in hostilities in Vietnam, appearing in the New York Times of June 13, 14 and 15, 1971. In my judgment the publication of these articles does not involve any injury to the national security of the United States. I base this judgment on the fact that this material printed by the New York Times on these dates deals with governmental decisions which have already been made and put into effect, which are generally known, both in this country and abroad, to have been put into

effect, and whose success or failure is now a subject of public debate in the United States. I am influenced in this judgment by a deep conviction that a free society benefits from an understanding of the process which produced these decisions.

ADRIAN S. FISHER

Sworn to before me this 17th day of June , 1971.

Notary Public

My Commission Expires May 14, 1975

UNITED STATES DISTRICT COURT
SOUTHERN DISTRICT OF NEW YORK

- - - - - - - - - - - - - - - - - - - -x

UNITED STATES OF AMERICA,

                Plaintiff,   :   71 Civ. 2662

             v.   :   NOTICE OF MOTION
                                  TO VACATE TEMPORARY
NEW YORK TIMES COMPANY, ARTHUR OCHS   :   RESTRAINING ORDER
SULZBERGER, HARDING F. BANCROFT,
IVAN VEIT, FRANCIS A. COX, JAMES C.   :
GOODALE, SYDNEY GRUSON, WALTER
MATTSON, JOHN McCABE, JOHN MORTIMER,   :
JAMES RESTON, JOHN B. OAKES,
A. M. ROSENTHAL, DANIEL SCHWARZ,   :
CLIFTON DANIEL, TOM WICKER, E. W.
KENWORTHY, FOX BUTTERFIELD, GERALD   :
GOLD, ALLAN M. SIEGAL, SAMUEL ABT,
NEIL SHEEHAN and HEDRICK SMITH,   :

               Defendants.   :

- - - - - - - - - - - - - - - - - - - -x

S I R S :

      PLEASE TAKE NOTICE that upon the annexed affidavit
of James L. Greenfield sworn to June 18, 1971 and on the pleadings
and proceedings heretofore had herein, the undersigned as
attorneys for defendants will move this Court, at 10:00 A.M.
on June 18, 1971 or as soon thereafter as counsel can be heard,
in Room 506, United States Courthouse, Foley Square, New York,
New York pursuant to Rule 65 of the Federal Rules of Civil
Procedure for an order vacating a Temporary Restraining Order

entered by this Court (Gurfein, J.) on June 15, 1971, and granting such other and further relief as to the Court may seem just and proper.

Dated: New York, New York
       June 18, 1971

                              Yours, etc.

                    CAHILL, GORDON, SONNETT, REINDEL & OHL

                    By _____
                              (A Member of the Firm)
                    Attorneys for Defendants
                      Office & P. O. Address:
                      80 Pine Street
                      New York, New York 10005
                      944-7400

UNITED STATES DISTRICT COURT

SOUTHERN DISTRICT OF NEW YORK

--x
                                          :
UNITED STATES OF AMERICA,   :
                                          :
                        Plaintiff,   :   AFFIDAVIT
                                          :
            -against-   :   71 Civ. 2662
                                          :
THE NEW YORK TIMES COMPANY,   :
et al.,   :
                                          :
                        Defendants.   :
                                          :
--x

STATE OF NEW YORK   )
                    :   SS.:
COUNTY OF NEW YORK)

        JAMES L. GREENFIELD, being duly sworn, deposes
and says:

        1. I am the Foreign Editor of The New York Times
("The Times") and am familiar with the facts of the instant
situation.

        2. On June 13, 1971, The Times began publishing
excerpts from a 47-volume history of the Vietnam War completed
in 1968 entitled "History of U. S. Decision-Making Process on
Vietnam Policy" and a summary of a document relating to the
Tonkin Gulf incident prepared by the Defense Department in
1965 (the "documents"). This was an exclusive feature of
The Times.

        3. On June 15, 1971, this Court entered a temporary
restraining order effective until 1:00 P. M. on June 19, 1971,

443

restraining The Times from further disclosing any portion of the documents. The Times has complied with this order and has stopped further publication of the documents.

4. I am making this affidavit in support of a motion to vacate this temporary restraining order.

5. Annexed to this affidavit is the Washington Post issue of June 18, 1971, story entitled, "Documents Reveal U. S. Effort In '54 to Delay Viet Election." This story indicated that the Washington Post has possession of some or all of the documents that are the subject of this order. Particularly, I am able to say it contains material that The Times has prepared for publication and would already have been published but for the restraining order. In addition, the Washington Post states clearly that today's article is the first in a series, thus clearly indicating the Washington Post possesses additional material.

6. The Washington Post has a News Service with some 275 subscribers. It is understood that the article referred to in paragraph 5 above was sent over the Washington Post - Los Angeles Times News Service wire to its subscribers. Further, attached hereto are releases with respect to the story of the Associated Press which is distributed to some 8,500 newspaper, television, and other media subscribers about the world.

7. Attached hereto are releases with respect to

-2-

the story of the United Press International which is distributed to some 6,000 newspaper, television, and other
media subscribers about the world.

8.   Attached hereto is a copy of The New York Post
of June 18, 1971, containing an article obviously taken from
the Washington Post News Service.

9.   Although we have no further evidence of how
many clients of the Washington Post - Los Angeles Times News
Service will use the material, its use throughout the world is
highly likely by many of the Services clients.

10.   Certain portions similar to The Times' prepared
but still unpublished material has from sources unknown also
appeared in The New York Daily News, issue of Friday, June 18,
1971.

11.   The Washington Post story is also being carried
by the British News Agency Reuters for world wide publication.

12.   From the aforegoing, it is evident that the
very material which is the subject of the restraining order
is receiving nation-wide and world wide dissemination from
sources other than The Times.

13.   If the restraining order continued in effect,
The Times will suffer irreparable pecuniary and professional
damage in that once the documents are published as aforesaid,

-3-

they will lose their newsworthy value to The Times as an exclusive story, and will cause The Times to lose all benefit from the large sums of money, time and energy expended by The Times in compiling this story. In fact, if the order continues in effect, The Times alone will be restrained from publishing its own carefully compiled story.

14. Furthermore, any arguable value to be derived from the restraining order is lost by virtue of the aforesaid publication by other sources, and it serves only as a restraint on The Times alone.

(signature)

Sworn to before me this
18th day of June, 1971.

(signature)

MARY ANN C. SIMPSON
Notary Public, State of New York
No. 41-3632775
Qualified in Queens County
Commission Expires March 30, 1973

The Washington Post

Times Herald

The Washington Post Co.

FRIDAY, JUNE 18, 1971

Documents Reveal U.S. Effort In '54 to Delay Viet Election

First of a Series

By Chalmers M. Roberts
Washington Post Staff Writer

The Eisenhower administration, fearful that elections throughout North and South Vietnam would bring victory to Ho Chi Minh, fought hard but in vain at the 1954 Geneva Conference to reduce the possibility that the conference would call for such elections.

But the following year it was South Vietnamese President Ngo Dinh Diem, far more than the American government, who was responsible for the elections' not taking place. Diem flatly refused even to discuss the elections with the Communist regime in Hanoi.

These are among the facts emerging from sections of the Pentagon study on the origins of the Vietnam war, made available to The Washington Post.

The chief architect of the American policy of opposition to elections, as was well known at the time, was President Eisenhower's Secretary of State, John Foster Dulles. But it was Eisenhower who had insisted on allied support if he were to ask Congress for authority to use American military force to save the French army in Indochina in early 1954. The United States did not get that allied support.

The origin of the idea of holding an election in divided Vietnam, called for in the Geneva accords of 1954, remains obscure. But there is nothing obscure about Dulles' attitude.

In July of 1954, he sent a cable to various American diplomats then struggling with the problem. It said in part:

". . . Thus since undoubtedly true that elections might eventually mean unification Vietnam under Ho Chi Minh this makes it all more important they should be only held as long after cease-fire agreement as possible and in conditions free from intimidation to give democratic elements best chance. We believe important that no date should be set now and especially that no conditions should be accepted by French which would have direct or indirect effect of preventing effective international supervision of agreement ensuring political as well as military guarantees."

Dulles went on to call attention to a joint statement by President Eisenhower and British Prime Minister Churchill in June, especially that part which spoke of achieving "unity through free elections supervised by the UN."

Later in July, shortly before issuance in Geneva of the "final declaration" of the long conference, a declaration that included the statement that "general elections shall be held in July 1956," Dulles cabled his unhappiness at the impending outcome.

He sent Walter Bedell Smith, the Under Secretary of State who had returned to the Geneva Conference to limit as much as possible what Dulles foresaw as the disastrous outcome, a cable that said in part:

"While we don't want to take responsibility of imposing our views on the French, I feel particularly concerned about provisions of paragraph 6 which gives the Control Commission constituted as per SECTO 666 authority also to control the general elections. The ink is hardly dry on the Declaration of President Eisenhower and Prime Minister Churchill of June 29 to the effect that 'In the case of nations now divided against their will, we shall continue to seek to achieve unity through free elections *supervised by the UN* to insure that they are conducted fairly.' It is rather humiliating to see that Declaration now so quickly go down the drain with our apparent acquiescence."

About a week before the above cable, and after French Premier Pierre Mendes-France had asked that Dulles return to Geneva and before Dulles agreed to send Smith as his stand-in, Dulles cabled some of his unhappiness to Mendes-France via the American Embassy in Paris.

Dulles complained to Mendes-France of "a whittling-away process, each stroke of which may in itself seem unessential, but which cumulatively could produce a result quite different from that envisaged" in a seven-point minimum program, agreed upon by Britain and the United States, that he then was trying to sell France.

Dwight D. Eisenhower with John Foster Dulles, architect of America's anti-Vietnam election policy, in 1954.

See DOCUMENTS, A16, Col. 1

Documents Reveal '54 U.S. Ef

DOCUMENTS, From A1

He included this paragraph as illustrative of that "whittling away process."

"Allowing Communist forces to remain in Northern Laos; accepting a Vietnam line of military demarcation considerable south of Donghoi; neutralizing and [one word indistinct] demilitarizing Laos, Cambodia and Vietnam so as to impair their capacity to maintain stable, noncommunist regimes; accepting elections so early and so ill-prepared and ill-supervised as to risk the loss of the entire area to Communism; accepting international supervision by a body which cannot be effective because it includes a Communist state which has veto power."

In the end the election was called for, but not without considerable argument at Geneva, where the United States worked through the French. But others had the important say.

Chief among these important people were Chou Enlai, then as now Chinese Premier, and V. M. Molotov, the Soviet Union's redoubtable foreign minister.

In June of 1954, American Ambassador to France Douglas Dillon cabled Dulles to report conversations with Jean Chauvel, a key diplomat at the conference. Chauvel reported that Chou had "said that he recognized that there were now two governments in the territory of Vietnam, the Viet Minh Government and the Vietnamese Government. According to Chauvel, this was the first time that Chou had recognized the valid existence of the Vietnamese Government."

An overall view of the 1954 Geneva Conference, where delegates finally called for an election in divided Vietnam in July, 1956. By the time the conference opened the United States had actively cons intervention. The U.S. Secret: Dulles is (2). France's George

and Turkey) could follow progressively. Such widespread alignment would seriously endanger the stability and security of Europe.

"c. Communist control of all of Southeast Asia and Indonesia would threaten the U.S. position in the Pacific offshore island chain and would seriously jeopardize fundamental U.S. security interests in the Far East.

· "d. The loss of Southeast Asia would have serious economic consequences for many nations of the free world and conversely would add significant resources to the Soviet bloc. Southeast Asia, especially Malaya and Indonesia, is the principal world source of natural rubber and tin, and a producer of petroleum and other strategically important commodities. The rice exports of Burma, Indochina and Thailand are critically important to Malaya, Ceylon and Hong Kong and are of considerable significance to Japan and India, all important areas of free Asia. Furthermore, this area has an important potential as a market for the industrialized countries of the free world.

"e. The loss of Southeast Asia, especially of Malaya and Indonesia, could result in such economic and political pressures in Japan as to make it extremely difficult to prevent Japan's eventual accommodation to communism."

While the NSC study stated that "overt Chinese

communist attack on any part of Southeast Asia is less probable than continued Communist efforts to achieve domination through armed rebellion or subversion," the possibility of war with China was explored. It was stated that "in the event the United States participates in the fighting, there is a substantial risk that the Chinese Communists would intervene."

The immediate aim was to help the French by expediting, "and if necessary" increasing aid, to "assist them in:

"a. An aggressive military, political and psychological program, including covert operations, to eliminate organized Viet Minh forces by mid-1955.

"b. Developing indigenous armed forces, including logistical and administrative services, which will eventually be capable of maintaining internal security without assistance from French units."

In the event of Chinese intervention, the NSC concluded, the United Nations should be asked to call on member nations to "take whatever action may be necessary . . . to meet such an aggression." Whether or not the U.N. did act, it was proposed, the United States either under U.N. auspices or in concert with France, Britain and "other friendly governments" should take such steps as interdicting Chinese communication lines "including those in China," and, "if appropriate," also establish a joint "naval blockade of Communist

China and "as desirable and feasible" utilize Chinese Nationalist forces "in military operations in Southeast Asia, Korea, or China proper."

The NSC paper noted that if such actions as those outlined indeed were taken, "the United States should recognize that it may become involved in an all-out war with Communist China, and possibly with the USSR and the rest of the Soviet bloc, and should therefore proceed to take large-scale mobilization measures."

Military studies suggested that if the United States were to be involved on the ground "seven U.S. divisions or their equivalent, with appropriate naval and air support, would be required to win a victory in Indochina if the French withdrew and the Chinese Communists did not intervene." These were the words of the "Army position" on one NSC action memorandum.

But President Eisenhower, although he had approved the planning, wanted both Congressional approval and allied participation for any American intervention. An April telegram from Dulles to Dillon reported that "Congressional action would be required. After conference at highest level, I must confirm this position." He added: "US is doing everything possible" to "prepare public, Congressional and Constitutional basis for united action in Indochina. However, such action is impossible except on coalition basis with active British Commonwealth's participation. Meanwhile US prepared, as has been demonstrated, to do everything short of belligerency."

But Dulles had trouble rounding up allies, especially the British. Dulles reported to Smith on an April 27 talk with Foreign Secretary Anthony Eden in London and found Eden worrying that military intervention would be "a bigger affair than Korea," where hostilities had ended less than a year earlier.

A few days later Dulles summarized his findings, in part, this way:

"UK attitude is one of increasing weakness. British seem to feel that we are dis-

fort to prevent the elections throughout all of Vietnam on taking place.

The Soviets had "proposed June 1955" according to one report from Geneva but they and the Chinese and the North Vietnamese had finally agreed to July 1956. But South Vietnam, which the telegrams make clear had been told almost nothing about the secret Geneva talks although there was a Saigon delegation present, never accepted the Geneva accords, then or to this day.

A summary paper done as part of the Pentagon papers by an unnamed analyst put the outcome this way:

"As the deadline for consultations approached (20 July 1955) Diem was increasingly explicit that he did not consider free elections possible in North Vietnam, and had no intention of consulting with the DRV concerning them. The U.S. did not—as is often alleged—connive with Diem to ignore the elections. U.S. State Department records indicate that Diem's refusal to be bound by the Geneva Accords and his opposition to pre-election consultations were at his own initiative.

"However, the U.S., which had expected elections to be held, and up until May 1955 had fully supported them, shifted its position in the face of Diem's opposition, and of the evidence then accumulated about the oppressive nature of the regime in North Vietnam. 'In essence,' a State Department historical study found, 'our position would be that the whole subject of consultation and elections in Vietnam should be left up to the Vietnamese themselves and not dictated by external arrangements which one of the parties never accepted and still rejects.'"

On Jan. 19, 1961, President Eisenhower met in the oval room of the White House with President-elect John F. Kennedy. The President said that "Laos is the key to the entire area of Southeast Asia." The President-elect asked "how long it would take to put a U.S. division into Laos."

There was no discussion of Vietnam. That would become the problem for President Kennedy—and President Johnson—and President Nixon.

...s meet the press ference. From left, Anthony Eden, Walter ... Geneva Con- Bedell Smith and George ...

idered the idea of military ary of State John Foster s Bidault is (1), Britain's

Anthony Eden (3), China's Chou En-lai (4) and North Korea's Gen. Nam II is (5). Later, Walter Bedell Smith, Under Secretary of State, replaced Dulles at the talks.

posed to accept present risks of a Chinese war and this, coupled with their fear that we would start using atomic weapons, has badly frightened them."

Dulles confessed to uncertainty by adding that "I do not underestimate the immense difficulty of our finding the right course in this troubled situation. Nor do I mean to imply that this is the moment for a bold or war-like course. I lack here the US political and NSC judgements needed for overall evaluation."

Summary statements in the papers available to The Washington Post do not include any Eisenhower decision not to intervene at any of the several points during 1954 when that was under consideration. The closest thing to a clear definition of the chief executive's thinking is a May memorandum to the Secretary of Defense and the Chairman of the Joint Chiefs by Robert Cutler, the special assistant to the President who handled NSC affairs.

Cutler reported on a meeting in the President's office with only President Eisenhower, Dulles and Cutler present, at which the chief executive approved instructions for Smith, then in Geneva. It was essentially an expression of unhappiness over Eden's proposals, which fell far short of intervention.

Point 3, however, was expressive of the President's frame of mind. It said: "The United States will not agree to a 'white man's party' to determine the problems of the Southeast Asian nations."

this should be reached by direct negotiations between the two governments in Vietnam ... Mendes at this point said that since the war had been going on for 8 years and passions were high, it would take a long time before elections could be held as the people must be given a full opportunity to cool off and calm down. Chou made no objection to this statement by Mendes and did not press for early elections."

On June 19, Smith called on Molotov at his Geneva villa. He filed a long report, with his comment, which included this:

"In private conversations with Mr. Eden and others, Communist delegates, in particular Chou En-lai, had taken an apparently reasonable view on Laos and Cambodia, but that here again, when we came to the point of trying to get open agreement on specific points we were unable to do so. I specifically mentioned Chou En-lai's statements to Eden in which he said that China would have no objections to recognizing the kingdoms of Laos and Cambodia or to these States having forces and arms sufficient to maintain security, or their remaining in French Union so long as they were not used as military bases by the United States. We could not disagree with any of this, although if we kept out the Chinese would have to keep out, and these small states would have to be allowed to join with their neighbors in whatever regional security arrangements would best protect their integrity without constituting a threat to any one else.

"Chou En-lai might be anxious about possibility of U.S. bases in Laos and Cambodia. We wanted on our part to be sure that these countries were not handed over to the Chinese. Molotov said that while he did not know about what attitude Chinese might have on other questions in future, he could assure me that Chinese attitude on this particular question was not at all unreasonable, and that there was nothing in it which would give rise to conflicts. He added, however, that if we continued to take a one-sided view and insist on one-sided solutions, he must 'in all frankness say that this would not succeed.'"

Smith told Molotov that "appearance of 'partition' was repugnant to U.S." and

NGO DINH DIEM
... refused to abide

to U.S. aversion to partition, he [Molotov] said that this problem could easily be solved by holding elections at once, which would decide 'one way or the other.'"

When Molotov indicated Smith might encourage the French to agree, "I replied," reported Smith "that US was not one of principals to Indochinese dispute and did not cast deciding vote, to which Molotov remarked 'maybe so, but you have veto, that word I hear you use so often.'"

In his "comment," Smith cabled:

"It is probable that initial Soviet tactics were to forestall US intervention in the Delta by some kind of a compromise formula involving Hanoi and Haiphong if it appeared that such intervention were imminent. The recent raising of the ante in negotiations here by the Communist side probably reflects an estimate on their part that our intervention is improbable and that they are safe to go ahead there, keeping, of course, a sharp eye out for indications of change in our attitude."

Dulles had fought any partition of Vietnam but Chauvel reported in Geneva in June to U. Alexis Johnson of the American delegation that "there had been conversations between Vietnamese and Viet Minh in which Viet Minh had made it clear that only two alternatives were coalition government or partition."

The same day Dulles cabled that the suggestion then surfacing for a line dividing Vietnam at the "Thakhek - Donghoi line, coupled with rapid Delta deterioration, is leading us to reexamine possible defacto partition Vietnam."

Both Dulles and the Joint Chiefs of Staff had opposed partition and/or elections. In April of 1954 Dulles cabled Dillon in Paris and American Ambassador Winthrop Aldrich in London a summary of what he had told French Ambassador Henri Bonnet on the eve of the Geneva Conference.

In part, it said that "division of Indochina impractical. QUOTE Mixed UNQUOTE government would be beginning of disaster." Both, he said, would lead to a "face-saving formula to cover surrender of French Union forces."

A March memorandum from the Chairman of the Joint Chiefs of Staff, Adm. Arthur Radford, to Secretary of Defense Charles Wilson on the JCS views about the then-impending negotiations said this about "establishment of a coalition government:"

"The acceptance of a settlement based upon the establishment of a coalition government in one or more of the Associated States [Vietnam, Laos and Cambodia] would open the way for the ultimate seizure of control by the Communists under conditions which might preclude timely and effective external assistance in the prevention of such seizure."

In a paragraph about "self-determination through free elections," the JCS said in part:

"The Communists, by vir-

bility in the field of propaganda, could readily pervert the issue as being a choice between national independence and French colonial rule. Furthermore, it would be militarily infeasible to prevent widespread intimidation of voters by Communist partisans. While it is obviously impossible to make a dependable forecast as to the outcome of a free election, current intelligence leads the Joint Chiefs of Staff to the belief that a settlement based upon free elections would be attended by almost certain loss of the Associated States to Communist control."

"Longer term" results of such a loss, said the JCS, "involving the gravest threats to fundamental United States security interests in the Far East and even to the stability and security of Europe could be expected to ensue."

By the time the Geneva Conference opened, as has been known for many years, the United States had actively considered the idea of military intervention. The documents made available to The Washington Post reflect this consideration at many points.

For example, a January, 1954, meeting of the President's Special Committee on Indochina discussed sending various aircraft to the French as well as 200 military mechanics. Deputy Defense Secretary Roger Kyes "questioned" whether sending the men "would not so commit the U.S. to support the French that we must be prepared eventually for complete intervention, including use of U.S. combat forces." State's Undersecretary Smith disagreed, saying "we were sending maintenance forces not ground forces. He felt, however, that the importance of winning in Indochina was so great that if worst came to the worst he personally would favor intervention with U.S. air and naval forces—not ground forces."

Kyes said he "felt this consideration was so important that it should be put to the highest level. The President himself should decide. General Smith agreed."

But there were contrary voices as well. Late in January, Sen. John Stennis (D-Miss.), then a low-ranking member and now chairman of the Armed Services Committee, wrote Secretary Wilson to say that "I have been impressed for some time that we have been steadily moving closer and closer to participation in the war in Indo-China."

He said he did not object to policy thus far but that "it seems to me that we should certainly stop short of sending our troops or airmen to this area, either for participation in the conflict or as instructors. As always, when we send one group, we shall have to send another to protect the first and we shall thus be fully involved in a short time."

The available papers do not include a response from Wilson to the senator.

Earlier that month, President Eisenhower approved but no later statement on air

the National Security Council table two days earlier on "United States objectives and courses of action with respect to Southeast Asia." It began with a sweeping statement of "general considerations," one foreshadowed in the Truman administration and to be continued in one form or another, as the documents show, into the Johnson administration.

"1. Communist domination, by whatever means, of all Southeast Asia would seriously endanger in the short term, and critically endanger in the longer term, United States security interests.

"a. In the conflict in Indochina, the Communist and non-Communist worlds clearly confront one another on the field of battle. The loss of the struggle in Indochina, in addition to its impact in Southeast Asia and in South Asia, would therefore have the most serious repercussions on U.S. and free world interests in Europe and elsewhere.

"b. Such is the interrelation of the countries of the area that effective counteraction would be immediately necessary to prevent the loss of any single country from leading to submission to or an alignment with communism by the remaining countries of Southeast Asia and Indonesia. Furthermore, in the event all of Southeast Asia falls under communism, an alignment with communism of India, and in the longer term, of the Middle East (with the probable excep-

Leading West...
showing...

Post-Disclosures 450. Three Takes Total 1-170

WASHINGTON AP — The Washington Post said today a Pentagon study asserts there was no connivance in 1955 between the United States and the Saigon regime to prevent elections throughout North and South Vietnam as agreed to by the Geneva Conference.

Then President Dwight D. Eisenhower and his secretary of State, John Foster Dulles, feared such elections as leading to a coalition government and eventual Communist takeover, but it was South Vietnamese President Ngo Dinh Diem who was responsible for their not being held, according to the Post account.

The story, written by Chalmers M. Roberts and appearing in the Post's later editions today, was described as based on "sections of the Pentagon study on the origins of the Vietnam war" made available to The Washington Post."

There was no indication in the Post story how the study was obtained or if it were the same or part of a secret, 47-volume Defense Department document used by The New York Times for a series on the conflict.

The Times account was ordered stopped by a federal judge Tuesday after publication of the third of a five- art series based on the secret study. The judge issued a temporary injunction in order to consider a government argument that further disclosure should be permanently banned in the interest of national security.

The Justice Department refused comment on the Post story.

The parts of the study disclosed by the Post today contained little not already known and published over the years since the Eisenhower administration.

But it did make these points:

—It was Diem, later assassinated, who was responsible almost alone for heading off the national elections, called for by the 1954 Geneva Conference, by refusing to deal with the Communists in the North.

—An Army report dealing with a National Security Council position paper in early 1954 on the need of preventing a Communist takeover in any of the Indochinese regions said the United States would need seven divisions plus air and naval support to win a ground war in Indochina.

At the height of U.S. involvement, April 1969, there were nine
American divisions and a total troop level of 543,000 men.

—That NSC position paper, approved by President Eisenhower, was
based on what is now called the "domino theory"—if one part of
Indochina fell to the Communists and there was no Western
intervention the rest would fall, leading to danger for U.S.
allies in the rest of Asia and Europe.

—Eisenhower, although approving the planning of the position paper,
refused to intervene on behalf of the French without allied
participation and congressional approval. The British refused.

As outlined by the Post, the Pentagon study indicates a reluctance
on the part of Eisenhower and particularly Dulles to any step
that they thought could lead to Communist domination.

MORE

AG617acd June 18

A048WX

     uivrgyr

WASH Post-Disclosures, AO47WX, Take 2! domination.

Regarding the elections, the Post quotes in part from what it
said was a July 1954 cable from Dulles to involved U.S. diplomats:

" . . . Thus since undoubtedly true that elections might eventually
mean unification under Ho Chi Minh this makes it all more
important they should be only held as long after
cease-fire agreement as possible and in conditions free from
intimidation to give democratic elements best chance.

"We believe important that no date should be set now and
especially that no conditions should be accepted by French which
would have direct or indirect effect of preventing effective
international supervision of agreement ensuring political as
well as military guarantees."

The Geneva accords starting in 1954 called for elections for
all of Vietnam, finally setting July 1956 as the date. Once the
elections were set the United States ceased active opposition,
but Dulles, according to the Post story, was unhappy nevertheless.

He is described by the Post account of the Pentagon documents as
saying a recent joint declaration by Eisenhower and British Prime
Minister Winston Churchill was going "down the drain with our
apparent acquiescence."

that declaration called for unifying divided nations with elections supervised by the United Nations, something not provided for by the Geneva agreements.

Although opposing the elections, the Post story said, Dulles also originally was against partitioning Vietnam. But the newspaper quotes a 1955 report from a French diplomat at the Geneva talks to U. Alexis Johnson of the U.S. delegation:

"There had been conversations between Vietnamese and Viet Minh Communists in which Viet Minh had made it clear that only two alternatives were coalition government or partition."

Dulles is quoted as saying at that same time U.S. opposition to de facto partition was being examined.

But in the end it was Diem almost alone who stopped the elections and any possibeb

pfeOf a a F 1 LR "T

But in the end it was Diem almost alone who stopped the elections andanf fbesibilitgonofsa coahsisunegrovernment with Hanoi, the Post

But in the end it was Diem ad∗so lone who sto5s C TA

But in the end it was Diem almost alone who stopped the elections and any possibility of a coalition government with Hanoi, the Post said of the Pentagon report.

The paper quoted what it called a summary part of the papers:

"As the deadline for consultations approached 20 July 1955 Diem was increasingly explicit that he did not consider free elections possible in North Vietnam, and had no intention of consulting with the Communists concerning them.

"The U.S. did not—as is often alleged—connive with Diem to ignore the elections. U.S. State Department records indicate Diem's refusal to be bound by the Geneva Accords and his opposition to pre-election consultations were at his own initiative.

"However, the U.S. which had expected elections to be held . . . shifted its position in the face of Diem's opposition, and of the evidence then accumulated about the oppressive nature of the regime in North Vietnam."

MORE

AC0g6aed June 18

ulvqyy

WASH Post-Disclosures, AO49XX: Take 5: Vietnam.''

The summary itself then quotes a State Department study, the
POST SAID, TO THE EFFECT THAT THE United States position was to
Interxxxxxctions up to the Vietnamese without any outside

Part of the problem facing the United States 19

The summary itself then quotes a State Department study, the
post said, to the effect that the United States position was to
leave elections up to the Vietnamese without any outside
interference.

Part of the problem facing the United States in Indochina through
the 1950s involved allied support for any possible U.S. intervention
on behalf of the crumbling French empire.

As the Post tells the story, the Pentagon documents show Dulles

$ 00 g Sel of the Br

As the Post tells the story, the Pentagon documents show Dulles
very critical of the British position regarding intervention.

After British Foreign Minister Anthony Eden is quoted as telling
Dulles in April 1954 he feared military intervention would be
''a bigger affair than Korea,'' the American secretary is said
to have summarized his feelings, in part:

''UK attitude is one of increasing weakness. British seem to feel
that we are disposed to accept present risks of a Chinese war and
this, coupled with their fear that we would start using atomic
weapons has badly frightened them.''

Although the Post account of the documents shows a generally
hard approach by the American government in line with Dulles'
thinking, the documents indicate Eisenhower had a careful and
constant state of mind.

In a memorandum the Post describes as written by Robert Cutler,
the president's special assistant for National Security Council
affairs Eisenhower is quoted as telling Dulles:

''The United States will not agree to a 'white men's party' to
determine the problems of the Southeast Asian nations.''

AO031xx1 June 13

THE NEW YORK COPS

__An Informal History by Gerald Astor • Today: The Pros • Page 35__

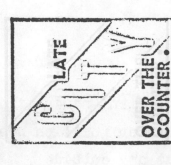

LATE
CITY
OVER THE
COUNTER.

New York Post

FOUNDED 1801. THE OLDEST CONTINUOUSLY PUBLISHED DAILY IN THE UNITED STATES.

Vol. 170
No. 181

NEW YORK, FRIDAY, JUNE 18, 1971
© 1971 New York Post Corporation

15 Cents

WEATHER
Sunny, high 80s.
Tonight: Clear,
high 60s.

Tomorrow: Sunny,
high 80s.

Fair and very warm
Sunday.

SUNSET: 8:30 PM
SUNRISE
TOMORROW: 5:25 AM

From the Pentagon Papers:

MORE WAR

MORE WAR SECRETS

By Chalmers M. Roberts

The Eisenhower Administration, fearful that elections throughout North and South Vietnam would bring victory to Ho Chi Minh, fought hard but in vain at the 1954 Geneva conference to reduce the possibility that the conference would call for such elections.

But the following year, it was South Vietnamese President Ngo Dinh Diem, far more than the U. S. government, who was responsible for preventing the elections.

Diem flatly refused even to discuss the elections with the Communist regime in Hanoi.

These are among the facts emerging from sections of the Pentagon study on the origins of the Vietnam war that have been made available to The Washington Post.

The chief architect of the American policy

The Washington Post has obtained access to sections of the Pentagon report on the Vietnam war, part of which appeared in The New York Times before the government got a temporary injunction to halt further publication. The first in a series of articles based on previously unpublished parts of the report begins here.

of opposition to elections, as was well known at the time, was President Eisenhower's Secretary of State John Foster Dulles.

But it was Eisenhower who insisted on getting allied support if he were to ask Congress for authority to use American military force to save the French Army in Indochina in early 1954.

The U. S. did not get that allied support.

The origin of the idea of holding an election in divided Vietnam, called for in the Geneva Accords of 1954, remains obscure. But there is nothing obscure about Dulles' attitude.

In July of 1954, he sent a cable to various American diplomats then struggling with the problem. It said in part:

"... Thus since undoubtedly true that elections might eventually mean unification Vietnam under Ho Chi Minh this makes it all more important they should be only held as long after ceasefire agreement as possible and in conditions free from intimidation to give democratic elements best chance.

"We believe important that no date should be set now and especially that no conditions should be accepted by French which would have direct or indirect effect of preventing effective

Continued on Page 2

2

Back to '54: Ike & Dulles

Continued from Page 1

international supervision of agreement ensuring political guarantees."

Dulles went on to call attention to a joint-statement by President Eisenhower and British Prime Minister Churchill in June, part which spoke of achieving "unity through free elections supervised by the UN."

Later in July, shortly before issuance in Geneva of the "final declaration" of the long conference — a declaration that included the statement that "general elections shall be held in July, 1956" — Dulles cabled his unhappiness at the impending outcome.

He sent a cable expressing his disappointment to Walter Bedell Smith, the Undersecretary of State who had returned to the Geneva conference to limit as much as possible that Dulles foresaw as the disasterous outcome. The cable said in part:

"While we don't want to take responsibility of imposing our views on the French, I feel particularly concerned about provisions of Paragraph 6, which gives the Control Commission constituted as per Secto 666 authority also to control the general elections.

"The ink is hardly dry on the declaration of President Eisenhower and Prime Minister

Churchill of June 29 to the effect that 'in the case of nations now divided against their will, we shall continue to seek to achieve unity through free elections *supervised by the UN* to insure that they are conducted fairly.'

"It is rather humiliating to see that declaration now so quickly go down the drain with our apparent acquiescence."

About a week before the cable, and after French Premier Pierre Mendes-France had asked that Dulles return to Geneva and before Dulles agreed to send Smith as his stand-in, Dulles cabled some of his unhappiness to Mendes-France via the American Embassy in Paris.

Dulles complained to Mendes-France of "a whittling away process, each stroke of which may in itself seem unessential, but which cumulatively could produce a result quite different from that envisaged" in a seven-point minimum program, agreed upon by Britain and the U. S., that he then was trying to sell France.

He included this paragraph as illustrative of that "whittling-away process:"

"Allowing Communist forces to remain in Northern Laos; accepting a Vietnam line of military demarcation considerable south of Dong

on Molotov at his Geneva villa. He filed a long report, together with his comments, which included these:

"In private conversations with Mr. Eden and others, Communist delegates, in particular Chou En-lai, had taken an apparently reasonable view on Laos and Cambodia, but that here again, when we came to the point of trying to get open agreement on specific points we were unable to do so.

"I specifically mentioned Chou En-lai's statements to Eden in which he said that China would have no objections to recognizing the kingdoms of Laos and Cambodia or to these states having forces and arms sufficient to maintain security, or their remaining in French union so long as they were not used as military bases by the U.S.

"We could not disagree with any of this although if we kept out, the Chinese would have to keep out and these small states would have to be allowed to join with their neighbors in whatever regional security arrangements would best protect their integrity without constituting a threat to any one else.

"Chou En-lai might be anxious about possibility of U. S. bases in Laos and Cam-

Smith told Molotov that "appearance of 'partition' was repugnant to U. S." and he reported that "in regard to U. S. aversion to partition, he [Molotov] said that this problem could easily be solved by holding elections at once, which would decide 'one way or the other.'"

When Molotov indicated that Smith might encourage the French to agree, Smith reported, "I replied that U. S. was not one of principals to Indochinese dispute and did not cast deciding vote, to which Molotov remarked, 'Maybe so, but you have veto, that word I hear you use so often.'"

In his "comment," Smith cabled:

"It is probable that initial Soviet tactics were to forestall U. S. intervention in the delta by some kind of a compromise formula involving Hanoi and Haiphong if it appeared that such intervention were imminent.

"The recent raising of the ante in negotiations here by the Communist side probably reflects an estimate on their part that our intervention is improbable and that they are safe to go ahead there, keeping, of course, a sharp eye out for indications of change in our attitude."

'Coalition Or Partition'

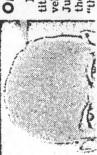

Dulles had fought any partition of Vietnam, but Chauvel reported in Geneva in June to U. Alexis Johnson of the American delegation that "there had been conversations

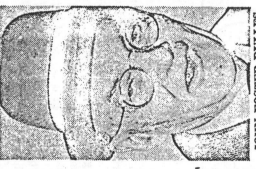

JOHN FOSTER DULLES
Opposed elections.

hoi; neutralizing and [one word indistinct] demilitarizing Laos, Cambodia and Vietnam so as to impair their capacity to maintain stable, non-Communist regimes; Accepting elections so early and so ill-prepared and illsupervised as to risk the loss of the entire area to communism; accepting international supervision by a body which cannot be effective because it includes a Communist state which has veto power."

In the end the election was called for, but not without considerable argument at Geneva, where the U. S. worked through the French. But others had the important say.

Chief among these important people were Chou En-lai, then as now Chinese premier, and V. M. Molotov, the Soviet

---

NEXT WEEK IN THE POST:
"THE ADVANCE MAN"

---

about provisions of para-graph 6, which gives the Control Commission constituted as per Secto 666 authority also to control the general elections.

"The ink is hardly dry on the declaration of President Eisenhower and Prime Minister considerable south of Dong

He included this paragraph as illustrative of that "whittling-away process:"

"Allowing Communist forces to remain in Northern Laos; accepting a Vietnam line of military demarcation

NEXT WEEK IN THE POST:
"THE ADVANCE MAN"

Jerry Bruno is a politician's advance man, the backstage virtuoso who guarantees that the crowds, the cheers, the local dignitaries are strewn like roses in the great man's path.

A pro's pro, Bruno worked for and with the Kennedys, John and Robert. Now, with Jeff Greenfield, he has written his account of those stirring years, plus a bonus of his expert's judgment on the Johnson and Humphrey campaigns.

"The Advance Man" is the inside story of presidential politicking. A digest of the book begins Monday in The Post.

which cannot be effective because it includes a Communist state which has veto power."

"Chou En-Lai might be anxious about possibility of U. S. bases in Laos and Cam-

Chief among these important people were Chou En-Lai, then as now Chinese premier, and V. M. Molotov, the Soviet Union's redoubtable foreign minister.

In June, 1954, U. S. Ambassador to France Douglas Dillon cabled Dulles to report conversations with Jean Chauvel, a key diplomat at the conference.

'Two Governments In Vietnam'—Chou

Chauvel reported that Chou had "said that he recognized that there were now two governments in the territory of Vietnam, the Vietminh government and the 'Vietnamese government.'" "According to Chauvel," Dillon wrote, "this was the first time that Chou had recognized the valid existence of the Vietnamese government."

As to elections, Dillon reported:

"Regarding the final political settlement, Chou said this should be reached by direct negotiations between the two governments in Vietnam . . . Mendes at this point said that since the war had been going on for eight years and passions were high, it would take a long time before elections could be held as the people must be given a full opportunity to cool off and calm down.

"Chou made no objection to this statement by Mendes and did not press for early elections."

ments would best protect their integrity without constituting a threat to any one else.

"Chou En-Lai might be anxious about possibility of U. S. bases in Laos and Cambodia. We wanted on our part to be sure that these countries were not handed over to the Chinese.

"Molotov said that while he did not know about what attitude Chinese might have on other questions in future, he could assure me that Chinese attitude on this particular question was not at all unreasonable, and that there was nothing in it which would give rise to conflicts.

"He added, however, that if we continued to take a one-sided view and insist on one-sided solutions, he must 'in all frankness say that this would not succeed.'"

EISENHOWER
Insisted on allied support.

'Coalition Or Partition'

Dulles had fought any partition of Vietnam, but Chauvel reported in Geneva in June to U. Alexis Johnson of the American delegation that "there had been conversations between Vietnamese and Vietminh in which Vietminh had made it clear that only two alternatives were coalition government or partition."

The same day, Dulles cabled that the suggestion then surfacing for a line dividing Vietnam at the "Thakhek-Donghoi line, coupled with rapid delta deterioration, is leading us to reexamine possible defacto partition Vietnam."

improbable and that they are safe to go ahead there, keeping, of course, a sharp eye out for indications of change in our attitude."

Both Dulles and the Joint Chiefs of Staff had opposed partition and/or elections. In April of 1954, Dulles cabled to Dillon in Paris, and to U.S. Ambassador Winthrop Aldrich in London, a summary of what he had told French Ambassador Henri Bonnet on the eve of the Geneva conference.

In part, the cable said that "division of Indochina impractical. 'Mixed' government would be beginning of disaster." Both, he said, would lead to a "face-saving formula to cover surrender of French union forces."

A March memorandum from the chairman of the Joint Chiefs of Staff, Adm. Arthur Radford, to Secretary of Defense Charles Wilson on the then-impending negotiations said this about "establishment of a coalition government":

"The acceptance of a' settlement based upon the es-

Continued on Page 3

The Post Carries me wire services of the Associated Press (AP), Chicago Daily News (CDN), Chicago Sun Times (CS-T), Los Angeles Times (LAT), Washington Post (WP) and London Express.

Published daily except Sunday 2d class postage paid at New York, N. Y. 76

1961: JFK Inherits the War

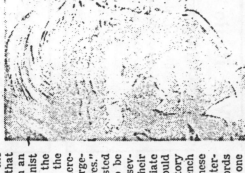

Continued from Page 2

tablishment of a coalition government in one or more of the Associated State [Vietnam, Laos and Cambodia] would open the way for the ultimate seizure of control by the Communists under conditions which might preclude timely and effective external assistance in the prevention of such seizure."

In a paragraph about "self-determination through free elections," the JCS said in part:

"The Communists, by virtue of their superior capability in the field of propaganda, could readily pervert the issue as being a choice between national independence and French colonial rule. Furthermore, it would be militarily infeasible to prevent widespread intimidation of voters by Communist partisans.

"While it is obviously impossible to make a dependable forecast as to the outcome of a free election, current intelligence leads the

use of U. S. combat forces."

Undersecretary of State Smith disagreed, saying that "we were sending maintenance 'forces, not ground forces." He felt, however, that the importance of winning in Indochina was so great that if worse came to the worst he personally would favor intervention with U. S. air and naval forces.

Stennis said he did not object to policy thus far but that, it seems to me that we should certainly stop short of sending our troops or airmen to this area, either for participation in the conflict or as instructors. As always, when we send one group, we shall have to send another to protect the first and we shall thus be fully involved in a short time."

Put to the Highest Level

The available papers do not include a response from Wilson to the Senator.

Keys said he "felt this consideration was so important that it should be put to the highest level. The President himself should decide. General Smith agreed."

But there were contrary voices as well. Late in January, Sen. Stennis (D-Miss.), then a low-ranking member and now chairman of the Armed Services Committee, wrote Secretary Wilson to say that "I have been impressed for some time that we have been steadily moving closer and closer to participation in the war in Indochina."

KENNEDY
Now it was up to him.

important areas of free Asia. "Furthermore, this area has an important potential as a market for the industrialized countries of the free world.

"E. The loss of Southeast Asia, especially of Malaya and Indonesia, could result in such economic and political pressures in Japan as to make it extremely difficult to prevent Japan's eventual accommodation to Communism."

While the NSC study stated that "overt Chinese Communist attack on any part of Southeast Asia is less probable than continued Communist efforts to achieve domination through armed rebellion or subversion," the possibility of war with China was explored. It was stated that "in the event the United States participates in the fighting, there a substantial risk that the Chinese Communists would intervene."

ously endanger in the short term, and critically endanger in the long team, United States security interests.

"A. In the conflict in Indochina, the Communist and non-Communist world clearly confront one another on the field of battle. The loss of the struggle in Indochina, in addition to its impact in Southeast Asia and in South Asia, would therefore have the most serious repercussions on U. S. and free world interests in Europe and elsewhere.

"B. Such is the interrelation of the countries of the area that effective counteraction would be immediately necessary to prevent the loss of any single country from leading to submission to or an alignment with communism by the remaining countries of Southeast Asia and Indonesia.

lined were indeed taken, "the U. S. should recognize that it may become involved in an all-out war with Communist China, and possibly with the USSR and the rest of the Soviet bloc, and should therefore proceed to take large-scale mobilization measures."

Military studies suggested that if the U. S. were to be involved on the ground, "seven U. S. divisions or their equivalent, with appropriate naval and air support, would be required to win a victory in Indochina if the French withdrew and the Chinese Communists' did not intervene." These were the words of the "army position" on one NSC action memorandum.

But President Eisenhower, although he had approved the planning, wanted both Congressional approval and allied participation for any American interventions.

An April telegram from Dulles to Dillon reported: "Congressional action would be required. After conference at highest level, I must confirm this position."

Dulles added that the "U. S. is doing everything possible" to "prepare public, Congressional and Constitutionl basis for united action in Indochina. However, such action is impossible except on coalition basis with active British Commonwealth's participation. Meanwhile U. S. prepared, as has been demonstrated, to do everything short of belligerency."

not underestimate the immense difficulty of our finding the right course in this troubled situation. Nor do I mean to imply that this is the moment for a bold or warlike course. I lack here the U. S. political and NSC judgments needed for overall evaluation."

Summary statements in the papers available to The Washington Post do not include any Eisenhower decision not to intervene at any of the several points during 1954 when that was under consideration.

The closest thing to a clear definition of the chief executive's thinking is a May memorandum to the Secretary of Defense and the Chairman of the Joint Chiefs by Robert Cutler, the special assistant to the President who handled NSC affairs.

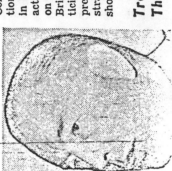

ANTHONY EDEN
He was worried.

Trouble With The British

The immediate aim was to help the French by expediting, "and if necessary," increasing aid, to assist them in:"

"A An aggressive military, political a n d psychological program, including covert op-

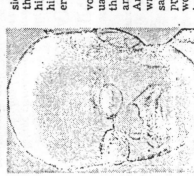

Continued on Page 23

highest level. The President himself should decide. General Smith agreed."

But there were contrary voices as well. Late in January, Sen. Stennis (D-Miss.), then a low-ranking member and now chairman of the Armed Services Committee, wrote Secretary Wilson to say that "I have been impressed for some time that we have been steadily moving closer and closer to participation in the war in Indo-China."

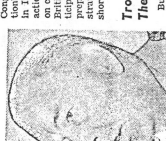

Joint Chiefs of Staff to the belief that a settlement based upon free elections would be attended by almost certain loss of the Associated States to Communist control."

"Long-term" results of such a loss, said the JCS, "involving the gravest threats to fundamental United States security interests in the Far East and even to the stability and security of Europe could be expected to ensue."

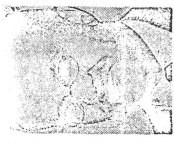

V. M. MOLOTOV
Urged immediate elections.

Intervention Is Considered

By the time the Geneva conference opened, as has been known for many years, the U. S. had actively considered the idea of military intervention. The documents made available to The Washington Post reflect this at many points.

For example, a January, 1954, meeting of the President's special committee on Indochina discussed sending various aircraft to the French as well as 200 military mechanics. Deputy Defense Secretary Roger Keys questioned whether sending the men "would not so commit the U. S. to support the French that we must be prepared eventually for complete intervention, including

possible" to "prepare public, Congressional and Constitutional basis for united action in Indochina. However, such action is impossible except on coalition basis with active British Commonwealth's participation. Meanwhile U. S. prepared, as has been demonstrated, to do everything short of belligerency."

Trouble With The British

But Dulles had had trouble rounding up allies, especially the British. Dulles reported to Smith that a late April talk with Foreign Secretary Anthony Eden in London had found Eden worrying that military intervention would be "a bigger affair than Korea," where hostilities had ended less than a year earlier.

ADM. RADFORD
Feared coalition government.

erations, to eliminate organized Vietminh forces by mid-1955."

"B. Developing indigenous armed forces, including logistical and administrative services which will eventually be capable of maintaining internal security without assistance from French units."

Preparing For Chinese Intervention

In the event of Chinese intervention, the NSC concluded, the UN should be asked to call on member nations to "take whatever action may be necessary...to meet such an aggression"

Whether or not the UN did act, it was proposed that the U. S., either under UN auspices or in concert with France, Britain and "other friendly governments," take steps such as interdicting Chinese communication lines "including those in China," and, "if appropriate," also establish a joint "naval blockade of Communist China and "as desirable and feasible," utilize Chinese nationalist forces "in military operations in Southeast Asia, Korea, or China proper."

"The rice exports of Burma, Indochina and Thailand are critically important to Malaya, Ceylon and Hong Kong and are of considerable significance to Japan and India, all

the most serious repercussions on U. S. and free world interests in Europe and elsewhere.

"B. Such is the interrelation of the countries of the area that effective counteraction would be immediately necessary to prevent the loss of any single country from leading to submission to or an alignment with communism by the remaining countries of Southeast Asia and Indonesia.

'An Alignment With Communism'

Earlier that month, President Eisenhower approved the policy statement set at the National Security Council table two days earlier on "United States Objectives and Courses of Action With Respect to Southeast Asia."

It began with a sweeping statement of "General Considerations," one foreshadowed in the Truman Administration and to be continued in one form or another, as the documents show, into the Johnson Administration:

"1. Communist domination, by whatever means, of all Southeast Asia would seri-

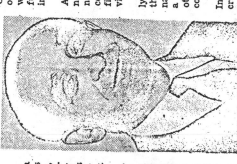

MENDES-FRANCE
Asked Dulles to return.

"Furthermore, in the event all of Southeast Asia falls under Communism, an alignment with Communism of India, and in the longer term, of the Middle East (with the probable exceptions of at least Pakistan and Turkey) could follow progressively. Such widespread alignment would seriously endanger the stability and security of Europe.

"C. Communist control of all of Southeast Asia and Indonesia would threaten the U. S. position in the Pacific offshore island chain and would seriously jeopardize fundamental U. S. security interests in the Far East.

"D. The loss of Southeast Asia would have serious economic consequences for many nations of the free world and conversely would add significant resources to the Soviet bloc.

"Southeast Asia, especially Malaya and Indonesia, is the principal world source of natural rubber and tin, and a producer of petroleum and other strategically important commodities.

Summary statement... papers available to The Washington Post do not include any Eisenhower decision not to intervene at any of the several points during 1954 when that was under consideration.

The closest thing to a clear definition of the chief executive's thinking is a May memorandum to the Secretary of Defense and the Chairman of the Joint Chiefs by Robert Cutler, the special assistant to the President who handled NSC affairs.

Cutler reported on a meeting in the President's office with only President Eisenhower, Dulles and Cutler present, at which the Chief Executive approved instructions for Smith, then in Geneva. It was essentially an expression of unhappiness over Eden's proposals, which fell far short of intervention.

U.S. Won't OK 'A White Man's Party'

Point 3, however, was expressive of the President's frame of mind. It said: "The United States will not agree to a 'white man's party' to determine the problems of the Southeast Asian nations."

In the available papers there is no evidence of a post-Geneva American effort to prevent the elections throughout all of Vietnam from taking place.

The Soviets had "proposed June, 1955" according to one report from Geneva but they and the Chinese and the North Vietnamese had finally agreed to July, 1956. But South Vietnam, which the telegrams make clear had been told almost nothing about the secret Geneva talks, although there was a Saigon delegation present, never accepted the Geneva accords, then or to this day.

A summary paper done as part of the Pentagon Papers

CHOU EN-LAI
An important voice.

But Dulles had had trouble rounding up allies... A few days later, Dulles summarized his findings, in part, this way:

"U.K. attitude is one of increasing weakness. British seem to feel that we are disposed to accept present risks of a Chinese war and this, coupled with their fear that we would start using atomic weapons, has badly frightened them."

Dulles confessed to uncertainty by adding that "I do

Continued on Page 23

4

Freedom of Press 'Not Absolute'—U.S.

By DICK BELSKY

The Justice Dept, seeking a permanent ban on The Times' publication of secret Pentagon Vietnam data, argued in federal court here today that "under certain circumstances the freedoms of speech and press must give way to compelling governmental need."

In a prepared brief for today's session before U. S. District Court Judge Murray Gurfein, government attorneys said:

"Of course the First Amendment to the Constitution guarantees the freedom of speech and press. But it is equally clear that these freedoms are not absolute.

"The issue to be decided in any particular case is whether the projected disclosure involved is so damaging to the national interest that prior restraint is permissible."

No Advance Copy

The Times, which did not release an advance copy of its brief, was expected to reiterate its argument that the government's attempt to halt further publication of the Pentagon documents constitutes a "classic case of censorship" forbidden by First Amendment free-press guarantees.

Meanwhile, the Washington Post today began publishing its own series on U. S. involvement in Vietnam and said it was based on the same secret material at issue here.

to halt the Washington Post law establishing its right to do so.

In distributing the series to newspapers which subscribe to its wire service, the paper included the following editors' note:

"Your attention is drawn to the fact that the study on which this article is based is the subject of the government's injunction against the New York Times in federal court in New York. In the judgment of the Washington Post editors, nothing in this article could be used to the injury of the United States."

Unusual Nature

Portions of today's court session here may be conducted behind closed doors. There were indications that the government might read portions of the secret documents to the court to establish its case that they are crucial to the national interest and must not be made public.

Yesterday, The Times voluntarily agreed to provide the government with a list of the documents on which its interrupted series was based. The U.S. Attorney's office here acknowledged last night that it had received such a list.

The unusual nature of the case was reflected in the government's brief, which did not cite a specific legal provision or an injunction to halt such material deemed secret and therefore not avail...

LBJ Often Gave Press A Peek at Secret Cables

By WILLIAM J. EATON

WASHINGTON (CDN)—Former President Lyndon B. Johnson showed top secret cables to reporters to justify his Vietnam policies and intervention in the Dominican Republic.

Johnson even gave some White House correspondents a peek at the list of bombing targets in North Vietnam during the controversy over U. S. air raids.

One reporter who was shown classified documents in the ex-President's office said he and other correspondents assumed they were not to write stories about what they saw.

And Johnson sometimes covered parts of the document or read excerpts from cables sent by U. S. commanders in Vietnam to the correspondents.

His practice was recalled as debate mounted over the halt publication by The New York Times of a top secret Pentagon study of U. S. involvement in Vietnam.

Meanwhile, two Democratic Congressmen — Bob Eckhardt of Texas and Abner J. Mikva of Illinois — said they would appear at today's session to make a formal motion to be allowed to intervene in the case. They say they are representing 21 members of the House of Representatives.

"This is the only way Congress can avail itself of this important information since...

LYNDON JOHNSON
Favorable secrets only.

Vietnam, and Gen. Maxwell D. Taylor, U. S. Ambassador to Saigon in the early stages of the Johnson Administration.

Unlike the documents disclosed by The New York Times, the ex-President rarely repeated to newsmen any gloomy reports.

"I don't remember anything unfavorable," said one reporter who frequently was present when Johnson divulged some of the contents of the cables from the war zone.

Another reporter recalled how Johnson read lengthy excerpts from cables filed by W. Tapley Bennett, U.S. Ambassador to Santo Domingo, when U.S. troops were sent to prevent a Communist takeover of the Dominican Republic.

Bennett's report was read to a group of reporters during a walking press conference around the South Lawn of the White House, the reporter said.

parently meaning that they were intended only for Johnson's viewing.

Johnson read excerpts of reports from Gen. William C. Westmoreland, who was then U. S. commander in

Ted: Let the People Judge

WASHINGTON (AP) —Sen. Edward M. Kennedy has called for the publication of secret government papers on the Vietnam policies of President Kennedy, so that the American people can be "the final judge" of any deception in U. S. involvement there.

"I don't have any idea what is in it, or how it will turn out," the Massachussets Democrat said in his statement.

But he added that papers published earlier this week in The Times dealing with government policies primarily under the Lyndon B. Johnson administration show "many government officials were deceiving the American people and ultimately deceiving themselves as we escalated the...

WASHINGTON (AP) —Sen. Edward M. Kennedy has called for the publication of secret government papers on the Vietnam policies of President Kennedy, so that the American people can be "the final judge" of any deception in U.S. involvement there.

"I don't have any idea what is in it, or how it will turn out," the Massachussetts Democrat said in his statement.

But he added that papers published earlier this week in The Times dealing with government policies primarily under the Lyndon B. Johnson administration show "many government officials were deceiving the American people and ultimately deceiving themselves as we escalated the violence.

The American people were misled," Kennedy said, "and they are entitled to this information."

---

release an advance copy of its brief, was expected to reiterate its argument that the government's attempt to halt further publication of the Pentagon documents constitutes a "classic case of censorship" forbidden by First Amendment free-press guarantees.

Meanwhile, the Washington Post today began publishing its own series on U. S. involvement in Vietnam and said it was based on the same secret material at issue here. There was no immediat word from the Justice Dept. on whether any new court action was being contemplated

Yesterday, The Times voluntarily agreed to provide the government with a list of the documents on which its interrupted series was based. The U.S. Attorney's office here acknowledged last night that it had received such a list.

The unusual nature of the case was reflected in the government's brief, which did not cite a specific legal provision for an injunction to halt such material deemed secret and therefore not available to the public.

But the government argued that an injunction could be granted without a specific

ized possession of The Times."

Johnson once told reporters about a number of clandestine military operations conducted against North Vietnam in 1964, one correspondent said. These American-sponsored raids were mentioned in the Times' articles.

"He gave the impression that it would be a matter of days or weeks before we would bring them to their knees," the correspondent recalled.

Some of the cables were marked "Eyes Only," ap-

Meanwhile, two Democratic Congressmen — Bob Eckhardt of Texas and Abner J. Mikva of Illinois — said they would appear at today's session to make a formal motion to be allowed to intervene in the case. They say they are representing 21 members of the House of Representatives.

"This is the only way Congress can avail itself of this important information, since the government has already refused to release it to a Senate committee," said Mikva.

secret Pentagon study of U. S. involvement in Vietnam.

HHH Fought Escalation: Aide

By DAVID S. BRODER.
WASHINGTON (WP) — A former member of Hubert H. Humphrey's Vice Presidential staff has offered the first detailed account of Humphrey's private efforts to moderate the Vietnam policies of the Johnson Administration—a record which he said shows Humphrey to be "an honest man" who supported the American role in Vietnam but opposed many of the steps to escalate the conflict.

Ted van Dyck, a top Humphrey speech writer and adviser from 1964 to 1968, said yesterday that Humphrey was "systematically exclued" from Vietnam policy talks for most of 1965 after strongly expressing his personal opposition to the escalation in the first meetings he attended as Vice President.

The recollections van Dyck poured forth in a two-hour interview constituted his rather poignant farewell salute to the Minnesota Senator. The 26-year-old writer and consultant will announce, Friday, that he is

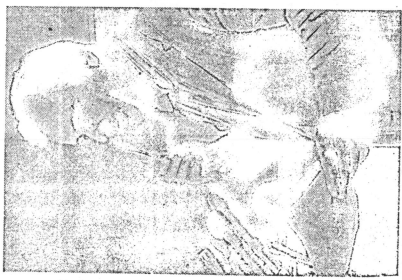

Rep. Bob Eckhardt (D-Tex.) tells reporters in Washington he will attempt to intervene in today's court session on behalf of The Times.

joining Sen. McGovern's Presidential campaign, having concluded that "I don't think Hubert Humphrey should become a Presidential candidate again," as he has hinted he might try to do.
'An Honest Man'

"I think the country and the party need a new start," Van Dyck said, "and I think George McGovern offers us that. But I want the record to show that Hubert Humphrey was no war criminal, nor did he duplicitously tell the American people what he knew to be untrue. He is an honest man."

Among the highlights in Van Dyck's recital of Humphrey's private record on Vietnam policy—confirmed by three other former staff members—were statements that:

¶In a memorandum to President Johnson, written in the spring of 1964, before Humphrey was picked for Vice President, the Senator opposed American withdrawal from Vietnam but contended that "direct U.S. action against North Viet-

nam, American assumption of command roles, or the participation in combat of U.S. troop units are unnecessary and undesirable."

¶In the first high-level Vietnam debates after joining the Administration in January, 1965, Humphrey argued fullscale against bombing of North Vietnam and the dispatch of more American ground troops.
Frozen Out of Talks

¶After Johnson in March, 1965, ordered into effect the policies Humphrey had opposed, the Vice President was "systematically excluded" and "just plain frozen out" of high-level Vietnam policy talks for almost a full year.

¶After a trip to Vietnam in early 1966, Humphrey told associates that the war was 'going to take a helluva lot longer than anybody had talked about, and the best we can hope for is a standoff" with the Communists.

¶Despite his continued support of American assistance to the Vietnamese throughout this period, Hum-

phrey was "almost physically nauseous" when, en route to the inauguration of President Nguyen Van Thieu and Vice President Nguyen Cao Ky in Saigon in October, 1967, an Army colonel described the widespread corruption of the government. "What you've told me," Van Dyck quoted Humphrey as saying, "means I've been telling a bunch of damn lies and defending a bunch of thieves of the American people."
Warning to Thieu

¶On that same trip, Humphrey warned Thieu "in very firm language" that governmental reform and "de-Americanization" of the war "had to take place immediately because American public opinion would not sustain the effort in Vietnam much longer."

¶When he returned from this journey, Humphrey sent Johnson a private report urging "a sharp cutback in American civilian personnel in Vietnam, particularly in the Agency for International throughout this period, Hum-

Continued on Page ??

Kennedy Inherits The Vietnam War

Continued from Page 3

by an unnamed analyst put the outcome this way:

"As the deadline for consultations approached (July, 1955) Diem was increasingly explicit that he did not consider free elections possible in North Vietnam, and had no intention of consulting with the DRV concerning them. The U. S. did not—as is often alleged—connive with Diem to ignore the elections. U. S. State Department records indicate that Diem's refusal to be bound by the Geneva Accords and his opposition to pre-election consultations were at his own initiative.

"However, the U. S., which had expected elections to be held, and up until May, 1955, had fully supported them, shifted its position in the face of Diem's opposition, and of the evidence then accumulated about the oppressive nature of the regime in North Vietnam. 'In essence'. a State Department historical study found, 'our position would be that the whole subject of consultation and elections in Vietnam should be left up to the Vietnamese themselves and not dictated by external arrangements which one of the parties never accepted and still rejects.'

On Jan. 19, 1961, President Eisenhower met in the Oval Room of the White House with President-elect John F. Kennedy. The President said that "Laos is the key to the entire area of Southeast Asia." The President-elect asked "how long it would take to put a U. S. division into Laos."

There was no discussion on Vietnam. That would become the problem for President Kennedy — and President Johnson — and President Nixon.

POST 6-18 WA

1ST LD 066A

WASHINGTON (UPI) --THE EISENHOWER ADMINISTRATION TRIED
TO DELAY 1955 ELECTIONS IN VIETNAM FOR FEAR THE LATE HO CHI
MINH WOULD WIN, AND WAS ACTIVELY CONSIDERING LIMITED MILITARY
INTERVENTION BEFORE THE 1954 GENEVA CONVENTION, ACCORDING TO
A SECRET PENTAGON DOCUMENT PUBLISHED TODAY BY THE WASHINGTON POST.

THE REPORT SAID PRESIDENT DWIGHT D. EISENHOWER'S SPECIAL
COMMITTEE ON INDOCHINA MET SIX MONTHS BEFORE THE CONVENTION TO
DISCUSS SENDING 200 MILITARY MECHANICS AND AIRCRAFT TO AID THE
FRENCH.

THE POST SAID THE DOCUMENTS "REFLECT THIS CONSIDERATION
(MILITARY INTERVENTION) AT MANY POINTS," BUT IT CITED ONLY THE
DISCUSSIONS RAISED IN THE JANUARY, 1954 MEETING OF THE COMMITTEE
ON INDOCHINA.

THE POST ALSO SAID THE PAPERS "DO NOT INCLUDE ANY EISENHOWER
DECISION NOT TO INTERVENE AT ANY OF THE SEVERAL POINTS DURING
1954 WHEN THAT WAS UNDER CONSIDERATION.

THERE WAS NO DIRECT INDICATION THE REPORT WAS THE SAME ONE USED
AS THE BASIS OF A NEW YORK TIMES SERIES ON THE VIETNAM WAR. THE
TIMES WAS PLACED EARLY THIS WEEK UNDER A TEMPORARY FEDERAL COURT
INJUNCTION NOT TO PRINT THE FINAL PARTS OF ITS SERIES.

THE POST, IN WHAT IT SAID WOULD BE THE FIRST OF A SERIES, SAID
IT HAD CULLED THE INFORMATION "FROM SECTIONS OF THE PENTAGON STUDY
ON THE ORIGINS OF THE VIETNAM WAR MADE AVAILABLE TO" THE POST.

THE POST SAID THAT EISENHOWER, UNDER THE PRODDING OF SECRETARY
OF STATE JOHN FOSTER DULLES, MADE HIS ATTEMPT TO DELAY THE
ELECTIONS DURING 1954 GENEVA CONVENTION.

DULLES SAID IN A TELEGRAM TO U.S. DIPLOMATS DEALING WITH THE
VIETNAM QUESTION IN 1954 THAT "SINCE (IT IS) UNDOUBTEDLY TRUE THAT
ELECTIONS MIGHT EVENTUALLY MEAN UNIFICATION (OF) VIETNAM UNDER
HO CHI MINH, THIS MAKES IT ALL THE MORE IMPORTANT THEY SHOULD BE ONLY
HELD AS LONG AFTER CEASE-FIRE AGREEMENT AS POSSIBLE AND IN
CONDITIONS FREE FROM INTIMIDATION TO GIVE DEMOCRATIC ELEMENTS
BEST CHANCE."

THE U.S. EFFORT TO HEAD OFF THE ELECTIONS FAILED AT THE
CONVENTION, WHICH WAS CALLED AFTER THE FRENCH WERE DEFEATED AT
DIENBIENPHU MAY 8, 1954.

BUT THERE WERE NO ELECTIONS IN 1955 BECAUSE SOUTH VIETNAMESE
PRESIDENT NGO DINH DIEM, WHO WAS EVENTUALLY ASSASSINATED DURING
THE MILITARY COUP OF NOVEMBER, 1963, REFUSED TO ALLOW THEM.

MORE E9AED

POST 6-18 WA

1ST ADD 1ST LD POST WASHINGTON 083A XXX ALLOW THEM.

THE POST SAID THAT AMONG THE DOCUMENTS IN ITS POSSESSION THERE
WAS NO CLEAR INDICATION HOW EISENHOWER FELT ABOUT THE POSSIBILITY
OF MILITARY INTERVENTION IN INDOCHINA.

"THE CLOSEST THING TO A CLEAR DEFINITION OF THE CHIEF EXECUTIVE'S
THINKING" SAID THE POST, "IS A MAY MEMORANDUM TO THE SECRETARY
OF DEFENSE AND THE CHAIRMAN OF THE JOINT CHIEFS BY ROBERT CUTLER,
THE SPECIAL ASSISTANT TO THE PRESIDENT" FOR NATIONAL SECURITY COUNCIL
AFFAIRS. THE MEMO, THE POST SAID, EXPRESSED "UNHAPPINESS OVER
(BRITISH PRIME MINISTER ANTHONY) EDEN'S PROPOSALS, WHICH FELL FAR
SHORT OF INTERVENTION."

THE DOCUMENTS INDICATE THAT EISENHOWER DID APPROVE A POLICY
STATEMENT OF THE NATIONAL SECURITY COUNCIL THAT SAID, "COMMUNIST
DOMINATION, BY WHATEVER MEANS, OF ALL SOUTHEAST ASIA WOULD SERIOUSLY
ENDANGER IN THE SHORT TERM, AND CRITICALLY ENDANGER IN THE LONGER
TERM, THE UNITED STATES SECURITY INTERESTS."

THE JOINT CHIEFS STATEMENT ADVOCATED SUPPORTING THE FRENCH IN
"AN AGGRESSIVE MILITARY, POLITICAL AND PSYCHOLOGICAL PROGRAM,
INCLUDING COVERT OPERATIONS, TO ELIMINATE ORGANIZED VIET MINH
FORCES BY MID-1955."

IT ALSO SAID A COMMUNIST TAKEOVER OF SOUTHEAST ASIA "COULD RESULT
IN SUCH ECONOMIC AND POLITICAL PRESSURES IN JAPAN AS TO MAKE IT
EXTREMELY DIFFICULT TO PREVENT JAPAN'S EVENTUAL ACCOMMODATION TO
COMMUNISM."

THE STATEMENT SAID "OVERT CHINESE COMMUNIST ATTACK" WAS NOT LIKELY UNLESS THE "UNITED STATES PARTICIPATES IN THE FIGHTING."

THE PENTAGON DOCUMENT, HOWEVER, SAID EISENHOWER, ALTHOUGH HE HAD APPROVED THE PLANNING OUTLINED IN THE NATIONAL SECURITY COUNCIL STATEMENT, WANTED THE APPROVAL OF CONGRESS AND THE SUPPORT OF U. S. ALLIES BEFORE IMPLEMENTING IT.

DURING THE 1954 MEETING OF THE COMMITTEE ON INDOCHINA, DEPUTY DEFENSE SECRETARY ROGER KYES SAID SENDING THE 200 MECHANICS TO HELP THE FRENCH MIGHT "SO COMMIT THE U. S. TO SUPPORT THE FRENCH THAT WE MUST BE PREPARED EVENTUALLY FOR COMPLETE INTERVENTION, INCLUDING USE OF U. S. COMBAT FORCES."

THE DOCUMENT SAID UNDERSECRETARY OF STATE WALTER BEDELL SMITH ARGUED THAT "THE IMPORTANCE OF WINNING IN INDOCHINA WAS SO GREAT THAT IF WORST CAME TO THE WORST HE PERSONALLY WOULD FAVOR INTERVENTION WITH U. S. AIR AND NAVAL FORCES--NOT GROUND FORCES."

AMONG THE VOICES RAISED AGAINST SENDING ANY U.S. FORCES TO INDOCHINA WAS SEN. JOHN C. STENNIS, D-MISS., WHO WAS THEN A LOW-RANKING MEMBER OF THE ARMED SERVICES COMMITTEE HE NOW HEADS.

"IT SEEMS TO ME THAT WE SHOULD CERTAINLY STOP SHORT OF SENDING OUR TROOPS OR AIRMEN TO THIS AREA, EITHER FOR PARTICIPATION IN THE CONFLICT OR AS INSTRUCTORS," STENNIS SAID IN A LETTER TO DEFENSE SECRETARY CHARLES E. WILSON.

"AS ALWAYS, WHEN WE SEND ONE GROUP, WE SHALL HAVE TO SEND ANOTHER TO PROTECT THE FIRST AND WE SHALL THUS BE FULLY INVOLVED IN A SHORT TIME."

INCLUDES PREVIOUS 066A. EDITORS WISHING MORE MATERIAL MAY PICKUP 9TH PGH 066A-076A: DULLES AND THE

E908AED..

Report '61 Study Urged:
Send 2 Divisions to Viet

By JOSEPH FRIED
Staff Correspondent of THE NEWS

Saigon, June 17—Nearly four years before American troops entered the Vietnam war, a top-level mission sent here by President Kennedy in 1961 urged that the United States immediately send two full combat divisions into South Vietnam to stem the mounting Communist threat.

Reliable sources disclosed for the first time today that the recommendation, made by Gen. Maxwell Taylor and Walt W. Rostow, two key Kennedy aides, advocated that some of the troops be assigned under the cover of "flood relief teams" in order partially to cushion the impact.

Taylor and Rostow flew here on Kennedy's orders in the autumn of 1961 to assess the deteriorating situation in South Vietnam and draw up proposals for further American assistance. At that time, U. S. military personnel in South Vietnam consisted of 3,200 advisers.

Cite Taylor's Role

The sources said Taylor, former chairman of the Joint Chiefs of Staff and later U.S. ambassador to South Vietnam, was a prime mover of the recommendation for early American combat commitment to South Vietnam. The proposal for two combat divisions—totaling about 40,000 men—followed the fact-finding mission here.

The Taylor-Rostow recommendation for combat troops cited what they said would be the advantages of such a move, including the demonstration of American commitment to South Vietnam, the boosting of the local morale and warning to North Vietnam against further support for the Viet Cong.

The sources said the recommendation specified that the divisions be split between the highlands and the populous Mekong Delta, the areas most threatened at that time by the enemy.

Delta Was Flooded

The Taylor-Rostow mission coincided with severe floods in the Mekong Delta, and the report to Kennedy recommended that some of the impact of the move could be softened by passing off one of the American divisions as intended to help the flood relief.

The proposal to send the two divisions here in 1961 headed the list of four alternatives in the Taylor-Rostow report, the sources said. Next in order was the dispatch of a single division. The third choice was to provide helicopter support and additional military advisers contingent on the Ngo Dinh Diem regime's agreement to make certain reforms in South Vietnam's deficient military system.

Made 2d Report

The fourth recommendation provided for a minimal immediate dispatch of helicopters and advisers without a firm advance commitment from the Diem regime for reforms, although it would mean working toward them.

After the report was submitted, the sources said, Rostow flew back to Washington and Taylor stopped off for rest in the Philippine resort of Baguio. While there, Taylor followed up with a second report to Kennedy in which he even more strongly urged the dispatch of U.S. combat troops as a deterrent to the Communists.

Sources said Kennedy was "appalled" by the proposal to dispatch combat troops and chose the fourth and least committing alternative: providing South Vietnam with limited helicopter and advisory support.

NNNN

NOR754

CK 0930

NOR755

CK 0945

DTNOR756 EPF154

0956 :DOCUMENTS - POST

(X825--FOUR TAKES)

WASHINGTON, JUNE.18, REUTER -- A NEW LEAK OF SECREFNTAGON
DOCUMENTS APPEARED TODAY WHEN THE WASHINGTON POST BEGAN
PUBLISHING ITS OWN VERSION OF THEM.

THERE WAS NO IMMEDIATE WORD FROM THE JUSTICE DEPARTMENT
WHETHER IT WOULD SEEK TO BLOCK FURTHER PUBLICATION OF THE
POST SERIES, AS IT DID WITH THE NEW YORK TIMES, WHICH FIRST
LEAKED THE DOCUMENTS.

THE POST SERIES, BY STAFF WRITER CHALMERS M. ROBERTS,
DEALT IN THE FIRST ARTICLE WITH THE YEARS OF THE EISENHOWER
ADMINISTRATION, WHEN PRESIDENT NIXON WAS VICE-PRESIDENT.

THE DOCUMENTS, AS PUBLISHED BY THE POST, RECALLED THAT THE
EISENHOWER ADMINISTRATION IN 1954, FEARFUL THAT ELECTIONS
THROUGHOUT NORTH AND SOUTH VIETNAM WOULD BRING VICTORY TO
HO CHI MINH, FOUGHT HARD AT THE GENEVA CONFERENCE TO TRY TO
AVOID A CALL FOR ELECTIONS.

THE POST SAID THE PENTAGON DOCUMENTS MADE AVAILABLE TO IT
REFLECT AT MANY POINTS THE CONSIDERATION OF THE EISENHOWER
ADMINISTRATION TO INTERVENE IN THE INDOCHINA WAR BEFORE THE
GENEVA PEACE CONFERENCE OPENED IN 1954.

"FOR EXAMPLE, A JANUARY, 1954, MEETING OF THE PRESIDENT'S
SPECIAL COMMITTEE ON INDOCHINA DISCUSSED SENDING VARIOUS
AIRCRAFT TO THE FRENCH AS WELL AS 200 MILITARY MECHANICS,"
THE DOCUMENTS WERE QUOTED AS SAYING.

"DEPUTY DEFENSE SECRETARY ROGER KYES QUESTIONED WHETHER
SENDING THE MEN WOULD NOT SO COMMIT THE U.S. TO SUPPORT THE
FRENCH THAT WE MUST BE PREPARED EVENTUALLY FOR COMPLETE
INTERVENTION, INCLUDING USE OF U.S. COMBAT FORCES," THE DOCUMENTS
SAID.

MORE:(NV) RH/TMR

NOR758   EPF155

1001   :DOCUMENTS -- PST 2 WASHINGTON

UNDERSECRETARY OF STATE WALTER BEDELL SMITH DISAGREED,
SAYING THEY WERE MAINTENANCE, NOT GROUND, FORCES.

"HE FELT, HOWEVER, THAT THE IMPORTANCE OF WINNING
IN INDOCHINA WAS SO GREAT THAT IF WORST CAME TO WORST HE
PERSONALLY WOULD FAVOR INTERVENTION WITH U.S. AIR AND NAVAL
FORCES -- NOT GROUND FORCES," THE REPORT SAID.

KYES WAS QUOTED AS SAYING HE FELT THIS CONSIDERATION
WAS SO IMPORTANT THAT IT SHOULD BE PUT TO THE HIGHEST LEVEL --
THE PRESIDENT.

THE DOCUMENTS ALSO QUOTED EISENHOWER AS APPROVING IN JANUARY,
1954, A POLICY STATEMENT OF THE NATIONAL SECURITY COUNCIL::NCS)
WHICH SAID COMMUNIST DOMINATION OF SOUTHEAST ASIA WOULD
SERIOUSLY ENDANGER THE UNITED STATES.

"FURTHERMORE, IN THE EVENT ALL OF SOUTHEAST ASIA FALLS
UNDER COMMUNISM, AN ALIGNMENT WITH COMMUNISM OF INDIA AND, IN
THE LONGER TERM, OF THE MIDDLE EAST: WITH THE PROBABLE EXCEPTIONS
OF AT LEAST PAKISTAN AND TURKEY) COULD FOLLOW PROGRESSIVELY.

"SUCH WIDESPREAD ALIGNEMENT WOULD SERIOUSLY ENDANGER
THE STABILITY AND SECURITY OF EUROPE," THE DOCUMENTS SAID.

"THE LOSS OF SOUTHEAST ASIA, ESPECIALLY OF MALAYA AND
INDONESIA, COULD RESULT IN SUCH ECONOMIC AND POLITICAL PRESSURES
IN JAPAN AS TO MAKE IT EXTREMELY DIFFICULT TO PREVENT JAPAN'S
EVENTUAL ACCOMMODATION TO COMMUNISM," THEY ADDED.

MORE::NV) RH/TMP

UNITED STATES DISTRICT COURT

SOUTHERN DISTRICT OF NEW YORK

--x
                        :

UNITED STATES OF AMERICA,   :

                        :

           Plaintiff,   :

                        :

           vs.   :   71 Civ. 2662

                        :

NEW YORK TIMES COMPANY, et al., :

                        :

           Defendants.   :

                        :

--x

Before:

          HON. MURRAY I. GURFEIN,

                  District Judge.

               New York, June 18, 1971,
                 10:00 a.m.

               APPEARANCES:

WHITNEY NORTH SEYMOUR, JR., ESQ., United States Attorney,
            for the government;
    By: Whitney North Seymour, Jr., Esq.,
            United States Attorney, and
        Michael D. Hess, Esq.,
            Assistant United States Attorney

CAHILL, GORDON, SONNETT, REINDEL & OHL, ESQS.,
                    Attorneys for New York Times Company;
        By: Floyd Abrams, Esq.,
             Lawrence J. McKay, Esq., and
             William E. Hegarty, Esq.,
                    and
        By: Alexander M. Bickel, Esq., of Counsel

THOMAS EMERSON, ESQ.,
                    Attorney for 27 members of Congress.

                            --

                THE COURT: I understand from the clerk

that there are some petitions for intervention.   I will

hear those first, very briefly, indeed.

                MR. EMERSON: My name is Thomas Emerson.

I represent 27 members of Congress.   I have two motions.

                THE COURT: Members of what?

                MR. EMERSON: Twenty-seven members of Con-

gress, the House of Representatives.

                I have two motions, one a motion for leave

to file a brief amicus.   And I have a copy of the

brief and I ask permission to file that with your Honor.

                THE COURT: Yes, that is granted.

                MR. EMERSON: The second motion is a motion

to intervene in the case as parties to the case.   I

have a motion, an answer and a brief in support of that

motion.

THE COURT: I haven't received any papers.

I can only act on papers.   It has to go to the clerk

and it has to come to me.

But if you do, then I will tell you in ad-

vance.   I am going to deny it for the same reason

that I denied the petition of the others yesterday.

I take it that the members of Congress are

acting as individual citizens, obviously, since they

cannot act for the one house of the legislative branch.

And I have a feeling in this case, as I said before, that

at least at this stage, Professor Emerson, the inter-

vention would not serve any useful purpose because

the Times counsel can adequately protect the interests.

But I will be happy to have briefs on any point.

MR. EMERSON: May I have a moment to argue?

THE COURT: Surely.

MR. EMERSON: I would point out to your

Honor that the interest of the members of Congress in

this case is quite different from the interest of mem-

bers of the public or of the Civil Liberties organization.

It is a very specific and a very definite interest and

a very special one.

The members of Congress have before them now

many types of legislation which involve questions of

fact, questions of information on which they need information of the sort that is available here.   They have to vote on those questions.   And they cannot get all information that is necessary from the executive.

As your Honor must know, anyone who depends on the executive to tell what is going on is in a bad way, and the members of Congress necessarily rely upon other sorts of information.   And these materials are as directly relevant as anything could possibly be to the performance of their functions as members of the legislature.

I think their petition, as distinct from those you have previously ruled on, comes clearly within the Federal Rules under the Flast case and the data processing case.   They have a very definite factual interest.   They have a very special interest which is not shared by members of the public.

THE COURT: Let me ask you one question, because this is what troubles me.   Are you contending that in any case between private parties or between the government and a party a single congressman has the right to intervene because there is something in the case that might affect his judgment in connection with legislation?   Is that what you are saying?

MR. EMERSON: No, your Honor.

THE COURT: Why is this different?

MR. EMERSON: I would certainly not make it that broad.   I would say in this situation, where there are important government materials involved, which are absolutely essential to an intelligent decision on their part, and when those are available, they are not even in the executive department any longer, at least these particular ones, they are available, in existence --

THE COURT: I have tried to indicate, Professor Emerson, that I recognize there is a balancing of interests here, and for that reason, without any prompting, I have permitted you to file an amicus brief. And I will see, as the proceeding goes on, how much more by way of argument I can have.   But I cannot allow an intervention which would permit conceivably the introduction of evidence and the introduction of documents and the cross examination of witnesses.   Our process just doesn't lend itself to it.

On the other hand, as I say, I am delighted to hear from you and I would like very much to read your briefs.   For that reason, as the Court of Appeals indicated yesterday in its affirmance of my earlier decision, I will stick to that.   Thank you so much.

MR. STAVIS: If the Court please, may I have
just a half minute of the Court's time?   My name is
Morton Stavis and I would like to present to the Court
an order to show cause for leave to intervene and suggest
that I am aware of the Court's ruling with respect to the
American Civil Liberties Union and the National Emergency
Civil Liberties Commission, but also suggest that the
parties whom I want to represent are quite different and
that their interest may not be fairly represented by the
New York Times.

I appear here to intervene on behalf of a
group of organizations, including the Vietnam Veterans
Against the War, the American Friends Service Committee,
the War Resistance League and a series of other organizations and individuals who state in their pleadings that
they do not take any neutral aspect about the matter
of the publication of this material, that they have for
a long time been in the forefront of the opposition to
the war and that they are entitled to it for reasons
beyond and reasons which may transcend the interests
of the New York Times.

That under the Lamont case they do have a
right to hear, in addition and different from the New
York Times' right to speak.   And I suggest, your Honor,

that whatever may have been your rulings with respect

to other organizations that may have sought to inter-

vene, the interests that we seek here to represent may

very well be different from the New York Times and that

our motion to intervene is as a matter of right under

Rule 24.

And I respectfully present to your Honor

an order to show cause which has been previously filed.

THE COURT: Have you given it to the clerk?

MR. STAVIS: Yes (handing).

THE COURT: I will sign it and deny it

now.

The public has an interest in this case,

and that's why I explain my reason again.   Every per-

son in the United States is interested in this case, and

the issue is not the Vietnam war as such, the issues

are far-reaching, perhaps.   We will see about that as

we go along.   But if I permitted everybody opposed

to the war, which could number thousands and thousands

of organizations, I would also have to permit everybody

in favor of the war, if anybody is in favor of a war, and

you would just have a courtroom more crowded than this

with intervenors.

I thought I would state that so that you

could see my decision is not arbitrary.   And on the

law I hold that you do not have standing under 24(h).

Thank you.

          MR. EMERSON: Your Honor, I take it I

have permission to file this motion to intervene (hand-

ing)?

          THE COURT: Yes.   I accept it with

thanks.

rms

MR. BICKEL: If it please the Court, I have a new matter I would like to put before your Honor --

THE COURT: Yes, Professor Bickel.

MR. BICKEL: First, may I take a moment to introduce --

THE COURT: We can't hear you, Mr. Bickel.

MR. BICKEL: May I take a moment to introduce Mr. Lawrence McKay, on Mr. Abrams' left, and next to him, Mr. William Hegarty, both members of the firm of Cahill, Gordon, associated with me in this case.

Your Honor, the new matter I wish to bring to your attention came to our attention first thing this morning. The Washington Post has begun publication, under a headline, and I will go into that in a moment more thoroughly, "Documents reveal U. S. effort in '54 to delay Viet election," heavily quoting from the same documents that the New York Times alleged to possess, and the publication proceeds from portions of those documents which the New York Times has not yet published. It is the first in a series.

Now, your Honor, the Washington Post runs a news service to 345 clients, including the New York Post among them, which has the article, "More War Secrets," and we have, if your Honor wishes to see, what went out

from the Washington Post News Service.

The New York Post in introducing the series, which it gets from the Washington Post News Service, says, "The Washington Post has obtained access to sections of the Pentagon report on the Vietnam War, part of which appeared in the New York Times before the Government got a temporary injunction to halt publication. The first in a series of articles based on previously unpublished parts of the report begins here."

These articles were published, those portions that the New York Times is under temporary restraining order not to publish. These stories have gone out on the wire services. There are three AP stories, one UPI story quoting heavily from the Post, so that I think, your Honor, without any exaggeration, we can assume this story is out and available, those portions of it which the New York Times had not printed before are out and available and will be made available by every news medium in the United States to the public. We suggest, your Honor, that this radically changes the posture of the case, it radically changes the position of the temporary restraining order that your Honor issued.

May I add, before I go on to that, the stories,

as we read them in the Washington Post, quote heavily

and at great length -- I see no difference from what the

Times itself did -- from documents of exactly the same

sort that the Times had, there are quotations from

National Security Council documents, there are ample

quotations, at length, for more than a column, with my

red markings on them, and perhaps your Honor will examine

it yourself, the length of these quotations, from cavils,

various documents of exactly the same sort, and it is

the portion of them that the Times has not yet printed.

THE COURT: Would the Times then voluntarily

show me what you have?   You still have not done any-

thing about that and I am in the dark and I don't know

whether it was the same document or another document.

MR. BICKEL: We have now given the Government

a list which I think is responsive to that request.

THE COURT: But it is not responsive to an

allegation that the Washington Post is publishing the

same thing.   I have nothing before me that indicates

that.

MR. BICKEL: Your Honor has the list which we

have made available to the Government of documents in the

possession of the New York Times, which I think will

confirm that the Washington Post, as it itself says, is

publishing from the same documents and from the portion

of the documents that the Times has not yet published,

what the New York Times has.

May I say parenthetically that your Honor is

aware, of course, that this is a different issue for us

because -- this is a separate issue for us because there

is a separate constitutional ground that the Times relies

on, the Caldwell ground, essentially, which disables

the Times, in its view, from making available the copies

of the documents that it has.

The Government is in a perfect position to

confirm what the Washington Post stories are and I think,

from the list, so is your Honor.

It seems to us that the radical change in the

situation is that there is now a situation which the

readers of the New York Times alone in this country are

deprived of this story.   This is a degree of irreparable

damage which varies, is different, it seems to me,

altogether from the situation that confronted your Honor

on Tuesday last when you granted the temporary restraining

order.

The Washington Post, I simply want to say, is

in our view doing exactly what is its right to do and,

indeed, is doing, in our view, its duty as a newspaper.

But the fact is that the readers of the New York Times,

probably by afternoon the single newspaper in the

country of which it can be said, are being deprived

and thus the Times and they are irreparably damaged, are

being deprived of access to a story which every other

medium in the country now has, or will have, 345 papers

directly from the Washington Post News Service, and as

your Honor knows there is also a question under an order

such as your Honor issued whether the Times is free or

in what position the Times is free to report the story

as it is appearing elsewhere.

From the Government's point of view, the sit -

ation is equally radically changed. We suggest to your

Honor that the case is simply, in the simplest terms,

moot, that there is no national security consideration,

if there ever was one, which we don't concede, left in

this case, there is nothing for your Honor to protect

with a temporary restraining order.

I will add only that it seems to us also that

the possibility of prevailing and getting a permanent

injunction, which is of course relevant on the hearing

this morning and relevant as well on the temporary

restraining order in an attenuated fashion -- that

possibility, it seems to us, has vanished.

It seems to us quite clear that if there was any further reason to demonstrate that all the Times did is what ever newspaper in the country would do given the opportunity, that the Times acted within the well understood usages of the newspaper profession and this proves it and in our view of the case that dfeats the Government's case, that makes it impossible to speak of this within the First Amendment as an unauthorized or unlawful publication within 793-E.

So, your Honor, I am moving now for an order to vacate your temporary restraining order and if your Honor desires, we are having papers prepared and will hand them up to the bench as soon as they become available.   But I move orally now that the order be vacated.

THE COURT: I will hear from the Government.

MR. HESS: Good morning, your Honor.

THE COURT: Good morning.

MR. HESS: To address myself to what the Professor just raised, first, I must admit that I have not seen these articles until this moment when the Professor handed them to me, but I was prepared to speak to your Honor anyway about the list.

Pursuant to your Honor's suggestion, the parties got together yesterday after court to discuss the possibility of our obtaining a list from the Times. I conferred with Mr. Abrams in my office, and he called me later in the afternoon at four o'clock and stated that they were going to give us a list, and he said that the list was being compiled, that it was going to be very detailed and quite long, and he mentioned the figure 40 pages long to me.   He also told me that he was calling your Honor's chambers to inform you that it would be a 40-page list.

We waited for that list, and at six p.m. a messenger did arrive and deliver a list to us.   The list that we got then was just four pages long.   The items on those four pages were stated in very broad terms, and, frankly, your Honor, they did not help us as much

lhs

as we had hoped.

We were prepared to proceed this morning on the basis of the four-page list, albeit we were unhappy with it, and we would do the best we can in putting in our proof with that four-page list. But I do think that it is relevant with regard to Professor Bickel's comments just now.

With regard to these articles, again, I have not looked at them carefully, but I think, as your Honor will see from the evidence that we are prepared to produce, that all the documents have not been published. It wouldn't be physically possible that they were published this morning.

THE COURT: What I am really asking you is, does the Government intend to move against the Washington Post, if you know?

MR. HESS: I do not know at this moment, your Honor, but we will show you that the case is certainly not moot and that there are serious problems of foreign relations that will result if the Times does publish, and that issue still remains in the case this morning. They are the defendants here, your Honor. They are the only ones before your Honor, and we wish to proceed as planned.

THE COURT: In denying these interventions I said that the Times could adequately represent the interests of the reading public, and I meant it. Now Professor Bickel makes the point that in the present situation the readers of the New York Times are the only readers who cannot read this material.

MR. HESS: Your Honor, I would say that the Times put themselves, in a way, in this position by opening the subject, being the first to announce that they were going to publish and coming into this court and asking this Court to decide. They said they would agree that the Court should decide. We would say that they put themselves in this unique position.

May I have a moment, please?

THE COURT: Yes.

(Pause.)

MR. HESS: Your Honor, I am informed that Mr. Robert Mardian, who is the Assistant Attorney General of the United States in charge of the National Security Division, is here in court and he has informed us that these articles in the Washington Post will be reviewed by the Justice Department and action will be taken, if it appears to be necessary.

MR. BICKEL: May I have another words, your

Honor?

           THE COURT: Yes, Professor.

           MR. BICKEL: First of all, your Honor, we are not in this court because we came into this court seeking its approval of our publishing enterprise.   We are in this court because the Government brought us in this court.   The Government obtained from your Honor a temporary restraining order on the basis that there was relatively no damage, no injury, to the Times in imposing a temporary restraint on publication, and, on the other hand, that there was serious damage impending to the Government.

           We suggest to your Honor that the position has changed radically on both sides.   There is now damage to the Times and from the Government's point of view the security interest is not visible with the naked eye any longer.   These things are coming out.

           The Government says it may move against the Washington Post.   It may move against the Washington Post -- when?

           We are talking about a publication of maybe two, three days, a series, and the Times' story is gone. That is simply not sufficient, your Honor, at this stage to outweigh the interest of the Times.

lhs

The Government's position in this court, your Honor, was that grave danger to the national security would occur if another installment of a story that the Times had were published.   Another installment of that story has been published.   The republic stands and it stood the first three days.

THE COURT: You told me that.   Apparently the remark that elicited the laughter is your statement that the republic still stands.   I don't see anything funny about that.

MR. BICKEL: I am surprised that it is a laughing matter.

THE COURT: So am I.

MR. BICKEL: Your Honor, as I say, we don't see how the national interest can now remain in danger in the Government's view of this case which prevailed with your Honor on Tuesday last.   This story is out. We have information that Congressman McCloskey has a copy and is about to put it in the Congressional Record. Every news medium in the United States has access to exactly what the Times is alleged to have.   How can it be said that the Times is in a special position of being the only one in the media under a restraining order and how can the damage that is thus done to the readership

of the Times be supportable?

THE COURT: You pose a very difficult problem. The question is still, so far as the United States security is concerned, I have been looking at it a little without the benefit of the documents, which I wish I had, and in studying the executive orders and classification, it seems to me that a rree and independent press ought to be willing to sit down with the Department of Justice and screen these documents that you have or the Washington Post has or anybody else has as a matter of simple patriotism to determine whether the publication of any of them is or is not dangerous to the national security.

If you disagree, then surely you would have the right and the Government has the right equally to go into a court and ask a Court to make that decision. I am concerned about things that come right to the surface. The lack of perhaps paraphrase of code messages, I use that as one illustration, I am concerned about material sent by foreign governments which do not belong to the United States under the rules of international law, as I know them, they are merely in our custody, and a few other limited categories of that type or perhaps the revelation of methods of intelligence gathering, all

lhs

of which as patriotic citizens I think the press as well

as anybody else agrees should be kept sacrosanct, not

to deprive anybody of a right to express an opinion,

mind you, but in order to protect what is dear to all

of us, the security of the country.

I say that only preliminary to my asking you

again in good faith whether the Times cannot supply

us, supply the Court -- and I can order it, you know,

I am trying to stay so closely within the ambit of your

constitutional protection that if I can do it without

an order, I would rather do it -- I don't understand,

though, frankly, why a patriotic press should not be

willing to subject these papers not to censorship

of any kind, except from a limited security point of

view.   I wish you would answer that because it is

troubling me.

MR. BICKEL: Your Honor, I see that as an

entirely separate issue from the motion that I have now

put, your Honor.   I will, of course, address myself

to it immediately.   It is a separate issue because we

are addressing ourselves to the basis of the TRO.

We are prepared, if your Honor so wishes, to

expand the list that we have handed the U. S. Attorney.

Beyond that, I think we can assume we are all, as the

lhs

light is given to us to see, equally interested in the national security and equally interested in the First Amendment.

THE COURT: I assume that and that is why I made the suggestion.

MR. BICKEL: Precisely. We know of no allegation in any of the Government's papers of nothing that is substantial and specific that suggests that anything that the Times put in print broke a code, compromised a code, came within five miles of an existing code that the United States is interested in the security of. We have nothing but the most generalized --

THE COURT: With all due respect, I may say that neither you nor I nor the New York Times is competent to pass on that subject as to what will lead to the breaking of a code.

MR. BICKEL: Your Honor, if it is true, it is true then dealing with historical documents going back even 40 years, 15, 10, every newspaper has to be concerned whether it is going to break a code, then, your Honor, I think that the balance between that kind of attenuated national security and the war interest --

THE COURT: I agree with that.

MR. BICKEL: That's the case here, your Honor,

because we are not dealing with anything that happened

today.

THE COURT: I am not sure.

MR. BICKEL: It is common knowledge that the

security of codes is insured by their being changed

with extreme rapidity in very short order.   To think

that the documents that stopped -- there is nothing

in there less than three years old.   To think that a

document like that could possibly compromise a code is

within my understanding ithin the understanding of

everybody at the Times, within the kind of common knowl-

edge that anybody can be expected to have and that must

govern the work of a newspaper.   It is absolutely out

of the question.

Your Honor suggests why we don't sit down

pleasantly with the Government and go over our story and

our materials, which might be a decent thing to do.

There are two reasons for that, your Honor, which I hope

will commend themselves to you.

One reason we see is that it is utterly incon-

sistent with the First Amendment on any matters, except

with the rare exceptions of wartime activities when it

is clear to everyone that the citizen, as such, cannot

have a judgment that is reliable, or in pitch national

crises, as during the Cuban missile crisis, when it

is again evident on its face of things that the judgment,

the news judgment of a newspaper, may get into dangerous

areas.

        With those exceptions, we cannot submit what

we are going to print in a newspaper in the regular course

to Government approval.

        THE COURT: Of course not, and nobody suggests

that.

        MR. BICKEL: Your Honor, I am afraid the

suggestion does amount to that, because as our affidavits

show what we are talking about is massive -- massive --

amounts of material of exactly the same sort, printed

in the New York Times, printed in every newspaper in

this country, although not all are as enterprising as the

New York Times, printed in books, this issue, the Vietnam

War, or any issue of foreign policy of that sort cannot

be intelligently discussed.

        Your Honor suggested that of course nobody

wishes to infringe the rights of discussion under the

First Amendment.   Your Honor, there cannot be intelligent

discussion without facts.

        THE COURT: There can be intelligent discussion

lhs

without reprinting verbatim a code message, of course there can be.

MR. BICKEL: Your Honor, we have no way of knowing and no reason to believe that there is any code message printed in the New York Times, that any compromising of any code has been done.

THE COURT: Do you have any reason to believe that it is not a compromising situation?

MR. BICKEL: Your Honor, that is not the burden of this case or a burden that can rest on an editor.

THE COURT: That's what I want to hear. I will say now, and I am not going to pass upon it, but nobody is suggesting that -- well, I will withdraw that. I will wait until afterwards.

I want to say this, that there are several categories that trouble me, and I want you to know it during whatever goes on today. For example, in the original Executive Order, 10501, by President Eisenhower -- this is by President Kennedy, 1961, there are categories of information which are listed --

MR. BICKEL: We will submit that none of them apply.

THE COURT: You haven't even submitted it in your brief. Neither side has given me this, but I

T4-jg

thought it might be interesting to see how the Government classifies its material, and it is a matter of public record.

MR. BICKEL: Your Honor, we haven't submitted it in our brief.   It is not our burden to prove that we have not published something that offends against the national security.

THE COURT: I say now that it not having been called to my attention, I am calling it to your attention to comment.

MR. BICKEL: I am just suggesting, your Honor, that the burden of proof in this case cannot get inverted against us.   The Government has to prove against us that we have violated the national security.

THE COURT: But I am saying that the Group I that President Kennedy formulated was information or material originated by foreign governments or international organizations and over which the United States Government has no jurisdiction.   They he had something about atomic energy, which I am leaving out, and then he said, ". . . an information or material requiring special handling, such as intelligence and cryptography. This information and material is excluded from automatic downgrading or declassification."

Then he has a second group and a third group,

which I am not going to be concerned with at the moment.

Limiting myself to Group 1, I am asking you

and the New York Times through you, assuming that some

of this material comes within what President Kennedy

designated as Group 1, do you still say that without any

control by the judiciary and anyone else the First

Amendment absolutely protects the publication of this?

MR. BICKEL: Your Honor, within the facts of

this case we say so most affirmatively and most firmly.

Our position would be that no President of the United

States can issue an Executive order with a vague

description, such as "Documents coming from a foreign

country," and, in 1971, under that Executive order,

consistently with the First Amendment, bind the news-

paper from printing documents that are 20 years old.

We say that if that is the intention, it is plainly

unconstitutional.

THE COURT: I am not up to the 20 years old

yet.

MR. BICKEL: Well, we are.   That is part of

our material, your Honor.

THE COURT: No.   I want to test you first.

You are claiming now, apparently, that there is

jgs

an absolute --

MR. BICKEL: No, sir, I didn't.

THE COURT: -- quality to the First Amendment.

MR. BICKEL: I say as applied to this case. I am not claiming, for example, if in time of war or national emergency a troopship leaves New York Harbor and the New York Times takes it into its head to publish the date of departure and the date of arrival and the probable course, thus leading to the destruction of that ship, that that is protected by the First Amendment. I am not claiming that.

THE COURT: Why isn't it?

MR. BICKEL: I am not claiming, as we said in our brief, that even the prior restraint element in the First Amendment is an absolute. I've spent some years of scholarship, if I may say so, resisting the idea of absolutes and I am not now turning around and embracing it.

But, your Honor, as applied to this case, as applied to the materials that have been published, to the materials that it was made clear we still have, by our affidavits, as applied to all and any of the Government's allegations, the application to censor us, on the circumstances of this case, on the ground that

the Government is discomfited and anything that

discomfits the Government because it may be put in an

unfavorable light with a foreign government as a result

of internal political discussion -- any application of

censorship to us on that ground, which is how we view the

case, is a flagrant violation of the First Amendment, in

our view.

        THE COURT: I understand that.   All right.

I will hear from the Government now on this.

        MR. BICKEL: May I remind your Honor that I am

leaving with you an oral motion and that we have

papers.

        THE COURT: I am going to take that under

advisement.   You raise a very serious question, there

is no doubt in my mind about it.

        MR. BICKEL: Would your Honor desire papers?

        THE COURT: If you think it would be helpful.

I am concerned about this, that I have nothing before

me except your very eloquent words at the moment.

        MR. BICKEL: And my motion, your Honor.

        THE COURT: Your very eloquent words and your

motion.

        No, I've got to have some papers from somebody.

        MR. BICKEL: We will file papers as quickly as

jgs

we can, your Honor.

MR. HESS: Your Honor, just briefly, so there
is no doubt, if what Professor Bickel says about these
new articles are true, the Government will move against
those articles so that the readers of the Times will
not be allegedly the only ones suffering.

THE COURT: With the speed of the presses,
you have to move fast.

MR. HESS: And, your Honor, with regard to
your recent discussion with the Professor, the Government
is prepared this morning to place the documents that we
have before the Court.   We will show you how classification occurs, how the classification of those documents occurred, and we will show you that many matters
in those documents fall within the group that your Honor
read in the Executive order.

Your Honor, one small matter.   Might I ask
permission of the Court for Mr. Seymour to share the
oral argument with me on behalf of the Government?

THE COURT: Delighted to have the distinguished
United States Attorney, always.

I just want to say this.   In the xontext of
what you are going to offer, President Eisenhower and
President Kennedy, both, in providing in these Executive

orders for certain classification, made it perfectly

clear that it was not the purpose of these classification

orders in any way to keep the public or the press from

getting whatever information was possible to give the

public and the press without endangering the serious

interests of the country, and let's keep that in mind.

MR. SEYMOUR: Your Honor, we are prepared to

proceed with the hearing on the merits whenever the

Court is.

THE COURT: Yes. I am ready.

MR. SEYMOUR: May it please the Court, as we

see it, the issue in this proceeding is a very simple one,

and that is whether, when an unauthorized person comes

into possession of documents which have been classified

under lawful procedures, that person may unilaterally

declassify those documents in his sole discretion.

The position of the Government in the proceeding

is equally simple. These are stolen documents. They

are classified. They compromise our current military

and defense plans and intelligence operations and

jeopardize our international relations.

Contrary to some of the suggestions in

counsel's argument, and in the brief, that what this

amounts to is a bald attempt at suppression and censor-

ship, we have attempted to approach the matter with the

highest regard for the constitutional rights of all

concerned and in an orderly, lawful process.

As your Honor will recall, the proceeding began

with the sending of a very polite telegram from the

Attorney General to the Times asking them if they would

voluntarily cease publication and return the documents.

The Times in its discretion refused to do so.

We then, with as much notice as we could

under the circumstances, approached the Court to have

the matter decided judicially under our system, and again,

during the course of those preliminary proceedings, your

Honor also asked the Times if they would voluntarily

suspend publication so that the matter could be considered

seasonably by the Court, and again the Times refused to

do so, and it was only in those circumstances that the

temporary restraining order was signed.

We are now at the point where we are presenting

the matter on the merits, and I think it is important

to recognize at the outset that our sole purpose here is

to present the evidence to the Court so that the matter

can be decided impartially and objectively on the facts

and on the merits and in accordance with the law.

We are prepared, in fact, to do what we believe

jgs

the defendants should have done in reverse, that is, to

submit to the Court, under appropriate protections,

the classified documents so your Honor yourself can

make the determination as to whether the Government's

position is sound.

In doing so, we remind your Honor that the

Congress in its wisdom has enacted the Freedom of

Information Act, which was precisely designed to take

care of the problems of access to Government documents,

that there in fact has been a specific test under that

Act and under the Congressional intention about the

declassification of documents, and that the present law

is that only if the classification has been arbitrary or

unsupportable will the documents be declared to be

declassified and available for unauthorized dis-

tribution.

THE COURT: That is a statutory matter, Mr.

Seymour.

MR. SEYMOUR: Yes, sir.

THE COURT: But we are talking of the

constitutional matter beyond that. I think that the

question then would be whether, assuming that in the

guise of security -- you must face that question -- a

government wishes to suppress matters that might be

embarrassing to it domestically, the Government has the right to do that under the First Amendment.

MR. SEYMOUR: I think that is very fair statement of the issue, and we are prepared to meet it head-on.

Contrary, again, to counsel's allegations both in the brief and in the argument that this is ar attempt by the Government to suppress the publication of historical data, or as I think he just said censorship to avoid matters which might cause discomfiture, the concern of the United States in this proceeding is a very fundamental one and it deals directly on the merits with the security of the United States, military matters, defense matters, intelligence matters, international relations, and we intend to show by live witnesses and documentary evidence that although some of these matters may have occurred a few years ago, some going back beyond that, that interwoven in the materials which have been the subject of these presentations are documents which still have current vitality, whose disclosure would currently adversely affect the military alliances, diplomatic efforts relating to a number of sensitive matters including military matters, and present and future military and defense plans and strategy.

Obviously we approach this proceeding on the

assumption that the Times acted in complete good faith and had no knowledge itself of these potential conse- quences, or indeed, if they had, they would have forebore from publishing it.   We wish we had had an opportunity to discuss it with them under less tense circumstances, but this was the only option that was ultimately left open to us when they refused to voluntarily suspend.

That good faith, however, does not alter the fundamental fact that the defendants had in their possession material that was classified, that they were not authorized to have that material, and they decided on their own to declassify it and to operate as if it were not protected under the Executive order and the statutes, without making any effort to determine whether there could be any objection to doing so.

The starting pint in the Government's proof today, your Honor, will of course be the Executive orders, Executive Order 1051 as amended, promulgated by Presidents Eisenhower and Kennedy, and the Government will offer proof, first of all, that the Times has already published verbatim texts of classified documents; secondly, that although it may not be obvious to the layman, to the trained intelligence man there are already disclosures which are harmful to the interests of the

United States; that the international relations of

the United States have already been impaired; and that

we are not dealing with matters of closed history but

matters which have very current vitality and signifi-

cance.

        The proof we will offer will be documents and

live witnesses.   And I should point out, your Honor,

that the witnesses that you will hear are career officers

of the military and diplomatic services.

        After preliminary testimony by the first witness,

about the nature of the documents in question and the

procedures that were followed, we will then move to have

testimony that relates to the specific classified material

heard en camera and the documents received en camera

under appropriate protections that maintain the classi-

fication of the documents.

        Obviously, as we approach the task, it is more

difficult because we have only this list as to what the

Times has in its possession.   And so, on the basis of

that, we are going to have to speculate to some extent

as to precisely what they do have.   But to get the

issue properly before your Honor, we are left with little

alternative.

        The witnesses we will call will be Dennis J.

Doolin of the Defense Department; Vice Admiral Francis J. Blouin of the Joint Chiefs of Staff; and William B. Macomber of the State Department.

We have documents here in the custody of a security officer, Brigadier General Jacob B. Glick of the United States Marine Corps, who is assigned to the Joint Chiefs of Staff, and at an appropriate point we will ask that the documents, once marked, when they have ceased being of service to your Honor, be returned to that custody under ordinary classification protection.

THE COURT: Unless they are printed in the Washington Post first.

MR. SEYMOUR: Yes.

I might say, when we are finished with the presentation, it will be perfectly easy to match up whether the Post disclosures cover the documents that are still available to be disclosed and the issue as to undisclosed documents certainly is not moot.

THE COURT: That is why I made that remark. It was not intended to be facetious.

MR. SEYMOUR: I understand that. We are prepared, your Honor, to start marking exhibits and calling witnesses, unless Mr. Bickel would like to make a statement.

MR. BICKEL: One word, your Honor. Two matters.

One is that we hear the names of these witnesses for the first time today, which I suppose is within their right, but in chambers before your Honor on Tuesday and twice on yesterday Mr. Hess assured us, Mr. Abrams chiefly, that we would know the names and general subject matter of testimony of witnesses to be proposed, and we feel ourselves handicapped by the failure to observe that agreement.

Secondly, your Honor, on the en camera point, the decision is, of course, your Honor's, but the entire position of the Times is that there is nothing secret here that cannot be heard in the open. If we do go en camera, we would respectfully request that the two representatives of the New York Times, Mr. Max Frankel, who is the Chief Diplomatic Correspondent, and Mr. Harding Bancroft, who is the Senior Vice President, be allowed to accompany counsel into chambers because especially in light of the surprise these witnesses constitute for us they are absolutely essential to us in any cross-examination.

Secondly, if your Honor does decide to go in chambers, which I repeat is not the position we take, we would respectfully suggest to your Honor's consideration the possibility of hearing these witnesses initially in chambers, partly or fully, and then your Honor deciding whether indeed there is matter which should be restricted in this fashion or whether the record of the hearing in chambers can afterwards be made public or whether we can come out.

THE COURT: Well, it is an unusual situation. I don't have to pass on the security of Mr. Frankel or any other person in the New York Times.   They have already seen these documents, and since they have seen them, they may as well be in the in camera part.   I can't see any objection to that.

MR. SEYMOUR: Your Honor, the practical problem of administering the security laws -- as I understand, Mr. Hess asked counsel who they would like to have present at the hearing yesterday so they could get quick clearance and they were supplied with four names and that clearance has been obtained but doesn't include these two gentlemen.

They were first suggested at this very moment.

In addition, your Honor, if Mr. Bickel is sug-

gesting our finally deciding who our witnesses were

going to be shortly before 2 p.m. this morning -- if he

would like a short adjournment --

THE COURT: I am going to recess in a few

minutes before we start, but having been in government

yourself, Professor Bickel, you know they have done a

remarkable job in getting three named persons in two

days.

MR. BIKEL: My only position is that I

commiserate with government counsel and I hope they

commiserate with me -- my sleep has been somewhat dis-

turbed of late -- but we couldn't do anything in a 10-

minute recess, your Honor.

THE COURT: I will take the responsibility

for their security, Mr. Seymour.   They are well-known

correspondents of a well-known newspaper and they have

access in Washington to all sorts of people.

MR. SEYMOUR: Your Honor's direction on that

subject will eliminate our problem.

MR. DORSEN: The American Civil Liberties

Union objects to going in camera at the present time on

the showing the United States Attorney has made, and if

the Court agrees to go in camera, we move that one of our

representatives be admitted into the hearing.   I can

rma3

assure the Court and the parties that there are members here who can secure top secret clearance.

The public here, which is essentially, as your Honor has pointed out on a number of occasions, the real party in interest, has an interest in hearing this material and in order that the ultimate balance between the national security and what we think is the over-arching value of the First Amendment to be determined -- I don't think the hearing can be held in camera without a representative of ours at the public hearing.

THE COURT: I will deny your application.

MR. RABINOWITZ: Victor Rabinowitz.

Your Honor, I would like to join in on that application.   I point out that when the applications for intervention were made, it was precisely because it was felt by those who made the application that the members of the public were the primary ones interested. Any in camera hearing in a matter of this importance and with such great significance which shuts out not only the large numbers of persons here listening but also the press, it seems to me to be denying to the people primarily interested in the situation the opportunity to know what is happening.   This is not a private litigation in which trade secrets are involved and in which the

public has no interest at all, this is a matter of profound public importance and the holding of an in camera hearing under these circumstances, it seems to me, is really not called for and is quite unjustified.

THE COURT: Nobody dislikes in camera proceedings more than I.   I just feel that in cases involving security there are situations where the Court must do it, and one reason I denied your intervention, Mr. Rabinowitz, is just for this reason: I cannot have people standing up in court and making motions. There are only two parties to the action now and therefore I will hear nobody else.   The court will recess for five minutes.

(Recess.)

MR. RABINOWITZ: Your Honor, it is with deference that I address your Honor again, but this discussion we had just before the recess is very troublesome and the fact that the amici are being barred from the in camera hearing seems to me contrary to the position taken by the Court of Appeals yesterday.

As your Honor may know, several of the intervenors did appear before the Court of Appeals yesterday in an effort to review your Honor's ruling that we would not be permitted to intervene and we were unsuccessful,

but the Court of Appeals in denying the application to
intervene did point out that as amici we would be
entitled to participate or at least to hear what was
happening and to present to your Honor our views on the
issues and evidence before you.   We cannot present to
your Honor the issues before you if we don't know what
is going on and we can't know what is going on unless
we are present in the proceeding.

I therefore would renew the application
that there be no in camera hearing in this case.   If
your Honor feels that there are any documents which ought
to be sealed, I suppose, in your Honor's discretion, that
can be done, but that is no reason for having a hearing
in camera.

I would also like to point out that your
Honor reserved decision on the application we made the
other day for an opportunity to present oral argument.
I would like to have the opportunity to argue this matter orally at this point preliminary and before the
hearing because I have an argument which I think goes
to the jurisdiction of the Court.   It is a threshold
argument, really, and which I would think that the Court
would take into consideration before ordering anything
as unusual as an in camera hearing and particularly

under the present circumstances, when public opinion is
so much concerned with this.

Mr. Seymour, in addressing your Honor just
a few moments ago, said, and I am quoting him pretty
accurately, I think, that the government doesn't doubt
the good faith of the New York Times in printing these
documents.

Now, if the government doesn't doubt the
good faith of the New York Times in printing these
documents, there is no applicable statute at all on
the basis of which this injunction can be brought and
no jurisdiction in the Court at all.

THE COURT: That is denied.   Next point.

MR. RABINOWITZ: Well, your Honor, the next
point that I would like to make is to renew the motion
made a few moments ago that there be no in camera hearing.
Alternatively -- and I assure you I suggest it as a
highly undesirable alternative -- that representatives
of at least some of the amici be permitted to attend
the hearing just to listen, so that our presentation
of the issues which the Court of Appeals thought and
which we contend we have a right to do --

THE COURT: Let me put it this way: I
agree with you that an in camera hearing is generally

speaking not in the American tradition of public trial.

I also point out to you that in the history of England

and the United States there are matters affecting

what are sometimes called secrets of state where it

has been, as I recall it, an unbroken rule that a judge

may hear in camera those matters which, if prematurely

divulged, might affect the public security.

Now, I am going to suggest to Mr. Seymour

that my presumption is against in camera, that I don't

want that used, and I know he won't in good faith use

that, as a pretext for not making most of this public,

and I would ask him to limit the in camera part of it only

to those most serious security things which in his

best judgment as a representative of the government he

feels should not be in the courtroom, and that is my

ruling.

MR. RABINOWITZ: Your Honor is quite right

about the English precedent and it is known in our history

as star chamber proceedings.   I don't believe this

is --

THE COURT: That is not a fair comment, Mr.

Rabinowitz.   You knew I didn't refer to star chamber,

didn't you?

Do you know of the doctrine of secrets of

state?

MR. RABINOWITZ: I have heard of secrets

of state.

THE COURT: Get Wigmore and go upstairs and

read it and then you will see.   I am not trying to be

facetious about it but I don't want any casual remarks

of this kind to impugne the good faith of the Court.

MR. RABINOWITZ: I am not impugning the good

faith of the Court, your Honor; I am merely arguing there

ought not to be any closed hearings.

THE COURT: I will limit them as much as

possible and thank you for your observations.

MR. DORSEN: Your Honor, I presumed when

your Honor denied the motions to intervene, including the

motion I made this morning, that when the Circuit Court

acted as it did yesterday afternoon, that was before

there was any suggestion that there would be in camera

hearings, because I first heard it from Mr. Seymour this

morning.

THE COURT: That is correct, yes.

MR. DORSEN: It seems to me appropriate

that your Honor reconsider and permit the Circuit Court

to reconsider the question of intervention.

THE COURT: I will it fast for you.   I

will deny it now, and run upstairs and see if you can

get a reversal of my order.   If you need it in writing,

I will give it to you.

          MR. DORSEN: May we be heard in opposition

to the in camera proceedings and simply suggest the

following: Mr. Seymour has made no showing other than

his mere assertion that there is a need for an in camera

proceeding, firstly.

          Secondly, it underscores the point I sought

to make earlier, that we may have a different interest.

I notice that Professor Bickel made no sharp opposition

by the New York Times.   He simply said, "We express

no view on it and leave it to the Court."   We have a

different point of view and again, your Honor, that is

why we state to you that our clients are not fully

represented or fairly represented by the New York Times.

lhg 1

THE COURT: We can't raise that at every procedural stage again. I have ruled on it and I think I
have ruled fairly. If you think I am wrong, go back to
the Court of Appeals.

I also point out to you that on a question of this
kind, which is a privilege, a governmental privilege or
an executive privilege, whatever you want to call it, that
it is like the Fifth Amendment. You can't ask a man too
much in advance as to why he claims the Fifth Amendment
because you would be invading his very privilege. For that
reason when Mr. Seymour states in very broad terms that it
requires a certain part of this to be held in camera, I
must take it on good faith as an official of the government
that he means what he says and I cannot force him to divulge in public what might divulge the whole thing.

MR. STAVIS: I appreciate that. You just understand the concern of organizations --

THE COURT: I appreciate it. I am very conscious
of it. I will state on the record for you that I will limit
it as much as possible, believe me.

MR. STAVIS: May I simply state, your Honor, part
of our problem, it is Civil Liberty organizations that are
our concern, issues mount upon issues. We started with a

lhg 2

prior restraint, itself unprecedented.   We now go to in camera hearings, not quite unprecedented.

THE COURT: I will take responsibility for that. That is my duty.   Thank you.

MR. HEGARTY: Your Honor, I think I on behalf of The New York Times may speak myself to some of the factual questions that Mr. Seymour purports to raise.   I take it from his presentation that he proposes to make a showing upon which your Honor could then rule as to the necessity of an in camera proceeding.

It is The New York Times position that certainly at this point no such showing has been made and we do oppose an in camera proceeding.   But we will abide the event and see what Mr. Seymour presents.

THE COURT: Preliminary.   All questions of privilege are preliminary.

You may proceed, Mr. Seymour.

MR. SEYMOUR: At the outset I'd like to mark a couple of basic documents as exhibits for this hearing, starting with the three New York Times stories that preceded the application.

As Government's Exhibit 1, the story on June 13th, 1971.

As Government's Exhibit 2, the story on June 14th,

lhg 3

1971.

Government's Exhibit 3, the story on June 15th, 1971.

MR. HEGARTY: I take it, Mr. Seymour, these are the complete texts of all that was published?

MR. SEYMOUR: They are and are intended to be and they are obviously subject to correction.

THE COURT: Any objection?

MR. HEGARTY: No, your Honor.

THE COURT: Received.

(Government's Exhibits 1, 2 and 3 received.)

MR. SEYMOUR: As Government's Exhibit 4, your Honor, I would like to offer a clean copy of the inventory, purported inventory, delivered to us by The New York Times late yesterday.

I also have a marked copy that we will get to in the course of one of the witnesses. But as to the basic document, I'd like to offer this as Government's Exhibit 4.

MR. HEGARTY: No objection.

THE COURT: Received.

(Government's Exhibit 4 received in evidence.)

MR. SEYMOUR: As Government's Exhibit 5, your

Honor, I'd like to mark at this time the Executive Order

10501 and the related documents that were issued at the

time those were made public.

THE COURT: Does that include the press release?

MR. SEYMOUR: Yes, your Honor, describing the

purposes behind the order, the order originally signed by

President Eisenhower and then subsequently amended in cer-

tain respects by President Kennedy.

MR. HEGARTY: I have no objection on Mr.Seymour's

representations, your Honor. Obviously I have not had a

chance to examine the particular document.

THE COURT: Received.

(Government's Exhibit 5 received in evidence.)

MR. SEYMOUR: Finally, your Honor, as Government's

Exhibit 6 I'd like to mark formally into the record the

telegram sent by Attorney General Mitchell to The New York

Times on the 14th of June.

THE COURT: Any objection?

MR. HEGARTY: No objection, your Honor.

THE COURT: Received.

(Government's Exhibit 6 received in evidence.)

MR. SEYMOUR: At this time, your Honor, the govern-

ment calls as its first witness Dennis J. Doolin.

. . .

D E N N I S   J A M E S   D O O L I N,   called

as a witness by the Government, having been first

duly sworn, testified as follows:

DIRECT EXAMINATION

BY MR. SEYMOUR:

Q   Mr. Doolin, would you please tell us what your

position is at the present time?

A   I am Deputy Assistant Secretary of Defense for

International Security Affairs.

Q   What are your responsibilities?

A   I have particular responsibility for the Office

of East Asian and Pacific Affairs.

THE COURT: Would you speak up a little so I can

hear you?

THE WITNESS: I have responsibility for the Office

of East Asian and Pacific Affairs, your Honor.

THE COURT: If you will face me rather than

Mr. Seymour, I think we will get along better.

Q   How long have you held your present position?

A   Since May of 1969.

Q   Prior to that did you hold other government posi-

tions?

A   Yes. Prior to that I served nearly two years with

the Central Intelligence Agency as a senior analyst in

Chinese Affairs, and I am still on leave at the present

time from Stanford University.

Q   Are you familiar with the classification procedures

followed by government agencies under Executive Order 10501?

A   Yes, I am.

Q   Are you also familiar with the preparation of a

document described as United States Viet Nam Relations

1945-1967 comprising 47 volumes?

A   I am.

Q   I wonder if you would tell the Court briefly the

history of that document and how it came into being, how

it was prepared and what were-- just in general terms--

the source documents on which it was based.

THE COURT: With dates, if possible.

A   Secretary-- then Secretary McNamara in 1967 di-

rected that a study be done of the entire decision-making

process with regard to U.S. involvement in Indo-China, spe-

cifically Viet Nam, with a view, I think, to seeing what

we did right and what we did wrong. This was done at his

request by a task force in the Office of the Assistant

Secretary for International Security Affairs, in the Office

of the Secretary of Defense.

It was headed by Dr. Leslie Gelb, who was at that

time a member of the staff in the Office of the Assistant

Secretary. He drew a staff, as I understand it, of some thirty to forty people, some in the Department of Defense, some in other departments in the executive branch, some outside contract assistants. They had the researchers, the task force had access to documents along a very high range of sensitivity, because they wanted to provide the Secretary with the best study possible.

The study was completed and submitted to the Secretary after Mr. McNamara left. It was submitted-- it was submitted after he had left.

THE COURT: To whom, Mr. Clifford?

THE WITNESS: It was -- the direction, sir, to continue the study was given to Mr. Clifford but it was not completed in its final form until after this administration took office.

Q   Can you give us a date for the completion of this?

A   I believe it was, in terms of dissemination, I believe it was July of 1969.

MR. HEGARTY: If your Honor please, I would like to move to strike the last two answers of the witness. Mr. Seymour asked the witness whether he was familiar with the preparation.

In his lengthy first answer he said "I understand."

He now says "I believe."

At least I think it should be established that he was a member of the task force, what role he held in the task force or whether indeed he is just giving departmental general knowledge.

THE COURT: I think that is a fair statement.

MR. SEYMOUR: Let me make this representation to the Court. Mr. Doolin is not here for the purpose of describing in fact the preparation except as a setting for the questions to follow having to do with classification, your Honor.

THE COURT: That is what I had assumed.

MR. SEYMOUR: Just general information.

THE COURT: If you need any more, you can examine on that.

MR. HEGARTY: I think I am compelled to renew my motion, your Honor. I think Mr. Seymour has confirmed that Mr. Doolin does not know.

THE COURT: Let me ask you a simple question.

Were you part of the task force?

THE WITNESS: No, I was not, your Honor.

THE COURT: Were you in the Secretary's Office at the time the thing was completed?

THE WITNESS: I was, but I was not involved. I

joined the office in May of 1969 but I was not involved.

THE COURT: What are you testifying from, not from memory, then?   What are you testifying from? How do you get your knowledge?

THE WITNESS: In November of 1969 The New York Times Sunday Magazine ran an article, an interview with former Secretary McNamara, in which he referred to the fact that the study had been done at his direction. This occasioned a request from Senator Fulbright to Secretary Laird for a set -- for the study.   The letter was referred to my office. I was directed to review the study and to propose a recommended position to the Secretary and a letter back to the Senator, which I did

I have been involved with the document since that time, since November of 1969.

MR. HEGARTY: Your Honor, if I may say again, I think the government has a severe burden here and I think it is important that its presentation be meticulous, we are in a court of law. I think it is perfectly clear that this gentleman's knowledge as to the preparation and as to Secretary McNamara's motivation as he purported to testify and the like--

THE COURT: It is a little preliminary. I am inclined to agree with you generally. He said he reviewed

the study. I think Mr. Seymour will now ask him how he

reviewed the study and what he found.

BY MR. SEYMOUR:

Q   Have you yourself, Mr. Doolin, actually examined

the text of the study in detail?

A   I have.

Q   Have you also examined the various source documents

referred to in the study and in some cases incorporated

in the study?

A   I have.

Q   On the basis of that examination, can you tell

us what agencies provided the documentary source material

as reflected in the study upon which the study was based?

A   The data base was derived with information from

the Department of State, Department of Defense, the Joint

Chiefs of Staff, the Central Intelligence Agency, the

National Security Agency and the White House.

Q   Can you also tell us, Mr. Doolin, whether you have

reviewed the list submitted to us by The New York Times

which has been previously marked here as Government's Ex-

hibit 4 to see whether that list relates to the documents

that are included in that study?

A   Sir, I have reviewed the list and it does relate

to the study.

Q   Let me hand you this document, Mr. Doolin, and ask

if that is in fact the copy that you used and on which you

have made certain notations.

A   That is correct.

MR. SEYMOUR: At this time, your Honor, I am going

to ask that this document, which I represent to be the

actual ribbon copy supplied to us by The Times but which

bears notations by this witness, be marked as Government's

Exhibit 4A but that it be sealed, because it actually

identifies within the particular volumes of classified

material where the documents fall.

THE COURT: Show it to counsel.

MR. HEGARTY: I hope, Mr. Seymour, that the

markings that you mentioned do not apply to all the docu-

ments.

MR. SEYMOUR: I intend to ask the witness about

that.

THE COURT: Let me see it, if I may.   Is there

any objection to the document as such?

MR. HEGARTY: I am not entirely persuaded that it

need be sealed, your Honor, from its description. I have

no objection to the document itself. It is apparently just

a handy way of refreshing this witness' recollection.

THE COURT: Yes, why should it be sealed?   It

just has numbers on it.

MR. SEYMOUR: The numbers refer to specific volumes in the classified material which will be handed up
to your Honor. It is in fact an index, and without the
other documents, obviously it does not present a problem.
With the other documents, it does.

THE COURT: You are sealing things you don't have
to seal. I will take it in evidence. It is merely a
descriptive thing for future purposes.

You may mark this, Mr. Clerk.

(Government's Exhibit 4A received in evidence.)

Q   Mr. Doolin, I wonder if you would describe to the
Court what the markings are -- what the markings reflect?

A   In some cases the title of the item is the title
of the volume. In other cases it is nearly exact. So what
I attempted to do was on the basis of this list determine
the volume numbers and to account for what was available.

THE COURT: It is nothing more than an index, is
it?

THE WITNESS: That's right, sir.

MR. SEYMOUR: Your Honor, this is to deal with
that problem that we have;because The Times has not produced
the actual documents, we are going to try to reconstruct
them for the Court.

THE COURT: I understand that.

Q   Mr. Doolin, as Mr. Hegarty has already noticed, there are certain items that you have not made marks next to in the margin.

Will you explain why that is, please?

A   Yes. The ones on-- some on page 2 and all the items with one exception, the last item on page 3 --

THE COURT: Hvae you got a copy of this, Mr.Seymour, so I can follow it?

MR. SEYMOUR: Do you have a copy?

THE WITNESS: I do, in my pocket.

MR. HEGARTY: It would be helpful for counsel to be able to follow this.

THE COURT: Yes.

MR. SEYMOUR: We are limited by the availability of copies, your Honor.

THE COURT: All right. We will do the best we can. As a matter of fact, it is more important for you to have it --

MR.HEGARTY: If the reporter will be good enough to read back the most recent answer, I think I can read an unmarked list and see what he is saying. I'd like to have the witness' prior answer.

(Record read.)

A   (continuing) -- I could not identify.

THE COURT: I don't understand that.

On my copy it doesn't show anything marked on page 3.

There are five items.   Did you mark anything on your

copy?

THE WITNESS: No, your Honor, I did not.

I was dealing with the study.

THE COURT: I mean all of page 3 is not marked,

is that right?

MR. SEYMOUR: Your Honor, let me try to

go back.   The interruption stopped the flow of what

he was saying.

THE COURT: Start again.

BY MR. SEYMOUR:

Q   Were there some items on the New York Times

list which you could not specifically identify into the

study?

A   That is correct.

Q   Would you tell us why that is?

A   For example, the third from the bottom on

page 2 refers to a chronological list and summary of

major internal policy documents for the Roosevelt,

Truman, Eisenhower, Kennedy, and Johnson administrations

on Indochina.   The Johnson administration chronological

list and summary is not a party of the study and we

do not hold it as such.   The last item on page 2,

documents relating to studies concerning the conference,

1950-54, including the Geneva conference, and the four

references on page 3 to what appear to me to be document-

ary collections, we do not hold as such and we cannot

determine from the title there just what is involved.

      Q   In other words, you are unable from this list

as presently worded to match up those descriptions with

the --

                THE COURT: May I have that again by subject?

                THE WITNESS: Yes, sir.

                THE COURT: Just give me the number.

                THE WITNESS: The third from the bottom on

page 2, sir, the reference to the Johnson administra-

tion --

                THE COURT: That I have covered, yes.

                THE WITNESS: That we don't have.   The

last one on the second page --

                THE COURT: The last one on the page?

                THE WITNESS: Yes, sir.   And the firsr

four on page 3.

                THE COURT: What about the fifth?   Oh,

that is a different study.

                THE WITNESS: That is a different study, sir,

not a part of this study.

MR. SEYMOUR: At this time, your Honor, I would like to renew the government's request of counsel to produce for the Court's inspection, if it needs to be limited to that, the documents in their custody that relate to this classified study so that the Court can adequately pass on the merits of this proceeding.

THE COURT: I will take that under advisement.

MR. HEGARTY: Will your Honor hear me on that if it should be necessary?

THE COURT: Yes.   In orderly procedure, with the witness on the stand, I thought I would reserve on that and then we can argue the subject later.

MR. SEYMOUR: In order to proceed with the witness, your Honor, in the absence of having the actual documents the Times has, I would like at this time to mark and offer to the Court a full set of this 47-volume study, but I do so with the request that if it is accepted by the Court that it be sealed and be for the Court's eyes only.

THE COURT: That I will do.

MR. SEYMOUR: And be returned to the custody

of the security officer.

THE COURT: Is there any cross examination?

MR. SEYMOUR: I am not finished yet, your Honor.

We have two cartons, your Honor, we would like to have marked as sealed exhibits for your Honor's inspection, and they would be government's exhibits --

THE COURT: Will that be preceded by a summary with specific comments relating to specific documents.

MR. SEYMOUR: I beg your pardon?

THE COURT: Will this be followed by a summary of the documents together with the government's view as to the security situation?

MR. SEYMOUR: Oh, yes, sir.   After putting them in evidence I will ask Mr. Doolin some general questions about it.

MR. HEGARTY: Your Honor, I am not entirely sure what it is Mr. Seymour is proposing.   I take it he is proposing to mark the two cartons as sealed exhibits, for your Honor's eyes only, and that presents no problem for me, on his personal representation that these are the, what shall I call them, printed definitive, final -- what exactly are they?

MR. SEYMOUR: Why don't we get the infor-

mation from the witness?

THE COURT: Isn't that what you refer to

as the 47 volumes of the Vietnam Archives?

MR. SEYMOUR: Yes, your Honor.

May they be marked Government's Exhibits 7

and 7A.

(Government's Exhibits 7 and 7A were received

in evidence.)

BY MR. SEYMOUR:

Q   Mr. Doolin, can you tell us, please, whether

included in these 47 volumes are any volumes which do not

specifically contain classified material?

A   Yes, your Honor, there are two volumes that con-

tain no classified material.   They are public positions

of the administrations on the subject of the study and

the material has no classification because they are un-

classified.

THE COURT: Where does it appear on my pages

of list?

MR. SEYMOUR: Your Honor, for the Court's

convenience, I believe I am correct thst the volumes you

will find in these boxes which are marked VA-1 and VA-2

are the unclassified volumes.

MR. HEGARTY: Again, your Honor, I am

at a disadvantage because I don't have the VA-1 and

VA-2.   Could that be identified for my use?

MR. SEYMOUR: I am not sure it does appear --

THE COURT: As long as it is unclassified,

you may as well tell him what it is.

BY MR. SEYMOUR:

Q   These are public policy statements made to

the world at large which are included as far as the back-

ground papers here?

A   That is correct.

Q   And I understand they are not identified by

the Times as material being in their possession?

A   That is correct.

Q   All of the material on the Times list which

you could identify that is contained in this study

is in fact classified?

A   That is correct.

Q   Can you tell us what the calssification is?

A   The highest classification -- the classifica-

tion of the study is top secret-sensitive.

THE COURT: You say the whole study except

for the two volumes is --

THE WITNESS: Classified top secret-sensi-

tive, yes, your Honor.

BY MR. SEYMOUR:

Q   Will you tell us, please, whether there is
any physical marking that appears on the pages of the
study to indicate that classification?

A   Yes.   The study is marked "Top Secret-
Sensitive" and it is so marked on the pages.

Now, in some of the documentary volumes
that are classified top secret-sensitive there is material
of a lower classification and it is so noted on an individual document, but the volume as a whole, under the law,
under the order, must have the highest classification,
the volume, of the highest document used in that volume,
which in each case is top secret.

THE COURT: That means it is only because
it is bound that it becomes top secret?   You take it
out of the book and it is no longer top secret?

THE WITNESS: If we broke up one documentary
volume there, your Honor, and the highest item that was
left in the collection as secret, then the volume would
be labeled secret or confidential in that case.   If
it was broken up each document would have its own individual classification.

THE COURT: Can you find out the date of

the classification, Mr. Seymour?

BY MR. SEYMOUR:

Q   Is it not a fact that each of the source
documents was classified at the time the source document
was prepared?

A   If the document was classified, that was
noted.

MR. HEGARTY: Your Honor, may I understand
whether the witness is testifying as to his own knowledge as to these particular documents?

THE COURT: I think that is a fair
question, a fair comment.

MR. SEYMOUR: Your Honor, I will approach
it a longer way around so we can have the whole procedure.

THE COURT: Right.

Please distinguish between what you know
as fact with relation to these documents, all right?

THE WITNESS: I am sorry, your Honor, I
didn't know I was not doing that.   I apologize.

MR. SEYMOUR: I am afraid it was my art-
less question, your Honor, and I will be specific
about it.

Q   I wonder if you would start at the beginning,

Mr. Doolin, and explain how the Executive Order 10501

works in actual practice.   That is, when a document

is prepared, who in the first instance determines whe-

ther it is to be classified or not?

       A   It would be the originator of the document.

       THE COURT: Could I interrupt for one point?

What is the last of the executive orders and when was it

promulgated, as of now, I mean?   The last one I found

is President Kennedy's in 1962.   Has there been any

further amendment of the Executive Order 10501 since?

       MR. SEYMOUR: Not to our knowledge, your

Honor.

       THE COURT: To your knowledge?

       THE WITNESS: No, sir.

       THE COURT: Has it been amended since

President Kennedy's date?

       MR. HEGARTY: There is one dated November

26, 1967, your Honor --

       THE COURT: That only dealt with different

departments --

       MR. HEGARTY: I can't assure the Court

one way or the other.

       THE COURT: When you speak of the classi-

fication procedures, are you speaking of them now under

existing law or as of the time when the Vietnam study
was made?

THE WITNESS: I am speaking in terms of
categories.   In other words, what was the criterion
for top secret then and now has not changed, nor has
it for secret or confidential.

MR. HEGARTY: Your Honor, I was rising to
make your Honor's point, in a sense.   I don't think
the witness has demonstrated that he is able to work
back from now to then.

THE COURT: But that is a matter of executive order, which anybody can read, and I assume since
he reads English he can read as well as you and I.

I think first he is saying what the practice
is, based upon the order itself.

MR. HEGARTY: As he has come to know it.

THE COURT: Then we can go further and
perhaps it will wait for cross examination and particular
documents.

THE WITNESS: If I may, your Honor, I was
in government at the time, although not with the Department of Defense, and I am familiar --

THE COURT: Try to keep that in mind when
testifying, what is practice and what do you know.

THE WITNESS: Yes, sir.

BY MR. SEYMOUR:

Q   Dealing specifically with the period since May of 1969, when you have been in your present position, can you tell us on the basis of your own personal knowledge whether the classification system which is described in Executive Order 10501 is in current practice in the various agencies?

A   It is.

Q   Can you tell us whether under that executive order there is a current and continuing procedure for reclassifying documents upon review?

A   There is.

Q   Can you tell us whether on the basis of your personal knowledge there exists in the various agencies a public officer known as a historian or other similar title who in fact is available to review with researchers the possibility of declassifying?

A   That is correct.

Q   Can you tell us on the basis of your personal knowledge what the procedure is as far as the documents are concerned when a declassification takes place?

A   When either a declassification takes place or a downgrading in the classification takes place, a

notice is sent to the original addressees, say, if it is

a cable, for example, that is later downgraded, they

are notified and the classification is changed on the

document.

        Other documents are downgraded at the end

of set calendar periods, three years, for example.

Certain documents are downgraded until they become

unclassified.   So there is an established procedure

and there are officers, for example, in the Department

of State, in the office of the Secretary of Defense,

in each of the military departments, the services, as well

as the Joint Chiefs of Staff, there are historians and

people to assist researchers, scholars on matters of this

type.

Q   And when the downgrading takes place, is there actually a physical change that is made on the face of the document itself?

A   Yes.   As I said, the classification will be changed or eliminated, if that is the case.

Q   And on the basis of your knowledge of the practice, are you able to tell the Court now whether, except for the two volumes you have indicated, this study contains documents classified as top secret?

A   The study does not contain volumes classified as top secret, yes.

Q   And individual documents within it?

A   That is correct.

THE COURT: Well, may I ask the witness, Mr. Seymour?

BY THE COURT:

Q   When an originating officer puts an original Top Secret on a document, is he not required to put down when it will become declassified?

A   No, sir.   Top secret documents are not automatically declassified at the end of a set period of time.

Q   Well, are any automatically declassified?

A   Top secret?   No, sir.   Some confidentials

will go down at three-year intervals and eventually be

declassified.

Top secret -- well, you referred, sir, to the

various groups?   Group 1 --

Q   Yes?

A   Group 1 --

Q   Never.

A   -- does not go down.

Q   Group 1 is never automatic.   Group 2 requires

a special exemption on an individual basis, does it not?

A   Yes, sir.

Q   Lest it be declassified automatically.

Did these documents have on them an exemption

on an individual basis against downgrading?

A   Some of the documents reproduced in here are

identified as Group 1, which would never be downgraded.

Q   I understand that.   I am asking you, are there

Group 2 documents in there as well?

A   I cannot say with -- I have never looked for

that specific point, your Honor.

Q   Group 3?

A   Again --

Q   You don't know.   Group 4?

A   Group 4?   I would assume so because there are

some documents in there which are confidential, which

would go down at three-year intervals, or secret

documents that would go down to the next level, con-

fidential, at the end of a certain period of time.

Q   I didn't understand it was as rigorous as that,

because if you had classifications merely of top secret,

secret and confidential, as they had during the war,

you wouldn't have categories called Group 1, 2, 3

and 4.

They are not synonymous, are they?

A   The groups are not synonymous, no, sir.

Q   They are not synonymous with top secret, secret

or confidential, are they?   They are defined in words.

A   Yes, sir.

Q   That's why I am asking you.

Group 2, for example, is that necessarily secret

or top secret?

A   I can't answer that, your Honor.   I don't know

whether they would be confidential, Group 2.   I just

never looked for that.

I may say, sir, that we deal mostly with

categories 1 and 4.

MR. SEYMOUR: May I pick up, your Honor?

THE COURT: I wish you would, yes.

BY MR. SEYMOUR:

    Q   Is it a fair statement, however, Mr. Doolin, based on your examination, that there are numerous documents in these studies which in fact are classified as top secret?

    A   Yes.

    Q   And they have not been reclassified.

    A   That is correct.

    Q   Now, I wonder --

    THE COURT: I'm asking, Mr. Seymour, whether they should have been declassified. That's what I am trying to get from the witness.

    MR. SEYMOUR: I think the witness' earlier answer was, your Honor, that on top secret documents there was no automatic time declassification. There is a review procedure that is available. But if that is implemented, then a physical change is made on the document, and the physical appearance of these documents indicates that there was not a reclassification of these particular top secret documents.

    THE COURT: Well, that's what troubles me. I don't see the top secret is free from automatic downgrading unless it happens to be information from foreign governments or material requiring special handling, such

as intelligence and cryptography or where the head of

the agency exempts it on an individual basis. That's

what troubles me.

BY THE COURT:

        Q   Can you answer that to my satisfaction?

        A   As to why it has a certain classification, sir?

I don't --

        Q   Why did the President make four groups when

all he had to do, from what I understand your testimony

to be, is say "I confirm top secret, secret and

restricted."?

        A   One reason, your Honor, would be that if you had

material in the top secret category that was, at the

end of a certain period, downgraded to secret, there are

people in government that hold secret clearances that

do not hold top secret clearances and therefore they

would have access to that document and they might have

no need to know.

        Q   That's not what I'm asking you. I am asking

you why the President limited Group 1 to information from

foreign governments, originating from foreign governments,

and material involving intelligence and cryptography.

        Well, that is a foolish question I am asking

you. You don't know why the President did it. But I

am asking you whether --

        A   I would say that is material that would not
be downgraded because it is so sensitive.

        Q   But there is other top secret material which
doesn't come within this category.

        A   Of Group 1, that is correct, sir.

        Q   And what happens to that material after a time?

        A   As I understand, sir, a judgment is made to
downgrade it because it is no longer, for example, time
sensitive or at the end of a 12-year period it would be
reduced to secret, which could be the case.

        Q   Where does it say that?   That's what bothers
me.

        A   I believe that is in Group 3.

        THE COURT: Group 3 also deals with information
which warrants some degree of classification for an
indefinite period.

        All right, you may proceed.   I didn't under-
stand this.

        MR. SEYMOUR: Your Honor, I am advised that we
have one of the experts on the intricacies of weaving
through the Executive order available.

        THE COURT: All right.   I just didn't want to
be misled by this witness, who apparently does not know

why these Group 4 categories were created and how they

differ from the old top secret, secret and confidential.

I just want you to be advised of that so you can fill in

your proof, if you want to.   But I am not satisfied.

BY MR. SEYMOUR:

Q   Mr. Doolin, I would like to make a distinction

in my next question as between source documents, as

original documents prepared some time in the past, and

the text of the study itself completed in 1969.

Referring, first of all, to the source materials,

to the extent that they are either in the exhibit or

are in existence, they will themselves physically show

their classification right on the face of the documents.

A   They will, yes, sir.

Q   And with respect to the analysis text of the

study, can you tell us from your examination whether there

is an interlacing of source material of different classi-

fications in the analysis that is contained therein?

A   That is right, throughout the studies.

Q   And is it possible, just as a broad gauge

question, to take sections or volumes of the study and

say simply that has no top secret material, this does, or

is it so interlaced that it cannot be separated that

way?

A   Well, with the exception of the two unclassified volumes, your Honor --

THE COURT: I don't know that. I mean, if you had a reference, for example, to a newspaper clipping in a document marked top secret, you also mark the newspaper clipping top secret, don't you?

THE WITNESS: Yes, sir.

THE COURT: Then why do you say it is interlaced? It isn't interlaced. You could have the newspaper clipping taken away from the top secret.

THE WITNESS: If I could explain, your Honor.

THE COURT: Yes, please.

THE WITNESS: And I'm approaching this now from the point of view of a researcher.

THE COURT: Yes.

THE WITNESS: In preparing this document for Mr. McNamara, they took materials of various levels of sensitivity; they used unclassified materials, yes. But the documentation on each specific point is not always quite rigorous, it is not always rigorous.

In other words, you could have a page of analysis, and this obtain in these volumes, where the researcher is making a judgment, he is quoting, and you all have a footnote for that page or part of a page that

will run the gamut, that will list top secret materials,

published books and newspaper articles.

We found this when you were reviewing Mr.

Fulbright's request, and it is hard to go back and

determine, on the face of it, what, for example, is the

opinion of a scholar and what was the opinion of a decision--

maker at that time.

MR. HEGARTY: Your Honor, I think I can only

put it in these terms:

I move to strike the answer because it is

apparent that in part the witness is speculating as to

how the things were compiled.   That is the first part of

his answer.   Then he is describing physically how a

particular page appears and the inference he draws from

that.

In this whole line of questioning, your Honor,

we are dealing with two large brown cartons, 47 volumes.

It is becoming clearer and clearer that much of it, I

think the Government is beginning to let it be known, is

of a very low security classification.

If we could address ourselves to particular --

THE COURT: Let him proceed.   It may well turn

out that you are right, I don't kno w, but at the moment

I've just got to listen.   I recommend that.

MR. SEYMOUR: I submit, the documents will speak

for themselves.   But just so we don't leave that

hanging:

BY MR. SEYMOUR:

Q   Mr.   , can you say, on the basis of your

personal examination of the documents contained in

Government's Exhibits 7 and 7-A, whether they contain

substantial quantities of top secret documents?

A   They do.

MR. HEGARTY: Your Honor, Mr. Seymour has asked

that they be seen by your Honor's eyes only, and now he

says they will speak for themselves.

THE COURT: Yes.   I think, Mr. Seymour, that

this I am going to read.   You need not ask the witness

about it.

BY MR. SEYMOUR:

Q   Can you tell us, Mr. Doolin, how many copies of

this study were prepared?

A   There were 15 sets of the finished volume that

was submitted here today prepared, 15 sets.

Q   And was security measures taken to cover their

distribution and safekeeping?

A   They were.

Q   And have you reviewed the material concerning

who has received clearance to have access to the documents

contained in Government's Exhibits 7 and 7-A?

    A   I have reviewed the list of recipients of

the documents.

    Q   Can you tell us, please, whether the New York

Times or any of the individual defendants named in this

proceeding have received authorization to have access to

those documents?

    A   They have not.

    Q   Now let me turn your attention to the last item

on Government's Exhibit 4-A.   That refers to the

New York Times list, and the item is described as a

Summary of the Command and Control Study on the Tonkin

Gulf Incident, and I believe you testified earlier that

you were not able to identify that document under that

specific title; is that correct?

    A   As a part of the 47-volume study, no.   It is

a separate study that was done, that is not a part of the

47-volume study.

Q   There is a separate study?

A   There is a study, yes, sir.

Q   Can you --

MR. SEYMOUR: Preliminary to that, let me again ask counsel for the defendants if they would produce for inspection by the Court the copy of the document described in that list as a summary of the command and control study on the Tonkin Gulf incident.

MR. HEGARTY: I believe your Honor has determined to reserve decision on that and I will state our position when your Honor requests argument on it.

MR. SEYMOUR: In the absence of that document, your Honor, our only alternative then is to ask that the government's copy in the courtroom of the command and control study be marked as Government's Exhibit 8 under the same circumstances as the earlier exhibit.

THE COURT: Yes.   Do you want to ask him how it is classified, by the way?

BY MR. SEYMOUR:

Q   Do you know how that study is classified?

A   It is top secret.

THE CLERK: Is this sealed, sir?

THE COURT: Yes.

(Government's Exhibit 8 was received in evi-

dence.)

Q   Can you tell us, Mr. Doolin, what personnel

are authorized to have access to Government's Exhibit 8?

A   Access to Government's Exhibit 8 is within

the office of the Joint Chiefs of Staff.

Q   Is that limited to the military personnel

only?

A   There are some civilians working within the

Joint Chiefs of Staff.   I don't know -- I would say as

a general rule, yes.   I know we do not have access

to it in my office.

MR. HEGARTY: Again, your Honor, the

witness says "we do not."   If that's the basis for his

testimony, it would be helpful, I think, to the record

if your Honor would again request the witness to use his

own knowledge.   The first part of his answer was

it is only available to the people in the office of the

Joint Chiefs of Staff, and then apparently he attempted

to bolster the answer by saying in his office he doesn't

have it.   The two points don't hang together.

THE COURT: No.   He was asked whether

only military personnel have it.   He said there may be

some civilians working for the Joint Chiefs of Staff who

have access.   That he doesn't know.   But he does know

2   that in the Department of Defense there is no access.

3   Is that what you are saying?

4   THE WITNESS: In the office of the Secretary

5   Defense, there is no access.

6   BY MR. SEYMOUR:

7   Q   Have you determined, Mr. Doolin, whether the

8   New York Times or any of the individually named defendants

9   in this action have been authorized to have access to that

10   document, Government's Exhibit 8?

11   A   On the basis of my previous answer, they

12   would not.

13   THE COURT: Were there lists of authorized

14   personnel on that study, the Gulf of Tonkin?

15   THE WITNESS: I do not have it, your

16   Honor.

17   THE COURT: Did you ever see a list?

18   THE WITNESS: No, sir.

19   THE COURT: All you know is that it says

20   top secret?

21   THE WITNESS: I was not aware of the

22   existence of this study because I had no need to know.

23   THE COURT: I don't think you can quite

24   ask him whether the New York Times was authorized,

25   except by inference.

MR. SEYMOUR: Your Honor, I am prepared to put on a witness on that subject.   I thought to save time -- I will betcounsel will even concede they are not authorized --

THE COURT: The inference is obvious but I don't think he can testify to it.

MR. HEGARTY: In view of the most recent answer, I would like to move to strike each of his answers on the subject of these documents.   I understood him to say he didn't know there was such a study.   How can he give the answers --

THE COURT: I think if you have another witness --

MR. SEYMOUR: We have a witness from the Joint Chiefs of Staff.   Why don't we suspend further questioning and put him on.

THE WITNESS: If I could say, your Honor, I have seen the document since it was noted that the New York Times has a summary of it.

MR. HEGARTY: Since it became the subject of litigation, your Honor.

THE COURT: I don't think it is too con-sequential.   They are going to follow up.   We are under the pressure of time for your reasons and ours,

and therefore let's not be too technical.

         MR. HEGARTY: I couldn't agree more, your Honor.   I don't wish to be technical.   It is very important to us that this be done with dispatch, as your Honor well knows, but I don't want to have a record which is based upon "My general understanding practices," and the like.   That would be unfair to the Court and --

         THE COURT: Are you finished with this witness?

         MR. SEYMOUR: I remind the Court that if the defendants would only produce their copy of the document we would obviate all of these problems, and it is in our effort to try to get material before the Court so that it can be intelligently passed on that we are here.

BY MR. SEYMOUR:

     Q   Based on the Times list, that is, Government's Exhibits 4 and 4A, and your knowledge of the documents contained in Government's Exhibits 7 and 7A, are you in a position to tell us whether public disclosure of any of the classified material contained therein, which has not yet been published, would compromise the present or future military or defense plans, intelligence operations or jeopardize international relations of the United

States?   Simply yes or no, whether you are in a posi-

tion to do so.

MR. HEGARTY: I object.   Opinion, con-

clusory.

THE COURT: I will take it.   I will con-

sider it myself, as long as I am going to read the volume ---

not that I am the greatest expert either -- but I will

let him answer it, for whatever it is worth.

MR. SEYMOUR: The first question is

whether he is in a position to do so, your Honor.

THE COURT: Are you in a position to do so?

THE WITNESS: I feel I am, your Honor.

BY MR. SEYMOUR:

Q   Do you have in your possession information

concerning specific fact situations in those various

areas which are intimately related to the classified

material in Government's Exhibits 7 and 7A?

A   Yes.

Q   Have you been limited in any way by your

superiors concerning your ability to testify on these

subjects in open court?

A   I have.

THE COURT: Who is your superior?   Name

him on the record.

THE WITNESS: My immediate superior, sir?

THE COURT: No.   What superior are you referring to in answer to Mr. Seymour's question.

BY MR. SEYMOUR:

Q   Who has directed you not to testify?

A   Mr. J. Fred Buzhardt.

THE COURT: What is his position?

THE WITNESS: The general counsel for the Department of Defense.

THE COURT: Just for the record.

MR. HEGARTY: Your Honor, I speak in ignorance.   Is that the hierarchy in the Department of Defense, the general counsel directs the assistant secretary, deputy assistant secretary, whatever the title is, in these security matters?

THE COURT: It is unusual, I must say.

MR. HEGARTY: The issue is security, not work product or the like.

THE COURT: There is also a question of whether a witness should claim a privilege on which he is entitled to the advice of counsel.   If he can claim the privilege himself, that's one thing.

I think you are right that normally you need the head of a department in a state secret matter to

authorize secrecy.   I haven't looked it up lately but

that's my feeling.

MR. SEYMOUR: I think the particular author-

ity here comes from the President of the United States

in the executive order which set up the limitations on

disclosure.   Why don't we approach it that way.

MR. HEGARTY: That's not the question you

asked and that requires an interpretation by the Court

of the order, I suppose.   What you asked was, has he

been directed by his superiors or superior, and the

answer was he was directed by the general counsel.

THE COURT: I may be wrong about this, by

the way, but I think I am right, I think that Mr. Seymour

on behalf of the government has the right to assert

the privilege for the government, and therefore with the

general counsel of the Defense Department advising Mr.

Seymour, practically there isn't anything much more

that he can do, is there?

MR. HEGARTY: I think on, so to speak, a

voir dire --

THE COURT: I can ask him to telephone the

Defense Secretary and ask him whether he approves, but

I know what the answer is going to be.

MR. HEGARTY: I will let the record sit

as it does.

       MR. SEYMOUR: Your Honor, we are at the threshold of trying to help the Court pass on the merits of this question, and I believe this witness is in a position to advise the Court, advise your Honor, of specific factual situations which indicate that there is a current clear and present danger of compromising the intelligence operations, the military and defense plans and international relations of the United States.   The problem is that he is not at liberty to testify to those subjects in open court.

       THE COURT: You need not dwell on that. I would do it on my own motion, if I had to.   All he is talking about now is this in camera business on specifics, I suppose.

       MR. HEGARTY: I take it what Mr. Seymour is really saying is not that -- I think he is being fairly technical.   He is saying that there exists an executive order.   For the purposes of argument I will assume it is absolutely valid, although I deny its relevance to this case, but to pass that, it is, let us assume, binding on this witness as an officer of the government, he must comply with it.   Mr. Seymour says therefore we must all go into camera.   He does not

quite say, which I think his original presentation was

when he suggested this would become necessary, that the

subject matters are such that the Court, exercising

its function as part of the United States Government, would

feel it appropriate that initially they should be disposed

of in camera so the Court will understand what's really

involved.   A different point is being made, I take it.

THE COURT: As I understand it, I don't know,

maybe we are not hearing him the same way, all he is

saying is, Mr. Seymour is saying now that there are

internal documents within the study which he believes

should not be declassified by public statement, which

would be its inevitable result if they were read or

discussed in a courtroom, and that he will by means of

those documents try to establish that there is what he

calls an interlacing of some of these volumes.   Whe-

ther he will succeed or not, I don't know at this point.

I wouldn't be alarmed about it at this

stage because that's all he is saying, and I don't think

he is saying any more.

MR. SEYMOUR: That is precisely it, your

Honor, and we are now at the crossroads on this legal

issue of whether the government has been arbitrary and

unsupported in its position that these are classified

documents and should not be disclosed.   We are pre-

pared to offer testimony on the merits on that issue,

but this witness is not authorized to offer that testimony,

for obvious reasons, in open court because it would

destroy the whole point.

THE COURT: I said that before.   I am not

going to listen to argument about this again.   I am

going to try to limit it as much as possible.

MR. HEGARTY: I understand.   I was only

rising to a point of how Mr. Seymour contemplates it

will be arranged.   Does he want to go witness by wit-

ness on the stand as now, then into camera, then the

next witness, and the like --

THE COURT: I would think the public

hearing would be better continued and then we can go

in camera perhaps skip lunch, or something, and then

come back to the courtroom.

MR. HEGARTY: I was just thinking, if that

would be the procedure, which I think seems to be pre-

ferable, would your Honor permit me to defer any cross

examination of this witness until we have had them all?

THE COURT: Yes, provided that you

agree to abide by the secrecy of the in camera part.

Otherwise, if you blurt out questions which destroy the

secrecy you have heard, that would destroy the whole

thing, wouldn't it?

MR. HEGARTY: No.   I would visualize if

there should be any cross examination, one public, one

private, if you will, your Honor.

THE COURT: All right.   I think we can

rely on counsel for that.   I did want to ask you one

question.

When you were asked to review this study, who

asked you to do that?

THE WITNESS: Secretary Laird.

THE COURT: Did anybody at that time re-

view the classifications on the document to determine

whether or not they should be downgraded or declassi-

fied?

THE WITNESS: We did an analysis for the

Secretary, your Honor, of the sensitivity of the docu-

ments.

THE COURT: You did do it?

THE WITNESS: Yes, sir.

THE COURT: Was that in writing, a report

in writing.

THE WITNESS: We submitted a report in

writing to the Secretary, yes, sir.

THE COURT: Is that available?   I want to save time, if you can do it by documents.

THE WITNESS: It was in terms of the study.

THE COURT: I am talking about the study. I am asking you a specific question.   Under the reviewing procedures or otherwise, was there a review at that time of whether or not these volumes or any parts of them could be declassified in the spirit of the executive order which says that the public must be in-formed wherever possible?   Was that done?

THE WITNESS: Yes, in the context of the response to Senator Fulbright.

THE COURT: All right.   Was that a written report analyzing the documents in the 47 volumes?

THE WITNESS: It was, yes, your Honor.

THE COURT: Where is that?

THE WITNESS: It is in the Defense Depart-ment, in Washington.

THE COURT: In Washington or New York?

THE WITNESS: In Washington.

THE COURT: You didn't bring it?

THE WITNESS: I did not bring it, no, sir.

THE COURT: That might save you a lot of

time.

        MR. SEYMOUR: Except, your Honor, that

that document was prepared in 1969 and we are really

talking about facts in 1971.

        THE COURT: But it is preliminary.   It

would help.

        MR. SEYMOUR: We would be glad to see if

it is feasible --

        THE COURT: If it would be possible to get

a courier bring it, I think it would be very helpful.

Somebody could make a telephone call.   It is easily

identifiable.

        Was there any other review that you know

of, before you leave the stand, on this phase of it,

made of whether or not the security should be down-

graded on these documents or any of them?

        THE WITNESS: Your Honor, we reviewed

it several times because we got repeated requests from

Senator Fulbright.   The Secretary would answer the

Senator, the Senator would then respond, the Secretary

said we would look at it again, we did.   We spent several

months looking at it again and came to the same conclu-

sion, that the set shouldn't be released.

        THE COURT: Who reached that conclusion,

the Secretary of Defense?

THE WITNESS: The Secretary, yes, sir.

THE COURT: Was there any attempt made to separate out the documents in any way to determine whether some of them could now be declassified and others not?

THE WITNESS: No, your Honor, because, as we explained -- as I explained earlier and as was also in our memo to Mr. Laird, that lumped together, as it were, it was awfully hard to do this, and the Senator never requested this.   The Senator never requested any classified version.   Nobody did.

THE COURT: But there is supposed to be a general review going on all the time.   Have these documents been reviewed from that point of view by the officer responsible in the Department of Defense?   Do you know?   If you don't know, don't answer.

THE WITNESS: I do not know, no, sir.   But if I may, your Honor, this was an internal document prepared for Mr. McNamara, at Mr. McNamara's direction, of which only 15 copies were made.   So it was not looked at in the same light because of the very close hold nature of the request and the product.

THE COURT: That's the problem we have, to

some extent.   There is an actual directive by the

President, is there not, that whatever can conceivably

be declassified for the purposes of public information

should be declassified as rapidly as possible, that's

a standing order, isn't it?

THE WITNESS: It is.

THE COURT: Dating from President Eisen-

hower's time, isn't that right?   I am asking you

whether pursuant to that order there has ever been any

review of these particular documents that are in issue

here, that you know of.

THE WITNESS: I can't say.   I have

only worked with this set.

MR. SEYMOUR: That's all I have of this

witness, your Honor, except for the in camera proceeding.

THE COURT: Do you want to go ahead now?

MR. HEGARTY: I thought I would suggest

that I might reserve for the three public witnesses.

THE COURT: Let's call your next witness

in the public session.   Would

Would you stay around for a while and then we

will have you in the in camera session.

THE WITNESS: Yes.

(Witness temporarily excused.)

MR. SEYMOUR: The government calls Admiral Francis J. Blouin, United States Navy.

F R A N C I S   J.   B L O U I N,   called as a witness by the government, being first duly sworn, testified as follows:

DIRECT EXAMINATION

BY MR. SEYMOUR:

Q   Admiral, what is your present position?

A   I am a Deputy Chief of Naval Operations for Plans and Policy, and that means that I do primarily JCS business.

Q   JCS referring to Joint Chiefs of Staff?

A   Joint Chiefs of Staff, yes.

Q   How long have you held your present position?

A   I have been in this position for three years.

Q   What are your present duties?

A   Primarily planning policy, military operations and in all of the interagency work in the military-political field.

THE COURT: What was that last part?

THE WITNESS: Interagency work that goes on in the military-political field.

Q   How long have you been in the Navy?

A   I entered the Naval Academy in 1929, graduated

in '33 and have been there ever since.

Q   You are a career officer?

A   I am a career officer.

Q   We previously started to offer into evidence,

Admiral, a document designated as Government's Exhibit

8, which has been described as the control study, I believe,

the command and control study, on the Tonkin Gulf in-

cident.   Are you familiar with that document?

A   I am familiar with that document.

Q   Can you tell us, please, of your own knowl-

edge, whether -- first of all, what the classification

of the document is?

A   Top secret.

Q   Can you tell us to whom the document is

accessible?

A   Normally a study of that kind prepared by

the Weapons Systems Evaluation Group is confined to the

Joint Chiefs of Staff, and if it is a matter of interest,

to the Secretary of Defense.   I know that this was a

very sensitive study and that the number of copies was

limited.   I don't have available with me just what the

distribution was, but I know that there are copies in

existence in the Joint Chiefs of Staff organization now.

Q   Do you also know --

MR. HEGARTY: Your Honor, I would suggest, your Honor, that the answer was really not responsive. The witness doesn't know to whom it was limited.   He tells us what normal practice is.

THE COURT: You know what he is going to say, that the New York Times was not authorized to get it, and you don't claim you were, I don't think.

MR. HEGARTY: I suggest to your Honor it is important, if Mr. Seymour thinks it is important to suggest it is a small group, we really know whether it is a small group or a large group.

THE COURT: I don't really thing it means a darn thing.   All it means is that the Joint Chiefs of Staff gets it and maybe a few others.   What difference does it make?

MR. SEYMOUR: For what it is worth, your Honor, the document shows on its face that there were 40 copies produced.

THE COURT: All right.   Let's not waste time on this little stuff.   We have big things to consider.

BY MR. SEYMOUR:

Q   Are you in a position, Admiral, to advise the

Court whether publication of the conyents of the

Tonkin study, that is, Government's Exhibit 8, would

compromise the present or future military or defense

plans or intelligence operations of the United States?

A   I believe it would.

Q   Are you in a position to explain in some detail

to the Court the ways in which that might occur, without

actually doing so at this time?

A   Well, I can say in open session here that

there is a summary in that report which describes what

happens, but then it goes on and gets into very intimate

details on the command organization of the United States,

and I feel that to go any farther in describing that or

the forces involved and how they are generated is very

definitely damaging to the best interests of the United

States.

Q   Have you also had an opportunity to review the
contents of the 47 volumes of the U.S. Viet Nam Study which
has been previously marked as Government's Exhibits 7 and
7A?

A   I might say that Wednesday night I was informed
that I was to get acquainted with that study and I have had
a little better than 24 hours to get acquainted with it and
I feel I am quite well-informed now as to the content.

Q   Do you have present information available which
would indicate to you whether the public disclosure of the
ceontents of that study would compromise the military or
defense plans of the United States or its intelligence
operations?

A   I don't think it would be an overstatement to say
that I think it would be a disaster to publish all of these
other documents, let alone the ones that have already been
published.

Q   Are you also in a position to explain to the Court
how past publication by The New York Times and the stories
which appeared earlier this week have already compromised
the intelligence operations of the United States?

A   I would rather not get into detail because I
think with the broad experience I have in the field that I
can detect things in there that perhaps, as you noted yourself

earlier, the ordinary layman would not detect, but I think as a matter of fact any intelligence organization will derive a great deal of benefit from the articles that have already been published and there is even more juicy material in the other volumes.

MR. SEYMOUR: Subject to asking some specific questions in camera, your Honor, that is all I have of this witness.

THE COURT: Has there ever been any review of the declassification of this Tonkin Gulf situation of any of the documents?

THE WITNESS: I am not in a position to know, your Honor, because I didn't have responsibility for the documents.

THE COURT: Who would declassify that themselves, the Joint Chiefs themselves?

THE WITNESS: The Joint Chiefs of Staff have a regular procedure for the review of all the documents.

THE COURT: Are you withholding cross-examination?

MR. HEGARTY: Yes, with your Honor's permission.

THE COURT: Mr. Seymour, we may excuse the Admiral.

(Witness excused.)

MR. SEYMOUR: Your Honor, the government now

calls William B. Macomber.

. . .

W I L L I A M   B U T T S   M A C O M B E R,   called

as a witness by the Government, having been first

duly sworn, testified as follows:

DIRECT EXAMINATION

BY MR. SEYMOUR:

Q   Mr. Macomber, what is your present position?

A   I am a Deputy Undersecretary of State for Administration in the Department of State.

Q   How long have you held that position?

A   Approximately -- well, a year and a half.

Q   How long have you been employed by the Department
of State?

A   Since 1953.

Q   Are you a career employee in that department?

A   I spent my entire professional life, with very
few exceptions, with that department.

Q   Would you describe what your present duties are?

A   I am in charge of the Administration of the State
Department, the principal categories of that being personnel and money.

Q   In connection with the preparation for your appearance here today, have you participated in a comparison

of various State Department classified documents?

A   I have.

Q   With The New York Times articles which appeared on the 13th, 14th and 15th of June?

A   Yes, sir.

Q   Have you found instances where verbatim excerpts of such documents were published in The Times articles?

A   I have.

THE COURT: I don't think you ought to go any further publicly, Mr. Seymour, on that subject.

MR. SEYMOUR: No, your Honor, what I am going to do, if I may, is mark as a sealed exhibit the classified documents which were in fact copied.

May I at this time, your Honor, offer as Government's Exhibit 9, as a sealed exhibit, subject to all of the same earlier conditions, the documents which were obtained from the files of the State Department and which contain portions quoted verbatim in The Times articles.

Q   Is that correct?

A   That is correct.

MR. HEGARTY: Your Honor, with respect to Mr. Seymour's statement that he is offering it as a sealed document subject to all the earlier conditions, I inquire whether he means in this respect for the eyes of the Court

only?

MR. SEYMOUR: I do, and obviously the representation in offering it is the Court will itself see from looking at the Times article and these documents--

MR. HEGARTY: In this particular respect, your Honor, I would request that this be available to counsel, counsel for the defendant.

MR. SEYMOUR: Then, your Honor, I will press our request for the production of the documents in the defendant's possession and that is, hands down, the best way to show what copied material they published.

THE COURT: That seems only fair, if you are going to get into this realm. I am assuming now that The Times should be, as anybody, interested in the security of the United States, and I am working on that assumption--

MR. HEGARTY: That is a correct assumption.

THE COURT: In connection with that, it seems to me if there are particular documents, this doesn't deal with the generality which could aid the Court in determining this question and it seems to me it is incumbent upon The Times in civil litigation to do this.

MR. HEGARTY: Your Honor, the government asked for production to itself, not in aid of the Court, but in aid of the government--

MR. SEYMOUR: My request now is that it be submitted to the Court. I don't want to see it.

MR. HEGARTY: You don't wish to see it?

MR. SEYMOUR: No. I would be satisfied if you
would submit it to the Court. We are trying to aid the
Court in arriving at a substantive ruling here.

MR. HEGARTY: I think you are attempting to at
least exemplify your general charge that this is security
of the United States and it seems to me that is your burden
and to put before the Court 7,000 pages and ask the Court
to read through that without selection on your part of
at least a showing that this document or that document
has the effect--

THE COURT: That is what he is doing now.

MR. HEGARTY: If it is confidential, still classified, I understand, and it should be in camera.

All I am asking is that I think I should see it
as well as the Court and counsel.

THE COURT: I think the cat is out of the bag, to
a certain extent, as far as any foreign intelligence
agents are concerned. I think all they have to do is look
at all of them and then eliminate. But I want to avoid
in a public court a specific reference to those which are
provable within the context of this Exhibit 9 and why you

should want to see it, I don't know.

MR. HEGARTY: I think it was a general proposi-
tion--

THE COURT: It is a purely technical question.

MR. HEGARTY: The issue is what appeared in The
New York Times and what the document before your Honor actually shows.

THE COURT: That I will look at.

MR. SEYMOUR: Let me offer to do this--

MR. HEGARTY: I want to match the two in detail.

MR. SEYMOUR: For as long as you care to do it,
we are prepared in camera to have the witness take the
document and show what appears there and I think a couple
of examples would suffice.

THE COURT: I am only requesting now, and I am
not going to order you, but I ask the good common sense of
The Times not to write a subsequent story which says the
documents that the State Department expert said were verbatim or could be copied were the following documents.

MR. HEGARTY: Oh, no, of course not, your Honor.

THE COURT: All right, let's understand that.

MR. HEGARTY; Assuming that the precise identification takes place in camera, we are bound by that.

(Government's Exhibit 9 received in evidence.)

BY MR. SEYMOUR:

Q   Mr. Macomber, are you familiar with the United

States-Viet Nam Study which has previously been marked

as Government's Exhibit 7 and 7A?

A   I have become familiar with it, yes, sir.

Q   Are you in a position to testify as to whether,

first of all, the actual publication of portions of that

study in The New York Times earlier this week has already

jeopardized international relations?

A   I am, sir.

Q   Are you in a position further to testify with

specifics as to how further publication of classified

material in that study would compromise present or future

military or defense plans, intelligence operations, or

jeopardize international relations?

A   Yes, sir.

Q   I wonder, Mr. Macomber, if you can tell also

tesll us, in a broader sense, whether there is any added

significance from the combination of certain of these docu-

ments as contrasted to the individual source documents

themselves?

A   Yes, sir.   From the point of view of a person who

has been in the work of diplomacy all his life, there is a

very great significance and I think a damaging one.

A historic and present absolute essential to the conduct of diplomacy is the capacity for governments to be able to deal in confidence with each other and to have confidence that when they are dealing in confidence, that confidence will not be violated.

If governments cannot deal that way, and I am not referring just to governments which have friendly relations with each other-- all governments are involved in this-- if they do not feelthis way, the communication which is the lifeblood of diplomacy is cut off and in fact diplomacy is crippled very severely.

This not only damages the capacity for the United States to pursue its security interests-- diplomacy is one way it does that-- but it damages the prospects that all nations seek to develop an enduring and just peace in the world.

If we cannot communicate privately with each other, the diplomatic process, which is the best hope we have to achieve this just and lasting peace, will be denied not only to this country but to others involved in this effort.

Q   Are you saying, Mr. Macomber, that the disclosure of originally presumed-to-be-confidential communications between nations in connection with the publication of this study would prejudice our international relations?

A   I am, sir.

Q   Can you tell us, Mr. Macomber, whether in connec-tion with your examination of the contents of these vol-umes, they contain information relating to current opera-tion plans which are still on the books?

A   Yes, sir, I am informed that they do, but they are in areas in which I am not expert and I would have to have someone else testify to that.

MR. HEGARTY: Your Honor--

THE COURT: I will strike that.

Q   Can you tell us whether there is classified material contained or eferred to in the studies which relate to current relations between countries involving sensitive diplomatic matters and treaty matters?

A   Yes, sir, that is correct.

Q   Can you tell us whether the disclosure of that material would have any impact on those diplomatic matters or treaty discussions?

A   Yes, sir, it would have an adverse impact.

MR. SEYMOUR: Except for going into detail, your Honor, on some of these matters, that is all I have of this witness.

I would like, if your Honor please, having in mind the introduction of that last exhibit in open court;

thatpossibly we might go at least through the formality

of offering similar exhibits back through Mr. Doolin and

then we can cross-examine in camera or offer the whole

thing in camera.

MR. HEGARTY: Your Honor, I have several very

brief questions for this gentleman and he is there --

THE COURT: You want to do it now?

MR. HEGARTY: I am prepared to, unless your Honor

wishes to recess very briefly.

THE COURT: If it is brief, go ahead.

CROSS-EXAMINATION

BY MR. HEGARTY:

Q   You testified, Mr. Macomber, that you have become

familiar with the 47-volume study.   When was that?

A   After the publication in The New York Times.

Q   When did you commence becoming familiar with it?

A   TNe day before yesterday.

Q   And your testimony you have given has been based

upon the familiarity you thus acquired, in part, at least?

A   In part, and the other part of it is based on a

life spent in diplomacy.

Q   But one part of the equation was the familiarity

you acquired from the study itself?

A   Yes.

Q   In response to questions which were to the effect, were you in a position to testify to various specified prejudices, you testified in the affirmative.

Is the position to which you are referring your present position in the State Department in charge of Administration, personnel and finance?

A   No, sir, it is based on what expertise I have based on diplomacy.

Q   So you would not be testifying, I take it, as a State Department official but as someone who has acquired past experience in that capacity?

A   No, sir, I would be testifying as a State Department official.

Q   Do you consider your present position with the State Department one that places you in the area of the testimony which you would be giving?

A   Yes, sir, among others, there are security reports to make.

Q   You at some length addressed yourself to your judgment of the effect upon international dealings and publication of confidential messages between nations.

I take it you are aware, Mr. Macomber, that such documents are ultimately published, are they not?

A   That is correct, a great many of them are, but

only after passage of considerable time and when the judgment has been reached that they no longer would be prejudicial and with the permission of the country or international organization that originated the documents.

Q   I take it by what you have just said in your reference to judgment, you mean the judgment of the State Department collectively or whoever particularly is responsible for it?

A   Yes, if it is a State Department document.

Q   I am assuming that for this purpose. And it is the State Department policy to obtain the agreement of the nation involved?

A   That is correct.

Q   But those are judgments formed by the State Department? You do concede, I take it, that there is a point in time, some point at which the confidential exchange between nations properly can be published and in the public interest should be published?

A   That is correct, if the nation that originated the document agrees.

MR. HEGARTY: Thank you.

THE COURT: Do you have any time period that is customary or is that an ad hoc decision?

THE WITNESS: No, sir, there is a program that

goes on, and has throughout our history, of publishing

basic documents that pertain to American-foreign policy.

That has traditionally been a good many years behind the

current date. We are presently publishing-- I believe we

are up to about 1946, sir.

       THE COURT: That is what I was going to ask you

about, 1945, 1946. You are up to that now?

       THE WITNESS: Yes, sir.

       THE COURT: That is 25 years later.

       THE WITNESS: Yes, sir.

       THE COURT: Some of these matters of state with

foreign governments also involve profound matters of

domestic policy, do they not?

       THE WITNESS: Yes, sir.

       THE COURT: Who determines in the ultimate what

the public is entitled to know about our negotiations with

foreign governments?   Is it the President?

       THE WITNESS: Yes, sir, on a very crucial matter

by the President himself, but ordinarily by senior offi-

cials below him.

       THE COURT: I would like to see counsel in the

robing room, if I may, and the Court will stand adjourned

until 2:15.

       (Luncheon recess.)

2

3   2:45 p.m.

4   MR. HESS: Subject to your Honor's pleasure,

5   could Mr. Doolin be recalled for brief cross-examination?

6   THE COURT: Yes.

7   ...

8   D E N N I S   J.   D O O L I N   recalled:

9   THE CLERK: Mr. Doolin, you are still under oath.

10   Please keep your voice up, Mr. Doolin.

11   CROSS-EXAMINATION

12   BY MR. HEGARTY:

13   Q   Mr. Doolin, in your testimony this morning you

14   gave a date in 1969 as the publication date, if that is the

15   correct term, of the Viet Nam Study. Is that correct?   Or

16   can you fix that date for us?

17   A   The date in 1969?

18   Q   That was my understanding of your testimony.

19   A   For the publication of the study?

20   Q   Yes.

21   A   Yes.

22   Q   When you say, and you accept my term "publication",

23   are we talking literally of the compilation, the putting

24   together of the final document?

25   THE COURT: Why do you call it publication? It

will be confusing.

MR. HEGARTY: Among the 15 people, it must be put together in some bound form, I assume?

THE COURT: Call it the report, when it was reported to the Secretary.

MR. HEGARTY: The crucial question, your Honor, is precisely there. It is my understanding that the report commissioned by Secretary McNamara was submitted to Secretary Clifford in 1968-

THE COURT: No. The witness testified that Secretary Clifford ordered it to be continued and it was finally submitted to Secretary Laird.

MR. HEGARTY: That is precisely the subject of my cross-examination, whether the report in the ordinary sense of the term was continued or whether it was simply a mechanical question of ofsetting, binding and the like. That is my question.

THE COURT: Don't use the word "publication" because that is confusing.

MR. HEGARTY: I understand that, your Honor.

Q   You understand my question?

A   Yes.

Q   Was further research work done in the period you are addressing yourself to?

MR. SEYMOUR: Your Honor, I remind counsel and the Court that he objected to this witness' competency to testify to these things.

I have no objection to his answering it, but I am not sure he knows.

THE COURT: Now that he has testified, I suppose he can cross-examine on it.

MR. SEYMOUR: Oh, certainly.

THE COURT: Go ahead.

MR. HEGARTY: He can't have it both ways, as it were.

THE COURT: Yes.

A   To my understanding, the research did continue.

Q   Given your familiarity with the document, can you tell us the latest date of any document, source document, contained in the study?

A   Not to a specific document, no.

Q   I am not asking you to tell me, to identify a document by subject matter or the like; can you tell us the most current date contained in the study?

THE COURT: By month, if you can't do it by date; by year if you can't do it by month.

A   The index refers to it continuing into 1968.

THE COURT: Not continuing into. What was the

last source document?

THE WITNESS: One chapter, your Honor, is 1965-1968.

Q   In your review for Secretary Laird to determine whether it could be provided, in response to the request of Senator Fulbright, did you consider the question of how current the data was?

A   The concern was the sensitivity of the data.

Q   Well, does sensitivity possibly decline with the passage of time?   Is it a relevant consideration?

A   It is certainly a relevant consideration, and in looking at the universe of this study, if my office had made a judgment that it should be released, we would have so recommended.

MR. HEGARTY: As your Honor will appreciate, that is not responsive.

THE COURT: I agree it is not responsive.

Pay attention to counsel. What he is trying to ask you, I gather, which I am interested in, too, is the source of it, not an ex-cathedra judgment that you exercised, but how did you determine that it was sensitive and in what way was it sensitive.

I think that is what counsel is getting to.

MR. HEGARTY: And was the dating of the most current document pertinent to that consideration?

THE COURT: Right. That is the question.

A   I did not approach it with date as a criterion. I approached it on the basis of the information in the study.

Q   In other words, I take it what you are saying is that, sitting there this afternoon, your best recollection as to the most current date in the document is a reference in the index to a month or a period in 1968 which you cannot recall, is that correct?

A   That is correct.   Although the title of the study is 1945-1967.

Q   On a different point, this morning you indicated that you did not consider the declassification of particuar sections, or documents, within the study, in doing such work as you did in response to Secretary Laird's direction because no request for that had occurred.

That I believe was your testimony.

MR. SEYMOUR: My recollection is different as to the witness' testimony.

Couldn't we possibly frame the question in a way to ask him what did happen.

THE COURT: My recollection is that that is what he said in response to a question of mine. I asked him whether he tried to separate the documents and he said

they never tried to do that.

MR. HEGARTY: Because there had been no request.

THE COURT: Because there had been no request, that's right.

Q   But I take it in coping with the question that had been presented to you, you were aware of governmental policy that to the extent possible documents are to be declassified and made available to the general public and, I should suppose, a fortiori, to the appropriate committees of Congress?

A   Yes. The point here is that we were looking at a study that ran 47 volumes, and I could go in on a given page and I could say this document is confidential.

When you put that particular document in with other documents and with the flow of the study, it became, we felt, my office felt, very difficult to separate it out. That was not our task. Our task was to determine whether the study should be provided to Senator Fulbright.

THE COURT: What criteria of judgment did you use in determining sensitivity?

THE WITNESS: We used the effect that it would have upon our diplomatic relations should the material become public, the effect that it would have on current military operations, as well as plans that were in force at the time, but contingency plans, and others.

THE COURT: And when was the last time that it was reviewed for current military operation impact?

THE WITNESS: We were reviewing this last week, your Honor.

THE COURT: And you reached the same conclusion?

THE WITNESS: Yes, in my office, yes, sir.

BY MR. HEGARTY:

Q   When you say "last week, you mean literally last week, before the publication in The New York Times on Sunday?

A   I mean literally last week because Senator Fulbright had renewed his request for the documents.

Q   Could you tell us with some more precision who the "we" is in your answer? Who reached the decision?

A   In terms of releasing the documents?

Q   In making the recommendation whether it should be, I take it. Who is the "we" that you are referring to?

A   My immediate superior.

Q   Who is he?

A   Mr. Nutter, the Assistant Secretary of Defense for International Security Affairs, signed the memo to Mr. Laird, initially giving our reasons why the study should not be released to Senator Fulbright and making this recommendation to the Secretary. The Secretary then, as

Secretary of Defense, as a member of the National Security

Council and bringing, I am sure, other information to bear

that we don't have, supported our recommendation and so

informed Senator Fulbright.

Q   Is the memorandum to which you just referred one that you drafted for your superiors?

A   I participated in the drafting.   It was done in my office.

Q   Other persons assisted you in that regard, other persons assisted you, participated in the draft?

A   Other persons assisted me in the preparation of the memorandum and then we coordinated our position with other offices in the Defense Department.

Q   Who is the other person?

A   Miss Kathryn Truex.

Q   What is her title?

A   At the present time she is deputy director of the office of special concerns in health, education and welfare.

Q   Is she on loan to the Department of Defense?

A   This is a permanent position.   She transferred. Miss Truex is now my wife.

MR. HEGARTY: Perhaps there is a privilege.

Q   Without attempting to infringe upon that privilege, was it done on office time in the office, the study? Was it done on office time in the office?   Was it official work, your evaluation?

A   Oh, very definitely.

Q   You are referring to a study that was most
recently given to her, as his Honor asked you, last
week?

A   She was not a party to that.

Q   My questions were directed to the most recent
review.

A   I am sorry.   My wife was a joint author of the
preparation of the original memo to the secretary recommending that the study not be released, the position
in that memo was since sustained in my office by further
review, the latest of which my wife, of course, did not
participate in.   She is no longer with the Department of
Defense.

Q   I had it confused as to the sequence.

In your review, did you weigh different documents
relating to, let us say, 1945 and 1946 as contrasted
with documents relating to more recent years?

A   We gave the greatest attention, of course, to
the documents in those years in which the United States
was actively involved in a combat situation, but we did
point out that -- and here we were looking at the fact
of privileged communications -- that there were communications in the earlier years between heads of state that
we felt in terms of type of material were just as sensitive

as ones of a later date.

Q   I take it it is fair to say that you have

testified that every volume of this study bears the

volume classification of top secret sensitive, as I recall,

and I take it that is the highest classification, or am

I treading on areas in which --

THE COURT: You are not treading on anything.

It is obvious that he has already testified that there was

top secret put on the volume.   That didn't mean that

all the documents in there were top secret, that nob ly

ever asked him to separate the documents.   That's where

it stands.

Q   One last question.   I take it, so that it

will be perfectly clear, a document dealing with the

period let us say 1945-1946, a volume, rather, containing

documents of that time period bears,   as a volume, the

classification you described?

A   It does.

MR. HEGARTY: Thank you.

THE COURT: In that 1945-46 volume, if you can

tell us without any breach of security, what type of

thing made that sensitive?   It is more than 20 years

old.

THE WITNESS: I could say in general, your Honor,

that there were exchanges in there between heads of state,

statements of U. S. positions that were since sustained.

THE COURT: U. S. Military positions?

THE WITNESS: No, U. S. positions with regard

to Southeast Asia that have since been sustained.

THE COURT: Were there any materials in there

which were generally speaking in the realm of what has

now become public debate?

THE WITNESS: I would say yes.   I am no expert

on this, I would have to go back to the individual

documents, but, as I said, we spent most of our eeffort

on the later materials, the materials in the '60s and --

'50s and '60s.   Primarily the 1960s.

THE COURT: I would suggest, Mr. Seymour, that

you bring out a little more clearly the criteria that the

witness used in determining the sensitivity, if you can.

If you cannot, I will just have to rest on it.

THE WITNESS: If I may add On this, your Honor,

again, we were looking at this as a universe, as detailed

a study as could be done on a particular problem,

namely U. S. relations in that part of the world during

this time frame.   That's the way we viewed it.   We

didn't get into the business of separating out this

document or that document.   That was not our job.

I think it would be very difficult to do this, sir.

REDIRECT EXAMINATION

BY MR. SEYMOUR:

Q   Why don't you deal with the question that the Court suggested as to what were some of the principal criteria that you used in arriving at your recommendation that the documents not be declassified?

A   In general terms, as I indicated earlier, it was our judgment and sustained by the Secretary that this would have had -- if made public would have had an extremely adverse impact on state-to-state relations, not only with friendly countries but with hostile countries, that it would have an impact --

THE COURT: Is that because of the content of what was in it or the fact that you would be divulging things that other governments believed would always remain secret?

THE WITNESS: It is, A, because of the divulging of the content, your Honor, and, B, as Mr. Macomber pointed out this morning, that if you can't guarantee confidentiality in certain sensitive situations, nobody is going to talk to you.

THE COURT: But suppose you had a document, say, of 1940, I am just trying to test the basis without

arguing about it, suppose you had a 1940 document which

was between heads of state, let's say, take the most

extreme case, would you still call that sensitive?

THE WITNESS: It may be.   As I said, I would

have to have a particular document from that time frame.

Obviously -- well, it would be my opinion that something

of later vintage would probably be more sensitive, but,

on the other hand, sir, I think that the materials in

the 1950's that were printed th is morning in the

Washington Post are themselves probably going to give

us more trouble than something that was written yester-

day on a less sensitive subject.

THE COURT: Is that because of the breach of

confidence or because the secret has been divulged of

another government?

THE WITNESS: I haven't reviewed that, sir, but

I would say both.

MR. HEGARTY: If I may.

RECROSS EXAMINATION

BY MR. HEGARTY:

Q   May I ask, if you recall, how much time you and

the fortunate lady, the lady who became your wife, spent

on this subject?

A   We had the volumes in my office, and this is just

a rough -- I would say for six months. We initially

responded to the Senator, the Senator -- Senator Fulbright

reclaimed the Secretary's decision. The Secretary

directed us to continue with the review, and we said

in our initial memo that "Here is our initial position,"

and my boss, Mr. Nutter, said, "However, I have instructed"

in this case me "to continue the review."

        So we kept on reviewing these volumes as press

of other business allowed, but I couldn't say definitely

how much time we put on, but it was quite a bit.

    Q   I am sorry, I must pursue this for one more

question.

        Was the initial response to Senator Fulbright,

that was given more promptly than six months, I take it?

    A   It was.

    Q   How long?

    A   I don't recall the exact date, sir, but I have

called down to my office as the Judge requested this

morning, and they are sending up our initial memo, and

subsequent memos.

    Q   At that point in time, if you can recall, when

that initial response was given, how many of the volumes

had you read?

    A   How many had we read in their totality?

Q   Yes.

A   I would say probably seven or eight, but we had surveyed the others.

THE COURT: Let's move along.

MR. SEYMOUR: Your Honor, just for housekeeping purposes, may I suggest that the Government request the reservation of the next exhibit number for inserting these documents when they appear.

REDIRECT EXAMINATION

BY MR. SEYMOUR:

Q   As I understand it, they are classified documents, Mr. Doolin?

A   The ones coming up?

Q   Yes.

A   Yes.   The cover memo, the response to Senator Fulbright, it is unclassified.

THE COURT: We will save No. 10, Mr. Seymour.

MR. HEGARTY: You said cover memo?

THE WITNESS: The memorandum that Mr. Nutter signed to Secretary Laird giving our reasons as to why the study should not be released to the Senator is classified.   The memo from Secretary Laird to Senator Fulbright is not.

MR. HEGARTY: I understand.

MR. SEYMOUR: I take it your Honor's request
was just the one of the Secretary or do you also want the
other document?

THE COURT: No, I don't think the other is
relevant. What I am trying to get at is the criteria
that are being used in the cases of older documents.

MR. SEYMOUR: I understand, your Honor.

BY MR. SEYMOUR:

Q   I understand these memoranda do reflect the
criteria as a part of the case?

A   Yes.

MR. SEYMOUR: I would ask your Honor

THE COURT: We will mark 10 for identification
at the moment, subject to their approval.

MR. HEGARTY: To be consistent and to complete
the story, I would think we should mark the response to
the Senator.

THE COURT: All right.

THE WITNESS: I have requested that.

MR. SEYMOUR: I request that the classified
document be a sealed exhibit.

MR. HEGARTY: With the understanding again that
that will be available to me.

MR. SEYMOUR: For inspection, yes.

THE COURT: Make the internal document 10 and

make 10-A the response to Senator Fulbright.

(Government's Exhibits 10 and 10-A were deemed

marked for identification.)

MR. SEYMOUR: Your Honor, there is one other

matter that we can deal with with this witness out in the

open proceeding, if you would like to, and that is that

he also can identify some classified documents which

are printed verbatim in the Times stories, if we could at

least have those marked --

THE COURT: Yes, let's do that, unless that's

a breach of security.   That is up to you.

MR. SEYMOUR: We will seal the document, your

Honor.

THE COURT: I am just interested in this.

Mr. Doolin, when you re-reviewed something at

somebody's request, what criterion did you use to see

whether your earlier determination is still valid?

THE WITNESS: We used basic one, to go back and

see if we made a mistake.

THE COURT: Just that?

THE WITNESS: That was the basic one, and we

kept reading farther into the study, and, to be perfectly

honest, your Honor, we became more convinced as we went

along, and especially as we worked through in some detail

in the later volumes, that our initial judgment was

not only correct but I would have written a much stronger

memo than the one that was prepared in my office.

MR. SEYMOUR: Mr. Doolin, would you please

describe the contents of the notebook that is before

you? Just generally, how it got to be assembled.

THE COURT: Why don't you mark it for identi-

fication? It might be easier.

MR. SEYMOUR: I was going to save that step,

your Honor. It will only take one minute. I will

then offer it. Maybe I can save you the time.

THE COURT: You can lead him.

Q Am I correct in my understanding, Mr. Doolin,

that this notebook contains classified documents, portions

of which appeared verbatim in the New York Times stories

of June 13, 14 and 15, which have previously been

received in evidence as Government's Exhibits 1, 2

and 3?

A That is correct.

Q These are all classified documents?

A Yes, these are all classified documents.

MR. HEGARTY: Do I understand this is a compil-

ation of such documents?

MR. SEYMOUR: These are the documents them-selves.

MR. HEGARTY: Put together, are they all the documents?

Q   They are not all, as I understand it, these are a substantial number of them?

A   A substantial number.   We haven't been able to find everything you published.

MR. SEYMOUR: The search goes on.

THE WITNESS: The search goes on.

MR. SEYMOUR: With the understanding that this is not everything but a substantial portion --

MR. HEGARTY: Is it everything that's been found?

MR. SEYMOUR: Everything that's been found.

THE COURT: Any objection?

MR. HEGARTY: No.

THE COURT: This will be sealed as well, Mr. Clerk.

(Government's Exhibit 11 received in evidence.)

MR. SEYMOUR: Your Honor, for clarification's sake, just for the record, it has been pointed out to me that these particular documents are not documents which are themselves contained in the study but are source documents which were, however, published by The New York Times and that are not contained in the earlier exhibits, Government's Exhibits 7 and 7A. These are additional classified documents.

THE COURT: Well, let me understand that. Does the 47 volumes contain source documents 7 and 7A?

MR. SEYMOUR: Source documents. These are additional source documents not contained in 7 and 7A.

MR. HEGARTY: Are they cross-indexed?

MR. SEYMOUR: I believe they are.

Q   Is that correct?

A   They are in the book under given days.

THE COURT: Which book?

THE WITNESS: In this volume here.

THE COURT: Aside from this book, where do they come from? Is that a secret?

THE WITNESS: No, sir. These came from department files, Department of Defense and Department of State.

THE COURT: But not contained in the 47-volume work?

THE WITNESS: The text of some of the-- some of
the texts published, yes, were quoted verbatim in the 47-
volume work, but if I may refer to the list that was provided by The New York Times-

Q   Referring to Government's Exhibit 4?

A   For example, as I said this morning, a chronological list and summary of major internal policy documents
for the Johnson Administration, that we do not hold as a
volume, nor do we hold the volumes, as I indicated to you,
that are called documents relating to studies, and so
forth, the last one on page 2 and the first four on page
3, so we had to go back to our files.

THE COURT: Do these documents in Exhibit 11
refer to these categories, the four on top of page 3,
for example?

THE WITNESS: They would fall under this general
framework, your Honor.

MR. HEGARTY: Your Honor, may I ask one question
about that?

THE COURT: Yes.

RECROSS-EXAMINATION

BY MR. HEGARTY:

Q   As I understand it, this is a compilation of
documents, whether they are documents published in full

text or referred to in The Times-- which is it, both?

A   The ones we could find were where The New York
Times ran the documents.

Q   Are you telling us in some measure those documents
while not forming part of the 47-volume study were referred
to in it?

A   That is correct.

Q   And in some other part they were, in your judgment,
apart from the study?

A   Yes. To give you one example, the conversation
between Ambassador Taylor and his deputy Johnson, and
General Thieu and General Ky, et al, that was in the text
in one of the volumes in the 47-volume study.   Others
we could find reference to in the footnotes to the study and
some we have not been able to find.

Q   Since the document was referred to in the footnote to the study, I take it you agree it was part of the
study in that text?

A   I would not, because I have the study but not
those documents.

Q   But you have in the study a footnote of a document dated a certain date from Smith to Jones --

A   I have not been able to locate them.

Q   But in some instances you have?

A   In some instances I have.

THE COURT: There is no use belaboring that. We understand it.

MR. SEYMOUR: That is all I have except for the in camera proceeding.

THE COURT: I don't know how long the in camera will take. It will not take place in this room. We presumably will be returning here and anybody who wants to sit around may do so, and that is the best announcement I can make.

MR. SEYMOUR: Your Honor, there is one other possible witness for the public side of the proceeding, if you want to call him now.

THE COURT: All right, get rid of that then.

(Witness excused.)

MR. SEYMOUR: George MacClain.

. . .

G E O R G E   M a c   C L A I N, called as a witness

by the Government, having been first duly sworn,

testified as follows:

DIRECT EXAMINATION

BY MR. SEYMOUR:

MR. SEYMOUR: Your Honor, just to keep you current on the legal proposition up and down the elevator

shaft, I should advise the Court that you were affirmed

again on the question of intervention by the Court of

Appeals, thanks to the effective advocacy of Mr. Hess.

BY MR. SEYMOUR:

Q   Would you please tell us what your present title

and responsibilities are?

A   My present title is the Director of the Security

Classification, Management Division.

THE COURT: Security Classification, Management

Division?

THE WITNESS: Yes, sir, in the office of the As

sistant Secretary of Defense for Administration, and in that

position we are responsible for the development and admin-

istration of the security classification system of the

Department of Defense.

Q   How long have you held your present position?

A   My present position since 1963.

Q   How long have you worked in the Department of

Defense?

A   Since 1955.

Q   And you are a career employee of the department?

A   Yes, I am.

Q   Were you present in court this morning, Mr.

MacClain, when the judge inquired of Mr. Doolin certain

questions about classification procedure and the different

groups of classifications?

A   Yes, I was.

Q   I wonder if you could at this time respond on

the basis of your knowledge to the questions the Court put?

A   Do you mean you would like to have me give you a

narrative statement?

Q   If you can, that are responsive to the questions

that the Court indicated.

THE COURT: Well, what I am interested in is that

the executed order defines things in terms of four groups,

whereas what has been discussed have been stamps, top

secret, secret and restricted and confidential, and the

question is what is the relationship between the two.

A   I would like to respond to that somewhat in nar-

rative if that is all right.

THE COURT: Yes, but try to be as brief as you

can.

A   Yes, sir.   Executed order 10501 which was issued

in 1953 did provide for security classification at the three

levels, top secret, secret and confidential. But at that

time there was no such thing as Group 1,2,3 or 4.

In later years, in the late 1950s, a study was

made within the Department of Defense to determine whether

an improved procedure for downgrading and declassification could be issued, and one was issued and thereafter by Executive Order 10964, in 1961, the Executive Order 10501 was amended to include this newly developed system.

Under this newly developed system, there are four groups, but the only one of the groups which is specifically related to a level of classification is Group 2.

Group 2 requires that the material be either top secret or secret. With respect to Groups 1, 3 or 4, however, the material can be either top secret, secret or confidential, and there is no real relationship outside of Group 2 between the sensitivity of the information per se and the particular level and the particular group.

Now, here is what happens—

THE COURT: Excuse me. That Group 2, does that actually state it is related to top secret and secret?

THE WITNESS: Within the Department of Defense, and I would have to check the Executive Order on this respect, but within the Department of Defense, Group 2 must be either top secret or secret. That is a requirement of the Department of Defense regulations.

I could check the Executive Order on that particular point, if you would like, but I suspect that that may not be too important in this case.

THE COURT: All right, you go ahead.

A   Group 1, or 3, or 4, may be top secret or secret or confidential and information in Group 4 may be top secret and may and can and does automatically become declassified.

I think this morning the impression may have been left that top secret information could not automatically become declassified.   The contrary is true.

The reason for having Groups 1, 2, 3 and 4 is to categorize information by subject matter rather than for any other reason, and Group 1, to which you referred, does refer to, for example, classified information furnished to the United States by other governments and as received, the United States, by the Executive Order, must protect it unless in that category.

Inasmuch as it comes from other governments, the Department of Defense cannot unilaterally change its classification and that is why if it is in Group 1, as it must be, no automatic change to it will occur. If any change is to occur to Group 1 information, it must come about, as indicated this morning, by a mutual understanding and agreement between the United States and those outside of the United States who would have furnished it to the United States.

The reason for grouping also is that there is a
time schedule for automatic processes to occur. Group 1
doesn't change at all. Group 2 doesn't change at all.
Group 3 will reduce one level on a 12-year period of time
until it reaches confidential and will not be further reduced automatically. Group 4 will be reduced on a three-
year time basis, so that it could go from top secret to
secret in three years, from secret to confidential in three
more years, and after twelve more years-- after six more
years after that, a total of twelve, the information then
would become automatically declassified.

THE COURT: I don't understand your Group 2,
though. May I read to you the Executive Order, as I
copied it down? It says "Extremely sensitive information
and material which the head of the agency or its designee
exempt on an individual basis from automatic downgrading
and declassification."

THE WITNESS: Yes, sir, that is true.

THE COURT: I thought you said all top secret
and secret are not automatically downgraded under 2?

THE WITNESS: Under 2, when the decision is made
by appropriate authority that the information belongs in
2, that decision has to be made with respect to a particular
document on a document-by-document basis. On the other

hand, you could put a total volume of documents into a

single category other than Group 2.

THE COURT: No. But isn't the rule that the originating classifier must indicate when the declassification is to take place or in what event?

THE WITNESS: Yes, sir. The original classifier
at the time of his determination to classify is required
both by the Executive Order and by the Department of Defense regulations, and I believe by other Executive Department regulations, to try to determine in advance whether
there is a particular future date or a particular future
event or any particular period of time upon the occurring
of which automatic change in classification could occur.

THE COURT: Would that apply to top secret and
secret as well?

A   Yes, it could, sir.

THE COURT: Was that done with respect to any
of the documents you are referring to?

THE WITNESS: I would not wish to comment on the
documents presented in evidence in this case because I
have only very general familiarity with some of them. But
I would say that some of those documents were created
prior to the time when this group system itself was created,
and so it is very natural that some of them would not have
been marked in that way.

THE COURT: But even under President Eisenhower's

directive there was a general requirement, wasn't there,
that you try to indicate when declassification would be
possible so that the public would get as much information
as possible?

THE WITNESS: Yes, sir, and that is still the case
today. Even though there is an automatic system for downgrading and declassification, there is a continuing obligation on the part of the Executive branch to review
classified material on as practical and frequent a time basis
as possible.   It could be done once a year. There is a
requirement that it could be done at a change of phase
in a development program. Indeed, it can be done and is
done for almost any reason.   And I would say that it has
been indicated here today that in connection with responding to Senator Fulbright's request, it would be natural,
not absolutely necessary, to examine in today's time frame,
at the time of answering the letter, what are the now considerations that would require this information to remain
classified if there are those considerations.

And I would like to point out that on any attempt
to downgrade or declassify, the judgment that has to be
made must be made in the current time frame, and in this
respect it doesn't really matter how old the document is or
how young it is. It is what has happened since the

classification occurred that may now affect the situation and permit downgrading or declassification.

THE COURT: What safeguards, if any, are there in the Department for avoiding the suppression of material which is, let's say, the subject of political debate, matters of that kind?

A   Sir, the basis for classifying information both by the Executive Order and the Department's regulations is that the information be so related to the interest of national defense that the unauthorized disclosure of that information would be harmful to those interests.

THE COURT: I am trying to get at who decides that in the last instance? Is it a declassification officer? Who is it?

THE WITNESS: Sir, the general rule is that the officials or their successors in interest or those who are higher in their own chain of command are the ones who should address that question, just as they were indeed the original classifiers.

The difference between declassification and classification is not a change of personnel or a succession of personnel but a person with authority and knowledge to address the question before you, does it still merit classification.

THE COURT: What I am trying to get at is, as a practical matter, it is obvious the Secretary of Defense has no time to review this stuff. Who really does it in the Department of Defense?

THE WITNESS: It will be done, sir, by staff personnel. But when the question comes up as to whether it may or may not be declassified, it often will be on a basis of recommendation by a staff officer but with an actual determination by an appropriately high official. And I would say that in the Department of Defense the Secretary of Defense has complete authority with respect to any information over which the Department of Defense has exclusive jurisdiction.

THE COURT: Anybody want to examine?

MR. SEYMOUR: I have no other questions, your Honor.

CROSS-EXAMINATION

BY MR. HEGARTY:

Q   I believe you gave your position, sir, as Director of the Security Classification, Management Division in the office of the Assistant Secretary of Defense for Administration, is that correct?

A   Yes, that is right.

Q   And what are your responsibilities in that position

apart from what the title implies?

A   Our total responsibility in that division is to
create and to administer what the Department of Defense
calls a security classification management program which
comprises the creation of standards and rules, procedures
and so forth for both classification and downgrading and declassification.

We are not the operators of the decision-making
process on individual cases. We are the people who make
sure that the people who should do that indeed do do it.

THE COURT: Excuse me. May I interrupt for one
minute?

Do you have a manual on that or something of that
order or directive?

THE WITNESS: Yes. I have a copy with me which happens to be a personal copy and I would be perfectly glad
to leave it here if you would like me to because--

THE COURT: Do you mind?   Do you want that sealed,
too?

THE WITNESS: Oh, no, no.

THE COURT: All right.

THE WITNESS: I'll identify it for the record.
It is called Department of Defense Instruction, 5210.47,
and the title of it is Security Classification of Official

Information.

It was issued on January-- December 31, 1964.
It has been amended severaltimes and my copy, which I will
be glad to leave here, is complete to this date.

MR. SEYMOUR: Could we ask the witness --

THE COURT: Any objection to that?

MR. HEGARTY: I am just curious.

Q   Is it itself classified?

A   No, indeed. We like to consider it as a best
seller.

Q   Within the government, I assume?

A   No, sir. We think of it as a best seller to any
one who may wish it.

THE COURT: Can you buy it for 50 cents?

THE WITNESS: I think it can be obtained free
of charge from Philadelphia.

BY MR. HEGARTY:

Q   Do I understand, sir, that it is the function
of your division to consider, I suppose, to propose re-
visions essentially of this document for use by other
branches of the department?

A   No, that is not our function.

For example, in this case the particular document,
as I understand it, was created within the Office of the

Joint Chiefs of Staff. If the Office of the Joint Chiefs of Staff wanted to talk with our office on the factors going to their judgment, we would be happy to advise them and consult with them. But they would make the decision. We would not.

THE COURT: Who wrote the manual? That's what we are trying to get at.

THE WITNESS: I personally had a lot to do with it. It was my particular office and it was promulgated by the Assistant Secretary of Defense.

THE COURT: May we put it in evidence?

We will try to give it back to you.

THE WITNESS: I don't need this particular copy (handing).

MR. SEYMOUR: The Government offers the manual referred to.

Government's Exhibit 12 marked for identification.)

MR. SEYMOUR: We offer it in evidence.

Government's Exhibit 12 received in evidence.)

THE COURT: You may proceed.

BY MR. HEGARTY:

Q   In your testimony, sir, in response to essentially his Honor's questions, you described the workings of these

four groups.

Just so I may be sure: A top secret document could appear in any one of the four, is that correct?

A   That's right.

Q   And if, for example, it appeared in the fourth group, I take it, it would be automatically downgraded at three-year intervals, the first three years secret and so on, is that correct?

A   Yes. Until it reached the confidential level, and then it would take six more years to go declassified.

Q   But taking Broup 4 as an example, applying it to top secret documents in that group, I take it that the order as written and as applied by the Department of Defense, recognizes that there is a pertinency to the passage of time in determining whether that material may be made available, is that correct?

A   The passage of time is one of the relevant factors, it is.

THE COURT: May I interrupt for just one minute?

Could you tell me, when you see a top secret stamp on something could you tell from the paper whether it was from Group 1, 2, 3 or 4?

A   Sir the requirement is that at the time the paper is created the stamp should be put upon it at the same

time as the classification stamp is.

THE COURT: You mean a group stamp?

THE WITNESS: Yes, sir.

Q   May I understand that? Do you mean a particular document determined to be top secret and meriting Group 1 should have two stamps, top secret, group 1? Is that correct?

A   It would have a top secret stamp which would say only "Top Secret." That would be that.

Q   Right.

A   It would also have another stamp, the specific language of which would mean that it is in Group 4 and, being in Grup 4, it would downgrade and declassify automatically on a time basis.

Q   Now, if there is a delicate question - don't answer it- is it a simple matter as Group 4 or is it a code that means Group 4? What I am trying to get at, if we look at the document, indeed if we look at the documents submitted to his Honor, can we tell which group they are in?

A   It should show.

Q   And in what fashion should it show?

A   By a stamp containing particular words.

Q   Can you tell us, and   pause before you do if

there is any problem about it, what the various words are

in relation to these four groups?

I don't know if you can or not.

A   I will try, but I could be very specific about it

and read them to you, if you like.

THE COURT: Excuse me. I think you testified that

this would only apply after 1961, is that correct?   There

was no group before then.

THE WITNESS: The system went into effect in 1961.

But ever since that time a custodian of a document which

does not bear a stamp, no matter what its date may be --

THE COURT: That's what I want to get to.

THE WITNESS: -- is authorized to address the ques-

tion, what group is it in.

Q   Could you give us the code, the group?

A   I believe that the group 1 will say group 1. I

believe group 2 will say group 2, group 3 will say group 3

and group 4, group 4.

But there are some additional words in group 1,

I think the words would say "Excluded from" the system.   In

Group 2 it would say "Exempted from" the system.   In Group

3 it would say something to mean downgraded to confidential,

no automatic declassification, and in Group 4 it would say

"Downgraded, declassified after 12 years."

MR. HEGARTY: Well, your Honor, with that testimony just before us, there was testimony this morning, I think, as to the classification with respect to the documents that were put to your Honor in these crates, and I think it was to the effect of top secret, sensitive I think was his testimony. I don't recall any language such as the witness has just testified to.

Obviously I have not seen it, so I don't know. But I think perhaps the government should clarify the record in that respect.

THE COURT: I understand it. I mean there is no jury yere. It seems perfectly simple. The only thing I did not understand was whether they retroactively put the second stamp on the documents which are involved here, which go before 1961, and the witness says yes.

MR. HEGARTY: I may be misremembering the testimony, but I don't believe there was testimony as to these documents, top secret group 1 or whatever.

THE COURT: But what happened was we dismissed the other witness because he didn't know and we got a fellow who knows.

BY MR. HEGARTY:

Q   Can you tell us, sir, with respect to Government's Exhibit 7, I believe, and 7A, what stamps appear on those

documents?

A   I could only if I had it.

MR. SEYMOUR: I submit the documents will speak
for themselves.

THE COURT: You have a record, don't you?

MR. MARTY: I can't speak to that, your Honor.

No, I can't speak to that.

THE COURT: I don't understand that. If you have
documents which are in the books that the government put
in, and if this gentleman is correct that there are stamps
marked Top Secret, Group 1, that should appear on each
document, or does it only appear on the book itself?

THE WITNESS: Sir, the rules for marking the
classification stamping Top Secret, Secret, or Confidential
are somewhat different from the rules for the group marking
themselves.   The ordinary place for a group marking
is on the outside of the front and back covers or perhaps
only the front cover. It doesn't have to appear on each
page at all.

I do want to make two more points, if I may, on
a voluntary basis.

Even though a particular document has been identified for the automatic system, a subsequent review of that
document before the time period has run can cause that

document to have its classificatoin changed at any period

of time during the course of time.

Furthermore, even though it is a requirement that

these documents shall be marked, one would hesitate to say

that that requirement is met 100 per cent everywhere, on all

occasions.

MR. HEGARTY: Your Honor, I cannot set the record

straight as to what we have --

THE COURT: I misunderstood. I thought you had

covers as well as papers.

MR. HEGARTY: I am not 100 per cent sure of the

fact, so I hate to make a representation to the Court.

THE COURT: I withdraw what I said.   If you have

a cover, you will find what this gentleman said. If you

don't have a cover, you won't.

MR.HEGARTY: Can't Mr. Seymour tell us without

violating the seal, what the documents he put in evidence

bear?

THE COURT: I think he will do that later. I am

sure he will.   You will hear it.

MR. HEGARTY: Fine.

MR. SEYMOUR: That is all I have, your Honor.

THE COURT: Thank you.

(Witness excused.)

THE COURT: Then we will proceed to the secrets of

state.

(9.50 p.m.)

THE COURT: In view of the lateness of the hour, I would like to announce that I have read the briefs and I think you can judge accordingly as to how much oratory we need.   I don't mean oratory in the derogatory sense.

Did you want to go first, Mr. Seymour?

MR. SEYMOUR: Whatever your Honor pleases. I think the amicus indicated they had an application to be heard first, but I will do it any way your Honor wants.

THE COURT: All right.

Please observe my admonition about brevity, if you can, without sacrificing fundamental rights.

MR. DORSEN: Your Honor, I represent the American Civil Liberties Union.   I would like to say this probably one of the most remarkable arguments I will have to make in view of the fact I am making the argument after having been absent for the most significant part of the testimony that is relevant to the determination of this case.

The American Civil Liberties Union regards this case as reflecting perh aps the most outrageous incursion on First Amendment rights the organization has witnessed over the past 20 years, and we do believe the role of the

amicus curiae has been emasculated by our inability to
be present at the hearing and I think it is instructive
to reflect upon the fact that the exclusion of the
organization representing primarily the public interest
here is really a microcosm, the exclusion of the ACLU is
a microcosm of what we see regarding society's role in
the determination of American policy during the Vietnam
War.

I must argue on what is publicly known --
publicly known --

THE COURT: How long are you going to take on
this, do you think?

MR. DORSEN: 20 minutes or so.

THE COURT: It is too long.   Take 10.   I can't
do 20 now, because we will all collapse.

You don't need the rhetoric for me.   If it is
for the press, give it to them later.

MR. DORSEN: I do not think this is rhetoric,
your Honor.

THE COURT: There are certain difficult issues
here and I would like to hear you on them.

MR. DORSEN: I will do the best I can, your
Honor.

Just as the public had to decide the Vietnam

policy without access to the facts, I am going to have

to argue without access to the facts and if my argument

is inapposite or inept, it will suggest the way the public

has been condemned to irrelevancy in the Vietnam debates.

The First Amendment values are well known and

I would not think it necessary to reiterate these at

this point in American history were it not for the fact

of this lawsuit.

The informed citizenry, of course, is the basis

of our society and as a former Attorney General said,

if government is to be truly of, by and for the people,

the people must know in detail the activities of the

government.   Nothing so diminishes democracy as

secrecy.   Self-government is meaningful only with an

informed public.   How can we govern ourselves if we

know not how we govern.

The line of cases, the line of history relating

to the authorities is, I assume, well known to the Court,

Chafee, Emerson, the leading freedom of the press cases,

Bridges, Craig and Harlan, New York Times and Sullivan,

Time, Inc., and, above all, the prior restraint cases,

Lovell, Stowe, Holmes, and a case I am not sure has been

brought to the Court's attention, Patterson against

Colorado, where he said --

THE COURT: I am familiar with it. You don't have to quote it. That is the one that cites Pickering.

MR. DORSEN: Yes. Near against Minnesota has a statement in it stating there are exceptions, there is not an absolute ban on prior restraints, and the Government suggests that that very, very narrow exception can be opened to include the kind of information made public in the New York Times and other newspapers.

Our position is that that is a very narrow exception, that it has to deal only with matters directly affecting military operations. Does the citizenry in order to be informed in order to govern does not have to know whether troops are on Hill A or Troopship B. That information is not necessary for the country to be governed by its people, but the people must know whether a policy decision has been made or is being made which would inevitably lead to shipment of troops, of war, of slaughter, or expenditure of vast fortunes, and the American people have to know exactly the kind of inform- ation that the documents published in the New York Times embody.

I would like to turn to what is probably the key issue, namely, the documents themselves, their classi-

fications, their relationship to nation defense.

I have not seen the papers or heard the testimony, but at bottom, I suppose, it is a question of whether or not one believes the experts, the experts in these matters, and I heard some of the experts today, although I did not hear them in camera, and I would like to suggest to the Court that it would be a terrible, terrible error, I respectfully urge, to allow the experts to govern. It is similar to the reliance on the experts that got us into the Vietnam War itself, similar to the reliance on the experts that the late President Kennedy said he was told all his life to avoid. The Bay of Pigs was directly traceable to the experts. The reason I suggest we did not have war during the Eisenhower era is because he knew enough about the experts to resist the generals, and I suggest that the word "expert" has a seductive and sometimes irresitible lure to people wh o are not of the particular persuasion or particular alleged wisdom, and I suggest that the Court should resist the experts and I suggest that the resistance of the experts in this case is not very far different from what another single District Judge did 21 years ago, in the District of Columbia, when he put himself as a barrier between the Government and people during another wartime era when

rms

the Government was attempting to seize the steel mills,
claimed it was an emergency, when the Government claimed
it knew the facts and the people did not know the facts,
but Judge Pine said, "You are wrong, sirs," and refused
to let the Government interfere with the property rights
of the steel companies.

We suggest that the District Judges in this
era at a time of equal grave emergency should likewise
resist what the experts, what the executive are prepared
to say is necessary to conduct the war, to win a war,
to conduct diplomatic relations.

Here we have First Amendment rights, basically.
There are some property rights involved, but they are
comparatively trivial, I say. The experts don't know
everything and I suggest it is the proper role of the
Federal judiciary, as it has been happily in many
instances from the beginning of the republic, to resist
the experts and to defend the all too overlooked right
embodied in the First Amendment.

This leads to what may seem like a side point,
although it is a point that did come up several times
during the gearing in public today, and that is patriotism. We are all patriotic men, it is suggested, and I am
suggesting that patriotism in this case means fidelity

to the First Amendment which is, in my judgment, based

upon the documents made public in the New York Times

so clearly -- so clearly where patriotism would lead us

in terms of the decision in this case.

I don't think it is irrelevant to ask who were

the patriots in 1964 and 1965 and 1966.   Who were the

patriots then, the generals, the politicians, or the

people who were the outsiders, the dissenters, the ones

who often were scoffed at?   Who were the patriots

then?   I suggest the New York Times has been the

patriots in this instance.

Now, this is a great case, this is a great

issue.   I respectfully suggest to the Court that it

is not a hard case, that the significance of the case

is far greater than the difficulty.   There is a basic

proposition that was settled at the beginning by the

founders of this country regarding prior restraints,

regarding the First Amendment, that in my judgment, on

the basis of the evidence that has come to light so far,

so obviously transcends the alleged and, it seems to

me, spurious arguments regarding national defense that

I think the Government should have been summarily dis-

missed the first moment they walked into the court.

The Government should be told in simple terms,

"No, you can't stop the publication of this kind of document."

I believe that is not only clearly the correct decision but it is the decision that history will redeem by whichever courts have strength and the vision to rend it.

Thank you.

THE COURT: Thank you very much. I appreciate the Civil Liberties Union's participation.

Who is next?

Mr. Seymour, I think you might be next.

MR. SEYMOUR: I will deal with the issue with brevity, your Honor.

Essentially the situation we are facing here is the existence of classified documents, stolen from the custody of the officials to whom they were consigned, classified top secret in general and in many specific instances.

There was no effort at all by the defendants to obtain a proper authorization to use them; instead a unilateral decision to publish them, to declassify them and treat them as if they were completely theirs to deal with with no questions asked.

I submit that this is not the commercial law

where one takes as a holder in due course and has no
obligations at all as to the source of the documents and
the intention of those who prepared them.

We have three basic points.

First, an injunction does lie to enforce the
congressional concept in Section 793, and particularly
in the situation such as here, where the criminal sanction,
that is, the after-the-fact criminal sanction is
essentially valueless; the damage is done and seeking
some form of nominal punishment has no real significance
at all.

THE COURT: Do any of your injunction cases
involve the press?

MR. SEYMOUR: I don't believe they do.   There
are, of course, a couple of cases that discuss the
question of prior restraint, but the principal --

THE COURT: I don't mean to cut you off, but
I think I can read those cases and I will have to
wrestle with them.   I have them in your brief.

MR. SEYMOUR: The factual thing I would like
to mention is that there have been only affidavits submitted in opposition from the defendants here.   They
have not been mentioned other than submitting them.
I think this much should be said about them.   They

refer to purported disclosures of classified information.

It is significant, at least to our reading, that in no case could we find an actual verbatim extract from a classified document as such, in strong contrast to this case, and, secondly, in those cases we are talking about a one-shot publication, where after the fact there was nothing that could be done, it was then too late, and if the Government had prosecuted, all they would have done was verified the authenticity of the information, which would have magnified the harm done.

So our position is that there is potential irreparable injury here and therefore is the perfect case for the injunction procedure.

There have been some references, from early morning until even the amicus argument, to the troopship similarly, and I think all concerned are prepared to acknowledge that the First Amendment privilege if not total, that there are some exceptions, and the one exception everyone seems to agree upon is that you don't publish the scheduling of a troopship movement, and we submit there has been now in the record before your Honor to consider enough specifics of that kind of situation that your Honor can make in such a finding precisely

here.

There is also some suggestion that, after all, all the Government was trying to do is to protect against the embarrassment of political figures, and we submit that the testimony of the career officers here who made a lifetime of doing the kind of work they were doing, testimony given in good faith, that what they were protecting was the interest of the United States, runs directly contrary to that suggestion.

Finally, on a practical plane, what damage would be done or what harm would be done to the New York Times? All of us who read it quite avidly, we think there are alternatives here.

No. 1, it is perfectly obvious that the Times, of all institutions, has public opinion available to it to try to bring about a reclassification of those documents that we are concerned with here that could properly be put in the public domain.

Already is the public opinion that they have generated in this direction obviously has brought all sorts of response pointing in that direction and we submit that is a proper way to go about the concept of balancing the need for national security against the need for public information.

rms

Secondly, the Congress of the United States

has in fact anticipated that kind of approach in the

Freedom of Information Act and the New York Times stands

on equal footing with any other citizen of this country

to be able to go in and seek the freeing up of classified

information which it believes in good faith was improvid-

ently classified.   It chose not to pursue either of

those routes here, and that being so, we think they have

to take the consequences of having the matter halted

until they do decide to follow the proper course.

THE COURT: What do you say, Mr. Seymour, to

Professor Bickel's argument that there is a constitutional

magnitude, if you will, on the proscription against pre-

censorship or prior restraint, which goes beyond the

particular acts that may have been done?   Do you have

any comment on that?

MR. SEYMOUR: I really think that Professor

Bickel's own concession, that he could see an injunction

against troopship movements, is really sufficient argument

in and of itself.

We submit, your Honor, we have met that burden

certainly with respect to specific types of situations

and that that is enough, really, to enjoin the publication

of all.

rms

In addition, of course, our basic position is that when the Congress and the Executive order have set up the system for treating classified documents, that the system that should be pursued.

THE COURT: As I understand it, they concede with the troop ip analogy that the First Amendment is not absolute and that if security to a sufficient degree is involved that there may be prior restraint.

MR. SEYMOUR: Correct.

THE COURT: You, on the other hand, concede that unless there is such security there is no prior restraint possible under the Constitution, First Amendment?

MR. SEYMOUR: I think clearly that is the law.

THE COURT: Then everybody then seems to agree. So the issue is the balancing of what the facts are.

Are we all agreed on that?

MR. BICKEL: Your Honor, when I am there (indicating) I will say that I entirely agree that we have found common ground between Mr. Seymour and myself.

We contend that nothing in the facts of this case we heard could possibly be --

THE COURT: You see what argument does and discussion, and it is an interesting thing that it seems

rms

to me the Government and the New York Times seem to agree on the law, fundamentally, as far as the con stitutional aspects are concerned, and it is merely a question of finding as to whatthe situation is.

MR. BICKEL: I do wish to reiterate, your Honor, and I am not sure whether I am up --

MR. SEYMOUR: I am finished, if I have answered your questions, your Honor.

THE COURT: I think you have.

MR. BICKEL: Let me indeed begin with just this. I do wish to repeat that in my view of the facts and considering the burden of proof that I think is applicable, a finding in this case that this is within the narrow exception it is, for the absoluteness of the First Amendment in a prior restraint case, unconstitutional.

THE COURT: Yes, I understand that.

MR. BICKEL: We agreed, however, that your Honor's task now is to fit the facts of this case into the paradigm of the ship leaving and the New York Times publishing the date and the ship being torpedoed.

Your Honor, I won't take long. We are all extremely grateful to Mr. Seymour, a gentleman and a brother, for taking as little time as he did and I will

rms

try to emulate him, although I fear I probably will take

a little longer, being a somewhat --

THE COURT: Don't overargue your case because

we have gotten down to fundamentals now. I am getting

tired, and everybody else is.

MR. BICKEL: We concede, which we think is all

the Government cases prove, that the Government has

standing to come into its own courts. We argue that

is a totally distinct issue from the separate issue as

to whether it has an inherent authority to come into

its court to do what it did. The issue is not whether

the Government had power to do something to commerce, the

issue is whether it had right to come into court and

get the Court to do it by injunction.

The question is whether the Government has

inherent power to put certain publications into a category

which justify their being restrained, and we say,

Youngstown Tool Company against Sawyer -- I should mention

another very recent case we cite in our brief, together

with the Sawyer case, the United States District Court

for the Eastern District of Michigan, United States

against United States, which is a wiretapping case, where

the Government claimed inherent authority to tap under

national security grounds, and that court held there is

rms

no such inherent authority.

As we see it, the case is one of statutory construction of 793-E, as Mr. Seymour says, within the constitutional rules that apply to this sort of an exercise of the statutory construction.

We cite in the brief the Rumely case, decided in 1953 by Justice Frankfurter, and I will, if I may, read one sentence we didn't quote in the brief, in which Justice Frankfurter describes the rule of construction and the avoidance of imprecision and vagueness in statutory construction and First Amendment cases that he followed.

"So to interpret," he says, after going through an analysis of the words and saying very candidly as a matter of English, you could go either way, and he comes out aginst an application of the statute and says:

"So to interpret is in the candid service of avoiding a serious constitutional doubt."

We suggest, your Honor, that that is the proper attitude for construing the applicable statute here, this being a prior restraint case.   I also on this point, if I may, will draw your Honor's attention -- this is not a First Amendment case but is a splendid example of the same attitude in a criminal case -- draw your Honor's

rms

attention to Justice Holmes' opinion in McBoyle v. United

States, and it is not cited in our brief, but it is

283 U.S. 25, and it was decided toward the end of

Justice Holmes' career, in 1931.

With that rule of statutory construction in

mind, I will not pursue, not try now to lead our way all

through the statute.

I do wish to draw your Honor's attention to

the legislative history materials we have in our brief,

starting at page 43, going to the question of whether

793-E, the applicable statute, can be constructed to

cover or should at least within the rule of construction

laid down by Rumely, be construed to cover newspaper

publication in a case like this.

We think we have excellent legislative history

to show on the three occasions on which Congress in deal-

ing with this statutory scheme addressed the issue of

whether it wished to cover newspapers, and its answer was

no, and its answer was no on First Amendment grounds.

The only aberration, so to speak, from that was

that in 1918, after the statute, that our legislative

history starting on page 43 deals with, or the bill that

our legislative history starting there deals with, to

punish publishing, was defeated in Congress.   This was

in 1917.   One year later the statute that it was applied

in the notorious Abrams case, which is cited in our

brief, and your Honor knows it well, Abrams against the

United States, was passed, only to be repealed in 1921.

The legislative record, so far as one can see

Congress addressing itself squarely to punishment,

"Do we want to publish publications and newspapers,

outside of such things as 794," which is now in the

statute, or 798, the one that deals with codes, specific

narrow statutes --

THE COURT: I want to understand one thing,

Professor Bickel, if I may.   If you concede that the

publication from the New York Times of the movement of a

troopship can be enjoined by the Government, under what

authority would that be?

MR. BICKEL: I concede it could be enjoined.

I would suppose that 794, as it now stands , would provide

the authority for that.   That was an abstract consti-

tutional concession.   I am conceding that Congress

could do that.   If the question is asked me is there a

law on the books now that would do that, I suggest 794

is that law.

THE COURT: Your point is that the President

under his powers, under the general Article 2 powers of

the executive function, the conduct of foreign relations, execution of laws, and what-not, nevertheless did not have power to create an Executive order which protects the security of documents in those realms?

MR. BICKEL: My position very clearly, your Honor, is that he has ample power to impose all sorts of rules on the internal operations of the Government; that he has no inherent power in any case remotely in the realm of the one here, no inherent power by himself to enjoin or otherwise prevent by process or by using force publications because they are of materials that are classified secret under his Executive order.

I would cite your Honor to Kent v. Dulles, in our brief, which held that under a statute which indeed said the Secretary may issue passports, the word "may" being subject to construction, he may or may not issue them. There is no such inherent power and the delegation is insufficient.

If that is so, your Honor, it would be a very striking thing to discover there is inherent power to say a document that somebody in the Defense Department -- after all, we say the President, but we mean some official infinitely lower on the scale, probably not even a political officer, probably a civil servant, classifies

the document as secret and that act of his means that any time that document is published the United States Attorney can go into court -- I can see the standing to go into court, but the question is can he win -- can go into court and enjoin the publication of that document.

That seems to me an extraordinary proposition, your Honor. Our argument is, without a statute there is nothing in this case. Hence, the statutory construction problem which arises within the First Amendment requires a kind of statutory construction typical perhaps only of First Amendment and criminal cases.

THE COURT: If it is a constitutional inhibition, why does Congress under Article 1 have more powers than the President under Article 2 in the field of foreign relations?

MR. BICKEL: I am arguing now a prior question. I am arguing to your Honor now that there is a prior question in this case which arises within the constitutional context but which doesn't require your Honor to come out with an opinion that attempts to define in ultimate terms the exact constitutional rights here involved. It is sufficient to premise that this is a prior restraint case and, secondly, premise the rule of statutory construction that prevails in such cases,

the premise, third, that the issue arises under a

statute or it doesn't exist because there is no inherent

to do that.

That leaves us, before we reach the consti-

tutional mountain, into the foothills of the construction

of this statute.

It seems to me, in light of its legislative

history, its words, the Rumely court would not have

construed this statute as applicable.

THE COURT: Section 771, 18 United States Code,

which deals with a law of Congress --

MR. BICKEL: I remember that, your Honor.

THE COURT: That deals with a law of Congress

preventing, which is obviously, I think, an advance,

the mailing of newspapers which violate 793 -- assume

for the moment that 793 is applicable to this type of

case, what do you make of that action by Congress in

relation to these statutes?

MR. BICKEL: As your Honor knows, I am

unfamiliar with the legislative history of that statute.

THE COURT: So am I.

MR. BICKEL: My initial reaction to it is that

if that statute forecloses the kind of statutory con-

struction I am proposing to your Honor, the result is,

to me, unconstitutional.

I do not think now we would hold what was held in the Milwaukee Leader case, that denying the second class mail privilege is not as bad as a prior restraint, and I think the holding now would be it is equally bad, and I think that applied to this situation, if the Government acted under that statute and we assumed 793 is applicable and had instead of coming in for a temporary restraining order acted out of the Post Office Department and simply excluded the Times the next morning -- of course it didn't do that because the Times doesn't rely on mail that much -- my judgment is that we would be in exactly the constitutional position we are in now.

THE COURT: I know that. I was just wondering on the statutory construction of 793 --

MR. BICKEL: I can only say, as I have said, the statute is somewhat baffling, but I think I understand it, I understand the scheme that says, and one must have in mind the frame of mind of the Congress that thought it could use the sanction of exclusion from the mails rather freely -- that is clearly the frame of mind.

Well, that Congress then said to itself, a

Congress as we see from our legislative history which was

rather conscious otherwise of the First Amendment --

we cite a long speech by Mr. Ashurst, the late Senator

from Arizona, in which the Blackstonian position that

prior restraints are the thing and that is about all that

is fully stated, and here is a Congress rather thinking

prior restraints they can't do, but thinking, on the

other hand, sanctions they can impose, and instead of

looking through the statute book for things a newspaper

could possibly do and wouldn't like and saying, "We will

kick you out of the mails for that," and you can see

any number of things in 793 a newspaper might do, plenty

of things a newspaper could do to which 793 would be

applicable.

It can go around and steal or purloin photo-

graphs of military installations, it can go around and

take plans and maps and obtain them unlawfully.   That

sentence triggers in me -- I will not hold your Honor

long --

THE COURT: Doesn't this statute talk of

documents and notes as well as maps and plans?

MR. BICKEL: It talks of stealing them, your

Honor.

THE COURT: You can aid and abet by receiving

rms

stolen goods, I suppose.   That is a common concept.

MR. BICKEL: I don't think that is shown in this case at all.

THE COURT: I didn't say it was.

MR. BICKEL: 793-B:

"Whoever for the purpose aforesaid" -- that is another thing.   The purpose that is involved here has to be obtaining information with intent or reason to believe that the information is to be used, your Honor, not "could be" used -- it is to be used to the injury of the United States or to the advantage of an foreign nation.

That is the predicate of these sections. It is a burden in this case that the evidence in the record does not -- not only doesn't begin to -- well, I am beginning to be cautious about what concessions I do hear from the Government, but I do believe I heard at some point a concession that the Times acted in good faith.

In any event, we know we acted in good faith and there is nothing in the record to deny that.   I don't see how we could be fitted into a formulation that we had reason to believe that the information is to be used to the injury of the United States or to the advantage of

any foreign nation.

Now, with that purpose and with like intent and reason to believe whoever copies, takes, makes or obtains, or attempts to copy, take, make or obtain any sketch, photograph, photographic negative, blueprint, plan, and so forth, and the next section, where receives, obtains or agrees to attempt to receive or obtain whatever documents, writings, code books, sketches, plans, this is an offense a newspaper could commit, and the Congress, wary of prior restraints, feeling, however, very much in possession of the power to deny access to the mails, thought that it would clobber any newspaper that did that in that fashion.

I don't see, in short, that it affects our case.

It does bring me to the point --

THE COURT: I want to cover E with you.

I agree, in a sense, that A and B deal with more than a prediction that it will be used by a foreign nation, and so on, but there is an even different language, it seems to me, in E, which is what the Government is talking about, where you say, "Has reason to believe could be used to the injury of the United States or to the advantage of any foreign nation."

MR. BICKEL: I was talking earlier about C and A

because I was making the point -- I was endeavoring to

explain the meaning of 1791, why the reference to 793.

I don't concede the reference to 793 would include E,

thus leading one to believe that Congress thought that E

covered publishing by a newspaper.   It is sufficient

to know that 793 -- no subsection is referred to -- that

793 has in it offenses that a newspaper could commit,

and once we know that, the further relevance of 771

is out.

As to the language "Has reason to believe could

be used," we say in our brief we think that modifies

only the word "information".   I don't insist on that

by any means -- and not the words "document writing,"

which I take it is meant to be applied to us here.

THE COURT: The document is even wider.

It says, "Relating to the national defense."   That is a

big one.

MR. BICKEL: That phrase we think, your Honor,

is the operative phrase under which the factual issue in

this cases arises for your Honor within the constitutional

context.   It is that phrase to which your Honor, we

believe, should apply the umely method of construction,

the method of construction applied in Rumely against

United States, which is a very cautious method candidly
aimed at not reaching great constitutional difficulties
and within that phrase we believe your Honor should
find that as applied to this case that phrase means if
the statute applies to us at all, which we do not concede --
as applied to this case, if it applies, that phrase must
mean grave danger, grave injury to the national security,
or, if Mr. Seymour and I agreed, the equivalent of the
troopship sailing and the newspaper publishing the
date.   That is the operative phrase.   If it were true
the phrase "Has reason to believe could be used to the
injury of the United States or to the advantage of any
foreign nation" were applicable, which I do not believe
it is, because I think that modifies "information," but
it is not a necessary part of my case and I don't insist
on it one way or the other -- if it is applicable, your
Honor, I think at that point the case is ours because I
think the record is bereft of anything, bare of any
showing whatever about the state of mind of the Times,
any showing whatever -- no showing has been made to your
Honor that the Times had reason to believe one thing or
another, except that we are to assume that the fact of
classification on a document is conclusive.

        THE COURT: The normal rule would be that you

rms

have to have scienter--

MR. BICKEL: That is how the Gorin case got out of the issue in an espionage case, avoided the issue, by reading in scienter, saying you have to show scienter, by which it meant bad faith.

If this record has a showing of bad faith, I have not heard it today, and I believe the record was made today, your Honor.

THE COURT: Let me ask you one other thing on statutory construction.

What do you make of the phrase "or wilfully retain the same and fails to deliver it to the officer or employee of the United States entitled to receive it"? You did get a telegram from the Attorney General?

MR. BICKEL: That is right, and I assume that that was intended to make out the wilfulness.

What I make of that phrase, your Honor, is that it entirely depends on wha we have construed in the statute beforehand. That is to say, we don't arrive at this offense if your Honor has not construed the relating to national defense as implying on the facts of this case -- as meaning on the facts of this case such a grave danger.

THE COURT: That may assume too much. I may

assume something is not related to the national defense

plight in good faith, but then when I am told about it

and I learn something about it, my state of mind may

change.

MR. BICKEL: I don't think your Honor is free

to do that under the statute. If I read the statute,

the offense of wilfully retaining cannot be made out if

the offense of, well communicating, whatever it is, is

not made out, and I see otherwise no definition whatever

for what it is that you have wilfully retained.

THE COURT: I take it what you think it means

is that either you give it to a person who is not entitled

to receive it or you keep it.

MR. BICKEL: It seems to me that "wilfully

retains the same" means that unless you have found facts

and construction down to that line, that the offense

described in this statute has been made out, unauthor-

ized possession and communication, and what-not -- unless

that is found, or unless the elements of it are found,

I suppose -- unless the element of that are found, there

is no offense of "wilfully retained," unless it relates

to the national defense, in the same sense we have just

been talking about, and there is no offense of wilfully

retained.

In addition to which, your Honor, in this case -- I must say the reason that must be so is that if it were possible separately to order in a case like this delivery of documents, to order them to be given back, that is the back door of censorship.

THE COURT: I am not arguing this. There is no doubt about that. It is just a question now of if you concede for a moment the constitutionality of the statutes, is there a difference between the wilfully retained part and the other part, I was asking -- all right, I think we have enough of that.

MR. BICKEL: They seem to me to coincide, your Honor. I am anxious not to overstay by leave, but I would like to go on to one or two points.

THE COURT: All right, go ahead.

MR. BICKEL: One point, your Honor, is what I view as the irrelevance to this case of the Information Act and of like arguments made essentially either by analogy to or under it, that there is an obligation on a newspaper to try -- an obligation of some sort to get permission or to try to get permission to publish something, that there is an obligation to get something declassified.

I think, your Honor, that is an unacceptable

argument, unsustainable argument in the First Amendment

area for all the reasons we have traversed as thoroughly

as we have.

It seems to me that Mr. Seymour says, and

perhaps rightly, that there are many cases of this sort

in which the criminal penalty which comes post facto,

the damage is done.

Your Honor, that s precisely why so much value

was placed on the difference between the prior restraint

and the criminal sanction imposed afterwards.

THE COURT: Well, you are begging the question,

because Mr. Seymour is talking about the security of the

United States and none of these other cases do, and you

have conceded there is a difference, with your troopship.

MR. BICKEL: I have conceded if he is in an

area, if he is in the sailing ship alalogy we have talked

about so long, he can probably have his prior restraint

under the applicable statute, but it is no argument to

make outside that to say, "Well, gee, unless I can

have prior restraint in some other matters in which I

can't have it, but I can have criminal penalties" --

well, I don't want to open that, but to say that the

criminal penalties are ineffective, of course, that is

why there is the kind of aversion to prior restraint,

rms

the idea is to be less effective in the First Amendment
area than we are with many other things that are
transgressions in this country.

Sure, the criminal penalty is less effective,
but that represents a value judgment --

THE COURT: There is no precedent on security
in the constitutional field.   It is a first-impression
situation?

MR. BICKEL: There are questions on security
in the constitutional field, but there are no precedents
on this case.

THE COURT: On free press as against security.

MR. BICKEL: There are prior restraint
precedents and there are, on the other hand, numerous
precedents in which the claim of national security was
raised against the First Amendment interest in other less
charged conditions and failed.

THE COURT: But not press?

MR. BICKEL: Yes, sir, press -- I am sorry?

THE COURT: Not free press situation?

MR. BICKEL: Well, no, but this is an a fortiorari
case.   If it is true that DeGregory against New Hampshire,
which we cite in our brief, that New Hampshire cannot --
in Watkins against the United States it was the Congress

of the United States which was not allowed to investigate

as a threat to national security a man's Communist

connections because his First Amendment rights by way

of construction or vagueness, as in Watkins, flat out

in DeGregory, prevailed, then we know the clashes between

these two instances most often come out on the First

Amendment side.

THE COURT: The speech cases involve security

only if there is a present and clear danger, but in

the press cases there are not any?

MR. BICKEL: It is not a bad analogy for this

case, your Honor, but I would add the burden of proof

on the Government in this case is even greater, but the

clear and present danger thought is not a bad analogy

to the finding of fact your Honor has to make.

THE COURT: I want to ask you another question,

and it may be hypothetical:

The 798 that you concede affects publication,

is that constitutional, in your opinion, dealing with

the cryptology?

MR. BICKEL: I find that very difficult to

answer without a factual situation.

THE COURT: Assume the fact there is a code

taken and published.

MR. BICKEL: My difficulty is this, your Honor:

I understand a layman's understanding that codes are broken, and so forth, all the time and that all the Government does is sort of pull another switch, and it cost money, but all it has done is change the code.

THE COURT: Let's say concerning the design of an appliance planned for use by the United States for communications in intelligence?

MR. BICKEL: Suppose it was the design of the appliance involved in Rosenberg against the United States, your Honor, I have no doubt of the constitution-ality of the application of the statute. Suppose it was a --

THE COURT: You agreed on the Rosenberg thing; would it apply to a newspaper like the New York Times if a newspaper had published what the Rosenbergs stole?

MR. BICKEL: I have no doubt the statute could be applied.

THE COURT: Why?

MR. BICKEL: It is the greatest danger to the national security, justifying the death sentence on the individuals.

THE COURT: It is subject to the same test of

clear and present danger --

MR. BICKEL: The standards in a prior restraint case are the highest. I don't know how to define it except as your Honor and I and Mr. Seymour are narrowing it down by picking one and another example. We have the troopship example and we now have the design of the atomic bomb example. That arises in such different circumstances, but it is an analogy.

I would think the burden in a case like this, where a prior restraint on the press, with all the favored position of the press against prior restraints -- I would think the burden of proof is on the Government to show a crisis, an emergency -- I would think that burden of proof is of the greatest.

We have affidavits in our submission, your Honor, which I think go both to the state of mind of the Times in publishing this and, perhaps more importantly, to the climate of discourse, to the universe of discourse under which this was done.

They go to argue the commonness, the every-day garden variety commonness of the Times' decision to publish. I don't deny this is a coup, a journalistic coup, but it falls -- and the Yalta thing was a coup --

THE COURT: Whoever did it gave it to the

rms

Washington Post --

MR. BICKEL: Not before he decided there would be difficulty having it published in the New York Times.

The proof in our affidavits goes to show how common this is, which it seems to me is entirely relevant to the statutory construction issue, to the vagueness issue, to the expectations that might have been entertained about the statute, relevant directly to the First Amendment issue, because something that goes on as commonly as this, and we think indistinguishably from this, can hardly suddenly have become a grave danger to the survival of the republic, which is virtually what we have to find.

Finally, your Honor, in conclusion, I would like to mention two points. Your Honor has a motion before you on the TRO, and, secondly, but without, I hope, violating anything that I would not remotely wish to violate, I hope I can say nothing I heard in camera struck me as justifying going in camera in this case and that I hope your Honor will take under consideration our suggestion that so much as your Honor believes of the record that was made in camera, so much of it as your Honor believes isn't touched by security considerations, should be made public.

rms

Thank you, your Honor.

THE COURT: Thank you very much.

Anybody else?

I guess we are finished.

Thank you all.

I will try to work out someth ing in the

morning.   Why don't you call my chambers about eleven

o'clock and see how I am doing.

WITNESS INDEX

Name	Direct	Cross	Redirect	Recross
Dennis James Doolin (Recalled)	52	118	129 132	130 138
Francis J. Blouin	100			
William Butts Macomber	106	114		
George MacClain	140	149		

EXHIBIT INDEX

Government	Identification	In Evidence
1		50
2		50
3		50
4		50
5		51
6		51
4A		59
7,7A		65
8		84
9		110
10 (deemed)	134	
10A (deemed)	134	
12	152	152